CONTEMPORARY. CURRENT. COMPLETE.

Stand-alone modules offer **flexibility** for instructors and **accessibility** for students.

Concrete **examples and pedagogy** throughout each module provide frequent opportunities for self-reflection and application.

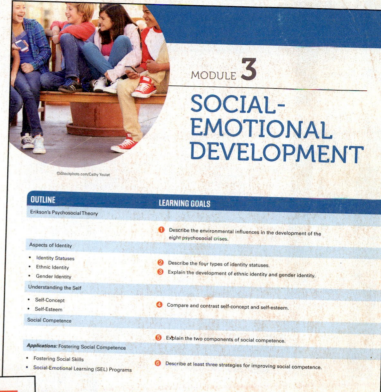

©iStockphoto.com/Cathy Yeulet

MODULE **3**

SOCIAL-EMOTIONAL DEVELOPMENT

OUTLINE	LEARNING GOALS
Erikson's Psychosocial Theory	① Describe the environmental influences in the development of the eight psychosocial crises.
Aspects of Identity	
• Identity Statuses	② Describe the four types of identity statuses.
• Ethnic Identity	③ Explain the development of ethnic identity and gender identity.
• Gender Identity	
Understanding the Self	
• Self-Concept	④ Compare and contrast self-concept and self-esteem.
• Self-Esteem	
Social Competence	
	⑤ Explain the two components of social competence.
Applications: Fostering Social Competence	
• Fostering Social Skills	⑥ Describe at least three strategies for improving social competence.
• Social-Emotional Learning (SEL) Programs	

APPLICATIONS: ADVANCING MORAL DEVELOPMENT

te to the moral development of children

W   es of moral development. You may have
n   using different terminology (see Table 4.2
fo   spects of these theories have been stud-
ie   provide suggestions on how to advance
m   (Eisenberg et al, 2009).

F
Al   ures who provide consequences, the
n   al code as they outgrow the need for
ex   000). More specifically, maternal sup-
port and responsiveness are related to empathy and prosocial behavior in children (Malti, Eisenberg, Kim, & Buchman, 2013). The children of parents who use consistent discipline that includes providing reasons for misbehavior and suggesting appropriate alternatives

Gender Differences in Motivation. Gender differences in competence beliefs are more pronounced in gender-stereotyped domains for boys and girls (e.g., sports for boys and reading for girls).

©iStockphoto.com/monkeybusinessimages
©iStockphoto.com/Choreograph

math as less useful for future goals (Frenzel, Pekrun, & Goetz, 2007; Gaspard et al., 2015; Steinmayr & Spinath, 2010). Despite their lower utility value for math, adolescent girls seem to have higher attainment value in the subject compared to boys (Gaspard et al., 2015). Girls consider it important to perform well in math classes even if they don't consider math to be important for their future. However, girls' value for math appears to be a double-edged sword because they also perceive math to have a higher cost compared to boys. They report more anxiety and hopelessness in math and feel that math requires more effort compared to that made by boys (Frenzel et al., 2007; Gaspard et al., 2015).

In elementary school, girls also begin to develop an entity belief about their ability in general (Dweck, 2000, 2002). Compared to boys:

DIVERSITY

CASE STUDIES

MIDDLE SCHOOL: ACHIEVEMENT GAP

PREPARE:

As you read the case, make notes:

1. WHO are the central characters in the case? Describe them.
2. WHAT is taking place?
3. WHERE is the case taking place? Is the environment a factor?
4. WHEN is the case taking place? Is the timing a factor?

Jarrod and Tamara Patterson met during college and are both teachers in the Chicago area. They live in the suburbs, where Jarrod teaches third grade. Tamara completed her student teaching at an inner-city school. She wanted to continue in a similar school district, so she takes the train into the city each day to teach history in a public middle school.

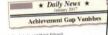
★ Daily News ★
January 2017
Achievement Gap Vanishes
iStockphoto.com/Haluk Köhserli

Over the years, Jarrod and Tamara have had a number of arguments about education—their disagreements stem from the developmental differences in their students—works with younger students—but their liveliest disagreements involve the difference suburban and urban classrooms. Ninety percent of Tamara's students are African Am live in households where the median annual income is around $33,000. In contra Jarrod's students are White, 9% are Latino, 8% are Hispanic, and only 3% are Africa The median annual income for households in Jarrod's school district is $83,000.

As they begin their drive into the city to run errands on Saturday morning, Tam Jarrod that she needs to stop by her classroom to pick up some papers. She yesterday and needs to finish grading them before Monday morning. Ja respond—he has taken the opportunity to read the newspaper while Tamara dr

"Listen to this," he begins. "A new study examined the 'achievement gap'—idea that African Americans perform more poorly compared to Whites. Says h researchers found that the differences in achievement levels between African Whites no longer exist."

Tamara responds skeptically, "How did they determine that?"

"Well, it says that the researchers found no differences in the GPAs of student ethnic backgrounds, including African American and White students," replies

Tamara pushes the issue. "Who were the students? How did they get in GPA? Did they use the official records?"

Jarrod replies, "It doesn't give that many details."

As they pull into the school parking lot, Tamara announces, "The newspap those statements without supplying more details." She grabs the r Jarrod's hands and says, "Come on. While we are inside getting my pape bly find more information about the study on the web."

"Do we have to do this today?" moans Jarrod, wishing he had kept his mouth shut.

"Yes," replies Tamara.

As they enter Tamara's classroom, Jarrod says, "I still can't get over how old everything seems in the building. When are they going to update the decor, not to mention your textbooks?"

Tamara ignores his comment. She turns on the only computer in the room and retrieves her papers while she waits for the computer to get up and running. Then she launches her Internet browser and begins to alphabetize her papers, because she knows it will take several minutes before the computer is ready.

Jarrod waits impatiently. "How long is this going to take?"

"Well, if we had new computers with wireless Internet connections like at your school, we'd be out of here by now. But I don't have those perks, so just give me a couple of minutes."

Tamara uses the researchers' names from the newspaper article to find the original study online. "Good, it was published early this year," she says, and sends the print job to the printer in the main office. "Come on. I'll grab the printout. I can read while you drive us."

As they walk to the office, Tamara can't help herself. "I suppose you have your own printer in your classroom and don't have to walk to the main office all the time."

"As a matter of fact, I do," replies Jarrod. "You know you could get a job in my school district anytime. Remember, you chose to work here. Don't give me a hard time because I chose not to."

As they drive to their next stop, Tamara begins to read and launches into a tirade: "Well, they used college students, not K-12 students. Oh, can you believe this? They didn't even use official records to find GPAs. They simply asked students to provide their GPA on a survey."

"Why do you care so much? It's just one newspaper article in the back of the paper," replies Jarrod.

Tamara continues her tirade. "Because parents and most other teachers won't take the time to read the actual study and see that the newspaper article is misleading. People won't realize that the achievement gap is still present in K-12 classrooms and will expect all teachers to have students with similar achievement levels. That's unrealistic. If journalists were actually trying to inform the public—instead of spewing out stories on movie stars in rehab—they would explain why the achievement gap exists. It's not even about ethnicity; it's about socioeconomic status."

© iStockphoto.com/Steve Debenport

"Maybe you should write a letter to the editor," suggests Jarrod.

"Maybe I will," Tamara says.

ASSESS:

1. How might the different schools in which Tamara and Jarrod work influence the importance each places on understanding achievement differences?
2. Should teachers be concerned with what type of students participate in research studies like the one reported in the newspaper article? Why or why not?
3. How would you respond to a parent whose child is not achieving as well as others but who believes that all students should perform equally well?

Tabs (right side): EARLY CHILDHOOD · ELEMENTARY SCHOOL · MIDDLE SCHOOL · HIGH SCHOOL

CASE STUDIES: REFLECT AND EVALUATE

EARLY CHILDHOOD: THE WORKSHEETS

These questions refer to the case study on page 268.

1. According to self-efficacy theory, what is Melissa's efficacy expectation for completing her schoolwork? How would you characterize Claire's self-efficacy? How would you characterize Martin's self-efficacy?

2. Explain why asking a peer to show Melissa how to complete the math sheet might improve her self-efficacy.

3. How can Mrs. Garvey improve the self-efficacy of students in her class?

4. Based on self-worth theory, which student—Melissa, Martin, or Claire—would be most difficult to motivate? Why? Which student would be easiest to motivate? Why?

5. Based on the case study, speculate on the degree of Mrs. Garvey's teaching efficacy.

CASE STUDIES

Case Studies for each unit include **all four grade levels**—early childhood, elementary, middle school, and secondary—and related pedagogy facilitates application for practice.

"I especially like that these case studies are realistic enough to create thoughtful discussions that connect to the lives of teachers and students."
—Robert J. Colesante, *Siena College*

"I like the fact that students can be in one class but enrolled in different education programs because the book includes questions from all three levels, elementary, middle school, and high school."
—Donna Farland-Smith, *The Ohio State University*

VIDEO CASES

Including footage with teachers and students, filmed in **real classrooms**, video clips are accessible in the interactive eBook and provide a firsthand look at the concepts and strategies presented in the modules.

Created specifically to support this text, the videos include footage from classrooms representing a range of grade levels.

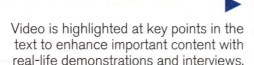 

Video is highlighted at key points in the text to enhance important content with real-life demonstrations and interviews.

All videos are supported by pedagogical aids including follow-up questions to assess understanding and prompt reflection.

THIRD EDITION

Ed Psych
Modules

THIRD EDITION

Ed Psych
Modules

Cheryl Cisero Durwin
Southern Connecticut State University

Marla Reese-Weber
Illinois State University

Los Angeles | London | New Delhi
Singapore | Washington DC | Melbourne

FOR INFORMATION:

SAGE Publications, Inc.
2455 Teller Road
Thousand Oaks, California 91320
E-mail: order@sagepub.com

SAGE Publications Ltd.
1 Oliver's Yard
55 City Road
London, EC1Y 1SP
United Kingdom

SAGE Publications India Pvt. Ltd.
B 1/I 1 Mohan Cooperative Industrial Area
Mathura Road, New Delhi 110 044
India

SAGE Publications Asia-Pacific Pte. Ltd.
3 Church Street
#10-04 Samsung Hub
Singapore 049483

Printed in Canada.

ISBN 978-1-5063-1075-6

Acquisitions Editor: Terri Accomazzo
Development Editors: Jessica Miller and
                          Lucy Berbeo
eLearning Editor: Allison Hughes
Editorial Assistant: Erik Helton
Production Editor: Olivia Weber-Stenis
Copy Editor: Tina Hardy
Typesetter: C&M Digitals (P) Ltd.
Proofreader: Ellen Brink
Indexer: Sheila Bodell
Cover Designer: Scott Van Atta
Marketing Manager: Kara Kindstrom

This book is printed on acid-free paper.

16 17 18 19 20 10 9 8 7 6 5 4 3 2 1

UNIT 2: THE DEVELOPING LEARNER

UNIT 3: LEARNING THEORIES

UNIT 4: COGNITIVE PROCESSES

BRIEF CONTENTS

DETAILED CONTENTS

UNIT 6: CLASSROOM MANAGEMENT AND INSTRUCTION

PREFACE

Teaching is about making instructional decisions. To be highly effective, teachers need to understand the science underlying all aspects of education and know how to apply concepts, principles, and conclusions from educational and psychological theories and research to particular situations they encounter. Students in education certification programs are often taught the "*what*" and the "*how*" of teaching. For example, they may be taught what to do when students are fighting or how to develop and deliver a lesson. Educational psychology is about the *why*. For example, why are teacher education students told to use a particular conflict resolution strategy or a particular teaching method in a certain situation? The effectiveness of these approaches can be determined only by evaluating what we know from psychological research. Teachers need to understand why particular approaches, strategies, and methods work under various circumstances to make effective decisions. We wrote this book to help students of educational psychology learn how to make better instructional decisions. This third edition of *EdPsych Modules* helps students to

- Understand the importance of learning evidence-based, best practices that guide how they will make informed decisions,

- Apply educational psychology theory and research findings to diverse instructional situations, and

- Understand student differences and learn ways to adapt instruction to individual student needs.

OUR APPROACH

FLEXIBLE: A book that adapts to your course.

- *EdPsych Modules* is the first and only text written with a modular approach rather than modified from a conventional chapter text. This intentionally designed format allows you flexibility in preparing and teaching your course. Our modules are succinct (about half the length of a typical chapter), stand-alone topics that represent every subject found in a traditional chapter textbook. The modules

are organized into themed units that correspond to chapters found in conventional textbooks. With this modular approach, instructors can arrange the topics in any order, and even skip entire modules or units if they choose.

- Our inclusion of case studies that span K-12 grade levels also allows you flexibility in designing your course. Each unit begins with four full-length case studies, one from each certification level: early childhood, elementary, middle school, and high school. Instructors can choose one particular educational level (only early childhood), several (elementary and high school), all levels, or may choose to skip the cases altogether.

Our stand-alone modules and cases allow you to tailor content to your particular course and student audience.

APPLIED: Opportunities for practical application of theories and concepts

In each module, our coverage of educational psychology theories and concepts includes examples that illustrate application and critical thinking about individual differences and instructional contexts.

- In every module, **Applications** sections help students tie theory and research to educational practice. Coverage is focused on evidence-based teaching methods and principles that are linked to research.

- **Case studies** – 33 in all – provide opportunities for students to apply theories and concepts. Our case studies are rich, detailed glimpses into classroom and school settings. Each unit begins with four case studies: early childhood, elementary school, middle school, and high school that are relevant to all modules in that unit.

  - At the end of each case study ASSESS questions prompt students to assess their existing knowledge and to identify assumptions, preconceptions, and personal beliefs prior to reading a particular module.

- Each module ends with REFLECT AND EVALUATE questions based on the case studies at the beginning of each unit. These questions encourage students to check their comprehension of important concepts, to apply what they have learned about the research presented in the modules, and to evaluate the situations and instructional decisions presented in the case.

- Our developmental approach of presenting cases at various certification levels enables students to meaningfully apply the concepts they are learning to the grade levels they intend to teach. Whether you use the cases studies out of class as homework or writing assignments or for in-class discussions, students will have the opportunity to practice applying what they've learned.

EXTENSIVE COVERAGE

Balance of classical and contemporary topics

We present research on traditional topics, such as cognitive development, learning, information-processing, and motivation, as well as more contemporary educational topics such as the role of the brain in learning, social-emotional learning, differentiated instruction, response-to-intervention, and underserved populations.

Depth of coverage

The scope of each module provides a deeper examination of core topics than the survey approach in traditional chapter textbooks. For example, while typical chapter textbooks combine behavioral and social cognitive learning theories into a single chapter, we treat each of these topics as separate modules to allow more meaningful discussion of the theory, research, and practice. We also offer more in-depth coverage of topics that may be only minimally covered in chapter textbooks such as constructivist teaching approaches, intelligence, grouping practices, and metacognition.

Integrated issues of diversity

Our book treats diversity—characteristics such as ethnicity, race, socioeconomic status, gender, and disabilities—not as a separate topic but as a facet of most instructional situations.

DIVERSITY ⟨ A marginal icon (see at left) indicates where pertinent coverage of diversity appears in the modules. We have chosen to emphasize information as a

diversity issue only if it is supported by sufficient research or theoretically relevant. Within the modules, we integrate diversity by covering research findings that

- indicate important similarities or differences among individuals of various diversity groups on psychological constructs such as intelligence, motivation, or language;

- reveal differences among individuals of various groups in values, practices, or social interactions;

- suggest differential responses to treatments, interventions, or teaching methods for individuals of varying diversity groups; and

- highlight differential treatment of individuals from various diversity groups within the classroom.

These findings are relevant because they provide essential information to help teachers make informed decisions that affect the success and well-being of their students.

You will also find diversity in the case studies. We include students and teachers of diverse backgrounds in the case studies, and where appropriate, we present Reflect and Evaluate questions at the end of the modules that probe students to re-evaluate their personal beliefs or assumptions about diversity.

NEW IN THIS EDITION

The third edition provides instructors and students with the same content as our previous edition in a more streamlined presentation. Our original motivation for writing a truly modular textbook was to ensure that our students actually read the pages that instructors assigned. Therefore, our intent has always been to provide students with an up-to-date treatment of theory and research on topics in a brief and easy-to-digest format. In our streamlined third edition, we have condensed 30 modules into 25 modules and have reduced the number of themed units from nine to eight. These changes include

- efficiently combining modules on "Social Development" and "Emotional Development" into one module called *Social-Emotional Development*;

- writing an entirely new module on *Brain Development* with updated research to replace the previous module called "The Brain and Development";

- writing an entirely new module on *Information Processing* with updated research;

- moving the topic of creativity with topics on critical thinking and problem solving to create a new module called *Higher-Order Thinking*, which replaces the old module called "Critical Thinking and Problem Solving;"

- creating a new module called *Classroom Management*, which covers many of the topics in the previous modules on "Creating a Productive Learning Environment" and "Understanding and Managing Student Behavior";

- combining topics on *Intelligence and Giftedness* into one module

- incorporating topics from the module on "Performance Assessment" into the module on *Assessing Student Learning*, which is also a newly written module, and

- incorporating topics from the module on "Issues in Standardized Testing" into the module on *Standardized Tests and Scores*, and moving this module to Unit 8 on Assessment, eliminating the need for a separate Unit 9 covering standardized testing.

Our third edition also features newly written case studies for Units 4, 6, and 8. These case studies provide a fresh new glimpse into classrooms that reflect the changes to modules within these units that we describe above. As in the previous editions of our textbook, the case studies are written based on real-life classroom situations.

In addition to these primary changes, we have ensured that all of our modules contain the most up-to-date research. We have included new research citations and have expanded our coverage of diversity throughout the book.

ACKNOWLEDGMENTS

The publisher and authors gratefully acknowledge the contributions of the following reviewers:

James A. Bernauer, Robert Morris University

Agnes Cave, The Catholic University of America

Robert Colesante, Siena College

Patricia Corbett, Great Bay Community College

Michael G. Curran Jr., Rider University

Jeff W. Dennis, Southwestern Michigan College

Maryann Dudzinski, Valparaiso University

Stella Erbes, Pepperdine University

Cynthia Erickson, University of Mobile

Donna Farland-Smith, The Ohio State University

Joseph D. Green, Pepperdine University

Alishia Huntoon, Oregon Institute of Technology

Miriam Lipsky, University of Miami

Christine Purkiss, Angelo State University

Martha Ravola, Alcorn State University

Deborah A. Scigliano, Duquesne University

Michael F. Shaughnessy, Eastern New Mexico University

Pam Tabor, Miami Dade College

Dawn N. Hicks Tafari, Winston-Salem State University

Katie Tuohey, Ursuline College

Kathy Vespia, Salve Regina University

Lois J. Willoughby, Miami Dade College–Kendall

DIGITAL RESOURCES

$SAGE coursepacks

SAGE coursepacks for Instructors makes it easy to import our quality content into your school's LMS (Blackboard, Canvas, Brightspace by Desire2Learn (D2L), and Moodle). **Don't use an LMS platform?** No problem, you can still access many of the online resources for your text via SAGE edge.

SAGE coursepacks offers:

- **Intuitive, simple format** that makes it easy to integrate the material into your course with minimal effort·

- Pedagogically robust **assessment tools including test banks and quizzing/activity options** that foster review, practice, and critical thinking, and offer a more complete way to measure student engagement·

- **Chapter-specific discussion questions** to help launch engaging classroom interaction while reinforcing important content

- **Assignable SAGE Premium Video** (available via the interactive eBook version, linked through SAGE coursepacks) that is tied to learning objectives, and curated and produced exclusively for this text to bring concepts to life and appeal to different learning styles

- EXCLUSIVE, influential **SAGE journal and reference content**, built into course materials and assessment tools, that ties important research and scholarship to chapter concepts to strengthen learning

- Editable, chapter-specific **PowerPoint® slides** that offer flexibility when creating multimedia lectures so you don't have to start from scratch but you can customize to your exact needs

- **Sample course syllabi** with suggested models for structuring your course that give you options to customize your course in a way that is perfect for you

- **Lecture notes** that summarize key concepts on a chapter-by-chapter basis to help you with preparation for lectures and class discussions

- **Integrated links to the interactive eBook** that make it easy for your students to maximize their study time with this "anywhere, anytime" mobile-friendly version of the text. It also offers access to more digital tools and resources, including SAGE Premium Video

- **All tables and figures** from the textbook

$SAGE edge™

SAGE edge for Students enhances learning in an easy-to-use environment that offers:

- Mobile-friendly **flashcards** that strengthen understanding of key terms and concepts, and make it easy to maximize your study time, anywhere, anytime

- Mobile-friendly practice **quizzes** that allow you to assess how much you've learned and where you need to focus your attention

- A customized online **action plan** that includes tips and feedback on progress through the course and materials

- **Learning objectives** that reinforce the most important material

- **Chapter-specific study questions** that allow you to engage with the material other content for use in independent or classroom-based explorations of key topics.

- **Video and multimedia resources** that bring concepts to life, are tied to learning objectives, and make learning easier.

ABOUT THE AUTHORS

Cheryl Durwin received her PhD in Educational Psychology at the University of Massachusetts, Amherst in 1996. She is Professor of Psychology at Southern Connecticut State University. She has taught educational psychology for over 20 years in various formats such as graduate level and undergraduate courses ranging from mid-size sections of 40 students to small, writing-intensive sections. Cheryl regularly teaches courses in research design, testing, motivation, cognition and memory, and learning disabilities. Her research interests include the development, assessment, and remediation of reading skills, efficacy of reading interventions in disadvantaged populations, and college-level teaching and learning.

Marla Reese-Weber received her PhD at The Ohio State University in 1998. She is Professor of Psychology and serves as the associate dean in the College of Arts and Sciences at Illinois State University. She has taught educational psychology for over 17 years in sections as small as 25 students and sections as large as 150 students. In addition, her course on educational psychology has included a focus on underserviced populations, particularly in urban areas. Marla also teaches adolescent development at the undergraduate and graduate levels as well as a course on developmental research methods. Her research interests include sibling and dating violence as well as romantic relationship development during emerging adulthood.

Though both of us have had varied experiences in teaching educational psychology, we came together because of a singular need. We wanted a textbook that was flexible enough to meet our very different circumstances. Cheryl has taught small, writing-intensive classes with a focus on case studies to help students apply what they are learning, while Marla has taught larger classes of 50 or more students with an emphasis on research design and the science behind educational psychology. In each of our courses, we select varied topics to emphasize and order the topics very differently, and we have unique teaching styles. We wanted a textbook that would fit each of our needs.

EdPsych Modules is the first textbook purposefully and intentionally written from a module approach. Our modules are succinct, stand-alone topics that are organized into themed units representing every subject matter found in a traditional chapter textbook. Because these are stand-alone, our modules can be combined or organized in any order, regardless of the order we decided to use in the table of contents. Instructors can even skip modules or entire units if they choose. For those who teach with case studies, we provide four detailed classroom situations at the beginning of every unit, one for each educational level: early childhood, elementary, middle school, and high school. Again, instructors can choose one particular educational level, several, all levels, or may choose to skip the cases altogether. We believe that if our textbook is flexible enough to meet our very diverse needs, it can meet the needs of any instructor, regardless of the type of teacher education program, class size, or course emphasis.

INTRODUCTION

USING SCIENCE TO INFORM CLASSROOM PRACTICES

CASE STUDY
MIDDLE SCHOOL: ACHIEVEMENT GAP, 2

MODULE 1: USING SCIENCE TO INFORM CLASSROOM PRACTICES

CASE STUDIES

MIDDLE SCHOOL: ACHIEVEMENT GAP

PREPARE:

As you read the case, make notes:

1. WHO are the central characters in the case? Describe them.

2. WHAT is taking place?

3. WHERE is the case taking place? Is the environment a factor?

4. WHEN is the case taking place? Is the timing a factor?

Jarrod and Tamara Patterson met during college and are both teachers in the Chicago area. They live in the suburbs, where Jarrod teaches third grade. Tamara completed her student teaching at an inner-city school. She wanted to continue in a similar school district, so she takes the train into the city each day to teach history in a public middle school.

★ *Daily News* ★
January 2017
Achievement Gap Vanishes

© iStockphoto.com/Haluk Köhserli

Over the years, Jarrod and Tamara have had a number of arguments about education. Some of their disagreements stem from the developmental differences in their students—as Jarrod works with younger students—but their liveliest disagreements involve the differences between suburban and urban classrooms. Ninety percent of Tamara's students are African American and live in households where the median annual income is around $33,000. In contrast, 79% of Jarrod's students are White, 9% are Latino, 8% are Hispanic, and only 3% are African American. The median annual income for households in Jarrod's school district is $83,000.

As they begin their drive into the city to run errands on Saturday morning, Tamara reminds Jarrod that she needs to stop by her classroom to pick up some papers. She forgot them yesterday and needs to finish grading them before Monday morning. Jarrod doesn't respond—he has taken the opportunity to read the newspaper while Tamara drives.

"Listen to this," he begins. "A new study examined the 'achievement gap'—you know, the idea that African Americans perform more poorly compared to Whites. Says here that some researchers found that the differences in achievement levels between African Americans and Whites no longer exist."

Tamara responds skeptically, "How did they determine that?"

"Well, it says that the researchers found no differences in the GPAs of students from several ethnic backgrounds, including African American and White students," replies Jarrod.

Tamara pushes the issue. "Who were the students? How did they get information about GPA? Did they use the official records?"

Jarrod replies, "It doesn't give that many details."

As they pull into the school parking lot, Tamara announces, "The newspaper shouldn't print those statements without supplying more details." She grabs the newspaper out of Jarrod's hands and says, "Come on. While we are inside getting my papers, we can probably find more information about the study on the web."

"Do we have to do this today?" moans Jarrod, wishing he had kept his mouth shut.

"Yes," replies Tamara.

As they enter Tamara's classroom, Jarrod says, "I still can't get over how old everything seems in the building. When are they going to update the decor, not to mention your textbooks?"

Tamara ignores his comment. She turns on the only computer in the room and retrieves her papers while she waits for the computer to get up and running. Then she launches her Internet browser and begins to alphabetize her papers, because she knows it will take several minutes before the computer is ready.

Jarrod waits impatiently. "How long is this going to take?"

"Well, if we had new computers with wireless Internet connections like at your school, we'd be out of here by now. But I don't have those perks, so just give me a couple of minutes."

Tamara uses the researchers' names from the newspaper article to find the original study online. "Good, it was published early this year," she says, and sends the print job to the printer in the main office. "Come on. I'll grab the printout. I can read while you drive us."

As they walk to the office, Tamara can't help herself. "I suppose you have your own printer in your classroom and don't have to walk to the main office all the time."

"As a matter of fact, I do," replies Jarrod. "You know you could get a job in my school district anytime. Remember, you chose to work here. Don't give me a hard time because I chose not to."

As they drive to their next stop, Tamara begins to read and launches into a tirade: "Well, they used college students, not K-12 students. Oh, can you believe this? They didn't even use official records to find GPAs. They simply asked students to provide their GPA on a survey."

"Why do you care so much? It's just one newspaper article in the back of the paper," replies Jarrod.

Tamara continues her tirade. "Because parents and most other teachers won't take the time to read the actual study and see that the newspaper article is misleading. People won't realize that the achievement gap is still present in K-12 classrooms and will expect all teachers to have students with similar achievement levels. That's unrealistic. If journalists were actually trying to inform the public—instead of spewing out stories on movie stars in rehab—they would explain why the achievement gap exists. It's not even about ethnicity; it's about socioeconomic status."

© iStockphoto.com/ Steve Debenport

"Maybe you should write a letter to the editor," suggests Jarrod.

"Maybe I will," Tamara says.

ASSESS:

1. How might the different schools in which Tamara and Jarrod work influence the importance each places on understanding achievement differences?

2. Should teachers be concerned with what type of students participate in research studies like the one reported in the newspaper article? Why or why not?

3. How would you respond to a parent whose child is not achieving as well as others but who believes that all students should perform equally well?

EARLY CHILDHOOD

ELEMENTARY SCHOOL

MIDDLE SCHOOL

HIGH SCHOOL

© iStockphoto.com/ lai9

USING SCIENCE TO INFORM CLASSROOM PRACTICES

OUTLINE	LEARNING GOALS

Educational Psychology: A Resource for Teachers

1 Explain why educational psychology is an important resource for teachers.

Educational Psychology: The Science

- Research Designs
- Samples
- Measures

2 Describe three elements of research studies that help determine which studies are worthy of consideration.

Educational Psychology: Classroom Practices

- Best Practices
- Addressing Diversity
- Using a Case Study Approach

3 Define best practices and explain why it is important for teachers to base them on scientific evidence.

4 Describe four diversity characteristics that can define an individual's group membership, and explain why teachers need to understand differences between groups.

EDUCATIONAL PSYCHOLOGY: A RESOURCE FOR TEACHERS

Master the content.
edge.sagepub.com/durwin3e

$SAGE edge™

❶ Explain why educational psychology is an important resource for teachers.

People who work outside educational settings may assume that good teaching practices are simply common sense. Yet common-sense approaches to classroom management and instruction often are ineffective or even counterproductive. Assume, for example, that an elementary student continues to get out of his seat during a lesson. A common-sense approach would be to politely ask the student to sit down. However, if the student is misbehaving to attract attention from the teacher and classmates, this approach might simply encourage the behavior.

Research suggests that a more effective approach would be to ignore the unwanted behavior, *depending on the individual characteristics of the student.* Hence, scientific evidence helps teachers determine the best practices for effective teaching. As a teacher, you will encounter situations for which, despite all your training, you are unprepared. When that happens, research can help you formulate an informed response.

When teachers need help dealing with issues of diversity, motivation, achievement differences, behavioral problems, and other concerns, they turn to the field of educational psychology. **Educational psychology** links the science of psychology to educational practice and provides teachers with evidence-based knowledge to support their day-to-day decision making in the classroom. Teachers who implement research-based practices have students with more academic engagement and fewer disruptive behaviors (Sanetti, Collier-Meek, Long, Kim, & Kratochwill, 2014). In short, educational psychology can help teachers become better teachers. We are writing this text to provide theories and empirical evidence you can use to develop a repertoire of skills and knowledge on your path to becoming an effective teacher.

gradyreese / E+ / Getty Images

Scientific Approaches Versus Common Sense. Research informs teachers about how best to approach situations in the classroom, such as children playing with one another rather than completing their work, as shown here. The common-sense approach does not always lead to best practices.

Video Case 1.1 ▲
New Teacher Advice

To make the most of educational psychology, teachers need both a basic understanding of scientific principles (the science) and an awareness of how these principles can apply to real situations (classroom practices). In this text, you will be considering the same major challenges that scholars face in this field:

- The science: formulating theories and conducting research studies.

- Classroom practices: developing applications of current theories and research to enhance teaching and learning.

EDUCATIONAL PSYCHOLOGY: THE SCIENCE

 Describe three elements of research studies that help determine which studies are worthy of consideration.

The science of educational psychology involves formulating **theories**—sets of ideas that are used to explain a phenomenon and make predictions about behavior—and then conducting research to determine how well those theories explain the phenomenon. The relationship between theory and research is reciprocal. Research findings may support a theory, but researchers also may alter theories or develop new ones based on accumulated evidence. This process is ongoing—scientists today are building upon (or tearing down) the work of twentieth-century scientists.

For today's teachers, the amount and variety of research material available can be intimidating. The first step in evaluating research is to find appropriate resources (see Guidelines 1.1: Finding Reputable Research). After you have located good research articles, you need to determine which studies are worthy of consideration. To evaluate the quality of research, you need to understand three elements of it:

1. Design: What was the purpose of the study (to describe, to show cause and effect)?

2. Sample: Who was being studied (elementary-aged children, college students)?

3. Measures: How were constructs of interest measured (surveys, observations)?

GUIDELINES 1. 1   Finding Reputable Research

Teachers need to become informed consumers of research. News stories and websites commonly misinterpret scientific findings. The first step in evaluating research is to find appropriate resources. To obtain reputable research:

- Don't use newspaper and magazine articles, because they are not research articles.

- Don't do Internet searches using search engines, because they may not yield credible sources.

- Do find peer-reviewed articles in scholarly journals at a local university library.

- Do find peer-reviewed articles in databases such as ERIC and PsycINFO.

- Do visit websites of professional associations to see if they have links to educational research groups such as the American Educational Research Association (AERA) and the American Psychological Association (APA).

Research Designs

Researchers must choose a method for investigating variables of interest. **Variables** are events, characteristics, or behaviors that can be measured, such as age, family divorce, medication, diagnosis of attention deficit hyperactivity disorder (ADHD), math scores, or aggression. To focus on a specific question about certain variables, researchers choose a particular **research design**—a method for investigating how and whether the variables selected are related. Table 1.1 describes four designs that are commonly used in educational research.

Video: Research Design

Descriptive designs provide basic information about variables in a population without making connections between behaviors, events, or conditions. For example, a descriptive research study might determine what percentage of school-age children are diagnosed with ADHD.

Two descriptive designs can provide in-depth perspectives:

- *Case study* research examines a single individual and creates a rich picture of that individual's psychological functioning. Researchers might observe a child diagnosed with autism both at home and at school, interview teachers and parents, and examine test scores, school records, and other sources of information.

- *Ethnographic study* research closely examines a particular group through direct participation within the group. For example, a researcher might attend a school of Latino students, taking extensive field notes to capture the unique educational values and social challenges of this ethnic group.

To move beyond simply *describing* behaviors, researchers use **correlational designs,** which answer questions about the connections between two variables. For example, in exploring the connection between study time and grades, the researcher might ask whether students who spend more time studying get better grades. These connections are expressed in a statistical computation called a *correlation coefficient,* a number between −1.0 and +1.0 that indicates the type and strength of the relationship between two variables.

TABLE 1.1	Summary of Research Designs			
	DESCRIPTIVE	**CORRELATIONAL**	**EXPERIMENTAL**	**QUASI-EXPERIMENTAL**
DEFINITION	To systematically explain a situation factually and accurately.	To assess how changes in one variable correspond with changes in another variable.	To establish a cause–effect relationship between variables.	To infer a cause–effect relationship between variables when the researchers cannot manipulate the independent variable.
RESEARCHER'S QUESTIONS	What percentage of students passed a state mastery test? Does the percentage differ by grade level or socioeconomic status?	To what extent are reading achievement scores correlated with socioeconomic status? How are science project scores correlated with parents' level of interest in science?	How is third-grade reading achievement affected by classroom reading-training? (Researchers randomly assign students into two groups, one with reading-training and one without, and then compare scores on reading achievement tests.)	How is third-grade reading achievement affected by classroom reading-training? (Researchers study two existing classrooms at the same school, one with reading-training and one without, and then compare scores on reading achievement tests.)
LIMITATIONS	Cannot show connections between different variables.	Can show connections between variables, but cannot prove one variable causes changes in the other.	Requires random assignment into experimental and control groups, which is often not possible.	Can show connections between variables and even infer causation, but cannot confirm that the results were due solely to the independent variable.

- The sign (positive or negative) indicates the type of relationship between the two variables. A positive correlation (+) between study time and grades means that as study time increases, grades also increase. A negative correlation (–) between school absences and grades means that as absences increase, grades decrease.

- The closer a correlation coefficient is to +1 or –1, the stronger the relationship between the two variables. For example, a correlation coefficient of –.56 indicates a stronger connection than a correlation coefficient of +.43 because the absolute value of the number is larger.

Although correlation studies measure the relationships between different variables, they *cannot* determine cause and effect. Although we may find that study time and grades are positively correlated, increased study time may or may not *cause* better grades. Instead, this positive correlation may suggest several possibilities: (a) more study time causes better grades, (b) better grades cause a person to enjoy academics and therefore to study more, or (c) some other variable, such as parental involvement, accounts for the high levels of study time and grades.

When researchers want to establish whether a cause–effect relationship exists, they turn to experimental and quasi-experimental designs. **Experimental designs** are used to establish a cause–effect relationship between an independent variable and a dependent variable. An independent variable is the variable of interest that is presumed to have an effect on the dependent variable, which is the outcome of the study. Researchers conduct experimental studies in two steps:

1. Randomly assign participants to one of two groups: an experimental group and a control group.

2. Manipulate the independent variable (a treatment or intervention) with the experimental group but not the control group.

Suppose researchers want to determine whether using computers in elementary classrooms (independent variable) affects the academic achievement of students (dependent variable). They might give an academic achievement test to students and then randomly assign some to a computer classroom (experimental group) and others to a no-computer classroom (control group). The experimental group would use computers in the classroom over a specified period of time, while the control group would not. At the end of the study, researchers would give the same academic achievement test to each student. If the experimental group showed greater improvement over time than the control group, researchers could make a claim about a cause–effect relationship: that the independent variable (the use of computers in the classroom) affected the dependent variable (academic achievement).

Video: Quasi-experiemental designs

In situations in which researchers cannot randomly assign individuals to groups or manipulate an independent variable, they use **quasi-experimental designs** to *infer* a cause–effect relationship. Obviously, researchers cannot randomly assign children to divorced and nondivorced families, abusive and nonabusive homes, male and female genders, or high and low socioeconomic groups. In other cases, researchers' actions may be limited by school district rules or by time or expense, making the manipulation of experimental and control groups impossible. As a result, quasi-experimental designs cannot establish that an independent variable directly affects a dependent variable, and therefore they leave open the possibility that the outcome of the study may be due to other variables the researcher could not control. Say, for example, that researchers study an existing group of students in a computer classroom and compare their achievement to that of students enrolled in a no-computer classroom. Changes in the academic achievement of students in the computer classroom (dependent variable) may not depend *solely* on the presence of computers (independent variable) but may also be affected by variables beyond the researchers' control: the computer classroom having more high-level readers, fewer behaviorally challenging children, or a teacher with more teaching experience than the teacher in the no-computer classroom. Researchers employ safeguards to account for and control all other possible variables that might affect the experimental and control groups, but their presence and the lack of random group assignment are limiting factors.

Despite these shortcomings, quasi-experimental research does allow researchers to examine questions involving differences between groups or differences over time. Two examples are cross-sectional studies and longitudinal designs, described here:

1. *Cross-sectional studies* examine two or more groups to compare behaviors. Researchers might examine whether middle school students have more or fewer hours of homework than high school students.

2. *Longitudinal designs* examine the same group of people repeatedly over time to provide information about how behaviors change or how earlier events can be connected to later events. A longitudinal study might follow children over time to determine whether children whose parents divorce in elementary school have more academic difficulties in adolescence than children whose parents did not divorce.

To use science effectively in decision making, teachers need to be informed consumers of research. When you encounter scientific evidence presented in the media, in journals, or at workshops, you should be aware of the various inferences that can be made with each research design, as shown in Figure 1.1. Experimental studies are the only type that can answer questions about cause-effect relationships. However, correlational and quasi-experimental designs are more common in educational research because they are more practical than experimental designs for investigating many hypotheses regarding teaching and learning. They also provide more information than descriptive designs. Nevertheless, you must be cautious when interpreting correlational and quasi-experimental designs. You should always question whether other variables not identified in the studies might account for the findings.

Samples

Once the research design is determined, researchers must identify the population of interest and select a sample. Suppose researchers want to study how students of different ages respond to the stress of transferring to a new school. Because the researchers cannot observe or survey all transferring students—the population of interest—they rely on a **sample,** a smaller set of individuals from the population of interest. The sample needs to be representative, meaning that it has gender, ethnicity, and age characteristics similar to the population of interest. The best method for ensuring a representative sample is to use a **random sample,** meaning every person in the population of interest has an equal chance of being included. Many computer programs can take a large list of individuals (for example, all students registered in a school district) and create a random subset of individuals to be included in a study.

FIGURE 1.1 **A Continuum of Research Designs.** Design dictates what inferences we can make from educational research studies.

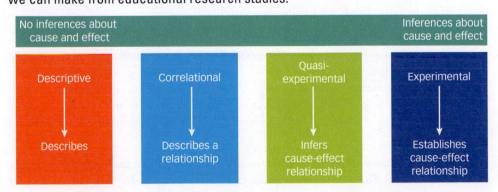

Research Measures. Observations allow researchers to view the behaviors of teachers and students during instruction, such as whether boys or girls are called on more frequently by teachers.

Even when a random sample of individuals within the population is selected, not all the people selected will agree to participate in the research study. (How many website surveys have you declined?) This is called **volunteer bias,** the tendency of those who choose to participate in research studies to differ in some way from those who do not participate. Typically, individuals who have strong feelings or opinions, or who are invested in the outcome of a particular research study, are more likely to participate than are those who do not have a vested interest. For example, a college student might be more willing to participate in surveys and interviews regarding opinions on the effectiveness of the university's financial aid office and less likely to participate in research on the effectiveness of the university president.

Measures

Once researchers have chosen a research design and representative sample, they must decide on a method for taking measurements, which will provide a framework for gathering information. If researchers are investigating the amount of time students spend during school hours completing assignments, they must decide whether to ask students verbally, have them complete a paper-and-pencil survey, or observe them within the school setting. Some measures commonly used in educational research are these:

- **Observations,** or watching or viewing the behavior of individuals, might be used to examine how many times a teacher calls on a girl versus a boy in relation to the number of students from each gender who raise their hands.

- **Interviews,** or questions presented to participants, can be highly structured lists of simple questions (*How many hours do you spend on homework each night?*) or can include open-ended questions (*How do you study for a test?*). Even though open-ended questions allow more information to be gathered, they often result in less consistency across participants. Participants might talk about the number of hours spent studying, the use of a study guide, or strategies they use for reading, note taking, memorizing, and testing themselves.

- **Tests and surveys** typically are paper-and-pencil measures that include a number of questions. Test and survey research can be done very easily with large groups of individuals in a relatively short amount of time. One requirement for participation in survey research is the ability to read and write. This might exclude younger children and individuals with language barriers.

When you examine research findings, consider the measurement strategy the researchers chose. Each measurement approach has limitations. In interviews, the researcher must speak the same language as the participant. On a test or survey, the participant must be able to read and write in the same language. Observation research is less valid for measurements of internal states of mind such as self-confidence or sadness.

Consider the research scenarios below and see if you can classify them according to research design.

1. There are two sections of a class. Both sections are taught by the same instructor, cover the same content, and have the same number of students. In one class the teacher uses a $150 textbook, and in the other class the teacher uses no textbook. The final exam scores are compared to determine which practice is a better option.

2. An educational psychologist examines how students' levels of motivation toward studying compare with their IQ scores.

3. In an effort to decrease obesity and increase movement among students, a superintendent has all the gym teachers in a district record the average number of hours in a week spent doing cardio work in gym class.

4. A researcher goes to an urban school and a rural school to observe differences. After much study, the researcher writes a report comparing and contrasting the two schools.

EDUCATIONAL PSYCHOLOGY: CLASSROOM PRACTICES

3 Define best practices and explain why it is important for teachers to base them on scientific evidence.

4 Describe four diversity characteristics that can define an individual's group membership, and explain why teachers need to understand differences between groups.

In addition to understanding educational research, teachers must be able to translate practical findings of specific research studies into school settings—diverse school settings. To do this, every teacher needs a systematic process for developing his or her personal educational philosophies.

Video Case 1.2 ▲
Teaching Philosophy

Best Practices

Effective teachers develop **best practices** for instruction, classroom management, and assessment. Best practices are evidence-based strategies determined by science to help inform decisions. They are not a list of specific strategies that one should and should not use. For example, many states are relying on a new set of academic standards, Common Core. However, the Common Core standards do not inform teachers *how* to teach and *what* material to teach. Instead, educators must develop a set of skills needed to determine best practices for having students reach these standards. Education programs training our next generation of teachers use the standards set forth by the *Interstate Teacher Assessment and Support Consortium* (InTASC) to evaluate skills and competencies of preservice teachers. Table 1.2 shows the standards set forth by InTASC.

Best Practices. Teachers need to examine current resources and up-to-date scientific evidence in making decisions about instructional methods and techniques, rather than relying on techniques used decades ago.

Note that best practices today may not be the same best practices in 5, 10, or 20 years from now. Best practices are fluid, changing with new research findings. We don't use the same teaching strategies, or best practices, from 50 years ago. It's likely we won't be using the best practices of today 50 years from now. The fluid nature of best practices means that teachers must continue to seek out evidence-based information, or current research, to assist them in making sound decisions regarding classroom management, instruction, and assessment.

Addressing Diversity

DIVERSITY ❮

Determining effective classroom practices is made more complex by the increasingly diverse nature of the student body in U.S. schools. Aspects of diversity will shape your teaching and the choices you make about the methods, techniques, and strategies you employ in the classroom. Because diversity can be found in all educational interactions, we discuss issues of diversity within specific educational contexts. An icon (like the one in the margin here) will point to pertinent coverage of diversity within a particular topic. To provide a basic understanding of diversity, some of the most important guidelines and concepts related to diversity and effective classroom practices are summarized here.

Effective teachers are aware of the diversity they are likely to encounter in the classroom. Individuals and environments can exhibit a wealth of diverse characteristics. To begin to understand individual and group differences, researchers often ask participants of studies to report their ethnicity or race, sex or gender, socioeconomic status, and disabilities. By grouping people based on these characteristics, researchers can divide any population into subsets for analysis. For example, in the 2010 U.S. Census, respondents were asked to report their race by choosing among the following categories:

Video Case 1.3 ▲
Addressing Diversity

© SAGE Publications

- White

- Black, African American, or Negro

- American Indian or Alaska Native

- Asian (with specific check box responses for Asian Indian, Chinese, Filipino, Japanese, Korean, Vietnamese, Other Asian, Native Hawaiian, Guamanian or Chamorro, Samoan, or Other Pacific Islander)

- Some other race (Individuals of "multiracial, mixed, interracial, or a Hispanic, Latino, or Spanish group" could respond in a write-in space under this category. Also, people of two or more races could fill in multiple race response check boxes and provide additional responses.)

TABLE 1.2 InTASC Core Teaching Standards 2011

The standards have been grouped into four general categories to help users organize their thinking about them:

THE LEARNER AND LEARNING

Standard #1: Learner Development. The teacher understands how learners grow and develop, recognizing that patterns of learning and development vary individually within and across the cognitive, linguistic, social, emotional, and physical areas, and designs and implements developmentally appropriate and challenging learning experiences.

Standard #2: Learning Differences. The teacher uses understanding of individual differences and diverse cultures and communities to ensure inclusive learning environments that enable each learner to meet high standards.

Standard #3: Learning Environments. The teacher works with others to create environments that support individual and collaborative learning, and that encourage positive social interaction, active engagement in learning, and self-motivation.

CONTENT

Standard #4: Content Knowledge. The teacher understands the central concepts, tools of inquiry, and structures of the discipline(s) he or she teaches and creates learning experiences that make the discipline accessible and meaningful for learners to assure mastery of the content.

Standard #5: Application of Content. The teacher understands how to connect concepts and use differing perspectives to engage learners in critical thinking, creativity, and collaborative problem solving related to authentic local and global issues.

INSTRUCTIONAL PRACTICE

Standard #6: Assessment. The teacher understands and uses multiple methods of assessment to engage learners in their own growth, to monitor learner progress, and to guide the teacher's and learner's decision making.

Standard #7: Planning for Instruction. The teacher plans instruction that supports every student in meeting rigorous learning goals by drawing upon knowledge of content areas, curriculum, cross-disciplinary skills, and pedagogy, as well as knowledge of learners and the community context.

Standard #8: Instructional Strategies. The teacher understands and uses a variety of instructional strategies to encourage learners to develop deep understanding of content areas and their connections, and to build skills to apply knowledge in meaningful ways.

PROFESSIONAL RESPONSIBILITY

Standard #9: Professional Learning and Ethical Practice. The teacher engages in ongoing professional learning and uses evidence to continually evaluate his/her practice, particularly the effects of his/her choices and actions on others (learners, families, other professionals, and the community), and adapts practice to meet the needs of each learner.

Standard #10: Leadership and Collaboration. The teacher seeks appropriate leadership roles and opportunities to take responsibility for student learning, to collaborate with learners, families, colleagues, other school professionals, and community members to ensure learner growth, and to advance the profession.

SOURCE: Council of Chief State School Officers. (2011, April). Interstate Teacher Assessment and Support Consortium (InTASC) Model Core Teaching Standards: A Resource for State Dialogue. Washington, DC: Author. Retrieved from http://www.ccsso.org/Documents/2011/InTASC_Model_Core_Teaching_Standards_2011.pdf

A group may be considered a **minority group** if it has less power than the majority group, even if the group is not smaller in number. For example, more women than men live in the United States, but women are considered a minority group due to their relative lack of power in business (lower paying jobs), politics (fewer political positions), and religion (in some religions, women still are not allowed to hold leadership positions). Let's examine group membership further:

- The terms *ethnicity* and *race* are often used interchangeably to express cultural differences, but they actually have different meanings (Spencer, 2014). Although each term has a definition that is so complex entire courses are taught to differentiate the two, our purpose here is to provide a basic distinction. **Ethnic group** includes people who share a similar culture—an environment with a unique history, traditions, rules, attitudes, and perhaps a specific language. In contrast, **racial group** categorizes people who share common biological traits (such as hair texture and skin color). The biological traits that distinguish races are socially defined. In other words, there is nothing particularly important about hair texture or skin color. Our society could have chosen, or defined as important, other biological traits (eye color, height, and so on). Certain traits were most likely chosen to establish social standing among groups (Moya & Markus, 2010). Most often, a person's ethnicity and racial group overlap. However, because ethnicity is based on environment and race is based on biology, they can diverge. For example, how would researchers categorize the race and ethnicity of an Asian-born child who is adopted and raised by a middle-class White family living in the rural Midwestern United States? Classrooms today are rich with such complexity.

- Like ethnicity and race, the terms *sex* and *gender* are often used interchangeably but differ technically. **Sex** refers to the biological status of male (penis) or female (vagina), whereas **gender** is the social definition, including behaviors learned in the environment about being either male (masculine) or female (feminine). Sexual orientation is another concept related to sex and gender that has been used to denote diversity. The term **sexual orientation** denotes homosexuality, heterosexuality, or bisexuality.

- Many people believe that **socioeconomic status** (SES) is based solely on income, with families who have higher incomes being considered high-SES and families with low incomes considered low-SES. A more accurate definition of SES relies on the educational level and occupation of family members rather than on their level of income. Although in most circumstances educational attainment and occupation are highly related to income (more education and/or more prestigious occupations lead to higher incomes), in many circumstances less-educated individuals have higher incomes than those who are highly educated. The typical example is the college professor who holds a doctoral degree but whose income is modest.

- **Disability** refers to being limited in one's ability to perform some behavior, task, or skill. The term can refer to physical disabilities (hearing impairment, cerebral palsy), cognitive disabilities (intellectual disabilities, learning disabilities, language delays), or behavioral or emotional disabilities (attention-deficit hyperactivity disorder, anxiety). We consider disability to be a diversity characteristic because a student's disability will result in different learning needs and perhaps different levels of achievement in comparison with students who have no disabilities.

Culturally responsive pedagogy: See Module 18

DIVERSITY

Effective teachers attempt to understand the possible causes of differences among groups. Teachers who understand why differences exist can learn to be sensitive to the individual needs of students from various backgrounds. Typically, environmental differences, not biological or genetic differences, are the root of group differences. Consider SES as an example. Students from high-SES homes tend to score higher on achievement tests, receive higher grades, and stay in school longer than students in lower SES homes (Dawson-McClure et al., 2015). These outcomes can be traced to several environmental differences (Goodman & Burton, 2012; National Center for Education Statistics, 2015):

- Poorer nutrition and more exposure to pollution in lower SES homes.

- Less exposure to school readiness materials such as books and computers in lower SES homes due to lack of financial resources or lack of knowledge about the importance of reading to children at a young age.

- Less parental involvement in lower SES homes, which may be due to work schedules or less education.

- Less well-qualified teachers and higher turnover rates among teachers in lower SES schools and preschools.

One might think these factors are most influential in early childhood, but the SES achievement gap for math actually widens around age 12, typically during the transition to middle school (Caro, McDonald, & Willms, 2009).

© iStockphoto.com/ Christopher Futcher

Achievement and SES. Achievement differences stemming from socioeconomic status may be due to differences in access to resources such as books and computers.

Social and political events have highlighted the connection between SES and academic achievement in underserved areas such as urban and rural communities. For example, in 2003 the University of Chicago Urban Education Institute began a two-year master's program for Urban Teacher Education. Similarly, the City University of New York (CUNY) Graduate Center has developed a doctoral program in Urban Education. Both programs focus on training individuals to work in urban educational systems and conducting research to determine the best classroom practices in these areas.

In a similar fashion, many universities have centers focused on rural education within their states. Washington State University has a Rural Education Center that focuses on exchanging information among rural schools and providing a voice in policy development. Likewise, Kansas State University established the Center for Rural Education and Small Schools, which focuses on improving education in those areas. Finally, the National Research Center on Rural Education Support (NRCRES) was established in 2004 with funding from the U.S. Department of Education. The research center examines issues related to retaining qualified teachers, increasing opportunities for advanced courses, and decreasing student dropout rates in rural schools. Knowledge of current research can help inform teachers' best practices. For example, teachers may take extra time with students who lack readiness skills, allow students to borrow books from the classroom for use at home, or find creative ways to involve parents in their children's education, particularly during the transition to middle school.

Effective teachers address and embrace diversity. Their teaching is not guided by assumptions about individuals from diverse groups. **Prejudice feelings** are rigid and irrational generalizations about a group or category of people. Prejudice feelings appear to emerge very early in life and peak at about 5 to 7 years of age, with more than half of 6-year-old White children and 85% of 5-year-old White children showing signs of pro-White, anti-Black biases (Doyle & Aboud, 1995; Katz, 2003; Raabe & Beelmann, 2011). Almost every individual has some prejudice feelings toward one or more groups, even though they may not be aware of those feelings. Teachers themselves may believe that lower achieving students need to focus on basic skills. They may assume that students from lower socioeconomic backgrounds are lower achievers, that girls are not as capable in math as boys, that Asian American students are naturally smarter than members of other ethnic groups, and that gifted students are socially immature. Prejudice feelings tend to become more intense over time due to confirmation bias and belief perseverance.

Confirmation bias is the tendency for people to seek evidence that confirms what they already believe to be true, rather than searching for facts that might refute their beliefs (Mercier, 2011; Nickerson, 1998). **Belief perseverance** is the tendency to continue or persevere our beliefs even when presented with contradictory evidence (Garcia-Mila & Anderson, 2008; Savion, 2009). For example, if a woman believes that green-eyed people are exceptionally intelligent, she will notice or pay attention to all instances in which a green-eyed person says something intelligent (confirmation bias). Likewise, she will ignore or assume it was just a fluke when a green-eyed person says something silly or unintelligent (belief perseverance).

Prejudice feelings can affect the way a teacher makes decisions about instruction, grouping, motivation, and assessment. Treating individuals differently based on prejudice feelings or biased beliefs about a particular group is **discrimination**. A recent study found that 6- to 7-year-old White children discriminated against Black children when distributing coins, even in the presence of an adult. Slightly older White children, 9 to 10 years of age, also discriminated against Black children in the same task, but only when the adult was out of the room (Monteiro, de Franca, & Rodrigues, 2009). Children are not the only ones who might discriminate.

Teachers and educators must identify their own feelings of prejudice and educate themselves on the scientific evidence regarding diversity issues. However, even scientific evidence that points to group differences should be interpreted with caution due to individual differences within each group. For example, Figure 1.2 shows that average math scores are higher for boys than girls, but the amount of overlap in scores is great.

 Consider your own experiences and group membership. Have you ever treated someone differently because of the person's race, socioeconomic status, gender, or disability? If you have experienced prejudice feelings—or been on the receiving end of prejudice feelings—how and why have those beliefs persevered?

Using a Case Study Approach

Did you read the opening case study on page 2? You may have skipped it, thinking, *Why do I need to read this? How will reading this before I read the content help me?* Case studies allow preservice teachers to develop decision-making skills by considering how to apply scientific evidence to specific classroom practices. In each unit, there are four cases: (1) early childhood, (2) elementary school, (3) middle school, and (4) high school. Your instructor may ask you to read one or more of the case studies, depending on which certification level you are pursuing. Reading one or more case studies before reading a module will provide you with a realistic classroom situation to consider as you learn about the theories, research, and their application as presented in the module. To get the most out of the case study approach, pay close attention to the different categories of questions we have provided. These prompts will help you uncover important elements, make connections between science and practice, and build problem-solving skills.

FIGURE 1.2 **More Similarities than Differences.** Comparing boys' and girls' math performance historically has found mean differences, but the overlap of scores between these two groups is great, emphasizing the enormous variability within groups.

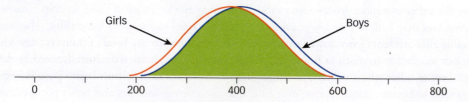

PREPARE

The Prepare questions that precede each case study will help you identify the relevant pieces of information within the case study:

- *Who?* Pay attention to characteristics of teachers, students, and parents and the relation-ships among them. These characteristics may include gender, ethnicity, disabilities, or the SES of students, parents, the teacher, or the school district.

- *What?* Attempt to identify the main problem described in the case study. Is it a behav-ioral problem, a learning problem, an instructional problem, or a classroom manage-ment problem? Each case may address more than one problem.

- *Where?* Consider where the events take place. Is it a traditional classroom, a chemistry lab, an art room, the gym, the hallway, or the principal's office? Try to envision that context and identify any characteristics that might contribute to the problem or to its solution.

- *When?* Identify time-relevant information. Does the story unfold in the morning or the late afternoon; at the beginning, middle, or end of the school year; before or after a holiday? Start thinking about how time might be related to the main problem.

ASSESS

At the end of each case study, you will find three or four Assess questions to help you evaluate your initial understanding and interpretation of the case. Because you will not yet have read the modules in the unit, you will not have the science and application to aid your thinking. Here, we will be asking you to use prior knowledge to make predictions or draw preliminary conclusions. These questions may focus on asking the following:

- *How* you might respond to the situation.

- *What* characteristics of the individuals involved contributed to the situation.

- *Why* solutions described did not work well.

REFLECT AND EVALUATE

At the end of each module, a series of Reflect and Evaluate questions will ask you to use the information presented in the module to formulate a more educated, scientific-based response to each case study:

- *How?* Rather than relying on your own opinions and experience, use the science and application discussed in the module to address the situation described in the case.

- *What?* Identify examples of key concepts in the modules.

- *Why?* Move beyond the facts of the case and focus on the characteristics and motivations of individuals. What aspects of the case study were most important, or why did one solution succeed when another failed?

- *What if . . . ?* Consider how the problem and solution presented in the case study would change if some aspect of the case were changed, such as the gender or ethnicity of stu-dents or teachers in the case study.

The Reflect and Evaluate questions will help you gauge your level of comprehension of important concepts. They will also encourage you to apply what you have learned in real-istic contexts, letting you practice the same type of informed decision making experienced teachers do.

SUMMARY

1 **Explain why educational psychology is an important resource for teachers.** Educational psychology links the science of psychology to educational practice and provides teachers with evidence-based knowledge to support their day-to-day decision making in the classroom. Teachers' choices of techniques and strategies should rely not on common-sense approaches but on scientific research.

2 **Describe three elements of research studies that help determine which studies are worthy of consideration.** First, the sample selection process for conducting research studies should attempt to use randomized samples and minimize volunteer bias. Second, measures should be selected based on how well the measure answers the research question. Third, the findings of research studies should be interpreted accurately given the limitations of the research design used, such as whether cause and effect can be established.

3 **Define best practices and explain why it is important for teachers to base them on scientific evidence.** Best practices are evidence-based strategies determined by science to help inform decisions. Because best practices of appropriate teaching methods have changed throughout

history and will continue to change in the future, teachers should become lifelong learners by using current scientific information to make decisions about best practices.

4 **Describe four diversity characteristics that can define an individual's group membership, and explain why teachers need to understand differences between groups.** (1) Ethnic groups share a common culture or environment, while race denotes a group of people who share common biological traits. (2) An individual's sex refers to his or her biology, whereas gender refers to the social definitions of masculine and feminine. (3) Socioeconomic status (SES) is defined by the educational level and occupational status of family members. (4) Disabilities also can be used as a characteristic of diversity, because individuals differ in physical, cognitive, and emotional capabilities. Teachers need to understand that group differences typically result from environmental differences and to be aware of their own prejudice feelings, which may easily be reinforced by attending to information that confirms their beliefs and by ignoring information that contradicts their beliefs or prejudice feelings.

KEY CONCEPTS

belief perseverance, 16

best practices, 11

confirmation bias, 16

correlational designs, 7

descriptive designs, 7

disability, 14

discrimination, 16

educational psychology, 5

ethnic group, 13

experimental designs, 8

gender, 14

interviews, 10

minority group, 13

observations, 10

prejudice feelings, 15

quasi-experimental designs, 8

racial group, 13

random sample, 9

research design, 7

sample, 9

sex, 14

sexual orientation, 14

socioeconomic status (SES), 14

tests and surveys, 10

theories, 6

variables, 7

volunteer bias, 10

CASE STUDY: REFLECT AND EVALUATE

MIDDLE SCHOOL: ACHIEVEMENT GAP

These questions refer to the case study on page 2.

1. Why are the resources available in school districts important for understanding differences among teachers and students?

2. Why is knowledge that the sample was college students important for interpreting the results of the study?

3. Why is the survey measure used in the study problematic? What might be an alternative measure?

4. What type of research design was used in the study? What type of information can be interpreted from this type of research design?

5. Based on the information presented in the module about prejudice feelings, why would some people have a difficult time believing that African American students and White students can achieve at equal levels?

6. If the study had been done with K-12 students in various school districts assessing their GPA from official records over several years, how would this alter the way the results might be interpreted?

APPLY AND PRACTICE WHAT YOU'VE LEARNED

▶ edge.sagepub.com/durwin3e

**CHECK YOUR COMPREHENSION
ON THE STUDENT STUDY SITE**

- **eFlashcards** to strengthen your understanding of key terms

- Practice **quizzes** to test your knowledge of key concepts

- **Videos and multimedia content** to enhance your exploration of key topics

UNIT ONE

PERSONAL DEVELOPMENT

EARLY CHILDHOOD: CRY BABY

PREPARE:

As you read the case, make notes:

1. WHO are the central characters in the case? Describe them.
2. WHAT is taking place?
3. WHERE is the case taking place? Is the environment a factor?
4. WHEN is the case taking place? Is the timing a factor?

Edward Abbott and Linda Harsted are teachers at a local child care facility in the 4-year-old preschool room. The 20 students are from diverse backgrounds with a range of levels of socioeconomic status. At this preschool, the children are taught letter recognition, colors, fine and large motor skills, and many other readiness skills. The teachers also spend a large portion of the day encouraging social behaviors such as sharing, helping, expressing assertiveness without aggression, and behaving respectfully toward others. Each year the teachers prepare kindergarten readiness reports to share with parents during a brief individual conference. To prepare for parent–teacher conferences, Ms. Harsted spent last week observing the children during centers to assess their educational skills while Mr. Abbott supervised the children. This week, Mr. Abbott will observe the children to assess their social behaviors while Ms. Harsted supervises. Centers include a number of activities, including playing house, having a snack, coloring, and playing with blocks and puzzles. Children in groups of four spend 15 minutes on each activity.

Mr. Abbott begins during snack time, when the children are having cheese crackers and juice. He quickly notices that Joe is helping Allison clean up her spilled juice that has soaked her crackers. Joe offers to share his crackers with Allison. Mr. Abbott thinks about how typical this behavior is of Joe. He is a very considerate child, always willing to help others. Mr. Abbott then turns his attention to Annie and Zada, who are arguing.

Annie says, "Zada, you aren't my best friend anymore!"

Zada replies, "Well, you didn't share your crayons with me before, so I don't have to share my crackers with you. You got your crackers! I don't have to give you some of mine."

Mr. Abbott has already commented in his notes for Annie and Zada that both girls tend to be natural leaders, which can result in problems, as both want to be "boss."

Ms. Harsted intervenes and asks Zada, "How did you feel earlier when Annie wouldn't share her crayons?"

Zada replies, "She was mean, so I was sad."

"Well, I bet that Annie is sad now because you won't share with her," states Ms. Harsted.

"Okay, she can have this one cracker, but only if I get to be the mommy when we play house," replies Zada.

Annie quickly responds, "Okay."

Mr. Abbott and Ms. Harsted exchange looks, because both know that Annie's home life is much different from Zada's. Zada's parents are married and middle class and spend much of their extra time with Zada and her brother. Both children were adopted when their parents were in their 40s. Yesterday, Zada told everyone about a recent family trip to a museum. Annie's parents are divorced. Her father lives halfway across the country with his new wife and Annie's new baby sister. Annie's mother works first shift at the local hospital as a nurse's aide and spends several evenings a week socializing with friends.

Mr. Abbott moves over to the block area. He notices that Tyler and Tanner are building a tall tower. Erica begins to place more blocks on the tower, but Tyler shouts, "That one doesn't go there!" The loud shout startles Erica, who bumps the tower, and all the blocks come tumbling down.

Tanner yells, "You did that on purpose. We told you that girls aren't supposed to play with blocks."

"Yeah," adds Tyler, "you ruined everything!"

Erica begins to cry. Tyler adds, "See, you are just a little cry baby. Cry baby. Cry baby . . . ."

"Boys, I want you to stop talking to Erica that way," interjects Mr. Abbott. "I saw the whole thing, and Erica didn't mean to knock down the tower. How do you think she feels when you make fun of her like that?"

Tyler jumps in, "Well, she's probably sad, but that's not our fault. We didn't knock down the tower."

"Maybe she's sad because you were blaming her for an accident and then calling her a cry baby," says Mr. Abbott. "Wouldn't you be sad too if someone blamed you and called you a cry baby?" he asks.

© iStockphoto.com/ vgajic

"I wouldn't care," answers Tanner.

Mr. Abbott comments in his observation notes that Tyler is always quick to blame others yet rarely takes responsibility for his own actions. Mr. Abbott thinks about how all the children have difficulty understanding how another child might feel, but some have more trouble than others.

ASSESS:

1. How typical are the behaviors in this classroom?

2. Why do you think some children are so eager to be helpful and to share while other children are so quick to assign blame and respond in a negative manner?

3. How do you think the gender of each child plays a role in his or her behaviors?

CASE STUDIES

ELEMENTARY SCHOOL: Team

Rocío Barone is one of two first-grade teachers at a small rural elementary school. She was raised in a large metropolitan area and is continually amazed at the connections her students share. For example, three students in the first grade this year—Patricia, Kelly, and Samantha—are all cousins. In addition to familial connections, many of the parents attended high school together and have been friends for years, with their children growing up highly connected to one another outside school. Ms. Barone has always had a soft spot for the children who lack those connections within the community. Kashi is a good example. She moved to the small rural community last year. Kashi is the only student in first grade who is African American. All the other students and almost everyone in the community are White. She had a rough transition to the school because her parents were getting a divorce that led to the move. Kashi seemed to have made friends and to have adjusted to the new curriculum last year. But this year she is struggling academically, and the children appear uninterested in playing with her on the playground or being her partner during classroom activities.

As Kashi enters the classroom, she squabbles with Patricia, one of the oldest but smallest children in the class, who also has experienced challenges adjusting to first grade. After kindergarten, Patricia was placed in a special pre-first-grade program for children who need extra time to develop academically or socially. Having her cousins in the same class has helped with the transition, but she continues to struggle with reading and math.

"Well, if you don't want to sit with me at lunch," says Kashi, "then you can't be on my team."

"I don't want to be on your team," Patricia replies. "My mom says I can do whatever I want on the playground. You know, Kashi, you aren't the boss!"

Ms. Barone intervenes and attempts to calm the situation. "Girls, please try to get along and speak nicely to each other. Now, take your seats so we can start our day."

As the day continues, Ms. Barone notes that Patricia and Kashi appear to have resolved their differences for the moment and are working on their science project together without bickering. This is typical for these two girls. One minute they are playing or working nicely together, referring to each other as "best friends," and the next minute one is telling on the other for saying or doing something "mean." Ms. Barone has always had trouble getting either of them to give specifics of the mean behavior.

As Ms. Barone asks the children to form their line and leave for lunch, two boys—Bill and Zach—begin pushing and shoving each other in the back of the line.

Bill shouts, "I am tired of you always bumping into me!"

Ms. Barone moves quickly to the back of the line and says, "Boys, please keep your hands to . . ."

Zach interrupts, saying to Bill, "Well, I didn't mean to bump you, and besides I am tired of you always cutting in line at lunch. You are such a bully to everyone—my dad says you are just like your dad was in school!"

"At least my dad isn't a sissy," says Bill, who is very tall and athletic. "I didn't hurt you or anyone else. You're just like a little girl."

Ms. Barone states firmly, "Both of you stop right now. You should be ashamed of yourselves for talking to each other that way."

Both boys keep looking at each other with angry faces, but they discontinue their verbal and physical assaults. Ms. Barone sends the other children to lunch and has a short talk with the boys.

"Now, Bill, accidents do happen, and Zach may not have meant to bump into you. And Zach, it is not nice to call others names. You both need to keep your hands to yourself."

The boys give a quick "okay" and walk to lunch.

During the lunch break, Ms. Barone checks her e-mail. Patricia's mom, Mary, has sent an e-mail to tell Ms. Barone that Patricia has been very upset about how Kashi treats her at school. The e-mail reads as follows:

> Ms. Barone,
>
> We have been having several conversations in the evening about Patricia and Kashi. Patricia tells me that Kashi has a "team" of girls and if Patricia doesn't do what Kashi asked then she cannot be on the "team." Her dad and I have tried to explain that Patricia should not allow others to boss her around and talk her into doing things she doesn't want to do. I am already somewhat concerned about Patricia's self-esteem and want her to have enough self-confidence to stand up for herself. I typically would have continued to try and work with Patricia at home on this issue, but now something else has happened and I thought you should be aware. Last week I was told by my friend who works in the cafeteria that Patricia doesn't always take all the food options because Kashi is whispering to her to only take the food that Kashi likes. I understand that a teacher cannot know everything that happens during the day, especially on the playground or at lunch, but I wanted you to know about this issue. Any advice you can give us to help Patricia deal with these issues would be helpful.
>
> Mary

©iStockphoto.com/carrollphoto

ASSESS:

1. How well do you think Ms. Barone handled the girls entering the classroom? How well do you think she handled the boys in the lunch line? Do you think gender played a role in her treatment of the incidents?

2. What examples of aggression did you notice?

3. What factors in the children's lives might have contributed to their behavior?

4. How would you respond to Mary's e-mail?

CASE STUDIES

MIDDLE SCHOOL: BASKETBALL STAR

PREPARE:

As you read the case, make notes:

1. WHO are the central characters in the case? Describe them.

2. WHAT is taking place?

3. WHERE is the case taking place? Is the environment a factor?

4. WHEN is the case taking place? Is the timing a factor?

Tyrone Martin is the middle school girls' basketball coach. The middle school is located in a suburb of a large metropolitan city, with students from mostly middle- to upper-middle-class homes. Mr. Martin has been teaching English at the school for three years. He was the coach for boys' basketball at his last job and enjoyed the out-of-class experience with his students. When he was asked by the principal to coach girls' basketball this year while the usual coach takes a leave of absence, he was excited about the opportunity. However, he has experienced some difficulties getting the girls to work as a team.

As Jill and Sierra enter the gym for practice, he overhears them whispering about Darla. Darla is very athletic but doesn't seem to fit in with the "popular" group of girls. Darla is already practicing and too far away to hear their conversation.

Mr. Martin overhears Jill saying, "If she thinks we are going to let her steal the show on the basketball court, she can forget it."

"The only reason she is any good is because her dad makes her play basketball every night for like three hours!" adds Sierra. "He thinks Darla is going to be some big star! Too bad she doesn't have a mother around to show her how to act."

Claudia, who appears to socialize with Darla, walks up behind the girls and overhears their conversation. She states loudly, "Well, Sierra, you have had three mothers now with all your dad's divorces and remarriages, and you're still not a lady. Maybe you should spend a little more time with your father. Oh, that's right, he's too busy to pay attention to anything you're doing."

Mr. Martin defuses the situation by announcing that the girls need to take their positions for a scrimmage. He begins to think about Darla. Mr. Martin has noticed in the past that Darla does not seem to have many friends. Claudia has repeatedly attempted to include Darla in social events, but Darla doesn't seem to respond with excitement, appreciation, or even a simple "Thanks, but no thanks." Rather, she seems to be uninterested in having friends or a social life.

Mr. Martin decides to have a talk with Darla after practice to see if he can help determine what might be the problem. He begins by asking Darla, "How do you like basketball this year?"

Darla replies, "I like it. I just wish the other girls were more dedicated to the game. They seem to think they are going to be movie stars or models."

"Well, what would you like to be when you grow up?" asks Mr. Martin.

"My dad says I should be a basketball player because I have a lot of natural talent. That's why I don't worry too much about those other girls and what they say about me. I know I am a good athlete. And I am going to take business classes in high school so that I can manage my own career and money when I make it big," says Darla with a slight smile.

Mr. Martin pushes her on the issue a bit. "Have you ever considered doing anything else?"

Darla replies quickly, "No way! My dad really wants me to be a basketball player. That's who I am. It's in my blood. Basketball is what makes me Darla. I am not good at many other things, especially school and making friends off the basketball court. So I'm sure I'll be a basketball player."

©iStockphoto.com/Craig Dingle

Mr. Martin ends the conversation, saying, "Well, Darla, I am glad you have such a clear vision of your future, but don't be afraid to change that vision. As people make their way through high school and college, most change their minds about what and who they want to be in the future. Just keep your options open, okay?"

"Okay, but I already know who I am and where I'm going," says Darla.

As Mr. Martin begins to put away the equipment, he thinks about a boy at his last school. Mark also didn't have many friends or the skills to make friends. Rather, he had a short temper and typically was in other students' faces about something they had done to him or, at least, what Mark thought they had done to him. He never thought his remarks or retaliatory behaviors were as bad as those of the other kids. Mark and Darla had similar backgrounds, in that their parents were divorced and each lived with their father. Mr. Martin wonders how two children from such similar backgrounds could act so different yet have so few friends.

ASSESS:

1. Darla seems to be a loner. Is this a bad thing? Why or why not?

2. What are some examples of appropriate social behavior? What are some examples of aggressive behavior?

3. How likely do you think it is that Darla will become a basketball player? Give the reasons for your answer.

EARLY CHILDHOOD

ELEMENTARY SCHOOL

MIDDLE SCHOOL

HIGH SCHOOL

CASE STUDIES

HIGH SCHOOL: Steal, Cheat, and Fight

PREPARE:

As you read the case, make notes:

1. WHO are the central characters in the case? Describe them.
2. WHAT is taking place?
3. WHERE is the case taking place? Is the environment a factor?
4. WHEN is the case taking place? Is the timing a factor?

Rebecca Durbin is the principal at one of the three high schools located in a small city with a population of approximately 100,000. The school enrollment is approximately 2,500 students. Recently, there have been a number of incidents related to cheating, stealing, and drinking, as well as a number of verbal and physical fights. Ms. Durbin decides to use next Friday's school improvement day to address these behavioral issues. To prepare for the workshop, she sends an e-mail to all the teachers and staff asking for examples of these behaviors and suggestions for how the school system should handle the issue. She receives a number of responses, including the following:

Mr. Smith (freshman English) wrote: Last week I wasted five minutes of class time breaking up an exchange between Lisa and Kiana. Basically, the girls were engaged in a verbal assault on each other, saying things such as "You're fat and ugly" and "Your mom is a slut." I was very disturbed by their comments, but I don't have many suggestions. I am just thankful they didn't start a cat fight during my lecture!

Ms. Baxter (advanced mathematics) wrote: I know we have several groups of students who don't apply themselves. For instance, there is that whole group of kids who stand across the street after school smoking (one of whom spent the night in jail last weekend for driving under the influence) and the group of girls who walk around the school like they are dressed for a night out on the town. However, I don't think it is the school's place to dictate how they dress or to meddle in their behavior outside the school. I am much more concerned about the students who are here to learn and their inability to determine their career paths. Many of them are very academically talented yet have no direction or ideas about where to go to college or what their major will be. I think our time is better spent guiding them into good colleges and career paths.

Ms. Presley (office staff manager) wrote: I have been working in high schools for over 20 years now and honestly believe that the school has little control over these teenagers. The problem is the breakdown of the family. So many of our students come from broken homes without a mother or a father, or they have the opposite problem—too many parents and stepparents. Plus, almost all of our mothers are out working full-time jobs, leaving no one at home to take care of these children when they leave school in the afternoon. I suggest we offer parenting classes and family counseling to keep families together.

Mr. Ruestman (biology) wrote: The problem is that we simply don't have the time to deal with all these issues. I have too much course content to cover to continually be dealing with the problems students have with their friends. Very few seem to know how to control their anger or how to think about how others might be feeling, and they don't understand that the world does not revolve around them. They all seem to be overly concerned about their friendships, who is friends with whom, who was and wasn't invited to the party, yet they lack the skills to make and keep friends. Maybe some form of social skills training would help, but not during my class time.

Mr. Cargill (physical education) wrote: Just yesterday, Jimmy was sent to the office for hitting Bob. Apparently, Bob was talking about another Jim, commenting on his sister. The whole thing was taken out of context, and Jimmy hauled off and hit him. If Jimmy would have taken two seconds to look at Bob and pay attention to his tone of voice and nonverbal behaviors, Jimmy would have realized that the comments were not inappropriate or derogatory, and they were not even about his sister but another Jim's sister. Bob was actually commenting on how nice this young lady had been, helping him with his math homework during study hall. These kids need a lesson in how to read others' intentions and behaviors as well as how to handle their own emotions.

Ms. Kennel (chemistry) wrote: I am mostly concerned about the girls and minority students in our school. The girls seem to be lacking in confidence, particularly in academics and even more so in math and science. I think we need to find a way to boost their egos and give them the confidence they will need out there in the real world. Maybe with a little more confidence they would stop worrying so much about their friends, boyfriends, and other relationships. The minority students may also need a boost, but even more they need to stop grouping together according to their ethnicity. Do you know we now have a whole group of students who are referred to as the "Spans" because they all speak Spanish? We need to incorporate all ethnic groups into our school and educate every student on the issues of diversity in our country.

Ms. May (special education) wrote:
The behaviors of stealing, cheating, and aggression in this school are due to a basic lack of respect for authority. We need to have firm policies on these issues and stick to them. Most students simply don't think it is a big deal to cheat, lie, or steal, and in many classes it is because teachers let them get away with these behaviors. We need every teacher on board to enforce the rules of the school.

Helen King/Corbis/Getty Images

ASSESS:

1. What are some of the recurring themes within these responses from the teachers and staff?

2. For each person's e-mail, give a score based on how much you agree with the view
(1 = *completely disagree*, 2 = *somewhat disagree*, 3 = *somewhat agree*, 4 = *completely agree*).
Briefly explain why you agree or disagree with each e-mail response and whether your rating is based on experience, observation, or opinion.

3. Do you think gender might be important in handling these issues? Why or why not?

4. Do you think it is appropriate for the principal and teachers to use school time to address issues related to social and emotional behaviors?

Peter Cade/The Image Bank/Getty Images

MODULE **2**

CONTEXTS OF DEVELOPMENT

OUTLINE	LEARNING GOALS
Bronfenbrenner's Bioecological Theory	
	❶ Describe Bronfenbrenner's bioecological theory.
Family Context	
• Parenting Practices • Divorce and Remarriage	❷ Describe how parenting styles and family transitions interact with the school system.
Peer Context	
• Friendships and Peer Groups • Peer Statuses	❸ Describe how aspects of the peer context interact with the school system.
Broader Contexts	
• Parental Employment • Cultural Factors	❹ Explain how broader contexts of development influence microsystems and individual outcomes.

BRONFENBRENNER'S BIOECOLOGICAL THEORY

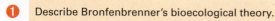

❶ Describe Bronfenbrenner's bioecological theory.

Who is the most influential person in your life now? Who was it five years ago? You can probably think of several people who have made a difference in your life. As children and adolescents, we grow and develop with the support and influence of people and places: our family members, friends, and teachers, and our neighborhoods and schools. Because of their influence on development, these people and places are considered *contexts of development.* Urie Bronfenbrenner's (1994, 2005) bioecological theory of human development, the best-known theory on the

FIGURE 2.1   Bronfenbrenner's Bioecological Model.

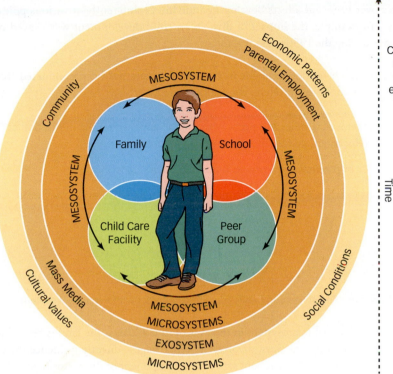

contexts of development, emphasizes the combined function of the person (or genetics) and the many systems that exist in the environment and interact to influence development, as shown in Figure 2.1. Let's examine this model more closely. It will be the framework for our discussion on the contexts of development throughout this module.

- The **microsystem,** the immediate environment surrounding an individual, includes the people, relationships, and systems that directly interact with the developing individual, such as family, peers, and school.

- The **mesosystem** links two or more microsystems. For example, the communication between parents and teachers links home and school environments or home and child care settings.

- The **exosystem** is the interaction among two or more environments, one of which does not directly include the individual. For developing children and adolescents, the exosystem includes links between home and their parents' places of work. The developing child typically has no direct interaction with a parent's workplace but is influenced by that environment indirectly. For example, parental work stress influences children's adjustment.

- The **macrosystem** includes many of the broader cultural patterns, such as beliefs, customs, knowledge, and morals. Bronfenbrenner suggests that this is not simply the ethnicity or social class of individuals but rather the social features that affect individuals. For example, low-income children may experience more stressors in their

Reference: Ecological Systems Theory

macrosystem—substandard housing, crowding, or community violence—than do middle-class children (Santiago, Wadsworth, & Stump, 2011).

- The **chronosystem** refers to the chronological nature of development within the individual as well as the history of the surrounding environment. The social environment changes over time and affects developing individuals differently at various points in history. For example, the impact of divorce on child development was viewed more negatively during the 1950s than it is today.

Much of the research on development in the past 30 years has been conducted from a bioecological perspective. In this module, we will examine:

- the microsystems of families and peers, with special emphasis on the interaction of these within the educational system (in other words, mesosystem);

- the influence of parental employment on development (exosystem);

- connections to ethnicity and socioeconomic status (macrosystem) as they relate to the microsystems.

FAMILY CONTEXT

② Describe how parenting styles and family transitions interact with the school system.

Arguably, the most influential microsystem in the lives of individuals is the family. Several basic aspects of families—parenting practices, divorce and remarriage—directly influence the child and how the family interacts with the school system as a component of the mesosystem.

Parenting Practices

Video: Parenting Principles

Reference: Parenting Styles

Parenting practices, also called parenting styles, are the patterns of discipline and affection parents display with their children. These have an important influence on child and adolescent development. Diana Baumrind (1966) described parenting practices as typically including two broad dimensions: control and responsiveness. **Control** is the manner and strictness with which parents provide their children with limits and discipline. **Responsiveness** includes the affection, acceptance, and caring involved in parenting. In short, control describes the *behavioral* aspects of parenting, while responsiveness describes the *emotional* aspects. Based on the levels of these two dimensions, Baumrind describes four parenting styles, as shown in Table 2.1.

- **Authoritative parenting** includes setting limits or having rules for children and adolescents and enforcing those rules. Parents and children also exhibit a high level of emotional connectedness that allows the parents to be flexible when necessary. For example, parents may be less strict than usual because they understand that their child is having difficulty with peers at school or is upset about not making the cheerleading squad.

- **Authoritarian parenting** includes a high level of control in which limits are set and rules are enforced yet emotional connectedness is lacking. Parents may be viewed as "dictators" who are inflexible, unable to bend the rules to accommodate special or unusual circumstances. For example, a parent might make a negative comment regarding the B on the child's report card when all the other grades are As.

- **Permissive parenting** involves less control, with parents either not setting rules for behavior or not enforcing rules. However, parents do have a close connection to their

TABLE 2.1   Baumrind's Parenting Practices

	RESPONSIVENESS	
	HIGH ⟵⟶ LOW	
HIGH ↑ CONTROL ↓ LOW	**Authoritative** Limits are set and rules are enforced, but parents are flexible when necessary. Parents and children exhibit a high level of emotional connectedness.	**Authoritarian** Limits are set and rules are enforced, yet emotional connectedness is lacking. Parents are inflexible, unable to bend the rules in special or unusual circumstances.
	Permissive Parents either do not set rules for behavior or do not enforce established rules. However, parents do have a close connection to their children.	**Uninvolved** Parenting lacks both control and responsiveness. Parents typically are unaware of their child's behavior, friends, difficulties, or achievements.

children such that observers might refer to them as "friends" rather than parents. For example, parents may show their affection by giving in to their child's tantrums in the grocery line and buying candy, or they may ground their adolescent but not monitor whether the teenager is home.

Video: Parenting Styles Quiz

- **Uninvolved parenting** lacks both control and responsiveness. Parents typically are unaware of their child's behavior, friends, difficulties, or achievements. For example, a parent may not know when reports come home from school or may be unable to name his or her child's friends. These parents are at risk of being neglectful or abusive.

Research studies consistently link authoritative parenting with positive outcomes. Children and adolescents with authoritative parents tend to have higher levels of healthy adjustment and fewer mental health issues or problem behaviors (De la Torre-Cruz, García-Linares, & Casanova-Arias, 2014; Luyckx et al., 2011; Windle et al., 2010). However, the optimal parenting style may depend on the broader cultural context within which the parents and children are living. Specifically, authoritarian parenting may be important for deterring antisocial behavior among young adolescents residing in low-income neighborhoods with high rates of unemployment and an insufficient police presence (Eamon, 2001; Shek, 2005).

> **DIVERSITY**

How do parenting practices interact with the school system? Remember that an interaction between two microsystems—in this case family and school—is called the mesosystem. The interaction between the family and school microsystems is evident because authoritative parenting is related to academic benefits among a variety of ethnic groups for both elementary-age students and high school students (Kang & Moore, 2011; Mandara, 2006; Nyarko, 2011; Pong, Johnston, & Chen, 2009). For example, students with authoritative parents tend to have higher achievement and better attitudes toward school, spend more time on homework, are more engaged with teachers and learning, and have lower levels of maladaptive behavior in the classroom (Duchesne & Ratelle, 2010; Simons-Morton & Chen, 2009; Walker & Hoover-Dempsey, 2006). Teachers are unlikely to be able to change the parenting practices a student experiences at home, but they can gain much insight into the reasons for children's and adolescents' behaviors in the classroom based on knowledge about those parenting practices.

Can you determine which parenting practice was used in your home? If you had two parents, were their parenting practices the same or different? How do you think parenting practices influenced your educational experiences or academic achievement?

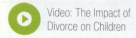 Video: The Impact of Divorce on Children

Divorce and Remarriage

Approximately 50% of all first marriages and 60% or more of second marriages end in divorce (Copen, Daniels, Vespa, & Mosher, 2012; Fine & Harvey, 2006). As a result, nearly half of all children in the United States will live in a single-parent family for some length of time (Hetherington et al., 1999). Although not all children and adolescents experience problems following divorce, some do. Children and adolescents may also experience difficulties prior to the divorce. In fact, they tend to have the greatest difficulties a few years before and after the divorce, as indicated by poorer academic performance (Sun & Li, 2011). The difficulties surrounding divorce are thought to be the result of changes in the *functioning* of the family rather than *structural* changes (Demo & Acock, 1996). Changes in the functioning of families include a number of possible issues:

1. *Family conflict* surrounding divorce is an important aspect of family functioning related to children's and adolescents' adjustment (Amato & Cheadle, 2008; Bing, Nelson, & Wesolowski, 2009). Although marital conflict occurs prior to the divorce, the level of conflict often increases around the time of divorce. Children living in high-conflict, intact families experience difficulties similar to those experienced by children in divorced families (Yu, Pettit, Lansford, Dodge, & Bates, 2010). In particular, school problems may arise as a result of attention difficulties. Children who are worried or concerned about the stability of their parents' relationship may be less able to focus, leading to poor peer relations and behavioral problems at school (Bascoe, Davies, Cummings, & Sturge-Apple, 2009).

2. *Disorganized parenting practices,* which may occur during divorce as parents are coping with their own distress, play a role in children's social and cognitive functioning as rated by their teachers (Forehand, Thomas, Wierson, Brody, & Fauber, 1990). Parents who once were authoritative may become overwhelmed by their own problems, have few cognitive resources available for their children, and become lax in their monitoring and supervision of children (Hetherington, 1991; Nair & Murray, 2005). Children tend to have fewer difficulties following divorce when parental discipline is consistent across homes (Amato, Kane, & James, 2011).

3. *Decreases in family economics* also can have a negative impact on the functioning of families (Amato & Keith, 1991; Esmaeili, Yaacob, Juhari, & Mansor, 2011; Pong, 1997, 1998). Parents who were not employed outside the home may need to obtain employment, or parents who were employed may need to work longer hours or earn a second income in order to sustain the level of economics within the home (exosystem). Postdivorce economics may lead to the family moving to a smaller home or a lower socioeconomic status (SES) neighborhood (macrosystem), which may lead to poorer school achievement.

DIVERSITY Some children—because of their developmental level, gender, personality, or relationships—may have a tougher time dealing with divorce than others do (Davies & Windle, 2001; Hetherington, Bridges, & Insabella, 1998), especially:

-   younger children;
-   boys more than girls;
-   children placed in custody with the opposite-sex parent (typically boys);

- children who have a difficult temperament or who have always been less able to adjust to change within their environment;
- children who do not have a supportive relationship with an adult outside the immediate family (for example, teacher, aunt, uncle, coach).

Although most difficulties occur around the time of divorce, children whose parents have been divorced for years may encounter problems again during adolescence; this is called the **sleeper effect** (Hetherington, 1993). Adolescents experiencing the sleeper effect exhibit difficulties such as drug and alcohol use, behavioral problems, poor school performance, and poor interpersonal relationships—including higher rates of divorce themselves later in life. The awakening of these difficulties is thought to occur because the period of adolescence introduces more opportunity to engage in drugs and alcohol use and to develop intimate relationships with peers and romantic partners, typically not a factor during childhood (Sarigiani & Spierling, 2011).

Some of the same family functioning issues surrounding divorce, such as family conflict and disruptions in parenting styles, continue to exist in remarried homes (Hetherington et al., 1998). Children's and adolescents' well-being suffers each time a transition or change occurs within the family. Remarriage adds a second transition to the family dynamics. As a result, adolescents from stepfamilies may have lower academic achievement and more involvement in delinquent acts than adolescents from single-parent homes (Amato & Keith, 1991; Hetherington, 1993; Sun & Li, 2009, 2011). Some children are particularly at risk for experiencing difficulties following remarriage, including (Hetherington et al., 1998; Sun & Li, 2009):

> **DIVERSITY**

- older children;
- girls more than boys;
- children with more difficult temperaments.

How do divorce and remarriage within the family interact with the school in the mesosystem? Children from both divorced and remarried families are more likely to have lower academic achievement and more problematic school behavior than children from intact families (Kurdek & Sinclair, 1988; Potter, 2010; Sun & Li, 2011). Understanding that family

Yellow Dog Productions/Iconica/Getty Images

Family Transitions. Children and adolescents experience fewer difficulties during family transitions when they have a supportive relationship with an adult outside the family, such as a teacher or coach.

functioning may be the reason for such difficulties and that particular children may be more likely to experience these difficulties allows educators the opportunity to provide the support necessary to assist these children during family transitions. Children and adolescents who have a supportive adult relationship outside the family—such as a strong relationship with a particular teacher—are less likely to experience difficulties (Dornbusch et al., 1985; Hetherington, 1993). On the other hand, teachers also may unwittingly form negative expectations about students based on their individual characteristics and family circumstances. This could lead to a **self-fulfilling prophecy**—an unfounded expectation that becomes true simply because it was expected. For example, a teacher who is aware of the relationship between divorce and achievement may expect less of children of divorce, which can lead to behaviors that cause the student to achieve less in school.

Teachers in today's classrooms encounter children from various family structures. Knowledge about family functioning and structure provides teachers with a context for understanding why some children may experience difficulties in the school setting. However, family background should not be used as a rationale to lower expectations for some students. Instead, it can provide information about who is most likely to need additional support and assistance within the microsystem of the school.

PEER CONTEXT

❸ Describe how aspects of the peer context interact with the school system.

After families, peers are considered the second most important microsystem influencing development. Let's examine the development of friendships and peer groups among children and adolescents, as well as how peer status can interact with the educational experience (mesosystem).

Friendships and Peer Groups

Friendships are important because having friends during childhood and adolescence is related to several positive outcomes. For example, children with close friendships tend to have more

Video: The Importance of Peer Groups

Friendship Development. Preschool-age friendships are based on moment-to-moment interactions.

© iStockphoto.com/SolStock

social competence, greater self-confidence, and higher self-esteem, as well as fewer difficulties with school transitions and better academic performance (Bagwell & Schmidt, 2011; Hartup, 1996). Parents and teachers therefore should attempt to promote friendships among children and adolescents while understanding that friendships undergo changes throughout development.

Friendships among preschool-age children are qualitatively different from friendships among adolescents. In early and middle childhood, children base their friendships on moment-to-moment interactions. For example, two preschool-age children might be playing well together and consider themselves best friends, but a moment of not sharing or an unwillingness to submit to the other's request can lead to anger, resulting in the children announcing that they are no longer friends. Within a few minutes, the children may resume interactions and once again announce that they are friends. Friendships among children in later childhood and early adolescence are based on more stable and similar qualities, such as typical play interests (we both like Barbies or video games) or typical qualities of sharing and kindness. In adolescence, friendships become based on common values and more complex interests, such as attitudes toward school, career aspirations, and achievement (Bagwell & Schmidt, 2011; Hartup, 1996). As a result, distinct peer groups begin to emerge during adolescence.

Over the past 25 years, much of the research on peer group formation during adolescence has been conducted and written by B. Bradford Brown and his colleagues (Brown, 1990, 2004; Brown & Braun, 2013; Brown & Klute, 2006). During middle school, groups of peers begin to form cliques and crowds. **Cliques** are small groups of two to eight people who know each other very well. Cliques provide opportunities to learn social skills, discover how to communicate in interpersonal relationships, and, for some, practice leadership roles within small groups. Many times these small groups have a social structure or place in which time is spent together. For example, one clique may hang out at the local restaurant, another may congregate at the school, and another may gather at one adolescent's home.

Clique members typically are very similar on a number of demographic characteristics, such as age, SES, and race, as well as on shared activities (for example, dress and music) and values (Hamm, 2000; Hartup, 1996; Schaefer, Simpkins, Vest, & Price, 2011). For example, members of a clique typically have similar beliefs about the importance of school and academic achievement, as well as similar levels of involvement in delinquent behavior and substance use (Becker & Curry, 2014; Brechwald & Prinstein, 2011; Jones, Audley-Piotrowski, & Kiefer, 2011). In addition, cliques typically include same-sex friends during middle school but develop into mixed-sex groups during high school (Xie & Shi, 2009). The similarities among clique members may be due to the following processes:

- *Peer selection process*—adolescents seeking out others similar to themselves.

- *Peer socialization process*—dissimilar adolescents becoming more similar over time.

In contrast to the small, interaction-based peer cliques, **crowds** are larger, reputation-based peer groups that typically have common labels across school districts and vary across gender (Sussman, Pokhrel, Ashmore, & Brown, 2007; Youniss, McLellan, & Strouse, 1994). They include the following:

- Populars/preps (elites)—having many friends, being well-known, being cool, being highly social (more likely to be girls than boys).

- Jocks (athletes)—participating in sports and physical activities (more likely to be boys than girls).

- Brains/nerds (academics)—being smart and showing high academic performance (equally likely to be girls or boys).

- Normals (others)—being average or normal, being cool, being highly social (more likely to be girls than boys).

Social competence and self-esteem: See Module 3

Video Case 2.1 ▲
Peer Factors in the Classroom

© SAGE Publications

Social skills: See Module 3

- Druggies/partiers/burnouts (deviants)—using drugs, alcohol, and physical aggression (more likely to be boys than girls).

- Loners—belonging to a small group, having few friendships, being nonconforming (more likely to be girls than boys).

Identity development:
See Module 3

Self-Esteem: See
Module 3

By ninth grade, most adolescents agree on who belongs to which crowd within the school system, and these labels provide adolescents with a basis for identity development—that is, understanding who they are and how they fit into society (Brown & Larson, 2009; Newman & Newman, 2001). Crowds tend to be hierarchical during middle school and hence are related to self-esteem, or how positively individuals feel about themselves. Adolescents in higher status crowds such as preps and jocks typically have higher self-esteem than individuals in lower status crowds such as druggies (Helms, Choukas-Bradley, Giletta, Cohen, & Prinstein, 2014; Prinstein & La Greca, 2002). The hierarchy of crowds changes over time, and membership within these crowds is more easily changed during the later years of high school, such that individuals may be members of more than one crowd (Youniss et al., 1994).

The interaction between the peer and school microsystems is another example of the mesosystem in Bronfenbrenner's bioecological model. As discussed earlier, children with friends tend to have better school performance and to handle school transitions, such as the move from elementary to middle school, better than children who lack friendships. Similarly, affiliation with cliques and crowds during adolescence promotes social skills and identity formation, both of which are related to higher levels of academic achievement (Denham et al., 2003; Flashman, 2012; Jones et al., 2011). As a result, teachers should attempt to foster friendships among peers early in students' development and should continue to support peer group formation throughout adolescence.

 Can you list the friends who were in your clique during high school? Which crowd label best represents you during high school? How did those peer groups help or hinder your academic progress?

Peer Statuses

In addition to friendships and peer groups, the social status of individuals among their peers is an important factor in the microsystem of peers. Peer social status typically is determined by both socially appropriate behaviors (for example, caring, leadership skills) and aggressive behaviors. Positive social behaviors and aggression are important determinants of peer status across developmental levels—with preschool-age children as well as elementary, middle, and high school students—and among rural African American adolescents (Burr, Ostrov, Jansen, Cullerton-Sen, & Crick, 2005; Farmer, Estell, Bishop, O'Neal, & Cairns, 2003; Rose, Swenson, & Carlson, 2004).

DIVERSITY

In discussing the peer context, aggression typically sparks ideas of physical or **overt aggression,** such as fighting, with the intent to harm another physically. Research has defined a second type of aggression: relational aggression (Crick & Grotpeter, 1995). **Relational aggression** refers to behaviors specifically intended to damage another child's friendships, social status, or feelings of inclusion in a peer group. Such behaviors include gossiping, rumor spreading, and excluding someone as a way to control them. In childhood and adolescence, boys are more likely to use overt aggression, whereas girls are more likely to display relational aggression, especially during middle school (Crick & Grotpeter, 1995; Mathieson & Crick, 2010; Ostrov & Crick, 2007).

Children and adolescents have been categorized into several peer statuses based on socially appropriate and aggressive behaviors with peers: popular, rejected, or neglected.

POPULAR

Using different approaches, researchers have determined that there are actually two separate forms of popularity (Brown & Larson, 2009; Cillessen & Rose, 2005). In the first type, **sociometric popularity,** students nominate peers whom they most like and most dislike within

© iStockphoto.com/Nesho

© iStockphoto.com/PeopleImages

Gender and Aggression. During middle school, boys are more likely to use overt aggression, and girls are more likely to use relational aggression.

their classroom or grade. In **perceived popularity,** students nominate peers who are the most popular or "cool" and those who are the least popular or "cool." Both sociometric and perceived popularity include characteristics of positive behavior, such as being cooperative and/or displaying socially appropriate behaviors. Unlike individuals with sociometric popularity, those with perceived popularity sometimes receive high numbers of nominations both for being liked and for being disliked—meaning that their popularity is controversial. The main difference between the two types of popularity, however, appears to be whether these peer status positions include displays of aggression. Sociometric popularity is not related to aggressive behaviors, whereas individuals with high levels of perceived popularity are likely to show higher levels of overt or relational aggression (LaFontana & Cillessen, 2002; Ojanen & Findley-Van Nostrand, 2014; Puckett, Aikins, & Cillessen, 2008). However, relational aggression appears to play a more important role in peer status than does overt aggression, and more so with girls' perceived popularity than with that of boys. Relational aggression can be used to obtain or maintain high peer status, which is more likely to occur following the transition from elementary school to middle school (LaFontana & Cillessen, 2002; Li & Wright, 2012). Middle school students with advanced social skills may be more effective in delivering threats of friendship withdrawal, excluding others from the peer group, or orchestrating rumor spreading (Adler & Adler, 1998; Dijkstra, Lindenberg, Verhulst, Ormel, & Vennstra, 2009; Xie, Cairns, & Cairns, 2005).

REJECTED

Not all individuals who display relational or overt aggression are perceived as popular (Rose et al., 2004; Vaillancourt & Hymel, 2006). Individuals who display aggressive behaviors but do not display the positive behaviors of cooperation and social skills typically are considered **rejected youth** (Zimmer-Genbeck et al., 2013). Rejected youth tend to be less well-liked by peers, including those within their own peer clique, and are members of smaller peer cliques (Bagwell, Coie, Terry, & Lochman, 2000). In addition, violence may beget violence in rejected students. For example, rejection status and the use of relational aggression are related to increases in relational aggression for girls. Similarly, rejection and overt aggression are related to increases in overt aggression for both boys and girls (Werner & Crick, 2004). Many consider a pattern of aggressive and coercive behavior over time to be *bullying.* Yet being the victim of aggression also may lead to higher levels of aggression, meaning victims of aggression may themselves become aggressive. For example, one study of African American eighth graders found that students who were the victims of overt or relational aggression by their peers also were more likely to be aggressive themselves (Sullivan, Farrell, & Kliewer, 2006). Unfortunately, students with mild disabilities may be more likely to be perceived as bullies and victims as compared with general education students who are more likely than gifted students to be perceived as bullies or victims (Estell et al., 2009).

Video Case 2.2 ▲
Student Popularity or
Social Status

© SAGE Publications

Bullying: See Module 17

› DIVERSITY

NEGLECTED

The final category of peer status includes those individuals who are neither popular nor aggressive but rather are considered **neglected youth.** Individuals who are considered neglected typically are not nominated as liked or disliked and do not show high rates of overt or relational aggression (Brown, 2004). Because little research evidence is available concerning this category of peer status, less is known about related characteristics among these individuals.

 Think about people at your high school who would have been considered popular because they were well-liked and those who were popular but not well-liked. Did aggressive behaviors contribute to these popular students being disliked by their peers?

How does peer status interact with the school in the mesosystem? Students perceived as popular but not necessarily well-liked tend to be less academically engaged, whereas students who are well-liked by peers are considered to be more academically engaged (de Bruyn & Cillessen, 2006; Ladd, 2013). Similarly, adolescents who experience victimization or peer rejection are likely to have lower school performance and more psychological distress (Beeri & Lev-Wiesel, 2012; Bellmore, 2011; Platt, Kadosh, & Lau, 2013; Risser, 2013). Because popularity and aggression are related to academic outcomes and psychological difficulties, teachers need to identify and eliminate aggressive behaviors. A study by Barone (1997) reported that counselors, teachers, and administrators tend to underestimate the amount of bullying that occurs within a school. When eighth graders were surveyed, 60% reported having been bothered by a bully in middle school; however, school personnel reported that they thought only 16% of the students had ever been bullied. When teachers recognize and react to overt aggression displayed by elementary-age boys, they typically assign more blame for the aggression to more popular boys than to less popular boys (Nesdale & Pickering, 2006). Teachers may attribute more blame to popular boys because of concerns that popular children will have more influence on the behaviors of other children. Even though popularity may influence teachers' views of who is to *blame,* the popularity of the aggressive boys does not affect the teachers' *punishment* of their behavior.

DIVERSITY

Research has not examined how teachers react to episodes of girls' overt aggression or relational aggression toward boys or girls. We might assume that teachers have more difficulty identifying acts of relational aggression and determining who is to blame because the behaviors are less obvious and more indirect. For example, teachers might clearly see overt aggression when one child hits, kicks, or slaps another child, but they might not "see" the rumor spreading or gossiping behaviors characteristic of relational aggression. Given the link between relational aggression and negative outcomes, teachers should be on the lookout for instances of relational aggression and react as swiftly to these aggressive behaviors as they do to instances of overt aggression. A recent intervention program for rural schools has been successful in improving teachers' abilities to identify students involved in bullying (Farmer, Hall, Petrin, Hamm, & Dadisman, 2010). Education and training of school personnel on the significance of relational aggression may also see benefits.

BROADER CONTEXTS

 Explain how broader contexts of development influence microsystems and individual outcomes.

Although the microsystems of families, peers, and schools most directly influence children, Bronfenbrenner's model also includes systems that have less direct influence on the developing individual—the exosystem and the macrosystem.

Parental Employment

In today's economy, both parents typically are employed outside the household, making parental workplaces a common element of a student's exosystem—that is, an indirect influence on development. Thirty to forty years ago, as more mothers began rejoining the workforce, researchers examined the effects on child and adolescent outcomes and did not find negative results. Instead, a number of positive outcomes were found, particularly for girls (Hoffman, 1974):

- Girls with working mothers tended to have higher achievement aspirations or greater desire to excel academically, as well as higher achievement in school, compared to girls with nonworking mothers.

- Girls with working mothers tended to have higher intelligence scores (IQ scores) compared to girls with nonworking mothers.

- Children of working mothers were not more likely to be involved in delinquent acts than were children of nonworking mothers.

- Children of working mothers had more household responsibilities than did children of nonworking mothers, a situation related to positive, rather than negative, outcomes, such as advanced social development.

> **DIVERSITY**

More recent research on parental employment as an exosystem suggests that having both parents employed outside the home does not generally affect children in either a negative or a positive manner (Crouter & McHale, 2005; Lucas-Thompson, Goldberg, & Prause, 2010). For example, working mothers spend slightly less time with their children than do nonworking mothers; however, fathers whose wives are employed become more involved in child rearing than do fathers whose wives are not employed outside the home. In short, parental employment appears to have little impact on children and may even be related to positive academic achievement, aspirations, and intelligence among girls.

Parental satisfaction or job stress may have an indirect influence in the lives of children and adolescents. Data from the 1970s suggested that children of working mothers who were satisfied with their jobs had more positive outcomes than did children of unemployed mothers who preferred to work or working mothers who did not want to work (Hoffman, 1974). Similarly, more recent research suggests that job stress may be related to parenting practices. Higher levels of job stress may lead to a mother's withdrawal from her preschool-age child or to conflict with her adolescent (Crouter, Bumpus, Maguire, & McHale, 1999; Crouter & McHale, 2005).

Because parental satisfaction and job stress are components of the exosystem, the interaction with the school system is less direct, but it is not completely absent. Parents who are employed and experience high levels of job stress and dissatisfaction may exhibit less effective parenting practices, which can influence the academic achievement of their children (see Figure 2.2). Teachers might not be able to change the employment, job satisfaction, or parenting styles of parents, but they need to understand that this aspect of the exosystem indirectly affects the students in their classrooms.

A more direct influence of parental employment on the school system is the need of many families to use child care facilities. Child care facilities are considered a microsystem within a child's life, but they exist within the broader context of parental employment. Approximately 50% of mothers with children under 1 year of age and 75% of mothers with school-age children use child care

Siri Stafford/DigitalVision/Getty Images

Parental Employment. Fathers with working wives become more involved in child rearing than do fathers whose wives do not work outside the home.

FIGURE 2.2 **Exosystem's Relevance.** The indirect influence of parental employment on academic achievement.

facilities (Scarr, 1998). A variety of options for child care are available, including home or center care, licensed or unlicensed care, and for-profit or not-for-profit organizations. The amount of time spent in child care is not as important as the quality of care (McCartney et al., 2010). Quality of care from birth through age 4 can have positive effects on academic achievement through adolescence (Vandell, Belsky, Burchinal, Steinberg, & Vandergrift, 2010).

Quality care typically means a safe environment with warm, supportive interactions that enhance children's development. Specific characteristics of quality care include the following:

- Small group sizes within homes or classrooms.

- Low teacher-to-child ratios within classrooms.

- Qualified teachers or child care providers with early childhood education or child development training.

- High stability or low turnover rates among teachers.

Although quality of care is an important microsystem to consider, other factors appear to have an even greater influence on later development. A government-funded study has examined child care since 1991, following children from birth through sixth grade. The most recent findings indicate that parenting practices as well as a child's temperament are better predictors of later cognitive and social development outcomes than are experiences in child care facilities (Belsky et al., 2007; Burchinal, Lowe Vandell, & Belsky, 2014; Pluess & Belsky, 2010). Broader contextual factors may also have a stronger impact on the cognitive and academic performance of children than quality of child care. For example, although quality of child care is related to language and cognitive development in children, this connection can be explained by family income and SES, because families living in higher socioeconomic (SES) neighborhoods have better access to quality child care (Brooks-Gunn, Han, & Waldfogel, 2002; Hatfield, Lower, Cassidy, & Faldowski, 2015; Scarr, 1998). Figure 2.3 depicts the complex nature of how microsystems, mesosystems, exosystems, and macrosystems together influence an individual.

DIVERSITY

Cultural Factors

Like parenting practices (microsystem) and parental employment (exosystem), even broader contextual factors—SES (macrosystem)—can shape child and adolescent development. More specifically, high-poverty school systems and highly segregated African American school systems can have a negative impact on educational outcomes beyond individual differences (Borman & Dowling, 2010). Similarly, cultural values regarding education can play a major role in children's and adolescents' academic performance. Almost all parents want their children to excel academically and become successful, yet parental expectations may vary based on ethnicity and SES. For example:

- Asian American students report that their parents have higher expectations and standards for school success than parents of White American students or Latino students (Chen & Stevenson, 1995; Naumann, Guillaume, & Funder, 2012).

FIGURE 2.3 **Interrelationships.** Systems are interdependent and exert direct and indirect influences on the individual.

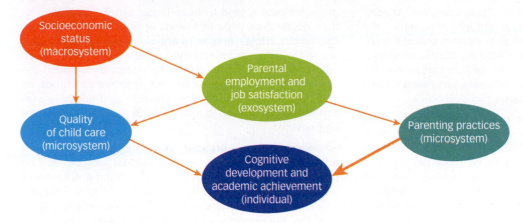

- African American students also report that their parents have high expectations for them, but the expectations are not as high as the parents of White American students (Ogbu, 2003).

These different expectations among parents may reflect their beliefs about the benefits of education. For example, African Americans are more skeptical of how helpful education will be, because many believe that even with an education their children will be discriminated against and their opportunities for success will be limited (Ogbu, 1994, 2003). Hence, African American students have fewer negative views of the future when they think about not being educated, whereas Asian American students have a greater fear of negative outcomes or failure when they think about not being well-educated (Steinberg, 1996).

Broader cultural beliefs about the benefits of education may lead to parents' being either more or less involved in their child's education. The connection between parental involvement and broader cultural beliefs is important because higher parental involvement is consistently linked to higher academic achievement (Choi, Chang, Kim, & Reio, 2015; Jeynes, 2008). African American parents have been found to participate less in school functions, such as parent–teacher organizations, workshops, and open houses, than White American parents and to be less likely to help their children with homework or check that homework has been completed (Ogbu, 2003). Lower parental involvement among African American parents most likely results from a misconception that the school does not need their help to educate their children, with the result that these parents may not understand the importance of their role at school or as homework facilitators (Ogbu, 2003; Steinberg, 1996). In contrast, Asian Americans are highly invested in the school system, and Asian American students spend substantially more time on homework than do White Americans (Steinberg, 1996). In short, families (microsystem) are influenced by cultural beliefs (macrosystem), particularly with regard to parental involvement in education and interactions with the school setting (mesosystem).

Teachers and educators need to be reminded that differences among beliefs in and support for education exist not only between ethnic groups but also within ethnic groups. The value each student's family places on education should be considered outside of his or her ethnicity. As with many of the contexts of development we have discussed, teachers may have little ability to change the cultural values or beliefs held by their students' parents. Teachers should, however, continue to provide encouragement and support for the importance of education among all students, regardless of race, ethnicity, or SES.

Video Case 2.3 ▲
Working with Families

❯ DIVERSITY

SUMMARY

① **Describe Bronfenbrenner's bioecological theory.** Bronfenbrenner's bioecological theory emphasizes the interaction between the biological person and the environmental systems, including microsystems, mesosystems, exosystems, macrosystems, and the chronosystem. Research examining families and peers has relied on this theory to help explain developmental outcomes.

② **Describe how parenting practices and family transitions interact with the school system.** The four parenting practices vary by level of control and responsiveness. Authoritative parenting appears to be most beneficial to children's and adolescents' academic achievement and school performance. Although children from both divorced and remarried families are more likely to have lower academic achievement and to exhibit more problem behaviors in school than children from intact families, not all such children experience difficulties. Difficulties do tend to increase with each family transition, meaning that academic achievement may be lower in remarried families than in single-parent families. Teachers should use information about the family context to help them understand children's difficulties and provide additional support to children and families.

③ **Describe how aspects of the peer context interact with the school system.** Children with friends or peer group affiliation tend to have better school performance than do children without friends or peer ties. In addition, children or adolescents who are well-liked by their peers are more likely to be engaged in school than are those who are disliked or neglected by peers. Because of the link between overt aggression and negative outcomes, as well as between relational aggression and negative outcomes, teachers need to identify both overt and relational aggression.

④ **Explain how broader contexts of development influence microsystems and individual outcomes.** The presence of an exosystem such as parental employment is not as important to a child's development as the indirect influence on the child via job satisfaction and stress. In addition, the presence of parental work outside the home may lead to an additional microsystem in the child's life—child care—but the child's development may be influenced more by the macrosystem of SES and neighborhood. The macrosystem also varies by ethnicity and cultural values such that parental expectations and support for educational achievement may vary across and within ethnic groups to help explain differences in academic performance among students.

KEY CONCEPTS

CASE STUDIES: REFLECT AND EVALUATE

EARLY CHILDHOOD: CRY BABY

These questions refer to the case study on page 22.

1. Based on the information provided in the case study, speculate on the parenting strategies most likely used by Annie's mom and Zada's parents.

2. How might the family structures of Annie and Zada influence their behavior?

3. How developmentally appropriate is Annie's comment about not being best friends with Zada?

4. How might Tyler's aggressive behavior become a problem with peers as he continues into elementary school?

5. How does the employment of Annie's and Zada's parents play a role in their development?

6. How does the value placed on education differ in Annie's and Zada's homes? What factors might account for these differences?

ELEMENTARY SCHOOL: Team

These questions refer to the case study on page 24.

1. How might Bronfenbrenner's bioecological theory be important in understanding Kashi's experiences?

2. Based on the information provided in the case study, speculate on the type of parenting strategy most likely used by Patricia's mom, Mary.

3. In what specific ways might the divorce of Kashi's parents have influenced her behavior?

4. What does Kashi's "team" most likely refer to regarding peer groups?

5. Based on the information provided in the case study, is Zach correct in labeling Bill a bully? Why or why not?

6. Does Ms. Barone handle the girls and boys differently? Based on the research presented in the module, how are teachers' reactions typically different based on types of aggression and children's gender?

MIDDLE SCHOOL: Basketball Star

These questions refer to the case study on page 26.

1. What parenting strategy is most likely used by Sierra's dad? Darla's dad?

2. How might the family structures of Sierra, Darla, and Mark influence their behavior?

3. Identify an example of a clique and a crowd in the case study. Would these be expected to be formed during middle school? How might they change over the next several years?

4. What are the peer statuses of Jill, Sierra, Darla, and Mark? Give specific examples of their behavior that indicate these statuses. How might their peer status affect their school performance?

5. What type of aggression is used by Jill and Sierra? By Claudia? By Mark? Why might teachers react differently to aggressive behaviors displayed by these students?

HIGH SCHOOL: Steal, Cheat, and Fight

These questions refer to the case study on page 28.

1. How could the content of these e-mails be combined to better reflect the bioecological model?

2. Ms. Presley believes that the family is responsible for these behaviors. To which aspects of family life might she attribute these behaviors?

3. How might Ms. Presley be accurate and inaccurate in her descriptions of divorce, remarriage, and parental employment?

4. What examples of cliques and crowds are given by the teachers and staff? Are these typical groupings in a high school? Why or why not?

5. What examples of relational and physical aggression are given by the teachers and staff? Based on the research presented in the module, is the gender of the adolescent who is displaying a particular type of aggression in the case study typical or atypical?

Visit **edge.sagepub.com/durwin3e** to help you accomplish your coursework goals in an easy-to-use learning environment.

- Mobile-friendly **eFlashcards**
- Mobile-friendly practice **quizzes**
- A complete online **action plan**
- Chapter **learning objectives**
- EXCLUSIVE! Access to full-text **SAGE journal articles**

$SAGE edge™

©iStockphoto.com/Cathy Yeulet

SOCIAL-EMOTIONAL DEVELOPMENT

OUTLINE	LEARNING GOALS
Erikson's Psychosocial Theory	
	❶ Describe the environmental influences in the development of the eight psychosocial crises.
Aspects of Identity	
• Identity Statuses	❷ Describe the four types of identity statuses.
• Ethnic Identity	❸ Explain the development of ethnic identity and gender identity.
• Gender Identity	
Understanding the Self	
• Self-Concept	❹ Compare and contrast self-concept and self-esteem.
• Self-Esteem	
Social Competence	
	❺ Explain the two components of social competence.
Applications: Fostering Social Competence	
• Fostering Social Skills	❻ Describe at least three strategies for improving social competence.
• Social-Emotional Learning (SEL) Programs	

ERIKSON'S PSYCHOSOCIAL THEORY

❶ Describe the environmental influences in the development of the eight psychosocial crises.

Cognitive development:
See Module 7

Erik Erikson (1959/1980) proposed one of the only theories of development that extends over the entire lifespan. Other theories typically begin in infancy and end during adolescence, including Piaget's cognitive development theory. Erikson's theory focuses on the social elements that influence individual development throughout a person's life, such as the importance of family and peer contexts, and identifies eight stages of development, as illustrated in Table 3.1. During each developmental stage, an individual faces and (ideally) masters a new psychological and social challenge, called a **psychosocial crisis**. Each psychosocial crisis has two developmental outcomes—one positive and one negative. The first five of Erikson's eight developmental stages apply directly to children in educational settings, whereas the latter three stages apply to adults, including teachers and administrators in educational settings. Let's examine each of these stages:

1. *Trust versus mistrust:* The first stage includes the period of infancy. Parents and primary caregivers are dominant environmental or social influences. Caregivers who dependably respond to the infant's needs provide a world in which the infant believes that his or her needs will be taken care of and learns to trust the world. Infants who experience lapses in having their needs met learn that the world may or may not meet their needs and develop a sense of mistrust. Similarly, attachment theory describes the importance of the mother-infant bond in providing infants with a warm, safe environment (Bowlby, 1969, 1973). Empirical data support the connection between secure attachment, or feelings of trust, and school readiness, as well as social-emotional development (Cassidy, Jones, & Shaver, 2013).

2. *Autonomy versus shame/doubt:* The second stage focuses on the period of toddlerhood, during which children continue to be most influenced by parents' and primary caregivers' responses. Toddlers are becoming more mobile and are attempting to do things on their own, such as toilet training, walking, and playing alone. Parents who provide opportunities for their children to explore their surroundings without guilt for

Master the content.
edge.sagepub.com/durwin3e
SAGE edge

Family and peer contexts: See Module 2

STAGE	DEVELOPMENTAL PERIOD	PSYCHOSOCIAL CRISIS	SIGNIFICANT RELATIONS	SIGNIFICANT EVENT
1	Infancy	Trust versus mistrust	Parents or primary caregivers	Feedings, diaper changes
2	Toddlerhood	Autonomy versus shame/doubt	Parents or primary caregivers	Toilet training, walking
3	Preschool	Initiative versus guilt	Family and early childhood educators	Learning to color, write; using pretend play
4	School-age	Industry versus inferiority	Parents, teachers, and peers	Learning to read and complete tasks
5	Adolescence	Identity versus identity diffusion	Peer groups and role models	More time with friends and romantic partners
6	Young adulthood	Intimacy versus isolation	Friends and romantic partners	Opportunities to try many new things
7	Middle adulthood	Generativity versus stagnation	Coworkers	Career choices and volunteer experiences
8	Late adulthood	Integrity versus despair	Mankind, society	Reflecting on one's life

TABLE 3.1 Erikson's Psychosocial Theory

SOURCE: A. Lefton Lester, *Psychology* (5th ed.). Boston, MA: Allyn and Bacon. Copyright 1994 by Pearson Education. Adapted from Erikson (1959), *Identity and the Life Cycle* (*Psychological Issues*, Vol. 1, no. 1).

accidents or mistakes are likely to instill a sense of autonomy in them. In contrast, parents who are either punitive—disciplining children for mistakes and accidents—or overly protective—not allowing their children to move forward on their own—will instill in their children a sense of shame or doubt about their own capabilities.

Parenting: See Module 2

As children's motor skills develop and language capacity increases, how and whether they comply with the wishes of parents and caregivers also becomes an important facet of their developing autonomy. Children can choose to follow adult directives, such as cleaning up toys when asked to do so, or they can choose to defy authority, typically by saying no. At this stage, toddlers begin to test parental limits, requiring parents and caregivers to establish rules and address the issue of discipline. The child's temperament and the parents' style of parenting affect how the child resolves the autonomy crisis. Basically, warm and responsive parenting—setting reasonable expectations and choices and providing suitable guidance (neither overcontrolling nor undercontrolling)—will allow the child to positively develop autonomy.

Application: Although parents primarily facilitate autonomy, the following guidelines can help teachers continue autonomy development during the preschool years:

- Provide reasonable choices (e.g., giving the child a choice between two activities, such as "Would you like a story or time to color?").
- Allow children to do things for themselves, and do not punish mistakes (e.g., accidents in toilet training).
- Be accepting of attempts to master skills even if the results are not perfect (e.g., a shirt that's on backward).
- Provide reasonable expectations for the child's age (e.g., don't expect a 2-year-old to sit quietly listening to stories for two hours).
- Provide opportunities for developing independence (e.g., toddler using utensils and cups, safety scissors, large crayons).
- Expect occasional noncompliance—the child is testing independence.

3. *Initiative versus guilt:* Stage three focuses on preschool-age children. Early childhood education contexts include increasing interaction with peers. Peers, along with parents and primary caregivers, influence the resolution of this stage's crisis. Preschoolers who are rewarded for trying new things— such as coloring, writing, and using their imagination in pretend play—are likely to develop a sense of initiative. Initiative gives children a sense of purpose and offers opportunities to master the environment, which may involve taking risks but not behaving impulsively. Therefore, parents, child care providers, and teachers must find a delicate balance between allowing children to try new things and potentially fail and doing things for children (that is, being overprotective). Adults who respond to failures by being overly critical or who ridicule children's creative and innovative behaviors are likely to instill guilt in children.

Application: The following guidelines can help teachers boost children's sense of initiative and decrease their feelings of guilt:

- Provide tasks and activities that are age-appropriate and in which children can experience success (e.g., helping pass out supplies or materials prior to doing a project, picking up toys, watering plants using a small cup, etc.).
- Refrain from providing unsolicited help, because this suggests that you believe they cannot do the task alone.

© Can Stock Photo Inc. / kiankhoon

Initiative Versus Guilt. Teachers can boost children's sense of initiative by allowing them to help with tasks and activities in the classroom.

- Avoid being overly critical of failures or setbacks, because this will lead to guilt. In response to failure, provide alternative strategies for tackling the task (e.g., "Maybe next time you can try . . .").
- Provide toys for pretend play.

4. *Industry versus inferiority:* The fourth stage of Erikson's theory focuses on children in elementary and middle school contexts who are learning to master many skills, such as reading, school subjects, physical skills (e.g., bike riding), and sports. Although parents continue to be an important context for development, teachers and peers within the school system become increasingly influential. Children will develop a sense of industry when they have parents, teachers, and peers who provide opportunities for them to successfully complete tasks, learn information, and become competent or skilled in particular areas. Children develop inferiority when they believe that they are not competent in areas of school-related functioning ("I can't read") or home functioning ("I can't make breakfast"). Unfortunately, children with learning disabilities are less likely to develop a sense of industry (Pickar & Tori, 1986), so teachers should be sensitive to these individuals' attempts to increase their feelings of success and competence.

> **DIVERSITY**

Application: Many aspects of the school environment can affect a sense of industry. The following guidelines may help teachers control some of these influences:

- Be aware that activities or teaching approaches that emphasize competition among students—such as spelling bees, competitive sports, and team captains picking players in physical education class—draw attention to skill-level differences among children, which could lead to feelings of inferiority.
- Minimize comparisons of ability among students, particularly ability grouping in elementary school. Most students are aware of their position in the hierarchy, and for students in lower ability groups, grouping can reinforce feelings of inferiority.
- Emphasize mastery of skills (academic, physical, and so on) over competition with other students (e.g., "You are in the reading level that *you* need to be in—the one that is right for *you.*").
- Have high expectations for all students. When teachers have different expectations for students, they convey these expectations in subtle ways, such as giving unsolicited help and praising for effort or a "good try." Such practices can lead students to believe that they lack competence (Jussim, 2013).

Ability grouping: See Module 19

5. *Identity versus identity diffusion:* Erikson's fifth stage focuses on adolescence. Beginning with this stage, the individual's own internal states play an important role, along with environmental contexts of development such as family, peers, and school. Identity is a sense of self or understanding about "Who am I?" In contrast, identity diffusion involves a lack of clear goals and aspirations about the self. During this period of development, adolescents need a **psychosocial moratorium,** a time with few responsibilities and many opportunities for exploring different roles. Many adolescents will be in a state of moratorium for many years as they contemplate familial and educational aspirations and career or occupational goals, as well as determine their own set of morals and values.

Application: Although peers become increasingly important during adolescence, teachers can also support adolescents in their formation of identity development. Strategies include the following:

- Allow students to enroll in a variety of courses and to engage in numerous extracurricular activities.

Identity Development. Teachers and parents can support adolescents' identity development by accepting individual preferences in the areas of clothing, body piercing, and hair style.

- Welcome individual or peer group preferences for music, clothing, and other minor issues.
- Prompt students to consider alternatives and consequences for multiple options (e.g., pros and cons of attending college versus gaining employment following graduation, or choosing one career path over another).
- Debate moral issues to provide students with multiple perspectives as they explore their own views and value systems.

6. *Intimacy versus isolation:* The period of young adulthood was considered by Erikson to be focused on developing close, personal relationships with others. Erikson did not limit this stage to the development of romantic relationships but included intimacy in close friendships and family relationships. In this sense, isolation is not necessarily about being a "loner" but is a characteristic demonstrated by individuals who move from one relationship to another and typically have an elevated fear of rejection, never becoming completely intimate with others.

7. *Generativity versus stagnation:* The seventh stage of development occurs primarily in middle adulthood and focuses on giving back to the next generation. Individuals who believe they have given to society in meaningful ways are likely to have a sense of generativity. In contrast, individuals who fail to contribute to society in meaningful ways may feel bored with life and develop a sense of stagnation. Most teachers and administrators will be in this stage of development during most of their careers. Providing educational opportunities to the next generation may be one way teachers and administrators can successfully resolve this psychosocial crisis.

8. *Integrity versus despair:* The final stage is focused on the elderly or the period of old age. Integrity is a feeling that life was worth living and that death is not a threat. Despair involves dissatisfaction with one's life, a strong desire for more time, and a fear of dying.

At first glance, you might think that the eight psychosocial crises imply an either-or situation, but these labels were intended to illustrate a continuum (Marcia, 1994), a spectrum of possibilities rather than a list of either-or choices. The way individuals resolve each crisis affects their view of themselves as well as their view of society.

Erikson clearly stated that a positive resolution of one crisis does not imply a positive resolution of the next crisis. Nor does a negative resolution of one crisis suggest that all the other crises will be negatively resolved. One exception, however, was the resolution of the intimacy versus isolation crisis. Erikson's early work suggested that an individual must have achieved a sense of self or identity to successfully resolve the crisis of intimacy. In other words, to achieve true intimacy, an individual must have developed a coherent identity. This aspect of Erikson's theory has been criticized for focusing on the development of men rather than women. In fact, early studies conducted with college men indicated that individuals with identity achievement had the highest levels of intimate relationships, whereas identity diffusion was characterized by the lowest levels of intimacy (Orlofsky, Marcia, & Lesser, 1973). Later research suggested that in women, intimacy may develop prior to identity formation, or identity and intimacy may codevelop (Josselson, 1988).

DIVERSITY

Which stage of Erikson's theory best represents your current stage of development? How will your own personal strengths and weaknesses, as well as your relationships with your family and peers, help support your resolution of this psychosocial crisis?

ASPECTS OF IDENTITY

❷ Describe the four types of identity statuses.

❸ Explain the development of ethnic identity and gender identity.

Identity Statuses

Developmental psychologist James Marcia (1966, 1987) conducted studies with adolescents and young adults to better understand the period of identity development described by Erikson. His research led him to discuss identity in terms of two variables: exploration and commitment. **Exploration** is a period of role experimentation and trying new behaviors, including contemplation of morals and values. **Commitment** is making decisions about areas of one's life such as educational and career goals, family obligations or goals, and political and religious beliefs. Marcia used the presence and absence of these two qualities to derive four identity statuses during adolescence, as shown in Table 3.2, that continue to be used today to assess identity development (Meeus, 2011). Identity statuses have been linked to parenting practices (Harter, 1990; Lam & Tam, 2011), school attendance, and math performance (Streitmatter, 1989), as well as self-esteem (Luyckx, Klimstra, Schwartz, & Duriez, 2013).

Parenting practices: See Module 2

- **Identity achieved:** These adolescents are provided with opportunities to explore many options involving occupations, academic skills, friendships, and values and to commit themselves to certain goals and values. They typically have parents who use an authoritative parenting style. Identity achievement is related to better performance on math achievement tests.

- **Identity foreclosure:** These adolescents are not given time to explore but have accepted the commitments laid out by their parents. They have parents who typically use an authoritarian style of parenting—telling them who they are, what they will become, or where they will attend college. These students are less likely to be absent from school but also are less likely to perform well academically.

- **Moratorium:** These adolescents are actively involved in the exploration process but have not yet made decisions or commitments. Moratorium would be considered developmentally appropriate for most high school students and early college students. Their parents may use an authoritative style of parenting, allowing them to try new things while deferring decisions. These students are more likely to be absent from school than are other students, but surprisingly they score well on math achievement tests.

- **Identity diffusion:** These adolescents either have not yet begun the process of exploration (as you might expect of younger children) or have been through the exploration process but were unable to make commitments to their goals and values. Their parents may be permissive, allowing them to explore but not asking them to make commitments. These individuals are more likely to be absent from school and to perform poorly on math achievement tests.

Ethnic Identity

Self-concept, self-esteem, and identity development all include a number of domain-specific areas. For many individuals, **ethnic identity,** or psychological attitudes toward and behaviors related to membership in an ethnic and racial group, is an important aspect of social

Video: Positive Ethnic Identity in Adolescence

TABLE 3.2 Marcia's Categories of Identity Achievement Commitment

	COMMITMENT	
	YES	**NO**
EXPLORATION — YES	**Identity achieved** Adolescents are provided with opportunities to explore many options involving occupations, academic skills, friendships, and values and to commit to certain goals and values. Parenting practice: Individuals who have achieved identity typically have parents who use an authoritative parenting style. Achievement: Identity achievement is related to better performance on math achievement tests.	**Moratorium** Adolescents are actively involved in the exploration process but have not yet made decisions or commitments. Moratorium would be considered developmentally appropriate for most high school and early college students. Parenting practice: Parents who use an authoritative style of parenting provide a moratorium for their children by allowing them to try new things while deferring decisions until they have had ample time to explore their options. Achievement: Students who are in a state of moratorium are likely to be absent from school but, surprisingly, they score well on math achievement tests.
EXPLORATION — NO	**Identity foreclosure** Adolescents have parents who typically use an authoritarian style of parenting, such as telling their adolescents who they are, what they will become, or where they will attend college. Parenting practice: Adolescents are not given time to explore but rather have accepted the commitments laid out by their parents. Achievement: Adolescents are less likely to be absent from school but also less likely to perform well academically.	**Identity diffusion** Adolescents either have not yet begun the process of exploration (as you might expect for younger children) or have gone through the exploration process but are unable to make commitments to their goals and values. Parenting practice: Parents are permissive and have allowed their adolescents to explore in the past but have never asked them to make commitments. Achievement: Individuals are more likely to be absent from school and to perform poorly on math achievement tests.

development in these areas (Phinney, 1990; Phinney & Balderlomar, 2011). Developmental psychologist Jean S. Phinney (1990) defined ethnic identity as having several components:

- *Self-identification,* or the ethnic label an individual uses regarding his or her group membership;

- A *sense of belongingness,* which includes the level of importance or concern given to one's ethnic group;

- *Positive or negative attitudes* toward one's ethnic group (essential to ethnic identity), typically in the form of acceptance (positive) or denial (negative) of one's ethnic group;

- *Ethnic involvement,* or the participation in social and cultural aspects of the ethnic group. Women of minority groups are more likely to achieve ethnic identity and to become active in cultural organizations and practices than are men of minority groups (Dion & Dion, 2004).

DIVERSITY

Research with Latino adolescents indicates that each of these components may develop at different rates but development typically occurs during the high school years (Umana-Taylor, Gonzales-Backen, & Guimond, 2009). The combination of these components determines the ethnic identity stage of an individual. Ethnic identity stages mirror those proposed by Marcia for general identity development. Phinney (1989) found that Asian American, Hispanic, and African American high school students tend to fall into one of three ethnic identity stages, which are highly related to global identity development:

FIGURE 3.1 **Ethnic Identity.** On questionnaire forms, individuals must self-identify an ethnic label regarding their group membership.

6. **What is this person's race?** *Mark* ☒ *onc or more boxes.*

☐ White
☐ Black, African Am., or Negro
☐ American Indian or Alaska Native—*Print name of enrolled or principal tribe.*

☐ Asian Indian   ☐ Japanese   ☐ Native Hawaiian
☐ Chinese   ☐ Korean   ☐ Guamanian or Chamorro
☐ Filipino   ☐ Vietnamese   ☐ Samoan
☐ Other Asian—*Print race, for example, Hmong, Laotian, Thai, Pakistani, Cambodian, and so on.*   ☐ Other Pacific Islander—*Print race, for example, Fijian, Tongan, and so on.*

☐ Some other race—*Print race.*

1. *Diffusion/foreclosure* includes individuals who have not yet examined their ethnicity.

2. *Moratorium* refers to those who currently are exploring the components described above.

3. *Achieved* describes those who are committed to their ethnic group membership.

Research suggests that strong, positive ethnic identities are related to better academic performance and may protect against peer and teacher discrimination (Brown & Chu, 2012). In particular, a sense of belongingness, such as having same-ethnicity peers, is related to higher achievement test scores (Benner & Crosnoe, 2011), and positive attitudes or affect towards one's ethnicity is related to self-esteem and academic achievement (Rivas-Drake et al., 2014).

Video Case 3.1 ▲
Creating a Classroom Community

© SAGE Publications

Gender Identity

Any discussion of gender must begin by defining a number of concepts used in developmental psychology. **Sex** typically is used to refer to the biological identity of male or female, whereas **gender** is a social definition that includes behaviors learned from the environment about being either male or female. The latter term has several facets:

〉DIVERSITY

Video Case 3.2 ▲
Identity and Gender Identity

© SAGE Publications

1. **Gender identity,** typically developed by age 4, refers to knowledge that one is biologically male or female.

2. In adolescence, gender identity often is referred to as **gender-role identity,** or the knowledge that one behaves appropriately according to societal expectations for one's gender. Gender-role identity may be defined as follows (Bem, 1974, 1975):

   • **Masculine:** stereotypical male behaviors such as being athletic, aggressive, dominant, self-reliant, and independent;
   • **Feminine:** stereotypical female behaviors such as being affectionate, warm, gentle, cheerful, and loyal;
   • **Androgynous:** having both masculine and feminine characteristics.

3. **Gender-role attitude** refers to approval or disapproval toward societal expectations for one's gender.

 Would you consider yourself masculine, feminine, or androgynous? What characteristics in your past, such as family or peer and media influences, may have contributed to your gender-role identity?

Let's examine the three main theories used to explain issues surrounding gender (for reviews, see Eisenberg, Martin, & Fabes, 1996; Galambos, Berenbaum, & McHale, 2009):

1. *Biological theories* suggest that males and females behave differently and have different expectations due to the biological differences between the sexes—for example, boys are more likely to engage in rough-and-tumble play based on hormonal differences. In actuality, most gender differences do not originate solely from biological differences but rather interact with cultural and environmental influences—such as parents using rough-and-tumble play with boys more than with girls.

Social cognitive theory:
See Module 9

2. *Social learning theory* suggests that children develop a sense of gender identity by observing the behaviors and attitudes displayed by their parents, teachers, peers, and people depicted in the mass media (television, movie, and book characters). Children imitate the behaviors and attitudes of others and find that they typically are rewarded for behaving in gender-appropriate ways; hence, they continue to display those behaviors, taking on that gender identity.

3. *Gender schemas,* as the theory with the most empirical support, focus on the thought processes included in gender identity. Gender schemas develop in three distinct steps:

   • In **gender labeling** (between ages 2 and 3), children can label themselves and others as male or female. First, children are able to correctly label *themselves* as either male or female. By age 2, children can correctly identify adults as either male or female. Finally, by age 3, they can also label other children correctly.
   • In **gender stability** (between ages 3 and 4), children form the knowledge that gender will not change over time. For example, they understand that a girl will grow up to be a woman, not a man.
   • In **gender constancy** (age 4 or 5), children understand that gender will remain the same regardless of behaviors, clothing, hairstyle, or other qualities. For example, a man holding a purse is still a man, not a woman.

Once children develop gender identity, they will begin to prefer the gender-role behaviors expected by society (Maccoby, 1990). Several factors influence the adoption of these behaviors, chief among them being the family and peer group. Typically, parents and siblings model and encourage gender appropriate behaviors in their toy selection during childhood and assigned

Gender Constancy. Around age 4 or 5, children understand that gender will stay the same. A man holding a purse is still a man.

chores during adolescence. For example, boys are more likely to receive trucks and sports equipment for gifts and to be asked to mow the grass and take out the garbage. Girls are more likely to receive dolls and kitchen sets for gifts and to be asked to help with dishes and laundry. Peers also provide models of gender-appropriate behaviors and will reward or punish (in the form of teasing) children for their displays of normal or contrary gender-role behaviors. For instance, if a kindergarten girl takes a Spiderman lunch box to school, her peers may tease her by saying that Spiderman is for boys. The girl would quickly learn to leave other Spiderman objects at home and to refrain from talking about "boy" things with her peers.

By adolescence, most individuals have a clear sense of the expected behaviors for males and females but develop **gender-role flexibility,** or the ability to alter expectations of their own and others' behaviors (Bem, 1974, 1975). Gender-role identity during adolescence includes incorporating that flexibility and choosing how closely to follow societal expectations. For girls and women, androgynous gender-role identity has the best outcomes for psychological well-being, as compared with masculinity or femininity (Galambos et al., 2009). The need for girls to have some masculine qualities is related to the higher value placed on those characteristics in our society. For example, strong leadership skills and a competitive nature are highly valued qualities for upper level administration and for skilled professions such as law and medicine. In contrast, professions characterized by feminine qualities of nurturing and caring, such as teaching and providing child care, receive less attention and fewer financial rewards in our society. Not surprisingly, given these societal expectations, adolescent boys and men who are considered predominantly masculine tend to have better psychological well-being than feminine or androgynous males.

UNDERSTANDING THE SELF

4 Compare and contrast self-concept and self-esteem.

Although the terms *self-concept* and *self-esteem* frequently are used interchangeably, they have quite different meanings. **Self-concept** refers to a cognitive aspect in which individuals have a perception about themselves, such as "I am a student." **Self-esteem** refers to an affective aspect in which an individual evaluates components of himself or herself, such as "I am a good student." Self-concept can influence self-esteem depending on how much the individual values the

Video Case 3.3 ▲
Importance of Getting to Know Your Students

© SAGE Publications

component being considered (Harter, 1990). For example, a secondary education student may perceive that she has weak creative writing skills. Because she plans to attend college to major in accounting and places little value on creative writing skills, her self-esteem may not be influenced. In contrast, a student who has career aspirations to become a journalist may devalue himself because he highly values creative writing skills. Let's take a closer look at how self-concept and self-esteem function in educational settings.

 Think about an aspect of yourself that is not particularly positive yet doesn't play an important role in your level of self-esteem.

Self-Concept

Reference:
Self-Concept

The structure of self-concept is related to educational settings because it includes the perceptions of one's knowledge and abilities in a number of activities, such as math, science, reading, athletics, and friendships (Bornholt, 2005; Byrne & Shavelson, 1986). Self-concepts or perceptions of oneself within particular domains are related to achievement in those domains. Contemporary educational psychologist Herbert W. Marsh and his colleagues (Liem, Marsh, Martin, McInerny, & Yeung, 2013; Seaton, Parker, Marsh, Craven, & Yeung, 2014) have repeatedly found that the relationship between academic self-concept and achievement is reciprocal: positive self-concept may lead to higher achievement, and higher achievement in turn will lead to an even more positive self-concept. The connection between academic self-concept and achievement has been found with children in elementary, middle, and high schools, as well as in a number of domain-specific areas such as math, science, and English. For example, Wilkins (2004) found that, in an international sample of over 40 countries, children with positive self-concepts for math and science were more likely to have high achievement in those areas as compared with children who had more negative self-concepts in math and science. Research with students in both rural and urban settings suggests that positive self-concepts in specific domains may lead to more interest and value for those domains, which in turn leads to greater participation and academic achievement (Bornholt & Wilson, 2007; Jones, Irvin, & Kibe, 2012). The connection between self-concept in specific domains and academic achievement may be due in part to teacher expectations. One study found that children's perceptions of feedback from teachers was predictive of academic self-concept (Chen, Thompson, Kromrey, & Chang, 2011). In addition, children's self-concepts of their math ability related to teacher expectations of students' math abilities (Bohlmann & Weinstein, 2013). Hence, student self-concept and teacher expectations may reciprocally influence each other and ultimately academic achievement.

DIVERSITY

Because self-concept is related to academic achievement through various means, educators should understand who is most likely to have a positive self-concept.

- Self-concepts tend to be more positive for young girls than young boys in elementary education, but the reverse is found in middle school, where boys have more positive self-concepts than girls (Bornholt, 2005). In particular, boys are found to have higher self-concepts for math and science than girls (MacPhee, Farro, & Canetto, 2013; Steffens, Jelenec, & Noack, 2010; Wilkins, 2004).

- Differences are also found for middle school children with speech and language impairments, who report less positive self-concepts for academic competence than do typically developing children (Lindsay, Dockrell, Letchford, & Mackie, 2002).

While some influences on self-concept, such as gender and learning difficulties, are beyond the control of educators, teacher–student interaction is important for the development of positive self-concepts. For example, teachers have been found to rate boys higher in mathematic ability, which may contribute to the gender difference in self-concept found among middle school students (Robinson-Cimpian, Lubienski, Ganley, & Copur-Gencturk, 2014). Specifically, teachers tend to ask ever more difficult questions of students for whom they have high expectations. They also tend to wait longer for a response, provide cues and prompts, and interrupt these students less often than they do students for whom they have lower expectations of success (Allington, 1980; Rosenthal, 1995). Positive teacher–student relationships have been linked to academic self-concept as well as academic motivation (Martin, Marsh, McInerney, Green, & Dowson, 2007). Hence, educators should focus on quality interactions in order to facilitate positive self-concepts among students, which in turn will facilitate students' academic motivation and achievement.

In addition to teacher–student interaction, specific aspects of the school context have been found to impact self-concept. For example, although you might expect students in high achieving or selective schools to have more positive academic self-concepts, a substantial body of research suggests the opposite. Termed the Big-Fish-Little-Pond Effect, Marsh and his colleagues (2015) have repeatedly found that elementary and secondary education students from various countries have lower academic self-concepts when their class average achievement is higher. This is most likely due to social comparisons such that students in high-achieving schools or classes view themselves as "little fish in the big pond." Research also finds that the transition to middle school, when ability grouping becomes more prevalent, is related to declines in several domains of self-concepts (Parker, 2010).

Ability grouping: See Module 19

Researchers who have examined the effectiveness of interventions designed to increase self-concept have made the following recommendations (O'Mara, Marsh, Craven, & Debus, 2006):

1. *Focus on domain-specific self-concept:* Help students focus on domain-specific aspects of self-concept, such as math or science but not both.

2. *Focus on praising students and providing feedback on their performance:* Praising students when they have succeeded on academic tasks conveys important information about their level of mastery and helps foster an intrinsic motivation to learn—that is, it motivates students to learn for the sake of curiosity, interest, and mastery (Deci, Koestner, & Ryan, 1999).

Intrinsic motivation and praise: See Modules 14 and 15

3. *Focus on at-risk populations:* Interventions have the best results for students with existing problems, such as behavioral disorders or learning disabilities.

Self-Esteem

We can look at self-esteem in two ways:

- as global self-esteem, a singular and relatively stable characteristic of the self, or

- as domain-specific self-esteem, separate components related to particular domains such as self-esteem in academics or self-esteem in relationships (Harter, Waters, & Whitesell, 1998).

Video Case 3.4 ▲
Students' Self-Confidence

© SAGE Publications

Global self-esteem develops around age 8 and is related to overall psychological well-being (Harter, 2012), whereas domain-specific self-esteem is related to specific behavioral outcomes. The latter may be more important for teachers, because academic self-esteem has a greater effect on academic performance than does global self-esteem (Rosenberg, Schooler, Schoenbach, & Rosenberg, 1995).

Like self-concept, self-esteem is influenced by a number of factors, including socioeconomic status (SES), gender, ethnicity, and generational factors:

> **DIVERSITY**

- Students from higher-SES families are more likely to have higher self-esteem (Falci, 2011; Twenge & Campbell, 2002).

- Girls tend to score higher than or equal to boys on levels of global self-esteem until adolescence, when girls score lower than boys (Falci, 2011; Moksnes & Espnes, 2013; Simmon, 1987). Although boys have higher self-esteem than girls following adolescence, the difference in levels of self-esteem is small, indicating that boys and girls actually are very similar (Kling, Hyde, Showers, & Buswell, 1999). This small difference may result from the importance of physical appearance for global self-esteem during adolescence, particularly for girls who report being less satisfied with their appearance (Gentile et al., 2009; Harter, 2012).

- While both boys and girls may be affected by the transition from elementary school to middle school, this has a more detrimental influence on self-esteem for girls (Dusek & McIntyre, 2006). Often, girls are experiencing biological changes (puberty) in conjunction with the social transitions of school, whereas boys typically begin puberty later and are not faced with two simultaneous changes (Galambos et al., 2009).

- African Americans tend to have higher levels of self-esteem than Whites (Bachman, O'Malley, Freedman-Doan, Trzesniewski, & Donnellan, 2011; Gray-Little & Hafdahl, 2000), including academic self-esteem, although their academic achievement is lower than that of Whites. African Americans tend to attribute their poorer academic achievement to causes outside their control, such as poor school systems and discrimination, an association that has less influence on their feelings about themselves (van Laar, 2000). Ethnic identity also plays a larger role in self-esteem for individuals from minority groups than it does for Whites, which also contributes to academic achievement (Corenblum, 2014; Gray-Little & Hafdahl, 2000; Hope, Chavous, Jagers, & Sellers, 2013).

- Overall levels of self-esteem have increased from previous generations. High school students in 2006 reported higher global self-esteem than high school students in 1975; however, few explanations have been tested to explain this difference (Twenge & Campbell, 2008).

SOCIAL COMPETENCE

5 Explain the two components of social competence.

Social competence comprises both social and emotional skills that lead to positive social outcomes, such as having friends and social status (Hubbard & Coie, 1994; Webster-Stratton & Reid, 2013).

First, social competence requires the development of an adaptive repertoire of social skills. **Social skills** include the ability to reason, think through situations, pick up cues, and make appropriate decisions with respect to interpersonal relationships. Sociability and prosociality are two important aspects of social skills (Chen, Li, Li, Li, & Liu, 2000). **Sociability** is one's level of social participation, such as maintaining relationships and interactions with others. For example, individuals high in sociability are likely to become active participants in social activities or conversations, whereas individuals low in sociability are likely to avoid social situations and inhibit behaviors to engage in conversations. **Prosociality** refers to focusing on others' needs and interests by helping or cooperating with individuals or groups based on social norms and expectations (e.g., sharing one's lunch when another doesn't have lunch money or offering to help someone carry heavy boxes to the classroom). Social skills are related to a number of social development outcomes, such as peer acceptance and social standing, as well as academic achievement and school competence (Montroy, Bowles, Skibbe, & Foster, 2014). However, the importance of sociability and prosociality may vary by outcome and culture. Prosociality has a stronger connection to academic outcomes than sociability, and sociability may be even less important in collective cultures such as China (Chen et al., 2000).

Because some children do not acquire social skills—which can lead them to be socially rejected by peers—teachers and educators should attempt to develop these skills in their students (Gresham, Vance, & Chenier, 2013). In particular, social skills programs may increase social competence in children with disabilities, including those diagnosed with autism spectrum disorder (Cotugno, 2009; Richardson, Tolson, Huang, & Lee, 2009).

Prosocial behavior:
See Module 4

DIVERSITY

Another aspect of social competence is the ability to express, understand, and regulate emotions within the self and others, called **emotional competence**. There are three major elements of emotional competence (Denham et al., 2003; Hubbard & Coie, 1994):

- *Emotional expressiveness* is the ability to express positive and negative emotions appropriately. Teachers are more likely to rate children who express more positive and less negative emotions as friendly and assertive, whereas children who express more negative emotions are viewed by teachers as aggressive and sad.

- *Emotional understanding* is having knowledge about others' emotions and using language to describe those emotions (e.g., "He looks sad"). As a result of understanding other people's emotions, children with emotional knowledge can respond more effectively to peers according to their emotional states (Liao, Li, & Su, 2014). Children as young as 2 to 3 years of age are able to understand other people's emotional expressions of distress and respond with appropriate behaviors.

TABLE 3.3   Characteristics of Social Competence During Childhood and Adolescence

DEVELOPMENTAL PERIOD	CHARACTERISTICS
Early childhood	• Beginning of strong reciprocity in social exchanges (matching, fitting, and coordinating social acts)
	• Rapid development in synchronizing interactions with peers
	• Movement from nonverbal signals to strong verbal communication patterns
	• Onset of self-classification of gender, age, and race
Early elementary	• High levels of mutuality in social responding
	• Responding simultaneously to more than one peer
	• Learning how to recruit others into ongoing activity
	• Increased reliance on verbal, rather than physical, strategies in interpersonal control
Late elementary	• Peer group formation and identification of role in the group
	• Continued reliance on authority figures to guide behavior, but with increasing reliance on peers as a mechanism of norm establishment
	• Continued reciprocity and increased integration of patterns of social exchange
Early adolescence	• Employment of peer group affiliation to achieve particular ends
	• Peers now taking primary role as a mechanism of norm establishment
Middle adolescence	• Sharp delineation between strategies for same-sex and opposite-sex relations, along with norms, behaviors, goals, and outcomes
	• Development of more rigid social structures and evolution of subgroup norms for behavior
	• Formation of transient cross-sex liaisons for mutual support or gratification
Late adolescence	• Divergence of interaction styles as a function of the social groups in which individuals engage (code switching)
	• Sharpening of sexual stereotypes
	• Employment of cognitive capabilities to enhance social relations (better social cognition)
	• More sophisticated use of skills to inhibit, remove, or control the behavior of others

SOURCE: Adapted from Cairns, 1986.

Social Competence.
Socially competent children and adolescents have good interpersonal skills that lead to many friendships and popularity among peers.

- *Emotional regulation* is the ability to cope with emotions, such as maintaining positive emotions and avoiding the display of inappropriate emotions by monitoring and modifying emotional reactions. Understanding when and where it is socially appropriate to express emotions is also referred to as emotion display rule knowledge (Matsumoto, 2009; Saarni, 1979), which does not develop until about age 7 (Hayashi & Shiomi, 2015). Display rules vary by ethnic group. For example, one study found that Asian Americans expressed emotions less often than Whites (Hwang & Matsumoto, 2012).

DIVERSITY

The presence of each of these three elements of emotional competence during the preschool years is related to social competence in elementary education students. Children who do not express positive affect, have difficulty regulating their emotions, or are unable to understand other people's emotional states are more likely to have peer difficulties later on (Denham et al., 2003). Although most studies on the importance of emotional competence have been conducted with preschoolers from middle-class families, preschoolers from low-income families are also found to benefit socially from emotional competence (Garner, Jones, & Miner, 1994). The benefit of emotional competence is important not only during preschool but has been found to be related to academic performance among adolescents as well (Morales & Zafra, 2013; Rodeiro, Emery, & Bell, 2012).

Family context: See Module 2

Social competence changes over time based on a wide variety of skills, processes, and social patterns that unfold across the life span. The family context was the original focus of most developmental research on social competence. The results of some significant family studies may help us understand which students are at highest risk for social competence deficits:

DIVERSITY

- Children with insecure attachment histories tend to show more withdrawal and negativity in peer relations and to display more problem behaviors across various cultures (Ding, Xu, Wang, Li, & Wang, 2014; Jaffari-Bimmel, Juffer, van Ijxendoorn, Bakermans-Kranenburg, & Mooijaart,, 2006; La Freniere & Sroufe, 1985; Park & Walters, 1989).

- Parental insensitivity and unresponsiveness may lead to impoverishment or distortion of the emotional and social resources needed to maintain peer relations (Attili, Vermigli, & Roazzi, 2010; Gagnon et al., 2014).

- Parenting stress has implications for social competence as well as for classroom behavior in preschool-age children (Anthony et al., 2005; Ostberg & Hagekull, 2013). Parents who experience high levels of stress such as poverty, a change in housing, or other major life events are less likely to have preschoolers who are rated by teachers as socially competent.

- Emotional expressiveness in the family is related to children's expression of emotions such that positive expressiveness by family members is related to higher levels of self-esteem, and the expression of anxiety by both fathers and mothers is related to higher levels of anxiety among their children (Moller, Majdandzic, Vriends, & Bogels, 2014; Reese, Bird, & Tripp, 2007). In particular, mothers who encourage their children to regulate negative emotions may be helpful in establishing emotional and social development (Eisenberg, Fabes, & Murphy, 1996).

The importance of fostering social competence in children and adolescents is evident from numerous research studies. For example, social competence correlates with a number of positive outcomes, including school readiness among preschoolers as well as peer status and academic achievement in elementary and middle school students (Arnold, Kupersmidt, Voegler-Lee, & Marshall, 2012; Denham, Way, Kalb, Warren-Khot, & Bassett, 2013; Zorza, Marino, de Lemus, & Mesas, 2013). Social competence is particularly important to academic achievement in ethnic minority, low socioeconomic, and urban school children (Elias & Haynes, 2008). Table 3.3 (p. 59) provides examples of social competence characteristics that develop during childhood and adolescence.

Can you think of someone you currently know or used to know who lacks social competence? Think of some specific behaviors or skills that the person seems to lack.

Video Case 3.5 ▲

External Factors Influence Student Learning

© SAGE Publications

> DIVERSITY

?

APPLICATIONS: FOSTERING SOCIAL COMPETENCE

6   Describe at least three strategies for improving social competence.

Fostering Social Skills

Research provides numerous suggestions for improving social skills (Elias & Weissberg, 2000; Han, Catron, Weiss, & Marciel, 2005; Sheridan, Hungelmann, & Maughan, 1999):

- *Select specific, critical social skills to be improved for individual children.* These can include interpersonal communication, perspective taking, self-control and self-management techniques, and most important, social problem solving (thinking of alternatives, decision making, and so on).

- *Provide modeling or direct instruction on the use of specific social skills.* Not only can teachers model appropriate behaviors for students, but peers can as well. By grouping children who lack social skills with children who are socially competent, educators can provide opportunities for children to learn by watching others.

Modeling: See Module 9

Direct instruction: See Module 18

- *Provide opportunities to practice learned social skills.* Teachers can implement role-playing in the classroom and encourage rehearsal strategies to help students remember and practice newly learned social skills. Reinforcement and feedback from the teacher are also necessary for social skills learning.

Transfer: See Module 12

- *Promote transfer of skills.* Give specific examples of how and when to apply the skill outside the classroom. Use reminders, prompts, and cues to help students employ specific social skills in naturalistic settings.

- *Point out student progress.* Through one-on-one interactions, help classmates recognize how and when a student's behavior is changing in positive ways, and guide them to respond to the student in more positive ways.

Video: Social-Emotional Learning Programs

Social-Emotional Learning (SEL) Programs

Social and emotional learning (SEL) is a relatively new way of thinking about social competence. In particular, Daniel Goleman's (1995) book, *Emotional Intelligence,* directed attention toward the importance of social and emotional competence to many areas of successful life, including interpersonal relationships and academic performance. In addition, the Collaborative for Academic, Social, and Emotional Learning (CASEL) was established in 1994 to advance research and provide evidence-based practices for enhancing SEL among children and adolescents (http://www.casel.org). From the work of CASEL, the book *Promoting Social and Emotional Learning: Guidelines for Educators* was published, providing a foundation for the study of SEL (Elias et al., 1997). Since that time, numerous SEL programs have been developed, and empirical support has been found for the connection of SEL to academic learning. Zins, Bloodworth, Weissberg, and Walberg (2004) provided an SEL framework with five competencies:

Perspective taking and empathy: See Module 4

1. *Self-awareness:* having an accurate view of one's self, such as one's strengths, weaknesses, and values.

2. *Social awareness:* having perspective-taking skills, empathy, and respect for diversity to effectively relate to others.

3. *Responsible decision making:* having the skills to identify problems, analyze the situation, and effectively solve problems; developing a sense of personal, moral, and ethical responsibility.

4. *Self-management:* having the skills to regulate one's emotions, such as coping with impulses and stress and being motivated to set goals and provide self-discipline.

5. *Relationship management:* implementing behaviors to facilitate interpersonal relationships, such as communication skills, conflict resolution skills, and cooperative and help-seeking behaviors.

A review of hundreds of studies examining universal, school-based SEL programs, including kindergarten through high school, as well as a two-year experimental study, found the following outcomes (Durlak, Weissberg, Dymnicki, Taylor, & Schellinger, 2011; Jones, Brown, & Aber, 2011):

- Increased prosocial behaviors such as the five competencies noted above;

- Decreased conduct problems such as less aggressive behaviors;

- Less emotional distress such as fewer depressive symptoms;

- Improved academic grades, particularly in the areas of math and reading;

- Improved achievement test scores by 11 percentile points.

Qualities of programs are important for acquiring positive outcomes. Best practices for SEL programs suggest the curriculum must be included across the entire school system and must include direct instruction about SEL (Elias et al., 1997). In addition, research suggests that programs are more successful if they are interactive in nature, including coaching and role-playing, and have structured activities to meet specific program goals (Durlak et al., 2011). Choosing a program for a school should be based on the specific needs of that school. With the "right" program and proper implementation and sustainability of the program, numerous positive outcomes are likely (Kress & Elias, 2013).

SUMMARY

❶ Describe the environmental influences in the development of the eight psychosocial crises. Erikson suggested that parents or caregivers are the most important influences for the first two stages (trust and autonomy) and continue to play an important role in the development of industry and identity. However, teachers and peers begin to become important during the third stage (initiative) and play an increasing role in the fourth stage (industry). Although environmental influences such as parents and peers continue to support the fifth and sixth stages (identity and intimacy), adolescents and young adults take a more active role in the resolution of these stages. The final two stages (generativity and integrity) are based almost exclusively on the individual's own processes.

❷ Describe the four types of identity statuses. Identity statuses are determined by the presence or absence of commitment and exploration. Identity-achieved adolescents have explored options and made commitments to personal values and future goals. Identity foreclosure status lacks exploration but involves a strong commitment to goals and values, typically based on parental aspirations. The status of moratorium includes actively exploring goals and values without yet having made commitments. Identity-diffused adolescents either have not begun exploration or, following exploration, have been unable to make commitments.

❸ Explain the development of ethnic identity and gender identity. Ethnic identity develops from self-identification with an individual's ethnic group, a sense of belongingness to the group, attitudes toward the ethnic group, and participation within the group. The stages of ethnic identity development mirror those of identity in other areas, as described by Marcia. Gender identity implies different meanings at different levels of development. For young children, gender identity is the knowledge of being biologically male or female. By adolescence, gender-role identity includes behaving appropriately according to the social expectations for one's biological status as male or female. Boys and men who consider themselves masculine tend to have the best psychological outcomes, whereas androgyny, not femininity, is related to better psychological well-being for girls and women.

❹ Compare and contrast self-concept and self-esteem. Although self-concept refers to the cognitive perceptions of the self and self-esteem to the affective evaluation of the self, both are influenced by the environment and are related to school achievement. Educators should be aware of the demographic variables related to these concepts and of strategies for improving self-concept and self-esteem among students.

❺ Explain the two components of social competence. One component of social competence is an adaptive repertoire of social skills, including sociability (social participation) and prosociality (focusing on other's needs) behaviors. Another component of social competence is emotional competence, including emotional expressiveness (expressing positive and negative emotions appropriately), emotional understanding (having knowledge about others' emotions), and emotional regulation (coping with emotions).

❻ Describe at least three strategies for improving social competence. Several strategies can be used to improve social competence, such as (a) selecting specific skills based on individual or school needs, (b) providing direct instruction, (c) modeling appropriate social behaviors, (d) using role-plays to practice skills, (e) coaching students to use skills in other contexts (transfer), (f) recognizing student progress, and (g) implementing and sustaining an evidence-based, school-wide SEL program.

KEY CONCEPTS

CASE STUDIES: REFLECT AND EVALUATE

EARLY CHILDHOOD: CRY BABY

These questions refer to the case study on page 22.

1. Based on Erikson's psychosocial theory, what crisis are most of these children experiencing?

2. What examples in the curriculum may help children with the psychosocial crisis for this stage?

3. Why would a preschool program spend so much time and effort on facilitating and observing social behaviors?

4. What types of developmentally appropriate social skills are evident in the classroom? Which social skills should be emphasized more?

5. Tanner seems to have clear ideas about gender appropriateness. Is this typical of children his age? How might these ideas change over time?

ELEMENTARY SCHOOL: Team

These questions refer to the case study on page 24.

1. Based on Erikson's psychosocial theory, what crisis are most of these children experiencing? What factors in Patricia's and Kashi's experiences can you identify that are important to their resolution of this crisis?

2. Can you think of ways Ms. Barone can help her students develop a sense of industry and avoid feelings of inferiority?

3. Why would Mary be concerned about her daughter's self-esteem? Is this a legitimate concern?

4. How might Kashi's ethnic identity be compromised in this particular school system?

5. Why would the comments made by Bill about Zach's father be hurtful given the boys' stage of gender identity?

6. How might comments such as Bill's about Zach's being "like a little girl" influence the gender identity of the girls and boys in his class?

MIDDLE SCHOOL: Basketball Star

These questions refer to the case study on page 26.

1. Based on Erikson's psychosocial theory, what crisis are most of these adolescents experiencing? What evidence is given that these adolescents are in that stage of development?

2. How might Mr. Martin attempt to foster Darla's social competence? Give specific suggestions.

3. Describe Darla's self-concept and self-esteem based on the information provided in the case.

4. What identity status does Darla appear to be in currently? To what factors is her status most likely attributed?

5. How does Mr. Martin attempt to foster identity development in Darla?

6. What is the gender-role behavior of Darla? How does Darla view the gender-role behavior of the other girls on the basketball team?

HIGH SCHOOL: STEAL, CHEAT, AND FIGHT

These questions refer to the case study on page 28.

1. Based on Erikson's psychosocial theory, what crisis are most of these adolescents experiencing? What evidence is given that these adolescents are in that stage of development? What evidence is given that they might also be entering the next stage?

2. Based on theory and research, is Principal Durbin correct in taking school time to consider social behavior? Is Mr. Ruestman correct in not wanting his class time to be used to address these behaviors by including social skills training?

3. How likely is it that Ms. Kennel's concern about the girls' self-concepts and self-esteem is accurate? What can be done?

4. Ms. Baxter is concerned that students should be making decisions about college and career paths. Is this a legitimate concern at this developmental level? Why or why not?

5. How might the ethnic identity of the Spanish-speaking students be enhanced or compromised by the creation of a peer group based on their ethnicity?

©iStockphoto.com/ mediaphotos

MODULE **4**

MORAL DEVELOPMENT

OUTLINE	LEARNING GOALS
Cognitive-Developmental Moral Reasoning	
• Piaget's Theory • Kohlberg's Theory • Gilligan's Criticism	**❶** Explain how thinking or reasoning about moral issues becomes more sophisticated over time, and identify any gender differences in moral reasoning.
Prosocial Behavior	
• Eisenberg's Theory • Perspective Taking • Empathy	**❷** Describe the importance of perspective taking and empathy to prosocial behavior, and identify any gender differences that exist in prosocial behaviors.
Aggressive Behavior	
• Social-Cognitive Domains • Social-Information Processing	**❸** Describe the cognitive deficits that may explain why some individuals are more likely than other individuals to use aggression.
Applications: Advancing Moral Development	
• Family Context • Peer Context • School Context	**❹** Explain how families, peers, and schools contribute to the moral development of children and adolescents.

COGNITIVE-DEVELOPMENTAL MORAL REASONING

❶ Explain how thinking or reasoning about moral issues becomes more sophisticated over time, and identify any gender differences in moral reasoning.

Do you think lying is wrong? We have all told "white lies," perhaps to spare people's feelings or shelter them from bad news. But how do we distinguish between a harmless fib and a more serious deception? When we think about such moral issues, a process called **moral reasoning,** we are seeking rationales for determining right and wrong.

As you already know, people might *think* about what is right and wrong, but they don't always *behave* consistently with those thoughts. However, individuals must be able to distinguish right from wrong before they can behave in appropriate ways. Hence, theories on moral reasoning focus on the thought processes individuals use to determine what is right or wrong, not on the moral (or immoral) behaviors individuals may exhibit. Before we can discuss how an understanding of moral development can serve teachers in the classroom, we need to summarize the prominent moral development theories.

Piaget's Theory

Developmental psychologist Jean Piaget is best known in the fields of education and psychology for his theory of cognitive development. In one of his early writings, *The Moral Judgment of the Child* (1932), he proposed a two-step process of cognitive moral development. According to Piaget, in the first stage of cognitive moral development, labeled **moral realism,** children believe that right and wrong are determined by the consequences of behavior as given by adult authority figures. Rules are absolute and are not meant to be broken or bent under any circumstances. At this stage, intentions are not important. As they develop more advanced thinking skills, children move into the stage of **morality of cooperation,** or autonomy, and understand that in certain situations or under particular circumstances rules can be bent. In other words, children begin to see the complexities of right and wrong, for example, understanding that lying may be necessary to spare someone's feelings or that killing someone may be acceptable in war or self-defense.

Kohlberg's Theory

Lawrence Kohlberg, one of Piaget's students, believed that moral reasoning was much more complex than the two-stage process proposed by Piaget. Kohlberg (1963, 1981) developed his own theory of moral reasoning, framing it in three levels, each of which encompasses two stages, as summarized in Table 4.1.

The **preconventional level** is defined by an egocentric, self-interested view of right and wrong and disregards the conventions or standards of society. **Egocentrism** is a focus on the self with little consideration for other people or their perspectives. Children in the first stage of this level, *punishment/obedience,* focus on the consequences of their behavior, similar to Piaget's moral realism. For example, "Cheating is wrong because I might get caught and fail the course." In the second stage, *naive hedonistic* or *personal reward,* children focus

Master the content.

edge.sagepub.com/durwin3e

SAGE edge™

Piaget's theory of cognitive development: See Module 6

Video Case 4.1 ▲
Moral Development

© SAGE Publications

TABLE 4.1	Kohlberg's Theory of Moral Reasoning	
LEVEL	**STAGE**	**DESCRIPTION**
Preconventional	Punishment/obedience Naive hedonistic	• Focus on the consequences of behavior • Focus on equal exchange, manipulative reciprocity
Conventional	Interpersonal authority Social authority	• Focus on conforming to rules of parents and other family members • Focus on conforming to laws and norms of society
Postconventional	Morality of social contract Morality of individual principles	• Focus on personal decisions to determine when and how rules should be bent • Focus on what will most benefit society as a whole or the greater good

on whether there will be a reward for their behavior: "What's in it for me?" Here individuals are concerned with the quid pro quo of behavior, a more or less equal exchange also called manipulative reciprocity. For example, "If you are nice to me, then I will be nice to you." An individual also may justify misbehavior by invoking manipulative reciprocity. For example, "Cheating is okay because the teacher's tests are unfair." Children need to be exposed to people and situations that introduce new ideas, outside their own perspectives, to advance beyond the preconventional level (Shaffer, 2000).

At the **conventional level,** the individual focuses on external authorities, such as the conventions and standards of society, in determining right and wrong. Because of their less egocentric focus and more advanced thinking skills, children at the conventional level are capable of judging the intentions of actions—for example, "He didn't mean to trip me." In the third stage, *interpersonal authority* has the highest priority, meaning that children want to hold the same beliefs as their parents and other family members. Therefore, they will conform to rules to gain the approval of authority figures and avoid disapproval—for example, "Cheating is wrong because my mother says you are only cheating yourself and should do your own work." The next stage of conventional reasoning, *social authority,* focuses on social systems in determining laws and norms of behavior. Here an individual may claim that cheating is wrong because it is against school policy.

The **postconventional level** moves beyond simple consequences and away from external authorities to an internal authority, as the individual establishes personal convictions about what is right and wrong. Again, advances in cognitive development allow individuals to move into the postconventional level of reasoning such that individuals who attend college or have more years of formal education show more complex reasoning than individuals who lack those educational experiences (Speicher, 1994). *Morality of social contract,* the fifth stage, includes personal decisions about when, why, and how rules should be bent or under which circumstances actions that typically are considered misbehaviors may actually be appropriate. For example, cheating is okay only if the task is unimportant (for example, playing a card game with friends) or when it benefits someone else (for example, cheating to let a younger child win to boost his or her confidence). In the sixth stage of moral reasoning, *morality of individual principles,* individuals focus on the system of morality that will most benefit society, or the greater good. For example, stealing should never be tolerated because societal chaos and disruption will follow.

Kohlberg measured an individual's level of moral reasoning by presenting moral dilemmas and rating responses according to the stages. Moral dilemmas have no right or wrong answer, so Kohlberg was interested not in the individual's choice to do or not do something but rather in a person's stage of moral development as determined by his or her rationale or reasoning for the choice.

The classic dilemma used by Kohlberg to measure moral reasoning follows. Read the dilemma below and think about whether you would make the same choice as Heinz, the character in the story. More important, explain why you would or would not make that choice.

Video: Interactive Animation of Heinz Dilemma

> In Europe, a woman was near death from a rare form of cancer. There was one drug that the doctors thought might save her, a form of radium that a druggist in the same town had recently discovered. The druggist was charging $2,000, ten times what the drug cost him to make. The sick woman's husband, Heinz, went to everyone he knew to borrow the money, but he could only get together about half of what the drug cost. He told the druggist that his wife was dying and asked him to sell it cheaper or let him pay later. But the druggist said no. So Heinz got desperate and broke into the man's store to steal the drug for his wife. (Kohlberg, 1981, p. 186)

Kohlberg believed that his theory of moral reasoning was universal across all cultures, but he was convinced that not all adults function at the highest levels of reasoning (Carpendale, 2000). While adults have been found to use a mix of moral reasoning strategies, children appear to progress developmentally from preconventional to postconventional thinking, as Kohlberg hypothesized (Colby, Kohlberg, Gibbs, & Lieberman, 1983; Kaplan, Crockett, & Tivnan, 2014; Rest,

Thomas, & Edwards, 1997). For example, high school students are likely to provide responses to moral dilemmas consistent with the interpersonal authority stage (conventional level), whereas college students provide responses consistent with the postconventional social contract stage (Boom, Brugman, & van der Heijden, 2001). However, some research indicates that individuals with intellectual disabilities do not progress as quickly through the stages and may not reach the advanced stages (Langdon, Clare, & Murphy, 2010). Support for Kohlberg's hypothesized order of cognitive-developmental moral reasoning has been found in Israel and Turkey, suggesting that, as he proposed, the theory applies universally across cultures (Colby & Kohlberg, 1987).

Gilligan's Criticism

Carol Gilligan has criticized several developmental theories for their lack of attention to women and exclusion of a feminine perspective. Most notably, Gilligan has criticized Kohlberg's theory of moral reasoning for focusing on justice as the overarching theme in determining the level of moral reasoning. Gilligan (1977) suggested that men, who typically are more focused on independence and individuality, will have a **justice orientation** that focuses on the rights of individuals. Women, however, who typically are more focused on interpersonal relationships, will have a **caring orientation** that focuses on responding to others' needs in intimate relationships. Gilligan suggested that the moral dilemmas presented to measure an individual's level of moral reasoning need to be real-life situations rather than the hypothetical situations presented by Kohlberg (Walker, 2006).

Early research using Kohlberg's methodology was conducted only with men, leading Gilligan to criticize the sample on which the theory was based. In addition, early studies using samples of women suggested that women's responses to the moral dilemmas were more likely to be scored in the third stage, interpersonal authority, while men's responses were scored more often in the fourth or fifth stage of moral reasoning (Walker, 2006). However, Kohlberg's

> DIVERSITY

HAZING
Soliciting, encouraging, aiding, or engaging in hazing is prohibited. Hazing means any intentional, knowing, or reckless act directed against a student for the purpose of being initiated into, affiliated with, holding office in, or maintaining membership in any organization, club, or athletic team whose members are or include other students. Students engaging in hazing will be subject to one or more of the following disciplinary actions:
1. Detention assignment.
2. Removal from the extra-curricular activities.
3. Conference with students and parents.
4. In-school suspension.
5. Referral to appropriate law enforcement agency.
6. If serious enough, possible recommendation for expulsion.

BULLYING/HARASSMENT
Bullying is defined, but not limited to: taunting, insults, teasing, aggression, exclusion, humiliation, alienation, harassment, intimidation, or any behavior repeated with the intent of hurting someone physically or emotionally.

CHEATING
Cheating is the most serious of academic crimes and an inarguable deceitful act which a school cannot afford to foster. Cheating will be defined as a student's intentional presentation of academic work which is not his/her own. Cheating will be constituted any time a student submits work which (1) has been fraudulently borrowed from another individual, including but not limited to current students and graduates; or (2) has been fraudulently borrowed from a published author. Furthermore, any student who knowingly lends his/her work to another in a circumstance where cheating exists will be considered an aide to cheating.

The consequences for those who cheat or are aides to cheating are as follows:
1. Resubmission of work in question.
2. No credit received for the work submitted, regardless of length and magnitude.
3. A semester's failing grade for the course.

Conventional Reasoning: Students at this stage may consider some behaviors wrong or immoral because the behaviors are against school policy as outlined in the student handbook.

scoring system for the moral dilemmas was revised following the first few empirical studies due to a number of problems. Walker (2006) reviewed the literature on gender differences in moral reasoning and found that, overall, men and women do not differ in their moral reasoning. Moreover, no evidence suggests that two separate orientations—justice versus caring—exist. Rather, most people use a combination of justice and caring to determine what is right and wrong in a given situation (Jorgensen, 2006). Although Gilligan's basic premise that men and women have different moral orientations has not been supported, her criticism did spark interest in moral development, issues of measurement in moral development, and the roles of caring and empathy in moral reasoning.

PROSOCIAL BEHAVIOR

2 Describe the importance of perspective taking and empathy to prosocial behavior, and identify any gender differences that exist in prosocial behaviors.

Separate from the cognitive-developmental perspectives of Piaget and Kohlberg, other researchers have studied the foundations of individual compassion and self-sacrifice. Why do people voluntarily care for and comfort one another? Why do they cooperate and share with one another? Psychologists call this human tendency **prosocial behavior,** and it encompasses those voluntary actions that are intended to benefit others through helping or sharing (Eisenberg, Spinrad, & Sadovsky, 2006).

Eisenberg's Theory

Nancy Eisenberg's theory of prosocial moral reasoning is different from the cognitive-developmental perspectives of Piaget and Kohlberg due to its focus on *positive justice* (Lapsley, 2006). In essence, positive justice focuses on why we do the right thing, such as helping others or sharing. Eisenberg (1986) developed levels of prosocial reasoning based on her longitudinal research. Although Eisenberg's levels refer to prosocial reasoning (thinking), many of the outcomes also include actions (behavior). She identified five levels of prosocial thinking:

- *Level 1—hedonistic or self-focused orientation:* Individuals focus on the consequence to the self or self-interest as a motive for prosocial behavior. "I will share my crayons because the teacher will be happy and say something nice to me."

- *Level 2—needs orientation:* Individuals focus on the needs of others even when those needs conflict with one's self-interest. "I will share my crayons with Jenny because she can't find hers today."

- *Level 3—approval/interpersonal orientation:* Individuals engage in prosocial behavior based on the stereotypical beliefs about a person, helping a person considered to be "a good person" and not helping a person considered to be "a bad person," to gain approval from or acceptance by others. "I will share my crayons with Billy because he is a nice person, but I won't share with Tommy because he is always mean to people."

- *Level 4—self-reflective empathetic orientation:* To determine whether their actions will result in positive feelings or feelings of guilt, individuals use empathy and perspective taking, the ability to understand another person's situation or psychological state, such as their thoughts or feelings (Damon, 1988). "I will share my lecture notes with Lisa, who missed class due to her grandfather's funeral, because I feel bad for her and I would want someone to help me."

- *Level 5—internalized orientation:* Individuals behave in prosocial ways due to their personal values rather than external authority or expectations. "Because I believe more fortunate people should help others, I will give some of my holiday bonus to the local charity that provides gifts for underprivileged children."

Prosocial Behaviors. Even preschool-age children can focus on others' needs by sharing.

Prosocial reasoning and behavior increase throughout childhood, with girls being more likely than boys to use prosocial behaviors, particularly in relationships (Carlo, 2014; Eisenberg & Fabes, 1998; Eisenberg, Morris, McDaniel, & Sprinrad, 2009). During adolescence, prosocial behavior declines between the age of 13 and 17 but then increases until at least age 21 (Kanacri, Pastorelli, Eisenberg, Zuffiano, & Caprara, 2013). Perspective taking and empathy are two components that help explain why older adolescents and girls are more likely to exhibit higher levels of prosocial reasoning and behavior (Eisenberg, Eggum, & Di Giunta, 2010; Taylor, Eisenberg, Spinrad, Eggum, & Sulik, 2013).

> **DIVERSITY**

Perspective Taking

Perspective taking is vital to the development of prosocial moral reasoning, which Kohlberg also considered important for cognitive-developmental moral reasoning. Individuals capable of **perspective taking** can appreciate that different people facing the same event may think or feel differently due to their unique backgrounds and qualities. For example, when two middle school students lose a homework assignment, their teacher understands that the incident will affect each child differently based on their commitment to education and the consequences they face at home for failure. Preschool children, however, are not yet able to grasp the perspectives of others, because children develop that ability gradually during their school years. Robert Selman (1971) proposed five stages of perspective-taking development from early childhood through adolescence and beyond:

- *Stage 0—egocentric viewpoint:* Preschool-age children (ages 3 to 6) understand that other individuals have thoughts and feelings but confuse their own emotions with those of others or have difficulty understanding the causes of others' feelings.

- *Stage 1—social-informational role taking:* Early elementary children (ages 6 to 8) understand that others have thoughts and feelings that may be different from their own but do not yet understand how different perspectives are related; hence, children are likely to focus on one perspective only. "I know she is sad, but I am happy I got the bigger piece of cake."

- *Stage 2—self-reflective role taking:* Older elementary children (ages 8 to 10) can understand the relationship between self and others' perspectives, enabling them to speculate on how another will feel or what another will think prior to the circumstances. "Johnny will be mad if I cut in line."

- *Stage 3—mutual role taking:* Early adolescents (ages 10 to 12) are also able to take the perspective of a third party to understand how two individuals influence each other in a mutual, simultaneous manner. "I can understand why both Jenny and Jill want first prize at the science fair and why each thinks the other's project is not as good as her own."

- *Stage 4—social and conventional system role taking:* By middle adolescence (ages 12 to 15) and beyond, individuals are capable of understanding social conventions that are relevant to everyone rather than to only one individual: "I can understand that you shouldn't cheat even if the teacher's tests are too hard."

Selman (1971) found that role-taking ability was related to Kohlberg's moral reasoning stages, with low role-taking ability related to preconventional reasoning and higher role-taking ability related to conventional reasoning. While perspective-taking abilities help individuals develop prosocial reasoning, those abilities do not necessarily lead to prosocial behavior. Some individuals may have the ability to take another's perspective but may not be motivated to consider the other person's perspective (Gehlbach, 2004). Others may use their perspective-taking abilities to their own advantage, understanding exactly what will anger or sadden another person and using that understanding to manipulate or con others (Damon, 1988).

Empathy

The development of prosocial behavior also relies on **empathy,** the ability to experience the emotions or feelings of another person, as when an individual feels sad because someone else feels sad (Eisenberg et al., 1987; Eisenberg et al., 2006). To experience empathy, an individual must have perspective-taking abilities (Hoffman, 2000), so both of these skills appear to be essential for prosocial moral development. Note that empathy differs from sympathy. *Sympathy* is the emotional response of concern for another person's emotional state (Eisenberg, Spinrad, & Morris, 2014). For example, we may express sympathy toward others when their loved one dies, yet we do not experience their grief. Psychologist Martin Hoffman (2000) has suggested that empathy development occurs in three stages early in life:

- *Stage 1—global empathy:* Infants may cry when other infants cry, but they are unable to differentiate between self and other. They will seek comfort for their own distress when they are exposed to another's cry or emotional distress.

- *Stage 2—egocentric empathy:* Toddlers begin to differentiate between self and others and may attempt to comfort others' emotional distress, but they do so from their own egocentric perspective. For example, a child may provide another person, including adults, with their comfort toy or blanket when, in actuality, it provides comfort only to himself or herself.

- *Stage 3—empathy for another's feelings:* Children as young as age 2 or 3 have an increasing awareness of others' emotions and different perspectives of needs. Hence, children begin to understand that what comforts them may not be what comforts others. With language and cognitive development, older children and adolescents can understand another person's emotions without having any direct experiences with that person (for example, reading about someone).

Research supports Hoffman's stages of empathy development as well as empathy's relationship to prosocial behavior (Eisenberg et al., 2014). For example, toddlers respond to both researchers' and mothers' injuries with empathy, and slightly older children will attempt to comfort siblings who are distressed (Eisenberg et al., 2006). Toddlers are even capable of responding with concern when someone is harmed but does not overtly express negative emotions (Vaish, Carpenter, & Tomasello, 2009). Empathy continues to develop throughout adolescence and has been linked to prosocial behaviors, such as being more likely to help a victim of cyberbullying (Van Cleemput, Vadenbosch, & Pabian, 2014).

Women and girls tend to be more empathetic than men and boys (Eisenberg & Fabes, 1998; Maite, 2009), yet research findings are not conclusive. The methods used to measure empathy may explain the gender differences found in some studies (Eisenberg et al., 2014). Studies that ask individuals to report their own levels of empathy or rely on reports from teachers or parents favor girls slightly. The expectation that girls will be more emotional and caring may bias these reports. Hence, girls may be expected to have higher levels of empathy, but in actuality they may have levels similar to those of boys.

> **DIVERSITY**

Think of some examples that illustrate how a person could have perspective-taking skills but not be empathetic. Is it possible for a person to be empathetic but not have perspective-taking skills? Why or why not?

?

AGGRESSIVE BEHAVIOR

3 Describe the cognitive deficits that may explain why some individuals are more likely than other individuals to use aggression.

Although some theories of moral development have focused on the positive, or prosocial, behaviors of individuals, aggression has also been a point of interest among scholars investigating moral development. Aggression typically refers to physical or *overt aggression,* in which a person intends to harm another person physically. Yet *relational aggression,* in which a person attempts to harm another person's relationships or social standing, can also be examined from a moral perspective. Regardless of the type of aggression used, the question becomes this: Why are some individuals more likely to use aggression than others? Possible answers to that question include the following:

Types of aggression:
See Module 2

📖 Reference: Relational Aggression

- Biological predispositions, such as genetics or hormones that may increase aggression;

- Family influences, such as direct experiences with violence and abuse from parents and siblings;

- Peer influences, such as having friends who are aggressive;

- Cultural differences;

- Other variables, such as exposure to violent television or video games.

Most often, the factors listed interact to increase the chance that a particular individual will become aggressive. The interaction among these factors can lead to differences in the ways individuals think about aggression. Much of the research on moral development has examined the cognitive deficits that accompany the use of aggression. Psychologist John C. Gibbs suggested that some individuals have a **sociomoral developmental delay,** or a self-centered, egocentric orientation that is not replaced by the more typical advanced moral development (Gibbs, 1991; Gibbs, Potter, & DiBiase, 2013).

Aggressive Behaviors. A number of factors can contribute to the development of aggressive behavior, such as exposure to violence in the home, on television, or in video games.

Stuart Pearce / age fotostock / Getty Images

This sociomoral developmental delay is maintained by two cognitive distortions:

1. *Externalizing blame:* Individuals see themselves as the victim, rather than those whom they have victimized. For example, students may explain their aggressive behavior toward a peer by declaring that the peer has always mistreated them.

2. *Mislabeling or minimizing:* Individuals will escape responsibility for their actions by viewing their behavior as less serious than social conventions might judge. For example, they might declare that an aggressive act was not that bad or that it did not really hurt the other person. This is also referred to as moral disengagement and is related to later criminal behavior (Fontaine, Fida, Paciello, Tisak, & Caprara, 2014).

Gibbs suggested that these cognitive distortions are used by individuals to decrease their feelings of **empathy-based guilt,** or the pain and regret felt for causing distress or pain in another person (Hoffman, 2000). To decrease their feelings of guilt and pain, individuals may rationalize their aggressive behaviors or believe that others do not experience negative emotions following victimization (Malti, Gasser, & Buchmann, 2009).

Social-Cognitive Domains

A common approach to evaluating aggressive behaviors is based on the social domain model, which examines how cognitions play a role in aggression (Rizzo & Bosacki, 2013; Turiel, 1983). Through their interactions with the environment, children and adolescents may consider social situations within three domains:

- The *moral domain* includes situations and circumstances related to the rights of others as well as the welfare of others.

- The *conventional domain* focuses on the rules of conduct necessary for social organization.

- The *personal domain* focuses on situations that affect the individual.

The moral domain is the area of the most serious infractions, and the personal domain encompasses the least. Conventional domain issues fall in the middle. When surveyed, elementary students typically view aggressive behavior as being in the moral domain because it affects human welfare and issues of fairness (Murray-Close, Crick, & Galotti, 2006). However, when adolescents judge moral infractions less strictly, or outside of the moral domain, they are more likely to be involved in antisocial behaviors (Bacchini, Affuso, & De Angelis, 2013.) Children and adolescents who view aggressive behavior as being in the conventional domain may have a cognitive deficit similar to minimizing (Tisak, Tisak, & Goldstein, 2006).

Social-Information Processing

Another theory used to explain aggressive behaviors in children and adolescents comes from the social-information processing model developed by Kenneth Dodge (Crick & Dodge, 1994). The model suggests that individuals process social information in six steps. Let's walk through those steps in the context of the commonplace event of an individual being bumped into by the school bully:

1. *Encoding cues:* Individuals pay attention to some information in their social environment and dismiss other information. (I noticed a shocked looked on his face when he bumped into me.)

2. *Interpretation of cues:* Individuals determine meaning for those cues and the causes of the behavior of others in the social environment. (His shocked look must mean that he was surprised to see me standing there.)

Social-Information Processing. Aggressive behaviors may occur because an individual interprets social information as intentional rather than accidental, such as bumping into someone.

3. *Clarification of goals:* Individuals determine goals or outcomes for the situation. (I don't want to make him mad.)

4. *Response access:* Individuals attempt to remember past responses to similar situations. (The last time he bumped into me, I just said, "Excuse me.")

5. *Response decision:* Individuals evaluate the past responses and select the most appropriate response based on the expected outcome. (If I don't want trouble, I should just walk away.)

6. *Behavioral enactment:* Individuals behave according to their decision to respond. (I'll walk away.)

Although this model focuses on the cognitive or thought processes of individuals, emotions are considered to be important as well (Palmer, 2005). For example, emotional arousal may be an internal cue encoded in the first step. Similarly, empathy-based guilt may be considered in the response decision step. However, aggressive children tend to process information differently from nonaggressive children (Tisak et al., 2006) and may be less attentive to cues—such as not noticing that the person who bumped into them was surprised. A specific difference is found between aggressive and nonaggressive children in the interpretation of cues. Aggressive individuals may have what is called a **hostile attributional bias,** or a tendency to interpret another person's intentions as hostile. For example, an aggressive student might interpret someone's bumping into them in the hallway as *intentional* when in fact the collision was *accidental.* Aggressive children are likely to have this bias (Bradshaw, Rodgers, Ghandour, & Garbarino, 2009; Crick & Dodge, 1996; Gagnon, McDuff, Daelman, & Fournier, 2015; Molano, Jones, Brown, & Aber, 2013), leading them to externalize blame for their own aggressive behavior. The cognitive deficits of externalized blame, minimizing or mislabeling the situation, and hostile attributional bias contribute to aggressive children's inability to process social information correctly (Palmer, 2005). A recent study found that these same types of processing deficits are associated with cyberaggression as well (Pornari & Wood, 2010).

Would you expect all individuals who have used aggression in the past to have cognitive deficits? Under what circumstances might someone without a cognitive deficit resort to aggression?

APPLICATIONS: ADVANCING MORAL DEVELOPMENT

 4 Explain how families, peers, and schools contribute to the moral development of children and adolescents.

We've made a fast and furious survey of the theories of moral development. You may have noticed that some of these theories overlap, despite using different terminology (see Table 4.2 for a developmental comparison of theories). Many aspects of these theories have been studied in the contexts of family, peers, and schools to provide suggestions on how to advance moral development among children and adolescents (Eisenberg et al., 2009).

Family Context

Although parents begin as external authority figures who provide consequences, the norms for behavior become the child's own moral code as they outgrow the need for external consequences (Dunn, 2014; Hoffman, 2000). More specifically, maternal support and responsiveness are related to empathy and prosocial behavior in children (Malti, Eisenberg, Kim, & Buchman, 2013). The children of parents who use consistent discipline that includes providing reasons for misbehavior and suggesting appropriate alternatives

Video Case 4.2 ▲

Supporting Students' Moral Development

© SAGE Publications

TABLE 4.2	Comparison of Moral Development Theories			
THEORIST	**EMPHASIS**	**INFANCY TO CHILDHOOD**	**CHILDHOOD TO ADOLESCENCE**	**LATE ADOLESCENCE TO ADULTHOOD**
Piaget	Cognitive	Moral realism	Morality of cooperation	
Kohlberg	Cognitive	Preconventional level	Conventional level	Postconventional level
Eisenberg	Prosocial reasoning	Hedonistic or self-focused orientation Needs orientation	Approval/ interpersonal orientation Self-reflective empathetic orientation	Internalized orientation
Selman	Perspective taking	Egocentric viewpoint Social-informational role taking	Self-reflective role taking Mutual role taking	Social and conventional system role taking
Hoffman	Empathy	Global empathy Egocentric empathy	Empathy for another's feelings	
Developmental trends across theories		Focus on the self, with little consideration for others (egocentrism)	Beginning to consider others through the perspective of external sources such as parents, society, and stereotypical views of others	Development of personal convictions and concern for society as a whole

are more likely to exhibit higher levels of empathy and social responsibility (Bronstein, Fox, Kamon, & Knolls, 2007; Eisenberg et al., 2006). In addition, siblings may play an important role in moral development by engaging in imaginative play that includes moral issues (for example, your Barbie stole something from my Barbie, so she has to go to jail) and by modeling empathy for younger siblings (Dunn, 2014; Eisenberg et al., 2006; Lam, Solmeyer, & McHale, 2012).

In examining the importance of family, psychologists have identified several parenting strategies that may help advance moral development (Berkowitz, 2012; Berkowitz & Grych, 1998; Patrick & Gibbs, 2012):

- *Induction,* in which parents explain discipline by verbally providing the consequences of choices as well as asking children to think about others' emotions (empathy);

- *Nurturance,* in which parents express warmth and affection toward their child as an indication of their concern for the child's emotional state (perspective taking);

- *Demandingness,* in which parents set high standards of behavior for their children and support them in their attempts to meet these standards;

- *Modeling,* in which parents "practice what they preach" such that they become examples of moral conduct;

- *Democratic processes,* in which parents include children in decisions, particularly those that require them to hear and appreciate another's perspective.

These parenting strategies can provide a model for teachers to follow in developing instructional strategies that promote moral development. For example, teachers should also ask children to consider others' feelings in order to promote empathy and perspective taking, two qualities essential to prosocial behavior. Also, teachers, like parents, are authority figures who model appropriate behavior and need to practice what they preach regarding moral conduct.

Parenting: See Module 2

How can parents and teachers balance the need to be demanding and set high standards for behavior with the need to follow a democratic process and allow children to participate in making decisions?

Peer Context

Peer relationships must include reciprocity—aspects of sharing, fairness, and equality—because most children will discontinue relationships with other children who refuse to share or play fair. According to Damon (1988), sharing in young children is an early sign of empathy and is considered an important aspect of prosocial behavior. He further suggested that the specific skill of perspective taking in prosocial behavior develops within peer interactions. Piaget and Kohlberg also both suggested that peer interaction is an essential component of moving into higher levels of cognitive moral reasoning and learning to cooperate with others to determine fairness and justice. Research has supported the link between peer interaction and moral development (McDonald, Malti, Killen, & Rubin, 2014).

Hence, parents and teachers should encourage peer interaction among children (Berkowitz, 2012). Teachers can ensure that children have adequate peer interaction by using cooperative learning strategies. Cooperative learning requires students to work collaboratively on projects and has been found to enhance both empathy and perspective-taking skills (Solomon, Watson, & Battistich, 2001). Therefore, requiring peer interaction among children and adolescents provides an opportunity for teachers to monitor and model the skills necessary for higher levels of moral reasoning.

Cooperative learning: See Module 19

School Context

Although teachers can benefit from the research in the family and peer contexts, several specific approaches to enhancing moral development in educational settings have also been proposed (Berkowitz, 2012; Lies, Bock, Brandenberger, & Trozzolo, 2012; Nucci, 2006; Spivak & Farran, 2012; Watson & Ecken, 2003):

1. *Climate of trust:* The classroom and school system should have a climate of trust and an ethic of caring. Children should feel safe to express emotions, knowing that they are supported and cared for by teachers and staff. Specific strategies have been suggested based on observational research:

   - Teachers can interact with students outside of instructional time, such as having lunch with students, engaging them in ordinary conversations about events, joking with students, and allowing them time to be "goofy."

   - Teachers can share minor personal information about family, pets, and hobbies with students as well as spend time learning about students' hobbies, interests, and family life.

   - Teachers can use a physical posture that relays a trusting, caring attitude, such as leaning down to a young child's level, standing close to a student, or putting a hand on a student's shoulder.

   - Teachers should be consistent and predictable in their responses and routine behaviors to impart a sense of trustworthiness.

2. *Developmental discipline:* Just as parents can use induction and a democratic process to establish standards and consequences as well as encourage empathy, teachers should employ those same strategies within the classroom:

   - Teachers should help students understand the reasons behind rules.

   - Rules should include prosocial behaviors such as sharing, taking turns, and respecting others.

   - Teachers can hold regular class meetings and include collaborative problem solving to stop misbehavior in the classroom.

   - Because adolescents will begin to view more and more issues as personal rather than conventional, desiring more power and control, teachers should give adolescents more opportunities to contribute to the development of rules and to make choices within the classroom (democratic governance).

Reference: Service Learning

3. *Service learning:* Service learning is a method of instruction that combines learning with service to the community. It can involve community service (typical volunteer activities such as tutoring, helping at a nursing home, or volunteering with an organization such as Race for the Cure), community exploration (experiential education, such as internships within the community or outdoor/environmental education), or community action (civic reform, community enhancement). Engaging in service learning has been linked to increases in prosocial behavior, decreases in aggressive behaviors, and increases in levels of civic skills, attitudes, and knowledge (Billig, 2013). For service learning to be effective, students should have choices in selecting activities and opportunities to reflect on their experiences in ways that help them prepare for, be successful in, and learn from those experiences (e.g., through journals or papers). Schools can reinforce the beneficial effects of service learning by offering some sort of acknowledgment and honoring of students'

©iStockphoto.com/Rick Rhay

Service Learning. Instruction that connects classroom learning with service to the community can increase prosocial behavior and decrease aggressive behavior among students.

contributions or of the student-community partnership (holding a party to celebrate a job well done, awarding certificates of appreciation, providing community-sponsored scholarships).

4. *Curriculum:* The moral curriculum should not be separated from academic content, but rather the two should be connected and intertwined within the classroom and school (Berkowitz, 2012):

- History lessons and classic literature typically include moral dilemmas, as do current events in social studies classes.

- Characters within an academic unit can be discussed from a moral standpoint (e.g., Martin Luther King Jr., Huckleberry Finn, Rosa Parks).

- Visual displays can be provided in classrooms to increase awareness of moral issues and to encourage charitable behavior, a positive attitude, and an awareness of environmental concerns.

5. *Challenging the status quo:* Students should not only be allowed but encouraged to challenge standards and social conventions to further their perspective-taking skills and advance their level of moral reasoning. Many times, ambiguity in situations can be used as an example of a moral dilemma, with students asked to provide information from various perspectives. Discussion of moral dilemmas within classrooms was a central component of Kohlberg's school program, Just Community, to advance cognitive moral reasoning (Berkowitz, 2012; Kohlberg, 1975; McDonough, 2005).

6. *School-based interventions:* School-based programs that include extensive teacher training can facilitate moral development. Many of these programs include role-playing to encourage the development of perspective-taking skills (Gibbs, 1991) as well as rehearsing prosocial solutions to moral issues, including modifying children's social-cognitive deficits and decreasing the likelihood of aggression (Espelage, Low, Polanin, & Brown, 2013; Jones, Brown, & Aber, 2011; Yeager, Miu, Powers, & Dweck, 2013).

SUMMARY

1 **Explain how thinking or reasoning about moral issues becomes more sophisticated over time, and identify any gender differences in moral reasoning.** Both Piaget and Kohlberg described stages of moral reasoning that become less reliant on the consequences of behavior and external authorities (family, law) and more heavily based on personal, internal views of right and wrong. Although initially women were considered to have lower levels of moral reasoning or different orientations with respect to moral reasoning, empirical evidence does not support gender differences in cognitive-developmental moral reasoning.

2 **Describe the importance of perspective taking and empathy to prosocial behavior, and identify any gender differences that exist in prosocial behaviors.** Prosocial behavior is voluntary behavior intended to benefit others by helping or sharing that increases throughout childhood and adolescence. The ability to understand another person's situation or psychological state (perspective taking), such as their emotions (empathy), is important to the display of prosocial behaviors. Perspective taking and empathy develop gradually throughout childhood and adolescence. Girls are more likely than boys to use prosocial behaviors, particularly in relationships. This gender difference may be due in part to expectations for girls to have more empathy than boys.

3 **Describe the cognitive deficits that may explain why some individuals are more likely than other individuals to use aggression.** Several theoretical models, supported by empirical data, suggest that aggressive individuals have cognitive deficits that increase their chances of using aggression. Cognitive deficits may include blaming the victim, minimizing the seriousness of the aggressive act, or believing that the aggression was justified because the other person was hostile first. In addition, aggressive individuals may not view aggression as harming others but simply as breaking a rule.

4 **Explain how families, peers, and schools contribute to the moral development of children and adolescents.** Families are considered important in two ways: (1) Parents can use specific parenting strategies to promote moral development, and (2) siblings can advance moral development during pretend play and by modeling prosocial behavior. Most theories of moral development, as well as empirical evidence, emphasize the importance of peer interaction for advancing moral reasoning in children. Finally, schools can promote moral development through the climate of the classroom; the discipline used; the curriculum, including moral issues and service learning; opportunities for students to debate moral dilemmas; and school-based programs to decrease aggression.

KEY CONCEPTS

caring orientation, 69

conventional level (of moral reasoning), 68

egocentrism, 67

empathy, 72

empathy-based guilt, 74

hostile attributional bias, 75

justice orientation, 69

moral realism, 67

moral reasoning, 67

morality of cooperation, 67

perspective taking, 71

postconventional level (of moral reasoning), 68

preconventional level (of moral reasoning), 67

prosocial behavior, 70

sociomoral developmental delay, 73

CASE STUDIES: REFLECT AND EVALUATE

EARLY CHILDHOOD: CRY BABY

These questions refer to the case study on page 22.

1. According to Kohlberg's cognitive-developmental moral theory, what stage does Zada appear to be in given her comments about sharing?

2. What examples of prosocial behavior are given in the case? Does the gender of the child displaying the prosocial behavior surprise you, based on current research?

3. How do Mr. Abbott and Ms. Harsted attempt to increase perspective taking and empathy in their students?

4. Based on Tyler's aggressive behavior and current level of thinking, what types of cognitive deficits might follow?

5. What other strategies can teachers use at this age to foster moral development?

ELEMENTARY SCHOOL: Team

These questions refer to the case study on page 24.

1. Based on the interactions between students in the case study, speculate on the children's level of moral reasoning, according to Kohlberg's cognitive-developmental moral theory.

2. How does Ms. Barone attempt to promote moral development in her students? Evaluate her attempt.

3. What specific examples of perspective taking and empathy are given by Ms. Barone?

4. Bill's response to Zach implies at least two cognitive deficits in his moral thinking. What statements are related to those specific deficits?

5. How might family factors play a role in the moral development of Bill? Of Kashi? Of Patricia?

MIDDLE SCHOOL: Basketball Star

These questions refer to the case study on page 26.

1. According to Kohlberg's cognitive-developmental moral theory, what stage of moral development does Claudia appear to be in based on her behavior and her comments? What stage of moral reasoning might Jill and Sierra be in?

2. Based on Mr. Martin's recollection of Mark, what stage of moral reasoning might Mark have been in, according to Kohlberg's cognitive-developmental moral theory?

3. What examples, if any, of prosocial behavior among the students are presented in the case?

4. Explain how Claudia uses her perspective-taking skills. How would you rate Darla's perspective-taking skills, based on Selman's theory and Darla's age?

5. Why might Mark blame others and downplay his own behaviors?

HIGH SCHOOL: Steal, Cheat, and Fight

These questions refer to the case study on page 28.

1. Based on the combination of responses, in which stage of moral development would Kohlberg most likely place these students?

2. According to Mr. Cargill, a number of skills would be necessary to eliminate these disruptive behaviors and replace them with more prosocial behaviors. Based on the information presented in the module, what skills should be promoted among these students to increase their prosocial behaviors?

3. Into which social-cognitive domain does Ms. May's evaluation of the students' behaviors fall? How might this influence her opinion of the seriousness of the behaviors?

4. Mr. Cargill describes Jimmy. What theories or concepts might explain Jimmy's aggressive behavior?

5. Ms. May believes the problem lies within the authority and discipline of the school. Assuming she is correct and many teachers do let students get away with these behaviors, what can be done? How might knowledge of parenting strategies be used within the school system to foster moral development?

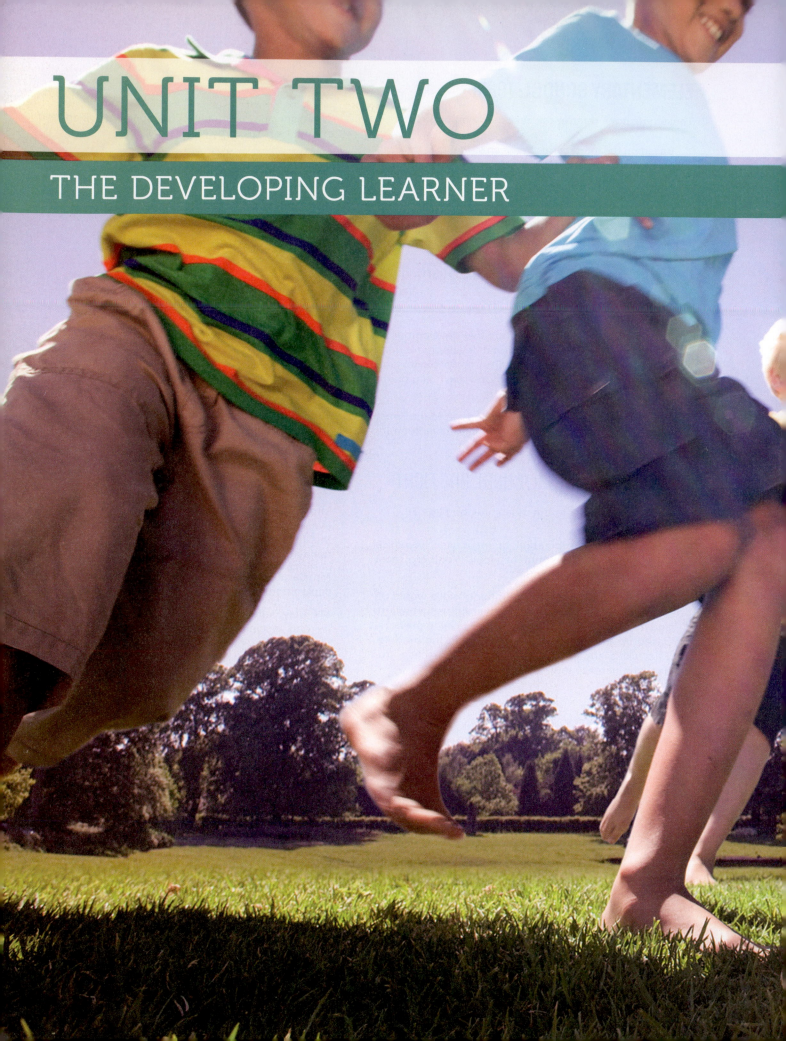

UNIT TWO

THE DEVELOPING LEARNER

Echo / Juniors Getty Images

CASE STUDIES

EARLY CHILDHOOD: FIRE SAFETY

It's Fire Safety Week at Rolling Hills Preschool, a half-day preschool in the small suburban town of Westview. Mrs. Grace Palmer, the head teacher for nearly 20 years, is supervising Angela Hodan, a student teacher from a university in a neighboring city. Miss Angela begins today's activities by explaining emergency situations for dialing 9-1-1 and having children practice how to dial 9-1-1 on

©jonalynnhansen/ Can Stock Photo Inc.

pretend phones. She also has the children recite basic safety information, such as their first and last names, address, phone number, and parents' names. The children trace the digits of their phone numbers on giant flashcards that Miss Angela prepared to help them recite the numbers, and then they color and decorate them.

"I'm going to pick pink first," says Michala. "I'm trying to stay in the lines."

"I like purple best," says her best friend, Brianna. "You know, my dad's a firefighter. He's coming to visit our school tomorrow."

As Miss Angela listens to the chatter and observes the coloring, she feels satisfied that things seem to be going smoothly.

On Tuesday morning, the preschool classroom is buzzing with excitement because the children are expecting a visit from the Westview Volunteer Fire Department. After snack time, Miss Angela announces, "Boys and girls, please find a spot on the carpet. We're going to read a story about fire safety while we wait for the firefighters to arrive."

Brianna and her best friend, Michala, rush to sit on the letter M on the alphabet rug, the coveted spot opposite the teacher. The girls begin pushing and shoving as each tries to occupy the letter M space. "I was here first!" Michala shouts.

"No you weren't!" Brianna responds.

"Well, M is for Michala, so I can sit here!" Michala yells, almost in tears.

Miss Angela asks the girls to apologize to each other and suggests that they sit on two different letters today, F for firefighter, and D for dragon, the main character in the story they are about to read. Brianna and Michala are happy that they can sit next to each other, because no one has chosen to sit on the E. Miss Angela eagerly announces, "I need all of you to put on your listening ears for our story." Once the children have settled down, Miss Angela sits in a tiny chair at the center of the carpet and begins to read *No Dragons for Tea: Fire Safety for Kids,* a rhyming book about a dragon who starts a fire at a girls' tea party. As Miss Angela finishes the story, distant sirens grow louder and louder. "The firefighters are here!" some of the children shriek, wriggling with excitement. Miss Angela leads them outside for a tour of the fire truck.

Back inside, the children take their seats while firefighters Dan and Tracy, in full gear, demonstrate what to do and what not to do in a fire situation. "If you hear a smoke alarm when you're in bed, should you hide under your covers?" Dan asks.

"Oooh! Oooh! I know," says Brenden. "You don't hide in your bed. The dragon in our story hided under a rug when he started a fire. That was bad."

"Right, that's not safe. You never hide in the house if there's a fire. You get out!" replies Tracy. The firefighters continue to demonstrate safety tips, such as feeling a door for heat before opening it, crawling low under smoke, and stop-drop-and-roll, with each child practicing in turn. When the firefighters leave, everyone receives a shiny red fire hat as a reward for learning the safety rules. The children eagerly line up to go outside. They can't wait to play firefighters on the playground.

In the last half-hour of preschool, Miss Angela reviews what they learned from the firefighters. "Who can tell me what we do if our clothes catch fire?" Several children happily drop to the floor and begin rolling around. "Okay, I see you remember stop-drop-and-roll. Now, what number do we call in a fire emergency?" Miss Angela asks.

"9-1-1!" they all shout.

"And where do we call 9-1-1?" she asks. The children look confused. "Where did the mommy in the story call 9-1-1? From her house?" asks Miss Angela.

Raising her hand, Dominique answers, "She goed to her neighbor's house."

"That's right. She went to a safe place to make the phone call," Miss Angela responds. "We need to give our address when we call 9-1-1 so the firefighters know where the fire is. Aakshi, can you tell me where you live?"

"Two-two . . . uhhm . . ." Aakshi pauses.

"2249 Hunter's . . ." Miss Angela hints.

"2249 Hunter's Ridge Road," Aakshi replies. The children all have a turn at recalling their addresses and phone numbers.

After the children leave, Grace and Angela discuss how the fire safety lessons are going. Grace listens as Angela describes what she thinks was effective and what wasn't working. Together they identify what needs to be changed and come up with some modifications of the lessons for the rest of the week. They agree to meet at the end of each day to evaluate the children's learning and Angela's teaching.

ASSESS:

1. Would you consider Rolling Hills Preschool a stimulating environment for four-year-olds? Why or why not?

2. In your opinion, are the lessons that Miss Angela prepared appropriate for preschool children? Why or why not?

3. Based on your knowledge of preschool-age children, describe their language skills. Can you find examples of preschool language skills in the case?

ELEMENTARY SCHOOL: PROJECT NIGHT

PREPARE:

As you read the case, make notes:

1. WHO are the primary participants in the case? Describe them.

2. WHAT is taking place?

3. WHERE is the case taking place? Is the environment a factor?

4. WHEN is the case taking place? Is the timing a factor?

©iStockphoto.com/ sturti

In March, students in Mr. Carlos Morales's fifth-grade class begin a project-based unit in social studies. They choose a topic for their project based on any of the social studies units they have completed during the school year. Mr. Morales has provided them with a long list of topics from five areas: Native Americans, explorers, colonial America, forming a government, and the westward movement. The students begin by conducting research in the school's media center with the help of Linda Porter, the library media specialist, who teaches them to find information on their topics using encyclopedias and Internet searches. Mr. Morales knows that his students need to develop and practice these important research skills.

After students have compiled and read information they collected on their chosen topics, Mr. Morales forms "research evaluation teams" to help them learn to identify important information and evaluate their sources. In research teams, students have an opportunity to explain to the others what information they think they should include in their projects and why it is important. To help team members evaluate the presenter's ideas, Mr. Morales gives them question starters:

- "Can you make your point clearer?"

- "An even better idea is . . ."

- "I'd like to know more about . . ."

Mr. Morales likes using this procedure. It helps improve the quality of the projects by giving students practice at evaluating their own and others' thinking. The question starters also have been especially helpful for the bilingual students who are not as fluent in English. Mr. Morales monitors students' progress in the research teams and assists when needed. Research teams continue for several weeks, until everyone has had a turn to present his or her project resources.

Students then meet individually with Mr. Morales to pick a project design. They have many choices, including the following:

- writing a skit,
- writing a poem,
- creating a painting or sculpture,
- developing storybooks,
- developing a board game,
- writing songs to illustrate an era, and
- writing a newspaper article or a letter from the perspective of a historical figure.

Mr. Morales thinks the range of options will allow both right-brained and left-brained students to use their strengths. He has arranged some time each week for students to work on their projects at school, and he has provided as many supplies as possible to support their projects (paints, clay, wardrobe items). Because his students come from diverse socioeconomic backgrounds, he wants every child to have equal access to resources and the same opportunity for success.

Project Night has finally arrived, and it's as much fun for Mr. Morales as it is for his students. It's a wonderful opportunity for students to show off their class projects to students in other grades, teachers, and parents. Mr. Morales enjoys viewing the projects of students in other grades, conversing with his students' parents, and beaming over the success of all his students. As Project Night winds down, Mr. Morales announces to his students, "Class, I want to congratulate you all on your hard work and achievement. Give yourselves a round of applause." Parents and children clap enthusiastically. "Make sure you enjoy some refreshments—you've earned it. Thanks everyone, and have a good evening."

Later that evening, Mr. Morales reviews the project self-evaluations students turned in before they left.

"I liked that we got to choose a project. So I picked something that interested me."—Ahmad

"My favorite subject is art. So I liked this project because I got to make something to show what I learned. I was happy I didn't have to take a test. I always do bad on multiple choice. Thanks, Mr. Morales."—Isaac (student with a learning disability)

"Working in the research teams was fun and helped me think more about what I wanted to do for a project. Doing projects is better than tests. I don't like memorizing a lot of facts."—Leah

"I learned a lot. The research was hard and it took a long time to read. But I had fun in the media center and in the research teams. It would be more fun to do group projects."—Sonia (a Spanish–English bilingual student)

Mr. Morales is surprised that many students made comments like Sonia's about wanting to work in groups. He is also disturbed that not much self-reflection is evident in the self-evaluations. But, as always, his students' comments give him much food for thought about how to improve the project unit next year.

ASSESS:

1. Was Mr. Morales correct in assuming that students are right-brained or left-brained? Is your response opinion speculation, or based on some source, such as a course, a textbook, or a news report?

2. In your opinion, is the lack of reflection in the students' self-evaluations typical of fifth graders? Why or why not?

3. Based on the students' comments, are their language skills typical of fifth graders? Why or why not?

CASE STUDIES

MIDDLE SCHOOL: FROGS

PREPARE:

As you read the case, make notes:

1. **WHO** are the primary participants in the case? Describe them.
2. **WHAT** is taking place?
3. **WHERE** is the case taking place? Is the environment a factor?
4. **WHEN** is the case taking place? Is the timing a factor?

As the second-period bell rings Monday morning at Exeter Middle School, eighth-grade students begin filing into their science labs. This morning in Ms. Morgan Thesdale's biology lab, students will be dissecting frogs. Dissection is a new addition to the district's curriculum, and Ms. Thesdale, who taught 10th-grade biology for three years, is eager to try dissection with middle school students. She's sure the students will enjoy the hands-on format.

©iStockphoto.com/Paolo Cipriani

After students take their seats, Ms. Thesdale briefly covers laboratory procedures, handling and storing the frogs, and the lab's objectives. She reminds students that one objective is to compare the frog's body systems to those of humans and discuss the similarities and differences between frogs and humans. She then divides students into six groups of three. Students will take different roles: cutting and probing, drawing the frog's body systems, and taking lab notes on their discussions. During the lab, Ms. Thesdale walks around the room to monitor the groups and join in their discussions.

Alanna, Yumi, and Keon have already made their first incision, have sketched the diagram of their dissection, and are discussing what they saw as Yumi takes notes. Ms. Thesdale stops to compliment them on their progress. Then she walks toward Haley, Kyla, and Erin, who are not as far along. "Kyla, like I heard Robert asked you out. Is that true?" Haley asks as Erin tries to draw the frog diagram and listen at the same time.

"Yeah, but my parents won't let me go out on a date yet. So we're going bowling this weekend like with a bunch of us. You wanna . . ." Kyla says, as Ms. Thesdale interrupts.

"Ladies, I'm not sure how this relates to biology. Keep your conversations on the frog, please," Ms. Thesdale warns.

Ms. Thesdale notices that Jay, Tyler, and Vincent are also talking. But they insist that they are already finished. However, when Ms. Thesdale asks them questions about the frog's digestive organs, it is clear that they have not done much discussing at all. Jay, who is outgoing and a natural-born leader, did the cutting, while Vincent sketched and Tyler took notes. Tyler, who has attention deficit hyperactivity disorder (ADHD) and a language impairment, receives special education accommodations such as extended-time tests and note takers. Ms. Thesdale is perturbed at the boys for assigning Tyler to a note-taking role, for speeding through the lab assignment without any discussion or collaboration, and for not taking Tyler under their wing. Ms. Thesdale finishes making her way around the room and tries to initiate and support students' discussions in the rest of the groups—she realizes that the students need a lot more assistance with the comparing and contrasting than she originally thought.

On Friday, students take a lab exam. They rotate through several stations set up in the classroom showing frogs at different stages of dissection. Students identify organs, indicated by tags, by filling in the diagrams on their exam sheets.

The following Friday, after the class finishes the unit on body systems, students take a written exam that includes questions about some of the same items from the lab exam, as well as multiple-choice and essay questions.

On Monday, Ms. Thesdale hands back the lab and the written exams. "Class, the good news is that everyone did pretty well on the lab exam. However, I'm very disappointed in the results of the written exam. Many of you did fine on the lab questions and multiple-choice questions. But I was disappointed by many of your essay responses. I expected to see a lot more explanation to show me that you were thinking, but I saw a lot of regurgitation of facts."

"But Ms. Thesdale, I studied a lot," says Keon. "I can even show you my flash cards."

"Yeah, Ms. Thesdale, some of us studied together. We quizzed each other on the definitions in the notes and the textbook," Haley chimes in, as Erin, Kyla, and others nod.

Vincent raises his hand and comments, "Your test questions are tricky. I mean . . . the multiple-choice questions are not exactly like the definitions in the book."

"I'm not sure I even understood some of the questions!" Alanna adds. "I mean, you know, what does *exemplify* mean, anyway, and I don't know how to even compare the *former* with the *latter*."

Ms. Thesdale and the students continue to discuss study techniques. She is glad she took the time to discuss this important issue. But she knows inside that in order to get students to learn material in a meaningful way, she has to make changes in her teaching as well.

ASSESS:

1. In your opinion, what role—if any—should knowledge of adolescent brain development play in teacher planning of curricula and teaching methods?

2. Should Ms. Thesdale have the same expectations for teaching biology in middle school and in high school? Why or why not?

3. How would you describe the language skills of the middle school students in this case?

HIGH SCHOOL: THE SUBSTITUTE

Tom & Dee Ann McCarthy / Corbis / Getty Images

As the first-period bell rings Monday morning, a hush falls over Mr. Reddy's British literature class as a young man in his 20s walks through the classroom door. A new substitute teacher! Mr. Reddy was to return to work after recent surgery, but due to complications he would be on medical leave for the remainder of the semester. Mr. Jake Matthews has been hired as a long-term substitute. "Good morning class. I'm Mr. Matthews. I'll be taking over Mr. Reddy's classes while he's on medical leave. I understand you're reading *A Tale of Two Cities,* one of my favorite novels," he says. Mr. Matthews, a newly certified secondary education teacher, exudes confidence and energy. The students definitely are not used to someone so young and vibrant.

Mr. Reddy is predictable and—well, boring. He assigns his junior class chapters of the book to read, they come to class, and he lectures for most of the 50-minute class about the progression of the plot or about Dickens's life while he was writing the novel. The students take notes and study for exams on the books they are reading.

But this morning, Mr. Matthews stands in front of the class, leaning against the teacher's desk. The students all look at him and then at each other, not sure what to expect. They are eager for a change of pace from Mr. Reddy's usual routine.

"Where did you leave off?" Mr. Matthews asks the class. Maya raises her hand sheepishly.

"The Jackal . . . page 89. That's where we are," she says.

"Great. Let's start by recapping where we are in the novel. Who wants to start off? You, sir, in the yellow shirt next to the window, what's your name?"

"Dylan," the boy says.

"Dylan, what's been happening in the plot?" asks Mr. Matthews. Dylan looks back at Mr. Matthews with a blank stare. He hasn't kept up with the reading and has fallen asleep in class several times. Dylan comes from a single-parent home and his mother works the late shift. Recently, he has been hanging out late at night with older adolescents, some of whom have dropped out of school. Rumor has it that he has started drinking and smoking. So he easily falls asleep at 8 a.m., especially when Mr. Reddy drones on.

"Who can help him out?" Mr. Matthews asks.

"We're not sure," says Collin, the outgoing junior class vice president. "Mr. Reddy doesn't really ask us any questions. We just listen to him and take notes."

"Hmmm," Mr. Matthews replies pensively. "Well, we're not going to do that. I know this is a challenging story with some archaic language. But the only way to understand it is to jump into it with two feet and enjoy it. Let's start by discussing the historical backdrop for the novel." Mr. Matthews is a history buff and is eager to begin by telling the students about the late 1700s in London.

"Excuse me, Mr. Matthews. Should we be taking notes? I mean . . . will this be on the test?" asks Felicia. Felicia has always been extremely anxious about taking tests and doing well.

"Don't worry about any tests for now. What's more important right now is that you listen and get a *feel* for the setting," replies Mr. Matthews.

The students sit on the edge of their seats, hanging onto Mr. Matthews's every word. He has a way of lecturing that is more like campfire storytelling. Even Dylan is staying awake.

As the bell rings for next period, Mr. Matthews announces, "Be sure you finish reading the next chapter for tomorrow. I have a special activity planned."

The next day, as students take their seats, wondering what Mr. Matthews has in store for them, he begins passing out booklets. They wonder if it's a quiz.

"Okay, everyone, these are scripts I prepared for today's class," Mr. Matthews announces. "Don't worry. You will all get a turn acting in a skit before we've finished the novel. For today, I'd like some volunteers. Who wants to be first?"

Jody, Mason, and Demeri raise their hands. Demeri, a bilingual student who recently transferred to this school, for the first time feels comfortable participating. Because the school does not have a separate bilingual program, Demeri was placed in British literature without any bilingual supports, even though his English reading skills are two grade levels below those of his peers.

"Great! An eager bunch!" Mr. Matthews says. "Now, the rest of you can follow along in your scripts." The students begin the skit as the rest of the class watches attentively. Mr. Matthews can tell they are enjoying themselves.

After the skit, Mr. Matthews arranges students in groups of four and hands out a sheet of guided questions, including these:

- Place yourself in the scene of the novel you acted out today.
- How do you feel—what are your thoughts, your reactions?
- How do you think the characters felt?
- What do you think will happen next? Why?

Mr. Matthews instructs, "I want you to first answer the questions by yourselves. Write down your responses in your notebooks. These won't be collected. They're only for your reference. Once each member of your group is done, discuss your points of view in your groups for about 15 minutes. You may take notes if you want." The students immediately begin writing. Soon the room is filled with noise.

ASSESS:

1. Imagine that you are a new high school teacher like Mr. Matthews. What might you want to know about the brain and its development in adolescence? Think of some specific questions you might have.

2. In your opinion, is British literature developmentally appropriate for juniors in high school? What about freshmen?

3. What aspects of language development should a high school teacher be concerned about?

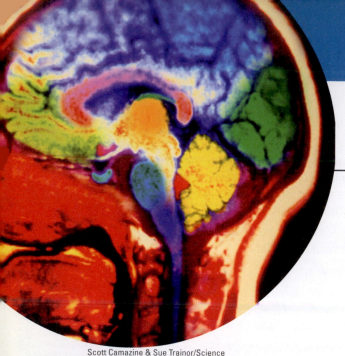

Scott Camazine & Sue Trainor/Science
Source/Getty Images

MODULE **5**

BRAIN DEVELOPMENT

OUTLINE	LEARNING GOALS
Influence of Neuroscience on Education	
	❶ Explain the direct and indirect influences of neuroscience on education.
Neuroscience 101	
• Brain Structures and Functions	❷ Identify the parts of a neuron and the four lobes of the cerebral cortex, and explain the function of these brain structures.
• Factors Affecting Brain Development	❸ Explain the role of experience, plasticity, and sensitive periods in brain development.
Brain Mechanisms During Learning	
• Executive Functioning	❹ Explain the developmental changes in the brain that occur for executive functioning, reading, and math.
• Reading	
• Math	❺ How do brain patterns of individuals with reading disability and math disability differ from those without disabilities?
Applications: How Neuroscience Informs Best Practices	
	❻ Explain the ways in which neuroscience can inform best practices for teachers.

INFLUENCE OF NEUROSCIENCE ON EDUCATION

❶ Explain the direct and indirect influences of neuroscience on education.

Without a doubt, the workings of the brain underlie everything we do. The brain is responsible for all aspects of our cognition—our ability to perceive the world, produce and understand speech, read and write, perform physical skills, learn and remember, solve problems, and evaluate our own thinking. The brain also underlies our affective responses, such as our expression of emotions like anger, fear, happiness, and anxiety, and behaviors such as aggression. In recent years, the field of neuroscience—the study of how the nervous system develops and how its structures and functions affect behavior—has made significant advances in our understanding of human cognition and behavior.

But why should teachers learn about the brain? To develop evidence-based practices, teachers not only need to evaluate research findings from the psychological literature to determine what works and what does not, but they also need to evaluate claims made about the brain and education. For example, have you heard of people saying they are left-brained or right-brained? In reality there is no evidence for this (Kroger et al., 2002; Uttal, 2001). Have you also heard that we only use 10% of our brains? This is also a neuromyth, a misconception resulting from a misinterpretation, misquoting, or oversimplification of results from neuroscience research to justify using brain research to inform educational practices (Organization for Economic Cooperation and Development, 2002).

How can neuroscience inform best practices in education? Neuroscience can influence education *indirectly*—providing support for existing research findings from the psychological literature by explaining brain mechanisms underlying various psychological phenomena (Bruer, 1997; Varma, McCandliss, & Schwartz, 2008). In this case, it is the psychological research that directly informs educational practices (Dubinsky, Roehrig, & Varma, 2013). In almost every other module of this textbook, we discuss research findings that help inform teaching. Neuroscience also can *directly* improve teachers' understanding of the dynamic role that the brain and environment play in shaping their students' development and learning (Dubinsky et al., 2013). We discuss the following areas of neuroscience research relevant to education: executive functioning, reading, and mathematics. Before we examine the neuroscience research in these domains, let's review some basics of neuroscience.

Master the content.

edge.sagepub.com/durwin3e

$SAGE edge™

Reflect on what you already know (or think you know) about the brain. Keep this in mind as you read the next section.

NEUROSCIENCE 101

2 Identify the parts of a neuron and the four lobes of the cerebral cortex, and explain the function of these brain structures.

3 Explain the role of experience, plasticity, and sensitive periods in brain development.

To understand the brain's role in important behaviors of children and adolescents, we first need to understand the basic structures and their functions.

Brain Structures and Functions

Let's begin our overview of brain structures and functions with the basic building block of the nervous system—the neuron. A **neuron** is a cell in the nervous system, and for that reason it is also called a nerve cell. Neurons transmit information to other nerve cells, muscle cells, or gland cells. Most neurons have the features shown in Figure 5.1:

- A cell body has a nucleus that contains genes.

- Dendrites are tiny "branch-like" extensions from the cell body that receive impulses from other neurons and carry the information to the cell body.

- An axon is the long "tail-like" fiber that carries electrical impulses away from the cell body and toward other neurons through branches at the end called axon terminals.

Fully-developed axons are covered by a **myelin sheath,** which is a fatty layer that protects and insulates axons. This insulation speeds up electrical transmission along axons and makes transmitting of nerve impulses quicker and more efficient. The myelin sheath is often called "white matter" because of the appearance of this fatty substance.

How is information carried from one neuron to another? There are small spaces between dendrites and axon terminals, called **synapses,** through which electrical impulses are passed. Electrical messages move down the axon and cause the release of certain chemicals into the synapse. These chemicals, called **neurotransmitters**, move across the space between the cells where the dendrites of the nearby cell receive the signal and transmit it to its cell body.

By the time we are born, we have almost all of the neurons we will ever develop—about 100 billion of them! Neurons are created through a process of proliferation, called neurogenesis, which occurs during the prenatal period (Rakic, 1995; Stiles, 2008). During peak proliferation, several hundred thousand neurons are generated each minute (Nelson, Thomas, & Dehaan, 2006). New neurons are typically not produced after birth, except in a few cases. For example, the adult brain continues to produce neurons in the hippocampus, which is a structure in the limbic system responsible for the formation of new memories (Shors, 2014). Also, new neurons are produced throughout life in the olfactory bulbs, which send smell information from the nose to the brain (Bjorklund, 2012).

Once neurons are formed, they migrate to their permanent position in the brain, where they collect with other cells to form the major parts of the brain, which we discuss next. Cells migrate at different times, and migration is complete by about seven months after conception (Johnson, 2007; Nelson et al., 2006). Neurons subsequently begin to grow, produce more and longer dendrites, and extend their axons farther and farther away from the cell body. **Myelination,** or the creation of myelin sheaths around axons, also begins prenatally and occurs rapidly in the first two years of life. It starts in the brainstem, which is the lower part of the brain (shown in Figure 5.2) that regulates vital functions, and then proceeds more slowly from lower parts of the brain to the cerebral cortex, the outer layer of neurons surrounding the rest of the brain. This is a process that continues steadily from childhood through adolescence and into adulthood (Bjorklund, 2012; Lenroot & Giedd, 2006).

With the growth and myelination of neurons, a period of "blooming and pruning" of neurons takes place. Blooming refers to the overproduction of synapses, called **synaptogenesis,** resulting in many more neuronal connections than the brain can use. Even though

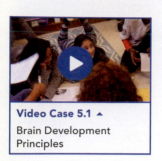

Video Case 5.1 ▲

Brain Development Principles

© SAGE Publications

FIGURE 5.1 **The Neuron.** A neuron is composed of a cell body, dendrites, and an axon covered in a myelin sheath, which speeds the transmission of impulses down the axon.

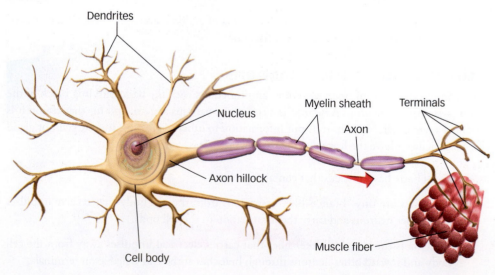

synaptogenesis continues throughout life in response to new information and experience, the most rapid synapse formation occurs before birth through the first few months after birth. The rate of synapse formation also varies in different parts of the brain. For example, peak synapse formation occurs between birth and four months in the visual area of the brain but extends from birth to about age three for language functions. **Pruning** refers to the systematic elimination of excess or redundant synapses. Like synaptogenesis, pruning occurs at different times in different areas of the brain (Huttenlocher & Dabholkar, 1997). Pruning in the visual area of the brain begins around 12 months and extends to age 10, whereas pruning in the higher parts of the brain (the frontal lobe area in Figure 5.2) progresses slowly over a longer period of time. In adolescence, the brain experiences a burst of synapse overproduction and pruning, similar to the blooming and pruning in infancy (Giedd et al., 1999; Gogtay et al., 2004). Later, we discuss how this period of development affects adolescents' emotions and executive functioning.

Now that we have an understanding of the cells that make up the brain, let's take a look at the various parts of the brain (structures) and their primary role in human behaviors (functions). The development of brain structures mirrors evolutionary development, starting with lower, more primitive parts of the brain and continuing with the parts responsible for more complex thinking and behavior. There are many more parts of the brain than we could possibly cover in this brief module. Therefore, we focus our discussion on these general areas: brainstem, limbic system, cerebrum, and cerebral cortex.

- **Brainstem:** The brainstem, also called the "primitive brain" because it developed first evolutionarily, comprises several structures found in the lower part of the brain that regulate vital functions, such as reflexes, respiration, digestion, states of arousal, regulation of temperature, metabolism, hormones, and drives, to name a few.

FIGURE 5.2 **Major Brain Structures.** A left hemisphere view of the lobes of the cerebral cortex.

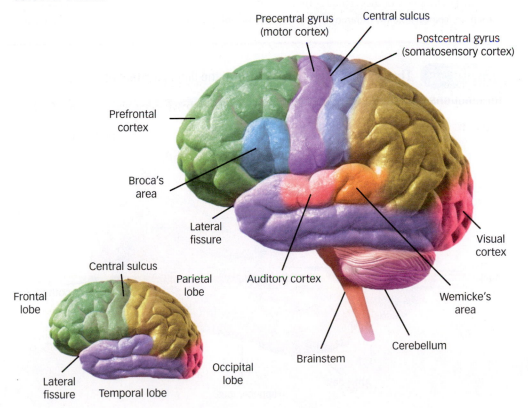

- **Limbic system:** The limbic system, shown in Figure 5.3, surrounds the brainstem and contains structures such as the **hippocampus** (which is responsible for formation of memories and retrieval of information from long-term memory) and the **amygdala** (which is responsible for emotions such as anger, fear, happiness, and anxiety).

- **Cerebrum:** The cerebrum, the largest part of the human brain, is the last to develop both evolutionarily and developmentally, and is responsible for many higher level functions—thinking, problem solving, planning, attention, and language, for example.

- **Cerebral cortex:** The cerebral cortex is a multilayered sheet of cells covering the cerebrum. It is often referred to as "gray matter" because it is composed mostly of unmyelinated neurons, which have a gray color.

The cerebrum is divided into two symmetrical halves called **cerebral hemispheres.** Typically, each hemisphere controls information and motor responses on the opposite side of the body. A thick bundle of fibers, called the **corpus callosum,** connects the left and right hemispheres, allowing communication between the two sides of the brain. The hemispheres are specialized for different types of processing, which is called **lateralization.** For example, the left hemisphere is considered to be lateralized for speech and language. Figure 5.3 shows two important language areas in the left hemisphere—Broca's area and Wernicke's area. **Broca's area** sends signals to other parts of the brain for planning the motor responses necessary for producing speech sounds and syntax (the ordering of words into an understandable sequence). Damage to this area results in speech that is slow and ungrammatical, lacks fluency, and may also involve the inability to use syntax to understand the meaning of others' speech (Caplan, 2006; Crewe et al., 2005). **Wernicke's area,** on the other hand, is responsible for understanding language and producing meaningful speech. Damage to this area results in speech that is fluent but lacks meaning, often sounding like gibberish. Even though the left hemisphere is lateralized for many language functions, the right hemisphere still plays a role. It is primarily responsible for understanding forms of figurative language, such as metaphors, sarcasm, and jokes (Code, 1987; Winner & Gardner, 1977).

Each hemisphere of the cerebral cortex is divided into regions, called lobes (shown in Figure 5.2), which are responsible for different functions. The **occipital lobe,** located at the back of the cortex,

Syntax: See Module 7

Figurative language: See Module 7

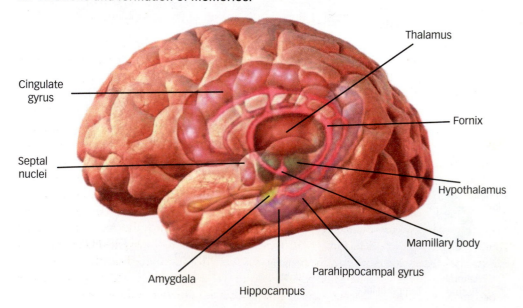

FIGURE 5.3 **The Limbic System.** Structures in the limbic system are responsible for emotions and formation of memories.

Thalamus

Cingulate gyrus

Fornix

Septal nuclei

Hypothalamus

Mamillary body

Amygdala

Hippocampus

Parahippocampal gyrus

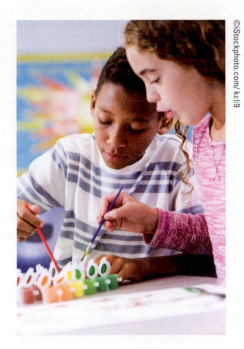

Experience-dependent plasticity. Everyday experiences stimulate neuronal connections in the brain.

is primarily involved in processing visual information. The **temporal lobe,** located on the sides of your brain (think of where your ears are), is responsible for functions such as hearing, language, and long-term memories. The **parietal lobe,** situated above the temporal lobe, is responsible for spatial processing and integration of information from the senses. The **frontal lobe,** one of the last brain regions to develop, is involved in a variety of executive functioning abilities, such as using working memory, planning, making decisions, solving problems, implementing strategies, and exhibiting inhibitory control (Casey, Giedd, & Thomas, 2000; Nolte, 2009; Segalowitz & Davies, 2004). Even though the hemispheres may be lateralized for different functions, and each of the lobes of the cerebral cortex have primary responsibilities, it is important to remember that the brain acts as a whole, with many areas being activated during a particular activity or skill (Kroger et al., 2002; Uttal, 2001). Therefore, it is incorrect to speak about individuals' strengths and weaknesses by referring to people as left-brained or right-brained.

Factors Affecting Brain Development

Brain development involves a genetically programmed unfolding of neuronal connections and a constant reorganization of brain networks as a result of learning and experiences (Butterworth, Varma, & Laurillard, 2011). The brain has a great deal of plasticity (or flexibility) to adapt to experiences, especially during optimal periods for growth called sensitive periods.

The brain's **plasticity,** or flexibility, is remarkable. It is described as "plastic" because of its ability to be modified by experiences (Kolb, 1995; Rakic, 2002). The development of neurons, myelination, synaptogenesis, and pruning are prewired to occur at different points in development for various brain regions. However, experience plays a powerful role in determining which new synapses form and which are eliminated as part of a competitive "use it or lose it" process. Synapses that are frequently activated create stronger connections between the neurons, described as "cells that fire together wire together" (Hebb, 1949; Shatz, 1992, p. 64). Synapses that are frequently activated in response to experiences are retained, and those that are rarely active are eliminated (Changeux & Danchin, 1976). Therefore, practicing newly acquired knowledge and skills is key to richly interconnected networks in the brain that function efficiently.

How do experiences determine which synapses are activated and which are not? Some experiences are called experience-expectant and some are experience-dependent.

- **Experience-expectant plasticity** refers to the forming of biologically preprogrammed connections among neurons in response to environmental stimulation that the brain expects to receive based on evolution. Creation of synapses in our sensory system is experience-expectant (Goswami, 2008). For example, our brains are prewired for certain experiences such as hearing and language, and early experience with hearing the sounds of one's language will enable neurons to develop and synapses to form and organize with other activated neurons in the temporal and frontal areas of the brain.

- Even though our brains may be prewired for language, they are not biologically set up for reading, which is a relatively new cultural invention of humans. Therefore, our brains must use the structures and connections already present for language and modify them in response to exposure to print and learning to read (Goswami, 2008). This is called **experience-dependent plasticity** because the connections that are formed occur in response to specific experiences of individuals. In addition to learning to read, schooling as well as informal educational experiences are examples of experience-dependent plasticity.

Language: See Module 7

Plasticity decreases with age, but it does not disappear completely. New learning can occur throughout adulthood as a result of experience-dependent plasticity (Goswami, 2008). However, the degree to which experience can modify brain structures and connections changes over time, with experience having less of an effect as time goes on. This gradual loss of plasticity can be explained by **sensitive periods,** which are windows of opportunity in which the brain is prepared for optimal learning. During a sensitive period, the brain is flexible and able to be modified by specific experiences that can have enhanced, long-term effects on brain development (Knudsen, 2004; Penhune, 2011). Connections among neurons become strengthened (the use it or lose it principle), and neurons become organized to perform certain functions, which makes processing more efficient (Butterworth et al., 2011). This creation of specialized subnetworks of neurons across the brain makes it difficult to reorganize a neuronal network when new learning occurs later in development (Goswami, 2008). It is still possible for learning to occur outside of a sensitive period, but it becomes more difficult because the brain's sensitivity to environmental input gradually diminishes over time (Knudsen, 2004; Lamendella, 1977). For example, if there is damage to the left hemisphere early in development, the brain is much more likely to reorganize itself than if damage to language areas of the brain occurs in adolescence or adulthood. The "crystallization" of networks that occurs during sensitive periods may also explain why it is more difficult to learn a second language later in life (Munakata & McClelland, 2003). Loss of plasticity that occurs after a sensitive period has ended should be considered adaptive and beneficial to the learner because it means that brain networks have become more efficient. For teachers, the key is to provide enriching experiences that will allow for experience-dependent neuronal connections to form.

Can you name all of the major structures of the brain we just discussed? If not, reread before continuing. Think about these structures as you read about their role in learning.

BRAIN MECHANISMS DURING LEARNING

4 Explain the developmental changes in the brain that occur for executive functioning, reading, and math.

5 How do brain patterns of individuals with reading disability and math disability differ from those without disabilities?

Now that we have an understanding of how the brain develops and operates, let's discuss the role of the brain and its development on some major functions, such as executive functioning skills, reading, and math skills.

Executive Functioning

Executive functioning is a set of skills that enables us to achieve goals, solve problems, and regulate our behavior. It includes functions such as metacognition (our knowledge about our thinking), planning, organizing, attention, working memory, and the ability to control emotions and inhibit responses (Dawson & Guare, 2010). For the most part these skills are processed by networks in the frontal lobe. Executive functioning skills are powerful predictors of school readiness and school achievement (Blair & Razza, 2007; Duncan et al., 2007).

Even though this set of skills is highly heritable (meaning that the traits are passed down through your genes), it is also influenced greatly by environmental factors, such as parent–child interactions, exercise, and teaching of executive skills (Friedman et al., 2008; Hillman, Buck, Themanson, Pontifex, & Castelli, 2009; Holmes, Gathercole, & Dunning, 2009; Hughes & Ensor, 2009). The slow development of the frontal lobes—in particular, the prefrontal cortex (the front-most part of the frontal lobe) from birth through adolescence, reaching full maturity in early adulthood—may allow the environment to have a significant impact on neuronal connections in this area and the subsequent skills that are displayed. Let's examine a few key skills involved in executive functioning—attention, control of emotions, and decision making.

ATTENTION

Attention may arguably be the most important executive functioning skill for learning. Learners must pay attention to incoming information in order to process it and store it in their long-term memory. To do this they need sustained attention in learning tasks, which is composed of two skills—resistance to interference and inhibition of responses. *Resistance to interference* refers to the ability to ignore competing demands for attention or distracting stimuli. For example, students who show poor resistance to interference may be distracted by events occurring outside a classroom window or might succumb to the temptation of watching a favorite TV show while trying to study. *Inhibition of responses* refers to an ability to actively suppress "inappropriate" physical or cognitive responses. Young children might not be able to suppress the act of taking cookies after mom has told them not to eat them until after dinner. School-age children might not be able to suppress unwanted thoughts, such as thinking about playing video games after school rather than listening to a lesson. Control of inhibition also helps students distinguish relevant information from irrelevant information and selectively attend only to relevant information in learning situations.

Metacognition: See Module 11

Working memory: See Module 10

Video: Executive Functioning

Attention: See Module 10

Resistance to interference. Paying attention to lessons and ignoring distractions are essential for learning.

©iStockphoto.com/J-Elgaard

Developmentally, children gradually improve their ability to sustain attention from childhood through adolescence. Older children are better able to inhibit responses compared to younger children (Harnishfeger & Pope, 1996; Lehman, McKinley-Pace, Wilson, Savsky, & Woodson, 1997). Resistance to interference capabilities improve from around 8 to 10 years of age through adolescence (Bunge, Dudukovic, Thomason, Vaidya, & Gabrielli, 2002; Rueda et al., 2004). Brain imaging research shows that several areas of the frontal lobe become increasingly activated on tasks involving inhibition of responses from childhood through adolescence (Booth et al., 2003; Giedd, 2004; Rubia et al., 2001). As a result of synaptic pruning that occurs in adolescence, neuronal networks in the frontal cortex also become reorganized, which leads adults to experience less activation in this area during executive functioning tasks because of increased efficiency (Blakemore & Choudhury, 2006; Casey, Jones, & Hare, 2008; Zelazo & Müller, 2002).

In some individuals, such as those with attention deficit hyperactivity disorder (ADHD), executive functioning skills are impaired compared to same-age peers (Barkley, 1997, 2007). Reduced activation has been found in various frontal regions, reflecting deficits in inhibitory control, selective attention, and decreased working memory (Dickstein, Bannon, Castellanos, & Milham, 2006). One reason for the reduced activation may be a developmental delay. Research indicates that development of the prefrontal cortex in children with ADHD may be delayed by three to five years compared to typically developing children, but motor cortex development may develop slightly earlier (Shaw et al., 2006, 2007). This may account for their inability to sustain attention and inhibit responses and may explain why some children "grow out of it" as they get older.

EMOTIONS

Empathy and perspective taking are two emotions that are essential for the development of prosocial behavior, and moral behavior in general. To help and cooperate with others, individuals need both perspective-taking skills and empathy. Perspective taking is appreciating that people may think or feel differently due to their unique backgrounds and qualities, which is necessary to feel empathy toward others. Empathy is the ability to experience the emotions or feelings of another person. The limbic system and frontal lobes are involved in these emotional skills.

Feelings of empathy involve reciprocal connections between the amygdala (which is in the limbic system; see Figure 5.3) and the prefrontal cortex (Bzdok et al., 2012; Gu et al., 2012; Morrison & Salzman, 2010). The primary role of the amygdala is to quickly extract the emotional significance of a stimulus, and the prefrontal cortex acts more slowly to guide our behavior (Fuster, 2000; Levy & Goldman-Rakic, 2000). The amygdala was originally thought to be the center for fear responses (Morrison & Salzman, 2010; Schumann et al., 2004). However, accumulation of research indicates that the amygdala also plays a role in more complex emotional responses such as:

- judging whether actions are rewarding or aversive (Bechara, Damasio, Tranel, & Damasio, 1997; Schoenbaum, Chiba, & Gallagher, 1998);

- associating learning with rewarding stimuli or positive emotions (Gallagher, 2000; Hamann, Ely, Hoffman, & Kilts, 2002);

- interpreting emotional and social signals, especially from the eyes and face (Blair, Morris, Frith, Perrett, & Dolan, 1999; Morris et al., 1996);

- judging trustworthiness and approachability (Adolphs, Tranel, & Damasio, 1998; Winston, Strange, O'Doherty, & Dolan, 2002); and

- racial stereotyping (Hart et al., 2000; Phelps et al., 2000).

All of these behaviors can contribute to whether an individual feels empathy toward another person.

ADHD: See Module 22

DIVERSITY ⟨

Working memory: See Module 10

Empathy and perspective taking: See Module 4

Reference: Empathy

To experience empathy, an individual must have perspective-taking abilities (Hoffman, 2000). Being able to take another person's perspective involves comparing one's own view with the contrasting views of the other person. Activation of the prefrontal cortex is key in the ability to identify how another person would feel (Amodio & Frith, 2006; Hooker, Verosky, Germine, Knight, & D'Esposito, 2008). In particular, mirror neurons in the inferior frontal gyrus (which is located in the frontal lobe) are involved in understanding the emotional state of others (Carr, Iacoboni, Dubeau, Mazziotta, & Lenzi, 2003). Mirror neurons become activated when a person performs an action and also when a person observes someone else doing the same action. These neurons enable the translation of an observed action into its corresponding internal emotional response. They are important for recognizing facial expressions and imitating them, which is necessary for recognizing and expressing emotions (Bodini, Iacoboni, & Lenzi, 2004; Keysers & Gazzola, 2006; Shamay-Tsoory, 2011).

As we already discussed, regions of the frontal lobe develop slowly over the course of childhood and adolescence, and components of the limbic system (such as the amygdala) begin to mature somewhat earlier (Casey et al., 2008; Konrad, Firk, & Uhlhaas, 2013). The differential rates of development of these brain areas may account for the gradual development of emotional skills such as empathy and perspective taking (Eisenberg, Morris, McDaniel, & Sprinrad, 2009). There also may be individual differences in development that result in the lack of ability to identify and feel others' emotions. For example, children with autism spectrum disorder (who have impairments in social interaction and communication skills) show reduced activation in the mirror neuron system of the inferior frontal gyrus during imitation of emotional expressions compared to typically developing children (Carr et al., 2003; Dapretto et al., 2006). This may help explain their inability to identify and understand others' emotions. As we will see next, the different time course of maturation for the frontal and limbic areas also helps explain the development of decision-making and risk-taking behaviors.

Autism spectrum disorder: See Module 22

> **DIVERSITY**

DECISIONS AND RISKS

Decision making is a complex cognitive skill that develops gradually through childhood and peaks in adolescence (Blakemore & Choudhury, 2006). During adolescence, individuals also begin to acquire formal operational thinking, according to Piaget's theory of cognitive development. Formal operational thinking refers to the ability to think abstractly, form hypotheses, consider alternative arguments, and weigh consequences (Brainerd, 2003; Zigler & Gilman, 1998). Development of this type of thinking is situational and requires extensive experiences in and out of school. According to Piaget's theory, individuals develop formal operational thinking at different rates (depending on experiences), and this process continues into early adulthood (Piaget, 1970, 1972; Zigler & Gilman, 1998). This is consistent with neuroscience research indicating that development of the prefrontal cortex—necessary for modulating attention, regulating emotions, inhibiting responses, foreseeing consequences, setting priorities, and making decisions—continues until around age 20 (Romer, 2010; Siegler, DeLoache,

Formal operational thinking: See Module 6

Adolescent decision-making. Immature frontal lobe development may lead teens to make risky decisions in peer situations.

Video: Brain
Development in
Adolescence

Eisenberg, & Saffron, 2014; Spear, 2010). Let's consider how the prolonged period of synaptogenesis, pruning, and reorganization of neural networks in the frontal lobes might affect decision-making behaviors, particularly with respect to risk taking.

Synaptogenesis and pruning in the prefrontal cortex are much slower than in other areas of the brain, occurring in childhood and beginning again at the onset of puberty (Konrad et al., 2013; Zecevic & Rakic, 2001). An extended process of neural reorganization in frontal lobes is supported by research indicating that adolescents show a different pattern of brain activation when making decisions regarding risks compared to adults. In one study, adolescents and adults were given scenarios and decided whether each behavior, for example swimming with sharks, was a good idea. Adolescents showed increased activation in the prefrontal cortex during decisions regarding the bad ideas and took significantly longer than adults in this case, whereas adults showed greater activation in the right occipital area (Baird, Fugelsang, & Bennett, 2005). This suggests that adolescents' decisions were effortful and relied on reasoning controlled by the prefrontal cortex, whereas adults' more efficient responses were due to quicker mental images of possible outcomes (Blakemore & Choudhury, 2006).

Whether adolescents make good or bad decisions about risks may depend on the environment and how that affects the corresponding brain mechanisms used. In situations that are not emotionally charged and where adolescents can take the time to decide about risks and consequences, teens may be able to make good decisions. For example, when adolescents are asked about the potential risk of situations in experimental studies, they make decisions as well as adults (Konrad et al., 2013). However, being in peer groups may result in higher states of arousal and emotion, leading to a different outcome for decision making. In support of this, adolescents tend to make more risky decisions in peer groups than they do alone (Gardner & Steinberg, 2005; Konrad et al., 2013; Steinberg, 2004).

The reason may lie in the activation of a more mature limbic system compared to the immature frontal lobes. In emotional situations, the limbic system may be activated and "take charge" because of a lack of activation in areas of the frontal lobe responsible for inhibitory control (Casey et al., 2008; Konrad et al., 2013). This may lead adolescents to make decisions and behave in ways that are more affected by rewards (such as positive attention from peers) and emotions than by rational decision making (Chein, Albert, O'Brien, Uckert, & Steinberg 2011; Galvan et al., 2006, Galvan, Hare, Voss, Glover, & Casey, 2007). Consistent with this explanation, research indicates that inhibitory control is one of the best predictors of adolescent risk taking (Aytaclar, Tarter, Kirisci, & Lu, 1999; Moffit et al., 2011). Also, research on preventive programs, such as "don't text and drive," indicates that providing information to adolescents about the risks involved is less effective than training them on social competence and skills for resisting temptations (Romer, 2003).

Social competence: See Module 3

Reading

Now that we've covered general cognitive functioning, let's examine specific cognitive skills, such as reading. Children learn language very naturally without formal instruction, whereas learning to read is *unnatural*. That is, children require formal instruction and practice to develop reading skills. Our brain has the necessary architecture for reading acquisition, such as the language and visual areas, but it is the act of learning to read and practicing reading that strengthens synapses and builds circuits within and across brain regions (Dehaene et al., 2010; Dubinsky et al., 2013). The role that certain brain areas play in reading depends on factors such as the type of print or the skill level of the individual. Different brain areas are involved if one is reading in an alphabetic language like English or a logographic language like Chinese. Also, brain areas deployed in skilled readers and adults are different from those in individuals with reading disability. Let's discuss these issues further by looking at the brain functions of skilled readers, children acquiring reading skills, and those with reading disability.

Reading disability: See Module 21

Skilled reading involves activation of three left hemisphere areas, shown in Figure 5.4 (Goswami, 2006; Shaywitz, Mody, & Shaywitz, 2006).

1. Areas of the frontal lobe are involved in reading, particularly Broca's area, responsible for the production of speech, and the inferior frontal gyrus, which contributes to understanding the meaning of words that are produced (Fiez, 1997; Tan et al., 2000).

2. The temporo-parietal region is responsible for hearing words and processing what words sound like, called phonological processing.

3. The occipito-parietal region (part of the visual cortex) was originally thought to be specialized for visual processing of objects and faces. However, more recent research indicates that it is also responsible for processing the visual form of words and the sequence of letters and translating the visual forms of letters into sounds (Cohen & Dehaene, 2004; Mechelli, Gorno-Tempini, & Price, 2003; Price, Winterburn, Giraud, Moore, & Noppeney, 2003). This region is called the *visual word form area*. Activation of this area is associated with rapid and effortless word identification (Dehaene, Cohen, Sigman, & Vinckier, 2005; Shaywitz et al., 2006).

In skilled readers, all of these areas work in concert to achieve fluent reading and comprehension.

There are differences in activation among these areas, depending on the type of print that readers process in their language. Skilled readers in languages that have one-to-one correspondences between letters and sounds (each letter is represented by a specific sound

‹ DIVERSITY

FIGURE 5.4 **Brain Areas Involved in Skilled Reading.** Individuals who have developed adequate reading skill show a pattern of activation in these three areas.

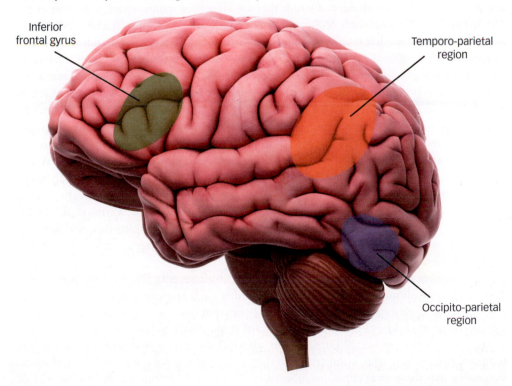

Inferior frontal gyrus

Temporo-parietal region

Occipito-parietal region

and only one sound), such as Italian or Spanish, have greater activity in the left planum temporale (located in the temporo-parietal region), which is involved in phonologically decoding letters into sounds (Paulesu et al., 2001). English does not have a strict one-to-one correspondence between letters and sounds. For example, sometimes the letter "c" makes a "k" sound, as in *cap,* and other times it makes an "s" sound, as in *city.* Also consider irregular words such as *people* and *their,* which cannot be decoded, or sounded out, by applying sounds to each of the letters. Skilled readers of English show greater activation of the visual word form area in the left occipito-temporal region (Paulesu et al., 2001). When reading Chinese characters, regions in the frontal and temporal lobes of the left hemisphere are activated like English and other alphabetic languages, but right hemisphere activation is also seen in the parietal and occipital regions (Tan et al., 2000). Therefore, the formation of synapses in the brain occurs in response to an individual's environmental exposure to, and practice with, a certain type of print.

We also see differences in patterns of brain activation as children acquire reading skills. Beginning readers (through about Grade 3) rely on the left hemisphere temporo-parietal area, which is involved in phonological decoding (Turkeltaub, Gareau, Flowers, Zeffiro, & Eden, 2003). As they become more skilled at reading, children show greater activation in the visual word form area (occipito-temporal region; Hruby, Goswami, Frederiksen, & Perfetti, 2011; Pugh, 2006). Children even show activation in this area when reading nonsense words, such as *gorp,* because the visual word form area is involved in storing information about common letter patterns in words and their corresponding sounds (Goswami, 2008; Hruby et al., 2011). Therefore, as children learn to read and acquire greater skill, the visual word form area, which is specialized for recognition of faces and objects, becomes rewired to recognize and process whole words (Dehaene et al., 2010). This is an example of experience-dependent plasticity at work.

Reading disability: See
Module 21

Children with reading disability do not show the typical progression from reliance on the left temporo-parietal area to activation in the visual word form area. Reading disability (RD) is characterized by a deficit in phonological processing that inhibits children's ability to decode words by applying sounds to printed letters and hinders their ability to acquire a large print vocabulary of words that are identified automatically (Fletcher et al., 1994; Lyon, 1995; Stanovich & Siegel, 1994). Typically developing readers show more activation in all three left hemisphere areas (shown in Figure 5.4) than children with RD (Shaywitz et al., 2006). Children with RD show reduced activation in the visual word form area (in the occipito-parietal area) and continued activation in right hemisphere temporo-parietal cortex (Richards & Berninger, 2008; Shaywitz et al., 2002). Over time, children with RD show greater activation in the frontal regions to compensate for reduced activity in the temporo-parietal and occipito-temporal areas (Shaywitz et al., 2002). The difference between older children with RD and older children without any reading problems lies in the activation patterns in the temporo-parietal and occipito-temporal areas (Shaywitz et al., 2002, 2006). This same pattern of brain activation that differentiates individuals with RD from those without disabilities also explains individual differences in the general population among readers of various skill levels (Shaywitz et al., 2002; Varma et al., 2008). Similar patterns of underactivation in the temporo-parietal and occipito-temporal areas for individuals with RD have been found in other alphabetic languages, such as Italian and French (Paulesu et al., 2001).

DIVERSITY

A promising line of research involves providing students with RD with intensive remediation of their phonological deficits and examining their reading skill improvement and brain processing. Research studies indicate that patterns of brain activation change along with improvement in children's reading skill (Aylward et al., 2003; Shaywitz et al., 2004; Simos et al., 2002; Temple et al., 2003). Children with RD show increased activation in the left temporal and parietal areas, consistent with their improved phonological processing abilities, suggesting that these areas appear to "normalize" (Richards & Berninger, 2008; Shaywitz & Shaywitz, 2005; Temple et al., 2003).

Math

Mathematics involves many skills, such as arithmetic, spatial reasoning, algebraic thinking, and problem solving. However, because the scientific research on mathematics is relatively new, much of what we know about the development of math skills and mathematics disabilities—and the brain processes underlying these outcomes—comes from research on numerical reasoning and arithmetic.

The frontal and parietal lobes and the visual word form area in the occipital lobe (which we discussed as an important region for reading) all play a role in different aspects of mathematical processing. The parietal lobes are involved in almost all numerical and arithmetical processes (Butterworth et al., 2011; Rivera, Reiss, Eckert, & Menon, 2005). There are two particular structures in the parietal area, shown in Figure 5.5, that are key to arithmetic performance.

- The intraparietal sulcus (a sulcus is a groove in the cerebral cortex) is activated when processing the magnitude of symbolic numbers, such as representing and manipulating quantity (e.g., is 9 bigger than 5?; Arsalidou & Taylor, 2011; Dehaene, Piazza, Pinel, & Cohen, 2003; Emerson & Cantlon, 2015). Children need to acquire knowledge about magnitudes of numbers, also called number sense, to develop adequate calculation skills (Geary, 1994).

Number sense: See Module 21

- The left angular gyrus is involved in retrieving previously learned facts from memory (Dehaene et al., 2003; Ischebeck, Zamarian, Schocke, & Delazer, 2009).

The left frontal lobe, which is specialized for language functions, is activated when making exact calculations because this task requires retrieval of well-learned information from long-term memory (Dehaene, Spelke, Pinel, Stanescu, & Tsivkin, 1999; Goswami, 2008). Information is also sent from the parietal lobes to the left frontal lobe when solving

FIGURE 5.5 **Areas of the Parietal Lobe Involved in Arithmetic Tasks.** The intraparietal sulcus and angular gyrus, shown here, are important for understanding and manipulating numbers and retrieving math facts from memory.

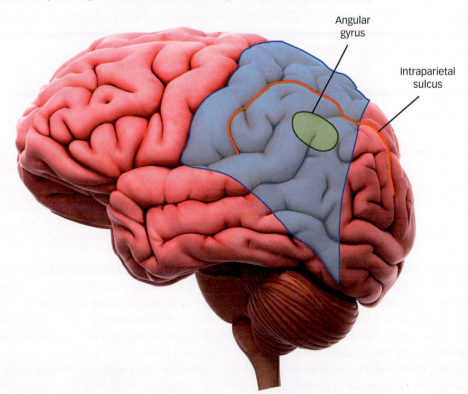

Angular gyrus

Intraparietal sulcus

more complex math tasks or when using reasoning to solve math problems (Blakemore & Choudhury, 2006; Nieder & Dehaene, 2009; Zamarian, Ischebeck, & Delazer, 2009). The visual word form area, which is involved in translating printed letters and words into sounds for word identification when reading, may also be responsible for mapping symbolic information in arithmetic (Rivera et al., 2005). For example, students need to read the digit "3" and connect this to the word "three."

As with reading, we see different patterns of brain activation, depending on the skill level of the individual. Learning new arithmetic facts involves the frontal lobes (responsible for executive functioning and working memory), intraparietal sulci in the parietal areas (for processing magnitudes), and the hippocampus (part of the limbic system), which is responsible for storage and retrieval of facts in long-term memory (Butterworth et al., 2011; Kuhn, 2015). Young children learning math skills show greater activation in the frontal lobe and hippocampus (Cantlon et al., 2008; Rivera et al., 2005; Squire, Stark, & Clark, 2004). Children's overreliance on the frontal lobe and hippocampus may reflect immature development of the parietal areas and suggests the use of developmentally immature strategies (Davis et al., 2009). For example, children may be using counting or other strategies to solve arithmetic problems rather than immediate fact retrieval. As children acquire more experience with math, they develop increased specialization for arithmetic in left parietal regions (Butterworth et al., 2011; Qin et al., 2014). Therefore, development represents a general shift from frontal lobe areas to parietal areas and visual word form areas (Butterworth et al., 2011; Qin et al., 2014; Rivera et al., 2005).

As with reading disability, the pattern of brain activation for students with math disability varies from those without disabilities. The most common characteristic of math disability is a deficit in the ability to commit facts to long-term memory and automatically retrieve them (Chong & Siegel, 2008; Jordan, Hanich, & Kaplan, 2003a, 2003b). Students with this type of deficit show less activation of the intraparietal sulcus when comparing numbers and performing arithmetic tasks (Ashkenazi, Rosenberg-Lee, Tenison, & Menon, 2012; Kucian et al., 2006). Compared to students with typically developing math skills, students with math disability also show fewer connections among networks in parietal regions and between the parietal and occipito-temporal areas (Ashkenazi et al., 2012; Rykhlevskaia, Uddin, Kondos, & Menon, 2009). These findings suggest that students with math disability have not developed the neuronal connections in various brain structures that are needed to coordinate functions for efficient processing of arithmetic, such as visual processing, magnitude processing, and fact retrieval (Butterworth et al., 2011).

DIVERSITY {

Math disability: See Module 21

Think about the grade level you intend to teach. How can information about the role of the brain in executive functioning, reading, and math help you as a teacher?

APPLICATIONS: HOW NEUROSCIENCE INFORMS BEST PRACTICES

6 Explain the ways in which neuroscience can inform best practices for teachers.

We began this module by discussing two roles of neuroscience for education: (1) to indirectly inform practice by providing an explanation of the brain mechanisms underlying behaviors as support for existing research findings from the psychological literature, and (2) to directly inform teaching by providing practices that are based on sound neuroscientific research. Let's discuss some guidelines for directly informing practice that we can glean from an understanding of neuroscience.

Learning is based on experiences. Much of our brain development underlying complex thinking processes relies on experiences. Synapse formation, especially in areas of the brain responsible for higher level cognitive functions, needs appropriate experiences to spur this growth. The very act of providing meaningful and enriching contexts for learning in school and outside of school will enable the brain to form connections (Goswami, 2008). Neuroscience research does not tell us what works in the classroom (Goswami, 2006). Neuroscience can tell us what the brain does in response to certain educational practices, as we have seen with research on remediation of reading deficits changing the way the brain processes print. Neuroscience findings can provide additional support for psychological research and will further enhance teachers' understanding of what works in the classroom. The convergence of neuroscience and educational psychology research will help educators determine best practices for student learning and corresponding brain growth.

Learning is incremental and continuous. The process of brain development is a long journey that begins prenatally and is seemingly endless, as certain areas of the adult brain continue to adapt to new learning experiences. Neurons form connections in response to specific experiences and eventually form whole networks of connections that become specialized for various functions, such as language, reading, attention, and so on. This process is achieved through incremental learning (Goswami, 2008). We have seen many examples of the incremental nature of brain development. Consider reading and math skills. There is a developmental progression in which the pattern of activation in certain brain areas changes from childhood to adulthood as a result of brain maturation, experience, and much practice with reading and mathematics tasks. Consider also the very long course of development in the frontal lobes from infancy through adulthood. The very nature of plasticity and the existence of sensitive periods for optimal brain development, which occur at different times for different functions, also support the incremental and continuous nature of brain development.

Teachers can support incremental learning in their students. For example, emphasize that learning takes time and practice. Homework is an opportunity to practice new skills and knowledge learned in school. Explain to students that the more practice they get, the more efficient their brains will be at processing information or performing certain skills. Teachers can also emphasize that ability is not fixed but incremental. Our brains form connections with every experience we have, so to say that "I will never be good at ____" is not an option. Teaching students about how their brains work at a developmentally appropriate level can also help them develop an incremental approach to learning and improve their intrinsic motivation to learn (Blackwell, Trzesniewski, & Dweck, 2007; Donohoe, Topping, & Hannah, 2012).

Be wary of claims about brain-based learning. Even though most of what we know from neuroscience research is correlational—indicating the brain structures and processes are associated with certain behaviors (such as reading, math, and attention)—the popular media often provides causal interpretations for the results of neuroscience studies (Goswami, 2008). However, those who are knowledgeable about research are well aware that "correlation does not imply causation." Publishers of commercial curricula and programs also make brain-based claims to "turn the brain on before a lesson," "increase information flow between the two hemispheres," or "promote neuroplasticity" (Goswami, 2008; Varma et al., 2008). These claims are based not on neuroscience evidence but are simple interpretations of what the brain already does while learning. Research by Weisberg, Keil, Goodstein, and Gray (2008) indicated that adults can be easily swayed to believe bogus explanations about psychological phenomena if they include neuroscience details. This suggests that we must not take educational claims made in the name of neuroscientific evidence at face value. Read, understand, and evaluate the research evidence for yourselves.

Be wary of claims about learning styles and preferences. Meeting the needs of students from many different backgrounds, experiences, and ability levels requires that teachers are aware of individual differences and how to accommodate them in the classroom. In short, they engage in culturally responsive pedagogy. An understanding of neuroscience can help teachers avoid misapplications of neuroscientific research in their teaching as

Video Case 5.3 ▲
Strategies to Engage Learners' Attention

© SAGE Publications

Intrinsic motivation: See Module 15

Correlational research: See Module 1

Learning styles: See Module 18

Culturally responsive pedagogy: See Module 18

they try to accommodate different learners. You may have heard teachers say that some students are left-brained, with strengths in language and analytical thinking, and others are right-brained, with strengths in spatial, musical, or creative thinking. In reality, however, individuals do not show a hemispheric preference or a strength of processing controlled by one hemisphere or another (Nielsen, Zielinski, Ferguson, Lainhart, & Anderson, 2013).

You also may have heard teachers say that students have different learning styles, for example, some are "visual learners" and others are "auditory learners." The way the brain processes information actually runs counter to these classifications. Recent research shows that if children are taught new information using several modalities, such as learning letters of the alphabet by looking at them, writing them, and naming them, the brain areas underlying each modality become activated even when children later process information using one modality, such as vision only (James, 2007). This suggests that rather than classify students as one type of learner or another, we should ask students to learn information in a variety of ways. This is consistent with research indicating that providing students with multiple contexts and opportunities to learn new information will enhance transfer for learning to new situations (Haskell, 2001; Perkins, Jay, & Tishman, 1993).

Transfer: See Module 12

Reflect on what you thought you knew before reading this module. How has your understanding of the brain and neuroscience research changed? How will you use this to become a better teacher?

SUMMARY

❶ **Explain the direct and indirect influences of neuroscience on education.** Neuroscience indirectly influences education by providing explanations of the brain processes underlying various psychological phenomena. In this case, it is the psychological research that directly informs educational practices and the neuroscience research that supports existing research. Neuroscience also can directly influence education by providing teachers with an understanding of the dynamic role that the brain and environment play in shaping their students' development and learning.

❷ **Identify the parts of a neuron and the four lobes of the cerebral cortex, and explain the function of these brain structures.** A neuron is a cell in the nervous system that consists of (1) a cell body with a nucleus containing one's genes, (2) an axon that transmits information to other neurons through a gap called a synapse, and (3) dendrites that receive information from the synapse and transfer it to the cell body. The brain is composed of neurons that develop, migrate to certain areas of the brain, and form richly connected networks that become specialized for different processes. A thin layer of neurons forms the cerebral cortex—a covering of the cerebrum, which is the largest part of the brain and is responsible for many higher level functions. The cerebral cortex is divided into areas, or lobes, that are responsible for different functions: (1) The occipital lobe is responsible for processing visual information;

(2) the temporal lobe is involved in functions such as hearing, language, and long-term memories; (3) the parietal lobe, responsible for spatial processing and integration of information from the senses, is important in the development of reading and math skills; and (4) the frontal lobe is involved in a variety of executive functioning abilities, including attention, emotions, and decision making.

❸ **Explain the role of experience, plasticity, and sensitive periods in brain development.** The brain has a great deal of plasticity (or flexibility) to adapt to experiences. The development of neurons, myelination, synaptogenesis, and pruning are prewired to occur at different points in development for various brain regions. This type of plasticity is called experience-expectant because biologically preprogrammed connections among neurons are formed in response to environmental stimulation that the brain expects to receive. However, experiences unique to each individual, called experience-dependent plasticity, also play a role in determining which new synapses form and which are eliminated. Examples include schooling and informal educational experiences. During a sensitive period, which is a window of opportunity in which the brain is prepared for optimal learning, the brain is flexible and able to be modified by specific experiences. Although plasticity declines with age, it is still possible for learning to occur outside of a sensitive period. It just becomes more difficult and may require more extensive experiences.

4 **Explain the developmental changes in the brain that occur for executive functioning, reading, and math.** Frontal lobe regions—which are responsible for many executive functioning skills, including attention, emotions, and decision making—develop slowly from childhood through adolescence compared to the limbic system (responsible for emotions and memory), which matures somewhat earlier. The differential rates of development of these brain areas may account for the gradual development of emotional skills, such as empathy and perspective taking, as well as poor decision making of adolescents in social situations involving risk taking. Reading involves a developmental progression from overreliance on the frontal regions and the left temporo-parietal area, which is involved in phonological decoding, to greater activation of the visual word form area in the occipital region, indicating greater efficiency of word recognition processes. Similarly, development of math skills shows a transition from greater activation in the frontal lobe and hippocampus to increased specialization for arithmetic in left parietal regions and the visual word form area.

5 **How do brain patterns of individuals with reading disability and math disability differ from those without disabilities?** Compared to typically developing readers, children with reading disability (RD) show reduced activation in the visual word form area and continued activation in the right hemisphere temporo-parietal cortex. Over time, children with RD show greater activation in the frontal regions to compensate for disruption in the temporo-parietal cortex and the visual word form area (occipito-temporal area). Similar patterns of underactivation in the temporo-parietal and occipito-temporal areas for individuals with RD have been found in other alphabetic languages. Similar to students with RD, students with math disability show fewer connections among networks in parietal regions and between the parietal and occipito-temporal areas compared to children who have no difficulties in math.

6 **Explain the ways in which neuroscience can inform best practices for teachers.** An understanding of the brain and its development based on neuroscience research can provide educators with some guidelines to consider when teaching. First, research on brain development reminds us that learning is based on experiences. Providing meaningful and enriching contexts for learning in school and outside of school will enable the brain to form connections. Additionally, the combination of neuroscience and educational psychology research will help teachers determine best practices for student learning and corresponding brain growth. Second, neuroscience research tells us that learning is incremental and continuous. Teachers should emphasize that learning does not occur overnight, and it takes practice and many experiences to form neuronal connections in the brain and lasting knowledge in their long-term memories. Lastly, teachers need to be informed consumers of research and be wary of claims regarding learning styles and commercial programs or curricula that claim to be "brain based" simply because explanations based on the brain are used.

KEY CONCEPTS

amygdala, 96

brainstem, 95

Broca's area, 96

cerebral cortex, 96

cerebral hemispheres, 96

cerebrum, 96

corpus callosum, 96

experience-dependent plasticity, 98

experience-expectant plasticity, 98

frontal lobe, 97

hippocampus, 96

lateralization, 96

limbic system, 96

myelin sheath, 94

myelination, 94

neuron, 93

neurotransmitters, 94

occipital lobe, 96

parietal lobe, 97

plasticity, 97

pruning, 95

sensitive periods, 98

synapses, 94

synaptogenesis, 94

temporal lobe, 97

Wernicke's area, 96

CASE STUDIES: REFLECT AND EVALUATE

EARLY CHILDHOOD: FIRE SAFETY

These questions refer to the case study on page 84.

1. Define *sensitive period* and explain why the preschool years may be a sensitive period for language development.

2. What types of activities, toys, and interactions would characterize a stimulating preschool environment, and how might this type of environment affect brain development? Based on this, evaluate whether Rolling Hills Preschool is a stimulating preschool environment.

3. Explain why Brianna and Michala entered into a heated argument over the letter M space on the carpet using what you know about brain development with respect to executive functioning skills.

4. Miss Angela asks the children to sit on the carpet and put their listening ears on. Explain, using components of attention, why this is an effective technique for new learning. How does research on age-related patterns of brain development in attention support the use of techniques such as this?

5. Miss Angela used several different ways to practice and remember phone numbers. Explain what happens in the brain when we learn information in various modalities. Why might a multimodal approach to instruction be beneficial for brain development and for learning?

ELEMENTARY SCHOOL: PROJECT NIGHT

These questions refer to the case study on page 86.

1. Evaluate Mr. Morales's assumptions about right-brained and left-brained students. Based on your reading of the module, what would you say to him?

2. Explain why practicing research techniques, such as using the Internet and an encyclopedia, is so important, using what happens in the brain as this occurs.

3. Based on the neuroscience research regarding development of executive functions, would you expect the fifth graders to have difficulty distinguishing important information from less important information in their project resources? Why or why not? Be sure to support your response with evidence from the module.

4. Mr. Morales uses question starters for his "research teams" approach because he says it helps students evaluate their own and others' thinking. Explain why this approach is important for students at this level, using research on brain development underlying executive functioning skills.

5. Some of Mr. Morales's students have learning disabilities or are English language learners who find it difficult to read. What can Mr. Morales say to encourage them to work on their reading skills, based on what the brain does when students acquire skills like reading and math?

MIDDLE SCHOOL: FROGS

These questions refer to the case study on page 88.

1. Tyler has ADHD and a language impairment. How would his brain functions differ from his peers? What accommodations might Ms. Thesdale need to make for the dissection activity and the class in general?

2. Ms. Thesdale believes that a sensitive period for language development means that there is not much she can do to help improve Tyler's language skills. Explain why her reasoning is flawed.

3. Ms. Thesdale's colleague has a student who has just been diagnosed as having a reading disability. He asks Ms. Thesdale to help him understand why this student has so much difficulty reading. Based on the neuroscience research in this module, what explanation might Ms. Thesdale give her colleague?

4. Ms. Thesdale and her students discuss study techniques to improve their performance on the essay exams. How might this help the development of executive functioning skills, and what effect will this have on brain development?

5. Use the saying, "cells that fire together wire together," to explain why students would be expected to become more efficient at dissecting skills if they repeated the steps multiple times.

HIGH SCHOOL: THE SUBSTITUTE

These questions refer to the case study on page 90.

1. Dylan appears to have begun engaging in some risk-taking behavior. Explain the brain changes taking place during adolescence that might contribute to risk-taking decisions.

2. Contrast Mr. Reddy's approach to Mr. Matthews's teaching style. Explain how the new experiences that Mr. Matthews introduces might shape brain development.

3. A teacher meets Mr. Matthews in the hall and says, "You've had quite an impact on your British literature students. I hear you're stimulating right-brained learning with creative skits and discussions." Explain why the teacher's comment is inaccurate. How should teachers use neuroscience research to support and inform their teaching?

4. If a student in Mr. Matthews's class had a reading disability, to what extent would it be possible to change the way that student's brain processes information during reading? Explain based on evidence from neuroscience research.

5. Demeri is a bilingual student who struggles with reading. Use the concepts of sensitive period and experience-dependent plasticity to explain why Demeri can still improve his language and reading skills. What areas of the brain might be activated while reading for Demeri, and how might this differ from skilled readers his age?

Jessica Nelson/Moment/Getty Images

MODULE **6**

COGNITIVE DEVELOPMENT

OUTLINE	LEARNING GOALS
Constructivist Theories of Cognitive Development	
• Individual and Social Constructivism	❶ Contrast individual and social constructivism.
• Piaget's Theory	❷ Describe cognitive development through Piaget's stages, and identify what causes changes in thinking.
• Vygotsky's Theory	❸ Describe intersubjectivity, internalization, and scaffolding within the zone of proximal development.
Issues in Cognitive Development: Piaget and Vygotsky	
• What Comes First: Development or Learning?	❹ Compare and contrast the views of Piaget and Vygotsky on issues in cognitive development.
• Role of Language in Cognitive Development	
• Role of Play in Cognitive Development	
Applications: Constructivist Principles for Effective Teaching	
	❺ Discuss how teachers can use constructivist theories to develop effective instruction.

CONSTRUCTIVIST THEORIES OF COGNITIVE DEVELOPMENT

❶ Contrast individual and social constructivism.

❷ Describe cognitive development through Piaget's stages, and identify what causes changes in thinking.

Constructivism is a paradigm in psychology that characterizes learning as a process of actively constructing knowledge. Individuals create meaning for themselves or make sense of new information by selecting, organizing, and integrating information with other knowledge, often in the context of social interactions (Bruning, Schraw, Norby, & Ronning, 2004; Mayer, 2003). Constructivist ideas about intellectual development can be traced back to the early 1900s and two notable theorists: Jean Piaget, a Swiss scientist and philosopher, and Lev Vygotsky, a Russian educational psychologist. Their work has significantly influenced U.S. educational practices. Many constructivist approaches continue to be studied by psychologists and used by teachers in today's classrooms.

During the 1940s and 1950s, schools typically used teacher-centered instructional approaches based on behavioral learning theories. Teachers were dispensers of information, and learning involved breaking down complex skills into subskills, learning those subskills in isolation, memorizing, and practicing. In the 1970s and 1980s, educational thinking began to shift toward teaching approaches that emphasized the teacher as facilitator and involved knowledge construction (rather than memorization) and peer interaction.

Individual and Social Constructivism

Constructivism is often defined as individual or social. In **individual constructivism,** a person constructs knowledge by using cognitive processes to gain knowledge from experience rather than by memorizing facts provided by others. In **social constructivism,** individuals construct knowledge through an interaction between the knowledge they bring to a situation and social/cultural exchanges within that context. For example, a child who is interested in how wheels and axles work may engage in individual construction of knowledge by tinkering with a bicycle, or she may socially construct knowledge by working alongside an adult who is fixing a bike.

While Piaget often is considered an individual constructivist and Vygotsky a social constructivist, the line between individual and social constructivism can easily become blurred:

- Even though Piaget was interested primarily in how meaning is *individually* constructed, he acknowledged *social experiences* as an important factor in cognitive development (Lourenço & Machado, 1996; Paris, Byrnes, & Paris, 2001).

- While Vygotsky was interested primarily in social and cultural interactions as triggers of cognitive change, his theory actually emphasizes knowledge construction as both *socially* mediated and *individually* constructed (Moshman, 1997; Palincsar, 1998; Windschitl, 2002).

Let's further explore Piaget's and Vygotsky's views on knowledge construction.

Piaget's Theory
BASIC TENETS

Piaget's first intellectual interests were the study of nature and *epistemology,* a branch of philosophy that is concerned with the origins of knowledge. These interests shaped his views of cognitive development, leading him to propose a theory of *genetic epistemology*—the idea that knowledge develops from an interaction between nature and nurture. He proposed that all children's thinking evolves as a result of four factors (Piaget, 1970):

1. Biological maturation (nature)
2. Active exploration of the physical environment (nurture)
3. Social experiences (nurture)
4. Equilibration (or self-regulation)

Master the content.

edge.sagepub.com/durwin3e

SAGE edge™

Constructivist teaching approaches: See Module 18

Behavioral learning theories: See Module 8

Biological maturation. Maturation implies a biological "readiness" to learn, opening the door for a person to profit intellectually from social experiences and active exploration. Our current level of cognitive functioning determines what knowledge we are able to construct from our experiences. On a trip to an aquarium, knowledge construction for a toddler or preschooler might be limited to acquisition of concepts (for example, dolphin, whale, turtle), whereas an older child might be able to classify aquatic life and an adolescent could engage in discussions about how aquatic life evolved.

Active exploration of the physical environment. Individuals construct new knowledge when they engage in active self-discovery, as they interact with objects in their environment. In infancy, the acquisition of **schemes**—organized patterns of physical action—is the basis of all further development. Infants' schemes, such as grasping and sucking or filling and emptying containers, allow them to learn about the world. Schemes in preschoolers, older children, and adolescents are performed mentally and are called **operations** (Zigler & Gilman, 1998). For example, figuring out 2 + 2 = 4 is an operation that involves mentally combining two objects and two more objects to get four.

Social experiences. Social interaction is necessary for the development of logic in older children and adolescents. Here the process (interactions) as well as the product (solution) is stored mentally (Piaget, 1976a). To be effective, the exchange of ideas and cooperation with others should occur between peers instead of between adults and children, because peers are more likely to cooperate as equals, can more easily see each other's point of view, and can more easily challenge each other (Karpov, 2006; Piaget, 1976b). In discussing opposing points of view, students are able to see multiple perspectives and may change their existing way of thinking (Brown & Palincsar, 1989). However, social interactions alone are not sufficient for intellectual development (Lourenço & Machado, 1996; Piaget, 1950).

Equilibration. Because Piaget (1950, 1985) believed that nature and nurture were insufficient in themselves to explain changes in thinking, he proposed equilibration to regulate—or control—all the individual influences on development. Intellectual development involves continual adaptation whereby individuals construct new and more sophisticated cognitive structures (schemes or operations). **Equilibration** is a process of maintaining a cognitive balance between our existing knowledge and new experiences. When individuals are confronted with new experiences, they have a sense of **disequilibrium,** a discrepancy between their existing way of knowing and the new experiences. This motivates them to explore and to reach a conclusion that restores balance in their cognitive system (Piaget, 1985). For example, a student learning the commutative property of addition—that changing the order of addends does not change the sum—may be confused by the assertion that 4 + 3 = 3 + 4, having learned these as separate and unrelated facts. This student's disbelief may lead him to test the commutative property with several addends (such as 5 + 7 and 7 + 5, or 8 + 9 and 9 + 8) to achieve a cognitive balance—knowledge that the commutative property "works."

Cognitive adaptation can be achieved through assimilation and accommodation, which work together to help the individual maintain equilibration (Piaget, 1970; Sternberg, 2003):

- **Assimilation** involves integrating new information or a new experience into an existing cognitive structure. For example, on a trip to the grocery store, a young girl might see a Granny Smith apple and call it "apple" because it looks like the McIntosh apple that she eats. Sometimes new experiences can be incorrectly assimilated, as when a preschooler learning the alphabet mistakes the letter R for the letter P, which he already knows and easily recognizes.

- **Accommodation** involves any modification of an existing scheme or formation of a new cognitive structure when it is not possible to fit information into an existing structure. For example, after many repeated experiences, the preschooler will develop the correct concept for the letter R.

 Think of some ways you could promote disequilibrium in your future students.

STAGE MODEL

In his book *The Psychology of Intelligence* (1950), Piaget explained how knowledge evolves through four stages, shown in Figure 6.1. Stage theories often suggest distinct and abrupt changes from one stage to the next, with children shifting to a qualitatively different way of thinking than before. In contrast to this stage view, Piaget considered children's progression from stage to stage as a continuous adaptation of cognitive structures, with each new capability growing out of the achievements of the previous stage. Each stage is defined by new cognitive abilities not evident in previous stages as well as cognitive limitations compared to later stages. While Piaget was not interested in the ages at which children acquire different levels of thinking, numerous studies indicate ages at which these cognitive abilities typically emerge. Let's take a closer look at Piaget's four stages:

Sensorimotor

Preoperational

Concrete operational

Formal operational

Sensorimotor stage. Acquiring a capacity for internalized thinking is the central goal of the sensorimotor stage. During much of infancy, intelligence is external and behavioral, with infants constructing knowledge from sensory perceptions and motor actions (Brainerd, 2003). Infants initially do not realize that they exist as separate entities apart from objects and people in their environment or that objects and people exist independent of their perceptions (Zigler & Gilman, 1998). Throughout the first year of life, infants gradually develop knowledge of themselves as separate entities, and by 8 to 12 months, they begin to acquire **object permanence**—an awareness that objects and people continue to exist even when they are not visible. Acquiring object permanence gives infants the capacity to represent objects, people, and events as entities that exist mentally, an important ability for the next stage. Children's acquisition and use of language allow them to progress cognitively from sensorimotor capabilities in infancy to mental representations in the preoperational stage (Piaget, 1970).

Preoperational stage. In the preoperational stage, children develop **semiotic functions.** Semiotic (or symbolic) function is an ability to represent an object or action with signs and symbols, such as language, imagery, drawing, symbolic games, and deferred imitation (mentally storing an action and reproducing it later). The term *preoperational* indicates that children are unable to engage in operations that involve two-way thinking, a characteristic of the next stage. Instead, their operations are limited to one-way thinking (Piaget, 1970):

- Preoperational children are **egocentric.** They think about the world primarily from their own physical and cognitive perspective and are unable to think of future actions or events that they have not seen or engaged in (Zigler & Gilman, 1998). They may hold up a drawing so that they can see it rather than turning the picture around to show the viewer, or they may nod while talking on the phone to grandma, not realizing that she cannot see them. Preoperational children typically engage in **egocentric speech,** talking aloud about things that interest them without regard for the interests and conversational contributions of the listener.

- Preoperational children exhibit **centration,** an inability to focus on two dimensions simultaneously. For example, the child in Figure 6.1 sorting blocks may start sorting them by shape, failing to see that they can also be sorted by color. A preschool child visiting a farm may say that a horse is "bigger" than the cow standing next to it because it stands taller, but she fails to take into account that the cow weighs more.

FIGURE 6.1 Piaget's Stages of Cognitive Development.

Sensorimotor (birth to 2 years)

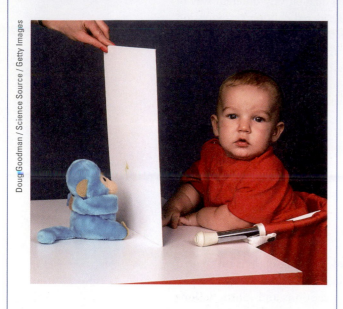

Infants explore their world using sensory and motor actions. Object permanence is a major attainment necessary for the next stage. If you distract an infant and remove a toy from his view as shown here, he will not look for it—"out of sight, out of mind"—but an older infant will search for the toy.

Preoperational (2–7 years)

One-way thinking is characteristic of this stage. Children at this stage typically show centration. This girl is selecting blocks by shape and ignoring color.

Concrete operational (7–11 years)

This student learning about weights and measures illustrates the ability of children in this stage to think logically using concrete materials.

Formal operational (11 years to adult)

This student, who is testing a hypothesis about evaluating which combination of solutions causes a chemical reaction, illustrates the abstract, logico-mathematical thinking of this stage.

- Preoperational children cannot engage in **reversibility** of operations. For example, they have not yet acquired **conservation,** the realization that quantity or amount remains the same (is conserved) despite changes in appearance. Consider Piaget's classic conservation tasks in Figure 6.2. A child who sees two rows of objects lined up as shown will acknowledge that each row has the same number of objects. When an adult spreads out one row of objects as the child observes and asks if the rows have the same number of objects, a preoperational child will say that the longer row has more, while a more cognitively advanced child will say that the rows have the same number because "you can put them back the way they were" (mentally reversing the operation). Similarly, a child whose mother cuts her sandwich in half and her brother's sandwich into fourths does not realize they are the same amount of sandwich.

In the classroom we see many signs of one-way thinking, as when children identify with a character in a story based on their own experiences or when they need to use manipulatives to solve an arithmetic problem.

Along with semiotic functions, **identity constancy** is an important milestone of the preoperational stage (Zigler & Gilman, 1998). Toward the end of this stage, children realize that an object remains qualitatively the same even if its appearance may have changed in some way (DeVries, 1969). For example, putting a ferocious dog mask on a cat does not change the cat into a dog. Identity constancy may be necessary for children to acquire conservation.

Concrete operational stage. In the concrete operational stage, children form mental representations that accurately reflect possible actions and events in the physical world (Zigler & Gilman, 1998). Unlike preoperational children, they are able to manipulate their operations— that is, to engage in two-way thinking. This in turn allows them to acquire reasoning skills (Brainerd, 2003). Concrete operational children who have acquired conservation will conclude that the two rows of objects, two pieces of clay, or two different-sized jars of liquid shown in Figure 6.2 have the same amount because they are able to mentally reverse the operation without having to test that hypothesis physically. While children's thinking becomes more logical and systematic, they are not yet able to manipulate abstract operations. In the classroom, we see signs of concrete operational thinking when students write a persuasive essay, solve a complex math problem, or test hypotheses in science using hands-on experiments. We also see difficulties related to concrete thinking, as when students have trouble making predictions in narratives or seeing the relevance of historical events to the present time.

Formal operational stage. While concrete operational thinkers are limited to concrete problems and tools, formal operational thinkers have achieved a characteristic way of thinking that allows them to solve many physical, logical, and mathematical problems:

- They exhibit abstract reasoning that is reflective and analytical (Brainerd, 2003), such as engaging in a debate, writing a critical analysis of a character in a novel, or considering future career plans.

- Formal operational thinkers can solve a problem without needing concrete representations like concrete operational thinkers. They may be able to find the area of various geometric forms using only an equation, whereas elementary school students may need the visual representation or manipulatives to aid their thinking.

- Students in the formal operational stage can consider implications and incompatibilities, think hypothetically, search for alternatives, and reject inappropriate solutions without physically needing to test them (Piaget, 1970; Zigler & Gilman, 1998). For example, they can evaluate how two different white powders are chemically different by systematically testing the color change of each powder when substances are added one by one and comparing the results for each powder, whereas children in the concrete operational stage might proceed in a haphazard manner or test some combinations and not others.

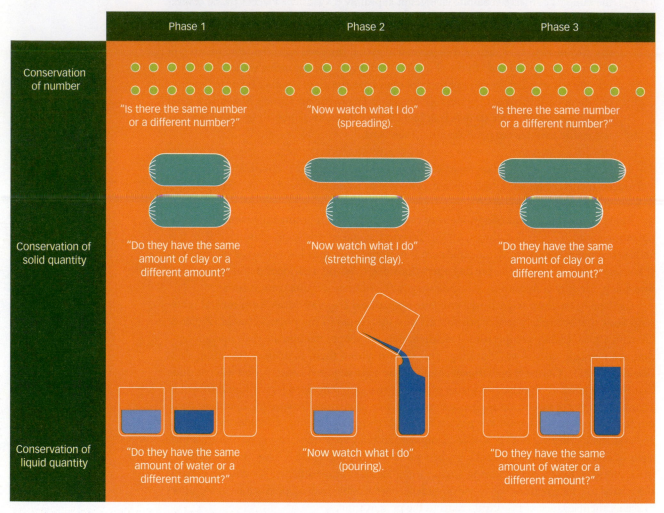

FIGURE 6.2 **Piaget's Conservation Tasks.** These tasks distinguish the preoperational stage from the concrete operational stage.

	Phase 1	Phase 2	Phase 3
Conservation of number	"Is there the same number or a different number?"	"Now watch what I do" (spreading).	"Is there the same number or a different number?"
Conservation of solid quantity	"Do they have the same amount of clay or a different amount?"	"Now watch what I do" (stretching clay).	"Do they have the same amount of clay or a different amount?"
Conservation of liquid quantity	"Do they have the same amount of water or a different amount?"	"Now watch what I do" (pouring).	"Do they have the same amount of water or a different amount?"

SOURCE: Siegler and Alibali (2005). Reprinted by permission of Pearson Education, Inc. New York, New York.

Piaget believed that cognitive development culminated in formal operational reasoning, the point at which we have developed all the cognitive processes necessary for thinking—from schemes and symbolic thinking to concrete and abstract operations (Inhelder & Piaget, 1955). However, does everyone reach formal operational thinking, and do individuals develop cognitively after this stage? Based on research indicating that in many cultures the development of formal operational reasoning depends on extensive schooling, Piaget acknowledged that differences in the acquisition of formal operational thinking can occur among individuals (Ashton, 1975; Goodnow, 1962; Laurendeau-Bendavid, 1977). An individual may acquire formal operational thinking in one domain but not another (Piaget, 1972a). Also, the rate at which individuals reach the formal operational stage, like any of the other stages, depends partly on cultural and educational factors (Piaget, 1970; Zigler & Gilman, 1998). While we may reach a final way of thinking about the world with formal operations, Piaget believed that we continue throughout adulthood to acquire new knowledge and accumulate more content in our cognitive systems (Piaget, 1972a; Zigler & Gilman, 1998). Research suggests that the formal operational stage provides a solid foundation for understanding the development of wisdom, moral reasoning, and expertise in adulthood (Baltes, 1987; Kohlberg, 1984; Sternberg, 1990).

Moral reasoning: See Module 4

Piaget made scientific contributions to fields such as biology, philosophy, and sociology, as well as psychology, and his writings gave rise to a proliferation of developmental research for several decades. The vast amount of research based on Piaget's theory has led to several criticisms, outlined in Table 6.1. It is important for teachers to be aware of *all* of the evidence—support for the criticisms and countersupport—to fully understand students' cognitive development. Also keep in mind that all theories are flawed. No single theory can perfectly explain or predict a psychological construct—in this case, cognitive development. Despite any criticisms, Piaget undoubtedly changed our understanding of the cognitive potential of children (Lourenço & Machado, 1996).

TABLE 6.1   Criticism of Piaget's Theory: Support and Counterarguments

CRITICISM OF PIAGET'S THEORY	SUPPORT FOR THE CRITICISM	COUNTERARGUMENTS
1. Underestimates children's cognitive abilities.	Infants achieve object permanence earlier than Piaget proposed. Preoperational children can pass concrete-operational tasks when they are modified to simplify instructions or reduce memory and language demands.	Research findings with younger infants may indicate only an awareness that the perceptual array has changed, rather than clear acquisition of object permanence. Children's success on simplified concrete operational tasks may be due to lower level cognitive competencies (e.g., using a counting strategy on number conservation) rather than logico-mathematical reasoning (reversibility).
2. Proposes that cognitive development cannot be meaningfully accelerated.	Preoperational children can learn conservation (not just memorize answers) through various methods, such as providing corrective feedback (right or wrong), directing their attention to the appropriate visual cues, modeling adult behavior, and working with peers who have mastered conservation.	Piaget was interested not in the rate of development, accelerations, and delays but in describing processes that account for developmental changes. The rate of progression through the stages will vary, depending on individuals' previous experiences.
3. Wrongly proposes that self-discovery is necessary for cognitive development.	There is little available evidence to support unguided, self-discovery as necessary for cognitive development.	Discovery can enhance thinking when students are given appropriate structure and guidance.
4. May not be stagelike.	Children master different conservation tasks at different ages—number conservation around age 7; mass, somewhat later; and liquid conservation, toward the end of concrete operations—even though conservation is a concrete operational acquisition.	Piaget's theory allowed for asynchrony in development, proposing continual transformations and integration of less advanced thinking into more complex forms of thinking. The stages give us a "big picture" of these transformations.
5. Is limited to Western cultures.	Critics argue that Piaget's theory is not universal as he originally proposed.	The sequence of development through the four stages has been found in cultures around the world, from Mexico and Australia to Thailand, Rwanda, Papua, Iraq, and Ghana. Research showing that the rate of development through stages varies across cultures supports Piaget's assertion that intellectual development depends on specific cultural and educational environments.

SOURCES: Au, Sidle, & Rollins, 1993; Baillargeon, 1991; Brainerd, 2003; Chandler & Chapman, 1991; Dasen, 1977; Greenfield, 1976; Lourenço & Machado, 1996; Miller & Baillargeon, 1990; Piaget, 1924, 1932, 1972b; Rogoff & Chavajay, 1995; Smith, 1993; Sternberg, 2003; Zigler & Gilman, 1998.

Vygotsky's Theory

Like Piaget, Vygotsky (1978, 1993) argued that cognitive development results from a complex interaction between heredity and environment—what he called the natural and the cultural lines of development, respectively. To understand how culture influences cognitive development, we need to know what cognitive structures the child already has developed and brings to the learning situation (Vygotsky, 1935/1994). Vygotsky considered the natural line to include genetic factors, but he did not discuss these as much as he did cultural factors (Tudge & Scrimsher, 2003). Rather, he emphasized the role of social interactions in the development of cognitive processes such as problem solving, self-regulation, and memory.

Video: Zone of Proximal Development

Zone of proximal development. To illustrate the social origins of individual cognitive functioning, Vygotsky (1978, 1935/1994) created a now-famous metaphor, the **zone of proximal development (ZPD)**. The ZPD is the difference between:

- children's actual developmental level (what they already can accomplish independently), and

- their level of potential development (the highest level they can reach with guidance from more capable individuals).

This zone includes all possible skills that children are on the verge of developing and can perform only with help from someone more cognitively advanced (rather than peers at the same cognitive level, as Piaget argued). Interaction with adults or more capable children (older children or those with higher ability) on tasks that are slightly above children's current level enables optimal learning to occur. With this type of interaction, children develop new skills and internalize more advanced ways of thinking, reaching a new level of potential development. When they reach this new level of thinking, this becomes their actual developmental level, and the cycle continues. For example, a first grader working alone may be able to write only a brief story with short sentences and simple vocabulary, but with help from a third-grade "buddy," she is able to write a longer, more elaborate story. With repeated experiences working with her buddy, she will eventually be able to write longer, more complex stories on her own. Let's examine the factors involved in cognitive growth within the ZPD.

Mechanisms of cognitive change. Within the ZPD, adults and learners engage in **intersubjectivity,** or co-construction of knowledge. Intersubjectivity is a process in which two individuals who begin a task with different knowledge and perspectives come to a shared understanding as each person adjusts to the perspective of the other (Newson & Newson, 1975; Vygotsky, 1978). Both the learner and the more skilled individual are active partners in coconstruction. In the first-grade example, even though the first grader and the third grader have different levels of writing skill and perhaps different ideas about what to include in the story, they must bridge the gap between them and *together* create the story.

Video Case 6.1 ▲
Scaffolding

© SAGE Publications

Video: Scaffolding in the Classroom

How do the more experienced and less experienced partners bridge the gap? During a joint activity, adults, older children, and more capable peers use **psychological and cultural tools** (what Piaget called *semiotic functions*) to mediate the child's thinking and shape the development of more complex thought (Rowe & Wertsch, 2002; Vygotsky, 1978). Broadly speaking, tools can be signs and symbols (primarily language), mnemonics, concepts, or any activities, interactions, or symbolic systems the culture provides (Das, 1995). To illustrate the adult's role, Wood, Bruner, and Ross (1976) used the metaphor **scaffolding,** based on Vygotsky's writings. Like the temporary platforms used in the construction of a building, scaffolding is a temporary social support to help children accomplish a task. It supports preschoolers as well as older students when they are learning new tasks (Barron et al., 1998; Brown & Kane, 1988).

As children master the use of psychological and cultural tools, a gradual **internalization** occurs, in which they slowly acquire more cognitive responsibility for the task, and scaffolding gradually is withdrawn (called *fading;* Vygotsky, 1962; Wood, 1989). Children shift from performing cognitive processes *socially* with an adult to performing them *mentally* by themselves

(Leontiev, 1961; Webb & Palinscar, 1996). The tools become part of children's repertoires, the children's new cognitive processes become part of their actual developmental level, and a new zone is created, with a new level of potential development (Karpov & Bransford, 1995; Vygotsky, 1978).

Teachers should keep in mind two points when applying the zone of proximal development to their classroom:

1. This zone in which optimal learning occurs will differ among students. Two same-age students can have the same actual developmental level but differ considerably in their learning potential in particular subjects or in their ability to benefit from external assistance (Sternberg, 2002; Vygotsky, 1978). Some students may have a narrower ZPD and may need more frequent and explicit assistance (Day & Cordon, 1993).

2. Scaffolding actually is driven by the learner rather than controlled by the more experienced person (Tudge & Scrimsher, 2003). To be effective, adults must match their communication and support to the learner's needs and current cognitive level (Dennen, 2004; Jacobs & Eccles, 2000). Vygotsky saw adults as both pushing and pulling development, yielding a co-constructive, bidirectional process within the ZPD rather than a one-way transmission from the adult to the learner (Tudge & Scrimsher, 2003).

It is difficult to critically evaluate Vygotsky's theory due to its smaller research base in comparison with Piaget's theory. Even though Vygotsky wrote extensively on the science of child development from 1928 until 1934, his career was cut short when he died at age 37 from tuberculosis. Also, in the Soviet Union, the study of child development and all references to it (including Vygotsky's theory) were denounced and banned from 1936 to the 1950s, and researchers and educators in the United States have only recently had access to translations of his writings (Tudge & Scrimsher, 2003). Researchers have begun to evaluate Vygotsky's theory and its impact on education by investigating the efficacy of various constructivist teaching methods based on his ideas about the co-construction of knowledge and intersubjectivity within the ZPD.

Constructivist teaching methods: See Module 18

Can you think of ways in which Piaget's and Vygotsky's theories are similar, different, and complementary?

ISSUES IN COGNITIVE DEVELOPMENT: PIAGET AND VYGOTSKY

3 Compare and contrast the views of Piaget and Vygotsky on issues in cognitive development.

Piaget and Vygotsky simultaneously developed theories of cognitive development during the early 20th century. Vygotsky wrote critiques of Piaget's work, but Piaget did not read any of Vygotsky's writings until years after Vygotsky's death (Piaget, 1962). Even though they never met in person, their views provide us with a dialogue on important issues in cognitive development. Let's examine these issues next.

What Comes First: Development or Learning?

Development involves acquiring concepts spontaneously through natural experiences, and learning involves applying the newly developed cognitive structures to new situations (Lawton & Hooper, 1978; Piaget, 1970). According to Piaget, development precedes learning because an individual must be developmentally ready to learn (Wink & Putney, 2002). A child's stage of development places constraints on what and how much he or she can learn from instruction (Brainerd, 1978; Inhelder, Sinclair, & Bovet, 1974). We must know a child's current stage before we can know what it is possible to teach the child (Piaget, 1970).

Vygotsky used the ZPD to explain how *theoretical learning,* a form of learning that occurs in school, pulls development to higher levels (Karpov & Bransford, 1995). Before children enter school, they engage in *empirical learning,* a simple form of learning that results in *spontaneous concepts.* Spontaneous concepts are unsystematic, unconscious, and sometimes incorrect ideas generalized from children's everyday concrete experiences (Davydov, 1972, 1988). Spontaneous concepts provide the conceptual framework—prior knowledge—for acquiring *scientific concepts,* or concepts acquired during theoretical learning (Karpov, 2006; Vygotsky, 1962).

During instruction, teachers should provide problem-solving activities that enable students to use scientific concepts in practical ways. This allows scientific concepts to meet students' personal, concrete experiences so their spontaneous concepts become structured and conscious (Karpov, 2006; Vygotsky, 1987). For example, elementary school students may begin school with knowledge of how a flower grows from a seed (an everyday experience). In school, they will learn the definitions of concepts related to plants and engage in scientific observation and recording of factors that affect plant growth (amount of water, sunlight, etc.). Their spontaneous concept or everyday knowledge about plant growth is transformed and restructured into scientific concepts.

Vygotsky cautioned that learning leads to development only if instruction has been organized properly to focus on cognitive functions not yet completely mastered (Karpov & Bransford, 1995). Teachers should create a ZPD in which social interaction and collaboration lead the student to use and develop new cognitive processes and skills (Vygotsky, 1978).

Role of Language in Cognitive Development

Piaget and Vygotsky shared similar views on the role of language in thinking. They agreed that internalized (not spoken) language:

- is needed for conscious thoughts—that we think in words (Das, 1995; Moll, 2001; Vygotsky, 1987);

- serves a reflective function, allowing individuals to refer to the past, present, and future (Das, 1995); and

- serves a planning function, whereby individuals practice a dialogue with a hypothetical other person before actually engaging in it (Piaget, 1926).

They also agreed on the role of language in logical thinking, but they differed in the importance they placed on language. For Vygotsky, language and thought are intertwined: Thinking is a mental process that needs language as its base (Leontiev & Luria, 1972). For Piaget, language plays a necessary but not primary role in logical thinking. During the concrete and formal operational stages, children use language as a tool for developing logical thinking, to think through problems and express what they know and do not know (Das, 1995; Inhelder & Piaget, 1955). However, because logical thinking involves a continual coordination of actions—from organizing sensorimotor schemes to coordinating logical operations—thinking comes *before* language (Piaget, 1970).

Piaget and Vygotsky also disagreed on the role of externalized speech in cognitive development. In Vygotsky's theory, social situations provide the initial context in which children develop planning and self-regulation strategies (Rowe & Wertsch, 2002). Adults and children use **socialized speech** (speech used to communicate with others) as a tool for coordinating their actions with those of others. Children gradually learn to regulate their thoughts and actions using **private speech,** a self-regulatory, internalized speech.

Video Case 6.2 ▲

Role of Language in Cognitive Development

Reference: Private Speech

In Piaget's theory, externalized speech takes the form of *egocentric speech* and is a cognitive limitation of preoperational thinking. Egocentric speech gradually diminishes as children progress through the preoperational stage and develop the two-way thinking characteristic of the concrete operational stage. Vygotsky, however, saw Piaget's egocentric speech as a necessary transition between socialized speech and private speech (Rowe & Wertsch, 2002). Vygotsky conducted research on Piaget's egocentric speech that showed substantial increases in egocentric speech during cognitively challenging activities (Kohlberg, Yaeger, & Hjertholm, 1968; Rowe & Wertsch, 2002). Recent research is consistent with Vygotsky's notion of private speech (Winsler, 2009; Winsler & Naglieri, 2003). School-age children use private speech when solving many academic tasks, such as arithmetic problems, when engaged in difficult tasks, and when deciding how to proceed after setbacks (Berk, 1986, 1992). Even adolescents and adults use private speech during challenging tasks, such as when organizing an essay or planning a study session. However, they may not always experience improved performance from private speech like children do (Behrend, Rosengren, & Perlmutter, 1989; Berk & Spuhl, 1995; Duncan & Tarulli, 2009). Therefore, externalized speech is a useful tool for independently planning and regulating a variety of actions.

Can you think of other examples when children and adolescents may need to talk themselves through a problem out loud?

Role of Play in Cognitive Development

The importance of play in the intellectual development of preschool-age children is evident in both Piaget's and Vygotsky's theories. Piaget (1945/1962) regarded pretend play as evidence of the child's ability to use and understand symbols, emerging at the end of the sensorimotor stage and developing throughout the preoperational stage (Smith, 2002). He also emphasized pretend play as an individual process, suggesting that the child alone invented and used symbols (Smolucha & Smolucha, 1998).

Reference:
Pretend Play

Vygotsky (1978) considered pretend play to be a more social phenomenon than did Piaget. Imaginative play creates a ZPD in which children behave beyond their current developmental level and advance to higher levels of cognitive functioning (Moll, 2001; Whitington & Floyd, 2009). In pretend play, children advance their thinking by:

- creating actions that originate from ideas ("Let's pretend we're dinosaurs"),

- detaching the meaning of objects from their typical appearance (a stick for a gun), and

- creating imaginary contexts for practicing roles, rules, and expectations they have experienced in their everyday life (playing a parent role and punishing a doll).

Sociodramatic play is a particular form of pretend play in which children jointly create and act out an imaginary context. In sociodramatic play, children learn to guide their behavior because they must think before acting (Vygotsky, 1978). They also use intersubjectivity by sharing a joint focus on the task, exchanging knowledge, and moving between pretend and reality to negotiate the play experience (e.g., stepping out of play to decide on roles; Goncu, 1993; Whitington & Floyd, 2009). This type of play advances cognitive development and prepares children for later symbol-based learning, such as reading and writing (Bodrova & Leong, 1997; Pellegrini & Galda, 1993). This type of symbolic learning may also lay the foundation for later hypothetical thinking that we see in the formal operational stage (Alexander, 1989; Harris, 2006).

Current research suggests that play experiences may continue to support children's cognitive development through the later elementary school years:

- Peer play in elementary school is related to academic success and the development of social skills (Bjorklund & Pellegrini, 2000; Hirsh-Pasek, Golinkoff, Berk, & Singer, 2008).

Pretend Play and Symbolic Thinking. Both Piaget and Vygotsky considered pretend play to be important to the development of symbolic thinking.

Executive functioning: See central executive in Module 10 and executive control functions in Module 11

Attention and memory: See Module 10

- Peer play and physical games during recess activities have positive benefits on executive functioning skills (such as attention, planning, organization, and monitoring) and achievement in school subjects (Best, 2012; Fedewa & Ahn, 2011). These activities reduce students' attention and memory demands and allow them to more efficiently process information when they return from the break (Pellegrini, 2009; Pellegrini & Bohn, 2005). Even when recess is held indoors with less opportunity for physical activity, elementary school students experience more attention after recess than before (Pellegrini, Huberty, & Jones, 1995; Pellegrini & Smith, 1993).

- Sociodramatic play with peers in middle childhood may contribute to the development of writing skills because it fosters the ability to imagine, to orally write and edit play "scripts," and to develop a sense of audience (Fromberg, 2002; Singer & Singer, 2006).

APPLICATIONS: CONSTRUCTIVIST PRINCIPLES FOR EFFECTIVE TEACHING

Video Case 6.3 ▲

Development of Conceptual Knowledge

© SAGE Publications

5 Discuss how teachers can use constructivist theories to develop effective instruction.

The constructivist theories we've discussed in this module can provide teachers with several guidelines for effective teaching.

Consider students' developmental level when designing curricula and activities. Both theorists recognized the importance of knowing a child's current level of thinking before planning instruction. Based on Piaget's theory, teachers can use a student's stage of cognitive development to determine appropriate instructional materials and activities (Brainerd, 1978; Piaget, 1970). Likewise, Vygotsky recommended that teachers identify what the child brings to the situation and then arrange activities to foster the development of cognitive processes on the verge of emerging (Tudge & Scrimsher, 2003; Vygotsky, 1998). Teachers can use dynamic testing to determine what students are able to learn with assistance (their ZPD) rather than rely on assessments that show only what a student already knows (Campione & Brown, 1990; Vygotsky, 1998). *Dynamic testing* is an interactive assessment in which teachers probe students' thinking and provide guidance and feedback during the testing. This points to students' learning potential by identifying how much they can achieve *above* their current level with appropriate support (Brown & Ferrara, 1985; Grigorenko & Sternberg, 1998).

Whether we consider stages or ZPD, students profit from experiences that are within their reach cognitively. When teachers design tasks that are moderately challenging, students will be operating in their ZPD—or, in Piagetian terms, they will experience disequilibrium.

Encourage students to be active learners. Encouraging students to be active learners does not mean that we must always use social interactions and group work (a common misapplication of Vygotsky's theory) or that all learning must be discovery based (an assumption based on Piaget's theory). Social interactions are beneficial only if they occur appropriately within students' ZPDs and if students are given the proper scaffolding. Also, unguided self-discovery is less effective than other teaching methods for learning and transfer of knowledge to new situations, because learning may not occur if students are given too much freedom in the discovery process (Mayer, 2004; van Joolingen, de Jong, Lazonder, Savelsbergh, & Manlove, 2005). Rather, **active learning** can be defined more broadly as any type of meaningful learning in which students construct a rich knowledge base (rather than memorizing facts) of interconnected concepts, prior knowledge, and real-life experiences (Bransford & Schwartz, 1999; Murphy & Woods, 1996; Renkl, Mandl, & Gruber, 1996).

Link new concepts to students' prior knowledge. Teachers can encourage meaningful learning (as well as the transfer of learning to new settings) by capitalizing on what students already know. According to Piaget, individuals first assimilate a new experience into their existing cognitive framework (thinking that a brick would fall faster than a feather in a lesson on gravity) and later may reorganize their cognitive structure to accommodate the new experience (realizing that they fall at the same rate after learning about air resistance; Piaget, 1970; Zigler & Gilman, 1998). Vygotsky likewise believed that children's spontaneous concepts from their everyday experiences form the basis for the development of more sophisticated concepts in school (Karpov & Bransford, 1995).

Use teaching methods based on constructivist principles. To encourage active, meaningful learning, teachers can use a variety of approaches based on constructivist principles:

- To teach reading comprehension, teachers can use methods such as *reciprocal teaching* and *instructional conversations*—methods based on Vygotsky's ZPD. Both methods contain elements of cognitive apprenticeships such as modeling and scaffolding. Reciprocal questioning, another method that relies on coconstruction of knowledge, can be used from elementary through high school to help students understand new concepts or skills through structured conversations.

- *Cognitive apprenticeships* involve opportunities to develop cognitive skills within the context of authentic activities. Students participate at a level commensurate with their abilities and move gradually toward full participation. Within cognitive apprenticeships, teachers use techniques such as modeling, scaffolding, and fading. Cognitive apprenticeships with teachers or other adults as mentors can be used at all levels of development, such as an elementary student learning about math and money while working at a school store, a middle school student refining writing skills while working at a school newspaper, or high school and college students completing internships within the community.

- Methods such as *inquiry learning,* in which students solve problems by following research steps, and *cooperative learning,* in which students work together to achieve a shared goal, can be used for any subject and with students from elementary through high school.

Discovery learning: See Module 18

Promoting meaningful learning: See Module 12

Prior knowledge: See Module 12

Reciprocal teaching: See Modules 11 and 18

Instructional conversations: See Module 18

Cognitive apprenticeships: See Module 18

Inquiry learning: See Module 18

Transfer: See Module 12

DIVERSITY

Provide multiple exposures to content. Returning to content at different times, in different contexts, for different purposes, and from different perspectives will enhance students' knowledge acquisition (Haskell, 2001; Spiro, Feltovich, Jacobson, & Coulson, 1992). Examining content from differing perspectives, such as in-class debates and discussions, may lead students to restructure or modify their existing knowledge. Revisiting content over time and in different contexts also encourages transfer of knowledge by preventing learned information from being tied to specific situations or contexts (Salomon & Perkins, 1989).

Recognize cultural context in learning situations. Consistent with Vygotsky's theory, teachers need to consider how the setting of particular instructional activities and the larger cultural context may affect learning (Griffin & Cole, 1999; Tharp & Gallimore, 1988). In arranging instructional activities that involve social interaction, such as collaborative projects or class discussions, teachers need to consider how styles of interaction may differ among students from different cultural backgrounds. For example, Native Hawaiian children, who tend to engage in negative wait time (children talking at the same time), and Navajo children, who wait a long time to be sure a speaker has finished talking, may have different needs during social interactions in the classroom (Tharp, 1989).

 Think about the grade level of students you expect to teach. How can you use the guidelines presented here in your classroom?

SUMMARY

❶ Contrast individual and social constructivism. In individual constructivism, a person constructs knowledge independently by using cognitive processes to abstract information from experiences. In social constructivism, individuals construct knowledge within a social/cultural context—the social interactions and what they bring to the learning situation are interconnected.

❷ Describe cognitive development through Piaget's stages, and identify what causes changes in thinking. In the sensorimotor stage, infants construct knowledge from sensory and motor experiences, preparing them for later symbolic thinking. While preoperational children are able to form mental representations, their thinking is one way. Operations develop further in the concrete operational stage, in which children can think logically and mentally reverse their thinking, albeit concretely. Formal operational thinkers can mentally manipulate abstract concepts. Maturational changes, active exploration, social interactions, and equilibration together cause thinking to evolve through the four stages.

❸ Describe intersubjectivity, internalization, and scaffolding within the zone of proximal development. In the ZPD, a child and an older individual engage in intersubjectivity, an active coconstruction of knowledge. As the adult provides scaffolding, the child gradually gains more skill and takes over more responsibility for the task. Cognitive processes that initially were shared between the adult and the child and were scaffolded by the adult gradually become internalized by the child, and the adult slowly removes the scaffolding.

❹ Compare and contrast the views of Piaget and Vygotsky on issues in cognitive development. Piaget argued that development precedes learning, while Vygotsky proposed that formal learning in school pulls development to a new level. Both theorists emphasized the importance of play in young children's cognitive development. However, Piaget considered pretend play to be an individual process, while Vygotsky considered it to be social as well as individual. The theorists also agreed on the role of language in logical thinking and shared similar ideas about the role of internalized language in thinking. They differed in their view of the role of externalized speech in planning actions and regulating thoughts—Piaget considered it a cognitive weakness of preoperational children, while Vygotsky viewed it as a tool for planning and regulating actions.

❺ Discuss how teachers can use constructivist theories to develop effective instruction. Teachers can begin by considering students' level of thinking when designing curricula and activities because students will benefit from experiences that are within their reach cognitively. During instruction, teachers should encourage students to be active learners and to link new concepts to their prior knowledge. Both Piaget and Vygotsky believed that children continually modify their existing thinking through active construction of knowledge. To encourage meaningful learning, teachers can choose among a variety of constructivist methods based on Piaget's and Vygotsky's theories. Examining content from different perspectives can also help students restructure or modify their existing knowledge, and revisiting content in different contexts will promote transfer. Finally, teachers should consider how the social settings within the classroom, as well as the larger cultural context, may affect students' learning.

KEY CONCEPTS

accommodation, 114

active learning, 125

assimilation, 114

centration, 115

conservation, 117

constructivism, 112

disequilibrium, 114

egocentric, 115

egocentric speech, 115

equilibration, 114

identity constancy, 117

individual constructivism, 113

internalization, 120

intersubjectivity, 120

object permanence, 115

operations, 114

private speech, 122

psychological and cultural tools, 120

reversibility, 117

scaffolding, 120

schemes, 114

semiotic functions, 115

social constructivism, 113

socialized speech, 122

zone of proximal development (ZPD), 120

CASE STUDIES: REFLECT AND EVALUATE

EARLY CHILDHOOD: FIRE Safety

These questions refer to the case study on page 84.

1. Using the concept of egocentrism, explain why Michala wanted to sit on the letter M on the carpet.

2. Use the case situation in which Brianna and Michala are coloring their flash cards to contrast Piaget's and Vygotsky's views on externalized speech.

3. According to Piaget's theory, why would demonstrations be an effective way to teach preschoolers about fire safety? Would demonstrations be effective for elementary school students, according to his theory?

4. Identify Miss Angela's use of scaffolding in the case, and explain how scaffolding helps children in the zone of proximal development.

5. Think of one original fire safety activity (not already mentioned in the case) that would be consistent with Piaget's theory of cognitive development. Think of another original fire safety activity that would be consistent with Vygotsky's theory of cognitive development. Describe how each activity is supported by the theory. What factors, consistent with these theories, do teachers need to consider when planning instruction at the early childhood level?

ELEMENTARY SCHOOL: PROJECT NIGHT

These questions refer to the case study on page 86.

1. Explain in your own words why the project-based unit would be considered a constructivist approach to learning.

2. Based on the students' current stage of cognitive development, why was it necessary for Mr. Morales to break down the project into smaller, more manageable steps?

3. Based on Piaget's stage theory of cognitive development, would you have expected students' self-evaluations to be so superficial? Why or why not?

4. How does the "research team" format exemplify Vygotsky's social construction of knowledge within the zone of proximal development?

5. Explain how the "research team" activity might stimulate disequilibrium in students. Explain how assimilation and accommodation would be involved in this activity.

MIDDLE SCHOOL: FROGS

These questions refer to the case study on page 88.

1. According to Piaget's theory of cognitive development, what factors should Ms. Thesdale consider in planning biology lessons?

2. Explain how Ms. Thesdale could stimulate disequilibrium in her students before the frog dissection and why disequilibrium is important for cognitive change.

3. Ms. Thesdale assumed that the social interaction of working together in groups on dissection would foster cognitive growth. Based on the processes that stimulate cognitive change within the zone of proximal development, evaluate the effectiveness of the group dissection activity.

4. Based on Vygotsky's zone of proximal development, was it appropriate for Ms. Thesdale to place Tyler with Jay and Vincent? Why or why not? What types of support would Tyler need from other students and from Ms. Thesdale in order to benefit from instruction involving social interaction?

5. How can Ms. Thesdale encourage active learning in her students? Provide specific suggestions, and explain whether each is supported by Piaget's or Vygotsky's theory.

HIGH SCHOOL: THE SUBSTITUTE

These questions refer to the case study on page 90.

1. Is it valid for a teacher to assume that high school students should be at the formal operational stage of development? Use Piaget's theory to support your answer.

2. Based on Piaget's theory of cognitive development, is a skit an effective method for helping Mr. Matthews's high school students understand *A Tale of Two Cities*? Why or why not?

3. From your reading of the case, what mistakes did Mr. Reddy make in teaching his British literature class, based on the four factors necessary for developmental change in Piaget's theory?

4. Explain how the group discussions at the end of the case exemplify intersubjectivity and internalization.

5. Assume that you are teaching a junior-level British literature course in high school. What would be your expectations of the students, and how would you approach teaching this subject? Explain how your response fits with either Piaget's or Vygotsky's theories, or both.

APPLY AND PRACTICE WHAT YOU'VE LEARNED

▶ edge.sagepub.com/durwin3e

**CHECK YOUR COMPREHENSION
ON THE STUDENT STUDY SITE**

- **eFlashcards** to strengthen your understanding of key terms

- Practice **quizzes** to test your knowledge of key concepts

- **Videos and multimedia content** to enhance your exploration of key topics

©iStockphoto.com/AnitaPatterson

MODULE **7**

LANGUAGE DEVELOPMENT

OUTLINE	LEARNING GOALS

Understanding Language Acquisition

- Biological Basis of Language
- Imitation and Reinforcement
- Social Interactions

❶ Explain the factors that contribute to language development.

Development of Language Skills

- Language Acquisition Through Early Childhood
- Language Acquisition Through Adolescence
- Bilingual Language Acquisition
- Individual Differences in Language Acquisition

❷ Describe changes in semantics, syntax, pragmatics, and metalinguistic awareness from birth through adolescence.

❸ Explain the advantages and disadvantages of the methods of teaching English language learners.

❹ Describe the language differences that emerge from early childhood through the early school-age years.

Applications: Encouraging Language Development in the Classroom

❺ Describe ways teachers can support language development in the classroom.

UNDERSTANDING LANGUAGE ACQUISITION

❶ Explain the factors that contribute to language development.

Language development forms the basis of much school learning from early childhood through secondary education. Language skills allow children to form concepts, engage in pretend play, and interact socially—all of which advance children's cognitive development. In elementary through secondary school, oral language skills enable students to learn from lessons and lectures, to demonstrate knowledge by answering questions, and to participate in discussions and group activities. Oral language also provides a foundation for reading and writing skills, as well as for acquisition of a second language in English language learners. Before we discuss the progression of language development and its impact on school-age learners, let's explore the factors responsible for language acquisition.

Biological Basis of Language

Our brains are well designed for the production and acquisition of language. The cerebrum, the largest portion of our brain, consists of two halves called hemispheres. Although both hemispheres are involved in language, in most individuals the left hemisphere has more responsibility for many language functions and becomes specialized for language functions early in infancy (Holowka & Petitto, 2002; Redcay, Haist, & Courchesne, 2008). When parts of the left hemisphere responsible for various language functions are damaged, the brain's *plasticity*—its ability to adapt to environmental experiences—allows other areas of the brain to take over many of the left hemisphere functions, leading to relatively normal language development (Stiles & Thal, 1993). Because plasticity decreases with age, however, it is more difficult for other areas of the brain to take on language functions after infancy (Huttenlocher, 2002; Stiles, 2008).

Humans may acquire language so readily and easily because we are genetically predisposed—that is, biologically ready—to acquire language (Ritchie & Bhatia, 1999; Spelke & Newport, 1998). From birth, infants prefer sounds that have characteristics of human speech: sounds in the frequency range of 1,000 to 3,000 Hz and sounds with a variation in frequencies rather than monotones (Schneider, Trehub, & Bull, 1979).

The similarities among cultures in many features of language also suggest an innate capacity for language:

1. Children around the world acquire language within a short period of time and at roughly the same rate despite differences in cultures (Kuhl, 2004). This is true both in cultures where children initiate and participate in conversations with adults and in cultures that discourage adults from conversing with children (Snow, 1986).

2. The sequence of language skills is similar across cultures for signed and spoken languages (Kent & Miulo, 1995; Petitto, Holowka, Sergio, & Ostry, 2001).

3. The sounds *b, p, m, d,* and *n* appear across many languages in infants' **babbling,** or repetitive consonant–vowel combinations (e.g., dadadadada; Gopnik, Meltzoff, & Kuhl, 1999; Locke, 1983).

4. All signed and spoken languages share similar first words, such as *daddy, mommy, milk,* and *dog* (Caselli et al., 1995; Tardif et al., 2008), and rules to indicate changes in tense and plurality and to organize words into grammatical sentences (Goldin-Meadow & Morford, 1985; Goldin-Meadow & Mylander, 1983).

Imitation and Reinforcement

Language learning partly involves imitation and reinforcement (Skinner, 1957). In response to adult modeling of language, children will attempt to produce language by spontaneously imitating sounds, words, and phrases. Parents also may encourage *elicited imitation* when they ask the child to produce a word spoken by the adult (say "bottle" instead of "ba-ba"). In many instances, children receive *positive reinforcement* (a positive consequence for behavior) for their efforts, as when a caregiver responds to infants' babbling with more dialogue or responds to a toddler's request ("want milk").

Modeling and imitation vary by culture. In cultures that do not encourage children to initiate conversations or to talk before a certain age, children are expected to learn by listening and by observing adult language (Schieffelin & Ochs, 1986). In the United States, elicited imitation is not

Master the content.

edge.sagepub.com/durwin3e

Brain development: See Module 5

> **DIVERSITY**

Positive reinforcement: See Module 8

> **DIVERSITY**

considered a crucial teaching method. Children implicitly discover the usefulness of imitation as a way to expand their communication skills. In recurrent, predictable events in their lives, children often repeat an utterance previously spoken by an adult during the same events (Snow & Goldfield, 1983). However, imitation and parental reinforcement cannot entirely explain children's development of grammatically appropriate language (James, 1990). Consider these findings:

- Children produce sentences they have never heard adults say ("I falled on the playground"). Also, children use imitation much less after age 2, even though they still have much more language to acquire (Otto, 2006).

- Reinforcement of children's grammar is not necessary for language development. Rather than correcting a child's grammar, parents tend to reinforce and correct children's utterances based on meaning or truth value (Brown & Hanlon, 1970). When a school-age child announces "I don't got no more money," a parent might respond, "Really, you *don't have* any more money? Where did you spend it?"

- We are motivated to learn to speak grammatically even though ungrammatical statements can convey our message just as well (Siegler & Alibali, 2005).

Social Interactions

Video: Child-Directed Speech

Reference: Expressive Language

Language acquisition is also a product of children's early social interactions with adults. Infants communicate and interact socially even before they are able to produce language. They make different babbling sounds in response to adults' pitch and intonation, move in rhythm to adults' intonations, and vocalize more when adults stop talking—a pattern similar to typical conversation (Ginsburg & Kilbourne, 1988; Locke, 1995; Masataka, 1992).

Adults also behave in certain ways that elicit communication and foster language development. They initiate communication in response to infants' eye contact, burping, or gurgling and respond to infants' babbling or first attempts at saying words. Adults in many cultures also encourage the development of language skills with additional techniques, described in Table 7.1. Caregiver techniques may not be universal, though. For example, even though caregivers in some cultures do not use **child-directed speech**, children acquire language as quickly and easily as those in cultures that do (Le, 2000; Ochs & Schieffelin, 1984). Therefore, while adult behaviors may not be *necessary* for language acquisition, they can *enhance* language development. Recent research suggests that several forms of caregiver responsiveness contribute to infants' development of expressive language: using expansions, describing objects, asking questions about objects ("What is that?"), using verbal prompts ("Let's feed the doll"), providing a rich vocabulary, and producing more complex sentences (Hoff, 2003a, 2003b; Tamis-LeMonda, Bornstein, & Baumwell, 2001). Parents who use more words, more complex sentence structures, and a diverse vocabulary when talking with their toddlers and preschoolers also encourage the development of their children's vocabulary, grammar, and comprehension skills (Hurtado, Marchman, & Fernald, 2008; Huttenlocher, Waterfall, Vasilyeva, Vevea, & Hedges, 2010; Rowe, 2012).

Adults' behaviors may have long-term benefits as well. Regardless of the family's socioeconomic status or ethnic group identity, parents who vary their speech, label objects, ask questions, respond to children's questions, and provide positive feedback for children's participation in conversations are more

DIVERSITY

Communication During the First Year. The mother shown here might be describing the flower and asking her child questions about the flower. Providing experiences such as these encourages expressive language in young children.

©iStockphoto.com/Jgalione

TABLE 7.1	Social Interaction Techniques of Caregivers		
CAREGIVER TECHNIQUE	**DESCRIPTION**	**OUTCOME**	**EXAMPLE**
Child-directed speech	Language directed to infants and children characterized by high pitch, exaggerated intonations, elongated vowels, short and simple sentences, and repetition.	Increases infants' attention to language, facilitating their comprehension and acquisition of language.	(playing peek-a-boo) "Where—is—Tommy?" (exaggerated intonation) "Peek—a—boo—I—see—you!"
Joint attention	Adults labeling and talking about objects on which the child's attention is focused.	Encourages vocabulary acquisition.	An adult noticing an infant looking at a bird and saying, "That's a bird. Do you hear it chirping?"
Expansion	Adults adding to—or expanding—the child's incomplete statement as a way to model more complex language.	Encourages the development of more complex grammar.	When a child says, "doggie sleep," an adult saying, "Yes, the doggie is sleeping. She's tired."
Recasting	Adults reproducing the child's utterance as a semantically similar expression that adds new information to model more complex language.	Encourages the development of more complex grammar.	A child saying, "We go home?" and the adult replying, "No, we're going to the store."

SOURCES: Brown & Bellugi, 1964; Campbell & Namy, 2003; Fernald, 1992; Nicholas, Lightbown, & Spada, 2001; Rollins, 2003; Sachs, 1989; Scherer & Olswang, 1984; Tomasello, 2005, 2006.

likely to have children with advanced language development (Hart & Risley, 1995; Snow, Tabors, & Dickinson, 2001). The amount of verbal interaction between caregivers and children is a significant predictor of a child's vocabulary, language skills, and reading comprehension at age 9 (Hart & Risley, 1999, 2003). Talking with children during activities and about activities should be a regular part of the day both at home and in early-childhood classrooms.

Imagine a child growing up in another part of the world. How might his language development be similar to that of a child in the United States? How might it be different?

DEVELOPMENT OF LANGUAGE SKILLS

2. Describe changes in semantics, syntax, pragmatics, and metalinguistic awareness from birth through adolescence.

3. Explain the advantages and disadvantages of the methods of teaching English language learners.

4. Describe the language differences that emerge from early childhood through the early school-age years.

Language Acquisition Through Early Childhood

Babbling is the first sign of an infant's ability to produce language, beginning at about 6 months. Around age 8 to 12 months, infants can more easily communicate with adults through gestures and **joint attention**. Joint attention—the adult labeling and talking about objects the child is gazing at—and the child's ability to point at interesting objects and make gestures provide a communicative context for language skills to develop (Behne, Liszkowski, Carpenter, & Tomasello, 2012; Rowe & Goldin-Meadow, 2009; Tomasello, 2006). Infants also become increasingly skilled at comprehending the meaning of words and can respond appropriately to commands (Benedict, 1979; Morrisette, Ricard, & Gouin-Decarie, 1995). With the acquisition of their first words at about 1 year of age, children gradually acquire the ability to use semantics, syntax, the pragmatics of language, and metalinguistic awareness.

SEMANTICS

Semantics (how words convey meaning) is evident in infants' first words. Their language is often referred to as **holophrastic speech,** because they use single words to express a larger meaning. For example, "juice" may mean "The juice is all gone" or "I spilled the juice." Children in the holophrastic stage will commit errors known as

- **overextensions,** or using a word to cover a range of concepts, such as saying "kitty" to refer to all four-legged animals; and

- **underextensions,** or limiting the use of a word to a subset of objects it refers to, such as using "kitty" only for the family cat.

Holophrastic Speech. "Juice" may mean "Daddy, I want some more juice."

SYNTAX

The development of **syntax** (the logical combination of words into meaningful sentences) begins with **telegraphic speech,** a way of ordering two or three words according to the grammatical rules of the child's language (Brown & Fraser, 1963). Such speech is called telegraphic because it resembles a telegram, an old communication system of paying per word in which messages consisted mostly of content words (nouns and verbs) and omitted function words (articles, conjunctions, etc.). Today's text messages resemble telegrams and illustrate telegraphic speech. A teen might text "need ride home" to his parent to indicate he needs someone to pick him up from school. Similarly, a toddler in the telegraphic language stage may say "sit floor mommy" to convey the request "sit on the floor with me, mommy." Children also develop several other forms of syntax throughout early childhood, including

- **morphemic inflections,** or word endings (dog*s*, dog*'s*, runn*ing*, bak*ed*);

- negations (I can't do it!);

- questions (What is Mommy doing?); and

- conjoining clauses (I went to a party *and* I ate cake).

Caregivers and early-childhood educators should not be concerned about children's **overregularizations** of past tense endings (e.g., saying "winned" for "won") because these are typical in this stage of development and continue through school age (Brown, 1973; Marcus et al., 1992).

PRAGMATICS

Pragmatics (knowledge about how to use language in communicative contexts) emerges in toddlerhood as children learn to use language for many purposes (Hulit, Fahey, & Howard, 2015):

- Regulating others' behaviors ("No!" or "Daddy, look!")

- Imagining (as in pretend play)

- Learning about their environment by asking questions ("Why?" "What's this?")

- Informing others ("I have a new baby sister")

Preschool children begin to use language for a wider range of purposes, such as asking permission, invoking social rules, expressing emotions, making judgments, joking and teasing, and making requests (Owens, 1988).

METALINGUISTIC AWARENESS

Metalinguistic awareness, our knowledge about language and how it works, is an important skill that emerges in early childhood and develops throughout the early elementary grades. Some early signs of metalinguistic awareness are:

- adjusting speech to different listeners, as when children as young as 2 years of age talk to a younger sibling differently from the way they talk to a parent (Warren-Leubecker & Bohannon, 1983);

- pretend reading of books, as when preschoolers turn pages and recite a story they have heard many times;

- asking "Are you making words?" to a parent typing on a computer; and

- "writing," in which preschoolers make marks on paper and ask an adult to read them (Schickedanz, York, Stewart, & White, 1990).

Phonological awareness, the knowledge that spoken words contain smaller units of sound, is a form of metalinguistic awareness that is important for later reading acquisition. Words can be divided into:

- *syllables,* the largest units of sound (cam-per);

- *onsets* and *rimes;* for example, in a word such as "bat," the onset is the sound corresponding to the initial consonant ("b"), and the rime is the vowel and the remaining consonant sound ("at"); and

- *phonemes,* the smallest units of sound that can change the meaning of a word (the word "tack," which has three phonemes /t/ /a/ /k/, can be changed to "tap" by replacing the last sound to get /t/ /a/ /p/, or to "pack" by replacing the initial phoneme to get /p/ /a/ /k/).

Children typically develop an awareness of global units, such as syllables and rhyming words, as a foundation for the acquisition of phonemic awareness, which is a more complex skill (Irwin & Moore, 2014). During kindergarten and first grade, children continue to develop awareness of phonemes as they acquire experience with printed words during reading instruction. Children with strong phonemic awareness skills when they enter school are more likely to become skilled readers as older children compared to those with weaker phonological skills (Liberman, Shankweiler, Camp, Blachman, & Werfelman, 1980; Shankweiler & Fowler, 2004). The guidelines in Table 7.2 can help early childhood educators determine whether a child is progressing adequately in phonological awareness development.

TABLE 7.2 — Benchmarks of Normal Development in Phonological Awareness

GRADE LEVEL	AVERAGE CHILD'S ABILITY
Beginning kindergarten	Can tell whether two words rhyme, can generate a rhyme for a simple word (e.g., cat or dot), or can easily be taught to do these tasks.
End of kindergarten	Can isolate and pronounce the beginning sound in a word (e.g., /n/ in nose or /f/ in fudge). Can blend the sounds in two-phoneme words [e.g., boy (/b/-/oi/) or me (/m/-/e/)].
Midway through first grade	Can isolate and pronounce all the sounds in two and three-phoneme words. Can blend the sounds in four-phoneme words containing initial consonant blends.
End of first grade	Can isolate and pronounce the sounds in four-phoneme words containing initial blends. Can blend the sounds in four and five-phoneme words containing initial and final blends.

Reprinted with permission from J. K. Torgesen & P. G. Mathes (2000). *A basic guide to understanding and teaching phonological awareness.* Austin, TX: Pro-Ed.

Phonological awareness and knowledge of letter names enable children to make progress in beginning reading instruction (Adams, 1990; Wagner, Torgesen, & Rashotte, 1994). Phonological awareness, in particular awareness of phonemes, helps children acquire the skill of **decoding,** or applying knowledge of the sounds of letters and letter strings to identify an unfamiliar word (Liberman, Shankweiler, & Liberman, 1989). Decoding helps children develop the ability to identify words while reading and enables them to develop a large print vocabulary of words in their long-term memory that they can recognize automatically (Dixon, Stuart, & Masterson, 2002).

Teachers can prepare children for reading through informal and formal instruction. Preschool and kindergarten teachers can teach phonological awareness skills through fun activities such as songs, nursery rhymes, and games (Irwin & Moore, 2014). Children who are exposed to activities such as these have better phonemic awareness as beginning readers (Whitehurst & Lonigan, 1998; Yopp & Yopp, 2009). Teachers in kindergarten and first grade can use direct instruction of phonemic awareness to help children learn to read and spell (National Reading Panel, 2000; Rupley, Blair, & Nichols, 2009).

Direct instruction: See Module 18

Language Acquisition Through Adolescence

Contrary to the assumption that children have mastered language by their fifth birthday, language acquisition continues throughout elementary school, with some language forms not mastered until adolescence.

SEMANTICS

As elementary school students learn many concepts in and outside of school, their vocabularies grow at a rate of several new words per day—ranging from about 6,000 words in first grade to as many as 40,000 words in fifth grade (Anglin, 1993; Johnson & Anglin, 1995). The understanding and use of figurative language, an aspect of semantics, also evolves from elementary through high school (Owens, 2012). By third grade, students appreciate puns and riddles because they realize that words can have two meanings (Ely & McCabe, 1994; Pepicello & Weisberg, 1983). Elementary school students also begin to understand similes (He eats like a pig), metaphors (She's an angel), sarcasm, proverbs (Haste makes waste), and idioms (Hold your tongue), and they begin to realize that figures of speech are not to be taken literally ("stealing" home base). However, children do not master the more complex figurative language found in proverbs, more abstract idioms, and sophisticated forms of humor until late adolescence (Cronk, Lima, & Schweigert, 1993; Nippold & Duthie, 2003). The ability to interpret figurative language is associated with prior knowledge and listening and reading comprehension skills (Dean Qualls, O'Brien, Blood, & Scheffner Hammer, 2003; Nippold, Moran, & Schwartz, 2001). Therefore, middle school and high school teachers should be aware that poetry and literature containing figurative language will be challenging for many students, and they should encourage students to read various genres to develop prior knowledge and comprehension skills.

SYNTAX

Children's sentences become more elaborate and consist of more complex grammatical structures in both oral and written language:

Metalinguistic Awareness. Preschoolers, like the girl shown here, know how to hold a book, turn the pages, and pretend to read.

- By age 10 or 11, students begin to produce subordinate clauses with complex conjunctions such as "because," "if," and "then" (Hulit et al., 2015; Wing & Scholnick, 1981).

- They begin to understand and use embedded sentences around age 7 (I saw a movie *that you would really like*). By age 12, they begin to understand embedding that occurs in the middle of sentences (The dog *that chased the cat* ran away) (Abrahamsen & Rigrodsky, 1984).

- Between ages 8 and 11, they also become better at understanding and producing passive sentences (Baldie, 1976; Horgan, 1978). For example, in the sentence "The boy was loved by the girl," younger children have difficulty determining who is the subject and who is the object of the loving.

Secondary education teachers should expect adolescents to continue to have difficulty with some aspects of syntax, particularly when writing. Even adults have difficulty producing the syntactic forms who/whom/that and I/me in oral language (Otto, 2006). Adolescent writers also have problems using pronouns to refer to nouns in their writing. Teachers commonly see errors in adolescents' writing, such as those shown in Figure 7.1.

PRAGMATICS

Elementary school students become more aware of the intent of indirect requests and the appropriate responses to such requests (Menyuk, 1988; Owens, 2005). Indirect requests are a more polite way of requesting an action from another person, such as "Can you turn off the TV?" rather than "Please turn off the TV." While preschoolers tend to respond literally by simply saying yes, 6-year-olds begin to respond appropriately to many types of indirect requests, with complete mastery occurring by adolescence (Cherry-Wilkinson & Dollaghan, 1979). By adolescence, most pragmatic skills related to common social experiences are well-developed (Berko Gleason, Hay, & Cain, 1988).

METALINGUISTIC AWARENESS

While knowledge about language and how it works dramatically increases between ages 5 and 8, development continues throughout adulthood (Bernstein, 1989). Students in upper elementary

FIGURE 7.1 **Syntax.** Even though adolescents' syntax continues to expand, they still may have difficulty with complex forms in their writing, as shown here.

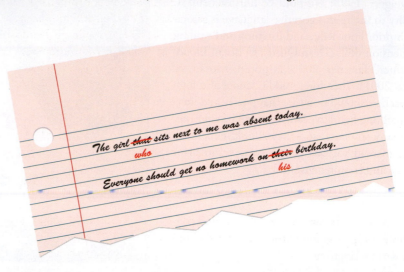

through secondary grades are better able to understand words with multiple meanings, to know when words are used incorrectly in sentences, and to understand how to construct sentences of varying types (active, passive, etc.). They also become better able to use reading and writing strategies, such as consulting a dictionary or thesaurus, monitoring their comprehension, and planning and revising their writing.

Reading and writing strategies: See Module 11

 How would you promote students' development of semantics, syntax, pragmatics, and metalinguistic awareness in the grade you intend to teach?

Bilingual Language Acquisition

Even though native English-speaking children and bilingual children (children speaking two languages) may have very different cultural and social experiences, they learn language in a very similar way (Bialystok, 2001):

- Children who acquire two languages from birth follow the same overall pattern and reach the same developmental milestones at the same rate as monolingual children (Genesee, Paradis, & Crago, 2004; Nicoladis & Genesee, 1997).

- Bilingual children say their first words and acquire a 50-word vocabulary at approximately the same age as monolingual children (Nicoladis & Genesee, 1997).

- Bilingual children have at least as large a vocabulary as monolingual children when vocabularies from both languages are combined (Nicoladis & Genesee, 1996; Pearson, 1998).

Becoming bilingual involves developing two separate language systems that interact with and complement each other. Even before children produce their first words, they have the capacity to differentiate between two languages, including sign languages (Petitto, Katerelos, et al., 2001). **Code mixing,** using words or phrases from one language as a substitute in the other language, is normal for bilingual children and adults and does not suggest confusion between the two languages (Genesee et al., 2004; Nicoladis & Genesee, 1997). It allows individuals to use competencies in each language to communicate in a way that is more complete than if either language were used alone (Genesee et al., 2004).

Video Case 7.1 ▲

Planning and Teaching a Bilingual Lesson

The developmental process of acquiring two languages simultaneously has more advantages than disadvantages. Even though bilingual children may start out having smaller vocabularies in both languages and a slight delay in development of syntax compared with monolingual children, by age 8 there are few differences between bilingual and monolingual children (Gathercole, 2002). Research indicates no distinct disadvantage of bilingual children in phonological awareness and even suggests an advantage in awareness of morphology (knowledge of word forms such as root words, prefixes, and suffixes) and syntax (Davidson, Raschke, & Pervez, 2010; Hirata-Edds, 2011; Loizou & Stuart, 2003). Elementary school children also are able to transfer their native-language competence in phonological awareness, vocabulary, and word recognition skills to their second language (Carlo & Royer, 1999; Cisero & Royer, 1995; Proctor, August, Carlo, & Snow, 2006). Therefore, bilingualism, itself, should not be considered a risk factor in language development, and it may facilitate growth of English vocabulary (Mancilla-Martinez & Lesaux, 2011).

The more important question is not whether bilingualism is advantageous but how best to facilitate development of English language skills in English language learners. Experts disagree about which instructional method is most effective for facilitating English language proficiency. Table 7.3 describes the aim of the major instructional methods.

Transitional bilingual education, which emphasizes the development of native language skills, was popular for almost 30 years. Because native language skills transfer to the second language, students experience greater academic success when they learn school subjects in their native languages in the early elementary grades along with English as a Second Language instruction

TABLE 7.3	Bilingual Instructional Approaches	
INSTRUCTIONAL METHOD	**AIM**	**LANGUAGE OF INSTRUCTION**
Transitional bilingual education	To ensure that English language learners do not fall behind academically by initially teaching school subjects in their native language.	Content instruction in native language; English as a Second Language instruction. Once proficient, students transitioned to content instruction in English, usually around Grades 3 through 5.
English immersion	To make English language learners fluent in English as soon as possible.	All instruction in English in classes with native English-speaking peers. Generally no modifications in instruction or materials.
Structured English immersion	To facilitate a rapid transition to English language instruction.	All instruction in English in classes separate from native English speakers typically for one year. Curricula and teaching methods designed to accommodate students who are learning the language. Minimal use of native language. Once "reasonably proficient" in English, students transitioned into classes conducted in English with native English-speaking peers.
Two-way immersion	To facilitate acquisition of two languages in English language learners and native English-speaking students.	Instruction in English and a non-English language for native English speakers and students who speak a non-English language (e.g., Spanish). Instruction and classwork in both languages, with the non-English language used at least 50% of the time. Only one language used, without translation, during periods of instruction.

SOURCES: Kim, Hutchison, & Winsler, 2015; Kogan, 2001; Lessow-Hurley, 2000; Lindholm-Leary, 2004–2005.

Two-Way Immersion. This bilingual instructional method leads to beneficial academic and nonacademic outcomes for native English speakers and English-language learners.

(Kim et al., 2015; Marsh, Hau, & Kong, 2002). In contrast, students struggle academically in **English immersion** classrooms *without any instructional modifications* because they find it difficult to understand the teacher and to demonstrate their knowledge (DaSilva Iddlings, 2005; Gutiérrez, Baquedano-López, & Asato, 2001). A variant of English immersion, **structured English immersion** provides appropriate supports to accommodate the needs of English language learners as they learn the language.

Recently, **two-way immersion** programs have been gaining popularity. These programs can start as early as preschool and usually run for about five years (through elementary school), but some continue through Grade 12 (Kim et al., 2015). Some recent research on two-way immersion (TWI) offers intriguing results:

Video: Two-Way Bilingual Immersion Classrooms

- In 3- and 4-year-olds, TWI improved the Spanish language skills of both the English language learners and monolingual children without any loss in English language skills (Barnett, Yarosz, Thomas, Jung, & Blanco, 2007).

- English language learners and native English-speaking students who attended TWI programs since the early elementary grades showed oral language, reading, and writing proficiency in both languages in the upper elementary grades (Howard, Christian, & Genesee, 2004; Howard, Sugarman, & Christian, 2003; Perez, 2004). They also scored at or above grade level in reading and math in both languages in middle school (Collier & Thomas, 2004; Lindholm-Leary, 2001).

- TWI programs have been successful in promoting positive attitudes toward school, especially among students from Hispanic backgrounds (Lindholm-Leary, 2001; Thomas & Collier, 2002).

Individual Differences in Language Acquisition

Typical language development varies considerably among young children in terms of the rate of acquisition and the style of acquiring words. Infants begin producing their first words at about 8 to 18 months and telegraphic speech at about 18 months to 3 years. Around 18 months, children typically experience a "vocabulary spurt" where the rate of learning new words appears to speed up (Bloom, 1973; McMurray, 2007). Children between ages 1 and 2 typically develop a vocabulary of 20 to 170 words (de Boysson-Bardies, 1999; Morrow, 1989). However, there is a lot of variability in development, with some 2-year-olds knowing fewer than 10 words and others knowing as many as 668 words (Fenson et al., 1994).

One explanation may be the caregiver-infant interactions discussed earlier. Children whose parents speak longer utterances with more complex sentence structures acquire new words at a faster rate and produce more complex language than those whose parents speak shorter and less complex utterances (Hoff, 2003a; Hurtado et al., 2008; Huttenlocher, 2002). Research suggests that children from lower socioeconomic families hear fewer words and less complex language, leading to less-developed vocabularies and language skills (Fernald, Marchman, & Weisleder, 2013; Huttenlocher et al., 2010). As a result of these experiences, children from lower socioeconomic backgrounds are more likely to have language delays as preschoolers (Nelson, Welsh, Vance Trup, & Greenberg, 2011; Roy & Chiat, 2013).

Video Case 7.2 ▲

Bilingual Vocabulary Lesson

© SAGE Publications

DIVERSITY

Children's distinct approaches to acquiring words may indicate that they have different ideas about pragmatics (Flavell, Miller, & Miller, 2002). Some children who acquire many words for the names of people and objects (milk, dog, cup) have a *referential style* that focuses on the informational aspect of language. Others who build a vocabulary of words used in social relationships (no, yes, want, please, love you) have an *expressive style* that focuses on the interpersonal aspect of language. Differences, however, are a matter of degree rather than kind, as all children learn both types of words (Goldfield & Snow, 2005).

Girls typically are faster than boys at acquiring first words, tend to have larger vocabularies, and are more likely to have a referential style of acquisition (Bauer, Goldfield, & Reznick, 2002; Flavell et al., 2002). Differences are small, however, and there are many exceptions. As with other cognitive abilities, males and females appear to be more alike than different.

> **DIVERSITY**

As children continue to develop through the preschool years and into the early elementary grades, many experience language problems involving articulation of sounds or lack of fluent speech that they eventually overcome. Others, however, experience more pervasive language difficulties. Children from toddlerhood through the preschool years produce many common articulation errors, as shown in Table 7.4 (Kostelnik, Soderman, & Whiren, 2004; McLean & Snyder-McLean, 1999). An **articulation disorder** is diagnosed when a familiar adult cannot understand a child's speech at age 3 or when articulation errors are still evident at age 8 (Patterson & Wright, 1990). Like articulation errors, **dysfluency** (a lack of fluency in speech production) typically is outgrown by the first year of elementary school (Weir & Bianchet, 2004). Dysfluency involves several types of errors, including the following (Gottwald, Goldbach, & Isack, 1985; Swan, 1993):

- Repetition of syllables, words, or phrases (that . . . that doll)

- Interjections (I saw . . . uh . . . a school bus)

- Pauses (Mommy, I want . . . some juice)

- Revisions (I went . . . we went to the doctor)

- Sound prolongation (r----abbit).

Children may experience dysfluency due to a heightened emotional state or hurried speech or, more likely, from experimentation with their rapidly expanding phonetic, syntactic, semantic, morphemic, and pragmatic knowledge (Otto, 2014).

TABLE 7.4	Common Articulation Problems in Early Childhood
ARTICULATION PROBLEM	**EXAMPLE**
Substituting one sound for another that is similar in manner of articulation.	Saying free for three. Other similar substitutions are s for sh sound, w for l sound, and th for s sound (a lisp).
Substituting across manners of articulation, using a sound produced with the teeth for a sound produced at the back of the mouth.	Saying tookie for cookie.
Omitting sounds, sometimes whole syllables.	Saying mote for remote or puter for computer.
Producing sound distortions.	Saying run as wun.
Mispronouncing consonant blends.	Saying pasketti for spaghetti.

Stuttering is the most common speech dysfluency. Approximately 80% of children who develop stuttering overcome it within 18 to 24 months after its onset (Ratner, 2004). Stuttering involves an involuntary repetition of isolated sounds or syllables, prolonged speech sounds, or a complete halt in the flow of speech (Cook, Tessier, & Armbruster, 1987). Speech problems that may indicate the onset of stuttering are (Yairi & Ambrose, 2005):

- sound and syllable repetitions that persist over time,

- repetition of part of a word more than twice or repetition of two sounds or syllables in 100 words, and

- frequent sound prolongations or sound prolongations of more than one second.

DIVERSITY

Unlike students with articulation problems or dysfluency, students with specific language impairment experience considerable delays in overall language development. Children with **specific language impairment (SLI)** have difficulties in receptive and expressive language, resulting in language development that is significantly below age level despite normal hearing, average non-verbal intelligence, and an absence of developmental disabilities (Montgomery, 2002; Tomblin, Zhang, Buckwalter, & O'Brien, 2003). Compared with normally developing children, children with SLI have smaller vocabularies, produce simpler sentences with more grammatical errors, and have difficulty with the pragmatic aspect of language (problems understanding others or being understood in conversations; Fey, Long, & Finestack, 2003; Fraser, Goswami, & Conti-Ramsden, 2010). SLI usually is first identified in the preschool years when a child shows difficulty in conversational settings and typically is not diagnosed until age 3. In elementary school, language impairment may be observed when children experience difficulty in comprehending and composing both oral and written language, reading, mathematics, or interacting with peers (Fraser et al., 2010; Fujiki, Brinton, Morgan, & Hart, 1999; Justice, Bowles, Pence Turnbull, & Skibbe, 2009).

 How would you respond to a parent who is concerned because her 2-year-old produces only a few words? How would you respond to a parent concerned about her 8-year-old's stuttering?

APPLICATIONS: ENCOURAGING LANGUAGE DEVELOPMENT IN THE CLASSROOM

5 Describe ways teachers can support language development in the classroom.

A responsive curriculum that recognizes language experiences as the foundation for academic learning will lead to beneficial student outcomes (García, 1992). Let's consider some general guidelines.

Talk, sing, and read to young children. Caregivers and early childhood educators can support language development by talking with children, singing songs with them, and reading to them.

- Stimulating verbal interactions promote expressive language skills and vocabulary development (Hart & Risley, 2003; Tamis-LeMonda et al., 2001).

- Singing songs encourages attention to rhythm, repetition, and expressive intonation (Squibb & Dietz, 2000). The rhymes in songs also promote the development of phonological awareness by calling attention to the component sounds in words (Maclean, Bryant, & Bradley, 1987).

- Engaging preschoolers and kindergarteners in dialogic reading can improve children's expressive language development and comprehension, especially for children from lower socioeconomic backgrounds (Arnold, Lonigan, Whitehurst, & Epstein, 1994; Whitehurst et al., 1994; Zevenbergen & Whitehurst, 2003). Dialogic reading is a shared book-reading technique in which the adult creates a dialogue with children about the stories while reading by (a) asking open-ended questions, (b) having children make personal connections to the story, (c) encouraging children to respond using more sophisticated language, (d) modeling language, (e) using **expansion** and **recasting** of children's language (see Table 7.1), and (f) praising their efforts. A similar approach called storybook sharing has been used with preschoolers and kindergartners who have specific language impairment to help them learn to communicate their thoughts, questions, and ideas (McNeill & Fowler, 1996).

All children, regardless of language or background, who are read to three or more times per week, have books in the home, and make frequent trips to the library have more advanced vocabulary and emergent literacy skills than children without these experiences (DeTemple, 2001; Payne, Whitehurst, & Angell, 1994; Santiago, 1994).

Encourage the development of listening skills. During class discussions and conversations, teachers can model effective listening strategies such as **active listening,** which involves listening in a non-defensive way and responding by clarifying the message rather than criticizing (Farris, Fuhler, & Walther, 2004; Wolvin & Coakley, 1985). Students need listening skills to help them understand oral directions and explanations of concepts, listen during class discussions, and listen to peers during collaborative group work.

Provide vocabulary instruction. Not only does reading practice influence vocabulary acquisition, but increased vocabulary knowledge contributes to students' reading comprehension (Aarnoutse & van Leeuwe, 1998; Verhoeven, van Leeuwe, & Vermeer, 2011). Teachers can foster vocabulary development through direct instruction with repeated exposure to words in varying contexts, as well as through indirect methods such as reading and class discussions involving critical thinking and exchanging of ideas (Ford-Connors & Paratore, 2015; Murphy, Wilkinson, Soter, Hennessey, & Alexander, 2009; National Reading Panel, 2000). Vocabulary development should extend

©iStockphoto.com/monkeybusinessimages

Reading. Reading to children regularly helps promote language and literacy skills.

beyond the elementary school years and can be easily incorporated into many academic subjects in middle school and high school (Boyd, Sullivan, Popp, & Hughes, 2012; Kelley, Lesaux, Kieffer, & Faller, 2010).

Provide opportunities for oral and written language use. Collaborative group activities, social interaction, and discussions can provide better opportunities for students to develop language and literacy skills than large group lessons, lectures, and independent activities or seatwork (Raphael & Hiebert, 1996). For example, open-ended discussions of culturally relevant books can facilitate meaningful dialogue and reading comprehension in English language learners as early as first grade (Martinez-Roldan & Lopez-Robertson, 2000). A teaching method known as *instructional conversations* can also be effective with English language learners. Here, teachers scaffold students in the interpretation of texts through conversations that resemble spontaneous discussions, rather than evaluate students'

Culturally responsive pedagogy: See Module 18

Instructional conversations: See Module 18

Reciprocal teaching: See Modules 11 and 18

PQ4R: See Module 11

Writing skills: See Module 11

Culturally responsive pedagogy: See Module 18

DIVERSITY ⟨

responses in traditional question-and-answer sessions (Bauer & Manyak, 2008; Saunders & Goldenberg, 1999). Middle school and high school teachers can improve their students' reading comprehension using approaches such as reciprocal teaching (developing strategies for summarizing, questioning, clarifying, and predicting) and PQ4R (preview, question, read, reflect, recite, review). Use of these strategies improves students' recall and understanding of important ideas presented in the text (Omoteso & Sadiku, 2013; Palincsar, 2003). Explicit grammar instruction and practice (e.g., writing stories, essays, and journals) help students of all grade levels develop oral language skills such as vocabulary, knowledge of morphology, syntax, and semantics. To further develop writing skills, middle school and high school teachers can improve students' planning, monitoring, and revision of writing through modeling, direct instruction of these strategies, and opportunities for practice (Bereiter & Scardamalia, 1987; Rijlaarsdam et al., 2012).

Be sensitive to individual differences among students. Rather than explicitly correcting language, teachers should focus on supporting language acquisition in *all* students by asking questions, clarifying, and expanding on students' utterances. Open-ended questioning helps elicit language participation from students with specific language impairment and builds their self-confidence and their competencies in responding to questions (McNeill & Fowler, 1996). Teachers also can encourage positive classroom experiences and promote language development in students who stutter or exhibit dysfluency by using the guidelines summarized in Table 7.5.

In addition, showing sensitivity to the needs of English language learners will promote their English language acquisition and improve their academic achievement. Teachers can encourage

Video Case 7.3 ▲
Supporting ELL in the Classroom

© SAGE Publications

| TABLE 7.5 | Guidelines for Promoting Language Development in Students With Dysfluency |

EARLY CHILDHOOD TEACHERS SHOULD	ELEMENTARY SCHOOL TEACHERS SHOULD
Reduce conversational demands on children by modeling slow, smooth speech.	Speak with students in an unhurried way.
Maintain eye contact and be patient so children do not feel that the teacher is uncomfortable talking with them.	Convey that they are listening to the content of students' utterances (rather than their grammar) by using appropriate eye contact, body language, and feedback.
Avoid telling children to slow down, start over, think, or take a deep breath, because these indicate that their speech is unacceptable, potentially increasing their anxiety and dysfluency.	Inform all students to take their time and think about their answers rather than answer questions in a hurry.
Discourage other children from interrupting or trying to finish an utterance for a child who is having difficulty talking.	Monitor social interactions so that peers do not tease or embarrass a student who stutters, and encourage all students to take turns when speaking.
Include group singing, choral responses, or choral reading in curricula, because these provide opportunities for children who stutter to participate in fluent speech. Recent neurological research has shown that choral speech is activated in the brain differently from speech that occurs in conversations.	Encourage all students to practice reading in pairs (taking turns or in unison) and to practice reading their stories at home before reading them orally to the class.

SOURCES: Büchel & Sommer, 2004; Scott, 2007; Weir & Bianchet, 2004.

language development by offering English language learners opportunities to read at their appropriate levels and to listen to rich, stimulating stories, in contrast with providing these experiences only when students show oral language proficiency (Bauer & Manyak, 2008). Teachers also need to recognize that the interaction styles of English language learners may be different from the type of communication they are expected to use in the classroom (Crago, 1992; Genesee & Nicoladis, 1995). For example, while native English-speaking children know that it is appropriate to initiate conversations with adults, compete verbally with other children, make eye contact during conversations, and demonstrate their knowledge, some Native American children are expected to remain silent in the presence of adults and to not make eye contact. Their behavior could be misinterpreted as a language delay or a lack of knowledge (Nicoladis & Genesee, 1997). Also, when teachers accept students' use of their native language for understanding content and answering questions, bilingual learners show positive attitudes toward both languages, leading to better linguistic, academic, and social achievement (Bhatnagar, 1980; Brisk, 1991; Jalava, 1988).

Think about the grade level of students you expect to teach. How can you use the guidelines we have discussed to promote language development in your students?

SUMMARY

❶ **Explain the factors that contribute to language development.** Humans are biologically ready to learn language, and our brains are well-equipped to produce and acquire language. Language acquisition also requires experiences that facilitate language learning. Caregivers model language for children, and children receive reinforcement for their language attempts. Caregivers also engage in verbal and nonverbal interactions that teach children about language. While cultures vary in their emphasis on techniques used to support language development, children in all cultures develop language at about the same rate.

❷ **Describe changes in semantics, syntax, pragmatics, and metalinguistic awareness from birth through adolescence.** Children rapidly acquire language skills during early childhood. They begin to babble at 6 months and acquire first words at about 1 year of age. From ages 2 to 5, children's syntax expands. Toddlers and preschoolers also acquire pragmatics by using their emerging language skills to achieve different goals. Preschoolers develop metalinguistic awareness as they begin to understand how reading, writing, and the sounds of their language work. From elementary through high school, students' semantic knowledge continues to expand as their vocabularies rapidly increase and they begin to understand figurative language. Students' sentences also become more elaborate and consist of more complex grammatical structures. Pragmatics and metalinguistic awareness improve through adolescence as students become better able to understand and use their language skills in reading, writing, and social interactions.

❸ **Explain the advantages and disadvantages of the methods of teaching English language learners.** Transitional bilingual programs encourage academic success because native language skills facilitate acquisition of English language skills and students do not fall behind academically. English language learners struggle in English immersion methods that have no curricular modifications to help them learn content in English. Structured English immersion improves on traditional immersion by providing accommodations to help students learn the language. Two-way bilingual immersion results in academic success in both languages and in positive attitudes toward school for students of all language backgrounds.

❹ **Describe the language differences that emerge from early childhood through the early school-age years.** Children exhibit differences in their rate of language development and in how they acquire words. Girls typically are faster than boys to acquire first words and tend to have larger vocabularies. Young children commonly exhibit articulation errors and fluency problems. A specific language impairment is identified in the preschool and early elementary grades when a child's receptive or expressive language development is significantly below age level despite normal hearing, average nonverbal intelligence, and lack of developmental disabilities.

❺ **Describe ways teachers can support language development in the classroom.** Teachers can promote language development by showing sensitivity to differences in children's language patterns, both with students who have language disorders and with students from different language backgrounds. They can support all students' language capabilities by asking questions, clarifying, and expanding on students' utterances rather than explicitly correcting language usage. Teachers also can model active listening strategies, incorporate vocabulary instruction into their curricula, and provide opportunities for oral and written language practice to encourage language acquisition in all students.

active listening, 143

articulation disorder, 141

babbling, 131

child-directed speech, 132

code mixing, 138

decoding, 136

dysfluency, 141

English immersion, 140

expansion, 143

holophrastic speech, 134

joint attention, 134

metalinguistic awareness, 135

morphemic inflections, 134

overextensions, 134

overregularizations, 134

phonological awareness, 135

pragmatics, 135

recasting, 143

semantics, 134

specific language impairment, 142

structured English immersion, 140

syntax, 134

telegraphic speech, 134

transitional bilingual education, 139

two-way immersion, 140

underextensions, 134

CASE STUDIES: REFLECT AND EVALUATE

EARLY CHILDHOOD: FIRE SAFETY

These questions refer to the case study on page 84.

1. Identify examples of *expansion* and *recasting* in the case study.

2. Identify the *overregularizations* of past-tense verbs in the case study. Is this typical of preschool children's language development? Based on research on language development, explain why correcting children's overregularizations and other grammatical errors may not be necessary.

3. Miss Angela read a rhyming book about fire safety. Explain how calling attention to rhymes can help promote phonological awareness and later reading development. In what other ways can preschool teachers promote the development of phonological awareness?

4. Story reading is a common practice in preschools. Explain how it helps foster language development.

5. Imagine that Miyu, a 4-year-old girl who recently immigrated to the United States from Japan and speaks little English, enrolled at Rolling Hills Preschool. Based on the research on bilingual two-way immersion programs, explain why it would be beneficial for the English-speaking preschoolers to learn Japanese while Miyu is learning English at preschool (assuming there is a Japanese-speaking bilingual teacher).

6. Suppose a parent approaches Miss Angela with a concern that her child has a language disorder. Many of the child's utterances are not understandable because he substitutes the "s" sound for the "sh" sound (saying *see* for *she*). What would you say to the parent about these articulation errors? How could you enhance the child's language development in the preschool classroom?

ELEMENTARY SCHOOL: PROJECT NIGHT

These questions refer to the case study on page 86.

1. Mr. Morales included writing a poem as a project option. Based on school-age children's language development, explain why poetry might be challenging for fifth-grade students.

2. How does Mr. Morales attempt to promote language development in his students? What changes could he make to the project unit to further support language development?

3. How well does Mr. Morales support the language development of his bilingual students?

4. How do the "research teams" help students develop more sophisticated language skills?

5. Based on your reading of the module, would you make any modifications to the research teams' activity for students with a specific language impairment or for English language learners?

MIDDLE SCHOOL: FROGS

These questions refer to the case study on page 88.

1. Describe the language achievements of children in the school-age years. Based on the information in the case, identify weaknesses in the eighth-grade students' language skills.

2. What changes can Ms. Thesdale make to the dissection lab to foster language development in her eighth-grade students?

3. What specific changes to her teaching can Ms. Thesdale make to support the language development of bilingual students in her class?

4. How can Ms. Thesdale support the language development of students, like Tyler, who have language impairments? Try to think of modifications you would make as a teacher to the biology lab activity and to your teaching in general.

5. Ms. Thesdale is attending a required workshop on children's language development but is frustrated at having to learn about the acquisition of language skills in young children. "What does this have to do with my adolescent students?" she thinks. Based on your reading of the module, explain to Ms. Thesdale how learning about language development from infancy onward can improve her understanding of adolescent language development.

HIGH SCHOOL: THE SUBSTITUTE

These questions refer to the case study on page 90.

1. Describe the language achievements of students from elementary through high school. Why might reading material such as *A Tale of Two Cities* be challenging for adolescents?

2. What techniques did Mr. Matthews use to foster language development in his students? What other recommendations would you suggest to Mr. Matthews?

3. What recommendations would you suggest to Mr. Matthews for supporting the language skills of bilingual students like Demeri?

4. What if some of the students in this case had language impairments? What recommendations would you suggest to Mr. Matthews for supporting the language skills of students with language impairments in his British literature class?

5. Imagine that you are at a school board meeting regarding bilingual education. Make a persuasive argument for K–12 two-way immersion based on the particular benefits to adolescents who have participated in programs.

UNIT THREE

LEARNING THEORIES

EARLY CHILDHOOD: PINCH

PREPARE:

As you read the case, make notes:

1. WHO are the primary participants in the case? Describe them.
2. WHAT is taking place?
3. WHERE is the case taking place? Is the environment a factor?
4. WHEN is the case taking place? Is the timing a factor?

Miss Rana (*RAH-nah*) is the head teacher at the local preschool for at-risk children. The preschool is state funded and typically includes children ages 3 to 5 from lower SES homes, from single-parent families, and/or with developmental delays. Arriving early one morning to prepare the art area for a sponge-painting activity, Miss Rana begins setting up space for pairs of children to share art materials. Miss Amber, the assistant teacher, arrives and provides the list of paired children she has prepared for the art project.

©iStockphoto.com/ kali9

Miss Rana reads the list and says, "I'm glad to see you paired Reagan and Emily for art. Emily has been so reluctant to participate in art ever since that day when she spilled the paint all over Billy's shoes."

"Yes," Miss Amber replies. "I thought it would be a good idea. Reagan loves art. I just hope she can keep her hands to herself today."

Reagan, a 3-year-old, is one of the youngest children in the preschool. Unlike the parents of many of the students, Reagan's parents are married and highly educated. Reagan qualified for the preschool due to a severe speech impairment. She was very hard to understand at the beginning of the school year, but her daily sessions with the school speech pathologist have resulted in markedly improved speech over the first three months of the school year. Although Reagan generally is a well-behaved child, during circle time she has a habit of pinching the children sitting next to her on the rug. Reagan does not attempt to conceal her misbehavior and readily admits to it if confronted by her teachers. Miss Rana and Miss Amber first tried ignoring the behavior, but that only resulted in a number of other children pinching their classmates. They have also tried telling her to stop pinching the other children and have even removed her from the rug area a few times, with no result. Recently, they decided to give Reagan a sticker at the end of the day contingent on no instances of pinching anyone. Stickers typically are used as special rewards when a child does something that deserves recognition. Only once during the past three weeks has Reagan earned the sticker—every other day she has pinched at least one child. Yesterday afternoon, Miss Rana and Miss Amber discussed the issue again and decided to try yet another strategy. They hope to "catch" Reagan early in circle time, before she has a chance to pinch, praise her for keeping her hands to herself, and then every couple of minutes praise Reagan and the other children for keeping their hands to themselves.

As the children begin to enter the classroom, Miss Rana gives her usual morning greeting: "Good morning, boys and girls!"

Emily enters the room and quietly walks to her space along the wall, where she hangs her coat on the hook and places her book bag below her name. As Emily sits down at her special spot on the rug, Miss Amber greets her. "Hello, Emily. I sure like the way you put your things away and sat down. You look ready to begin this morning."

As usual, Emily does not respond to this praise. However, a number of other children who were wandering off to inspect the art supplies quickly scramble to their own special spots on the rug. Reagan has just sat down, and Miss Rana quickly says, "Reagan, I like the way you have your hands in your lap—look everyone—Reagan is giving a wonderful example of how to sit with our hands to ourselves during circle time." Reagan's face clearly displays her pride at being the good example.

Circle time includes doing the calendar and weather, followed by Miss Amber reading the morning book. Miss Amber holds the children's attention during the story by asking them to clap each time they hear the word *leaf*. The teachers praise Reagan a number of times—along with many of the other children—for sitting with her hands to herself and for clapping along with the story. After she finishes reading, Miss Amber says, "Yesterday we read a different story about leaves. How is today's story like that one? How is it different from the one we read yesterday?" Several children raise their hands to share their ideas. Following circle time, the children are told who will be their partner for art that day and are sent to the space designated for them.

Miss Amber stands in front of four pairs of children, while Miss Rana stands in front of the other four pairs of children. "Eyes up here," Miss Rana says, as she notices some of the children whispering to each other. Each teacher holds up the art supplies and demonstrates how to gently put the leaf-shaped sponge into the paint tray and then gently place the sponge on their large piece of paper. Miss Rana tells the children to begin painting and quietly observes the interactions between Reagan and Emily.

Reagan asks Emily, "Do you want the red paint first?"

"Um, you pick," Emily quietly replies.

"Red is my favorite color," says Reagan. When Emily does not respond, Reagan asks, "What is your favorite color?"

Emily answers, "I don't know. I guess pink."

Emily has too much paint on her sponge and gets too much paint on her paper. Under her breath, she says: "I can't do it."

Miss Rana approaches and offers a few words of encouragement.

Reagan, mimicking the teacher, offers similar comments, such as "I like it too."

The two children continue to talk and share the art supplies. As Miss Rana walks around the room to provide assistance, she notices that Reagan and Emily are talking and giggling. She thinks about how she has never heard Emily giggle during class.

Miss Rana quickly takes the opportunity to encourage Emily: "You are doing a wonderful job! You are quite a little artist!"

ASSESS:

1. Why do you think the initial attempts to stop Reagan from pinching were unsuccessful?

2. Do you think the teachers would have reacted the same way if a boy were pinching other children? Why or why not?

3. Why do you think Miss Amber makes a point of getting the children's attention when a new activity begins? What might happen if she failed to do this?

CASE STUDIES

ELEMENTARY SCHOOL: SILLY STUDENTS

©iStockphoto.com/monkeybusinessimages

Aidan Lindsay is in his first year of teaching at a small rural school where most students are from lower to middle SES homes. His fourth-grade class has 25 students, with about equal numbers of boys and girls. Mr. Lindsay designed his room so that desks are arranged in clusters of three or four, which allows students to work together on some projects. The students seem to like this arrangement. However, some disruptive behaviors have occurred during the first few weeks of the school year.

Mr. Lindsay is seeking the assistance of the other fourth-grade teachers, Anna Vargas and Elsa Klendworth. During their lunch break in the teachers' lounge, he asks, "What do the two of you do with a group of three children who do not seem interested in anything but talking with one another and giving silly answers to questions?"

Ms. Klendworth presses him for more information. "What exactly do you ask of your students, and how do they respond?"

"Many times I will show the students how to do something, such as multiplication, on the whiteboard and then ask them to complete worksheets," Mr. Lindsay says. "I inform them that they should not copy the work of others in their group, but I encourage them to ask others for help. This typically works well. I have seen students showing other students how to complete the problems. However, these three children, Billy, Jason, and Megan, all pretend to help each other by talking and pointing to the worksheets, but as I walk past they obviously are talking about other things and typically end up getting little work done. In addition, their laughing and giggling disrupt the other students, particularly the fourth child in their group, Sara. Of course, given this silly behavior, it is not surprising that Billy, Jason, Megan, and Sara all received low scores on the math quiz I gave last week."

Ms. Vargas asks, "What have you tried to get them back on track?"

"Well, of course, I have repeatedly told them to calm down and get back to work. I have also tried ignoring their laughing and giggling, but they are just too disruptive to the other children around them. So yesterday I started taking away their recess time when their work is not completed, but I don't know yet how well that is going to work," says Mr. Lindsay.

"I would suggest that you give them extra time to talk with one another *only* if their project is completed," Ms. Vargas suggests.

Ms. Klendworth adds, "Yes, you might even begin by telling them that if they can just be quiet and not disrupt the other children you will give them a few minutes at the end of the period to talk with one another quietly."

Mr. Lindsay leaves the teachers' lounge somewhat skeptical about rewarding students for doing what all the other students already are doing, but he decides to try these suggestions because Ms. Klendworth and Ms. Vargas have been teaching much longer than he has and have been very supportive and helpful over the past several weeks.

As the children enter the classroom after their lunch and recess time, Mr. Lindsay asks them to sit in their seats. On the whiteboard he demonstrates the day's lesson on multiplication. As the children begin working in their groups, he walks over to the table where Billy, Jason, Megan, and Sara are working.

"I have a new idea," Mr. Lindsay says. "If the three of you can work quietly for the next 10 minutes while others are also trying to complete their math worksheets, I will give you three minutes to talk with one another. You can use quiet voices to help one another, but you need to stay focused on the math work. Sound good?"

The following week at lunch in the teachers' lounge, Ms. Klendworth asks, "So, how is that problem with your group of silly students going?"

"Oh, your suggestions worked like a charm. The three misbehaving students are paying more attention and actually helping one another finish their work so they have time to talk together. However, now the problem is the fourth student in that group, Sara. She has become increasingly frustrated that the other students finish before her. Many times I hear her say 'I can't do it' or 'This is too hard.' She even went so far as to throw her pencil down on the table and start crying.

"I have tried to explain to her that she does good work and should ask for help if she needs it, but Sara insists that she is not good at math. Do you have any suggestions?" asks Mr. Lindsay.

"What if you make the three minutes contingent on all *four* students completing the assignment?" Ms. Klendworth suggests. "Then the students will be more interested in helping Sara, and Sara will not need to ask for their help."

"Yes," Ms. Vargas agrees. "I would also suggest that you take as many opportunities as possible to prove to Sara that she is doing well. You can continue to tell her that she is doing well, but you should also remind her of previous work she has completed well—maybe even start a bulletin board where you can spotlight the students' work."

ASSESS:

1. Do you think having fourth-grade students "help" each other is a good idea? Why or why not?

2. Do you think Mr. Lindsay's reliance on the other teachers is a sign of incompetence? Why or why not?

3. If you were the teacher in this classroom, what strategies would you use to help the three disruptive students focus on their schoolwork?

MIDDLE SCHOOL: STUDY HALL

Milos Havel is one of three seventh-grade teachers at a middle school in a small but ethnically diverse city. The three seventh-grade teachers cover reading and social studies in their own "homeroom" classes, but each one instructs all the seventh graders in one subject area (math, English, or science). Mr. Havel's specialty is English.

©iStockphoto.com/Steve Debenport

Mr. Havel is worried about Jamie, a student in his homeroom class. Jamie appears to be a very bright child when he applies himself. He readily participates in class by explaining difficult concepts and providing good examples of the material, particularly during his favorite subject, social studies. His difficulties appear to be in the sixth-period mathematics class. Although Gladys DeBrick does not complain about Jamie's compliance in her class, his academic performance is weak. He rarely finishes his homework on time and appears to have fallen behind in the subject. For example, he lacks an understanding of basic mathematical principles taught the previous year in sixth grade.

During their weekly Thursday morning meeting, the three seventh-grade teachers discuss their students' performance. It turns out that Ms. DeBrick's student Jasamine is having problems completing her English assignments for Mr. Havel's sixth period. Much like Jamie, Jasamine does not have many behavioral problems within the classroom, nor does she appear to struggle with the content of Mr. Havel's English class. Nevertheless, Jasamine typically doesn't have the homework completed.

Mr. Havel and Ms. DeBrick develop a plan. Mr. Havel will help Jamie with his math homework during the study hall period immediately following Jamie's sixth-period math class. In turn, Ms. DeBrick will help Jasamine with her English homework during the study hall period immediately following Jasamine's sixth-period English class. Although both need to attend to other students during the study hall period, Mr. Havel and Ms. DeBrick will try to give Jamie and Jasamine as much extra help with homework as possible.

Several issues arise while trying to implement this plan with Jamie. On the first day, Mr. Havel walks by Jamie's desk and states, "I will be around to help you with your mathematics homework, so take out the assignment and get started."

Jamie replies, "I thought we could talk about the social studies lesson you gave today, like we usually do."

"No, I think your time is much better spent completing your math homework while you are here and have my help available to you," says Mr. Havel.

"I don't think I have the worksheets Ms. DeBrick gave us to complete. I guess I will have to do them tomorrow. So we can discuss social studies, right?" asks Jamie.

This pattern of forgetting the homework assignment and diverting the conversation to social studies continues for several days. Finally, Mr. Havel tells Jamie that he will not discuss social studies with him during study hall until his math homework is complete. After only one day of Mr. Havel's refusing to talk with him about social studies, Jamie begins to bring his math homework. Although he struggles with completing the problems, he puts forth effort to complete the assignments so he will have a few extra minutes at the end of the class study hall period to discuss social studies with Mr. Havel.

In Ms. DeBrick's homeroom, the plan works wonderfully from the start. Jasamine seems to enjoy the extra attention she receives in completing her English assignments. Ms. DeBrick notices that Jasamine does not seem to have difficulty completing the work once she has given Jasamine an example or two to get her started. Ms. DeBrick decides to pair Jasamine with a student who excels in English, so that Ms. DeBrick is able to spend her time helping the other children and preparing her lessons for the next day.

ASSESS:

1. Why do you think the initial plan to get Jamie to complete his math homework during study hall was unsuccessful? Why did the same plan work so well for Jasamine's English homework?

2. Do you think Ms. DeBrick's plan to have another student help Jasamine will be as effective? Why or why not? Would this strategy work for Jamie?

3. How might memory play an important role in completing math problems for Ms. DeBrick's class?

4. How might memory be important for completing assignments for Mr. Havel's English class?

EARLY CHILDHOOD

ELEMENTARY SCHOOL

MIDDLE SCHOOL

HIGH SCHOOL

CASE STUDIES

HIGH SCHOOL: BENDING THE RULES

©iStockphoto.com/monkeybusinessimages

Dan Hardy is a teacher of U.S. history, the only subject he has taught during his five years at a high school in an upper socioeconomic community. The students are highly motivated to do well and to continue their education at the top universities in the state. Mr. Hardy is well liked by most of his students. He spends a lot of class time providing examples of how to relate concepts in history to current events. He also uses group work during class, such as debating a controversial historical issue and predicting what would have happened if a particular event had not occurred. Mr. Hardy assigns homework that typically involves thinking and writing about issues discussed during class. Because his assignments are thought-provoking and because most of his students are eager to learn, Mr. Hardy rarely has problems with students completing the assignments.

At the beginning of Mr. Hardy's third class period, he asks students to pass their homework forward to the front person in each row. As he reaches the third row, he notices that Jason's assignment is missing from the stack. This is the fourth day in the past two weeks that his assignment has not been completed. Jason was told after missing his last assignment that one more incomplete grade would earn him a trip to detention.

After class Mr. Hardy asks Jason to stay for a minute. Mr. Hardy asks, "Why didn't you turn in your homework assignment today?"

"I don't know," Jason answers. "I guess I forgot about it, Mr. Hardy."

Mr. Hardy wonders whether he really forgot about it or instead was having difficulty understanding the material or organizing his thoughts. "Well, you will need to spend one hour in detention after school today to complete the missed work. Please be sure to stop by the office and notify your parents that you will be home late today," Mr. Hardy requests.

"I can't stay today—I have basketball practice," Jason replies. "If I miss practice, I will have to miss the game Friday night."

"Well, I warned you after your last missed homework assignment that you would be sent to detention if you missed another assignment," Mr. Hardy states. "You were aware of this class-room rule. I suggest you spend your hour today completing your missing assignments for the class."

When the last bell rings at the end of the day, Jason walks to Coach Gil Hanson's office and tells him why he will not be at basketball practice. Coach Hanson, upset that Jason's detention would mean facing the school's archrival without a star player, offers to discuss the issue with Jason's teacher and with the principal, Ms. Alice Krug.

In the principal's office, the coach makes his case to Mr. Hardy and Principal Krug. "I understand that Jason has missed some assignments in history class and is now in detention," he says. "As a result, he is missing basketball practice today and, by the rules, cannot play in Friday night's game. Is there something we can work out as a compromise?"

Principal Krug turns to Mr. Hardy and says formally, "What is your class rule about completing assignments and detention?"

"The rule is four incompletes result in detention until the student no longer has four incompletes. I rarely need to enforce this rule, but Jason is missing four assignments," Mr. Hardy explains. "I gave him a warning when he had missed three assignments, but he came to class again today without his homework."

"Can't you make an exception in this case?" Coach Hanson suggests. "Jason is overall a good student and an excellent athlete."

Principal Krug interjects, "I believe that a rule is a rule. If this is the system that Mr. Hardy has set up for his class, then we must all support his efforts. Jason will not be at practice and hence cannot play in the game Friday night."

"Well, the no practice/no game rule is my own team rule, not a school rule. I am willing to bend the rule in this case. The rule has been bent before for cases of illness and family vacations," Coach Hanson replies.

"I was not aware of that," the principal says. "I suggest that you change the rule to better reflect the practice. However, you and I can discuss this issue at a later date, in private."

Back in detention, Jason begins to gather his notes for the assignments he did not complete during the past few weeks. He quickly realizes that he has not taken good notes and cannot remember clearly Mr. Hardy's demonstration of how to complete the assignment, nor has he really participated with his classmates during the group work. Jason remembers that he did not do well in history during middle school because he wasn't good at keeping dates and facts straight.

ASSESS:

1. Was the strategy of placing Jason in detention helpful to Jason? Why or why not?

2. Do you think the teachers would have reacted the same way if a girl had been experiencing the same problems with homework and missing an extracurricular event? Why or why not?

3. What strategies would you use to help you remember dates and facts in history, and what types of skills or strategies would you need to complete Mr. Hardy's homework assignments?

Peter Dazeley/Photographer's Choice/Getty Images

MODULE **8**

BEHAVIORAL LEARNING THEORIES

OUTLINE	LEARNING GOALS
Assumptions of Behavioral Learning Theories	
	1 Describe the basic assumptions of traditional behavioral learning theories.
Classical Conditioning	
	2 Explain classical conditioning and its relevance to educational settings.
Operant Conditioning	
• Basic Tenets of the Theory	**3** Explain how reinforcement and punishment influence future behavior and how often each should be used to be effective.
• Using Consequences Effectively	**4** Explain how teachers can use consequences effectively.
Applications: Applied Behavior Analysis	
• Strategies for Increasing Appropriate Behaviors	**5** Describe strategies teachers can use to increase appropriate behaviors and decrease inappropriate behaviors.
• Strategies for Decreasing Inappropriate Behaviors	

ASSUMPTIONS OF BEHAVIORAL LEARNING THEORIES

1 Describe the basic assumptions of traditional behavioral learning theories.

How did you *learn* to write your name? How did you *learn* to raise your hand during class? Although most psychologists and educators might define **learning** as a change in either behavior or knowledge, traditional behavioral theories have focused on learning *behaviors,* with little focus on knowledge, mental processes, or memories.

As behavioral psychologists have studied how learning occurs, their theories traditionally have fallen into one of two categories: classical conditioning or operant conditioning.

We'll examine each of these theories separately, but first let's consider their shared assumptions about how learning occurs:

Master the content.
edge.sagepub.com/durwin3e

- *Learning must include a change in behavior.* To show that learning has occurred, traditional behaviorists assert that new information must cause behavior to change (Watson, 1913). If one cannot determine that behavior has changed, learning has not occurred.

- *Behavior occurs due to experiences in the environment.* British philosopher John Locke (1632–1704) stated that children are born as blank slates who can be taught to do, or not do, any behavior based on experiences in their environment (Locke, 1690/1892).

- *Learning must include an association between a stimulus and a response* (Kimble, 2000). Stimuli are events that individuals link or associate with certain responses. Learning by associations, called **contiguity learning,** is important for learning the vast amount of information children and adolescents are presented with. For example, letter and word recognition in early childhood is based on repeated exposure.

- *The stimulus and the response must occur close together in time.* Remember that time is relative. Immediate consequences are needed for young children, who view 30 minutes as an eternity. In contrast, cross-cultural studies have found that older children and adults are more likely to delay small rewards and wait much longer in exchange for larger rewards (Jimura et al., 2011; Rotenberg & Mayer, 1990; Vanderveldt, Green, & Myerson, 2014). Although this developmental trend implies that older children and adolescents can wait longer, immediate feedback in educational settings is optimal. For example, studies repeatedly find that immediate feedback is more effective than delayed feedback with respect to performance on classroom quizzes and success with learning materials (Kulik & Kulik, 1988).

Contiguity Learning. Young children learn to associate golden arches with fast food.

- *Learning processes are very similar across different species.* Rats, pigeons, and humans learn in similar ways. Because traditional behaviorists believe most learning processes are the same across species, few behavioral studies have focused on differences across ethnicity, gender, socioeconomic status (SES), or other issues of diversity within the human species. According to traditional behaviorists, it does not matter whether you are Black, White, female, or male—all humans (and all animals) learn behaviors through similar mechanisms.

> DIVERSITY

Can you think of examples of contiguity learning from your own experiences, both in and outside school?

CLASSICAL CONDITIONING

2 Explain classical conditioning and its relevance to educational settings.

We are all aware of involuntary behaviors, such as the body's many reflexes. For example, people automatically blink when an object quickly moves toward their eyes (the "you flinched" game played by children). These involuntary behaviors include two elements:

Video: Classical Conditioning

Philippe Lissac/Corbis Documentary/Getty Images

Behavioral Perspective.
Behaviorists assume that learning processes are very similar between animals and humans.

- an **unconditioned stimulus,** the behavior or event that evokes an automatic response (e.g., moving your hand quickly toward someone's face); and

- an **unconditioned response,** the automatic behavior caused by the stimulus, which can be physiological (e.g., someone flinching when your hand approaches) or emotional (e.g., fear).

In short, we don't learn to connect an unconditioned stimulus with an unconditioned response; rather, we inherit these involuntary behaviors.

Classical conditioning, or classical learning, is based on the pairing of these involuntary behaviors with events that do not evoke an automatic response. These **neutral stimuli** include shapes, behaviors, sounds, and smells. In classical conditioning, learning will occur when a neutral stimulus is paired repeatedly with an unconditioned stimulus, as in the famous study by Ivan Petrovich Pavlov (1849–1936), a physiologist who was studying the digestive systems of dogs. (Note that he was not a psychologist.) In Pavlov's (1927/1960) study, his researchers would release the alarm on the doors to the dogs' cages, sounding a bell, and then bring food to the dogs. After they had done this repeatedly, Pavlov noticed that the dogs started to produce saliva when the bell sounded rather than when the food was presented.

Classical conditioning states that an unconditioned stimulus (in this case, the presentation of food) and its unconditioned response (the dogs salivating automatically) can be paired with a previously neutral stimulus (a bell sounding). As a result, the previously neutral stimulus becomes a **conditioned stimulus,** or a learned stimulus that evokes a **conditioned response,** or a learned response. The dogs produced saliva (conditioned response) when they heard the bell (conditioned stimulus), not when presented with food. According to the first assumption we discussed, the change in behavior showed that learning had occurred.

While Pavlov's study illustrates a physical response, classical conditioning also demonstrates how emotions, particularly fear, can be learned (Watson & Rayner, 1920). In one study, researchers began by placing an infant, Little Albert, in the middle of a table and then made a loud noise behind him (unconditioned stimulus, UCS), automatically producing a startled fear response (unconditioned response, UCR). A neutral stimulus—a white rat—was paired repeatedly with the loud noise. After several pairings, Little Albert learned to be afraid of the white rat

Video: Little Albert Experiment

FIGURE 8.1 **Watson's Classical Conditioning of Little Albert.** A once neutral stimulus, the white rat, became a conditioned stimulus (CS). Fear of the white rat became a conditioned response (CR).

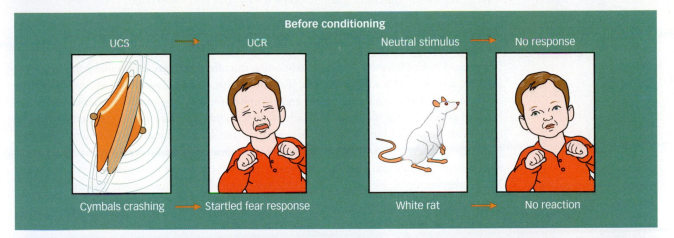

Before conditioning

UCS → UCR

Cymbals crashing → Startled fear response

Neutral stimulus → No response

White rat → No reaction

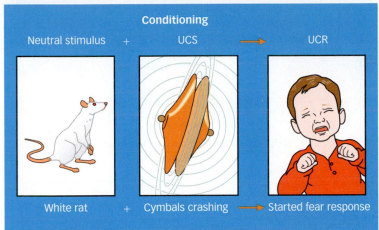

Conditioning

Neutral stimulus + UCS → UCR

White rat + Cymbals crashing → Started fear response

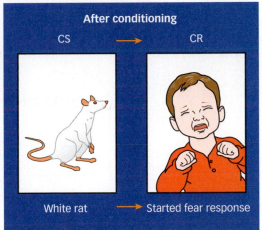

After conditioning

CS → CR

White rat → Started fear response

and would cry and attempt to crawl away when the white rat appeared, even in the absence of the loud noise. The once neutral stimulus, the white rat, became a conditioned stimulus (CS), and the fear of the white rat became a conditioned response (CR), as depicted in Figure 8.1. Again, the change in behavior confirmed that learning had occurred. (It is important to note that current ethical guidelines would not allow similar studies to be conducted.)

Once learning—or a change in behavior—has occurred, the behavior can be expanded on, altered, or eliminated. These additional learning opportunities are referred to by traditional behavioral theorists as generalization, discrimination, and extinction, respectively.

- **Generalization:** Conditioned learning can be expanded beyond a specific stimulus to other, similar stimuli. After conditioning with the white rat, Little Albert was presented with a white rabbit and more quickly learned to fear the rabbit as well—he generalized the meaning of "white rat" to the white rabbit.

- **Discrimination:** Species can learn to differentiate between similar but different stimuli. For example, Little Albert could have been taught to discriminate between white rabbits and white rats by being presented with white rabbits *without* the loud noise. Little Albert would have learned to distinguish, or discriminate, between the animals.

- **Extinction:** If the conditioned stimulus is presented repeatedly without the unconditioned stimulus, the previously learned behavior will disappear or become extinct.

Consider the example of Pavlov's dogs. Researchers could have presented the bell repeatedly without food. Eventually, the dogs would no longer respond to the bell by producing saliva. The conditioned response would have become extinct.

Although classical conditioning is widely used in modern psychology in the areas of cognitive science and neuroscience, there are fewer examples of how it may be applied in classroom settings (Rescorla, 1988). However, classical conditioning can affect students' emotional states regarding teachers, schools, and academic subjects. (Remember that emotions are automatic responses.) For example, a child who has been harassed and victimized on the playground by other children may begin to associate recess with fear. High school students may associate a teacher who is critical and harsh with feelings of humiliation or may associate the subject matter with fear and inferiority (e.g., math anxiety). In contrast, students may associate a teacher who is positive and supportive with feelings of pride and may learn to associate the subject matter with pleasure and happiness. Many other examples, including test anxiety and school phobia, illustrate how specific situations, people, and events often come to be associated with certain emotions.

Can you think of examples from your educational experiences that might have led to feelings of anxiety or fear about a particular subject? What might have been the unconditioned stimulus, the conditioned stimulus, and the conditioned response in those experiences?

OPERANT CONDITIONING

3 | Explain how reinforcement and punishment influence future behavior and how often each should be used to be effective.

4 | Explain how teachers can use consequences effectively.

Operant conditioning, like classical conditioning, includes a pairing of events. However, operant conditioning does not depend on involuntary behaviors such as physiological responses or emotional states. Rather, it includes new, voluntary behaviors such as raising your hand in class.

Basic Tenets of the Theory

Operant conditioning originated with Edward Thorndike (1874–1949), who, like many behaviorists, was conducting experiments with animals. The results of his experiments led to the **law of effect,** which states that behaviors associated with good consequences (satisfiers) are more likely to occur again in the future, whereas behaviors associated with bad consequences (annoyers) are less likely to occur again (Thorndike, 1898). For example, when a child is praised for class participation (good consequence), he or she is *more* likely to participate in the future. In contrast, when a child is laughed at or humiliated by the teacher or by other students when he or she attempts to participate in class (bad consequence), that child is *less* likely to participate in the future. B. F. Skinner (1904–1990) expanded on these ideas to form the ABCs of learning (Skinner, 1953). The antecedent (A) occurs prior to the behavior (B) and leads to the consequence (C) of the behavior. Remember, from the assumptions stated earlier, that the antecedent, behavior, and consequence must occur close together in time.

Antecedents can be cues or prompts. **Cues** refer to nonverbal events that signal that a behavior is expected. For example, many kindergarten teachers use the nonverbal cue of shutting off the lights (A) to signal children to quiet down and return to their seats (B). Similarly, many middle schools and almost all high schools use a bell (A) to cue students that a new class period has begun. Teachers' nonverbal cues are very important in maintaining classroom management and increasing the level of student performance (Woolfolk & Brooks, 1985). **Prompts** typically are verbal reminders that accompany a cue. The first few times the kindergarten teacher turns off the lights, he or she also says, "Please quietly sit down in your seats." Prompts may be particularly effective in teaching students with special needs. For example, studies have found that prompts can be used effectively to teach children with autism how to initiate conversations during play activities as well as stay on task during learning activities (Oliver & Brady, 2014; Seaver & Bouret, 2014; Shabani et al., 2002).

The consequence (C) of the behavior can either increase or decrease the behavior in the future. **Reinforcement** is a consequence of a behavior that increases the future occurrence of that behavior. When a teacher praises a student for participating in class and the student considers the praise good, he or she is likely to participate again—in order to receive more praise. **Punishment** is a consequence of a behavior that decreases the future occurrence of that behavior. Most children, after participating in class, would consider being laughed at and humiliated by their teacher and peers a bad thing, making them less interested in participating in the future—to avoid such consequences. It is important to remember that the definitions of reinforcement and punishment are based on the outcome (increase or decrease in behavior) and not the intent of the consequence (DeLeon, Bullock, & Catania, 2013). For example, a teacher might offer social time for completing homework, assuming that social time will be a reward or increase the likelihood of completing homework. However, if a child does not have many friends or is socially uncomfortable, the child may view this consequence as "bad" and it may decrease his or her likelihood of completing homework. For this child, social time is a punishment, not a reinforcement.

Reinforcement and punishment can occur by adding (+) something desirable or by taking away (–) something undesirable, as shown in Figure 8.2.

> **DIVERSITY**

Reference: Positive Reinforcement

FIGURE 8.2 **Examples of Reinforcement and Punishment.**

	Increasing Behavior	Decreasing Behavior
Stimulus presented	**Positive reinforcement** — Example: More time to socialize	**Positive punishment** — Example: Saturday detention
Stimulus removed or withheld	**Negative reinforcement** — Example: Not needing to wash the dishes	**Negative punishment** — Example: Not being allowed to play video games

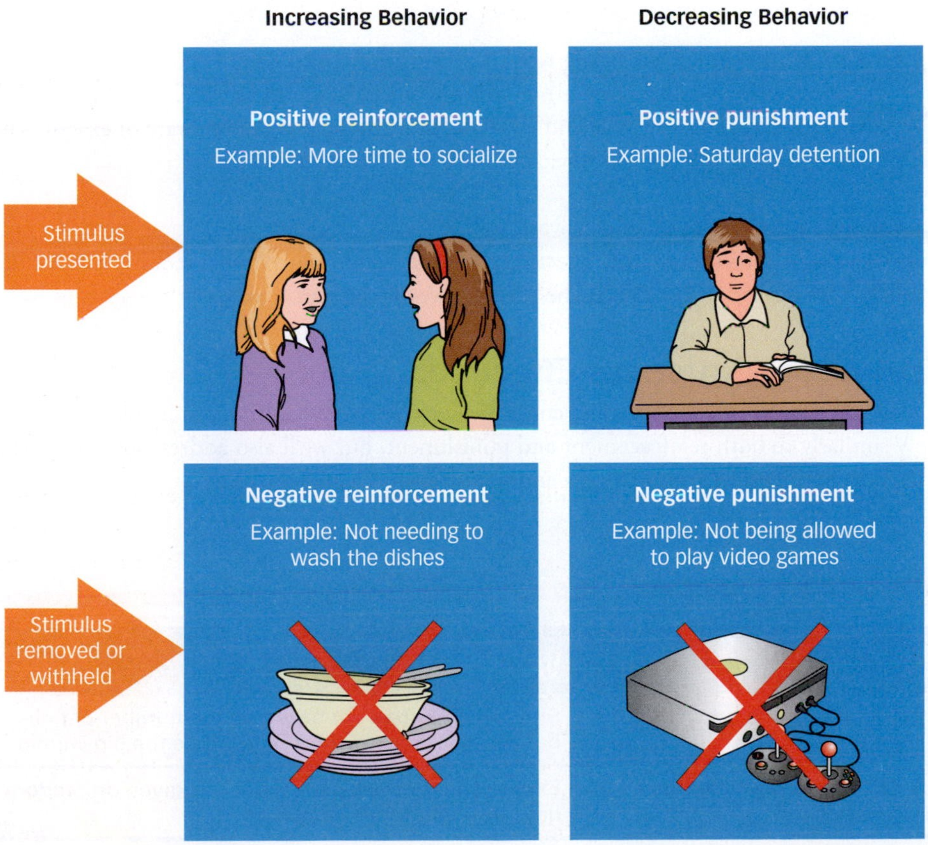

Video: Operant Conditioning, Positive Reinforcement

Video: Operant Conditioning, Negative Reinforcement

- *Positive reinforcement* is adding (+) something that is desired by the individual, such as praise, candy, or wanted attention.

- *Negative reinforcement* is taking away (–) something undesired by the individual, such as an annoying noise, an unpleasant chore, or unwanted attention.

- *Positive punishment,* also called presentation punishment, is adding (+) or presenting something undesired by the individual, such as physical pain, unpleasant chores, or unwanted attention.

- *Negative punishment,* also called removal punishment, is taking away (–) something desired by an individual, such as toys, free time, or wanted attention.

Regardless of whether the reinforcement is positive or negative, reinforcement *increases* the behavior, whereas both positive and negative punishments *decrease* the behavior.

When a behavior is first being developed, consequences are needed every time the behavior occurs for individuals to make the association and perform the behavior consistently—a **continuous schedule.** After the behavior has been well established, reinforcement is needed only periodically to continue supporting the behavior (DeLeon et al., 2013; Skinner, 1954). Reinforcement can occur on an **intermittent schedule.** Intermittent reinforcement schedules, shown in Table 8.1, may be:

- *ratio* schedules, based on the number of times a behavior occurs, such as every third time the child raises his or her hand;

- *interval* schedules, based on the time elapsed after the behavior has occurred, such as providing praise for every five minutes a student is quietly working on an assignment;

- *fixed* schedules, occurring exactly every third time the behavior occurs (fixed ratio) or exactly every five minutes (fixed interval), such that individuals know when to expect the reinforcement; or

- *variable* schedules, providing reinforcement every third time (variable ratio) or every five minutes (variable interval) on average but varying across time. Variable schedules typically are more effective and efficient because students are unaware of exactly when the reinforcement will be provided.

Although intermittent schedules work well for reinforcement, punishment needs to occur after every single infraction to work effectively. In other words, punishment requires a continuous schedule. Let's examine more closely the effective use of consequences.

Using Consequences Effectively

Here we present several tips for using consequences effectively, summarized in Table 8.2. Many apply similarly to both reinforcement and punishment, but we'll also address some important differences in the use of reinforcement and punishment.

TABLE 8.1	Examples of Intermittent Schedules	
	FIXED	**VARIABLE**
Ratio	Feedback on book reports is given for every third book report completed.	Slot machines pay out based on the number of pulls, but you don't know which pull will be the big winner.
Interval	Every Friday, popcorn is given to all students who meet their weekly reading goal.	Extra credit for class participation is given on random days throughout the semester.

TABLE 8.2 · Guiding Principles for Using Consequences Effectively

GUIDING PRINCIPLES	TIPS
Know the developmental level of the individual.	Younger children may like pencils, candy, and stickers. Older children and adolescents may prefer time to socialize with friends or listen to music.
Know the individual's likes and dislikes.	Although we assume most young children will like candy and stickers, some won't. Know what is considered desirable by particular students.
Understand the function of attention.	Some students will want the teacher's attention (praise and criticism alike), whereas other children may not want attention or may want only positive attention, such as praise.
Know when and how often to provide consequences.	Reinforcement can be given on an intermittent schedule without needing to catch every appropriate behavior. Punishment must be given on a continuous schedule by catching every infraction.
Use reinforcement more than punishment.	Because reinforcement is more efficient on an intermittent schedule, reinforcement should be used often and punishment sparingly.
Do not use certain punishments.	Physical or psychological punishment, extra homework, withdrawal of recess, and out-of-school suspensions all are ineffective punishments.

Know the developmental level of the individual. To use consequences effectively, teachers should understand what typically is considered good and bad by students in a particular developmental period. Stickers and smiley faces may be desired consequences for early childhood and elementary students, but they will not be as effective for influencing the behavior of middle school and high school students, who may instead desire free time to talk with friends.

Know the individual's likes and dislikes. To provide reinforcement and punishment, teachers must know what individual students consider to be positive and negative. One student may love chocolate and another may not, so chocolate might work great as positive reinforcement for one student's behavior but not another's. Individuals choose different reinforcements due to preference and are more likely to increase their behavior for a highly preferred reinforcement than for other reinforcements (Damon, Riley-Tillman, & Fiorello, 2008; DeLeon et al., 2013). Teachers must find out what is preferred by the students in their classrooms. Some examples of specific classroom strategies based on student preferences are described in Table 8.3.

Understand the function of attention. Just as students have individual preferences for tangible rewards, attention given to students can be a powerful consequence, as either reinforcement or punishment (Maag, 2001). For example, a teacher who repeatedly asks a student to sit down and be quiet may actually be increasing the behavior by providing the student with attention for the misbehavior—positive reinforcement. Peers can also reinforce inappropriate behaviors by providing attention, such as looking and laughing at disruptive behaviors (Flood, Wilder, Flood, & Masuda, 2002). In contrast, a teacher who repeatedly praises a student publicly for appropriate behavior may be decreasing the likelihood of that behavior because the student does not want the attention—positive punishment. By increasing or decreasing the amount of attention given, the teacher can alter problem behavior in the classroom (McComas, Thompson, & Johnson, 2003). Teachers must assess whether the attention they give to problem behavior is increasing or decreasing that behavior for each individual student and alter the amount of teacher and peer attention accordingly.

Know when and how often to provide consequences. As we discussed earlier, behavior and consequence must occur close together in time. The sticker given to a preschooler one day after the child has sat quietly for a story is no longer associated with the child's behavior the day before due to the elapsed time. Also, remember that scheduling how often to provide a consequence differs for reinforcement and punishment. Intermittent reinforcement can be as effective as continuous reinforcement in children and adolescents (Freeland & Noell, 1999; Milo, Mace, & Nevin, 2010). Although teachers can use either schedule with similar results,

TABLE 8.3   Classroom Strategies Targeted to Students' Preferences

STRATEGY	DESCRIPTION	NOTE OF CAUTION
Token economy	Students are given a token for appropriate classroom behavior or good academic work. The tokens are exchanged periodically for toys or prizes that children can choose based on their own preferences (i.e., bouncy ball, stickers, pencil).	Managing this complex system of tokens and exchanges is very time consuming.
Contingency contract	Teachers write a contract for each student specifying goals for behaviors that will be reinforced and what reinforcement will be given based on student preferences. Students should be involved in setting the goals and determining the rewards (i.e., free time, computer time, phone privileges).	Teachers must be able to remember the goals and rewards specified for numerous students.
Group consequences	Reinforcement is based on the behavior or academic achievement of the class as a whole. The students may help choose the class reward (i.e., excess recess, pizza party).	Individual students who struggle in the subject area or who have behavioral difficulties can be singled out as holding back the whole class.

an intermittent schedule of reinforcement is more efficient because it does not require teachers to "catch" every instance of positive behavior. In contrast, teachers *do* need to catch every instance of misbehavior if punishment is to be effective. Students who "get away" with a negative behavior learn that punishment can be avoided.

Use reinforcement more than punishment. Because it is difficult to use punishment on a continuous schedule, punishment is considered less effective than reinforcement. Also, punishment alone tends to teach a student only what *not* to do rather than encourage a more appropriate behavior (Alberto & Troutman, 2012). Given these limitations of punishment, psychologists tend to agree that teachers should focus on using reinforcement to increase wanted behaviors and less on punishing unwanted behaviors (Cheyne & Walters, 1970; Maag, 2012). Historically, teachers were more likely to use disapproval (punishment) than approval (reinforcement) in the classroom. Many teachers may learn to use punishment. For example, the first time a teacher yells, students typically react with immediate silence and obedience; hence, the teacher experiences positive reinforcement for her yelling. Yet the students eventually adjust to the yelling, and the punishment becomes less effective. More recent studies have found that teachers use approval more often than disapproval. Although this signals an important shift in the behaviors of teachers, research also indicates that approval is used primarily for academic learning and rarely to increase appropriate social behavior. Teachers would also benefit from using reinforcement for appropriate classroom behavior to increase on-task time for academic learning (see Beaman & Wheldall, 2000, for a review of approval and disapproval).

Do not use certain punishments. Several types of punishment are considered ineffective. First we need to define what we mean by effective and ineffective punishment. If effective punishment means simply getting the individual to stop engaging in some behavior, then most punishments work extremely well when given on a continuous schedule. However, most scholars think that effective punishment should not only stop the unwanted behavior but also lead to an understanding of why a behavior should not be used, enabling individuals to generalize to other, similar behaviors (Pfiffner & Barkley, 1998). In addition, effectiveness usually implies that the reasons for using the punishment outweigh its negative effects (Alberto & Troutman, 2012). The following five types of punishment do not meet this requirement of effectiveness:

1. *Physical punishment.* Physical punishment typically is viewed as spanking, but it also includes washing someone's mouth out with soap or making someone remain in a physically uncomfortable environment (e.g., extremely cold, extremely hot). One negative

effect of physical punishment is that it teaches individuals that it is acceptable for older or more powerful individuals to hit, push, or slap others. One longitudinal study found that children who were spanked, even at low levels, when they were 5 years old were more likely to have behavioral problems and lower verbal skills at age 9 (Mackenzie, Nicklas, Waldfogel, & Brooks-Gunn, 2013). Although empirical data do not support the use of physical punishment, many educators still believe it is a necessary evil, and changing their belief has proved difficult (Robinson, Funk, Beth, & Bush, 2005). Specifically, teachers in Botswana, Africa, have been found to strongly believe that physical punishment (e.g., caning) is inherent in their culture (Tafa, 2002).

> DIVERSITY

2. *Psychological punishment.* Psychological punishment can include public humiliation, such as a teacher ridiculing a student in front of the class, and may lead to loss of self-esteem (Davis & Thomas, 1989). The negative impact of this type of punishment on an individual's long-term well-being far outweighs the potential effect of decreasing an unwanted behavior. Hence, scholars agree that psychological punishment should not be used (Shea & Bauer, 2012).

3. *Extra homework.* By giving additional homework as a punishment, teachers send the message that homework is undesirable. Teachers should be sending the message that learning is important, essential, and positive—not negative, bad, or unwanted (Corno, 1996).

4. *Withdrawal of recess.* Recess may be necessary for children to focus attention and behave appropriately, in addition to the usefulness of physical activity for health purposes (Cook-Cottone, Tribole, & Tylka, 2013). Attention appears to decrease after long periods of confinement in classrooms and to improve following recess (Holmes, Pellegrini, & Schmidt, 2006; Mahar, 2011). In addition, classroom behavior, as rated by teachers, is better among children who have at least some recess during the day (Barros, Silver, & Stein, 2009). One study examining the importance of recess for children with ADHD found inappropriate behaviors more likely to occur on days when the children did not have recess (Ridgway, Northup, Pellegrin, LaRue, & Hightshoe, 2003). In addition to increasing attention and decreasing inappropriate behaviors, activities typically

> DIVERSITY

©iStockphoto.com/laflor

A Necessary Break. Recess provides positive outcomes, such as increased attention. The withdrawal of recess should not be used as a punishment.

engaged in by students during recess help foster cognitive development and social skills (Bohn-Gettler & Pellegrini, 2014) as well as higher scores on reading and math assessments (Becker, McClelland, Loprinzi, & Trost, 2014). The American Academy of Pediatrics has stated that recess is necessary for child development and should not be withheld as a form of punishment (American Academy of Pediatrics, 2013).

5. *Out-of-school suspensions.* In most cases, students who are given out-of-school suspensions do not view missing school as a punishment. Most of those students will see the suspension as negative reinforcement—taking away something undesired (attending school). In addition, empirical data suggest that out-of-school suspensions are given disproportionately to children from lower SES homes and minority ethnic groups and to boys more than girls (Gibson, Wilson, Haight, Kayama, & Marshall, 2014; Krezmien, Leone, & Achilles, 2006; Skiba et al., 2011). An alternative approach is in-school suspensions that can be used to more closely supervise students and to provide assistance for their academic struggles (Gootman, 1998; Huff, 1988). However, in-school suspensions also may serve as a negative reinforcement—as some students may misbehave because they do not want to be in class. In addition, teachers and administrators must be careful not to give in-school suspensions disproportionately to lower SES students, ethnic minority students, or boys.

? **Think of some ways you might use positive and negative reinforcement in a classroom. What are some things that students would consider desirable or undesirable to have taken away? (Remember, don't assign additional academic work—you don't want to imply that you consider it bad.)**

APPLICATIONS: APPLIED BEHAVIOR ANALYSIS

5 Describe strategies teachers can use to increase appropriate behaviors and decrease inappropriate behaviors.

We've discussed many examples regarding the use of operant conditioning in classroom settings. However, teachers can use specific strategies based on operant conditioning to influence behaviors in their classrooms. These specific strategies typically are referred to as applied behavior analysis or behavior modification. Many of these strategies focus on increasing appropriate behaviors, while others focus on decreasing inappropriate behaviors. Let's examine some of these strategies more closely.

Strategies for Increasing Appropriate Behaviors

Premack principle: Using the Premack principle (Premack, 1959, 1965), a teacher may increase one behavior of students by providing an activity as reinforcement (e.g., playing a game, socializing with friends, drawing) rather than giving tangible rewards (e.g., stickers, smiley faces). Early studies found the Premack principle extremely effective for teaching young children (3-year-olds) to sit quietly and look at the teacher by using free time as reinforcement (Homme, DeBaga, Devine, Steinhorst, & Rickert, 1963). The principle applies to older students as well. Middle school or high school students who complete an assignment early could use the rest of the class period to listen to music on an iPod or talk quietly with their friends.

Shaping: Shaping is used when a behavior is not currently being displayed and therefore cannot be reinforced, such as when a student *never* brings pencil and paper to class (DeLeon et al., 2013). The teacher does not have the opportunity to reinforce the behavior

Video Case 8.1 ▲
Increasing Appropriate Behaviors

© SAGE Publications

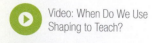
Video: When Do We Use Shaping to Teach?

Premack Principle. Reinforcement can include preferred activities such as listening to music or talking with friends.

because it doesn't occur. Shaping involves reinforcing small steps that move toward the behavior until the entire behavior is displayed (Skinner, 1953, 1954).

Teachers can use shaping for both academic learning and classroom behavior. For a child who struggles with learning to read, teachers can shape behavior by first praising the student for attempts to sound out a difficult or unfamiliar word, then for each time the child correctly sounds out words, then for increased reading fluency, and finally for answering comprehension questions. In middle school or high school classrooms, class participation can be shaped by reinforcing any effort at participation by students, such as making eye contact, raising their hand, or providing an answer, even if it is incorrect (Hodge & Nelson, 1991).

Reinforcing incompatible behaviors: In this strategy, teachers use reinforcement to increase the appropriate behavior (e.g., working on the assignment) while decreasing the behavior it is incompatible with (e.g., passing notes). While this strategy is effective for a number of behaviors, it must be used correctly, with consistent and frequent reinforcement of the appropriate behavior, so students do not return to the original, inappropriate behavior (Alberto & Troutman, 2012).

Praise-and-ignore: Like the strategy of reinforcing incompatible behaviors, the praise-and-ignore strategy suggests that teachers ignore inappropriate behaviors displayed by an individual while praising the appropriate behaviors of others. For example, the teacher may ignore a student who blurts out the answer to a question while praising the other students for raising their hands and being patient. Several early studies found this technique to be very effective for increasing appropriate behaviors (Becker, Madsen, Arnold, & Thomas, 1967; Madsen, Becker, & Thomas, 1968). Remember, however, that certain students may consider public praise a positive reinforcement, while others may consider it a positive punishment. In addition, some behaviors cannot be ignored, such as physically harming others or destroying property. Ignoring such behaviors would be unsafe and unethical.

Positive practice: In using positive practice, the teacher has a student perform the right or appropriate behavior (Kazdin, 2001). Students may write words they misspelled to practice the correct way to spell them. Teachers also can have students who run down the hallway return to the end of the hall and practice walking, decreasing the likelihood that the student will run in the hallway again and increasing the likelihood that the student will walk. Research has found positive practice to be an effective strategy for children with autism spectrum disorder (Anderson & Le, 2011; Peters & Thompson, 2013)

Strategies for Decreasing Inappropriate Behaviors

Satiation: In this strategy, the teacher asks the student to perform the negative or inappropriate behavior repeatedly, until it is no longer rewarding. Satiation diminishes the desirability of an inappropriate behavior by requiring the student to perform it over and over (Krumboltz & Krumboltz, 1972). For example, a student caught throwing spitballs is required to spend the entire class period creating those balls and spitting them at a specified target. At first, the other students may reinforce the behavior with their laughing and attention to the student (as they probably have done in the past), but eventually the spitball making and spitball watching behaviors will become satiated and no longer fun, entertaining, or desirable. The trick is to make sure that everyone has had enough. Don't give up too quickly. When the student appears bored with the behavior, let it go on a bit longer. Satiation should be used only when the behavior is not seriously harmful to the individual (Krumboltz & Krumboltz, 1972). In other words, do not use satiation with behaviors that may result in harm, such as smoking or lighting matches.

Satiation also can occur unintentionally, making a particular reinforcement no longer effective. Suppose, for example, a high school teacher reinforces students' completion of their homework with class time for talking and socializing. If other teachers begin to use the same reinforcement strategy in their classrooms, the importance and desirability of social time may be reduced. So teachers should continually reevaluate the effectiveness of the reinforcement strategies they use and alter them when the original reinforcement is satiated or no longer desirable enough to effect a change in behavior.

Extinction: Similar to its use in classical conditioning, extinction means that the behavior ceases or is eliminated. However, according to operant conditioning, extinction occurs because reinforcement no longer is given for that behavior (Skinner, 1953). Extinction can be useful for addressing a number of inappropriate behaviors (for a review, see Alberto & Troutman, 2012). For example, suppose a teacher stops giving a disapproving look to a student who continually speaks out of turn. The teacher is eliminating the positive reinforcement (attention), and the inappropriate behavior (speaking out of turn) should decrease or cease altogether. Like satiation, however, extinction should be used only when the undesired behavior can easily be ignored and is not harmful or dangerous, such as aggression (Krumboltz & Krumboltz, 1972).

A word of caution on using extinction: When a teacher withdraws reinforcement that has been given on an intermittent schedule, the student is likely to display an *extinction burst*—an initial increase in behavior due to the withdrawal of reinforcement. Consider the student who continually speaks out of turn. The teacher has been providing the positive reinforcement of attention (a disapproving look) to the student's unwanted behavior (talking out of turn). When the teacher eliminates the reinforcement, the student likely will increase the unwanted behavior in hopes that the teacher will "give in" and again provide the previous reinforcement. Over time, the student will learn that talking out of turn will no longer gain the teacher's attention, and the behavior will decrease. Individuals are less likely to display an extinction burst when extinction is used in conjunction with other behavioral methods, such as reinforcing the appropriate behavior (Lerman & Iwata, 1995).

Overcorrection: Overcorrection includes making restitution for inappropriate behavior (Alberto & Troutman, 2012). A student who writes on a desk in the classroom may be

Video Case 0.2
Decreasing Inappropriate Behaviors

asked to remove the markings not only from that desk but from all the other desks in the classroom—overcorrecting for his or her own behavior.

Reprimand: Reprimands are verbal criticisms of behavior intended to be positive punishment. When teachers confront a student in class for an inappropriate behavior, they are providing attention. Some students will find this attention desirable, because they enjoy being in the spotlight, while other students will find it undesirable. Teachers must assess whether their reprimands (attention) are increasing or decreasing the behavior. When giving a verbal reprimand, teachers should make eye contact with the student and stand close to the student rather than several feet away. The quiet, private approach allows the teacher to point out the behavior without providing the spotlight effect (O'Leary, Kaufman, Kass, & Drabman, 1970; Van Houten, Nau, MacKenzie-Keating, Sameoto, & Colavecchia, 1982).

Response cost: The concept of response cost is illustrated by the substance abuse policies of many athletic programs. Student athletes who use drugs or alcohol face the response cost of being suspended for a certain number of games or banned from the team. Response cost, a type of negative punishment, always involves taking away something the individual desires. For adolescents, the cost may be social time with peers, such as not being allowed to eat lunch in the cafeteria with friends or not being able to attend the class field trip. Response cost interventions effectively decrease disruptive behavior and tend to have lasting effects (Sullivan & O'Leary, 1990). One study of children with ADHD found that losing free time as a response cost was more effective in increasing on-task behavior and academic learning than was the use of the prescription medicine Ritalin (Rapport, Murphy, & Bailey, 1982). The effectiveness of this strategy may be one reason why teachers prefer this type of punishment to others (McGoey & DuPaul, 2000). The key in using response cost is to determine—both at the developmental level and at the individual level—what is desired and to consistently take that away following inappropriate behavior.

Social isolation (time-out): The time-out strategy includes removing an individual from one setting, where reinforcement is given, to another setting, where reinforcement is denied (Donaldson, Vollmer, Yakich, & Van Camp, 2013; Shea, & Bauer, 2012). In the best-known form of time-out, the student either is moved to an empty, uninteresting room or is removed from an activity to sit alone. When implementing time-out, teachers should consider these guidelines for using it effectively:

- Time-out should be used only when other strategies have failed and after careful consideration of time and age guidelines (Everett, Hupp, Olmi, 2010; Morawska & Sanders, 2011). The duration of the time-out should not exceed one minute per year of age and should not be used with children younger than age 2. Hence, 5-year-olds should not be in time-out longer than five minutes. The use of a timer will increase the consistency and fairness of the strategy and serve to alert both teacher and student to the duration (Shea & Bauer, 2012).

- Time-out is effective only if reinforcement is not present and the student desires to be with others in the classroom. Children who prefer to be alone and do not want attention from others may view removal from the classroom as desirable, making it a negative reinforcement (Shea & Bauer, 2012). Also, in child care centers and preschools, time-out may be ineffective because the teacher is not able to place the child in a separate room away from other children. Thus the child may draw attention from other children or from the teacher if he or she is being supervised by the teacher. In such cases, the attention associated with the time-out actually may be a positive reinforcement rather than a punishment.

> **DIVERSITY**

Video Case 8.3 ▲
Addressing Disruptive Behaviors

© SAGE Publications

Think about the grade level you want to teach. How could you use the Premack principle and response cost with this group of students? Think of specific examples.

SUMMARY

❶ Describe the basic assumptions of traditional behavioral learning theories. Learning processes are very similar across species and include associations between a stimulus and a response that occur close together in time. The association between stimulus and response results in a behavioral change, which indicates that learning has occurred.

❷ Explain classical conditioning and its relevance to educational settings. Classical conditioning is the pairing of an unconditioned stimulus with a neutral stimulus, resulting in learning by association. Classical conditioning provides an explanation for why some children may experience anxiety or fears related to school. Emotions—which are unconscious, involuntary responses—can be linked to important aspects of educational settings, such as particular teachers, a certain subject, or school more generally.

❸ Explain how reinforcement and punishment influence future behavior and how often each should be used to be effective. Reinforcement following a behavior will increase the likelihood that the behavior will occur again. When a behavior is first being developed, reinforcement must be given continuously. Once the behavior is established, only intermittent reinforcement is needed to maintain the behavior. Punishment following a behavior will decrease the likelihood that the behavior will occur again. For punishment to eliminate a behavior and keep the behavior from occurring in the future, every instance of the behavior must be followed by the punishment.

❹ Explain how teachers can use consequences effectively. Teachers must understand how developmental level and individual preference influence the use of reinforcement and punishment—in particular, the preference for attention from the teacher. Reinforcement should be given more often than punishment yet can be used on an intermittent schedule. Some punishments should not be used, and all others should be used consistently and continuously to be effective.

❺ Describe strategies teachers can use to increase appropriate behaviors and decrease inappropriate behaviors. A number of strategies can be used to increase appropriate behaviors. The Premack principle focuses on using activities for reinforcement, and shaping uses reinforcement of small steps toward a goal behavior. Reinforcing incompatible behaviors and praise-and-ignore strategies focus on reinforcing appropriate behaviors and ignoring other behaviors. Positive practice increases appropriate behaviors by having students practice the appropriate behaviors and providing reinforcement. Strategies to decrease inappropriate behaviors are also available. Satiation, extinction, overcorrection, and social isolation eliminate previous reinforcement of inappropriate behaviors in various ways. Reprimands, or verbal criticism, are a specific case of positive punishment. Response cost, a specific case of negative punishment, involves taking away something desired by the student following an inappropriate behavior.

KEY CONCEPTS

CASE STUDIES: REFLECT AND EVALUATE

EARLY CHILDHOOD: PINCH

These questions refer to the case study on page 150.

1. Why didn't the verbal reprimands of Miss Rana and Miss Amber deter Reagan from pinching others? Why was Reagan so eager to admit to her behavior?

2. Why was providing the sticker for reinforcement at the end of the day ineffective in decreasing Reagan's inappropriate pinching behavior? What could have been done differently to increase the effectiveness of the sticker strategy?

3. It may be difficult for Miss Rana and Miss Amber to continue to provide Reagan with so much praise for keeping her hands to herself. How might they change this strategy over time?

ELEMENTARY SCHOOL: SILLY STUDENTS

These questions refer to the case study on page 152.

1. What strategies were originally used by Mr. Lindsay with the three students who were being disruptive? According to operant conditioning, why didn't those strategies work well for decreasing their disruptive behavior?

2. Mr. Lindsay focused on punishment as a behavioral strategy, whereas the other fourth-grade teachers suggested a focus on reinforcement. Explain why this shift in focus toward reinforcement most likely increased appropriate behavior.

MIDDLE SCHOOL: STUDY HALL

These questions refer to the case study on page 154.

1. What types of reinforcement could be included in the English, mathematics, and study hall periods to increase homework completion?

2. How might the same reinforcements have different outcomes for different students? How might these reinforcements be different from rewards used with elementary students?

HIGH SCHOOL: BENDING THE RULES

These questions refer to the case study on page 156.

1. Does this school appear to focus on reinforcement or punishment? What are some specific examples of reinforcement and punishment within the school?

2. Do some teachers use behavioral strategies better than others? Which strategies are used, and why are they effective or ineffective?

4. Could shaping be used to increase Emily's behavior during art or Reagan's behavior during circle time? If so, explain how.

5. What techniques for increasing appropriate behavior and for decreasing inappropriate behavior were used in the preschool classroom?

3. Although taking away recess time may have decreased the students' disruptive behaviors, why is this a poor option?

4. Providing students with three minutes of "free time" to talk after each subject will decrease the time available for Mr. Lindsay to present lessons and/or decrease the time available for students to complete work. How might Mr. Lindsay change the three-minute reward over time?

5. Do you think the same reinforcement would have been equally effective with younger and older children? Why or why not?

3. How was the Premack principle used with Jamie?

4. How is the importance of receiving attention from the teacher illustrated in this case? How might attention be used as a reinforcer within the English and mathematics class periods to enhance performance?

5. What other strategies could be used to increase homework productivity for Jamie? For Jasmine? How might the strategies be different for these two students, and why?

3. How and why might bending the rules influence Jason's future completion of homework? What about other students' completion of homework?

4. What other specific strategies could the teacher, the coach, and the principal implement to increase appropriate behavior and decrease inappropriate behavior?

5. Are the behavioral strategies used in the classrooms and the school appropriate, given the developmental level of the students? Why or why not?

Visit **edge.sagepub.com/durwin3e** to help you accomplish your coursework goals in an easy-to-use learning environment.

- Mobile-friendly **eFlashcards**
- Mobile-friendly practice **quizzes**
- A complete online **action plan**

- Chapter **learning objectives**
- EXCLUSIVE! Access to full-text **SAGE journal articles**

Cultura RM Exclusive/Annie Engel/Cultura
Exclusive/Getty Images

MODULE **9**

SOCIAL COGNITIVE THEORY

OUTLINE	LEARNING GOALS
Assumptions of Social Cognitive Theory	
	❶ Describe the basic assumptions of social cognitive theory.
Observational Learning	
• Model Characteristics	❷ Describe those characteristics of models, imitators, and the environment needed for observational learning.
• Imitator Characteristics	
• Environmental Characteristics	
Personal Factors in Learning	
• Self-Efficacy	❸ Explain how self-efficacy and self-regulation are related to positive outcomes for students.
• Self-Regulation	
• *Applications:* Improving Students' Self-Efficacy and Self-Regulation	❹ Explain how teachers can promote self-efficacy and self-regulation among their students.

ASSUMPTIONS OF SOCIAL COGNITIVE THEORY

❶ Describe the basic assumptions of social cognitive theory.

Maybe you've heard a young child say a swear word and thought to yourself, *Well, she heard that somewhere.* Would you ever consider teaching children how to shoot a basketball or write their name without showing them how? Many times children imitate our behaviors when we don't necessarily want them to, such as when they repeat swear words, but often we want them to imitate our behaviors as a way for them to learn. In the 1960s, Albert Bandura began to study how individuals could learn by observing others' experiences in the environment. His ideas about observational learning were first termed *social learning theory.* As the theory evolved and included more personal characteristics such as cognition, it was relabeled *social cognitive theory.* Let's examine several assumptions of Bandura's (1986) social cognitive theory before we address the specifics of it:

- *Learning can occur by observing others.* An individual does not need to directly experience environmental stimuli, such as through reinforcement and punishment of behavior. Instead, an individual can observe others' environmental experiences to learn new behaviors or which behaviors will receive rewards or punishments. Learning by observing others' behaviors is called vicarious learning, or **observational learning.**

- *Learning may or may not include a behavior change.* Learning can include observing others' behaviors and gaining knowledge but not performing those behaviors. For example, an individual may learn how to put a pencil in the sharpener and sharpen it through observation but might not sharpen the pencil if it is already sharp.

- *Personal characteristics are important in learning.* Behavior is not simply a direct effect of the environment but also includes personal characteristics, such as beliefs in one's ability. For example, a student who believes she can succeed on a history test is more likely to learn the material. Personal characteristics can be enhanced by the environment to promote learning, as when the student's high score on the history test further solidifies her belief in her success.

The best-known example of observational learning is the classic experimental study examining aggressive behaviors (Bandura, Ross, & Ross, 1961). Preschool-age children in the experimental group were taken individually to a toy room and exposed to an adult model exhibiting aggression toward a Bobo doll. Preschool-age children in the control group were taken individually to the same toy room and exposed to an adult model playing quietly and ignoring the Bobo doll. Then the adult model exited the room, and the children's behavior in the toy room was observed for aggression. As expected, the children exposed to the aggressive model exhibited more aggressive behaviors—both physical and verbal—than did children in the control group.

Master the content.

edge.sagepub.com/durwin3e

Stimuli: See Module 8

Video: Bandura and Social Cognitive Theory

Video: Bobo Doll Experiment

Albert Bandura

Classic Bobo Doll Study. This study showed that children can learn aggressive behaviors through observational learning.

Think of some instances when you have learned through observation. Did your learning include a change in behavior? What factors were important in your observational learning?

OBSERVATIONAL LEARNING

2 Describe those characteristics of models, imitators, and the environment needed for observational learning.

Observational learning includes several components that influence what information will be learned. Both specific characteristics of the model performing the behavior and specific characteristics of the imitator influence whether learning will occur. Even with the most effective models and imitators, environmental conditions also influence whether behaviors will be performed.

Model Characteristics

Video Case 9.1 ▲
Observational Learning and the Bobo Doll Experiment

© SAGE Publications

For observational learning to occur, someone must perform a behavior while being observed by another individual. The **model,** the individual whose behavior is being observed, performs (or models) a behavior that can be imitated by others. Models can be either live or symbolic (Bandura, 1986, 2002). **Live models**—individuals who are observed directly—can be the observer's friends, parents, siblings, fellow students, or teachers. **Symbolic models**—individuals who do not live within the same environment as the observer—can be observed through various media such as movies, books, and television programs. Both live and symbolic models provide individuals with many opportunities to observe the behaviors of others.

Certain characteristics of models, whether live or symbolic, increase the likelihood that their behaviors will be observed:

1. *Relevance:* The behavior of models must be relevant for the individual observing the behavior—the individual must be interested in the behavior being performed, and the model must be similar to the individual (Schunk & Hanson, 1989). For example, some children may not be interested in chess and will not pay attention to the behavior of the stellar chess player in school. Also, individuals are more likely to imitate the behaviors of models who appear similar to them based on age, gender, race, socioeconomic status (SES), and so on. Students who observe a peer of the same age

Symbolic Models. Models can be found in the media, such as singer Meghan Trainor and athlete Stephen Curry.

will increase their level of mathematical performance more than students who observe a teacher (Schunk & Hanson, 1989).

2. *Competence:* The model must be viewed as competent in the behavior being observed. Students learning math will pay more attention to the behavior of other students who have strong academic performance in math than to that of students who are failing or struggling in math.

3. *High status:* The model is more likely to be imitated if he or she is someone with high status. High status can include power:

   - within the family (parents and older siblings),
   - within the peer group (the popular students at school),
   - of authority (teachers and principals),
   - within the popular media (celebrities), or
   - within a particular culture (political or religious figures).

4. *Gender-appropriateness:* An effective model is more likely to be someone of the same sex who is performing gender-appropriate behaviors. Gender-appropriate behaviors are those viewed by mainstream society as specific to either males or females (Bussey & Bandura, 1999). In the classic Bobo doll study described earlier, boys and girls were more likely to imitate a male model being aggressive than they were a female model. The strongest relationship was between a male model and male child, most likely because physical aggression is deemed more appropriate for males than for females by society (Bandura et al., 1961).

Gender: See Module 3

Teachers provide an excellent example of models in the classroom. Teachers may not have all the characteristics described, such as being of the same gender or race, but they can facilitate observational learning by making sure they are competent in the subject matter and maintaining their high status as authority figures. Teachers must be careful not to model inappropriate behaviors, which also can be imitated by students.

Imitator Characteristics

Many times, teachers with several of the characteristics described model academic skills or appropriate social behaviors, yet those behaviors are not imitated by students. In addition to requiring certain characteristics of models, observational learning requires the imitator to meet several conditions (Bandura, 1986; Schunk, 2012):

1. *Attention:* The imitator must be paying attention to the model. Teachers can perform behaviors that are intended to be imitated by students, such as completing mathematical equations on the whiteboard, but students must pay attention to the behavior in order to perform the behavior themselves later. Teachers can enhance student attention by keeping the content relevant and interesting.

Attention: See Module 10

2. *Retention:* Students not only must pay attention to the teacher who is completing the mathematical equation on the whiteboard, but they also must be able to remember the behavior later that evening while they are completing the homework assignment. Providing students with memory strategies such as numbering the steps in a math equation or creating a mnemonic for a list of items can increase the likelihood that the information will be retained for later imitation.

3. *Production:* The imitator must be able to produce the behavior. For example, many individuals paid attention to Michael Jordan's legendary basketball skills in the 1990s and even memorized his physical moves; however, few people could produce those same behaviors.

Live Models. Teachers can model learning tasks and behaviors for students, such as completing mathematical equations on a whiteboard, but students must be paying attention in order to perform the behavior themselves later.

Motivation: See Modules 14, 15, and 16

4. *Motivation:* An imitator who pays attention, retains the information, and can produce the behavior also must have the motivation to perform that behavior in the future. A math student may have attended to and retained the model's behavior and may be able to produce the behavior but may not be motivated to complete the math homework. Recent research suggests that a program using students' personal information (name, friends' names, favorite store) can create math word problems that are more interesting to students. Nigerian students provided with this personalized program had much higher achievement scores than those using the traditional math word problems (Akinsola & Awofala, 2009). By keeping the information personally interesting, teachers can increase a student's motivation to imitate the behavior or performance.

Students may be more or less likely to meet these conditions. For example, although even infants can imitate their mothers' behaviors (Markova & Legerstee, 2015; Paulas, 2014), infants and young children do not have the same attention span or memory strategies as older individuals. As cognitive development becomes more advanced, individuals are able to imitate more complex behaviors. Similarly, physical strength and ability grow throughout childhood and adolescence, allowing some behaviors to be more easily produced at a later time. In addition, children with autism spectrum disorder may have deficits in their ability to imitate modeled behavior (Edwards, 2014). Finally, some cultures, such as the country of Samoa, use observational learning as a primary mode of teaching social behavior, a strategy that may give students practice in using the skills involved in learning by observation (Odden & Rochat, 2004).

DIVERSITY

Environmental Characteristics

Assume that we have a model who has all the necessary characteristics to be effective and an imitator who also has all the necessary characteristics to be effective. Will all the modeled behaviors be imitated? No. Environmental conditions increase or decrease the likelihood that a modeled behavior actually will be imitated by an individual (Bandura, 1986; Schunk, 2012). Let's look at some of these environmental conditions:

- *Response facilitation effect:* A behavior is imitated more frequently if a model has been reinforced for that behavior—called **vicarious reinforcement.** An adolescent who views another student receiving free time to talk with friends because she has completed her homework during class time is more likely to complete the homework (increase behavior) to receive that same reinforcement.

- *Response inhibition effect:* A behavior is imitated less frequently if a model has been punished for that behavior—called **vicarious punishment**. An elementary student is less likely to swear in class if a classmate has been sent to the principal's office for swearing in class.

Reinforcement and punishment: See Module 8

- *Response disinhibition effect:* A behavior is imitated more frequently if a model's behavior is not punished when the behavior typically is punished. For example, cheating on an exam typically results in punishment. If some students are successful in cheating on an exam without receiving punishment, other students are more likely to perform that same cheating behavior.

Researchers continue to find support for learning by observation. For example, a study of aggression, based on natural observations of preschoolers in a low-income, urban day care center, found that aggression occurred more frequently after an aggressive act resulted in a positive outcome—vicarious reinforcement—than after aggression was followed by a negative outcome—vicarious punishment (Goldstein, Arnold, Rosenberg, Stowe, & Ortiz, 2001). Support has also been found for using observational learning in academic domains, such as preschool-age reading and middle school writing (Braaksma, Rijlaarsdam, van den Bergh, & van Hout-Wolters, 2004; Horner, 2004). Teachers should not only model academic skills and appropriate behaviors themselves but also reinforce students' appropriate behaviors, as other students may imitate their peers.

> DIVERSITY

Celebrities and athletes are symbolic models with extremely high status who may not model appropriate behaviors and may not be punished for inappropriate behaviors. How can teachers compete with such models?

PERSONAL FACTORS IN LEARNING

3 Explain how self-efficacy and self-regulation are related to positive outcomes for students.

Bandura (1986) expanded his theory of observational learning to move beyond the historical link between environment and behavior and include variables unique to individuals. The advances in his theory led to the *triadic reciprocal determinism model of causality* to explain the interaction among three aspects (see Figure 9.1):

1. *Behavior,* including choices in actions and performance.

2. *Environment,* consisting of the various contexts (family, school, mass media) and the socialization factors within those contexts (parents, teachers, symbolic models).

3. *Person,* including personality, temperament, emotions, and physical characteristics (gender and race) as well as internal cognitive processes (goals, beliefs, and attitudes).

Note two features of this model. First, the influence of these three aspects on one another is bidirectional, or reciprocal. A teacher's instructional style (environment) may influence a student's performance (behavior), and the student's performance may influence the teacher's instruction. Second, personal characteristics are important and interact with environment to influence behavior. A student with high levels of anxiety (personal characteristic) who is

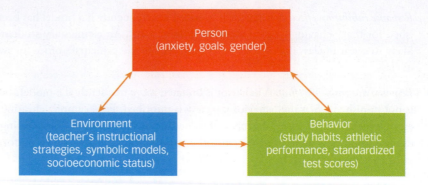

Video Case 9.2
Reciprocal Determinism

© SAGE Publications

attending a school in a low-SES district with few resources (environment) may score lower on a standardized test than a student with high levels of confidence (personal characteristic) who is attending a school in a high-SES district with the best teachers and resources (environmental characteristic). Although many personal characteristics contribute to learning, two that have received much attention in the educational field are self-efficacy and self-regulation.

Self-Efficacy

Self-Efficacy: See Module 16

Self-efficacy, an individual's belief about his or her capabilities for success, has been studied extensively (Bandura, 1977, 1997). Individuals with high self-efficacy believe that they are capable of success, whereas individuals with low self-efficacy believe that they are likely to fail or that they are not capable of success. Self-efficacy develops from four influences (Schunk, 2012; Schunk & DiBenedetto, 2014):

1. *Past performance:* Individuals who have been successful in a given domain in the past are likely to have high self-efficacy for it. For example, a student who has performed well in math is likely to expect to achieve success in math in the future. In contrast, the student who has struggled with math or has had many instances of failure likely expects to fail again in the future. Teachers who provide students with ample opportunities to be successful may enhance a student's self-efficacy for more challenging tasks.

Reference: Modeling

2. *Modeling:* When individuals see others similar to themselves experience success, they are likely to have high self-efficacy and to believe that they too can be successful.

3. *Verbal persuasion:* Individuals who are told that they can be successful are more likely to believe in their own success and to develop high self-efficacy. Students who are told that they are unlikely to succeed may develop low self-efficacy and a belief that they will fail. Here, simple words of encouragement may increase a student's self-efficacy.

4. *Physiological states:* Physical strength or fatigue can influence levels of self-efficacy. A student who is physically weak may have lower self-efficacy in areas of athletic performance than a student who is physically strong; or students who are tired may be less likely to view their capabilities as leading to success.

Cultural differences also may influence the development of self-efficacy (Bandura, 2002; Schunk & DiBenedetto, 2014; Schunk & Pajares, 2002). Teachers and media figures often are less likely to represent a minority group. Because students from minority groups may have fewer similar models available, they may have lower self-efficacy. For example, one study found that minority students predicted their own performance on standardized tests—as well as that of others in their minority group—to be below average. Similarly, women had lower self-efficacy than men for performance on a standardized test (Mayo & Christenfeld, 1999). Historically in American culture, girls had few female role models in successful careers, and verbal persuasion toward participation in certain academic areas, particularly math and science, was not encouraging but rather discouraging (Bussey & Bandura, 1999). Research suggests that this pattern may be disappearing in some cultures. A cross-national study found that middle school-age girls had *higher* self-efficacy for academic activities than boys in Eastern and Western European countries (Pastorelli et al., 2001). Teachers can counter the limited models available for minority students and girls by using verbal persuasion and providing examples of successful similar models whenever possible.

Self-efficacy is considered an important cognitive process in learning because it influences choice of behavior, effort and persistence, and achievement (Bandura, 1982, 1989, 1997; Schunk & DiBenedetto, 2014). Let's examine each of these more closely.

- *Choice of behavior:* Individuals will choose more difficult behaviors for which they have high self-efficacy, whereas individuals with low self-efficacy will avoid those behaviors. For example, the student with high self-efficacy for reading will choose more difficult books to read, while the student with low self-efficacy for reading will avoid it (Mucherah & Yoder, 2008). Similarly, one study found that middle school students who had high self-efficacy for math and science were more likely to continue taking classes in those areas (Fouad & Smith, 1996).

- *Effort and persistence:* Students with high self-efficacy will increase their effort and persistence for success even when they are struggling. For example, students with high self-efficacy for mathematics who do not perform well on the first homework assignment will put more time and energy into the next assignment. These students will continue to strive for success because they believe that they can be successful. In contrast, students with low self-efficacy for mathematics will view their first failure or struggle in math as verification that indeed they cannot be successful, and they will give up more easily (Bandura, 1982).

- *Achievement:* Individuals with high self-efficacy tend to have higher levels of academic achievement than individuals with low self-efficacy (Tella, Tella, & Adeniyi, 2009; Weiser & Riggio, 2010; Zimmerman & Labuhn, 2012). Specifically, self-efficacy for learning is related to mathematical performance, reading, and writing skills (Basak & Ghosh, 2014; see Schunk, 2003, for a review).

Whitehouse.gov

Minority Status. The election of President Barack Obama was significant for many people, as he provided the first presidential model of diversity in our nation's history.

High Self-Efficacy.
Individuals with high self-efficacy believe that they are very capable of success and would be more likely to participate in class by raising their hand.

©iStockphoto.com/monkeybusinessimages

 Think about your own self-efficacy. Do you have high self-efficacy in some academic areas and low self-efficacy in others? What factors most influenced your self-efficacy in those areas?

Self-Regulation

Self-Regulation: See Module 15

Another personal characteristic in the triadic reciprocal model that has received much attention in educational settings is **self-regulation**—the ability to control one's emotions, cognitions, and behaviors by providing consequences for oneself. Bandura (1989) proposed that individuals need to learn self-regulation because the external environment cannot always provide reinforcement and punishment. Because learning processes can be very different in different domains and contexts, self-regulation is not a general trait but rather is highly situational and context specific (Zimmerman & Schunk, 2011). For example, a student may have the ability to master his learning rather than relying on others in the subject of math but not in American literature.

Self-regulation for learning includes a cyclical process with three major components, as shown in Figure 9.2 (Bandura, 1986; Schunk, 2012; Zimmerman, 2001).

1. **Self-observation,** or self-monitoring: viewing one's own behavior and possibly recording one's own behavior.

2. **Self-judgment:** comparing one's performance to a predetermined goal or standard.

3. **Self-evaluation:** determining the quality of the judgment (good or bad) and possibly providing self-imposed consequences (reinforcement or punishment).

Let's examine these three components using the example of a student studying for an exam. The student would self-observe her study strategies, including recording the number of hours spent reading the text or taking notes. Then, assuming the student set a goal of an 80% score and achieved a 90% score on the exam, she would self-judge that she had met

FIGURE 9.2 **Self-Regulation.** Cyclical process between major components of self-regulation.

the goal. Finally, she would evaluate her performance positively and possibly self-impose a reward, such as going to a movie with a friend. The cyclical process suggests that the student would use the self-judgment and self-evaluation processes to conclude that her study strategies are effective and should be used in the future. When the judgment and evaluation processes are less favorable, the student may choose to change study strategies and start the process of self-observation again.

The development of self-regulation begins in social interactions with parents, teachers, and peers who model learning strategies and provide verbal persuasion (Schunk & DiBenedetto, 2014). The learning processes demonstrated in these social experiences become more self-directed through internal standards, beliefs, and self-reinforcement. Achieving self-regulation is more difficult for younger children than for older children, because younger children:

- have a shorter attention span,

- possess fewer memory strategies,

- tend to overestimate or underestimate their progress (exhibit poor self-judgment and self-evaluation), and

- need more immediate consequences.

Given these limitations, self-regulation does not begin to develop until the elementary school years (Schunk & Zimmerman, 1997; Zimmerman & Schunk, 2001). Self-regulation skills continue to grow throughout development, with high school students having higher levels of self-regulation than middle school students (Schunk & DiBenedetto, 2014; Zimmerman & Martinez-Pons, 1990).

A higher level of self-regulation skills in students is related to a number of positive outcomes in educational settings across various cultures, including (Lee, Yu, & Choi, 2012; Zimmerman, 1998; Zimmerman & Schunk, 2011):

- higher self-efficacy,

- the setting of higher academic goals,

- the use of effective learning strategies,

- the monitoring of one's learning progress, and

- the attribution of academic success to one's own learning strategies.

Teacher efficacy: See
Module 15

APPLICATIONS: IMPROVING STUDENTS' SELF-EFFICACY AND SELF-REGULATION

Given the link between self-efficacy and academic achievement, educators need to promote self-efficacy. To do this, teachers can provide students with accurate, specific feedback rather than undeserved positive feedback (Linnenbrink & Pintrich, 2003; Zimmerman & Labuhn, 2012). Self-efficacy that is based on accurate appraisals of an individual's capabilities is more beneficial for positive outcomes than that based on inaccurate appraisals. This is especially true for younger children, who are less likely to assess their capabilities accurately due to their limited cognitive abilities and limited past performances (Schunk & Pajares, 2002). Teachers also can provide verbal persuasion for their students, particularly young children, to enhance accurate appraisals and increase self-efficacy (Schunk & DiBenedetto, 2014).

Teachers should also model self-efficacy (Bandura, 1989). **Teacher efficacy** is a teacher's belief in his or her capability to transmit knowledge as well as manage the classroom well. Teacher efficacy is important because it influences student self-efficacy and can affect student achievement (Woolfolk & Hoy, 1990). Teachers with high efficacy develop more challenging lessons, spend more time on academic activities, and are more persistent in working with students who are struggling. Conversely, teachers with low efficacy tend to have a pessimistic view of student motivation, are more easily stressed by students' misbehaviors, and have lower job satisfaction (Bandura, 1997; Schunk & DiBenedetto, 2014; Viel-Ruma, Houchins, Jolivette, & Benson, 2010). Teacher efficacy can be increased by observing other teachers, practicing performance (e.g., student teaching), and gaining more knowledge in one's subject areas.

Student self-efficacy and teacher self-efficacy can be increased through collective efficacy within school systems (Viel-Ruma et al., 2010). **Collective efficacy** is the belief in success with respect to a group or social system, such as beliefs about teachers and administrators in a school system as a whole (Schunk & DiBenedetto, 2014). Research has found that the SES of a school is related to the level of collective efficacy such that lower SES is related to lower levels of collective efficacy (Belfi, Gielen, De Fraine, Verschueren, & Meredith, 2015). Research suggests a number of characteristics needed for collective efficacy in a school system (Bandura, 1997; Kurt, Duyar, & Calik, 2011; Moolennaar, Sleegers, & Daly, 2012):

- Administrators acknowledge the expertise of others in the school.

- Administrators seek to improve instruction.

- Administrators and teachers have high expectations and standards.

- Teachers collaborate with one another.

- Teachers provide activities that promote self-efficacy in students.

- Classroom behavior is well managed, resulting in more time spent on instruction and less on discipline issues.

- The school encourages a collaborative effort with parents, including open communication.

Self-regulation also can be enhanced by modeling learning strategies and guiding the practice of learning strategies (Chatzistamatiou & Dermitzaki, 2013; Schunk & Zimmerman, 2007). Teachers first need to act as models and to provide feedback (Labuhn, Zimmerman, & Hasselhorn, 2010). Teachers then can provide students with opportunities for independent practice that require more self-evaluation, such as homework. Training in self-regulation processes (goal setting, self-reflection) has been found to lead to remarkable improvements in learning skills and self-efficacy (Schunk, 2001), including increases in performance and learning processes in individuals with learning disabilities (Butler, 1998).

> DIVERSITY

SUMMARY

❶ **Describe the basic assumptions of social cognitive theory.** Learning can occur through observation as well as through direct experiences with the environment but may not always lead to a change in behavior. Learning is not simply a product of the environment but includes individual, personal characteristics such as cognitive beliefs.

❷ **Describe those characteristics of models, imitators, and the environment needed for observational learning.** Models are more likely to be imitated if they are similar to the imitator, have a high status, and competently display gender-appropriate behaviors that are of interest to the imitator. Observational learning can take place only when the imitator is paying attention, can remember the behaviors observed, can actually produce the behaviors, and is motivated to imitate the behaviors. Behaviors are more likely to be imitated if the model was reinforced for the behavior and less likely to be imitated if the model was punished for the behavior. When the model is not punished for behaviors that typically are punished, the behavior is likely to be imitated.

❸ **Explain how self-efficacy and self-regulation are related to positive outcomes for students.** Self-efficacy, or beliefs about one's ability to be successful, are related to choice of behavior, effort and persistence, and achievement. Self-regulation involves a cyclical process among self-observation, self-judgment, and self-evaluation that enhances self-efficacy and promotes the setting of higher goals, the attribution of academic success to the self, and enjoyment of learning activities.

❹ **Explain how teachers can promote self-efficacy and self-regulation among their students.** Teachers can provide students with successful models and accurate, positive feedback on their performance to increase self-efficacy. In addition, teachers who have high self-efficacy for instruction and are involved in school systems with collective efficacy are more capable of increasing student self-efficacy. Teachers can increase self-regulation among students by first providing a model and feedback and then giving students opportunities for independent learning.

KEY CONCEPTS

collective efficacy, 184

live models, 176

model, 176

observational learning, 175

self-efficacy, 180

self-evaluation, 182

self-judgment, 182

self-observation, 182

self-regulation, 182

symbolic models, 176

teacher efficacy, 184

vicarious punishment, 179

vicarious reinforcement, 178

CASE STUDIES: REFLECT AND EVALUATE

EARLY CHILDHOOD: PINCH

These questions refer to the case study on page 150.

1. Identify an example of vicarious reinforcement being used in the preschool classroom.

2. Although ignoring misbehaviors can be effective at times, why did that strategy lead to increased pinching by other students?

3. Why did Miss Rana and Miss Amber both demonstrate how to use the sponge for painting?

4. What are some reasons why Emily was unable to use the sponge and paint in the way it was demonstrated by her teachers?

5. How did self-efficacy influence Emily's art project? How did pairing Emily with Reagan help improve Emily's self-efficacy? What else can Miss Rana and Miss Amber do to increase Emily's self-efficacy?

ELEMENTARY SCHOOL: SILLY STUDENTS

These questions refer to the case study on page 152.

1. What are some examples of how modeling is used within Mr. Lindsay's classroom? How might these be improved upon?

2. What characteristics of imitators needed to be improved upon for the students to increase their ability to complete the work?

3. What methods of increasing Sara's self-efficacy were suggested by Ms. Vargas? What else can Mr. Lindsay do to increase her self-efficacy?

4. Mr. Lindsay asks the other two fourth-grade teachers for help quite often during their lunchtime. Why is this type of interaction among teachers important for Mr. Lindsay and for the school system?

5. In what specific ways did Mr. Lindsay attempt to increase self-regulation among his students?

6. How might the knowledge that Mr. Lindsay is African American and his students are predominantly White change your expectations for modeling and increasing self-efficacy? Why?

MIDDLE SCHOOL: STUDY HALL

These questions refer to the case study on page 154.

1. What modeling characteristics were important for Jamie to complete his math homework and for Jasamine to complete her English homework?

2. Do you think this plan would work as well if Jamie were a girl and Jasamine were a boy? Do you think this plan would work as well if Mr. Havel were a woman and Ms. DeBrick were a man? Explain your answers.

3. Is Ms. DeBrick's idea of having Jasamine work with another student a good idea? Why or why not, based on effective modeling?

4. How might Jamie's past performance in mathematics influence his ability to complete the homework? How might Jasamine's past performance in English influence her ability to complete the homework? What other factors might influence their performance?

5. How might "helping" Jamie and Jasamine with their homework increase or decrease self-regulation? What strategies could be used to increase self-regulation?

HIGH SCHOOL: BENDING THE RULES

These questions refer to the case study on page 156.

1. What specific aspects of observational learning does Mr. Hardy include in his classroom?

2. According to social cognitive theory, what specific characteristics of imitators make completing the homework assignments easy for most of the students? What characteristics of imitators give Jason difficulty? How could these characteristics be changed?

3. How and why might bending the rules influence the other basketball players' future completion of homework?

4. What factors might be influencing Jason's self-efficacy? How might his self-efficacy be changed?

5. How would you describe the collective self-efficacy within this school system? How might it be changed?

©iStockphoto.com/ Redrockschool

MODULE 10

INFORMATION PROCESSING

OUTLINE	LEARNING GOALS
Assumptions of the Information Processing Approach	
	❶ Describe the assumptions that underlie the information processing approach.
Perception and Attention	
	❷ Explain how perception and attention are important processes for learning information.
Memory	
• Encoding, Storage, and Retrieval	❸ Describe the function, capacity, and duration for three types of memory.
• Sensory Memory	
• Working (Short-Term) Memory	
• Long-Term Memory	
Applications: Teaching Effective Processing	
• Increase Attention	❹ Discuss the methods for getting and maintaining students' attention.
• Enhance Memory	❺ Summarize the instructional strategies for helping students enhance memory.

ASSUMPTIONS OF THE INFORMATION PROCESSING APPROACH

❶ Describe the assumptions that underlie the information processing approach.

Do you remember the Pledge of Alliance? Do you remember any of the geometry theorems you learned in high school? How about your great-grandmother's maiden name? What did you eat for breakfast on June 5, 2015? The information you can and cannot remember is most likely due to the ways in which you attempted to remember (or not) that information. The information processing model helps us understand how various cognitive processes such as attention and memory can influence our ability to learn information. Before explaining these processes, let's first consider some basic assumptions about how learning occurs:

Master the content.
edge.sagepub.com/durwin3e

- *Learning is influenced by how we process information.* Some information is more easily or quickly learned because of *how* we think about that information. Other information is more difficult to pay attention to or memorize because of *how* we process the information. As educators, you need to be aware of these different processes and help students be effective in processing, or learning, information.

- *Attention is an important process for learning.* We cannot possibly pay attention to all the information surrounding us; thus, we focus or pay attention to some information and ignore other information. Teachers need to assist students in paying attention to important information or class material while helping them ignore distractions or unimportant stimuli.

- *Humans are active processors of information.* Other learning theories focus on how the environment influences learning (more passive), whereas the information processing approach assumes that humans are active participants in the learning. Students will purposefully study, memorize, and learn information.

- *Prior knowledge and experience provide a meaningful context for new information to be learned.* Learning about the three branches of the government might be easier for a student who has already visited Washington, DC, and toured the White House and Capitol building. Likewise, visiting Washington, DC, might be more interesting if a child has already learned about the U.S. government. Teachers can help students learn information by attempting to connect new information to students' individual experiences or prior knowledge.

Attention: See Module 9

Have you ever discussed a past event with a friend or family member to discover he or she remembers the event very differently from you? Have you ever discovered that you can't remember the details of a conversation that happened earlier that same day?

PERCEPTION AND ATTENTION

❷ Explain how perception and attention are important processes for learning information.

As you read this module, you are most likely experiencing several senses at work—seeing (the words on this page), tasting, and smelling (if you happen to be eating a snack), and possibly hearing (if you have some music or the television on). You are most likely experiencing some touch as well, even if it is simply the clothes you have on touching your body. All of your sense organs—eyes, tongue, nose, ears, and skin—are used to perceive the world around you. **Perception** is the interpretation of the sensory information we encounter that helps us understand the environment. It is very much an "interpretation," as not everyone experiences the same sensory information in the same way. For example, some people love the taste of beets, but I hate them. My husband insists that the recliner in our living room is brown, but it's sage green! (In his defense, he is color-blind.) The point here is that we all "process" or interpret sensory information in our own way. Next we examine two types of processing that help explain perception.

- **Bottom-up processing** means that we begin with specific features of stimuli and automatically piece those features together without using conscious awareness to experience an entire object. For example, we use basic features to help interpret a word when reading. Those basic features might include lines and curves, and when put together, the lines and curves are interpreted as a word. Figure 10.1 provides an example for the word "safe." Lines can also help us interpret distance and size. Photo 10.1 shows a women standing in front of a skyline. Even though she is a larger object in the photo, we interpret her as smaller than the buildings but closer in distance.

- We perceive the woman as smaller than the buildings because we use prior knowledge that skyscrapers are much taller than women to help us interpret the size and distance of the objects in Photo 10.1. Conscious use of our prior knowledge, expectations, or context to perceive stimuli is called **top-down processing.** For example, we can misspell a word when writing a paper and read over that paper a dozen times without noticing the misspelled word. This is because we use our prior knowledge of what we know the word should be and process the word as it was intended, not as it was misspelled. Here is another example:

Aoccdrnig to a rscheearch at Cmabrigde Uinervtisy, it deosn't mttaer in waht oredr the ltteers in a wrod are, the olny iprmoetnt tihng is taht the frist and lsat ltteer be at the rghit pclae. The rset can be a toatl mses and you can sitll raed it wouthit porbelm. Tihs is bcuseae the huamn mnid deos not raed ervey lteter by istlef but the wrod as a wlohe.

The example above suggests that what we pay attention to when reading is mostly the first and last letters of a word. This example also shows us that although we make the distinctions between top-down and bottom-up processing, the two often work in concert.

Attention: See Module 9

Attention is an important aspect of how we perceive the environment and how we process information. **Attention** is the process of focusing on certain aspects of the environment. Because we cannot possibly attend to all the stimuli in our environment at one time, we select a small amount to focus on or attend to. One model of attention describes our limited amount of cognitive or mental resources (Kahneman, 1973). In this model, more difficult tasks require more cognitive resources, making it less likely for us to attend to multiple stimuli. For example, I have about a 30-minute commute to work each day and almost always have the radio on

FIGURE 10.1 **An Example of Bottom-Up Processing.**

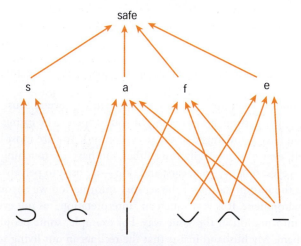

Basic features of letters are detected by the visual system.
Then this information goes through a hierarchy of letters and then words from the bottom up to eventually identify words.

Perception Processing. Distance of objects can be determined from retinal image size and knowledge about the objects, such that people are smaller than buildings.

while thinking about my "to-do" list for the day. Because each of these tasks, driving, listening to the radio, and planning my day are fairly easy and familiar to me, I am able to attend to all three at once. However, I recently drove into Chicago for the day where I was on less familiar roads with much more traffic than my typical drive. As a result, I needed to turn off my radio and focus my attention on driving. Fairly easy or familiar tasks are considered to use **automatic processing,** whereas difficult or new tasks require **effortful processing,** or conscious attention (Treisman & Gelade, 1980; Treisman, Sykes, & Gelade, 1977). Students who are learning new material or reading a difficult passage may need to limit disruptions so they can stay focused. However, when reviewing already learned material, students may be more apt to attend to other stimuli, such as chatting with a friend during class or listening to music while studying.

Attentional capacity changes throughout childhood and adolescence. **Selective attention** is the ability to focus on one stimuli and ignore others. Compared to younger children, older children and adolescents are better able to ignore many distractions that could be present in the classroom or hallway. For example, one study found that kindergarten children learning a science lesson were more distracted, spent less time on-task, and had lower learning scores when the classroom walls were highly decorated than when no decorations were present (Fisher, Godwin, & Seltman, 2014). Adolescents are also better than children at **divided attention,** or the ability to focus on multiple stimuli (Mizuno et al., 2011). However, educators should be cautious of students claiming they can "multitask." Most often students are not doing two tasks at once but rather are switching their attention back and forth between tasks. This switching is inefficient such that tasks take longer and are completed with more mistakes in both education contexts (Kirschner & van Merrienboer, 2013) and applied contexts, such as driving and talking on a cell phone (Strayer & Johnston, 2001). In short, multitasking tends to led to poorer learning and performance. Teachers need to be aware of these attentional limitations and plan lessons accordingly.

As a student, what strategies do you use to keep your attention focused on the course material during a lecture? How to you attempt to eliminate distractions when studying for an exam?

MEMORY

 Describe the function, capacity, and duration for three types of memory.

Encoding, Storage, and Retrieval

Memory is referred to as both a structure and a process. When we think about storing a memory for later retrieval, we tend to be thinking about memory as a storage space or structure. Yet when we think about the best ways to try to remember something for later, we are referring to memory as a process. Three important aspects of memory are encoding, storage, and retrieval. **Encoding** is the process by which information or stimuli enter our memory. Attention, as described earlier, is important to the process of encoding information. We cannot encode information we were not paying attention to. However, some information may be attended to and remembered unintentionally. For example, you probably remember what you had for breakfast yesterday morning because you were paying attention, but you didn't necessary intentionally try to encode that information. **Retrieval** is the process by which information is obtained from memory. Many times we intentionally try to remember some information, for example, when asked a question such as "When is your birthday?" Other times, we retrieve information unintentionally, such as when a song sparks a memory from a special event.

For encoded information to be retrieved later, the memory needs to be stored. **Storage** is the process in which information is held or kept between encoding and retrieval. We use the term "process" to define storage, but most of us also think about storage of memories as a structure or place we keep memories. It is important to know that memories are not kept in specific brain regions. Rather, multiple brain areas are needed to retrieve one memory. The efficiency of these three memory processes is based in part on our use of prior knowledge. For example, learning about the government in Canada, a parliamentary democracy, would be easier if students already understand the British parliament and more difficult if they are familiar only with a government that does not have a parliament. In other words, we better encode information that we can relate to prior knowledge. We also tend to store similar information together to make the retrieval process easier. Later we discuss specific ways to improve these memory processes. But now we turn our attention to Atkinson and Shiffrin's (1968) modal model of memory. This model, as depicted in Figure 10.2, describes how encoding, storage, and retrieval processes work with the three types of memory—sensory memory, working (short-term) memory, and long-term memory.

Video Case 10.1 ▲

Using Retrieval Cues to Support Learning

© SAGE Publications

Brain development: See Module 5

FIGURE 10.2 Atkinson and Shiffrin's (1968) Modal Model of Memory.

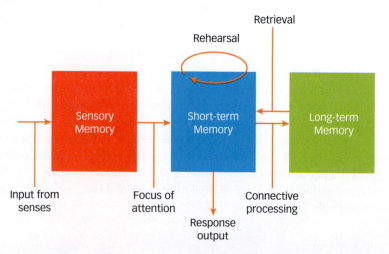

Source: Atkinson, R. C., & Shiffrin, R. M. (1968). Human memory: A proposed system and its control processes. In K. W. Spence & J. T. Spence (Eds.), *The psychology of learning and motivation: Advances in research and theory* (Vol. 2, pp. 89–195). New York: Academic Press.

Sensory Memory

Sensory memory is all the sensory information experienced before that information is processed. This is information that you aren't even consciously aware of. For example, as you walk along the quad at your university or through the mall during the holiday season, you "see" many people passing by. You even look directly at some of them. Yet if I stopped you and asked "what color shirt was that women who just passed you wearing?" you would probably not be able to tell me.

A well-known study of visual sensory memory (also called iconic memory) conducted in 1960 found that the capacity of visual sensory memory is quite large, but the duration of visual sensory memory is very brief, lasting only about one second (Sperling, 1960). More recent research has confirmed the short duration of visual sensory memory (Bradley & Pearson, 2012). Other research has found that auditory memories, memories based on information presented orally (also called echoic memory), last about four seconds (Darwin, Turvey, & Crowder, 1974). Interestingly, research has found that visual sensory memory doesn't seem to be underdeveloped in individuals with autism spectrum disorder (McMorris, Brown, & Bebko, 2013), but auditory memory may not fully develop in those individuals (Erviti et al., 2015). Memories of touch (also called tactile memory) last about five seconds (Sinclair & Burton, 1996). Hence, the duration of sensory memory typically lasts about one to five seconds.

Autism spectrum disorder: See Module 22

> **DIVERSITY**

Working (Short-Term) Memory

Atkinson and Shiffrin's (1968) modal model of memory suggests that the sensory memories we attend to will be moved into short-term memory. For example, if the women who passed you in the mall had been wearing the exact shirt you just bought your mother, you would have attended to that visual stimuli and the information would have made it into short-term memory. **Short-term memory** is the structure that temporarily holds information from sensory memory that we are attending to, until the information is either no longer attended to or moved to long-term memory. Because our attention is limited, the capacity and duration of short-term memory are also limited. Early studies on short-term memory found that the capacity of short-term memory is about five to nine "bits" of information (Miller, 1956) and the duration is about 18 seconds (Peterson & Peterson, 1959). So, what is a bit? Think about the telephone number 347-930-5778. You could think about this information as 10 separate bits of information (bit = one number). However, most people think of it as three bits of information such that 347 is one bit, 930 is another bit, and 5778 is a third bit. This strategy is called **chunking,** or organizing information into smaller units or meaningful bits of information. This strategy effectively reduces the number of bits you have to remember.

Can you think of other examples where you have used chunking to reduce the number of "bits" you have to remember?

Because information in short-term memory is what we are paying attention to or currently thinking about, the capacity and duration are limited by our attention. For example, students taking a test whose attention is focused on thoughts such as "I didn't study enough. This is so hard. I'm never going to pass" don't have as much "space" to process the question being asked or the answer choices. Research has found that anxiety does tax the limited capacity of short-term memory and negatively affects performance (Ashcraft & Rudig, 2012). One limitation in keeping information active in short-term memory is due to **interference,** when new information from sensory memory comes into short-term memory and interferes with old information. Back to our mall example, as you are thinking about the woman with the shirt like the one you bought for your mother, you notice your aunt and cousins walking toward you. You begin to talk with them, and as result, you are no longer thinking about the woman's shirt. That old information (woman's shirt) has been replaced with new information (aunt and cousins) that now has your attention. One strategy used to block interference and extend the duration of short-term memory is **maintenance rehearsal,** which involves repeating information over and over again to keep attention activated. For example, if I want to remember a phone number

Anxiety: See Module 15

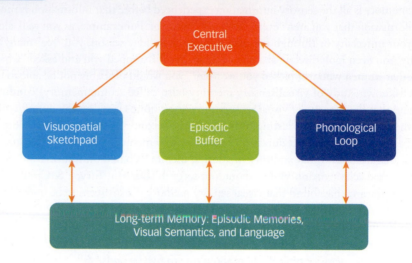

FIGURE 10.3 **Baddeley's (2000) Working-Memory Model.**

Central Executive

Visuospatial Sketchpad

Episodic Buffer

Phonological Loop

Long-term Memory: Episodic Memories, Visual Semantics, and Language

until I can find a piece of paper and pen, I repeat the number over and over again either in my head or out loud. Maintenance rehearsal is the first memory strategy that children use to remember information learned in school, and they become increasingly better at it, mostly likely due to their increased verbal skills (Bebko, McMorris, Metcalfe, Ricciuti, & Goldstein, 2014; Tam, Jarrold, Baddeley, & Sabatos-DeVito, 2010). Another strategy that we use is called **elaborative rehearsal.** Consider again the example of the phone number 347-930-5778. I might try to remember this number by linking "347" to the house number where I grew up, "930" to the time I teach every morning, "57" to the year my mother was born, and "78" to the year my brother was born. The additional meaning I have given these numbers makes them easier to remember while I search for that pen and paper.

The information we are thinking about or attending to at the moment in short-term memory is also considered our **working memory.** Cognitive psychologists might separate the terms short-term memory and working memory by saying that short-term memory is the storage or structure, whereas working memory is the process or system used to encode, store, and retrieve information. The most well-known model of working memory was proposed and later revised by Baddeley (Baddeley, 1992, 2000, 2012; Baddeley & Hitch, 1974). The model suggests that within working memory there are subsystems to process different types of information. Figure 10.3 depicts the four subsystems of working memory, discussed next.

Look at Photo 10.2. You processed that photo both as visual information but also as verbal information as you most likely saw the image (visual) but also thought "computer" (verbal). The **visuospatial sketchpad** subsystem in Baddeley's model is responsible for briefly processing visual information (an image or picture of the computer), whereas the **phonological loop** subsystem is responsible for briefly processing verbal or auditory information (the word "computer"). In addition to the brief duration of these subsystems, both have limited capacities, yet their capacities may not interfere with one another. For example, research has found that the recall of information for two tasks with the same type of information (both visual) is less accurate than recall of information for two tasks with different types of information (one visual and one verbal;

Processing Visual and Verbal Information. When you visually see an object such as this computer, you also think the verbal word "computer."

Baddeley, 1998; Quinn & McConnell, 1996). This research suggests that processing two tasks in the same subsystem is more limited than processing two tasks in separate subsystems because each subsystem has its own limited capacity.

A third subsystem of Baddeley's model, the **episodic buffer,** is responsible for integrating information from the visuospatial sketchpad and phonological loop as well as linking information in working memory to long-term memory. For example, research has found that memory of visually presented digits (visuospatial sketchpad) is enhanced when presented with a keypad, such as one used at an ATM or to unlock a smartphone, because the keypad is familiar (stored in long-term memory; Allen, Havelka, Falcon, Evans, & Darling, 2015). Think about the example in the mall. Attending to that women's shirt is most likely included in the visuospatial sketchpad (image of shirt), the verbal words (woman, shirt, mom) and the stored information in long-term memory about what you had bought your mother. The integration of that information is stored in the episodic buffer. Recent research has found that the ability to integrate information in the episodic buffer develops between 6 and 9 years of age (Darling, Parker, Goodall, Havelka, & Allen, 2014) and may be delayed in children with intellectual disabilities (Henry, 2010).

Intellectual disabilities:
See Module 20

> **DIVERSITY**

The **central executive** subsystem of Baddeley's model does not store information but manages or oversees the flow of information between the other three systems (Brown & Wesley, 2013). The central executive subsystem focuses our attention on important relevant information while ignoring other information. Hence, the central executive is limited by the limits of our attention. Baddeley (1998) suggested that our automatic functioning is attended to in the central executive. For example, as you read the words on this page, the episodic buffer is hard at work integrating the visual information consisting of letters and words on the page into verbal information that is interpretable because the meanings of these words are stored in long-term memory. The central executive subsystem is focusing your attention on the relevant words and ignoring some information (maybe the year 1998 a few lines up). However, all of this processing of information is being done relatively automatically in the central executive unless you encounter a word that you may not remember or know the meaning of, or read a sentence that doesn't make sense. Then, the central executive allocates attention to the task and deploys strategies such as rereading or using context to help determine the meaning of a word. As described in our mall example, as well as our reading example, the working memory system is closely tied to our long-term memories.

©iStockphoto.com/Krystian Nawrocki

Episodic Buffer. The PIN number for our phone or debit card (stored in long-term memory) is easier to remember when presented visually with the keypad (visuospatial sketchpad).

Long-Term Memory

Long-term memory holds all the information we have learned or experienced. Unlike the other memory systems, long-term memory does not seem to have capacity or duration limitations. It is believed that people can store an unlimited amount of memories for an unlimited duration. However, whether we can retrieve those memories is another story. Have you ever saved a file on your computer but then couldn't seem to find it? You most likely didn't name the file well or didn't place it in the correct folder on your computer (poor encoding). The information is stored, but you can't find it (lack of retrieval). Our long-term memory can be the same way. Next we discuss ways information is encoded or stored in long-term memory as well as how information is retrieved or forgotten.

Several theories have been developed to explain how information from working memory is encoded and stored in long-term memory. Here are three prominent theories:

Video Case 10.2 ▲
Short to Long Term Memory

© SAGE Publications

- **Dual-coding theory** suggests that we remember information better if we encode it as both verbal and visual (Clark & Paivio, 1991). Remember our earlier example in working memory of the computer being encoded as both visual (image of a computer) as well as verbal (the word "computer")? We also encode information in long-term memory using both visual and verbal cues. Consider the words on this page: You are encoding the visual words printed on the page, but you are also encoding the verbal sound and meaning of the words.

- **Network theory,** which is also referred to as semantic network, propositional network, and concept map, suggests that information is encoded in relation to other information (Anderson, 1983). Figure 10.4 illustrates how "red" and "street" can be connected within a network of information through a process of **spreading activation,** where accessing one concept can lead to activation of other related concepts in the network.

 Have you ever been studying for a test and then found yourself remembering a vacation from years past or other personal experience? Could you trace the network of thoughts/memories that led you from one thought to another?

Schemes: *See Module 6*

- **Schema theory** suggests that information contained within a script, or typical pattern of events, is easier to understand and encode (Anderson & Bower, 1973). What would happen if you began reading a mystery novel at Chapter 10, then read Chapters 1 through 3, then Chapter 31, and then back to Chapter 11? Most likely the story wouldn't make much sense because the typical order of events is not being presented (if you have seen the movie *Pulp Fiction,* this is exactly what happens). When information is not connected to a schema, that information is more difficult to encode and store in long-term memory.

FIGURE 10.4 **Network Theory. Two concepts that seem unrelated, such as red and street, are connected through the process of spreading activation.**

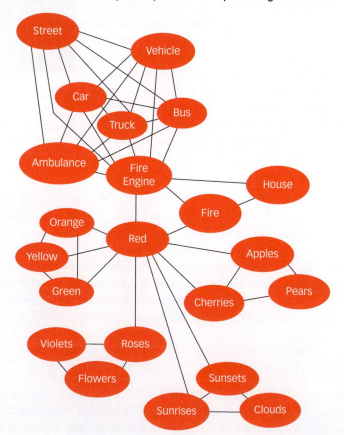

Regardless of the way in which we might represent information in long-term memory, the general conclusion is that the more deeply we encode information, the easier it is to activate and retrieve it when we need it.

Although we might have learned information and stored it in long-term memory, we can't always retrieve it. For example, what year did the Civil War in the United States begin? Most of us have learned that information at some point in time and it is still stored in our long-term memory, but we may not be able to remember the answer. Would it help if I gave you three choices: 1854, 1861, or 1865? Your ability to remember without being given these choices is referred to as **recall.** Being able to choose the correct answer from a list of choices is referred to as **recognition.** You may have connected the Civil War with Abraham Lincoln and tried to remember in what year he was killed to help you remember the year the war started. The activation of one piece of information (Lincoln's death) can activate memories of connected information (year the Civil War began) through spreading activation. (By the way, the Civil War began in 1861.)

Which testing strategies require the recall of information? Which testing strategies require the recognition of information?

I suspect that many students reading this module were not able to answer the question about when the Civil War began even with the list of choices provided. Yet I am also confident that those students were taught that information at some point in elementary school. Why did they forget that information? One reason for forgetting is *interference.* As discussed with working memory, interference works the same way in long-term memory. People simply have a vast amount of information they encounter each and every day that serves as interference for remembering other information. Another reason we forget information is due to a lack of consolidation. **Consolidation** is the neural process that strengthens memories over time and can take days, weeks, and months to complete (Wixted, 2010). Research has found that sleep is important for consolidation such that sleeping between studying and testing increases storage and enhances testing (Jenkins & Dallenbach, 1924; Stickgold, Hobson, Fosse, & Fosse, 2001).

Information that is encoded, stored, and retrieved in long-term memory is typically considered as one of three main types of long-term memories:

- **Episodic memory** includes information from "episodes" of your own life. This personal information can include a feeling of being taken back in time to a particular event, called *autobiographical memory.* Some episodic memories are considered *flashbulb memories* because they tend to be frozen in time as they have a heavy emotional component. For example, I would consider my memory of the morning of September 11, 2001, as a flashbulb memory. Although people think their autobiographical and flashbulb memories are exact replicates of the actual events, research suggests that these memories can be misremembered just like any other information we have stored in long-term memory (Talarico & Rubin, 2003).

- **Semantic memory** involves information we have that is not tied directly to our personal experiences. You probably know that there are 365 days in a year, but you don't have a personal memory of learning that information. Semantic memory includes information about language and the meaning of concepts.

- **Procedural memory** is information about how to perform certain tasks, such as writing your name, walking across the floor, or putting contacts in your eyes. Many tasks or skills are performed automatically with little attention or intention. Think about when you were first learning to drive a car. You probably had to put forth a lot of cognitive effort or attention to the details (e.g., where to put your hands, how soon to press on the brake as you approached the stop sign, how much pressure to put on the brake). This is called

Automaticity: See Module 12

effortful processing. Now, because of much practice, you probably don't really "think" about those things at all when you're driving. The procedural memory of how to perform those skills has *automatic processing.* The automatic nature of some procedural knowledge has long been substantiated by studies of people with amnesia who can't retrieve episodic or semantic memory but are still able to read, write, talk, and walk based on their procedural memory (Warrington & Weiskrantz, 1970).

When we discuss our memories, we are also referring to our knowledge. The different kinds of knowledge we acquire map well onto the three types of long-term memory discussed earlier.

- **Declarative knowledge** is information about facts, both personal facts, such as the first time you saw the ocean was in 1992 (episodic memory), and general facts, such as the 16th president of the United States was Abraham Lincoln (semantic memory).

- **Procedural knowledge** is information about how to perform tasks and skills. Many times procedural knowledge and procedural memory are considered the same.

- **Conditional knowledge** is information about under what conditions information (episodic and semantic memories) or skills (procedural memories) can be used. Conditional knowledge is knowing when it is appropriate to laugh, when to refer to people by their first name versus the more formal "Ms. Smith," or when to use certain memory strategies to study for a test. In addition, conditional knowledge is understanding why information is important, necessary, or useful. For example, why do we retain more of what we read when we take short breaks to summarize the material or take notes on the main points?

Brain development: See Module 5

DIVERSITY

Research has suggested that the capacity and duration of working memory increase between childhood and adolescence and continue to increase over the adolescent period (Sprondel, Kipp, & Mecklinger, 2011). Similarly, improvements in long-term memory are also found among adolescents in comparison to children (Keating, 2004). These increases during adolescence are mostly likely due to continued brain development (Jolles, Kleibeuker, Rombouts, & Crone, 2011). Other research examining gender differences has found that women, at various ages, have larger working memory capacities than men, as well as better episodic memory (Halpern, 2000; Halpern & LaMay, 2000).

APPLICATIONS: TEACHING EFFECTIVE PROCESSING

4 Discuss the methods for getting and maintaining students' attention.

5 Summarize the instructional strategies for helping students enhance memory.

There are several ways in which teachers can help facilitate the processing of information. Research has found strategies to improve attention and encoding and retrieval of information. We summarize some of those strategies next.

Increase Attention

As stated very early in this module, what we don't pay attention to will not be remembered—or learned. If a student in a classroom is focused on the other children outside the window or on his or her thoughts about going to the movies with friends that evening, the student is not paying attention to the teacher's lesson. Hence, teachers must help students stay focused on the content to be learned.

Video Case 10.3 ▲
Increasing Students' Attention

© SAGE Publications

Get their attention. Teachers can begin lessons with interesting facts or activities to spark students' attention. In planning for attention, teachers need to consider the developmental level of students and what might interest that specific group of students. For example, using a math activity that focuses on how much money it might take to have their own apartment and pay for living expenses is much more applicable and of interest to senior high school students than to elementary school students. Focusing students' attention on the lesson also means limiting distractions. A teacher may quickly realize that two students have a hard time paying attention when sitting near each other so a change in seating arrangements might be needed.

Keep their attention. Once you have developed a lesson plan with interesting and novel information to attract their attention, you then have to keep their attention. Attention spans are typically quite short, even for adults. A common estimate is that adults have about a 10- to 15-minute attention span, but research evidence suggests that attention spans are hard to determine due to individual differences and strategies to keep attention (Wilson & Korn, 2007). One strategy to lengthen attention spans is to change the activity or shift the topic to pull students back into the lesson. You might consider having pairs of students talk briefly about the content covered, write a short reflection about the material covered, or come up with their own examples for the content, such as creating their own word problem in math to be used in a fraction lesson. Keeping attention can also be done by asking questions of students. For example, rather than providing the information, ask students to try and predict what comes next in a story or what might happen when two chemicals are mixed together.

Assess their attention level. Effective teachers are constantly assessing the level of attention students are giving to a lesson. Teachers should focus on body language that might suggest their attention has waned, such as staring out the window.

Help students attend to the most important information. Teachers can use various methods to assist students in figuring out the specific aspects of a lesson that need their attention. For example, teachers might repeat information or have important concepts listed on a PowerPoint presentation.

Video Case 10.4 ▲
Strategies for Memorization

© SAGE Publications

Studying: See Module 11

Enhance Memory

In addition to our need to pay attention, our ability to *learn* information is based on how well we can remember—encode, store, and retrieve—that information. Teachers can help students better remember information by providing them with strategies for encoding information and strategies for retrieval of information. Next we review a few strategies that have been found to enhance memory.

Use space encoding. Research has found that encoding or studying for shorter periods of time across multiple days (distributed practice) enhances memory in comparison to studying for a long period of time, called massed encoding (Cepeda et al., 2009; Cepeda, Pashler, Vul, Wixted, & Rohrer, 2006; Melton, 1970). This holds true even when the total amount of time studied is equal. For example, students who study for one hour each day for five days perform better on tests than students who study for five hours the day before the test. Teachers may not be able to control when their students study outside the classroom, but they can review material daily (e.g., study the material) to enhance students' memory of the information.

Facilitate consolidation. Remember, consolidation is the neural process that strengthens memories over time, and sleep is important for consolidation. Teachers can facilitate consolidation by making sure that information is reviewed across multiple days so that sleep periods occur during the learning process.

Encourage deep processing. Memory is enhanced when information is encoded according to meaning, or what is called deep or meaningful processing (Craik & Tulving, 1975;

Roberts et al., 2014). For example, asking students to memorize the Gettysburg Address is easier when they actually understand the meaning of those words (e.g., "four score and seven years ago" is not meaningful unless students know that "score" refers to a unit of 20 years). Information is typically more meaningful when based on prior knowledge. One study had students read a passage about a baseball game and then verbally retell the story. Students who had prior existing knowledge about baseball remembered more information (Recht & Leslie, 1988), whether or not they were considered "good" or "poor" readers. That is, students with low reading comprehension scores but good baseball knowledge had an advantage over those good readers with little baseball knowledge. Hence, teachers can help connect new information to be learned with already existing knowledge to enhance memory.

Use explanatory questioning. Some say the best way to learn information is to teach the information to others. Explanatory questioning is related to this idea. Students who are able to explain *why* an answer is correct are better able to remember that information (Roediger & Pyc, 2012). Teachers can enhance memory by having students explain information in writing or verbally, to the teacher or fellow students.

Teach mnemonics. **Mnemonics** are strategies used to help remember large amounts of information. There are numerous mnemonic devices, some of which are summarized in Table 10.1. Research has found that not only does the use of mnemonics enhance memory but that being taught mnemonics enhances memory better than creating one's own mnemonic (Miller, 1967). Hence, teachers should create mnemonics and teach those memory strategies to students.

Present important information first. People are better at remembering the first information presented to them, and to a lesser extent, the last information presented to them (Glanzer & Cunitz, 1966; Hu, Hitch, Baddeley, Zhang, & Allen, 2014). Since information presented in the middle of a lesson is the least likely to be remembered, teachers can plan lessons such that the most important information is presented first. In addition, students should be taught to change the order of material they are studying, such as shuffling flash cards to avoid order effects.

Give quizzes and practice tests. Several studies have found that retrieving information strengthens the ability to retrieve that information, which is called testing effects (Bjork & Bjork, 1992; Blunt & Karpicke, 2014; Pyc & Rawson, 2012). In other words, practicing the

TABLE 10.1	Mnemonic Strategies for Enhancing Memory
MNEMONIC	**DESCRIPTION**
Acronym	Creating an abbreviation, such as "ROY G BIV" for the colors of the rainbow.
Chain or rhyme	Connecting items to be memorized in a jingle, such as "i before e, except after c" for a common spelling rule.
Loci method (bizarreness effect)	Imaging a familiar location with items in unusual places. For example, to memorize a grocery list, you might picture bread in your bathroom sink, milk in the microwave, cereal scattered over your bed, and toothpaste smeared on the dining room table.
Spelling mnemonics	Using a word to help remember the spelling, such as dessert has two of the letter "s'" because most people want double the sweet treat rather than desert (area of land).
Image mnemonics	Visualizing a picture to help remember the meaning of a word or phrase. For example, you might picture a women standing before a crowd about to give a speech with a "plum" in her hand to remember that the word "aplomb" means complete confidence and poise.

retrieval of information will enhance memory and meaningful learning, especially when the practiced retrieval occurs repeatedly over time (Karpicke, 2012; Karpicke & Bauernschmidt, 2011). Teachers can use practice tests and quizzes to give students ample opportunities to retrieve the information to be learned (Karpicke & Grimaldi, 2012).

Use similar study and testing conditions. The encoding specificity principle suggests that encoding and retrieval conditions that are matched or similar enhance memory (Smith & Vela, 2001). Hence, students should study and test under similar conditions. During testing, teachers should attempt to keep the classroom conditions, such as seating arrangements, lighting, and noise level, similar to the conditions when the information was first presented and later reviewed.

Which of these strategies to enhance memory would work best for the grade level or subject area you intend to teach?

SUMMARY

❶ Describe the assumptions that underlie information processing theory. (1) Because cognitive processes influence learning, teachers must understand that information can be processed in different ways and consider that *how* students process information influences learning. (2) Information that is not attended to cannot be learned, and individuals can pay attention to only a limited amount of information. Teachers need to focus students' attention on important information. (3) Learning new information is enhanced when connected to prior knowledge or experiences. Teachers should connect information to be learned with individual experiences or prior knowledge.

❷ Explain how perception and attention are important processes for learning information. Information can be interpreted or perceived differently by different people, which influences what we learn or how we remember information. In addition, information that is not attended to will not be learned, so teachers must help keep students focused and eliminate distractions during learning.

❸ Describe the function, capacity, and duration for three types of memory. Sensory memory processes raw information acquired through the sensory organs and has an unlimited capacity but a very short duration of only one to five seconds. Working memory is the

information we are currently thinking about, so it has a limited capacity of only five to nine bits of information and a duration of about 18 seconds. Long-term memory is where all the information we have learned is stored and has both an unlimited capacity and duration.

❹ Discuss the methods for getting and maintaining students' attention. Teachers need to be planful in acquiring students' attention. In addition, teachers must be aware of attentional limitations and thus monitor students' attention levels regularly. When attention wanders, teachers must be effortful in their strategies to reestablish attention. Finally, teachers must help students identify the information that is most important and in need of the students' attention by using verbal or visual signals.

❺ Summarize the instructional strategies for helping students enhance memory. Teachers can present and review information over several days to facilitate consolidation and space encoding. Teachers must also attempt to connect new information to prior knowledge, including the creation and teaching of mnemonics. Having students practice retrieving the information by providing practice quizzes and tests as well as having students explain the material themselves will also enhance memory. Finally, teachers should present the most important information first and test students under conditions similar to those in which the material was learned.

KEY CONCEPTS

attention, 190
automatic processing, 191
bottom-up processing, 190
central executive, 195

chunking, 193
conditional knowledge, 198
consolidation, 197
declarative knowledge, 198

divided attention, 191
dual-coding theory, 195
effortful processing, 191
elaborative rehearsal, 194

CASE STUDIES: REFLECT AND EVALUATE

EARLY CHILDHOOD: PINCH

These questions refer to the case study on page 150.

1. Why does Miss Amber have the children clap at certain points during her story?

2. When the children are asked to compare today's story with the one from yesterday, what memory system(s) is(are) being activated? Explain.

3. What does Miss Rana do to focus the children's attention on her instructions for the art project? Why is this important?

4. How do the teachers help the children acquire *procedural knowledge* for the painting activity?

5. Emily has been reluctant to paint since she accidentally spilled paint on Billy's shoes. From an information processing perspective, why might this incident be very memorable for Emily?

ELEMENTARY SCHOOL: SILLY STUDENTS

These questions refer to the case study on page 152.

1. How did the cluster seating arrangement affect the attention levels of Billy, Jason, Megan, and Sara?

2. Billy, Jason, Megan, and Sara receive low scores on the math quiz. What might explain their inability to successfully retrieve the information they needed to answer the questions on the quiz?

3. What strategies could Mr. Lindsay use to help his students increase attention and enhance memory during his math lesson?

4. Sara began to feel frustrated in trying to complete her math problems. What strategies could Mr. Lindsay have used to help her acquire the *procedural knowledge* necessary to successfully complete the problems?

5. Under what conditions would it have been appropriate for Mr. Lindsay's students to use a calculator? How would the use of a calculator affect the way they process information in working memory?

MIDDLE SCHOOL: STUDY HALL

These questions refer to the case study on page 154.

1. What strategies could Mr. Havel use to help Jamie develop the *procedural knowledge* necessary to complete the math problems?

2. Assume Jamie's difficulties are due to a lack of interest in the mathematical principles being covered. How could Ms. DeBrick present mathematical concepts in a way that increases attention and memory of the material?

3. What memory strategies could Jasamine's classmates share to help Jasamine complete her English homework successfully? What memory strategies could Mr. Havel incorporate into his English lessons to enhance memory?

4. What strategy for enhancing memory is being used when Jamie readily participates in class by explaining difficult concepts and providing good examples during social studies?

5. How might the examples Ms. DeBrick gives Jasamine serve as retrieval cues for her?

HIGH SCHOOL: BENDING THE RULES

These questions refer to the case study on page 156.

1. Jason has forgotten Mr. Hardy's demonstration of how to complete the assignment. Explain the role of attention in his inability to retrieve this information.

2. What strategies could Mr. Hardy implement to help focus students' attention during his lessons?

3. What strategy for enhancing memory is being used when Mr. Hardy has students debate a topic or write about an issue?

4. What types of strategies, consistent with information processing, would you use to study for a history test, such as keeping dates and facts straight? Give specific examples.

5. What types of knowledge are being acquired in Mr. Hardy's class? Give examples for each type.

UNIT FOUR

COGNITIVE PROCESSES

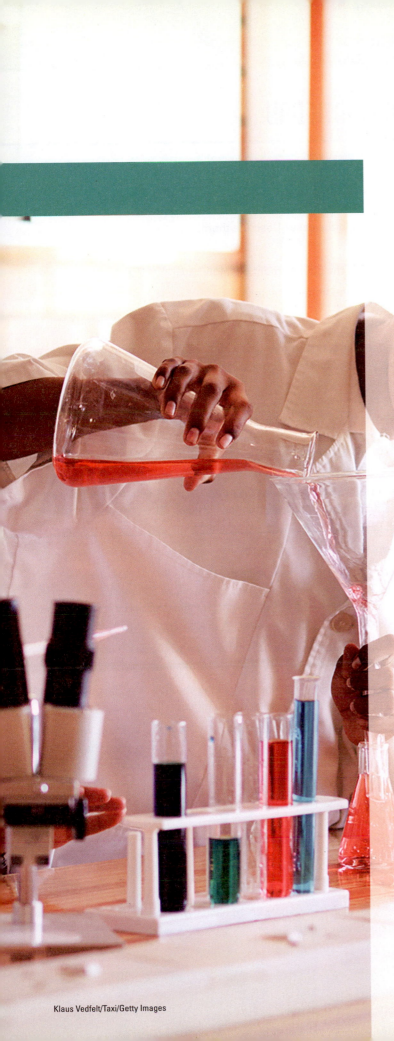

Klaus Vedfelt/Taxi/Getty Images

EARLY CHILDHOOD: 100TH DAY

Ms. Prendergast is a kindergarten teacher at one of many suburban elementary schools. She has an excited bunch of eager learners this year and has been looking forward to today—the annual 100th day celebration. From the beginning of the school year, children have been counting the days of school as a way to learn about number concepts, sequencing, and grouping. Each year on the 100th day of the school year, students are asked to bring 100 of something. Projects in the past have included 100 safety pins on a shirt, 100 buttons glued on a shirt in the shape of "100," or 100 pennies in a bag. Much of the day is spent counting the children's projects to be sure there are 100. Ms. Prendergast loves to see how creative the children can be with their projects.

"Good morning boys and girls," says Ms. Prendergast. She claps three times and the children clap back in unison to indicate they have heard her and are paying attention. "Please have a seat on the carpet. I have a special book to read today."

Jose asks, "Ms. P, when are we goin' get to show our projects?"

Ms. Prendergast replies, "We are going to take turns throughout the day. But first, I want to read you this special book." She lifts the book high in the air and reads the title, "*100 Days of School* by Trudy Harris." Many of the children seem excited but quickly sit down in their designated spots on the carpet. Ms. Prendergast begins by asking with a smile, "What do you think this book is about?"

Sophia waves her hand enthusiastically to indicate she knows the answer. Once called upon, she says, "My mom has this book so I know it tells how to count lots of things to 100—even legs on icky bugs!"

Ms. Prendergast says, "Well, let's get started." She reads the book to the children, stopping periodically to ask what they think will happen next or to ask one of the children to summarize the previous few pages.

Sophia seems to forget that the rest of the class hasn't read the book. When Liam guesses what might happen next, Sophia says in an irritated tone, "That's not right. You know the next thing they count is dots on the clown!" Ms. Prendergast gently reminds Sophia that Liam wouldn't know that because he hasn't read the story before.

One example in the book includes 10 children taking off their shoes. Ms. Prendergast asks, "How many toes would there be?"

Liam shouts out, "100!"

She then asks, "What if I have 10 children raise one hand in the air? How many fingers would there be?"

Liam quickly shouts out again, "100!"

Ms. Prendergast smiles and says, "Well, there would only be 10 hands with *five* fingers. So who else thinks they might know how many fingers would be in the air?"

After a few seconds of silence, Aubrey, a very shy but bright girl, slowly raises her hand. When called on, she says, "50 because that's half of 100 and there are half as many fingers as toes."

"That's correct. What a good strategy to figure out the answer!" says Ms. Prendergast. She then continues reading. When they have finished reading the book, Ms. Prendergast randomly selects five names from her "hat" to decide who will show their 100th day projects first.

Lily is the first name drawn. She brings to the front of the carpet area a rather large box. She pulls out five stacks of red plastic cups and carefully counts 20 cups in each stack. Next is Jaxson. He brings four small bags of bubble gum and counts 25 pieces in each bag. Ms. Prendergast is impressed and notes to the other children that these students separated the items into smaller piles. The third name drawn is James. Ms. Prendergast is immediately concerned because James seems to have little support from his parents with out-of-school work and projects. Last week when Ms. Prendergast asked each of the children to privately come up to her desk and whisper what they were planning for their 100th day project, James didn't have any ideas. As James walks to the front of the room, without a box or bag, she really starts to wonder what he is going to do.

James starts pointing to some of the children asking them to join him: "Oliver, come stand up here with me." When he has invited nine students, he asks them to put both their hands straight out in front of them. He begins to count their fingers until he hits 90 and then uses his own fingers for the last 10. Most of the students seem annoyed that he didn't bring something to class, but Ms. Prendergast begins to clap for James and says, "How very creative, James!"

Ms. Prendergast announces that as a treat for today, she has 100 stickers to give them. "Boys and girls, there are twenty of you. How many stickers do I give each of you so that everyone gets the same number? How many stickers do each of you get?" The children look bewildered. This seems like a totally different problem than grouping objects to make 100. "Does anyone have a way to solve it?" Ms. Prendergast asks the class.

Monish suggests, "Why don't we pass out one sticker to each of us and keep going until there are no more left?

"I like your thinking, Monish," Ms. Prendergast replies. "Before we do that, does anyone see how one of the 100th day projects presented today could be used to help solve our problem?" The children still don't seem to catch on. "Ok, I'll give you a hint— red cups," she says.

"Oh!" many of the children exclaim.

Lily shouts, "Five stickers! Just like my plastic cups!"

"Great thinking, Lily," Ms. Prendergast compliments. "Because you and Monish had such wonderful ideas, you can both pass out the stickers." The classroom fills with chatter as the pair distributes stickers.

AP Photo/Hazleton Standard-Speaker, Ellen F. O'Connell

ASSESS:

1. Why would having the students create their projects of 100 help them understand the concept of counting?

2. How would you help children who don't receive much support from parents?

3. How creative do you think the children are with their projects?

ELEMENTARY SCHOOL: INVENTION CONVENTION

PREPARE:

As you read the case, make notes:

1. WHO are the primary participants in the case? Describe them.
2. WHAT is taking place?
3. WHERE is the case taking place? Is the environment a factor?
4. WHEN is the case taking place? Is the timing a factor?

Ms. Tina Bury and Mr. Richard Grant are fourth-grade teachers at an elementary school composed of students from an affluent, suburban neighborhood. Each year the two require all their students to create an invention that is showcased at the Invention Convention. The project includes determining a problem, writing a proposal for how to solve the problem, and then creating or building the product.

About a week before the big event, Ms. Bury asks Mr. Grant, "How are your students coming along on their inventions? Will they all be ready for Invention Convention night next week?" Mr. Grant rolls his eyes and replies, "It will be a miracle if they are. This group is not very creative and seems to want to come up with solutions without knowing the problem. How about your group?"

"Well, my class seems to have some great ideas, but their writing skills need a lot of work" replies Ms. Bury. "I have worked with each one of them trying to get them to tell me about their ideas verbally so I can help them determine what to write. I think I am going to create a 'cheat sheet' with some specific questions to help guide their writing and maybe even . . ."

Mr. Grant interrupts, "Hey, remember they're just kids. Most of them can't verbalize their thoughts, let alone write them down in a coherent way!"

"I know. I just want them to think ahead a bit about the problem-solving process and write out the steps" says Ms. Bury. "They seem to be all over the place without a clear plan."

Later in the afternoon, Mr. Grant is talking with some of his students about their ideas, or lack of ideas, for their projects. One student, Riley, says, "I just can't seem to come up with anything. I guess I am just not very creative."

Another student, Allen, says, "Mr. Grant, I have a great idea. I am going to make an unlevel plate."

"Um . . . what problem would you be solving with an unlevel plate?" asks Mr. Grant.

"Well, I hate it when runny food on my plate gets into my other food, like gravy at Thanksgiving. If you had an unlevel plate then all the gravy would run to one side of the plate and your other food wouldn't get messy," explains Allen.

Mr. Grant replies, "That's a pretty good idea, Allen. Where did you get that idea?"

"I saw my aunt roll up a napkin and put it under one end of her plate at breakfast the other morning. She said she didn't want syrup from her pancakes getting on her eggs" answers Allen.

Meanwhile, Ms. Bury was making some progress with her students as well. She had found a book with real-life stories about inventions. She had decided to have the class read the book together to help them see how inventions are created but more importantly how those ideas can be described in writing. While reading the book, Ms. Bury stops and asks students to guess what might happen with a particular invention. Did it succeed or fail? When she finishes with the book,

she asks all the students to work quietly at their desks on writing their proposals. She had provided them with a list of questions to answered in their proposals.

Ms. Bury also informs them that tomorrow they will be switching papers with a partner and giving feedback on their partner's idea and written proposal. Immediately Isaac starts to fidget. While everyone else is quietly working, he walks up to Ms. Bury and whispers, "Do I have to share my paper with someone else? I am afraid it won't be good enough and everyone will make fun of me."

Ms. Bury answers, "Oh Isaac, I am sure your idea will be as good as the others. Getting feedback from someone else will help you make the project even better. Everyone is going to trade with someone else."

As he walks back to his desk, Isaac is thinking, "I bet no one will have the whole class laughing at them for a stupid idea."

ASSESS:

1. Do you think Ms. Bury's expectations for her students are reasonable? Why or why not?

2. Do you think it is a good idea to have peers give feedback? Provide your reasons.

3. How creative do you think we should let children be?

MIDDLE SCHOOL: PRESIDENT OR QUEEN FOR A DAY?

James van der Laan, or Mr. Van as his students call him, walks into his eighth-grade social studies classroom on Friday afternoon and asks, "Who wants to be President today?"

Kirsten calls from her desk, "I do!"

"Great, you come up here and sit at my desk as if we were in the Oval Office," replies Mr. Van. "Now, who can tell me how many people I need to fill the Supreme Court?" he asks.

Niall raises his hand and answers, "Eight plus the Chief Justice. Can I be the Chief Justice today?"

"Well, given that you got that question right, yes you can. How about I let you choose your eight members?" says Mr. Van.

"Wait a minute!" yells Kirsten, "I am the President. I get to nominate the justices."

"Technically, Kirsten, you are correct. But for the sake of time today, I am just going to have Niall choose his justices and divide the rest of the class into senators and representatives."

After providing each student with his or her role for the class, Mr. Van assigns the senators the task of coming up with a bill. The students go through the process of how a new bill might be become law and how the Supreme Court might review a law to determine whether it is constitutional. Mr. Van reminds them as they leave to review the government of England because Monday they would be enacting that governmental structure.

On Monday morning, Mr. Van begins by asking, "Who would like to be Queen today?"

Kirsten again yells "I do!" but Mr. Van selects Maria.

"Maria, do you know what your first duty as Queen must be if we are to enact the governmental structure of the United Kingdom?" asks Mr. Van.

"Yes, I get to select my Prime Minister. I choose Bridgett," answers Maria.

Laura asks, "So the Prime Minister is kind of like a Supreme Court Justice if the Queen gets to choose, right?"

"No," answers Niall, "the Prime Minister is like the President of the United States."

Laura replies, "That doesn't make any sense. Isn't the Queen like the President? If the Prime Minister is like the President, what does the Queen do?"

Mr. Van interjects, "Who can explain to Laura the similarities and differences in these two different governmental systems?"

Several students attempt to make comparisons and match the branches of the government. Mr. Van reminds them of the comparison they did last week on the Smart Board. "Where are your notes from last week? We put on the Smart Board the links between specific roles in the U.S. government and the UK government." It becomes clear that some students did not copy the information from the Smart Board into their notes. Mr. Van goes through the diagram again, making connections between the governmental systems.

Kirsten asks, "Mr. Van, are we going to need to know all these terms for the test? I am just not very good at memorizing all this information, especially when it is about government. I think it is just easier for other kids."

"Well Kirsten, I don't want you to just memorize the terms. I really want you to understand how these various governmental systems work. This is why I am going to have you do several activities in class, like the one today, as well as write several papers. I would hope that those strategies would help you learn the material," replies Mr. Van.

Directing his attention to the whole class, Mr. Van announces, "For homework this week, I want you to write a position paper. You must decide which governmental system you believe works better and provide evidence for your position."

"Well, of course the United States has a better system. That will be easy," states Niall.

Mr. Van then states, "Well, let me give you a heads up. Next week you will have to write a position paper making a case for the other governmental system."

Many of the students begin to complain and comment, "Why do you always make us take both positions? You did the same thing when we discussed the Civil War."

Ute Grabowsky / Contributor / Photothek / Getty Images

Mr. Van replies, "Because I want you to *think,* not just spit back information to me. I also want you to think beyond what we already know. So I will also be asking you to work in groups over the next few weeks to design your own governmental system. You can use pieces and ideas from the other systems we have discussed, but yours will need to be unique and original in some ways."

ASSESS:

1. Do you think the strategy of assigning students to specific governmental roles worked? Why or why not?

2. Do you think it is a good idea to have students provide opinions for opposing sides? Provide your reasons.

3. Why would having the students create their own governmental system help them understand the systems being used today?

HIGH SCHOOL: BROWN-EYED GIRL

Ms. Overocker is the biology teacher at a small-city high school of about 1,000 students. She teaches several sections of introductory biology to the freshmen each year. Today's lesson is on genetics, using the Punnett square. Ms. Overocker asks the class to take out a clean piece of paper for a pop quiz. The students begin to grumble and Ms. Overocker says, "You can use your notes from yesterday, so if you took good notes, you'll be fine."

"Using your notes from yesterday on brown and blue eyes as a model, write the Punnett square for green and blue eyes, given that green is a dominant gene and blue is recessive. Assume that one parent is homozygous dominant and the other is heterozygous."

Many of the students whisper how easy it is but a few students seem to be lost. Ms. Overocker walks over to Garrett and asks, "Where are your notes from yesterday?"

Garrett responds, "I have them right here, but I didn't copy down the Pruit Square or whatever you called it."

Akilah, who is sitting next to Garrett, says in a somewhat irritated tone, "You can look at my notes for now and copy them later. The Punnett square is what we'll be working on the next week or so. Didn't you hear her say that yesterday?"

Ms. Overocker continues, "Who can tell me the eye color of each parent in this example?"

Everyone starts to look around for someone else to answer. Finally, Akilah says, "I think they both have green eyes."

"That's right," says Ms. Overocker. "How do you know that?"

Akilah answers, "Because both parents would have a dominant gene for green."

"Correct. Now, who can tell me the probability of an offspring with these parents having blue eyes?" asks Ms. Overocker.

Wyatt quickly answers, "Zero!"

Xander replies, "No, it's 25%, just like yesterday with the brown and blues eyes."

---

*3rd hour Biology—Overocker
2/23/17*

Punnett Squares

	B	b
B	BB	Bb
b	Bb	bb

B = Brown eyes (dominant gene)
b = blue eyes (recessive gene)

BB = Homozygous dominant (Brown eyes)
Bb = Homozygous recessive (blue eyes)
Bb = Heterozygous (Brown eyes)

Wyatt fires again, "No, it's zero because one parent is pure green eyed and the other is hybrid. So every combination has a dominant gene of green. Yesterday both parents had brown eyes but they were both hybrids."

"Very good, Wyatt," replies Ms. Overocker. "Now, I want each of you to come up with your own example of a Punnett square. You can use anything that might be considered to have a genetic basis. These don't have to be real examples, so be creative."

Xander whispers to Camrie, "I hate it when she makes us come up with our own examples. It's so hard when you don't know the first thing about genetics. What the hell does pure and hybrid mean?"

Camrie answers, "I know. I am a test taker. Give me some multiple-choice questions and I can do it, but the assignments in this class are too hard. You've done better than me on these assignments. I'll probably be the only freshman who has to retake biology."

Akilah decides to use straight hair and curly hair because she knows from reading the chapter that straight hair is a dominant gene and curly hair is a recessive gene. She is one of the only students who actually reads the required text before coming to class. She finds it easier to listen and take notes in class if she has already read the material.

After a few minutes, Ms. Overocker asks, "Is anyone willing to share their example?"

Wyatt, as usual, is the first to reply. "I have a good one Ms. O! I decided to be creative like you said and use wings as genetic characteristics of unicorns. In my example, wings is the dominant gene and not having wings is the recessive gene. I used capital W for the dominant gene and little w for the recessive gene. One parent has wings but the other doesn't. That would mean that all their offspring would have wings." Wyatt holds up his Punnett square to show Ms. Overocker.

Akilah is quick to clarify, "That's only true if the parent with wings is homozygous. If the parent with wings is heterozygous, then there is a 50-50 chance the offspring will have wings."

Xander sighs, "I have no idea what you are talking about. What is homozygous and heterozygous?"

Several other students begin to nod and collectively agree that they are confused.

Ms. Overocker spends the remainder of the day reviewing how to use the Punnett square and the meaning of key concepts such as homozygous (pure), heterozygous (hybrid), dominant, and recessive. This time she is careful to point out to the students what they should be including in their notes. The same problems seem to occur in her other freshman class and require her to repeat information and provide additional examples. She thinks to herself: *It is no wonder I am so exhausted at the end of the day. The other teachers don't spend all day with freshman who have limited reading and writing skills. Does anyone else at this school make them do these time-consuming projects?*

Over the next few days, most of the students seem to catch on and are able to create their own Punnett squares for various genetic characteristics, real and imaginative. Ms. Overocker then announces that their next unit will use this knowledge of genetic characteristics to discuss whether genetic testing should be used.

Wyatt asks, "Wouldn't everyone want to know if they were carrying a genetic abnormality?"

"Well, these are the types of questions we are going to read about, write about, and debate over the next few weeks," answers Ms. Overocker.

Camrie looks over at Xander, rolls her eyes and says, "Here we go again with these impossible assignments that have no right answer. Why do I have to debate a topic? Can't she just tell us what she wants us to know?"

ASSESS:

1. Is it a good idea to let students use imaginary creatures as examples? Why or why not?

2. What should the teacher do when many of the students in class do not understand the material?

3. Are you surprised that some students were not able to apply previously taught material (brown and blue eyes) to new examples (green and blue eyes)? Why or why not?

©iStockphoto.com/DragonImages

MODULE **11**

METACOGNITION

WHAT IS METACOGNITION AND WHY IS IT IMPORTANT?

❶ Describe the two main components of metacognition.

As you begin to read this module, you might have a pencil, pen, or highlighter in hand, ready to begin identifying important concepts and examples. Did you look over the outline on this page? How many of the six learning goals can you recall without looking above? Do you plan to

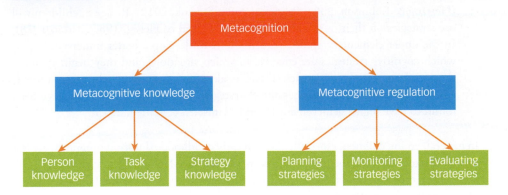

FIGURE 11.1 **Components of Metacognition.**

memorize the key concepts? These questions are prompting you to engage in **metacognition**—thinking about your own thinking processes, including study skills, memory capabilities, and the ability to monitor your learning (Baker, 2013; Hertzog & Robinson, 2005; Metcalfe, 2000).

Metacognition is important for both teaching and learning. The more students know about *what* learning strategies are and *how, when,* and *where* to apply different learning strategies effectively, the more likely they are to use such strategies and thereby increase their academic achievement (Baker, 2013; Peterson, 1988). Rather than expect students to spontaneously acquire metacognition on their own, teachers need to explicitly teach students metacognitive skills along with content instruction (Kistner et al., 2010). Teaching students about their metacognition and how to use it requires an understanding of its two main components: metacognitive knowledge and metacognitive regulation (see Figure 11.1).

Metacognitive knowledge is knowledge about our own cognitive processes and an understanding of how to regulate those processes to maximize learning. Metacognitive knowledge falls into three categories (Flavell, Miller, & Miller, 2002; Manning, 1991):

1. **Person knowledge,** also called *declarative knowledge,* refers to understanding our own capabilities: "I am good at memorizing lists" or "I am poor at comprehending what I read in textbooks." This type of knowledge changes considerably from kindergarten through high school. Older school-age children become much more accurate in determining how much information they can learn within a specific time frame (Flavell et al., 2002).

2. **Task knowledge,** or *procedural knowledge,* relates to how we perceive the difficulty (or ease) of a task. In school, students may make this judgment based on the following aspects of the task:

   - Content ("This is a review of irregular verbs in Spanish.")

   - Length ("This chapter is very long.")

   - Type of assignment ("Essay exams require recall of information rather than recognition, as in multiple-choice exams.")

Very young children understand that fewer items will be easier to learn than more items and that learning a list of similar concepts (three colors) is easier than learning concepts with little connection to one another (Flavell et al., 2002). Older children also understand that the difficulty level of a task will influence the study strategies they use (e.g., studying to summarize information versus studying to repeat the information verbatim; Schunk, 2012).

Video Case 11.1 ▲
Metacognition

3. **Strategy knowledge,** or *conditional knowledge,* describes our capability for using strategies to learn information. In general, young children are not good at using strategy knowledge (Flavell et al., 2002). Three-year-olds can be taught a learning strategy for a specific task but will not spontaneously apply that strategy in a similar learning task (Hertzog & Robinson, 2005; Palincsar, 2003; Schunk, 2012). By age 8, children will use strategies on their own without prompting (Beal & Fleisig, 1987; Ritter, 1978). In the upper elementary grades, students start to develop a better understanding of which cognitive strategies are effective in which situations, and they begin to apply them with increasing consistency (Flavell et al., 2002). Secondary education students who have knowledge of metacognitive strategies and use those strategies have been found to have higher achievement (Merki, Ramseier, & Karlen, 2013).

In general, young children, especially those in early childhood education programs, are less likely to accurately estimate memory abilities (person knowledge), judge task difficulty (task knowledge), or apply appropriate strategies in new contexts (strategy knowledge).

Metacognitive regulation is the purposeful act of attempting to control our own cognitions, beliefs, emotions, and values. It allows us to use our metacognitive knowledge to function efficiently in learning situations. Metacognitive regulation requires using *executive control functions,* a collection of mental processes that includes planning, monitoring, and evaluating strategies (Brown, 1987; Flavell et al., 2002; Tajika, Nakatsu, Nozaki, & Maruno, 2007).

1. **Planning** involves scheduling learning strategies and selecting which strategies to use in different contexts.

2. **Monitoring** involves periodically checking on how well the planned strategy is working. For example, we can monitor our performance through self-testing and self-explanation.

3. **Evaluating** involves appraising the outcomes of the cognitive strategies used. More than just "getting a good grade," this process measures to what degree our performance is affected by our planning and monitoring of selected learning strategies.

Children in early childhood are less likely to plan the use of memory strategies. They also are less accurate at monitoring their learning progress, being more likely to insist that they understand or have learned material that in fact is not yet well learned (Chi, 1987). Monitoring skills increase with age, with 11- to 12-year-olds becoming much more accurate in their monitoring than younger children (Krebs & Roebers, 2010). Young children also are not good at evaluating the effectiveness of learning strategies and memory skills (Hertzog & Robinson, 2005). Children need explicit instruction and feedback about the outcomes of strategy use to increase experience and hence metacognitive regulation (Askell-Williams, Lawson, & Skrzypiec, 2012; Baker, 2013). Some research has highlighted how metacognitive knowledge continues to develop during the secondary education level (Karlen, Merki, & Ramseier, 2014).

 Where did you learn metacognitive knowledge and regulation? Did your teachers provide information to help you develop metacognitive skills?

SPECIAL CASES OF METACOGNITION

❷ Explain four characteristics of children's theory of mind.

❸ Explain two consequences related to adolescent egocentrism.

Theory of Mind in Childhood

As early as age 2, children begin to recognize that others have their own minds. This recognition helps them understand why others' perceptions and feelings differ from their own. This early understanding of the mind and the "mental world" is called **theory of mind** (Flavell et al., 2002) and may predict constructive beliefs about learning and memory later in childhood (Lecce, Caputi, & Pagnin, 2015; Lockl & Schneider, 2007). Studies on theory of mind have defined four characteristics:

1. **False beliefs:** the understanding that a belief is only one of many mental representations, which can be false or accurate. Three-year-olds are not capable of understanding that someone could have a false belief. Rather, they perceive only one belief—the correct one. However, by age 4 or 5, most children understand that people can believe one thing but be wrong (Flavell et al., 2002). The candy box experiment described here provides an example of false beliefs (Flavell et al., 2002).

    Video: False Belief Tasks

   Trial 1, with 5-year-old:

   > A developmental psychologist shows a 5-year-old a candy box and asks her, "What is in it?"

   > "Candy," she says. She then looks inside the box and to her surprise discovers that it actually contains pencils, not candy.

   > "What would another child who had not yet opened the box think was in it?" the experimenter asks.

   > "Candy!" says the child, amused at the trick.

   Trial 2, with 3-year-old:

   > The experimenter then tries the same procedure with a 3-year-old, asking her, "What is in the box?"

   > "Candy," she says. She then looks inside and is also surprised to discover the pencils.

   > "What would another child who had not yet opened the box think was in it?" the experimenter asks.

   > "Pencils," says the child, who also insists that she had originally thought the box held pencils.

   Conclusion:

   > The 3-year-old does not understand that other people or the child herself can have a false belief.

2. **Appearance-reality distinctions:** a person's ability to understand that something may look one way (appearance) but actually be something else (reality), such as a well-designed plastic spider (reality) that appears to be alive (appearance). One experiment presented preschool-age children with a fake egg (appearance). Once the children learned that the "egg" was actually a painted rock (reality), they insisted that it looked like a rock, not an egg (Flavell, Flavell, & Green, 1983). Similar experiments have been conducted with numerous stimuli, such as sponges (reality) that look like rocks (appearance). The findings suggest that, until they reach age 4 or 5, children are not capable of understanding that appearances can be deceiving or false.

3. **Visual perspective taking:** understanding that views of physical objects differ based on one's perspective. Researchers have been able to establish the development of perspective taking in preschool as occurring on two levels (Flavell et al., 2002):

Visual Perspective Taking. Children understand that another person may see the same object from a different view, such as a game board that faces the child and not his or her opponent.

- Level 1 (2 to 3 years of age): Children understand that another person can see something if the person's eyes are open and looking in the appropriate direction without any visual obstructions. At this level, perspective taking involves determining *whether* something is seen (e.g., "Mom can see the game board.").

- Level 2 (4 to 5 years of age): Children understand that another person can see something in a different way or from a view that differs from how they see it. Here perspective taking involves determining *how* something is seen (e.g., "Mom's view of the game board is upside down because she is sitting across from me at the table.").

4. **Introspection:** children's awareness and understanding of their own thoughts (Flavell, 2000, 2004; Flavell, Green, & Flavell, 1995, 2000). By age 5, children are likely to both overestimate and underestimate the amount of thinking they and others are capable of. For example, 5-year-olds believe that people know when they are sleeping (overestimate) yet believe that a person can go days without thinking (underestimate). Even when they do understand that thoughts are occurring within the mind, 5-year-olds are not clear about what is being thought about within their own mind or that of another person. For example, children who are asked to think about where in their house their toothbrush is kept will deny having been thinking about their bathroom (Flavell et al., 1995). By age 8, children are better able to describe their own stream of thoughts and understand that it is very hard, if not impossible, to stop thinking for any length of time (Flavell et al., 2000).

Hence, the theory of mind becomes increasingly sophisticated over the preschool- and school-age years.

Egocentrism in Adolescence

As the awareness of thoughts within one's own and others' minds develops, early adolescents become increasingly *self-conscious,* having a heightened sense of the self and a concern for how and what others think of them. Egocentrism in young children involves difficulty differentiating between their view of an object and another's view of an object, while **adolescent egocentrism** is difficulty differentiating between one's own thoughts and the thoughts of others. Elkind (1967) proposed two specific consequences of adolescent egocentrism:

1. **Imaginary audience:** The adolescent imagines or believes that he or she is the focus of attention in social settings due to a lack of differentiation between self and others' thoughts. For example, an adolescent boy may believe that others' thoughts are focused on him, just as his own thoughts are (e.g., "I can't stop thinking about the zit on my chin, and everyone else is looking at it too!"). Imaginary audience can manifest itself in two ways:

   - An adolescent girl might be highly critical of herself and expect others to judge her negatively as well. Let's say she tries a new hairstyle and is very concerned that it does not look good on her. When no one in her group of friends comments on the hairstyle, she might ask, "What do you think of my new haircut?" and be unconvinced by the answer "We didn't even notice."

   - An adolescent boy might be self-admiring and assume that others also will find his qualities endearing and positive. Perhaps he believes that his joking, sarcastic style of classroom behavior is a flattering and attractive quality. He will have difficulty understanding why his parents and teachers do not approve of this behavior.

2. **Personal fable:** Adolescents mistakenly believe that they are unique, such that no one else can understand their situation. For example, most adolescents do not believe that their teachers can understand the difficulty they might have in studying or receiving good grades. They might believe that their friends do not experience the same pressure to do well or have the same feelings of disappointment (e.g., "None of my friends have this much trouble in math class.").

Imaginary Audience. Adolescents may believe or imagine that other people are watching or thinking about them, especially about their appearance.

Two separate explanations for the rise of the imaginary audience and the personal fable during adolescence have been offered. The first, based on Piaget's theory of cognitive development, suggests that imaginary audience and personal fable are negative consequences that arise as the individual moves into formal operational thinking (Alberts, Elkind, & Ginsberg, 2007; Elkind, 1967). The development of formal operational thinking not only enables adolescents to use metacognition but also leads them to think too much about themselves and about what others think of them. The second explanation proposes that imaginary audience and personal fable are not negative side effects but rather adaptive coping processes that arise because of the changing relationship between adolescents and their parents (Lapsley, 1993). In the course of adolescence, as the child becomes an adult, the relationship between child and parent must be renegotiated to balance separateness and connectedness (Gavazzi & Sabatelli, 1990; Sabatelli & Mazor, 1985). Imaginary audience helps adolescents maintain their connectedness with others, whereas personal fable helps them maintain their separateness and uniqueness. Imaginary audience and personal fable may continue to be used as coping mechanisms throughout adulthood, although less often and intensely than during adolescence (Frankenberger, 2000; Lapsley, 1993; Quadrel, Fischhoff, & Davis, 1993).

Piaget's theory of cognitive development: See Module 6

Think of a time when you thought no one could possibly understand your situation or emotions.

©iStockphoto.com / MachineHeadz

FACTORS AFFECTING THE DEVELOPMENT AND USE OF METACOGNITION

4 Explain the factors that influence the development and use of metacognitive skills.

A number of factors influence the development of metacognition, including biological differences and environmental differences (Flavell et al., 2002). Neurological impairments can impede the development of metacognition. For example, children with autism are considered to have neurological deficits in their ability to understand the mind and thoughts of people (Hamilton, Brindley, & Frith, 2009; Schuwerk, Vuori, & Sodian, 2015), and children with intellectual disabilities have difficulty with processes such as planning, monitoring, and evaluating strategies for task performance (Nader-Grosbois, 2014). In addition, frontal brain damage can impair metacognitive abilities (Shimamura, 1994; Szczepanski & Knight, 2014).

Our environment—in particular, our family experiences—also plays a role in the development of metacognition. Children learn about metacognition by listening to parents' and siblings' conversations about beliefs, emotions, knowledge, how to learn, and how to study (Laranjo, Bernier, Meins, & Carlson, 2014). Family conversations may be more influential for girls than for boys because parents tend to express their thoughts and emotions more with daughters than with sons (Flavell et al., 2002).

Students also possess individual characteristics that determine whether they choose to use the metacognitive skills they have developed:

Belief about the nature of the task (task knowledge): Students who believe that the information to be learned is easy will not use more advanced skills and strategies such as planning, monitoring, and evaluating (Schunk, 2012). Also, when the task involves memorization rather than connections between important ideas or elaboration of ideas, students are more likely to use lower-level strategies (e.g., rote memorization) or to alter their strategies to reflect the type of exam or task identified by the teacher (Van Meter, Yokoi, & Pressley, 1994).

Motivation: Students who are highly motivated to learn are more likely to invest time and energy in metacognitive strategies than are students who are less interested in learning (Karlen et al., 2014; Schunk, 2012).

Prior knowledge about the topic: The more students know about a topic, the better they are able to understand, organize, and retain new information (Engle, Nations, & Cantor, 1990; Kuhura-Kojima & Hatano, 1991). For example, research has found that reading comprehension is better for a weak reader who knows the topic or content of the passage well as compared to a strong reader who does not know the topic well (Hirsch & Hansel, 2013). Students who are aware of what they know and do not know are better able to use planning strategies to increase their study time for information not well understood (Brown, Bransford, Ferrara, & Campione, 1983).

Prior success using metacognitive skills: Successful use of metacognitive skills will lead to increased use of those skills. Students who do not understand how metacognitive strategies improve their learning are less likely to use those strategies in the future (Schunk, 2012).

DIVERSITY

Intellectual disabilities: See Module 21

Brain development: See Module 5

Motivation: See Modules 14, 15, and 16

Prior knowledge: See Modules 10 and 12

Think of some specific ways teachers can help students understand the importance of metacognitive skills and encourage them to use these skills.

APPLICATIONS: LEARNING STRATEGIES

⑤ Describe how teachers can assist students with reading comprehension and writing skills.

⑥ Explain the importance of note taking and study time and describe how teachers can help students improve these learning strategies.

Students typically equate learning or study strategies with basic memory skills that help them remember information (see Table 11.1). Several other learning strategies are related to metacognition, notably reading comprehension, writing skills, note taking, and study time. Reading and writing are introduced early in educational settings, whereas note taking and studying typically are not required until later elementary school or middle school. Let's examine each of these learning strategies more closely.

Memory: See Module 10

Video Case 11.2 ▲
Reading Comprehension Strategies

© SAGE Publications

Reading Comprehension

Learning strategies include extracting information from reading materials, or reading comprehension. Reading comprehension increases with age, partly due to increases in metacognitive skills and knowledge (Artelt & Schneider, 2015; Palincsar, 2003; Schunk, 2012). Two popular instructional techniques are used to increase reading comprehension: reciprocal teaching, commonly used with younger children, and the PQ4R strategy, typically used with older students.

TABLE 11.1	Memorization Strategies
MEMORY STRATEGY	**DESCRIPTION**
Rehearsal strategies	
Maintenance rehearsal	Simply repeating the information over and over.
Elaborative rehearsal	Connecting new information to prior knowledge.
Chunking	Grouping individual pieces of information in a meaningful way.
Mnemonic devices	
Acronym	Forming a word from the first letter of each word to be remembered or forming a phrase or sentence from the first letter of each item in a list to be remembered.
Chain mnemonic	Connecting the first item to be memorized to the second, the second to the third, and so on, or incorporating items to be remembered into a catchy jingle.
Keyword method	Associating new words and concepts with similar sounding cue words and images.
Method of loci	Imagining a familiar place, picking out particular locations, and using those locations as pegs on which to hang items to be remembered from a list.

Reciprocal teaching is a structured conversation in which teachers and students discuss sections of a text (Palincsar, 2013; Palincsar & Brown, 1984), as depicted in Table 11.2. Reciprocal teaching involves four steps:

1. *Summarizing:* Students must verbally summarize the text, which requires them to attend to the main points and check or monitor their understanding.

2. *Questioning:* Students must create questions based on the text, a form of monitoring their understanding.

3. *Clarifying:* Students are asked to clarify difficult points to critically evaluate their understanding of the material.

4. *Predicting:* Students are asked to make predictions about future content to test their inferences between main points.

As with many learning strategies, teachers first need to model good reading comprehension skills using this strategy. Then students begin to use the strategy with the support of teachers, who provide cues, prompts, and feedback (Palincsar, 2003, 2013). Teachers' prompts can be derived from a related instructional strategy, "Questioning the Author" (Beck & McKeown, 2001). Examples of teacher prompts include questions such as the following:

- What is the author trying to say?

- What does the author want us to know?

Teachers can provide follow-up to student responses by asking questions such as these:

- That is what the author said, but what did he or she mean?

- Why does he or she want us to know that?

Teacher training on reciprocal teaching and Questioning the Author approaches suggest that teachers first use the strategies with a focus on the procedures but later learn to use these instructional strategies as a springboard for more analytical discussions that foster reading comprehension (Kucan, Palincsar, Khasnabis, & Chang, 2009). Results of using these instructional strategies to improve reading comprehension are substantial across various age groups, from elementary students to adults, as well as among elementary and middle school students with learning disabilities (Gajria, Jitendra, Sood, & Sacks, 2007; Lundberg, & Reichenberg, 2013; Rosenshine & Meister, 1994; Schünemann, Spörer, & Brunstein, 2013). The strategy is also effective when used in peer interaction or cooperative learning instruction (Palincsar, Brown, & Martin, 1987).

A traditional system for teaching older students reading comprehension skills involves a series of steps known as **PQ4R** (Robinson, 1961; Thomas & Robinson, 1972). These steps are described here:

1. *Preview:* Consistent with the executive control process of planning, the first step in reading comprehension is to survey or preview the material to be read. Students read chapter outlines, scan the chapter for general topics, and identify major sections within the reading assignment.

2. *Question:* Developing questions based on the outline or section headings allows students the opportunity to plan or identify the important information that will be obtained from the reading assignment. For example, the heading "Theory of Mind" might be rephrased as the question "What is theory of mind?"

DIVERSITY

Learning disabilities: See Module 21

Video: PQ4R

TABLE 11.2	Reciprocal Dialogue Example
Text:	In the United States, salt is produced by three basic methods: solar (sun) evaporation, mining, and artificial heat evaporation. For salt to be extracted by solar evaporation, the weather must be hot and dry. Thus, solar salt is harvested in the tropic-like areas along our southern ocean coasts and at Great Salt Lake.
Chris:	Name three different basic methods for how salt is produced.
Angela:	Evaporation, mining, evaporation . . . artificial heat evaporation.
Chris:	Correct. Very good. My summary on this paragraph is about ways that salt is being produced.
Teacher:	Very good. Could you select the next teacher?
	(Chris selects another student to read.)
Text:	The second oldest form of salt production is mining. Unlike early methods that made the work extremely dangerous and difficult, today's methods use special machinery, and salt mining is easier and safer. The old expression "back to the salt mine" no longer applies.
Logan:	Name two words that often describe mining salt in the old days.
Ken:	Back to the salt mines?
Logan:	No, Ken. Angela?
Angela:	Dangerous and difficult.
Logan:	Correct. This paragraph is all about comparing the old mining of salt and today's mining of salt.
Teacher:	Beautiful!
Logan:	I have a prediction to make.
Teacher:	Good.
Logan:	I think it might tell when salt was first discovered; well, it might tell what salt is made of and how it's made.
Teacher:	OK. Can we have another teacher?
Text:	Table salt is made by the third method—artificial evaporation. Pumping water into an underground salt bed dissolves the salt to make a brine that is brought to the surface. After purification at high temperatures, the salt is ready for our tables.
Ken:	After purification at high temperatures the salt is ready for what?
Chris:	Our tables.
Ken:	That is correct. To summarize, after its purification, the salt is put on our tables.
Teacher:	That was a fine job, Ken, and I appreciate all that work, but I think there might be something else to add to our summary. There is more important information that I think we need to include. This paragraph is mostly about what?
Angela:	The third method of artificial evaporation.
Brian:	It mainly tells about pumping water from an underground salt bed that dissolves the salt to make a brine that is brought to the surface. Angela hit it right on the money. This paragraph is mostly about the method of artificial evaporation and then everything else in the paragraph is telling us about that process.
Teacher:	OK. Next teacher.

SOURCE: Palincsar & Brown, 1984.

3. *Read:* While reading the assigned chapter, article, or book, students attempt to answer the questions developed from the outline or the section headings.

4. *Reflect:* The process of monitoring one's reading comprehension includes taking breaks from the reading material to relate information to prior knowledge and create examples beyond those provided in the text. Reflection includes asking questions such as these: "Did I grasp the main points?" "Do I understand the content?" "How does this relate to other information in the text?" "Can I think of an example?"

5. *Recite:* Reciting or rehearsing the information in the text is an attempt to store the information in long-term memory. One strategy is to answer the questions developed from the outline or section headings (Step 2) without looking back at the text material.

6. *Review:* Although it might be thought that review implies rereading, it actually requires the student to mentally, rather than physically, think through the chapter contents to monitor how much of the material has been learned.

DIVERSITY ⟨

Learning disabilities: See Module 21

Empirical studies have consistently found that the use of reading comprehension strategies such as reciprocal teaching and PQ4R improves students' recall and understanding of important ideas presented in the text (Anderson, 1990; Omoteso & Sadiku, 2013; Palincsar, 2003). This also applies to children with learning disabilities (Schewel & Waddell, 1986).

Writing Skills

Writing skills increasingly require metacognitive skills such as planning, monitoring, evaluation, and revision (Bereiter & Scardamalia, 1987; Rijlaarsdam et al., 2012). However, even kindergarten children are capable of answering questions about their planning strategies or their ability to put thoughts onto paper. When interviewed about their writing skills, kindergarten children typically use words such as "thought," "remembered," and "idea." They also are increasingly able to answer questions about where or how they formulated ideas for their writing assignments (Jacobs, 2004). Revision becomes an important part of the writing process in middle school and high school as students become better able to engage in monitoring and evaluation of their writing and develop an increasing ability to think abstractly (Berninger, Mizokawa, & Bragg, 1991; Rijlaarsdam et al., 2012).

Direct Instruction: See Module 18

Modeling: See Module 9

Intervention strategies suggest that direct instruction and modeling of metacognitive skills can improve writing skills (Conner, 2007; Hooper, Wakely, de Kruif, & Swartz, 2006; Rijlaarsdam et al., 2012). Teachers can:

- provide instruction in and modeling of planning strategies such as (a) determining the audience, (b) identifying the main ideas, (c) outlining the organization, and (d) making rough drafts and revising. *Procedural facilitations,* shown in Table 11.3, are a set of prompts used during planning and revision (Bereiter & Scardamalia, 1987; Scardamalia & Bereiter, 1985). Elementary students using procedural facilitations spend more time planning and improve the quality of their writing (Scardamalia, Bereiter, & Steinbach, 1984). Similarly, middle school students who plan their writing by developing rough drafts perform at levels comparable to those of some college students (Brown, Day, & Jones, 1983).

- provide assistance in monitoring and evaluating progress. With younger children, this might include asking them to think aloud or answer questions about their ideas as they engage in writing assignments (Jacobs, 2004). For older children and adolescents, teachers might ask students to reread (aloud or silently) and substantially revise, not simply edit, their papers.

TABLE 11.3 Sample Procedural Facilitations: Planning Cues for Opinion Essays

New Idea	An even better idea is . . .
	An important point I haven't considered yet is . . .
	A better argument would be . . .
	A different aspect would be . . .
	A whole new way to think of this topic is . . .
	No one will have thought of . . .
Improve	I'm not being very clear about what I just said, so . . .
	I could make my main point clearer by . . .
	A criticism I should deal with in my paper is . . .
	I really think this isn't necessary because . . .
	I'm getting off the topic, so . . .
	This isn't very convincing because . . .
	But many readers won't agree that . . .
	To liven this up I'll . . .
Elaborate	An example of this . . .
	This is true, but it's not sufficient, so . . .
	My own feelings about this are . . .
	I'll change this a little by . . .
	The reason I think so . . .
	Another reason that's good . . .
	I could develop this idea by adding . . .
	Another way to put it would be . . .
	A good point on the other side of the argument is . . .
Goals	A goal I think I could write to . . .
	My purpose . . .
Putting It Together	If I want to start off with my strongest idea I'll . . .
	I can tie this together by . . .
	My main point is . . .

SOURCE: Adapted from Scardamalia, Bereiter, & Steinbach, 1984.

Note Taking

As students continue to develop metacognitive skills, note taking becomes necessary in many middle school and high school classes. Learning the best practices of note taking is important because the amount of information and the techniques used during note taking are related to academic achievement for students, including students with learning disabilities (Boyle & Rivera, 2012).

Functions of note taking: Before we examine best practices for note taking, we need to understand the three functions of taking notes (Kiewra, 1985; Kiewra et al., 1991).

1. Encoding: The process provides assistance in the encoding of material because writing down ideas from lecture material is a second form of encoding that goes beyond simply listening to the lecture. Some research supports the encoding function, suggesting that taking notes, even without time for review, leads to

> **DIVERSITY**

Learning disabilities: See Module 21

superior academic performance over not taking notes (Kiewra, 1985; Peverly, Brobst, Graham, & Shaw, 2003).

2. Encoding plus storage: While taking notes may serve an encoding function, reviewing notes provides the additional benefit of returning to the lecture material for review and storage of the information in memory. Empirical studies consistently find that students who take notes and review their notes have higher achievement levels than students who do not review notes (Kiewra, 1985; Kiewra et al., 1991).

3. External storage: External storage—or the review of notes borrowed from another student—can still benefit the storage of information. While less beneficial than encoding or encoding plus storage for tasks of recall, external storage may actually have more benefit than merely encoding (listening to lectures) for tasks that ask students to integrate or synthesize ideas (Kiewra et al., 1991).

Amount of information recorded: One important aspect of note taking is the amount of information included in students' notes. Increased amounts of noted lecture material are related to higher achievement. For example, information that is recorded in notes has about a 50% chance of being recalled on an examination, whereas nonnoted information has only a 15% chance of being recalled (Aiken, Thomas, & Shennum, 1975). However, most students record only about 30% of the important information (Kiewra, 2002). Students may not record important information because they lack the metacognitive knowledge to understand the usefulness of note taking as well as to determine what is and is not relevant information (Garcia-Mila & Anderson, 2007; Haynes, McCarley, & Williams, 2015). In addition, the amount of information recorded during note taking may also be influenced by individual differences in working memory abilities (Bui & Myerson, 2014).

Teachers can increase the amount of important information that is identified and recorded by students in a number of ways (see Kiewra, 2002, for a complete review):

- Provide lecture notes, which offer a model for identifying important concepts. However, many teachers, particularly those in secondary education and beyond, believe that students should be responsible for their own note taking. Providing detailed notes to students does not encourage them to develop and improve their note-taking skills.

- Provide skeletal notes that contain the main points plus space for students to add detail. Skeletal notes provided by teachers and completed by students include over 50% of the important information, compared to only 30% of important information contained in notes taken without assistance.

- Provide lecture cues to signal important ideas, such as writing concepts on the board, verbally repeating information, pausing after stating the information, or explicitly identifying the organization (e.g., "There are three categories."). Organization cues increase the percentage of important information recorded to close to 65%, while approximately 80% of the information presented on the board is recorded in students' notes.

- Allow—and even encourage—students to audiotape or videotape lectures as an opportunity to hear the lecture a second time and add to their existing notes. Audiotapes or videotapes should not be used as a substitute for note taking during the lecture, except when students are unable to take notes—such as in cases of physical or learning disabilities. Students who hear or view a lecture can recall 30% of the important information, while students who hear or view it twice recall more than 50%.

Working memory: See Module 10

- Allow students the opportunity to compare notes with other students to make corrections or add details they missed. Reconstructing notes with a partner increases the amount of important information recorded to 50%.

Note-taking techniques: Several studies have compared the use of conventional outline notes to the use of matrix notes (Figure 11.2 gives a sample of each technique). Matrix notes consistently have resulted in greater learning (Kiewra, 2002; Risch & Kiewra, 1990). The advantage of matrix notes may be due to their completeness: Students' matrix notes typically include 47% of the lecture ideas, compared with only 32% of lecture ideas contained in conventional outline notes. In addition, matrix notes allow connections and comparisons to be made between key concepts and ideas, possibly resulting in improved integration and synthesis of the information presented in lectures (Kiewra et al., 1991). Teachers can assist students in creating matrix notes in a number of ways:

- Completed matrix notes can be prepared by the teacher and provided to students.

- The matrix framework can be prepared by the teacher and provided to students for them to complete.

- Teachers can train students to construct matrix notes through direct instruction, modeling, feedback, and practice.

Studying

Students can read the class material, complete writing assignments, and take notes, but quizzes and tests also require *studying*. The developmental level at which studying begins varies considerably. Early elementary students typically are quizzed in spelling and math. In later elementary grades, social studies tests may be added and spelling tests may become vocabulary tests, with students needing to study definitions as well as spelling. At the middle school level, science tests are included and social studies tests are common. However, great variability exists among schools, classrooms, and teachers regarding the introduction and difficulty level of study skills required.

Video Case 11.3 ▲
Teaching Students to Study

© SAGE Publications

FIGURE 11.2 **Note-Taking Techniques.** Outline notes and matrix notes provide the same information but organize that information very differently.

Wildcats: Outline Notes

I. Tiger
  A. Call
    1. Roar
  B. Weight
    1. 450 pounds
  C. Life span
    1. 25 years
  D. Habitat
    1. Jungle
  E. Social behavior
    1. Solitary
II. Lion
  A. Call
    1. Roar
  B. Weight
    1. 400 pounds
  C. Life span
    1. 25 years
  D. Habitat
    1. Plains
  E. Social behavior
    1. Groups

III. Cheetah
  A. Call
    1. Purr
  B. Weight
    1. 125 pounds
  C. Life span
    1. 8 years
  D. Habitat
    1. Plains
  E. Social behavior
    1. Groups
IV. Bobcat
  A. Call
    1. Purr
  B. Weight
    1. 30 pounds
  C. Life span
    1. 6 years
  D. Habitat
    1. Forest
  E. Social behavior
    1. Solitary

Wildcats: Matrix Notes

	Tiger	Lion	Cheetah	Bobcat
Call	Roar	Roar	Purr	Purr
Weight	450	400	125	30
Life span	25	25	8	6
Habitat	Jungle	Plains	Plains	Forest
Social behavior	Solitary	Groups	Groups	Solitary

SOURCE: Kiewra, 2002.

More advanced metacognitive abilities include **study-time allocation,** or the amount of time devoted to studying as well as whether studying will take place over a long period of time or be crammed into a few hours. Specifically, study-time allocation has been closely linked to procedural knowledge or judgments about the difficulty of learning. For example, one student might believe that the list of vocabulary words for this week's English quiz is easy, whereas another student judges the list to be very difficult to learn. According to the *discrepancy reduction model,* individuals with advanced metacognitive skills will determine the difficulty level of items to be studied and allocate more study time to more difficult items (Dunlosky & Hertzog, 1998). However, the extra time spent on difficult items is not consistently related to better performance on tests or evaluations (Metcalfe, 2002).

In an alternative view of study-time allocation, a student should focus on material that is not easy or extremely difficult but just out of grasp, an area Vygotsky termed the *zone of proximal development* (ZPD). A model based on Vygotskian theory, the **region of proximal learning,** suggests that individuals will study items close to being learned but not yet mastered (Metcalfe, 2002). Study-time allocation gradually shifts toward more difficult items, as reflected in changes in the individual's region of proximal learning. Experimental studies have confirmed that allocating study time based on one's own region of proximal learning, rather than on the most difficult items (as the discrepancy reduction model proposes), results in better performance (Kornell & Metcalfe, 2006; Metcalfe & Finn, 2013; Metcalfe & Kornell, 2005).

For the region of proximal learning to be effective, students must engage in metacognitive regulation, particularly in planning and monitoring skills.

- *Planning:* Students must be able to make accurate judgments about what they know and do not know and must plan or prioritize the information to be learned (Metcalfe & Finn, 2008, 2013). Teachers can assist students in planning study time by asking them to make a list of items to be learned, arranging the items from easiest to most difficult.

- *Monitoring:* Students must be able to monitor their learning by continually making judgments about what has and has not been learned during their study time. However, even college students are not good at monitoring their level of preparedness for exams (Peverly et al., 2003). Teachers can assist middle school and high school students in monitoring their progress during study time by teaching them the metacognitive skill of **self-interrogation,** or asking themselves questions to help them gauge whether newly learned material has been mastered. Students can learn to turn headings in their textbook chapters into questions for self-testing. Teachers also can provide sample questions, give quizzes, or ask students to write practice exam questions (Kiewra, 2002).

One study strategy that combines many of the ideas presented here and has been found to be effective is the **SOAR method** (Jairam, Kiewra, Rogers-Kasson, Patterson-Hazley, & Marxhausen, 2014). Although this strategy was designed to be used with college students, it can be taught to high school students as well. The SOAR method includes four components that directly address common study errors (Jairam & Kiewra, 2009, 2010):

- **S** – *Selection.* The teacher provides complete notes, skeletal notes, or cues to combat the common student tendency not to record all of the important information. Many times students highlight text material as a form of selection, but they often select too much or too little material. Teachers' assistance in identifying important material within the text, such as providing an outline of the text material, can be particularly beneficial.

Zone of proximal development: See Module 6

- **O** – *Organization.* Students receive or create graphic organizers such as matrix notes or hierarchies rather than lists or linear notes. Teachers can present visual material in the form of matrices and hierarchies to model this strategy.

- **A** – *Association.* Students identify similarities between items to be learned (comparisons) and differences between items to be learned (contrasts) rather than studying each item separately, one at a time. Again, teachers can model this skill by presenting concepts or material in comparison with other concepts or materials.

- **R** – *Regulation.* Students move beyond simple rehearsal of the material and use self-testing, which involves asking themselves questions to help gauge whether newly learned material has been mastered. Students can learn to turn headings in their textbook chapters into questions for self-testing. Teachers also can provide sample questions, give quizzes, or ask students to write practice exam questions.

Instruction for the specific learning and study strategies just discussed should follow these general guidelines (Baker, 2013; Bruning, Schraw, & Ronning, 1995):

- Explain the value of the learning strategy. Many students do not use strategies because they do not understand how strategy use improves learning and performance.

- Introduce only a few learning strategies at one time to decrease the probability of cognitive overload.

- Explicitly teach and model strategy use for students.

- Provide ample opportunity for students to practice learning strategies.

- Provide feedback to students about their use of learning strategies and improvement in their use.

- Encourage reflection on strategy effectiveness.

Transfer: See Module 12

- Note opportunities for the transfer of learning strategies to other classes or domains.

How will you promote the use of learning strategies in the grade level you expect to teach?

SUMMARY

❶ Describe the two main components of metacognition. Metacognitive knowledge, the first component of metacognition, refers to knowledge about our own cognitive processes. It is divided into person (declarative), task (procedural), and strategy (conditional) knowledge. Metacognitive regulation is the purposeful act of controlling our own thinking, emotions, and values and includes the functions of planning, monitoring, and evaluation. Both metacognitive knowledge and metacognitive regulation develop over time and are related to higher academic achievement.

❷ Explain four characteristics of children's theory of mind. Theory of mind, which describes a child's early understanding of the mental world, involves four characteristics that begin in preschool and become increasingly sophisticated throughout the school-age years: (1) false beliefs, an understanding that beliefs can be accurate or inaccurate; (2) appearance-reality distinctions, the understanding that objects may look one way but actually be something different; (3) visual perspective taking, an ability to understand that another person may visually see something differently from the way you do; and (4) introspection, an awareness of thoughts within one's own and others' minds.

❸ **Explain two consequences related to adolescent egocentrism.** Egocentrism in adolescence includes (1) imaginary audience, the belief that others' thoughts are focused on the individual, and (2) personal fable, or the belief that the individual is so unique that no one else can understand his or her emotions or thoughts. Egocentrism in adolescence begins in an attempt to renegotiate parent–child relationships so they become more adult–adult by balancing separateness and connectedness. The balance of separateness and connectedness continues into adulthood, as does the use of imaginary audience and personal fable, albeit less intensely.

❹ **Explain the factors that influence the development and use of metacognitive skills.** Metacognitive development is influenced by several factors. Biological factors such as neurological deficits and brain damage and familial factors such as conversations between children and their parents and siblings about thinking, learning, and knowledge influence the development of metacognition. Once metacognitive skills begin to develop, individual factors will determine whether those skills are used in learning situations. These factors include the nature of the task and the individual's level of motivation, prior knowledge, and prior success with metacognitive skills.

❺ **Describe how teachers can assist students with reading comprehension and writing skills.** Teachers can improve students' reading comprehension by using reciprocal teaching with younger students and the PQ4R strategy with older students. Both of these strategies require the use of metacognitive skills such as planning, monitoring, and evaluating and improve students' recall and understanding of important ideas. Teachers can improve students' writing skills by encouraging the use of planning techniques such as making rough drafts. They can also assist students in increasing their monitoring skills by asking younger children to think aloud or answer questions about their ideas and by asking older students to reread their initial drafts and make revisions.

❻ **Explain the importance of note taking and study time and describe how teachers can help students improve these learning strategies.** Note taking and study time are both related to higher achievement. Although greater amounts of note taking are related to higher achievement, most students do not record the bulk of important information. Teachers can improve the amount of information students record by teaching them specific note-taking strategies such as using matrix notes. Study time should be based on an individual's region of proximal learning, which requires being able to make accurate judgments about prior knowledge and to-be-learned knowledge. Teachers can assist students in planning and monitoring their study time by asking them to list items to be learned from easiest to most difficult, teaching them self-testing skills, and providing them with sample questions.

KEY CONCEPTS

adolescent egocentrism, 219

appearance-reality distinctions, 217

evaluating, 216

false beliefs, 217

imaginary audience, 219

introspection, 218

metacognition, 215

metacognitive knowledge, 215

metacognitive regulation, 216

monitoring, 216

personal fable, 219

person knowledge, 215

planning, 216

PQ4R, 222

reciprocal teaching, 222

region of proximal learning, 228

self-interrogation, 228

SOAR method, 228

strategy knowledge, 216

study-time allocation, 228

task knowledge, 215

theory of mind, 217

visual perspective taking, 217

CASE STUDIES: REFLECT AND EVALUATE

EARLY CHILDHOOD: 100TH DAY

These questions refer to the case study on page 206.

1. What strategies did Ms. Prendergast use to aid students' reading comprehension?

2. What characteristic of theory of mind is illustrated by Sophia? What does this tell you about Sophia's theory of mind?

3. The nature of the task can influence the way students use metacognitive strategies. How do you think students viewed the nature of the 100th day project task? How might this view have affected their use of metacognitive strategies?

4. How did Ms. Prendergast incorporate planning and monitoring into her students' 100th day projects? Why are those skills important?

5. How could Ms. Prendergast's students use the strategy of evaluation to assess how well their 100th day ideas work?

ELEMENTARY SCHOOL: INVENTION CONVENTION

These questions refer to the case study on page 208.

1. Explain what type(s) of metacognitive knowledge would be needed to complete the assignment for Invention Convention night?

2. Explain the phenomena Isaac is experiencing when he thinks he will be singled out as having a poor project.

3. What reading comprehension strategies were being used by Ms. Bury?

4. How might Ms. Bury have helped the students working at their desks to monitor their writing progress?

5. Was the use of a "cheat sheet" or list of questions to answer in their proposals a good instructional tool? Explain.

MIDDLE SCHOOL: PRESIDENT OR QUEEN FOR A DAY?

These questions refer to the case study on page 210.

1. What categories of metacognitive knowledge did Kirsten display when discussing the difficulties she might have when taking the test?

2. Which student provides an example of a personal fable in this case? How so?

3. What factors in this lesson might have helped or hindered students from using metacognition?

4. What can Mr. Van do to help his students write their position papers? Provide specific strategies.

5. What can Mr. Van do in the future to increase the amount of information recorded in students' notes? Could matrix notes have been used in this lesson? How so?

HIGH SCHOOL: BROWN-EYED GIRL

These questions refer to the case study on page 212.

1. What types of metacognitive knowledge are evident in the students' responses and actions during the lesson?

2. What factors may have led to students not using metacognitive skills?

3. In what way does Ms. Overocker display characteristics of having a personal fable? Is it realistic to think

that a teacher would have a personal fable? Which student also has a personal fable?

4. Some students used their notes from previous class sessions to help them better understand the material, but other students didn't have good notes. What might Ms. Overocker do to increase the usefulness of notes for her students?

5. How could Ms. Overocker have helped students use monitoring and evaluation during the lessons?

©iStockphoto.com/ Wojciech Kozielczyk

MODULE 12

TRANSFER OF SKILLS AND KNOWLEDGE

WHAT IS TRANSFER AND WHY IS IT IMPORTANT?

1 Contrast the specific versus general view of transfer with the high-road versus low-road view.

As teachers, we would all like our students to take what they have learned in our classrooms and find ways to apply that knowledge in other courses and in other contexts of their lives—that is, to transfer their learning. But the transfer of skills and knowledge is easier said than done. Researchers have found it difficult to demonstrate that we spontaneously and successfully transfer our learning from instructional situations to other contexts (Haskell, 2001; Perkins & Salomon, 2012). The research findings tell us that we cannot teach students and *expect* them to find a way to use the information outside school. Rather, we must teach *for* transfer. To do this, teachers must clearly understand the nature of transfer and carefully design instruction with transfer in mind (Perkins & Salomon, 2012).

Transfer can be defined broadly as the influence of prior knowledge, skills, strategies, or principles on new learning. We should be careful not to assume that all transfer is **positive transfer,** in which previous learning facilitates learning on new tasks. Learners can also experience **negative transfer,** in which previous learning hinders learning on new tasks. For example, an elementary school student's misconception that a whale is a fish may lead to making incorrect animal classifications in science class. Learners also may experience **zero transfer,** in which previous learning has no effect on the performance of a new task. For example, a high school student might not apply knowledge learned from a business course to managing money earned from a part-time job.

How, exactly, does prior knowledge influence our behavior in new situations? Psychologists have long debated whether transfer involves specific responses or more general principles and strategies. This debate has led to different definitions of transfer.

Specific Versus General Transfer

An idea popular at the turn of the 20th century, the **doctrine of formal discipline,** advocated a *general* view of transfer in which the study of subjects such as Latin and geometry could improve individuals' general cognitive abilities (such as logical thinking and problem solving), and their improved cognitive functioning then would transfer to other disciplines. In the early 1900s, Edward Thorndike (1923, 1924) provided evidence against the doctrine of formal discipline, showing that students who studied Latin or geometry did not perform better on tests of intellectual reasoning than students who studied other subjects.

Thorndike's alternative to the doctrine of formal discipline, called the **theory of identical elements,** is a *specific* view of transfer. According to this theory, transfer will occur between two learning tasks if the new skill or behavior contains elements that are identical to a skill or behavior from the original task. For example, mastering single-digit addition helps the learning of two-column addition because adding 53 and 26 requires that the individual know 3 + 6 and 5 + 2 and can apply these skills to the problem (Mayer & Wittrock, 1996). According to the specific view of transfer, the more a new learning situation resembles the context in which a skill was learned, the more likely it is that transfer will occur. In contrast, the general view proposes that broad-based cognitive faculties can "leap" across very different learning situations because these general abilities are the same in both contexts.

Today, researchers no longer characterize transfer simply as specific or general. Rather than focusing on this oversimplified dichotomy, experts are interested in investigating:

- how transfer differs depending on the content to be transferred, such as specific knowledge or skills, or more general principles, strategies, and abilities; and

- the extent to which learning transfers from one situation to another, or not.

Keep these issues in mind as we discuss a more contemporary view of transfer next.

Low-Road Versus High-Road Transfer

Salomon and Perkins (1989) provided a more detailed account of transfer than did earlier theories of specific and general transfer. Unlike these earlier theories, their model of transfer specifies *what* exactly transfers and *how* it transfers. Let's explore the types of transfer in their model.

Low-road transfer involves the "spontaneous, automatic transfer of highly practiced skills, with little need for reflective thinking" (Salomon & Perkins, 1989, p. 118). Low-road transfer results from extensive practice of a skill in a variety of contexts until it becomes

Reference: Low-Road Transfer

Master the content.
edge.sagepub.com/durwin3e
SAGE edge™

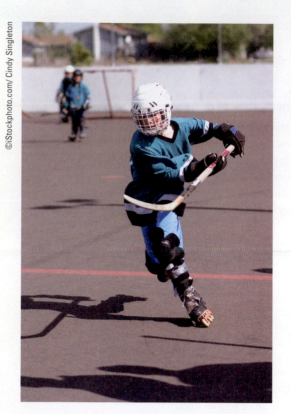

Low-Road Transfer. Acquiring automaticity at ice skating enables low-road transfer to the sport of in-line skating, allowing players to practice hockey during warm weather.

Automaticity: See Modules 10 and 21

Metacognition: See Module 11

Problem solving: See Module 13

flexible and developed to automaticity (Salomon & Perkins, 1989). **Automaticity** occurs when a person performs a skill very quickly, very accurately, and with little attention or other cognitive load. Developing automaticity of a skill allows a person not only to perform the skill without much thought but also to transfer the skill to other, similar situations. Reading and arithmetic are examples of automatic skills that transfer to many situations in and outside school because they have been extensively practiced in varied contexts.

In **high-road transfer,** an individual purposely and consciously applies general knowledge, a strategy, or a principle learned in one situation to a different situation (Salomon & Perkins, 1989). For example, a child who has mastered a puzzle may approach a new and more challenging puzzle by first thinking of the strategies used with the original puzzle. Just as automaticity is the key characteristic of low-road transfer, **mindful abstraction** is the defining feature of high-road transfer. Abstraction is the process of retrieving meaningful information (that has been consciously and actively learned rather than memorized) and applying it to a new learning context. Abstraction is *mindful* when it is guided by metacognition (our awareness, monitoring, and regulation of our thinking), allowing the learner to recognize transfer situations and apply abstract knowledge across contexts (Fuchs et al., 2003). In the puzzle example described, the child reflects on what he or she knows about puzzle solving and applies this knowledge to the new puzzle.

The puzzle example illustrates a type of high-road transfer called **problem-solving transfer,** in which we recall a general strategy or principle that we have learned from solving one type of problem and apply it to solve another type of problem. **Analogical transfer,** another example of high-road transfer, involves creating or using an existing analogy to aid in understanding a new concept, as when science teachers compare the orbit of an electron in an atom (new knowledge) to the orbit of a planet in the solar system (existing knowledge).

High-road transfer can also be described in simple chronological terms. **Forward-reaching transfer** involves learning a principle or strategy so well that an individual selects it quickly and easily when it is needed in future situations. For example, a high school student who has developed a deep, conceptual understanding of geometry might easily think of ways he could use geometric principles in other classes, real-life situations, or future careers. **Backward-reaching transfer,** in contrast, occurs when an individual deliberately looks for strategies or principles learned in the past to solve a current problem or task. A high school student building a birdhouse in a woodworking class might think *back* to last year's geometry class for knowledge that could help him or her calculate the dimensions for the birdhouse.

 Think of your own learning experiences. When have you used transferred knowledge successfully and when have you failed to do so? When have you used forward-reaching or backward-reaching transfer?

DO WE READILY TRANSFER WHAT WE LEARN?

2 Explain why high-road transfer is more difficult to achieve than low-road transfer.

Problem-Solving Transfer. Strategies the child is learning about solving puzzles, such as starting with the edge pieces first, can be consciously retrieved and applied to solving new and more challenging puzzles.

The answer to the question of whether we readily transfer what we learn is not yes or no. Rather, it depends on the content to be transferred, on the situation, and on the initial learning, as we will see. As you read, keep in mind the following questions. In what contexts and under what circumstances do we transfer our learning? What types of knowledge or skills transfer and how *well* were they learned?

The Success of Low-Road Transfer

Consider all the skills you are able to perform automatically. As elementary school students you learned how to read, and as college students you apply those reading skills broadly, to textbooks, magazines, Twitter feeds, and so on. These examples illustrate the success of low-road transfer: Once students develop a skill to automaticity, they can transfer it readily to novel situations. Just as experts such as chess players, musicians, and athletes must engage in thousands of hours of practice at their craft, students must devote an extensive amount of time to honing their skills in areas such as reading, mathematics, computer use, speaking a foreign language, athletics, and playing a musical instrument (Anderson, 1982; Hayes, 1985).

Keep in mind that extensive practice alone is not sufficient for effective transfer to occur. Extensive practice using **rote memorization** (memorizing without understanding) leads to discrete bits of information or skills in long-term memory (permanent storage for all of the information we have learned) that are not meaningfully connected and fade over time, making transfer less likely. To ensure that low-road transfer occurs, students should engage in reflective and deliberate practice rather than rote memorization (Haskell, 2001). **Reflective practice** involves developing a conceptual understanding. For example, students must practice $2 \times 3 = 6$ to automaticity, but they also need to understand the concept behind this fact. **Deliberate practice** involves an intrinsic motivation to engage in extensive, focused, long-term repetition with the goal of learning the skill and improving performance, not just "going through the motions" of practicing (Duckworth, Kirby, Tsukayama, Berstein, & Ericsson, 2011; Ericsson, 2006). Extensive, deliberate practice is needed to sufficiently develop skills that readily transfer. A minimum of 100 hours of practice is needed for development of modest levels of skill proficiency and about 10,000 hours are needed for development of expert performance (Anderson, 1982; Ericsson & Ward, 2007).

Long-term memory: See Module 10

Automaticity: See Module 21

Deliberate Practice. Musicians engage in many hours of deliberate practice to acquire skill proficiency.

The Problem of High-Road Transfer

To understand the problem of high-road transfer, first read the following story and problem, used in research by Mary Gick and Keith Holyoak (1980, 1983):

MILITARY STORY

A small country was ruled from a strong fortress by a dictator. The fortress was situated in the middle of the country, surrounded by farms and villages. Many roads led to the fortress through the countryside. A rebel general vowed to capture the fortress. The general knew that an attack by his entire army would capture the fortress. He gathered his army at the head of one of the roads, ready to launch a full-scale direct attack. However, the general then learned that the dictator had planted mines on each of the roads. The mines were set so that small bodies of men could pass over them safely, since the dictator needed to move his troops and workers to and from the fortress. However, any large force would detonate the mines. Not only would this blow up the road, but it would also destroy many neighboring villages. It therefore seemed impossible to capture the fortress. However, the general devised a simple plan. He divided his army into small groups and dispatched each group to the head of a different road. When all was ready he gave the signal and each group marched down a different road. Each group continued down its road to the fortress so that the entire army arrived together at the fortress at the same time. In this way, the general captured the fortress and overthrew the dictator. (Gick & Holyoak, 1980, p. 351)

MEDICAL PROBLEM

Suppose you are a doctor faced with a patient who has a malignant tumor in his stomach. It is impossible to operate on the patient, but unless the tumor is destroyed the patient will die. There is a kind of ray that can be used to destroy the tumor. If the rays reach the tumor all at once at a sufficiently high intensity, the tumor will be destroyed. Unfortunately, at this intensity the healthy tissue that the rays pass through on the way to the tumor will also be destroyed. At lower intensities the rays are harmless to healthy tissue, but they will not affect the tumor either. What type of procedure might be used to destroy the tumor with the rays, and at the same time avoid destroying the healthy tissue? (Duncker, 1945, pp. 307–308)

Did you solve the medical problem? If not, reread the military story for a hint. In the study, college students read the medical problem after reading the military story, which provides an analogous solution to the medical problem. When prompted to use the military story to help solve the medical problem, the majority of students arrived at the correct solution: Use the convergence of several rays at lower intensities from different angles. However, significantly fewer students were able to generate the solution without the hint given by the military story. This example, like several other classic experimental studies, illustrates a well-known finding—students often fail to *spontaneously* transfer what they have learned from a previous problem to a structurally similar problem, even when the new problem is presented immediately after the original problem (Gick & Holyoak, 1983; Hayes & Simon, 1977; Reed, Ernst, & Banerji, 1974).

Experimental studies indicate that high-road transfer involving problem solving and analogies is rare because students lack one or more of three skills needed for successful transfer across seemingly different learning situations (Mayer & Wittrock, 1996; Perkins & Salomon, 2012):

1. *Recognition.* Very simply, this refers to the ability to detect a link between the new situation and prior knowledge. Students often fail to recognize that they have an analogous solution in their memory that they can apply to solving a new problem. In the study described earlier, for example, most students did not think of the convergence solution to the tumor problem unless the researcher explicitly directed them to search previously read stories for a hint about the solution. A primary reason for recognition failure is that students have acquired inert knowledge—discrete facts and concepts that are not deeply learned or richly connected to other knowledge (Chi & VanLehn, 2012; Perkins & Salomon, 2012). Overcoming recognition failure requires instruction that promotes reflective and elaborative processing, which encourages students to connect new learning in meaningful ways to their prior knowledge (Perkins & Salomon, 2012).

    Elaborative rehearsal: See Module 10

2. *Abstraction.* Students often fail to abstract the general principle or strategy. In the study described, reading two stories with the same solution enhanced students' ability to abstract the analogy for the tumor solution, compared to reading one story with the solution and one irrelevant story. This suggests that students may need a lot of varied exposure to problems for them to become successful at recognizing and abstracting analogous strategies.

3. *Mapping.* Students may fail to transfer because of difficulty mapping—making appropriate connections between the original and the new problem—especially when the problems appear very dissimilar on the surface (Holyoak & Koh, 1987; Reed, 1987). Consider the training and transfer problems that follow, which are adapted from research by Reed (1987):

    i. *Training problem:*

    A nurse mixes a 6% boric acid solution with a 12% boric acid solution. How many pints of each are needed to make 4.5 pints of an 8% boric acid solution?

    ii. *Transfer problem:*

    A grocer mixes peanuts worth $1.65 a pound and almonds worth $2.10 a pound. How many pounds of each are needed to make 30 pounds of a mixture worth $1.83 a pound?

The two mathematical problems involve an identical solution but look very different—one is about mixtures of boric acid, and the other is about mixing peanuts and almonds. The difference between experts and novices in problem solving is that experts can see past the surface features to detect underlying principles because of their richly connected knowledge base (Chi & VanLehn, 2012). For novices, learning how to solve one problem often does not help them solve a new problem that looks different but has the same solution because their more superficial knowledge base prevents successful mapping (Gick & Holyoak, 1983; Hayes & Simon, 1977; Reed, 1987). At the end of the module, we discuss approaches to encourage successful transfer of problem solving.

Research on the transfer of school learning to other contexts is equally discouraging. Although some research demonstrates successful transfer of strategies from one subject to a different learning context in school (Adey & Shayer, 1993; Chen & Klahr, 1999), other research shows a general failure of students to apply what they have learned in school to novel tasks (Brown, Campione, Webber, & McGilly, 1992; Nickerson, Perkins, & Smith, 1985). For example, students typically do not exhibit transfer of mathematical problem solving (Bransford & Schwartz, 1999; Mayer, Quilici, & Moreno, 1999). This is especially true for elementary school students who have difficulty applying computational skills when problems change in minor ways, as in the training and transfer problems described earlier (Durnin, Perrone, & MacKay, 1997; Larkin, 1989). Likewise, children and adults rarely apply

TABLE 12.1	Distinguishing Between Near and Far Transfer		
DOMAIN	**DESCRIPTION**	**NEAR EXAMPLE**	**FAR EXAMPLE**
Subject matter	Knowledge may transfer to a similar or very different subject matter.	Using knowledge from a calculus class to solve equations in a physics class	Using knowledge of the scientific method (science class) as part of a persuasive writing assignment (English class)
Physical context	Knowledge may transfer from one context to a similar physical context or to a different environment.	Applying knowledge about liquid measures to solving word problems at school	Applying knowledge about liquid measures to bake a cake at home
Functional context	Knowledge learned for one purpose may transfer to a similar purpose or to a very different purpose.[a]	Using knowledge of calculating percentages in math class to solve word problems (both academic purposes)	Using knowledge of calculating percentages (academic) to figure out batting averages of favorite baseball players (recreational)
Temporal context	Near and far transfer can be distinguished by the length of time between learning and transfer.	Transferring knowledge over a short period of time (same or next day)	Transferring knowledge over a longer time lapse (weeks, months, or years later)
Social context	Knowledge in the learning and transfer situations may involve a similar social context or different social contexts.	Working alone in both learning and transfer situations	Using what has been learned from a group activity to do independent research
Modality	Knowledge in learning and transfer situations may involve the same or a different modality.	Listening to a lecture on fetal pig dissection and being able to describe the process to a friend (oral modality for both)	Listening to a lecture on fetal pig dissection and being able to perform the dissection (oral versus hands-on)

SOURCE: Adapted from Barnett and Ceci, 2002.

[a] Physical and functional contexts sometimes overlap. For example, baking a cake at home can be far transfer in terms of physical context (outside school) and functional context (real-life purpose). However, physical and functional context can also be distinct. A student may use percentages to calculate his or her favorite players' batting averages at an afterschool program at school (similar physical context, different purpose).

school-taught procedures to problems they encounter in real life, such as determining a better buy in a supermarket (Lave, 1988; Saxe, 2002; Schliemann & Acioly, 1989).

Why do individuals seldom transfer school-learned knowledge to real-life contexts? One line of research suggests that they may not have learned the knowledge in a sufficiently meaningful and lasting way in the first place (Bereiter, 1995; Chi & VanLehn, 2012). Instruction that relies primarily on rote memorization or *convergent thinking* (obtaining the one right answer to a question) produces a narrow ability to answer only certain kinds of questions rather than encourages students to acquire flexible knowledge that can be recognized, abstracted, and mapped to new situations. Experimental studies have shown that learners who understand concepts and procedures are more likely to transfer their learning to novel contexts than students who learn by rote memorization (Adams et al., 1988; Bransford et al., 2000). For example, fourth- and fifth-grade students were more likely to engage in transfer of mathematical problems if they learned conceptual principles rather than simply memorizing procedures (Perry, 1991).

Convergent thinking: See Modules 13 and 18

Another line of research suggests that high-road transfer of school-learned knowledge may be limited by the extent to which the learning and transfer contexts are similar (Barnett & Ceci, 2002). As Table 12.1 illustrates, learning and transfer contexts may differ on several dimensions, including subject matter, physical features, and purpose. We may readily engage in **near transfer,** which involves applying prior knowledge to new situations that are very similar, but not identical to, the learning context. However, we may be less likely to engage in **far transfer,** or applying prior knowledge to a context that is very different from the learning context. We may not realize that our knowledge is relevant in a context that is very different from the learning context (Perkins & Salomon, 2012; Singley & Anderson, 1989). We also may find it difficult to recognize uses for our school-learned knowledge when faced with real-life tasks if the content taught in school is disconnected from a clear goal or purpose for learning it (Barnett & Ceci, 2002; Perkins & Salomon, 2012). Transfer across very different contexts may occur rarely simply because it requires so much effort (Gage & Berliner, 1992).

Think about your school experiences. Were you encouraged to memorize, or to think, solve problems, and practice using your knowledge? How might teaching methods have affected transfer opportunities?

APPLICATIONS: HOW TO FACILITATE TRANSFER

3 Identify four teaching principles that support transfer, and explain how each facilitates transfer.

Teachers can use several research-based principles, discussed next, to help them design instruction that will foster transfer. Similarly, these guidelines can help students adopt learning strategies that lead to more efficient transfer.

Develop Automaticity of Skills

To facilitate low-road transfer of academic skills, teachers should provide students with many opportunities to practice and achieve automaticity of academic skills. To be effective, practice needs to (Haskell, 2001):

- be reflective rather than rote,
- occur in a variety of contexts, and
- involve **overlearning,** in which students engage in continued practice after they have demonstrated mastery. Skills continue to improve long after individuals achieve complete accuracy (Schneider, 1985).

Video Case 12.1 ▲
Counting by Fives: Developing Automaticity

© SAGE Publications

Developing automaticity does not necessarily mean that teachers need to use drill and practice, a method that relies on flash cards and rote memorization. The use of drill and practice has declined since the 1970s, after it acquired a reputation as "drill and kill," meaning that its lack of meaningful context or purpose for learning *killed* students' motivation. However, extensive practice leading to automaticity can occur within the context of meaningful and fun academic tasks such as problem solving, collaborative activities, computer games, and classroom games.

Word recognition: See Modules 7 and 21

Developing automaticity can also facilitate high-road transfer. Students who attain automaticity of lower level skills, such as word recognition (the ability to accurately and automatically identify words in text) and arithmetic computation, are able to focus more cognitive resources on higher level cognitive skills, such as comprehension, planning, monitoring, and problem solving (Case, 1985; Geary, 1994; Perfetti, 1992). Greater attention to higher level skills during learning will increase the likelihood of high-road transfer in elementary as well as middle and high school students. For example, a high school student who can automatically perform the arithmetic operations of algebra is more likely to understand and transfer algebraic problem solving than is a student who struggles with arithmetic operations.

DIVERSITY ⟨

Even though automaticity enables the development of higher level cognitive skills such as reading comprehension, problem solving, and reasoning, a lack of automaticity should not be used as an excuse for delaying students' exposure to complex cognitive skills. Often, lower achieving students will continue to receive basic skills instruction and drill and practice as a prerequisite for progressing to instruction in higher level skills. As a result, lower achieving students receive less instruction in these higher order thinking skills and fall farther behind their peers as they move through higher grades, when complex cognitive skills become increasingly important (Means & Knapp, 1994).

Higher order thinking: See Module 13

Teachers can prevent lower achieving students from falling farther behind their peers by following two simple principles.

1. *Create problem-solving tasks that remove the constraint of automaticity.* Students can use calculators for mathematical problem solving, dictate essays to remove grammatical constraints, and draft essays or journals without worrying about handwriting, spelling, or punctuation (Glynn, Britton, Muth, & Dogan, 1982; Scardamalia, Bereiter, & Goelman, 1982).

Reciprocal teaching: See Modules 11 and 18

Scaffolding: See Module 6

2. *Supplement basic skills instruction with teaching methods that focus on higher level cognitive skills.* For example, teachers can use *reciprocal teaching,* a method of teaching metacognitive strategies important for reading comprehension. In this method, the teacher models strategies of summarizing, questioning, clarifying, and predicting and provides *scaffolding* (support, hints, and prompts) to help students acquire and later demonstrate these strategies on their own, without the teacher's assistance. Reciprocal teaching has improved the reading comprehension of students with poor reading skills from elementary through secondary education (Kelly, Moore, & Tuck, 1994; Palincsar & Brown, 1984; Rosenshine & Meister, 1994). It is also effective when used with:

Learning disabilities and intellectual disabilities: See Module 21

- students with learning disabilities from elementary through middle school (Gajria, Jitendra, Sood, & Sacks, 2007; Lederer, 2000),

- students with mild intellectual disabilities (Lundberg & Reichenberg, 2013), and

English language learners: See Module 7

- students who are English language learners (Choo, Eng, & Ahmad, 2011; Ghorbani, Gangeraj, & Alavi, 2013; Ostovar-Namaghi & Shahhosseini, 2011).

Promote Meaningful Learning

High-road transfer relies on active, meaningful learning in which students possess deep-level knowledge structures (not discrete facts acquired by rote memorization) that are connected to similar concepts, prior knowledge, and real-life experiences (Bransford & Schwartz, 1999; Day & Goldstone, 2012; Salomon & Perkins, 1989). Teachers can use a variety of techniques for encouraging meaningful learning.

Take inventory of students' prior knowledge before beginning a new lesson or topic. Teachers can prevent negative transfer by determining what students already know about a topic, identifying inaccurate prior knowledge, and correcting it before teaching new information. Tapping into students' prior knowledge will also help students see the relevance of new material and enable them to integrate it with their existing knowledge, facilitating forward-reaching transfer (Engle, Lam, Meyer, & Nix, 2012; Schwartz, Bransford, & Sears, 2005). Teachers can do this by asking students to brainstorm what they know about a topic, and students can adopt a strategy of asking themselves "What do I know about this topic already?" when they read a textbook or research a topic. **KWL,** a popular method used in schools, shown in Figure 12.1, taps into prior knowledge by requiring students to list their *Knowledge* about a topic and *What questions* they have before instruction begins (Ogle, 2009). To complete the process, students list what they *Learned* from instruction. Research indicates that KWL can improve students' metacognition, reading comprehension, and achievement (Al-Khateeb & Idrees, 2010; Cantrell, Fusaro, & Dougherty, 2000; Tok, 2013). Teaching students to use this strategy can transfer to varied subjects.

Require students to construct relationships between new information and their prior knowledge. Teachers can ask students to think of their own examples of a concept rather than memorizing the example given in a textbook. Such methods have been used successfully in subjects that include reading, mathematics, science, economics, and geography (Mackenzie & White, 1982; Osborne & Wittrock, 1983; Peled & Wittrock, 1990) and with students from lower socioeconomic backgrounds (Kourilsky & Wittrock, 1992). In subjects that involve calculating a solution to a problem, such as math or science, teachers can encourage students to construct their own representations or models of the problems to aid their understanding with proper support so that students do not develop incorrect knowledge. Elementary school students might draw five groups of six circles to help calculate a story problem involving the operation 5 × 6, or high school students might draw an incline and other attributes of a physics problem. Constructing one's own

Meaningful learning: See Module 18

Video Case 12.2 ▲
Promoting Meaningful Learning

© SAGE Publications

Video: The KWL Strategy

❯ **DIVERSITY**

Video Case 12.3 ▲
Transferring Knowledge to New Situations

© SAGE Publications

FIGURE 12.1   **Tapping Into Prior Knowledge.** KWL, shown here, can help prevent negative transfer by assessing students' prior knowledge before a lesson.

K What I *know*	W What I *want* to learn	L What I have *learned*
Magnets stick to metal. Magnets are black.	How do they attract things? Why don't they attract some objects?	Opposite poles attract; same repel. Magnets work in water. Magnets don't attract plastic or aluminum.

problem representation improves students' learning and transfer of their knowledge to new, complex problems, benefiting both low and high achievers (Terwel, van Oers, van Dijk, & van den Eeden, 2009).

Encourage the use of question-answering and self-explanation strategies. Teachers can encourage students to generate questions while reading their textbooks and answer them. Questions that focus on acquiring deep, conceptual knowledge, rather than finding answers to factual questions, are best because they facilitate students' transfer of knowledge to new examples or new problems (Bugg & McDaniel, 2012; Chi & VanLehn, 2012). Generating questions and their corresponding answers can improve recall more than just rereading the text alone (Weinstein, McDermott, & Roediger, 2010). Because it takes additional time to generate and answer one's own questions, a comparable strategy is to have teachers supply the questions to be answered (Weinstein et al., 2010). Teachers can also encourage self-explanation, as when students explain concepts in expository texts, or describe their solutions or their steps taken in solving problems in math and other subjects. Students show deeper learning and greater transfer when using self-explanation because it promotes the integration of new content with existing knowledge (Chi, 2000; Tajika & Nakatsu, 2005; Tajika, Nakatsu, Nozaki, Neumann, & Maruno, 2007).

Use manipulatives. These are materials that encourage active learning and help students make a connection between a concrete situation and a more abstract principle (Mayer & Wittrock, 1996). Hands-on activities involving experiments can be used in science at all grade levels, and beads, Dienes blocks, or any other concrete objects can help elementary school students learn computational principles in math (Champagne, Gunstone, & Klopfer, 1985; Montessori, 1964). The acquisition of deeper conceptual knowledge by using manipulatives can facilitate transfer (Bugg & McDaniel, 2012; Chi & VanLehn, 2012).

Teach by analogy. Science educators are increasingly using analogies as a way to tap students' prior knowledge about topics (Haskell, 2001). For example, teachers can use the solar system as an analogy for learning about the atom, or use the flow of water through pipes to introduce the concepts of current and voltage in electrical circuits (Brooks & Dansereau, 1987; Vendetti, Matlen, Richland, & Bunge, 2015). Simply presenting an analogy is often ineffective (Richland, Zur, & Holyoak, 2007). Therefore, there are several techniques teachers can use to encourage analogical reasoning and improve transfer.

- Because students have difficulty mapping—making appropriate connections between the analogy and a new problem—teachers should check students' understanding of prior concepts to prevent incorrect application of the analogy (negative transfer).

- Presenting cases or examples simultaneously rather than sequentially also improves transfer because it enables students to see similarities between the cases and abstract a general principle (Alfieri, Nokes-Malach, & Schunn, 2013; Nokes-Malach, VanLehn, Belenky, Lichtenstein, & Cox, 2013).

- Highlighting both the similarities and differences among the source example (the solar system in the previous example) and the target information (the atom) can improve learning and transfer. If the difference can potentially lead to incorrect mapping, teachers should explain where the analogy "breaks down" (Vendetti et al., 2015).

Use worked-out examples for practice in problem solving. In a worked-out example, students can see the solution and the steps involved in reaching the solution. Using worked-out examples enhances learning and transfer (Renkl, 2005; Renkl & Atkinson, 2010). This effect has been found for well-defined domains such as math and science as well as more ill-defined subjects such as music, writing, and psychology (Hübner, Nückles, & Renkl, 2010; Kyun, Kalyuga, & Sweller, 2013; Owen & Sweller, 2008; Sweller, Ayres, & Kalyuga, 2011).

Well-defined and ill-defined problems: See Module 13

Reading and studying a worked example may result in near transfer, where students can successfully solve new problems that have similar features to the ones they studied (Nokes-Malach et al., 2013). To encourage far transfer, where students are able to solve new problems that have different features, teachers can follow these guidelines:

- Use worked-out examples that differ in only one key feature from the current problem (Jee et al., 2013; Smith et al., 2014). This is especially important for younger learners (Gentner, Loewenstein, & Thompson, 2003; Reed, 1987).

- Have students actively attempt to understand the worked example using self-explanation, the drawing of analogies between problems, or problem-solving activities (Nokes-Malach et al., 2013; Renkl, Atkinson, & Maier, 2000; Wittwer & Renkl, 2008).

- Ask students to compare two examples rather than examine a single example or study two examples independently (Gentner & Namy, 2004; Silver, Ghousseini, Gosen, Charalambous, & Strawhun, 2005).

- Present multiple dissimilar examples, which encourages students to recognize their underlying similarities and can help them acquire general principles that can be applied across contexts (Day & Goldstone, 2012).

Present similar concepts in multiple contexts. Presenting similar concepts in different contexts prevents students from tying knowledge only to the context in which it was learned and encourages far transfer (Engle et al., 2012; Salomon & Perkins, 1989). Teachers can introduce new concepts in the context of relevant previous knowledge (backward-reaching transfer) and in the context of potential uses for the new knowledge (forward-reaching transfer; Engle et al., 2012). Periodically, they should return to topics or concepts but on different levels and in different contexts (Haskell, 2001). Teachers also can encourage students to learn general strategies or principles in many contexts so they can flexibly apply what they have learned to a variety of situations (Perkins, Jay, & Tishman, 1993; Prawat, 1989).

Teach Metacognitive Strategies

Because successful transfer requires the ability to identify appropriate transfer situations, it is important to teach students metacognitive strategies for recognizing situations in which they can use their knowledge. Recent research with elementary and middle school students indicates several benefits of teaching metacognitive strategies.

- Explicitly teaching elementary school students what transfer is leads to greater far transfer on novel problems in comparison with students not instructed about transfer (Fuchs et al., 2003). Teachers in this study taught students the concept of transfer (meaning to move), gave examples of how students transfer skills (moving from two-digit horizontal problems to two-digit vertical problems), and reviewed the meaning of transfer in every unit. Both lower and higher achievers benefitted from this instruction, in contrast to earlier research suggesting that transfer is difficult for low-achieving students (Fuchs, Fuchs, Kams, Hamlett, & Karzaroff, 1999; Mayer, 1998; Woodward & Baxter, 1997).

- Providing students with practice using metacognitive strategies can facilitate transfer. In the elementary grades, practice at classifying different types of problems, solving partially worked-out examples, and being prompted to think of previous solutions when solving new problems can facilitate transfer (Fuchs et al., 2003). Practice with multiple types of problems can help students overcome their difficulties

Video Case 12.4 ▲
Teaching Real-Life Math Skills

© SAGE Publications

Metacognition: See Module 11

 **DIVERSITY**

both in *abstracting* principles or solutions and in *mapping* solutions from previously learned problems to new ones. Also, teaching middle school students planning, monitoring, and evaluation skills in the context of solving various problems can lead to near and far transfer compared with conventional instruction (Zepeda, Richey, Ronevich, & Nokes-Malach, 2015).

- Teaching adolescents a general problem-solving strategy may be more effective for promoting both near and far transfer than conventional instruction. In recent research, students who were taught a general strategy for geometry, such as "find as many angles as you can in any order," performed better than those who were taught the conventional method of finding the value of a certain angle, and lower achieving students benefitted most from this general strategy (Youssef-Shalala, Ayres, & Schubert, 2014).

Teachers can incorporate metacognitive strategies in their lessons in many ways, from simple cuing to more explicit instruction. They can begin by having students cue themselves: "Do I know anything from [other subjects or problems] that might help here?" (Salomon & Perkins, 1989). Cuing the relevance of recently learned information or the similarities across tasks facilitates backward-reaching transfer (Catrambone & Holyoak, 1989; Ross, 1987, 1989). To get students to independently recognize transfer situations without the aid of external cues, teachers can explicitly teach metacognitive strategies—such as the scientific method, Internet research, reading comprehension strategies, and problem-solving strategies—in many different subjects. Both in-class activities and out-of-class assignments can provide students with opportunities for practicing strategies in the context of subject-matter instruction. Explicit instruction in reading and mathematics strategies can encourage high-road transfer, especially among lower achievers (Fuchs et al., 2003; Gajria et al., 2007).

Motivate Students to Value Learning

Motivation to learn: See Module 14

Students' motivation to learn and to take advantage of transfer opportunities can lead to higher levels of transfer (Colquitt, LePine, & Noe, 2000; Pea, 1987). Teachers can facilitate transfer by using several techniques to encourage students to take an interest in and value learning.

Mastery goals: See Module 15

Encourage students to set mastery goals. Students with **mastery goals** focus on mastering a task, growing intellectually, and acquiring new skills and knowledge (in contrast with learning for the sake of passing a test or getting a good grade). As a result, they are more likely to (Grant & Dweck, 2003; Wolters, 2004):

- engage in meaningful learning (or deep-level processing),

- use metacognitive strategies, and

- show high levels of effort.

All of these behaviors have been linked to greater likelihood of transfer (Elliot & Murayama, 2008; Pugh & Bergin, 2006). Students with mastery goals are more likely to engage in backward-reaching transfer—looking for learned information that may be helpful to their current understanding—and forward-reaching transfer—looking for ways to apply their newly learned knowledge. Part of being a good student is acquiring a tendency to independently look for transfer opportunities (Salomon & Perkins, 1989).

Capitalize on students' natural interests when teaching new topics. Students who come to school with **individual interest**—an intrinsic interest in a particular subject or activity because it is considered to be personally meaningful and enjoyable—are more

Video Case 12.5 ▲
Motivating Students to Value Learning

© SAGE Publications

likely to use deep-level processing in learning content (Ainley, Hidi, & Berndorff, 2002; Linnenbrink-Garcia, Patall, & Messersmith, 2013). A student who is interested in a particular topic may consciously look for ways the material can be applied in other contexts, facilitating forward-reaching transfer (Salomon & Perkins, 1989). For example, a high school student who wants to become a doctor might be interested in ways science topics can be applied to medicine and therefore be more likely to engage in forward-reaching transfer in science classes.

Use techniques to create situational interest. Because many students will not show individual interest in subjects or topics, teachers can spark **situational interest**—an immediate interest in a particular lesson—to encourage meaningful learning and transfer (Covington, 2000; Linnenbrink-Garcia et al., 2013). Introducing new material using enthusiasm, novelty, and surprise, and providing choice for learning activities, can trigger situational interest (Ciani Ferguson, Bergin, & Hilpert, 2010; Palmer, 2009; Tsai, Kunter, Ludtke, Trautwein, & Ryan, 2008). Situational interest also can be achieved by using social interactions and hands-on activities during lessons (Del Favero, Boscolo, Vidotto, & Vicentini, 2007; Palmer, 2009).

Situational interest: See Module 14

For situational interest to benefit learning and transfer, it must be maintained over the course of instruction. In some cases, students experience a fleeting sense of situational interest—momentary engagement and attention—from the instructional methods rather than the content of the instruction (Linnenbrink-Garcia et al., 2010). Such situational interest might *not* lead to transfer because it can be superficial and unrelated to learning goals (Bergin, 1999; Linnenbrink-Garcia et al., 2013). Consider these examples:

- When elementary school teachers use manipulatives to make math fun, this approach may not foster deep thinking about mathematical principles (Moyer, 2002).

- When lessons or textbooks include **seductive details**—highly interesting but non-essential information to engage students in the learning process—students may or may not recall the important information and are very unlikely to transfer learned material (Day & Goldstone, 2012; Harp & Mayer, 1998; Mayer, Griffith, Jurkowitz, & Rothman, 2008). These details activate prior knowledge that is not directly related to the material to be learned, making it less likely that students will deeply process the important points (Mayer et al., 2008; Pugh & Bergin, 2006). Using seductive details in lessons and lectures can attract students' immediate interest, but it may undermine effective learning that would lead to transfer.

Encourage students to acquire critical dispositions (attitudes and values) about thinking and learning. High-road, far transfer requires students to develop a conscious and purposeful approach to acquiring knowledge (Langer, 1993; Salomon & Globerson, 1987). If students are taught to think scientifically and critically about concepts in particular subjects such as science, math, or literature, they will learn to value this type of thinking and will be more likely to transfer this disposition to other subjects and to real-life experiences (Bereiter, 1995). When learning, students also must be motivated to look for connections to prior knowledge and to potential uses for their newly acquired concepts and skills (Perkins & Salomon, 2012). Encouraging students to see that what they are learning has relevance in the future, such as in subsequent courses they may take or in career goals, and can promote a sense of value in learning, increase intrinsic motivation, and lead to deep-level learning and transfer (Engle et al., 2012; Hulleman, Durik, Schweigert, & Harackiewicz, 2008).

Intrinsic motivation: See Module 14

Think of some specific ways you can implement these guidelines in the grade you intend to teach.

SUMMARY

❶ Contrast the specific versus general view of transfer with the high-road versus low-road view. The general view of transfer proposes that certain school experiences allow transfer of general mental functions to new situations, while the specific view claims that specific behaviors transfer but only to the extent that the original and new situations share common elements. The low-road versus high-road distinction provides a more detailed account of transfer than earlier theories of specific and general transfer. This distinction specifies *what* exactly transfers and *how* it transfers. In low-road transfer, highly practiced skills are automatically applied from one situation to the next, whereas high-road transfer involves the conscious and reflective application of abstract knowledge from one context to a very different context.

❷ Explain why high-road transfer is more difficult to achieve than low-road transfer. Low-road transfer—the spontaneous transfer of automatic skills—is relatively easy to achieve because students have extensively practiced skills in a variety of contexts and have developed them to automaticity. High-road transfer—a conscious retrieval of abstract knowledge, principles, or strategies from one situation to a very different situation—is more difficult to achieve because knowledge sometimes is not learned in a meaningful way. Also, applying knowledge from one context to very dissimilar physical, functional, or social contexts requires a lot of cognitive effort.

❸ Identify four teaching principles that support transfer, and explain how each facilitates transfer. (1) Require students to develop automaticity of skills. This leads to low-road transfer and frees up cognitive resources for use on higher level tasks. (2) Promote meaningful learning, in which students form a rich, interconnected knowledge base of concepts, principles, and strategies. Deep-level knowledge is more likely to transfer to a variety of situations. (3) Teach metacognitive strategies so students recognize high-road transfer situations. (4) Motivate students to value learning, which may enhance the likelihood of transfer. Students with individual interest in a topic and with mastery goals are more likely to process information deeply and to look for ways to apply their knowledge.

KEY CONCEPTS

CASE STUDIES: REFLECT AND EVALUATE

EARLY CHILDHOOD: 100TH DAY

These questions refer to the case study on page 206.

1. How do the 100th day activities encourage reflective practice of arithmetic concepts? How does reflective practice facilitate low-road transfer?

2. Are the 100th day projects that the children complete an example of near transfer or far transfer? Use the information in Table 12.1 to support your answer.

3. Do you consider the 100th day activities meaningful learning? How does this affect transfer?

4. Based on the research on high-road transfer, explain why the children can't see that Lily's red plastic cups are a way to solve the sticker problem. Did you have a similar experience with the medical problem and military story in the module?

5. Evaluate Ms. Prendergast's teaching using the four principles for facilitating transfer.

ELEMENTARY SCHOOL: Invention Convention

These questions refer to the case study on page 208.

1. Ms. Bury expects her students to readily transfer their writing skills to writing the proposal for the Invention Convention. Based on low-road transfer, is this a realistic expectation? Why or why not?

2. Explain whether Allen's idea of the unlevel plate is an example of near or far transfer.

3. Explain how Ms. Bury's use of a story about inventions can be a worked-out example. What benefits do worked-out examples have for transfer?

4. What metacognitive strategies did Ms. Bury and Mr. Grant encourage in their students? How does teaching metacognitive strategies promote transfer?

5. Evaluate whether the assignments that Ms. Bury and Mr. Grant gave for the Invention Convention promoted meaningful learning. What could they have done differently, and how would this affect the students' ability to transfer their knowledge to the projects?

MIDDLE SCHOOL: President or Queen for a Day?

These questions refer to the case study on page 210.

1. Do Mr. Van's class activities promote meaningful learning? Why or why not? How does meaningful learning relate to transfer?

2. Use Table 12.1 to evaluate whether comparing the systems of government between the United States and the United Kingdom represents near or far transfer.

3. Laura seems to have forgotten from a previous lesson how the government in the United Kingdom compared to that of the United States. What might account for her failure to transfer this knowledge?

4. The students are concerned with memorizing information for an upcoming test. Explain to the students the disadvantages of rote memorization for learning and transfer.

5. Using the principles for promoting transfer discussed at the end of the module, evaluate Mr. Van's teaching. What does he do well, and how does that promote transfer? What can he improve upon?

6. Can you think of other ways to foster transfer of knowledge in middle school social studies? What about other subjects? Think of at least one way in which teachers can facilitate transfer in a subject such as English, math, or science.

HIGH SCHOOL: Brown-Eyed Girl

These questions refer to the case study on page 212.

1. Does the Punnett square activity promote meaningful learning? Why or why not? How does meaningful learning relate to transfer?

2. Xander and Wyatt disagree about the outcome of the green-eyed/blue-eyed Punnett square problem. Explain why Xander is having difficulty transferring knowledge from yesterday's brown-eyed/blue-eyed example, using the concepts of *recognition, abstraction,* and *mapping.*

3. Using Table 12.1, explain whether the pop quiz is considered near transfer or far transfer.

4. Ms. Overocker asks students to create their own examples of a Punnett square. Does this activity require near or far transfer? Does the activity involve low-road or high-road transfer? Does it involve forward-reaching or backward-reaching transfer?

5. Some of Ms. Overocker's students prefer taking multiple-choice tests. Explain to the students how the use of rote memorization to study for tests affects learning and transfer.

6. Ms. Overocker seems frustrated by her students' inability to complete the class activities such as creating an original Punnett square and debating the ethics of genetic testing. Use the guidelines for facilitating transfer to provide Ms. Overocker with suggestions for improving her activities.

APPLY AND PRACTICE WHAT YOU'VE LEARNED

▶ edge.sagepub.com/durwin3e

**CHECK YOUR COMPREHENSION
ON THE STUDENT STUDY SITE**

- **eFlashcards** to strengthen your understanding of key terms

- Practice **quizzes** to test your knowledge of key concepts

- **Videos and multimedia content** to enhance your exploration of key topics

©iStockphoto.com/ davidf

MODULE 13

HIGHER ORDER THINKING

WHAT IS HIGHER ORDER THINKING AND WHY IS IT IMPORTANT?

❶ Define higher order thinking and explain why it is important in the current educational climate.

Not all thinking is equal. Some cognitive process are viewed as lower level that require basic facts and skills. These can be accomplished by memorization and reproduction of behaviors.

Higher order thinking refers to more advanced or complex cognitive processes that may include integrating facts, applying knowledge and skills, as well as analyzing and evaluating information. Levels of thinking abilities are most often viewed from Bloom's taxonomy (Anderson & Krathwohl, 2001; Bloom, Englehart, Frost, Hill, & Krathwohl, 1956). Figure 13.1 depicts the six levels of Bloom's taxonomy. The first three are typically considered lower level thinking and the next three are considered higher order thinking.

Lower Level Skills

- *Remember:* Remembering facts or information learned earlier without necessarily understanding or being able to use that knowledge (e.g., list or define)

- *Understand:* Understanding or making sense of information without connecting the information to prior knowledge (e.g., explain or summarize)

- *Apply:* Selecting and using information to solve a problem or specific task (e.g., demonstrate, compute)

Higher Level Skills

- *Analyze:* Breaking information or knowledge into parts and possibly making connections between those parts (e.g., compare, contrast)

- *Evaluate:* Making judgments about the value of information for a particular situation (e.g., assess, critique)

- *Create:* Creating or generating new ideas by combining information (e.g., produce, develop)

Master the content.

edge.sagepub.com/durwin3e

Bloom's taxonomy: See Module 18

Video: Bloom's Taxonomy

FIGURE 13.1 **Higher Order Thinking.** Bloom's taxonomy presented here is often used to distinguish lower level thinking skills from higher order thinking skills.

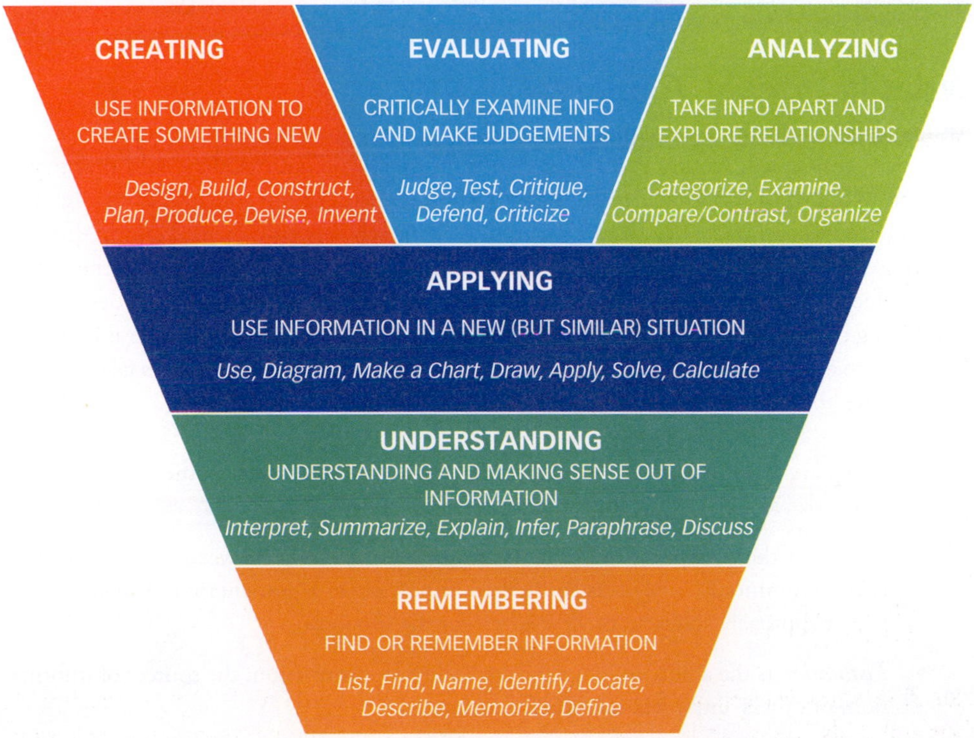

CREATING	EVALUATING	ANALYZING
USE INFORMATION TO CREATE SOMETHING NEW	CRITICALLY EXAMINE INFO AND MAKE JUDGEMENTS	TAKE INFO APART AND EXPLORE RELATIONSHIPS
Design, Build, Construct, Plan, Produce, Devise, Invent	*Judge, Test, Critique, Defend, Criticize*	*Categorize, Examine, Compare/Contrast, Organize*

APPLYING
USE INFORMATION IN A NEW (BUT SIMILAR) SITUATION
Use, Diagram, Make a Chart, Draw, Apply, Solve, Calculate

UNDERSTANDING
UNDERSTANDING AND MAKING SENSE OUT OF INFORMATION
Interpret, Summarize, Explain, Infer, Paraphrase, Discuss

REMEMBERING
FIND OR REMEMBER INFORMATION
List, Find, Name, Identify, Locate, Describe, Memorize, Define

Lower and higher order thinking skills are not mutually exclusive. To the contrary, higher level thinking most often also includes lower level thinking skills. For example, writing a research paper on the historical importance of World War I on World War II requires memorization (lower level) of dates and events but also critical analysis (higher level) of World War I events. Experimental research has found that the use of higher level test questions on quizzes and exams facilitates both lower level and higher level thinking among students (Jensen, McDaniel, Woodard, & Kummer, 2014). Hence, Bloom's taxonomy is not only used to better understand cognitive processes but is useful for determining learning objectives and assessment of those objectives in learning contexts.

Assessment: See Module 23

Higher order thinking skills are important because we not only want students to learn facts and information but we want them to learn how to learn. For example, most math curriculum today, even starting in the elementary grades, requires students to explain their answers. It is no longer good enough to get the correct answer; students must be able to explain *how* they got the correct answer. In addition, most states have adopted the Common Core standards, which focus on developing higher order thinking skills needed for success in college and careers (see the Common Core website at http://www.corestandards.org for more information). Recently, scholars in the field have attempted to provide guidance on how to promote higher order thinking within the context of Common Core (Alexander, 2014; Beghetto, Kaufman, & Baer, 2015; Sternberg, 2015). Although there are numerous examples of higher level thinking skills that could be discussed in this module, we focus on three specific cognitive processes: critical thinking, problem solving, and creativity.

CRITICAL THINKING

2 Explain what critical thinking means.

3 Identify five instructional strategies that can be used to foster critical thinking.

What Is Critical Thinking?

Assume that one of your college professors entered the classroom on the first day of classes and said, "This course will require you to use critical thinking." What exactly would that mean? What thinking skills would you need to have to be successful in the course? **Critical thinking** has not been well-defined in the research literature. Some scholars have defined critical thinking as purposeful and goal-directed thinking that utilizes reasoning (Halpern, 1998). Other scholars have focused on defining critical thinking based on the specific cognitive abilities needed. Combining both of these views, critical thinking can be defined as a set of cognitive abilities that allows one to evaluate and judge the accuracy and importance of information. Let's take a look at the cognitive abilities considered essential to critical thinking (Facione, 2013).

Video Case 13.1 ▲
Critical Thinking

© SAGE Publications

- *Interpretation* is the ability to explain or clarify the meaning of something as well as categorize and determine the significance of information.

- *Analysis* is the ability to determine the connections or links between ideas and experiences. Commonly, analysis is considered important to argumentation or determining which approach, solution, or view is best for the situation.

- *Evaluation* is the ability to judge the credibility of information, the sources of information, or others' interpretation of information.

- *Inference* is the ability to draw reasonable conclusions based on limited information.

- *Explanation* is the ability to provide justification for one's judgements and conclusions.

- *Self-regulation* is the ability to monitor one's own thinking, including the aforementioned skills, such as interpretation, analysis, evaluation, and inference.

Self-regulation: See Module 9

Most simply, critical thinking has been defined as reasoning, or the process of determining an outcome. For example, the math teachers at a high school may examine several online programs to use to supplement their textbook and lesson plans. Each teacher may analyze the various programs, evaluate the quality of activities, and make inferences on how well the program will assist students. Finally, the members will likely explain their own preferences and collectively determine a program. The outcome, or which program was selected, is not an example of critical thinking, but the reasons for their choice or the process used to determine the outcome did include critical thinking. There are two specific types of reasoning. First, **deductive reasoning** is the use of logic to determine specific outcomes or expectancies based on general information. Consider this example.

All butterflies are insects.

All insects are animals.

All butterflies are animals.

Here you have deducted that all butterflies are animals from the set of arguments provided.

The second type is **inductive reasoning,** or the use of specific information to make generalizations (see Figure 13.2). Inductive reasoning focuses on the probability of a conclusion rather than the absolute truth. Consider this example.

All volleyball players in your school are tall.

All volleyball players must be tall.

How likely is this generalization? As teachers, you will be asked to base your lessons and teaching strategies on science or evidence-based practices. The scientific process includes a specific form of inductive reasoning referred to as hypothesis testing. **Hypothesis testing** is the method of using data to determine if a suspected outcome or idea can be confirmed. Consider this example from a task used extensively in research (Wason, 1960; Wason & Johnson-Laird, 1972).

You are given a sequence of numbers—2, 4, 6—and are asked to come up with other sequences of three numbers that follow the same rule. You might hypothesize that the rule is "even numbers" and provide the sequence of 8, 10, and 12. You are told that the sequence follows the rule, but the rule is not "even numbers." Next, you hypothesize that the rule is "you add 2 to each number" and provide a sequence of 3, 5, and 7. You are told that the sequence follows the rule, but the rule is not "add 2 to each number." The correct rule is "list numbers smallest to largest." In the original study using this task, 29% of people never determined the correct rule, and 50% determined the rule after making at least one other hypothesis, leaving only 21% of people to get it correct on their first try.

Why is teaching critical thinking so important in a climate of standardized testing? How can critical thinking assist students on standardized tests?

FIGURE 13.2 **Critical Thinking.** Inductive and deductive reasoning are two critical thinking processes used to determine outcomes.

Inductive

Specific case(s) → General rules or principles

Deductive

APPLICATIONS: FOSTERING CRITICAL THINKING

Critical thinking is one of the skills necessary to become a good student, learner, and teacher. Not only should teachers attempt to foster critical thinking among their students; they should also attempt to enhance their own critical thinking skills. Recently, Abrami and colleagues (2015) examined over 300 findings regarding strategies for teaching critical thinking. The results suggest that critical thinking skills can be developed among students at various education levels. Three strategies were found to be effective individually and collectively (Abrami et al., 2015).

1. *Dialogue* is an instructional method that includes discussion of a problem or issue. Typically, the teacher begins by presenting a question to the students, but the discussion can also begin because a student poses a question to the teacher. The discussion that follows can take a number of forms, including whole-class discussions or debates, or small-group discussions or debates. The discussions can be verbal or written, such as online discussion forums. Empirical data suggest that students given a facilitation prompt during online discussions are more likely to user a higher level of thinking, such as critical thinking, than students not given a similar prompt (Giacumo, Savenye, & Smith, 2013). Hence, dialogues can be teacher-led or occur with at least some teacher participation.

2. *Authentic or situated problems* is an approach that begins with presenting a real-world problem or issue to students. These problems or issues can be presented as

Facilitation prompt: See Module 11

Situated cognition: See Module 18

Dialogue. Critical thinking can be fostered by providing students with opportunities to discuss or debate problems or issues.

©iStockphoto.com/ kali9

case studies, ethical dilemmas, or simulations, such as having students manipulate content, most often with computer programs. The process for students can include playing games, role-playing various solutions, or providing written responses. The Reflect and Evaluate questions based on the case studies presented in this textbook are a good example of an authentic method.

3. *Mentorship* is one-on-one instruction, including coaching, modeling, or tutoring by an expert. The expert is most often a teacher but can also be a peer. Specifically, an expert might model critical thinking skills for a particular assignment and then provide guided practice with feedback.

Modeling: See Module 9

Another method for fostering critical thinking is to help your students overcome two common barriers to critical thinking (Paul & Elder, 2014). First, people tend to be *egocentric,* or view most everything from only their perspective or interests. As a result, we judge situations and content based on our own desires and beliefs. For students, this can manifest itself as arrogance (unwilling to listen to another perspective) or inferiority (recognizing that the content is difficult and not being interested in working hard to understand or learn). Second, people are sociocentric, or view most everything from their group's perspective. This can include an assumption that one's own group is superior and judges others from that viewpoint. For example, students can be less likely to challenge their peers and instead simply accept the viewpoint of peers within their group. Teachers need to recognize these barriers in themselves, as well as their students, and challenge the type of egocentric and sociocentric thinking that prevents students from thinking critically.

Egocentric thinking: See Module 6

Can you think of teachers or specific courses that have challenged you to think critically using one or more of the methods just discussed?

PROBLEM SOLVING

4 Identity the five steps of the IDEAL method, including specific problem-solving strategies.

5 Identify five strategies that can be used to foster problem-solving skills.

What Is Problem Solving?

A **problem** occurs when there is a desired goal that is different from the initial state. **Problem solving** involves attempting to find a means of moving from the initial state to the desired goal. Problem solving does not include an already available means of achieving the goal, nor is it simply the retrieval of information from memory, such as $2 + 2 = 4$. Problem solving does include some behavioral or cognitive operation, such as manipulating information mentally. For example, what will the final cost be if 20% is taken off of $14.99? Some people would solve this problem by:

- rounding the $14.99 up to $15

- determining that 20% of $10 is $2,

- determining that 20% of $5 would be $1

- adding $2 + $1 = $3 is 20% of $15

- subtracting the $3 from $15, indicating that the final cost would be approximately $12

As shown in this example, problem solving usually requires several steps or subgoals. Table 13.1 summarizes one general method of problem solving labeled IDEAL (Bransford & Stein, 1993).

Video Case 13.2 ▲
Problem Solving in Math
© SAGE Publications

TABLE 13.1	IDEAL Problem-Solving Method
STEP	**DESCRIPTION**
I—Identify the problem.	Identify the initial state, goals, and constraints.
D—Define goals and represent the problem.	Determine how best to ask the question or consider the problem.
E—Explore possible solutions.	Identify possible options and strategies that might be used to solve the problem. Do not yet evaluate those strategies.
A—Anticipate outcomes and act.	Consider consequences of possible strategies and choose a strategy.
L—Look back and learn.	Determine how well that strategy worked and consider how to approach similar problems in the future.

SOURCE: Bransford & Stein, 1993.

Identify the Problem. Identifying the problem may seem very simple, but sometimes this can be very difficult. **Well-defined problems** have clear initial states, goals, and constraints with only one correct answer. For example, $8x + 1 = 65$ has a goal of solving for x with only one correct answer. **Ill-defined problems** do not have clear goals or may have multiple correct answers. For example, if the government had a surplus of money, it would need to decide what the money should be used for. Politicians from various parties would have very different ideas about how to solve this problem. Ill-defined problems for students can include constructing a mobile of the solar system, writing a fictional story, or creating a presentation to summarize historical events in the 1980s.

Define Goals and Represent the Problem. Defining and representing the problem suggests that problems can be viewed from various perspectives. Determining the important factors in a

Well- and ill-defined problems: See Module 12

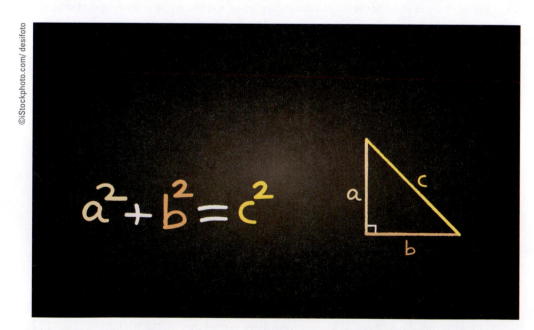

©iStockphoto.com/desifoto

Algorithms. The Pythagorean theorem is an algorithm that always finds the square of the hypotenuse when used correctly.

problem helps determine how best to solve the problem. Consider how the solution to a problem might be different because of how the question is phrased. For example, "how do we ensure we don't bury anyone alive?" is different than determining "how do me make sure everyone we bury is dead?" We can make sure everyone we bury is dead by injecting them with poison before burial, but that doesn't solve the problem of determining whether someone we *think* is dead is *actually* alive.

Explore Possible Solutions. Exploring possible solutions might include examining algorithms or heuristics. **Algorithms** are problem-solving strategies that provide a specific set of steps, which, if followed, will result in a solution. Examples would include how to calculate the mean scores of a test or how to use the formula for the Pythagorean theorem. **Heuristics** are simple rules of thumb that work in some situations but not others. For example, someone flips a coin and the result is heads. He or she flips the coin again and asks you to guess the outcome. Most people would make an educated guess of tails due to one's knowledge of probabilities. However, that strategy would not always work. Some effective heuristics include the following:

- **Means-ends analysis** is a strategy that focuses on dividing the problem into subgoals. Students who have a large project due will benefit from setting smaller goals or tasks that work toward the final project. For example, in writing a review paper on the economic changes over the past 20 years, a student might set subgoals, such as (1) find sources, (2) read each source, (3) create notes for each source, (4) find patterns of information across sources, (5) develop outline, (6) write draft of each section, and (7) revise draft for final paper.

- **Working backward** is a strategy that begins with the end goal and determines the steps needed to get there by thinking backward. Using the previous example, (7) if the final review paper is due May 1, (6) a draft is needed by April 25, (5) an outline should be completed by April 1, (4) patterns of information should be determined by March 20, (3) notes should be taken by March 10, (2) sources should be read by March 1, and (1) sources should be found by February 15.

- **Analogical thinking** is a strategy that focuses on exploring possible solutions that are similar to solutions used with similar problems. For example, a student who has been assigned his or her first oral presentation might think about strategies or solutions that are similar to writing a review paper.

Anticipate Outcomes and Act. Anticipating outcomes and acting on the strategy refer to choosing a solution based on possible consequences. It is important to note that the previous step does not include evaluating possible solutions. When demonstrating this to my own class, I typically ask students to come up with all the ways they might use to get class cancelled without considering the consequences (Step 3 discussed earlier—"Explore Possible Solutions"). Over the years they have been very creative with suggestions, such as posting a note on the door that class was cancelled, pulling the fire alarm, and even poisoning me! In this step, I ask them to consider what solution has the best outcome with the fewest negative consequences (they usually choose posting the note on the door!).

Look Back and Learn. Looking back and evaluating the effectiveness of your chosen strategy allows one to learn how to solve similar problems in the future.

Think about a recent problem you had. Once the problem was resolved, did you actually look back and evaluate the effectiveness of the solution? Teachers need to reflect on problem solving with their students as well as their own problem solving in learning activities.

APPLICATIONS: FOSTERING PROBLEM-SOLVING STRATEGIES

Video Case 13.4 ▲
Problem-Solving

© SAGE Publications

Fostering problem-solving skills includes instruction on what *not* to do as well as explicit instruction on what to do. Teachers should understand that problem-solving skills develop across childhood and adolescence, with some research finding that these skills are more likely to be developed between Grades 6 and 8 (or about 12–14 years of age; Molnár, Greiff, & Csapó, 2013; Scherer & Tiemann, 2014).

As learners, it is important to recognize and avoid the obstacles to successful problem solving. Consider these instances.

- Avoid **functional fixedness,** which is the inability to find a solution because we are "fixed" on using objects for their intended purpose and ignoring other potential uses (Duncker, 1945; Maier, 1931). For example, I recently needed to hang a picture in my new office and didn't have a hammer. I could have become fixated on needing a hammer and given up hanging the picture that day. Instead, I quickly took off my shoe and used the bottom to hammer a nail into the wall.

- Avoid **response sets** or tendencies to make assumptions that represent a problem in one way, usually in a manner that is familiar to us, rather than seeing all additional options. For example, Figure 13.3 asks you to connect all the dots with only four lines and not lift your pencil. The solution can be seen in Figure 13.5.

- Avoid **belief perseverance** or the tendency to continue or persevere in beliefs even when presented with contradictory evidence (Garcia-Mila & Anderson, 2008). As an example, I have had students come to my office after not doing well on a test insisting that their study strategies work.

As teachers, there are several things you can do to foster problem-solving skills in your students.

- Provide explicit instruction on both general and specific problem-solving strategies. General problem-solving strategies include the IDEAL method discussed earlier that can be used within a large range of situations and circumstances. Specific problem-solving strategies are those used in a particular content area, such as converting fractions to percentages. Both general and specific problem-solving strategies need to be taught and practiced within the classroom.

FIGURE 13.3 **Response Sets.** Assume you are given a sheet of paper showing these nine dots. Connect the nine dots with four straight lines. You must draw all four lines without lifting your pencil from the paper. You may not fold, cut, or tear the paper in any way.

- Provide opportunities for **problem-based learning (PBL).** Problem-based learning, unlike traditional strategies, includes a series of steps that begin with a problem rather than teaching content knowledge (see Figure 13.4). This strategy allows students an opportunity to construct their own knowledge from real-world, complex problems. The formation of the PBL strategy was to foster the following (Loyens, Kirschner, & Paas, 2012; Schmidt, 1983):

  o a flexible knowledge base
  o collaboration with others
  o problem-solving skills
  o intrinsic motivation for learning
  o self-directed learning

Research evidence indicated that problem-based learning is effective for the development of both knowledge and applied skills (Schmidt, van der Molen, Te Winkel, & Wijnen, 2009). There has also been a focus on integrating technology into PBL, such as using video case studies. More specifically, Liu and colleagues (Liu, Horton, Olmanson, & Toprac, 2011; Liu, Rosenblum, Horton, & Kang, 2014) have developed an interactive game, *Alien Rescue*, which uses a PBL approach to teach middle school students science knowledge in a variety of areas. Results on the effects of this PBL approach have found that students, especially girls, have increased science knowledge and enhanced intrinsic motivation to learn (Liu et al., 2011; Liu et al., 2014). In addition, student engagement has been found to be higher within PBL environments in comparison to lecture-based instruction (Delialio Iu, 2012; Muehlenkamp, Weiss, & Hansen, 2015). The effectiveness of PBL has been documented in cross-cultural contexts such as Thailand, South Africa, the Netherlands, the United Kingdom, and the United States (Hmelo-Silver, 2012).

Intrinsic motivation: See Module 14

DIVERSITY

Student engagement: See Module 17

Before we begin the next section, think about someone you consider to be "creative." What qualities does that person have? What ideas or tasks of this person do you consider creative?

FIGURE 13.4 **Problem-Based Learning.** This figure depicts a series of steps that can be used to construct knowledge from real-world problems.

Problem Presentation	**Collaborative Learning**	**Self-Directed Learning**	**Second Collaborative Learning**
Prior to teaching content knowledge, teachers present students with an ill-defined, real-world problem.	Groups discuss the problem and formulate learning issues. A teacher or tutor can help facilitate the discussion by asking questions to ensure relevant information is included.	Individual students gather information and sources to help understand and solve the problem.	Group members share information and resources, critically evaluate all information, and determine the best solution.

How can we decrease the amount of waste put into landfills each year?

Adapted from Loyens, Kirschner, & Paas, 2012.

FIGURE 13.5 **Response Sets.** If you had not seen this problem before, you probably assumed the four lines had to remain inside the perimeter of the dots. The solution requires you to use an "out of the box" option.

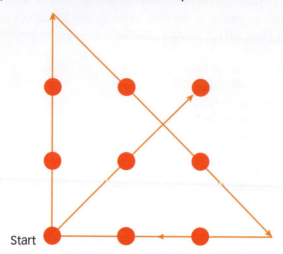

Start

CREATIVITY

6 Explain what creativity is.

7 Identify five strategies for promoting creativity.

What Is Creativity?

Reference: Creative Thinking

Creativity and problem solving are both cognitive processes and considered examples of higher order thinking. However, each requires a different type of higher order thinking. Problem solving requires more **convergent thinking,** or combining several pieces of information to resolve a problem or reach a single conclusion or "right answer." In contrast, creativity typically includes **divergent thinking,** or identifying several outcomes or solutions, usually from a single starting point (see Figure 13.6). In the earlier example, was using a shoe as a hammer creative? The use of a shoe in more than one way (not to walk on but to hammer with) and determining more than one solution to the problem (not limiting the solution to only a hammer) are examples of divergent thinking; hence, one might consider it creative. We can also determine whether using the shoe as a hammer was creative based on the two essential elements used to define creativity (Amabile, 1996; Kaufman & Beghetto, 2013):

- *Novelty:* Creativity typically refers to something new or unique. Using a shoe as a hammer is unusual.

- *Appropriateness:* New or unique ideas and tasks must be viewed as appropriate in the context. The shoe worked well as a hammer.

Creativity can be viewed on a continuum where high levels include extraordinarily intelligent people (Einstein, Mozart) producing notable ideas and products in specific fields of study to low levels in which typical people produce novel and appropriate everyday ideas and products (Amabile, 1996; Kaufman & Beghetto, 2009). The extremes of this continuum are typically referred to as *Big C creativity* (e.g., great works) and *little c creativity* (e.g., everyday creativity). As educators, you are more likely to be interested in

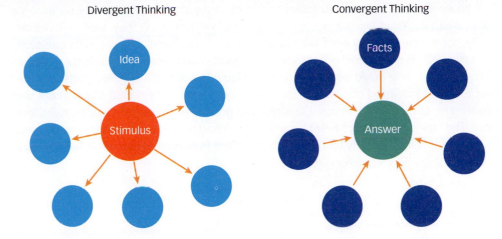

FIGURE 13.6 **Convergent and Divergent Thinking.** Problem-solving requires more convergent thinking, whereas creativity typically includes divergent thinking.

Divergent Thinking

Idea

Stimulus

Convergent Thinking

Facts

Answer

identifying and fostering little c creativity. So, how do you know if a student is creative or has produced something creative?

Identifying creativity can occur in many ways. There are some standardized measures of creativity, such as the Torrance Tests of Creative Thinking (TTCT; Torrance, 1972), that assess both verbal (e.g., think of as many uses for a water bottle as possible) and graphic (e.g., create as many designs as possible with 30 circles) creativity. In addition, creativity can be identified by **consensual assessment,** which requires observers or judges to agree that an idea or product is creative (Amabile, 1996). Finally, identifying creative students can include examining specific qualities that suggest one is more likely to be creative (Amabile, 1996; Sternberg, 2006; Strom & Strom, 2013).

1. *Intellectual abilities,* such as synthesis and analysis, are necessary for creativity.

2. *Domain-specific knowledge* is necessary for creative thought. A person must have a significant amount of knowledge in an area to "think outside the box."

3. Certain *personality characteristics* also facilitate creativity, in particular, an individual's willingness to take reasonable risks and tolerate ambiguity and the determination to continue in frustrating or difficult tasks. Creative individuals are also more likely to be highly imaginative, daydream more, and spend more time alone than less creative individuals.

4. *Intrinsic motivation* for the domain area or task is found among individuals likely to be creative. In short, people who have an internal desire or interest in the domain are more likely to produce creative ideas or products.

5. *Environmental conditions* can help or hinder individuals' abilities to be creative. Individuals working in environments that allow them to express ideas openly while suspending judgment as well as reward creative ideas are more likely to be creative.

Research has found that even children as young as preschool-age can be taught creativity, including both divergent and convergent thinking skills (Alfonso-Benlliure, Meléndez, & García-Ballesteros, 2013). Actually, creativity is more likely to be highlighted in the curriculum of younger students, rather than adolescents, not only in the United States but also in China (Yi, Hu, Plucker, & McWilliams, 2013).

Intrinsic motivation: See Module 14

> DIVERSITY

Video Case 13.5 ▲
Fostering Creativity
in Math

**Bias and prejudice
feelings:** See Module 1

**Instructional
approaches:** See
Module 18

Intrinsic motivation: See
Module 14

APPLICATIONS: FOSTERING CREATIVITY

Ask yourself this: Do I want to foster creativity in my students? You may be thinking "Of course, I do. What teacher wouldn't?" Most teachers would say they want to foster creativity, but in actuality they don't like students who portray creative qualities. In one study, Torrance (2000) asked teachers to indicate the ideal characteristics of students as well as characteristics they would discourage in their students. Interestingly, the results indicated that teachers preferred obedience over asking questions, acceptance of judgment over challenging authority or traditional thought, and good memory skills rather than intuitiveness. The lack of excitement over characteristics linked to creativity may be due to several myths surrounding creativity that can hinder teachers from putting forth time and energy to foster creativity (Plucker, Beghetto, & Dow, 2004).

1. *Creativity is an innate trait—you either have it or you don't.* Research evidence finds just the opposite—creativity can be taught.

2. *Creativity is related to deviance.* Many people, including teachers, equate creativity with nonconformists, drug users, or loners. Although some creative people do have these tendencies, and that fuels this myth, many noncreative people are also nonconformists, drug users, and loners. Teachers should be aware of their potential bias against students high in creativity or even a bias against creativity for fear it will lead to deviant behaviors.

3. *Creativity is a fuzzy concept not grounded in scientific study.* In contrast, there is a large field of study surrounding the concept of creativity. Although there may be some disagreement about the definition of creativity or best theoretical perspective to explain creativity, that can also be said of many other concepts, such as intelligence, social skills, and motivation.

4. *Groups are more creative than individuals.* Collectively working through problems may ultimately lead to more innovative ideas, but research suggests that first brainstorming ideas individually is important in the creative process.

In addition to avoiding these myths about creativity, teachers can also promote creativity in their students in a number of ways (Beghetto & Kaufman, 2011, 2014; Colzato, Szapora, Pannekoek, & Hommel, 2013; Hammond, Skidmore, Wilcox-Herzog, & Kaufman, 2013; Hung, 2015; Pang, 2015).

- Children exposed to *play-based curriculum* in early childhood have been found to have higher levels of creativity and higher academic achievements. The benefit of play-based programs to higher academic achievement seems to continue into elementary school.

- *Physical exercise* can also improve creative thinking (both convergent and divergent thinking). Hence, teachers might implement short breaks to stand, stretch, or walk.

- Research suggests that *indirect instructional approaches,* which focus on the creative process rather than the final product, are more effective than direct instruction for fostering creative thought. Specifically, teachers should encourage exploration and offer choices in activities and in creative assignments.

- The focus should be on *intrinsic motivation,* or personal interest in a topic or task, rather than rewards. Teachers can provide choices to students that allow them to focus on areas of study or type of assignments that are of most interest to them.

- Using PBL, as described earlier, also can facilitate creativity.

- Teachers should provide *authentic feedback* on creative ideas and products. Feedback should be positive but also include evaluation and constructive criticism.

- Teachers must value creativity and tolerate ambiguity. Many teachers focus on structure and organization in their classrooms. *Disciplined improvisation* is balancing the need for classroom structure such as rules, procedures, and specific content to be covered with more fluid, spontaneous, and unique curriculum that leads to unexpected discussions and insights.

Think about the grade level you wish to teach. How can you demonstrate to your students that you value creativity?

SUMMARY

❶ Define higher order thinking and explain why it is important in the current educational climate. Higher order thinking refers to more advanced or complex ways of thinking. According to Bloom's taxonomy, those thinking skills include analyzing, evaluating, and creating. Higher order thinking skills are important for students to learn how to learn, rather than just memorizing facts and information. With a focus on Common Core in most current educational systems, higher order thinking skills will become increasingly important.

❷ Explain what critical thinking means. Critical thinking is the ability to evaluate and judge both the accuracy of information as well as the importance of that information. There are several cognitive abilities associated with critical thinking, such as interpretation, analysis, evaluation, inference, explanation, and self-regulation. These reasoning skills can result in deductive reasoning, inductive reasoning, or hypothesis testing.

❸ Identify five instructional strategies that can be used to foster critical thinking. (1) Dialogue is an important strategy for promoting critical thinking, such as discussing a problem or issue. (2) Authentic problem solving is another strategy that allows students to critically consider a real-world problem. (3) Teachers or peers can also provide mentoring, or one-on-one instruction that models and prompts critical thinking. (4) Teachers should help students identify how their own values and beliefs may be clouding their ability to judge information. (5) Similarly, teachers should help students recognize biases they may have due to being within a certain group.

❹ Identify the five steps of the IDEAL method, including specific problem-solving strategies. I—Identify the problem, including both well-defined and ill-defined problems. D—Define or represent the problem by determining the important factors. E—Explore possible solutions, such as algorithms, heuristics, means-end analysis,

working backward, or analogical thinking. A—Anticipate or consider the consequences and outcomes of each solution. L—Look back and evaluate how well a solution worked to solve a specific problem and consider how that same solution could be used in the future

❺ Identify five strategies that can be used to foster problem-solving skills. There are several cognitive obstacles to problem solving that need to be avoided, including (1) functional fixedness, or the tendency to focus on one purpose of an object without considering alternatives; (2) response sets, or representing the problem in only one, usually familiar, way, rather than identifying additional "out of the box" ideas; and (3) belief perseverance, or the tendency to hold onto our beliefs even when the evidence is contrary. In addition, (4) teachers need to provide direct instruction on problem-solving strategies, both general and specific, as well as (5) consider problem-based learning (PBL) approaches to instruction.

❻ Explain what creativity means. Creativity is defined by an idea or outcome being both unique and appropriate, which is usually judged as such by agreeing on the uniqueness and appropriateness of the idea or outcome. Creativity can include great works that have a large influence on the world, labeled Big C creativity, or everyday creativity activities, such as students' creative writings, poems, or innovative ways of problem solving, labeled little c creativity.

❼ Identify five strategies for promoting creativity. Teachers can promote creativity by including (1) play-based curriculum in early childhood, (2) providing opportunities for physical activity, (3) providing choices in assignments, (4) providing problem-based learning (PBL) opportunities, and (5) giving authentic feedback on creative ideas and products. In addition, teachers should focus on students' intrinsic motivation for a topic or task as well as value creativity themselves.

algorithm, 257

analogical thinking, 257

belief perseverance, 258

consensual assessment, 261

convergent thinking, 260

critical thinking, 252

deductive reasoning, 253

divergent thinking, 260

functional fixedness, 258

heuristics, 257

higher order thinking, 251

hypothesis testing, 253

ill-defined problems, 256

inductive reasoning, 253

means-ends analysis, 257

problem, 255

problem-based learning (PBL), 259

problem solving, 255

response sets, 258

well-defined problems, 256

working-backward strategy, 257

CASE STUDIES: REFLECT AND EVALUATE

EARLY CHILDHOOD: 100TH DAY

These questions refer to the case study on page 206.

1. Which skill levels from Bloom's taxonomy are demonstrated in this case? Explain.

2. Describe how Ms. Prendergast used questioning techniques to promote critical thinking.

3. Was the 100th day project an example of a well-defined or an ill-defined problem? Explain.

4. Identify at least two strategies Ms. Prendergast used to promote creativity.

5. Was Ms. Prendergast's assessment of James's project being creative consistent with the definition of creativity given in the module?

ELEMENTARY SCHOOL: INVENTION CONVENTION

These questions refer to the case study on page 208.

1. Which features of higher order thinking, if any, did you see represented by the students in Ms. Bury and Mr. Grant's classes?

2. What strategies were used by these teachers to foster critical thinking?

3. What steps of the IDEAL problem-solving method could have been represented on Ms. Bury's "cheat sheet"?

4. How could these teachers have used means-end or working backward strategies to help their students with this project?

5. Would Allen's invention be considered creative? Why or why not?

MIDDLE SCHOOL: PRESIDENT OR QUEEN FOR A DAY?

These questions refer to the case study on page 210.

1. Which levels of Bloom's taxonomy are represented in the learning events that transpired in Mr. Van's classroom? Provide examples.

2. How do the writing assignments promote students' critical thinking about governmental systems? What barriers to critical thinking were evident in this case?

3. What heuristics might help students complete their assignments on governmental systems?

4. Does the classroom activity of getting a bill passed through the U.S. governmental system represent problem-based learning? Why or why not?

5. How does Mr. Van attempt to foster creativity in his students? What other strategies might he use as well?

HIGH SCHOOL: BROWNED-EYED GIRL

These questions refer to the case study on page 212.

1. What higher level skills were displayed by the students in Ms. Overocker's class? Give specific examples.

2. How would you describe Xander's thinking about genetic testing?

3. Did the type of problems Ms. Overocker assigned require the use of algorithms or the use of heuristics? Explain.

4. Is genetic testing a well-defined or ill-defined problem? Is using these types of controversial issues useful? Why or why not?

5. Based on the two essential elements used to define creativity, would you consider Wyatt's example of unicorns with or without wings to be "creative"? Explain.

UNIT FIVE

MOTIVATION

Daniel Grill/Getty Images

EARLY CHILDHOOD: THE WORKSHEETS

©iStockphoto.com/ monkeybusinessimages

Elizabeth Garvey, a second-year teacher at Fitzgerald Elementary School, enjoys teaching kindergarten because the children are eager to learn new things and approach each new experience with excitement. As with any kindergarten class, it is typical for some students to have trouble adjusting to the structured, academic environment of elementary school. Mrs. Garvey tries to balance formal instruction with opportunities for social interaction and play. This year seems especially challenging, as she has a large class of 21 students with diverse backgrounds. Three students are English language learners, many students have had no preschool experience, and there are large disparities in readiness skills among the children.

After the morning meeting, during which Mrs. Garvey and the children go over the date, the day's weather, the lunch count, and any special news or events, she begins a lesson on math concepts that includes a game of "Numbers I Spy." After the group lesson, the children return to their seats to complete some worksheets. Mrs. Garvey gives them instructions to match digits on the left side of the page to sets of objects on the right side of the page. She shows them how to complete the first one, drawing a line from the number 5 to the five hats. "When you're finished, use the color key at the bottom of the page to color the sets of objects," Mrs. Garvey says, pointing to the bottom of the page.

As the children begin working, Mrs. Garvey walks around the room to check on their progress. She notices Melissa coloring instead of doing the worksheet. "Melissa, why haven't you started your math sheet?" whispers Mrs. Garvey.

"I can't do it," replies Melissa, slouching in her chair.

"I know you can do it if you just try," says Mrs. Garvey with a reassuring smile. Melissa tends to need a little extra coaxing and then ends up doing fine work. "I'll come back and check on you."

Melissa has been raised by her grandmother since she was a year old. From the age of 3, she has attended Head Start, a preschool program for economically disadvantaged children. Her academic skills are steadily improving, but she still lacks confidence in her abilities.

As Mrs. Garvey continues moving around the room, she notices Emanuel, Kristina, and Martin at the building center playing with Legos. She approaches the children and says, "Now is not the time for building."

"But we're already done with our math sheets!" exclaims Martin. "I already know numbers and adding so I don't need to do baby worksheets. My mom says I'm smart at math."

"Yes, I know you three are good at doing math," Mrs. Garvey says. "Show me your worksheets so I can check to see if they are correct and neatly colored, and then you can play with the blocks while the others finish."

Because Mrs. Garvey needs to follow the district's curriculum, she often lets advanced students play while others finish their work. She's not sure whether their playing affects other students' motivation, though. She always has a few students who want to rush through their work so they can play as well.

Mrs. Garvey walks past the next table and says, "Nice work, Alannah and Mahiro!" She then stops at Kayvon, and leans over his shoulder saying, "The seven fish don't go with that number, Kayvon. It's this one. Count them with me."

Tugging at her shirt is Claire. Claire is anxiously waiting for Mrs. Garvey to check her answers, as she does with all her work, even art projects. Claire never wants to get anything wrong.

"Mrs. Garvey, I'm done with the numbers. Are they all right? I want to color the pictures now," says Claire. Mrs. Garvey glances at the sheet and gives her a nod. *Everyone looks like they're doing fine,* she thinks as she goes back to check on Melissa and Kayvon.

ASSESS:

1. How motivated do you think Melissa, Martin, Kayvon, and Claire are to learn in this case study? What evidence supports your point of view?

2. In your opinion, should Mrs. Garvey allow Martin and the others to play while they wait for other students to finish their work? Why or why not?

3. Which student's motivation would you be concerned with most? Why?

ELEMENTARY SCHOOL: WRITER'S BLOCK

PREPARE:

As you read the case, make notes:

1. WHO are the central characters in the case? Describe them.
2. WHAT is taking place?
3. WHERE is the case taking place? Is the environment a factor?
4. WHEN is the case taking place? Is the timing a factor?

Yuiko Okuda is a third-grade teacher at White Eagle Elementary School who believes that hands-on experiences are essential to students' understanding and skill development. Mrs. Okuda uses many different activities to help her students improve their writing skills. Every week, she has them write a letter home to their parents about what they have learned in school that week, any

upcoming events they are looking forward to, and any exciting activities they will be participating in. Most of the students enjoy writing letters home to their parents. Every Thursday morning Mrs. Okuda uses another activity, called "free writing," in which students are given 30 minutes to write about a given subject, such as a favorite season or family traditions. She gives the essays a grade based on whether they are completed. She displays them all on the bulletin board outside the classroom.

This Thursday morning Mrs. Okuda announces, "The topic of the day today will be your favorite pastime during summer vacation. After you've completed your assignment, you may read, use the computer, or play a board game quietly at the back of the class." James, Zara, Ronnie, and Shanti begin chatting as they quickly take out a piece of paper to start writing.

"I love writing!" says Shanti, eagerly beginning her assignment.

"I like that we get to show the other kids in the school our writing work," whispers Zara.

"I just like to write about things I like. It's more fun than other subjects like reading," adds James. "Plus we don't get graded on it." James dislikes reading and would much rather be doing math, playing sports, or using the classroom computer. But he generally likes school and is a good student because his parents have tried to instill in him the value of hard work and a good education.

Carter takes out a piece of paper and a pencil, writes his name at the top of the page, and then turns pale, quietly staring at the blank paper. Carter is a high-achieving and popular student who turns in letters to parents, journals, and other writing assignments that are above average. But he seems to have difficulty when it comes to the free writing activity. Lately he has asked to go to the nurse after Mrs. Okuda announces the topic, but she has caught on to his attempt to avoid the assignment.

Mrs. Okuda notices Carter's demeanor and asks, "What's wrong, Carter?"

"I don't know what to write about," Carter replies, as he typically says at every free writing activity. "I want this to be the *best* story, but I don't know where to start."

Mrs. Okuda sits down with Carter and begins to help him brainstorm. "What was the most fun for you during your last summer vacation?"

"I went on a sailboat for the first time!" Carter replies. A smile spreads across his face and he begins to write.

Before Mrs. Okuda returns to her desk, she walks by Mason to see how he is doing. Mason has a learning disability in reading and spelling and usually needs some help with writing, although he never asks for it. She is happy to see Mason working hard. "Here's a suggestion. Try to use more adjectives so that the story is more descriptive," Mrs. Okuda says as she glances over his shoulder.

After about 15 minutes, Shanti and James place their essays on Mrs. Okuda's desk. Shanti heads to the reading corner with a book from the shelf, and James hurriedly walks over to the computer before anyone else gets there. Mrs. Okuda glances over their essays and gets up.

At the reading corner, she whispers, "Great use of vocabulary in your story, Shanti." She then goes over to the computer, kneels by James, and sternly says, "James, your thoughts are very incomplete and you've forgotten about the rules of punctuation. Go back to your seat and finish your work. I know you can do better than that."

ASSESS:

1. Which student do you identify with and why? In your own words, describe this student's motivation.

2. Do you think it is okay for Mrs. Okuda to allow the students to read, use the computer, or play a board game quietly at the back of the class after completing their assignments? What might be some problems with this? What might be some alternatives?

3. In your opinion, is Mrs. Okuda's practice of hanging all the papers on the bulletin board outside the classroom a good idea? Why or why not?

EARLY CHILDHOOD

ELEMENTARY SCHOOL

MIDDLE SCHOOL

HIGH SCHOOL

MIDDLE SCHOOL: THE MATH REVIEW

PREPARE:

As you read the case, make notes:

1. WHO are the central characters in the case? Describe them.
2. WHAT is taking place?
3. WHERE is the case taking place? Is the environment a factor?
4. WHEN is the case taking place? Is the timing a factor?

As the bell rings for the start of third period at Washington Middle School, Jack Pantera announces to his eighth-grade class, "Today we'll be doing a math review for the state mastery test next week." The room fills with groans and sighs. Mr. Pantera understands the students' reaction, but he also realizes the importance of this

©iStockphoto.com/ Chris Schmidt

test. Last year Washington Middle School did not meet its annual goals for math, with only 27% of the eighth graders in the district performing at the proficiency level.

"Come on, everyone, we're going to make this fun," he explains. "I've assigned all of you to four-member teams. Each of you will be given a set of problems and will first work on the problems by yourselves. When everyone on the team is done, you will compare answers and work together to make sure everyone understands how to solve the problems. The first team to finish all the problems correctly gets a prize, and . . ."

"What is it?!" Jeremy interrupts.

"That's a surprise," Mr. Pantera replies. "Let me finish. If *all* teams complete the problem set correctly by the end of the period, the entire class will get a surprise."

Mr. Pantera hopes the prize will encourage students to work together and help one another. Some students in the class are very skilled in math, and others either struggle with math concepts or have anxiety about math.

While students are working in their teams, Mr. Pantera moves around the room to monitor their progress. As Mr. Pantera approaches the first team, he notices Aaron missing. Aaron had gone to sharpen pencils and stopped to talk to Ben. "Aaron, this isn't time for socializing.

You should be helping your team. I see you haven't even started the problems yet," says Mr. Pantera, a bit exasperated. Aaron appears to lack a strong work ethic, although he gets good grades.

"Team Two looks like a contender for the first prize. Everyone's working hard!" Mr. Pantera announces. He stops at the next team because he notices Jesse erasing all her answers. "Jesse, what are you doing?" he asks.

"I'm no good at math. All my answers are wrong," she replies, holding back tears. "How do you know they're wrong? Jesse, you just need a little confidence in yourself," says Mr. Pantera, a bit perplexed. "You get As on all your homework assignments and you got a B– on the midterm exam. I'd say you're doing fine," Mr. Pantera says, trying to be reassuring.

"That's just it. I think I know the stuff. But when it comes time for an exam or a competition like this, I go blank! I must not be smart at math," Jesse sighs.

"Math is about working hard and practicing. Just try a little harder and I'm sure it will pay off," says Mr. Pantera.

"But Aaron doesn't try at all and he gets As," Jesse retorts.

Knowing that he has to check on the other groups, Mr. Pantera discourages Jesse from comparing herself to other students, asks her to finish the problems, and suggests that they talk further after class.

Mr. Pantera overhears some arguing and heads over to Team Five to check out the disturbance. "Hurry up, you guys! I want to win this prize," Jeremy shouts to Gabriel and Rachel.

"I want to be sure I understand how to do the problems myself before we all go over them. It's not all about the stupid prize, you know!" Rachel replies.

"Rachel's right," says Mr. Pantera, looking over Jeremy's shoulder. "Jeremy, you used all the correct procedures. But you should double-check your work. You made simple computation errors on three of the problems. Slow down and concentrate on what you're doing."

Mr. Pantera looks around at all the students and musters a serious tone. "I want to see everyone working together."

"We're all done," announces Renee from Team Four, with her hand raised. Mr. Pantera goes over to check the team's answers.

"We have a winner!" Mr. Pantera announces. "The remaining teams should keep working. We have 15 minutes left, and we can still get the class prize."

ASSESS:

1. In your opinion, was it a good idea for Mr. Pantera to encourage his students to do math problems by making it into a friendly competition? Why or why not?

2. In your opinion, how effective was Mr. Pantera in motivating Jesse? What would you have done differently?

3. What experiences have you had with statewide or district-wide testing? How did these experiences affect your own motivation?

HIGH SCHOOL: Exam Grades

PREPARE:

As you read the case, make notes:

1. WHO are the central characters in the case? Describe them.
2. WHAT is taking place?
3. WHERE is the case taking place? Is the environment a factor?
4. WHEN is the case taking place? Is the timing a factor?

Image Source/Getty Images

It's Monday morning at Davis High School, which is located in a large, metropolitan city and boasts a variety of programs, such as Advanced Placement (AP) classes, vocational/technical classes, and the arts. Today, Curtis Womack, a first-year teacher, is handing back exams in his classes. As the bell rings for his second-period sophomore general science class, Mr. Womack begins distributing the exams and says, "Class, I'm very disappointed that the highest grade was a C+. But I must say that I'm not very surprised. Many of you turned in exams after only 20 minutes. With 25 multiple-choice questions and one essay, that meant you weren't putting a lot of effort into answering the questions. I don't know what's going on. Can you help me with this?"

"A C+ sounds pretty good," Reggie says with a sly smile.

"Yeah, pretty good for not studying," Tamika adds. "I mean we can drop the lowest grade we get, and we can even do an extra credit project at the end of the marking period."

"But those options are supposed to help you get the *best* grade you can," replies Mr. Womack, "not make it easy for you to get out of work."

"Mr. Womack, I'm not trying to get out of work," Carla explains. "I just want to focus on my other classes, ones that are more important to my arts program, no offense!"

"Yeah, why do we need to know this stuff anyway?" adds Reggie. "It's not like we're going to be engineers or scientists or something."

Mr. Womack's concern over his students' motivation is apparent. He spends almost half the period discussing their aspirations, motivation, and work habits. He is eager to understand their perspectives on school and ways to motivate them. But the day's schedule leaves him

little time to think about it further. The bell rings, signaling the end of the period, and he begins gathering another set of exams to hand back to his next class, AP Physics.

"Good morning, everyone. I have exams ready to hand back," Mr. Womack announces. The classroom fills with groans and sighs.

"Not to worry," says Mr. Womack, "the scores were actually quite good. The highest grade was an A–, congratulations to Madelyn, and the lowest grade was a C–. There's definitely room for improvement, but you all are doing fine."

As Mr. Womack continues distributing the exams, Nicholas leans over to his longtime friend Chelsea and whispers, "What'd you get?"

Chelsea hesitates, "C+. I can't believe it. I've never gotten a C in my life," she admits. "What'd you get?"

"I got a C+ too," he says. "I guess we'll have to study harder next time if we want to get a good grade."

"That's just it. We've always gotten As and hardly ever studied," says Chelsea. She doesn't tell her best friend that she *did* study and wondered whether he did too.

After class, Chelsea approaches Mr. Womack about her grade. "Mr. Womack, I'm not sure what to do. I studied for the exam and am not happy with my grade. I think I want to drop AP Physics and take another science class," Chelsea says.

"I wouldn't make such a drastic decision based on one test score, Chelsea. I'm sure you'll improve next time. Maybe you just need to study more," replies Mr. Womack. "Tell me, why did you choose AP Physics in the first place?"

"Because I like math and science, and my dad's an engineer, and ever since I can remember I've wanted to be an engineer too. I figured AP Physics might be good preparation for an engineering major in college."

"So you want to give up your dream?" Mr. Womack persists.

"No, uh, I don't know. I know I don't want to fail or hurt my GPA. That will hurt my chances of getting into a good college. That is, if I even want to choose engineering. I must not be as good at science as I thought. I was always the 'smart' kid in the class. Getting a C+ must mean I'm stupid compared to the other kids."

"No, I wouldn't say that at all," says Mr. Womack in a reassuring tone. "I say sleep on this and let's talk more tomorrow."

ASSESS:

1. Which student do you identify with in terms of motivation? Why?

2. What recommendations would you give to Mr. Womack for dealing with Chelsea and for dealing with students in general science?

3. Do you think it was a good idea for Mr. Womack to announce who received the highest grade in the AP Physics class? Why or why not?

©iStockphoto.com/Christopher Futcher

MODULE **14**

BEHAVIORAL THEORY

A DEVELOPMENTAL VIEW OF MOTIVATION

1 Explain how motivation changes from elementary through middle school, and discuss what factors might account for this trend.

Many students pursue careers in teaching because they were once inspired by a teacher. For teachers, can anything be more gratifying than sparking students' interest in school subjects and fostering a love of learning in young minds? The importance of motivation to student success begins early and remains significant through adolescence (Gottfried, Fleming, & Gottfried, 2001; Vansteenkiste, Simons, Lens, Sheldon, & Deci, 2004).

Defining Intrinsic and Extrinsic Motivation

Most early research on motivation was rooted in the study of behavioral learning theory, specifically the theory of operant conditioning. It suggests that an individual who receives **reinforcement,** a positive consequence for a behavior, would be likely to perform the behavior again under similar circumstances (Skinner, 1953). Reinforcement, in other words, can motivate behavior. Early researchers called this **extrinsic motivation,** meaning it is "external" to the behavior—in other words, participants engage in an activity to obtain an outcome that is distinct from the activity itself (deCharms, 1968; Lepper & Greene, 1978). Extrinsic motivators can be tangible, such as trophies, awards, stickers, prizes, and grades on report cards, or they can be intangible, such as praise, attention, or recognition.

Of course, individuals do not need external incentives for some activities, such as reading or playing video games. When the reward is an intrinsic part of the activity itself, it is called **intrinsic motivation.** Humans and many animals engage in many exploratory and curiosity-driven behaviors in the absence of reinforcement (White, 1959). For example, young children build towers of blocks, color, and play dress-up with no need for extrinsic rewards. Elementary school children enjoy recreational reading, adolescents tweet or listen to music, and adults engage in hobbies. In school, teachers strive to encourage **academic intrinsic motivation,** which is an orientation toward learning characterized by curiosity; persistence; attraction to challenging, novel tasks; and a focus on mastery of knowledge and skills (Gottfried, Fleming, & Gottfried, 1994; Gottfried & Gottfried, 1996).

Think of some ways in which you are intrinsically and extrinsically motivated.

Factors Influencing Intrinsic and Extrinsic Motivation

Researchers now believe that discussing motivation as intrinsic or extrinsic may oversimplify what's really happening. Many learning activities are both intrinsically and extrinsically motivating. Students reading this textbook might work hard in their course because they enjoy learning about educational psychology *and* because they want to get a good grade. The issue may not be whether a student is extrinsically *or* intrinsically motivated but whether students' intrinsic motivation outweighs their extrinsic motivation (Corpus & Wormington, 2014; Hayenga & Corpus, 2010; Wormington, Corpus, & Anderson, 2012). Compared to students with high levels of extrinsic motivation, students with high intrinsic motivation and low extrinsic motivation exhibit higher academic achievement and more self-regulatory behaviors, are more likely to engage in extracurricular activities, and are likely to feel like they belong in the classroom (Hayenga & Corpus, 2010; Vansteenkiste, Sierens, Soenens, Luyckx, & Lens, 2009; Wormington et al., 2012). Therefore, the question teachers should ask is this: In what situations and to what degree is the student intrinsically motivated?

Video: Extrinsic v. Intrinsic Motivation

Operant conditioning: See Module 8

Self-Regulation: See Module 9

DIVERSITY

Students' upbringing and cultural background can significantly influence their motivation:

- Children's early experiences at home may affect their motivation. Regardless of the family's socioeconomic level, cognitively stimulating home environments encourage academic intrinsic motivation through early adolescence. Conversely, parental reliance on extrinsic motivational practices to promote achievement may lower academic intrinsic motivation (Gottfried et al., 1994; Gottfried, Fleming, & Gottfried, 1998).

- Extrinsic and intrinsic motivation may be more interrelated in cultures that emphasize interdependence. Asian American children view the desire to please adults (extrinsic) and intrinsic motivation as interrelated, whereas White children tend to view external pressures from adults and intrinsic motivation as distinct forces (Lepper, Corpus, & Iyengar, 2005).

Extrinsic rewards may not be necessary in early childhood because children at this developmental level generally are curious, inquisitive, and motivated to learn new things (Corpus & Wormington, 2014; Harter, 1978). Students tend to become less intrinsically motivated as they move from upper elementary grades through middle and high school (Hayenga & Corpus, 2010; Wormington et al., 2012). They prefer less challenging tasks and show less interest in and curiosity about learning (Dotterer, McHale, & Crouter, 2009; Harter & Jackson, 1992). Students also tend to like reading, math, and science less as they advance in grade level (Gottfried et al., 2001; Jacobs, Lanza, Osgood, Eccles, & Wigfield, 2002).

The structure and climate of classrooms and schools in middle and high school compared to elementary school may help explain the developmental trend toward extrinsically motivated learning.

- Middle school and high school students may experience *decontextualized learning*, where learners do not see the relevance of academic material (Lepper et al., 2005). Teachers in middle and high schools have many students to teach and tend to use more lecture and fewer hands-on activities. This may lead students to view learning as acquiring discrete bits of information. For example, high school students spend about one-third of their academic learning time passively absorbing information through instructional methods such as lecture (Shernoff, Csikszentmihalyi, Schneider, & Shernoff, 2003).

- Students have multiple teachers, switch classes, and often have schedules with academic subjects organized into short periods. This creates an environment in which students are anonymous, feel little belongingness in the classroom, and become disengaged with the subject matter (Martin, 2009; Otis, Grouzet, & Pelletier, 2005; Rolland, 2012).

- Middle and high schools also have stricter academic and behavioral policies than elementary schools, leading to a more extrinsic and controlling atmosphere (Eccles, Wigfield, & Schiefele, 1998; Lepper & Henderlong, 2000). As a result, students may make fewer independent decisions, encounter more rules and discipline, and experience poorer teacher–student relationships (Anderman & Maehr, 1994).

- As students progress beyond elementary school, they also experience a greater emphasis on performance goals, such as looking smart and getting the highest grades rather than mastery and learning for the sake of learning (Haselhuhn, Al-Mabuk, Gabriele, Groen, & Galloway, 2007; Randall & Engelhard, 2009). This increasing emphasis on competition among students can be seen in honor rolls, class rankings, and standardized testing.

- As children develop, they also spend more time comparing their own skills and performance in academic subjects with those of their classmates, which could lead to the increased competition and focus on performance goals that we see during adolescence (Wigfield, Eccles, Schiefele, Roeser, & Davis-Kean, 2006; Wigfield & Wagner, 2005).

Video Case 14.1 ▲
Motivational Factors

© SAGE Publications

Belongingness: See relatedness in Module 16.

Mastery and performance goals: See Module 15

Competition and Extrinsic Motivation. This boy looking to see if he made the honor roll illustrates the increased academic competition in middle school and high school that can lead to greater extrinsic motivation.

All of these experiences lead students to become more extrinsically motivated and perhaps shift from an internal to an external locus of control. **Locus of control** is a belief that the result of one's behavior is due to either external factors outside one's control, such as luck or other people's behaviors (i.e., external locus), or internal factors under one's control, such as ability or effort (i.e., internal locus; Rotter, 1966, 1990). Keep in mind that not all extrinsic motivators lead to an external locus of control or are detrimental to motivation. Extrinsic motivators can be an important part of teachers' motivational techniques when used appropriately. Let's look at two extrinsic approaches teachers use to encourage motivation for learning: rewards and praise.

REWARDING STUDENTS FOR LEARNING

❷ Explain why task-contingent rewards tend to diminish intrinsic motivation and performance-contingent rewards tend to enhance intrinsic motivation.

Educators often attempt to stimulate students' intrinsic motivation for academic tasks by using extrinsic motivators. Teachers give tangible rewards such as stickers or smiley faces on classwork or homework that is well done, no-homework passes, or opportunities to pick a prize from a treasure box. They also use intangible rewards, such as extra time for recess or chatting with classmates, and rewards for completing required assignments or tasks (Premack, 1959, 1963). How do extrinsic motivators such as these affect students' intrinsic motivation?

Consider a common incentive in schools in which a principal sets a reading goal and promises a school-wide activity, such as a school carnival or field trip to an amusement park. The goal may be a certain number of pages, minutes, or books read. According to the operant conditioning model, rewarding reading in this way will increase the likelihood that the behavior (reading) will be performed again, enhancing motivation to produce the behavior in that environment (Skinner, 1953).

The question, however, is whether students continue to read after they no longer receive rewards (once the school carnival or field trip has passed). Operant conditioning predicts that when the reward is withdrawn, individuals will perform the behavior just as frequently as they did before (Skinner, 1953). However, in classic experimental research, Deci (1971) provided the first evidence that individuals performed a task *less frequently* after withdrawal of extrinsic rewards than they did before rewards were introduced. Therefore, rewards actually *undermined* intrinsic motivation.

To use rewards effectively for enhancing intrinsic motivation, teachers should consider not only *what* rewards to offer and *why* but also *how* and *when*. Rewards can have different effects on intrinsic motivation depending on several factors:

- the purpose of the reward,

- how students perceive the reward, and

- the context in which the reward is given.

Task-Contingent and Performance-Contingent Rewards

Task-contingent rewards are given for *participating in* an activity (a certificate or extra free time for working on a science project) or for *completing* an activity (a sticker for completing a set of math problems). Students tend to perceive task-contingent rewards as controlling—the student must only do what the teacher wants to get the reward. Such rewards undermine intrinsic motivation. When given task-contingent rewards, students show less interest in the activity and choose to engage in the activity less often than before the reward (Deci, Koestner, & Ryan, 1999a, 2001).

Like task-contingent rewards, educational practices that students perceive as controlling may also lead to diminished intrinsic motivation. These practices include

- close monitoring by the teacher (Plant & Ryan, 1985),

- deadlines and imposed goals (Amabile, DeJong, & Lepper, 1976; Manderlink & Harackiewicz, 1984),

- threats and directives (e.g., "get started," or "no, do it this way"; Assor, Kaplan, Kanat-Maymon, & Roth, 2005; Koestner, Ryan, Bernieri, & Holt, 1984),

- external evaluation (Harackiewicz, Manderlink, & Sansone, 1984; Hughes, Sullivan, & Mosley, 1985), and

- competition (Reeve & Deci, 1996; Vansteenkiste & Deci, 2003).

The effect of any of these educational practices, though, depends on the context and emphasis (Stipek, 2002). For example, goals may enhance intrinsic motivation if students are encouraged to participate in establishing the goals and if the emphasis is on mastery or personal growth (Deci, Koestner, & Ryan, 1999b; Stipek, 2002). In a competition, how students feel about the outcome is of primary importance. When students feel pressure to win above all else, even the winners experience diminished intrinsic motivation (Vansteenkiste & Deci, 2003). When students lose competitions, such as spelling bees or science fairs, or even receive a lower grade than other students, they still can feel enhanced intrinsic motivation if they receive positive feedback about their performance. Positive performance feedback, which provides students with information about mastery, can facilitate intrinsic motivation more than winning a competition (Vansteenkiste & Deci, 2003).

In contrast with task-contingent rewards, **performance-contingent rewards** are those given for doing well or achieving a certain level of performance (receiving a sticker for *correctly* completing all math problems). Students perceive such rewards to be informational—conveying meaningful feedback about one's achievement on a given task. Compared with task-contingent rewards, performance-contingent rewards are less likely to undermine intrinsic motivation. Students who receive performance-contingent rewards for successful performance on an activity continue to express interest and enjoyment in that activity, although they may choose to engage in the activity less frequently (Deci et al., 1999a). Performance-contingent rewards may enhance intrinsic motivation by providing positive feedback about students' competence (Cameron, 2001; Deci et al., 1999b).

Even performance-contingent rewards can undermine intrinsic motivation in certain situations. When students expect a performance-contingent reward for achieving a certain level of mastery, the anticipation of being evaluated may interfere with their intrinsic interest in the subject (Harackiewicz et al., 1984). For example, elementary school students may be told in advance that if they earn an A on their math test, they will receive a no-homework pass, or high school students may know that if they pass a standardized test at the end of their AP History course, they can receive college credit. These students may be more focused on the anticipated evaluation and outcome than the subject matter itself.

Also, feedback that is negative may not enhance intrinsic motivation because the feedback suggests a lack of ability (Stipek, 2002). For example, in research that closely reflected what happens in classrooms, where only the top-performing participants received a reward and lower performing participants received a smaller reward or no reward at all, performance-contingent rewards clearly undermined intrinsic motivation for individuals receiving lesser rewards (Deci, Koestner, & Ryan, 2001).

Rewards. Rewards can take many forms, such as extra recess, stickers, no-homework passes, or the opportunity to choose a toy from a treasure box, as shown here.

Think of some instances when you have received rewards for learning in or out of school. Were these rewards task contingent or performance contingent, and did they increase or decrease your intrinsic motivation?

APPLICATIONS: USING REWARDS EFFECTIVELY

Educators can adopt the following research-based guidelines for using rewards in ways that are minimally detrimental to intrinsic motivation (Deci, Ryan, & Koestner, 2001):

Occasionally use unexpected rewards. Unexpected rewards, such as surprising students with a movie after a job well done on a group activity, do not significantly affect intrinsic motivation. Students are not specifically working for the opportunity to receive a reward and are more likely to be intrinsically motivated by the task itself (Cameron, 2001; Deci, Ryan, & Koestner, 2001).

Use expected tangible rewards sparingly. Expected tangible rewards (e.g., prizes or certificates) generally undermine intrinsic motivation, especially for children in elementary school (Deci et al., 1999a; Deci, Koestner, & Ryan, 2001). Rewarding students in this way can cause them to shift from an internal to an external locus of control (Deci & Ryan, 1985). For example, if students who initially were interested in recreational reading receive rewards for reading, they may at first believe that they received rewards for their ability to read well (internal locus of control) but eventually may consider rewards as externally imposed constraints by the teacher (external locus of control). Over time, students may believe that their successful performance is due more to the reward than to internal causes such as ability, effort, or interest (Brockner & Vasta, 1981; Pittman, Cooper, & Smith, 1977). One exception may be tangible rewards that are related to the activity being rewarded, such as receiving a book as a reward for reading (Marinak & Gambrell, 2008).

Withdraw rewards as soon as possible. Rewards may be useful in situations where school tasks are necessary but seem to have little intrinsic value or interest to students.

Elementary students may groan at practicing spelling words, middle school students may not particularly enjoy working through sets of math problems, and high school students may not initially appreciate reading the Greek tragedies. In these instances, educators can use rewards to draw students into an activity because students who develop an initial interest in a topic or activity are more likely to develop intrinsic motivation (Hidi, 2000). However, when teachers use rewards to encourage engagement in a task for which students have little initial interest, they should withdraw rewards as soon as possible to prevent students from engaging in the activity solely to get the reward (Stipek, 2002).

Use the most modest reward possible. Individuals will attribute their involvement in an activity to the most obvious explanation. Receiving a reward leads individuals to attribute their successful performance more to the reward itself—a very obvious reason for engaging in an activity—and less to internal causes such as intrinsic interest, enjoyment, or ability (Deci et al., 1999a, Deci & Ryan, 1985). As a result, individuals may shift from an internal to an external locus of control. The use of smaller rewards, however, will not become the primary reason for students' participation in a learning activity because they are not very prominent as explanations for student behavior (Stipek, 2002).

Make rewards contingent on quality of work (Deci, Eghrari, Patrick, & Leone, 1994). Remember that performance-contingent rewards are informational—conveying feedback about one's achievement on a given task. Teachers can give performance-contingent rewards to reinforce effort as well as achievement. Rewarding students' efforts toward mastering a particular task fosters intrinsic motivation (Harter, 1978). Performance-contingent rewards for increased effort and improvement over past performance may be especially beneficial to students who do not recognize that effort has an effect on task success (Seligman, 1994; Urdan, Midgley, & Anderman, 1998). Teaching them that effort leads to greater achievement will increase their achievement level (Craske, 1985; Van Overwalle & De Metsenaere, 1990).

Minimize the use of an authoritarian style. Authoritarian teaching styles that involve controlling language, directives, threats, and close monitoring have been shown to decrease students' intrinsic motivation (Deci et al., 1994; Koestner et al., 1984). Teachers should avoid using disapproval as a way to motivate students when they fail to achieve mastery on tasks. Punishment for failing to master a task inhibits intrinsic interest (Harter, 1978). Disapproval or punishment for failures also leads students to prefer easy tasks and thus to avoid risking the failure that sometimes occurs when initially attempting a challenging task (Stipek, 2002).

PRAISING STUDENTS FOR LEARNING

③ Discuss the conditions under which praise can enhance or diminish intrinsic motivation, and explain individual and developmental differences in the effectiveness of praise.

In some situations, the performance of a skill or behavior itself provides an individual with direct reinforcement (Stipek, 2002). A 5-year-old who successfully ties her shoes and an adolescent who beats his highest score on a video game have immediate feedback about mastery of their skills. In other situations, reinforcement of an individual's performance requires social input. Knowing that your batting swing has improved, your term paper is persuasive, or your homework assignment is correct requires feedback from an adult. In these cases, **praise,** or positive feedback in the form of written or spoken comments, is useful for providing individuals with feedback.

In developmental terms, praise has a limited window of effectiveness. Children younger than age 7 interpret praise as affirmation that they are pleasing authority figures, rather than as

Video Case 14.2 ▲
Use of Praise

© SAGE Publications

feedback about their performance (Brophy, 1981). However, even in toddlers and preschool-age children, the type of praise they hear, as we see in the next section, affects their later beliefs about ability and their motivation (Gunderson et al., 2013). Elementary school students tend to benefit from praise because they come to realize that praise should occur only after certain types of behavior, such as compliance and academic success. By the time students reach high school, however, they interpret praise from the teacher as an indication of low ability (Henderlong & Lepper, 2002). For praise to be effective with older students, it has to be sincere, provide positive information about one's competence, and not be given for tasks that are too easy (Henderlong & Lepper, 2002).

Praise may also benefit some students more than others because of the way they perceive the praise.

> **DIVERSITY**

- Students with an external locus of control—a belief that teacher praise is caused by external factors (teacher's attitude or liking of them) rather than internal factors (their own success)—are more receptive to praise (Brophy, 1981).

- Lower achieving students and students from lower socioeconomic backgrounds tend to benefit academically from praise. Students who are more likely to be discouraged academically may interpret teacher praise as more meaningful (Brophy, 1981).

Praise is widely recommended as a reinforcement method because it is free and has the potential to provide encouragement and enhance self-esteem (Brophy, 1981). Praise also may have positive effects partly because it is unexpected, leading students to believe that they genuinely have done something praiseworthy (Brophy, 1981; Deci et al., 1999a). However, like the rewards discussed earlier, praise can enhance or undermine intrinsic motivation depending on the type of praise, how it is given, and how it is perceived.

Process, Performance, and Person Praise

Teachers can give students process praise or performance praise as feedback to encourage improvement. **Process praise** is an evaluation of the process taken to complete a task—"What a careful job you did coloring inside the lines!" This form of praise may result in a belief that ability is controllable and able to be improved—called an incremental belief about ability. When parents use process praise with their toddlers, their children tend to develop an incremental belief about ability as elementary school students (Gunderson et al., 2013). Process praise also fosters intrinsic motivation and feelings of competence in students from childhood through late adolescence (Corpus & Lepper, 2007; Haimovitz & Corpus, 2011; Mueller & Dweck, 1998). **Performance praise** (or outcome praise) is an evaluation of the end product—"The argument in your term paper is clear and compelling" (Corpus & Lepper, 2007). Researchers refer to process or performance praise as *informational praise* because it provides students with information about what they have done well and what to do the next time.

Informational praise enhances students' intrinsic motivation. Specific praise that provides detailed information about one's competence promotes a sense of mastery, leading to the following outcomes (Corpus & Lepper, 2007; Dweck, 2006; Zentall & Morris, 2010):

- increased interest,
- more positive self-evaluations,
- more positive attitudes about the activity,
- persistence after experiencing failure, and
- a greater likelihood of choosing the activity during free time.

Person praise involves a favorable judgment about a person's attributes or behaviors, such as "You're so good at math" (Corpus & Lepper, 2007). In contrast with process and

Incremental view of ability: See Module 15

Need for competence: See Module 16

performance praise, this form of praise does not indicate specifically what the student does well. It is also considered by researchers to be *controlling praise.* The teacher's favorable evaluation, rather than students' intrinsic interest or self-evaluation, provides the motivation. Students work to receive another favorable evaluation.

Person praise may be detrimental to intrinsic motivation. This form of praise may result in a belief that ability is fixed and uncontrollable—called an entity view of ability (Corpus & Lepper, 2007; Pomerantz & Kempner, 2013). Parents who use person praise with their elementary-age children tend to have children who hold an entity belief about ability and avoid challenging schoolwork (Pomerantz & Kempner, 2013). Use of person praise may lead students to acquire learned helplessness when faced with repeated failures (Kamins & Dweck, 1999). They attribute their failures to causes beyond their control and give up trying (Seligman & Maier, 1967). Person praise may also foster a poor sense of self-worth because it leads to feelings of shame after failure and may teach students to make inferences about a global sense of worth based on their performance (Brummelman et al., 2014; Kamins & Dweck, 1999).

Like person praise, positive feedback given using controlling language, such as *should* and *ought,* tends to undermine intrinsic motivation even when teachers are attempting to give students encouragement (Kast & Connor, 1988; Ryan, Mims, & Koestner, 1983). An example is "Thank you for turning in neat homework. You should keep up the good effort." Instead, a teacher could say "I've noticed your homework is neater; I appreciate your efforts."

Girls and boys react differently to person, process, and performance praise. In comparison with girls, elementary school boys are more intrinsically motivated by person praise, particularly praise of their ability when they succeed (Corpus & Lepper, 2007; Koestner, Zuckerman, & Koestner, 1989). Elementary school girls are more intrinsically motivated by performance and process praise, particularly praise for effort on their successes (Corpus & Lepper, 2007; Koestner et al., 1989). Girls also tend to perceive praise as controlling even when the praise is relatively ambiguous with respect to its informational or controlling qualities (Kast & Connor, 1988; Koestner, Zuckerman, & Koestner, 1987).

Entity view of ability: See Module 15

Learned helplessness: See Module 15

Self-Worth: See Module 16

DIVERSITY

APPLICATIONS: USING PRAISE EFFECTIVELY

Teachers' appropriate use of praise can encourage students to focus on the intrinsic value of learning. Table 14.1 provides do's and don'ts for effective praise. Keep in mind these recommendations for using praise effectively to foster intrinsic motivation in students.

Make praise specific to the particular behavior being reinforced. Teachers should refrain from using vague phrases such as "Nice work," "Good job," or "You're so smart!" Instead, they should use process or performance praise to identify exactly what is *good* about the behavior. Specific praise is more credible and is informational, providing feedback about students' performance. Also, praising children and adolescents for being smart leads them to believe that learning is about looking smart and not making mistakes (Dweck, 2006). These children believe intelligence to be innate and fixed, and they experience lowered motivation when they are confronted with failure. When using specific praise, teachers also should *not* include social comparisons—comparing a student's performance to that of other classmates—because it may undermine students' later perseverance (Henderlong & Lepper, 2002). If students learn to judge their personal success by comparing themselves with others rather than focusing on individual mastery, they may not learn to cope with situations in which others show superior performance.

Be sure praise is sincere. Teacher praise must be credible for students to believe that their performance is praiseworthy. Praise can undermine intrinsic motivation, so teachers need to be careful to

- not praise everyone, because students will be less likely to attribute praise to anything special (Brophy, 1981).

Video Case 14.3 ▲
Praise and Rewards

© SAGE Publications

TABLE 14.1 — Examples of Effective Praise and Ineffective Praise

EFFECTIVE PRAISE . . .	INEFFECTIVE PRAISE . . .
is delivered contingently.	is delivered randomly or unsystematically.
specifies the particulars of the accomplishment.	is restricted to global positive reactions.
shows spontaneity, variety, and other signs of credibility; suggests clear attention to the student's accomplishment.	shows a bland uniformity that suggests a conditioned response made with minimal attention.
rewards attainment of specified performance criteria (which can include effort criteria, however).	rewards mere participation, without consideration of performance processes or outcomes.
provides information to students about their competence or the value of their accomplishments.	provides no information at all or gives students information about their status.
orients students toward better appreciation of their own task-related behavior and thinking about problem solving.	orients students toward comparing themselves with others and thinking about competing.
uses students' own prior accomplishments as the context for describing present accomplishments.	uses the accomplishments of peers as the context for describing students' present accomplishments.
is given in recognition of noteworthy effort or success at difficult (for this student) tasks.	is given without regard to the effort expended or the meaning of the accomplishment.
attributes success to effort and ability, implying that similar successes can be expected in the future.	attributes success to ability alone or to external factors such as luck or low task difficulty.
fosters endogenous attributions (students believe that they expend effort on the task because they enjoy the task and/or want to develop task-relevant skills).	fosters exogenous attributions (students believe that they expend effort on the task for external reasons—to please the teacher, win a competition or reward, and so on).
focuses students' attention on their own task-relevant behavior.	focuses students' attention on the teacher as an external authority figure who is manipulating them.
fosters appreciation of, and desirable attributions about, task-relevant behavior after the process is completed.	intrudes into the ongoing process, distracting attention from task-relevant behavior.

SOURCE: J. Brophy (1981), "Teacher praise: A functional analysis." *Review of Educational Research, 51*(1), 5–32. Copyright © 1981 American Educational Research Association. Reprinted by permission of Sage Publications.

- not praise students for easy tasks, because students see the praise as undeserved (Marzano, Pickering, & Pollack, 2005). They perceive praise for performing an easy task as an indication of low ability (Miller & Horn, 1997; Weiner, 1990).

- not praise students for completing a task quickly and easily because it conveys that "being smart" does not involve effort (Dweck & Master, 2008). This promotes a perception that ability is fixed and uncontrollable. Instead, teachers should say that the task is too easy and offer a more challenging one, which conveys that teachers value challenging tasks that require effort (Dweck & Master, 2008).

Entity view of ability: See Module 15

Give praise that is contingent on the behavior to be reinforced. When teachers give praise that is contingent on success, students interpret it as feedback that success has been achieved (Brophy, 1981; O'Leary & O'Leary, 1977). However, praise is often noncontingent because of the unsystematic way teachers apply praise during lessons (Beaman & Wheldall, 2000). Teachers have been found to

- give praise for success relatively infrequently—only about 10% of the time— suggesting that they do not consistently offer praise despite observing many examples of successful performance in their students (Brophy, 1981);

- shift their criteria for "success," leading them to praise a student for a certain achievement on one occasion and not on another (Mehan, 1974); and

- praise incorrect responses in addition to correct responses (Anderson, Evertson, & Brophy, 1979). For example, teachers gave similar praise to students who demonstrated errorless oral reading and to students whose oral reading contained mistakes.

DIVERSITY

Avoid the use of person praise. As we discussed, person praise has detrimental effects on students' intrinsic motivation for learning. This form of praise is perceived as controlling, and it may also lead students to believe that ability is fixed and to give up in the face of failure. This is especially true for learners with low-self-esteem. In one study, adults gave children with low self-esteem twice as much person praise compared to children with high self-esteem, whereas they gave children with high self-esteem more process praise (Brummelman et al., 2014). Adults may provide person praise to students with low self-esteem with good intentions—as a way to correct for children's insecurities about their low ability. However, the approach backfires when children consequently feel shame for their failures (Brummelman et al., 2014).

Think of some instances when you have been praised. Did the praise increase your intrinsic motivation or decrease it? Why do you think this happened?

WHEN THE REWARD IS THE ACTIVITY ITSELF

4 Discuss methods teachers can use to create an intrinsically motivating learning environment.

Flow Theory

Some students are intrinsically motivated by the nature of the task in which they are involved and do not need any external reward. Have you ever been surprised by how much time has passed when you've been engaged in an interesting experiment or activity in one of your college classes? If so, you were in a state of flow, also called optimal experience or, using a sports metaphor, being "in the zone." **Flow** is a feeling of intrinsic enjoyment and absorption in a task that is challenging and rewarding, making a person feel at one with the task. Mihalyi Csikszentmihalyi (1990, 2000) created flow theory to describe the subjective experiences of individuals who are motivated to engage in an activity for its own sake. For flow to occur, individuals must experience concentration, interest, and enjoyment simultaneously (Csikszentmihalyi, 1997).

Some activities are more likely than others to create the level of engagement and absorption characterized by flow. Playing chess, rock climbing, sailing, and playing a musical instrument are activities conducive to flow. In general, experiences that promote flow tend to

- have rules that require the learning of new skills,

- establish goals,

- provide feedback,

- allow the participants to have a sense of control, and

- facilitate a high level of concentration and involvement.

Based on these characteristics, what classroom experiences do you suspect might be flow inducing? At the upper elementary level, vocabulary relay races in which teams of students compete against one another to define a set of vocabulary terms could have flow-inducing components: rules of the relay, immediate feedback (as each vocabulary word's definition is checked), heightened concentration, and active participation. At the middle school or high school level, flow might be induced by a living history assignment in which students learn about the Civil War and then spend time planning and implementing a live reenactment of a certain battle.

Flow state is difficult to achieve and maintain (Schweinle, Turner, & Meyer, 2008). To achieve a state of flow, an individual must have the right balance between the degree of challenge in the activity and the degree of mastery of the necessary skills for engaging in the activity (Brophy, 2008; Shernoff et al., 2003). A student whose skills exceed the requirements of the activity likely will find the task boring and not conducive to flow. Likewise, a student who lacks skills for a particular activity may find it frustrating and will not experience a state of flow. If individuals are willing to devote an extensive amount of time and practice to mastering new skills, an activity that at first requires conscious focus and effort can become conducive to flow (Csikszentmihalyi, 1990). For that reason, flow experiences may be easier to attain in older students. Older students might better understand that time and sustained effort devoted to a challenging task are needed for improving skills. They also may have a more sophisticated view of challenge as a vehicle for helping them improve their skills, which can lead to enhancing an area of talent (Schweinle et al., 2008).

APPLICATIONS: CREATING AN INTRINSICALLY MOTIVATING LEARNING ENVIRONMENT

Teachers can create an intrinsically motivating learning environment through the way they introduce material, design learning tasks, group students for activities, and display students' work. Let's explore each of these components.

Introduce a lesson by conveying its importance or relevance. Students often ask teachers "Why do I have to know this?" When students know why it is important to learn something and when and where to use this new knowledge, they will be more likely to value what they are learning, which can lead to increased intrinsic motivation (Brophy, 2008;

Turner & Paris, 1995). Relating information to students' interests is particularly effective in conveying the value of to-be-learned material (Brophy, 2008; Covington, 2000). For example, if a high school physics teacher begins a lesson on mass and velocity by telling students how it relates to driving a car or another use relevant to their lives, this should pique their interest and intrinsically motivate them to learn. When students have a personal interest in material, they are more likely to process information meaningfully and to learn more (Ainley, Hidi, & Berndorff, 2002; Cordova & Lepper, 1996).

Another way to emphasize the importance of lessons is to ground them in authentic learning activities that are real-life tasks, such as designing experiments in science, writing letters to members of Congress in an English class, or conducting an interview for a social studies class. Authentic activities encourage the acquisition of skills for solving problems and completing tasks that are important in the real world (Brown, Collins, & Duguid, 1989; Collins, Hawkins, & Carver, 1991). Students may be motivated in these instances because learning has real-world significance.

Use enthusiasm, novelty, and surprise. Introducing new material through the use of enthusiasm, novelty, and surprise can spark *situational interest* in learning—an immediate interest in a particular lesson (Hidi, 2000; Silvia, 2005, 2006). Using novelty and surprise is consistent with Piaget's (1954, 1963) notion of *disequilibrium,* a state of cognitive imbalance in which new information does not fit with an individual's existing way of thinking. In Piaget's theory of cognitive development, individuals are motivated to learn in order to resolve their disequilibrium.

Design tasks of optimal difficulty (Covington, 2000; Stipek, 1996). Providing tasks that are just slightly beyond the skill level of students is an effective way to challenge them (Piaget, 1985; Vygotsky, 1978). Optimal challenge fosters feelings of competence and self-esteem. Teachers must be careful to tailor tasks to the ability levels of their students (Stipek, 2002). Work that is too difficult increases anxiety, but tasks that are too easy can lead to boredom. The right balance between challenge and skill level can also foster flow experiences. When middle school or high school students are allowed to choose their classes, such as electives or foreign languages, this presents them with an opportunity to choose courses at an appropriate difficulty level for their skills and may facilitate flow experiences in these classes (Schweinle et al., 2008).

Authentic tasks: See situated learning in Module 18 and authentic assessment in Module 23

Situational interest: See Module 12

Disequilibrium: See Module 6

Using Surprise When Teaching. Novelty or surprise, as shown here by the teacher demonstrating a chemical reaction, can spark intrinsic motivation.

©iStockphoto.com/Steve Debenport

Provide students with choices for learning activities (Deci & Ryan, 1992; Ryan & Stiller, 1991). Even though students might develop feelings of competence in response to praise and extrinsic rewards, they might not become intrinsically motivated unless they have a sense of autonomy, or self-determination (Ryan & Deci, 2000). In other words, students should feel that they have control over their learning. Teachers who promote autonomy by offering students opportunities to make choices that affect their learning create more responsible, independent, self-regulated learners (Patall, Cooper, & Robinson, 2008; Patall, Cooper, & Wynn, 2010). Keep in mind that choice is beneficial for tasks that students consider uninteresting (Patall, 2013). Also, students with a high level of individual interest prefer to make choices in learning, and this further enhances their motivation (Patall, 2013). If students are provided with too many choices, however, they can become overwhelmed. An effective teacher must be selective about how and under what circumstances to allow student choice in learning tasks. For example, a teacher might *require* groups of students to develop social studies projects about a particular country but *allow* groups to choose which country to research based on their personal interests.

Self-determination: See Module 16

Create tasks that involve collaborative grouping. Collaborative group activities can focus students' attention on the intrinsic value of learning (Turner & Paris, 1995). Learning in a social context not only challenges students to think in more advanced ways but also can satisfy students' need for affiliation (Deci & Ryan, 2000; Vygotsky, 1978). Collaboration works best when:

Collaborative grouping activities: See Module 19

- students depend on one another to reach a desired goal,

- all students must contribute to the group toward the goal,

- they are shown how to work together effectively, and

- group performance is valued or rewarded in some way (Driscoll, 2005).

Display student work to emphasize effort, creativity, and pride in accomplishments. Displaying students' work on an art wall, bulletin board, or website or at events like a science fair can lead to an increase in intrinsic motivation, depending on what teachers choose to display (Malone & Lepper, 1983).

Putting only A papers on a bulletin board can undermine feelings of competence in students who did well but did not earn an A. This competitive focus can foster feelings of incompetence in students who have performed well but did not outperform classmates (Stipek, 2002). In contrast, displaying students' work is effective if it is intended to show improvement over past performance or conveys the message that there is more than one way to complete a project (Fryer & Elliot, 2008). This recognition process creates positive feelings about effort, ownership, achievement, and responsibility (Turner & Paris, 1995).

Imagine a grade level you intend to teach. How would you use these guidelines to create an intrinsically motivating classroom environment?

SUMMARY

❶ **Explain how motivation changes from elementary through middle school, and discuss what factors might account for this trend.** Students' motivation shifts as they grow, from an intrinsic focus to an extrinsic focus. With extrinsic motivation, students may engage in an activity to obtain an external reward, while intrinsic motivation means the activity is itself rewarding. Students' intrinsic motivation for academic tasks declines from elementary through middle school. This may be due to changes in the structure of the classroom environment, a greater focus on grades and evaluations of performance, decontextualized learning, and the overuse of extrinsic rewards for learning.

② **Explain why task-contingent rewards tend to diminish intrinsic motivation and performance-contingent rewards tend to enhance intrinsic motivation.** Task-contingent rewards, given for merely completing a task or an activity, diminish intrinsic motivation. Students perceive task-contingent rewards as controlling and work only to get the reward. Performance-contingent rewards are less likely to undermine intrinsic motivation and may even enhance it, because they provide information about a student's level of mastery. However, even performance-contingent rewards can undermine intrinsic motivation if the feedback is negative.

③ **Discuss the conditions under which praise can enhance or diminish intrinsic motivation, and explain individual and developmental differences in the effectiveness of praise.** Praise generally enhances intrinsic motivation because it is unexpected and provides feedback about a student's competence. However, praise may diminish intrinsic motivation if teachers use it as feedback for easy tasks or convey it in a controlling or insincere manner. Praise is more likely to benefit students in the middle elementary grades, lower achieving students, students from lower socioeconomic backgrounds, males, and students with an external locus of control.

④ **Discuss methods teachers can use to create an intrinsically motivating learning environment.** Teachers have several options for creating intrinsically motivating environments. In general, they can convey the importance of a new lesson or concept and spark interest in academic subjects by using enthusiasm, novelty, and surprise. Teachers can create tasks that involve collaborative learning, provide students with a choice in learning tasks, and be sure that tasks are optimally challenging for all students. Teachers can appropriately display students' work, making sure that these create positive feelings about effort, achievement, and responsibility.

KEY CONCEPTS

academic intrinsic motivation, 277

extrinsic motivation, 277

flow, 286

intrinsic motivation, 277

locus of control, 279

performance-contingent rewards, 280

performance praise, 283

person praise, 283

praise, 282

process praise, 283

reinforcement, 277

task-contingent rewards, 280

CASE STUDIES: REFLECT AND EVALUATE

EARLY CHILDHOOD: THE WORKSHEETS

These questions refer to the case study on page 268.

1. Is the kindergarten class as a whole extrinsically motivated or intrinsically motivated? Are there any students for whom your answer would be different? Based on the research presented in the module, would you expect the same type of motivation in a sixth-grade class? Explain.

2. Mrs. Garvey is rewarding Emanuel, Kristina, and Martin by allowing them to play after satisfactorily completing their seat-work. What type of reward is this called? Is this reward effective in promoting students' intrinsic motivation, according to the research evidence?

3. Does Claire have an external locus of control or an internal locus of control? How do you know? How might that influence the effect that praise has on her motivation?

4. What guideline did Mrs. Garvey violate when praising Alannah and Mahiro? What alternative praise would you suggest Mrs. Garvey use? Give an example.

5. Some of the children want to rush through their work so they can play like Martin and his friends. How can you use rewards to motivate these children to focus on their schoolwork?

6. How can Mrs. Garvey encourage Martin to have an intrinsic motivation to learn math?

ELEMENTARY SCHOOL: WRITER'S BLOCK

These questions refer to the case study on page 270.

1. Identify the instances of extrinsic and intrinsic motivation in this case.

2. Mrs. Okuda announces that students may select an activity of their choice after they've completed their writing. What type of reward is this called? Is this effective in promoting intrinsic motivation, according to the research evidence?

3. Based on the research evidence, explain why Mrs. Okuda's freewriting activity might discourage intrinsic motivation. What could she do differently to enhance students' intrinsic motivation for writing?

4. What type of praise did Mrs. Okuda use with Shanti—controlling or informational? According to the guidelines for praise discussed in the module, is the praise given to Shanti effective? Why or why not?

MIDDLE SCHOOL: THE MATH REVIEW

These questions refer to the case study on page 272.

1. Do the eighth graders appear to be intrinsically or extrinsically motivated in math class? According to the research evidence presented in the module, is their motivation typical of middle school students?

2. Based on the research evidence discussed in the module, are the first prize and class prize likely to enhance students' intrinsic motivation for math? Why or why not?

3. Is the feedback Mr. Pantera gives to Jeremy likely to be perceived as informational or controlling? How might that affect Jeremy's motivation?

HIGH SCHOOL: EXAM GRADES

These questions refer to the case study on page 274.

1. Contrast the motivational orientation—intrinsic or extrinsic—of students in general science and students in AP Physics.

2. Is the motivational orientation of students in Mr. Womack's classes typical of high school students? What factors might contribute to their motivational orientation?

3. According to the research presented in the module, is praising Madelyn for the highest grade on the physics exam an effective motivator? Why or why not?

5. Based on your reading of the module and the information presented in the case, does the practice of displaying students' writing on the bulletin board motivate them? If so, which students and in which way, intrinsically or extrinsically? How would you display students' work in your own classroom?

6. Outside of writing activities, identify strategies Mrs. Okuda can implement to foster intrinsic motivation in her third graders.

4. Based on the guidelines for effective praise, evaluate Mr. Pantera's interaction with Jesse. Imagine that Mr. Pantera and Jesse talk further after class. What can Mr. Pantera say to increase Jesse's intrinsic motivation for math?

5. What should the first prize and class prize be? How would that enhance students' intrinsic motivation?

6. Instead of creating a competition, what else could Mr. Pantera do to foster intrinsic motivation for math?

4. How can Mr. Womack encourage students like Chelsea to focus more on learning and less on grades?

5. If Mr. Womack wants to use rewards to stimulate students' intrinsic motivation and interest in science in his general science class, what types of rewards would you recommend? Be sure your answer is supported by the research evidence discussed in the module.

6. Aside from offering rewards, how can Mr. Womack create an intrinsically motivating environment in his general science class?

©iStockphoto.com/ Rawpixel Ltd

COGNITIVE THEORIES

OUTLINE	LEARNING GOALS

Cognitive Theories of Motivation

- Expectancy-Value Theory
- Goal Theory
- Attribution Theory

❶ Define expectancies and values, and explain how they influence students' motivation.

❷ Compare and contrast the two types of mastery and performance goals.

❸ Identify attributions that enhance motivation and those that lower motivation.

Developmental and Cultural Differences in Motivation

- Developmental Changes in Motivation
- Gender Differences in Motivation
- Ethnic Differences in Motivation

❹ Explain the major developmental changes in motivation.

❺ Identify gender and ethnic differences in motivation.

Serious Motivational Problems

- Learned Helplessness
- Anxiety

❻ Explain how learned helplessness and anxiety affect students' motivation to learn.

Applications: Enhancing Students' Motivation

- Student-Level Techniques
- Classroom-Level Techniques

❼ Identify student-level and classroom-level strategies for enhancing motivation.

COGNITIVE THEORIES OF MOTIVATION

❶ Define expectancies and values, and explain how they influence students' motivation.

❷ Compare and contrast the two types of mastery and performance goals.

❸ Identify attributions that enhance motivation and those that lower motivation.

What does *thinking* have to do with motivation? According to cognitive theories of motivation, changing students' motivation to learn requires changing the way they think. To do this, we need to understand students' expectations for success and valuing of learning tasks, their goals for learning activities, and their attributions (or explanations) for their successes and failures. In this module, we discuss:

- expectancy-value theory,
- goal theory, and
- attribution theory.

But before we discuss *how* to motivate student learning, let's review *what* motivation is. When students study for a test to get a good grade, they are exhibiting **extrinsic motivation,** which focuses on external rewards for their behavior. When students study out of interest or enjoyment, they show **intrinsic motivation,** in which learning is the reward itself. And some learning may be prompted by both, as when a student wants a good grade (extrinsic motivation) *and* enjoys the subject matter (intrinsic motivation).

Our goal as teachers is to foster **academic intrinsic motivation,** in which students exhibit curiosity and persistence and focus on mastery of knowledge and skills (Gottfried, Fleming, & Gottfried, 1994; Gottfried & Gottfried, 1996). From elementary school through high school, students with high academic intrinsic motivation have positive views of their ability, display lower anxiety and greater persistence, and show deeper learning and higher achievement than students with lower academic intrinsic motivation (Gottfried, Fleming, & Gottfried, 2001; Vansteenkiste, Simons, Lens, Sheldon, & Deci, 2004). To encourage academic intrinsic motivation in all students, we first need to understand the thinking that underlies students' motivation. Let's begin with expectancy-value theory.

What factors motivate you to succeed in school? Reflect on these factors as you read about the motivational theories.

Expectancy-Value Theory

What motivates students to participate in class, study, or complete homework assignments and projects? According to the expectancy-value model, the answer involves two components (Eccles, 2005; Wigfield & Eccles, 2000, 2002):

1. **Expectancy:** Students' expectation for success (Can I do this task?)

2. **Value:** Reasons for undertaking a task (Why should I want to do this task?)

Expectancies and values are related to each other. Individuals tend to value what they are good at (Jacobs, Lanza, Osgood, Eccles, & Wigfield, 2002; Wigfield et al., 1997). Expectancies and values also predict motivational behaviors, such as choice of activities as well as performance, effort, and persistence on activities (Denissen, Zarrett, & Eccles, 2007; Wigfield, Tonks, & Klauda, 2009).

EXPECTANCIES

Students have different expectancies for success. Some children and adolescents with positive expectancies believe that they can succeed on a task when they are presented with a new challenge, while others with negative expectancies believe that they are likely to fail. Expectancy depends on the student's **competency belief,** a judgment about one's relative ability in one

Master the content.
edge.sagepub.com/durwin3e
$SAGE edge™

domain compared to the ability of other individuals and compared to one's ability in other domains (Eccles et al., 1983). For example, a student may say, "Math is my strongest subject and I am better at it than my friends." Competency beliefs are determined by past experiences, our interpretations of those experiences (why we think we've succeeded or failed), and social and cultural factors, such as parental beliefs and gender-role stereotypes (e.g., the idea that males are better at math and females are better at reading; Eccles, 2005; Wigfield & Cambria, 2010a). Note that competency belief differs from an individual's sense of self-efficacy. Self-efficacy is a belief about a particular task and does not involve a comparison of one's ability to others' ability or to one's ability in other skill areas (Wigfield & Cambria, 2010a).

Self-efficacy: See Module 16

VALUES

Why do students choose to complete academic tasks? Individuals may choose to engage in tasks because of:

- **intrinsic value**—satisfying interest, curiosity, or enjoyment (completing a science project because the topic is interesting);

- **attainment value**—the *intrinsic* importance of being good at a task (studying spelling words to be a good speller); and

- **utility value**—*extrinsic* usefulness for meeting short-term and long-term goals (choosing to take calculus to prepare for college).

Ideally, we want students to engage in tasks for intrinsic reasons (intrinsic or attainment value). However, even though utility value provides an extrinsic reason for undertaking tasks, it also has motivational benefits. Students who consider academic tasks to have high utility value show greater effort and achievement compared to those with lower value for the tasks (Cole, Bergin, & Whittaker, 2008; Hulleman, Durik, Schweigert, & Harackiewicz, 2008; Malka & Covington, 2005).

Students also might choose to engage in tasks or to avoid tasks because of their **cost,** or the expense of engaging in the activity. A cost may be the amount of effort needed to complete a task, time away from other activities (e.g., going to the mall), or psychological risks, such as anxiety, fear of failure, or social consequences of success (e.g., being labeled a nerd).

Many factors influence how we value a task (Wigfield, Eccles, Schiefele, Roeser, & Davis-Kean, 2006). For example, a high school girl may decide to take calculus because she likes math (intrinsic value), is good at it (attainment value), and needs it for college (utility value). She has developed these values based on her view of herself (self-schema), long- and short-term goals, competency beliefs about math, and past experiences. Her parents' beliefs about math and their expectations for her success, as well as gender roles and cultural stereotypes, are environmental factors that also affect task values (Meece, Glienke, & Askew, 2009). Parents' values and expectancies for their child's success are related to adolescents' valuing of many school subjects (Simpkins, Fredricks, & Eccles, 2012).

The values students ascribe to academic tasks or subjects influence their achievement-related choices. For example, the value elementary school students place on reading, math, and science is predictive of the number of courses they will choose in high school in English, math, and science, respectively (Durik, Vida, & Eccles, 2006; Simpkins, Davis-Kean, & Eccles, 2006). Values are also related to adolescents' achievement-related choices, such as course selection decisions, involvement in sports, occupational choices, and anticipated college major (Eccles, Wigfield, & Schiefele, 1998; Simpkins et al., 2012).

Goal Theory

Individuals form goals for a variety of academic and nonacademic pursuits. An **achievement goal** includes both (a) the reason for undertaking a task and (b) the standard that individuals construct to evaluate their performance (Ames, 1992; Pintrich, 2000). For example, an adolescent may decide to earn better grades to get into college and may decide that this means earning Bs in all classes. Our *goal orientation,* or what drives our behaviors and choices, can be described by two types of mastery goals and two types of performance goals, as shown in Table 15.1.

Mastery-approach goals and performance-approach goals are grounded in a need for achievement. Students with these goals are motivated to approach situations in which they have an opportunity to achieve. Students with **mastery-approach goals** focus on improving intellectually, acquiring new skills and knowledge, and developing competence (Elliot & Murayama, 2008; Hulleman & Senko, 2010). Students who hold **performance-approach goals** are motivated simultaneously by a need to achieve and a fear of failure (Elliot & Church, 1997; Vansteenkiste, Lens, Elliot, Soenens, & Mouratidis, 2014). Because these students fear failure and have perceptions of low ability, their goal is to demonstrate their ability to others and outperform others (Hulleman et al., 2010; Urdan & Mestas, 2006).

TABLE 15.1	Comparing Mastery and Performance Orientations	
	MASTERY	**PERFORMANCE**
Approach State	Focus: mastering task, learning, understanding Standards: self-improvement, progress, deep understanding of task Outcomes: • intrinsic motivation, interest, enjoyment • deep-level learning strategies to enhance understanding and recall • preference for challenging tasks and moderate risk taking • adaptive help seeking • effort and persistence • positive self-efficacy and self-regulation	Focus: being superior, being the smartest, besting others Standards: getting best or highest grades, being best performer in class (comparing to the norm) Outcomes: • intrinsic motivation • effective, but often superficial, learning strategies (e.g., rote memorization) • effort and persistence • low anxiety and positive self-efficacy • acceptance of cheating
Avoidance State	Focus: avoiding misunderstanding, avoiding not learning or not mastering task Standards: not being wrong, not performing incorrectly relative to task Outcomes: • disorganized studying • increased test anxiety • negative feelings about failure • avoidance of help seeking • less intrinsic motivation	Focus: avoiding inferiority, not looking stupid or dumb in comparison to others Standards: not getting the worst grades, not being lowest performer in class (comparing to the norm) Outcomes: • surface-level learning strategies (e.g., memorizing, studying only what is likely to be on the test) • disorganized study habits • self-handicapping strategies (e.g., not trying, procrastinating, minimizing participation, making excuses for incomplete work, possibly cheating) • anxiety and negative feelings about failure • avoidance of help seeking • disengagement • lower performance

SOURCES: Anderman, Cupp, & Lane, 2009; Cury, Elliot, Da Fonseca, & Moller, 2006; Daniels et al., 2008; Darnon, Butera, Mugny, Quiamzade, & Hulleman, 2009; Elliot & Church, 1997; Elliot, McGregor, & Gable, 1999; Elliot & Moller, 2003; Harackiewicz, Barron, Pintrich, Elliot, & Thrash, 2002; Harackiewicz, Barron, Tauer, Carter, & Elliot, 2000; Hulleman et al., 2010; Hulleman & Senko, 2010; Jansen, 2006; Karabenick, 2003; Leondari & Gonida, 2007; Maatta & Nurmi, 2007; Middleton & Midgley, 1997; Moller & Elliot, 2006; Murayama & Elliot, 2009; Payne, Youngcourt, & Beaubien, 2007; Rolland, 2012; Valentiner, Mounts, Durik, & Gier-Lonsway, 2011.

Performance-Approach Goals. Some students are motivated to show others their ability, like the boy showing off his soccer trophy.

Mastery-approach and performance-approach goal orientations result in positive outcomes such as persistence and effort (Hulleman, Schrager, Bodmann, & Harackiewicz, 2010; Hulleman & Senko, 2010). Performance-approach goals are often linked to students' use of superficial learning strategies, such as memorizing, although this behavior nonetheless results in achievement most of the time. However, mastery-approach goals are not always linked to high achievement despite the use of deep-level learning strategies, such as planning and organizing material, relating information to prior knowledge, and monitoring comprehension while learning (Diseth, 2011; Hulleman et al., 2010). Particularly in elementary school, where there is an emphasis on learning factual knowledge, deeper processing may not be the most adaptive approach for mastery-oriented students who are high achieving (Rončević & Kolić-Vehovec, 2014).

While some individuals may be motivated to *approach* achievement situations, others may be motivated to *avoid* situations that may lead to failure. Students with **mastery-avoidance goals** want to avoid situations in which they might fail to achieve mastery. They judge their competence by personally created, absolute standards, such as avoiding a strikeout when coming up to bat or avoiding the possibility of answering a question incorrectly. Perfectionists are considered mastery avoidant because they set high personal standards and never want to be wrong or incorrect (Elliot & McGregor, 2001; Fletcher, Shim, & Wang, 2012). In contrast, students with **performance-avoidance goals** are concerned with judging their competence relative to others, such as failing a test they believe others will succeed on (Elliot & Church, 1997; Elliot & McGregor, 2001). To avoid failure, these students use several self-handicapping strategies listed in Table 15.1, which are a useful way to attribute failure to causes other than low ability, leading to less shame (Stipek, 2002).

Self-Handicapping strategies: See Module 16

Attribution Theory

Think about a time when you studied for a test and were surprised to find out that you received a lower grade than expected. What caused this outcome? According to attribution theory, we all try to explain our performance through **causal attributions,** interpretations of events based on past performance and social norms (Weiner, 2010). To better understand how attributions influence students' motivation, consider the three dimensions of attributions.

1. **Locus:** where we place the cause of the outcome. Do we believe our success or failure results from *internal* causes, such as ability and effort, or due to *external* causes, such as asking the teacher for help? Compared to external attributions, ability and effort attributions for success lead to higher levels of pride, confidence, satisfaction, and self-esteem (Graham & Weiner, 1996).

2. **Stability:** whether we perceive the cause as being stable or unstable over time. We expect future success when we attribute success to a *stable* cause (the typical effort you make every time you study). However, our expectation decreases when we attribute failure to a stable cause, such as our belief that a teacher's tests are too difficult (Weiner, 1982). Our expectations for future success are not hampered when we attribute failure to an *unstable* cause—say, missing several classes because of illness.

3. **Controllability:** our personal responsibility for the cause of the success or failure. Was success or failure *controllable* (the amount you studied) or *uncontrollable* (unfairness of the test)? Attributing success or failure to amount of effort generally leads to positive

expectations for future performance, because we believe that effort is under our control (Weiner, 1994). Our future motivation is not likely to be affected by attributing success to uncontrollable causes, such as luck. However, when we attribute failure to uncontrollable causes, such as believing we have low ability that cannot improve, we might experience shame and avoid situations that may lead to failure (Covington & Omelich, 1984a; Graham & Weiner, 1996).

Figure 15.1 shows common attributions students make and characterizes them according to locus, stability, and controllability. Two students who get the same grade on the same test might make completely different attributions for their performance. The attributions we make are affected not only by our own beliefs about our ability but also by the evaluations others make about our academic performance. Let's examine these two factors next.

BELIEFS ABOUT ABILITY

Attributing success and failure to ability has different effects on motivation, depending on our belief about ability.

Individuals with an **incremental view of ability** perceive ability as unstable and controllable; they consider it to be ever-changing (Dweck & Leggett, 1988). When students with an incremental view attribute success to their ability, they will be motivated to continue to improve their knowledge and skills. When they attribute failure to low ability, they will become motivated to find alternative strategies for succeeding next time.

Students with an **entity view of ability** believe that ability is stable and uncontrollable; they see it as fixed and unchangeable (Dweck, 2000; Molden & Dweck, 2000). Individuals with an entity view are motivated by gaining favorable judgments or avoiding negative judgments of their ability (Haimovitz, Wormington, & Corpus, 2011). When such students experience success, they want to continue to demonstrate their competence if they believe that competence is

FIGURE 15.1 **Locus, Stability, and Controllability Dimensions of Attributions.**
Students can make different attributions for past successes and failures, each of which has a different effect on their future motivation.

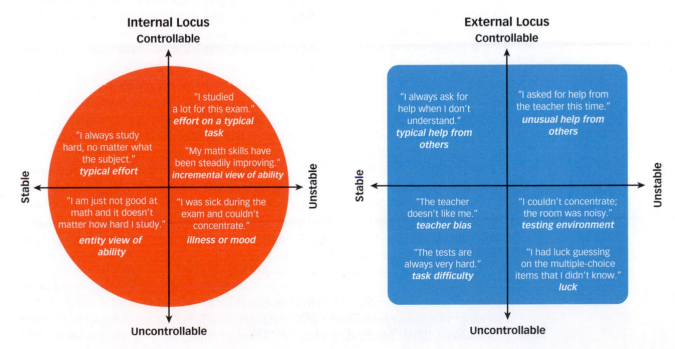

valued by others, such as teachers and peers (Stipek, 2002). When they attribute failure to lack of ability, their expectations for future success diminish, negatively affecting their motivation to learn (Haimovitz et al., 2011; Hong, Chiu, Dweck, Lin, & Wan, 1999).

For students with an entity view, preventing a negative impression of their ability is more important than actually succeeding (Dweck & Master, 2008). When they experience failure, they often engage in self-handicapping behaviors, such as not trying, procrastinating, and making excuses, which further undermine their performance (Cury et al., 2006). Because students with an entity view believe that exerting effort indicates a lack of ability, they tend to use lack of effort as an excuse for failure ("I failed because I didn't study"), which suggests to others that lack of effort is the reason for failure, not low ability (Blackwell et al., 2007; Hong et al., 1999). Making low effort excuses can result in more peer approval, especially during adolescence when being popular and minimizing the importance of effort go hand in hand (Juvonen, 2000).

Self-Handicapping behaviors: See Module 16

TEACHER REACTIONS AND EVALUATIONS

When evaluating student performance, teachers' beliefs and reactions affect students' attributions (Reyna & Weiner, 2001; Weiner, 2000). Many teachers tend to have an entity view of ability, believing it to be fixed and unchangeable (Oakes & Guiton, 1995; Reyna, 2000). Adults with this belief tend to pass judgment more quickly on the basis of initial performance, have low expectations for a student's improvement, express pity for low performance, and resist changing their judgments when students' performance contradicts their initial assumptions (Plaks, Stroessner, Dweck, & Sherman, 2001; Rattan, Good, & Dweck, 2012). If teachers with an entity view of ability hold low expectations for students, their initial perceptions may lead students to attribute failure to low ability or teacher bias (stable and uncontrollable attributions), with serious motivational consequences. Students from lower socioeconomic backgrounds and minority students are especially susceptible to low-ability messages from teacher expectations and behaviors (Banks & Banks, 1995; Graham, 1990; McLoyd, 1998).

DIVERSITY 〈

Teachers may not be consciously aware of their own beliefs, but they can be mindful of the types of reactions to student performance that can lead to diminished motivation. Students tend to adopt an entity view of ability when teachers praise or reward them for easy tasks, offer unsolicited help, express pity for failures, or fail to blame students for poor performance (Dweck, 2000; Graham & Barker, 1990; Rattan et al., 2012). Also, when teachers tell students to work harder after poor performance, students may adopt entity beliefs about ability if they believe they are already trying as hard as they can (Ames, 1990). In contrast, high school students—but not elementary school students—tend to make high-ability attributions when teachers react to successes with neutral feedback ("Yes, that's correct.") or more demanding criteria ("I know you can do better!"; Brophy, 1981; Meyer et al., 1979).

Praising students for being *smart* or telling them they have natural ability also fosters an entity view of ability and can lower students' intrinsic motivation because it implies that learning is about looking smart and not making mistakes (Dweck, 2000; Dweck & Master, 2008). Children who are praised for being smart believe intelligence to be innate and dislike when tasks become more challenging (Mueller & Dweck, 1998). Middle school students of *all* ability levels who believe that intelligence is fixed think that poor performance in school implies low intelligence and that making an effort means they lack intelligence. They also report that they would consider cheating if they did poorly on a test (Blackwell et al., 2007; Henderson & Dweck, 1990). The negative effects of praising for intelligence have been found in children from preschool age through adolescence, in urban and rural settings, and with students from all ethnic backgrounds (Dweck, 2007).

DIVERSITY 〈

Have you noticed that expectancy-value, goal, and attribution theories overlap? Students develop competency beliefs and expectations for success (expectancy-value theory) based partly on the attributions they make (Wigfield & Cambria, 2010a; Wigfield et al., 2009). They also adopt mastery or performance goals based on their beliefs about ability (Linnenbrink & Fredericks, 2007; Maehr & Zusho, 2009). For example, students with an entity view

TABLE 15.2 Integrating Cognitive Theories of Motivation

		STUDENTS WITH AN INCREMENTAL VIEW OF ABILITY	STUDENTS WITH AN ENTITY VIEW OF ABILITY
Attribution theory	Success		
	Attributions due to:	Effort (unstable, uncontrollable)	Unstable factors (luck) external factors (help from others)
	Feelings:	Pride and satisfaction	Lack of pride, lack of personal responsibility
	Failure		
	Attributions due to:	Lack of effort (unstable, controllable) or low incremental ability (unstable, uncontrollable)	Stable causes (low entity ability)
	Feelings:	Guilt	Shame
Expectancy-value theory	Competency beliefs:	Perceive ability to be high	Perceive ability to be low
Goal theory	Goal orientation:	Mastery-approach goals (try to improve skills)	• Performance-approach goals (try to look smart); or • Performance-avoidance goals (try to avoid looking inferior)
	Types of strategies:	• Increasing effort • Trying new learning strategies • Seeking help	• Avoiding help seeking • Selecting very easy tasks (to ensure success); or • Selecting very difficult tasks (failure would be due to task difficulty, not low ability) • Using self-handicapping strategies

SOURCES: Ames, 1992; Covington & Omelich, 1979; Cury et al., 2006; Dweck & Master, 2008; Linnenbrink & Fredericks, 2007; Maatta & Nurmi, 2007; Maehr & Zusho, 2009; Stipek, 2002; Tollefson, 2000; Turner, Meyer, Midgley, & Patrick, 2003; Urdan, 2004; Weiner, 1982.

of ability tend to have a fear of failure that becomes the basis for mastery-avoidance and performance-avoidance goals (Cury et al., 2006). The types of strategies that students use—adaptive or nonadaptive—also depend on their goal orientations and beliefs about ability. As Table 15.2 illustrates, these theories are complementary—they work together to give us a more complete understanding of students' motivation.

DEVELOPMENTAL AND CULTURAL DIFFERENCES IN MOTIVATION

4 Explain the major developmental changes in motivation.

5 Identify gender and ethnic differences in motivation.

To influence students' motivation, teachers need to understand the developmental changes in motivation and individual differences among students. Let's consider these factors next.

Developmental Changes in Motivation

Most children are intrinsically motivated when they begin school. They tend to value learning, have positive competency beliefs, endorse mastery-approach goals, and attribute successes to effort and ability and failures to low effort or unstable causes. As students progress from elementary through secondary education, their competency beliefs and their values, goals, and attributions gradually change.

CHANGES IN EXPECTANCIES AND VALUES

Children begin elementary school with positive competency beliefs and high intrinsic value. As early as first grade, children are able to make judgments about their competencies in school subjects, music, and sports, and typically have perceptions of their abilities that are overly optimistic (Wigfield & Cambria, 2010a; Wigfield & Eccles, 2000). Of course, there are always exceptions. Some preschoolers show negative attitudes about their ability after failure and may be more at risk for motivational problems as they progress through school (Dweck, 2002).

Children in the early elementary grades also value a task primarily according to how much it interests them (Wigfield & Cambria, 2010b). Elementary school boys in the United States, Taiwan, and Japan more highly value sports, while girls in these countries more highly value reading and music (Debacker & Nelson, 2000; Jacobs et al., 2002). As students move from elementary through middle school, they begin to make achievement-related choices not only based on interest (intrinsic value) but also attainment value, utility value, and cost (Wigfield & Cambria, 2010b). For example, a boy might decide to play baseball out of enjoyment, but as he grows older and the game becomes more competitive, requiring greater skill (cost), he might choose not to play.

Both competency beliefs and academic values decline from elementary school through high school, with the greatest changes occurring after the transition to middle school (Watt, 2004; Wigfield & Eccles, 1994). Students' beliefs about their abilities in math, language arts, and sports decline from elementary school through high school (Fredericks & Eccles, 2002; Jacobs et al., 2002; Watt, 2004). The values students place on these domains as well as the value they place on achievement and effort also decline (Jacobs et al., 2002; Watt, 2004).

Competitive Classroom Practices. Competitive classroom practices, such as earning a star for each new book read, can lead students to adopt performance goals.

CHANGES IN GOAL ORIENTATIONS

Children experience a general shift from a mastery orientation to a performance orientation, and this shift may be due to changes in the learning environment. Many children come to school with mastery goals that reflect what they think their parents' goals are (Friedel, Cortina, Turner, & Midgley 2007; Gonida, Voulala, & Kiosseoglou, 2009). In early childhood, parents and teachers encourage a mastery approach to learning through an emphasis on effort and work habits and through feedback such as praise, happy faces, and stickers (Blumenfeld, Hamilton, Bossert, Wessels, & Meece 1983; Blumenfeld, Pintrich, Meece, & Wessels, 1982; Turner & Johnson, 2003).

In the middle elementary grades (Grades 3 to 5), children's abilities are more systematically evaluated through reading groups, standardized test scores, grades, and so on (Wigfield et al., 2009). The other three goal orientations begin to emerge, but performance-approach and performance-avoidant goals are not as distinct as in older students (Bong, 2009). Elementary school students tend to be intrinsically motivated to learn and approach learning tasks to master them (mastery approach) or to show off their abilities (performance approach), rather than approach learning as a way to avoid misunderstanding (mastery-avoidance) or to avoid inferiority (performance-avoidance; Corpus & Wormington, 2014; Dekker et al., 2013; Sungur & Senler, 2010).

From childhood through early adolescence, children's goals become less related to their parents' goals, and their mastery orientations decrease (Dekker et al., 2013; Kim, Schallert, & Kim, 2010; Wigfield & Cambria, 2010b). In middle and high school, they often encounter performance-oriented environments characterized by ability grouping, harsher grading practices, and competitive recognition practices, such as honor rolls and class rankings (Anderman & Maehr, 1994; Midgley, 2002; Wolters & Daugherty, 2007). As a result, students become socialized to adopt performance goals in response to competitive classroom environments that emphasize performance-approach goals (Luo, Hogan, & Paris, 2011; Maehr & Zusho, 2009).

- Students with high perceived competence will tend to adopt performance-approach goals.

- Students with low perceived competence, who begin to doubt their performance, will tend to adopt performance-avoidance goals in addition to performance-approach goals (Barron & Harackiewicz, 2001; Law, Elliot, & Murayama, 2012; Sungar & Senler, 2010). They may be more likely to engage in negative behaviors, such as cheating, avoiding help seeking, and using self-handicapping strategies, especially if they already have lower achievement (Anderman et al., 2009; Leondari & Gonida, 2007; Rolland, 2012).

Compared to performance-oriented goal structures, classrooms at all grade levels that emphasize mastery-approach goal structures are more likely to have students who adopt or maintain personal mastery-approach goals and who express interest, enjoyment, and intrinsic motivation (Benita, Roth, & Deci, 2014; Murayama & Elliot, 2009).

Adolescents also begin to endorse multiple goal orientations (Rončević & Kolić-Vehovec, 2014). For example, high school students consider both grades and interest to be their major motivators (Hynd, Holschuh, & Nist, 2000). We don't yet understand how adoption of both mastery and performance goals may affect motivation. Some research indicates benefits, such as greater interest and intrinsic motivation, higher self-regulation and self-efficacy, and better grades, whereas other research indicates potential psychological distress and emotional exhaustion of balancing extrinsic and intrinsic goals over time (Barron & Harackiewicz, 2000; Corpus & Wormington, 2014; Midgley, Anderman, & Hicks, 1995; Tuominen-Soini, Salmela-Aro, & Niemivirta, 2008).

Many adolescents, especially boys, also may adopt a **work-avoidance goal** orientation—a motivation to avoid academic work (Dekker et al., 2013; Steinmayr, Bipp, & Spinath, 2011). Students motivated by work avoidance often use surface-level learning strategies and engage in behaviors such as (Dowson & McInerney, 2001; Meece & Miller, 2001)

- pretending they don't understand something,

- complaining about assignments,

- engaging in off-task behavior,

- taking the easiest path when given choices, and

- not contributing their fair share in group activities.

Students exhibit these behaviors because they believe that putting forth effort indicates low ability, a trait they consider to be stable and unchanging. Therefore, they value performance goals and try to avoid exerting effort on academic tasks (Dweck & Leggett, 1988;

Self-Regulation: See Module 9

Self-Efficacy: See Module 16

›DIVERSITY

Dweck & Sorich, 1999). Adolescents are more likely to adopt a work-avoidance orientation if (Kumar & Jagacinski, 2011; Peixoto, 2011; Rončević & Kolić-Vehovec, 2014):

- they perceive their parents as having performance-approach goals for them;
- their teachers use a performance-approach orientation; or
- they experience a decline in their perceived ability as a result of more challenging subjects.

CHANGES IN ATTRIBUTIONS

Many children show a developmental progression from an optimistic, incremental view of ability to a more pessimistic entity belief. Children in preschool and early elementary school (Folmer et al., 2008; Graham & Williams, 2009; Schunk, 2008; Stipek & Daniels, 1990; Stipek & Tannatt, 1984)

- think of *ability* broadly, as comprising social behavior, conduct, work habits, and effort;
- believe that individuals who try hard are smart;
- have a limited ability to reflect on and compare their performance to that of their peers; and
- don't understand the compensatory relationship between effort and ability—that those with lower ability need greater effort to succeed compared to those with higher ability.

As a result, they have high expectations for success and are resilient after failure (Stipek, 1984). Around age 7 or 8, children begin to understand normative comparisons and to compare themselves to others more (Dweck, 2002). In middle school, students are able to use normative criteria to judge their ability and understand the compensatory relationship between effort and ability (Dweck, 2002; Tollefson, 2000). They now believe that exerting greater effort on a task compared to others implies lower ability (Folmer et al., 2008). As a result, adolescents' self-assessments become more realistic, leading them to have more negative beliefs than before (Wigfield & Cambria, 2010a).

 Think about how your own competency beliefs, values, goals, and attributions have changed throughout your schooling.

GENDER DIFFERENCES IN MOTIVATION

DIVERSITY

Boys and girls in both Eastern and Western cultures generally have similar beliefs about their overall academic competence (Stetsenko, Little, Gordeeva, Granshof, & Oettingen, 2000). However, students' attributions, beliefs about ability, expectancies, and values differ by gender.

Elementary school boys and girls differ in their competency beliefs and values for different domains. Boys have more positive competency beliefs about math, science, and sports, while girls have more positive beliefs about music, reading, and language arts (Eccles, Barber, Jozefowicz, Malenchuk, & Vida, 2000; Freedman-Doan et al., 2000; Parker et al., 2012). As students transition to middle school and high school, girls more highly value English, and boys more highly value math and sports (Jacobs et al., 2002; Nagy, Trautwein, Baumert, Köller, & Garrett, 2006; Stephanou, 2008). Middle school and high school boys in several countries, including the United States, report a higher intrinsic value for math compared to girls of the same age (Gaspard et al., 2015; Watt, 2004; Watt et al., 2012). Even though there generally are no gender differences for the utility value of math across various countries and grade levels, girls in the United States typically perceive

Gender Differences in Motivation. Gender differences in competence beliefs are more pronounced in gender-stereotyped domains for boys and girls (e.g., sports for boys and reading for girls).

math as less useful for future goals (Frenzel, Pekrun, & Goetz, 2007; Gaspard et al., 2015; Steinmayr & Spinath, 2010). Despite their lower utility value for math, adolescent girls seem to have higher attainment value in the subject compared to boys (Gaspard et al., 2015). Girls consider it important to perform well in math classes even if they don't consider math to be important for their future. However, girls' value for math appears to be a double-edged sword because they also perceive math to have a higher cost compared to boys. They report more anxiety and hopelessness in math and feel that math requires more effort compared to that made by boys (Frenzel et al., 2007; Gaspard et al., 2015).

In elementary school, girls also begin to develop an entity belief about their ability in general (Dweck, 2000, 2002). Compared to boys:

- girls are less likely to attribute success to ability and tend to rate their ability lower even when they outperform boys (Freedman-Doan et al., 2000; Stetsenko et al., 2000);

- girls are more likely to attribute failures to lack of ability and show decreased persistence and motivation after failure (Mok, Kennedy, & Moore, 2011).

Even girls who are gifted and high achieving hold an entity view of ability more often than do boys (Eccles et al., 2000; Freedman-Doan et al., 2000). While results are not consistent across studies, this effect tends to be true for gender-stereotyped subjects, such as math and science (Gunderson et al., 2013; Meece & Painter, 2008).

Cultural norms, such as the expectation that math and science are male achievement domains, may lead to sex-role stereotypes—the idea that boys are better at math and girls are better at language arts. These societal values may in turn contribute to gender differences in competency beliefs and values. Boys may value math and sports because they have been socialized to believe these are male achievement domains (Eccles, 2005; Wigfield & Cambria, 2010a).

- Some parents may unknowingly convey their belief that boys are more competent than girls in math and science (Meece et al., 2009). They may offer different types of encouragement to boys and girls in math, and they may subtly influence children's choices of activities, such as being more likely to buy math and science items for boys than girls (Bleeker & Jacobs, 2004; Meece et al., 2009; Wigfield et al., 2006).

- Teacher–student interactions also may convey different expectations for boys and girls (Brophy & Good, 1974). Teachers tend to praise boys only for successful performance while praising girls for success as well as easy or unimportant achievements, such as neatness or following instructions, leading to a perception of low ability among girls (Dweck, Davidson, Nelson, & Enna, 1978).

Nevertheless, we should interpret these gender differences in motivation with caution. No clear gender differences in students' achievement goal orientations have been found, and

)DIVERSITY

Giftedness: See Module 20

Gender differences in math: See Module 20

gender differences in causal attributions are small (Meece, Glienke, & Burg 2006). Gender differences in *actual* achievement domains such as math also are very small (Lindberg, Hyde, Peterson, & Linn, 2010; Reilly, 2012).

ETHNIC DIFFERENCES IN MOTIVATION

Ethnic differences in motivation have been found across cultures as well as within our own culture. Let's explore some findings.

Students from Asian cultures tend to have a motivational outlook different from that of most students in Western cultures. Students in Western cultures, such as the United States, Canada, and England, typically have higher competence beliefs in various subjects than do students in East Asian cultures (Wigfield & Cambria, 2010a; Zusho & Pintrich, 2003). This is possibly due to the emphasis that East Asian cultures place on self-criticism versus the emphasis Western cultures place on self-enhancement (Heine & Hamamura, 2007). For example, Chinese parents tend to de-emphasize their children's successes and provide more negative emotional responses to their failures (Ng, Pomerantz, & Lam, 2007). Japanese and Chinese students attribute outcomes more to effort and less to ability than do American students (Heine et al., 2001). Asian parents' negative reactions to failures may lead their children to focus on self-improvement (Ng et al., 2007). This attitude is consistent with the Asian philosophy emphasizing the importance of striving for improvement and the belief that ability is malleable (Stipek, 2002).

Within American culture, African American and Hispanic adolescent boys may be most at risk motivationally. African American elementary school students believe in personal responsibility for their achievements and failures and have high expectations for success (Graham, 1984). During adolescence, however, African American and Hispanic boys are more likely than other groups to reject achievement-related values and become disengaged in education (Mau & Bikos, 2000; Taylor & Graham, 2007). The tendency of minority students to devalue academic achievement may result from several factors:

- an increasing tendency to make external attributions for academic success—believing that school success is determined by external forces beyond their control (van Laar, 2000);

Ethnic Differences in Motivation. In some cultures, students attribute school success more to effort, such as studying, than to ability.

©iStockphoto.com/ DragonImages

- their belief that education has limited usefulness for long-term social and economic success because discrimination will narrow their opportunities (Mickelson, 1990; Ogbu, 1994, 2003);

- low teacher expectations and negative classroom climates (Meece et al., 2009; Wood, Kaplan, & McLoyd, 2007); and

- a disconnect between the values and norms promoted by schools—that performance in school will lead to future success—and the cultural values, beliefs, and norms regarding schooling that are endorsed in their homes or communities (Brown-Wright & Tyler, 2010; Tyler et al., 2010).

A discrepancy between home and school values and a general devaluing of achievement may lead minority students in middle school and high school to adopt performance-avoidance goals or work-avoidance goals, engage in academic self-handicapping, such as cheating, display lower academic self-efficacy, and consequently achieve lower grades (Arunkumar, Midgley, & Urdan, 1999; Brown-Wright & Tyler, 2010; Tyler et al., 2010).

Researchers are unsure why this shift in motivational orientation by minority students occurs at adolescence. The changes students experience in their transition from elementary school to more advanced grades may affect students' values about education, regardless of their ethnicity. Some White adolescents from middle and upper socioeconomic backgrounds also have expressed doubt in the utility of school despite their average school performance. These anti-academic values appear to be rooted in a sense that teachers were not supportive, curricula were not meaningful, and the school environment was competitive and stifled autonomy (Roeser, Eccles, & Sameroff, 1998, 2000).

As with gender differences, we should interpret ethnic differences in motivation with caution. Even though research cites *average* differences in motivational orientations among ethnic groups, we should be careful not to make stereotypical assumptions about a student's motivation based on ethnicity. Students' motivation is more likely due to their achievement experiences, the beliefs and values of their families, and the classroom climate than to their ethnic or racial identification. Much more research needs to be conducted for us to understand ethnic differences in motivation.

Home and school values: See Modules 2 and 18

Self-Handicapping and self-efficacy: See Module 16

〉DIVERSITY

SERIOUS MOTIVATIONAL PROBLEMS

6 Explain how learned helplessness and anxiety affect students' motivation to learn.

Learned Helplessness

Learned helplessness occurs when students who have experienced repeated failures attribute their failures to causes beyond their control (Seligman & Maier, 1967). They might attribute failure to *external,* stable, and uncontrollable causes such as teacher bias ("the teacher doesn't like me") or task difficulty ("math is too hard for me"). Or they might attribute failure to *internal,* stable, and uncontrollable causes such as lack of ability (entity; Dweck, 2000; Dweck & Goetz, 1978). Teachers can use the following characteristics to identify learned helplessness in students (Stipek, 2002):

- says "I can't,"

- doesn't pay attention to the teacher's instructions,

- doesn't ask for help, even when it is needed,

- does nothing (e.g., stares out the window),

Video: Learned Helplessness

- guesses or answers randomly without trying,

- doesn't show pride in successes,

- appears bored or uninterested,

- is unresponsive to the teacher's encouragement to try,

- is easily discouraged,

- doesn't volunteer in class, or

- gets out of or avoids work (e.g., has to go to the nurse's office).

Learned helplessness can be domain-specific, occurring in one subject but not another (Sedek & McIntosh, 1998). Even high-achieving students can experience learned helplessness (Dweck, 2000). Because learned helplessness results from experiences of failure, it is less common in preschool children, who typically receive reinforcement and encouragement of their efforts and products (Rholes, Blackwell, Jordan, & Walters, 1980).

Teachers should be aware that simply providing opportunities for success will not alleviate learned helplessness. For several reasons, it is difficult to convince students with learned helplessness that they can succeed in the future, because they (Ames, 1990; Diener & Dweck, 1978):

- believe others performed better than they did,

- do not take responsibility for their successes (i.e., believe successes are uncontrollable),

- underestimate their performance when they do succeed, and

- interpret a new failure as further evidence of their lack of ability.

Creativity: See Module 13

To reduce learned helplessness, teachers can use a combination of the motivational techniques that are discussed in the last section. In general, learned helplessness is less common in classrooms where teachers emphasize understanding (rather than memorizing), stimulate creative thinking, and value students' opinions (Sedek & McIntosh, 1998).

Anxiety

Anxiety: See Module 22

All students occasionally experience anxiety in achievement situations in which their abilities are being evaluated. For most students, a small amount of **anxiety** does not impair performance and may even facilitate it, especially if the task is not too difficult (Ball, 1995; Sieber, O'Neil, & Tobias, 2008). However, for other students, anxiety can significantly impair motivation and academic performance. Students with anxiety experience mental worry, which most directly interferes with learning and task performance (Tobias, 1992; Zeidner & Nevo, 1992). They also experience negative emotions, such as nervousness or tension, which are indicated physically by increased heart rate, sweaty palms, and so on.

Anxiety is more common in school-age children and adolescents than in preschool children because parents and early childhood educators frequently reinforce young children's efforts and rarely criticize failures (Stipek, 1984). In school-age children, anxiety can interfere with performance at three points during the instructional process, shown in Table 15.3.

DIVERSITY

Girls typically show higher anxiety levels than boys (Eccles et al., 2000; Zalta & Chambless, 2012). Also, girls and boys may become anxious for different reasons. Girls may be more sensitive to social approval from adults (worrying about making parents or teachers proud of them), while boys may be more concerned with peer evaluation (Dweck & Bush, 1976; Maehr & Nicholls, 1980). As they progress through the grades, girls may become more anxious about certain school subjects, such as math and English, because of the stereotypes these subjects elicit (Beilock, Gunderson, Ramirez, & Levine, 2010; Meece, 1981).

TABLE 15.3	Understanding and Reducing Anxiety in Students		
STAGE OF LEARNING	**ANXIETY IMPAIRS ABILITY TO**	**EXAMPLE OF OUTCOMES**	**REDUCE ANXIETY BY**
Preprocessing	learn new material	Impaired ability to • pay attention • take notes • listen carefully to teacher's explanation	• providing clear, unambiguous instructions • presenting organized lessons • allowing students to reinspect material, such as a video that was shown in class
Processing	retain information after material is presented	• less effective study skills • poor performance even when studying more	• teaching effective study skills
Output	retrieve information in evaluative situations (i.e., *test anxiety*)	• divided attention between the task and thoughts about one's performance • lack of attention to important information during testing • more off-task behavior • poor test-taking strategies	• using relaxation techniques prior to testing situations • teaching test-taking strategies • relaxing time limits • describing tests in a way that de-emphasizes ability • providing instructions that reduce students' worries about being evaluated

SOURCES: Bruch, Juster, & Kaflowitz, 1983; Linn & Gronlund, 2000; Naveh-Benjamin, 1991; Naveh-Benjamin, McKeachie, & Lin, 1987; Nottlemann & Hill, 1977; Plass & Hill, 1986; Sapp, 1999; Stipek, 2002; Tobias, 1992; Topman, Kleijn, van der Ploeg, & Masset, 1992; Vagg & Spielberger, 1995; Wigfield & Eccles, 1989.

Teachers' own anxieties or their own personal entity views of ability in certain subjects may send subtle but powerful messages to students, especially girls (Reyna, 2000). For example, a recent study by Beilock et al. (2010) showed that in Grades 1 and 2 classrooms with female teachers who had math anxiety, girls but not boys were more likely to endorse the stereotype that "boys are good at math" at the end of the school year. They also generally performed more poorly in math on end-of-year assessments compared to boys. Because there was no link between a teacher's math anxiety and her students' math achievement at the beginning of the school year, one might conclude that the teachers' math anxiety subtly influenced the beliefs of their female students.

Teachers can use varied approaches for reducing students' anxiety, depending on when students experience anxiety during the instructional process, as Table 15.3 outlines. Developmental level is also an important consideration in choosing methods to reduce anxiety in students. Because younger children are more responsive to praise and feedback from adults than are older children, teachers can alleviate anxiety by providing additional support and encouragement and by ensuring that academic tasks are at an appropriate level of difficulty so students do not experience multiple failures (Wigfield & Eccles, 1989). Older students may benefit more from techniques that focus on changing their negative views of ability and attributions for failure and worries, in addition to study skills training (Wigfield & Eccles, 1989). Relaxation techniques involving writing about one's emotions prior to the stressful activity, such as taking an exam, have been shown to reduce negative thoughts that might overburden working memory and increase performance in high school and college learners (Frattaroli, Thomas, & Lyubomirsky, 2011; Park, Ramirez, & Beilock, 2014; Ramirez & Beilock, 2011).

> DIVERSITY

Teaching efficacy: See Module 16

Can you remember a time when you felt anxiety or helplessness? Think about what may have caused these feelings and what you did to overcome them.

Video Case 15.1 ▲
Student Motivation

© SAGE Publications

APPLICATIONS: ENHANCING STUDENTS' MOTIVATION

7 Identify student-level and classroom-level strategies for enhancing motivation

The cognitive theories we've examined provide many useful strategies for improving students' motivation. Teachers can use certain techniques to stimulate the motivation of individual students and structure their classrooms and tasks to encourage motivation in all students.

Student-Level Techniques

Change students' attributions for success and failure. We should not assume that individuals with an entity view are doomed to have low overall motivation and performance. Entity and incremental views of ability are domain specific (Dweck, Chiu, & Hong, 1995), meaning students may believe that they have fixed ability in math but malleable ability in other subjects or in sports.

The first step is to determine what attributions students currently make for their successes and failures. To do this, teachers can ask students about their expectancies and their views about skill improvement and difficulty level of tasks, as shown in Guidelines 15.1. The next step is to encourage students to shift from making an entity attribution for

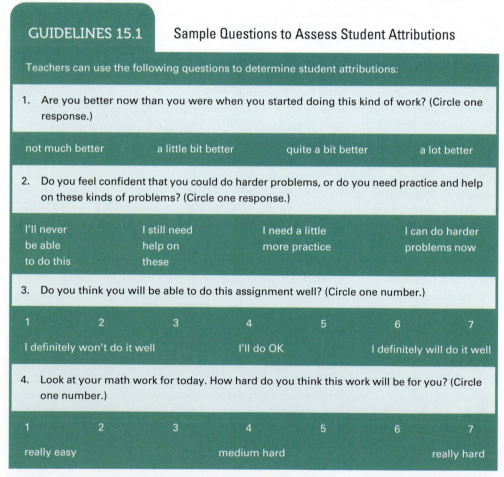

GUIDELINES 15.1 — Sample Questions to Assess Student Attributions

Teachers can use the following questions to determine student attributions:

1. Are you better now than you were when you started doing this kind of work? (Circle one response.)

not much better   a little bit better   quite a bit better   a lot better

2. Do you feel confident that you could do harder problems, or do you need practice and help on these kinds of problems? (Circle one response.)

I'll never be able to do this   I still need help on these   I need a little more practice   I can do harder problems now

3. Do you think you will be able to do this assignment well? (Circle one number.)

1   2   3   4   5   6   7
I definitely won't do it well   I'll do OK   I definitely will do it well

4. Look at your math work for today. How hard do you think this work will be for you? (Circle one number.)

1   2   3   4   5   6   7
really easy   medium hard   really hard

SOURCE: D. Stipek (2002). *Motivation to Learn: Integrating Theory and Practice*. Boston: Allyn & Bacon. Reprinted with permission from the publisher.

failures to making more positive attributions that will encourage them to continue trying and be intrinsically motivated. Teachers can encourage students to view ability as incremental by providing feedback to students that attributes future success to effort, offers concrete strategies for improving, and avoids pity for poor performance, such as "It's OK, we all can't be good at . . ." (Rattan et al., 2012). Also, training students to attribute failure to lack of effort rather than to low ability can be accomplished by having them read persuasive articles or participate in discussions that focus on strategies for dealing with challenges and emphasize ability as improvable (Blackwell et al., 2007; Niiya, Crocker, & Bartmess, 2004). Reattribution training in academic settings has led to improvement in grades, decreases in attributions to uncontrollable factors, and increased motivation (Blackwell et al., 2007; Horner & Gaither, 2006; Good, Aronson, & Inzlicht, 2003).

Teach students to value challenge, improvement, and effort. Encourage students to view challenge as necessary for learning instead of something low-achieving students experience (Dweck & Master, 2008). Also, help students realize that success should be defined as improvement in knowledge or skills rather than looking smart or outperforming others. This conveys the message that effort is important for everyone, not just for students with low ability (Dweck & Master, 2008; Snyder, Malin, Dent, & Linnenbrink-Garcia, 2014). Some students are not aware that effort can affect task success (Urdan, Midgley, & Anderman, 1998). Other students, especially high-achieving and gifted students, view academic success as the result of high-entity ability rather than effort (Snyder et al., 2014). Teaching all students that increased effort leads to greater achievement increases their actual achievement (Craske, 1985; Van Overwalle & De Metsenaere, 1990).

Provide short-term goals and strategies for making progress toward goals (Ames, 1990). When teachers help students set short-term, mastery goals, students are more willing to put forth effort because they learn that both effort and ability contribute to success (Schunk, 1989; Tollefson, 2000). This technique will prepare elementary school students to accept that students with different levels of ability need different amounts of effort to obtain the same level of achievement. In middle school and high school, encouraging mastery and providing students with opportunities to experience success at achieving academic goals may prevent adolescents from viewing academic tasks as a measure of their ability and discourage the adoption of work-avoidance goals (Kumar & Jagacinski, 2011; Tollefson, 2000).

Classroom-Level Techniques

Reduce the competitive atmosphere of the classroom. Students at all levels of K-12 education, regardless of their motivational orientation, consider school to be competitive (Maehr & Midgley, 1991; Thorkildsen & Nicholls, 1998). When the classroom atmosphere is competitive, students are likely to adopt performance-approach goals and may endorse performance-avoidance goals if they experience failure and perceive themselves to lack competence (Law et al., 2012; Luo et al., 2011). Competitive classroom contexts are likely to draw students' attention away from the learning activity toward more extrinsic goals and reduce their intrinsic motivation (Vansteenkiste, Matos, Lens, & Soenens, 2007). Therefore, experts advise teachers to advocate a mastery-approach structure and to avoid the use of a performance-approach orientation because teachers cannot guarantee that all students will feel competent all of the time (Law et al., 2012). Teachers can reduce competition and enhance students' motivation by using any academic tasks that foster a mastery orientation because students will have less opportunity or need to engage in social comparisons of performance (Marshall & Weinstein, 1984; Rosenholtz & Simpson, 1984). For example, teachers may consider using mastery learning, a method in which students work at their own pace on curricular units once teachers present material and repeat the units until they have achieved a certain level of mastery. Also, teachers can use cooperative learning, an approach in which students of varying ability levels work together to achieve a single goal on a task or project. Because cooperative learning helps students

Video Case 15.2 ▲
Increasing Student Engagement and Participation

© SAGE Publications

Video Case 15.3 ▲
Planning by Students' Interests

© SAGE Publications

Mastery learning: See Module 18

Cooperative learning: Module 18

achieve social goals, as well as academic goals, this approach may reduce the tendency for students to adopt work-avoidance goals and may help sustain intrinsic motivation (Kumar & Jagacinski, 2011).

Use appropriate methods of evaluation and recognition. Consider these methods when evaluating students' learning:

- Praise students only when they learn or do something well, not for being smart, perfect at a task, or completing a task quickly or easily (Dweck, 2000; Dweck & Master, 2008). Saying something positive just to praise a student backfires because usually it is about something that is unimportant or irrelevant to the task requirements, implying that the student has low ability (Ames, 1990). Such praise will undermine intrinsic motivation.

- Take developmental level into account when using praise. In young children, praise for effort enhances self-confidence and is considered an indicator of high ability because young children do not differentiate between ability and effort (Schunk, 2008). However, in middle and high school students, who have differentiated concepts of ability and effort, praising effort and praising for success on easy tasks can be interpreted as signs of low ability (Barker & Graham, 1987; Henderlong & Lepper, 2002).

- Offer opportunities for improvement so students know that effort is important and that performance is not due solely to fixed ability (Covington & Omelich, 1984b).

- Be aware that motivational strategies such as announcing highest and lowest scores, posting grades, displaying students' work, and charting progress emphasize social comparisons. When ability comparisons are heightened, this can decrease intrinsic motivation and lead high achievers to experience anxiety about keeping up their success and low achievers to give up when they fail (Rose, 1989; Weinstein, 1993). Such practices need not undermine intrinsic motivation, though. For example, if the reason for displaying student work is to show improvement over past performance or reaching a standard of performance, the display would promote feelings of mastery (Fryer & Elliot, 2008).

Emphasize the value of learning. When teachers emphasize the relevance of to-be-learned knowledge, students will appreciate its utility value—its usefulness to students' goals in or out of school (Brophy, 2008). Students who see utility value in what they are learning are more likely to engage in meaningful learning—learning that results in rich, interconnected knowledge structures rather than discrete facts—which can lead to increased effort, interest, and achievement (Brophy, 1999; Wagner et al., 2006). Teachers can foster an appreciation for learning by modeling interest and enthusiasm, making abstract content more concrete and personally relevant to students, connecting content to students' interests and backgrounds, and emphasizing the utility value of content for tasks outside of school (Brophy, 2008).

However, simply informing students about the usefulness of content to their future goals may not be effective, especially for students who believe they have low ability (Canning & Harackiewicz, 2015; Durik, Shechter, Noh, Rozek, & Harakiewicz, 2015). For example, if students struggle with math, why would they view it as helpful to their future? Instead, having students generate ways the content is relevant to them may be more effective (Canning & Harackiewicz, 2015; Hulleman & Harackiewicz, 2009). Students may find calculating percentages important for understanding batting averages or for figuring out sale prices at the mall. Teachers also can have students write about the personal relevance of a topic or school subject, which can improve interest and grades even in students with

Meaningful learning: See Module 12

low perceptions of competence (Hulleman & Harackiewicz, 2009; Hulleman et al., 2010). Because much of the research on utility value has been conducted with adolescents in high school and college, we do not know about the efficacy of this approach with students in lower grades.

Think of some specific ways you can implement these guidelines in the grade you intend to teach.

SUMMARY

❶ Define expectancies and values, and explain how they influence students' motivation. Expectancies are an individual's expectations for success on a task, which are based partly on one's competency beliefs. Values are the reasons for choosing to do a task (attainment value, intrinsic value, utility value, and cost). Expectancies and values, in combination, determine an individual's motivation to engage in a particular task.

❷ Compare and contrast the two types of mastery and performance goals. Mastery-approach goals (improving knowledge) and performance-approach goals (besting others) both lead students to be intrinsically motivated and are associated with many beneficial outcomes. Mastery-avoidance and performance-avoidance goals both involve avoiding situations that show one's incompetence, but the standard for incompetence is absolute (e.g., best/worst) for mastery avoidance and normative (compared to others) for performance avoidance. Performance-avoidance goals are related to poor intrinsic motivation.

❸ Identify attributions that enhance motivation and those that lower motivation. Attributing success and failure to amount of effort increases motivation to learn. Attributing success to controllable causes leads to further motivation, while attributing failure to stable and uncontrollable causes, as with an entity view of ability, hinders motivation. Teachers who give praise for easy tasks, express sympathy or pity for failures, or offer unsolicited help may inadvertently convey a sense of low ability in students. Praising intelligence also leads to an entity view of ability, which could lower motivation when students encounter failure or difficult tasks.

❹ Explain the major developmental changes in motivation. Young children begin school with a mastery orientation. They have an incremental belief about ability, have high expectancies, and choose tasks based primarily on intrinsic value. As children progress from elementary through high school, they shift toward a performance orientation. Adolescents place less emphasis on mastery and effort and believe that ability is fixed. As a result, they have lower competency beliefs, expectancies, and intrinsic values for academic tasks.

❺ Identify gender and ethnic differences in motivation. Girls tend to hold an entity view of ability and to rate their ability lower than that of boys, especially in math and science. While research suggests that African American and Hispanic adolescents may be most at risk motivationally compared to other ethnic groups, motivation is the result of many cultural and environmental factors rather than simply the product of a person's ethnicity.

❻ Explain how learned helplessness and anxiety affect students' motivation to learn. Students with learned helplessness believe that they have no control over learning outcomes and therefore expect to do poorly, lowering motivation. Anxiety may affect an individual's performance while learning, studying, or retrieving material. The expectation of performing poorly as a result of anxiety lowers motivation to learn.

❼ Identify student-level and classroom-level strategies for enhancing motivation. Teachers can improve the motivation of individual students by changing their attributions for success and failure and by providing short-term goals and strategies for progressing toward goals. They can use classroom-level techniques, such as emphasizing values that promote intrinsic motivation, reducing the competitive atmosphere of the classroom, and using appropriate methods of evaluation and recognition.

KEY CONCEPTS

CASE STUDIES: REFLECT AND EVALUATE

EARLY CHILDHOOD: THE WORKSHEETS

These questions refer to the case study on page 268.

1. According to expectancy-value theory, what is Melissa's expectancy for completing her schoolwork? Based on evidence from the case study and the module, what attribution do you think Melissa might make for her math ability?

2. Kristina, like Emanuel and Martin, appears to like math and to be good at math. Based on the research evidence in the module, predict how her competency beliefs in math and the value she places on math might change as she progresses through the upper elementary grades and middle school. How might her attributions change?

3. Imagine that you are having a parent–teacher conference with Martin's mother. Explain to her why she should not praise him for being smart. What effect might this have on Martin's subsequent motivation?

4. Which student(s) might be the most difficult to motivate based on goal theory? Which student(s) might be the most difficult to motivate based on attribution theory? Cite evidence from the case study to support your position.

5. Based on research evidence regarding the effects of praise, explain why Mrs. Garvey encouraging Melissa to try harder would be appropriate for a kindergartner but not for a student in middle school or high school.

ELEMENTARY SCHOOL: WRITER'S BLOCK

These questions refer to the case study on page 270.

1. According to expectancy-value theory, what is Carter's expectancy for completing his writing assignment? Which type of value—intrinsic value, attainment value, or utility value—does Carter have for writing?

2. Based on the information in the case study regarding goal orientations, which student—Shanti, Zara, or Carter—would be most difficult to motivate? Why? Which student would be easiest to motivate? Why?

3. Reread Mrs. Okuda's interactions with James and Mason. Based on these interactions, what attribution might James and Mason make for their writing performance? Are they likely to have motivation for freewriting in the future?

4. What information do students at this developmental level use in making attributions for their performance?

5. Carter appears to have anxiety about writing when he starts his assignments. What can Mrs. Okuda do to help reduce his anxiety about writing?

MIDDLE SCHOOL: THE MATH REVIEW

These questions refer to the case study on page 272.

1. In your own words, define *expectancy* and *value*. What is Aaron's expectancy for and value of the math game activity? Which type of value—intrinsic value, attainment value, or utility value—do Jeremy and Rachel have for the math activity?

2. According to goal theory, which student—Jesse, Jeremy, or Rachel—would be most difficult to motivate? Why? Which student would be easiest to motivate? Why?

3. What attribution does Mr. Pantera likely make for Aaron's performance in his class? Does Mr. Pantera view math performance to be the result of an entity view of ability or an incremental view of ability?

4. What attribution does Jesse make for her math performance? Cite research evidence related to gender differences in attributions that might help explain Jesse's attributional pattern.

5. What error did Mr. Pantera make in his feedback to Jesse?

6. At what point in the instructional process does Jesse's anxiety affect her performance? What specific strategies can Mr. Pantera use to help reduce Jesse's anxiety?

HIGH SCHOOL: EXAM GRADES

These questions refer to the case study on page 274.

1. What is Chelsea's expectancy for success in physics? Speculate on the social, cultural, and individual factors that might contribute to this expectancy.

2. Explain how physics holds *intrinsic value, attainment value,* and *utility value* for Chelsea. If Chelsea decides not to drop AP Physics, what are the *costs* resulting from this decision?

3. Explain why students in AP Physics are likely to adopt performance goals. What factors in their environment might contribute to this orientation?

4. What type of goal orientation do students in general science have? Support your answer with details from the case. Explain how this goal orientation is typical of adolescents.

5. What attribution do Nicholas and Chelsea make for their C+ grades in AP Physics? Based on the research on gender differences in attributions, why is Chelsea's attribution not surprising?

6. What specific suggestions would you give Mr. Womack for intrinsically motivating students in general science? Would your suggestions differ for students in AP Physics? If so, why and how? If not, why not?

Visit **edge.sagepub.com/durwin3e** to help you accomplish your coursework goals in an easy-to-use learning environment.

- Mobile-friendly **eFlashcards**
- Mobile-friendly practice **quizzes**
- A complete online **action plan**

- Chapter **learning objectives**
- EXCLUSIVE! Access to full-text **SAGE journal articles**

©iStockphoto.com/ nojustice

SELF THEORIES

OUTLINE	LEARNING GOALS
Self-Efficacy Theory	
• Self-Efficacy and Motivation • Teacher Efficacy	**1** Describe outcome expectations and efficacy expectations with respect to student and teacher efficacy.
Self-Worth Theory	
• Self-Worth and Motivation • Types of Students	**2** Explain how self-worth affects the motivation of success-oriented students, overstrivers, and failure-avoiding and failure-accepting students.
Self-Determination Theory	
• Self-Determination and Motivation • Becoming Self-Determined	**3** Explain how autonomy, competence, and relatedness can facilitate intrinsic motivation. **4** Define internalization and explain how educational contexts can facilitate internalization of behaviors.
Integrating the Self Theories	
• Self Theories Compared • *Applications:* Fostering Self-Efficacy, Self-Worth, and Self-Determination	**5** Describe techniques teachers can use to enhance students' intrinsic motivation, and identify which self theory supports each technique.

The *self* in self theories of motivation refers to characteristics within individuals that cause them to be motivated: self-efficacy, self-worth, and self-determination. We examine each of these characteristics as theories of motivation and consider how they apply to students' intrinsic motivation for learning. All three theories have two things in common. They all focus on:

Intrinsic motivation: See Modules 14 and 15

- a *competence* that underlies the self and an individual's motivation, and
- **intrinsic motivation,** a tendency to engage in an activity for its own sake or out of interest, which can be achieved through feelings of competence. This contrasts with **extrinsic motivation,** engaging in a behavior (in this case, learning) for external reasons such as rewards, praise, grades, or recognition.

Extrinsic motivation: See Modules 14 and 15

However, the theories differ in several respects, as we discuss in the following pages.

SELF-EFFICACY THEORY

Master the content.

edge.sagepub.com/durwin3e

$SAGE edge™

1 Describe outcome expectations and efficacy expectations with respect to student and teacher efficacy.

Albert Bandura's (1986, 2001) social cognitive theory provides us with the concept of efficacy as a way to understand student motivation and achievement. Let's explore how self-efficacy and teacher efficacy affect students' intrinsic motivation.

Social cognitive theory: See Module 9

Self-Efficacy and Motivation

Self-efficacy, an expectation that we are capable of performing a task or succeeding in an activity, influences our motivation for the task or activity. To be motivated, we must have high outcome and efficacy expectations. **Outcome expectations** are beliefs that particular actions lead to particular outcomes—in this case, success. **Efficacy expectations** are beliefs that we have the requisite knowledge or skills to achieve the outcome. An elementary school student might believe that learning spelling words makes students better spellers (outcome expectation), but to be motivated to achieve she also needs to believe that *she* has the ability to memorize the assigned spelling words (efficacy expectation). Likewise, a middle school or high school student might believe that studying leads to performing well in school, but he also must believe that *he* has the appropriate study skills to achieve success in school subjects. Students with high efficacy and outcome expectations approach difficult school tasks as challenges to be mastered, set moderately challenging goals, and persist when tasks are difficult—that is, they are motivated. Students with low efficacy and outcome expectations are easily discouraged by failure and therefore are not motivated to learn (Bandura & Schunk, 1981; Schunk & Pajares, 2009).

Self-efficacy is a critical determinant of behavior in school, sports, and social relationships (Bandura, 1977, 1997). It is domain specific, meaning that a student may have high self-efficacy in math but not in other subjects, or in athletics but not in academics. Boys tend to have higher self-efficacy in math and science, while girls tend to have higher self-efficacy in writing (Anderman & Young, 1994; Pajares & Valiante, 2001; Pintrich & De Groot, 1990). Gender differences may be due partly to cultural expectations that influence parents' perceptions that boys are better at math and science (Meece, Glienke, & Askew, 2009). Because cultural expectations also affect parental behaviors, they may indirectly influence children's self-efficacy and motivation. In one study, for example, mothers were more likely to buy math and science items for boys than for girls, regardless of the child's age (Bleeker & Jacobs, 2004).

Students from various ethnic backgrounds also show differences in self-efficacy, depending on subject matter. Students from minority groups tend to have self-efficacy for reading that is comparable to that of their White peers (Mucherah & Yoder, 2008). However, self-efficacy for math appears to be lower for African American and Hispanic students (Pajares & Kranzler, 1995; Stevens, Olivárez, Lan, & Tallent-Runnels, 2004). Also, Hispanic students tend

Self-Efficacy. *The Little Engine That Could* is a good example of self-efficacy, with the engine saying, "I think I can, I think I can . . ." as it climbs the hill.

DIVERSITY

Video: Self-Efficacy Theory

Four influences on self-efficacy: See Module 9

to have lower writing self-efficacy than White students (Pajares & Johnson, 1996). Because self-efficacy is domain specific, the challenges of second language acquisition may partly explain the lower self-efficacy of Hispanic students in writing. Despite any group differences in self-efficacy for certain subjects, we should remember that students from diverse ethnic and cultural backgrounds tend to have positive overall academic self-efficacy (Graham, 1994; Lay & Wakstein, 1985; Stevenson, Chen, & Uttal, 1990). Also, group differences in self-efficacy may be less important for teachers' understanding of self-efficacy than knowing about the experiences that shape self-efficacy and the relative importance of these experiences for different cultural groups.

How do individuals develop beliefs about their own self-efficacy? For example, why does a high school student think she's good at physics? Research shows that, over time, individuals develop self-efficacy beliefs as they interpret information from four influences (Bandura, 1982; Usher & Pajares, 2008):

1. *Past performance.* Students' self-efficacy improves when they achieve mastery and attribute their success to ability or effort (Scholz, Dona, Sud, & Schwarzer, 2002; Zimmerman, 2000). Mastery experiences are the most influential of all four sources of information for developing self-efficacy (Pajares, Johnson, & Usher, 2007; Usher & Pajares, 2006a, 2006b).

2. *Vicarious experiences.* Vicarious experience, or observing the performance of someone else, can help an individual develop self-efficacy. When students lack personal experience with a task, it is especially important that the model be similar to them (Schunk & Miller, 2002). For example, observing peers complete a task leads students to greater self-efficacy than does observing a teacher (Schunk & Hanson, 1985). However, if the model is more able or more talented, observers will not have high-efficacy expectations after viewing the model's performance (Zimmerman, 2000).

3. *Verbal persuasion.* Reassuring individuals that they will succeed or encouraging their efforts can foster positive self-efficacy. Parents who encourage their children to try different activities and provide them with support for doing so encourage their children's self-efficacy (Bandura, 1997). Verbal persuasion is less effective than both past mastery performance and vicarious experiences because success outcomes are merely described, not witnessed or experienced, and depend on the credibility of the persuader (Zimmerman, 2000).

4. *States of emotional arousal.* Fatigue, stress, and anxiety often are interpreted as indicators of lack of competence (Scholz et al., 2002; Tollefson, 2000). Confidence and eagerness, in contrast, are emotional signs of competence. Individuals with higher self-efficacy show decreased stress, anxiety, and depression when they are confronted with demanding school tasks, while those with lower self-efficacy tend to exhibit depression, anxiety, and helplessness (Bandura, 1997; Scholz et al., 2002).

DIVERSITY

Students of varying backgrounds are influenced differently by the sources of information described earlier, and these varied experiences may be the cause of gender and ethnic differences in self-efficacy.

- For example, boys report stronger mastery experiences and lower anxiety in math and science while girls have stronger mastery experiences and lower anxiety in writing (Britner & Pajares, 2006; Lent, Lopez, Brown, & Gore 1996; Pajares et al., 2007). General academic efficacy is influenced more by vicarious experiences for boys and by verbal persuasion for girls (Usher & Pajares, 2006a, 2006b). This suggests that the right type of praise and encouragement could be effective in motivating girls.

- The self-efficacy of White students seems to be influenced by all four sources of information, while African American students' self-efficacy is influenced mainly by mastery

©iStockphoto.com/ HelpingHandPhotos

Vicarious Experiences. The most effective model for this young girl learning to tie her cleat is a child of a similar age, like her brother shown here.

experiences and verbal persuasion (Usher & Pajares, 2006a, 2006b). In contrast, Mexican American students may be more influenced by vicarious experience than their White peers (Stevens, Olivárez, & Hamman, 2006).

- Students with learning disabilities and students in lower ability groups have lower self-efficacy than their peers and report fewer mastery experiences, vicarious experiences, and verbal persuasions. They also have higher anxiety than students with average or above-average achievement (Hampton & Mason, 2003; Usher & Pajares, 2006b).

To better understand how to increase students' self-efficacy, we need to discuss how school experiences help shape self-efficacy. Young children's beliefs about their ability are overly optimistic (Wigfield & Cambria, 2010). They interpret praise as an indication of exceptional performance and pay little attention to social comparisons of performance (Usher & Pajares, 2008). Self-efficacy declines developmentally (Anderman & Midgley, 1997; Eccles & Midgley, 1989). As children progress through school, their cognitive development and school practices that involve evaluation (grades, displaying best work, etc.) lead them to make comparisons of their performance with others. These comparisons may lead to more realistic perceptions of ability and consequently decreased self-efficacy.

School transitions from elementary to middle school and from middle to high school can cause further declines in self-efficacy (Friedel, Cortina, Turner, & Midgley, 2010; Schunk & Meece, 2006). Middle school students perceive school as more focused on performance-approach goals (competing for grades, showing off ability) than mastery-approach goals (focusing on learning and improving; Midgley, 2002). In response to the increasing emphasis on grading and evaluation that they experience as they transition to middle school, adolescents continually reassess their self-efficacy in various subjects (Schunk & Miller, 2002).

Regardless of grade level, classroom practices can influence self-efficacy. In classrooms where teachers make explicit comparisons of ability, lower achieving students have lower self-efficacy. For example, ability grouping, which involves placing students into homogeneous groups based on their achievement level (e.g., for reading or math in elementary classrooms), can undermine the self-efficacy of students in the lower groups (Schunk & Miller, 2002). Explicit comparisons are less likely in middle school and high school, because in many schools students are assigned to curriculum tracks in which all students within a class are of the same ability level.

Learning disabilities: See Module 21

Ability grouping: See Module 19

Praise: See Module 14

Performance-Approach goals and mastery-approach goals: See Module 15

Ability grouping: See Module 19

During any particular grade, outcome and efficacy expectations may also change over the school year. Students may have high outcome and efficacy expectations on the first day of school. But as the school year progresses and they receive feedback about their performance, they may come to believe that while it is possible for students to be successful (outcome expectation), they personally do not have the requisite skills, abilities, or work ethic to achieve success in that particular environment (efficacy expectation; Tollefson, 2000).

Self-efficacy influences self-regulation in learners (Bong & Skaalvik, 2003; Pintrich & Schunk, 2002). **Self-regulation** is the ability to control one's emotions, cognitions, and behaviors by providing consequences to oneself. Students with high self-efficacy are more likely to engage in self-regulatory processes, such as goal setting, self-monitoring, self-evaluation, and effective strategy use (Zimmerman, 2000). Many of these processes are linked to intrinsic motivation. For example, students with high self-efficacy tend to:

Self-Regulation: See Module 9

Goal theory: See Module 15

- choose more difficult tasks and set mastery goals (Seijts & Latham, 2001; Zimmerman, Bandura, & Martinez-Pons, 1992). Intrinsically motivated students set moderately challenging goals that allow them to achieve mastery of knowledge or skills.

- respond more positively to negative feedback and persist when faced with failure (Pugh & Bergin, 2006; Seijts & Latham, 2001). Intrinsically motivated students do not fear failure; rather, they consider feedback to be useful information for improving themselves.

- choose more effective strategies, such as organizing information, making connections, rereading material, making outlines, and monitoring performance (Bouffard-Bouchard, Parent, & Larivee, 1991; Pintrich & De Groot, 1990). This is true of students at all levels of K-12 education (Zimmerman & Martinez-Pons, 1990). Students who are intrinsically motivated to achieve mastery are more likely to use effective learning strategies (Pintrich & De Groot, 1990; Pintrich & Garcia, 1991). As a result, students with high self-efficacy attain higher achievement through their efficient use of self-regulatory skills (Bandura & Locke, 2003; Valentine, DuBois, & Cooper, 2004).

Think of a subject that you find enjoyable and one that you find challenging. Describe your self-efficacy in each. How do your outcome and efficacy expectations differ in each subject?

Teacher Efficacy

Reference: Teacher Efficacy

Teacher efficacy is a belief by teachers that they have the skills necessary to teach all students effectively. Teacher efficacy is positively related to student achievement, motivation to learn, self-esteem, positive attitudes toward school, and expectations for academic success (Caprara, Barbaranelli, Steca, & Malone, 2006; Hines & Kritsonis, 2010; Ross, 1998). Over time, teachers develop outcome expectations (a belief that all students can learn the material) and efficacy expectations (beliefs about their own ability to help all children learn; Ashton & Webb, 1986; Gibson & Dembo, 1984).

Like students, teachers possess different levels of efficacy. Teachers may have low teaching efficacy for a variety of reasons. New teachers, who tend to feel overwhelmed and sometimes unprepared, might believe that all teachers can have a positive effect on the education of students (outcome expectation) but that *they* lack the skills required to teach students effectively (efficacy expectation; Stipek, 2002). Teachers also may have low efficacy because they believe that

- a lack of school resources or administrative support hinders their ability to teach effectively (Stipek, 2012);

- student behavior problems and lack of motivation are impediments to teaching and learning (Collie, Shapka, & Perry, 2012);

- a lack of parental support for academics contributes to students' low achievement (Stipek, 2012); or

- students' low ability contributes to their poor achievement.

Many teachers tend to have an entity view of ability—the belief that ability is stable and uncontrollable (Oakes & Guiton, 1995; Reyna, 2000). Adults with an entity view tend to pass judgment more quickly on the basis of initial performance, have low expectations for the student's improvement, express pity for low performance, and resist changing their judgments when they are confronted with evidence that contradicts their initial assumptions (Plaks, Stroessner, Dweck, & Sherman, 2001; Rattan, Good, & Dweck, 2012). In contrast, other teachers have an incremental view of ability, in which ability is seen as improvable (unstable and controllable).

Teachers who believe that low student ability, low levels of effort, and lack of parental involvement are stable factors leading to poor academic achievement may develop low outcome expectations for both their students and themselves (Tollefson, 2000). This, in turn, may affect their expectations for and interactions with students. Teachers with low teacher efficacy tend to call on low achievers less often, give them less praise and more busy work, and interact more with high achievers (Ashton & Webb, 1986). Also, teachers are more likely to give students from lower socioeconomic and minority backgrounds low-ability messages, such as expressing pity for students' failures, praising students for easy tasks, or offering unsolicited help (Graham, 1990; McLoyd, 1998). As a result, students may develop an entity belief about their ability—believing that they have low ability and cannot change it—and may experience lower intrinsic motivation (Dweck, 1999; Graham & Weiner, 1993).

To understand how teacher efficacy can enhance students' intrinsic motivation, consider these characteristics of highly efficacious teachers. Teachers with higher efficacy:

- spend more time on planning and organizing (Gibson & Dembo, 1984; Tschannen-Moran & Woolfolk-Hoy, 2001).

- are more willing to try new instructional methods (Cousins & Walker, 2000; Supovitz & Turner, 2000). They tend to use more self-directed activities and small group discussions (Tschannen-Moran, Woolfolk Hoy, & Hoy, 1998). They also are more open to using interactive approaches, such as cooperative learning, peer tutoring, and problem-based learning, because they believe these types of activities enhance learning (outcome expectation; Tollefson, 2000; Wahlstrom & Louis, 2008).

- focus more on mastery than performance goals (Wolters & Daugherty, 2007). They modify curricula so that students with different levels of ability can achieve success with moderate effort (Tollefson, 2000).

- use classroom management strategies that keep students on task and promote achievement (Ross & Bruce, 2007; Woolfolk, Rosoff, & Hoy, 1990).

- foster positive self-esteem in students (Ross & Bruce, 2007).

- show persistence when helping students who are having difficulty (Malmberg, 2008; Schunk, Pintrich, & Meece, 2008).

In sum, teachers with high efficacy tend to have a mastery-oriented focus to teaching practices, meaning that they emphasize the importance of learning, improving, and overcoming challenges over performance goals, such as outperforming other students (Wolters & Daugherty, 2007).

Entity view of ability and incremental view of ability: See Module 15

> **DIVERSITY**

Cooperative learning: See Modules 18 and 19

Problem-Based learning: See Module 13

Classroom management: See Module 17

SELF-WORTH THEORY

 Explain how self-worth affects the motivation of success-oriented students, overstrivers, and failure-avoiding and failure-accepting students.

According to self-worth theory, humans naturally strive to maintain a sense of **self-worth**, or an appraisal of one's own value as a person (Covington, 1998, 2009). They are motivated to protect their self-worth by maintaining a belief that they are competent (Ames & Ames, 1984; Covington, 2009).

Self-Worth and Motivation

Video: Self-Worth Theory

Because schools value and reward competencies (being able, smart, successful), students' perceptions of ability contribute to their self-worth (Covington, 1998). Proving their ability, therefore, becomes a primary focus of students' learning. This leads students to be motivated to avoid a negative consequence—such as looking less competent than their peers (Covington & Müeller, 2001). Consequently, students become *extrinsically motivated*—that is, motivated by external factors—and their intrinsic motivation to learn becomes compromised.

Students may be both intrinsically and extrinsically motivated but appear extrinsically motivated because of external pressures to prove their self-worth. When college students (like you) were asked why they would do extra, unassigned work for a course, they most often reported that it would satisfy their curiosity and interest (intrinsic motivation). In practice, however, college students didn't pursue topics that interested them because it would take time away from studying for exams (extrinsic motivation; Covington & Müeller, 2001).

Intrinsic and extrinsic motivation: See Module 14

DIVERSITY

As students progress from elementary school through middle school and high school, they experience greater emphases on competition and performance evaluation, and their self-worth increasingly depends on their ability to achieve competitively (Gottfried, Fleming, & Gottfried, 2001; Harari & Covington, 1981). Extrinsic rewards for learning, such as good grades and high performance on standardized tests, are symbols of success that maintain self-worth. However, because success is defined by comparing one's performance with that of others, the self-worth of low-achieving students, including students with disabilities and students with limited English proficiency, may be threatened when they face standards that are too high for them to have success (Stipek, 2002). Students from lower socioeconomic backgrounds and minority students, who traditionally have performed poorly on standardized tests, also may experience low self-worth (Kim & Sunderman, 2005). A focus on extrinsic factors, such as grades and test scores, therefore may decrease students' intrinsic motivation (Lepper, Corpus, & Iyengar, 2005; Lepper, Sethi, Dialdin, & Drake, 1997).

Types of Students

Success-Oriented students: See mastery-approach goals in Module 15

Goal theory: See Module 15

Overstrivers: See performance approach-goals in Module 15.

According to self-worth theory, the distinction between "approaching success" and "avoiding failure" is central to understanding students' motivation (Covington, 2009; Covington & Beery, 1976). This distinction allows us to understand the motivation of four different types of students, as shown in Figure 16.1, based on how much each student is driven to approach success and to avoid failure.

Success-oriented students are intrinsically motivated. Because they value ability as a tool to achieve mastery on personally meaningful goals, they define success in terms of becoming the best they can be, regardless of the achievements of others. Students in the other three categories define success (and their resulting self-worth) as doing better than others, so they are motivated to avoid failure or to avoid looking as if they have low ability (Covington & Müeller, 2001).

Like success-oriented students, **overstrivers** are driven by high hopes for success, but unlike success-oriented students, they have an excessive fear of failure (Covington & Omelich, 1991; Martin & Marsh, 2003). Therefore, they are motivated to channel their fears into increased

FIGURE 16.1 **Four Types of Students.** Students have different types of motivation, according to self-worth theory.

SOURCE: From M. V. Covington and K. J. Müeller (2001), "Intrinsic versus extrinsic motivation: An approach/avoidance reformulation." *Education Psychology Review, 13*(2), 157–176. Copyright © 2001. Reprinted by permission of Springer.

effort to ensure they perform better than others (De Castella, Byrne, & Covington, 2013). To do this, they use several strategies to ensure their success (Covington, 1984; Stipek, 2002):

1. *Attempting only very easy tasks.* This guarantees success with little learning.

2. *Having low aspirations.* A student might announce that he is not prepared for a test and hopes simply to pass. Doing better than passing (success) with minimal effort implies that the student has high ability.

3. *Rehearsing responses.* An elementary school student might rehearse a section of text that she expects to read aloud to minimize any reading errors. Likewise, a student in a high school foreign language or math class might practice the answer to a question before being called on.

4. *Paying excessive attention to detail.* Overstrivers doubt their actual abilities and attribute success to extreme effort, such as being overprepared or showing excessive attention to detail (Covington, 1984; Covington & Beery, 1976). An elementary school student might ask the teacher if she is on the right track with a math worksheet after every few problems, or a middle or high school student might ask the teacher for clarification or feedback several times while working on an individual project.

5. *Cheating.* Students might cheat as an extreme measure to ensure success because they believe that asking for help indicates low ability (Butler, 1998).

Overstrivers are motivated by a sense of pride stemming from their success and by the temporary relief of not failing (of avoiding negative consequences), creating a continual cycle of having to prove themselves (Covington & Müeller, 2001). This continual cycle may lead overstrivers to feel anxiety and a lack of control (Martin, Marsh, & Debus, 2001a, 2001b). When overstrivers experience failure, they consider this proof that they lack competence and may adopt strategies to avoid failure (Covington, 1992; Martin & Marsh, 2003).

Failure-avoiding students: See performance-avoidance goals in Module 15.

Self-handicapping strategies: See Module 15

Failure-avoiding students also are highly motivated to avoid failure, but unlike overstrivers they do not have high expectations for success. Failure-avoiding students are motivated to temporarily avoid a negative outcome—the anxiety of being identified as incompetent—and learn to internalize feelings of relief rather than pride (Covington & Müeller, 2001). To avoid looking incompetent, they engage in defensive pessimism—setting unrealistically low expectations for performance, which reduces the likelihood that ability will be judged as inadequate (Martin & Marsh, 2003). Defensive pessimism is a common failure-avoiding tactic among adolescents (Martin, 2001). Additionally, failure-avoiding students may choose to use several self-handicapping strategies that prevent any real learning (Covington, 1984; Rhodewalt & Davison, 1986):

1. Minimizing or withdrawing participation (not raising one's hand, sitting at the back of the room out of the teacher's view, note taking with head down, pretending to pay attention with a pensive look, or being absent on the day of a test);

2. Making excuses (for missing or incomplete homework; "forgetting" a presentation at home);

3. Procrastinating (studying or starting a term paper the night before an exam or due date);

4. Setting unattainable goals or selecting very difficult tasks;

5. Not trying or making others think one didn't try.

DIVERSITY >

From elementary school through high school, students with lower achievement tend to use more self-handicapping strategies than students who are doing well in school (Leondari & Gonida, 2007). Success-oriented students and overstrivers in Eastern and Western cultures are less likely to engage in self-handicapping behaviors than failure-avoiding students (De Castella et al., 2013). However, when teachers convey the belief that ability is fixed and unchangeable, even gifted students may engage in self-handicapping, leading them to underperform in school (Snyder, Malin, Dent, & Linnenbrink-Garcia, 2014). Research on gender differences in self-handicapping is inconclusive, with some studies showing boys using these strategies more often than girls, while other studies find no gender difference (Leondari & Gonida, 2007; Urdan, Midgley, & Anderman, 1998).

To failure-avoiding students, self-handicapping strategies are a useful way to attribute failure to causes other than low ability, enabling them to feel less shame (Stipek, 2002). If a student puts in a lot of effort to succeed on a task—one that others master with less effort—the student would feel this implies low ability. Worse, according to the student's perception, failure after putting in effort would be a public admission of low ability (Covington & Omelich, 1979). Failure without effort, though, does not reflect negatively on the student's ability (Covington & Beery, 1976).

However, lack of effort can become a "double-edged sword" (Covington & Omelich, 1979). Because teachers value effort, students who purposely do not try risk teacher disapproval and punishment (Urdan et al., 1998; Weiner, 1994). Teachers may require elementary school students to complete work during recess or as a homework assignment, and in the upper grades they may give detentions or failing grades. Therefore, the student is stuck between two competing alternatives: being punished for not trying, or trying and risking a demonstration of low ability.

Unlike the other three types of students, **failure-accepting students** neither approach success nor avoid failure. Rather, in response to repeated failures to perform up to their expectations, they accept failure and give up the struggle to demonstrate their ability and maintain their self-worth (Covington & Omelich, 1985). Failure-accepting students (Covington, 1984)

- take little credit for success and believe that success is determined by external, uncontrollable factors;

- blame themselves (i.e., their low ability) for failure; and

- view a new failure as confirmation of their belief that they lack ability.

Failure-accepting students are similar to students with *learned helplessness,* those who are not motivated to learn because they believe that past failures are due to causes they do not control. Therefore, these students are the most difficult to motivate because positive reinforcement for successes does not work, and convincing them that they could succeed in the future is difficult (Ames, 1990; Covington & Omelich, 1985).

Learned helplessness:
See Module 15

Failure-avoiding and failure-accepting students, whose sense of ability is threatened, may attempt to maintain positive self-worth by discounting the importance of school success (Harter, Whitesell, & Junkin, 1998). Some adolescents use this strategy as a last resort. They shift their attention to developing competencies in nonacademic areas such as sports, music, art, social relationships, or delinquent behavior (De Castella et al., 2013; Stipek, 2002). It is important for teachers to identify students with failure-avoiding or failure-accepting orientations so they may help them develop more positive mastery behaviors.

Which type of student do you consider yourself? Has your motivational orientation changed during your schooling? If so, how has it changed?

SELF-DETERMINATION THEORY

3 Explain how autonomy, competence, and relatedness can facilitate intrinsic motivation.

4 Define internalization and explain how educational contexts can facilitate internalization of behaviors.

According to self-determination theory, humans possess *universal,* innate needs for autonomy, competence, and relatedness (deCharms, 1976; Ryan & Deci, 2000b). We need to feel *autonomy*—that our behavior is internally controlled or self-regulated and that we have choices in our actions rather than being controlled or pressured (Deci & Ryan, 1985; Vansteenkiste, Niemiec, & Soenens, 2010). We also have a *need for competence,* that is, an innate desire to explore and attempt mastery of skills (White, 1959). To feel safe enough to explore our environment, though, we also need to feel *relatedness,* or a sense of being securely connected to others (Ryan, Deci, & Grolnick, 1995). When these needs are supported in our environment, we feel a sense of **self-determination,** or a freedom to pursue goals and activities that are personally relevant and interesting to us. These needs are important for psychological well-being of individuals in Western cultures and Eastern collectivistic cultures, including Bulgaria, South Korea, Russia, and China (Vansteenkiste et al., 2010).

DIVERSITY

Self-determination theory's focus on needs may remind you of **Maslow's hierarchy of needs.** In Abraham Maslow's (1943, 1987) theory, individuals are motivated by basic human needs:

1. physiological needs (food, water, shelter, and clothing),

2. safety needs (feeling nonthreatened and having a sense of order and stability),

3. love and belongingness (a need to give and receive love and to experience friendship, appreciation, and belonging),

4. esteem needs (desire for achievement and for respect from others), and

5. **self-actualization,** a need to satisfy their full potential.

Video: Maslow's
Hierarchy of Needs

Maslow proposed that the needs are organized according to their biological urgency, with the most urgent ones needing to be satisfied first. Lower level needs, such as physiological and safety needs, need to be at least partially satisfied for an individual to focus on higher level needs. The four basic needs (physiological comfort, safety, love, and self-esteem) are all **deficiency needs** (Maslow, 1954), meaning we are motivated to obtain them when they are lacking in our environment. The fifth, self-actualization, is a **growth need,** because individuals are continually motivated from within by a need for growth, maturation, and fulfillment (Maslow, 1954). Even though Maslow never used a pyramid or triangle to depict the hierarchy, these needs are often shown in this way, as in Figure 16.2 (Wininger & Norman, 2010).

A common misconception of Maslow's theory is that individuals need to fully satisfy one need before addressing the next need in the hierarchy (Wininger & Norman, 2010). However, the hierarchy is not rigid; the order in which needs are met may vary (Maslow, 1954, 1987). For example, a student who desires to do well in school and attend a prestigious college may spend

FIGURE 16.2 **Maslow's Hierarchy of Needs.** Maslow's hierarchy provides teachers with an understanding that when certain needs are extremely deficient in a student, these can become obstacles to learning and self-fulfillment.

countless hours studying (motivated by esteem needs) and neglect spending time with family and friends (love and belongingness needs). Also, the satisfaction of needs is not "all-or-none." Most individuals in our society have all of their basic needs partially satisfied to different degrees (Maslow, 1987; Wininger & Norman, 2010).

Very little systematic research has been conducted to validate Maslow's theory (De Bruyckere, Kirschner, & Hulshof, 2015). However, the theory remains popular in practice because it gives teachers a way to understand the possible obstacles to learning and motivation. Maslow's theory proposes that if lower needs are *mostly* unmet, this would interfere with students' interest in learning. Similarly, self-determination theory suggests that if needs for autonomy, competence, and relatedness are not supported, students will not be intrinsically motivated. Let's explore this idea further.

Self-Determination and Motivation

As we discussed with regard to self-efficacy and self-worth theory, feelings of competence can facilitate intrinsic motivation. Engaging in optimally challenging tasks fulfills the need to feel competent, encouraging intrinsic motivation (Deci & Ryan, 1992; Grolnick, Gurland, Jacob, & DeCourcey, 2002). When cognitive tasks are slightly above children's skill levels, they spend more time on them, show more intrinsic motivation, and exhibit intense joy and pride when they master the tasks (Harter, 1978; McMullin & Steffen, 1982). Increases in feelings of academic competence from elementary school to middle school result in increased intrinsic motivation for schoolwork, while lowered feelings of competence over the years decrease intrinsic motivation (Harter, 1992; Harter, Whitesell, & Kowalski, 1992). High school students whose perceptions of competence increased over the semester found the subject they were learning more interesting at the end of the semester than at the beginning (MacIver, Stipek, & Daniels, 1991).

Video Case 16.1 ▲
Self-Directed Learning

Feelings of competence enhance intrinsic motivation only when they are supported by autonomy (Patall, Cooper, & Robinson, 2008; Patall, Cooper, & Wynn, 2010), meaning that behaviors are internally regulated. Earning an A on an exam (feeling competent) will lead you to be intrinsically motivated if you believe that your actions—studying—were autonomous. Highly autonomous students are more engaged in school, achieve higher academic performance, and stay in school until graduation (Grolnick et al., 2002; Soenens & Vansteenkiste, 2005). However, if you study hard because your parents expect you to do well in school or because you want to impress the teacher, your studying behavior is not internally regulated, leading you to be more extrinsically motivated.

Intrinsic motivation also is more likely to flourish when students feel relatedness (Ryan & Deci, 2000a). Students who feel secure in their environment and connected to others are more likely to seek out mastery experiences, promoting a sense of competence. They may develop intrinsic motivation for academic tasks and activities if these are modeled or valued by others with whom they feel (or want to feel) attached (Ryan & Deci, 2000a). For example, students may become intrinsically motivated to learn if they have "bonded" with a teacher who shows them the value of learning. Students who believe their teachers to be caring and supportive of them have higher intrinsic motivation (Wormington, Corpus, & Anderson, 2012). When students feel relatedness in the classroom, both in Eastern and Western cultures, they also tend to consider teachers' behaviors as less controlling and are more willing to internalize teachers' values and expectations (Zhou, Lam, & Chan, 2012). Relatedness may positively affect the motivation of girls more than that of boys. Girls report closer relationships with teachers, and teachers consider their relationships with girls to be closer than their relationships with boys (Howes, Phillipsen, & Peisner-Feinberg, 2000; Valeski & Stipek, 2001).

〉 **DIVERSITY**

Becoming Self-Determined

Like self-efficacy, self-determination is specific to a particular activity or subject (Grolnick et al., 2002). Individuals can develop self-determination for behaviors such as schoolwork, chores,

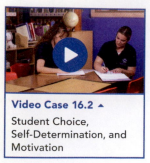

DIVERSITY ⟨

or attending religious functions (Grolnick, Deci, & Ryan, 1997). Individuals develop self-determination through a developmental process called **internalization,** where they acquire beliefs, attitudes, and behaviors from external sources and progressively transform them into personal attributes, values, and self-regulatory behaviors (Grolnick et al., 1997). Figure 16.3 shows the developmental continuum from non-self-determined behavior (no self-regulatory behavior) to self-determined behavior (fully autonomous and intrinsically regulated behavior). Let's remember that self-determination theory does not imply movement through each form of motivation (Vansteenkiste, Lens, & Deci, 2006). Rather, individuals may show different types of motivation that vary in their degree of autonomy, depending on how successful they are at internalization (Deci & Ryan, 1985; Ryan & Deci, 2000a). To intrinsically motivate students, it is important for teachers to know what type of motivation along the continuum students currently exhibit.

Amotivation is a lack of motivation. Individuals with this orientation do not show any self-regulation. Instead, they simply "go through the motions" or are unwilling to act at all. Students may be amotivated because the academic task is unappealing to them or they do not value the learning activity (Legault, Green-Demers, & Pelletier, 2006; Ryan, 1995). Students may also be amotivated because they do not feel competent to do the activity or they do not feel they can put forth the effort needed to succeed (Bandura, 1986; Legault et al., 2006). Amotivation may be more likely to occur in boys than girls (Alvernini, Lucidi, & Manganelli, 2008).

External regulation is the least autonomous form of extrinsic motivation. Externally regulated individuals perform behaviors in response to external contingencies such as rewards, praise, punishments, and deadlines. An elementary school student who studies to get money for As on her report card exhibits external regulation of behavior, as does a high school student who completes homework assignments to avoid detentions.

Introjected regulation is a form of extrinsic motivation in which individuals engage in an activity to comply with external pressure. Because individuals have partially internalized the behavior and have not taken ownership of it, they perform the behavior to avoid guilt or anxiety or to achieve a sense of pride (Ryan & Deci, 2000a; Vansteenkiste et al., 2010). A middle school student who studies before going to baseball practice (because he would feel guilty if he put sports ahead of schoolwork) is showing introjected regulation, as is a high school student who feels intense pressure to ace an exam to prove her self-worth (because she has not yet accepted studying as part of her internal values).

FIGURE 16.3 **A Taxonomy of Human Motivation.** The degree of autonomy we have affects our level of motivation from non-self-determined to self-determined.

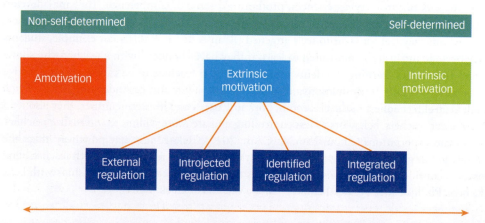

SOURCE: Adapted from R. M. Ryan, & E. L. Deci (2000a). "Self-determination theory and the facilitation of intrinsic motivation, social development, and well-being." *American Psychologist, 55*(1), 72, January 2000. Copyright © 2000 American Psychological Association. Used with permission.

Identified regulation is a slightly internalized form of regulation that approximates intrinsic motivation. Individuals identify with the value of an activity, have accepted regulation of the activity as their own, and more willingly engage in the activity because they see its personal relevance. Elementary school students tend to have high levels of identified regulation because they are motivated by tasks that are personally relevant to them (Sungur & Senler, 2010). For example, an elementary school student who says, "I do my schoolwork because learning new things makes you smarter," exhibits identified regulation, as does a high school student who chooses to learn a foreign language because of its importance for career goals.

Integrated regulation occurs when individuals have fully accepted extrinsic regulations by integrating them with other aspects of their values and identity (Ryan, 1995). A high school student might study regularly because it has become a part of his identity as a student.

Finally, the most self-determined and autonomous form of motivation is **intrinsic motivation.** A high school student might study regularly because it satisfies her curiosity, interests, or need for competence.

Amotivation and external and introjected regulation are considered controlled (pressured or coerced), while intrinsic motivation and well-internalized forms of extrinsic motivation (identified and integrated regulation) are considered autonomous, or self-determined (Vansteenkiste et al., 2010). Girls tend to be more self-determined in school than boys, showing higher levels of identified and introjected regulation (Vallerand et al., 1993). Consistent with research showing a general decline in intrinsic motivation from elementary through high school, amotivation and external regulation are typically found more often in high school students (Alvernini et al., 2008; Legault et al., 2006). Supportive home and peer contexts, which promote feelings of relatedness, can help prevent students from becoming amotivated (Legault et al., 2006).

What level of self-determination do you have? How have your parents or teachers influenced your self-determination?

Home or school contexts that fulfill individuals' needs for competence, autonomy, and relatedness—called autonomy-supportive contexts—can facilitate internalization and encourage intrinsic motivation (Grolnick et al., 1997; Ryan & Deci, 2000a). Autonomy-supportive parents spend time with their children, know about their daily life, and provide them with opportunities to explore and master their environment (Grolnick et al., 1997). As a result, their children tend to be mastery oriented and to have increased self-esteem, connection to school, and academic achievement (Eccles, Early, Frasier, Belansky, & McCarthy, 1996; Grolnick et al., 1997). Teachers with a strong sense of autonomy in their teaching tend to be more autonomy supportive (Reeve, 2009; Roth, Assor, Kanat-Maymon, & Kaplan, 2007). Their behaviors lead to numerous positive outcomes for students, as outlined in Table 16.1. The advantages of autonomy-supportive environments have been found in Western and non-Western cultures (Chirkov, Ryan, & Willness, 2005; Jang, Reeve, Ryan, & Kim, 2009; Vansteenkiste, Zhou, Lens, & Soenens, 2005).

Autonomy-supportive learning contexts are beneficial for students from preschool through high school, including students with special needs (Deci, Hodges, Pierson, & Tomassone, 1992; Reeve, 2009). This type of context may be especially important during adolescence, when students are experiencing important changes, such as going through puberty, establishing their independence and identity, and transitioning to middle and high school. Ironically, schools seem to become more controlling just as students' autonomy needs begin to increase (Eccles et al., 1993; Midgley & Feldlaufer, 1987). In middle school, students face more rules and discipline, have fewer opportunities to make decisions, and experience harsher grading practices (Anderman & Maehr, 1994). In high school, teachers tend to rely on extrinsic motivators to engage students in learning, use controlling language without explanations for their requests, and reject students' complaints and negative emotions (Jang et al., 2010; Reeve et al., 2004).

TABLE 16.1	Autonomy-Supportive Teaching Practices and Beneficial Student Outcomes

WHAT AUTONOMY-SUPPORTIVE TEACHERS DO	BENEFICIAL OUTCOMES OF AUTONOMY-SUPPORTIVE TEACHING
• empathize with the students' perspectives, showing an understanding of their complaints and negative emotions • encourage students to express opinions and preferences • allow students to work at their own pace • solicit students' opinions • provide classroom structure, conveying their expectations for students in a noncontrolling way and providing sufficient information and support for meeting those expectations • give feedback about students' competence and express confidence in students' abilities • avoid the use of controlling educational practices such as controlling language, directives, threats, imposed deadlines, and close monitoring	• better time management and concentration • deep, meaningful learning • greater creativity • better academic performance • greater identified regulation for schoolwork • higher intrinsic motivation • enhanced well-being

SOURCES: Assor, Kaplan, Kanat-Maymon, & Roth, 2005; Deci, Eghrari, Patrick, & Leone, 1994; Jang, Reeve, & Deci, 2010; Koestner, Ryan, Bernieri, & Holt, 1984; Levesque, Zuehike, Stanek, & Ryan, 2004; Patall et al., 2010; Reeve, 2009; Reeve, Jang, Carrell, Barch, & Jeon, 2004; Sierens, Vansteenkiste, Goossens, Soenens, & Dochy, 2009; Soenens & Vansteenkiste, 2005; Vansteenkiste, Lens, Dewitte, De Witte, & Deci, 2004; Vansteenkiste et al., 2010; Vansteenkiste, Simons, Lens, Sheldon, & Deci, 2004; Vansteenkiste et al., 2005.

The structure of middle schools and high schools—in which students have multiple teachers, switch classes, and often are grouped by ability—also may discourage relatedness (Martin, 2009; Otis, Grouzet, & Pelletier, 2005; Rolland, 2012).

INTEGRATING THE SELF THEORIES

 Describe techniques teachers can use to enhance students' intrinsic motivation, and identify which self theory supports each technique.

Have you noticed similarities among the theories? You may have asked yourself why we need three separate theories related to the self. While the theories do overlap, they each bring a unique perspective to understanding intrinsic motivation. As a teacher, it is important to become familiar with these differing perspectives and to understand how each can inform best practices for enhancing motivation.

Self Theories Compared

Table 16.2 presents the self theories side by side to illustrate where they overlap and where they diverge. As our examination of self-efficacy, self-worth, and self-determination has shown, all three theories place importance on competence and intrinsic motivation. Self-efficacy depends on whether individuals believe they have the knowledge or skills to succeed on a task. Self-worth relies on a basic need to protect our perception of competence. Self-determination has at its core the individual's need to feel competent.

However, while self-efficacy and self-worth theories both focus on *perceived* competence—on whether individuals *think* they have ability—self-determination theory emphasizes the *need* for competence, the individual's need to develop mastery of knowledge and skills.

TABLE 16.2   Self Theories Compared

	SELF-EFFICACY	SELF-WORTH	SELF-DETERMINATION
Description	Expectations for success on a particular task	Overall evaluation of our worth as individuals	Feeling that we have choice in our actions
Core needs	To believe we have the knowledge or skills to succeed on a task	To protect our perception of competence	To feel autonomous, competent, and related
Domain specific	Yes	No	Yes
Focus	Perceived competence		A need to develop competence

Both self-efficacy and self-determination are domain specific, meaning they refer to specific learning situations (e.g., biology lab) or subjects (e.g., calculus). For self-efficacy, that means our expectations about accomplishing a specific goal. Likewise, for self-determination, it means our *feelings* of autonomy, competence, and relatedness can vary depending on the situation. However, remember that our *strivings* for autonomy, competence, and relatedness (like our need to protect self-worth) represent universal human needs. Despite differences among the theories, they provide similar suggestions for enhancing students' intrinsic motivation, which we explore next.

APPLICATIONS: FOSTERING SELF-EFFICACY, SELF-WORTH, AND SELF-DETERMINATION

Students with high self-efficacy, positive self-worth, and self-determination are more likely to be intrinsically motivated than are students with lower levels of these traits. According to the self theories, teachers can enhance students' intrinsic motivation by following the guidelines described here.

Capitalize on interest and relevance. When teachers point out the relevance of new material, students are more likely to become self-determined in their learning (Assor, Kaplan, & Roth, 2002; Deci et al., 1994). This is especially true when students have low initial interest. Students also are more likely to value what they are learning and to enjoy it more when they are studying something of personal interest. In one study, students valued learning more when it involved a topic of interest to them, even when they experienced failure (Covington & Müeller, 2001). One way to make content relevant to students is to ground it in authentic learning activities that are real-life tasks, such as designing experiments in a science class, writing a persuasive letter to a local politician for English class, or creating a plan to reduce pollution in a civics class. Authentic activities encourage the acquisition of skills for solving problems and completing tasks that are important in the real world (Brown, Collins, & Duguid, 1989; Collins, Hawkins, & Carver, 1991). Students may be intrinsically motivated because learning has real-world relevance.

Provide realistic choices among tasks. Teachers can enhance students' autonomy by giving all students realistic choices, as when elementary school students choose which book they want to read or when middle and high school students select their own topics for research projects. When students have choices such as these, they tend to enjoy tasks more, feel more competent, and have higher achievement (Patall et al., 2010). Giving students control over the process or the product of a task also fosters autonomy, promotes self-determination, and enhances intrinsic motivation (Deci, Vallerand, Pelletier, & Ryan, 1991; Reeve & Jang, 2006). To be effective, teachers should do the following:

Video Case 16.3 ▲
Self-Efficacy and Motivation

© SAGE Publications

Situated cognition: See Module 18

- provide choices when tasks are not intrinsically interesting (Patall, 2013);

- match choices to students' interests and goals and ensure that choices are consistent with their cultural values (Katz & Assor, 2007; Vansteenkiste et al., 2010); and

- offer a moderate number of choices at an optimally challenging level (Katz & Assor, 2007).

Teach and model skills necessary for success. Rather than expect that students will acquire learning strategies on their own, teachers need to explicitly teach strategies, such as study skills, mnemonic techniques, and math algorithms. Students who learn strategies improve their self-efficacy as well as their academic skills (Pintrich & De Groot, 1990; Zimmerman & Martinez-Pons, 1990). Teacher modeling of cognitive strategies can also promote higher self-efficacy and achievement than independent learning, where students read and answer questions without guidance (Schunk, 1981).

Mastery goals: See Module 15

Focus on mastery. When students complete tasks that are moderately difficult—just slightly beyond their capabilities—they are more likely to prefer the tasks and be motivated to master them (Harter, 1974). Emphasizing mastery encourages students to be success oriented rather than failure avoiding. Covington (1992) described a mastery approach called the "grade-choice arrangement," in which students can earn any grade they choose by accruing credits (a specific number for an A, fewer for a B, etc.), but the higher the grade they choose to aim for, the more they must accomplish and the better they must perform. Students compete not against one another but for a standard of performance. Students working under this approach learned more and were more motivated than students in a typical competitive environment (Covington, 1998; Covington & Omelich, 1984). Teachers should not allow students to select a grade option that allows them to minimize effort, protect self-worth, or avoid failure (Ryan, Connell, & Deci, 1985). For example, allowing students to choose a C grade option when you know they are capable of B or A work reinforces their attempt to minimize effort and avoid failure rather than encourages them to strive for mastery.

Help students set appropriate goals. Teachers can break down tasks and assignments into smaller components; provide short-term, moderately difficult goals; and offer strategies for making progress toward goals. Mastering small components of tasks teaches students to accept credit for their successes (Covington, 1984). Also, when students learn to set short-term, realistic goals and learn ways to make progress toward goals, they (Schunk & Miller, 2002; Tollefson, 2000)

- learn that effort as well as ability contribute to success,

- are more willing to put forth effort,

- improve their academic skills, and

- develop positive self-efficacy and self-worth.

However, assigning easy tasks or helping students complete an assignment they could not have done independently will not necessarily enhance efficacy expectations, because students will not attribute their success to their own ability or effort.

Provide appropriate feedback. When teachers give students feedback indicating that their success was due to increased effort, students feel greater self-efficacy and higher motivation (Schunk, 1987; Schunk & Miller, 2002). Be aware, however, that telling students to work harder following poor performance may lower their self-efficacy, especially if they believe they already are trying as hard as they can (Ames, 1990; Tollefson, 2000). Whenever possible, teachers should use informational feedback, which conveys what the student has done well and what to do the next time. One form of informational feedback is performance (or outcome) praise, which evaluates the end product, such as "The argument in your paper is clear and compelling" (Corpus & Lepper, 2007). Another form of

Process, performance, and person praise: See Module 14

informational feedback is process praise, such as "I like the way you approached that math problem," which evaluates the process taken to complete a task. Process and performance praise foster intrinsic motivation and feelings of competence in students from childhood through late adolescence (Corpus & Lepper, 2007; Haimovitz & Corpus, 2011; Mueller & Dweck, 1998). In contrast, giving positive feedback in a controlling manner undermines intrinsic motivation (Kast & Connor, 1988; Ryan, Mims, & Koestner, 1983). Person praise, which involves a favorable judgment about a person's attributes, such as "You're so good at math" is considered controlling because it is the teacher's favorable evaluation that drives students' motivation. Also, when teachers use words like *should* and *ought,* as in "Excellent, you *should* study that hard all the time," even when it is intended to be positive and motivating, students perceive the language as controlling.

Limit the use of external constraints in teaching. Some educational practices—such as close monitoring, the use of threats and directives, and the imposition of goals and deadlines—can be perceived as controlling and lead to diminished intrinsic motivation (Ryan & Deci, 2000b; Sierens et al., 2009). However, the way such tools are introduced, expressed, or administered makes a difference. For example, goals and deadlines are a necessary part of instruction, but the more students see them as a valued component of the learning process and the more autonomy they have in learning, the more likely goals and deadlines will support intrinsic motivation. Limiting controlling practices does not mean that instruction should lack structure. Autonomy support and structure are complementary. In classrooms where teachers used a highly structured instructional approach, students experienced a high level of engagement in learning and autonomy support by teachers (Jang et al., 2010). Teacher-provided autonomy support enhances students' perceived autonomy, and teacher structure enhances students' perceived competence, both having beneficial effects on students' intrinsic motivation and achievement (Jang et al., 2010).

Foster relatedness in the classroom. Show students that you care about them as individuals. Feelings of relatedness promote internalization, the integration of extrinsic values, and intrinsic motivation (Deci et al., 1994). Also, show students that you trust them. For example, an elementary school student might be trusted to bring the lunch count to the main office, and high school students might be asked to abide by an "honor system" when the teacher leaves the classroom during an exam. Last, use strategies to build a sense of community in the classroom. Adolescents who believe they are valued and respected members of the classroom tend to have higher self-efficacy and mastery goals, show greater responsibility, and attain higher levels of achievement (Anderman & Anderman, 1999; DeBacker & Nelson, 1999). Ideas for creating a classroom community include highlighting group achievements, increasing opportunities for students to interact with one another during the school day, and engaging students in relationship-building activities (Burden, 2003).

Controlling educational practices: See Module 14

SUMMARY

❶ Describe outcome expectations and efficacy expectations with respect to student and teacher efficacy. A student may believe that studying leads to good grades (outcome expectation) and that *he* has adequate study skills to obtain good grades (efficacy expectation). Teachers also have outcome expectations about the ability of all students to learn, as well as efficacy expectations, which are beliefs about their own teaching effectiveness.

❷ Explain how self-worth affects the motivation of success-oriented students, overstrivers, and failure-avoiding and failure-accepting students. Because our sense of competence

contributes to our overall feeling of self-worth, we are motivated to protect our self-worth by maintaining a positive feeling of competence. Success-oriented students, who are intrinsically motivated, value learning as an opportunity to improve their ability and are not discouraged by failure. Overstrivers have high hopes for success but fear failure, so they use strategies to ensure that they will perform better than other students. Failure-avoiding students use many self-handicapping strategies to avoid situations that lead to failure or to avoid looking incompetent. Failure-accepting students neither approach success nor avoid failure because they have learned to accept failure.

3 **Explain how autonomy, competence, and relatedness can facilitate intrinsic motivation.** Individuals are more likely to be intrinsically motivated to perform activities over which they feel they have autonomy. Autonomy supportive contexts lead to many benefits, including increased autonomy, perceived competence, and intrinsic motivation. Feelings of competence are associated with increased intrinsic motivation for schoolwork. Optimally challenging tasks enable students to feel competent, increase students' sense of pride, and stimulate intrinsic motivation. Students also are more likely to be intrinsically motivated to engage in school activities if teachers have a connectedness with their students.

4 **Define internalization and explain how educational contexts can facilitate internalization of behaviors.** Within the context of motivation, internalization is a developmental process in which individuals move from less self-determined (more extrinsically motivated) to more self-determined behavior. Educational contexts can facilitate internalization and encourage students' intrinsic motivation if they allow for the satisfaction of autonomy, competence, and relatedness needs.

5 **Describe techniques teachers can use to enhance students' intrinsic motivation, and identify which self theory supports each technique.** Teachers can encourage intrinsic motivation with these techniques: (a) capitalizing on interest and relevance, (b) providing realistic choices of tasks, (c) teaching skills necessary for success, (d) focusing on mastery, (e) helping students set appropriate goals, (f) providing appropriate feedback, (g) limiting external constraints in teaching, and (h) fostering relatedness. Pointing out the relevance of new material and providing students with choices among tasks may make students more self-determined. Teaching students the skills needed to achieve success will increase their self-efficacy. When teachers focus on mastery and help students set moderately challenging, short-term goals, students become success oriented and develop positive self-efficacy and self-worth, increasing their intrinsic motivation. Feedback that is informational and focuses on effort also increases self-efficacy and intrinsic motivation. Limiting external constraints and fostering relatedness in the classroom also will enhance self-determination.

KEY CONCEPTS

amotivation, 326
deficiency needs, 324
efficacy expectations, 315
external regulation, 326
extrinsic motivation, 314
failure-accepting students, 322
failure-avoiding students, 322
growth needs, 324

identified regulation, 327
integrated regulation, 327
internalization, 326
intrinsic motivation, 314
introjected regulation, 326
Maslow's hierarchy of needs, 324
outcome expectations, 315
overstrivers, 320

self-actualization, 324
self-determination, 324
self-efficacy, 315
self-regulation, 318
self-worth, 320
success-oriented students, 320
teacher efficacy, 318

CASE STUDIES: REFLECT AND EVALUATE

EARLY CHILDHOOD: THE WORKSHEETS

These questions refer to the case study on page 268.

1. According to self-efficacy theory, what is Melissa's efficacy expectation for completing her schoolwork? How would you characterize Claire's self-efficacy? How would you characterize Martin's self-efficacy?

2. Explain why asking a peer to show Melissa how to complete the math sheet might improve her self-efficacy.

3. How can Mrs. Garvey improve the self-efficacy of students in her class?

4. Based on self-worth theory, which student—Melissa, Martin, or Claire—would be most difficult to motivate? Why? Which student would be easiest to motivate? Why?

5. Based on the case study, speculate on the degree of Mrs. Garvey's teaching efficacy.

ELEMENTARY SCHOOL: WRITER'S BLOCK

These questions refer to the case study on page 270.

1. Contrast Carter's and Shanti's self-efficacy for writing. What failure-avoiding tactics does Carter use during freewriting?

2. Using your response to the previous question, explain why you would expect to see a failure-avoiding motivational pattern in Carter and not in Shanti, according to the research on gender differences discussed in the module.

3. What specific things can Mrs. Okuda do to increase Carter's self-efficacy for free writing? Would your suggestions for increasing self-efficacy change if the student you were considering were Mason? Why or why not?

MIDDLE SCHOOL: THE MATH REVIEW

These questions refer to the case study on page 272.

1. How would you describe Jesse's self-efficacy for completing the math problems?

2. Speculate on whether Mr. Pantera has high teaching efficacy. Use details in the case to support your answer.

3. What can Mr. Pantera do to promote positive self-efficacy in his students?

HIGH SCHOOL: EXAM GRADES

These questions refer to the case study on page 274.

1. How would you describe Chelsea's self-efficacy? Compare this with Nicholas's self-efficacy. Based on research evidence regarding gender differences, how typical is this motivational pattern?

2. Based on the comments of Reggie, Tamika, and Carla, describe the self-efficacy of students in the general science class. Assuming that general science is a class for students with lower achievement than students in AP Physics, explain how this practice of ability grouping (assigning students to different levels of classes) might affect students' self-efficacy. What are the outcome expectations in science for students in the general science class?

4. According to self-worth theory, how can Mrs. Okuda encourage James and Carter to be more intrinsically motivated for writing activities?

5. How are *self-regulation* and *internalization* similar? Which students in Mrs. Okuda's class are most self-regulated? How can Mrs. Okuda encourage all her students to become self-regulated in writing? How will this affect their self-determination?

6. What changes can Mrs. Okuda make to increase her students' autonomy? How will this affect their motivation?

4. According to self-worth theory, which student—Aaron, Jesse, or Rachel—would be most difficult to motivate? Why? Which student would be easiest to motivate? Why?

5. The eighth graders feel external pressures due to the need to perform on the state test. Provide Mr. Pantera with suggestions for creating a classroom that promotes student autonomy to improve their motivation. How can Mr. Pantera promote feelings of competence and relatedness in his classroom in general?

3. Is Mr. Womack's reassurance to Chelsea that she will do better next time likely to improve her self-efficacy? Why or why not?

4. According to self-worth theory, which student—Nicholas, Chelsea, or Reggie—would be most difficult to motivate? Why? Which student would be easiest to motivate? Why?

5. Mr. Womack realizes that the general science class and the AP Physics class have different motivational needs. Help Mr. Womack create a motivational plan for each class for increasing students' self-efficacy, enhancing their self-worth, and facilitating their self-determination. Provide specific examples that are consistent with each theory. How do the motivational plans differ for the general science class and the AP Physics class?

UNIT SIX

CLASSROOM MANAGEMENT AND INSTRUCTION

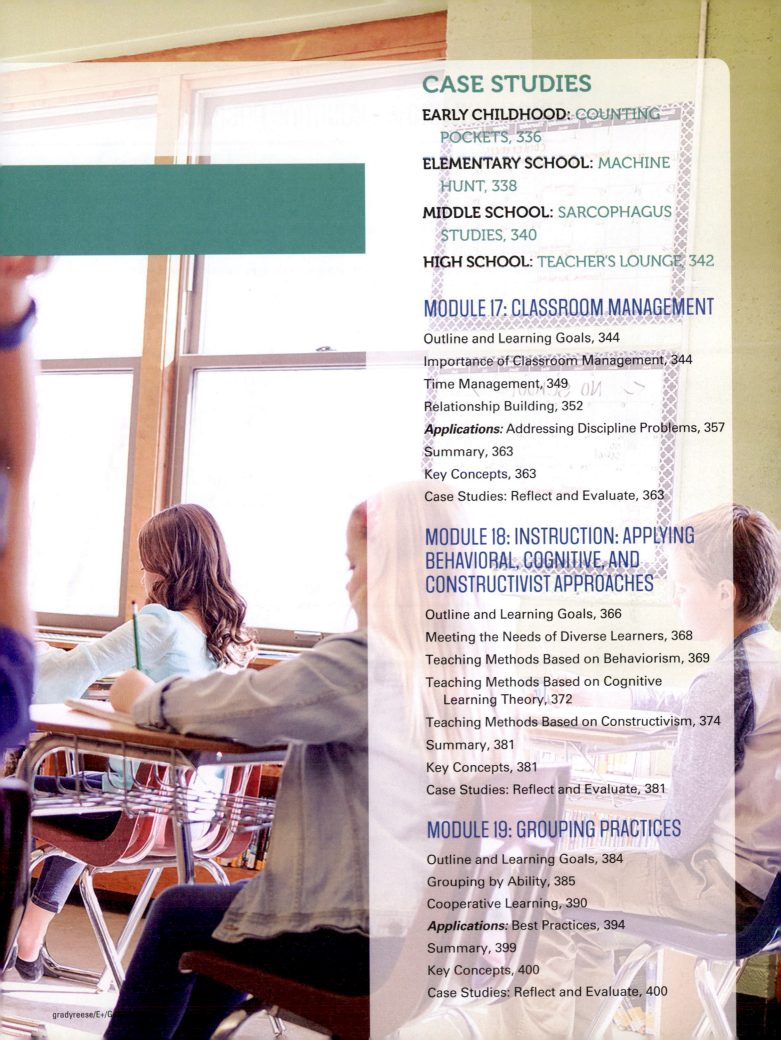

gradyreese/E+/G

EARLY CHILDHOOD: COUNTING POCKETS

PREPARE:

As you read the case, make notes:

1. WHO are the primary participants in the case? Describe them.
2. WHAT is taking place?
3. WHERE is the case taking place? Is the environment a factor?
4. WHEN is the case taking place? Is the timing a factor?

Ms. Abby Miller teaches three- and four-year-olds in a preschool situated within a large, comprehensive high school in a diverse suburb outside a metropolitan area. The preschool is free for the high school teachers and for low-income families in the community. Ms. Abby finds the mix of different backgrounds and languages a rewarding aspect of teaching, and she also enjoys mentoring high school students who earn credit toward their Child Development class by assisting in the classroom during their study hall.

©iStockphoto.com/ Christopher Futcher

Today, on a cold February morning, Ms. Abby and the two high school students, Miss Maggie and Miss Addison, huddle in a circle on the carpet with the children for "morning meeting." Ms. Abby likes to use the morning meeting to encourage language, number concepts, and general knowledge through fun, hands-on activities. After the children sing the hello song and talk about the weather the way they do every morning, Ms. Abby asks them to stand up. "Today we're going to count pockets! Noah, how many pockets do you have?"

Noah quickly looks at his clothes and proudly shouts, "Six!" He has four pockets on his jeans and two on his shirt.

"That's right," Ms. Abby replies, as she draws six squares next to his name on the easel to represent the pockets and writes a "6."

"Diego, how many pockets do you have?" she asks, as Miss Addison points to Diego's pockets.

Diego counts, "Uno, dos, tres—three."

"Great counting!" says Ms. Abby. "Now say, I have three pockets." Diego repeats it exactly.

Ms. Abby continues, "Ok, now we're going to count more pockets. You're going to work with a buddy and count each other's pockets. Then draw your pockets up here," as she points to the children's names on the easel, "and write the number the way I did."

She begins to assign pairs: Casey and Mariah, Anika and Ella, Jayden and Aarush, and so on. Ms. Abby is careful to pair children of different backgrounds and abilities so they can learn from and help each other. She is also grateful to have Miss Addison and Miss Maggie to circulate the room and help children count and write the numbers on the easel. Some children know how to count, write numbers, and add, while others can't count yet.

As Ms. Abby is circulating the room, she overhears Caleb and Hunter shouting back and forth, "No you don't!" "Yes, I do!"

Caleb shoves Hunter and knocks him down. Caleb is 4 years old and big for his age. He often resorts to using his fists "instead of his words," as Ms. Abby constantly reminds him.

Hunter jumps up angrily and wipes tears from his eyes.

"What's the problem, boys?" Ms. Abby asks.

"Caleb is cheating. He has two pockets, not three!" Hunter shouts.

"No, I have three!" Caleb shouts back.

Ms. Abby reminds them both to use their inside voices.

"I have two pockets on my pants and a pocket on my hoodie. That's three," Caleb says.

"Hoodies don't count," Hunter retorts. "That's a pouch, not a pocket."

"Well, I see the problem," says Ms. Abby. "I think you're both right. It can be called a pouch, but if it can hold things, then we can call it a pocket, too. Agreed?" They both nod hesitantly.

"Caleb, apologize to Hunter for pushing and knocking him down, and both of you shake hands," says Ms. Abby.

Seeing that most children were done with the task, Ms. Abby calls them back to the carpet. "Now let's continue our game. Who has the *most* pockets?"

Ella raises her hand and waits to be called on. "I like how you raised your hand, Ella. You may answer," says Ms. Abby.

Ella responds, "Noah has the most cuz six is the biggest number."

"Good thinking, Ella," replies Ms. Abby. "Who has the fewest pockets? Aarush, I haven't heard from you yet today."

She knows he is still learning his letters and numbers. He speaks very little English and his parents speak Hindi to him at home. Aarush is reluctant to answer.

"Can you come up and point to the smallest number?" Ms. Abby asks.

He goes to the easel and points to the number one next to Casey's name.

"Hmmm. One is a very small number. That's the number we start with when we count 1, 2, 3. But there's an even smaller number," says Ms. Abby.

Some children start shaking their heads in confusion. Ms. Abby continues, "This is a tricky one. Can someone help Aarush?"

Anika is called on. She points to Ella and says, "Ella has the smallest. It's zero because she's wearing a dress!" Everyone chuckles.

"That's right, Anika! Zero means none, so it's the smallest number," replies Ms. Abby. "Now put on your listening ears. I've put a sheet in your cubbies to take home to your families. Have someone help you count the pockets of each person in your family, draw the number of pockets for your family, and write the number. Bring back the sheet tomorrow."

The children seem so excited to get "homework." Many of them have older siblings, and they want to do homework like them. Ms. Abby ends the activity by saying, "One, two, three, eyes on me."

The children reply, "Three, two, one, we are done!"

Ms. Abby announces that it's time for free play and begins calling on children who are sitting quietly to go to the center of their choice. Outside the classroom, the high school bell rings, signaling that it's time for Miss Maggie and Miss Addison to go back to their classes.

ASSESS:

1. Did Ms. Abby handle the situation with Caleb and Hunter appropriately? What would you have done differently?

2. Do you agree with Ms. Abby's approach to teaching the children number concepts? Why or why not? Should children in preschool experience more formal instruction?

3. Should Ms. Abby work with the children who know their numbers separately from those who are still learning these basic concepts? Why or why not?

EARLY CHILDHOOD

ELEMENTARY SCHOOL

MIDDLE SCHOOL

HIGH SCHOOL

ELEMENTARY SCHOOL: MACHINE HUNT

PREPARE:

As you read the case, make notes:

1. WHO are the primary participants in the case? Describe them.
2. WHAT is taking place?
3. WHERE is the case taking place? Is the environment a factor?
4. WHEN is the case taking place? Is the timing a factor?

Brian Finnegan loves teaching at West Heights Elementary School, the only K-5 elementary school in a rural school district of about 3,000 people. Mr. Finnegan finds teaching here particularly rewarding and also challenging because he teaches a split-grade class of fourth and fifth graders—13 fourth graders and 12 fifth graders, to be exact. He deals with a range of abilities within each traditional grade level. Even though the children's ages range from 9 through 11, most of the time they all get along.

After the Pledge of Allegiance and morning announcements, Mr. Finnegan's class gets right to work with the first subject of the day, math. Mr. Finnegan is introducing fraction concepts to some of the fourth graders—Sabrina, Brandon, Austin, and Avery—while other students are doing various assignments. Other fourth graders and some fifth graders are practicing addition, subtraction, multiplication, and division of fractions. Ellie, Connor, and Nathan, fourth graders with advanced math skills, and fifth graders Layla, Chloe, Henry, and Milo, along with some other students, are all working at their seats on a summative test to assess their mastery of factors and multiples. Each group of students will have its turn working with Mr. Finnegan. He has established an efficient system in which he works with each group of students on a rotation while other groups do independent work—either a formative assessment (pretest), worksheets for practice, an independent project, or a summative (mastery) test. Each child has an "in-box" where he or she can pick up new work, so the students do not interrupt Mr. Finnegan while he's working with a group, and students have a "buddy" they can ask for help if they have a question. There is also a completed work basket for students to turn in their work before getting another assignment. Mr. Finnegan's math class runs like a well-oiled machine!

Mr. Finnegan rings a bell on his desk, which signals that math has ended and science is beginning. Students put away their work. Mr. Finnegan claps twice, and most students clap twice; he claps once, and they all clap once. He knows they are ready to listen. He announces, "Today we're starting a new science unit on simple machines." He then hands out a sheet listing each simple machine, its purpose, and an example.

"You're going to walk around the school with your buddy, and jot down every example you can find of simple machines. Then you'll come back to the classroom and compare your findings in groups. Does everyone remember the rules for outside the classroom?" Mr. Finnegan asks, as he points to the list on the wall stating, "walk, quiet whisper, stay with your buddy."

Everyone nods. "OK, 1, 2, 3, get in line with your buddy," he says. And off they go.

When they return, Mr. Finnegan has created the groups. As he usually does in science and social studies, he creates groups with students who are mixed in age, gender, and ability, and even personality. Children come in and hurry to find their groups, eager to share what they learned, and Mr. Finnegan circulates the room listening and helping when needed. They all agree on the common objects, such as the ramp at the entrance (inclined plane), a light bulb (screw), and the fan in the cafeteria (wheel and axle). However, there are many disagreements about other items.

Nathan rattles off a bunch of items: "I found a lot of levers: the door handle, the light switch, the staple remover . . ."

"I don't think those are levers," Henry replies. "They don't look like the lever on the sheet."

"You don't just go by the way it looks," Nathan retorts. "You also need to think about what it does. A lever is for lifting." Henry still doesn't agree.

Mr. Finnegan says to Henry, "Henry, go get my staple remover and the stack of papers on my desk." Henry returns with the items. "Now, use the staple remover to take out the staple." Henry does.

"Ohhh . . . I get it. It lifted it. Cool!" Henry exclaims.

Mr. Finnegan notices that Austin, Sabrina, Milo, and Layla are arguing about wedges. He doesn't mind because he knows that the differences of opinion indicate that their thinking is being challenged.

Milo says, "So, we all agree that the doorstop is a wedge, right?"

"Yes," the others respond.

Sabrina adds, in a somewhat arrogant tone, "I also found scissors, tacks, and staples."

"How are those wedges?" asks Austin. "They don't look like the doorstop."

"And they don't separate anything like a wedge is supposed to," adds Layla.

"Well, the doorstop holds the door in place. It doesn't separate anything," Milo reasons.

Although Mr. Finnegan doesn't notice, Sabrina rolls her eyes, and then very politely says, "The sheet says wedges are for holding things together too!"

Mr. Finnegan chuckles and says, "I'm glad you all got that figured out. That's some great problem solving." But the other children look annoyed with Sabrina.

Milo whispers to Austin, "Princess Sabrina sure has everyone fooled into thinking she's so sweet. Sure wish he would catch her making fun of everyone at lunch. Just once I'd like a teacher to see how she really acts!"

Mr. Finnegan continues moving around the room until all the groups have finished. He flicks the lights on and off to get everyone's attention and says, "Tomorrow we start a group project that we will work on for the rest of this science unit. Your group will design and build a toy or game that contains at least three of the simple machines. Your homework tonight is to brainstorm ideas about what toy or game you'd want to build and what simple machines it will contain. Come prepared tomorrow to share with your group."

Brandon asks, "Mr. Finnegan, can we bring materials from home for the project?"

Mr. Finnegan responds, "Yes, you may. That's up to you and your group members. But let's not get ahead of ourselves. Start with the brainstorming and we'll go from there."

With that, he rings the bell and the children chatter about possible ideas as they pack up their things and get ready to go to lunch. Mr. Finnegan takes their enthusiasm as a good sign that he accomplished his learning objective.

ASSESS:

1. What strategies does Mr. Finnegan use to keep his classroom running smoothly?

2. Do you agree with Mr. Finnegan's approach to teaching math and science? Why or why not? What improvements, if any, would you suggest?

3. What challenges does a mix of abilities within a classroom present for a teacher? How would you respond to those challenges?

EARLY CHILDHOOD

ELEMENTARY SCHOOL

MIDDLE SCHOOL

HIGH SCHOOL

MIDDLE SCHOOL: Sarcophagus Studies

PREPARE:

As you read the case, make notes:

1. **WHO** are the primary participants in the case? Describe them.
2. **WHAT** is taking place?
3. **WHERE** is the case taking place? Is the environment a factor?
4. **WHEN** is the case taking place? Is the timing a factor?

Mrs. Stacey DeSantis has been teaching social studies at Riverbend Middle School for several years. She enjoys the unit on ancient Egypt each time she teaches it in her seventh grade classes. She has about 100 seventh graders: Periods 2 and 3, which consist of students who have lower achievement, particularly in language arts; Period 5, which consists of advanced students; and Period 7, which consists of on-grade-level students. Mrs. DeSantis begins the unit with a field trip to the local museum of natural history and then ends with a group project where students make their own sarcophagus. This morning students file into the auditorium carrying a notebook and a pen or pencil to prepare for the trip. Teacher aides pass out a checklist to each student. On it, there is a list of clues, such as, "What is the alphabet of ancient Egypt?" "What did Egyptians write on?" and "Who was the Egyptian god of the afterlife?" This turns the museum visit from a passive viewing of artifacts into a scavenger hunt that will be used as a basis for the lessons back at school.

Mrs. DeSantis begins with instructions and reminders about behavior. "Students, I know you're all excited to get to the field trip, but before we go a few reminders are in order. Remember that you and your parents signed a contract about expected behaviors for the trip. You will be exploring the museum in groups of five, and each group has an assigned chaperone. Parents, thanks for taking time out of your busy lives to accompany us on the trip. Students, you are to adhere to our school's code of conduct at all times. I expect to see walking—not running or shoving—and using a quiet whisper inside the museum. You may explore each of the exhibit rooms on your own, in pairs, or with your assigned group, but the rule is that when exiting an exhibit room and entering another, you must be in your assigned group so chaperones can get a head count. Any student who violates the contract will not be able to go on the school-wide field trip to the amusement park in June. Are there any questions?" Students begin whispering to each other, but no one raises a hand. Mrs. DeSantis begins dismissing students in groups to the buses waiting outside.

Just then, Dwayne, a 5-foot-9-inch 13-year-old, who seventh graders call "mean" and "scary" and try to avoid, starts pushing and intimidating the students at the front of the line. "No one sits in the back but me, got it?!"

Mrs. DeSantis, who seems to have eyes in the back of her head, calls him out of line.

"Dwayne, did you hear what I said in there about expected behaviors? We have a zero-tolerance policy about aggressive behavior. You just lost the privilege to go on the field trip. I will be sending a note home to your parents to let them know and they will need to sign it so I know they actually read *this* note. As for today, take the front seat in the bus. You will be going through the museum with Vice Principal Johnson. Lucky you," she says in a sarcastic tone with a smirk.

Several weeks later, Mrs. DeSantis's Period 5 class, her advanced level, begins the sarcophagus project.

She begins, "Class, for this project, you will be assigned to a group of four members. Each group will decide on a team name and what materials to use for creating the sarcophagus. Remember that the sarcophagus needs to be able to hold four items that the group would want to take to the afterlife, one item for each member. Let's discuss how you will decorate the sarcophagus. The top should have a headpiece, and it should have a face with eyes. Why are the eyes important?"

Several hands go up. "Dillon?" says Mrs. DeSantis.

"So the dead people can see out of the coffin," Dillon replies.

Mikaya adds, "Because the eyes were like a window to the afterlife."

"That's right, you two," Mrs. DeSantis responds in a pleasant tone. "OK, so you need eyes. You will also need to draw five memories that you will take with you to the afterlife, one memory for each of you and a collective group memory—maybe something you all remember from elementary school. Last, you will need to write your team's name in hieroglyphics. We're going to work on the project this week and each team will present its sarcophagus on Monday. Then Tuesday we'll review for the unit test."

The room is abuzz with chatter as teams get busy planning their projects.

Dillon, Julia, Xanthe, and Owen choose the name Eagles after Dillon's favorite football team, even though Julia and Xanthe really aren't into football.

"I want to draw the eyes!" Julia eagerly exclaims.

"Wait a sec," retorts Dillon. "Don't we need to decide what we're going to make it out of first?"

"Yeah," the others chime in, almost ganging up on Julia.

Mrs. DeSantis notices a few disagreements like this one, so she reminds the class about showing respect for each other's ideas, taking turns talking and listening, and handling conflicting ideas. She's confident that a reminder is all they need because she spent a lot of time at the beginning of the year going over classroom rules and specifically teaching them the behaviors they need for working in groups. They have had a lot of practice so far.

Meanwhile, another group—Mikaya, Andre, Ralph, and Cody—has gotten right to work. They have decided to have each student write down thoughts about the team name, materials, artifacts, and decorating the outside. Then they will take turns sharing ideas, and the group will vote. They have also assigned themselves roles. Cody will take notes because she has neat handwriting; Andre will be in charge of finding materials because his dad is a contractor; Mikaya will make sure everyone gets and does a fair share of the work; and Ralph will lead and monitor the group's discussions.

Mrs. DeSantis is always amazed at how some groups just work better than others no matter how hard she tries to balance group members in terms of abilities, talents, and personalities. Of course it takes a bit more planning, structure, and monitoring with her lower level classes.

ASSESS:

1. Was Ms. DeSantis's response to Dwayne appropriate? What would you have done differently?

2. What are the potential benefits of doing the sarcophagus project as a group project rather than individually? What are the potential disadvantages or obstacles?

3. Why might Riverbend Middle School group its students into separate classes based on their achievement? Do you agree or disagree with the approach?

CASE STUDIES

HIGH SCHOOL: TEACHER'S LOUNGE

Gary Burchell/Taxi/Getty Images

Mr. Horace Webster, a veteran teacher of 27 years, sits in the teacher's lounge at Concourse High School, which serves over 2,000 students as the only high school in the diverse suburban town. Horace is sipping his coffee and grading homework assignments for his third period English Grammar and Composition class, which is a course that freshman usually take if they needed remedial instruction in language arts in elementary or middle school. Horace sighs exasperatingly and says out loud to himself, "I must be getting burnt out and too old for this job. These kids can't write, they don't know the least bit of grammar, and they don't even want to be in school!"

"Tough day, Ace?" asks Bryce Williams, a fellow English teacher who has been teaching for eight years.

"Tough year," replies Horace. "It seems like I haven't had such an unskilled and unmotivated class like this one in years. Have you experienced that—that they don't even care? They stroll into class after the bell rings, if they come at all. I tried giving out extra homework for those who are late, but that didn't work. I think I'm going to start passing out detention slips when the bell rings and send students directly to the office, so if they're not here—too bad. Maybe that will wake them up and make them want to get to class on time."

"Well, I wouldn't go that far. It might create more administrative work at the main office," replies Bryce. "Have you tried bell work?"

"Eh?" replies Horace.

Bryce explains: "Bell work is when you put a question on the board for the start of class. Students know they have to answer this as soon as they come in and sit down. This gives them something to do right away. You can have them write down their responses and then connect it to the class discussion, or you can have them turn in their responses for bonus points—as a surprise, of course, not every time. Students love that! That might get them coming to class on time, especially if they want to earn bonus points or a participation grade."

"Hmmm . . . I doubt it," says Horace. "I don't know if they'll come to class on time if they don't even want to be there for the lesson. They sit with their arms crossed and don't bother to take notes. Believe me, I know that noun-verb agreements and dangling modifiers are not the most interesting subjects, but I'm supposed to teach this and they're supposed to learn it. Like just the other day, I was lecturing on how to construct a typical 'five-paragraph essay' and I noticed Logan sitting at his desk in the back row with his eyes shut and Dehlia was filing her nails!"

"Well, maybe the problem is that they're bored," Bryce suggests in a hesitating tone. After all, Horace is a senior faculty member at the school and Bryce does not want to overstep.

"Of course they're bored," snaps Horace. "But it's not like I can expect them to read pieces of literature, discuss, and write about it, like my first period AP American Literature class."

"Why not?" asks Bryce.

Horace interrupts, "Oh, you're kidding me, right?"

"No, hear me out. I get that they don't have the same level of skills. I have the same issues with my upper level and lower level English classes. But I bet if you raised the bar and tried a different teaching approach, they might be motivated to learn—well, at least some of them. To give you an example, in my English Grammar and Composition class, I have them write persuasive essays and cover letters regarding the jobs or careers they want after high school. Of course, there's reading involved too, because they first have to research jobs they might want by reading newspapers, trade magazines, and sources like that. So, I can correct and teach grammar in the context of what mistakes they're making in writing. Don't get me wrong, we still need to do some lectures and assign homework and quizzes, but this gives them a more meaningful context and maybe a reason to come to class."

"Hmmm . . ." Horace mutters, as he taps his red pen to his chin.

"Hey, Ace, I hope you don't think I'm rude or anything by giving you some suggestions," Bryce says.

"No, no, of course not," Horace replies.

Bryce interrupts, "I'm not claiming to be an expert, or anything. I just remember my Ed Psych class in college. We talked a lot about keeping students interested with meaningful assignments. Anyway, the bell's about to ring for my next period. Gotta go."

"Yeah, see ya," responds Horace. "Ed Psych . . . I think I remember taking that class," he mutters, as he ponders some of the suggestions.

ASSESS:

1. Why do the students in Bryce Williams's class seem to be more interested and motivated than the students in Horace Webster's class?

2. Which teacher, Horace Webster or Bryce Williams, has the better approach to teaching the English Grammar and Composition class? Why?

3. Do you agree that upper level and lower level classes should be taught differently because they have different skill levels? Why or why not?

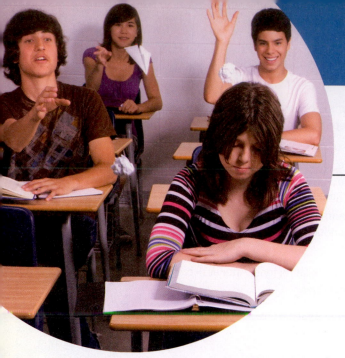

©iStockphoto.com/fotogeek4

CLASSROOM MANAGEMENT

OUTLINE	LEARNING GOALS

Importance of Classroom Management

- Preparing for the First Day
- Establishing Rules and Procedures

❶ Provide at least three strategies needed to become an effective classroom manager.

Time Management

- Increasing Academic Learning Time
- Increasing Student Engagement

❷ Explain how time management can increase academic performance.

Relationship Building

- Teacher–Student Relationships
- Parental Involvement

❸ Provide strategies for building positive relationships with both students and parents.

Applications: Addressing Discipline Problems

- Providing Consequences
- Bullying

❹ Provide steps for handling misbehaviors, including bullying.

IMPORTANCE OF CLASSROOM MANAGEMENT

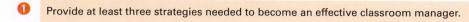

❶ Provide at least three strategies needed to become an effective classroom manager.

Much research over the past several decades has indicated that classroom management is one of the most important factors impacting students' learning and achievement (Brophy, 1998; Freiberg, 2013; Wang, Haertel, & Walberg, 1993; Marzano, Marzano, & Pickering, 2003). A well-managed classroom allows students to focus on the learning process rather than time-wasting transitions, disruptions from others, or a student's own internal disruptions such as day-dreaming. In short, effective teachers keep their classroom focused on learning. There are several ways teachers can facilitate classroom management, and it doesn't include being dictatorial, harsh, or even unemotional. Quite the opposite. As you will see in this module, effective classroom managers are planful in structuring a productive learning environment, they are proactive in managing time, and they also build relationships with students and parents.

To become an effective classroom manager, you must start at the beginning—the first day of school. This includes setting up the physical space of the classroom effectively and quickly establishing rules and procedures. These first important steps, and much else we review in this module, need to be considered within a developmental perspective.

What rules and procedures might you have for first graders? What about sixth graders? What about tenth graders? Why would you need different sets of rules and procedures for different developmental levels?

Preparing for the First Day

Think about the first day of classes in most college courses. What happens? Instructors usually introduce themselves and provide a syllabus with the expectations for academic success and classroom behavior. This includes information about exams, assignments, due dates, turning in late work, use of cell phones, and how to communicate best with the instructor (office hours and e-mail address). Similar information is needed in the K-12 grades, though the specific information and how it is presented may be different based on grade level.

To get started, let's review some guidelines for the first day of class (Harris & Garwood, 2015; Marzano et al., 2003):

- Effective teachers greet students and direct them to their assigned seats (seating arrangements are discussed later). New students should be introduced to one or two students to make them feel comfortable and welcome.

- Once everyone arrives, teachers can provide an introduction that includes some personal information. For example, a teacher might let students know that the Chicago Bears is her favorite team or that she went to college at The Ohio State University. The idea here is for students to begin to see the teacher as a "person" who they can relate to and feel comfortable talking with about assignments and problems.

- The teacher should also introduce the classroom. This may be more important for elementary school students who need to know where to provide their lunch count and where to put their coats and bags. However, introducing the classroom is also important in middle school and high school so that students know where to look for information about assignments (e.g., left-hand corner of the whiteboard) and where to turn in assignments (e.g., basket on the bookshelf under the window).

- Rules and procedures need to be established and communicated to students on the first day. For elementary school, rules and procedures should be posted in the classroom, and for middle and high school students, a hard copy should be provided. We discuss guidelines for setting rules and procedures later in the module.

- A calendar and/or course outline should be provided to the students. For elementary school students this would include reviewing the daily schedule. For middle school and high school students, this would resemble a course syllabus with information about dates, topics, and assignments.

- Communication with parents should be established on the first day. Give students something to take home that introduces the teacher to their parents, provides the basic

Master the content.

edge.sagepub.com/durwin3e

$SAGE edge™

Video Case 17.1 ▲
Considering Classroom Arrangement

© SAGE Publications

Video Case 17.2 ▲
Involvement with Parents and Communities

© SAGE Publications

FIGURE 17.1 **Physical Space.** A traditional arrangement of desks in rows works well for direct instruction, whereas small group work or pair-share discussions benefit from cluster arrangements. Teachers should choose the seating that best matches the type of instruction they intend to use.

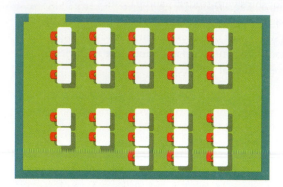

The traditional *auditorium arrangement*, with all desks in rows facing the teacher, is most effective when the teacher wants students' attention to be focused on direct instruction and wants to minimize interaction between students (Renne, 1997).

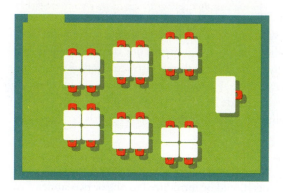

In general, face-to-face seating (such as *clusters*) leads to higher student distraction; however, this seating arrangement is ideal to facilitate collaboration during small-group activities.

rules and procedures, and indicates how best to contact the teacher. This would include the teacher's web page, e-mail address, and office phone number, as well as the time of day when the teacher is most likely to be available to talk or answer e-mail, such as a free period.

Preparing for the first day of class includes determining the best use of the physical space a teacher has been given (see Figure 17.1). Here are some suggestions to consider when creating the seating chart and room arrangements (Fisher, Godwin, & Seltman, 2014; Harris & Garwood, 2015; Marzano et al., 2003):

- The room should be arranged so that the teacher can see all students from anywhere in the classroom, especially from his or her own desk.

- The teacher's desk and whiteboard could be on opposite ends of the classroom to provide proximity to students in the front and back of the classroom.

- The room should be arranged for easy transitions in and out of the classroom as well as easy access to the teacher and frequently used materials (e.g., basket for homework assignments).

- Classes that will include mostly direct instruction might benefit from a seating arrangement that focuses attention on the teacher, such as traditional rows.

- Classes that will include substantial amounts of small group work or pair-share discussions might benefit from a seating arrangement in which three to four students can all see each other, such as clusters of desks.

- The walls and bulletin boards should not be overstimulating. Research with kindergarten children has found that they are more likely to be off-task in classrooms that are highly decorated. Items need to be included for the purpose of learning, not simply to make the room look pretty.

Room arrangements and seating charts can be changed throughout the year. However, these changes should be done for the purpose of enhancing learning, not just for the sake of change. One likely change is adjusting the seating chart after the first few weeks of school. For example, the teacher may want to separate two girls who talk to one another often or move disruptive students closer to the teacher. Guidelines 17.1 provide a summary for preparing for the first day.

Establishing Rules and Procedures

Historically, preservice teachers were not taught classroom management skills, yet it was clear that some classrooms functioned more smoothly than others. Research in the 1970s by Jacob Kounin was conducted to determine how teachers handle disruptions and misbehaviors. Even though the results indicated that effective and ineffective classroom managers were not that different in how misbehaviors were handled, the occurrence of misbehaviors differed. In other words, prevention of **misbehaviors** was the clear distinction. Effective classroom managers set appropriate expectations and clearly communicate those expectations to students on the first day of class. In particular, effective classroom managers have been found to use both rules and procedures (Weinstein & Romano, 2015). **Rules** are clear expectations for general conduct, such as being polite, raising one's hand, or arriving to class on time. **Procedures**, or routines, are instructions for carrying out specific tasks that occur regularly, such as lining up for lunch, turning in homework assignments, or keeping busy when work is finished early.

Researchers have provided the following guidelines for creating classroom rules (Harris & Garwood, 2015; Marzano et al., 2003; Weinstein & Romano, 2015):

- *Allow students to help develop the rules.* Rules and procedures are more likely to be remembered and followed when students provide input into their creation. If teachers decide to have student input in creating the rules, the best time to do this would be on the first day.

- *Know the purpose of a rule.* The purpose of a rule should be to keep students safe, keep them focused on learning, or build social skills. Consider the rule, "Raise your hand and

Video Case 17.3 ▲
Establishing Rules and Procedures

© SAGE Publications

Social skills: See Module 3

GUIDELINES 17.1	Preparing for the First Day

Arrange the room to optimize teacher visibility and proximity to all students.

Arrange the room to minimize disruptions and distractions, especially during transitions.

Arrange desks to best accommodate the most likely type of instruction to be used.

Use wall space for educational resources.

Greet students on the first day.

Introduce yourself.

Introduce the classroom.

Establish rules and procedures.

Provide a developmentally appropriate schedule.

Begin communication with parents.

wait to be called on before speaking." This rule keeps students focused on learning by eliminating disruptions but also builds social skills, such as being polite. Students who understand why the rule is necessary are more likely to follow the rule. Rules that seem meaningless are more difficult to explain and enforce. For example, a teacher may have a rule that students cannot wear hats in class. How does not wearing a hat keep one safe or focused on learning or help build social skills? What exactly is the harm in wearing a hat during class?

Behavioral learning theory: See Module 8

Cognitive development: See Module 6

- *Rules should be stated positively.* State rules as a list of do's, rather than a list of don'ts. For example, the rule should be "Arrive to class on time," rather than "Don't be late to class." Focusing on the positive behavior rather than the negative allows teachers to also focus on praising or reinforcing positive behaviors, rather than drawing attention to negative behaviors. The importance of using reinforcement more than punishment is grounded in behavioral learning theory and discussed in more detail later.

- *Rules should be developmentally appropriate.* Expectations for early childhood, elementary, middle, and high school students vary based on students' cognitive abilities and social skills. For example, classroom rules for high school students may include turning all homework in online or not accepting homework late. Elementary school students would not be expected to submit work online and would be given more lenient expectations for turning homework in late.

- *Classroom rules should align with the school rules and be limited in number.* Rules created within a classroom should support school-wide rules and not be in contradiction to those rules. In addition, a long list of 10 to 20 rules will not be easily remembered. Rules are about general expectations, so each rule should be written to cover many situations. For example, the rule "be polite" covers how one treats peers and teachers and uses manners, such as saying "please" and "thank you." Therefore, only a few rules are needed—a good guideline is about five rules.

Video Case 17.4 ▲

Managing Centers and Rotations

Researchers also have studied procedures or routines, and the general findings provide us with important guidelines. In particular, scholars in the field of classroom management have found there are three main types of routines that need clear procedural guidelines (Marzano et al., 2003; Weinstein & Romano, 2015).

1. **Class-running routines.** Although these procedures will save time, which in turn may enhance learning, they are not directly related to learning. Rather, these procedures are about nonacademic or more administrative issues. For example, class-running routines would include hanging your coat and bag, taking a lunch count, leaving the room as a class (recess) or individually (restroom), and storing personal electronic devices during the day.

2. **Lesson-running routines.** These procedures directly relate to learning and academic issues. For example, lesson routines would specify behaviors about students being prepared when class begins (have your tablet on and loaded to the correct web page), turning in homework assignments (put your homework in the basket prior to the beginning of class), and keeping busy if finishing early (take out a book to read or work on homework for another subject/class).

3. **Interaction routines.** These procedures provide students with instruction on how to communicate in the classroom, such as when and how to speak. These procedures may be different for different types of classroom lessons. For example, raising one's hand may be important during direct instruction but not necessary during small group discussions. There may also be different procedures for free time (e.g., whisper to friends) than during instructional time.

Direct instruction: See Module 18

Rules and procedures are at the heart of classroom management. In fact, some research indicates that time off-task is reduced by 50% when rules and procedures are provided clearly and within the first days of school. In turn, time on-task is related to increases in academic achievement (Harris & Garwood, 2015). Hence, teachers who develop a good set of classroom rules and procedures are more likely to have students engaged in the learning process.

TIME MANAGEMENT

❷ Explain how time management can increase academic performance.

Academic learning time, which may also be referred to as instructional time, makes up only about 64% of the time spent in school. Even less time, approximately 50%, includes students who are actually engaged in the learning process (Smith, 2000; Weinstein & Romano, 2015). **Student engagement** has been defined as a student's motivation and effort to learn, interest in specific topics, and connectedness to the school or classroom (Ackerman, 2013). So, why does so little school time include student engagement? First, about a third of school time is used for noninstructional activities, such as transitions, lunch, recess, and homeroom. Second, even when instructional activities are the focus, students may or may not be attending to those activities but instead may be daydreaming or doodling, indicating low student engagement (Smith, 2000). The point is that the actual time spent learning is significantly less than the hours spent in school.

Research across many studies has consistently found that classroom management facilitates both academic learning time and student engagement, which in turn is related to higher academic achievement (Brophy, 1998; Freiberg, 2013; Wang & Holcombe, 2010). Hence, teachers need to attempt to increase their own instructional time as well as enhance student engagement.

Think about the students and/or subject areas you plan to teach. What strategies might you use to keep them focused on learning rather than the multitude of distractions that can occur in a classroom?

Increasing Academic Learning Time

Researchers have provided us with several strategies that teachers can use to increase the amount of school time focused on instructional activities (Good & Brophy, 2008; Kounin, 1970; Marzano et al., 2003; Weinstein & Romano, 2015).

- *Maintain activity flow.* It is important for teachers to keep the flow of instruction moving forward. This means teachers need to avoid moving back and forth between activities, spending too much time on an activity or providing instructions when students already know or understand the content, or becoming distracted with less important tasks. Rather, teachers should have quick activities prepared to keep students focused on the lesson. For example, assume that an elementary school teacher is reading a book to her class, or a high school teacher has students read a chapter for homework. The teachers are getting ready to review the last few pages or chapters with the class when an unexpected interruption occurs (e.g., secretary calls from the office). Do the teachers leave the students waiting with nothing to do? No. They should have already prepared a quick assignment to give during interruptions or transitions, such as talk to the person to your left about the passage we just read (for lower grades) or take out a piece of paper and write down the two most important things that happened in the last chapter (for older students). In math classes, teachers might always have a challenging math problem waiting to be given to students to work on during these interruptions or transitions.

Inclusion: See Module 21

Special service: See Modules 21 and 22

Prompts: See Module 8

- *Manage expected interruptions.* Classrooms today are much more inclusive and integrate all students within a general classroom, even those with disabilities. Teachers need to manage the routine interruptions associated with inclusive education, such as additional staff entering the classroom to assist specific students and students leaving for special services. Principals should encourage their teachers to work with one another to schedule these routine interruptions simultaneously. For example, Jim will leave at 1:20 for the gifted reading group, and Mr. Wieberg will enter at the same time to assist Dexter with his math assignment.

- *Minimize transition time.* Not all, but most, misbehaviors, problems, and complaints occur during transition times. There is typically less structure and hence there are more opportunities for disruptions. As we discussed earlier, teachers need to have very clear procedures for transitions. For younger grades, these procedures can include singing during transitions. For example, kindergarten students might be asked to sing the ABC's as they line up for lunch. Middle school and high school students might have a quick assignment or problem written on the whiteboard at the beginning of class to get them started as soon as they are seated. Teachers need to include prompts or reminders about the routine (e.g., remember to sing as we line up from lunch), time to practice the routine (e.g., let's pretend you are going to recess), and positive outcomes when the routine is followed and the transition occurs smoothly (e.g., you were all so good at getting started on time this morning).

- *Provide clear instructions.* Teachers who initially provide clear instructions and expectations for assignments spend less time answering basic questions about those assignments (e.g., When is this due? Can we work on it in groups? Does it have to be typed? Does it need to be submitted online?). A good strategy is to have a student repeat the instructions, such as stating, "Dominick, just to be sure everyone understands, I would like you to please repeat the instructions for this assignment to the class." In addition, instructions for assignments and projects in middle school and high school should be provided in writing or online so students can refer back to the specific directions.

Transitions. Many problems and misbehaviors in the classroom occur during transitions, such as lining up to leave the classroom for lunch or recess.

©iStockphoto.com/Steve Debenport

- *Monitor student behavior and progress.* Teachers need to pay attention to students, even when they are working independently. For example, effective classroom managers have been found to rarely sit down. Rather, they are slowly walking around the room, making eye contact with students, checking on student progress, and answering questions. These behaviors define the disposition of effective classroom mangers labeled **withitness,** or what students might refer to as "she has eyes in the back of her head." Teachers with a high level of withitness will anticipate disruptions to instructional time and intervene before large amounts of time are wasted.

Increasing Student Engagement

In addition to planning that increases academic learning time, teachers must also attempt to increase students' interest in and attention to those learning activities or subject areas—that is, increase student engagement. As indicated earlier, student engagement is a student's motivation, interest, and connectedness to the school or classroom. This important construct has been further defined to include three specific components (Fredricks, 2013):

Intrinsic motivation: See Module 15

- a behavioral component, which includes classroom participation, following rules or the absence of disruptive behavior, and participation in extracurricular activities;

- an emotional component, which includes affective qualities, such as interest and motivation; and

- a cognitive component that includes attention and concentration to the learning process.

Video Case 17.5 ▲
Increasing Student Engagement

© SAGE Publications

Empirical evidence suggests there are a number of ways in which teachers can attempt to enhance these components of student engagement (Cooper, 2013; Gilboy, Heinerichs, & Pazzaglia, 2015; Harbour, Evanovich, Sweigart, & Hughes, 2015; Hsu & Mascolo, 2015; White, 2011).

- *Teachers should provide support and encouragement and model enthusiasm for the material.* Research indicates that teachers who provide frequent, positive feedback to students have students who are more engaged in the lesson and have higher achievement. In addition, teachers who are enthusiastic about their content have students who are also more interested in the content.

Modeling behavior: See Module 9

- *Lessons should be meaningful and interesting.* Teachers should explain why the content or skill being learned is important. Connecting the material to students' interest will also increase student engagement. Facilitating interest in course content can be achieved in numerous ways, such as focusing on current issues (relate the lesson to the new iPhone about to hit the market), providing novelty or surprise (a shocking fact about the author of a piece of classic literature), or giving students choices that are tailored to their own specific interests (write a biography regarding a celebrity of your choosing).

Meaningful learning: See Module 12

- *Lessons should be appropriately challenging.* Students who are given easy tasks will quickly become bored and unengaged. Similarly, students who are given extremely difficult tasks will become overwhelmed and unengaged. Teachers should provide instruction at a cognitive level that is developmentally appropriate for the grade level they are teaching. For example, elementary school teachers should not expect their students to be able to find sources and write a research paper.

Task and activities: See Module 18

Cognitive development: See Module 6

- *Lessons should include a variety of tasks and activities.* Teachers can use a mix of individual work, group work, and class discussions to keep students interested and engaged. In particular, group work and class discussions that provide opportunities for students to respond have been found to increase student engagement. Group work can include think-pair share activities, peer feedback, or jigsaw classrooms that give each group

Group work: See Module 19

Student Engagement.
Students are more engaged when teachers use a mix of instructional strategies such as flipped classrooms that include small group work and class discussions.

DIVERSITY

member a piece of the assignment to become the expert and teach other members. Class discussions can take the form of small group discussions, whole class discussions, or debates. Teachers should be aware that some students are less likely to participate in discussions based on cultural and language barriers. Additional encouragement and support may be needed for some students.

- *Flipped classroom models can be used to increase student engagement.* The flipped classroom includes switching the location of traditional classwork and homework. Specifically, students would be asked to read materials and possibly watch videos or view the teacher's lectures at home. Class time would be used to complete activities that include group work or classroom discussions. One advantage to this model is that it fosters the development of higher level thinking skills (analyzing, evaluating, and creating) in the classroom with teacher support and encouragement. Because of the cognitive development needed to carry out the independent learning activities at home and to engage in higher level thinking skills in the classroom, a flipped classroom structure is most appropriate at the middle school and high school levels.

Higher order thinking:
See Module 13

Cognitive development:
See Module 6

RELATIONSHIP BUILDING

3 Provide strategies for building positive relationships with both students and parents.

Parental involvement:
See Module 2

Intrinsic motivation: See Module 14

Much research has been done in two areas of relationship building—teacher–student relationships and parental involvement—both of which are related to fewer behavioral disruptions, higher student engagement, more intrinsic motivation, and increased academic achievement (Grolnick, Raftery-Helmer, & Flamm, 2013; Murray, 2015; Wentzel, 1998). Effective classroom managers are purposeful in their ability to build good, supportive relationships with all students, as well as encourage and support parental involvement in their child's education.

Do you remember a former teacher who you felt particularly connected to? What characteristics did that person have that helped form the connection? Do you have those characteristics? How might you display those characteristics to your students?

Teacher–Student Relationships

Positive, productive teacher–student relationships are related to a large number of positive social and academic outcomes. Specifically, these important relationships have been linked to student engagement, higher achievement, and more prosocial behaviors, such as sharing or helping others, whereas negative teacher–student relationships are related to higher levels of behavioral problems (Marzano et al., 2003; Murray, 2015; Pianta, 2006; Wentzel, 1998). The influence of teacher–student relationships to various outcomes appears to be even more important for students at risk; however, those who need these supportive relationships the most are often the students least likely to have the interpersonal skills to develop positive, productive relationships (Murray, 2015). In addition, supportive teacher–student relationships are especially important during educational transitions, such as moving from the middle school to the high school (Wentzel, 1998). Hence, effective classroom managers spend valuable time and energy building supportive relationships with their students.

> **DIVERSITY**

Prosocial behaviors: See Module 4

There are teacher characteristics and behaviors that can facilitate developing good, supportive relationships with students. In particular, Wubbels and colleagues (Wubbels et al., 2006; Wubbels & Levey, 1993) identified two important dimensions of the teacher–student relationship. First, teachers need to have moderate levels of dominance. **Dominance** is providing a clear purpose and strong guidance or support for both academic content as well as expected behavior (rules and procedures). For example, teachers need to display assertiveness both in tone and behavior but also be aware and concerned for specific student needs. Second, teachers need to have a spirit of cooperation with students rather than opposition (i.e., them vs. us). In this context, **cooperation** can be defined as being concerned for students' views and opinions and working as a team member rather than being a dictator. For example, during instructional time, teachers can provide hints to questions or rephrase questions to provide support and not leave students fearful of answering questions incorrectly. During noninstructional time (i.e., before or after class), teachers can chat with students about their personal interests, such as extracurricular activities (e.g., "I hear we won the volleyball match last night"). Talking informally with students may be even more important for middle school and high school students as teacher–student relationships tend to become more formal and less personal following elementary school (Harter, 1996).

Video Case 17.6 ▲
Creating Teacher-Student Communities

© SAGE Publications

Research suggests that novice teachers tend to be low on dominance and high on cooperation, whereas experienced teachers have increased dominance and lower levels of cooperation (Marzano et al., 2003; Wubbels et al., 2006). Effectively building good, positive relationships with students includes moderate levels of both dominance and cooperation. Some specific guidelines for building teacher–student relationships have been identified (Harris & Garwood, 2015; Marzano et al., 2003; Weinstein & Romano, 2015):

- Greet students in the morning.

- Call students by name or preferred name, especially the first few days of class.

- Make eye contact with students often.

- Use a calm, assertive tone when speaking to students.

- Welcome student mistakes as they are opportunities for learning.

- Really listen to your students. Look directly at them when they speak, nod when appropriate, and try paraphrasing what they have said.

- Talk informally with students during noninstructional time. These chats should be mostly about their interests, but teachers should also share their own interests without oversharing or attempting to be their friend—just be a real person.

- Do not treat all students equal—some want attention and others don't; some like encouragement while others view it as an indication that they are incapable. Effective classroom managers know their students and use different strategies with different students.

Parental Involvement

Parental involvement:
See Module 2

In addition to building positive relationships with students, teachers also need to build relationships with parents and encourage parental involvement in their child's education. **Parental involvement** can be defined as parents' participation in their children's education to promote academic success. High parental involvement can be displayed in many ways, including *school-based involvement,* such as volunteering at the school for academic or extracurricular activities and communicating with teachers about problems and concerns, as well as *home-based involvement,* such as parents having high expectations for their child's academic achievement and supporting their child's learning at home (Epstein, 1987). Parental involvement in elementary school may include more school-based involvement, whereas in middle school and beyond, parental involvement may be more focused on home-based involvement (Hill & Tyson, 2009). A particular aspect of parental involvement—academic socialization—seems to be linked to academic achievement for middle school students. **Academic socialization** includes openly discussing parents' values and expectations for academic success, assisting with learning strategies, and fostering future plans based on academic strengths and interests (Hill & Tyson, 2009).

Self-Efficacy: See Module 9

Intrinsic motivation: See Module 15

Parental involvement is important because empirical data has consistently found that higher parental involvement is related to higher academic achievement among students (Choi, Chang, Kim, & Reio, 2015; Hill & Tyson, 2009; Hopson, Schiller, & Lawson, 2014). In particular, academic socialization has been tied to self-efficacy and engagement in academics, as well as higher levels of intrinsic motivation for academics (Grolnick et al., 2013; Hill & Tyson, 2009). Each of these student characteristics is directly related to academic achievement, as depicted in Figure 17.2.

FIGURE 17.2 **Parental Involvement.** Parents' involvement in their child's education has important implications on student characteristics, and those student characteristics have important implications for academic outcomes.

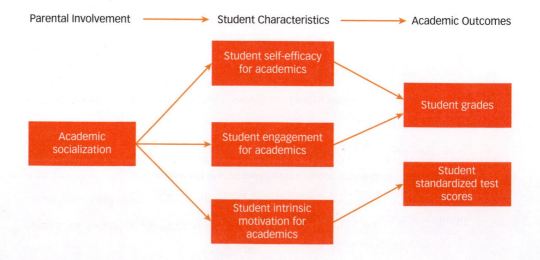

Almost all parents want their children to excel academically and become successful, yet academic socialization, particularly parental expectations, may vary based on ethnicity and socioeconomic status. For example:

- Asian American students report that their parents have higher expectations and standards for school success than parents of White American students or Latino students (Chen & Stevenson, 1995; Naumann, Guillaume, & Funder, 2012).

- African American students also report that their parents have high expectations for them, but the expectations are not as high as the parents of White American students (Ogbu, 2003).

These different expectations among parents may reflect their beliefs about the benefits of education. African Americans tend to be more skeptical of how helpful education will be, because many believe that even with an education their children will be discriminated against and their opportunities for success will be limited (Ogbu, 1994, 2003). Hence, African American students have fewer negative views of the future when they think about *not* being educated, whereas Asian American students have a greater fear of negative outcomes or failure when they think about not being well educated (Steinberg, 1996).

In addition to parental expectations and values, other forms of parental involvement also vary by ethnicity and socioeconomic status. Specifically, African American and Latino parents have been found to participate less in school functions, such as parent–teacher organizations, workshops, and open houses, compared to Caucasian American parents, and they tend to be less likely to help their children with homework or check that homework has been completed (Gonzalez, Borders, Hines, Villalba, & Henderson, 2013; Ogbu, 2003). Lower parental involvement among African American and Latino parents most likely results from a misconception that the school does not need their help to educate their children, with the result that these parents may not understand the importance of their role at school or as homework facilitators (Gonzalez et al., 2013; Ogbu, 2003; Steinberg, 1996). Asian American parents are likely to have high parental involvement at home—Asian American students spend substantially more time on homework than do Caucasian—but are less likely than Caucasian parents to volunteer at school activities or initiate communication with teachers (Steinberg, 1996; Yamamoto, 2015). Parents from lower socioeconomic neighborhoods and homes may want to be involved but simply not have the resources to do so. For example, they may be unable to take time off from work to attend school activities and functions or may be less available to help with homework due to varying work shifts.

How might teachers encourage and support parental involvement? The foundation of parental involvement is communication between the school and parents as well as the teacher(s) and parents (Karibayeva & Boğar, 2014; Weinstein & Romano, 2015). The following are some guidelines for encouraging parental involvement.

- *Establish communication early in the school year.* This might include sending a note home the first day with the school phone number, teacher's school e-mail address, times the teacher is most likely to be available to call or return e-mail, and the preferred mode of communication (e.g., "I will return phone calls, but I can return answers to quick questions best by e-mail.").

- *Use multiple modes of communication.* Technology can provide avenues of communication not available historically. Teachers can send mass e-mails, create and maintain web pages, and use social media sites to provide information or reminders. Three points of caution are necessary when considering modes of communication.

  1. Provide the same information in multiple ways because not all parents have access to all forms of communication.

Socioeconomic neighborhoods: See Module 2

Video Case 17.7 ▲
Parental Involvement

© SAGE Publications

2. Be sure the information is updated regularly and presented in a professional manner. Parents will become frustrated quickly if the information posted on the class web page or social media site is outdated. Similarly, provide grammatically correct and edited written forms of communication (e.g., e-mail).

3. Only communicate sensitive or personal information, including grades, in verbal forms, such as on the phone or face-to-face.

DIVERSITY

- *Hold an open house for the classroom.* The school may hold an open house and the classroom's open house can certainly be that same day and time. If the school doesn't sponsor an open house, teachers should consider doing so for their specific classrooms. Parents from diverse backgrounds might benefit from a personal invitation to attend the open house and specific information about how their involvement is essential to their child's success.

Parent–Teacher conferences: See Module 23

Culturally responsive suggestions: See Module 18

- *Be prepared for parent–teacher conferences.* This does not mean that the teacher needs to have pages of notes to cover for each child. Actually, a teacher might begin by posing a few starter questions to get the parents to speak first (e.g., How do you think Billy likes the class? Do you have any concerns about the class or Billy's performance?). Then, an opportunity for the parents to ask questions should be provided (e.g., Do you have any questions about the classroom rules, procedures, or activities?). Finally, the teacher might have some notes or specific points to cover about the class generally or the specific student. Teachers should begin with stating some positives about the student. When discussing weaknesses or problem areas, teachers need to speak calmly and discuss possible solutions with a tone of assurance that the issue can be improved or resolved.

DIVERSITY

- *Provide additional support for students from diverse backgrounds.* As indicated earlier, parents from diverse backgrounds may be less likely to become involved in their child's education, especially at school or communicating with teachers. This may be particularly true for English language learners (Tarasawa & Waggoner, 2015). Panferov (2010) has provided several culturally responsive suggestions for improving parental involvement of English language learners, as summarized in Guidelines 17.2.

GUIDELINES 17.2	Culturally Responsive Suggestions for Parental Involvement

Provide information in multiple forms—both written and verbal.

When speaking to parents of English language learners, pause after two to three sentences to allow them to process the information. If an interpreter is present, be sure to speak to the parent, not the interpreter.

Whenever possible provide information in both languages—English and their native language.

Pair new parents of English language learners with an existing parent of an English language learner to answer questions.

Ask parents to provide information about their culture and background to help you better understand their child and his or her needs.

Invite parents to participate in the classroom as a guest—possibly to teach the students about their culture.

SOURCES: Panferov, 2010; Weinstein & Romano, 2015.

APPLICATIONS: ADDRESSING DISCIPLINE PROBLEMS

4 Provide steps for handling misbehaviors, including bullying.

Even the most effective classroom managers, who prepare well, manage time, and build strong relationships, will have disruptions. Students are humans (try not to forget that), so they are going to make mistakes, not only academically but in their decision making regarding appropriate behavior. What do teachers do when students misbehave? They must provide discipline. Some teachers believe that discipline takes time away from learning. However, the Latin root for the word **discipline** is to give instruction, to teach and to learn. Thus, discipline, by definition, is exactly what teachers are tasked with doing—give instruction and teach! Rather than viewing the need to provide discipline for misbehaviors as something "extra" or "beyond my pay grade," teachers should view discipline as a portion of their responsibilities and duties as a teacher—as an opportunity to teach. They may not be using that time to teach academic subject matter, such as reading or math skills, but they are using that time to teach very important social skills, interpersonal skills, and professional skills.

Of course, teachers want to limit the time needed to deal with misbehaviors and increase academic learning time. Teachers should determine whether the infraction or misbehavior is a minor issue or more serious, which will help determine the appropriate reaction (Weinstein & Romano, 2015). Determining the level of seriousness and reacting accordingly typically needs to occur rather quickly. As such, teachers should consider ahead of time what specific misbehaviors they consider to be minor or severe and how best to handle those misbehaviors. Here are some suggestions for considering the severity of misbehaviors:

- Minor misbehaviors might include being noisy, talking during quite time, or daydreaming.

- More serious misbehaviors can include arguing with the teacher or other students, being defiant when given instructions, or being rude.

- Intolerable misbehaviors would include lying, cheating, bullying, or aggressive behavior.

Video Case 17.8 ▲
Dealing with Conflict

© SAGE Publications

Think about the grade level you would like to teach. What are some examples of behaviors you would consider mild misbehaviors versus more serious misbehaviors versus intolerable misbehaviors? What type of consequences would you provide to students regarding these misbehaviors?

Providing Consequences

Once teachers have established the rules and procedures for their classroom, as well as determined what they consider minor versus more serious infractions, they will have to enforce those rules with consequences. Not only does this mean that when the rules are broken, consequences should follow, but when rules are followed, teachers should provide consequences such as praise and rewards.

Consequences are usually considered to be either reinforcements or punishments. **Reinforcements** are consequences of a behavior that increase the future occurrence of that behavior (e.g., praise and rewards). **Punishments** are consequences of a behavior that

Consequences: See Module 8

decrease the future occurrence of that behavior (e.g., free time taken away). It is important to remember that the definition of reinforcement and punishment is based on the outcome (increase or decrease in behavior) and not the intent of the consequence (Deleon, Bullock, & Catania, 2013). For example, a teacher might offer social time for completing homework, assuming that social time will be a reward or increase the likelihood of completing homework. However, if a child does not have many friends or is socially uncomfortable, the child may view this consequence as "bad" and it will decrease his or her likelihood of completing homework. For this child, social time is a punishment, not a reinforcement. Here we present several tips for providing consequences effectively.

- *Know the developmental level of the individual.* Teachers should understand what typically is considered good and bad by students in a particular developmental period. For example, they can provide stickers and smiley faces for early childhood and elementary students but social time for most middle school and high school students.

- *Know the individual's likes and dislikes.* Teachers must know what individual students consider to be positive and negative. As discussed earlier, one student may love social time and another may not. Teachers must find out what is preferred by the students in their classrooms.

- *Understand the function of attention.* Attention can be a powerful consequence, as either reinforcement or punishment (Maag, 2001). For example, a teacher who repeatedly asks a student to sit down and be quiet may actually be increasing the behavior by providing the student with attention for the misbehavior—reinforcement. Likewise, a teacher who repeatedly praises a student publicly for appropriate behavior may be decreasing the likelihood of that behavior because the student does not want the attention—that is, it is considered punishment. By increasing or decreasing the amount of attention given, the teacher can alter problem behavior in the classroom (McComas, Thompson, & Johnson, 2003). Teachers must assess whether the attention they give to problem behavior is increasing or decreasing that behavior for each individual student and alter the amount of teacher attention accordingly.

- *Know when and how often to provide consequences.* A behavior and its consequence need to occur close together in time. The sticker given to a preschooler one day after the child has sat quietly for a story is no longer associated with the child's behavior the day before due to the elapsed time. Research suggests that reinforcements do not need to be given for every good behavior, but they should be given often (Freeland & Noell, 1999; Milo, Mace, & Nevin, 2010). In contrast, teachers *do* need to catch every instance of misbehavior if punishment is to be effective. Students who "get away" with a negative behavior learn that punishment can be avoided and are more likely to engage in that same negative behavior in the future.

- *Use reinforcement more than punishment.* Because it is difficult to catch every instance of misbehavior and provide a punishment, punishment is considered less effective than reinforcement. Also, punishment alone tends to teach a student only what *not* to do rather than encouraging more appropriate behavior (Alberto & Troutman, 2012). Hence, research suggests that teachers should focus more on using reinforcement to increase wanted behaviors and less on punishing unwanted behaviors (Cheyne & Walters, 1970; Maag, 2012).

- *Avoid using certain punishments.* Several types of punishment are considered ineffective and should not be used by teachers. These are listed and explained in Table 17.1.

TABLE 17.1	Ineffective Punishments
Physical punishment	Physical punishment typically is viewed as spanking, but it also includes washing someone's mouth out with soap or making someone remain in a physically uncomfortable environment (e.g., extremely cold, extremely hot).
Psychological punishment	Psychological punishment can include public humiliation, such as a teacher ridiculing a student in front of the class, and may lead to loss of self-esteem (Davis & Thomas, 1989; Shea & Bauer, 2012).
Extra homework	By giving additional homework as a punishment, teachers send the message that homework is undesirable. Teachers should be sending the message that learning is important, essential, and positive—not negative, bad, or unwanted (Corno, 1996).
Withdrawal of recess	Recess may be necessary for children to focus attention and behave appropriately, in addition to the usefulness of physical activity for health purposes (Cook-Cottone, Tribole, & Tylka, 2013). Attention appears to decrease after long periods of confinement in classrooms and to improve following recess (Holmes, Pellegrini, & Schmidt, 2006; Mahar, 2011). The American Academy of Pediatrics has stated that recess is necessary for child development and should not be withheld as a form of punishment (American Academy of Pediatrics, 2013).
Out-of-school suspension	In most cases, students who are given out-of-school suspensions do not view missing school as a punishment. Most of those students will see the suspension as reinforcement (e.g., staying home and not having to go to school is a good thing). In addition, empirical data suggest that out-of-school suspensions are given disproportionately to children from lower socioeconomic homes and minority ethnic groups, and to boys more than girls (Gibson, Wilson, Haight, Kayama, & Marshall, 2014; Krezmien, Leone, & Achilles, 2006; Skiba et al., 2011).

These suggestions provide some general guidelines for providing consequences, but what do teachers do when specific problematic behaviors occur? Of course, the seriousness of the infraction should be considered when determining a course of action. However, in most cases of minor misbehaviors, the following steps can be used quite effectively (Marzano et al, 2003; Weinstein & Romano, 2015):

1. Praise the students who are behaving appropriately and ignore the misbehavior, called praise-and-ignore. Obviously a teacher cannot ignore more serious misbehaviors such as aggression, but minor disruptions can be ignored. Drawing attention to them may add to the disruption.

2. Provide nonverbal prompts and cues. These might include using eye contact, moving closer to the student, or using a hand gesture such as a finger to one's lips.

3. Talk directly and calmly to the student. Provide a specific description of the misbehavior as well as the alternative, expected behavior (e.g., "You are talking when you are supposed to be working on the assignment.").

4. Provide a direct consequence for the misbehavior. This might include moving a student's desk closer to the teacher (elementary students) or giving a detention (high school students).

5. Notify parents or the principal about misbehaviors if the student continues to be disruptive, for example, if the student is late to class for several days and direct consequences are not effective in changing the misbehavior.

TABLE 17.2 Applied Behavior Analysis Strategies

STRATEGY	DEFINITION	EXAMPLE
Premack Principle	Provide a desired activity as reinforcement rather than a tangible item.	"Once you finish your assignment, you can quietly chat with friends."
Shaping	Provide reinforcement for small steps toward a desired behavior.	Reinforce sitting, even if still talking, for several days. Then, reinforce when sitting and not talking.
Positive Practice	Have the student perform the correct behavior.	After running downing the hallway, have the student go back and walk down the hallway.
Overcorrection	Have the student make restitution and more for his or her misbehavior.	"Clean the desk you wrote on and all the other desks in the classroom."
Satiation	Have the student perform an inappropriate behavior repeatedly until it is no longer reinforcing.	Have a student toss crumpled paper into the trash can from his or her desk for the entire class period (and even continue after school if needed).
Response Cost	Take away something rewarding (type of punishment).	Do not allow the student to eat lunch with his or her friends but make that student eat in the office or a classroom.
Token Economy	Students are given a token for appropriate behavior and later exchange them for prizes.	Give a ticket to students who have raised their hands or lined up quietly. Provide various prizes, such as pencils, stickers, or bracelets, that can be bought with a certain number of tickets.
Group Consequences	Reinforcement is based on the behavior of the whole class.	If all students are seated and ready to begin when the bell rings Monday through Friday, they can have five minutes at the end of the period on Friday to talk and socialize.

In addition to these general guidelines regarding the use of consequences and the specific steps to deter minor misbehaviors, there are many specific strategies developed to change behaviors in the classroom, based on behavioral theories of learning. These specific strategies typically are referred to as applied behavior analysis or behavior modification. Table 17.2 provides a summary of several applied behavior analysis strategies.

 What misbehaviors are you most worried about handling in the classroom? How were similar misbehaviors addressed when you were in school? How do you plan to manage those misbehaviors in your own classroom?

Bullying

One specific type of misbehavior that has received much attention in recent years is bullying. By definition, **bullying** is intentional, repetitive aggression toward a person perceived as having less power (Hymel & Swearer, 2015). Let's discuss these three aspects of bullying in more detail (Goodstein, 2013):

- *Intentional*—Behaviors that are done on accident cannot be considered bullying. For example, a child who sincerely forgets to invite the new student to his or her birthday party is not engaging in bullying behavior.

- *Repetition*—Behaviors that only occur once do not constitute bullying. The cumulative effect of repeatedly being harmed is important in understanding bullying.

- *Power*—The bully has some real or perceived power over the victim, which may exist due to age, size, social status, or some other strength or quality of value.

Scholars have reviewed the large body of research on bullying and concluded that approximately 10% to 40% of students report being the victim of bullying (Baly, Cornell, & Lovegrove, 2014; Finkelhor, Turner, Ormord, & Hamby, 2010). The rates vary depending on age, as well as how bullying is defined. For example, although peer aggression begins as early as preschool, bullying is most prevalent during middle school. In addition, researchers found that boys were more likely to report being perpetrators than girls, whereas girls were more likely to report being the victims of bullying than boys (Ayenibiowo & Akenbode, 2011; Cook, Williams, Guerra, Kim, & Sadek, 2010).

Knowing bullying occurs somewhat frequently doesn't help teachers identify bullying behavior. Bullying occurs in many forms. Some are quite obvious, such as physical aggression, and other forms are very difficult to notice, such as relational aggression. **Physical aggression** is defined as behaviors that intend to harm another physically. **Relational aggression** refers to behaviors specifically intended to damage another person's friendships, social status, or feelings of inclusion in a peer group. Such behaviors include gossiping, rumor spreading, and excluding someone as a way to control them. Relational aggression can occur in physical space, such as the cafeteria, hallways, or classrooms, but it can also occur in cyberspace. **Cyberbullying** typically includes relational aggression via texts, e-mails, and social media. Some research suggests that students may be more likely to use cyberbullying when their teachers are viewed as highly capable of handling more direct forms of bullying (Elledge et al., 2013). In other words, students who find that their traditional modes of bullying will lead to negative consequences may turn to less direct methods such as cyberbullying.

Research suggests that during childhood and adolescence, boys are more likely to use overt, physical aggression, whereas girls are more likely to display relational aggression, especially during middle school (Crick & Grotpeter, 1995; Mathieson & Crick, 2010; Ostrov & Crick, 2007). Interestingly, some of the students who are most likely to use relational aggression are also very socially skilled. In fact, those with advanced social skills may be more effective in delivering threats of friendship withdrawal, excluding others from the peer group, or orchestrating rumor spreading (Adler & Adler, 1998; Dijkstra, Lindenberg, Verhulst, Ormel, & Vennstra, 2009; Xie, Cairns, & Cairns, 2005). These advanced social skills allow these individuals to present themselves rather positively to adults.

Aggression: See Module 4

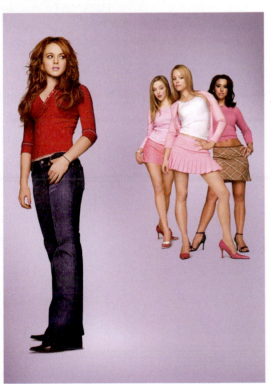

ZUMA Press, Inc. / Alamy Stock Photo

Bullying. The movie *Mean Girls* provides numerous examples of relational aggression used to bully others.

Anxiety and depression:
See Module 22

DIVERSITY

In other words, students who use relational aggression to bully others are likely to be some of the teacher's favorite students.

The importance of bullying behavior to educators is evident by the numerous studies connecting bullying to negative outcomes. Not only victims but perpetrators have also been found to have lower academic achievement, lower self-esteem, higher anxiety and depression, and higher levels of suicidal ideation (Ayenibiowo & Akenbode, 2011; Baly et al., 2014; Feldman et al., 2014; Goodstein, 2013). Research has also repeatedly found that African American youth and students with disabilities, including autism spectrum disorder, are more likely to be perpetrators and victims of bullying behavior (Albdour & Krouse, 2014; Chen & Schwartz, 2012; Rose, Espelage, & Monda-Amaya, 2009; Rose & Monda-Amaya, 2011). Although we typically think about a person being either a perpetrator or a victim, some students are both perpetrators and victims, termed **bully victims** (Hymel & Swearer, 2015; Olweus, 1978). These individuals are viewed as being most at risk. Specifically, they are likely to have more negative views of themselves, have more limited social problem-solving skills, be more likely to experience peer rejection, and have lower academic performance (Cook et al., 2010). The important question for those working closely with children and adolescents is this: How do we decrease the occurrence bullying?

There are several school-wide bullying prevention programs available, yet little research has been done on these programs to provide evidence-based practices. Recently, Bradshaw (2015) examined the existing research and concluded that prevention programs do reduce negative outcomes. Specifically, several promising features of these programs have been identified that can be used in schools and individual classrooms to address traditional bullying as well as cyberbullying (Bradshaw, 2015; Cook et al., 2010; Couvillon & Ilieva, 2011; Goodstein, 2013):

- Present school-wide and classroom rules about bullying, including cyberbullying.

- Present policies about Internet and phone use.

- Inform parents about school and classroom policies regarding bullying and cyberbullying.

- Use class time to define bullying.

- Never ignore bullying behavior.

- Build strong, positive relationships with students.

- Consistently provide expectations of positive behavior.

- Consistently provide a good model of positive behavior. Don't insult or belittle students (e.g., "You're in high school. Stop acting like a third grader."). Use a positive tone when speaking to students.

- Provide specific suggestions for bystanders of bullying behaviors. For example, be sure students know that reinforcing the bully by laughing or smiling is also unacceptable. Rather, students are expected to defend victims of bullying and report bullying behavior to teachers.

Social-emotional learning: See Module 3

- Provide social-emotional learning (SEL).

- Provide additional supervision in contexts likely to include bullying (i.e., playgrounds, lunchrooms, bathrooms, school buses).

 Can you remember who the bullies were at your school? What behaviors did they use? Did teachers also view them as bullies?

SUMMARY

❶ Explain why classroom management is important and what major strategies can be used to become an effective classroom manager. Classroom management is one of the most important factors influencing students' learning and achievement. To become an effective classroom manager, teachers need to prepare well for the first day of classes, including setting up a functional physical space. In addition, rules and procedures should be established early to increase student learning. Increasing student engagement begins with increasing the academic learning time and providing meaningful and interesting learning experiences for students. Also important to effective classroom management are the relationships teachers have with both students and parents. Finally, effective classroom managers understand misbehaviors and have clear consequences for those misbehaviors.

❷ Explain how time management can increase academic performance. Much of school time is not used on learning activities. To increase academic performance, teachers need to increase the time spent on instruction by maintaining the flow of activities, managing interruptions, minimizing transition time, providing clear instructions, and monitoring student behavior and progress. In addition, instruction time should be designed to increase student engagement, such as modeling enthusiasm and making lessons meaningful, interesting, and appropriately challenging, as well as including a variety of activities. Increased time of instruction in which students are highly engaged is related to higher academic achievement.

❸ Provide strategies for building positive relationships with both students and parents. Teachers need to have moderate levels of both dominance and cooperation to facilitate good, positive relationships with students. Specific behaviors would include greeting students, making eye contact, talking calmly but assertively, listening to students, and talking informally with students about their interests. Teachers should also build strong relationships with parents, such as encouraging parental involvement while being aware and sensitive to cultural differences. Specifically, teachers can establish clear communication with parents using multiple modes of communication. They might hold an open house and should be prepared for parent–teacher conferences.

❹ Provide steps for handling misbehaviors, including bullying. Minor misbehaviors are best handled by the following steps: (1) Praise students who are behaving appropriately and ignore misbehaviors. (2) Provide nonverbal prompts and cues. (3) Talk directly and calmly with the student. (4) Provide a consequence for the misbehavior. (5) Notify parents or the principal. Bullying behavior has received much public attention and is best handled by prevention programs that present clear, school-wide policies about behavior and use of technology, as well as provide good models of positive behaviors and expectations for positive behaviors.

KEY CONCEPTS

CASE STUDIES: REFLECT AND EVALUATE

EARLY CHILDHOOD: COUNTING POCKETS

These questions refer to the case study on page 336.

1. Based on the information provided in the case, evaluate whether Ms. Abby has the physical space of her classroom set up appropriately for this age group and types of activities.

2. What strategies does Ms. Abby use with the children to keep them focused on the instructional activity and engaged/interested in learning number concepts?

3. How does Ms. Abby's reaction to wrong answers help build strong relationships with her students? What

type of parental involvement is being encouraged by assigning the "homework"?

4. What type of misbehavior was the interaction between Caleb and Hunter? Do you think Ms. Abby handled the

misbehavior appropriately? What could have been done differently?

5. What are three examples of reinforcement provided by Ms. Abby to a child?

ELEMENTARY SCHOOL: Machine Hunt

These questions refer to the case study on page 338.

1. Which classroom arrangement would work best for Mr. Finnegan's variety of activities? Explain.

2. What procedures or routines are used in Mr. Finnegan's classroom that help increase academic learning time?

3. The students in Mr. Finnegan's class seem to be highly engaged in the activity of finding examples

around the school. Why might this particular activity lead to high student engagement?

4. How could the homework assignment have more explicitly involved parents?

5. Why do Milo and Mr. Finnegan have such different views of Sabrina? What type of behavior is Sabrina likely displaying to her classmates at lunch?

MIDDLE SCHOOL: Sarcophagus Studies

These questions refer to the case study on page 340.

1. Are the classroom rules of showing respect for each other's ideas, taking turns talking and listening, and knowing how to handle conflicting ideas specific enough? Why or why not?

2. How does providing a list of questions for the museum visit help increase both academic learning time and student engagement?

3. What behaviors did Mrs. DeSantis display that suggested she did or did not have positive productive relationships with her students?

4. Was it necessary to have parents sign the contract about expected behaviors? Why or why not?

5. How would you classify Dwayne's misbehavior? How well did Mrs. DeSantis handle his misbehavior? Did she need to involve his parents and the principal?

HIGH SCHOOL: Teacher's Lounge

These questions refer to the case study on page 342.

1. What are some examples of high and low student engagement in Mr. Webster's and Mr. Williams's classes?

2. What are two purposes or positive outcomes of "bell work?"

3. What types of misbehaviors are occurring in Mr. Webster's class? How should he handle these misbehaviors? Give examples.

4. Why is Mr. Webster's punishment of assigning homework to those who are late ineffective?

5. What rules and procedures might be needed in a high school classroom that seem to be lacking in Mr. Webster's class?

APPLY AND PRACTICE WHAT YOU'VE LEARNED

▶ edge.sagepub.com/durwin3e

CHECK YOUR COMPREHENSION ON THE STUDENT STUDY SITE

- **eFlashcards** to strengthen your understanding of key terms

- Practice **quizzes** to test your knowledge of key concepts

- **Videos and multimedia content** to enhance your exploration of key topics

©iStockphoto.com/monkeybusinessimages

INSTRUCTION: APPLYING BEHAVIORAL, COGNITIVE, AND CONSTRUCTIVIST APPROACHES

OUTLINE	LEARNING GOALS

Meeting the Needs of Diverse Learners

❶ Explain why it is not necessary to individualize instruction for every student, and identify the situations in which teachers need to differentiate instruction.

Teaching Methods Based on Behaviorism

- Direct Instruction
- Mastery Learning

❷ Describe the goals of mastery learning and direct instruction, and discuss the advantages and disadvantages of each approach.

Teaching Methods Based on Cognitive Learning Theory

- Discovery Learning and Guided Discovery
- Expository Teaching

❸ Explain how discovery learning and expository teaching foster meaningful learning.

Teaching Methods Based on Constructivism

- Inquiry Learning
- Cooperative Learning
- Methods of Fostering Comprehension

❹ Describe the techniques based on cognitive apprenticeships that are used in constructivist teaching.

A major concern of both novice and expert teachers is being able to meet the diverse needs of every learner in their classrooms. One way to achieve this goal is to choose appropriate instructional approaches. In this module, we explore evidence-based teaching methods that can be considered teacher centered or student centered in their approach to instruction. In *teacher-centered approaches,* the learning environment is structured and teachers control the amount and pace of information. In *student-centered approaches,* teachers create a learning environment that enables students to construct meaning from their interactions with subject matter and peers. In this approach, teachers often facilitate student learning rather than dispense information. Effective teachers do not choose a teaching method because it is student centered or teacher centered but because it is best suited to:

- particular **learning objectives** (what teachers want students to know and be able to do);

- how students will demonstrate their learning of the material; and

- the subject matter itself, on occasion.

Learning objectives for a lesson can range from lower level to higher level skills, and the assessment that teachers use for evaluating students' mastery of the material should match the learning objectives. Consider **Bloom's taxonomy** shown in Table 18.1, which is useful for determining learning objectives and assessment of those objectives (Anderson & Krathwohl, 2001; Bloom, Englehart, Frost, Hill, & Krathwohl, 1956). For example, students in a high school chemistry class who listen to their teacher lecture and take notes (teacher-centered approach) would be expected to demonstrate lower level skills such as knowledge and understanding, perhaps on a multiple-choice test. These students might not perform as well on an essay test that assesses higher level skills, such as analyzing compounds, evaluating the validity of experimental results, or creating problem solutions, because it is inconsistent with the way they learned the information. As you read about the variety of instructional methods, think about whether the teacher-centered or student-centered approach of each method is best

Master the content.

edge.sagepub.com/durwin3e

$SAGE edge™

Match between teaching and testing: See Module 23

Bloom's taxonomy: See Module 13

TABLE 18.1	Levels of Bloom's Taxonomy	
CATEGORY	**DESCRIPTION**	**INSTRUCTIONAL ACTIVITIES**
Remember	Remembering facts or information learned earlier without necessarily understanding or being able to use that knowledge	state, define, list, label, name
Understand	Understanding or making sense of information without connecting it to prior knowledge	explain, describe, summarize, paraphrase
Apply	Selecting and using information to solve a problem or specific task	demonstrate, compute, solve, or apply knowledge
Analyze	Breaking information into parts; making connections between those parts	compare, contrast, categorize, classify
Evaluate	Making judgments about the value of information for a particular situation	justify, critique, recommend
Create	Creating or generating new ideas by combining information	produce, develop, invent, design, hypothesize

suited for the particular students you are working with and your learning objectives. Before we delve into teaching methods, let's first address the concern of effective teachers—meeting the needs of diverse learners.

MEETING THE NEEDS OF DIVERSE LEARNERS

❶ Explain why it is not necessary to individualize instruction for every student, and identify the situations in which teachers need to differentiate instruction.

In any given classroom, even when students are similar in ability or achievement level, you will encounter students who have varying cultural, socioeconomic, linguistic, and family backgrounds, different levels of prior knowledge, work ethics, and motivation, and different interests, to name a few characteristics. It is unrealistic to consider creating individualized instructional methods for students based on their specific characteristics.

However, there are times when it is important to implement *differentiated instruction,* providing a different learning experience to address particular students' needs. For example, differentiation might be necessary for students with language impairments or who are English language learners, students with learning disabilities or intellectual disabilities, or students who are gifted. It also might be helpful to group students who have similar levels of skill for the groups to optimally benefit from instruction, such as grouping students with different levels of reading skill. These forms of differentiation are discussed in more detail in several other modules.

You also may have heard of matching instruction to a student's *learning style.* I have heard many of my own students tell me that they are verbal learners or visual learners and therefore learn best when instruction matches their learning preference. The visual–verbal distinction is only one model of more than 70 approaches to thinking about learning styles or preferences (Coffield, Moseley, Hall, & Ecclestone, 2004). With so many ways to define learning style, it would be impossible to accurately say that any one model is correct. The notion of learning styles is likely to be an urban legend in education, a popular and widely accepted belief with little empirical support (Kirschner & van Merriënboer, 2013). Most of the studies examining learning styles used questionable research designs, and of those that used a valid research design, results were primarily negative (Rohrer & Pashler, 2012). Also, an examination of the research literature indicates no conclusive evidence for a benefit of modifying instruction to match students' learning styles (Pashler, McDaniel, Rohrer, & Bjork, 2009; Rohrer & Pashler, 2012).

Although it may not be necessary to match instruction to the learning preferences of individual students, it is important to teach with the unique backgrounds and interests of your students in mind. This is known as *culturally responsive pedagogy.* Culturally responsive pedagogy involves instruction that uses students' cultural beliefs, values, family and community backgrounds, language, and prior knowledge to create learning experiences characterized by active construction of knowledge and connections to personal experience (Brown-Jeffy & Cooper, 2011; Gay, 2010; Nieto & Boder, 2008; Utley, Obiakor, & Bakken, 2011). The intended result is an environment of equitable learning for all. Guidelines 18.1 list the major principles of culturally responsive instruction. As you can see, these principles are discussed in many modules throughout this textbook because they are principles of effective teaching in general.

Teachers who implement these principles will enable students of all backgrounds to reach their potential regardless of the specific teaching methods they may choose for different lessons. Now let's turn to the various approaches to instruction.

Language development: See Module 7

Cognitive disabilities: See Module 21

Giftedness: See Module 20

Grouping practices: See Module 19

Research designs: See Module 1

Video Case 18.1 ▲
Differentiated Instruction

© SAGE Publications

 Think about your K-12 educational experiences. Which teachers were effective in encouraging you to reach your potential? What were some of the teaching principles they may have used?

GUIDELINES 18.1 — Principles of Culturally Responsive Pedagogy and Links to Other Modules

Teaching Principle	Module
1. Be aware of your own background and cultural assumptions.	Modules 1, 2
2. Convey the message that you care about each student.	Modules 16, 17
3. Create positive relationships with students and their families and communities.	Modules 2, 16, 17
4. Provide a nurturing and supportive classroom environment that encourages connectedness among students.	Modules 16, 17
5. Be aware of students' cognitive and psychosocial development and motivation, and implement developmentally appropriate practices.	Modules 3, 4, 5, 6, 7
6. Have high expectations for all students.	Module 15
7. Ensure that learning is rigorous, interesting, and challenging for all students at all levels.	Modules 6, 12, 13, 14
8. Use active teaching methods.	Modules 6, 10, 11, 12, 13
9. Make learning meaningful and relevant to students' lives.	Modules 10, 11, 12
10. Show cultural sensitivity by incorporating students' culturally valued knowledge into curriculum and instruction.	Modules 2, 10
11. Appreciate bilingualism and multiculturalism as assets in learning rather than deficits.	Module 7
12. Differentiate instruction when applicable and necessary.	Modules 7, 20, 21, 22

SOURCES: Brown-Jeffy & Cooper, 2011; Gardner & Mayes, 2013; Gay, 2010; Klingner & Soltero-González, 2011; Nieto & Boder, 2008; Polleck & Shabdin, 2013; Schmidt & Ma, 2006; Utley et al., 2011.

TEACHING METHODS BASED ON BEHAVIORISM

 Describe the goals of mastery learning and direct instruction, and discuss the advantages and disadvantages of each approach.

Behavioral learning theory proposes, simply, that learning leads to a change in an individual's behavior. This school of thought has its roots in *operant conditioning*, which proposes that an individual's behavior is the result of two environmental stimuli: antecedents and consequences. Antecedents are stimuli or situations that signal that a behavior is expected, whereas consequences are stimuli that either strengthen the likelihood that the behavior will occur again or reduce the future occurrence of the behavior. For example, a typical classroom interaction would involve a teacher asking a question (antecedent), a student providing a response (behavior), and the teacher offering feedback (consequence). Behavioral learning theory is equated with teacher-centered instructional approaches in which teachers serve as dispensers of information and structure the learning environment to help students progress from simple to more complex skills. Two examples of this approach are direct instruction and mastery learning, in which teachers create an antecedent for learning and consequences that strengthen students' knowledge and skills.

Operant conditioning:
See Module 8

Direct Instruction

The goal of **direct instruction** is to maximize the time that students spend in appropriate tasks by emphasizing completion of learning tasks and by minimizing off-task behavior such as puzzles, games, and teacher–student interactions not directly related to academic tasks (Joyce, Weil, & Calhoun, 2004; Rosenshine, 1979). With this approach, teachers use a high degree of control

Reference: Direct Instruction

to create a structured learning environment and monitor student progress. Direct instruction assumes students learn best when teachers structure the learning environment to present accurate information in small chunks and offer many opportunities for practice and feedback (Kirschner, Sweller, & Clark, 2006; Mayer, 2004; Rosenshine, 1985). This approach also requires all students to move through the content at the same pace. Let's examine the typical components of direct instruction by discussing what occurs before, during, and after a lesson.

Teachers using direct instruction would begin a lesson by reviewing the previous day's lecture and checking student work. This allows teachers to identify misconceptions or errors so that they can reteach the material to the entire class. Next, teachers would introduce new content by activating prior knowledge through discussion of the learning objective or an overview of the lesson (Joyce et al., 2004; Rosenshine, 1985). Identifying the learning objective or lesson overview provides students with a purpose for learning the material and an overall procedure for how material is to be learned. Preparing students for the lesson using these steps improves student achievement (Fisher et al., 1980; Medley, Soar, & Coker, 1984).

During a lesson, teachers control the pace and presentation of new material. They present information in small steps to be mastered one step at a time, provide varied examples, use modeling, and reexplain challenging concepts. They also check for understanding by asking convergent questions that call for a right answer or questions that require students to explain their answers (Rosenshine, 1985).

Convergent thinking: See Modules 12 and 13

Once students have learned material, they have an opportunity to progress through four structured types of practice.

1. In *controlled practice,* the teacher leads students through examples, providing immediate corrective feedback. This stage requires careful monitoring to prevent students from learning incorrect procedures or concepts. Rather than simply giving the right answers, effective teachers provide feedback, telling students what they have done correctly, prompting them for clarification or improved answers, and reteaching when necessary (Fisher et al., 1980; Rosenshine, 1971).

Reinforcement: See Module 8

2. In *guided practice,* students practice on their own while the teacher provides reinforcement and corrective feedback. For example, high school students might complete a worksheet conjugating Spanish verbs as teachers move through the classroom to check on their progress.

Feedback: See Module 14

3. Students move to *independent practice* when they are able to practice knowledge or skills with about 85% to 90% accuracy. Homework is an example of independent practice.

Distributed practice: See Module 10

4. Students also need to engage in *distributed practice,* a process of spreading out practice over a period of time. These short and frequent practice periods are more effective than fewer but longer practice opportunities, especially for children in early elementary grades (Cepeda et al., 2009; Cepeda, Pashler, Vul, Wixted, & Rohrer, 2006). To foster long-term learning, teachers also provide weekly and monthly reviews and reteach as necessary.

Direct instruction is a popular method in the early elementary grades, where much of instruction is focused on basic skills, such as reading, mathematics, spelling, handwriting, and early science and social studies knowledge. Direct instruction is effective

*   for lower level objectives in Bloom's taxonomy and for improving students' basic skills in reading and mathematics (Brophy & Evertson, 1976; Denham & Lieberman, 1980; Poncy, McCallum, & Schmitt, 2010);

DIVERSITY

*   as an initial instructional strategy for lower achieving students (Good, Biddle, & Brophy, 1975); and

*   for teaching basic skills to students with disabilities (Reddy, Ramar, & Kusama, 2000; Turnbull, Turnbull, Shank, Smith, & Leal, 2002).

Direct instruction can also be used for teaching more complex skills and subjects. Elementary school students have learned how to design controlled experiments in science through direct instruction (Klahr & Nigam, 2004; Lazonder & Egberink, 2014). Direct instruction is effective for teaching multistep procedures typically found in high school subjects, such as algebra, geometry, and computer programming (Anderson, Corbett, Koedinger, & Pelletier, 1995; Klahr & Carver, 1988). The key to the effectiveness of this approach is to provide students with worked examples and timely feedback, such as on homework assignments and quizzes (Alfieri, Brooks, Aldrich, & Tenenbaum, 2011).

However, direct instruction is not effective for all students and all situations (Joyce et al., 2004). This method may not benefit high-achieving students or task-oriented students who are intrinsically driven to perform and succeed on tasks (Ebmeier & Good, 1979; Solomon & Kendall, 1976). Also, direct instruction should not become the sole instructional method for lower achieving students. Rather, as these students achieve more success, teachers should transition to less structured learning experiences and emphasize more complex knowledge and skills (McFaul, 1983; Means & Knapp, 1991). Furthermore, direct instruction may not be sufficient alone for encouraging long-term retention and transfer of complex skills (Dean & Kuhn, 2007). Teachers should follow direct instruction with opportunities for extended practice with problem solving and application of strategies. For a more balanced emphasis on basic and complex learning skills, direct instruction can effectively be used together with more student-centered approaches (Dean & Kuhn, 2007; Kierstad, 1985).

Mastery Learning

Mastery learning is based on the idea that *all* students can learn curricular material if given sufficient time (Carroll, 1971). Teachers set a prespecified mastery level, such as 80% on a unit test. Students who do not master a certain unit are allowed to repeat it or an equivalent version at their own pace and to take another unit test until they have mastered the material (Joyce et al., 2004). The approach consists of (Bloom, 1971; Guskey & Jung, 2011):

- developing major learning objectives representing a course or unit;

- dividing major learning objectives into smaller units from simple to complex, with each unit having its own learning objectives;

- conducting a *formative assessment*—a brief diagnostic test to assess students' current level of performance before instruction and to determine areas needing improvement;

- presenting material to students, who typically work individually and independently;

- providing students with feedback about their progress (reinforcement of learning); and

- conducting a *summative assessment*—a test to determine what the student has learned.

This sequence of instruction has been used with students at all grade levels and for curricula ranging from basic skills to complex material (Joyce et al., 2004). Mastery learning is also appropriate for students of varying achievement and ability levels. Students who need extra time and teacher feedback to achieve mastery are allowed this opportunity, while those who master the material after initial teaching can be given enrichment or extension activities (Bloom, 1971; Guskey & Jung, 2011). Keep in mind that enrichment should be rewarding and challenging, does not need to be related to the subject matter in the current lesson, and should not involve busy work or more difficult work in the same lesson (Guskey & Jung, 2011). Compared to traditional instruction, well-implemented mastery learning leads to higher school achievement and increased confidence and academic self-concept, a perception of one's knowledge and abilities in school subjects (Guskey & Pigott, 1988; Kulik, Kulik, & Bangert-Drowns, 1990). However, mastery learning may not improve performance on standardized tests compared to other teaching methods (Kulik et al, 1990; Slavin, 1990;

Video Case 18.2 ▲
Mastery Learning
Math Lesson

© SAGE Publications

Formative and summative assessment:
See Module 23

Academic self-concept:
See Module 3

Mastery Learning. In mastery learning, shown here, students work independently at their own pace.

©iStockphoto.com/ Lise Gagne

Wambugu & Changeiywo, 2008). Also, this method may widen the *achievement gap* between students rather than narrowing it. While lower achieving students are given extra time to repeat content in order to achieve mastery, the enrichment activities of higher achieving students may further enhance their achievement.

Think about the grade level you intend to teach. Would you consider using mastery learning or direct instruction? Why or why not?

TEACHING METHODS BASED ON COGNITIVE LEARNING THEORY

3   Explain how discovery learning and expository teaching foster meaningful learning.

Cognitive learning theory proposes that learning involves actively constructing knowledge. Teaching methods based on this perspective are considered student centered because they focus on the *mental processes* students use in knowledge construction rather than the external stimuli teachers use in behaviorist approaches. An important concept in cognitive learning theory is **meaningful learning**—actively forming new knowledge structures by (Mayer, 2003):

Meaningful learning: See Modules 10 and 12

- selecting relevant information,

- organizing the information into a coherent structure, and

- integrating the information with relevant prior knowledge.

Teachers can foster meaningful learning using one of two distinct teaching methods—discovery learning and expository teaching—or both. Today's K-12 teachers consider these two methods to be complementary, as each has features that encourage meaningful learning when used appropriately.

Discovery Learning and Guided Discovery

Discovery learning encourages students to discover and internalize a concept, rule, or principle through unstructured exploration of to-be-learned information (Bruner, 1961). For example, high school students might be given various inclines and objects and be expected to experiment with the materials—without explicit guidance from the teacher—to "discover" certain physics principles.

However, discovery learning without any guidance from the teacher generally does not benefit learning because students need a sufficient amount of prior knowledge (Alfieri et al., 2011; Bruner, 1961; Fletcher, 2009). Without it, students may not be able to integrate the to-be-learned principle into their memory or may activate inappropriate knowledge (Klahr & Nigam, 2004). Students also may fail to stumble across the principle at all because of too much freedom in the discovery process (Mayer, 2004). As a result, the discovery process often leads to gaps in understanding and results in *negative transfer* (incorrectly applying prior knowledge to the problem) or *zero transfer* (failing to recognize when they can apply their knowledge).

A form of discovery learning called **guided discovery** is considered more effective than pure discovery in facilitating the learning and transfer of knowledge (Alfieri et al., 2011; Mayer, 2004). In this approach, the teacher provides enough guidance to ensure that students discover the rule or principle to be learned. For the high school students discovering physics principles, the teacher would provide general guidelines for experimentation, ask them to explain their thought processes to themselves or others, and provide feedback and support to steer their activities in the right direction when needed. The structure and guidance allow students to focus cognitive resources on integrating and reorganizing knowledge and making inferences rather than on figuring out how to carry out the discovery process itself (Alfieri et al., 2011; Chi, 2009; Fletcher, 2009). To be successful using guided discovery, teachers must consider the individual abilities and needs of students in determining how much and what type of guidance to provide (Mayer, 2004). It is also helpful to teach students the procedure for discovery learning because this provides them with a "tool" for engaging in active learning in many other domains (Bruner, 1961; Chi, 2009; Kirschner et al., 2006). Recent research suggests that a guided discovery approach can be effective for:

- development of conceptual knowledge in preschoolers (Fisher, Hirsh-Pasek, Newcombe, & Golinkoff, 2013); and

- learning and transfer of new scientific knowledge for students from elementary through high school (Akinbobola & Afolabi, 2009; Balim, 2009; Dean & Kuhn, 2007).

Expository Teaching

In **expository teaching** (also called *meaningful verbal learning*), the goal is not to have students independently discover to-be-learned content but to ensure that new information will be integrated into the learner's memory in a meaningful way (Ausubel, 1963, 2000).

Teachers begin by emphasizing the relevance of the new content to what students already know and to real-life examples and situations. To do this, they use an **advance organizer,** a tool that presents general information and provides a structure into which new information can be integrated. Take a moment to flip back to the beginning of this module and examine the outline on page 366. It is one example of an advance organizer. Advance organizers are not just outlines. They can be visual presentations, such as a flowchart that introduces a process, or an *analogy* that compares a new concept (a molecule) to a familiar one (a solar system). Advance organizers that consist of concrete models or analogies presented either verbally or graphically, rather than abstract examples or principles, are most effective (Mayer, 1992; Robinson, 1998). Advance organizers also enhance learning and promote transfer (application of knowledge to new situations), especially when new material is unfamiliar or difficult (Corkill, 1992; Luiten, Ames, & Ackerson, 1980; Morin & Miller, 1998).

Video Case 18.3 ▲
Guided Learning Math Lesson

© SAGE Publications

Transfer: See Module 12

Analogical transfer: See Module 12

Transfer: See Module 12

After activating students' relevant knowledge, teachers present topics in a highly organized process that moves from general, or prerequisite, knowledge to more specific topics. This structuring provides a relevant foundation on which students can build. Teachers also offer students opportunities to practice their knowledge in many different contexts to be certain they develop a thorough understanding of the new content. Implemented in this way, expository teaching is an efficient method for teaching subject matter content, such as science, math, social studies, or health, especially with students from the upper elementary grades through high school (Ausubel, 2000; Luiten et al., 1980).

 Have you ever experienced discovery learning, guided discovery, or expository teaching? Reflect on how effective these methods were for your learning.

TEACHING METHODS BASED ON CONSTRUCTIVISM

4 Describe the techniques based on cognitive apprenticeships that are used in constructivist teaching.

Teaching methods based on constructivism are considered student centered because constructivism emphasizes the individual's active role in exploring and socially interacting within his or her environment. Many constructivist theories of learning are based on *situated cognition,* a conceptual framework with roots in the writings of Russian educational psychologist Lev Vygotsky, Swiss psychologist Jean Piaget, and philosopher/educator John Dewey (Cobb & Bowers, 1999; Rogoff, 1990). Situated cognition is about learning in authentic contexts, such as apprenticeships, in which individuals work alongside experts and acquire necessary skills for solving problems and completing tasks that are important in the real world (Brown, Collins, & Duguid, 1989; Collins, Hawkins, & Carver, 1991).

Piaget's and Vygotsky's theories: See Module 6

Educators can bring situated cognition into schools by creating what are called **cognitive apprenticeships,** in which students develop cognitive skills through guided participation in authentic activities (Brown et al., 1989; Collins, Brown, & Newman, 1989; Lave & Wenger, 1991). Students participate in activities at a level commensurate with their ability and move gradually toward full participation. For example, young children at first may only be able to participate in conversation around the dinner table by talking about their day at school, but they will gradually move on to discussing current events and social issues with increasing cognitive and language development and with support from family members. Cognitive apprenticeships involve many techniques (Dennen, 2004; Enkenberg, 2001):

Modeling: See Module 9

- *modeling* (performing a behavior for others to imitate) by the adult or the more experienced individual,

- *explaining* (discussing one's reasoning or the need for certain strategies),

- *coaching* (monitoring students' activities and assisting and supporting them when necessary),

- practicing,

Scaffolding and fading: See Module 6

- *scaffolding* (providing support to students so they can accomplish a task) and *fading* (gradually withdrawing scaffolding),

- *exploration* (forming and testing hypotheses; finding new ideas and viewpoints), and

- *reflection* (assessing and analyzing one's learning performance), and *articulation* (verbally expressing the results of one's reflection).

Cognitive Apprenticeships.
Cognitive apprenticeships, like actual apprenticeships (shown here), involve guided participation in authentic activities.

These techniques are found in many of the constructivist teaching methods described next. As you read, try to identify the techniques in each teaching method.

Think about your learning in and out of school. Have you experienced any of the aforementioned techniques?

Inquiry Learning

In **inquiry learning,** students construct knowledge and develop problem-solving skills through a process of formulating and testing a hypothesis (Yilmaz, 2011). The process begins with the teacher presenting a complex and perplexing situation. This creates disequilibrium in students where they may be confused by the new information and motivated to solve the problem and acquire new knowledge in the process (Yilmaz, 2011). Inquiry typically involves several phases:

Problem-Solving skills:
See Module 13

Disequilibrium: See Module 6

1. formulating appropriate research questions,

2. collecting and organizing data,

3. analyzing and evaluating data, and

4. communicating the research results in a presentation.

Video: Inquiry-Based Learning

More than a finite list of steps, however, the process of inquiry, shown in Figure 18.1, usually is practiced as a continuous cycle, which can take several days, weeks, or even months (Bruner, 1965; Yilmaz, 2011). While this approach appears similar to the *scientific method,* inquiry learning assignments can be designed for any discipline and any developmental level.

In inquiry learning, teachers serve as facilitators, using their expertise to guide the inquiry lesson and to evaluate students' progress and the direction of the inquiry process. This approach requires the teacher to design and monitor inquiry groups to ensure that students are working collaboratively. If some students are allowed to take over the inquiry process of the group, the opportunity for all students to "construct" knowledge for themselves may be reduced. Students with intellectual disabilities, who generally show a weakness in independent insight and inductive thinking relative to typically achieving students, may require additional coaching and scaffolding to benefit from the inquiry process (Mastropieri, Scruggs, & Butcher, 1997; Mastropieri et al., 1996).

DIVERSITY

Inquiry learning is effective for elementary and secondary students (Gillani, 2003). Inquiry activities that are properly structured and guided by the teacher lead to better student learning compared to unstructured student-led inquiry or traditional lessons such as lectures (Furtak, Seidel, Iverson, & Briggs, 2012). Providing students with opportunities to engage in the inquiry process before reading or instruction facilitates greater transfer compared to traditional instruction alone (Parker et al., 2011).

Video: Cooperative Learning

Cooperative Learning

Cooperative learning involves students working together to achieve a shared goal. In a high school U.S. history course, for example, a cooperative learning group might create a presentation on the Bill of Rights in which group members work together to develop the content of the presentation, each member presents a portion, and the group is graded on the final product. In a fifth-grade language arts class, a teacher may have each cooperative group conduct an author analysis in which groups compare and contrast the themes and writing styles of the author's books and create a presentation or product to showcase the results of their analysis. Cooperative learning can be used for any subject and with students from elementary through high school (Johnson & Johnson, 1986). It also can be a component of other active learning approaches, such as problem-based learning, class projects, inquiry learning, and team-based learning (Johnson, Johnson, & Smith, 2014). Regardless of the approach, a cooperative group activity must contain these five elements (Johnson & Johnson, 1999, 2009):

Transfer: See Module 12

Cooperative learning: See Module 19

Problem-based learning: See Module 13

1. *Positive interdependence:* Members of the group work together and depend on one another so that all group members succeed.

2. *Individual and group accountability:* Each member must contribute to the group for the group to succeed and be rewarded.

3. *Interpersonal skills:* Trust, communication, decision making, leadership, and conflict resolution are all important to the success of cooperative learning.

4. *Face-to-face interaction:* Offering effective help and feedback, exchanging resources effectively, challenging one another's reasoning, and motivating one another to achieve goals are all necessary for effective learning.

5. *Group processing:* Reflecting on how well the group is functioning and how to improve is important for successful cooperative learning.

Video Case 18.4 ▲
Using Cooperative Learning

© SAGE Publications

Teachers can use Guidelines 18.2 to create activities that incorporate these five essential elements.

Decades of research show that cooperative learning yields many beneficial academic and social outcomes, including the following:

- higher level reasoning, creative thinking, and long-term retention and transfer of learned information (Johnson & Johnson, 1998);

- higher achievement in reading and mathematics (Rohrbeck, Ginsburg-Block, Fantuzzo, & Miller, 2003; Slavin, Lake, Chambers, Cheung, & Davis, 2009);

- increased self-esteem, especially in students with disabilities (Johnson & Johnson, 1998);

- greater intrinsic motivation for learning (Johnson & Johnson, 1985); and

- improved peer relationships in general, among students with disabilities and nondisabled students, and between students of different ethnicities (Johnson & Johnson, 2000, 2002; McMaster & Fuchs, 2002).

Transfer: See Module 12

Students with disabilities: See Modules 21 and 22

Intrinsic motivation: See Modules 14, 15, and 16

Methods of Fostering Comprehension

Teachers can use several methods to promote students' comprehension, all of which foster the construction of knowledge through social interactions and embody several characteristics of cognitive apprenticeships.

RECIPROCAL TEACHING

Based on Vygotsky's zone of proximal development, **reciprocal teaching** teaches metacognitive strategies necessary for skilled reading comprehension. Using this method, a group of students would be jointly responsible for understanding and evaluating an assigned text (which is why it is called *reciprocal*). The teacher would first model four comprehension strategies (questioning about the main idea, clarifying, summarizing, and predicting) and then provide scaffolding to students, who take turns leading discussions (Brown & Palincsar, 1987; Palincsar, 2003). Scaffolding by the teacher (and later by the students) may involve asking questions and rephrasing or elaborating on statements (Brown & Palincsar, 1989; Rosenshine & Meister, 1994). Students are given as much support as they need to complete the activity (Collins et al., 1989). Students with lower reading ability can participate and contribute to the level of their ability while learning from those with more ability or experience (Brown & Palincsar, 1989). As students acquire skill, they take greater responsibility over the reciprocal teaching process, and scaffolding gradually fades.

Reciprocal teaching is most appropriate at the elementary school level, when instruction in reading focuses on the acquisition of comprehension skill. The method results in substantially improved reading comprehension in students of all ages (Rosenshine & Meister, 1994; Slavin et al., 2009). It also improves the comprehension skills of elementary and middle school students with intellectual disabilities and learning disabilities (Alfassi, Weiss, & Lifshitz, 2009; Gajria, Jitendra, Sood, & Sacks, 2007). Because students are required to articulate what makes a good question, prediction, and summary, their strategies become decontextualized, meaning students are able to use them in many domains, which improves transfer (Collins et al., 1989). Even though reciprocal teaching focuses on metacognitive skills involved in reading comprehension, this approach also has been used to improve students' vocabulary and their ability to solve story problems in math (Mandel, Osana, & Venkatesh, 2013; Meyer, 2014; Reilly, Parsons, & Bortolot, 2009).

Zone of proximal development: See Module 6

Reciprocal teaching: See Module 11

> **DIVERSITY**

Students with disabilities: See Module 21

Tips for Effective Use of Cooperative Learning

Characteristic	Teaching tips
Positive interdependence	• Establish a group goal stating that all group members must reach their learning goals. • Provide rewards based on the success of the group (e.g., a group grade, bonus points, or tangible rewards). • Distribute limited resources. • Assign each member a specific role. • Divide the work so that one member's assignment is necessary for the next member to complete his or her assignment.
Individual and group accountability	• Randomly select one student's product to represent the group. • Test all group members and average the scores.
Interpersonal skills	• Teach communication skills, especially in the elementary grades. • Include interpersonal objectives for a cooperative lesson. • Inform students of the collaborative skills needed to work successfully in their groups.
Face-to-face interaction	• Monitor group members' use of resources and level of challenge and feedback. • Monitor and scaffold interactions and collaboration, especially for students in elementary grades.
Group processing	• Allow time for groups to reflect on their functioning so students do not assume that speed and finishing early are more important than meaningful learning. • Have students identify what was helpful and unhelpful in their interactions. • Use information about group processing to make decisions about what to change for the next task or what changes to make in group placements.

SOURCES: Johnson & Johnson, 1986, 1990; McCaslin & Good, 1996.

INSTRUCTIONAL CONVERSATIONS

In many elementary school classrooms, students' verbal contributions during reading lessons are limited to known answers (Gallimore & Goldenberg, 1992), as when a teacher asks, "Who is the main character in this story?" Teachers can move away from the traditional role of evaluating students' responses toward *assisting* students in interpreting texts by using **instructional conversations,** a method that assumes that (a) students have something important to say and (b) their input is valued (Gallimore & Goldenberg, 1992). This method consists of 10 elements (see Table 18.2) that reflect Vygotsky's notion of assisted learning in the zone of proximal development.

Teachers and students engage in a joint conversation about a text that looks like a spontaneous discussion where each person contributes to the dialogue by building on, extending, or challenging a previous comment. However, the discussion is a planned interaction with instructional and conversational purposes (Gallimore & Goldenberg, 1992; Gallimore & Tharp, 1990). The instructional purpose focuses on learning objectives—what the teacher wants students to acquire from reading the text (e.g., vocabulary, comprehension, themes). The conversational purpose involves creating a joint understanding and interpretation of the text through genuine communication.

Teachers have used instructional conversations to promote elementary school students' interaction with and comprehension of stories during reading lessons (Gallimore & Goldenberg, 1992; Saunders & Goldenberg, 1999). Students participating in instructional conversations have achieved grade-level or higher reading skills and mastery of more complex, differentiated concepts than children receiving traditional reading comprehension instruction

Zone of proximal development: See Module 6

Video Case 18.5 ▲
Lecture and Discussion Methods

© SAGE Publications

TABLE 18.2 Components of Instructional Conversations

INSTRUCTIONAL ELEMENTS	HOW TO IMPLEMENT
1. Thematic focus	• Select a theme or idea as a starting point for focusing the discussion. • Make a general plan for how the theme will unfold.
2. Activation and use of background knowledge	• Provide students with necessary background knowledge for understanding the text by weaving the knowledge into the discussions.
3. Direct teaching	• When necessary, teach a skill or concept directly.
4. Promotion of more complex language and expression	• Elicit more complex language by asking students to expand on their thoughts, questioning them, and restating their contributions using more complex grammar and vocabulary.
5. Promotion of bases for statements or positions	• Encourage students to use text, pictures, and reasoning to support an argument or a position. • Probe for the bases of students' statements (e.g., ask "How do you know?").
6. Fewer "known-answer" questions	• Focus on questions for which there might be more than one correct answer.
7. Responsiveness to student contributions	• Be responsive to students' statements and the opportunities they provide for further discussion, while maintaining the focus and coherence of the discussion and the initial plan for the discussion.
8. Connected discourse	• Be sure the discussion involves interaction and turn taking so that succeeding contributions build on and extend previous ones.
9. A challenging but nonthreatening atmosphere	• Create an open, supportive environment that challenges students to negotiate and construct the meaning of the text.
10. General participation	• Encourage students to volunteer to speak or to influence the selection of speaking turns rather than directly determining who speaks.

SOURCE: Adapted from Goldenberg, 1992/1993.

(Saunders & Goldenberg, 1992; Tharp & Gallimore, 1988). These findings have primarily come from research with culturally diverse populations, as the instructional conversations method was initially developed and used with native Hawaiian children in grades K–3 in urban Honolulu and was later adapted for use with Latino students in Los Angeles, California (Au, 1979; Goldenberg, 1987). Although research results are promising, more empirical support for this approach is needed (Gallimore & Goldenberg, 1992). The effectiveness of instructional conversations with other grade levels and other student populations has yet to be tested. Another potential obstacle to the widespread adoption of this method is that effective implementation requires one year of teacher training (Moll, 2001).

> **DIVERSITY**

RECIPROCAL QUESTIONING

Reciprocal questioning, which is a method of reinforcing new concepts, information, or procedures that students have learned in class, encourages structured conversations among students. Because each student's understanding of new material may differ from that of others, the social negotiation of conflicting perspectives can lead to a restructuring of knowledge (Bearison, 1982; Glachan & Light, 1982).

For example, after high school students participate in a history lesson on the consequences of the Missouri Compromise of 1820, they would independently generate two or three questions using question stems, shown in Table 18.3, and then take turns in cooperative groups asking and answering each other's questions. This approach is called *reciprocal* because students help each other achieve an understanding of material.

TABLE 18.3 Question Stems for Reciprocal Questioning

TYPE OF PROMPT	PURPOSE	EXAMPLES
Comprehension checking	To enable students to test themselves	• What does . . . mean? • Describe in your own words . . . • What is a new example of . . . ?
Knowledge constructing	To construct new knowledge and integrate it with prior knowledge by: • explaining • making evaluative, comparative, or evidential connections within the material	• Explain why . . . . • Explain how . . . . • How do you account for . . . ? • How does . . . tie in with what we learned before? • What conclusions can you draw about . . . ? • What would happen if . . . ? • How would . . . affect . . . ? • What do you think causes . . . ? • What are the strengths and weaknesses of . . . ?
Thought provoking	To create cognitive conflict through expression of different points of view	• What do you think would happen if . . . ? • Do you agree or disagree with this statement? Why or why not? • What is the best . . . and why?
Metacognitive	To monitor thinking and learning	• What made you think of that? • What is your reasoning?

SOURCE: Adapted from King, 2002.

The question stems are the most important aspect of this approach, because they guide discussions by encouraging students to do the following things (King, 1990, 2002):

- provide explanations to others,

- think about the material in new ways by confronting different perspectives, and

- monitor their own thinking through metacognitive questions.

Autism spectrum disorder: See Module 22.

DIVERSITY

Providing students with more instruction on how to generate the questions is better than offering less instruction. In research by King (1990, 2002), students trained in the use of "why" and "how" questions asked more critical thinking questions and gave and received more elaborated explanations than untrained students.

Reciprocal questioning results in several positive academic outcomes. Students using this technique generate more high-level (critical thinking) questions than those involved in group discussion (King, 1990, 2002). Students who give explanations of lesson content in peer groups also improve their own comprehension of the material (Dansereau, 1988; Webb, 1989). Research with students in elementary school through college shows that reciprocal questioning improves comprehension more effectively than group discussion, unguided peer questioning (i.e., no question stems provided), and a general review of material (Fantuzzo, Riggio, Connelly, & Dimeff, 1989; King, 1991). Reciprocal questioning may also be appropriate for students with disabilities. A recent study with children with autism spectrum disorder indicates that these students were able to increase the frequency of questioning and responding while reading in peer groups after being taught reciprocal questioning (Whalon & Hanline, 2008).

❶ Explain why it is not necessary to individualize instruction for every student and identify the situations in which teachers need to differentiate instruction. With so many individual differences among students, it would be impractical to individualize instruction for each student. Also, there is no conclusive evidence to support the existence of individual learning styles, which means that modifying instruction to individual styles is not necessary. Teachers may need to differentiate instruction to meet the needs of English language learners, students with language impairments, students with disabilities, and students who are gifted.

❷ Describe the goals of mastery learning and direct instruction, and discuss the advantages and disadvantages of each approach. Mastery learning encourages *all* students to achieve mastery of course content by adjusting the amount of time and feedback provided to meet students' needs as they progress through individual curricular units. Mastery approaches are applicable to all grade levels and to material of varying complexity, but they may widen the achievement gap between lower and higher achieving students. Direct instruction maximizes academic learning time through use of teacher control, structured lessons, practice, and feedback. The approach is effective for teaching basic skills, especially with lower achieving students and students with disabilities, but it may not be beneficial when used with high-achieving or task-oriented students or as a teacher's only instructional method.

❸ Explain how discovery learning and expository teaching foster meaningful learning. Both approaches promote *meaningful learning,* in which students form new knowledge by selecting and organizing information and relating it to prior knowledge. In discovery learning, students actively discover and internalize a concept, rule, or principle through unstructured exploration of lesson content. Expository teaching promotes meaningful learning by (a) activating students' prior knowledge through advance organizers, (b) emphasizing how new material relates to what students already know and to real-life examples and situations, and (c) providing opportunities for students to practice their knowledge in many different contexts.

❹ Describe the techniques based on cognitive apprenticeships that are used in constructivist teaching. Inquiry learning, cooperative learning, instructional conversations, reciprocal teaching, and reciprocal questioning are all constructivist teaching methods that use a variety of techniques based on cognitive apprenticeships. Students engage in exploration, practice of skills, explanations of their reasoning, reflection, and articulation. Teachers use explanation whenever necessary, as well as modeling, coaching, scaffolding, and fading. More experienced students also use scaffolding and fading of cognitive strategies to assist their less experienced peers.

KEY CONCEPTS

advance organizers, 373

Bloom's taxonomy, 367

cognitive apprenticeships, 374

cooperative learning, 376

direct instruction, 369

discovery learning, 373

expository teaching, 373

guided discovery, 373

inquiry learning, 375

instructional conversations, 378

learning objectives, 367

mastery learning, 371

meaningful learning, 372

reciprocal questioning, 379

reciprocal teaching, 377

CASE STUDIES: REFLECT AND EVALUATE

EARLY CHILDHOOD: COUNTING POCKETS

These questions refer to the case study on page 336.

1. Explain how the two high school students who are assisting in the preschool classroom represent a cognitive apprenticeship.

2. How does the counting pockets activity reflect a guided discovery approach?

3. Make a prediction about what would happen if Ms. Abby allowed children to learn number concepts through a pure discovery approach.

4. Is there any room for pure discovery in a preschool classroom? Why or why not?

5. To what extent should Ms. Abby use a direct instruction approach in her classroom?

6. Use a theory or teaching approach in the module to explain why Ms. Abby pairs the children for the counting pockets activity.

ELEMENTARY SCHOOL: THE MACHINE HUNT

These questions refer to the case study on page 338.

1. What type of instructional approach does Mr. Finnegan use for math? Why might this approach be effective for this group of students?

2. Explain how the walk around the school and the small group discussions afterward represent a guided discovery approach.

3. Why might guided discovery be effective for a lesson about simple machines? What must teachers do to ensure that guided discovery is successful?

4. Identify the techniques involved in cognitive apprenticeships that are present in the case.

5. What instructional approach does Mr. Finnegan use for the group project involving designing a toy or game using simple machines? Identify some factors for Mr. Finnegan to consider to ensure that this group project is successful.

6. Should Mr. Finnegan use a different teaching approach to teach about simple machines? If not, provide a rationale. If so, which approach do you suggest and why?

MIDDLE SCHOOL: SARCOPHAGUS STUDIES

These questions refer to the case study on page 340.

1. Explain how the museum trip represents the concept of meaningful learning.

2. How does the museum scavenger hunt reflect a guided discovery approach? How does the scavenger hunt serve as an advance organizer?

3. Using the five elements of cooperative learning, evaluate how well the sarcophagus project represents cooperative learning. What suggestions for improvement would you give Mrs. DeSantis?

4. After the museum trip and before the group project, Mrs. DeSantis covers information on ancient Egypt.

Should she use direct instruction or expository teaching for her Period 5 class? Justify your response.

5. Refer to your response to Question 4 above. What teaching approach should Mrs. DeSantis use for her Period 3 class? Provide a rationale for your position. (Note: This is an open-ended question.)

6. Assume Period 5 students go to English class where they are learning about symbolism and themes in novels. Choose an instructional approach that would be most appropriate for this type of lesson and provide a rationale for your response.

HIGH SCHOOL: TEACHER'S LOUNGE

These questions refer to the case study on page 342.

1. Mr. Williams suggests that Mr. Webster use "bell work" at the start of class. Explain how bell work can be a component of direct instruction and expository teaching.

2. Mr. Webster uses lecture to teach students about constructing a typical "five-paragraph essay." Identify the type of instructional approach he is using and explain why it may be ineffective in this situation.

3. How does Mr. Williams teach writing in his class? Explain how this approach represents situated cognition.

4. Imagine that you are observing Mr. Williams's English class, where he is teaching writing by having students write cover letters for jobs. Using the components of cognitive apprenticeships, elaborate on what this lesson might look like.

5. Assume that Mr. Webster wants to try a new approach to teach his students grammar. Explain how he could use cooperative learning and its five elements to accomplish this. What benefits does this approach yield?

6. As a teacher, you want to introduce the English Grammar and Composition class to novels. What instructional approach or approaches based on constructivism would you choose? Provide a rationale for your response.

APPLY AND PRACTICE WHAT YOU'VE LEARNED

▶ edge.sagepub.com/durwin3e

CHECK YOUR COMPREHENSION ON THE STUDENT STUDY SITE

- **eFlashcards** to strengthen your understanding of key terms

- Practice **quizzes** to test your knowledge of key concepts

- **Videos and multimedia content** to enhance your exploration of key topics

©iStockphoto.com/Christopher Futcher

GROUPING PRACTICES

OUTLINE	LEARNING GOALS

Grouping by Ability

- Within-Class Ability Grouping
- Between-Class Ability Grouping
- Flexible Grouping Methods

❶ Discuss the pros and cons of within-class and between-class ability grouping.

❷ Discuss the advantages of flexible grouping methods.

Cooperative Learning

- Characteristics of Cooperative Learning
- Effectiveness of Cooperative Learning

❸ Identify the characteristics of cooperative learning and discuss the effectiveness of this approach.

***Applications:* Best Practices**

- Elementary School: Using Within-Class Ability Grouping Effectively
- Middle School and High School: To Track or Not to Track
- Using Cooperative Learning Effectively

❹ Describe effective practices for addressing student differences in elementary and secondary education and for implementing cooperative learning.

A primary challenge for teachers is resolving how to deal with differences in their students' prior knowledge and achievement levels. When students in a group show variation on an attribute, such as achievement or ability, it is called **heterogeneity.** When little variability occurs among students on an attribute, it is referred to as **homogeneity.** Historically, the first attempt at reducing heterogeneity among children was the transition from the one-room schoolhouse to grouping by age, now called grades. Grouping by age, an innovation of the 19th century, still left a great deal of variability in student ability within each grade (Goodlad & Anderson, 1987).

Starting around 1900 and through most of the 20th century, ability grouping was a common practice for reducing heterogeneity (Barr, 1995; Mills & Durden, 1992). **Ability grouping** is a method of creating groups of students who are homogeneous in achievement or ability. **Cooperative learning,** a more recent approach, is a method of grouping students to work collaboratively, usually with students of different achievement levels within each group. Although students within ability groups also may work collaboratively, ability grouping creates a more competitive atmosphere than cooperative learning. The segregation of students into distinct groups of higher and lower achievers often results in the groups experiencing different teacher expectations and working toward different learning goals, usually with different curricula (Weinstein, 1993).

The distinction between ability grouping and cooperative learning does not necessarily mean that one grouping structure is better than the other. When choosing a grouping structure to address heterogeneity in student ability, teachers need to consider many factors, both academic and socioemotional. Let's examine the different approaches and discuss some best practices for grouping students.

Master the content.

edge.sagepub.com/durwin3e

 SAGE edge™

GROUPING BY ABILITY

❶ Discuss the pros and cons of within-class and between-class ability grouping.

❷ Discuss the advantages of flexible grouping methods.

The aim of ability grouping is to enhance learning for students of all ability levels by allowing teachers to adapt learning goals, activities and materials, and the pace of instruction to meet the specific needs of students within each particular group or class. When ability grouping is implemented correctly, students of *all* ability levels show achievement gains (Fielder, Lange, & Winebrenner, 1993; Shields, 1995; Slavin & Madden, 1989). Students from minority groups and economically disadvantaged backgrounds also benefit from well-implemented ability grouping (Lynch & Mills, 1990).

Reference: Ability Grouping

> **DIVERSITY**

Within-Class Ability Grouping. This method is commonly used in elementary schools for teaching reading and math.

©iStockphoto.com/ Christopher Futcher

Teachers may decide whether to use ability grouping based partly on their beliefs about the approach (Chorzempa & Graham, 2006). Beliefs aside, to objectively evaluate the benefits of ability grouping, we should consider two key questions:

1. How effective is ability grouping?

2. Are the advantages (and disadvantages) of ability grouping the same for all students?

Within-Class Ability Grouping

Within-class ability grouping is the practice of dividing students within a self-contained class-room into groups that are homogeneous in ability. This type of grouping is common practice in the elementary grades for reading instruction and sometimes math instruction. For example, a teacher might divide the class into high-, average-, and low-achieving groups for reading, devoting time to each group for read-aloud and comprehension activities while students from other reading groups complete independent seat work. Within-class ability grouping has sharply increased from the 1990s to the 2000s for reading and has steadily increased for math, with 71% of fourth-grade teachers grouping for reading and 61% for math (Loveless, 2013).

Research has shown that within-class ability grouping has positive effects on student learning compared to other methods.

Video Case 19.1 ▲
Grouping Arrangements and Co-Teaching

© SAGE Publications

Mastery learning: See Module 18

- Within-class ability grouping generally is more effective than traditional teacher-led whole-class instruction, heterogeneous grouping, or individual seat work (Kulik & Kulik, 1992; Lou et al., 1996).

- It is also more effective than individualized mastery learning (Lou et al., 1996). *Mastery learning* is a practice in which teachers present a lesson and test students. Students who fail to meet a preset mastery criterion (e.g., 80% on the test) receive additional instruction, while students who exceed the criterion do enrichment activities.

- Ability grouping for reading in kindergarten and for math and science in upper elementary grades is more effective than heterogeneous instruction (Adelson & Carpenter, 2011; Lou et al., 1996). In subjects such as these, in which new concepts and skills often build on earlier content, within-class ability grouping allows teachers to specifically tailor instruction to the current skill level of students in each group.

While ability grouping does not appear to have detrimental effects on students' self-esteem, it does promote the achievement of some students over that of others (Kulik & Kulik, 2004). Students from higher ability groups and gifted students benefit most from within-class ability grouping (Adelson & Carpenter, 2011; Kulik & Kulik, 1992). Average students tend to benefit somewhat from ability grouping, while lower achieving students benefit more from heterogeneous grouping (Lou et al., 1996; Saleh, Lazonder, & Jong, 2005). Thus, a major criticism of ability grouping is that it widens the gap between high and low achievers (Condron, 2008; Lleras & Rangel, 2009; Tach & Farkas, 2006).

The gap between ability groups may widen partly because students in lower and higher groups receive different levels and paces of instruction. Compared with students in higher reading groups, students in lower reading groups spend more time reading orally and being read to by the teacher, spend less time reading silently, and spend more time on rote learning of skills than on comprehension, discussion, and interpretation (Allington, 1983; Chorzempa & Graham, 2006). Teachers also tend to interrupt oral reading to correct errors more often with students in lower reading groups, slowing the pace of instruction (Allington, 1980, 1983). As a consequence, students in different ability groups get different amounts of practice (Biemiller, 1977/1978; Juel, 1988; Nagy & Anderson, 1984). Students in higher groups read about three to four times as many words per day as those in lower groups (Allington, 1984; Biemiller, 1977/1978). Grouping students for reading, coupled with more out-of-school reading practice by good readers than by below-average readers, creates a so-called **Matthew effect**—above-average readers increase their reading achievement at a faster rate than below-average readers (Stanovich, 1986).

> DIVERSITY

Boys, minority students, and students from lower socioeconomic backgrounds may be particularly disadvantaged by this grouping method because they are more likely to be placed in lower ability groups. Teachers place more boys than girls in lower groups for reading (Catsambis, Mulkey, Buttaro, Steelman, & Koch, 2012). Similarly, students from lower income families or from minority groups typically are placed in lower ability groups, whereas students from higher socioeconomic backgrounds usually make up the highest ability groups (Saleh et al., 2005; Tach & Farkas, 2006). In schools with large populations of students from lower socioeconomic or minority backgrounds, within-class ability grouping does not improve student achievement (Nomi, 2010). Within-class ability grouping may also widen the achievement gap for English language learners (Chang, Singh, & Filer, 2009).

Several factors may influence placement decisions, such as teacher expectations, past performance, and standardized test scores. Lower school readiness at kindergarten entry (e.g., knowledge of letters, sounds, numbers, and counting) is one reason that boys and children from impoverished and culturally diverse backgrounds may be placed in lower groups (Catsambis et al., 2012; Tach & Farkas, 2006). Placement of boys into lower reading groups is also based on teachers' subjective evaluations of boys' reading ability and behaviors (Catsambis et al., 2012). Lower initial teacher expectations for boys and students from minority and lower socioeconomic backgrounds may lead to a *self-fulfilling prophecy*, where a groundless expectation leads teachers and students to act in ways that make the expectation come true (Merton, 1948). Initial teacher expectations—especially in classrooms where students perceive there is differential treatment—may contribute to an achievement gap in the early grades, which can be sustained through middle school and high school (Kuklinski & Weinstein, 2001; McKown & Weinstein, 2008; Sorhagen, 2013).

Self-Fulfilling prophecy:
See Module 20

Between-Class Ability Grouping

> DIVERSITY

Between-class ability grouping (also called *tracking*) is a common practice in high school and sometimes middle school, in which students are placed into homogeneous classes based on their level of achievement. Tracking has changed over time from a rigid practice of assigning students to curriculum tracks (e.g., honors, college prep, remedial/vocational), in which all their subjects are with students of similar ability, to a more flexible method of skill-based sorting, where students can take courses in different levels, such as an advanced English class but lower level math class (Kalogrides & Loeb, 2013). In skill-based sorting, every student experiences the same curriculum, with classes at the lower skill level covering content at a slower pace. Assignment of students to courses using either form of tracking is based on past performance, such as grades or standardized test scores. Students' ability group placement in elementary school is often another criterion for determining tracking placement in middle school or high school (Moore & Davenport, 1988; Rist, 1970; Rosenbaum, 1980). A student who was in the low reading group in elementary school is likely to be placed in a lower track in middle school or high school.

One criticism of tracking is that it reinforces racial and socioeconomic segregation. Like within-class ability grouping, tracking results in students from lower socioeconomic and minority backgrounds being placed into lower ability classes (Buttaro, Catsambis, Mulkey, & Steelman, 2010; Gamoran, 2010; Kalogrides & Loeb, 2013). As discussed earlier, students from minority groups and impoverished backgrounds are more likely to be placed into lower ability groups in elementary school. Low expectations for students in lower ability

©iStockphoto.com/FangXiaNuo

Matthew Effect. Good readers, like the boy shown here, read more often outside of school and increase their reading skills at a faster rate than below-average readers.

DIVERSITY ⟨

groups in elementary school may lead to a self-fulfilling prophecy that extends through high school. Recent research indicates that students who were expected to perform at a lower level in elementary school actually performed worse on standardized reading and math tests in high school than their elementary school scores would have predicted and that this effect was more pronounced for high school math achievement of students from lower socioeconomic families (Sorhagen, 2013).

Before discussing the effects of tracking on students, we should remember that the effects are caused not by tracking itself but by the different experiences students have in their respective tracks. Tracking affects higher and lower achieving students differently partly because of the different approaches teachers use (Gamoran, 2010). Table 19.1 contrasts the experiences of students in higher and lower tracks. As a result of these experiences, students in gifted programs, honors classes, and advanced placement courses clearly benefit from tracking (Kulik & Kulik, 2004; Preckel, Götz, & Frenzel, 2010). In contrast, students in middle and lower tracks experience a small academic disadvantage (Kulik & Kulik, 2004). Looking at the overall effects of tracking—by comparing higher track and lower track students—does not give the entire picture. The effects of tracking also vary depending on factors such as subject matter and gender.

Tracking may be beneficial to many students when it is used for subjects that are hierarchical, such as math. In tracked classes, teachers can focus instruction on the skill level of students, whereas in mixed-ability classes they need to cover some material that lower ability students have not yet learned and higher ability students have already mastered. Recent research on 24 countries including the United States indicates that middle school math instruction in homogeneous classes benefits all students except for students with very low ability (Huang, 2009). This finding supports previous research indicating that tracking for middle school math may benefit all but the lowest performing students and that rigorous and challenging instruction is the key factor in positive outcomes for students at all levels (Epstein & MacIver, 1992).

Tracking also may affect males and females differently. In middle school, high-achieving males tend to have lower aspirations than high-achieving females when tracked for English and math (Catsambis, Mulkey, & Crain, 1999, 2001). In math—a subject considered to be a "male domain"—high-achieving females spend more time on homework, perhaps because

Giftedness: See Module 20

DIVERSITY ⟨

| TABLE 19.1 | A Comparison of Higher and Lower Track Experiences |

HIGHER TRACK EXPERIENCE	LOWER TRACK EXPERIENCE
• Experienced teachers	• Novice teachers
• Challenging curricula	• Lack of stimulating content
• Faster pace of instruction	• Slower pace of instruction
• More effort by students	• Less effort by students
• Discussion and interactive teaching methods	• Worksheets and rote instruction
• Demanding and longer reading assignments	• Fewer writing assignments
• Use of independent projects and writing assignments to evaluate students	• Greater use of tests to evaluate students
• Completion of more advanced courses	• Election to take fewer English, math, and science courses

SOURCES: Applebee, Langer, Nystrand, & Gamoran, 2003; Banks, 2006; Carbonaro, 2005; Darling-Hammond, 1995; Gamoran, 2010; Loveless, 1999; Oakes, 1992, 2005; Watanabe, 2008.

they work harder to compete with their male peers. In contrast, males—who place a greater emphasis on social comparisons in male achievement domains—may no longer feel superior to other students when they are placed in higher tracks because they now are grouped with peers of comparable ability (Catsambis et al., 2001; Schwalbe & Staples, 1991). Low-achieving male students placed in low tracks have more positive feelings than do low-achieving females (Butler, 2008; Catsambis et al., 2001).

Before drawing your own conclusions about tracking, let's consider some effects on non-academic outcomes, such as academic self-concept—a perception of one's abilities and skills in school subjects—and self-esteem—an evaluation of oneself. In general, tracking has been associated with lower academic self-concepts for students in higher tracks and positive academic self-concepts for students in lower classes (Goldsmith, 2011; Thijs, Verkuyten, & Helmond, 2010). Students placed in separate classes for the gifted also experience slight decreases in academic self-concept (Preckel et al., 2010). This may be due to greater competition for grades and comparing their performance with that of other same-achieving students (Chiu et al., 2008; Mulkey, Catsambis, Steelman, & Crain, 2005; Preckel et al., 2010). However, students in gifted classes still have higher self-concepts than those in lower tracks (Preckel et al., 2010). Additionally, when students' actual grades in their courses are taken into account, there is little difference between students of higher tracks (including gifted classes) and lower tracks in academic self-concept or self-esteem (Chiu et al., 2008; Preckel et al., 2010).

Imagine that you teach at a school that uses ability grouping. What are the disadvantages of ability grouping at the grade level you teach? How might you reduce these negative effects when teaching your students?

Flexible Grouping Methods

Flexible grouping methods can be used as alternatives to ability grouping. Like ability grouping, flexible grouping methods reduce the heterogeneity in skill level among students, allowing teachers to tailor instruction to the needs and ability levels of students. Unlike within-class grouping and tracking, however, flexible approaches allow for greater movement of students between ability groups as their achievement changes and thereby avoid the stigmatization of becoming stuck in a low group.

Regrouping is a method in which students receive reading or math instruction in homogeneous groups based on their current skill level but remain in heterogeneous classrooms for all other subjects (Slavin, 1987b). For example, if two second-grade classes have reading at the same time each day, students would go to separate classes, each designed for a specific reading level. Students may be grouped and regrouped continuously as their achievement changes. Regrouping reduces the number of reading or math groups to one whole-class group, alleviating common problems of within-class ability grouping, such as the need to manage various groups and assign independent seat work and the stigmatization of students in rigid ability groups (Gutiérrez & Slavin, 1992; Slavin, 1987b). Regrouping has positive effects on achievement when it is implemented for only one or two subjects and when the curriculum and the pace of instruction are modified to meet students' ability levels (Gutiérrez & Slavin, 1992; Mason & Good, 1993; Slavin, 1987a).

Several **nongraded plans** organize students flexibly into homogeneous groups across grade or age levels (Gutiérrez & Slavin, 1992). **Cross-grade grouping** is the simplest nongraded plan. Students from different grades are assigned to homogeneous groups based on their reading or math achievement level, and each group works with different curricular materials and different methods (Kulik & Kulik, 1992). Because cross-grade grouping involves many more groups than within-class ability grouping, it allows for group placement and instruction that closely

Self-Concept and self-esteem: See Module 3

Giftedness: See Module 20

Video Case 19.2 ▲

Methods to Group Students

© SAGE Publications

match students' skill levels (Kulik & Kulik, 2004). For example, in the first and best-known cross-grade grouping plan—the **Joplin plan** (Floyd, 1954)—students in Grades 4 through 6 were assigned to homogeneous groups that ranged from second- to ninth-grade reading levels (Kulik & Kulik, 2004). Students in cross-grade grouping, particularly lower achieving students, show small achievement gains over students in mixed-ability instruction (Kulik & Kulik, 2004). Gifted students benefit from cross-grade grouping because it enables them to interact with peers of the same ability level (Kulik, 1992; Rogers, 1993).

On a wider scale, students may be grouped flexibly for multiple subjects, or entire schools may be structured as nongraded, multiage classrooms (Gutiérrez & Slavin, 1992; Slavin 1987a). In **multiage classrooms,** students of varying ages (e.g., 8, 9, and 10) are grouped within a classroom based on their current achievement, motivation, and interests. This structure reduces heterogeneity among students and fosters a developmentally appropriate curriculum (Gutiérrez & Slavin, 1992; Lloyd, 1999). Consistent with the aims of nongraded plans, this grouping approach benefits student achievement and does not negatively affect socialization or psychosocial adjustment (Gutiérrez & Slavin, 1992; Rogers, 1991). Students in nongraded, multiage classes like school better and have a more developed interpersonal intelligence than do students in graded classes (Anderson & Pavan, 1993; Goodlad & Anderson, 1987; Veenman, 1995).

Interpersonal intelligence: See Module 20

Note that *multiage* classes are distinct from *multigrade* classes. **Multigrade classes,** also called combination classes or split-grade classes, are an administrative tool for combining grades to address declining enrollments or uneven class sizes (Lloyd, 1999; Quail & Smyth, 2014). Students in these classes are exposed to different curricula and therefore maintain separate grade levels. No achievement benefits are to be gained from multigrade classrooms in which students from different grades are taught by the same teacher but separate curricula and grade levels are maintained (Quail & Smyth, 2014; Veenman, 1997).

? As a student, would you prefer flexible grouping methods over ability grouping? What about as a teacher? Why or why not?

COOPERATIVE LEARNING

3 Identify the characteristics of cooperative learning and discuss the effectiveness of this approach.

Cooperative learning as a constructive teaching method: See Module 18

Cooperative learning, a method of grouping students to work collaboratively, has become an increasingly popular approach in education, used for learners from preschool age through college (Johnson, Johnson, & Smith, 2007; Tarim, 2009; Tsay & Brady, 2010). It is used in some form by 79% of elementary school teachers and 62% of middle school teachers (Puma, Jones, Rock, & Fernandez, 1993). This approach differs from **group work,** in which students work in groups but do not necessarily need to work cooperatively. Also, in cooperative learning, as opposed to group work, groups typically are heterogeneous, consisting of low-, average-, and high-achieving students (Johnson & Johnson, 1986; Slavin, 1980).

Characteristics of Cooperative Learning

For group work to be considered cooperative learning, it must contain these five elements (Johnson & Johnson, 1998):

1. Positive interdependence

2. Individual and group accountability

3. Face-to-face interaction

4. Interpersonal skills

5. Group processing

Positive interdependence is the most important factor to consider when structuring a cooperative learning task (Johnson & Johnson, 1998; Slavin, 1991). **Positive interdependence,** a sense of "sink or swim together," can be implemented by doing the following things (Johnson & Johnson, 2009):

- establishing a group goal specifying that all group members must achieve their learning goals,

- providing rewards based on the success of the group (e.g., giving a group grade, bonus points, or tangible rewards when all group members achieve their goals),

- distributing limited resources so that cooperation is required,

- assigning each member a specific role in the group project, or

- dividing the work so that completion of one member's assignment is necessary for the next member to complete his or her assignment.

Structuring tasks so that students work toward a single goal or reward increases student productivity and achievement (Johnson & Johnson, 2009). However, having students rely on each other for resources, roles, or tasks—without establishing a group goal or reward—may undermine achievement and productivity because students focus on obtaining resources from each other without sharing their own (Johnson & Johnson, 2009).

Individual and group accountability, the second most important element in cooperative learning, refers to a sense of personal responsibility to the group (Johnson & Johnson, 1990). Because students are graded or rewarded as a group (group accountability), individual students are held accountable for completing their share of the work and for helping others work toward achieving the group goals (individual accountability). Accountability can be achieved in a variety of ways, such as randomly selecting one student's product to represent the group or testing all members on the material they were learning in the group and then averaging the scores (Johnson & Johnson, 1986).

Cooperative learning also requires face-to-face interaction and interpersonal skills. Beyond simply working together, **face-to-face interaction** requires students to provide each other with *effective* help and feedback to improve performance, exchange resources effectively, challenge each other's reasoning, and motivate each other to achieve goals (Johnson & Johnson, 1990). To that end, students need to have **interpersonal skills,** such as trust, communication, decision making, leadership, and conflict resolution. Rather than assume that students possess these skills, teachers should teach and monitor them, especially in the elementary grades (Boekaerts, 2009; Johnson & Johnson, 2009). They also should include interpersonal skills as objectives of a cooperative learning activity and discuss the collaborative skills needed for students to work successfully in their groups. Elementary school children need to be taught specific skills, such as asking for and offering help, managing conflict among group members, and self-regulating emotions and behaviors (Ladd et al., 2013).

Cooperative learning ends not with the completion of the activity but with group processing. In **group processing,** students identify what was helpful and not helpful and make decisions about what to change before moving on to the next task. Allowing time for group processing is necessary if cooperative learning is to be effective (Johnson & Johnson, 2009). Including group processing as part of cooperative learning improves achievement, even at the elementary school level (Bertucci, Johnson, Johnson, & Conte, 2012).

A cooperative approach can be used for any subject and with students from elementary through high school (Johnson & Johnson, 1986). It also can be a component of other active

Constructivist teaching methods: See Module 18

Problem-Based learning: See Module 13

learning approaches, such as inquiry learning, problem-based learning, class projects, and team-based learning (Johnson, Johnson, & Smith, 2014). Teachers can structure cooperative group activities differently for different purposes (Slavin, 1987b):

1. *Johnson methods* (named after creators David and Roger Johnson): Students work together on a joint activity in groups having the characteristics just discussed (Johnson & Johnson, 1975, 1978). For example, a middle school English teacher who has just finished a lecture on poetic devices and figurative language may arrange students in cooperative groups and assign each group a set of poems to compare and contrast, ending with a group presentation to the class. To be effective, groups should be heterogeneous and consist of three or four students (Lou et al., 1996; Marzano, Pickering, & Pollack, 2005). Teachers can create mixed groups based on such criteria as ability, interests, gender, or ethnicity.

2. *Jigsaw method:* Jigsaw was designed to provide an opportunity for interdependence and cooperation among students from culturally diverse backgrounds (Aronson, Blaney, Stephan, Sikes, & Snapp, 1978). Each group member becomes an "expert" on one piece of an assignment and teaches the other members so the assignment can be completed collaboratively. Everyone's contribution is important, and each member contributes to the attainment of a common goal (Aronson, 2000; Aronson et al., 1978). For example, fourth-grade students studying the Underground Railroad might be assigned different topics for a cooperative project, such as the lives of slaves, routes that slaves took to freedom, roles of the abolitionists, and the role of Harriet Tubman.

3. *Skills-focused methods:* Students in mixed-ability groups study reading, mathematics, or other academic material and are rewarded based on the achievement of all group members. Examples of several of these methods are shown in Table 19.2.

 Have you participated in group work or cooperative learning? Did you find either of these beneficial? Why or why not?

Effectiveness of Cooperative Learning

Cooperative learning benefits student achievement more than competitive teaching methods, which have students compete for high grades or best scores, and more than individualistic methods, which have students work alone on tasks (Johnson & Johnson, 1998; Johnson, Maruyama, Johnson, Nelson, & Skon, 1981). Also, students in cooperative learning situations (Gillies, 2008; Johnson & Johnson, 1990, 1998):

- spend more time on tasks,

- are willing to take on more difficult tasks,

- show persistence on tasks despite difficulties,

- exhibit positive attitudes,

- demonstrate higher level reasoning, creative thinking, and critical thinking, and

- achieve better long-term retention and transfer of what was learned.

But is cooperative learning beneficial for everyone?

DIVERSITY Cooperative learning tends to benefit low-achieving students most and gifted students least. Low-achieving students from elementary through high school benefit from cooperative learning both academically and socially in subjects such as English, math, science, and social studies (Schachar, 2003). Gifted students, however, do not benefit from cooperative learning activities

TABLE 19.2

Skills-Based Cooperative Methods

COOPERATIVE METHOD	SUBJECT	CHARACTERISTICS
Student Teams–Achievement Division (STAD)	Various	• Four-member teams are heterogeneous in ability, gender, SES, and ethnicity. • Group members study together until all members master the material. • Based on improvement over past quiz scores, each student contributes points to an overall team score. • Individual high scores and team rankings are recognized in a classroom newsletter.
Teams-Games-Tournament (TGT)	Various	• Students earn points for their team by playing in weekly tournaments against members of other teams with similar ability. • Individual winners and highest scoring teams are recognized in a newsletter.
Team-Assisted Individualization (TAI)	Grades 3–6 mathematics	• Four to five-member teams heterogeneous in ability. • Team members complete a series of math units at their own pace, with teammates working in pairs to check each other's worksheets. • Test scores and number of tests completed in a week contribute to a team score. • Certificates are given for improvement over preset team standards of performance.
Peer-Assisted Learning Strategies (PALS)	Beginning reading (K-3)	• Students who need help with specific skills are paired with another student for assistance. • Students are paired as "coaches" (tutors) and "players" but alternate the role of tutor while reading aloud, listening, and providing feedback in structured activities.
Cooperative Integrated Reading and Composition model (CIRC)	Upper elementary reading and writing/ language arts	• Heterogeneous groups are formed by matching pairs of students from one reading level (e.g., above average) with pairs of students from another reading level (e.g., average). • Students in cooperative groups complete independent reading requirements and work on reading assignments and integrated language arts/writing assignments.

SOURCES: DeVries & Edwards, 1974; Slavin, 1978, 1986; Slavin, Lake, Chambers, Cheung, & Davis, 2009; Slavin, Leavey, & Madden, 1984; Slavin, Madden, & Stevens, 1990; Stevens, Madden, Slavin, & Farnish, 1987; Webb, 2008.

involving groups of mixed abilities (Feldhusen & Moon, 1992; Fielder et al., 1993). Rather, gifted students who spend at least part of the school day in homogeneous groups show greater achievement than gifted students who are grouped heterogeneously (Kulik & Kulik, 1987).

Socioeconomic status and ethnicity also are factors to consider when evaluating the effectiveness of cooperative learning. Students living in urban settings, students from low-income families, and minority students show higher achievement as a result of participating in the cooperative learning approaches listed in Table 19.2, such as peer-assisted learning (Rohrbeck, Ginsburg-Block, Fantuzzo, & Miller, 2003; Sáenz, Fuchs, & Fuchs, 2005). Students who are African American, Native American, Mexican American, Puerto Rican, Southeast Asian, or Pacific Islander tend to benefit from cooperative learning activities because these classroom structures more closely match the family values and practices of these groups, emphasizing cooperative rewards and group achievements (Allen & Boykin, 1992; García, 1992; Lomawaima, 2003). Cooperative activities also may be helpful for second-language learners, because these learners have more opportunity to practice language in this context (Smith, 2006).

DIVERSITY

FIGURE 19.1 **Jigsaw Method.** Each group member is responsible for a piece of the assignment.

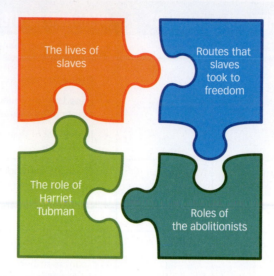

Cooperative learning has many nonacademic benefits as well (Solomon, Watson, & Battistich, 2001):

- More than 80 studies have shown that cooperative learning enhances self-esteem, especially in students with disabilities (Johnson & Johnson, 2009; Smith, Johnson, & Johnson, 1982).

- Cooperative learning encourages greater academic intrinsic motivation (learning driven by curiosity, interest, and a focus on mastery) than competitive or individualistic approaches (Johnson & Johnson, 1985).

- Students who learn math in cooperative groups show decreased math anxiety and greater help-seeking behaviors (Lavasani, Afzali, & Afzali, 2011).

- Because students in cooperative groups must give and receive personal and academic support, cooperative learning promotes peer relationships, enhancing students' empathy, tolerance for differences, feelings of acceptance, and friendships (Johnson & Johnson, 2009; Solomon et al., 2001). It fosters relationships between students with disabilities and nondisabled students and between students from different ethnic groups (Aronson, 2000; Johnson & Johnson, 2009).

Academic intrinsic motivation: See Module 14

Anxiety: See Module 22

DIVERSITY

APPLICATIONS: BEST PRACTICES

4 Describe effective practices for addressing student differences in elementary and secondary education and for implementing cooperative learning.

Video Case 19.3 ▲

Grouping by Level of Student Support

© SAGE Publications

Elementary School: Using Within-Class Ability Grouping Effectively

Although flexible grouping methods may be more effective than within-class ability grouping for reducing heterogeneity among students and increasing student achievement, within-class grouping remains the norm in many elementary schools. The formation of within-class ability groups requires careful consideration—and frequent reassessment—of each student's current achievement level. The following guidelines can help ensure that within-class ability grouping is used appropriately and effectively so that students of all levels benefit.

Adapt instructional methods and materials to meet the needs of students within each group. Ability grouping fails when students, regardless of ability group, receive the same instruction (Lou et al., 1996). For example, elementary school teachers tend to spend equal amounts of time with all reading groups even though the pace of instruction often differs among the low, middle, and high groups, with higher achieving readers moving faster through curricula (Allington, 1983; Barr & Dreeben, 1983). This implies that additional instructional time for students in the lower groups is necessary to close the achievement gap (Allington, 1984).

Keep group size small. Teachers historically have formed three homogeneous groups when implementing within-class grouping: below average, average, and above average. However, today's larger class sizes pose a problem for within-class ability grouping because they lead to larger groups. Larger group size has been found to negatively affect achievement, with students in larger groups learning less than students in smaller groups (Hallinan & Sorensen, 1985). The optimal size for within-class ability groups is three or four members (Lou et al., 1996). And recent trends show teachers moving in this direction by forming more groups with fewer members—an average of four groups per classroom (Chorzempa & Graham, 2006).

Change group placement frequently (Smith & Robinson, 1980). In within-class ability grouping, students know that a hierarchy of groups exists, and most students are aware of their position in the hierarchy even when steps are taken to disguise it (e.g., calling groups "dolphins" and "sharks"; Eder, 1983; Filby & Barnett, 1982). In the early elementary grades, students also are beginning to compare their abilities to those of others. A fixed hierarchy reinforces feelings of inferiority for students in the lower groups. By changing group placement frequently, teachers can counter the negative effects of students' comparing their group placement to that of other students. This may also prevent the **sustaining expectation effect,** which refers to teachers inadvertently keeping low-achieving students' from progressing by holding them in their current group placement. Once groups have been formed, teachers tend to generalize expectations to all members of a group (Amspaugh, 1975). As a result, they sometimes fail to notice a student's improvement in a skill and thus fail to change their expectations for that student. The sustaining expectation effect, along with the self-fulfilling prophecy discussed earlier, may explain why teacher expectations of students' skill level in reading and math in the early elementary grades strongly predict their achievement years later, even into high school (Hinnant, O'Brien, & Ghazarian, 2009; Sorhagen, 2013). However, recent data suggest that teachers tend to change students' reading groups more frequently than in the past, when students remained stuck in the group in which they originally were placed (Chorzempa & Graham, 2006; Rowan & Miracle, 1983).

Industry versus inferiority: See Module 3

Middle School and High School: To Track or Not to Track

Tracking in middle school and high school appears to have mixed effects, with students in higher tracks, advanced placement courses, and gifted programs experiencing greater academic benefits than students in lower tracks. To address the variability of student abilities in middle schools and high schools, educators have attempted at least two options: skill-based sorting and detracking. Let's consider the pros and cons of each.

Skill-based sorting. In recent years, schools have moved to a more flexible tracking method of skill-based sorting. As we discussed earlier in the module, in this approach every

DIVERSITY

student experiences the same curriculum but can choose courses at different levels. For example, all high school students would be required to pass algebra and geometry but students can choose whether they take an advanced level, medium difficulty, or low-level class. Skill-based sorting is consistent with the Common Core State Standards, recently adopted by 42 states, and aimed at increasing the readiness of *all* students for college and career. However, student choice does not eliminate the gap between students with higher and lower achievement levels or the overrepresentation of students from lower socioeconomic and minority backgrounds in the lower tracks (Watanabe, 2007). Students tend to sort themselves in the same way as more formal methods of tracking, and minority students tend not to select higher level classes because they prefer classes in which they are not racially isolated (Watanabe, 2007; Yonezawa, Wells, & Serna, 2002). Keep in mind that the type of instruction students experience would also still vary among the levels.

Therefore, experts have argued that to reduce the educational disparities among students, educators need to improve the quality of instruction in the lower tracks. Researchers have identified several criteria for improving the achievement level of students in lower tracks (Gamoran, 1993, 2010; Gamoran & Weinstein, 1998):

- high expectations for students,

- a rigorous curriculum,

- encouragement of class discussions and other interactive teaching methods, and

- assignment of innovative and experienced teachers to lower track courses.

Tracked middle schools and high schools that were effective in providing high-quality instruction for *all* students emphasized intellectually stimulating content, higher order thinking, and in-depth discussions of material, even in the lower tracks. These successes were due partly to teachers' passion for their subject and a commitment to ensure equity across classes (Gamoran & Weinstein, 1998).

Detracking. Other experts have argued that eliminating tracks altogether, called detracking, is the only way to ensure equity in educational experiences among students. Case studies of schools or school districts have found that effective approaches to detracking involve several key components, such as (Boaler & Staples, 2008; Gamoran & Weinstein, 1998; Gamoran, 2010; Oakes, 2005; Rubin, 2008)

- a shared belief among faculty and administrators;

- training of teachers on differentiated instruction and inclusive practices;

- small classes or learning communities (15 students or less);

- a college-prep curriculum;

- active learning methods, including class discussions and projects; and

- additional support for struggling students, such as supplemental tutoring or double-period instruction.

Results suggest that successful implementation of these elements can lead to improved attendance, increased number of course credits earned, and higher rates of promotion to the next grade (Kemple, Herlihy, & Smith, 2005). One promising approach within detracking is the *double-dose* method. Double-dose means that lower achieving students receive an extra period of instruction each day in a subject such as math or English (Nomi & Allensworth, 2009). This might be implemented as a second "support" course

FIGURE 19.2 **Interpersonal Objectives.** Teachers need to state interpersonal objectives to foster cooperative learning, as shown here in this PowerPoint slide.

For this activity, all group members will need to

- Listen attentively
- State ideas clearly
- Take turns
- Give constructive criticism
- Clarify what others are saying
- Clarify your own understanding

or as a blocked schedule where students get two periods instead of one (Chait, Muller, Goldware, & Housman, 2007; Nomi & Allensworth, 2009; Oakes & Wells, 2002). Use of the double-dose method as a district-wide policy for high school algebra has resulted in more challenging coursework, higher teacher expectations, and improvement in algebra test scores (Nomi & Allensworth, 2009). However, this strategy may not be effective for students with the lowest skills, such as those who receive special education services (Nomi & Allensworth, 2009).

Educators also should be aware that there may be some disadvantages of detracking in urban schools. Research generally has found negative effects of detracking for high-achieving minority students (Gamoran & Weinstein, 1998; Rosenbaum, 1999; Rubin, 2008). Detracking may be difficult to implement successfully in urban schools because low-achieving students greatly outnumber high-achieving students, making mixed ability classes less challenging. High achieving students also may not have adequate academic support outside of school (Gamoran, 2010).

Using Cooperative Learning Effectively

In general, cooperative learning is misused when tasks given to groups are not well structured or when teachers group students out of convenience without ensuring that all elements of cooperative learning have been met (Gillies, 2003; Marzano et al., 2005). Students will not benefit from a cooperative activity if they are not given specific guidance about the objectives of the lesson and about the expectations for individual contributions and the end product. Also, cooperative learning can be overused when students spend most of their instructional time in groups, with little time to independently work on and demonstrate their new knowledge and skills (Marzano et al., 2005). Research on cooperative learning has yielded several guidelines that teachers can use to help them effectively implement this approach (Johnson & Johnson, 1986).

Preparing students for a cooperative activity. When preparing students for a cooperative task, specify the academic and interpersonal objectives for the lesson so students are aware of the goals of the task. Teachers often fail to inform students of the collaborative skills needed to work successfully in their groups. They may also incorrectly assume that students have the requisite social skills for effectively working with peers (Ladd et al., 2013). Teachers also need to clearly explain positive interdependence to students so they understand that they must work together to achieve success. Teachers can also help groups function effectively during a cooperative activity by:

> **DIVERSITY**

> **DIVERSITY**

Differentiated instruction and culturally responsive pedagogy: See Module 18

Video Case 19.4 ▲
Grouping Practices

© SAGE Publications

- teaching collaborative skills, such as how to ask for and offer help and how to manage conflict among group members,

- monitoring student behavior, and

- providing assistance to groups (e.g., answering questions and clarifying instructions).

Forming cooperative groups. Forming groups of mixed abilities is not a critical element of cooperative learning (Mills & Durden, 1992). However, cooperative groups should be heterogeneous in general. Heterogeneous grouping can be based on a variety of criteria, such as ability, interests, motivation, or even random assignment (Johnson & Johnson, 1986; Marzano et al., 2005). Also, groups of three or four tend to work best—such groups are small enough to ensure that each student actively participates (Lou et al., 1996). However, when students have little experience with cooperative learning or when the teacher has limited time or materials, groups of two or three should be formed (Bertucci, Conte, Johnson, & Johnson, 2010; Johnson & Johnson, 1986).

Teachers need to pay careful attention to the gender composition of groups. Balancing the number of girls and boys in a group provides the best opportunity for equal participation (Webb, 1985). When girls outnumber boys, they tend to defer to the boys for input; when boys outnumber girls, they tend to ignore the girls (Webb, 1984, 1985, 1991).

Integration of students with disabilities into cooperative groups also requires careful consideration. Cooperative learning may not be useful for students with disabilities when

FIGURE 19.3 **Surveying Group Processing.** Teachers can give students surveys like this one to help cooperative group members reflect on the functioning of their group.

Each of the statements below will ask you how the group worked. Next to each statement is a number. Circle your answer.

Circle number 1 if this almost never happened.
Circle number 2 if this seldom happened.
Circle number 3 if this sometimes happened.
Circle number 4 if this often happened.
Circle number 5 if this almost always happened.

1. All group members felt free to talk.	1	2	3	4	5
2. People listened to one another.	1	2	3	4	5
3. Group members were asked to explain their ideas.	1	2	3	4	5
4. Some members tried to boss others.	1	2	3	4	5
5. Group members tried to help others.	1	2	3	4	5
6. Everyone had a say in the decisions that were made.	1	2	3	4	5
7. The members worked well as a group.	1	2	3	4	5
8. Each member had a job to do.	1	2	3	4	5
9. I felt good about being in this group.	1	2	3	4	5

SOURCE: Adapted from R. M. Gillies (2007). *Cooperative learning: Integrating theory and practice.* Los Angeles, CA: Sage Publications.

they are learning new or challenging concepts (Kirk, Gallagher, Anastasiow, & Coleman, 2006), so it should be used only when it is appropriate for the instructional objectives. When implementing cooperative learning to include students with disabilities, the most common concerns teachers encounter are (Johnson & Johnson, 1986):

> DIVERSITY

- feelings of fear or anxiety on the part of students with disabilities,

- nondisabled students' apprehension about their grades, and

- ways to encourage active participation by the students with disabilities.

You can address these concerns by adapting lessons so that students of all ability levels can participate successfully in the cooperative group. To adapt a lesson, use different criteria for success for each group member, or vary the amount of material each member is expected to master. This approach should alleviate the concerns of the nondisabled students as well as the anxieties of the students with disabilities. Also, to lessen the anxiety of students with disabilities, explain the procedures that the group will follow and give these students specific roles or sources of expertise that the group will need, thereby encouraging their active participation (Johnson & Johnson, 1986).

Providing time for group processing. When students evaluate the functioning of their group and plan for improvements, they are less likely to believe that speed and finishing early are more important than meaningful learning (McCaslin & Good, 1996). At the end of an activity, teachers can give students a survey, such as the one in Figure 19.3, to help them identify what was helpful and not helpful. Teachers then can use this information to make decisions about what to change for the next task or what changes to make in group placements.

In sum, remember that both ability grouping and cooperative learning are vulnerable to inappropriate use (Clark, 1990; Robinson, 1990; Slavin, 1990). Whether a grouping strategy is effective depends on the appropriateness of the content and the instruction (Mills & Durden, 1992).

Imagine that you are being interviewed by a school principal for a teaching position. Based on the grade level you intend to teach, provide a statement of your philosophy about ability grouping and cooperative learning.

SUMMARY

❶ Discuss the pros and cons of within-class and between-class ability grouping. In both within- and between-class ability grouping, high achievers and gifted students benefit academically more than students in lower groups, and students from impoverished backgrounds and minority students are disproportionately placed into lower groups. Tracking leads to beneficial nonacademic outcomes, such as greater engagement in school, better grades, and positive attitudes toward academic subjects. Within-class ability grouping tends not to affect self-esteem, but tracking yields a small self-esteem benefit for lower achieving students.

❷ Discuss the advantages of flexible grouping methods. Cross-grade grouping and nongraded plans tend to have positive effects on achievement, especially for lower achieving

students. Flexible methods are effective because they reduce the heterogeneity of skills among students and allow teachers to tailor instructional materials and paces to meet the needs of students. Flexible plans also result in many positive nonacademic outcomes.

❸ Identify the characteristics of cooperative learning and discuss the effectiveness of this approach. To be truly cooperative, tasks must contain five elements: (1) positive interdependence, (2) individual and group accountability, (3) interpersonal skills, (4) face-to-face interaction, and (5) group processing. Cooperative learning benefits students academically more than competitive and individualistic approaches. Girls and minorities tend to benefit more from cooperative learning, while gifted students do not benefit. Cooperative learning also enhances self-esteem, motivation, and peer relationships among students from diverse backgrounds and students with and without disabilities.

④ **Describe effective practices for addressing student differences in elementary and secondary education and for implementing cooperative learning.** For within-class ability grouping to be effective, teachers should adapt instruction to meet the needs of students in each group, use many small groups, and change group placement frequently. To meet the needs of middle school and high school students of all ability levels, schools need to eliminate the remedial focus in the lower tracks and emphasize high expectations and higher level thinking skills for all students. For effective cooperative learning at any grade level, teachers should specify objectives for interpersonal skills, emphasize positive interdependence, form heterogeneous groups, use small groups, and facilitate group functioning. Teachers also must carefully consider several factors when integrating students with disabilities into cooperative groups.

KEY CONCEPTS

ability grouping, 384

between-class ability grouping, 387

cooperative learning, 385

cross-grade grouping, 389

face-to-face interaction, 391

group processing, 391

group work, 390

heterogeneity, 384

homogeneity, 384

individual and group accountability, 391

interpersonal skills, 391

Joplin plan, 390

Matthew effect, 387

multiage classrooms, 390

multigrade classes, 390

nongraded plans, 389

positive interdependence, 391

regrouping, 389

sustaining expectation effect, 395

within-class ability grouping, 386

CASE STUDIES: REFLECT AND EVALUATE

EARLY CHILDHOOD: COUNTING POCKETS

These questions refer to the case study on page 336.

1. Within-class ability grouping typically is used in elementary school for reading and math. Is there any reason to form homogeneous groups in preschool? Why or why not?

2. Assume that you are in favor of ability grouping. On what criteria would you group preschool students (ability, prior knowledge, age, etc.) and for what types of lessons?

3. Review the guidelines for effective use of within-class ability grouping in the section, "Elementary School: Using Within-Class Ability Grouping Effectively." Explain why these guidelines would be easier to implement in a preschool classroom than in an elementary school classroom.

4. What are the benefits of using cooperative learning, especially in a class as diverse as Ms. Abby's?

5. Keeping in mind the developmental level of the children, what specific things would you need to do to implement the five elements of cooperative learning discussed in the module? Be sure to give specific examples of how you would implement each of the five elements, and address any challenges you would expect with this age group.

ELEMENTARY SCHOOL: THE MACHINE HUNT

These questions refer to the case study on page 338.

1. Mr. Finnegan's class is a split-grade, or multigrade class. Explain how this differs from a multiage class.

2. Why might within-class ability grouping for reading or math be beneficial for the students in Mr. Finnegan's class?

3. What flexible grouping methods may work for the advanced math students in Mr. Finnegan's class?

4. In a diverse class such as Mr. Finnegan's, lower achievers who are grouped by ability may experience a *self-fulfilling prophecy* and *sustaining expectation effect*. Identify some ways that Mr. Finnegan can prevent these from occurring.

5. Based on the five characteristics of cooperative learning, explain why the group discussion after the simple machines hunt through the school was *not* cooperative learning.

6. Use the guidelines for implementing cooperative learning effectively and evaluate Mr. Finnegan's use of the simple machines project involving creating a game or toy.

MIDDLE SCHOOL: SARCOPHAGUS STUDIES

These questions refer to the case study on page 340.

1. Riverbend Middle School uses tracking. Discuss the advantages and disadvantages of tracking for these students. Why might students' gender, socioeconomic status, and ethnicity be important factors to consider when evaluating the effectiveness of tracking?

2. Based on the guidelines regarding detracking in the Applications section, provide some suggestions to Mrs. DeSantis for ensuring that her lower level classes experience high-quality instruction even within the tracked system.

3. Evaluate the sarcophagus project using the five characteristics of cooperative learning. What suggestions for improvement do you have for Mrs. DeSantis?

4. Explain to Mrs. DeSantis why group processing is important.

5. Explain why balancing the number of girls and boys is important for Mrs. DeSantis to consider when forming groups for the project.

6. What modifications might Mrs. DeSantis need to make to the group project for a student with a disability?

7. The school board is discussing whether to detrack Riverbend Middle School. Provide a convincing argument for detracking. Create an original plan for meeting the needs of both higher achievers and lower achievers within a detracked curriculum.

HIGH SCHOOL: TEACHER'S LOUNGE

These questions refer to the case study on page 342.

1. Assume that Dehlia is Latina. Based on the research on tracking, explain why it would not be surprising to find students from minority groups in a lower level English class.

2. Imagine that you are giving Mr. Webster teaching advice. Describe how you would use cooperative learning to teach grammar in his third-period class. Be sure to give specific examples of how you would implement (a) positive interdependence, (b) individual and group accountability, (c) face-to-face interaction, (d) interpersonal skills, and (e) group processing.

3. Mr. Webster wants to introduce literature in his third-period English class. Explain how he could use the jigsaw approach.

4. Explain to Mr. Webster the benefits of cooperative learning compared to his typical instructional approach, particularly for students like those in his third-period class.

5. Explain why allowing high school students, regardless of prior achievement or ability, to choose the difficulty levels of classes will not solve many of the problems inherent in tracking.

6. You are at a faculty meeting at Concourse High School to discuss detracking. State a convincing case for detracking, and describe a new curriculum that would address the needs of students in higher tracks as well as students in the lower tracks.

UNIT SEVEN

LEARNER DIFFERENCES

EARLY CHILDHOOD: LETTER *P* DAY

PREPARE:

As you read the case, make notes:

1. WHO are the primary participants in the case? Describe them.
2. WHAT is taking place?
3. WHERE is the case taking place? Is the environment a factor?
4. WHEN is the case taking place? Is the timing a factor?

It is Monday morning, and the children in Mrs. Anita Cahill's kindergarten class are eagerly waiting to hear what centers they will be assigned for today's language arts lesson. Mrs. Cahill, who also has taught preschool and first grade, is a veteran kindergarten teacher who was chosen to be the school's first teacher for the new full-day kindergarten this year.

Mrs. Cahill has an interesting way of teaching literacy skills. Each Monday, children are introduced to a new letter of the alphabet. Language arts begins with children sitting on a carpet in the reading corner, listening attentively to Mrs. Cahill reading a nursery rhyme or tongue twister featuring the letter of the week. Today she is reading "Peter Piper" to introduce the letter *P* and its sound.

When she has finished reading, Mrs. Cahill announces, "Boys and girls, I have put name cards at each center. Find your name. That is the center you will be working at this morning. Craig, Adriana, and Marcie, you look like you're ready to begin. You may get up and look for your names."

Mrs. Cahill continues calling children. Joanna Gallagher, a parent volunteer, is helping the children find their center and get started.

Mrs. Cahill has set up four learning centers—publishing, art, building, and science—each with different activities. The children are able to choose which activity they want to do.

- At the "publishing" center, Miguel, Darnell, and Pat are drawing pictures of words that begin with *P* and writing the words, and Craig is looking through the book *Hop on Pop*, by Dr. Seuss, to find words that contain the letter *P*. Jillian has started writing a "story" in her daily journal, using her favorite words that begin with *P*.

- At the "art" center, children can make the shape of the letter *P* using art supplies. Sam, Tonya, and Marcie are gluing cotton balls onto paper to form a puffy *P*, and Teran and Nicholas are gluing pieces of pink tissue paper to form a pink *P*.

- At the "building" center, Tomás, Adriana, Peter, and Emily are constructing letter *P* shapes with blocks.
- At the "science" center, Daniel, Ryan, Cassie, and Marcus are busy cutting out pictures of objects and classifying them into foods that begin with *P* and animals that begin with *P*.

Mrs. Cahill rotates the children through the centers so that each week they have a different experience rather than picking their favorites each time. She overhears some interesting conversations as she makes her way around the tables.

"I'm glad it was my turn at publishing," Pat says excitedly. "Drawing is my favorite." Pat would rather color, cut and paste, and build than do many other activities and is able to draw very realistic and colorful figures.

"Well, I love to write stories," replies Jillian. She typically spends more time than any other student creating detailed responses to journal prompts in her daily journal. Jillian can already write in complete, but short, sentences.

"How's my puffy *P*?" Marcie asks at the art center.

"My favorite color is purple," Nicholas adds, as he presses sticky pink tissue to his paper.

Teran, who is very quiet, almost seems to ignore Marcie and Nicholas as she glues pink tissues with the help of Mrs. Cahill. Her language and fine motor skills are delayed, and she needs extra time to understand and complete most academic tasks.

Children at the building center are working diligently on their projects, except for Peter. Mrs. Cahill has noticed, as is typical of Peter, that he has gotten up from the center twice during the activity and now is making towers of blocks and loudly knocking them down. She redirects him and heads over to the reading corner, where Nolan is looking at books. Mrs. Cahill gently taps his shoulder, whispering, "Shouldn't you be making the letter *P*?"

"Mrs. C," replies Nolan, "I already know *P* and all my letters. This is boring. I want to learn to read."

"You'll get to reading soon enough," says Mrs. Cahill, smiling reassuringly.

Mrs. Cahill makes her way around to the centers, recalling a parent–teacher conference she recently had with Nolan's mother. His mother reports that when Nolan discovers a new topic of interest, he will spend weeks learning all he can about it by having his parents read books to him, watching educational programs, and going on "field trips" with them. He also likes to spend hours on puzzles and on classifying and counting his dinosaur collection. He is an only child, and his mom, who does not work outside the home, spends a great deal of one-on-one time with him. Although she is an experienced teacher, Mrs. Cahill is unsure how to accommodate the varied skill levels of the children, especially the many students who are still adjusting to the routine of full-day kindergarten.

ASSESS:

1. What are the benefits of Mrs. Cahill's approach to language arts? What are the disadvantages? Would you do anything differently?
2. What should Mrs. Cahill do regarding Nolan's academic needs?
3. How typical is Teran of most young children you know? Should Mrs. Cahill give Teran any special assistance or make special accommodations? Why or why not?
4. Did Mrs. Cahill handle Peter's behavior appropriately? Why or why not?

CASE STUDIES

Elementary School:
Cheetahs, Lions, and Leopards

PREPARE:

As you read the case, make notes:

1. WHO are the primary participants in the case? Describe them.
2. WHAT is taking place?
3. WHERE is the case taking place? Is the environment a factor?
4. WHEN is the case taking place? Is the timing a factor?

It is 9 a.m. on a cold Tuesday morning in February at Glendale Elementary School. Mrs. Diana Fratelli calls a group of her third graders to a corner of the classroom to do oral reading. "Cheetahs, get your books and come to the reading circle," calls Mrs. Fratelli. "The rest of you can work quietly at your tables on the phonics worksheets in your folders until it's time for your group."

Mrs. Fratelli has been teaching at Glendale Elementary for the past 18 years. Glendale is one of nine elementary schools in a large metropolitan city and serves a diverse population of students. Mrs. Fratelli has a class of 24 students this year, a bit larger than usual. She uses whole-class instruction for most subjects. However, to manage the diverse levels of reading skill among the students, she has assigned them to one of four reading groups:

- Cheetahs, reading at the fourth-grade level;
- Lions, reading at the end-of-third-grade level;
- Tigers, reading at the beginning-of-third-grade level; and
- Leopards, reading at the end-of-second-grade level or below.

As Mrs. Fratelli is reading with the Cheetah group, most of the other children are busy completing their seat work.

Travis is in a dimly lit corner of the classroom working with the help of his aide, Mrs. Cormier. Travis has autism spectrum disorder and is very sensitive to the bright lights of the classroom and the noise of the traffic on the busy street below. Most of his classmates have gotten so used to Travis's behavior—rocking back and forth in his chair and muttering certain expressions—that it hardly distracts them at all.

By now, Denise has finished her worksheets and leans over to whisper to Marcela. "I wish I could be in the Cheetah group and read chapter books like they are. Their stories are so interesting," Denise whispers. "Not like our books. I could do it if Mrs. Fratelli would give me a chance. I just don't read as good when I have to do it in front of the other kids. I get all nervous and make lots of mistakes. Sometimes I feel like my heart is going to jump out of my chest!"

"At least you're not in the 'dummy' reading group," replies Marcela.

Marcela is in the Leopard group, which is below grade level in reading skill. She struggles with reading fluency. She has difficulty sounding out words and needs some extra help with phonics. Marcela's family immigrated to the United States from Peru when she was 3 years old because her father had landed a prestigious engineering position. Marcela's parents speak only Spanish at home, but she quickly picked up English at her new preschool. Despite her struggle with reading, Marcela is a bright student with a natural curiosity about the world, especially science.

Carl, who is sitting between Denise and Marcela, whispers, "Shhhhh! You two are gonna get our table in trouble!"

Carl is not at all concerned that he is in the Leopard reading group because he likes that the work is easy for him. He finishes his work quickly so he can spend time doodling detailed futuristic sketches of robots, spaceships, and spacemen. Mrs. Fratelli considers him to be very careless in his schoolwork. To encourage his creativity, though, she often sends home pencils and paper for Carl's artwork. Carl's family is struggling financially because his father lost his job when a large factory in town closed. Carl receives free lunch and has few school supplies.

After all reading groups have had a turn in the reading circle, Mrs. Fratelli collects the worksheets and announces that it's time for science.

"Boys and girls, we are starting a new science unit today on solids, liquids, and gases," says Mrs. Fratelli. "Our first experiment is to test which materials dissolve in water and which don't. Each of you has a cup with water and a plastic spoon. On each table there are several materials for you to share."

Mrs. Fratelli passes out small plastic containers of sand, flour, lemon juice, vegetable oil, and sugar. She explains what to do and tells the students to record their results on their worksheets so they can discuss their findings when everyone is done. As students begin the activity, chatter spreads through the classroom.

"I want to try the lemon juice," exclaims Marcela.

"I want the sand," Denise states.

"I like it when we do experiments," Carl adds. "It's more fun than worksheets!"

ASSESS:

1. Based on this case, what are areas of strength for Denise, Marcela, and Carl? How do you think Mrs. Fratelli would rate their capabilities?

2. Which students, if any, do you think could be considered gifted? Why?

3. What characteristics would you look for in third-grade students when trying to identify those with a specific reading or math disability?

4. Should Mrs. Fratelli include Travis in the science experiment with the other children? Why or why not?

EARLY CHILDHOOD

ELEMENTARY SCHOOL

MIDDLE SCHOOL

HIGH SCHOOL

MIDDLE SCHOOL: MATH TROUBLES

It is first period at Chesterfield Middle School, and Miss Elizabeth Barton is teaching the order of operations in seventh-grade prealgebra. Miss Barton has a diverse class in many respects, especially with regard to ability.

Erik Isakson/Getty Images

Lindsey struggles with math. She repeated first grade because of difficulties in both reading and math. Even though Lindsey was able to improve her skills with extensive private tutoring and does well in most subjects, she still is easily frustrated and often will not participate in math class. In other situations, Lindsey is very outgoing. She takes on leadership roles in group projects, designs sets for school plays, and is the seventh-grade vice president.

Sam, on the other hand, loves math and is very good at it. In math class, Sam is easily distracted, likes to finish work quickly to talk with friends, and seems to be a step ahead of the other students. When Miss Barton is reviewing problems with the class, Sam will ask about Problem 6 while Miss Barton and the class are on Problem 3. This behavior often annoys Miss Barton and breaks the other students' concentration.

Today Miss Barton has assigned students to work on practice problems in groups of four and has begun moving around the room to monitor their progress.

"Did everyone try the first problem on the page?" Miss Barton asks as she approaches the first group.

Derek and Emma already have the question correctly done, while Lindsey and Jessica are still working. Miss Barton notices that the students seem to be working independently and are not helping each other. She had hoped that group work would help Lindsey with her math skills.

"Do you two have the answer yet?" Miss Barton asks. Lindsey doesn't reply.

"Let me see what you've got there, Lindsey. That's actually incorrect; you needed to multiply before you added those two numbers. Do you understand?"

"Yes," Lindsey nods.

"Let's all try the next problem," says Miss Barton. "It follows exactly like the first."

Emma and Derek finish it quickly. Jessica takes a bit longer. She has always struggled academically in most subjects and is a bit slower at mastery of concepts than her peers. And, again, Lindsey is the last one done. Everyone got the correct answer except Lindsey. While Miss Barton tries to explain the problem to Lindsey, she notices Sam fooling around.

Miss Barton approaches Sam. "Has your group finished *all* the problems already, Sam?" she asks incredulously.

"No, but I'm already finished," Sam quickly responds.

"But you know you should be working with your group members," says Miss Barton. "Yeah, but working with them is boring," Sam responds.

A bit exasperated, Miss Barton keeps Sam busy by assigning some extra math problems and begins circulating around to the groups again. She returns to Lindsey's group and notices that Lindsey and Jessica are talking and not concentrating on the problems. Miss Barton gently redirects them: "Lindsey and Emma, are you talking about math? Please get back to the problems."

"Why should I?" Lindsey mutters to herself as she begins doodling. "I'm sure I'll get the answers wrong anyway," she sighs.

Later in the teacher's lounge, Miss Barton shares her experience with Dexter Sharp, who teaches the eighth-grade algebra classes. "I feel like I'm losing some of these kids," she says. "I have a few students who struggle with the concepts and others who don't. And I have one student who is completely bored and not challenged by the work we are doing. I need to find a way to keep everyone engaged."

Mr. Sharp pauses to think for a minute before he replies. "Last semester I created a word problem contest," he explains. "If students finished their work and had a little time to spare, they could develop a word problem and the answer using our math concepts from that week and submit it in the problem box on my desk. They could also create problems at home to submit. The rules of the contest required that students write out the problem and the correct solution. Every other Friday I created a review sheet with the problems they had submitted, excluding the answers, and let the students vote on the best problem."

ASSESS:

1. In your opinion, is finishing one's work quickly a sign of being "smart"?

2. Should Miss Barton give Sam more challenging work or treat Sam differently from the rest of the class? Why or why not?

4. In your opinion, what are Miss Barton's expectations of Lindsey?

5. Should Miss Barton give Jessica any special attention academically?

EARLY CHILDHOOD

ELEMENTARY SCHOOL

MIDDLE SCHOOL

HIGH SCHOOL

HIGH SCHOOL: NOON SUPERVISED STUDY

Mr. Beau Hardy is starting his second year at Shreveport High School, where he teaches ninth-grade U.S. history. Students typically enjoy Mr. Hardy's classes because he is an enthusiastic and charismatic lecturer. From time to time, he has been known to begin class by reenacting a famous event dressed as an important historical figure. Students in his classes take notes on the lectures and have an exam on each unit.

The bell rings for fourth period. Mr. Hardy begins by collecting homework. Noticing that Jason has not turned in his homework, he asks, "Jason, why didn't you turn in homework today?"

Roy Mehta/Iconica/Getty Images

"I don't know, Mr. Hardy. Guess I forgot about it," Jason responds.

"You know that you'll need to attend Noon Supervised Study today," says Mr. Hardy.

Jason replies, "But I'm already in there for two other classes from yesterday!"

"Jason," Mr. Hardy explains, "you're just going to have to start doing your work at home then. It's critical for you to have your assignments done in time before each class period. How can I be sure that everyone is reading and understanding the material if I don't check homework?"

"But Mr. Hardy, you know I understand it!" Jason argues.

Mr. Hardy gives Jason a slip for Noon Supervised Study, called NSS for short. As Jason leaves the room, Mr. Hardy is disturbed at the many times he has sent Jason to NSS. Jason is an active and energetic participant in class. Although he takes few notes, he enjoys analyzing historical events and discussing alternative routes that history could have taken.

Later at NSS, Jason sits for 40 minutes attempting to finish his homework assignments. He has one from Mr. Hardy, two from his English teacher, and one more from his health teacher. All of them are past due, and he's not sure where to start or even what the instructions were. He realizes he cannot possibly get all the assignments done in 40 minutes, so he starts his health assignment that was due three days ago. He looks around and notices that Tommy, Gabe, Anthony, and Sarah are all back in NSS with him. After NSS is over, the students head to lunch.

Throughout the day, Mr. Hardy can't stop thinking about Jason, Anthony, and Sarah—all U.S. history students from fourth period whom he has sent to NSS several times for not completing their work. At the end of the day, perplexed by this situation, he decides to look through their academic records for answers.

According to Jason's records, he excelled all through elementary school, but his school performance began to decline in fifth and sixth grades. Mr. Hardy wonders why. Anthony, an African American student, was identified as eligible for special education in third grade for a reading disability. Mr. Hardy is aware that Anthony received extended time for tests but had no idea about the extent of his disability. Anthony's disability has not hampered his social prowess. He has many friends and is captain of the freshman football team and vice president of the freshman class.

Mr. Hardy is not surprised to find that Sarah, who gets As on quizzes and tests despite not doing her homework, skipped first grade and was in a gifted and talented program for mathematics in Grades 3 through 6. Her record states that, on transferring to Shreveport High, Sarah chose a lower level track for math and science, which meant that all other subjects also needed to be on a basic level to fit into her schedule. Mr. Hardy wonders why she chose that track.

ASSESS:

1. Which students in your own high school did you consider to be "smart"? What characteristics made them smart?

2. Why do you think Jason and Sarah don't do homework?

3. What types of learning accommodations do you think high school teachers need to make for students with disabilities?

4. What types of emotional, social, and behavioral problems do you think high school teachers face with their students?

©iStockphoto.com/ shulz

MODULE **20**

INTELLIGENCE AND GIFTEDNESS

OUTLINE	LEARNING GOALS

Intelligence and Giftedness: More Than "Being Smart"

- Theories of Intelligence
- Theories of Giftedness

❶ Explain how intelligence and giftedness are more than just high cognitive ability.

Assessing Intelligence and Giftedness

- Intelligence Measured as IQ
- Interpreting IQ Scores
- Assessing Giftedness

❷ Describe what IQ tests measure and indicate the concerns with using IQ scores to identify giftedness.

Biological, Social, and Cultural Issues

- Heredity or Environment?
- Socioeconomic and Cultural Factors

❸ Describe how environment, socioeconomic status, and gender influence IQ.

Applications: Intelligence and Giftedness in the Classroom

- Teaching for Multiple Intelligences
- Teaching for Successful Intelligence
- Teaching Students Who Are Gifted

❹ Explain how theories of intelligence and giftedness can be used to enhance the learning of all students regardless of their ability level.

INTELLIGENCE AND GIFTEDNESS: MORE THAN "BEING SMART"

❶ Explain how intelligence and giftedness are more than just high cognitive ability.

What do you think of when you hear the words *intelligent* and *gifted?* You probably think they refer to being "smart" and scoring very high on an IQ test or similar test of cognitive ability.

However, as you will see in this module, intelligence and giftedness are much more than exceptional cognitive ability.

Almost all psychologists agree that intelligence involves adaptation to the environment (Sternberg, 2014). Psychologists throughout the past century have emphasized the importance of cognitive skills in adaptation: abstract reasoning, representation, problem solving, decision making, and speed of processing (Hogan, 2015; Sternberg, Conway, Ketron, & Bernstein, 1981). However, the skills that are considered adaptive vary across cultures. For example, in African cultures, such as Kenya and Zimbabwe, facilitating and maintaining social relationships is an important aspect of intelligence (Greenfield, 1997; Sternberg & Kaufman, 1998). In Asian cultures, such as Cambodia, Vietnam, and the Philippines, motivation, social skills, and practical skills are just as important as cognitive skills in defining intelligence (Okagaki & Sternberg, 1993; Sternberg, 2004). Even within the United States, there are different views of intelligence among cultural groups (Sternberg, 2007). Asian and Anglo individuals emphasize the importance of cognitive skills, in contrast with the emphasis on social-competence skills in Latino cultures (Okagaki & Sternberg, 1993).

When we think of giftedness, we typically think of someone who is extremely smart and performs at an exceptional level in school and on standardized tests. A person may be "smart" in this way but not gifted because giftedness, like intelligence, involves much more than just high cognitive ability. Giftedness can be thought of as an exceptional ability to reason and learn in an academic subject, such as language, science, or mathematics, or extraordinary skills in nonacademic domains, such as art, athletics, dance, and music. Giftedness may also be represented as a high level of competence in social skills and leadership. Therefore, like intelligence, the definition of giftedness varies according to what individuals within and across cultures value. To understand intelligence and giftedness and how to identify these traits in school-age children, let's begin by exploring theories of each.

How do you define intelligence and giftedness? As you read the next section, compare your views with the theories.

Theories of Intelligence

Modern theorists have debated about the definition of intelligence for more than a hundred years—and the debate continues. The debate over whether intelligence is a single trait or many abilities originated with a theory of intelligence advanced by Charles Spearman. Spearman (1904, 1927), after examining the relationship among many cognitive tests, proposed the **two-factor theory of intelligence** shown in Figure 20.1. The two factors are:

- g, which is our overall ability to perform on a variety of cognitive tasks, and
- s, which refers to specific skills, such as vocabulary and mathematical skills.

Other 20th-century theorists proposed that intelligence consists of multiple factors. One theorist identified seven factors in intelligence, called primary mental abilities (Thurstone, 1938, 1947). Another proposed 120 distinct abilities but later revised that number to 180 (Guilford, 1956, 1988). Several other theorists have proposed hierarchical theories of intelligence—a compromise between one intelligence, g, and many intelligences. In one of the most influential hierarchical theories, g is the overall ability and encompasses two secondary abilities (Cattell, 1963; Horn, 1994):

- *general crystallized intelligence* (Gc), our overall knowledge base resulting from formal and informal education (think of it as an individual's pool of knowledge or facts), and
- *general fluid intelligence* (Gf), or abilities that allow us to reason, think, and learn new things (think of it as an individual's potential for learning).

> **DIVERSITY**

Video: Theory of Successful Intelligence

FIGURE 20.1 **Spearman's Two-factor Theory of Intelligence.** Intelligence comprises general ability as well as specific skills.

While some contemporary theories still focus on g (e.g., Carroll, 1993; Gustafsson, 1994; Horn, 1994), psychologists Howard Gardner and Robert Sternberg argue that g becomes less important if we define intelligence using a broad range of abilities rather than a limited set of academic-related tasks (Sternberg, 2003). They have proposed multidimensional theories of intelligence that are distinct yet complementary.

GARDNER'S THEORY OF MULTIPLE INTELLIGENCES

In his **theory of multiple intelligences** (MI theory), Gardner (1983, 1999) proposes that we have eight intelligences:

1. *Linguistic* (using words to describe or communicate ideas).

2. *Logical-Mathematical* (reasoning, perceiving patterns in numbers, using numbers effectively).

3. *Spatial* (accurately perceiving and transforming the visual-spatial world).

4. *Bodily-Kinesthetic* (having expertise in using one's body).

5. *Musical* (recognizing components of music, expressing musical forms, using music to express ideas).

6. *Interpersonal* (accurately perceiving and appropriately responding to the emotions of other people).

7. *Intrapersonal* (being introspective, discriminating one's emotions and perceptions, knowing one's strengths and limitations).

8. *Naturalistic* (recognizing and classifying living things, having a sensitivity to features of the natural world).

The intelligences are independent of one another, but they interact—or work together—in activities (Gardner & Moran, 2006). For example, playing basketball involves bodily-kinesthetic and spatial intelligences, while ballet dancing incorporates bodily-kinesthetic, spatial, and musical intelligences. Linguistic and logical-mathematical intelligences typically are assessed on IQ tests, but the other intelligences are not.

Think about your own abilities. How would you describe yourself in terms of multiple intelligences? Your answer—whether it be musical, bodily-kinesthetic, or some combination of intelligences—likely comes from a variety of sources:

- activities in which you excel,

- past experiences and successes, and

- interests or preferences.

Just as you determined your intelligences based on these external sources, Gardner (1993) believed that multiple intelligences exist in the context of a person's interaction with objects and people in the environment, not as abstract entities in the person's mind. For example, we observe intelligence as it is applied every day in *authentic tasks*—that is, tasks that reflect real-life problems, roles, or situations, such as when an elementary school student solving word problems and a high school student designing and conducting a physics experiment show logical-mathematical intelligence.

Gardner's theory has received much attention in K-12 education. Many schools have translated MI theory into practice (see Table 20.1), and some, such as the Key Community School in Indianapolis, have developed an entire curriculum using Gardner's ideas. Keep in mind, though, that while Gardner's theory is very appealing to educators, it lacks empirical

Authentic assessments:
See Module 23

Video Case 20.1 ▲
Learner Profiles

© SAGE Publications

TABLE 20.1	Gardner's Multiple Intelligences	
INTELLIGENCE	**EXAMPLES**	**INSTRUCTIONAL ACTIVITIES**
1. Linguistic	writer, comedian, journalist, editor, professor	Write a poem, short story, or play about . . . Create an interview of . . .
2. Logical-Mathematical	mathematician, scientist, computer programmer	Design and conduct an experiment on . . . Describe the patterns in . . .
3. Spatial	interior decorator, architect, artist	Illustrate, draw, or sketch . . . Create a slide show or piece of art about . . .
4. Bodily-Kinesthetic	actor, athlete, mime, dancer	Build or construct a . . . Use hands-on materials to demonstrate . . .
5. Musical	composer, director, performer, musical technician	Sing a song to explain . . . Indicate rhythmical patterns in . . .
6. Interpersonal	pastor, counselor, teacher, manager, coach	Participate in a service project for . . . Teach someone about . . .
7. Intrapersonal	religious leader, counselor, writer, philosopher	Write a journal entry on . . . Assess your own work in . . .
8. Naturalistic	hunter, farmer, environmentalist	Create observation notebooks of . . . Use observational tools (microscope, binoculars) to explore . . .

SOURCES: Campbell, 1997; Johnson, 2000.

support. To date, there are no published studies reporting evidence for the validity of MI theory (Gardner & Connell, 2000; Sternberg & Grigorenko, 2004; Waterhouse, 2006). Educators should be cautious about implementing any theory that has not been thoroughly tested and is not supported by research evidence.

STERNBERG'S THEORY OF SUCCESSFUL INTELLIGENCE

Like Gardner, Sternberg (1999, 2010a) does not limit intelligence to capabilities that allow individuals to succeed in school. Rather, he considers intelligence to be a person's ability to succeed in life. According to his **theory of successful intelligence,** an individual defines success based on personal goals, which may be focused on career, extracurricular activities, personal interests, or community service. Our sociocultural context also contributes to defining success, because the types of knowledge needed for success—and what is valued as success—differ across cultural contexts. In Usenge, Kenya, for example, children develop expertise in identifying natural herbal medicines to survive in an environment where they are exposed to many parasitic illnesses, just as children in Western cultures engage in formal education because it allows them to be successful within their own cultural context (Sternberg, 1999, 2004).

Sternberg proposes that we all possess analytical, creative, and practical abilities to differing degrees and that individuals who are successfully intelligent find ways to balance the strengths and weaknesses in their abilities (Sternberg, Grigorenko, & Zhang, 2008).

- **Analytical abilities** involve identifying and defining a problem, choosing a strategy for solving the problem, and monitoring the outcome. Analytical skills, typically measured on IQ tests, involve analyzing, evaluating, judging, or comparing and contrasting.

- **Creative abilities** involve generating novel ideas for solving problems. Individuals with creative abilities are risk takers because they often generate ideas that initially are unpopular and must convince others of the value of their ideas. Assessing creative intelligence involves evaluating how well people deal with novelty.

- **Practical abilities** involve applying knowledge to real-life contexts, implementing options and solutions, and making them work. Students who are practical learners are better able to learn information if they can see its relevance to their own lives (Sternberg, 1997).

Successful individuals are able to balance their abilities by effectively adapting to, shaping, and selecting their environment (Sternberg, 2002; Sternberg et al., 2008). An elementary student may decide to read more at home to better his oral reading skills in class (adapting to the environment). A middle school student who is excelling academically may ask the teacher for more challenging work (shaping the environment). An adolescent may decide to attend a high school arts academy because it matches her interests and abilities in music and art (selecting the environment). External factors, such as socioeconomic status, education, and cultural background, affect individual students' opportunities to adapt, shape, and select their environments. For example, students from lower socioeconomic backgrounds may not have access to the same resources (books, newspapers, and magazine subscriptions in the home; rigorous curricula; money for private schools) as students from higher socioeconomic backgrounds, limiting their options. Educators need to remember to evaluate students' success within the context of the opportunities afforded them (Sternberg, 1999).

Traditional methods of instruction and assessment in schools have enabled students with strengths in analytical or memory abilities to be successful, conveying the skewed message that only these abilities are valued in society (Sternberg, 1999; Sternberg et al., 2008). In reality, many people who have been successful in creative or practical domains were in fact mediocre students (Sternberg, 1997). Designer Tommy Hilfiger, actor/producer Henry Winkler, and Charles Schwab, CEO of the largest brokerage firm in the United States, all have achieved great

DIVERSITY <

Creativity: See Module 13

DIVERSITY <

DIVERSITY <

success in life based on their creative or practical abilities, despite struggling in school academically. A narrow focus on analytical skills also tends to overlook students from culturally diverse backgrounds. By including creative and practical abilities in our conception of intelligence, educators can identify more culturally and socioeconomically diverse students as "smart" (Stemler, Grigorenko, Jarvin, & Sternberg, 2006; Stemler, Sternberg, Grigorenko, Jarvin, & Sharpes, 2009; Sternberg, 2010a).

Unlike MI theory, the theory of successful intelligence is supported by a body of research evidence. Sternberg and colleagues developed tests based on successful intelligence to identify gifted students, assess achievement, and help determine college admissions (Chart, Grigorenko, & Sternberg, 2008; Sternberg, 2006, 2010b; Sternberg & Coffin, 2010). Findings generally indicate that performance on these assessments is consistent with the theory of successful intelligence and that the tests better predict success than traditional tests alone. Researchers also studied whether instruction that balances analytical, creative, and practical abilities is more effective than traditional instruction. Students from elementary school through high school who were taught using a balanced approach typically outperformed those taught by conventional methods on tests of factual memory and on performance assessments where students demonstrate their knowledge in authentic formats (Grigorenko, Jarvin, & Sternberg, 2002; Sternberg, Grigorenko, Ferarri, & Clinkenbeard, 1999; Sternberg et al., 2008; Sternberg, Torff, & Grigorenko, 1998a, 1998b).

Performance assessment: See Module 23

Theories of Giftedness

Like intelligence, **giftedness** is multidimensional, as you can see from examining the characteristics of giftedness here. Students who are gifted:

Reference: Giftedness

- master knowledge or skills in a particular domain earlier than their peers (Steiner & Carr, 2003);

- tend to have above-average ability in a particular subject, such as reading, mathematics, science, art, or music, or above-average ability overall (Renzulli, 2002);

- process information more efficiently, learn at a faster pace, use more effective strategies, and monitor their understanding better than peers (Davidson & Davidson, 2004; Housand & Reis, 2008);

- require less direct instruction and support from teachers than peers (Hammond, McBee, & Hébert, 2007; Winner, 1996);

- show flexibility and creativity in the way they apply their knowledge (Ferrando, Ferrandiz, Prieto, Bermejo, & Sainz, 2008).

- possess a high level of interest and intrinsic motivation (Winner, 2000);

- display unusual curiosity, a high level of questioning, and an intense desire to learn (Creel & Karnes, 1988; Gross, 1993);

- seek out challenging tasks and exhibit boredom at tasks they consider too easy (LoCicero & Ashbly, 2000; Parker, 1997); and

- set high personal standards for their performance, sometimes to the point of perfectionism (LoCicero & Ashbly, 2000; Parker, 1997).

Experts agree that giftedness is multidimensional, but they differ in the specific traits or abilities they emphasize to define it. Let's explore the abilities that comprise giftedness in the theories of intelligence we just discussed and in a popular theory of giftedness.

As we have seen, both Gardner and Sternberg view intelligence as multidimensional, comprising several independent but interacting abilities, and therefore giftedness is multidimensional as well. According to MI theory, all individuals have strengths and weaknesses in eight separate intelligences (Gardner, 2006). Individuals who are gifted rapidly move through a domain (math, writing, etc.) because they have certain strengths among their intelligences and have had environmental opportunities to nurture those strengths (Gardner, 1993). According to the theory of successful intelligence, all individuals possess differing degrees of analytical, creative, and practical abilities (Sternberg, 1996). Because individuals differ in their patterns of strengths and weaknesses in these abilities, various patterns of giftedness are possible, depending on whether an individual demonstrates a high level of competence in only one of these abilities or a combination of them (Sternberg, 2000).

Like Sternberg, Joseph Renzulli (2002, 2011) proposes that giftedness is a set of traits that collectively defines the behavior of individuals who are gifted. In Figure 20.2, which shows Renzulli's **three-ring conception of giftedness,** giftedness is represented as the shaded area—the interaction among the three distinct and equally important traits.

Video: Three-Ring
Conception of Giftedness

1. Above-average ability, defined as:

   - general ability, the capacity to process information, synthesize information, or think abstractly; or

   - specific ability, the capacity to acquire knowledge or skill in a specialized domain such as mathematics, poetry, or science.

2. High level of task commitment, or an individual's energy or passion for a particular task, problem, or domain. Higher levels result in behaviors such as perseverance, endurance, hard work, practice, and self-confidence in one's ability to engage in a productive endeavor (Renzulli, 1990).

3. High levels of creativity, the ability to generate many interesting and feasible ideas with respect to a particular problem or domain.

Research on highly talented and productive individuals in their respective fields showed that they display all three of these traits (Renzulli, 2011). Therefore, it is not sufficient to

FIGURE 20.2 **Renzulli's Three-Ring Conception of Giftedness.** Giftedness is the interaction among the three traits, shown as the shaded area in the figure.

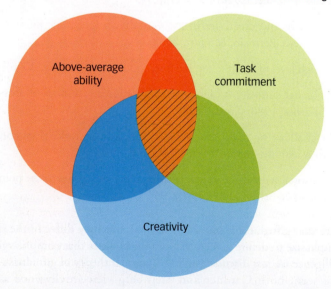

SOURCE: Renzulli, J. S. (1978a). What makes giftedness? Reexamining a definition. *Phi Delta Kappan, 60,* 180–184, 261.

define giftedness solely by high cognitive ability. Yet when identifying students for gifted programs, educators tend to emphasize superior cognitive ability at the expense of the other two traits (Renzulli, 2011). Educators emphasize **schoolhouse giftedness,** which characterizes students who have high overall cognitive ability and school achievement, who excel in a particular domain such as reading or science, or who are very efficient at processing information and learning new things. Often, they overlook students who exhibit **creative-productive giftedness,** who enjoy engaging in exploration, creating, and problem solving.

Reflect on the theories of intelligence and giftedness. What similarities do they have? How do they differ?

ASSESSING INTELLIGENCE AND GIFTEDNESS

❷ Describe what IQ tests measure and indicate the concerns with using IQ scores to identify giftedness.

Historically, the primary method of assessing intelligence and giftedness has been an IQ test, which is a set of cognitive tasks that measures general cognitive ability in children and adults. The main purpose of IQ tests is to predict school achievement.

Intelligence Measured as IQ

The Wechsler Intelligence Scale for Children, Fifth Edition (WISC-V; Wechsler, 2014) and the Stanford-Binet Intelligence Scales-V (Roid, 2003) are the most common individually administered IQ tests used in school settings. **Individually administered IQ tests** measure individuals' cognitive abilities with a battery of subtests that require no reading and are administered one-on-one by a trained examiner. As an example, the WISC-V includes 10 subtests to measure five general cognitive abilities: verbal comprehension, working memory, visual-spatial reasoning, fluid reasoning, and processing speed. Table 20.2 provides a description of one subtest from each of these areas. School and clinical psychologists use individually administered tests to predict school achievement for very specific purposes, such as:

- determining eligibility of students for gifted programs, and
- identifying intellectual and learning disabilities.

Intellectual and learning disabilities: See Module 21

Group administered IQ tests contain objective items, such as multiple choice, and are administered in a group setting using a paper-and-pencil format. At one time, schools used group IQ tests as screening tools to help teachers make decisions about instruction and placement of students into ability groups (Cohen, Swerdlik, & Sturman, 2013; Sternberg, 2003). Today, schools use these tests less frequently than they did about 20 years ago (Cohen et al., 2013). Experts recognize that placement decisions should not be based on a single test score.

Objective items: See Module 24

When IQ is used to identify students for special services or programs, individually administered tests are preferred. Because group administered tests are given to large groups of students at once, they have several features that may affect students' scores and lead to a narrow interpretation of students' intellectual functioning. These tests rely on a test taker's understanding of the directions, on reading skills, and on test-taking strategies. Group test taking may cause distractions and increase a student's anxiety. Individually administered IQ tests provide a more accurate picture of a student's cognitive ability because they require no reading and are given one-on-one with a psychologist, who can establish rapport and determine a student's level of anxiety, motivation, and distractibility.

Ability groups: See Module 19

Anxiety: See Module 15

TABLE 20.2   Description of Selected WISC-V Subtests

COGNITIVE AREA	DESCRIPTION OF A WISC-V TASK
Verbal Comprehension	*Vocabulary:* Student gives definitions of words presented by the examiner as a question ("What is a . . . ?").
Visual-Spatial Reasoning	*Block Design:* Student views a picture of a design and must recreate it within a specified time period using red and white blocks.
Fluid Reasoning	*Matrix reasoning:* Student views a grid with a missing piece and selects the item from several choices that best completes the matrix.
Working Memory	*Digit Span:* Examiner says a series of digits (ranging from 2 to a maximum of 9), and the student repeats the digits in the exact order.
Processing Speed	*Symbol Search:* Within a specified time period, student indicates whether a specified target symbol appears in an array of symbols. For example:
	Target: ♠ Array: ⊥ ≤ ▫

Simulated items similar to those in the *Wechsler Intelligence Scale for Children–Fifth Edition.* Copyright © 2014 by NCS Pearson, Inc. Reproduced with permission. All rights reserved.

Interpreting IQ Scores

Norm-Referenced testing: See Module 25

IQ scores reveal a test taker's relative standing on an IQ test as compared with the scores of other, similar individuals on the same test. This is called a **norm-referenced** interpretation—judging how the student performs compared to others in the **norm group** (all other test takers with similar characteristics). Psychologists make a norm-referenced interpretation by converting a test taker's *raw score,* the number of items correctly answered, to a **deviation IQ,** a score that indicates how far above or below the average a student scored on the IQ test compared to same-age individuals. To interpret a student's deviation IQ, we must compare it to the normal (or bell-shaped) curve

Individually Administered IQ Tests. These IQ tests are given one-on-one by a trained examiner.

shown in Figure 20.3. For any group of same-age individuals, most IQ tests set the average score at 100, with a standard deviation (SD) of 15. **Standard deviation** measures how much a score strays from the average.

Standard deviation: See Module 25

By using the SD, we can partition the bell curve to allow norm-referenced interpretations. Figure 20.3 shows the following:

- Approximately 68% of test takers have IQ scores within 1 SD of the average—that is, between 85 and 115. Performance in this range is considered average.

- Approximately 13.5% of individuals have scores between 115 and 130 (i.e., between 1 and 2 SDs above the average). Similarly, about 13.5% of individuals have scores between 70 and 85 (i.e., between 1 and 2 SDs below the average).

- Almost 2.5% of the population has scores more than 2 SDs away from the mean in either direction. IQ scores at these extremes of the distribution help to define intellectual disabilities (formerly called mental retardation) at the low end of the distribution and giftedness at the high end of the distribution, as we discuss later.

Intellectual disabilities: See Module 21

Because IQ tests are used in high-stakes situations in which important educational decisions are made based in part on test scores, educators must be cautious in interpreting students' IQ scores, for several reasons.

- IQ tests represent a finite sample of a person's cognitive skills. They capture certain, but not all, abilities that are part of intelligence.

- Different IQ tests do not measure the same skills. Because IQ tests are developed based on different theories of intelligence, each test uses a slightly different set of subtests rather than a standard set of tasks.

- IQ is a snapshot of a person's ability *at a given point in time*. Children's IQ scores indicate only their performance at the time of the test administration (Jarvin & Sternberg, 2003). Educators should use caution when they make predictions about future academic

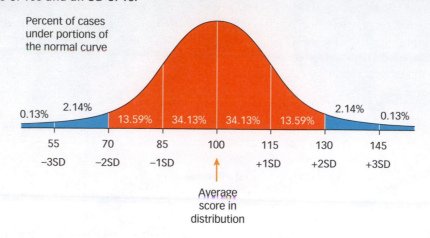

FIGURE 20.3 **Normal Distribution of IQ Scores.** The IQ distribution has an average score of 100 and an SD of 15.

Percent of cases under portions of the normal curve

| 0.13% | 2.14% | 13.59% | 34.13% | 34.13% | 13.59% | 2.14% | 0.13% |

| 55 | 70 | 85 | 100 | 115 | 130 | 145 |
| −3SD | −2SD | −1SD | | +1SD | +2SD | +3SD |

Average score in distribution

performance based on IQ scores. Scores on tests used in early childhood are not very stable from infancy through preschool years (Sternberg, 2002). A person's performance on IQ tests can change over time as a result of formal or informal education (Garlick, 2003; Jarvin & Sternberg, 2003).

Remember that even though individuals can improve their performance as a result of instruction and environmental input, their performance *relative to the norm group* generally does not change drastically over time. Therefore, IQ scores generally are stable from elementary school through adulthood (Beaver et al., 2013; Garlick, 2003).

To ensure *validity*—fairness of the test and accuracy of the results—several precautions also should be taken with culturally and linguistically diverse students. Students must be tested in their native language on an IQ test that has been developed for use with individuals in their culture. If a test is given in English to a student who does not speak the language, the test score will not be a valid assessment of the student's ability. Use of translated tests and interpreters also may compromise the validity of the test score (American Educational Research Association, American Psychological Association, & National Council on Measurement in Education, 2014; Kaplan & Saccuzzo, 2013). There is no guarantee that translated tests are comparable to the original English version or that interpreters will not inadvertently bias the test administration. When interpreting test results, educators need to take into account the student's sociocultural and linguistic background (Donovan & Cross, 2002; Harry & Klingner, 2006). For example, it is important to consider whether a student has had an opportunity to learn the content being tested.

DIVERSITY

Validity in testing: See Module 25

Test bias: See Module 25

Assessing Giftedness

In 1926, Lewis Terman, creator of the Stanford-Binet IQ test, narrowly defined giftedness as an IQ score in the top 1% of the population, and for most of the 20th century many experts equated giftedness with a score on an IQ test. IQ tests remain a primary tool for identifying students as eligible for gifted programs (Gubbins, Callahan, & Renzulli, 2014). As shown in Figure 20.3, students with IQ scores above 132 (top 2% of the population) or above 135 (top 1% of the population) may be eligible for gifted programs. However, guidelines vary from state to state (Coleman, Gallagher, & Job, 2012; Gallagher, 2005). Many states also use standardized achievement tests and state mastery tests and rely on teacher nominations for selecting which students should receive further testing, making test scores a deciding factor (Gubbins et al., 2014).

Using teacher nominations may introduce bias into the selection process based on teacher perceptions of ability (Bianco, Harris, Garrison-Wade, & Leech, 2011). Students with creative or practical talents in areas such as the arts or leadership are often overlooked when teachers focus on the identification of schoolhouse giftedness (Renzulli, 2011). When this single-test score criterion approach is used, females, students with learning disabilities, students from impoverished backgrounds, and minority students typically are underidentified as eligible for gifted programs (Bianco et al., 2011; Davis, Rimm, & Siegle, 2011; Worrell, 2009), for several reasons:

- IQ scores have the potential to discriminate against students from minority groups who typically do not score well on standardized tests (Schoon, Jones, Cheng, & Maughan, 2012; Subotnik, Olszewski-Kubilius, & Worrell, 2012). Similarly, students from low-income families are at risk of being overlooked for gifted programs because they lack family and community resources to help them develop their talents (Borland & Wright, 1994; VanTassel-Baska, 1998).

- Teachers often overlook students from different ethnic backgrounds in favor of White, middle-class students, because the characteristics of the latter more closely match teachers' expectations of what giftedness looks like—high academic achievement and good behavior (Bonner, 2000).

- Similarly, girls are less likely to be referred for gifted programs because teachers may base their decisions on characteristics often seen in boys, such as boredom with subject matter, individuality, and ability to succeed in a competitive environment (Bianco et al., 2011). This contrasts with typical practices of rewarding girls for conformity to rules and expectations, diligence in classwork, and cooperation with others.

- Students with learning disabilities who also are gifted typically are overlooked for gifted programs because their giftedness may be "masked" by their disability, making them appear to have average abilities (Davis et al., 2011; VanTassel-Baska, Feng, Swanson, Quek, & Chandler, 2009).

Despite the popularity of IQ tests for identifying students for gifted programs, current theory and research support a multifaceted approach, as illustrated in the definition of giftedness found in the No Child Left Behind (NCLB) Act of 2001 (PL 107–110):

The term "gifted and talented," when used with respect to students, children, or youth, means students, children, or youth who give evidence of high achievement capability in areas such as intellectual, creative, artistic, or leadership capacity, or in specific academic fields, and who need services or activities not ordinarily provided by the school in order to fully develop those capabilities. [Title IX, Part A, Section 9101(22)]

To identify students who are gifted—especially those from diverse backgrounds—educators need to move away from using standardized tests and include information from nontest sources (Renzulli, 2002). Experts recommend using a variety of criteria, as outlined here (Pfeiffer & Blei, 2008; Renzulli, 1990; Renzulli & Reis, 1991):

1. Educators first identify the traditional schoolhouse giftedness using IQ or achievement test scores. According to the three-ring conception of giftedness, students would be considered to have above-average ability if they perform in the top 15% to 20% in a certain subject or skill domain (Renzulli, 1978b, 2011). This differs markedly from requiring an IQ score in the top 1% or 2% of the population, as discussed previously. Demonstration of above-average performance in this case, however, should not be measured solely by tests.

Creativity: See Module 13

2. Teachers may nominate students who display behaviors not measured by tests, such as creativity, task commitment, interest, or special talents. Students who are creative can come up with many different solutions to problems, as assessed on tests of creativity. Students who have high levels of task commitment are highly fascinated by a certain topic or subject matter and have a strong drive to achieve in that domain (Renzulli, 1978b, 2002).

3. A selection committee then considers students who do not qualify based on test scores or teacher nominations by evaluating alternative criteria, such as parent or peer nominations, self-nominations, tests of creativity, or evaluations of products (e.g., special projects, grades, or portfolios).

4. The selection committee also may consider nominations from previous-year teachers to prevent overlooking students who may not have been identified by present teachers.

Implementation of such a multidimensional identification model would solve the limitations of the single-test score criterion approach and would be consistent with the multimethod approach proposed by federal guidelines for identifying giftedness. Parents, teachers, administrators, and students have reported satisfaction with this type of approach (Renzulli, 1988).

 Your friend has received a very high score on a group administered IQ test. He believes he is intelligent and also should be considered gifted. Explain to your friend the flaws in his reasoning.

BIOLOGICAL, SOCIAL, AND CULTURAL ISSUES

③ Describe how environment, socioeconomic status, and gender influence IQ.

Heredity or Environment?

Heredity and environment interact to produce all types of behaviors, including intelligence and giftedness (Sternberg, 2014; Subotnik, Olszewski-Kubilius, & Worrell, 2011). We must be careful not to conclude that genetics predetermines that an individual will have a certain level of intelligence. The environment has been shown to have a dramatic effect on the development of intelligence.

Children's IQ scores may be affected by several factors related to their home environment prior to entering school (Bradley & Caldwell, 1984; Korenman, Miller, & Sjaastad, 1995):

- emotional and verbal responsiveness of parents (responding to children's requests, answering questions),

- parents' involvement with their children (playing with them, reading to them), and

- availability of appropriate play materials, activities, and resources in the home.

DIVERSITY Consider the importance of parent–child interactions from the classic research of Hart and Risley (2003). Home observations of 1- and 2-year-old children indicated that parents from lower socioeconomic families spoke about 616 words per hour to their children, middle socioeconomic parents about 1,251 words per hour, and higher socioeconomic parents about 2,153 words per hour. Early language experience influenced rate of vocabulary growth, which in turn predicted vocabulary, language skills, and reading comprehension at age 9 (Hart & Risley, 2003). We should be careful not to assume that socioeconomic status itself is the primary factor affecting children's cognitive development. Recent research indicates that of primary importance is the difference among parents in behaviors such as the amount and quality of parent's language when speaking with their children, caregiver responsiveness to children's communication, amount of encouraging feedback, and parenting style (asking rather than telling a child what to do; Rindermann & Baumeister, 2015).

Also, most experts believe that intelligence can be shaped and even improved through various interventions (Grotzer & Perkins, 2000; Mayer, 2000). The Abecedarian Project, in which children from impoverished families were provided with an enriching educational environment from age 6 weeks to kindergarten, showed IQ and achievement advantages through age 12 (Ramey, 1994). Head Start, a program that provides at-risk preschoolers with experiences to promote intellectual development, has helped children become cognitively ready for school and has improved their school achievement through middle adolescence (Barnett, 2004; Lazar & Darlington, 1982; Zigler & Berman, 1983).

Another example of the effect of environment on cognitive abilities is the **Flynn effect** (Flynn, 1984, 2007), a phenomenon in which IQ scores have increased over successive generations throughout the world (about 3 IQ points per decade since the 1930s). Possible explanations for the increase in IQ include (Baker et al., 2015; Kaufman, 2010; Nisbett et al., 2012; Resing & Tunteler, 2007):

- better nutrition,

- increased schooling,

- greater educational level of parents,

- fewer childhood diseases,

- improved parent–child interactions,

- greater familiarity with taking tests, and

- minor changes in content, instructions, and administration of IQ tests from one version to another.

However, factors such as improved nutrition and fewer diseases are less likely to contribute to IQ gains now than they were 50 years ago (Nisbett et al., 2012).

Socioeconomic and Cultural Factors

SOCIOECONOMIC STATUS (SES)

The connection between IQ and socioeconomic status (SES) is well documented (White, 1982). When SES is defined by parents' income, occupation, and educational level, children from higher SES families tend to have higher IQs than children from lower SES families (Schoon et al., 2012). The lower performance of children from poor families may be due to the following influences (Duncan & Brooks-Gunn, 2000; McLoyd, 1998; Sternberg, 2002):

- fewer resources (books, computers, access to high-quality preschool),

- poorer nutrition,

- poorer health care, and

- strained parent–child relationships due to high levels of parental stress.

However, this correlation does not show the entire picture. When we define a child's home environment based on factors such as parental attitudes about education and parent–child interaction patterns, home environment is a stronger predictor of performance on IQ tests

Caregiver responsiveness: See Module 7

Parenting styles: See Module 2

> **DIVERSITY**

SES as a context of children's development: See Module 2

Self-Fulfilling prophecy:
See Module 19

than is a student's socioeconomic status (Bradley & Caldwell, 1984; Suzuki & Valencia, 1997). Children from families in which parents value education, talk with their children, read to their children, and make time for learning—regardless of the financial and occupational status of the family—tend to have higher IQ scores.

What does this research mean for teachers? Teachers form expectations for students based on many sources of information, of which SES is one. Teachers might assume from a student's appearance that he or she is from a lower SES background and unconsciously form lower expectations for the student, leading to a **self-fulfilling prophecy**—a groundless expectation that leads teachers to act in ways that make the expectation come true (Merton, 1948; Rosenthal & Jacobson, 1968). Teachers should regularly monitor their own expectations of student performance to avoid making assumptions or behaving in ways that negatively affect students.

ETHNICITY

DIVERSITY

Like the connection between SES and IQ, the correlation between ethnicity and IQ scores is well documented. Compared with White students:

- African American students score approximately 15 points below average (about 1 SD below the norm; Pesta & Poznanski, 2014; Rushton & Jensen, 2005);

- Hispanic students score approximately average on nonverbal portions of IQ tests but about 7 to 15 points lower (½ to 1 SD below average) on verbal subtests (Hogan, 2015); and

- students from Chinese and Japanese cultures score about average on verbal subtests and about 1 SD above the average on nonverbal portions (Hogan, 2015).

Remember that these scores represent group averages, which can fluctuate over time (Sternberg, 2002).

What accounts for these differences among ethnic or racial groups? The differences may be due to a **stereotype threat**—an unconscious, automatic activation of prior knowledge about a stereotype that hinders performance on cognitive tasks. For example, African Americans have performed significantly worse on a test when they were told that it was an intelligence test compared to when they were given different instructions about the test (Brown & Day, 2006; Steele & Aronson, 1995). The stereotype they invoked about their ethnic group and intelligence while taking the test may have hindered their performance. Similar stereotype threat effects have been found for individuals from lower SES groups and Hispanic students (Croizet, Desert, Dutrevis, & Leyens, 2001; Schmader & Johns, 2003).

Also, the differences among ethnic or racial groups are more the result of socioeconomic and environmental influences than of race itself. When we compare the IQ scores of racial or ethnic groups within the same SES level—for example, African American, Hispanic, and White students all from higher SES families—group differences are minimized (Suzuki & Valencia, 1997). It is important to remember that the differences between ethnic groups in IQ scores can occur for many reasons. Therefore, teachers should be careful not to make assumptions about a student's ability based on ethnicity or any other visible characteristic.

GENDER

DIVERSITY

In general, no gender differences are found in overall performance on IQ tests because test makers are careful to remove any items leading to gender bias and to maintain a balance of items that more males answer correctly and more females answer correctly (Halpern, 2011; Halpern & LaMay, 2000). Even though males and females do not differ on average, males show more variability in performance on cognitive tests, especially at the extremes of the distribution, leading to more males than females at the highest and lowest levels of measured intelligence (Hyde, Lindberg, Linn, Ellis, & Williams, 2008; Lindberg, Hyde, Petersen, & Linn, 2010).

When examining performance on specific cognitive abilities, such as language or spatial skills, we also find few gender differences.

- Females show a slight advantage in verbal skills, and males and females show no differences in vocabulary, reading comprehension, or essay writing (Hyde, 2014).

- Despite the stereotype that males have better spatial skills, few gender differences also exist. Males show advantages on some tasks measuring spatial abilities, such as spatial navigation and timed tests of mental rotations, illustrated in Figure 20.4 (Geiser, Lehmann, & Eid, 2008; Iaria, Petrides, Dagher, Pike, & Bohbot, 2003; Postma, Jager, Kessels, Koppeschaar, & van Honk, 2004; Titze, Jansen, & Heil, 2010). However, the advantage is much smaller when mental rotations tasks are untimed (Maeda & Yoon, 2013; Voyer, 2011). Also, girls' performance is comparable to that of boys or better than boys on tasks that assess memory for the spatial location of objects (Postma et al., 2004; Silverman, Choi, & Peters, 2007).

- Evidence that brief interventions can substantially improve spatial performance in both boys and girls suggests that gender differences may be more the result of environmental experiences rather than biology (Uttal et al., 2013).

The gender stereotyped notion that "males are better at math" also does not always hold true and may have been exaggerated by the popular media (Hyde, 2005). Recent research suggests that there are small to nonexistent gender differences in conceptual understanding and calculation skills during elementary school in the United States and internationally (Else-Quest, Hyde, & Linn, 2010; Lindberg et al., 2010; Reilly, 2012). At the high school level, boys show a small advantage for quantitative skills and complex problem solving, which historically may have been due to more exposure to the content and practice than a reflection of gender (Lindberg et al., 2010; Reilly, Neumann, & Andrews, 2015; Robinson & Lubienski, 2011). The gap in the number of high-achieving boys and high-achieving girls in math and science has been decreasing over the last several decades, partly due to girls taking more advanced courses (Wai, Cacchio, Putallaz, & Makel, 2010). Currently, male and female high school students take approximately the same number of math and science courses (Lindberg et al., 2010; National Science Foundation, 2012).

Even though overall differences between adolescent boys and girls are small, there may be cognitive factors that account for this difference.

- Differences in strategy use might lead to performance differences. Boys tend to favor a spatial imagery strategy when solving mathematical word problems, whereas girls are more likely to use a verbal computation strategy (Geary, Saults, Liu, & Hoard, 2000; Klein, Adi-Japha, & Hakak-Benizri, 2010).

FIGURE 20.4   **Mental Rotations.** Individuals are given a target shape and asked to identify the mirror image of that shape from a set of comparison shapes, as shown.

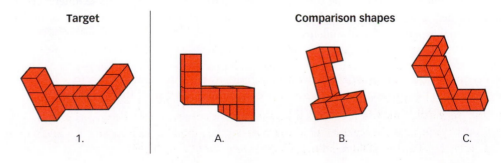

- The stereotype threat that "girls are bad at math" may also hinder females' performance on tasks that assess complex mathematical abilities (Halpern, 1997). For example, females who were told that a math test produced gender differences favoring males performed worse than when they were told the test was insensitive to gender differences (Steele, 1997). This effect has consistently been found in research with college students, and more recent research has identified the effect as early as middle school (Miyake et al., 2010; Muzzatti & Agnoli, 2007; Spencer, Steele, & Quinn, 1999).

The belief of parents and teachers that math is a male domain may also lead them to behave in ways that provide different experiences in and out of school for boys and girls as they develop from early childhood through adolescence, leading to different levels of mathematical ability at the high school level.

- Parents provide children with different activities and offer different feedback about their performance on those activities (Wigfield & Cambria, 2010a; Wigfield, Eccles, Schieffele, Roeser, & Davis-Kean, 2006). For example, one study reported that mothers were more likely to buy math and science items for boys than girls, which affected subsequent math and science interests (Bleeker & Jacobs, 2004).

- Parents and teachers also tend to rate boys as having higher math ability (Lindberg, Hyde, & Hirsch, 2008). These experiences lead children to develop expectancies about what they are good at and what they value as important to them (Jacobs, Davis-Kean, Bleeker, Eccles, & Malanchuk, 2005; Lindberg et al., 2008). Despite a lack of gender differences in elementary school math, girls develop more negative beliefs about their math competence, even when they are high-achieving or gifted and when they outperform boys (Eccles, Barber, Jozefowicz, Malenchuk, & Vida, 2000; Else-Quest et al., 2010; Freedman-Doan et al., 2000).

- Teachers also can subtly and inadvertently convey the message that girls are not as good as boys at math. A recent study of first- and second-grade female teachers with math anxiety showed that by the end of the school year, girls, but not boys, were more likely to believe that boys are better at math. Girls who endorsed this stereotype had lower math achievement in comparison with girls who did not endorse the stereotype and with boys overall (Beilock, Gunderson, Ramirez, & Levine, 2010).

- As students transition to high school, they may acquire additional gender-stereotyped experiences. Teachers tend to assign high-ability boys to top math groups more frequently than high-ability girls (Hallinan & Sorensøn, 1987). High school math teachers also tend to interact less with girls and provide them with less feedback (Oakes, 1990; Sadker, Sadker, & Klein, 1991).

Anxiety: See Module 15

Let's remember, as we did for ethnic and SES differences, on average gender differences are rather small. Teachers should be careful not to make assumptions about any student's abilities based on membership in a particular gender, ethnic, or socioeconomic group. It is important to understand differences among students and the factors that may cause these differences so that teachers can develop curriculum, methods, and interactions that provide an equitable educational experience for all students.

 Why might research on socioeconomic, ethnic, and gender differences in intelligence be important for teachers? How will knowledge of this research influence your teaching philosophy?

④ Explain how theories of intelligence and giftedness can be used to enhance the learning of all students regardless of their ability level.

Teaching for Multiple Intelligences

Teachers can reach all types of learners using MI theory if they follow general guidelines and avoid common misapplications, shown in Table 20.3. MI theory can be implemented either on a school-wide basis or in individual classrooms.

School-Wide approach. Educators can use MI theory to identify the skills and abilities that are valued in society and cultivate those abilities (Gardner, 1995). At the Key Community School in Indianapolis, a group of teachers worked with Gardner and his colleagues to develop a curriculum based on MI theory. The Key School emphasizes the use of all kinds of abilities by students. The curriculum is integrated through the use of school-wide themes that span all grades and all subjects and are studied in depth for nine weeks.

Schools at all levels can create a curriculum that reflects MI theory. In early childhood and elementary classrooms, the curricula should provide students with a variety of experiences to help them discover their interests and talents (Johnson, 2000). Some elementary schools have adopted a themed curriculum, like that of the Key School, integrating language arts, science, mathematics, and social studies. This allows children to experience topics in greater depth and to recognize how they can apply knowledge and skills to multiple subjects. Middle schools and high schools can adapt their existing curricula to reflect an emphasis on MI by adding a stronger arts program, implementing learning stations in classes, using community experts to mentor students in their areas of expertise, or constructing school-wide interdisciplinary units (Campbell, 1997).

TABLE 20.3	Multiple Intelligences Theory: Guidelines and Misapplications
GENERAL GUIDELINES	**COMMON MISAPPLICATIONS**
Differences among students are taken seriously so that curricula and assessments are constructed to be sensitive to those differences.	Attempting to teach *every* lesson in eight ways
Knowledge about differences is shared with students and parents.	Using MI theory as a mnemonic aid (e.g., using dance or mime to help students remember material from a lesson)
Lessons are presented in a way that allows all students the opportunity to master the material and demonstrate what they have learned.	Promoting musical intelligence by playing background music during learning activities
Students gradually take on responsibility for their own learning.	• Using intrapersonal intelligence as a rationale for self-esteem programs • Using interpersonal intelligence as a rationale for cooperative learning

SOURCE: Gardner, 1995.

Individual classrooms. Teachers should recognize and identify students' different strengths and weaknesses in their intelligence by directly observing students in authentic tasks—real-life activities that are themselves valued (Gardner, 1991, 1999). For example, a teacher might identify spatial intelligence by observing students as they design a new gymnasium or linguistic intelligence by evaluating the process and product of students' writing given a writing prompt.

To meet the needs of learners with diverse strengths and weaknesses, teachers should introduce subject matter in more than one way (Gardner, 1991, 1999). For example, as teachers, we can learn about intelligence through:

- a narrative (reviewing the history of the development of intelligence theories and tests),

- hands-on experiences (looking at IQ tests, learning how to administer them), or

- logical-quantitative techniques (practicing the interpretation of IQ scores),

Teaching the same topic using different approaches will provide students with opportunities to learn a topic using their strengths and to develop skills in their weaker areas of intelligence (Kornhaber, Fierros, & Veenema, 2004).

As a result of teaching material through multiple methods, teachers will cover fewer topics, but the topics will be covered in greater depth and more students will be successful (Gardner, 1995). This is not a new concept. International comparisons of mathematics performance indicated that mathematics instruction in top-performing countries focuses on fewer concepts in greater depth (Schmidt, McKnight, & Raizen, 2002). Schools that have used MI-inspired practices for several years documented both qualitative and quantitative evidence of the benefits to students' learning (Gardner & Moran, 2006). Of 41 schools implementing MI-inspired curricula, 49% have shown improvement in achievement test scores, 54% have reported fewer discipline problems, and 60% have documented increased parental involvement (Kornhaber et al., 2004).

Teaching for Successful Intelligence

Consistent with an MI approach to teaching, the goal of teaching for successful intelligence is to ensure that *all* students can achieve higher levels of learning. Teachers must use instructional approaches that focus on (Sternberg, 1997, 2010a):

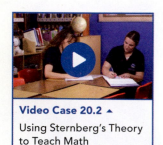

Video Case 20.2 ▲

Using Sternberg's Theory to Teach Math

© SAGE Publications

- analytical learning (analyze, compare and contrast, evaluate, judge, assess),

- creative learning (create, invent, imagine, suppose, discover), and

- practical learning (use, apply, employ, put into practice, implement, demonstrate).

Table 20.4 illustrates how teachers can use instructional approaches for analytical, creative, or practical thinking in any subject and at any grade level.

Teaching for successful intelligence should empower students to cultivate an ability to adapt to, select, and shape their environments. Guidelines to help students develop successful intelligence include the following (Sternberg, 1998, 2002):

1. Balance instruction over the course of a unit so that lessons emphasize creative and practical abilities as well as analytical abilities, but remember that it is not necessary to teach each lesson in three different ways.

2. Include memory-based instruction (factual knowledge or recall) in a balanced approach to teaching; students cannot think analytically, creatively, or in a practical manner if they have no knowledge base.

3. Vary the methods used to assess student learning rather than relying on a single mode of evaluation, such as written tests.

4. Provide students with opportunities to *shape* their environment by choosing activities, paper topics, projects, or portfolio items.

5. Teach in a "zone of relative novelty" where material is challenging but not too much so. This approach not only encourages students to develop their creative abilities (responding to novelty) but also is consistent with Piaget's (1972) and Vygotsky's (1978) theories of cognitive development.

6. Encourage *automaticity* of information-processing skills such as reading and mathematics. Individuals with successful intelligence have information-processing skills that are automatic, allowing them to engage more efficiently in analytical, creative, and practical thinking.

When teachers apply successful intelligence in the classroom, students learn more. In studies of elementary through high school classrooms, students performed better when teachers provided instruction that matched students' strengths *at least some of the time,* compared with students in classes that involved traditional memory-based instruction or instruction that did not match student abilities (Grigorenko et al., 2002; Sternberg et al., 1999). This finding holds true for different subjects and types of assessment (factual knowledge or higher order thinking).

Piaget's and Vygotsky's theories of cognitive development: See Module 6

Automaticity: See Modules 12 and 21

Video Case 20.3 ▲

Using Sternberg's Theory to Plan Groups and Instruction

© SAGE Publications

TABLE 20.4	Teaching to Analytical, Creative, and Practical Abilities		
SUBJECT AREA	**ANALYTICAL**	**CREATIVE**	**PRACTICAL**
Language Arts	Compare the personality of Tom Sawyer with that of Huckleberry Finn.	Write a very short story with Tom Sawyer as a character.	Describe the general lesson about persuasion that can be learned from Tom Sawyer's way of persuading his friends to whitewash Aunt Polly's fence.
Mathematics	Solve a mathematical word problem (using the D = RT formula).	Create your own mathematical word problem using the D = RT formula.	Show how to use the D = RT formula to estimate driving time from one city to another near you.
Social Studies	Compare, contrast, and evaluate the arguments of those who supported slavery versus those who opposed it.	Write a page of a journal from the viewpoint of a soldier fighting for one or the other side during the Civil War.	Discuss the applicability of lessons of the Civil War for countries today that have strong internal divisions.
Science	Analyze how the immune system fights bacterial infections.	Suggest ways to cope with the increasing immunity bacteria are showing to antibiotic drugs.	Suggest three steps that individuals might take to reduce the likelihood of bacterial infection.

Reprinted with permission from Sternberg, 1997.

Differentiated instruction: See Module 18

Video Case £0.4 –
Gifted Students

© SAGE Publications

Teaching Students Who Are Gifted

The current definition of giftedness in the NCLB Act states that to fully develop their potential, students who are gifted need special activities or services not typically provided by schools. However, few states require differentiated curriculum or experiences for gifted students (VanTassel-Baska, 2015). Teachers have several approaches available to them in deciding how to meet the needs of students who are gifted.

Advanced instruction in topics or subjects. Teachers can provide students who are gifted with more advanced instruction commensurate with their level of ability. Because a large proportion of the curriculum content in a given school year includes information and skills that gifted students already have mastered, gifted students benefit academically from accelerated instruction (Kulik & Kulik, 2004; Reis & Purcell, 1993; Rogers, 1993). *Acceleration* refers to adjusting the pace of instruction within the student's grade, moving students quickly through grades (i.e., skipping grades), or providing instruction above grade level in one or two subjects and allowing students to remain with same-age peers for other subjects. Contrary to common beliefs, skipping grades does not appear to be as harmful to social and emotional well-being as once thought (Colangelo & Assouline, 2009; Subotnik et al., 2011).

Enrichment. Because students who are gifted need opportunities for developing critical thinking and problem-solving skills, they benefit greatly from enrichment activities (Johnson, 2000; Miller & Gentry, 2010; Reis & Boeve, 2009). *Enrichment* activities allow them to broaden and deepen their knowledge beyond the regular curriculum. For optimal learning, teachers should create enrichment activities that satisfy the criteria listed in Table 20.5.

The decision to use acceleration or enrichment activities must take into account the student's interests and learning preferences (independent work, hands-on activities, collaboration, etc.). When teachers uniformly give students more advanced and challenging work without regard for their needs and interests, students quickly learn that if they do their "best work" they are rewarded with more and harder work, perhaps dampening their motivation (Renzulli & Reis, 2004).

When choosing accelerated content or enrichment activities, teachers can use *curriculum compacting,* a useful tool for streamlining the material that needs to be covered with

TABLE 20.5	Criteria for Successful Enrichment Activities
ENRICHMENT ACTIVITIES SHOULD:	**EXAMPLES:**
Take into account the interests of the student	Allowing a third-grade student who is gifted to pursue an interest in astronomy by researching galaxies and creating a PowerPoint presentation
Be situated within the context of a real problem for meaningful learning to occur	Doing a project on alternative fuel sources to help solve global warming
Encourage the use of authentic methods and resources, those used in real life to investigate problems	Using computers, microscopes, library resources, interviewing, experiments
Lead to tangible solutions or products as a result of the activity	Creating models, posters, presentations, plays

SOURCE: Renzulli, 1999.

students who are gifted. This method involves evaluating students' existing knowledge of the content in an instructional unit through a pretest and then teaching only material aimed at those instructional objectives not met by the student (Gilman, 2008; Reis & Renzulli, 2004; Renzulli, 1978a). For example, in a high school history class, the student might read the assigned material for a particular unit, demonstrate mastery by taking a test, and then contract with the teacher to do an independent project related to the student's particular interests within the course.

Grouping gifted students with same-ability peers. Research shows that gifted students from elementary through high school benefit from being grouped with students of the same ability level (Adelson & Carpenter, 2011; Preckel, Götz, & Frenzel, 2010). Educators can use grouping methods such as cross-grade grouping and cluster grouping to tailor instruction for gifted students. *Cross-grade grouping* is used to provide accelerated instruction for gifted students who excel in a single subject such as reading or math. In this method, gifted students are assigned to classes for reading or math with other students at different grade levels who have similar achievement levels. For example, a gifted second-grade student might go to a fourth-grade class for reading and spend the rest of the day with peers, or a gifted ninth grader might be allowed to take AP Calculus with seniors and take the rest of his classes with peers.

Ability grouping: See Module 19

Cross-Grade grouping: See Module 19

In *cluster grouping,* gifted students—regardless of their background, language, or gifted talents—are grouped together in one classroom that contains nongifted students at various achievement levels (Gentry & MacDougall, 2008; Winebrenner & Brulles, 2008). To effectively use this method, the participation of all classrooms at a particular grade level is needed. The achievement levels of students within the classrooms at the same grade level are balanced so that no classroom contains students at the high and low extremes of the achievement continuum (Brulles, Peters, & Saunders, 2012). For example, one fifth-grade class may contain a cluster group of gifted students, average students, and below-average students, whereas the other fifth-grade class would contain high-achieving, average, and very low-achieving students. Grouping in this way reduces the variability in achievement levels within each classroom and allows the high-achieving students in the class without the gifted students to become the academic leaders (Gentry & MacDougall, 2008). Also, in the class containing the gifted cluster, teachers are better able to (Brulles et al., 2012; Brulles, Saunders, & Cohn, 2010; Brulles & Winebrenner, 2013; Gentry & MacDougall, 2008):

- plan differentiated instruction, which may include curriculum compacting, acceleration, or enrichment;

- offer a faster instructional pace and more challenging content to the gifted students; and

- provide more individual attention and focused instruction for the lower achieving students.

Differentiated instruction: See Module 18

Research indicates that gifted students benefit from this method and there is no disadvantage to the nongifted students in the same class (Brulles et al., 2010, 2012; Kulik, 2003; Pierce et al., 2011).

Think of the grade level you intend to teach. How would you use the theories of intelligence and giftedness and their applications to ensure that you challenge all students in your classroom?

SUMMARY

① Explain how intelligence and giftedness are more than just high cognitive ability. Current theories of intelligence propose that intelligence is more than an IQ score. Gardner proposed eight intelligences, only two of which are measured by IQ tests, whereas Sternberg's theory involves a balance among three abilities—analytical, creative, and practical—of which only analytical skills are measured on IQ tests. Gardner's and Sternberg's theories of giftedness also emphasize that giftedness should not be defined solely by exceptionally high test performance. Because individuals have strengths and weaknesses in different abilities or domains, they can be gifted in a certain ability or domain. Similarly, Renzulli's theory of giftedness proposes that high ability alone does not constitute giftedness; individuals need task commitment and creativity as well.

② Describe what IQ tests measure and identify the concerns with using IQ scores to identify giftedness. IQ tests measure a specific set of skills, which vary from test to test, and they assess an individual's cognitive ability at a specific point in time rather than capturing all of the abilities that are part of intelligence. When interpreting IQ scores of students from linguistically and culturally diverse backgrounds, educators must be certain that students have had the opportunity to learn content assessed by the test and that the test is given in their native language. Otherwise, scores may not be an accurate reflection of their ability. Using IQ tests as the sole measure for identifying giftedness excludes students from disadvantaged and minority backgrounds and students with learning disabilities because they typically do not score well on standardized tests.

③ Describe how environment, socioeconomic status, and gender influence IQ. Many factors in children's home environments prior to school entry are related to their IQ. Children tend to have higher IQ scores if their parents are responsive to their needs and provide opportunities that stimulate their cognitive development. Children from higher SES families also have higher IQs. Although ethnic groups differ in their average IQ scores, we must be cautious in interpreting these differences. SES also may account for a large proportion of the ethnic differences in IQ. Few gender differences in intelligence exist. Researchers are now examining the cognitive and social processes that might account for any gender differences in cognitive skills such as math.

④ Explain the similarities between the theory of multiple intelligences and the theory of successful intelligence in their applications to the classroom. The goal of both MI theory and the theory of successful intelligence is to reach more learners than traditional education does. Both theories emphasize that teachers should be sensitive to individual differences among students. They also advocate approaching a subject in a variety of ways to capitalize on students' strengths and help them develop in their weak areas. Both theories also stress the importance of allowing students to choose assignments and tasks in a way that helps them demonstrate their strengths and work on their weaknesses.

⑤ Explain how theories of intelligence and giftedness can be used to enhance the learning of all students regardless of their ability level. Using either MI theory or the theory of successful intelligence, teachers can reach all types of learners by approaching a subject in a variety of ways to capitalize on students' strengths and help them develop in their weak areas. They can also allow students to choose assignments and tasks in a way that helps them demonstrate their strengths and work on their weaknesses. Because students who are gifted need specific opportunities for challenge and a faster instructional pace, teachers can provide enrichment experiences or accelerate instruction through curriculum compacting, cross-grade grouping, or more advanced work at the same grade level using cluster grouping.

KEY CONCEPTS

CASE STUDIES: REFLECT AND EVALUATE

EARLY CHILDHOOD: LETTER P DAY

These questions refer to the case study on page 404.

1. How does Mrs. Cahill's language arts activity reflect Sternberg's theory of successful intelligence? How does Mrs. Cahill's language arts activity reflect Gardner's theory of multiple intelligences?

2. Contrast the capabilities of Jillian and Pat using the theory of multiple intelligences and the theory of successful intelligence.

3. Nolan's IQ score is 143. Use the normal curve in Figure 20.3 to interpret what this score means. Based on Nolan's IQ score, would you expect him to have a high IQ in later grades? Why or why not?

4. Based on the information given in the case, would you consider Nolan to be gifted according to Renzulli's three-ring conception of giftedness? Why or why not? Would you need additional information about him?

5. If Nolan were assessed and found to be gifted, discuss whether you would choose acceleration or enrichment activities for him. Give specific developmentally appropriate examples of how you would implement your chosen approach.

ELEMENTARY SCHOOL: CHEETAHS, LIONS, AND LEOPARDS

These questions refer to the case study on page 406.

1. How would you describe Marcela and Carl according to Gardner's theory of multiple intelligences? How would you describe each student using Sternberg's theory of successful intelligence?

2. Based on the information given in the case, would you consider Marcela or Carl to be gifted according to Renzulli's three-ring conception of giftedness? Why or why not? Would you need additional information?

3. Carl appears to come from a lower socioeconomic family. How might this affect his chances of being identified as gifted, according to the research evidence presented in the module?

4. According to the research on sociocultural issues in intelligence, how do you think Marcela's family background has influenced her interest in science?

5. What strategies could Mrs. Fratelli use to meet the needs of a gifted student in reading and science? How might these strategies be different or similar?

MIDDLE SCHOOL: MATH TROUBLES

These questions refer to the case study on page 408.

1. At the beginning of middle school, Lindsey and her classmates took a paper-and-pencil group-administered IQ test. Her IQ score was 113. Use the normal curve in Figure 20.3 to interpret what this score means. How certain are you that this IQ score accurately reflects her cognitive ability?

2. How would you characterize Sam according to Gardner's theory of multiple intelligences? According to Sternberg's theory of successful intelligence, would you say that Lindsey has strengths in analytical, creative, or practical abilities, or in some combination of these?

3. Do you think Sam may be gifted? Using the characteristics discussed in the module, identify details from the case to support your answer.

4. Provide Miss Barton with suggestions for incorporating Gardner's theory of multiple intelligences into her prealgebra class and for using Sternberg's theory of successful intelligence in her teaching approach.

5. Explain how factors such as *gender stereotyping* and *stereotype threat* may be affecting Lindsey's motivation and performance in prealgebra.

HIGH SCHOOL: NOON SUPERVISED STUDY

These questions refer to the case study on page 410.

1. Sarah was administered the WISC-V as part of the process of selecting students for the gifted and talented program in elementary school. The IQ score in her academic record is 132. Use the normal curve in Figure 20.3 to interpret what this score means.

2. What expectation do you think Jason has for success in school? How might this create a *self-fulfilling prophecy*?

3. Evaluate whether Anthony could be gifted according to the federal definition of giftedness. Discuss what factors might cause educators to overlook students like Anthony for eligibility in gifted programs.

4. According to the research on identification of students for gifted programs, would it surprise you that Sarah chose to be in lower level math and science classes? Why or why not?

5. Evaluate Mr. Hardy's use of exams and homework assignments. Which intelligence in MI theory would Gardner say Mr. Hardy is emphasizing? Which ability or abilities in the theory of successful intelligences would Sternberg say Mr. Hardy is emphasizing? Using MI theory and the theory of successful intelligence, give Mr. Hardy some suggestions for additional methods of assessing students' learning rather than relying solely on exams and homework assignments.

APPLY AND PRACTICE WHAT YOU'VE LEARNED

▶ edge.sagepub.com/durwin3e

CHECK YOUR COMPREHENSION ON THE STUDENT STUDY SITE

- **eFlashcards** to strengthen your understanding of key terms

- Practice **quizzes** to test your knowledge of key concepts

- **Videos and multimedia content** to enhance your exploration of key topics

©iStockphoto.com/Christopher Futcher

COGNITIVE DISABILITIES

OUTLINE	LEARNING GOALS

Cognitive Disabilities in Today's Classrooms

- Special Education Referral and Eligibility
- Planning and Placement

1 Describe how cognitive disabilities are identified and served under the Individuals with Disabilities Education Improvement Act.

Intellectual Disabilities

- Identification of Intellectual Disabilities
- *Applications:* Guidelines for Teachers in the General Education Classroom

2 Discuss the impairments you would expect to see in students with intellectual disabilities and the curricular approaches useful in addressing these deficits.

Specific Learning Disabilities

- Identification of Specific Learning Disabilities
- Reading Disability
- Mathematics Disability

3 Explain how learning disabilities are identified using the IQ-achievement discrepancy and the response-to-intervention approach.

4 Explain the characteristic deficits you would look for in identifying students with reading and mathematics disabilities and how you would approach remediating these deficits.

COGNITIVE DISABILITIES IN TODAY'S CLASSROOMS

1 Describe how cognitive disabilities are identified and served under the Individuals with Disabilities Education Improvement Act.

Teachers play a central role in the education of students with disabilities. They not only refer students for special education evaluations but also assist in determining the eligibility of students for special education and implement curricular modifications in the classroom. Who are the students with disabilities? Let's first look to federal special education law for an answer.

The **Individuals with Disabilities Education Improvement Act of 2004 (IDEA),** the most recent revision of the first special education law, adopted in 1975, defines a student with a disability as a child:

(i) with mental retardation, hearing impairments (including deafness), speech or language impairments, visual impairments (including blindness), serious emotional disturbance (referred to in this title as "emotional disturbance"), orthopedic impairments, autism, traumatic brain injury, other health impairments, or specific learning disabilities; and (ii) who, by reason thereof, needs special education and related services. [PL 108-446, Section 602.3(A)(i-ii)]

Students with cognitive disabilities—specific learning disabilities and intellectual disabilities (formerly called mental retardation)—together represent a large segment of the K-12 special education population, as the pie chart in Figure 21.1 illustrates (U.S. Department of Education, 2014). In this module, we discuss the learner characteristics and educational needs of students with cognitive disabilities. Other categories of disability shown in the pie chart are topics of other modules.

Master the content.

edge.sagepub.com/durwin3e

 SAGE edge™

Video: IDEA: History and Summary

FIGURE 21.1   **An Overview of Disabilities.** This pie chart shows the percentage of K-12 students with various disabilities receiving special education and related services under IDEA.

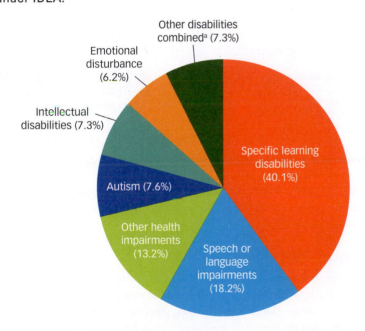

a"Other disabilities combined" includes *deaf-blindness* (less than 0.03 percent), *developmental delay* (2.1 percent), *hearing impairments* (1.2 percent), *multiple disabilities* (2.2 percent), *orthopedic impairments* (0.9 percent), *traumatic brain injury* (0.4 percent), and *visual impairments* (0.4 percent).

NOTE: Percentage was calculated by dividing the number of students ages 6 through 21 served under *IDEA*, Part B, in the disability category by the total number of students ages 6 through 21 served under *IDEA*, PART B, then multiplying the result by 100.

SOURCE: Adapted from U.S. Department of Education (2014). *Thirty-sixth annual report to Congress on the implementation of the Individuals with Disabilities Education Act, 2014, Vol. 1.* Office of Special Education and Rehabilitative Services, Washington D.C.: U.S. Government Printing Office.

Speech and language impairments: See Module 7

Special Education Referral and Eligibility

IDEA requires states to provide a "free" and "appropriate" public education for children with disabilities between the ages of 3 and 21. An appropriate public education involves curricular methods and modifications designed to provide educational benefit to the student. Specifically, this means special education and related services, such as speech and language therapy, counseling, physical therapy, social services, and transportation.

Determining a student's eligibility for special education and related services begins with a referral, typically by the student's teacher and sometimes by the parent. Parents must consent to the educational evaluation of the student. Once the evaluation is completed, the next step is to determine whether the student meets eligibility criteria as specified by IDEA and, if so, to develop a special education plan. Under IDEA, schools must create an **Individualized Education Plan (IEP),** a plan outlining curricula, educational modifications, and provision of services intended to enhance or improve the student's academic, social, or behavioral skills. IEPs contain several important features:

1. The student's present levels of academic achievement and functional performance.

2. Measurable annual goals and short-term instructional objectives.

3. An explanation of how the student's progress toward annual goals will be measured and when progress will be reported to parents.

4. Any appropriate accommodations for test taking on statewide and district-wide assessments, and when alternative assessments are needed, an explanation for why this assessment was selected and why it is appropriate for the student.

5. The types of special education and related services provided to the student, how long the services will be needed, and how much of the student's education will *not* be in the general education classroom.

6. Measurable postsecondary goals related to education, training, or employment for students age 14 and older.

7. A statement of transition services needed to reach goals involving independent living, continuing education, or employment after high school for students age 16 (or younger, if appropriate).

A multidisciplinary team called the **IEP team**—consisting of the student's parents (and sometimes the student), teachers, the school psychologist, and other relevant members (e.g., speech-language pathologist, occupational therapist, reading specialist)—determines eligibility and develops and annually revises the IEP. All those involved in writing the IEP must be informed about the rights of students and their parents. Guidelines 21.1 outline these rights that educators must follow.

Planning and Placement

IDEA ensures a free and appropriate education by requiring students with disabilities to be placed in the general education classroom "to the maximum extent appropriate," known as the **least restrictive environment (LRE).** Special classes, separate schools, or other pull-out programs should be used only when the nature or severity of the disability prevents the student from functioning in the general education classroom with supplementary aids or services. LRE should not be confused with *mainstreaming* and *inclusion,* which are LRE approaches that have evolved out of different interpretations of the law over the past four decades.

- In **mainstreaming,** students with special needs are placed with typically achieving peers when appropriate. For example, students may spend most of their day in a special education classroom and be integrated with their peers for subjects such as music, art, and social studies and for activities such as lunch, recess, library, and field trips.

- **Inclusion,** a more recent and popular approach, refers to integrating all students within the general education classroom, even those with severe disabilities (with the assistance of paraprofessionals), for most or all of the school day.

Video Case 21.1 ▲
Inclusion

© SAGE Publications

Reference: Inclusive Classroom

Experts continue to debate whether inclusion is the best environment for every student (Gordon, 2006; Zigler, Hodapp, & Edison, 1990). Only about 17% of students with intellectual disabilities spend most of the day in general education classes, while two-thirds of students with specific learning disabilities in elementary through high school spend most of the school day in the general education classroom (U.S. Department of Education, 2014). In any case, the decision to place students with disabilities in their LRE must be made on a case-by-case basis and in accordance with the intent of the law.

Did you ever have an IEP during your schooling? Did you know someone who had an IEP? Can you remember what services or accommodations were offered to you or to this individual?

INTELLECTUAL DISABILITIES

 Discuss the impairments you would expect to see in students with intellectual disabilities and the curricular approaches useful in addressing these deficits.

Identification of Intellectual Disabilities

IDEA serves approximately 7% of students ages 6 to 21 for intellectual disabilities, a relatively new term that replaced the term *mental retardation* (U.S. Department of Education, 2014). The American Association on Intellectual and Developmental Disabilities (AAIDD) defines **intellectual disability** as a disability that develops before age 18 and involves significant impairments in intellectual functioning and adaptive behavior, which include conceptual, social, and practical skills (Schalock et al., 2010). Determining whether a student has an intellectual disability involves evaluating whether the student exhibits significant impairment on measures of cognitive ability and adaptive behavior.

IQ tests: See Module 20

Psychologists assess impairments in cognitive ability using individually administered IQ tests, such as the Wechsler Intelligence Scale for Children-V (Wechsler, 2014) or the Stanford-Binet Intelligence Scales-V (Roid, 2003), both of which measure a range of cognitive skills. On such tests, the typical criterion for identifying an intellectual disability is an IQ score of 70 or lower, which is 2 standard deviations below the average IQ score. This means that a student is performing significantly below his or her age group (only 2% to 3% of individuals in the population obtain scores of 70 or below).

Standard deviation: See Modules 20 and 25

It is important not only to assess students' cognitive functioning with IQ tests but also to assess their everyday functioning, or adaptive behavior. *Adaptive behavior*—acting independently and in a socially responsible manner—includes conceptual, social, and practical skills (American Psychiatric Association, 2014):

Video Case 21.2 ▲

Testing for Intellectual Disabilities

© SAGE Publications

- *Conceptual skills,* such as reading, writing, understanding currency, and communicating, are necessary to function in society.

- *Social skills* include using good manners, showing responsibility, following rules and societal laws, demonstrating interpersonal skills, and being neither naive nor gullible.

- *Practical skills* comprise daily living skills and work skills, such as dressing, bathing, grooming, cooking, cleaning, shopping, managing money, working at a job, and using public transportation.

To evaluate adaptive behavior, psychologists use standardized instruments that assess the three dimensions of adaptive behavior outlined earlier. The Vineland Adaptive Behavior Scales, Second Edition (Sparrow, Cicchetti, & Balla, 2005), a popular instrument for this purpose, uses parent and teacher interviews to gather information about the individual's typical behaviors in areas such as communication, daily living skills, socialization, and motor skills. For example, the interviewer might ask whether a kindergartner brushes his teeth every day (daily living) and whether he can hold a pencil (motor skills).

A deficit in adaptive behavior may be identified by a significant impairment in one of the three dimensions or by a low overall score. The specific criteria for deficiency are:

- a score that is 2 standard deviations below average on a standardized instrument of adaptive behavior in one of the three dimensions (conceptual, social, or practical), or

- an overall score on the instrument that is 2 standard deviations below the average, which indicates that the individual is functioning substantially below the norm.

DIVERSITY 〈

Diagnosis of a disability should involve multiple modes of assessment and include standardized instruments that are culturally fair to students from ethnically diverse or lower socioeconomic backgrounds. Since the 1960s, students from culturally and linguistically diverse backgrounds have been disproportionately identified as having disabilities and placed in special education classes in elementary through high school (McKinney, Bartholomew, & Gray, 2010; Scott, Hauerwas, & Brown, 2014). For example:

- African American students are more likely to receive services for an intellectual disability than are students from all other ethnic groups (Hosp & Reschly, 2004; U.S. Department of Education, 2014).

- Students from impoverished backgrounds are more likely to receive special education services for cognitive or behavioral disabilities (Caspi, Taylor, Moffitt, & Plomin, 2000; Evans & English, 2002).

We should be cautious *not* to interpret these data to mean that race, ethnicity, or socioeconomic status (SES) is associated with a greater risk for cognitive disabilities. Many environmental factors contribute to a child's intellectual development. For example, children from lower SES families may have lower IQs because they lack the resources that middle and upper SES families provide to promote cognitive development, such as books, computers, and high-quality preschool. Also, students from lower SES and culturally diverse backgrounds historically have not performed as well as White, middle-class students on IQ and other tests of cognitive ability due to discrimination and bias.

The effects of environment on intelligence: See Module 20

APPLICATIONS: GUIDELINES FOR TEACHERS IN THE GENERAL EDUCATION CLASSROOM

When deciding how to teach students with intellectual disabilities in the general education classroom, educators must first remember that students with and without disabilities are more alike than they are different (Westwood, 2003). For example, two 10-year-old boys, one with an intellectual disability and one without, may both like sports, enjoy gym and art, and prefer to work in groups rather than independently. With this in mind, teachers should start by asking the following questions (Ashman, 1998):

Video Case 21.3 ▲
Co-Teaching

© SAGE Publications

- In which setting will the student learn most successfully?

- What skills need to be taught?

- What are the most effective approaches to teaching those skills?

Teachers can use several guiding principles to maximize learning opportunities for students with intellectual disabilities.

Teach using direct instruction. Direct instruction is a structured instructional method that involves teaching in small steps, providing ample opportunities for guided and independent practice, giving explicit feedback, and reteaching when necessary (Rosenshine, 1979, 1988; Rosenshine & Stevens, 1986). This method is effective when used with students with disabilities, especially for teaching basic skills (Kroesbergen & Van Luit, 2005; Turnbull, Turnbull, Shank, Smith, & Leal, 2002). However, keep in mind that skills such as reading need not be taught solely through drill and practice. For example, adolescents with intellectual disabilities improved their reading comprehension using an approach called *reciprocal teaching,* which teaches metacognitive skills that support comprehension, such as summarizing, questioning, clarifying, and predicting (Alfassi, Weiss, & Lifshitz, 2009).

Focus on overlearning, or practicing a skill past the point of mastery. Many students with intellectual disabilities have difficulty storing information in long-term memory, possibly due to attentional problems or lack of effective memorization strategies (Hallahan & Kauffman, 2000; Westwood, 2003). These students need extensive repetition and practice of skills, which can help them easily and automatically retrieve information from long-term memory (Westwood, 2003).

Encourage hands-on learning. Students with intellectual disabilities typically have difficulty with abstract thinking and need concrete examples (Reddy, Ramar, & Kusama, 2000).

Direct instruction: See Module 18

Reciprocal teaching: See Modules 11 and 12

Overlearning: See Module 12

Long-term memory: See Module 10

Learning math should include not only traditional methods, such as textbooks and work-sheets, but also real-life situations, such as shopping, measuring, cooking, and so on. Similarly, reading skills should be practiced in a variety of realistic contexts, such as reading instructions for a game, recipes, brochures, street signs, and newspapers.

Use cooperative learning when applicable. Cooperative learning requires heterogeneous (mixed) groups of students to work together to achieve a common goal. Teachers should adjust the curriculum content, however, to reflect the different cognitive needs and educational objectives of students with disabilities and typically achieving students. For instance, in a middle school social studies activity, typically achieving students might be learning content related to geography and history while students with disabilities are learning vocabulary or social skills from the same cooperative activity. Cooperative learning can raise the self-esteem of students with disabilities and promote positive peer relationships between students with and without disabilities (Acton & Zabartany, 1988; Johnson & Johnson, 2009; Salend & Sonnenschein, 1989).

Foster generalization. Students with intellectual disabilities have difficulty generalizing what they have learned, that is, transferring newly acquired information to new contexts (Meese, 2001; Taylor, Sternberg, & Richards, 1995). Often, the teacher needs only to remind students that they have successfully performed the skill in the past. For example, when a student is figuring out how much money to give the clerk at the school store, the teacher may need to remind her that she has practiced counting money in the classroom. Other examples of fostering generalization include (Mastropieri & Scruggs, 1984; Westwood, 2003)

- providing immediate feedback following performance of the skill;
- practicing the skill several times (which also would encourage overlearning);
- providing reinforcement for demonstrating the skill (e.g., privileges, free time, tokens);
- reteaching the same skill in different contexts, gradually increasing the range of contexts in which to practice the newly acquired information; and
- requiring students to decide whether a particular skill or strategy could be used to solve a new problem.

Cooperative learning: See Modules 18 and 19

Transfer: See Module 12

Reinforcement: See Module 8

Hands-On Learning. Hands-on learning is effective for teaching students with intellectual disabilities.

©iStockphoto.com/ EVAfotografie

Keep in mind that transfer is difficult for *all* learners when they are acquiring new information and that the aforementioned approaches are useful for encouraging generalization in *all* students.

Think about whether you will be teaching in early childhood or elementary school, or whether you plan to teach a certain subject in middle school or high school. How would you use these guidelines in your classroom?

SPECIFIC LEARNING DISABILITIES

❸ Explain how learning disabilities are identified using the IQ-achievement discrepancy and the response-to-intervention approach.

❹ Explain the characteristic deficits you would look for in identifying students with reading and mathematics disabilities and how you would approach remediating these deficits.

Identification of Specific Learning Disabilities

Specific learning disabilities (LD) represent the largest special education category under IDEA (Reid & Knight, 2006; U.S. Department of Education, 2014). Refer back to the pie chart in Figure 21.1. When first introduced in 1963, LD referred to students who had learning difficulties but were not eligible for special services under already existing categories such as mental retardation (MacMillan & Siperstein, 2002). Today, excluding mental retardation, now called intellectual disabilities, remains a component of the definition of LD in IDEA 2004:

> The term "specific learning disability" means a disorder in one or more of the basic psychological processes involved in understanding or in using language, spoken or written, which may manifest itself in imperfect ability to listen, think, speak, read, write, spell or do mathematical calculations. Such term includes such conditions as perceptual disabilities, brain injury, minimal brain dysfunction, dyslexia, and developmental aphasia. Such term does not include a learning problem that is primarily the result of visual, hearing, or motor disabilities, of mental retardation, of emotional disturbance, or of environmental, cultural, or economic disadvantage. [PL 108-446, Section 602.30(A-C)]

For the past several decades, the primary method for determining special education eligibility for a learning disability has been the **IQ-achievement discrepancy.** This method is based on the notion that students with LD have a learning problem that is *not* due to low intelligence (the exclusion of mental retardation as a causal factor in LD in the definition). Students would be identified as learning disabled if their achievement in one or more academic areas was significantly below what would be expected from their IQ. Individually administered IQ and achievement tests, typically given by a psychologist, are used for this purpose.

Consider an example of the IQ-achievement discrepancy, shown in Table 21.1, for a 9-year-old boy suspected of having a reading disability. The boy's reading and spelling scores are two standard deviations below average, meaning that he is far below average for his age group on these skills. These skills are significantly below what we would expect from his average IQ, while his mathematics scores are average, in line with his IQ score. The boy probably would be considered eligible for special education services in reading and spelling using the discrepancy approach.

Standard deviation: See Modules 20 and 25

TABLE 21.1

IQ and Achievement Scores for a 9-Year-Old Boy. These scores illustrate the IQ-achievement discrepancy. The boy's reading and spelling scores are severely discrepant from his average IQ.

Boy, age 9	
TEST	**STANDARD SCORES**[*]
WISC-V Full-Scale IQ	105
Kaufman Test of Educational Achievement II	
Spelling	70
Reading Composite	68
Calculations	92
Applied Problems	93

[*] Standard scores have an average of 100 and a standard deviation of 15. Scores below 70 (2 standard deviations below the average) are considered extremely low.

Since the adoption of the IQ-achievement discrepancy, researchers have accumulated evidence challenging the adequacy of this method on theoretical, statistical, and practical grounds (Fletcher, Lyon, Fuchs, & Barnes, 2007; Stanovich, 1991a, 1991b). Several practical problems are important to keep in mind.

- Researchers have found wide variation among states and even among districts within a state in how the IQ-achievement discrepancy is implemented (Mercer, Jordan, Allsopp, & Mercer, 1996; Vaughn, Linan-Thompson, & Hickman, 2003). For example, states differed as to the amount of discrepancy between a student's IQ and achievement performance required for eligibility (Reschly & Hosp, 2004).

- Finding a discrepancy between IQ and achievement scores does not provide instructionally useful information to help educators develop remedial plans (Aaron, Joshi, Gooden, & Bentum, 2008; Semrud-Clikeman, 2005). Collection of additional data (e.g., other tests, student work samples, etc.) is needed to determine students' strengths and weaknesses.

DIVERSITY

- Using this approach, minority students and English language learners tended to be placed in special education for LD at a higher rate than White students (Blanchett, 2006; U.S. Department of Education, 2009; Shifrer, Muller, & Callahan, 2011). The disproportionate representation may be due to a variety of factors, including standardized test bias, discrimination, and factors related to socioeconomic status (Shifrer et al., 2011).

- IQ-achievement discrepancy is considered by many to be a "wait to fail approach" in which students continue to struggle academically until the discrepancy becomes significant enough to result in eligibility (Fuchs & Fuchs, 2006; Hale, Wycoff, & Fiorello, 2011).

The limitations of the IQ-achievement discrepancy method have led to recent and important revisions. Since the changes in IDEA in 2004, LD identification does *not* require use of an IQ-achievement discrepancy and now includes an additional method called **response-to-intervention (RTI).**

Using RTI, educators determine whether a student responds to "scientific, research-based intervention." A major goal of RTI is to reduce the number of referrals for special education in pre-K through Grade 12 by identifying and correcting academic problems at an early stage (Al Otaiba & Fuchs, 2006; Carreker & Joshi, 2010). RTI also attempts to reduce the number of students who are incorrectly identified as having an LD, especially students from minority and linguistically diverse backgrounds who are disproportionately placed in special education (Finch, 2012). For example, students may have reading difficulties that are not due to an actual reading disability involving specific cognitive deficits (discussed next) but instead are the result of:

> DIVERSITY

- socioeconomic disadvantage (i.e., they have poor readiness skills due to lack of resources, non-English-speaking parents, and so on), or

- lack of appropriate instruction (i.e., they were not taught necessary reading or math skills).

RTI involves screening and monitoring of progress on academic skills for *all* students within a district and providing increasingly intensive interventions to students who perform below grade-level expectations. Currently, all 50 states use RTI as a prevention model, meaning that instruction and interventions are provided as part of general education (Zirkel & Thomas, 2010). Some states use RTI as both a general education initiative and as part of special education eligibility decisions (Hauerwas, Brown, & Scott, 2013). This means that the data collected through RTI documenting a student's continued failures to respond to increasingly intensive interventions can be used to make a referral for special education eligibility. While there is no single RTI model mandated by IDEA, the typical model has three tiers, as shown in Figure 21.2:

Tier 1. The preventive tier involves whole-class, general education instruction that is considered effective based on research evidence (Cakiroglu, 2015). Experts estimate that general education instruction should be effective for about 80% of students (Cates, Blum, & Swerdlik, 2011; Denton, 2012). In this tier, educators assess all students using screening measures to identify which students may need additional intervention.

FIGURE 21.2 **A Three-Tiered Model of RTI.** Models such as this are used by schools in all 50 states.

Tier 2. The secondary intervention tier involves small-group, short-term, and intensive interventions, and targets about 15% of students who were not making adequate progress in Tier 1 (Fuchs & Fuchs, 2007).

Tier 3. The tertiary intervention tier is the most intensive intervention. It is typically provided one-on-one by highly trained personnel to about 5% of students who did not respond to Tier 2 interventions (Denton, 2012).

The type of intervention (oral reading fluency, comprehension, math computations) and how often each week students receive the intervention will vary depending on students' needs. An intervention should last about 10 to 15 weeks, during which progress is monitored frequently (Cates et al., 2011).

To accurately identify a student as needing more intensive and more frequent instruction (movement to Tier 2 or Tier 3), a **dual discrepancy method** should be used (Cates et al., 2011). The student's academic performance should be below average, or discrepant, compared with grade-level expectations, *and* the student should show a slow rate of improvement toward benchmarks such that the gap widens over time between the student's performance and the benchmark (Cates et al., 2011). Consider Figure 21.3, showing a student's oral reading fluency (number of words correctly read per minute). The student correctly identified 24 words per minute compared with the benchmark of 60 indicating grade-level performance, meaning that the student is below grade-level expectations. The student's performance throughout the intervention shows very little progress toward the benchmark, indicating a slow rate of learning that is not sufficient to close the gap between current performance and grade-level expectations.

Keep in mind that RTI often involves trying multiple interventions within a tier during a grade or over several grades and does *not* require a student to move through all tiers before a special education referral can be made. A student can be referred for special education evaluation at any point in the RTI process even though in most states the process begins after Tier 3 (Berkeley, Bender, Peaster, & Saunders, 2009; Van Der Heyden & Burns, 2010). However, recent research suggests that students can be accurately identified for special education services at Tier 1 or Tier 2 without needing to fail to respond to multiple interventions (Al Otaiba et al., 2014; Compton et al., 2012).

FIGURE 21.3 **Oral Reading Fluency Graph.** This graph shows the performance of a student who is not responding to intervention.

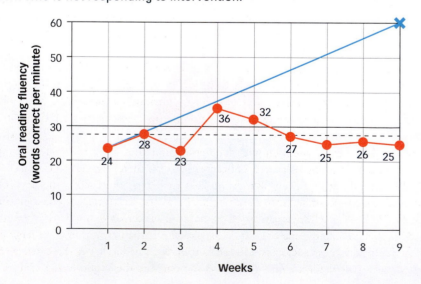

Like the IQ-achievement discrepancy, RTI is not without its problems. A major practical problem is the wide variation among states in aspects of implementation, such as the following (Callinan, Cunningham, & Theiler, 2013; Hauerwas et al., 2013; Mellard, McKnight, & Jordan, 2010):

- frequency of the Tier 2 and Tier 3 interventions and the size of the instructional groups in each tier;

- requirements for monitoring treatment fidelity (tracking how well the teachers or teacher aides are implementing particular lessons according to the guidelines provided in curriculum manuals, software, or research literature);

- frequency of progress-monitoring assessments;

- criteria to determine responsiveness to interventions; and

- timetable for when the process of determining special education eligibility begins.

As a result, RTI may result in as much or greater variation in the number of students identified as having LD than the variation produced by the IQ-achievement discrepancy (Fuchs & Deshler, 2007).

Another practical problem concerns the reliability of the RTI approach. Selecting students for tiered interventions using a single screening measure may increase the possibility of identification errors—identifying students who do not need intervention and overlooking those who do (Lipson, Chomsky-Higgins, & Kanfer, 2011). Also, schools measure "failure to respond" using different assessments for screening and progress monitoring and different criteria (cutpoints for determining benchmarks and ways to measure progress), leading to inconsistent results (Beach & O'Connor, 2015). A student may be considered nonresponsive to intervention using one set of tests and criteria and responsive using a different set.

Additionally, experts argue that RTI may not be a valid method for determining learning disabilities and therefore should not be used for special education eligibility (Kavale, Kauffman, Bachmeier, & LeFevers, 2008; Reynolds & Shaywitz, 2009). Classifying students as responding or not responding to an intervention based on progress monitoring, without the use of any additional information, may not be a valid indicator of the presence of a learning disability (Fletcher, Barth, & Stuebing, 2011). This method only tells us that a student did not respond to educators' best attempts at intervention, but we do not know why the student failed to respond (Hale et al., 2011). This approach would identify both students who are slow learners and students with cognitive deficits indicative of a learning disability (Kavale, 2005). This method also, by itself, cannot differentiate specific learning disabilities from intellectual disabilities and emotional/behavioral disorders and may overlook students who can compensate for their learning difficulties, such as students with giftedness (Mastropieri & Scruggs, 2005; Volker, Lopata, & Cook-Cottone, 2006).

A final practical problem with RTI is that it may not correct the problem of the IQ-achievement discrepancy method as a "wait to fail" approach. Critics of the discrepancy method argue that educators waited for children to fall behind in reading, math, or other academic skills until their achievement was sufficiently discrepant from their overall cognitive ability. In a similar fashion, RTI has been deemed a "watch them fail" approach (Reynolds, 2008, p. 20). To qualify for Tier 2 and 3 interventions, students need to continually score below grade level on progress monitoring measures, indicating their failure to respond to various interventions (Callinan et al., 2013). Even though students are being helped along the way, RTI may result in more students identified with a learning disability than the discrepancy method (Fuchs & Deshler, 2007). This "watch them fail" problem becomes exacerbated in schools where a majority of students score below grade level, such as schools in urban areas that serve large populations of students from lower socioeconomic backgrounds. In such schools, there may be 60% to 80% of students who perform below grade level compared to the hypothesized 20% in typical

Reliability: See Module 25

Validity: See Module 25

Emotional, social, and behavioral disorders: See Module 22

Giftedness: See Module 20

> DIVERSITY

RTI models (see Figure 21.2). When demand far outweighs the staff needed for RTI, resources become strained and all students who need intervention cannot be adequately served (Abbott & Wills, 2012; Abbott et al., 2008).

Rather than using failure to respond to identify learning disabilities, experts recommend administering tests to pinpoint the cognitive processing deficits that contribute to students' learning difficulties (Callinan et al., 2013; Hale et al., 2011). For example, research indicates that skills such as phonological awareness, alphabetic principle, word identification, and fluency, which are necessary for adequate reading development, consistently predict a student's responsiveness to intervention in RTI (Al Otaiba & Fuchs, 2002; Lam & McMaster, 2014). These are the same skills, as we see next, that are important for identifying a reading disability. Once educators identify the cognitive processing deficits that impair students' reading, math, or other academic skills, they can develop evidence-based intervention plans to help students improve their skills. Therefore, it is important for teachers to know what a reading disability or mathematics disability "looks like" to effectively plan instruction and remediate students' difficulties. Let's turn to these topics next.

Reading Disability

Students with a reading disability, or dyslexia, represent only 3% to 10% of the school-age population (Compton, Miller, Elleman, & Steacy, 2014; Duff & Clarke, 2011). Yet they are the focus of much research because their difficulties are often severe and resistant to remediation using typical instructional methods. As we will see, reading disability is characterized by a deficit in phonological processing that affects the development of reading skills and ultimately reading comprehension. A **deficit** is an impairment in specific cognitive processes that affect a certain skill area, such as reading or math. A deficit suggests that students acquire skills in a *qualitatively different* way from other students and that skill impairments may not be easily remediated with conventional instruction or interventions (Stanovich, 1993). This contrasts with the notion of a **developmental delay,** in which a student acquires cognitive skills in the same way as other students but at a slower rate. This suggests that the student will catch up given proper intervention.

CHARACTERISTICS

Individuals with a reading disability (RD) have a deficit in phonological processing that inhibits their ability to learn to recognize and decode words, which can affect their reading comprehension (Stanovich & Siegel, 1994; Vellutino, Fletcher, Snowling, & Scanlon, 2004). To understand RD, let's first review some important concepts in the development of skilled reading.

Skilled reading begins before formal reading instruction with the acquisition of two foundational skills, phonological awareness and knowledge of letter names (Adams, 1990; Wagner, Torgesen, & Rashotte, 1994). **Phonological awareness** refers to knowledge that spoken words contain smaller units of sound. For example, the word *cup* has three distinct sounds, called *phonemes,* which are the smallest units of sound that can change the meaning of a word. The words *cup* and *pup* differ in only one phoneme, the initial "c" or "p" sounds. Phonological awareness, in particular awareness of phonemes, along with knowledge of letters help children develop the **alphabetic principle,** an awareness that printed letters are represented by sounds. The alphabetic principle allows beginning readers to acquire a strategy called **decoding,** or applying the sounds of letters or letter strings to printed words, that is "sounding out" words. This is necessary for beginning readers to acquire skill in **word recognition,** or identifying individual words in text. Skilled readers have developed word recognition and decoding skills to the point of *automaticity,* which means they can perform the skill very quickly, accurately, and with few cognitive resources such as attention and strategies (Perfetti, 1992; Stanovich, 1990). Automaticity allows a reader to use cognitive resources for understanding what is being read, as you are doing while you read this paragraph. Conversely, slow and inaccurate word recognition and decoding consume cognitive resources and lead to difficulties in reading comprehension (Perfetti, 1985; Snowling & Hulme, 2013).

Phonological awareness and letter name knowledge: See Module 7

Word recognition and decoding: See Module 7

Automaticity: See Module 12

Compared to typically achieving students, students with RD show deficits in phonological awareness as young children, which limits their ability to acquire efficient word recognition and decoding skills (Compton et al., 2014; Snowling & Hulme, 2013). From elementary through college level, students with RD lack automaticity of word recognition and decoding (Cisero, Royer, Marchant, & Jackson, 1997; Compton & Carlisle, 1994). They have difficulty holding a phonological representation of a word (e.g., the sounds of letters in a printed word and the name of the word) in working memory to decode it during reading. As a result, many words do not become stored in long-term memory as representations that then can be automatically retrieved—even words that students with RD have encountered frequently. Consequently, individuals with RD experience a lack of automatic word recognition and decoding that often results in a breakdown in reading comprehension (Snowling & Hulme, 2013).

The cognitive deficits involved in RD are distinct from those involved in comprehension impairment, which affects about 5% to 10% of the school-age population (Compton et al., 2014; Snowling & Hulme, 2013). Students with comprehension impairment, also called *poor comprehenders,* have adequate phonological processing skills and can decode and spell words, but they have difficulty with reading comprehension (Duff & Clarke, 2011; Snowling & Hulme, 2013). Reading comprehension difficulties may stem from difficulties in a variety of oral language skills, such as listening comprehension, vocabulary, figurative language (for example, similes, metaphors, and idioms), ability to make inferences about the text, comprehension monitoring strategies, and knowledge of story structure (Cain, 2010; Duff & Clarke, 2011). Students' comprehension also may suffer because they lack prior knowledge about the world, which is necessary for supporting their understanding of texts and their ability to make inferences while reading (Compton et al., 2014).

Teachers and school psychologists can use information about the characteristic deficits of RD and comprehension impairment to choose appropriate assessments for determining whether a student is eligible to receive special education services for an RD.

- For children in kindergarten and first grade, an evaluation should include measures of phonological awareness, letter and word recognition, and rapid naming (quickly retrieving labels for objects, letters, colors, and numbers from long-term memory).

- For older children and adolescents, an evaluation should consist of measures of word recognition, decoding, vocabulary, and listening and reading comprehension. Timed measures of word recognition and decoding are particularly important because they provide an indication of automaticity.

APPLICATIONS: REMEDIATING READING DISABILITY

Research studies on RD and comprehension impairment suggest different types of interventions for remediating these distinct reading problems. For students with RD, experts recommend interventions that improve the underlying cognitive deficits that contribute to difficulties in oral reading and comprehension, whereas for students with comprehension impairment, experts recommend a variety of methods to address their particular comprehension problems.

Research indicates that extensive and systematic instruction in phonics can help elementary school students with RD acquire word identification and decoding skills (Foorman, Francis, Winikates, Schatschneider, & Fletcher, 1997; Torgesen et al., 2001; Torgesen, Wagner, & Rashotte, 1997; Torgesen, Wagner, Rashotte, Herron, & Lindamood, 2010; Torgesen et al., 1999). **Systematic phonics instruction** focuses on teaching children to recognize and manipulate phonemes and to apply that knowledge to letter-sound correspondences. In addition to explicit instruction, students practice decoding new words to mastery. **Fluency**—the ability to read text quickly, accurately, and with proper expression—is also problematic for many students with RD and is difficult to remediate in older students (Lyon, Shaywitz, & Shaywitz, 2003; Torgesen, 2005). One approach to increase fluency is **repeated reading,** which involves reading a text multiple times. For optimal fluency improvement, teachers should use texts that have a

Working memory and long-term memory: See Module 10

Figurative language: See Module 7

Making inferences: See Module 13

high percentage of common words, many words that are easily decodable, and few multisyllabic words that are less common (Hiebert, 2003; Hiebert & Fisher, 2002; Pressley, Gaskins, & Fingeret, 2006). Also, repeated reading is more effective with the assistance of an adult or more capable peer rather than a student reading alone (Kuhn & Stahl, 2003).

Several caveats must be considered before research findings on RD can be successfully translated into educational practice:

1. Even though research suggests that systematic phonics instruction may be beneficial for students with RD, this does not mean that the same approach leads to similar levels of improvement for each student. Even the most systematic and intensive interventions used in research tend to result in 10% to 15% of students who fail to acquire adequate word recognition and decoding skills (O'Connor & Fuchs, 2013; Torgesen, 1998, 2000).

2. In research studies, children receive an extensive amount of instruction. For example, research interventions ranged from 67 hours of individual instruction to over 80 hours of small-group or individual instruction (e.g., Torgesen et al., 2001; Torgesen et al., 2010). Outside of research studies, students are unlikely to receive such a considerable amount of remedial instruction. Many schools do not have the financial and personnel resources to provide sufficient time and intensity of interventions during the school day to accelerate the reading development of students with RD so that they achieve average-level skills (Torgesen et al., 2001; Torgesen et al., 2010).

Low-road transfer: See Module 12

3. Teachers should not expect mastery of letter-sound correspondences and phonemic skills to transfer automatically to improved word recognition and decoding. Studies of systematic phonics instruction by researchers have shown that this approach can improve decoding skills of students with RD, but these skills do not necessarily transfer to word recognition (Foorman et al., 1997; McCandliss, Beck, Sandak, & Perfetti, 2003; Torgesen et al., 2001; Torgesen et al., 1997). Word recognition and decoding skills must be practiced to the point of overlearning so that automaticity of word identification can support higher level reading processes such as comprehension (Cisero et al., 1997; Royer, 1997; Royer & Sinatra, 1994). Some research suggests the possibility that **automaticity training** of word recognition can improve the reading skills of students with RD (Royer, 1997). Also, systematic phonics is most effective when it is provided within a broad literacy curriculum that includes many opportunities to practice reading text (Stuebing, Barth, Cirino, Francis, & Fletcher, 2008).

4. Teachers must remember to offer opportunities for students to read rich, connected text in addition to practicing phonics (Stahl, 1998; Torgesen, 2000). Research indicates that providing simple reading material to students with RD may send the wrong message—that teachers think they are incapable of reading more challenging material and that reading is merely decoding. Also, students may expect to fail when they are given material that they have already encountered without success (Stahl, 1998). Using novel instructional materials helps circumvent this problem and motivates students by providing them with fun and interesting activities.

Research studies have found a variety of techniques to be effective in improving outcomes of students with comprehension impairment.

- Vocabulary instruction integrated within content courses, such as science or social studies, can improve reading comprehension (Clarke, Snowling, Truelove, & Hulme, 2010; Elleman, Lindo, Morphy, & Compton, 2009). Some simple classroom techniques are providing definitions and examples and nonexamples of concepts and using semantic maps (Kim, Vaughn, Wanzek, & Wei, 2004).

- Inference training has been found to improve reading comprehension (McGee & Johnson, 2003; Yuill & Oakhill, 1988). Teachers can ask students to select words from the text and explain how they contribute to the overall meaning. Students can also generate questions and make predictions about the text and then revisit their predictions to affirm or refute them after reading.

- Instruction that teaches students strategies for comprehending text have yielded positive results (Gersten, Fuchs, Williams, & Baker, 2001; National Institute of Child Health and Human Development, 2000; Rosenshine & Meister, 1994). Teachers can improve students' reading comprehension by activating prior knowledge through previewing headings or key concepts and making predictions (Klingner, Vaughn, & Boardman, 2007; Roberts, Torgesen, Boardman, & Scammacca, 2007). Encouraging students to summarize and make connections to prior knowledge, other subjects, or real-life applications also enhances reading comprehension. Reciprocal teaching, a method for teaching metacognitive strategies necessary for skilled reading comprehension (questioning about the main idea, clarifying, summarizing, and predicting), can be used for this purpose. These approaches can be used with students who have comprehension impairments as well as students with RD.

Reciprocal teaching: See Modules 11 and 12

Mathematics Disability

A large proportion of students in your classroom may struggle with various aspects of mathematics. Approximately 7% of students are typically identified as having a mathematics disability (MD), and an additional 10% of students are considered to have very low achievement in math (Geary, 2011; Geary, Hoard, Nugent, & Bailey, 2012). Our understanding of MD currently is limited to arithmetic skills in elementary school (Geary, 2004). However, when working with students in middle school and high school, a teacher should know the cognitive bases of the math difficulties to better plan appropriate curricula and accommodations for students. Let's explore the characteristics of MD and how they might differ from low math achievement.

CHARACTERISTICS

Research evidence indicates that MD is likely to be a heterogeneous disability and cannot be defined by classifying students into distinct categories, as once thought (Bartelet, Ansari, Vaessen, & Blomert, 2014; Geary, 2010; Rubinsten & Henik, 2009). Recent research has focused on students with different profiles of cognitive abilities: those with a specific MD and those with low math achievement (Geary, 2011, 2013):

- Students with a specific MD have mathematics achievement scores below the 10th percentile for two consecutive years and IQ scores that are within the average range.

Percentile scores: See Module 25

- Students with low math achievement also have IQ within the average range, but they have less severe problems, as indicated by below average math achievement (percentile scores ranging between 11 and 25) over two or more consecutive years.

IQ scores: See Module 20

The poor performance of both types of students is not the result of low intelligence or reading ability (Geary, 2011). Students with low achievement typically are average readers (Geary, 1993; Jordan, Hanich, & Kaplan, 2003b). Many students with an MD, but not all, also have an RD (Moll, 2014). To understand MD and low achievement, researchers have focused on three areas related to the development of arithmetic skill: (1) deficits in the ability to store and retrieve facts in long-term memory, (2) delays in the development of counting and arithmetic procedures, and (3) a disruption in the development of the number sense system. Let's explore each of these skill areas.

Fact-retrieval deficit. The characteristic most consistently found in research is a **fact-retrieval deficit,** an inability to commit facts to long-term memory and automatically retrieve them

Working memory and long-term memory: See Module 10

(Geary, 1990; Jordan, Hanich, & Kaplan, 2003a; Jordan et al., 2003b; Mazzocco, Devlin, & McKenney, 2008). When learning arithmetic facts such as 3 + 2 = 5, students must hold number-words (e.g., the words *three* and *two*) in working memory long enough for a memory representation of the problem (3 + 2) and the answer (= 5) to be associated in long-term memory. For individuals with MD, many arithmetic facts do not become stored in long-term memory for automatic retrieval, even after extensive drilling (Geary, 1993, 2004). Compared to students without disabilities, students with this deficit (Chan & Dally, 2001; Geary, 2004):

- retrieve fewer arithmetic facts from long-term memory,

- commit many more errors when using fact-retrieval as a strategy,

- overuse counting strategies (e.g., finger counting and verbal counting) rather than using retrieval, and

- exhibit variability in rates of retrieval of math facts (some slower, some faster), especially compared with younger, typically achieving students.

Both students with MD and students with low math achievement have difficulties learning basic arithmetic facts and retrieving them from long-term memory (Andersson, 2010; Chan & Ho, 2010, Geary, 1993; Jordan et al., 2003b). However, the origin of this deficit may be different for each type of student (Geary, 2011). Researchers are currently investigating possible sources of this deficit.

Procedural delays. Students with MD and students with low math achievement also have **procedural delays,** a lag in the development of counting procedures characterized by performance that is often similar to that of younger, typically achieving children (Geary et al., 2012). Students with this delay often use immature procedures for solving arithmetic problems. For example, children begin solving arithmetic problems by using the *counting all* strategy, which means that they begin counting from 1. For example, to solve 3 + 4, they would say "1, 2, 3, 4, 5, 6, 7" to get the answer 7. By first or second grade, typically achieving children will shift to *counting on* (also called the min strategy; Jordan & Montani, 1997; Ostad, 1998). In this strategy, the student identifies the larger addend (4) and mentally counts on from there, "5, 6, 7," to get the answer. Low-achieving students use their fingers to *count on,* but students with MD continue to use their fingers while performing *counting all* (Geary, 2011; Jordan et al., 2003a). The achievement gap represents a one-year delay for low-achieving students and a two- to three-year delay for students with MD (Geary, 2011). In addition to simple arithmetic problems in the early elementary grades, older students with this delay also exhibit problems with (Geary, 1990; Geary, Hoard, Byrd-Craven, Nugent, & Numtee, 2007; Jordan et al., 2003b; Russell & Ginsburg, 1984):

- more complex arithmetic, such as 367–142;

- multistep problems, such as 38 × 13; and

- story problems.

Number sense. **Number sense,** or the ability to represent exact quantities or approximate magnitudes of objects, develops in young children and is important for development of counting and arithmetic skills. For example, young children develop the understanding that three dots (***) represent the quantity 3 and that six dots (******) represent a greater quantity than three dots (***). Many students with MD show severe deficits in these number sense abilities (Halberda, Mazzocco, & Feigenson, 2008; Mazzocco, Feigenson, & Halberda, 2011; Piazza et al., 2010; Stock, Desoete, & Roeyers, 2010). However, this deficit is *not always* found in students with MD (Iuculano, Tang, Hall, & Butterworth, 2008; Mazzocco et al., 2011; Rousselle & Noël, 2007). In contrast, students with low math achievement are less likely to have number

Number Sense. Number sense is important for arithmetic development and may play a role in fact-retrieval deficits and procedural delays.

sense problems, and when they do, they eventually catch up developmentally and are similar to typically developing students on these skills (Geary et al., 2012; Mazzocco et al., 2011). The pattern indicating a deficit for students with MD and a delay for students with low achievement may suggest that there are different mechanisms underlying the number sense difficulties of these two types of students (Geary, 2013).

Some researchers believe that number sense difficulties may be at the root of fact-retrieval deficits and procedural delays (Jordan et al., 2003a; Raghubur et al., 2009). Difficulty developing number sense may impair a child's ability to map representations (***) onto Arabic numerals (3) and number-words (three; Geary, 2010). Some children with MD and children with low achievement are slower than peers at mapping quantities onto number-words and Arabic numerals (Geary et al., 2012; Mazzocco et al., 2011; Rousselle & Noël, 2007). The difficulty mapping may in turn lead to problems counting and performing arithmetic. However, experts believe that there may be different mechanisms underlying the number sense deficits of children with MD and those with low achievement, and this research is ongoing (Geary, 2013).

Much research is still needed to understand the underlying causes of number sense problems, procedural delays, and fact-retrieval difficulties of students with MD and low math achievement. Regardless, teachers can use knowledge regarding these characteristics to identify children who may need differentiated instruction, RTI, or referral for special education. Diagnostic evaluations by school psychologists typically include individually administered standardized achievement tests that measure a range of skills, from factual knowledge about math to mathematical calculation (from elementary through secondary level) and problem solving. School psychologists should choose standardized tests that assess mathematical computations in a timed format to assess automaticity of fact retrieval.

In addition, school psychologists or classroom teachers can conduct informal assessments of mathematical competence. An informal assessment requires working one-on-one with students and interviewing them about their knowledge and how they arrived at answers to problems.

Differentiated instruction: See Module 18

- For students from kindergarten through second grade, teachers can give students a variety of arithmetic problems to determine what types of counting strategies they are using (Jordan, 1995).

- For students in the upper elementary grades, teachers can conduct an error analysis (Fleischner, 1994). For example, mathematical errors sometimes involve simple misalignment of numbers while writing down partial answers. Students also may make errors due to carrying or borrowing—called procedural bugs (Brown & Burton, 1978). Consider the following problems, indicating that the student lacks knowledge of carrying and does not understand place value.

$$
\begin{array}{r} 93 \\ +57 \\ \hline 1410 \end{array} \qquad \begin{array}{r} 46 \\ +39 \\ \hline 715 \end{array}
$$

APPLICATIONS: REMEDIATING MATH DISABILITY

To effectively remediate mathematics disability, interventions need to target the specific deficits that students exhibit in contrast to a one-size-fits-all approach (Geary, 2011). Depending on students' difficulties, teachers may focus interventions on number sense, counting strategies, or encouraging automatic fact retrieval.

To improve students' number sense, teachers can use two free, research-based, online games—*The Number Race* (Wilson, Revkin, Cohen, Cohen, & Dehaene 2006) and *GraphoGame-Maths*—that were developed to target difficulties representing the magnitudes of number sets and manipulating them. Both games are computer adaptive, meaning that they adjust the difficulty level to make trials easier if the student shows a pattern of incorrect responses or more challenging if the student makes many correct responses.

- *The Number Race* teaches children to judge approximate magnitudes. Users are shown two arrays of dots and are told to select the larger array. The program starts with large differences between two sets (e.g., 9 vs. 4 dots) and progresses to smaller differences over time (9 vs. 8 dots) as the child gains mastery. The game can be used with kindergarteners and as a remedial intervention for children ages 4 to 8 who have an MD (Kroeger, Brown, & O'Brien, 2012; Price & Ansari, 2013).

- *GraphoGame-Maths* teaches children to compare exact quantities of small sets that can be counted, and focuses on mapping the quantities to number-words (Butterworth, 2005; Price & Ansari, 2013).

Research indicates that the computer programs improve number sense, but benefits do not transfer to counting and arithmetic (Räsänen, Salminen, Wilson, Aunio, & Dehaene, 2009; Wilson, Dehaene, Dubois, & Fayol, 2009).

For students who use immature counting strategies, teachers can focus on ways to help them shift to more mature strategies. Students who rely on the *counting all* strategy might practice the *counting on* strategy with their fingers or with manipulatives (objects used for counting; Garnett, 1992). Using manipulatives facilitates students' understanding of mathematical principles (Gersten et al., 2009). Students also may practice identifying the larger addend and using the commutative property (e.g., 5 + 4 = 4 + 5).

To encourage automatic fact retrieval, teachers should remind their students to ask themselves "Do I know this one?" For example, when faced with the problem 6 + 8, students should first ask whether this is a known problem that they can directly retrieve from memory, rather than relying on a counting strategy. Overreliance on counting strategies impedes the development of direct fact retrieval.

Teachers also can introduce shortcut strategies to help students develop fact-retrieval skill (Jordan et al., 2003b; National Research Council, 2001; Robinson, Menchetti, & Torgesen, 2002). For example, if students know 3 + 3 = 6, they can derive the answer to 3 + 4. Another shortcut is the commutative property (3 + 4 = 4 + 3). Shortcut strategies link similar problems to facilitate storage of facts in long-term memory—and thus direct retrieval. Table 21.2 provides two different ways to organize instruction for students with MD. Even though the approaches differ, the intent is the same—reducing the load on working memory in solving arithmetic problems and allowing sufficient practice with calculations so that facts are committed to memory.

Some experts argue against rote memorization of arithmetic facts because it places a heavy load on working memory—a weakness in many children with MD (Geary, 1994). However, other researchers have found success in remediating the fact-retrieval deficit by using rote drill, or more specifically, automaticity training. In one study involving an at-home intervention for students with MD, six weeks of nightly practice involving speeded retrieval of addition, subtraction, and multiplication facts improved the speed and accuracy of fact retrieval (Royer & Tronsky, 1998). The speeded practice forces students to abandon their less efficient counting strategies and use fact retrieval instead. In the classroom, teachers can use a method called Detect-Practice-Repair (DPR; Poncy, Skinner, & O'Mara, 2006). This approach has several stages (Axtell, McCallum, & Bell, 2009; Poncy et al., 2006):

Working memory: See Module 10

- a timed assessment to identify the math facts that are not yet automatic;

- multiple repetitions of these facts in sets of five in which students cover the math fact (3 + 2 = 5), copy it from memory, and then compare their result to the example; and

- a timed assessment and graphing of scores to show progress.

TABLE 21.2	Ways to Organize Number Facts Instruction for Students With Math Disabilities	
APPROACH	**INSTRUCTIONAL SEQUENCE**	**EXAMPLE**
Garnett (1992)	+1 principle and	2 + 1, 3 + 1, etc.
	+0 principle	2 + 0, 3 + 0, etc.
	ties	5 + 5, 6 + 6, etc.
	ties + 1	5 + 6, 6 + 7, etc.
	ties + 2	5 + 7, 6 + 8, etc.
	+10 number facts	1 + 10, 2 + 10, 3 + 10, etc.
	+9 number facts	6 + 9 is one less than 6 + 10
	remaining facts	2 + 5, 2 + 6, 2 + 7, 2 + 8
		3 + 6, 3 + 7, 3 + 8
		4 + 7, 4 + 8
		5 + 8
Thornton and Toohey (1985)	count-ons	+1, +2, +3 facts
	+0 principle	2 + 0, 3 + 0, 4 + 0, etc.
	doubles (i.e., ties)	5 + 5, 6 + 6, etc.
	10 sums	6 + 4, 7 + 3, etc.
	+9s	4 + 9, 9 + 3, etc.
	near doubles	4 + 5, 3 + 4, etc.
	remaining facts	7 + 5, 8 + 4, 8 + 5, 8 + 6

DPR has several advantages over traditional classroom methods. Most classroom approaches use a combination of known and unknown facts, which wastes instructional time because much of the practice is on material the student already knows (Axtell et al., 2009; Poncy, Skinner, & Axtell, 2010). DPR reduces the amount of material students need to practice. Additionally, DPR can be implemented as a class-wide intervention, can be used to differentiate Tier 1 instruction, and requires little effort from teachers (Parkhurst et al., 2010; Poncy et al., 2010). Research indicates that this method uses very little instructional time and improves the fact-retrieval skills of elementary and middle school students with very low performance in math (Axtell et al., 2009; Parkhurst et al., 2010; Poncy, Fontenelle, & Skinner, 2013; Poncy et al., 2010; Poncy et al., 2006).

 The research and practical applications regarding reading and mathematics disabilities focus on elementary school students. How might middle school and high school teachers assist their students who have been identified with reading or mathematics disabilities?

SUMMARY

1 Describe how cognitive disabilities are identified and served under the Individuals with Disabilities Education Improvement Act. Students with intellectual disabilities and learning disabilities are eligible for special education and related services under IDEA as specified by the law. Students undergo a diagnostic evaluation by a school psychologist after parents give consent. Based on the evaluation results, a multidisciplinary team determines whether the student is eligible for special education. IDEA requires the development of an educational plan and placement of the student in the least restrictive environment.

2 Discuss the impairments you would expect to see in students with intellectual disabilities and the curricular approaches useful in addressing these deficits. Individuals with intellectual disabilities have a significant deficiency in intelligence and one or more areas of adaptive behavior (conceptual, social, and practical behavior). Diagnosis is made based on a score that is two standard deviations or more below the average on a standardized IQ test and on a standardized measure of adaptive behavior. Teachers can use direct instruction and cooperative learning methods, encourage hands-on learning, focus on repetition of knowledge and skills, and foster generalization of skills to a variety of contexts.

3 Explain how learning disabilities are identified using the IQ-achievement discrepancy and the response-to-intervention approach. Learning disabilities may be identified using an IQ-achievement discrepancy, where a student's achievement in one or more achievement areas is significantly below what would be expected from his or her IQ. Learning disabilities also may be identified using a response-to-intervention approach, in which students are referred for evaluation if they were identified as at risk and failed to respond to increasingly intensive research-based interventions.

4 Explain the characteristic deficits you would look for in identifying students with reading and mathematics disabilities and how you would approach remediating these deficits. Students with reading disability experience a lack of automaticity of word recognition and decoding, which in turn impairs reading comprehension. Students with mathematics disability have a fact-retrieval deficit, experiencing great difficulty storing and retrieving math facts from long-term memory even after extensive drilling. They may also experience extreme procedural delays in counting strategies and deficits in number sense. Systematic phonics may be used successfully with some students who have reading disability, while interventions that encourage development of number sense, more mature counting strategies, and automaticity of fact retrieval may be effective for students with mathematics disability.

KEY CONCEPTS

alphabetic principle, 450

automaticity training, 452

decoding, 450

deficit, 450

developmental delay, 450

dual discrepancy method, 448

fact-retrieval deficit, 453

Family Educational Rights and Privacy Act, 441

CASE STUDIES: REFLECT AND EVALUATE

EARLY CHILDHOOD: LETTER *P* DAY

These questions refer to the case study on page 404.

1. The case study does not specify what disability, if any, Teran has. Based on the information given in the case, how likely is it that Teran has an intellectual disability? What additional information would you need to be certain?

2. Describe conceptual, practical, and social skills that you would expect to find among kindergartners. What difficulties in these areas would you expect to see in a kindergartner with an intellectual disability?

3. Jillian appears to be somewhat advanced in literacy skills. What difficulties would you expect to see in a kindergartner who may be at risk for later reading disability?

4. Consistent with the response-to-intervention approach to identifying learning disabilities, what type of instruction and activities in language arts does Mrs. Cahill need to provide to document that research-based approaches have been tried with students having academic difficulties? Evaluate whether Mrs. Cahill's language arts activities are consistent with the response-to-intervention approach.

5. Using the guidelines discussed in the module, describe what specific types of skills or strategies Mrs. Cahill should focus on in math instruction to document that research-based approaches have been tried with students having academic difficulties.

ELEMENTARY SCHOOL: CHEETAHS, LIONS, AND LEOPARDS

These questions refer to the case study on page 406.

1. Assume that Travis also has an intellectual disability. Speculate on the possible deficits in conceptual behavior, social skills, and practical skills that Travis may experience in the classroom.

2. If Travis has deficits in adaptive behavior but not intellectual abilities, could he be considered to have an intellectual disability? Why or why not?

3. Provide Mrs. Fratelli with specific suggestions for teaching Travis. Do these suggestions differ from recommendations you would make for teaching a nondisabled student?

4. Evaluate whether Marcela could have a specific reading disability based on the characteristic deficits of reading disability. Based on the IQ-achievement discrepancy, describe the IQ and achievement test results you would expect to find if she has a reading disability.

5. Assume that Marcela does have a specific reading disability. What recommendations would you give Mrs. Fratelli for helping Marcela improve her reading skills?

MIDDLE SCHOOL: MATH TROUBLES

These questions refer to the case study on page 408.

1. Like Lindsey, Jessica also seems to struggle in math. Which student would you consider to have a *deficit* and which student a *delay?* Why?

2. Jessica does not have any identified disabilities. What characteristics would you look for if you suspected that she has an intellectual disability?

3. Based on the definition of intellectual disabilities discussed in the module, is it likely for Jessica to

be identified with an intellectual disability as a 12-year-old?

4. Assume that Lindsey has a math disability. What types of interventions and/or services would you expect to see on her IEP? How might these differ if she were in fourth grade?

HIGH SCHOOL: NOON SUPERVISED STUDY

These questions refer to the case study on page 410.

1. Why would you expect to find few students with intellectual disabilities in a ninth-grade history class? Discuss the issue of least restrictive environment.

2. A student with a mild intellectual disability who is highly functioning is assigned to Mr. Hardy's history class. He has an IQ of 68 and a significant deficit in social skills but fewer problems with conceptual and practical skills. Discuss potential modifications Mr. Hardy may need to make to address this student's specific academic needs.

5. If Lindsey has a math disability, what strategies or teaching methods can Miss Barton use to help Lindsey succeed in math? If Jessica has an intellectual disability, how can Miss Barton address her specific cognitive needs? Is there any overlap of the teaching strategies Miss Barton would use for a math disability and those she would use for an intellectual disability?

3. What characteristic reading deficits would you expect Anthony to show? How might these affect his performance in history class?

4. Discuss how Anthony's ethnicity may have played a role in his being identified as eligible for special education. How might the response-to-intervention approach prevent students from being incorrectly identified for special education?

5. At the high school level, Anthony is unlikely to receive remedial intervention in reading. Brainstorm ways Mr. Hardy can help Anthony read and understand the text in history class.

Visit **edge.sagepub.com/durwin3e** to help you accomplish your coursework goals in an easy-to-use learning environment.

- Mobile-friendly **eFlashcards**
- Mobile-friendly practice **quizzes**
- A complete online **action plan**

- Chapter **learning objectives**
- EXCLUSIVE! Access to full-text **SAGE journal articles**

$SAGE edge™

APPLY AND PRACTICE WHAT YOU'VE LEARNED

▶ edge.sagepub.com/durwin3e

©iStockphoto.com/ KaeArt

EMOTIONAL, SOCIAL, AND BEHAVIORAL DISORDERS

OUTLINE	LEARNING GOALS

Emotional, Social, and Behavioral Disorders in
   Today's Classrooms

- Special Education Referral and Eligibility
- Planning and Placement

❶ Describe how students with emotional, social, and behavioral disorders are identified and served under IDEA and Section 504.

Characteristics of Disorders

- Anxiety and Depression
- ADHD and Conduct Disorder
- Autism Spectrum Disorder

❷ Explain how anxiety and depression affect students' academic and social functioning.

❸ Explain how ADHD and conduct disorder affect students' academic and social functioning.

❹ Describe the characteristics of autism spectrum disorder, and explain how these affect academic and social functioning.

Applications: Interventions

- Types of Interventions
- Effectiveness of Interventions

❺ Describe interventions that are effective in treating emotional, social, and behavioral disorders.

EMOTIONAL, SOCIAL, AND BEHAVIORAL DISORDERS IN TODAY'S CLASSROOMS

❶ Describe how students with emotional, social, and behavioral disorders are identified and served under IDEA and Section 504.

Students with emotional, social, or behavioral disorders face unique problems that interfere with their academic progress (Nelson, Benner, & Bohaty, 2014). Their problems are distinct from those of students with cognitive disabilities—intellectual disabilities (formerly referred to as mental retardation) and specific learning disabilities. To clarify, the term *disability* implies an impairment in some aspect of functioning (hearing, reading, cognitive processing, and so on), whereas *disorder* is used to describe a collection of symptoms or behaviors. Students with emotional, social, communicative, or behavioral disorders are likely to have poor peer relationships, poor classroom interactions, and low academic performance. The specific disorders most relevant to school-aged children and adolescents include anxiety, depression, attention deficit hyperactivity disorder (ADHD), conduct disorder, and autism, and they represent a heterogeneous category of students who receive special education services under federal law.

Consider Figure 22.1, which shows the percentage of K-12 students receiving special education under the **Individuals with Disabilities Education Improvement Act of 2004 (IDEA),** a federal law that provides special education funding for 13 categories of disability. Autism, represented in the pie chart in Figure 22.1 as "Other disabilities combined," is its own IDEA category, albeit a small one, whereas ADHD is not one of the 13 categories of disability under IDEA. Students with ADHD who meet eligibility criteria for special education (which is not always the case, as we discuss later) may qualify under the "Other health impairments" category or the "Emotional disturbance" category. Students with anxiety, depression, severe aggression,

Cognitive disabilities:
See Module 21

FIGURE 22.1 **An Overview of Disabilities and Disorders.** This graph shows the percentage of elementary through high school students with various disabilities and disorders receiving special education and related services under IDEA.

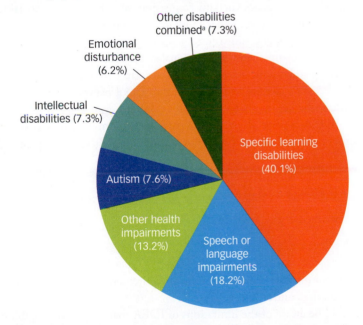

a"Other disabilities combined" includes *deaf-blindness* (less than 0.03 percent), *developmental delay* (2.1 percent), *hearing impairments* (1.2 percent), *multiple disabilities* (2.2 percent), *orthopedic impairments* (0.9 percent), *traumatic brain injury* (0.4 percent), and *visual impairments* (0.4 percent).

NOTE: Percentage was calculated by dividing the number of students ages 6 through 21 served under *IDEA*, Part B, in the disability category by the total number of students ages 6 through 21 served under *IDEA*, PART B, then multiplying the result by 100.

SOURCE: U.S. Department of Education, *EDFacts* Data Warehouse (EDW), OMB #1875-0240: "*IDEA* Part B Child Count and Educational Environments Collection," 2012. These date are for the 50 states, DC, BIE schools, PR, the four outlying areas, and the three freely associated states. Data were accessed fall 2013. For actual data used, go to http://www.ed.gov/about/reports/annual/osep.

and conduct disorder also are represented in the "Emotional disturbance" category. **Emotional disturbance** is defined as:

> a condition exhibiting one or more of the following characteristics over a long period of time and to a marked degree that adversely affects educational performance—
>
> A. An inability to learn that cannot be explained by intellectual, sensory, or health factors;
> B. An inability to build or maintain satisfactory interpersonal relationships with peers and teachers;
> C. Inappropriate types of behavior or feelings under normal circumstances;
> D. A general pervasive mood of unhappiness or depression; or
> E. A tendency to develop physical symptoms or fears associated with personal or school problems.
>
> [Code of Federal Regulations, Title 34, Section 300.7(c)(4)(i)]

Teachers refer students for special education evaluation, serve on committees to determine the eligibility of students for special education, and implement behavioral and curricular modifications to address the unique problems of these students in the classroom. To carry out these tasks effectively, teachers need to be aware of the laws that govern special education eligibility and, most important, the characteristic behaviors of students with emotional, social, or behavioral disorders that affect the way students learn and interact with peers.

Special Education Referral and Eligibility

Students with disabilities or disorders have the right to receive a "free and appropriate public education" through the provision of special education and related services, including academic interventions, speech and language therapy, counseling, physical therapy, social services, and transportation. Determining a student's eligibility for these programs begins with a referral, typically by the student's teacher and sometimes by the parent. Parents must consent for a school psychologist to conduct a comprehensive educational evaluation, which includes multiple sources of information (achievement tests, behavioral measures, etc.). Then a multidisciplinary team— consisting of the student's parents and teachers, the school psychologist, and other relevant members—evaluates whether the student meets the eligibility criteria specified by federal law.

According to IDEA, a prior diagnosis of a particular disorder such as anxiety, depression, ADHD, or conduct disorder in itself does not warrant eligibility. The student's disability or disorder must:

* persist over a long period of time,

* exist to a marked degree, and

* adversely affect academic performance.

If the disability or disorder fails to meet these requirements, the student is not eligible for special education services under IDEA.

Teachers should be aware of the limitations of IDEA that may affect eligibility decisions. The ambiguous language in the definition may lead to inconsistent diagnoses. For example, the definition says that the disability or disorder must persist over a long period of time and exist to a marked degree. How long is long enough? And how do we measure a "marked degree"? The requirement that the disorder "adversely affect academic performance" can also be interpreted in many ways. As a result, the determination of eligibility can vary across states and from one school district to another (Osher et al., 2004; Parrish, 2002).

DIVERSITY {

In addition, students from various ethnic groups are identified for special education disproportionately under the IDEA category. In comparison with White students, African American males and Native American students are overrepresented, while Asian and Latino students tend to be underrepresented (U.S. Department of Education, 2014; Wiley, Brigham, Kauffman, & Bogan, 2013). We should be cautious *not* to interpret these findings to mean that race or ethnicity is associated with a greater risk for placement into special education. Disproportionate identification may be the result of educators' failure to consider cultural context when making special education referrals based on interpretations of students' classroom behaviors (Carrero & Lusk, 2014; Cartledge, Kea, & Simmons-Reed, 2002). A pattern in which students shout out answers and do not respect turn-taking rules in class discussions may reflect culturally specific, valued actions rather than disruptive behaviors, while the verbally unassertive behaviors of other students may be interpreted incorrectly as a lack of motivation or a resistance to instruction.

Students with special needs who do not meet the IDEA eligibility requirements may be eligible under **Section 504 of the Rehabilitation Act of 1973,** a federal antidiscrimination law protecting the rights of individuals with disabilities or disorders who participate in any program or activity that receives federal funds from the U.S. Department of Education, including public schools. Students with a physical or mental disability are not automatically eligible for special services under Section 504; their disability or disorder must interfere with learning. Nevertheless, the eligibility requirements under Section 504 are more flexible than those specified by IDEA.

Planning and Placement

While both IDEA and Section 504 protect the right to "free and appropriate education," the term *appropriate* implies different accommodations under each law. Under Section 504, *appropriate* means an education that is comparable to that of students who are not disabled. For example, providing books on tape would allow a student who is blind equal access to the same information that is available to his or her sighted peers. Schools develop a **Section 504 plan,** which outlines the type of education (general classroom or special education) and services for allowing the student to function as adequately as nondisabled students. Under IDEA, *appropriate* refers to a curricular program designed to provide educational benefit to the student. Schools develop an **Individualized Education Plan (IEP),** which outlines curricula, educational modifications, and provision of services intended to enhance or improve the student's academic, social, or behavioral skills. IEPs contain several important features, such as:

1. The student's present levels of academic achievement and functional performance.

2. Measurable annual goals and short-term instructional objectives.

3. An explanation of how the student's progress toward annual goals will be measured and when progress will be reported to parents.

4. Any appropriate accommodations for test taking on statewide and district-wide assessments, especially those required by the No Child Left Behind Act. In cases where educators determine that the student will take an alternative assessment, the IEP needs to specify why this assessment was selected and why it is appropriate for the student.

5. The types of special education and related services provided to the student and how long the services will be needed. The IEP also needs to specify how much of the student's education will not be in the general education classroom.

6. Measurable postsecondary goals related to education, training, or employment for students age 14 and older.

7. A statement of transition services needed to reach goals involving independent living, continuing education, or employment after high school for students age 16 (or younger, if appropriate).

Both IDEA and Section 504 require educators to place students with disabilities or disorders in the general education classroom "to the maximum extent appropriate," known as the **least restrictive environment (LRE)**. Two LRE approaches have evolved from different interpretations of the law over the past four decades.

- In **mainstreaming,** students with special needs are placed with typically achieving peers when appropriate. For example, they may spend most of their day in a special education classroom and be integrated with their peers for subjects such as music, art, and social studies and for activities such as lunch, recess, library, and field trips.

- **Inclusion,** a more recent and popular approach, refers to integrating all students within the general education classroom, even those with severe disabilities (with the assistance of paraprofessionals) for most or all of the school day.

DIVERSITY ⟨

About 45% of elementary through high school students served under IDEA for emotional disturbance spend most of the school day in the general education classroom (U.S. Department of Education, 2014). Special education classrooms or *pull-out programs,* in which students are pulled out of the general education classroom for remediation or therapy, are more common at the middle school and high school level. Students with disabilities or disorders who are eligible for services under Section 504 may be placed in special education classes or remain in general education classrooms with accommodations and supports, or both, depending on their individual needs. Research does indicate that African American and Latino students are more likely to be placed in more restrictive settings than their nonminority peers (Skiba, Middelerg, & McClain, 2014).

? Did you or someone you know receive special education services for an emotional, social, or behavioral disorder? Do you recall the type of disorder and what services or accommodations were offered to you or this individual?

CHARACTERISTICS OF DISORDERS

2 Explain how anxiety and depression affect students' academic and social functioning.

3 Explain how ADHD and conduct disorder affect students' academic and social functioning.

4 Describe the characteristics of autism spectrum disorder, and explain how these affect academic and social functioning.

We examine several specific disorders and the collection of behaviors or symptoms that are used to make a diagnosis for these disorders. Before we summarize these specific disorders, it is helpful to examine how they fit within the broad categories of disorders. Two common categories used to describe disorders include (1) *internalizing disorders* and (2) *externalizing disorders* (Achenbach, 1992). Internalizing disorders are those that include emotional states and cognitive distress, such as fear, anxiety, and depression. Externalizing disorders are those that include more behavioral characteristics, such as impulsivity and aggression. Teachers must be alert to both, especially internalizing symptoms that may not be as readily identified in a busy classroom. Although these two broad categories can be very distinct from one another, some children and adolescents exhibit co-occurring emotional (internalizing) and behavioral (externalizing) problems (Fanti & Henrich, 2010). A third category comprises *developmental disorders* that include symptoms in which a child does not meet expected levels of basic skills, most often related to communication and socialization skills.

In the following sections, we examine the specific internalizing disorders of anxiety and depression, the specific externalizing disorders of ADHD and conduct disorder, and a group of developmental disorders—autism spectrum disorder—that have received increased public attention over the last five to ten years.

Anxiety and Depression

In IDEA's emotional disturbance definition, anxiety is suggested by the criterion "physical symptoms or fears associated with personal or school problems," and depression is suggested by the criterion, "a general pervasive mood of unhappiness or depression." What are the academic and personal characteristics of students with anxiety and depression, and how do these affect their academic and peer relationships? Let's explore these questions further.

ANXIETY

Approximately 20% of children and adolescents suffer from an **anxiety disorder**, which includes a variety of disorders: generalized anxiety disorder, obsessive-compulsive disorder, selective mutism, specific phobia, social anxiety disorder, and separation anxiety disorder (American Psychiatric Association, 2013; Swan, Cummings, Caporino, & Kendall, 2014). The description of each of these disorders is beyond the scope of this text, but we can discuss some general features of anxiety disorders.

Anxiety: See Module 15

Anxiety disorders are much more than the occasional anxiety we all feel from time to time. They involve distressingly unpleasant and maladaptive feelings, thoughts, behaviors, and physical reactions (Higa-McMillan, Francis, & Chorpita, 2014). Students with anxiety often worry about their competence, even when they are not being evaluated. Because they tend to be overly conforming, perfectionist, or unsure of themselves, they may redo tasks due to excessive dissatisfaction with what they have produced. Students with anxiety also may worry about catastrophes, violence, and bullying by peers and may engage in avoidance behaviors such as absence from school (American Psychiatric Association, 2013; DeVoe et al., 2003). The following behaviors can help teachers identify cases of anxiety that may require referral to a psychologist for further evaluation (Albano, Chorpita, & Barlow, 2003; Cullinan, 2007; Egger, Costello, Erkanli, & Angold, 1999; Nishina, Juvonen, & Witkow, 2005):

- Thoughts about being threatened, criticized, or appearing incompetent
- Thoughts about losing control of one's thoughts and actions
- Thoughts about the hypothetical death of a loved one
- Increased heart rate, fast breathing, or excessive sweating
- Headache, stomach ache, nausea, or bowel problems
- Muscle tension

Developmental differences. Anxiety is more common in adolescents, with girls twice as likely to experience an anxiety disorder as boys (American Psychiatric Association, 2013). However, the type of problem varies by age. Separation anxiety—an anxiety related to separating from parents and caregivers—is typical in infants and younger children, while social anxiety disorder—anxiety that is evoked in certain social or performance situations—occurs more frequently in adolescents (American Psychiatric Association, 2013; Higa-McMillan et al., 2014). Some research has suggested that anxiety at very young ages, such as separation anxiety, is related to later mental health problems, particularly depression (Higa-McMillan et al., 2014).

Effect on school performance and relationships. Students with anxiety experience impairments in academic and social functioning. They tend to perform below their ability level, receive lower

Anxiety. High levels of anxiety decrease a student's ability to concentrate and perform on assignments or tests.

©iStockphoto.com/ Antonio_Diaz

grades, and score lower on IQ tests (Davis, Ollendick, & Nebel-Schwalm, 2008; Nail et al., 2015; Wood, 2006). Students' heightened state of arousal impairs concentration on academic tasks and interferes with learning and/or recall of subject matter (Owens, Stevenson, Hadwin, & Norgate, 2012). Students who are highly anxious also experience difficulties with peers, which in turn may increase their social anxiety (Tillfors, Persson, Willén, & Burk, 2012). The long-term effect of anxiety was found in a longitudinal study following African American children over seven years: Anxiety symptoms in the first grade were related to academic and social difficulties in the eighth grade (Grover, Ginsburg, & Ialongo, 2007).

DIVERSITY

 Look at the characteristics of anxiety listed earlier. What changes can you make to your teaching and to the general classroom environment to help students with anxiety in the grade you intend to teach?

DEPRESSION

We all occasionally feel blue or sad, but this is not depression. **Major depressive disorders** involve at least two weeks of depressed mood or loss of interest, along with at least four additional depressive symptoms, and can last about two months (American Psychiatric Association, 2013). To be considered a major depressive episode, symptoms also must cause significant distress or impairment in social, occupational, or other types of functioning and cannot be the result of medication, a medical condition, bereavement, or drug abuse (American Psychiatric Association, 2013). Teachers can use the following list to help them accurately identify possible cases of depression in students who may require referral to a psychologist for further evaluation (American Psychiatric Association, 2013; Garber & Horowitz, 2002; Gresham & Kern, 2004; Harrington, 2002; Lewinsohn & Essau, 2002; Weller, Weller, Rowan, & Svadjian, 2002).

- pervasively sad mood
- general irritability
- inability to sustain attention, think, or concentrate
- decline in school participation and performance
- loss of interest in activities

- drastic change in weight (or failure to gain weight in children) or appetite

- drastic change in energy level

- prolonged, unpredictable crying

- hopelessness

- strong feelings of worthlessness or guilt

- social withdrawal

Developmental differences. Depressive disorders are very rare in young children. While only about 2% of students have experienced some type of depressive disorder by early adolescence, rates of depression rise to about 20% during adolescence; in particular, the likelihood increases with the onset of puberty (American Psychiatric Association, 2013; Hammen, Rudolph, & Abaied, 2014). In late adolescence, females are twice as likely as males to experience some form of depression, in contrast with equal incidence rates for the genders before adolescence (Hammen et al., 2014).

Effect on school performance and relationships. Depressive symptoms are linked to lower academic performance as well as a higher dropout rate (Owens, et al., 2012; Quiroga, Janosz, Bisset, & Morin, 2013). Like anxiety, a bidirectional relationship exists with peer relationships such that depression may lead to peer isolation and suicidal behaviors in adolescence and peer isolation then leads to increased depression (Hammen et al., 2014; Marcotte, Lévesque, & Fortin, 2006).

ADHD and Conduct Disorder

Rather than identifying specific types of behavioral disorders, the IDEA definition of emotional disturbance broadly lists "inappropriate types of behavior or feelings under normal circumstances." Educators often interpret this criterion as aggression and/or impulsivity. We discuss two types of behavioral disorders that fit this criterion: attention deficit hyperactivity disorder (ADHD) and conduct disorder.

ADHD

Individuals with **ADHD** have a neurological condition that impairs self-regulation as compared with same-age peers (Barkley, 1997; Vaidya, 2013). Examination of several studies found that gray matter in the brains of individuals with ADHD is reduced in areas essential to cognitive control or self-regulation (Ellison-Wright, Ellison-Wright, & Bullmore, 2008; Vaidya, 2013). Self-regulation involves maintaining attention, inhibiting impulsive or inappropriate responses, maintaining executive control over planning, monitoring progress, and selecting appropriate strategies in working memory (Thomas, 2013). Approximately 5% of U.S. children and adolescents have a diagnosis of ADHD, with boys diagnosed more than twice as often as girls (American Psychiatric Association, 2013). Media coverage as well as information provided by some experts suggests that ADHD is overdiagnosed, yet empirical data have been inconsistent in substantiating or disproving this claim (Chilakamarri, Filkowski, & Ghaemi, 2011; Sciutto & Eisenberg, 2007).

Individuals can have one of three subtypes of ADHD:

1. The *predominantly inattentive* subtype is characterized by symptoms of inattention, such as difficulty sustaining attention, forgetfulness, or difficulty organizing tasks.

2. The *predominantly hyperactive-impulsive* subtype is represented by symptoms of hyperactivity or impulsivity, such as fidgeting, constant physical activity, excessive talking, and difficulty playing quietly.

3. The *combined* subtype consists of both inattentive symptoms and hyperactivity-impulsivity.

Brain development: See Module 5

Self-regulation: See Module 9

 DIVERSITY

Executive control: See Module 11

Working memory: See Module 10

Characteristics of ADHD.
Adolescents with ADHD
may show disorganized
thinking and planning.

Rubberball/Mike Kemp/Brand X Pictures / Getty Images

For a diagnosis of ADHD, symptoms must persist for at least six months. Additional criteria for an ADHD diagnosis are these:

Reference: ADHD

- Individuals must show some symptoms before age 12. However, this does not mean that the child must be diagnosed prior to age 12. ADHD typically is first diagnosed in elementary school when school adjustment is impaired. Many ADHD-like behaviors of toddlers and preschoolers are normal for their age or developmental stage, making it difficult to distinguish ADHD symptoms from age-appropriate behaviors in young, active children (American Psychiatric Association, 2013).

- Some symptoms must be present in two or more settings. If a teacher (school setting) believes the child exhibits inattentive or impulsive/hyperactive behaviors but the parents (home setting) do not see those same behaviors, the problem most likely is differences in the environment and not a function of the individual.

- The inattentive or impulsive/hyperactive behaviors must cause *clinically significant impairment* in academic or social functioning. Students who exhibit behavioral symptoms of ADHD but receive good grades and form solid relationships with peers would not qualify for the diagnosis of ADHD.

- Symptoms are not due to other disorders. Several other disorders may cause an individual to exhibit difficulties in inattention, impulsivity, or hyperactivity. In those cases, ADHD is not the diagnosis.

Specific learning disabilities: See Module 21

Comorbidity. Approximately 40% to 60% of children with ADHD have at least one coexisting disorder (Pliszka, 2015). Although any disability or disorder can coexist with ADHD, common ones include conduct disorder, mood disorder, anxiety, and specific learning disabilities (American Psychiatric Association, 2013; DuPaul & Stoner, 2014; Jensen et al., 2001).

Developmental differences. ADHD affects individuals differently at different ages. Children may be initially identified as having the hyperactive-impulsive subtype and later identified as having the combined subtype as their attention problems surface (American Psychiatric Association, 2013). Impulsiveness also manifests differently in younger and older children. A preschooler may appear fidgety, have a high energy level, have difficulty playing quietly, and have difficulty taking turns, behaviors that tend to continue into elementary school in the form of problems with impulsivity, aggression, and social adjustment. By elementary school, students with impulsivity may show disorganized thinking and planning, noncompliance, and academic failure and may become increasingly aggressive and be rejected by their peers (Curchack-Lichtin, Chacko, & Halperin, 2014). Adolescents diagnosed with ADHD tend to make friends with other unpopular adolescents, leading to detrimental choices with respect to peer groups, such as defiant and aggressive behaviors, delinquency, reckless behaviors, substance abuse, and illegal acts (McQuade & Hoza, 2015).

Effect on school performance and relationships. Table 22.1 illustrates typical problems that students with inattentiveness or impulsivity may experience during school. Students with ADHD tend to have difficulties in reading, math, and writing and have lower overall achievement than their peers (DuPaul & Langberg, 2015; Martin, 2014). Working memory deficits may be partly responsible for poor academic achievement (Holmes, Hilton, Place, Alloway, Elliott, & Gathercole, 2014; Martinussen, Hadyen, Hogg-Johonson, & Tannock, 2005). Teachers can improve students' classroom performance by providing frequent breaks between periods of concentration and structured work (Ridgway, Northup, Pellegrini, LaRue, & Hightshoe, 2003).

Working memory: See Module 10

ADHD also affects students' social lives. Students with ADHD exhibit several socially incompetent behaviors, including the following (Cullinan, 2007; King et al., 2009; Wehmeier, Schacht, & Barkley, 2010):

- lack of cooperation,
- unwillingness to wait their turn or play by the rules,
- defiance or opposition, and
- aggression.

| TABLE 22.1 | Identifying Behaviors of ADHD in School Settings |

INATTENTIVE BEHAVIORS IN SCHOOL SETTINGS	IMPULSIVITY/HYPERACTIVITY BEHAVIORS IN SCHOOL SETTINGS
Difficulty attending to instructions, explanations, or demonstrations	Attending only to activities that are entertaining or novel
Missing important details in assignments	Moving from one task to another without finishing
Difficulty sustaining attention, daydreaming	Appearing fidgety
Avoidance or dislike of tasks requiring sustained mental effort	Difficulty staying seated
Procrastination about assignments	Difficulty playing quietly
Difficulty organizing assignments	Verbal or physical disruptions in class, blurting out answers
Misplacing needed items	Difficulty taking turns
Lack of attention to details, careless mistakes	High energy level

SOURCES: Barkley, 2003; Cullinan, 2007; Schachar & Tannock, 2002; Weiss & Weiss, 2002; Zentall, 1993.

The inability of children with ADHD to control their behavior may lead to social rejection by peers and to relationships with parents and teachers characterized by conflict (Johnston & Chronis-Tuscano, 2015; McQuade & Hoza, 2015). As a result, students with ADHD are more likely to be suspended or expelled and to develop peer relationship problems in adolescence. The lack of positive peer relationships among children with ADHD can lead to problems later, such as delinquency, cigarette smoking, substance use, anxiety, and depression (McQuade & Hoza, 2015; Mrug et al., 2012)

 Examine the characteristics of ADHD in school settings listed in Table 22.1. Think of some ways you would handle these behaviors in the grade you intend to teach.

CONDUCT DISORDER

Approximately 4% of U.S. children and adolescents exhibit aggressive patterns typical of a conduct disorder (American Psychiatry Association, 2013; Connor, 2002; Hinshaw & Lee, 2003). An individual with a **conduct disorder** shows persistent behaviors, such as the following (American Psychiatry Association, 2013):

- aggression toward people and animals (e.g., bullying, fighting, being physically cruel),

- destruction of property (e.g., setting fires),

- deceitfulness or theft (e.g., burglarizing homes or businesses, conning others), and

- serious violation of rules (e.g., being truant, running away).

Individuals must show three or more symptoms over a 12-month period. The characteristic behaviors typically are evident at home, at school, and in the community (American Psychiatry Association, 2013; Jensen, 2005). Also, these behaviors must be due to an underlying psychological disorder rather than to behavior patterns that children and adolescents acquire as protective strategies in threatening environments, such as neighborhoods with high poverty levels or high crime rates (American Psychiatry Association, 2013).

DIVERSITY

Developmental differences. Conduct disorder may emerge as early as preschool (American Psychiatry Association, 2013). Childhood onset of conduct disorder is identified when children demonstrate at least one characteristic behavior before age 10 (typically fighting and hostility). Boys are more likely to develop the childhood-onset type of the disorder and to display aggression through fighting, stealing, vandalizing, and having discipline problems in school (American Psychiatry Association, 2013; Foster, 2005; Hinshaw & Lee, 2003). This type of conduct disorder generally is stable and resistant to change and predicts more severe antisocial, aggressive behaviors through adulthood (Frick, 2012; Tobin & House, 2016). Without early intervention, antisocial behaviors may escalate from childhood through adolescence to more deviant forms of behavior, such as stealing, destroying property, and victimizing others (Frick, 2012).

DIVERSITY

Individuals with conduct disorder who do not show any characteristic behaviors before age 10 develop the adolescent-onset subtype, more commonly found in females. Girls with this disorder typically engage in behaviors such as lying, running away, being truant, abusing substances, and being sexually promiscuous (American Psychiatry Association, 2013). Those with the adolescent-onset subtype are less likely to have persistent conduct disorders or to develop more serious antisocial disorders in adulthood than those with the childhood-onset type (American Psychiatry Association, 2013).

Effect on school performance and relationships. Elementary and middle school students with conduct disorder tend to have lower verbal skills and lower academic achievement overall (Frick, 2012; Gresham, Lane, & Beebe-Frankenberger, 2005). However, experts are not certain whether poorer academic achievement is one of several causal factors leading to conduct problems or an outcome of the conduct problems themselves (Zimmermann, Schütte, Taskinen, & Köller, 2013). Like students with ADHD, students who show highly aggressive and antisocial behaviors gradually become isolated from their peers. By fourth and fifth grades, children who are excluded by their peers may gravitate toward a negative peer group, leading to more serious behaviors in adolescence, such as delinquency, substance abuse, involvement with gangs, and other criminal activities (Jensen, 2005). Delinquent patterns of behavior that continue through adolescence are predictive of adult criminality (Howard, Finn, Jose, & Gallagher, 2012).

Autism Spectrum Disorder

Autism is a developmental disorder that has received considerable attention in the last several years. The classic diagnosis of autism has been replaced with the label **autism spectrum disorder,** which encompasses both severe and milder forms of the symptoms. As a group of developmental disorders, autism spectrum disorder affects social interaction, communication, and behavior in many ways. Table 22.2 provides specific impairments as well as examples. The prevalence rates of autism are difficult to specify because some studies include only the classic disorder of autism, which has very low rates, whereas most refer to the prevalence of the broader category of autism spectrum disorder. In addition, the rates have increased over the last 15 years, which may be due to (a) other disorders now being labeled as autism, (b) better detection of the spectrum of disorders, or (c) an actual increase in rates of autism (Coo et al., 2008). The most recent data suggest that the rates for autism spectrum disorder are on average 1 in 110 children in the United States,

| TABLE 22.2 | Identify Impairments Among Students With Autism Spectrum Disorder |

IMPAIRED SOCIAL COMMUNICATION AND INTERACTION	EXAMPLES
• Deficit in socio-emotional reciprocity	Not initiating or responding to social interaction; lack of sharing interest or emotions
• Deficit in nonverbal communication behaviors	Abnormal eye contact; lack of facial expressions
• Deficit in developing and maintaining relationships	Difficulties engaging in shared imaginative play; general lack of interest in peers

RESTRICTED, REPETITIVE BEHAVIORS, INTERESTS, AND ACTIVITIES	EXAMPLES
• Repetitive motor movement	Lining up toys over and over again; repeating phrases; hand flapping
• Insistence on sameness	Extreme distress over small changes to routines; eating the same food and the same time everyday
• Fixated interests	Preoccupation with unusual objects
• Hyper- or hypoactivity to sensory input	Adverse reaction to certain sounds or textures; adverse reaction to being touched

SOURCES: APA, 2013; Matson & Nebel-Schwalm, 2007; Swinkels et al., 2006; Schaaf & Lane, 2015

Communication Skills. Individuals with autism, like the character Raymond in the hit 1988 movie *Rain Man,* often exhibit repetitive language and are unable to sustain conversations.

Intellectual disabilities:
See Module 21

DIVERSITY

or about 1% (American Psychiatric Association, 2013; Centers for Disease Control and Prevention, 2009). Similar rates are found in many cultures (Mansell & Morris, 2004; Naoi, Yokoyama, & Yamamoto, 2007). Yet students from ethnic minorities are underrepresented across the United States, especially those from Hispanic backgrounds (Morrier & Hess, 2012). This disparity among ethnic groups may be due to the assessments used as well as cultural differences in some behavioral symptoms (eye contact, social communication).

Comorbidity. Comorbidity refers to the coexistence of two or more disorders. About 75% of individuals with autism also have an intellectual disability (Tobin & House, 2016). One criterion for a diagnosis of intellectual disability is significantly lower performance on IQ tests than that of same-age peers (another criterion is deficits in adaptive behavior). Individuals with autism tend to have weaker verbal than nonverbal performance on IQ tests because of their deficits in communication (American Psychiatric Association, 2013).

Developmental differences. The degree of social and communicative impairment may change over time, but delays in social interaction, communication, or imaginative play must occur in early development to be considered an autism spectrum disorder (American Psychiatric Association, 2013). Infants with autism may appear unresponsive emotionally and socially—not making eye contact, cuddling, showing physical affection, or responding to parents' voices. The first symptoms can be delays in language, usually in the second year of life (American Psychiatric Association, 2013). As children develop, though, they may become more interested in and willing to passively engage in social interaction. However, even in these cases, children with autism tend to interact with others in unusual ways, such as being inappropriately intrusive in interactions or having little understanding of others' boundaries. At adolescence, some individuals experience deterioration in behaviors, while others experience improvements. About two-thirds of individuals with autism do not develop independent living skills by adulthood and continue to struggle with the social aspects of jobs and daily functioning (American Psychiatric Association, 2013; Howlin, Mawhood, & Rutter, 2000).

While autism is three to seven times more likely to occur in boys than in girls, the gender difference in rates of occurrence depends on IQ (American Psychiatric Association, 2013; Centers for Disease Control and Prevention, 2009; Towle, Visintainer, O'Sullivan, Bryan, & Busby, 2009). Individuals who have more severe cognitive impairments in IQ, especially girls, are more likely to be identified with autism (Bryson, 1997; Ehlers & Gillberg, 1993). Girls who have mild cognitive impairments may be diagnosed less frequently than boys because their communicative abilities might make them appear more socially adept than boys with the same level of cognitive ability, masking some symptoms of autism (Kirkovski, Enticott, & Fitzgerald, 2013).

Effect on school performance and relationships. Because of their intellectual disabilities, students with autism spectrum disorder face major academic challenges in the general education classroom. Their problems in communication and social interaction present added challenges to learning and impair their ability to develop age-appropriate peer relationships. Contrary to common belief, individuals with autism do not prefer to be alone, even though they lack social and communication skills that would allow them to develop friendships. Development of a few close friendships can be very beneficial, as the quality of friendships—not the number—affects whether individuals with autism feel lonely (Burgess & Gutstein, 2007).

❺ Describe interventions that are effective in treating emotional, social, and behavioral disorders.

Students with all types of disorders need to learn how to function in the general education classroom. Often, students are prescribed medications by their physicians to reduce anxiety or depressive symptoms and to increase attention and reduce impulsivity, which can improve students' academic and social functioning at school. Pharmacological interventions are outside the teacher's control and therefore are beyond the scope of this text. However, teachers can play a central role in shaping positive student behaviors in the classroom through several behavior modification approaches.

Types of Interventions

As part of their general classroom discipline, teachers can use contingency management techniques with students who have disorders. **Contingency management** involves the use of consequences that are tied to specific behaviors exhibited by students. When shaping appropriate classroom behaviors, teachers are encouraged to use *positive reinforcement*—applying a positive consequence (praise, stickers, and so on)—for appropriate behaviors. They also should avoid positively reinforcing misbehaviors by paying attention to them. Calling on, or even reprimanding, a student who is blurting out an answer positively reinforces the inappropriate behavior. Teachers can implement positive reinforcement in a concrete way by using a *token economy* in which students earn tokens for good behavior and cash them in for a small toy or favored activity when they have accumulated a certain number. A student can lose tokens for inappropriate behaviors, a consequence known as *response cost*.

Psychologists also can train teachers to use **cognitive-behavioral treatment (CBT),** a technique that teaches students to regulate their own behavior using a series of instructions that they memorize, internalize, and apply to different school tasks. The goal of CBT is self-management through the development of new thinking patterns and good decision-making skills. CBT techniques include self-monitoring, self-assessment, self-evaluation, and self-reinforcement (Lee, Simpson, & Shogren, 2007). For example, if the goal is for the student to work independently and quietly at his desk on a worksheet, the student can periodically check on his behaviors, assess whether he is achieving the goal, and, if so, put a token in a jar. If not, he can evaluate what he needs to do to get back on track. As a result, students gain an ability to control their own behavior rather than having the behavior be controlled by an adult through consequences.

School psychologists also may use systematic desensitization to reduce fears and anxieties in students with anxiety. **Systematic desensitization**—a technique based on the assumption that anxieties and fears are a conditioned (or learned) response to certain stimuli—combines relaxation training with gradual exposure to the anxiety-provoking stimulus. For example, a student who has anxiety about participating in class would engage in relaxation techniques as she moves from answering a question with a class partner to speaking in small groups to giving a response amid all her classmates.

Research has also focused on **multimodal interventions,** interventions that combine more than one approach. For example, students may receive both medication and CBT or both medication and contingency management. Schools increasingly have implemented CBT to augment pharmacological treatment of anxiety and depression. Because medication is a common form of treatment for ADHD, students with ADHD often are exposed to multimodal interventions consisting of medication, behavior modification, and sometimes academic interventions as well.

Contingency management: See Module 8

Video: Token Economy

Video Case 22.2 ▲
Behavior Management Strategies

© SAGE Publications

Conditional learning: See Module 8

Effectiveness of Interventions

Because the nature and severity of students' disorders vary, no single intervention is universally effective for every student. Educators need to be aware of the efficacy of interventions for different types of disorders so they can make informed decisions regarding which practices to implement in school settings.

Internalizing disorders. Systematic desensitization is effective in reducing a variety of fears in children and adolescents, including test anxiety, public speaking, and school phobia (Lane, Gresham, & O'Shaughnessy, 2002). Contingency management techniques and CBT also can be used effectively to reduce students' fears and anxieties (Lane et al., 2002; Read, Puleo, Wei, Cummings, & Kendall, 2013; Swan et al., 2014). CBT can also be adapted to meet the needs of ethnic minority students whose values may vary as a function of culture (Wood, Chiu, Hwang, Jacobs, & Ifekwunigwe, 2008)

DIVERSITY

Multimodal interventions consisting of CBT and pharmacological intervention are particularly beneficial in treating anxiety and depression because they help change the student's thoughts, feelings, and behaviors (Kendall et al., 2016; Treatment for Adolescents with Depression Study Team, 2004; Walkup et al., 2008). Regarding depressive symptoms, studies have found that adolescents who use poor coping strategies, such as consistently talking about negative feelings with peers without the purpose of seeking their support or trying to avoid the problem by never talking with peers or others about their feelings and thoughts, have an increased risk of depressive symptoms (Eacott & Frydenberg, 2009; Stone, Uhrlass, & Gibb, 2010). Intervention programs aimed at increasing productive coping strategies—such as teaching adolescents to share their problems or feelings with others as a means of gaining support or using problem-solving or planning strategies to eliminate the problem—have been found to decrease depressive symptoms, specifically among rural adolescents who typically have fewer options in obtaining services for mental health disorders (Eacott & Frydenberg, 2009).

DIVERSITY

Externalizing disorders. Preschool prevention programs have significantly improved behaviors and delayed the development of more serious behavior problems of children at risk for behavioral disorders (Graziano, Slavec, Hart, Garcia, & Pelham, 2014). Token economies and response cost have reduced the number of aggressive and disruptive behaviors in school-aged children (McGoey, Schneider, Rezzetano, Prodan, & Tankersley, 2010). Multimodal approaches that include parent training have also been found to decrease disruptive behaviors and increase social skills of children with externalizing problems. The changing of disruptive behavior has been found effective in diverse, urban school settings as well as cross-cultural settings. However, most interventions tend to be less effective in improving academic performance (Broadhead, Hockaday, Zahra, Francis, & Crichton, 2009; Walker et al., 2009). Some interventions that are more effective for academic improvement include one-on-one work with a peer, computer-assisted instruction, and interventions that specifically focus on working memory and basic skills, such as reading and math (Holmes et al., 2010; Jitendra, DuPaul, Someki, & Tresco, 2008).

DIVERSITY

Contingency management techniques and parent training of contingency management have been found to reduce the incidence of disruptive behaviors among school-age children and adolescents with ADHD and other behavioral disorders. For example, daily report cards that list children's target behaviors and whether goals were met on that day are found to be effective in reducing disruptive behavior (DuPaul, Eckert, & Vilardo, 2012; Fabiano et al., 2010). Students with ADHD respond positively to a combination of academic interventions, behavior management, and modifications of the classroom environment (Fabiano et al., 2009). Research findings on multimodel interventions include these (Smith & Shapiro, 2015):

- Combined behavioral and medication treatments tend to have the best overall decrease in symptoms.

- Using combined behavioral and medication treatments allows the dosage of medication to be lower, decreasing side effects of the medication.

Video Case 22.3 ▲
Physical Environment
Interventions

© SAGE Publications

- Multimodal interventions improve outcomes such as aggression, internalizing symptoms, social skills, and academic performance.

- Teachers, parents, and physicians need to work together to effectively deliver combined treatments.

Developmental disorders. Because individuals with autism spectrum disorder experience multiple deficits, they often need a variety of interventions, such as speech and language therapy, social-skills training, occupational therapy, and behavior modification techniques. Intensive contingency management techniques have led to improved overall functioning of children with autism spectrum disorder (Eikeseth, 2009). CBT that focuses not only on the symptoms of autism spectrum disorder but also addresses issues related to social anxiety appears to be effective as well (Lang, Mahoney, El Zein, Delaune, & Amidon, 2011; Wood et al., 2009). Teachers can improve the social skills of students with autism by including such students in activities with nondisabled peers, providing multiple opportunities to practice social skills in varied settings, and positively reinforcing attempts at appropriate social skills (Kohler, Anthony, Steighner, & Hoyson, 2001). Preschool children, older children, and adolescents with autism have also improved their social skills through cognitive-behavior management (Lee et al., 2007). In short, there is no single effective intervention for individuals with autism. What may be more important than the type of intervention is the timing and length of the intervention. Children with autism benefit from early and intensive interventions—those begun between ages 2 and 4 and involving 15 or more hours per week of treatment over a one- to two-year period with low adult-to-child ratios (Filipek et al., 1999).

Imagine the grade level you intend to teach. Think of some ways you could use contingency management to reduce anxieties and disruptive behaviors and to increase appropriate classroom behaviors in students with internalizing or externalizing disorders.

SUMMARY

❶ Describe how students with emotional, social, and behavioral disorders are identified and served under IDEA and Section 504. Students with emotional, social, or behavioral problems may be eligible for special education or related services under IDEA. They must present symptoms to a marked degree that exist over a long period of time and significantly impair educational performance. Section 504 provides more flexible criteria for eligibility, but eligibility is not guaranteed. Both laws require placement in the least restrictive environment.

❷ Explain how anxiety and depression affect students' academic and social functioning. Students with anxiety perform below their ability, earn lower grades, avoid peer interactions, and may appear less competent in social interactions because of a heightened state of arousal in academic and social situations. Students with depression tend to have lower academic performance and are more likely to be isolated from peers, have suicidal behaviors, and drop out of school during adolescence.

❸ Explain how ADHD and conduct disorder affect students' academic and social functioning. Students with ADHD display many behaviors that impair school performance, such as fidgeting and excessive activity in younger children and problems with organization, planning, and decision making in older children. These problems lead to difficulties in reading, math, and writing and to lower overall achievement. Impulsive and hyperactive behaviors may lead to conflict with adults and social rejection by peers, especially in adolescence. Children with conduct disorder tend to have lower levels of verbal skill and academic achievement, gradually become excluded by their peers, and develop delinquent patterns of behavior in adolescence.

❹ Describe the characteristics of autism spectrum disorder, and explain how these affect academic and social functioning. Autism includes deficits in social interaction, communication, and behavior. Because many individuals with autism spectrum disorder have some degree of intellectual disability, they face major academic challenges in the general education classroom. Their problems in communication and social interaction pose added challenges to learning and to the development of peer relationships. Few individuals with severe autism are able to function independently in society.

⑤ Describe interventions that are effective in treating emotional, social, and behavioral disorders. Systematic desensitization and contingency management techniques are effective strategies for reducing students' fears and anxieties. Children with autism spectrum disorder need a variety of interventions and benefit most from early and intensive therapies. They respond positively to intensive contingency management and cognitive-behavioral management. Cognitive-behavioral and contingency management techniques also work well for reducing disruptive behaviors. Students with ADHD respond most positively to a combination of interventions.

KEY CONCEPTS

ADHD, 469

anxiety disorder, 467

autism spectrum disorder, 473

cognitive-behavioral treatment (CBT), 475

conduct disorder, 472

contingency management, 475

emotional disturbance, 464

inclusion, 466

Individualized Education Plan (IEP), 465

Individuals with Disabilities Education Improvement Act of 2004 (IDEA), 463

least restrictive environment (LRE), 466

mainstreaming, 466

major depressive disorders, 468

multimodal interventions, 475

Section 504 of the Rehabilitation Act of 1973, 465

Section 504 plan, 465

systematic desensitization, 475

CASE STUDIES: REFLECT AND EVALUATE

EARLY CHILDHOOD: Letter P Day

These questions refer to the case study on page 404.

1. Based on the information given in the case, is it likely that Peter has ADHD? Why or why not? If Peter were a girl, would that change your decision?

2. What behaviors should Mrs. Cahill look for to determine whether Peter may have ADHD? How might these symptoms differ from symptoms that students might show in higher grades?

3. What specific strategies based on contingency management can Mrs. Cahill use to keep Peter on task?

4. Imagine that Devin is a student with conduct disorder in Mrs. Cahill's class. Using the information presented in the module, describe how Devin might behave during the language arts activity.

5. Does Nolan exhibit symptoms of depression? Why or why not? Use characteristics listed and the research discussed in the module to support your answer.

6. Why wouldn't you expect to see many anxiety problems in kindergarten? Compare this situation to middle school or high school. What factors might contribute to the development of anxiety in middle school or high school?

ELEMENTARY SCHOOL: Cheetahs, Lions, and Leopards

These questions refer to the case study on page 406.

1. Assume that Travis has autism spectrum disorder. What challenges might Mrs. Fratelli face in addressing Travis's learning and social needs?

2. Based on the information presented in the module, evaluate whether Denise might have an anxiety disorder.

3. Several days this week, one of the students in Mrs. Fratelli's class has come into school very sullen. She's not eating very much or paying attention the way she normally does. What factors does Mrs. Fratelli need to consider to help her determine whether this student has symptoms of a major depressive disorder? What additional information would she need to gather?

4. Based on information in the module, give Mrs. Fratelli specific suggestions for adapting the science experiment so that it helps Travis improve his social functioning.

5. Based on information in the module, give Mrs. Fratelli specific suggestions for easing Denise's anxiety about reading aloud.

MIDDLE SCHOOL: MATH TROUBLES

These questions refer to the case study on page 408.

1. Use the characteristics listed in this module to evaluate whether Lindsey could have an anxiety disorder. What additional information would you need to help you decide? If Lindsey were a boy, would that make a difference?

2. Use the characteristics in Table 22.1 to evaluate whether Sam could have ADHD. What additional information would you need to help you decide?

3. Did you assume Sam was a boy? How did that affect your evaluation in Question 2?

HIGH SCHOOL: NOON SUPERVISED STUDY

These questions refer to the case study on page 410.

1. How might anxiety affect a student's performance in Mr. Hardy's class? Think of specific examples related to in-class performance, performance on assignments, and peer interactions.

2. Mr. Hardy regularly uses student presentations in his class but finds that several students have severe anxiety about public speaking. What specific methods discussed in the module are used to reduce anxiety? Brainstorm additional strategies for reducing student anxiety that Mr. Hardy can use with his students.

3. Why would you expect to find few students with autism spectrum disorder in a ninth-grade history class?

6. This case does not include any students with ADHD. Using information in the module, create and describe an elementary school student with ADHD for this case.

4. Assume that Sam is African American. How might that affect your evaluation in Question 2? What does the research say about identification of emotional and behavioral disorders in students from minority and lower socioeconomic backgrounds?

5. How can Miss Barton address Sam's disruptive behaviors? Give specific strategies based on contingency management.

6. How can Miss Barton prevent students like Jessica and Lindsey from developing anxiety about math? Give specific suggestions based on information discussed in the module.

4. Use Table 22.1 to evaluate whether Jason could have ADHD. What additional information would you need to help you decide?

5. This case does not include any students with conduct disorder. Using information discussed in the module, create and describe a high school student with conduct disorder for this case. Specifically, provide behaviors that Mr. Hardy would see in class or information he would be given by school administrators.

6. Give Mr. Hardy specific suggestions based on contingency management for how to increase homework completion in students like Jason, Anthony, and Sarah.

UNIT EIGHT

ASSESSMENT

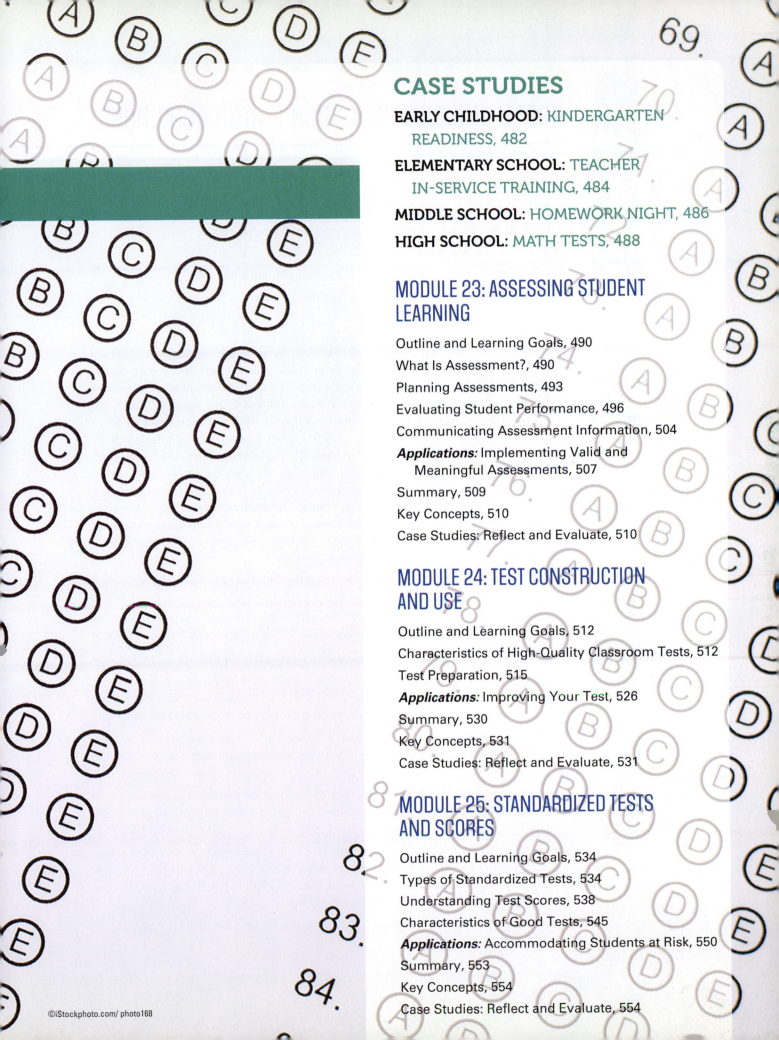

EARLY CHILDHOOD: KINDERGARTEN READINESS

Ms. Jane Walters and Ms. Sidney Theesfield are the kindergarten teachers at Bentley Elementary School in Arizona. During this week in April, the teachers are busy conducting readiness testing for the new incoming kindergarten class. The testing helps the teachers determine the strengths and weaknesses of each child so they can adapt instruction and social experiences to meet the needs of their students when the school year begins in August. Ms. Walters and Ms. Theesfield have scheduled 30-minute appointments with the parents of potential incoming kindergarten students. The teachers alternate roles, one conducting a one-on-one readiness assessment with the child while the other meets with the parent or guardian to hand out brochures about kindergarten readiness and to answer questions. Amy Shelby, a student teacher under Ms. Walters's supervision during the spring semester, will be observing some of the test administrations and parent meetings. Ms. Walters and Ms. Theesfield are doing some final preparations before the appointments begin and are preparing Amy for what to expect.

Ms. Walters begins, "Now, Amy, you aren't yet qualified to give the BRIGANCE K & 1 Screen-II that we use for testing, but you will be observing. I asked you to practice giving the test so you can ask good questions when we have finished the screening. You know we need to follow the instructions exactly as written on the testing materials, right?"

"Yes, I have been practicing at home reading the instructions to my roommate," replies Amy.

Ms. Theesfield interjects, "Well, giving the test is actually the easy part. The harder part is answering parent questions. Ms. Walters, do you remember Ms. Jackson from last November at parent–teacher conferences who wanted her daughter to skip the rest of kindergarten?"

Ms. Theesfield turns to Amy and continues, "She assumed that because her daughter had a grade equivalent score of 1.2 on our district literacy assessment that she should be in first grade."

Ms. Walters replies, "Yes, it took 30 minutes to convince her that grade equivalent scores were not that meaningful and shouldn't be used to move students up or down grade levels. I am glad we decided to stop providing those scores to parents. It just causes confusion."

Amy replies, "Test scores can be hard to explain to anyone. Last night I was trying to explain the scores to my roommate. She couldn't understand why a child wouldn't be considered above average if she scored two points above the mean for the test. I tried to explain that *average* typically refers to a range of scores, not the exact mean."

"Well, we typically don't need to explain test scores to parents at this meeting," Ms. Walters replies.

Just then she hears a family entering the classroom. "Good morning, I am Ms. Walters. You must be Maria Sanchez. I'll bet you're excited to be a kindergartener!" Ms. Walters says with a smile and a wink.

Maria doesn't say a word. She sheepishly looks toward the two ladies who have accompanied her to the screening.

The older woman turns to the younger one and speaks to her in Spanish. The younger woman replies in Spanish and then turns to Ms. Walters. "My name is Ana. I am Maria's sister. I am the only one in our family who speaks English. I came along today to translate for my mother and sister. Is that okay?"

Ms. Walters replies, "Well, I am very glad you're here. We do have the Spanish version of the screening we use and an individual who is trained to give the screening to Spanish-speaking children. So we won't need you to help with the screening, but you are welcome to help interpret for your mother during the parent meeting."

Ana turns to her mother, and they converse in Spanish for a minute or two. Ana asks, "Do you mean that I can't go in with Maria during her testing? My mother is concerned that she will be considered behind the other kids because of her English."

Ms. Walters assures Ana, "Please tell your mother that the entire test is given in Spanish, so the test score will be based on Maria's abilities, not her English skills. Okay?"

Again, Ana translates for her mother. The mother nods at Ms. Walters but doesn't look convinced.

In the next room, Ms. Theesfield is administering the BRIGANCE K & 1 Screen-II to another child, Kaden, who has attended preschool the last two years. Kaden seems surprised that he is asked to do such simple tasks as naming body parts and standing on one foot. He is even a bit annoyed when he is asked to identify the color of some objects and draw a circle on the page. These are such easy tasks for him that he wonders if kindergarten will be boring. When asked to count as high as he can, Kaden seems pleased because he knows he can count all the way to 100. He is also excited to name the various letters shown to him (A, U, K, d, l, j). Kaden states timidly, "I can read some words too."

Ms. Theesfield responds, "That's wonderful. You will learn how to read lots of words next year in kindergarten."

© Bill Aron/ PhotoEdit

When Kaden has finished the test, Ms. Theesfield escorts him over to Ms. Walters's room to talk with his parent. Ms. Theesfield returns to record her observations: (1) He is left handed; (2) he grasps the pencil with his fingers, not his fist; and (3) he talks or interacts very little. She notes that social skills may be something to assess more completely when the school year begins.

ASSESS:

1. In your opinion, should educators conduct readiness testing for entering kindergarteners? Why or why not?

2. Why might Maria's mother be concerned about how her daughter's scores will be used by the school?

3. Do the tasks being assessed by Ms. Theesfield seem to be reasonable assessments for kindergarten readiness?

CASE STUDIES

ELEMENTARY SCHOOL:
TEACHER IN-SERVICE TRAINING

PREPARE:

As you read the case, make notes:

1. WHO are the primary participants in the case? Describe them.

2. WHAT is taking place?

3. WHERE is the case taking place? Is the environment a factor?

4. WHEN is the case taking place? Is the timing a factor?

Ms. Alexandria Bowman has been the principal at Lincoln Elementary School for the past two years. The inner-city school includes a diverse group of students from various ethnic backgrounds. The school's standardized achievement test scores in reading were up two years ago from the previous year, but they have fallen this past school year below the state cutoff level in the third, fourth, and fifth grades. Before leaving for the day, Ms. Bowman sends an e-mail memo to all teachers and teacher assistants:

TO:	Lincoln Elementary teachers
FROM:	Ms. Bowman
Subject:	Suggestions for Spring testing
Date:	October 29, 2017

Good afternoon,

Tomorrow is our teacher in-service training and we will be covering assessment and standardized achievement test scores. Our standardized testing scores for reading across several grades fell last year in comparison to the previous year and are below the state cutoff level. I would like each of you to be thinking about (1) how you assess reading in your classes, (2) possible reasons for the decline in standardized test scores, and (3) specific suggestions that we can implement over the next several months to prepare for the spring testing session. We will discuss your ideas tomorrow.

Sincerely,

Ms. Bowman

The next morning the teachers convene in one of the larger classrooms. They all seem eager to express their opinions about the decline in reading scores. Ms. Bowman provides some structure to the conversation by saying that each person can provide a quick overview of his or her thoughts before breaking into smaller work groups.

Ms. Fernández (fourth-grade teacher) begins, "Our test scores have fallen because we have so many students with learning disabilities who are not being provided with the appropriate accommodations. I have to routinely create two different assessments for just about everything I evaluate in my class—one version for the typical students and another version for students with learning disabilities. For example, I give my students with learning disabilities a true–false test but create a longer test with short answer questions for my other students. I get so tired of making two assessments for everything that sometimes I just decide to use the same assessment but grade them differently."

Ms. LeBlanc (the reading specialist) agrees, "I work with students every day who have difficulty reading a few sentences. The standardized achievement tests require a lot of reading in a short amount of time. We need to allow certain students extra time to complete the tests. I am not sure how to decide which students should get extra time or how much extra time should be allowed, but there is no way some of these children can finish the test in the time allotted."

Mr. Whitney (fifth-grade teacher) addresses the group next, "I assess reading every quarter by having the students write a short report on all the books they read. They have to read at least three but can get extra credit for doing more. I am pretty lenient in the grading. If the report seems like they read it, they get the points. The problem with the standardized test is that we are using a norm-referenced test and then imposing criterion-referenced test interpretations. If our scores are only slightly below average compared to the national norm, then it shouldn't matter that our scores have fallen slightly below the state cutoff for mastery. We are still within the average range. I don't think we should panic just yet. In other words, I am not sure there is a problem here to be fixed."

Ms. Cong (third-grade teacher) clearly disagrees, "Well, I am very glad we are taking this so seriously. I know this is only my first year teaching, but when I saw that we had an average percentile score of 48, I was astonished. If our students didn't even get half of the questions correct on the test, we simply are not doing our jobs. I don't understand why something wasn't done the previous year when our average percentile score was even lower—46th percentile. I think we should be discussing radical changes in the curriculum or our assessment procedures."

Ms. Seifert (fifth-grade teacher) looks in Mr. Whitney's direction and says, "I don't know why any teacher today would be asking students to write a report on a book. That is not what they will be asked to do on these state achievement tests. Our students need more test preparation. Many students are not familiar with the test format and don't understand how to complete the computerized answer sheets. We should be using classroom assessments that resemble the standardized tests. For example, almost every assessment I give now is based on multiple-choice items. I select questions from the test bank that comes with our language arts curriculum."

Mr. Johnston (fourth-grade teacher) responds, "I would never use test bank questions. I don't think they can possibly be valid because the test writer doesn't know what material I've covered or how I've covered that material. I always create my own test items and keep them simple. I use matching exercises on vocabulary words and then create true–false questions on reading passages. Those standardized tests always have reading comprehension portions. My students should do very well on those types of items. I can't imagine why their scores would be lower than last year."

Ms. Rivadeneyra (special education teacher) seems very annoyed and dismisses Mr. Johnston's comments. Instead she reverts to an earlier comment, "I agree with Mr. Whitney. I am just not sure there is really a problem here to be solved. Last year's test scores are not an accurate reflection of our students' abilities. Remember that the week before the testing session we had the shooting two blocks down and had to lock down the school until almost 5 p.m. that day. I would assume that many students were still shaken up about the event and didn't perform as well as expected. My guess is that the test scores would have been much better if the testing session had taken place prior to the shooting. I don't think we should get too concerned yet."

There are still several teachers yet to speak and Ms. Bowman already knows it is going to be a very long day.

ASSESS:

1. Do you like one teacher's classroom assessment procedures better than another? Why?
2. After reading the teachers' responses, in your opinion, how concerned should Ms. Bowman be about the fallen standardized test scores?

CASE STUDIES

MIDDLE SCHOOL: HOMEWORK NIGHT

PREPARE:

As you read the case, make notes:

1. WHO are the primary participants in the case? Describe them.
2. WHAT is taking place?
3. WHERE is the case taking place? Is the environment a factor?
4. WHEN is the case taking place? Is the timing a factor?

Before she leaves work, Karen receives a text from her daughter, Payton, who is in the eighth grade. The text reads, "I am going to need your help tonight. I have a ton of homework and I don't understand any of it! 😡 "

Karen decides to look at Payton's grades in the online system before shutting down her computer. In her opinion, Payton should be an A/B student because she always scores above the mean on the standardized tests. She actually had a percentile score of 87 on the math portion of last year's test. However, she sees Payton is getting a C− in social studies and a C+ in science. Karen also notices that several grades are missing for Payton's math class. She will definitely need to ask Payton about those missing scores.

As Karen enters the back door of their house she sees Payton at the kitchen table with her school laptop open and says, "What are you working on first?"

Payton replies, "Social studies. It is the easiest because all we have to do is find the answers in the book."

Karen knows that the social studies teacher basically runs an online course. There is no hard copy of the textbook and the homework is all online assignments that ask them to answer questions on a section in a chapter. Karen notices that Payton has the e-book open on one side of the screen and the homework assignment open on the other side. She watches as Payton uses the mouse to copy a sentence from the e-book and paste it into the assignment. Karen quickly reacts, "Payton, you can't just copy and paste from the book!"

Payton responds, "Mom, that's how he wants it. If we don't copy it word for word we don't get full credit. That's why I scored so low on the last two homework assignments."

Karen sighs, "Well, just know that if you do that next year in high school or when you go to college, you will get an F. In college, they may even suspend you."

Karen changes gears, "I'll start dinner while you finish that. What other homework do you have tonight?"

"Well, I have math and I have to practice my speech on why students shouldn't have to take standardized tests. Remember, for literature, we had to pick a controversial topic and do research and now we have to present it to the whole class," Payton explains as she signals she is not thrilled about talking in front of everyone.

After dinner, Payton begins her math homework. "Mom, why does Ms. Bowden make us do all these math problems every night if that's not what is going to be on the test?"

"What do you mean? What's on the test if it's not these questions?" Karen asks.

"The tests usually have word problems and we have to *explain*, in *words*, how we got our answers," Payton replies, clearly annoyed. "Why can't she just give us the basic problems on the test like the ones we have to do for homework?"

Karen replies, "Well, actually, I think she should be giving you the word problems and asking you to explain your answers on the homework. That's probably how the questions appear on the state achievement test."

"Oh, you're right. She told us that's why our tests are designed that way. She wants them to be like the standardized test we have to take in March," Payton answers.

"That reminds me," Karen says. "I checked your grades today and you're missing several scores for assignments in Ms. Bowden's class. Why is that? Aren't you turning in your homework?"

"No, I am turning them in. She just loses them all the time. It happens all the time. So she just doesn't count them. That's why I'm missing some and my grade is still good."

Somewhat shocked, Karen says, "So you aren't getting any feedback on those assignments either? How are you supposed to know what you did wrong to work on before the test?"

"I don't know," Payton answers. "Anyway, I am done with math. Will you listen to my speech? I can't believe he is making us get up in front of everyone!"

Karen answers, "Sure. But, before you start, tell me the specifics. Like, how long are you supposed to talk? Are you supposed to ask your audience questions or just talk?"

"I can show you the rubric. Mr. Lorton has it all laid out with exactly how many points we will get for each specific thing. He even has stuff like eye contact and voice tone on it, whatever that means," replies Payton.

"It means that you shouldn't be reading from your notes but need to look up at your audience and that you should speak loudly and clearly," Karen explains.

Before starting her speech, Payton adds, "Well, I think the only reason he is making us do a presentation is because Kylie keeps getting such horrible scores on the written assignments so he wants to give her a chance to get a good grade. I mean, Mom, she gets Ds and Fs all the time on our written assignments, but when we talk in class about the stories we have to read, she seems to know more than anybody else. It's weird."

Karen thinks that's weird too. Last month when she picked up Payton from school for an orthodontist appointment, she overheard the teachers talking about the school's standardized tests scores. They were saying that the school's overall score was half a standard deviation below the mean and that Kylie scored higher than anybody in the whole school on the reading portion of the test.

ASSESS:

1. What aspects of Ms. Bowden's and Mr. Lorton's classroom assignments are good and what aspects should be changed?

2. Do you think it is a good practice to give students the exact rubric for an assignment with specific points for certain aspects noted? Why or why not?

3. What might it mean that Kylie has the highest standardized test score in the school but receives such poor scores on the classroom assignments?

CASE STUDIES

HIGH SCHOOL: MATH TESTS

PREPARE:

As you read the case, make notes:

1. WHO are the primary participants in the case? Describe them.
2. WHAT is taking place?
3. WHERE is the case taking place? Is the environment a factor?
4. WHEN is the case taking place? Is the timing a factor?

Ms. Alexia Fortner arrived early this Monday morning to prepare upcoming lessons for her senior math class. Several of her students should have received their SAT scores over the weekend. She is sure much of today's discussion will surround their scores and plans for college now that they have their test scores. Over the past several weeks, Ms. Fortner tried to help prepare her students by giving them multiple-choice math tests with Scantron answer sheets, along with tips for decreasing test anxiety, and letting them use one class period to take a practice math subscale of the SAT test from the official website. Ms. Fortner is particularly excited to hear from Lu Tuong, who typically is given special accommodations on the state achievement tests due to her limited English proficiency.

Ms. Fortner greets her first student. J. T. announces in his confident, somewhat arrogant voice, "I got a 600 on the math portion. I'm sure I'll be able to get into the state university." He continues in a more concerned tone, "Bethany only got a 400. She cried all day yesterday and started seriously looking into community colleges. I wouldn't be surprised if she doesn't come to class today to avoid everyone asking her about it."

Lu enters the room with a shy smile and says in her choppy English, "Ms. Fortner, I got 500 on math. I think will be enough!"

Ms. Fortner replies, "Oh, that's great! You must have used some of the techniques we covered in class about relaxing, taking your time to think, and . . ."

Trevor interrupts as he enters the room, "Don't ask. Just don't anybody ask me about the SAT!"

Ms. Fortner scans the room and sees that some students are excited about their scores and ready to talk but others don't look so eager. Here comes Bethany with her head down, avoiding all eye contact. Ms. Fortner decides it's best to leave the SAT scores out of the discussion for the day. "Okay, good morning everyone, we're going to go over the homework assignment from last week . . . ."

After school, Ms. Fortner runs into Mr. Tom Harris, one of the school counselors, in the hallway. "Hey, did you hear anything about Trevor?" asks Ms. Fortner. "He seemed to be very upset this morning about his SAT score."

Mr. Harris replies, "Oh, it isn't that bad. I heard him telling somebody that he got a 600 on the math subscale. He thinks that will keep him from getting into his top pick for college. I have to admit that I was surprised his score was so low—not that 600 is low— but he is such an outstanding student and typically scores extremely high on our state achievement tests. I don't really think that score accurately represents his ability. Do you?"

Ms. Fortner replies, "Well, I know he was very sick with the flu the week he took the SAT. It could be that his illness had something to do with his low score. Well, anyway, I am on my way to the office to meet with a disgruntled *parent*. She says my tests are too hard." Ms. Fortner rolls her eyes.

"Good luck," yells Mr. Harris.

Ms. Fortner walks into the small conference room in the main office area. Ms. Camponi, Tony's mom, is waiting with Principal Wieburg and has a less than friendly look on her face.

After the polite greetings, Principal Wieburg begins, "I understand that the two of you met a few weeks ago about Tony's math grade. Ms. Camponi, you were not satisfied with the outcome, so as I indicated on the phone, I thought it might be helpful for all three of us to meet. I had originally thought Tony should also join us. However, given the issue seems to be more about Ms. Fortner's grading procedures in general and not Tony's performance specifically, I decided not to include him. Ms. Camponi, would you like to start?"

"Yes," answered Ms. Camponi. "As I had mentioned before, I don't think that Ms. Fortner's grading procedures allow for my child, or other children, to be fairly evaluated on their math skills. She gives them hours of homework each night that only count for a very small percentage of their grade and then gives them particularly challenging exams that count for huge percentages of their grade. My Tony, for example, has an 89% on his homework assignments. But, he did so poorly on one exam that his overall grade in the class is 72%. Now, Principal Wieburg, does that sound like a fair grading procedure?"

Principal Wieburg turns to Ms. Fortner and says, "I would actually like Ms. Fortner to respond first."

"Well," starts Ms. Fortner, "as I said to Ms. Camponi a few weeks ago, my grading policies are clearly laid out on the class syllabus. Homework assignments only count for 30% of the overall grade and exams count for 70%. My philosophy is that students should be able to demonstrate their math skills in multiple contexts, including exams."

Ms. Camponi quickly replies in a sarcastic tone, "Multiple contexts." She continues, "You used those same words when we spoke last time. If you want them to demonstrate their math skills in multiple contexts then you have to teach them in multiple contexts. You are known for giving your students straightforward problems on the homework assignments and then giving them extremely difficult word problems on the exams. Of course they don't know how to do the word problems because no one has taught them those skills."

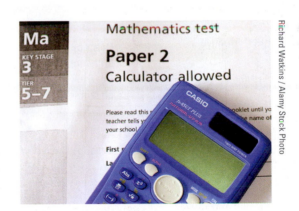

Principal Wieburg interjects before the meeting gets too heated, as she can tell Ms. Camponi is furious. "I would like us to take a step back. Ms. Camponi, did you say you brought along some of Tony's work to show me?"

ASSESS:

1. Do you think Ms. Fortner does a good job of assessing her students' learning? Why or why not?

2. What type of math tests do you prefer, multiple choice or problem solving? Why?

3. Based on the four students' math SAT scores provided in the case, do you think the students at this school typically are below average, average, or above average? Is there too much difference in scores to decide?

EARLY CHILDHOOD

ELEMENTARY SCHOOL

MIDDLE SCHOOL

HIGH SCHOOL

©iStockphoto.com/ Filmwork

MODULE 23

ASSESSING STUDENT LEARNING

WHAT IS ASSESSMENT?

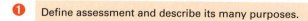

❶ Define assessment and describe its many purposes.

In education, you hear the term *assessment* used in many contexts. Elementary school teachers may conduct an assessment of a student's oral reading fluency by listening to the child read aloud. Students in all grades take tests and quizzes or submit portfolios as assessments to demonstrate mastery of the subject matter. Principals may even conduct classroom observations of teachers to assess teachers' effectiveness. As you can see, an **assessment** is more than just a test. It is any procedure for obtaining information about students (Brookhart & Nitko, 2014).

Sometimes professionals use the term *assessment* interchangeably with the terms *measurement* and *evaluation*. However, measurement and evaluation are part of the assessment process. A teacher may listen to a student read orally to assess reading fluency, but the score that she assigns to indicate the student's level of fluency is considered a measurement. **Measurement** is the assignment of numerical values to performance, such as an oral fluency score, a grade on a classroom test, or a ranking of contestants in a speech contest. The values indicate the degree to which the individual possesses the trait being assessed (e.g., reading fluency, mastery, public speaking), and it should indicate an ordering of the trait from best to worst. Teachers can also make an **evaluation,** which is the act of making a value judgment about a student's product or performance. Evaluations do not necessarily need to be based on measurement (Brookhart & Nitko, 2014). For example, when a teacher writes a recommendation letter for a student, part of the teacher's evaluation of the student's ability to succeed in graduate school is based on the student's measured performance, such as on tests and papers, but the teacher's evaluation also includes his or her informal observation of the student's maturity level, initiative, and motivation to succeed. In this module, we explore all aspects of assessment, from planning and choosing assessments, to evaluating performance and communicating these results to students and parents. Let's begin with an overview of the many uses of assessment in education.

Purposes of Assessment in Education

Assessments are used for making many types of decisions in education. They inform educational policies at the district, state, and national level (Brookhart & Nitko, 2014). Historically, standardized test performance and international rankings have been used to inform educational policies such as the No Child Left Behind Act of 2001, and more recently, the Common Core State Standards (CCSS), which have been adopted by 42 states. To evaluate student, school, and state performance on the CCSS, states have chosen one of two new assessment systems— the Partnership for Assessment of Readiness for College and Careers (PARCC) or the Smarter Balanced Assessment Consortium (SBAC)—and began pilot testing in the 2014 to 2015 school year. Assessments also can be used for making decisions about the efficacy of curricula and programs (Brookhart & Nitko, 2014). A district-wide test might be used to evaluate a new curriculum for teaching high school algebra, and educators might use the assessment results to decide whether to continue using the curriculum. Finally, educators use assessments to make many decisions about individual students, such as those shown in Table 23.1 (Brookhart & Nitko, 2014).

Some of these assessments used for decision making about individual students are formative assessments and others are summative assessments. **Formative assessments** guide the instructional process and improve student learning by providing data to help teachers (Shepard, 2006; Van der Kleij, Vermeulen, Schildkamp, & Eggen, 2015):

- plan instruction by assessing what students already know about a topic,

- place students into groups or levels for more focused attention, and

- monitor student progress toward learning goals.

A successful formative assessment includes high-quality feedback and involves students in evaluating their progress toward learning goals (Bonner, 2013; Brookhart, 2011). In contrast, **summative assessments** are used to make decisions about students' content knowledge or

Master the content.

edge.sagepub.com/durwin3e

⑤SAGE edge™

Video Case 23.1 ▲
Purposes of Assessment

© SAGE Publications

Standardized tests: See Module 25

Common Core State Standards: See Modules 1 and 25

Formative assessments: See Modules 18 and 25

Summative assessments: See Module 25

TABLE 23.1	Examples of Assessments for Making Decisions About Students
ASSESSMENT DECISIONS	**EXAMPLE**
Selection	Admissions tests for entry to college or private high schools
Placement	Assignment of students to elementary reading groups, ability groups, or tracks in high school
Diagnosis	Standardized test scores used to identify learning disabilities
Counseling and guidance	Interest inventories and aptitude tests for exploring students' career options
Instructional planning	Pretests or surveys to assess what students know prior to instruction
Progress monitoring	Scores on standardized or classroom tests to provide feedback for improvement or monitor progress toward learning objectives
Outcomes evaluation	Grades on a report card or scores on standardized or classroom tests to determine students' achievement or mastery

SOURCE: Brookhart & Nitko, 2014.

achievement, such as grades on a report card or standardized achievement test scores (Sanders, 2011). The difference between formative and summative assessments is in their purpose (Bennett, 2011). For example, a high school chemistry teacher may ask students to write a paragraph explaining what they know about atoms before a lesson and then may ask them to write an essay after the lesson summarizing what they learned. Both assessments involve essay writing, but the former is a formative assessment and the latter is summative.

Types of Assessments

Because assessments are broadly defined as any means of obtaining information about students, there are many different methods of collecting such data. Assessments can be formal, such as tests, papers, or projects, or they can be informal, such as an observation of a student's behavior on the playground. **Informal assessments** can take place in many situations, such as the classroom, playground, or home. They typically have a formative purpose, involve an observation or interview, and do not involve scores or a comparison students. In contrast, **formal assessments** typically occur in more structured environments, like the classroom or testing centers, and their purpose is to obtain summative data of students' performance that can be compared to other students.

Another way to think of assessments is whether they are objective or subjective. Informal assessments typically collect **subjective data,** which means the data are open to interpretation. For example, two school counselors observing a student's social interactions in a peer group may make very different interpretations. In contrast, formal assessments often collect **objective data,** which refer to a score having one interpretation, such as right or wrong. Multiple-choice and true–false tests are objective because these items have one correct answer. However, formal assessments can be subjective, such as essays or performance-based assessments, which require students to demonstrate their knowledge by creating a product (writing a lab report) or carrying out a process (demonstrating how to perform CPR). Because performance-based assessments are open to interpretation, teachers attempt to quantify characteristics of performance (such as organization, clarity, and grammar in an essay) by applying scores to each criterion using a rubric, which we discuss in more detail later in the module. The result is a score that may translate to a letter grade, but the assessment is not purely objective.

We can also distinguish assessments by whether they are standardized. Often, formal assessments are standardized, which means that the assessment is administered under standard conditions (the same way for each student) and there is a standard method of scoring. IQ tests and achievement tests administered by psychologists are **standardized tests,** and paper-and-pencil

Video Case 23.2 ▲
Assessment Types

© SAGE Publications

Multiple-Choice and true–false: See Module 24

Essays: See Module 24

IQ tests: See Module 20

achievement tests that you have probably taken through most of your schooling are also standardized tests. **Classroom tests** are also formal assessments but may not be administered and scored in a standard fashion. They can be formative or summative, whereas standardized tests typically provide summative information. One similarity between classroom and standardized tests, however, is that they both need to demonstrate characteristics of "good" tests, such as validity (that the test score accurately reflects what the test is intended to measure) and reliability (that the test produces consistent results).

Achievement tests: See Modules 21 and 25

Standardized vs. classroom tests: See Module 25

Reflect on the assessments from your past schooling. As you read, think about the assessments that were most meaningful to you as a student. Why were they meaningful, and what did they indicate about your performance or achievement?

Validity and reliability: See Modules 24 and 25

PLANNING ASSESSMENTS

 Contrast the major advantages and disadvantages of objective assessments and performance assessments.

Assessment, like instruction, requires careful planning and development. There are several factors to consider when choosing an assessment that is right for your instructional purpose, grade, and subject matter. Knowing about the advantages and disadvantages of objective and performance-based assessment formats also can be helpful when choosing an approach.

Choice of Assessments

A primary factor to consider when choosing an assessment is purpose. Is the purpose to recall memorized facts, show problem-solving ability, or demonstrate a skill? More importantly, the purpose of the assessment must match the teacher's learning objective and teaching method (Bonner, 2013; Brookhart & Nitko, 2014). According to Bloom's taxonomy, learning objectives can range from lower level—such as remembering, understanding, and applying information—to higher level skills, such as analyzing or evaluating information, or creating new information or a product based on one's learning (Anderson & Krathwohl, 2001; Bloom, Englehart, Frost, Hill, & Krathwohl, 1956). If a learning objective focuses on memorizing and recalling information, then tests containing objective items such as multiple choice, true–false, matching, or short answer are a good option (Brookhart & Nitko, 2014). If learning objectives emphasize logical thinking, understanding and applying concepts, or reasoning, these skills also can be assessed effectively with objective formats that are well-constructed. However, performance-based formats also may be used to assess higher level skills, as we discuss later.

Match between instruction and assessment: See Module 18

Bloom's taxonomy: See Modules 13 and 18

Constructing objective items: See Module 24

Once you decide on the learning objective and the level of knowledge you want students to acquire, be sure to choose an instructional method and assessment that match the objective. For example, if you want students in your American Government class to analyze the pros and cons of the right to free speech, then an appropriate instructional method might be a class debate or a small group activity in which they discuss articles on both sides of the argument. To evaluate students on this objective you might ask them to write a persuasive essay, give an oral presentation, or create a video. In this case, the learning objective, instruction, and assessment all match. In contrast, providing factual knowledge on the topic through a lecture (passive learning of lower level knowledge) and assigning a persuasive essay on the pros and cons of free speech (higher level analysis skill) will not lead to optimal student performance. Student performance is enhanced when the method of instruction and learning match the way in which students are assessed (Morris, Bransford, & Franks, 1977; Tulving & Thomson, 1973).

Constructing and scoring essays: See Module 24

Finally, teachers need to consider whether the assessment yields an accurate reflection of students' actual mastery or achievement. For this, we need to ensure that the test, essay,

Characteristics of high-quality assessments: See Modules 24 and 25

or performance conforms to several criteria of high-quality assessments, such as validity, reliability, fairness, and practicality.

- **Validity** is the extent to which an assessment actually measures what it is intended to measure (e.g., calculating long division, writing a persuasive argument, building a birdhouse). A valid assessment yields accurate and meaningful interpretations of a student's ability or achievement based on the score or letter grade.

- To be valid, an assessment also needs to have **reliability,** yielding consistent measurements. For example, if a teacher scored an essay twice a few days apart and gave the same student a C on one day and a B on another, which grade accurately reflects the student's knowledge? Because the assessment yields inconsistent results, we cannot be sure. Therefore, validity is compromised. When judging the reliability of classroom assessments, it is important for teachers to determine what type of consistency is important for different assessments (Parkes, 2007). For essays and performance-based assessments, the consistency of ratings across time or across raters (e.g., two teachers) is important. When determining grades, it is important to have consistency in one's decisions. Is a B grade always given for the same level of performance?

Reliability of objective tests: See Modules 24 and 25

- **Fairness** in classroom assessment reflects the extent to which all students have an equal opportunity to learn content and demonstrate their knowledge (Tierney, 2013). For example, is it a fair assessment to require all students to write a term paper even though some students in your class have a learning disability and struggle with writing? Similarly, the dilemma regarding how to handle makeup work from absences may be a fairness issue. Have you ever had a professor who gave a *really difficult* makeup exam simply because you were sick on the day of the test? Was this a fair assessment of your learning?

- **Practicality** refers to how time-consuming the assessment is to create, administer, and score. The key issue is whether the time involved in the assessment, whichever you choose, is a worthwhile cost given the learning objective you want students to achieve.

As you read further about objective and performance-based assessments, compare these assessment formats on the characteristics of high-quality assessments, such as validity, reliability, fairness, and practicality.

Objective and Performance Assessments

Objective assessments and performance assessments differ in how student learning is assessed. Objective assessments are tasks in which students produce a response that can be scored as correct or incorrect with little interpretation. Elementary school students may complete a set of arithmetic problems for homework or take a spelling test, middle school students may be quizzed on Spanish vocabulary, and high school students may take multiple-choice unit tests. Objective tasks like these are common assessments in K-12 education.

In contrast to assessments that require students to obtain one correct answer, **performance assessments** require students to demonstrate their knowledge, which can be accomplished through creating a product, such as writing a children's story to show knowledge of an historical period, or through demonstrating a process, such as setting up materials in a chemistry lab. Performance assessments sometimes have been called *alternative assessments* to contrast this type of assessment with objective tests. They also have been referred to as *authentic assessments,* which are tasks that are situated in a realistic context and directly meaningful to students' education (Brookhart & Nitko, 2014). However, a performance assessment may or may not be directly meaningful. Requiring elementary school students to count change by counting images of coins on a worksheet is a performance assessment, but it is not a realistic context and may not be

Situated cognition: See Module 18

directly meaningful. In contrast, observing students making change with actual money in a school store would be a more directly meaningful and realistic assessment. Of course, the extent to which various contexts are realistic and meaningful can be debated. For this module, we refer to performance assessments as all assessment tasks that require a process or product, whether or not they are considered authentic.

Table 23.2 presents types of performance assessments and the methods used in these tasks. Some examples of performance assessments used frequently by teachers are term papers, presentations, and projects. Portfolios also can be considered a performance assessment because students create a product in the form of a collection of work samples, such as test results, writing samples, drawings, research reports, and self-reflections (Randel & Clark, 2013). Portfolios can be used to demonstrate students' overall achievement or progress over time (Brookhart & Nitko, 2014; Waugh & Gronlund, 2013).

- **Best work portfolios** contain artifacts that demonstrate mastery and may impress others. A student seeking admission to an art academy may need to submit a portfolio of his or her best art work.

- **Growth portfolios** contain student work samples that are not final products, along with teacher comments and student self-reflections. Students typically decide what to include with help from the teacher. Growth portfolios have a formative purpose to monitor students' progress, identify weaknesses, and guide new learning by encouraging students to understand and evaluate their own progress.

To decide whether to use an objective task or a performance assessment, teachers can compare the two approaches on several characteristics summarized in Table 23.3. Each approach has advantages and disadvantages to consider.

Assessment is a complex and dynamic process that involves many factors, such as learning objectives, instructional approaches, practical issues involving implementation and scoring,

Video: How to Use Portfolios in Your Classroom

Guidelines for constructing objective items: See Module 24

TABLE 23.2	Types of Performance Assessments	
TYPE OF PERFORMANCE ASSESSMENT	**DESCRIPTION**	**EXAMPLES OF METHODS USED**
Structured, on-demand tasks	Students receive materials, instructions, and expectations for the task, and they prepare for the assessment. These tasks can be used for individual students or groups.	• Paper-and-pencil tasks • Demonstrations using equipment (e.g., microscope, pottery wheel, musical instrument)
Naturally occurring performance tasks	An adult observes students in natural settings, such as at recess, day care, or home, and records observations.	• Typically none
Long-term projects	These involve complex tasks that have multiple components, which may require research and take several weeks or months to complete. They can be used for individual students or groups.	• Term papers or lab reports • Experiments • Oral presentations and skits • Created products (e.g., sculptures, dioramas)
Simulations	These are contrived activities that mimic naturally occurring events, such as a mock election or trial or a driving simulation.	• Actors to play "roles" • Computerized simulations

Adapted from Brookhart and Nitko, 2014.

TABLE 23.3 Contrasting Objective and Performance Assessments

	OBJECTIVE ASSESSMENTS	PERFORMANCE ASSESSMENTS
Breadth/Depth of assessment	Breadth of assessment; can assess many learning objectives at once	Depth of assessment; typically assesses one or only a few learning objectives in one assessment
Objectives	Typically measures lower level objectives (e.g., knowledge and comprehension) but well-constructed items can measure higher level objectives	Typically assesses higher level objectives
Development	• Time-consuming to create good items • Items often poorly constructed	May be difficult and time-consuming to create
Time	Takes little class time (typically 10 to 30 minutes)	• Can take up valuable instructional time if assessments are done in class (e.g., presentations, group projects); possibly days or weeks • Some performance assessments (products) evaluated outside of class time
Scoring	Quick and accurate; can be scored with optical scanning sheets ("bubble sheets")	Time-consuming
Reliability and validity	Generally high reliability and validity when teachers follow research-based guidelines for construction of objective items	• Lower reliability than objective assessments; rubrics improve reliability but often poor quality; factors outside of the learning expectations, such as creativity, neatness, and originality, may affect teachers' consistency in applying the criteria of the rubric • Possible reduced validity if performance assessments contain aspects of the task, such as reading or writing ability or creativity, that are not directly relevant to the learning objective

SOURCES: Brookhart, 2015; Hambleton & Murphy, 1992; Lane, 2013; Lane, Parke, & Moskal, 1992; Linn, 1993; Miller & Seraphine, 1993; Reynolds & Livingston, 2012; Rudner & Boston, 1994; Shavelson & Baxter, 1991; Waugh & Gronlund, 2013.

validity, reliability, and fairness. Neither type of assessment, objective or performance, can satisfy all of these criteria. Experts recommend a balanced approach to take advantage of the benefits of both types of assessment (Brookhart & Nitko, 2014). Most importantly, teachers need to choose the assessment that is appropriate for learning goals and the type of instruction, and they must take the time to evaluate their assessment practices for reliability, validity, and fairness (Bonner, 2013; Randel & Clark, 2013).

Video Case 23.3 ▲
Addressing Cheating

© SAGE Publications

EVALUATING STUDENT PERFORMANCE

❸ Describe the tools used to score performance tasks, and explain the limitations of scoring performance assessments.

❹ Describe the three main types of grading procedures and explain their advantages and limitations.

Planning assessments requires teachers to have a clear idea about how the assessments will be scored or graded and how grades on individual assignments will factor into report card grades. Let's first discuss procedures for scoring performance assessments (objective assessments do not require procedures because they are marked correct or incorrect). Then we turn to general practices for grading assessments and determining final grades.

Scoring Procedures for Performance Assessments

Providing valid and meaningful information about a student's achievement using performance assessments requires that scoring is as objective and reliable as possible (Waugh & Gronlund, 2013). To accomplish this, experts recommend the following steps (Brookhart & Nitko, 2014; McKenzie, 2005; Moss, 2013).

- Before instruction, have an idea of what students are expected to know and do on the performance assessment, and clearly state these requirements in the assignment.

- Plan how the assessment will be scored and develop guidelines for scoring before instruction.

- Communicate the expectations and scoring criteria to students prior to the assessment so they know exactly what they are expected to do and how to achieve the learning objective.

These actions will lead to better student products and increased consistency in scoring.

To score performance assessments, teachers have a choice of checklists, rating scales, holistic rubrics, or analytic rubrics. The choice depends on the level of detail teachers need to judge the quality of the process or product. **Checklists** provide no judgment of the quality of the performance. They simply list the behaviors or characteristics of a process or product, and teachers check if the behavior is present (Brookhart & Nitko, 2014; Quinlan, 2012). Checklists are useful for tasks comprising behaviors in a chronological sequence, such as shooting a free throw in basketball, or tasks containing subtasks, such as driving a car (Brookhart & Nitko, 2014). Sometimes, teachers may want to evaluate the quality of a process without assigning a numerical score by using an *expanded checklist* (Quinlan, 2012). Teachers might place a check if the behavior is observed, a check-plus for consistent or superior performance of the behavior, a check-minus for inconsistent execution of the behavior or a need for improvement, and a zero for not observed. An expanded checklist would be appropriate for homework assignments, informal writing such as journal entries, or artistic products. **Rating scales** provide a numerical score for varying levels or degrees of performance on one or more dimensions, such as rating students on the quality of their class presentations, as shown in Figure 23.1 (Brookhart & Nitko, 2014).

Rubrics provide the most detailed information about students' performance because they list multiple dimensions or aspects of performance and provide a descriptive rating for each of them. **Holistic rubrics,** such as the one shown in Figure 23.2, allow teachers to evaluate the overall quality of a student's performance on a task project when it is not possible to define the specific characteristics of "good work" ahead of time (Brookhart & Nitko, 2014; Quinlan, 2012). They are called holistic because teachers assign a score to the description that best matches the student's overall performance. Holistic rubrics provide a quick method of scoring and are appropriate for final exams, essays, papers, final portfolios, or projects where feedback and an opportunity to revise work are not necessary (Waugh & Gronlund, 2013). However, the lack of detailed feedback may leave teachers without a sound justification for scoring. For example, in Figure 23.2, could teachers confidently justify why they assigned a 3 rather than a 4 on students' essays?

Compared to holistic rubrics, **analytic rubrics** allow teachers to give detailed feedback regarding students' strengths and weaknesses, which students can use to improve their performance (Brookhart & Nitko, 2014). Analytic rubrics are displayed as a grid with the major criteria or dimensions for evaluating the performance in the left column and the rating scale containing performance levels for each of these criteria across the top, as shown in Table 23.4. The cells of the grid contain exemplars, or descriptors, which are statements that describe the degree of success or mastery for each dimension in a way that both the teacher and student can understand (McKenzie, 2005). An analytic rubric can have as many dimensions as needed,

FIGURE 23.1 **Sample Rating Scale for an Oral Presentation.** Rating scales such as this can improve teachers' consistency in scoring.

	Poor	Fair	Average	Good	Excellent
	1	2	3	4	5

Name: _____   Date: _____

Topic: _____

	Poor 1	Fair 2	Average 3	Good 4	Excellent 5
The content of the presentation:					
• demonstrates knowledge of the topic	1	2	3	4	5
• flows in a logical, coherent order	1	2	3	4	5
• contains an interesting introduction and conclusion	1	2	3	4	5
• contains supporting details and examples	1	2	3	4	5
The delivery of the presentation:					
• is engaging	1	2	3	4	5
• uses audio or visual aids	1	2	3	4	5
• does not heavily rely on notes	1	2	3	4	5
The presenter:					
• makes adequate eye contact with audience	1	2	3	4	5
• is able to answer questions from the audience	1	2	3	4	5

FIGURE 23.2 **Sample Holistic Essay Rubric.** Teachers can use holistic rubrics to provide an overall impression of students' performance.

Sample 4-point Holistic Rubric

4   Advanced (in-depth understanding)—exemplary performance or understanding; shows creativity

3   Proficient (general understanding)—solid performance or understanding; meets the standard

2   Basic (partial understanding)—performance is emerging or developing; makes errors; has a grasp, but not thorough

1   Below basic (minimal understanding)—makes an attempt but has serious errors or misconceptions

0   No attempt made

Adapted from Quinlan, A. M. (2012). *A complete guide to rubrics: Assessment made easy for teachers of K-college* (2nd ed.). New York: Rowman & Littlefield.

and it does not have a preset number of performance levels, although the typical is three to five levels (Quinlan, 2012; Stevens & Levi, 2013). The whole range of performance should be represented in the rubric with adequate descriptors, even though you might not expect some performance levels from your students, such as the very lowest rating (Brookhart & Nitko, 2014).

TABLE 23.4	Sample Analytic Rubric. Analytic rubrics can provide students with feedback on how to improve.				
DIMENSION	**4**	**3**	**2**	**1**	**SCORE**
Thesis Statement	The thesis statement clearly identifies the topic and previews the main points.	The thesis statement identifies the topic but main points are unclear.	The thesis statement outlines some or all of the main points but does not identify the topic.	The thesis statement does not identify the topic and does not preview the main points.	
Evidence and Examples	All of the evidence and examples are specific and relevant. The writer thoroughly explains how each piece of evidence supports his/her position.	Most of the evidence and examples are specific and relevant. The writer explains how each piece of evidence supports his/her position.	Some pieces of evidence and examples are relevant. The writer attempts an explanation for each piece of evidence or example.	Evidence and examples are not relevant and/or are not explained.	
Depth of Understanding	The essay demonstrates excellent understanding of major concepts.	The essay shows a solid grasp of major concepts.	The essay shows a minimal grasp of concepts.	The essay demonstrates a lack of understanding of most concepts.	
Organization	Arguments and support are presented in a logical order that is easy to follow.	Arguments and support are presented in a fairly logical order that is reasonably easy to follow.	A few arguments or supportive details are not in a logical order, making the essay a little confusing in a few places.	Many of the arguments or supportive details are not in a logical order, making the essay seem very confusing.	
Grammar and Spelling	The essay contains no major errors that distract the reader from the content.	The essay contains a few errors that distract the reader from the content.	The essay contains many serious errors that prevent the reader from following the content.	The essay contains errors throughout that make it difficult for the reader to understand the content.	

Well-constructed rubrics have several advantages for assessment and student learning outcomes. Rubrics make scoring easier and improve the reliability of grading. Sharing rubrics with students ahead of time helps them optimally perform on assessments because they know what to do to perform well (McKenzie, 2005; Quinlan, 2012). Rubrics can also serve an important role in formative assessment by providing students with information about their level of progress toward learning objectives and what knowledge or skills still need to be mastered (Quinlan, 2012). Research indicates that use of rubrics can improve student achievement in writing, math, science, and social studies (Brookhart & Chen, 2015).

When scoring assessments using rating scales and rubrics, keep in mind their limitations, which can reduce the reliability and validity of the assessment. The numeric score applied to various dimensions or characteristics of performance gives the impression of precision and objectivity even though it reflects a subjective judgment (Bean, 2011). Because judgments are subjective, scoring may be influenced by subtle biases, which may lead to the following scoring errors (Brookhart & Nitko, 2014; Cohen, Swerdlik, & Sturman, 2013).

- Teachers might make a leniency error—using only the ratings at the high end of the scale—or a severity error—using only the ratings toward the lower end of the scale.

- A central tendency error occurs when only the middle part of the scale is used, scoring everyone as average. This may happen when evaluating characteristics that are difficult to quantify, such as creativity or motivation.

- Teachers also may experience a **halo effect,** in which their overall impression of a student subtly influences their ratings. For example, teachers who believe certain students are "good students" may grade their essays more favorably than those of other students. A halo effect can also occur when using analytic rubrics (Humphry & Heldsinger, 2014). A teacher may give a high rating to a student's thesis statement in an essay and therefore may also rate the essay's organization more highly than deserved because the previous rating causes a general positive impression. To remedy this problem, teachers can more heavily weight certain dimensions that may be more important in the assessment (Humphry & Heldsinger, 2014; Quinlan, 2012). This allows raters to make independent judgments of each dimension, resulting in better differentiation of performance among students (Humphry & Heldsinger, 2014).

Grading Procedures

Grading is part of *evaluation,* applying a value judgment to the score on an assessment or set of assessments. A student may earn a 4 out of 6 on a performance assessment, or a 78 out of 100 on a test. But what do these numbers mean? Did the student master the learning objective? Is the student's performance or score above average, average, or below average compared to peers? Our interpretation of the measurement depends on our point of reference. To make an evaluation of achievement, teachers can compare the student's performance to other students in the class (norm-referenced grading), to a predetermined level of mastery for various objectives (criterion-referenced grading), or to the student's own past performance (self-referenced grading).

NORM-REFERENCED GRADING

Norm-referenced grading, a method of assigning grades based on how a student's performance compares with classmates, can be accomplished using two methods. In the **grading on the curve method,** teachers arrange scores from highest to lowest and then assign grades based on the ranked scores, with highest scores receiving an A grade, and so on (Brookhart & Nitko, 2014). In the **standard deviation method,** instructors compute the average score (called a mean) and a standard deviation (which indicates the variability of scores around the mean), and then they use the standard deviation to mark segments of the score distribution corresponding to letter grades (Brookhart & Nitko, 2014). Figure 23.3 illustrates the standard deviation method.

These grading methods can be used for grading individual assessments or for determining final grades (combining several components or course requirements) for a semester or marking period. However, to use norm-referenced grading, both individual grades and the final grade should be norm-referenced (Brookhart & Nitko, 2014). It is not appropriate to use another grading method, such as criterion-referenced grading, for assessments and then use a norm-referenced approach for determining final grades.

Experts discourage the use of norm-referenced grading methods (Guskey, 2009; Marzano, 2006). Classroom assessments rarely result in a normal distribution of scores, such as those in Figure 23.4 (Waugh & Gronlund, 2013). Therefore, if teachers use a normal distribution to assign grades when the scores do not have a normal curve shape, they may be unfairly assigning students grades of D or F (as when giving an F to the lowest score of 72) or may be assigning A grades to scores that do not necessarily indicate exceptional performance (a score of 85 may be the highest score for the class, but it is not worthy of an A). In contrast to the normal distribution, the ideal distribution for classroom assessment is one with a long tail to the left (called a negative skew), as shown in Figure 23.4.

Norm-referenced grading: See also norm-referenced tests in Module 25

Mean and standard deviation: See Module 25

FIGURE 23.3 **Norm-Referenced Grading.** This normal distribution shows segments corresponding to letter grades.

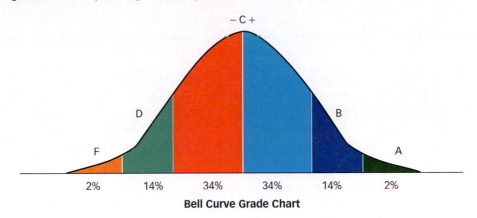

Bell Curve Grade Chart

FIGURE 23.4 **Ideal Distributions for Classroom Assessment.** Negatively skewed distributions indicate mastery.

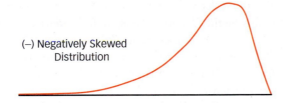

(−) Negatively Skewed Distribution

This is appropriate because it indicates that most students have achieved some level of mastery (Rodriguez & Haladyna, 2013). Norm-referenced grading should not be used with this type of distribution (Waugh & Gronlund, 2013).

CRITERION-REFERENCED GRADING

Criterion-referenced grading is a method of assigning grades in which scores on an assessment or a set of assessments are compared to a predetermined criterion (or standard) for what is considered A performance, B performance, and so on. Two common methods are the fixed percentage method and total points method.

- In the **total points method,** teachers decide the maximum number of points for each component of the final grade during the planning process. A teacher would plan the number and type of assessments for the entire course and the total amount of points to be earned, as in the following example:

  Quizzes (five, 10 points each) = 50 points
  Tests (four, 25 points each) = 100 points
  Project (one, 100 points) = 100 points

  The maximum number of points for each component reflects the weight assigned to each. In this example, tests count twice as much as quizzes in the final grade or are more heavily weighted. Letter grades are then assigned based on the number of total points a student accumulated over a marking period using the maximum possible total points to set letter-grade boundaries. For example, a teacher may

> **Criterion-referenced grading:** See also criterion-referenced tests in Module 25

set the boundary for an A grade at 230 to 250 total points. Therefore, if a student accumulated 237 points, he would earn an A for the marking period. Letter grades are only assigned for the sum of all components, not for individual components (Brookhart & Nitko, 2014). Students and parents find it easy to understand the weight of assessments toward the final grade because it is obvious from the maximum number of points for each component (McMillan, 2014).

- In the **fixed percentage method,** the scores on each course component that contribute to the final grade are converted to a percentage correct (or a percentage of total points). Then the percentages are combined and converted to letter grades using percentage ranges that are determined by the teacher, school, or district, as in the following:

A	95–100%
B	85–94%
C	75–84%
D	65–74%
F	below 65%

The percentage ranges corresponding to each letter grade must be the same for each course component (Brookhart & Nitko, 2014). For example, the criterion for an A must be 95% to 100% on quizzes, tests, lab reports, and essays.

Before choosing a criterion-referenced method, teachers should be aware of the limitations of each. In the total points method, setting a maximum number of points for a course or subject before instruction may reduce teachers' flexibility in creating assessments or making adjustments, such as adding or removing assessments while a course is ongoing (Brookhart & Nitko, 2014; McMillan, 2014). In the earlier example where quizzes are 10 points each, tests are 25, and the project is 100, a teacher may only need seven quiz items for adequate content coverage and would need to "make up" a 3-point deficit to keep all quizzes at 10 points each. Or teachers might decide to add some quizzes to help students improve their learning, which means that the sum of the quizzes will carry more weight than originally intended.

Compared to the total points method, the fixed percentage method is more flexible, allowing teachers to add, modify, or remove assessments while instruction is ongoing. However, grading criteria may vary among teachers, with one teacher choosing 95% to 100% for an A and another 90% to 100% (Brookhart & Nitko, 2014). Also, the fixed percentage method has the potential to distort students' actual achievement.

- Almost two-thirds of the percentage scale, from 0 to 65%, represent an F grade. Therefore, calculating final grades using this method may be an unfair assessment of students' actual achievement, as in the case of a low grade on a test that was difficult for the entire class or a zero for a missed assignment (Brookhart & Nitko, 2014; Marzano & Heflebower, 2011; McMillan, 2014; Wormeli, 2006). This has led many school districts to adopt a policy prohibiting teachers from giving zeros, requiring them to issue the highest possible failing score for an assessment rather than a zero (Brookhart & Nitko, 2014; Carey & Carifio, 2012). For example, consider the following two sets of scores for a student, one with a zero and one with a 65 as a failing score instead of zero:

	92	92
	95	95
	83	83
	0	65
Average:	71.4	84.4

With the zero, the student would receive a C as a final grade, whereas with the 65, the student would get a B.

- Many teachers fail to use weighting of various components when combining scores on assessments to determine letter grades in the fixed percentage method (Moss, 2013). A simple average of students' percentages can distort their actual achievement by overestimating or underestimating the final grade (Waugh & Gronlund, 2013). Consider the following example in which Student 1 performs better on homework assignments and quizzes than tests, and Student 2 shows an opposite pattern:

	TESTS (WORTH 60%)	QUIZZES (WORTH 20%)	HOMEWORK (WORTH 20%)	FINAL GRADE (SIMPLE AVERAGE)	FINAL GRADE (WEIGHTED AVERAGE)
Student 1	70%	98%	100%	89% (B)	82% (B)
Student 2	90%	70%	70%	76% (C)	82% (B)

A simple average would yield a higher overall grade for Student 1. However, a weighted average—taking into account how much tests, quizzes, and homework are worth toward the final grade calculation—indicates that the two students perform similarly. Consider the same two students using a total points system. In this system, the total for all course requirements is 200. Tests are worth 120 points toward the total (or 60% of the total), quizzes are worth 40 points (20% of the total), and homework is worth 40 points (20% of the total).

	TESTS (120 POINTS)	QUIZZES (40 POINTS)	HOMEWORK (40 POINTS)	FINAL GRADE
Student 1	84	39	40	163/200 = 81.5% (B)
Student 2	108	28	28	164/200 = 82.0% (B)

In this example, the students earned the same grades on tests, quizzes, and homework assignments as in the weighted average example shown earlier (for example, 84 points out of 120 is 70%). However, the grading is more transparent and easier for students and their parents to understand.

SELF-REFERENCED GRADING

Self-referenced grading, also called growth-based grading, is a method in which teachers assign grades by comparing students' performance to past performance or to the teacher's perceptions of their ability. This approach is helpful for lower achieving students and students with disabilities because it prevents them from being penalized by a single grading structure that is used for all students regardless of their ability level (Brookhart, 2013; McLesky & Waldron, 2002). When determining a grade for a lower achieving student, a teacher might take into account the student's effort, motivation, and improvement, and assign a grade of B when the student actually earned a C+. However, this approach might be detrimental to higher achieving students in the same classroom because they would have less improvement to make. Also, a teacher may lower a grade (let's say from a B to a B-) if he or she believed the student was not putting forth his best effort based on his ability. These examples of self-referenced grading raise issues of fairness because the approach may create a situation in which grading structures are not evenly applied to all students in the class.

In addition to fairness, self-referenced grading also may raise issues regarding the reliability and validity of grades (Nitko & Brookhart, 2011).

> **DIVERSITY**

- This approach relies on teacher judgments to estimate nonacademic factors, such as effort and motivation, and may be influenced by subtle biases, leading to an evaluation of student achievement that is unreliable.

- Also, parents and students want to know what students actually earned and where they stand in relation to instructional objectives in an absolute sense without factoring in nonacademic behaviors. The question is, "Does an A grade really mean A-level knowledge and skills?"

 As a student, what type of grading approach would you prefer? Why? Think of the grade level or subject you intend to teach. As a teacher, what type of grading approach would you choose? Why?

COMMUNICATING ASSESSMENT INFORMATION

⑤ Describe the different types of report cards, and explain how teachers can open the lines of communication with parents regarding their children's progress.

Report cards and parent–teacher conferences are the primary ways teachers communicate students' academic progress to parents. Because parents interpret report card grades differently than teachers, and few report cards provide an explanation of what grades mean, it is important for teachers to clearly communicate how they calculate grades and what the grades mean (Brookhart, 2013). At the elementary school level, this information can be provided in an overview at back-to-school nights, and at the middle and high school level, teachers can convey this to parents in course syllabi.

Report Cards

The information presented in report cards has changed dramatically over the past 200 or so years since formal schooling began, from detailed explanations, to numerical scales, letter grades, and more recently standards of performance.

Prior to the 1770s, teachers used **narrative reports** to communicate student performance to parents (Quinlan, 2012). Narrative reports are written descriptions of students' effort and mastery of curriculum. In these reports, teachers have the freedom to include observations and personalized information about the student that would not appear on typical letter-grade report cards. This contrasts with the "canned" comments in many typical report cards, such as "pleasure to have in class." In narrative reports, teachers can elaborate on the characteristics and behaviors that make a student a pleasure to have in class. Despite the potential benefit of an individualized evaluation, narrative reports have several disadvantages (Bagley, 2008; Brookhart & Nitko, 2014).

- They are time-consuming to write.

- Teachers may need extensive professional development to learn how to write sensitive and constructive comments.

- This approach may not be feasible for teachers in large schools with many students.

- Narratives can be too lengthy for parents to read and get a sense of their child's progress, and they may be an ineffective means of communicating students' performance to parents with low reading levels or language barriers.

- Students generally consider narrative reports as more stressful than letter grades.

DIVERSITY

It was not until the 20th century with the proliferation of public schools that teachers transitioned from informal means of reporting students' achievement to the grading systems we recognize today. Two common forms are the percentage grade system (0 to 100%) and the letter grade system (A through F). The percentages or letter grades are composites, representing a combination of scores or grades on formative and summative assessments over a marking period. As we discussed, teachers can arrive at these composites using norm-referenced, criterion-referenced, or self-referenced grading practices.

With the increasing emphasis on how students are performing relative to national standards—first initiated by the No Child Left Behind Act of 2001 and more recently prompted by the Common Core State Standards—some schools have shifted to **standards-based grades** in report cards. This report card lists:

- the standards for each subject. For example, the math section of a fifth-grade report card would list standards for algebraic thinking, numerical reasoning, rational numbers, spatial reasoning, and statistics.

- performance level descriptors for each standard, such as "advanced," "proficient," "basic," or "below basic," which are similar to descriptors used on state standards-based assessments (Brookhart, 2013).

Compared to letter or percentage grades, standards-based grades may be easier for parents to understand. However, even though standards-based grade reporting is intended to align with state standards, the "grades" on a report card may not match state assessments (Brookhart & Nitko, 2014). A student may be given a "proficient" level in math on her report card but only achieve a "basic" level on the state standards-based assessment. Also, for high school students seeking entry to college, there needs to be a way to quantify performance categories for reporting GPA and class rank to colleges (Brookhart & Nitko, 2014). Because standards-based grading is so new, there is little research at this time (Brookhart, 2013).

Parent–Teacher Communication

High-quality communication between teachers and parents provides information for helping students make continued progress on learning objectives (Randel & Clark, 2013). Teachers communicate formally through report cards, which we have discussed, and through regular parent–teacher conferences several times per year. They also communicate informally through electronic media.

Parent–teacher conferences are an opportunity for teachers to update parents on their child's progress and also gain unique insights from parents about their children. Parents' observations about their children's effort, work habits, and motivation might be very helpful to the teacher's understanding of how the student approaches learning in class. Therefore, the first priority is to put parents at ease by setting a tone that invites this two-way communication (Wright, 2008). Teachers can begin by identifying positive aspects of the child's academic progress, work habits, behaviors, and social interactions. Showing student work samples also can provide a context for discussing the student's learning progress, strengths, and weaknesses in a manner that is supportive and nonconfrontational (Waugh & Gronlund, 2013). Encourage parents to discuss their observations and concerns, listen, and take brief notes as necessary. Also, be prepared to explain what grades mean on report cards, how these grades were derived, and what standardized test scores mean. Parents may interpret grades differently than teachers and are not as familiar with the many types of assessments and how they are scored and interpreted (Brookhart, 2013). Finally, so that teachers as well as parents do not feel pressured to resolve any issues discussed during a brief conference, teachers should reassure parents that they will follow up with additional conversations. The conference is a means to open the lines of communication between school and home (Wright, 2008).

Common Core State Standards: See Modules 1 and 25

Parent–Teacher conferences: See Module 17

Standardized test scores: See Module 25

Ariel Skelley/Blend Images/Getty Images

Teachers can continue communicating with parents through many avenues, such as additional meetings after school, phone calls, progress reports, and e-mail. Recent research indicates that e-mail is parents' preferred method of communication (Thompson, Mazer, & Grady, 2015). Teachers can use e-mail to follow up on a parent–teacher conference, provide information parents requested, or answer questions. Also, the wide availability of web-based software that allows parents to view their children's grades in real time opens up the possibility of increased communication with teachers regarding questions about their children's performance (Brookhart & Nitko, 2014). Be sensitive to cultural differences and language barriers that may prevent effective communication with and cooperation from parents (Guo, 2010; Ogbu, 1982; Osborne, 1996). Parents may not be able to communicate with teachers in oral or written form if they do not speak the language, and in some cultures parental involvement is considered a Western value and practice (Naylor, 1993).

DIVERSITY

Recent research on other forms of electronic media indicates that text messaging can provide parents with effective communication from teachers regarding their child's academic progress while instruction is ongoing. When teachers sent parents text messages about the missing assignments of their adolescent, lower socioeconomic high school students showed significant gains in GPA, tests scores, and school engagement (Bergman, 2015). In another study, parents of high school students in a credit recovery program for graduation received a weekly one-sentence message from teachers emphasizing what their children needed to improve. Parents who did not speak English received messages translated into their native language. Weekly communication with parents improved students' readiness for graduation, and the largest effects were obtained for students with limited English proficiency (Kraft & Rogers, 2014).

Teachers have a legal obligation to respond to parents' requests for information about their children's grades, test scores, and other aspects of their educational record, and they also have a responsibility to keep students' educational records confidential beyond communication with parents. The **Family Educational Rights and Privacy Act** of 1974 (FERPA), also called the Buckley Amendment, provides parents with several rights regarding the educational records of their children under age 18. Under this legislation, parents have the right to

FERPA: See Module 21

506   Unit 8: Assessment

- review their children's education records within 45 days of a request,

- take steps to amend records believed to be inaccurate, and

- consent to disclose personally identifiable information in their children's education records.

FERPA prevents any persons or entities from accessing any personally identifiable information in educational records, such as students' names and social security numbers, without a parent's or guardian's consent except in cases when such information is requested through a court order or subpoena.

Any practice of revealing students' identity, especially when their identity is linked to their grades or test scores, is also prohibited under FERPA. Therefore, teachers need to ensure that they maintain anonymity of student identity and confidentiality of student records in practices such as announcing grades in class and posting grades. Teachers cannot publicly post or announce individual grades that will identify the students' identities and their corresponding grades using names, social security numbers, or student ID numbers. Sending information to parents in e-mail is generally safe if the teacher is sure that the e-mail address belongs to the parent, which can be verified in the student's educational record.

Teachers also need to be aware of the FERPA guidelines for situations in which students reach the age of 18 while still in high school. In this case, FERPA allows parents to have access to their children's educational records if:

- the student is a dependent for income tax purposes;

- there is a health or safety emergency involving the student;

- the student, who is under age 21, has violated any law or institutional policy concerning the use or possession of alcohol or a controlled substance and the school must take disciplinary action for the violation; or

- the information requested by the parent is based on a school staff's personal knowledge or observation of the student.

In most cases, 18-year-old high school students will still be dependents, allowing parents a right to access their records. When in doubt regarding FERPA or other educational legislation, it is always best to consult with the principal or legal staff in the district for specific information.

Think about the grade level you intend to teach. What methods would you choose for communicating to parents?

APPLICATIONS: IMPLEMENTING VALID AND MEANINGFUL ASSESSMENTS

6 Describe the principles for implementing valid and meaningful assessments.

Assessments that are reliable and valid, relevant to learning objectives, and provide useful feedback to students become more than a vehicle for "giving a grade." They become an integral part of the teaching and learning process and foster a sense of meaningful learning in students. Let's consider some principles for valid and meaningful assessment.

Meaningful learning: See Module 12

Use feedback appropriately to promote mastery. Feedback is an essential component of formative assessment, and when used properly it can encourage students' progress toward learning goals (Brookhart, 2012; Brookhart & Nitko, 2014).

Process, performance, or person praise: See Module 14

Intrinsic motivation: See Module 14

- Provide immediate feedback containing comments that identify students' strengths and give at least one suggestion for improvement toward the learning objectives (Brookhart, 2012).

- When making comments, avoid person praise and focus on the process or product of the assessment. Person praise—a favorable judgment about a person's attributes or behaviors, such as "You're a math whiz"—can be detrimental to intrinsic motivation to learn, which is natural interest and enjoyment in the task (Corpus & Lepper, 2007; Pomerantz & Kempner, 2013). Instead, using feedback that emphasizes the process students took to accomplish a task (e.g., praising the student's strategy use in solving a math problem) or the product (e.g., the essay is focused and clearly written) promotes intrinsic motivation and feelings of competence (Corpus & Lepper, 2007; Zentall & Morrris, 2010).

- Learning will only be enhanced if students are given an opportunity to take comments into consideration and revise their work. A grade on a paper or test is not sufficient feedback to encourage students to strive for improvement the next time they complete an assessment (Brookhart & Nitko, 2014).

Take steps to improve the validity and reliability of assessments. To ensure that all types of assessments—objective and performance—are valid for indicating mastery of content, create assessments that align to instructional objectives, teaching methods, and time spent on material (Cizek, 2009). Because performance assessments are subjective, teachers need to make scoring as objective and reliable as possible so that they provide valid information about students' performance (Waugh & Gronlund, 2013). Directions for performance assessments should be clear, which will help students produce work that can be more easily scored. Also, rubrics and rating scales should be well-constructed and include procedures for avoiding rater errors (Brookhart & Nitko, 2014). To obtain data on the reliability of performance assessments, teachers can ask a colleague to grade a small sample of assessments using the teacher's rubric or rating scale (Brookhart & Nitko, 2014). High **interrater reliability** for the rubric or rating scale would be obtained if similar scores resulted from two teachers independently rating a batch of assessments. When interrater reliability is not possible to obtain, teachers can improve **intrarater reliability,** consistency within the same rater over time, by grading assessments without student names (which will reduce biases and increase rater consistency) and periodically returning to assessments that were graded earlier to verify that regrading them would result in the same score (Brookhart & Nitko, 2014).

For information on reliability of objective assessments: See Modules 24 and 25

Ensure that grades are a valid reflection of students' achievement. A valid grade reflects only students' achievement or mastery of content and does not include nonachievement factors, such as attitudes, effort, or behavior (Brookhart & Nitko, 2014).

- When assigning grades, avoid combining achievement with effort and work habits (Brookhart, 2013; McMillan, Myran, & Workman, 2002; Randall & Englehard, 2010). Combining tardiness with achievement, as when teachers deduct points on late assignments, also lowers the validity of the grade. It is generally poor practice to control students' behavior by lowering achievement grades because of factors unrelated to achievement (Brookhart & Nitko, 2014).

- Provide students with multiple opportunities to be assessed using multiple measures, for example, do not always use tests (Tierney, 2013). This enables teachers to collect sufficient information about students' progress and achievements and helps ensure the fairness of assessment (Tierney, 2013). Multiples measures also help improve reliability and validity, especially since teachers do not typically evaluate the reliability and validity of their assessments (Gullickson & Ellwein, 1985; Mertler, 2000).

Use technology to increase the efficiency of grading and improve communication with parents. Over the past 10 years, electronic grading systems have become popular technologies to assist teachers with recording and calculating grades (McMillan, 2014). Many school districts provide web-based programs that teachers can use and that can be accessed by students, parents, and administrators. Before you develop your assessment plan, become familiar with the features of the grading program and its limitations. For example, does it allow you to drop the lowest grade or weight course components in a user-friendly manner? How will it handle zeros or grading on improvement? Teachers may be constrained by the grading programs purchased by their school or district. However, they have freedom to choose many different technologies for communicating with parents about their children's grades and progress. E-mails and automated text message reminders can be helpful in keeping parents informed about students' progress, completion of assignments, and classwork, and they can improve student learning.

Think about the grade level or subject you plan to teach. What types of assessments would you use, for what purposes, and how would you communicate your expectations and your students' performance to your students and their parents?

SUMMARY

❶   Define assessment and describe its many purposes. Assessment is any process of gathering information about students' mastery and achievement. There are many types of assessments that serve different purposes. Assessments can inform educational policies at the district, state, or national level, provide information for making decisions about the efficacy of curricula and programs at the district or school level, and provide data for making many decisions about individual students. Assessments can be used for student selection (such as for college admissions), placement decisions (such as classes grouped by ability), diagnosis of disabilities, career planning, and for teacher decision making when planning instruction, monitoring student progress, and evaluating student outcomes on learning goals.

❷   Contrast the major advantages and disadvantages of objective assessments and performance assessments. One advantage of objective assessments is their breadth of coverage compared to the depth of coverage for performance approaches. Compared to performance assessments, objective assessments tend to measure lower level objectives, take less class time, and can be scored relatively quickly with high reliability and validity. However, objective assessments are often poorly constructed, which can reduce the validity of the interpretation.

❸   Describe the tools used to score performance tasks and explain the limitations of scoring performance assessments. Teachers can use checklists, rating scales,

and rubrics. Checklists provide no judgment of the quality of the performance but simply list behaviors or characteristics for teachers to determine whether they are present. Rating scales provide a numerical score for varying levels or degrees of performance on one or more dimensions. The purpose of holistic rubrics is to evaluate the overall quality of a student's performance on a task project when it is not possible to define the specific characteristics of "good work" ahead of time. Analytic rubrics provide the most detailed scoring and feedback of all scoring tools. They allow teachers to give specific feedback regarding strengths and weaknesses and are useful for any task in which students have an opportunity to improve their performance. Providing students with rubrics or rating scales ahead of time helps students know what to do to perform well. Teachers should be aware of limitations when scoring performance assessments caused by subtle biases, such as the leniency error, central tendency error, and halo effect, all of which can reduce the reliability of the assessment score.

❹   Describe the three main types of grading procedures and explain their advantages and limitations. The three main grading procedures are norm-referenced grading, criterion-referenced grading, and self-referenced grading. Norm-referenced grading is a method of assigning grades based on how a student's performance compares with classmates. Experts discourage this approach because classroom assessments rarely result in a normal distribution of scores, and applying this method without a normal curve would unfairly assign grades to students. Criterion-referenced grading involves assigning grades by comparing students' scores on an assessment or a set of assessments to a predetermined criterion for each letter grade. Two types are the total points method and the fixed percentage method. The total points method gives teachers less flexibility in creating assessments or making adjustments. While the fixed percentage method is more flexible, it has the potential to distort students' actual achievement. In self-referenced grading, teachers assign grades by comparing students' performance to past performance or to the teacher's perceptions of their ability. This approach is helpful for lower achieving students and students with disabilities. However, self-referenced grading also may raise issues regarding the reliability, validity, and fairness of grades.

5 **Describe the different types of report cards, and explain how teachers can open the lines of communication with parents regarding their children's progress.** Conveying information about student progress can be accomplished through narrative reports (descriptive accounts of students' achievements and behaviors),

letter grades, percentage grades, or standards-based grades that align with the standards of state assessments. Teachers communicate with parents about their children's progress formally through report cards and parent–teacher conferences and informally through electronic media. Research indicates that parents prefer e-mail contact and that use of text messages by teachers to inform parents about students' progress and work completion can improve learning. When communicating students' grades, teachers should be aware of student privacy laws.

6 **Describe the principles for implementing valid and meaningful assessments.** Assessments that are reliable and valid, relevant to learning objectives, and provide useful feedback to students foster a sense of meaningful learning in students. To achieve this goal, teachers can implement the following principles: (a) Use feedback appropriately to promote mastery, (b) take steps to improve the validity and reliability of assessments, (c) ensure that grades are a valid reflection of students' achievement, and (d) use technology to increase the efficiency of grading and improve communication with parents.

KEY CONCEPTS

analytic rubrics, 497

assessment, 497

best work portfolios, 495

checklists, 497

classroom tests, 493

criterion-referenced grading, 501

evaluation, 491

fairness, 494

Family Educational Rights and Privacy Act (FERPA), 506

fixed percentage method, 502

formal assessment, 492

formative assessment, 491

grading on the curve method, 500

growth portfolios, 495

halo effect, 500

holistic rubrics, 497

informal assessment, 492

interrater reliability, 508

intrarater reliability, 508

measurement, 491

narrative reports, 504

norm-referenced grading, 500

objective data, 492

performance assessment, 494

practicality, 494

rating scales, 497

reliability, 508

self-referenced grading, 503

standard deviation method, 500

standardized tests, 492

standards-based grades, 505

subjective data, 492

summative assessment, 491

total points method, 501

validity, 494

CASE STUDIES: REFLECT AND EVALUATE

EARLY CHILDHOOD: Kindergarten Readiness

These questions refer to the case study on page 482.

1. Examine Table 23.1. What assessment purpose does the BRIGANCE K & 1 Screen-II serve for the kindergarten teachers?

2. Would you consider the BRIGANCE K & 1 Screen-II a formative assessment or a summative assessment? Explain your reasoning.

3. What are examples of summative assessments that are appropriate for kindergarteners?

4. What types of technology would you use to inform parents about their child's progress and mastery?

5. What type of report card grades do you think is most appropriate for kindergarteners? Why?

ELEMENTARY SCHOOL: Teacher In-Service Training

These questions refer to the case study on page 484.

1. Ms. Fernández says she gave different tests to her students with learning disabilities and her other students. Evaluate the fairness of this practice for both groups of students.

2. Ms. LeBlanc, the reading specialist, says that many students she works with need extra time on the standardized achievement tests. Evaluate the fairness of this accommodation. How might it affect the validity of the test scores?

3. Do you think Mr. Whitney's approach of assigning a book report is a more valid assessment of students' reading than Ms. Seifert's use of tests? Why or why not?

4. Explain to Mr. Whitney the advantages of using a rating scale or rubric to evaluate students' performance on their book reports.

5. Assume you are a teacher at the meeting in favor of using a performance assessment to evaluate students' reading progress. Explain what type of performance assessment you would use and how you would score it.

MIDDLE SCHOOL: Homework Night

These questions refer to the case study on page 486.

1. Evaluate the validity of Payton's social studies homework as an indication of her academic progress.

2. Is the math test containing word problems a fair assessment of students' mastery if they had no opportunity to practice problem solving on homework assignments? Why or why not?

3. Give Payton's math teacher, Ms. Bowden, suggestions for improving homework assignments as a formative assessment. Give Payton's social studies teacher tips for improving the online homework.

4. Explain the benefit of providing a rubric to students along with the assignment.

5. Pick one of Payton's subjects—math, social studies, or literature. Provide the teacher with examples of performance assessments that could be used in place of their existing assignments, and explain whether they would be considered formative or summative assessments.

HIGH SCHOOL: Math Tests

These questions refer to the case study on page 488.

1. What was Ms. Fortner's rationale for giving her students multiple-choice math tests to prepare for the SAT? Would this be considered good assessment practice?

2. Mr. Harris questions the accuracy of Trevor's SAT score. Explain the concept of validity in this situation.

3. Tony had one exam in Ms. Fortner's class, which brought down his grade. Is one exam sufficient for making interpretations about a student's mastery? Why or why not?

4. Ms. Camponi's complaint identifies a flaw in Ms. Fortner's approach to assessment. Identify the flaw.

5. How can Ms. Fortner improve her communication with parents regarding students' grades? Give specific suggestions.

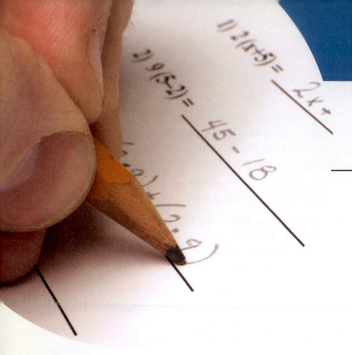

©iStockphoto.com/ Jim Jurica

TEST CONSTRUCTION AND USE

OUTLINE	LEARNING GOALS
Characteristics of High-Quality Classroom Tests	
• Validity • Reliability • Fairness and Practicality	❶ Explain why validity, reliability, fairness, and practicality are important for classroom tests.
Test Preparation	
• Developing a Test Blueprint • Creating Selected-Response Items • Creating Constructed-Response Items	❷ Explain why a test blueprint is important for test planning and construction. ❸ Compare and contrast the usefulness and scoring considerations of selected-response and constructed-response item formats.
***Applications:* Improving Your Test**	
• Test Administration Considerations • Item and Distractor Analyses	❹ Explain how item and distractor analyses can be used to improve the validity of a classroom test.

CHARACTERISTICS OF HIGH-QUALITY CLASSROOM TESTS

❶ Explain why validity, reliability, fairness, and practicality are important for classroom tests.

Formative and summative assessment:
See Module 23

Tests and quizzes are common classroom assessments that teachers use for formative and summative purposes. Before a lesson, teachers might use a quiz as a *formative assessment*, which gauges what students already know about content and what strengths and weaknesses they may have. Once a lesson or unit is completed, teachers use a test as a *summative assessment* for obtaining information about what students have mastered. Classroom tests, whether used for formative or summative purposes, need to be held to the same high standard of quality as standardized tests.

Creating high-quality tests requires that teachers follow research-based principles for designing tests and creating test items. In this module, we cover the essentials of test planning and item construction for formats such as true–false, multiple choice, matching, short answer, and essays. First, let's examine the criteria for judging the quality of tests.

Validity

Have you ever taken a test that you thought was *not* an accurate reflection of your knowledge or mastery of a subject? If so, you questioned the test's validity. **Validity** is the extent to which an assessment measures what it intended to measure and only what it intended to measure, yielding accurate and meaningful interpretations from the assessment. One issue affecting the validity of the test score interpretation is how well a test reflects the entire topic or lesson that was taught, and another issue is the extent to which the test does *not* measure other factors that might affect test performance, such as test-taking skills or processing speed. A test assessing knowledge of this module would be valid if it contained items that reflected only the content of this module and not content of another module that students were not required to study. The test would also be valid if the items represented all of the content of the module rather than only a few key concepts (unless your instructor identified in advance that only a few concepts were important to know). Therefore, an important characteristic of a "good" classroom assessment is **content validity,** the extent to which an assessment accurately reflects the subject matter, leading to meaningful interpretations of students' mastery and achievement.

Content validity is one type of evidence supporting the validity of the test score interpretation. There are many other types of validity evidence that researchers use when evaluating whether standardized tests are "good" tests. However, in this module we focus on only content validity because it is the most important type of evidence for classroom assessments.

Regardless of whether the assessment is a classroom test or standardized test, there are four important points to remember about validity.

1. Validity refers to the test *score,* not the test itself (the collection of items on a test). When we say, "The test is valid," we mean the interpretation of the test score is valid.

2. Validity is not an all-or-none characteristic (valid or invalid). Validity of a test score varies from more valid to less valid. Consider the example of an algebra test intended to measure computation and problem solving. If a teacher requires students to memorize formulas, then the validity of the test as a measure of algebra knowledge would be reduced (less valid) because it also measures memorization ability.

3. Validity can never be conclusively *proven.* Rather, it varies depending on the extent of the research evidence supporting a test score's validity.

4. Test score validity refers to the *intended purpose* of the test (Shepard, 2013). For classroom assessment, this means that the purpose of the test should align with instructional objectives (what you want students to learn and be able to do) and with the method of instruction and learning (Bonner, 2013; Brookhart & Nitko, 2014). A fifth-grade geography quiz asking students to list the states located in different regions of the country would not be a very valid measure if the learning objective was to locate states on a map.

As we will discuss, teachers can take steps to ensure the validity of classroom tests during instructional planning, during test development, and once the test is administered and scored.

- Valid assessment begins with instructional planning. Teachers need to ask themselves, "what do I want students to know or do," and plan instructional activities and the

Master the content.

edge.sagepub.com/durwin3e

Video: Formative Assessment

Content validity: See Module 25

Types of validity evidence: See Module 25

Standardized tests: See Module 25

Match between instructional objectives and tests: See Modules 18 and 23

assessment to match the objective. Student performance is enhanced when the assessment matches how the material was learned (Morris, Bransford, & Franks, 1977; Tulving & Thomson, 1973).

- When developing tests, teachers need to adhere to research-based principles for constructing items such as multiple choice, true–false, matching, short answer, and essays. Creating "good" items will result in a more valid test.

- After a test is developed and scored, teachers need to examine how well the individual items in a test are performing. Are they too easy or too difficult? Do they differentiate the students who really know the material from those who do not? Items that are moderately difficult and differentiate among test takers contribute to a valid test score.

Reliability

For a test to be valid, it must have **reliability**, or consistency in its measurement. If a teacher were to administer the same test on Monday and Friday, we would expect students to obtain the same scores or nearly the same scores (assuming they did not study more in between). If the test scores are not similar, then the measurement lacks consistency and therefore the scores lack validity—they cannot be meaningfully interpreted. For example, if scores for a student on Monday and Friday are 67 and 88, respectively, which is the true reflection of the student's ability?

Because classroom tests are used to make decisions about mastery or achievement, it is important that teachers create reliable tests for those decisions to be valid. To ensure reliability of an assessment, we need to identify and reduce factors that can lead to *measurement error*, which is an accumulation of imperfections that are found in all measurement tools, including tests. For example, measurement error can result from poorly written multiple-choice or true–false items or teachers' subjective biases when scoring essays.

Measurement error: See Module 25

Fairness and Practicality

Fairness and practicality are other characteristics of "good" tests that affect the validity of test score interpretations and should be considered when planning assessments. **Fairness** reflects the extent to which all students have an equal opportunity to learn the required content and

Measurement Tools. Tests, like other measurement tools, must have reliability of measurement.

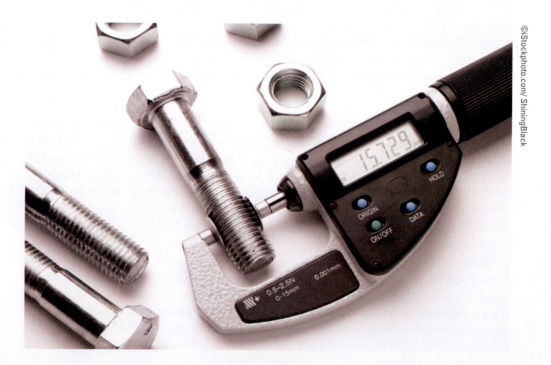

@iStockphoto.com/ ShiningBlack

demonstrate their knowledge (Tierney, 2013). Teachers should ask themselves whether the items on the test they created are consistent with what they taught and what students actually learned. Is it a fair assessment to ask questions on content that was not covered in class or assigned as reading? Also, students need to be given an adequate opportunity to demonstrate their knowledge on tests. Is an essay test a fair assessment for third graders who are still developing their writing skills? Is a multiple-choice test containing so many items that high school students cannot finish in the allotted time a fair reflection of their mastery? When evaluating fairness, it is also important to consider individual differences among students within your classroom. Students with disabilities or students with limited English proficiency might require testing modifications or a different type of assessment altogether to demonstrate their mastery.

Practicality issues are just as important to consider when planning assessments. Ask yourself the following questions:

- How time-consuming is the assessment to create?

- How long will the assessment take to administer? How much class time will be used?

- How easy and efficient is the assessment to score?

All test item formats have advantages and disadvantages. Creating well-written objective items, such as multiple choice and true–false, generally takes more time than constructing essay questions. However, objective items can cover many more learning objectives within a single test, take less class time, and can be quickly and accurately scored compared to essay tests. Despite practical limitations of essay tests, they might be preferred in certain situations in which learning objectives cannot be adequately measured by objective items. For example, if the learning objective is to integrate information from various perspectives, an essay test may be the best way for students to demonstrate that skill or knowledge.

Video Case 24.2 ▲
Fair Tests

© SAGE Publications

Reflect on your own education. When have you encountered assessments that violated validity, reliability, fairness, or practicality?

TEST PREPARATION

❷ Explain why a test blueprint is important for test planning and construction.

❸ Compare and contrast the usefulness and scoring considerations of selected-response and constructed-response item formats.

Many teachers use commercially prepared tests for classroom assessment, such as a bank of test items that accompanies a chosen textbook (Cizek, Fitzgerald, & Rachor, 1995; Frey & Schmitt, 2010; McMillan, Myran, & Workman, 2002). Whether teachers choose test bank items or create their own items, they need to select items that represent the content they expect students to know and the way in which they expect students to demonstrate their learning. They also need to use sound principles for construction of items to evaluate and edit the prepared test bank items or to create their own so that the test is of high quality and leads to valid score interpretations.

Developing a Test Blueprint

Test development begins with a test blueprint, or a plan for the content the test will cover and the ways in which students will demonstrate mastery of the content (Randel & Clark, 2013). Test blueprints are often represented as a **table of specifications,** a matrix that specifies the number and type of items to include on a test given the number of learning objectives and the

Bloom's taxonomy: See
Modules 13, 18, and 23

Match between
instructional objectives
and tests: See Modules 18
and 23

class time spent on each of the objectives (Fives & DiDonato-Barnes, 2013). As the table of specifications in Table 24.1 illustrates, content areas or learning objectives are listed in the left column, and the cognitive processes that students are expected to use on the test are shown across the top, with the cells containing the number and type of items for each content/process combination (Gregory, 2013). Often, Bloom's taxonomy is used to represent the cognitive processes in the table of specifications. The taxonomy specifies that learning objectives can involve lower level processes, such as remembering, understanding, and applying information, or higher level processes, such as analyzing or evaluating information or creating new information or a product based on one's learning (Anderson & Krathwohl, 2001; Bloom, Englehart, Frost, Hill, & Krathwohl, 1956).

A table of specifications helps teachers align objectives, instruction, and assessment, which improves the validity of the assessment (Fives & DiDonato-Barnes, 2013; Notar, Zuelke, Wilson, & Yunker, 2004). Sometimes teachers create tests that represent the learning objectives and the content of instruction but require students to respond in ways that are inconsistent with how they learned the information (Fives & DiDonato-Barnes, 2013). For example, a teacher who lectures on the influence of Greek culture on the Roman Empire might expect students to be able to answer objective items (such as multiple choice) measuring their factual knowledge but should not expect them to answer an essay comparing and contrasting Greek and Roman cultures. Similarly, a class that completes a group activity comparing Greek and Roman life might not perform as well answering basic factual questions on a multiple-choice exam.

In the table of specifications, the cognitive processes are sometimes confused with the type of item, such as multiple choice or essay (Fives & DiDonato-Barnes, 2013). All multiple-choice items (or other objective items) do not necessarily require low-level cognitive processes, and all essays do not necessarily involve high-level processes. For example, an essay question that reads, "Discuss the factors leading to the fall of the Roman Empire," appears to assess higher level thinking that requires students to analyze or evaluate the situation. However, if students took lecture notes on a list of factors, then it is a low-level question assessing knowledge or comprehension.

Teachers need to decide what types of items match the content that was taught, the learning objectives, and the cognitive processes in the table of specification (Rodriguez & Haladyna, 2013). They have a wide array of items available to them, from selected-response to constructed-response formats. **Selected-response** items provide students with information and

---

TABLE 24.1 Sample Table of Specifications. A table of specifications can improve the validity of an assessment.

| | TIME SPENT ON TOPIC (MIN) | MAJOR CATEGORIES OF COGNITIVE TAXONOMY | | | | | | |
		REMEMBER	UNDERSTAND	APPLY	ANALYZE	EVALUATE	CREATE	
Topic A	50	2	2	2	1			7
Topic B	50	2	2	1	1	1		7
Topic C	50	1	2	1	2	1		7
Topic D	90		2	2	3	1	1	9
Total		5	8	6	7	3	1	30 items

require them to select a response, such as the correct answer in a multiple-choice item, circling true or false, or linking information in a matching exercise. In contrast, **constructed-response** formats require students to construct, or create, a response to a question or prompt. Next we discuss how to create items from both of these formats.

Creating Selected-Response Items

Selected-response formats, such as multiple choice, true–false, and matching, are staples of classroom assessment (Haladyna, Downing, & Rodriguez, 2002). Tests containing these items are called **objective tests** because the items have one correct answer and can be scored objectively without interpretation or judgment. We begin with multiple choice, which is a popular format for teachers because it can assess lower level and higher level learning objectives (Reynolds & Livingston, 2012).

Objective tests: See Module 23

MULTIPLE-CHOICE ITEMS

There are two types of **multiple-choice items,** correct-answer and best-answer formats (Reynolds & Livingston, 2012). In the correct-answer format, there is clearly only one correct answer. In the best-answer format, there may be more than one correct answer and the aim is to identify the best one. Compare the following two items.

Video Case 24.3 ▲
Creating Tests

© SAGE Publications

Correct-answer format:

On IQ tests, the average score is _____.

a) 85

b) 95

c) 100*

d) 115

Best-answer format:

It is most accurate to say that IQ is _____.

a) stable throughout infancy and early childhood

b) unlikely to change over time as a result of education

c) indicative of a person's ability at the time of testing*

In the correct-answer item, there is clearly a correct answer—the average IQ score is 100. In the best-answer format, the object is to choose the most accurate statement.

Multiple-choice items have two parts: the **stem,** which asks a question or presents an incomplete statement, and the **alternatives,** or choices. Among the alternatives, one is the correct answer and the rest are called **distractors.** Guidelines 24.1 provide the basic principles for constructing stems and alternatives.

When creating alternatives, keep in mind that using fewer distractors that are well-written and plausible is better than creating more distractors that are not as effective. Many instructors use multiple-choice items with four alternatives (three distractors) or five alternatives (four distractors) because the greater number of alternatives decreases the chance of correctly guessing the answer when the test taker knows nothing about the content (Reynolds & Livingston, 2012). However, research indicates that test takers usually do not blindly guess the answer but are strategic, eliminating less plausible items before guessing (Rodriguez & Haladyna, 2013). Because it is difficult to write highly plausible distractors, adding distractors that are clearly incorrect does not reduce the chance of guessing correctly (Reynolds & Livingston, 2012). Consider the following item.

GUIDELINES 24.1   Rules for Constructing Multiple-Choice Items

Constructing the stem:

- The stem should make a single statement or ask a single question that is of central importance to a learning objective.

- Use simple, clear language.

- Put as much wording in the stem as possible, rather than in the alternatives, to minimize reading.

- Use negatively worded items (except, least, never, not) only to measure a relevant learning objective, such as what to avoid, what is not true, or several characteristics of a trait. The negative word should appear in capital letters and boldface font.

- Limit the use of *always* and *never* because good test takers will rule out distractors based on these words.

Constructing alternatives:

- Use three to five alternatives.

- Alternatives should be unambiguous so the correct response can be clearly identified.

- Alternatives should fit the stem grammatically.

- Alternatives should be of equal length and grammatical complexity because there is a tendency to make the correct answer longer.

- Place alternatives in a logical or numerical order, such as placing numbers in ascending order, dates in chronological order, and names in alphabetical order.

- Make the distractors plausible (no giveaways that can be easily eliminated) and use common misconceptions of students to create distractors.

- Avoid *all of the above.*

- Sparingly use *none of the above.*

SOURCES: Brookhart, 2015; Brookhart & Nitko, 2014; Haladyna et al., 2002; Reynolds & Livingston, 2012; Rodriguez & Haladyna, 2013; Waugh & Gronlund, 2013.

Which theorist was the founder of attachment theory, which posits that early childhood experiences shape our interactions with others later in life?

    a)   Bandura

    b)   Bowlby*

    c)   Freud

    d)   Mickey Mouse

Here, the giveaway distractor, Mickey Mouse, can be easily eliminated, increasing the chance of guessing from 25% to 33%. Therefore, the four-alternative item does not reduce the chance of guessing when distractors are poorly written. For this reason, experts recommend that a three-alternative item with two well-written distractors would work just as well and save time in creating additional distractors (Haladyna et al., 2002; Rodriguez & Haladyna, 2013). Obviously, the above multiple-choice item is an exaggeration. However, it makes the point that it is not the number of distractors that will differentiate students who know the material and those who do not; it is the quality of the distractors (Rodriguez & Haladyna, 2013).

Using the alternatives *all of the above* and *none of the above* is also not recommended. *All of the above* allows students to answer the item based on partial information (Reynolds & Livingston, 2012; Rodriguez & Haladyna, 2013). In a four-alternative item, if students know that two alternatives are correct, they can guess that *all of the above* might be the correct answer, or if they know that at least one alternative is incorrect, they can rule out *all of the above* as the correct answer. Experts disagree regarding the usefulness of *none of the above*. Some argue that when it is used as the correct answer, it does not assess whether students actually know the correct answer and may only assess whether they can identify incorrect answers (Gronlund, 2003). Others argue that being able to identify *none of the above* as correct (rejecting three false statements) may require greater understanding than recognizing that one answer is correct (Rodriguez & Haladyna, 2013). The disagreement among experts is why we recommend using this option sparingly. *None of the above* should be used only for correct-answer formats (not best-answer items), should be consistent with learning objectives, and should be used for items that would otherwise be too easy. It is also appropriate to use *none of the above* in math because it may encourage students to make accurate calculations and avoid estimation (Rodriguez & Haladyna, 2013).

Once all the items are constructed, there are a few additional guidelines for assembling them into a test (Haladyna et al., 2002; Reynolds & Livingston, 2012; Waugh & Gronlund, 2013).

- Display alternatives vertically, as we show in this module, so students can more easily read and compare the alternatives.

- Make sure the items are independent of each other so that students cannot answer one item correctly because a previous item provided a clue or the correct answer. For example, recall our previous item on page 518 about the founder of attachment theory. It appears again here. This item, if it occurred earlier in a test, gives a clue to the item below it.

  Which theorist was the founder of attachment theory, which posits that early childhood experiences shape our interactions with others later in life?

  a) Bandura

  b) Bowlby*

  c) Freud

  d) Mickey Mouse

  Which of the following accurately summarizes the basic premise of attachment theory?

  a) People learn by observing other people and imitating their behaviors.

  b) There are psychosocial crises for the 8 major stages in life from birth until death.

  c) Early childhood experiences shape our interactions with others later in life.*

  d) Our psychological development is grounded in our sexual development.

- The correct answer should appear in each alternative position an approximately equal number of times, and it should appear randomly throughout the test (for example, not AAACCC). To check this, assemble the test and count the number of times the correct answer occurs in each alternative position (A, B, C, D). If a particular position is overrepresented or underrepresented, move the correct answer of an item to a different position in the list of alternatives. For example, in a 20-item test, if there are 5 As, 3 Bs, 7 Cs, and 5 Ds, choose two items with C as the correct answer and move the correct answer from C to B. Then examine the test to make sure the correct answer also appears randomly throughout (for example, CDBA, etc.) and make adjustments as necessary.

- Proofread for spelling, grammar, and punctuation, and edit the test.

A well-written multiple-choice test can be an efficient assessment. It requires very little reading and can target many learning objectives in a short testing time. Well-written items also are easy to score and highly reliable. However, poorly written items can be superficial and measure only lower level processes, such as factual knowledge and comprehension (Brookhart & Nitko, 2014). To use multiple-choice items for measuring higher level processes, teachers can create interpretive exercises in which multiple-choice items are used to analyze, evaluate, or interpret a map, chart, figure, photo, or paragraph (Brookhart, 2015; Rodriguez & Haladyna, 2013).

TRUE–FALSE/ALTERNATIVE-RESPONSE ITEMS

The true–false item is a declarative statement to which students respond whether the statement is correct. The typical response is true or false, but other variations are "yes" or "no," "agree" or "disagree," "right" or "wrong," or "fact" or "opinion." These variations on the true–false format are called **alternative-response items** (Waugh & Gronlund, 2013). Experts recommend the following guidelines when creating alternative-response items (Brookhart & Nitko, 2014; Reynolds & Livingston, 2012; Waugh & Gronlund, 2013).

- Begin by creating a true and false item for the same concept even though you will use only one statement. This helps you check on whether each statement is clearly worded. If you can only write a false item by inserting the word "not" in the true statement, then it is not a good item (Frisbie & Becker, 1990).

- Similar to the stem in a multiple-choice item, use only one central idea in each statement. Avoid double-barreled statements, such as, *"A dendrite, which has origins in the Greek word 'tree,' receives information from other cells."* Students will not know whether to evaluate the truth of the Greek origin or the function.

- Keep the statements short and use simple vocabulary and sentence structure. Also, use precise wording so that statements can be unequivocally judged true or false. If a statement requires students to make evaluative judgments ("The best . . ." or "The most important . . ."), rephrase it as a comparative statement ("Compared to B, A is better . . ."). Also, statements of opinion should be attributed to some source ("According to your textbook author, . . .") unless the statements are of the fact–opinion format.

- Avoid **specific determiners,** which are words that provide cues to the correct answer. Words such as *never, always, none,* and *all* occur more frequently in false statements and provide a cue for students who may not know the answer because the statements are too broad to be true. Similarly, words such as *seldom, frequently, often,* and *usually* serve as cues to students who do not know the answer because statements with these words are more likely to be true.

- Similar to multiple-choice stems, use negative statements sparingly and avoid double negatives. As with distractors in multiple-choice items, write false statements that reflect misconceptions of students.

- Like alternatives in multiple-choice items, make sure true and false statements are about equal length. There is a tendency to write true statements that are longer than false ones, which can serve as a cue to the correct answer.

- When assembling the test, include approximately equal numbers of true and false statements because sometimes students develop a pattern of responding in which they select true every time they are unsure of the correct answer, or they select false every time.

Alternative-response items have many of the same advantages and disadvantages as multiple-choice items. Very little reading is involved and many learning objectives can be assessed within a short testing time. Scoring also is easy, objective, and reliable when items are well-constructed (Brookhart & Nitko, 2014; Reynolds & Livingston, 2012; Waugh & Gronlund, 2013). However, because it is difficult to write unambiguous items that assess more complex learning objectives, alternative-response items tend to focus on lower level factual knowledge (Reynolds & Livingston, 2012; Waugh & Gronlund, 2013). Experts recommend using alternative-response formats only in situations that are limited to two possible responses, such as classifying objects, determining whether a rule does or does not apply, distinguishing fact from opinion, and indicating whether arguments are valid or invalid (Waugh & Gronlund, 2013). Teachers also can use alternative-response items to measure more complex objectives by embedding them in interpretive exercises in which students are given a context (map, figure, paragraph) and interpret the information using alternative-response statements (Waugh & Gronlund, 2013).

MATCHING EXERCISES

Matching exercises contain two columns of words or phrases. The left column contains a numbered list of *premises,* which are words or phrases for which students seek a match, and the right column contains a lettered list of *responses,* which are words or phrases that are available for matching to the left column (Brookhart & Nitko, 2014; Reynolds & Livingston, 2012). A simple matching exercise might look like this:

Directions: In the left column are brain functions, and in the right column are areas of the brain. Match the brain area to its function. Do <u>not</u> use a brain area more than once.	
1. Making decisions, controlling impulses, judgments	a. Amygdala
2. Memory and learning	b. Cerebellum
3. Coordination and balance	c. Hippocampus
4. Emotional responses such as anger and fear	d. Prefrontal cortex
	e. Temporal lobe

Matching exercises function like a series of multiple-choice items. The premises are similar to a stem in a multiple-choice item and the responses are similar to multiple-choice alternatives. Like distractors in a multiple-choice item, all of the responses in a matching exercise should be plausible or likely to match any of the premises (Brookhart & Nitko, 2014; Waugh & Gronlund, 2013). For example, including body parts in the list of responses in the aforementioned matching exercise would not be plausible, and students could easily eliminate them.

No research evidence exists on matching exercises (Rodriguez & Haladyna, 2013). However, testing experts recommend the following principles for creating matching items (Brookhart & Nitko, 2014; Reynolds & Livingston, 2012; Waugh & Gronlund, 2013).

- The list of premises and responses should have a common theme. For example, a matching item on psychologists and their theories should include only the names of psychologists and theories and should not include other scientists (Albert Einstein) or scientific theories (theory of relativity).

- Keep the list of items short (about 5 to 8, but no more than 10).

- Make sure that the responses in the right column are brief. Students should read longer premises, and then scan the briefer responses.

- Similar to alternatives in multiple-choice items, the responses should be listed in alphabetical or numerical order.

- Use a larger, or smaller, number of responses than premises, and allow the responses to be used more than once or not at all. This reduces the chance of narrowing down options and successfully guessing. An even match between premises and responses allows students to correctly guess the last pair if they know all of the other premise-response pairs.

- Make sure all of the matching items appear on the same page for ease of reading.

- Provide clear instructions about the basis for matching and whether each response may be used once, more than once, or not at all. This will prevent misunderstanding of the task and improve the validity of the assessment.

Rote memorization: See Module 12

Matching exercises share the same advantages as multiple-choice and alternative-response items. Little reading is involved and the test can cover many learning objectives in a short time (Waugh & Gronlund, 2013). Scoring is also quick, objective, and reliable (Reynolds & Livingston, 2012). Matching also shares similar limitations, such as focusing on knowledge-level learning objectives (Brookhart & Nitko, 2014; Reynolds & Livingston, 2012; Waugh & Gronlund, 2013). Use of matching exercises may also encourage rote memorization (memorizing without necessarily understanding) of associations such as names and dates (Brookhart & Nitko, 2014).

Creating Constructed-Response Items

Constructed-response items, which require students to formulate a response to a question or prompt, range from simple completion or short-answer items to restricted essays and extended essays. Tests containing these types of items are considered **subjective tests** because the response may vary from student to student; therefore, judging the correctness of the response is open to interpretation. Short-answer/completion items are the least subjective and extended essays are the most subjective.

SHORT-ANSWER/COMPLETION ITEMS

This type of item requires students to write a word, phrase, number, or symbol to complete an incomplete statement or to answer a question. Items that use a direct question are called **short-answer items,** and those that use an incomplete statement with a blank in it are called **completion items** (Reynolds & Livingston, 2012). The following examples show each type using the same content:

What is the capital of Texas? <u>Austin</u>

The capital of Texas is <u>Austin</u>.

Direct questions are preferred because they state the problem more clearly and have only one correct answer (Reynolds & Livingston, 2012). However, incomplete statements are sometimes preferred because they are more concise. If that is the case, teachers can improve the clarity of incomplete statements by first creating a question and then converting it into an incomplete statement. Short-answer/completion items are appropriate for assessing factual knowledge and mathematical computations (Waugh & Gronlund, 2013).

These items are easy for teachers to create using the following guidelines (Reynolds & Livingston, 2012; Waugh & Gronlund, 2013):

- State the item so that only a single, brief answer is possible.

- Try to use direct questions, rather than incomplete statements, whenever possible.

- Use only one blank, which should relate to the main point of the statement.

- Whenever possible, place blanks at the end of the statement, which prevents rereading the statement and causes less confusion.

- Avoid extraneous clues to the answer. For example, the length of blanks should all be uniform so that the length of a blank does not give a clue to the word or response that fits. Also, using the indefinite article "a" or "an" before a blank might be a clue to the answer or allow students to eliminate some possible incorrect answers.

- For numerical answers, indicate the degree of precision and units expected in the response (inches or feet, seconds or minutes).

Short-answer/completion items are easy to create and score objectively, especially when the expected response is a one-word answer. Guessing is also less likely than with selected-response items. However, teachers should be prepared for unexpected responses and have a plan for scoring these. For example, "Which country in Africa is the largest?" might lead to different answers, such as Algeria (if responding by area) or Nigeria (if responding based on population). A scoring key is helpful for deciding whether students receive full or partial credit and can increase the reliability of the assessment by ensuring consistency in grading.

ESSAYS

Teachers have two choices for essay tasks, restricted-response essays and extended-response essays. Restricted-response essays are restricted in content and length of response. They provide a narrowly defined problem that can be addressed with a brief response containing certain concepts or information that teachers are looking for as a "correct answer," and they are often limited by word count or page length. In contrast, extended-response essays allow students the freedom to construct an open-ended response to a complex question or problem. Many appropriate answers to the essay question are possible, and students are not limited to a brief word count or page limit. However, there may be a maximum page count or a time limit if the essay is administered in class. Extended-response essays allow students to demonstrate higher level thinking skills, whereas restricted-response items are limited to lower level skills, such as factual knowledge, comprehension, and application (Waugh & Gronlund, 2013).

TABLE 24.2 Question Starters for Essay Questions Assessing Higher Level Learning Outcomes

OUTCOME	SAMPLE TERMS
Comparing	compare, classify, distinguish between, explain, outline
Interpreting	convert, draw, estimate, illustrate, interpret, restate, translate
Inferring	derive, draw, estimate, extend, extrapolate, predict, propose, relate
Applying	arrange, compute, demonstrate, illustrate, rearrange, relate, apply
Analyzing	break down, diagram, differentiate, divide, list, outline, separate
Creating	compose, design, devise, draw, formulate, make up, present, propose
Synthesizing	arrange, combine, construct, design, rearrange, regroup, relate
Generalizing	construct, develop, explain, formulate, generate, make, propose
Evaluating	appraise, criticize, defend, describe, evaluate, explain, judge

SOURCE: Adapted from Waugh & Gronlund, 2013 (Table 8.2, p. 136).

Creating well-written, unambiguous essay questions that will elicit the desired response teachers expect is more difficult than one might think (Gronlund, 2003). To improve the quality of essay questions, experts recommend the following principles (Reynolds & Livingston, 2012; Waugh & Gronlund, 2013):

- Each question should be created to assess a particular learning objective.

- The question should present a clear task to be performed. That is, what do you want students to do? For extended-response items, avoid starting the question with *who, what, where, when, name,* or *list* because these elicit knowledge-level responses. Table 24.2 (on p. 524) provides examples of question starters for assessing higher level learning outcomes with essays.

- Try not to make the question too rigid because this removes students' freedom to retrieve their knowledge, organize it, and present it in a manner that makes sense to them. Rather, inform students of the responses you are expecting by providing explicit criteria that will be used to evaluate the answer. For example, you might state, "In your response, be sure to address the following issues . . . ." This provides students with guidance regarding how essays will be evaluated while allowing them freedom to organize the response according to their individual preferences.

- Write a model answer. This helps instructors check on whether the phrasing of the essay is clear and also provides an idea of the time needed to complete the essay. This suggestion works better for restricted-response essays than extended-response essays, because in the extended-response format, there will be a variety of appropriate answers. In this case, a rubric will be helpful, as we discuss next.

- Avoid giving students a choice in the essays they are to complete. Essay questions are restricted in terms of the content they sample (one question may relate to only one learning objective), and choices will further limit the sampling of content, which may reduce the validity of the assessment. Also, because students will select the essays they are most prepared for, their performance may overestimate their mastery of content compared to completing all of the questions. Therefore, to accurately compare achievement among students, it is best to require all students to answer the same questions. However, teachers can allow choice if they are assessing writing ability or creativity.

- When deciding how many essays to include in a test, be sure to allow enough time for thinking and writing. If too many essays are given in a single test administration, the resulting score will reflect writing speed as well as achievement, which will reduce the validity of the assessment. Teachers also sometimes give students multiple class periods spanning several days to complete essays, which could lead to contamination of the test score (additional studying or preparing in between days) and wasted class time. Instead, use more restricted-response essays in place of fewer extended-response essays, and write model responses to estimate the time students will need.

Because restricted-response and extended-response essays are subjective, it is important to follow recommended guidelines for scoring to ensure reliability and validity of the assessment. Be sure scoring of essays is based on the learning outcomes and is not affected by extraneous factors, such as creativity, writing ability, handwriting, or neatness (Brookhart & Nitko, 2014). Because the possible set of answers for restricted-response essays is constrained, teachers can create a model essay and assign points to components of the essay. This will improve the reliability of the assessment, making the teacher's ratings more consistent across essays. Because extended-response essays have many possible responses, it is not possible to create a model answer and score it point by point with a scoring key. Instead, teachers can develop a rating scale or rubric for judging the quality of extended

Rubrics: See Module 23

essays (Brookhart & Nitko, 2014; Reynolds & Livingston, 2012). Rating scales provide a numerical score for varying levels of performance (good, average, fair, poor) on one or more dimensions of an essay, such as quality of the argument, supporting evidence, organization, grammar, and spelling. **Rubrics,** like the one shown in Table 24.3, provide the most detailed method of scoring essays because they list multiple dimensions or aspects of performance, along with a descriptive rating for each dimension.

When grading essay exams, it is important to ensure consistency and objectivity in scoring. To prevent any scorer bias, score essays anonymously by having students put their names at the end of the exam or essay (Brookhart & Nitko, 2014). When teachers know students' identity, scoring may yield a **halo effect,** in which a teacher's overall impression of a student subtly influences the rating on the essay. For example, teachers who believe certain students are "good students" may grade their essays more favorably than those of other students. Also, score all answers to one essay question before proceeding to the next question. This prevents a **carry-over effect** in which a teacher's evaluation of a student's response to Question 1 affects the evaluation of the student's response to Question 2, either positively (scoring Question 2 more favorably based on Question 1) or negatively (scoring Question 2 more harshly based on the previous

Rating scales and rubrics: See Module 23

Halo effect: See Module 23

TABLE 24.3	Sample Essay Rubric. Rubrics such as these can improve the reliability of essay tests.

DIMENSION	4	3	2	1	SCORE
Position Statement	There is a clear, convincing statement of the writer's position on the topic.	There is a clear statement of the writer's position on the topic.	There is a position statement, but the position is not clear.	There is no position statement.	
Introduction	There is an attention-grabbing introductory paragraph that clearly states the position.	The attention-grabbing introductory paragraph is weak.	The introductory paragraph is interesting but the topic is not clear.	The introductory paragraph is not interesting and is not relevant to the topic.	
Support for Position	Provides 3 or more pieces of relevant evidence, and provides at least 1 counter-argument.	Provides 3 or more pieces of relevant evidence, but no counter-arguments are given.	Provides 2 pieces of evidence that adequately support the position.	Provides 1 or fewer pieces of evidence.	
Organization	Ideas are clearly connected in a logical order using a variety of thoughtful transitions.	Ideas are orderly and connected, but there is little variety in transitions.	Ideas are orderly but some are not well connected and there are few transitions.	Ideas are not presented in a logical order and transitions are unclear or nonexistent.	
Conclusion	The closing paragraph effectively restates the position.	There is a recognizable conclusion that attempts to restate the position.	There is a closing paragraph with a vague restatement of the position.	There is no conclusion; the paper just ends.	
Grammar and Spelling	The essay contains no major errors.	The essay contains a few errors.	The essay contains many serious errors.	The essay contains errors throughout.	

Intrarater reliability and interrater reliability: See Module 23

question; Brookhart & Nitko, 2014; Waugh & Gronlund, 2013). Because raters tend to change the way in which they apply scoring criteria over time, it is also important to periodically return to previously scored essays to ensure that regrading them would result in the same score. This increases **intrarater reliability,** or consistency within the same rater over time (Brookhart & Nitko, 2014). Whenever possible, have a colleague score a subsample of essays using the rating scale or rubric to ensure **interrater reliability,** or consistency between raters. Preventing biases, such as the halo effect and carry-over effect, and ensuring reliability of scoring, will improve the validity of the essay test.

 Think about the grade level you intend to teach. If you were designing a test for a particular lesson or topic, what test item formats would you choose? Why?

APPLICATIONS: IMPROVING YOUR TEST

 Explain how item and distractor analyses can be used to improve the validity of a classroom test.

Tests are measurement tools much like scales, rulers, and thermometers, and all measurement tools contain some degree of error in measurement. Once tests are created, teachers can take additional steps to improve their tests for the next time, which will reduce measurement errors and improve the test's reliability and validity.

Test Administration Considerations

Validity evidence for standardized tests: See Module 25

In classrooms, it is often not possible to collect evidence regarding the validity of assessments the way researchers and test developers do for standardized tests. What can teachers do, once they have developed their tests, to ensure that the tests lead to valid interpretations?

Double-check and proofread. Use the guidelines for constructing items in this module as a checklist. When you have created items, turn the guidelines into questions and ask yourself, for example, "are all of my distractors plausible?" (Rodriguez & Haladyna, 2013). Double-checking that you have followed these guidelines, and proofreading for ambiguous instructions, spelling, and grammar will improve the validity of your test.

Adjust the length of the test. To ensure a valid interpretation of students' performance, be sure that the length of the test matches the time allotted for the assessment. There should be sufficient time for brainstorming on essay items and checking answers on selected-response items (Fives & DiDonato-Barnes, 2013). Teachers can use the estimates in Table 24.4 to help them determine the optimal amount of time needed for their tests.

Make essay scoring as objective as possible. Use model answers and scoring keys for restricted-response essays and rubrics for extended-response essays to reduce biases and improve the reliability of scoring (Waugh & Gronlund, 2013). This will help make the test scores more valid.

Ask for student opinions about the test. Have students reflect on their thought processes on particular items that were problematic (Rodriguez & Haladyna, 2013). For example, sometimes students in my classes might say, "I thought the answer was B because when I read it, I thought it meant . . . ." This gives me important insights into how students interpreted the item and helps me improve it for the next time. Experts support this practice as an effective way to gain insights into student thinking, which will contribute to improved teaching and improved test construction (Waugh & Gronlund, 2013).

TABLE 24.4   Optimal Time Needed to Complete Test Items

TYPE OF ITEM	APPROXIMATE TIME PER TASK (ITEM)
True–false items	20–30 seconds
Multiple choice (factual)	40–60 seconds
One-word completion	40–60 seconds
Multiple choice (complex)	70–90 seconds
Matching (five premises/six responses)	2–4 minutes
Short answer	2–4 minutes
Multiple choice (with calculations)	2–5 minutes
Word problems (simple arithmetic)	5–10 minutes
Restricted-response essays	15–20 minutes
Extended-response essays	35–50 minutes

SOURCE: Brookhart & Nitko, 2014.

Item and Distractor Analyses

Once the test is completed and graded, don't forget about it until the next time. Before you move on, evaluate how "good" your items are. To determine this, teachers can use item analyses and distractor analyses. *Item analysis* is a term used to refer to two statistics for evaluating how well items are functioning—item difficulty and item discrimination. **Item difficulty** is a calculation that gives us the proportion of students *correctly* answering an item. **Item discrimination** is a statistic that indicates how well the item differentiates students who know the content of the item and those who do not. **Distractor analysis** looks at how many students selected each alternative in a multiple-choice item. These statistics, together, provide information about how "good" each item is, which can then be used to improve the items for next time and ultimately improve the reliability and validity of the test.

ITEM DIFFICULTY

The item difficulty index is a simple calculation to obtain the proportion of test takers who correctly answered the item. Let's say we have 30 students in class, and 21 students correctly answered a multiple-choice item. Our item difficulty index, denoted as p for proportion, is .70 (or 21 out of 30). Is this a good item difficulty? First, it is important to know that an item difficulty index ranges from 0 (no student correctly answered the item) to 1.00 (all students answered correctly). Item difficulty indexes that are close to zero indicate that the item is too difficult, and indexes close to 1.00 indicate that the item is too easy. In general, the optimal item difficulty should be .50 to ensure a test that reliably differentiates students (Reynolds & Livingston, 2012). However, this does not mean that all items need to have a difficulty level of .50. A test should have items with a range of difficulty, and experts recommend that item difficulty indexes between .30 and .70 are adequate (Gregory, 2013). Item difficulty indexes also need to be adjusted to take into account that students will sometimes be using guessing to get the item correct. Testing experts use a simple calculation to determine the optimal difficulty adjusted for guessing by determining the halfway point between chance performance and 100%. For example,

TABLE 24.5	Optimal Item Difficulty Indexes Adjusted for Guessing
ITEM TYPE	**OPTIMAL ITEM DIFFICULTY**
True–False	.75
Multiple choice: three alternatives	.67
Multiple choice: four alternatives	.625
Multiple choice: five alternatives	.60
Essay test	.50

SOURCE: Wright, 2008.

on a four-alternative multiple-choice item, the chance of guessing correctly is 25%, so halfway between 25% and 100% is 62.5%, or .625 written as a proportion. Table 24.5 contains optimal item difficulty indexes adjusted for guessing for various types of tests. Teachers can use this table to evaluate the item difficulty indexes for items in their tests, keeping in mind that a range from .30 to .70 is acceptable.

Clearly in Table 24.5 the optimal item difficulty for essay tests does not include an adjustment for guessing because there is no guessing on essays. Also, the item difficulty index for essays is calculated somewhat differently from selected-response items. Find the average score for the class on a particular essay question and divide this by the maximum possible score for the question. For example, say an essay question is worth 25 points on an exam. If the average score is 19.5, the item difficulty index would be 19.5/25, or .78.

ITEM DISCRIMINATION

The item discrimination index, denoted as D, ranges from -1 to $+1$ with positive values of D, indicating greater discrimination among students who know the item content and those who do not. In general, item discrimination indexes greater than .30 are acceptable. A reliable test will have items with high positive item discrimination indexes. Positive item discrimination indicates that students who did well on the test tended to answer the item correctly and students who did poorly on the test tended to answer incorrectly. Any items with a low item discrimination index do not discriminate among students very well, with zero indicating no discrimination at all. Also, a negative item discrimination index indicates that the item discriminates among students but *not* in the expected direction. Instead, students who did poorly on the test tended to correctly answer the question and students who scored well on the test answered incorrectly. This is an item that needs to be significantly revised or replaced.

There are two methods of obtaining item discrimination indexes. One is a correlation between the item and the total score on the test (called item-total correlations), which may not be practical for teachers to do. The other method is a shortcut that teachers can calculate relatively quickly. The shortcut method involves comparing the *item difficulty indexes* of the students who performed in the top third of the class on the test (highest third of the total test scores) and the students who performed in the bottom third of the class on the test (lowest third of the total test scores), setting aside the middle scorers (Waugh & Gronlund, 2013). For example, let's say the item difficulty is .80 for students in the high group and .40 for students in the low group. The item discrimination is .40 (.80 − .40 = .40).

A similar approach can be used for essay items when all students respond to the same question (Brookhart & Nitko, 2014; Wright, 2008). This involves finding the average score on an essay question for students in the high group and the low group and subtracting the

TABLE 24.6 — Sample Item Analysis Chart Showing Distractor Analysis

	ITEM ANALYSES		PROPORTION OF STUDENTS CHOOSING EACH ALTERNATIVE		
ITEM	ITEM DIFFICULTY	ITEM DISCRIMINATION	ALTERNATIVE	HIGH GROUP (TOP THIRD)	LOW GROUP (BOTTOM THIRD)
1	.61	.52			
			A	0.07	0.55
			B*	0.87	0.35
			C	0.06	0.10
			D	0.00	0.00
2	.58	.05			
			A	0.12	0.10
			B	0.22	0.31
			C*	0.60	0.55
			D	0.06	0.04

* denotes correct answer

average of the low group from the average of the high group. Then this result is divided by the range of possible scores on that essay. For example, on a 25-point essay, if the high scorers averaged 21 points out of 25 (or 84%) and the low scorers averaged 19 out of 25 (or 76%), the difference between the averages is 8 (84–76). If the essay scores ranged from 14 to 25 points (or a range of 11), the item discrimination is .72 (8 divided by 11). This essay question discriminates students who know the content and those who do not.

DISTRACTOR ANALYSES

Distractor analysis tells teachers how many students chose each alternative on a multiple-choice item (Reynolds & Livingston, 2012). It is important to examine how well distractors are functioning because well-written distractors increase item discrimination and improve the reliability and validity of the test (Rodriguez & Haladyna, 2013). If multiple-choice items are written with common student misconceptions as distractors, then distractor analysis also can be diagnostic by identifying concepts that may need to be retaught (Rodriguez & Haladyna, 2013). The general rule of thumb is that at least one student who performed poorly on the test should choose the distractor, and more lower performing students than higher performing students should choose it (Brookhart & Nitko, 2014; Reynolds & Livingston, 2012).

Let's examine item analysis statistics shown in Table 24.6 for two multiple-choice items to examine the pattern of responding on distractors:

- First, both items have acceptable item difficulty indexes. The item difficulty indexes of .61 and .58 for Items 1 and 2, respectively, indicate that these items are moderately difficult and close to the optimal item difficulty of .625 for a four-choice multiple-choice item.

- Also, note that the item discrimination index for Item 1 (.52) is acceptable, indicating that it discriminates the higher performers on the test from the lower performers. Notice that for the correct answer, B, 87% of higher performers chose this option, and only 35% of lower performers chose it. Remember that more lower performers should choose the distractors (A, C, D) than higher performers. This is the case for options A and C. No student selected option D, which means that everyone eliminated it and it is not effective. Remember the giveaway alternative, *Mickey Mouse*, in the multiple-choice item on the founder of attachment theory on page 519 ? This would be a distractor with no students choosing it, as in option D here.

- The item discrimination index for Item 2 (.05) indicates that this item does not differentiate students who know the material and students who do not. Approximately equal proportions of high-performing students and low-performing students chose the correct answer, C (60% and 55%, respectively). Also, approximately equal proportions of students in the high group and low group chose distractors A and D. There should be more lower performing students choosing each distractor. All of the alternatives in this item need significant revision.

When interpreting item and distractor analyses, it is important to remember that these statistics are very accurate with large samples (such as 100 or more test takers), but they may be unstable with smaller samples (Rodriguez & Haladyna, 2013). This means that if the test were administered again, the analyses might yield slightly different statistics. Therefore, interpret the statistics with caution in small classes. High school teachers who teach several sections of the same class may be able to pool their sections for a larger sample. Even in small classes, item analyses should still be conducted. However, make decisions based on these small-class data cautiously. Do not eliminate an item from a test just because of poor item statistics based on one class. Instead, use the data to improve the item, and if you think the item is questionable, give all students credit for it. Then collect additional data on the item (perhaps try it again the next year) and examine all of the data over time to determine whether to revise or replace the item. Remember that the item could be poorly constructed, or it may be that students did not grasp the concept. Item statistics are a tool, but teachers still need to use their best judgement when evaluating and revising their test items.

Have you ever been marked wrong on a multiple-choice item that was poorly worded or confusing, or have you ever been graded harshly on an essay test with an ambiguous question? Explain how item analyses could have helped the teacher produce better items.

SUMMARY

❶ Explain why validity, reliability, fairness, and practicality are important for classroom tests. Validity, reliability, fairness, and practicality are characteristics of "good" tests and therefore are just as important for classroom tests as they are for standardized tests. For classroom tests, validity refers to a test score accurately reflecting the subject matter, meaning that accurate interpretations of students' mastery can be made. For classroom tests to be valid, they must also be reliable or have consistency in measurement. Fairness, or the extent to which all students have an equal opportunity to learn the required content and demonstrate their knowledge, affects the validity of classroom tests. Finally, practicality issues, such as the time it takes to create, administer, and score assessments, should be considered when deciding on the type of assessment that is most appropriate for learning objectives.

❷ Explain why a test blueprint is important for test planning and construction. A test blueprint helps teachers plan for the content that the test will cover and the ways in which students will demonstrate mastery of the content. Test blueprints are often represented as a table of specifications, a matrix specifying the number and type of items to include on a test based on the number of learning objectives and the class time spent on each of the objectives. Test blueprints ensure that objectives, instruction, and assessment are aligned, which improves the validity of the assessment.

❸ **Compare and contrast the usefulness and scoring considerations of selected-response and constructed-response item formats.** Selected-response items, such as multiple choice, alternative response, and matching, share advantages, such as requiring very little reading, being useful in assessing many learning objectives within a short testing time, and providing easy, reliable, and objective scoring. Disadvantages of these item types include the fact that they are often poorly constructed, and they tend to focus on lower level learning objectives. Constructed-response items, such as short answer, restricted-response essays, and extended-response essays, require students to write responses and cover fewer learning objectives.

Because responses are subjective, teachers need to use rating scales or rubrics to improve the reliability of scoring and make their evaluations as objective as possible.

❹ **Explain how item and distractor analyses can be used to improve the validity of a classroom test.** Item analyses consist of two statistical analyses, item difficulty and item discrimination. Item difficulty refers to the proportion of test takers who answer an item correctly. Item discrimination refers to how well an item can differentiate students who know the content and students who do not. Distractor analyses are used to examine how many students chose each of the distractors in a multiple-choice item. Each of these statistics can provide information about how well an item is functioning. Items with moderate item difficulty (not too challenging and not too easy) and items with good discrimination will result in a more valid test. Distractors that no students choose result in items that do not discriminate well and therefore will reduce the validity of the test. Teachers should examine these statistics and use the data to revise test items to improve the validity of their assessment.

KEY CONCEPTS

alternative-response item, 520

alternatives, 517

carry-over effect, 525

completion items, 522

constructed-response, 517

content validity, 513

distractor analysis, 527

distractors, 517

extended-response essay, 523

fairness, 514

halo effect, 525

interrater reliability, 526

intrarater reliability, 526

item difficulty, 527

item discrimination, 527

matching exercise, 521

multiple-choice item, 517

objective tests, 517

practicality, 515

reliability, 514

restricted-response essay, 523

rubrics, 525

selected-response, 516

short-answer items, 522

specific determiners, 520

stem, 517

subjective tests, 522

table of specifications, 515

validity, 513

CASE STUDIES: REFLECT AND EVALUATE

EARLY CHILDHOOD: Kindergarten Readiness

These questions refer to the case study on page 482.

1. Maria's mother is concerned about the testing. Explain the issue of test fairness in this situation.

2. Define what it means to be "ready" for kindergarten. Is the BRIGANCE K & 1 Screen-II a valid indicator of kindergarten readiness?

3. Are Ms. Theesfield's observations a formative assessment or summative assessment?

4. Evaluate the practicality of a kindergarten screening measure like the BRIGANCE. Would the teachers be able to obtain the same information with a paper-and-pencil assessment?

5. What test item formats, if any, would be appropriate for kindergarten students?

ELEMENTARY SCHOOL: TEACHER IN-SERVICE TRAINING

These questions refer to the case study on page 484.

1. Evaluate the validity of Ms. Fernández's true–false test as a measure of reading ability.

2. What advice would you give to Ms. Seifert about ensuring that the multiple-choice items she is selecting from a test bank are good items?

3. Are Mr. Johnston's matching exercises on vocabulary words and true–false questions on reading passages a valid assessment of reading? Why or why not?

4. Assume Mr. Whitney's book report is an example of an extended-response essay. Contrast this format with Mr. Johnston's assessment approach using concepts of validity, reliability, fairness, and practicality.

5. Explain to the teachers how item analyses can be used to improve their tests.

MIDDLE SCHOOL: HOMEWORK NIGHT

These questions refer to the case study on page 486.

1. Explain to Payton's math teacher, Ms. Bowden, how a table of specifications can improve the validity of her math tests.

2. Evaluate the validity and fairness of Payton's social studies homework assignment.

3. Assume you are giving advice to Payton's social studies teacher about constructing a unit test. What type of test items would you recommend? What are the advantages and disadvantages of these items?

4. Assume Payton's social studies teacher wants to change the online homework assignments to 20-minute online quizzes. What item format(s) would you recommend? Why? How many items would you need?

5. Payton's social studies teacher ran an item analysis report on a new online quiz. The results are shown here for the first few items. Based on the results, give the teacher advice about which items are good and which are poor.

ITEM	ITEM DIFFICULTY	ITEM DISCRIMINATION
1	.77	.43
2	.82	.22
3	.89	−.12

HIGH SCHOOL: MATH TESTS

These questions refer to the case study on page 488.

1. Explain how taking multiple-choice math tests beforehand might benefit students when they take the SAT.

2. How can a table of specifications help Ms. Fortner improve the assessment of her students' math skills?

3. Explain to Ms. Fortner why she needs to conduct item analyses on her multiple-choice math tests.

4. Ms. Fortner wants to give students a pop quiz in math. What item format(s) would you recommend and approximately how many items should she use?

5. Ms. Fortner wants students to demonstrate their thought processes on math problems, so she creates a "Creative Word Problem Assignment" in which students create a word problem and explain its solution in a brief essay. Give her specific recommendations for grading the essays that will help improve the reliability and validity of scoring.

6. The item difficulty on the "Creative Word Problem" essays was .37. What should Ms. Fortner do based on this data?

APPLY AND PRACTICE WHAT YOU'VE LEARNED

▶ edge.sagepub.com/durwin3e

CHECK YOUR COMPREHENSION ON THE STUDENT STUDY SITE

- **eFlashcards** to strengthen your understanding of key terms

- Practice **quizzes** to test your knowledge of key concepts

- **Videos and multimedia content** to enhance your exploration of key topics

©iStockphoto.com/ kali9

STANDARDIZED TESTS AND SCORES

OUTLINE	LEARNING GOALS

Types of Standardized Tests

- Categories of Standardized Tests
- Criterion-Referenced and Norm-Referenced Tests

1 Describe the purpose of four broad categories of standardized tests and how standardized tests are used by teachers.

2 Explain the difference between criterion-referenced and norm-referenced tests.

Understanding Test Scores

- Central Tendency and Variability
- Normal Distribution
- Types of Tests Scores

3 Explain the basic properties of a normal distribution.

4 Describe four types of test scores, and explain the advantages and limitations of each.

Characteristics of Good Tests

- Validity
- Reliability

5 Explain why validity and reliability are two important qualities of tests and why teachers need this information about tests to interpret test scores.

Applications: Accommodating Students at Risk

6 Explain how accommodations improve the validity of test scores for students at risk.

TYPES OF STANDARDIZED TESTS

1 Describe the purpose of four broad categories of standardized tests and how standardized tests are used by teachers.

2 Explain the difference between criterion-referenced and norm-referenced tests.

How many standardized tests have you taken in your life? Can you remember why you took them? Perhaps you took the SAT or ACT to apply for college, or the Praxis I exam to be admitted to your undergraduate education program. Before we consider why educators at all levels use standardized tests, we first need to define exactly what makes a test standardized. **Standardized tests** are distinguished by two qualities (Gregory, 2013):

1. They are created by testing experts at test publishing companies.

2. All students are given the test by a trained examiner under the same (hence "standardized") conditions. For example, all students are given the same directions, test items, time limits, and scoring procedures.

You're probably very familiar with tests that are *not* standardized, such as the classroom tests you have taken since elementary school. Classroom tests, often created by individual teachers, measure specific learning that occurs within a classroom and typically focus on the district's curriculum. Teachers may use classroom tests as a formative or a summative assessment of students' knowledge. *Assessment* includes any and all procedures used to collect information and make inferences or judgments about an individual or a program (Brookhart & Nitko, 2014). *Formative assessments,* such as homework assignments and quizzes, enable teachers to plan for instruction and monitor student progress throughout a grading period. To assess student achievement at the end of an instructional unit or grading period, teachers use *summative assessments,* such as tests and cumulative projects.

Like some classroom tests, standardized tests typically are used for summative assessments, but they focus on broader areas of learning, such as overall mathematical achievement rather than mathematical progress within a grading period. For a summary of the differences between classroom and standardized tests, see Table 25.1.

What standardized tests do you remember taking in elementary through high school? What purpose do you think they served? Think about these tests as you read about the categories of standardized tests.

Master the content.

edge.sagepub.com/durwin3e

$SAGE edge

Classroom assessments: See Module 23

Classroom tests: See Module 24

TABLE 25.1	Comparison of Classroom Tests and Standardized Tests	
	CLASSROOM TEST	**STANDARDIZED TEST**
Purpose	Formative and summative	Typically summative
Content	Specific to a content covered in the classroom over a specific time frame	Specific or general topics across many districts or states
Source of items	Created or written by the classroom teacher	Created by a panel of professional experts
Administration procedures	Can be flexible for students with disabilities and special needs	Standardized across all settings and individuals
Length	Usually short—less than an hour	Usually very long—several hours
Scoring procedures	Typically teacher scored	Typically machine scored
Reliability	Typically low	Typically high
Scores	Individual's number or percentage correct (raw score)	Compared to predetermined criteria or norm group (converted from raw score)
Grading	Used to assign a course grade	Used to determine general ability or achievement; not used to assign course grade

SOURCE: Haladyna, 2002.

Categories of Standardized Tests

Standardized tests have several purposes. Some standardized tests—called single-subject survey tests—contain several subtests that assess one *domain-specific* content area, such as mathematics. Other standardized tests contain a battery of several tests used in conjunction with one another to provide a broader, more *general* picture of performance that may include competencies such as vocabulary, spelling, reading comprehension, mathematics computation, and mathematics problem solving. Standardized tests fall into one of four broad categories based on their purpose (Chatterji, 2003), as described here (see Table 25.2).

1. **Standardized achievement tests** assess *current knowledge,* which can include learning outcomes and skills either in general or in a specific domain. Standardized achievement tests do not necessarily match the curriculum of any particular state or school district. Instead, they are used to identify the strengths and weaknesses of individual students as well as school districts. *Readiness tests,* like achievement tests, measure young children's current level of skill in various academic (reading, math, vocabulary) and nonacademic (motor skills, social skills) domains and are used to make placement and curricular decisions in the early elementary grades. Recently, college and career readiness has emerged as a major concern of educators, which has led many states to adopt a set of Common Core State Standards (CCSS) that outline

Common Core State Standards: See Modules 1 and 23

TABLE 25.2	Standardized Tests in Four Broad Areas	
	NAME	**TYPE/PURPOSE**
Standardized achievement tests	Iowa Test of Basic Skills (ITBS)	Battery of achievement tests for Grades K–8
	Tests of Achievement and Proficiency (TAP)	Battery of achievement tests for Grades 9–12
	Metropolitan Achievement Test (MAT)	Battery of achievement tests for Grades K–12
	Smarter Balanced Assessment Consortium (SBAC)	Computer-adaptive test (difficulty level of items is adjusted to match students' ability) to assess achievement in Grades 3–8
Standardized aptitude tests	Differential Aptitude Test (DAT)	Battery of tests to predict educational goals for students in Grades 7–12
	Scholastic Assessment Test (SAT) American College Testing (ACT)	Single test to predict academic performance in college
	General Aptitude Test Battery (GATB)	Battery of aptitude tests used to predict job performance
	Armed Services Vocational Aptitude Battery (ASVAB)	Battery of aptitude tests used to assign armed service personnel to jobs and training programs
Career or educational interest inventories	Strong Interest Inventory (SII)	Instrument used with high school and college students to identify occupational preferences
	Kuder General Interest Survey (KGIS)	Instrument used with students in Grades 6–12 to determine preferences in broad areas of interest
Personality tests	NEO Five-Factor Inventory (NEO-FFI)	Instrument to assess an individual on five theoretically derived dimensions of personality
	Minnesota Multiphasic Personality Inventory-2 (MMPI-2)	Instrument used to aid in clinical diagnosis

SOURCE: Chatterji, 2003.

what students are expected to know and be able to do at each grade level. To assess students' achievement on the standards, many states have chosen to use one of two computer-administered tests specifically aligned to the CCSS: the Partnership for Assessment of Readiness and College Careers (PARCC) and the Smarter Balanced Assessment Consortium (SBAC).

2. **Standardized aptitude tests** assess *future potential*—or capacity to learn—in general or in a specific domain. Aptitude tests are used for admission or selection purposes to place students in particular schools (e.g., private schools or colleges) or specific classrooms or courses (e.g., advanced mathematics). Standardized intelligence tests are considered aptitude tests because their purpose is to predict achievement in school.

3. Career or educational interest inventories assess individual *preferences* for certain types of activities. These inventories typically are used to assist high school and college students in planning their postsecondary education, as well as to assist companies and corporations in selecting employees. Some of these tests are also considered aptitude tests because they may predict future success.

4. Personality tests assess an *individual's characteristics,* such as interests, attitudes, values, and patterns of behavior. Personality tests are limited in their educational use because psychologists and counselors with graduate-level training primarily use them for diagnosis of clinical disorders and because most personality tests are appropriate only for individuals age 18 or older.

Most standardized tests administered by teachers are given in a group format. *Group-administered tests* are relatively easy to administer and score, making them cost-effective. *Individually administered tests,* such as personality tests and IQ tests, require expert training, time to administer, and time to score and interpret, all of which lead to greater cost. Although teachers typically are not trained to administer these individual tests, they will encounter the test scores of individually administered tests in meetings to determine the eligibility of students for special education and related services.

Criterion-Referenced and Norm-Referenced Tests

The interpretation of test scores includes understanding not only what the test measures—general versus specific knowledge or current knowledge versus future potential—but also how test scores should be evaluated. A test score is a **measurement** that assigns a quantitative or descriptive number during the process of assessment. But a test score in itself cannot be detached from how it is evaluated. **Evaluation** is the subjective judgment or interpretation of a measurement or test score. For example, a student might take a test and answer 20 of 30 questions correctly (measurement), but whether that score is interpreted as a "good" score, an "improvement" from a previous score, or "substantially below" the expected score is a matter of evaluation. Standardized tests typically are designed so that any test score can be evaluated by comparing it either to a specific standard (criterion) or to data compiled from the test scores of many similar individuals (norm).

- **Criterion-referenced tests** compare an individual's score to a preset criterion, or standard of performance, for a learning objective. Many times criterion-referenced tests are used to test mastery of specific skills or educational goals to provide information about what an individual does and does not know. On criterion-referenced tests, test developers include test items based on their relevance to specific academic skills and curricula.

Video Case 25.1 ▲

Preparing for Standardized Tests

> **DIVERSITY**

IQ tests: See Module 20

Video: Criterion- and Norm-Referenced Tests

The criteria are chosen because, together, they represent a level of expert knowledge. Lawyers, doctors, nurses, and teachers must take standardized tests and meet a specified criterion to become licensed or certified for their profession.

- **Norm-referenced tests** compare the individual test taker's performance to the performance of a group of similar test takers, called the norm sample. A **norm sample** is a large group of individuals who represent the population of interest on characteristics such as gender, age, race, and socioeconomic status (SES). For example, a norm sample for a standardized test can be all fifth graders nationally, all fifth graders in a state, or all fifth graders in a district. Norm samples for nationally used standardized tests, such as the achievement tests listed in Table 25.2, need to be large (about 100,000 test takers) and representative of the population of students to allow accurate interpretations. The test items on norm-referenced tests are designed to differentiate, to the greatest degree possible, between individual test takers. For example, a norm-referenced mathematics achievement test might be used to select the top elementary school students in a school district for a gifted program with limited seats or space.

The major difference between the two types of tests is the purpose or situation for which each type of test is most useful, as summarized in Table 25.3. Many standardized group-administered achievement tests provide teachers with both a criterion-referenced and a norm-referenced interpretation of scores, as shown in Figure 25.1. When dual interpretation is not available, the type of test that is used will depend on the purpose. Criterion-referenced tests provide information about mastery of material but do not allow comparisons among test takers. In contrast, norm-referenced tests do not provide information about the mastery or the strengths and weaknesses of a particular individual, but they do provide ample information for comparing test scores across individuals using several basic concepts of measurement, as discussed next.

UNDERSTANDING TEST SCORES

Video: Do Standardized Tests Matter?

3 Explain the basic properties of a normal distribution.

4 Describe four types of test scores, and explain the advantages and limitations of each.

To interpret test scores accurately, teachers must understand some basic concepts of measurement that are used in conjunction with one another to evaluate individual students as well as to evaluate groups of students, such as classrooms or school districts.

TABLE 25.3	Comparison of Criterion-Referenced and Norm-Referenced Tests	
	CRITERION-REFERENCED	**NORM-REFERENCED**
Purpose	To determine mastery at a specified level	To compare a score to the performance of similar test takers
Content	Specific to a domain or content area	Broad domain or content area
Item selection	Similar level of difficulty	Wide variability in difficulty level
Scores	Number or percentage correct as compared to criteria	Standard score, percentile, or grade-equivalent score as compared to the norm group

SOURCE: Gregory, 2013.

FIGURE 25.1 **A Sample Standardized Test Score Report.**

Performance on Objectives

Obj. No. Objective Titles	Student	Natl OPI	Diff	Moderate Mastery Range	Objectives Performance Index (OPI)*
Reading					
02 Basic Understanding	91	79	12	48–70	
03 Analyze Text	92	84	8	52–75	
04 Evaluate/Extend Meaning	65	66	–1	50–70	
05 Identify Rdg. Strategies	70	74	–4	45–73	
Language					
07 Sentence Structure	63	68	–5	45–70	
08 Writing Strategies	59	74	–15	50–75	
09 Editing Skills	78	63	15	55–75	
Mathematics					
10 Number & Num. Relations	71	69	2	47–77	
11 Computation & Estimation	83	72	11	45–75	
13 Measurement	66	86	–20	45–60	
14 Geometry & Spatial Sense	71	72	–1	50–78	
15 Data, Stats., & Prob.	61	83	–22	52–78	
16 Patterns, Funcs, Algebra	77	88	–11	44–73	
17 Prob. Solving & Reasoning	71	74	–3	52–75	
18 Communication	69	68	1	43–73	
Science					
19 Science Inquiry	47	74	–27	50–75	
20 Physical Science	49	69	–20	52–77	
21 Life Science	46	83	–37	45–78	
22 Earth & Space Science	52	84	–32	48–73	
23 Science & Technology	48	78	–30	52–69	
24 Personal & Social Persp.	52	56	–4	50–73	
Social Studies					
26 Geographic Perspectives	79	91	–12	48–70	
27 Historical & Cultural	84	92	–8	52–75	
28 Civics & Government	66	65	1	50–70	
29 Economic Perspectives	74	70	4	45–73	

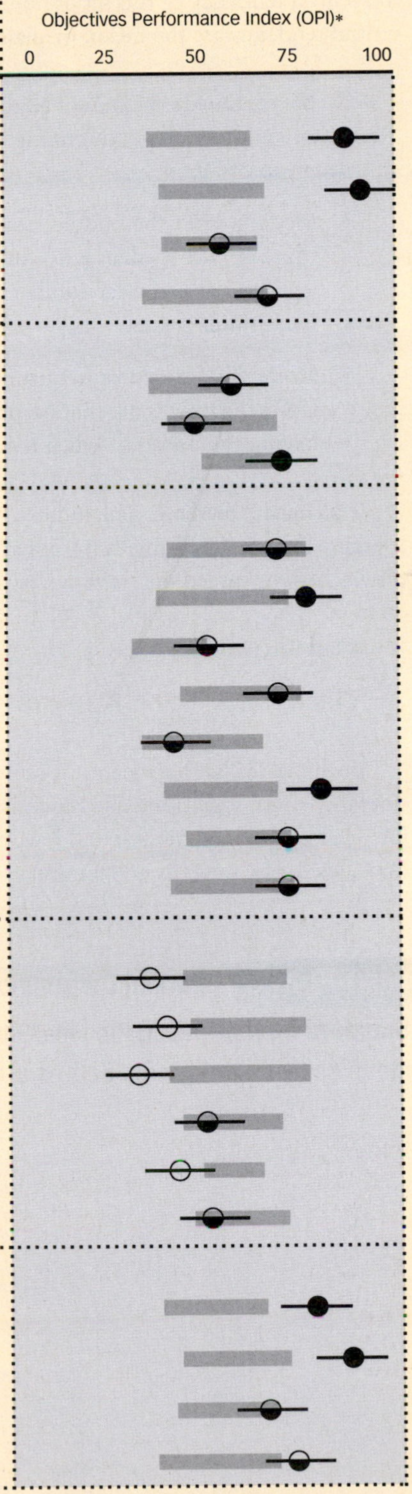

OPI scale markers: 0, 25, 50, 75, 100

SOURCE: Data Recognition Corp.

Central Tendency and Variability

One basic measure needed to form evaluations or make comparisons is **central tendency**—the score that is typical or representative of the entire group. Let's examine a set of classroom or standardized test scores. Suppose you teach a class of 11 students who receive these scores on their first exam: 63, 65, 72, 75, 76, 78, 83, 87, 87, 92, and 98. What measure will tell you the central tendency of this set of numbers? The three most common statistical descriptions of central tendency are the mean, median, and mode:

1. **Mean:** Divide the sum of all the scores by the total number of scores to find the mean, or simple average. Summing the 11 scores (sum = 876) and dividing by 11 gives a mean of 79.64.

2. **Median:** Find the middle score in a series of scores listed from smallest to largest. In this case, the median is 78, the middle value, because five scores are on either side. In a group with an even number of scores, the median is the midpoint, or average, of the two middle scores.

3. **Mode:** Find the most frequently occurring score in the group. In this group, the mode is 87, the only score that occurs more than once. A group of scores can be bimodal—having two modes—when two different scores occur frequently.

The mean, median, and mode all provide information about the typical score within a group but do not provide information about the **variability**—how widely the scores are distributed, or spread out, within a particular group. Compare these two groups of test scores:

Class 1 scores: 6, 7, 7, 8, 8

Class 2 scores: 4, 7, 7, 8, 10

Both classes have a mean test score of 7.2, but the scores in the second class show considerably more variation. The **range** is a simple measure of variability calculated as the difference between the highest and lowest scores. For Class 1, the range is 2 (8 minus 6), while for Class 2, the range is 6 (10 minus 4).

FIGURE 25.2 **Normal Distributions With Large (blue) and Small (orange) Standard Deviations.** In the small standard deviation, most scores are close to the mean score of the group. Scores are more spread out in a large standard deviation.

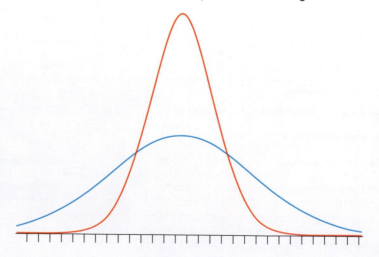

The most commonly used measure of variability among scores, **standard deviation (SD),** is the degree of variability in a group of scores. The SD is more difficult to compute than the range: It equals the square root of each score's deviation from the mean. This sounds more complex than it is. The computation is less important than understanding the SD for test score interpretation. Figure 25.2 shows the difference in variability for two groups of scores with small and large SDs.

- A *small* SD indicates that most scores are close to the mean score of the group. For a classroom test, the teacher might hope that all students would score well and close to one another, indicating that all students are mastering the course objectives.

- A *large* SD suggests that the scores are more spread out. On standardized achievement tests, a large degree of variability is not only typical but optimal, because the test items are designed to make fine discriminations in achievement among a large population of students.

In the example with Class 1 and Class 2, the SDs are .84 (Class 1) and 2.17 (Class 2). With a small set of numbers, the variability may be obvious. However, with large groups of scores, such as the thousands of scores of students taking a standardized achievement test, the SD provides a scientific measurement of the distribution of scores.

Normal Distribution

Understanding and interpreting test scores also means understanding a normal distribution of scores. We begin by explaining a frequency distribution. A **frequency distribution** is the simple list of all scores for a group. The scores can be depicted visually in a histogram, or bar graph. For example, Figure 25.3 depicts the final grades in an educational psychology course. Final grades are indicated along the horizontal axis (x-axis), and the number of students receiving each final grade is indicated along the vertical axis (y-axis). As Figure 25.3 shows, 7 students failed the course, 17 students received a grade of D, 45 students received a C, 37 students received a B, and 15 students received an A. In this figure, more scores fall to the right (higher scores) and fewer scores fall to the left (lower scores) of the midpoint, indicating that the scores are skewed.

FIGURE 25.3 **Histogram of Final Grades in an Educational Psychology Course.**

Final grades are indicated along the horizontal axis (x-axis), and the number of students receiving each final grade is indicated along the vertical axis (y-axis).

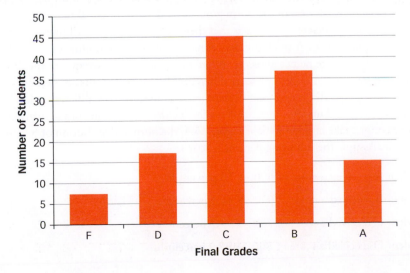

Skewness, or the symmetry or asymmetry of a frequency distribution, tells how a test is working. Negatively skewed distributions (with long tails to the left), such as in Figure 25.3, indicate that the scores are piled up at the high end. Positively skewed distributions indicate that the scores are piled up at the low end (long tail to the right). Classroom tests with negative skewness are what teachers hope to achieve (i.e., mastery by most students). In standardized testing, positively skewed distributions suggest that the test had too many difficult questions, and negatively skewed distributions suggest that the test had too many easy items.

For standardized tests, we expect a frequency distribution that is symmetrical and bell-shaped, called a **normal distribution** (see Figure 25.4). Normal distributions are apparent in scores on the SAT and on IQ tests. A normal distribution has several properties:

- The mean, median, and mode are equal and appear at the midpoint of the distribution, indicating that half the scores are above the mean and half the scores are below the mean.

- Approximately 68% of scores occur within 1 SD above and below the mean.

- Two SDs above and below the mean include approximately 95% of scores.

- Three SDs above and below the mean include approximately 99% of scores.

Types of Test Scores

Both classroom and standardized tests first yield a **raw score,** which typically is the number or percentage of correct answers. For evaluating the results of classroom tests, raw scores typically are used. For standardized criterion-referenced tests, raw scores are compared to the preset criterion for interpretation (e.g., pass/fail, mastery/nonmastery). For standardized norm-referenced tests, raw scores more commonly are converted or transformed by the test developers to help provide consistent evaluation and ease of interpretation of scores by parents and teachers. Next we consider several common norm-referenced test scores.

PERCENTILE SCORES

Percentile scores (or ranks) are derived by listing all raw scores from highest to lowest and providing information on the percentage of test takers in the norm sample who scored below or equal to that raw score. For example, a percentile score of 80 means that the test taker scored as well as or better than 80% of all test takers in the norm sample. Be careful not to confuse the percentage of correct answers on a test with the percentile score, which compares individual scores among the norm sample. For example, an individual could correctly answer 65 out of 100 questions (65%) on a test, but the percentile ranking of that score would depend on the performance of other test takers. If a raw score of 65 is the mean in a normal distribution of scores (the middle value in the bell curve), then the raw score of 65 would have a percentile score of 50, meaning that 50% of the norm group scored below or equal to 65.

One problem with percentile scores is that they are not equally distributed across the normal curve (Gregory, 2013). A small difference in raw scores in the middle of a distribution of scores can result in a large percentile score difference, while at the extremes of the distribution (the upper and lower tails) larger raw score differences between students are needed to increase the percentile ranking. This means that percentile scores overestimate differences in the middle of the normal curve and underestimate differences at either end of the normal distribution.

As an example, take another look at Figure 25.4, the normal distribution of SAT scores for each subscale. Assume the following percentile scores:

Student A received a score of 500 → 50 percentile

Student B received a score of 600 → 84.1 percentile

Student C received a score of 700 → 97.7 percentile

Student D received a score of 800 → 99.9 percentile

FIGURE 25.4
Normal Distribution Curves. For standardized tests, a symmetrical, bell-shaped frequency distribution is considered normal. Normal distributions are found on the SAT and most IQ tests.

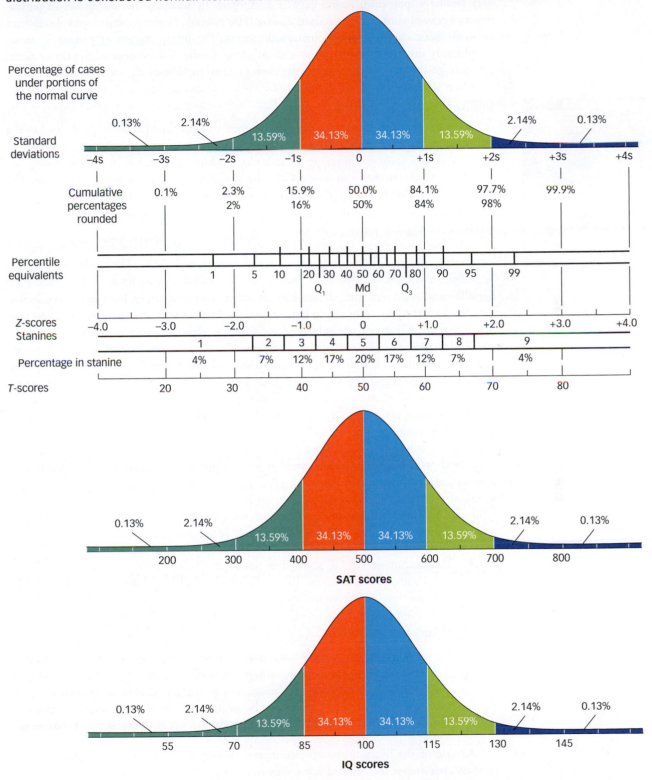

SAT scores

IQ scores

Based on percentile scores, student B appears to have markedly outperformed student A (percentile score of 84.1 compared to 50), and students C and D appear to have performed very similarly (percentile scores of 97.7 and 99.9). In actuality, the difference in performance between students is exactly the same (100 points). Hence, comparisons should not be made between two students' percentile scores. The interpretation of percentile scores should only involve comparing one student's score to the performance of the entire norm group (e.g., student A performed better than or equal to 50% of all test takers).

GRADE EQUIVALENT SCORES

Grade-equivalent (GE) scores are based on the median score for a particular grade level of the norm group. For example, if the median score for all sixth graders in the second month of the school year in a norm group taking a standardized achievement test is 100, then all students scoring 100 are considered to have a GE score of 6.2, or second month of sixth grade. The 6 denotes grade level, and the decimal represents the month in the school year. Suppose the median score for all sixth graders in the seventh month of the school year is 120. Then a student earning a score of 120 would have a GE score of 6.7.

GE scores often are misused because individuals assume they are mathematical statistics for interpreting students' performance. However, GE scores function more like labels—they cannot be added, subtracted, multiplied, or divided. Because each GE score for a test (or a subtest of a test battery) is derived from the median raw score of a norm group, median raw scores will vary from year to year, from test to test, and from subtest to subtest within the same test battery. Therefore, GE scores cannot be used to compare students' improvement from year to year, students' relative strengths and weaknesses from test to test, or even students' scores on subtests of a standardized test. GE scores can be used only to describe whether a student is performing above grade level, at grade level, or below grade level.

There is a risk of misinterpreting GE scores. A person might conclude that a student who scores above his or her actual grade level is able to be successful in an advanced curriculum or that a student who scores below grade level should be held back a grade. Suppose a second-grade student has a GE score of 5.2 on a reading achievement test. We would say that the second-grade student scored as would an average fifth-grade student in the second month of school, *if* the fifth-grade student took a reading test appropriate for second graders. In other words, all we can say is that the second grader is above average for his or her grade in reading achievement, not that the second grader "reads on a fifth-grade level." The limitations of GE scores include the following (Sullivan, Winter, Sass, & Svenkerud, 2014):

- The computation of GE scores does not use any information about the variability in scores within a distribution. The median score of all beginning sixth graders may be 100, but there is great variability in scores among the students. Not all beginning sixth graders will score 100. An expectation by the school district, teacher, or government that all students should reach that score is unrealistic.

- The variability in GE scores increases as grade level increases, with students at lower grade levels relatively homogeneous in performance and students at middle and high school levels showing a wide variation. So a first-grade student who scores one year below grade level may be substantially below peers in achievement, while a ninth-grade student who scores one year below grade level actually may be average in achievement.

Because of the likely misinterpretation and misuse of GE scores, most educators and psychologists do not recommend using them.

STANDARD SCORES

Standard scores are used to simplify score differences and, in some instances, more accurately describe them than can either percentiles or GE scores. For example, standard scores are used in interpreting IQ tests and the SAT by converting the raw scores using the mean and SD. When the scores are converted, the mean for IQ tests is 100 and the SD is 15, while for each subscale of the SAT, the mean score is approximately 500 and the SD is 100.

A common standard score is calculated by using the mean and the SD to convert raw scores into **z-scores.** When raw scores are converted into z-scores using the simple formula

$$z = \frac{(\text{raw score} - \text{mean})}{\text{SD}}$$

the z-score distribution always has a mean score of 0 and an SD of 1, leading to z-scores that range from –4.00 to +4.00, as shown in Figure 25.4. Because z-scores are based on units of SDs, comparisons across student scores are more precise than with percentiles or GE scores and are less likely to be misinterpreted.

Because negative numbers can create some concern and confusion—and also have a negative connotation when interpreting students' ability or achievement—another common standardized score is the T-score. The **T-score** is also based on the number of SDs, but it has a mean of 50 and an SD of 10 (z-scores are multiplied by 10, and then 50 is added to the product). Again, looking at Figure 25.4, we see that a T-score of 60 represents 1 SD above the mean (+1.00 z-score), and a T-score of 40 represents 1 SD below the mean (–1.00 z-score). T-scores typically are not used with standardized achievement or aptitude tests, but they are commonly used with personality tests and behavioral instruments, particularly those that assist in the diagnosis of disorders (Gregory, 2013).

Stanine scores are derived by ranking raw scores from lowest to highest and converting the scores to a single-digit system from 1 to 9 that can be easily interpreted using the normal curve, as shown in Figure 25.4 (Gregory, 2013). The statistical mean is always 5 and comprises the middle 20% of scores, although scores of 4, 5, and 6 are all interpreted or evaluated as average. Stanines of 1, 2, and 3 are considered below average, and stanines of 7, 8, and 9 are considered above average. Because the scores are based on percentile rank, they do *not* provide better comparisons across scores than do z-scores and T-scores.

Teachers typically are asked to interpret standardized test scores for parents. Given a choice, which type of test score would you prefer to use in providing your interpretation and why? How comfortable would you be explaining the various other test scores?

CHARACTERISTICS OF GOOD TESTS

⑤ Explain why validity and reliability are two important qualities of tests and why teachers need this information about tests to interpret test scores.

Several characteristics of tests and test scores are important for appropriate test-score interpretation, including:

- standardized test administration (as mentioned at the beginning of this module),

- large and representative norm samples for norm-referenced tests, and

- the use of standard scores when interpreting performance.

Video Case 25.3 ▲
Standardized Tests

© SAGE Publications

Teachers should evaluate two additional characteristics before selecting tests to use or interpreting test scores: validity and reliability. Without adequate evidence that test scores are reliable and valid, test score interpretations are meaningless. Let's explore each concept in more detail.

Validity

Validity of classroom assessments: See Modules 23 and 24

How do we know that a test score accurately reflects what the test is intended to measure? To answer this question, we need to be able to evaluate the validity of the test score. **Validity** is the extent to which an assessment actually measures what it is intended to measure, yielding accurate and meaningful interpretations from the test score. Keep in mind that validity refers to the test *score,* not the test itself (the collection of items in a test booklet). Consider these examples:

- Just because a test score is intended to predict intelligence, such as an IQ score of 120, does not mean that it fulfills that purpose.

- A test may have valid scores for most individuals, but the test score might be invalid for a particular individual. For example, a standardized achievement test score would not be valid for a student who takes the test without wearing his or her prescription eyeglasses. Similarly, a non-English-speaking student taking a test written in English is unlikely to receive an accurate interpretation of his or her achievement in a particular subject area based on the test score.

Validity is not an all-or-none characteristic (valid or invalid), and it can never be *proven.* Rather, it varies depending on the extent of the research evidence supporting a test score's validity. All validity is considered **construct validity,** or the degree to which an unobservable, intangible quality or characteristic (construct) is measured accurately. The construct validity of a test score can be supported by several types of evidence:

1. **Content validity** evidence provides information about the extent to which the test items accurately represent all possible items for assessing the variable of interest. For example, do the 50 items on a standardized eighth-grade math achievement test adequately represent the content of eighth-grade mathematics? The issue of content validity is also relevant to classroom tests because most teachers choose a subset of questions from a pool of possible questions they could ask to represent the knowledge base for a particular learning goal.

2. **Criterion-related validity** evidence shows that the test score is related to some criterion— an outcome thought to measure the variable of interest. For example, aptitude tests used to predict college success should be related to subsequent GPA in college, an outcome measure related to a student's general aptitude (Gregory, 2013). Two types of criterion-related validity are:

   - **concurrent validity** evidence, based on the test score and another criterion assessed at approximately the *same time,* such as a math achievement test score and the student's current grade in math; and

   - **predictive validity** evidence, based on the test score and another criterion assessed in the *future,* such as an aptitude test and later college GPA.

3. **Convergent validity** evidence shows whether the test score is related to another measure of the construct. For example, a new test designed to measure intelligence should be correlated with a score on an established intelligence test.

4. **Discriminant validity** evidence demonstrates that a test score is not related to another test score that assesses a *different* construct. For example, a reading test would not be expected to correlate with a test of mental rotations or spatial abilities.

5. **Theory-based validity** evidence provides information that the test scores are consistent with a theoretical aspect of the construct (e.g., older students score higher than younger students on an achievement test).

Validity can be compromised on standardized tests in many ways. Two commonly discussed issues related to validity are test fairness and test bias. The terms test fairness and test bias are sometimes used interchangeably, and both refer to judgments about test design and implementation. However, these two terms actually have distinct meanings and implications. **Test fairness** is the broader term, addressing the ethical issue of how to use tests appropriately (Gregory, 2013). Test fairness includes aspects of test bias, equal treatment in the testing process, equal treatment of outcomes, and equal opportunities to learn the material presented on standardized achievement tests (American Educational Research Association, 2014). **Test bias** is some type of systemic error in a test score (American Educational Research Association, 2014) that may or may not be a function of cultural variations. The **cultural test bias hypothesis** states that standardized tests and testing procedures were designed in such a way as to have a built-in bias against groups categorized by some aspect such as gender, ethnicity, race, or socioeconomic status. The difference in group test scores is thought to be a result of the test itself and not of differences in actual group skill or ability.

The classic example used to denote cultural test bias is the difference in average IQ scores among racial groups. The average IQ score of African Americans is about 1 SD (or 15 points) below the average score of Caucasians. When variations in socioeconomic status are controlled, African Americans' average IQ score is .5 to .7 SD (or 7–10 IQ points) below that of Caucasians. Similarly, Hispanics score .5 SD below Caucasians, whereas Asian Americans score equal to or better than Caucasians on standard IQ tests. These average differences in test scores across racial groups are used as evidence to support the cultural test bias hypothesis.

Two problems become evident when average group differences are used as evidence of cultural test bias. First, because the construct being measured is an unobservable characteristic (e.g., intelligence, achievement, mental ability) rather than an observable characteristic (e.g., weight, height), there is no way to substantiate that the average differences are not due to actual differences in intelligence or achievement rather than to cultural test bias (Reynolds et al., 2009). Second, test scores will vary more among individuals within the same group (within-group variability) than between two groups (between-group variability). Figure 25.5 depicts the normal distribution of scores for two groups. As you can see, the overlap between the two groups is quite large, suggesting that the between-group differences are not profound.

If the cultural test bias hypothesis cannot explain the average differences found between groups on standardized tests, what else might account for the disparities? One hypothesis ascribes the differences to genetics, but little theoretical or empirical evidence supports a connection between DNA and standardized test scores. The most likely explanation is differences in environment. Minority students are more likely to be enrolled in lower SES school districts where the quality of instruction is lower, leading to actual ability differences among groups of students. For example, more White, middle-class kindergarten

DIVERSITY

FIGURE 25.5 **Similarities Outweigh Differences.** Comparing boys' and girls' math performance historically has found mean differences, but the overlap of scores between these two groups is quite great, emphasizing the enormous variability within groups, as opposed to between groups.

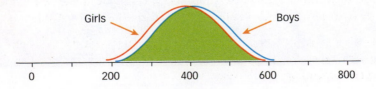

students may correctly answer the question, "What is 2 plus 2?" It is hard to argue that this question is culturally biased; rather, the quality of instruction may have been poor in the lower SES homes and school districts, leading those students to answer the question incorrectly (Popham, 2006).

 Prior to reading this section, did you believe that standardized tests were biased against certain groups? On what basis did you form your opinion (personal experiences, media coverage, previous courses)? Have you changed your mind? If so, what evidence had a strong impact on your thinking?

Reliability

Reliability of classroom assessments: See Modules 23 and 24

If a standardized aptitude test is given to a student on Monday and again on Friday, would you expect the test scores to be different, similar, or exactly the same? We would expect both test scores to be similar, because it would be highly improbable for the student to receive exactly the same score twice or to have two wildly divergent scores. This consistency, called the **reliability** of the test score or measurement, is measured on a continuum from high to low. A reliability index can be computed in a number of ways depending on the type of test and the test-scoring procedures. For example, administering the same aptitude test on Monday and Friday is a type of reliability procedure called *test–retest*. The computed relationship between the test and retest scores provides a reliability index. All reliability indexes, or reliability coefficients, range from 0 to 1, with higher numbers indicating higher reliability (Gregory, 2013):

- .90 or above is considered highly reliable,

- between .80 and .90 is considered good, and

- below .80 is considered questionable.

Measurement Error. All measurements, including weights on bathroom scales and scores on standardized tests, have imperfections.

©iStockphoto.com/ PhotoTalk

To better understand reliability, let's consider another form of measurement—your bathroom scale. Have you ever stepped on the scale to weigh yourself, read the number, and then thought, "That can't be right"? You step right back onto the same scale, and a slightly different weight registers (maybe one you prefer, maybe not). The difference in the weights is due to measurement error. **Measurement error** is the accumulation of imperfections that are found in all measurements. Test scores, like all other measurements, are an imperfect type of measurement. Measurement error on tests can result from a number of sources (Gregory, 2013):

- item selection (e.g., clarity in the wording of questions),

- test administration (c.g., a test administrator who has a harsh tone of voice and increases student anxiety),

- individual factors (e.g., anxiety, illness, fatigue), or

- test scoring (e.g., subjective, judgment-based assessments such as essays).

Even though these sources of measurement error are unpredictable, developers of standardized tests estimate the amount of error expected on a given test, called the **standard error of measurement (SEM;** also called the margin of error in public surveys, such as political polls). The statistical calculation for determining the standard error of measurement is based on the reliability coefficient of the test and the SD of test scores from the scores of a norm group. This calculation is not as important as how SEM can be used to interpret test scores. With an individual test score, SEM can help determine the **confidence interval,** or the range in which the individual's true score (i.e., true ability) lies. Consider this example:

A student receives a raw score of 25 on a standardized achievement test with SEM 4.

If we calculate a 68% confidence interval (the raw score plus or minus the SEM), the student's score range is 21 to 29.

We can say with 68% confidence that the student's true score is between 21 and 29 on this standardized achievement test.

We have used a 68% confidence interval with a raw score as a simple explanation of how SEM helps determine a student's true score (also see Figure 25.6). However, remember that most standardized test results will report a 95% or 99% confidence interval and that

FIGURE 25.6   **Error in Political Polls.**

The standard error of measurement (SEM), or margin of error, provides information used to determine a confidence interval or range in which the true score would fall. In this political poll, the president's actual approval rating is somewhere between 32% and 42%.

THE PRESIDENT'S APPROVAL RATING

APPROVE 37%

DISAPPROVE 63%

± 5% margin of error

the confidence intervals will use standard scores (z-scores, T-scores, stanines, etc.) rather than raw scores. Many psychologists and test developers recommend using confidence intervals to remind professionals, parents, and researchers that measurement error is present in all test scores (Gregory, 2013).

One note of caution is needed regarding the relationship between validity and reliability. Say, for example, that your bathroom scale is very reliable but you later discover that its measurement is consistently off by 10 pounds. This shows that consistent results (reliability) can be found with a measure that does not accurately assess the construct of interest (validity). In short, reliability does not lead to validity. Reliability is necessary—any test that is valid also must measure the construct of interest consistently—but it is not sufficient for achieving validity. A bathroom scale can consistently read 350 pounds for a person who actually weighs 110 pounds. In this case, the scale is reliable but not valid. If a standardized aptitude test accurately predicts success in college (validity), the results should be consistent (reliability) across multiple testing sessions, such as early or late in 12th grade. If the test results lack reliability, validity also is undermined.

Teachers need to evaluate the validity and reliability of a test before attempting to make test score interpretations. Most standardized tests publish the validity evidence and reliability coefficients that are used by teachers and school districts to determine which tests are "good."

 Assume that your school district is using a highly reputable standardized test with a reliability coefficient above .90. One of your students performs well, as you would expect, at the beginning of the year but then performs very poorly on the same test at the end of the year. Is this student's test score valid? What might affect the reliability and validity of it?

DIVERSITY

APPLICATIONS: ACCOMMODATING STUDENTS AT RISK

6 Explain how accommodations improve the validity of test scores for students at risk.

Accommodations are changes in the way standardized tests are administered or scored that do *not* change what is being measured. The test scores of students who are given accommodations are a more valid measure of their achievement than are the test scores of students with disabilities or limited English proficiency (LEP) who are not given accommodations, and they lead to similar inferences or meaning across all students (Lissitz & Schafer, 2002). For example, students with LEP may do poorly on a math achievement test not because they have poor math skills but because they had difficulty understanding the questions and answer options given in English.

Students at risk need accommodations to have an equal opportunity to perform as well as students not at risk (Reynolds et al., 2009). The term **students at risk** refers to a group of students considered to be at risk for not meeting standard achievement levels at school. The U.S. government uses four factors to identify children at risk: (1) a mother with less than a high school education, (2) a family using food stamps or other forms of public assistance, (3) a single-parent household, and (4) a home where the parents' primary language is not English. The first three factors are used to assess poverty, and the last factor is used to determine limited English proficiency. Students with disabilities are missing from this list of risk factors but should be included. Hence, students who are at risk for receiving low scores on high-stakes achievement tests include three groups (Haladyna, 2002):

1. *Students living in poverty.* Approximately 21% of students live in poverty. Family income levels and standardized achievement test scores are highly correlated, with students living in poverty having substantially lower test scores on a number of standardized achievement tests. Reasons for lower standardized achievement test scores among students living in poverty include poorer nutrition, less learning outside school due to lower parental education and lack of school readiness resources, a high rate of moving from one school to another, and lower quality instruction at schools in low-income school districts. Many students living in poverty drop out of school in response to high-stakes pressure to raise their standardized achievement test scores.

2. *Students with limited English proficiency (LEP).* Limited English proficiency (LEP) is the U.S. government's term for individuals whose native language is not English. Several other terms also are used within the educational context, including English language learner (ELL) and English as a second language (ESL). According to the federal law regarding bilingual education, students are considered LEP if they meet one of three criteria: (1) The student was born outside the United States in a country where the native language is not English, (2) the student comes from a home environment in which English is not the spoken language, or (3) the student comes from an isolated culture (e.g., Native Americans and Alaska natives). Approximately 14% of students in U.S. schools fall into the category of LEP. Students with LEP can be given accommodations during high-stakes testing to provide a more valid assessment of their achievement.

3. *Students with disabilities.* Approximately 11% of students in schools have some type of cognitive, behavioral, or social disability that puts them at risk for scoring lower on standardized achievement tests. Students with cognitive, emotional, or behavioral disabilities experience impairments in learning and lower academic achievement than their same-age peers. Federal laws provide guidelines for teaching and testing students with disabilities.

When using tests with students at risk, educators can consider typical accommodations from four broad categories, shown in Table 25.4 (Lissitz & Schafer, 2002; Reynolds et al., 2009):

1. *Presentation format:* The student may be presented with different directions or be given assistive devices for help in understanding the questions. For example, a student with LEP might be provided with an English-translation dictionary or an interpreter.

2. *Response format:* The format of responding to questions and providing answers may be altered. For example, a student with a motor impairment might provide oral responses to a scribe, who transfers them to the corresponding "bubbles" on a computer-scored answer sheet.

3. *Timing or scheduling:* The student might be given more time—or more sessions—to take the test but not unlimited time. The extended time may be particularly necessary when other accommodations require more time, such as having a reader or translator.

4. *Setting:* Students may be given the test in a special setting, such as in a separate room or a special seat, rather than in the standardized group format. For example, a student with a physical disability might need to sit at a table rather than in a desk.

TABLE 25.4   Accommodations for Students at Risk

PRESENTATION FORMAT	RESPONSE FORMAT
Oral exams to written exams	Oral exams to written exams
Written exams to oral exams	Written exams to oral exams
Braille format	Braillewriter to record responses
Sign language	Responding in sign language
Large print	Pointing to answer
Reader services	Having an aide mark answers
Increased spacing between items	Using a tape recorder to record responses
Reduced number of items per page	Increasing spacing on the answer sheet
Rephrased directions	Marking responses on the test booklet, not a Scantron sheet
Restated directions	
Additional examples	
Specialized computer programs to read text	

TIMING	SETTING
Extended time	Individual administration
More frequent breaks	Small-group administration
More sessions	Preferential seating
Sessions over more days	Study carrel to minimize distractions
Changing time of day test is given	Special lighting

SOURCE: Reynolds et al., 2013.

When considering accommodations, keep in mind that accommodations are *not* appropriate when the test being used measures skills related to the student's disability or language limitations. For example, reading the test questions out loud to a student is an acceptable accommodation in some cases but not if the test measures reading comprehension. In this case, giving the student such an accommodation would provide an unfair advantage in the skill being measured.

Accommodations vary greatly from state to state and most often are not explicitly determined by research evidence. For example, some accommodations, such as reading aloud the test questions and directions, may actually be a disadvantage to younger children (Finch, Baron, & Meyer, 2009). Further research on how well accommodations work for various items and developmental levels is needed. Typically, school officials make recommendations for how a particular student should be accommodated during standardized testing, as required by law. This is part of the student's *Individualized Education Plan (IEP)*—the legal contract between the parents and school officials detailing the provision of regular or special education and related services designed to meet the student's educational needs. The degree of accommodation allowed depends on the degree of risk. For example, in the area of English proficiency, most states require that students first take a basic English proficiency exam, and their score on that exam then determines the number and types of accommodations allowed. Although there are no definite criteria, some general guidelines for making accommodations include the following (Lissitz & Shafer, 2002; Reynolds et al., 2009):

Individualized Education Plan: See Modules 21 and 22

- providing accommodations routinely given during classroom assessments,

- providing accommodations only when needed and promoting independence when possible, and

- continuing to evaluate the need for the accommodation and altering or ceasing the accommodation when possible.

Imagine that you are at an IEP meeting for an LEP student in the grade level you intend to teach. What factors should the group members consider in deciding on testing accommodations for the state mastery test?

SUMMARY

❶ Describe the purpose of four broad categories of standardized tests and how standardized tests are used by teachers. Standardized achievement tests are used to assess the degree of current knowledge or learning in either broad or domain-specific areas. Standardized aptitude tests assess an individual's future potential to learn in general or in domain-specific areas. Career or educational interest inventories assess preferences related to certain types of activities. Personality tests are used to assess individual characteristics. Teachers are most likely to administer group tests, which are both relatively easy to administer and cost-effective. Teachers may encounter individually administered test results when determining special education eligibility.

❷ Explain the difference between criterion-referenced and norm-referenced tests. Although some standardized tests provide both criterion-referenced and norm-referenced interpretations, the type of test or interpretation used is based on the purpose of the test. Criterion-referenced tests provide information about the mastery and the strengths and weaknesses of individual students, such as whether a particular student meets certification requirements. In contrast, norm-referenced tests allow comparisons among student scores that may be used in making decisions, such as selecting the top students from a group.

❸ Explain the basic properties of a normal distribution. The normal distribution is a special type of frequency distribution. Although some frequency distributions may be skewed, with more scores falling on the higher or lower end, the normal distribution is bell-shaped and symmetrical. The three central tendencies—mean, median, and mode—are equal to one another and appear at the midpoint of a normal distribution. The variability among scores is standard such that 68% of scores are within 1 SD of the mean, 95% of scores are within 2 SDs of the mean, and 99% of scores are within 3 SDs of the mean.

❹ Describe four types of test scores, and explain the advantages and limitations of each. (1) Raw scores are the number of correct answers or percentage of correct answers. They provide adequate information for classroom tests but are more difficult to interpret when comparing scores across students or groups of students. (2) Percentile scores are based on the percentage of test takers who scored below or equal to a student's raw score. Percentile scores provide information about how well an individual performed in comparison to a group but should not be used to compare different students' scores. (3) GE scores represent the median score for particular grade levels, indicating whether a student is scoring at grade level, below grade level, or above grade level. GE scores are commonly misinterpreted; hence, experts do not recommend their use. (4) Standard scores are derived from percentile rank scores by converting them into a single-digit system (i.e., stanines) or from raw scores by converting them into scores based on a specified mean and SD (i.e., z-scores and T-scores). Standard scores typically are used for ease of interpretation, and those based on the mean and SD also allow accurate comparisons among scores.

❺ Explain why validity and reliability are two important qualities of tests and why teachers need this information about tests to interpret test scores. To determine the quality of a test, teachers should evaluate the validity evidence and reliability of test scores. Validity refers to the extent to which a test measures what it is intended to measure. Reliability of test scores refers to the consistency of the measurement, with highly reliable tests having minimal measurement error and low quality tests having high measurement error. Teachers can use information about validity and reliability evidence to determine the quality of a test and to make decisions about whether the test should be used. The standard error of measurement also can be used to determine a confidence interval, rather than depending on a single raw or standard score. Confidence intervals remind teachers and other professionals that some measurement error is present in all tests—even high-quality tests.

❻ Explain how accommodations improve the validity of test scores for students at risk. Test scores of students at risk who are given accommodations are a more valid measure of their achievement than are test scores of students with disabilities or LEP who are not given accommodations. Accommodations include changing (a) the presentation format, such that students may be given different directions or assistive devices for help in understanding questions; (b) the response format, such that students provide answers differently from the standardized format; (c) the timing or scheduling of the test, allowing more time or more sessions to take the test; and (d) the setting, allowing students special seating. Changes in the way standardized tests are administered or scored provide students at risk an equal opportunity to succeed.

KEY CONCEPTS

CASE STUDIES: REFLECT AND EVALUATE

EARLY CHILDHOOD: Kindergarten Readiness

These questions refer to the case study on page 482.

1. The BRIGANCE K & 1 Screen-II measures gross and fine motor skills, color recognition, knowledge of body parts, counting, oral comprehension, and many literacy and numeracy skills. In what way is this standardized readiness test like a standardized achievement test?

2. What basic concepts of measurement are used to create the range Amy refers to when explaining to her roommate that *average* typically means a range in scores?

3. Explain why grade-equivalent scores can be confusing to parents like Ms. Jackson. What types of scores could be used to better compare achievement differences among students?

4. Maria's mother is concerned about how Maria's test score will be interpreted and used. What characteristic of "good tests" is a concern for Maria's mother? Is her concern justified? Why or why not?

5. Suppose Maria's ranking on the BRIGANCE is at the 38th percentile. How would you interpret this score in relation to other students? What if another student scored at the 49th percentile? How would you compare the performance of this student to Maria's?

6. Define *validity* in your own words. Explain whether Maria's readiness test results would be valid if she took the English version of the BRIGANCE. What if she took the English version with her sister as interpreter?

ELEMENTARY SCHOOL: TEACHER IN-SERVICE TRAINING

These questions refer to the case study on page 484.

1. Mr. Whitney mentions the difference between norm-referenced and criterion-referenced tests. Explain whether he is accurate in his interpretation about how the test scores are used.

2. If the test scores had been half a standard deviation above the national mean, would Principal Bowman have been as concerned? Why or why not?

3. Explain what is wrong with Ms. Cong's interpretation of percentile scores.

4. Explain how the average percentile score could have increased from 46 to 48 while average scores fell below the state cutoff levels.

5. Ms. Rivadeneyra suggests that the test scores do not accurately reflect the students' abilities. What characteristic of good tests is involved here? Explain how this characteristic was influenced by the events near the school last year.

MIDDLE SCHOOL: HOMEWORK NIGHT

These questions refer to the case study on page 486.

1. Karen uses the fact that Payton's standardized test scores are always above the mean to assume that she should be an A/B student. Is this a reasonable assumption? Why or why not?

2. If you were Payton's teacher, how would you explain the meaning of a percentile score of 87 on the math portion of the test to Karen?

3. Based on the normal distribution and the information Karen notes regarding the standardized test scores being half a standard deviation below the mean, how poorly are the students at Payton's school doing in comparison to students across the country?

4. Explain how Kylie could be getting the highest standardized test scores in the school but receiving Ds and Fs on her written assignments?

5. Given that Kylie consistently receives Ds and Fs on her assignments, does that mean her scores on the written assignments are valid? Explain.

HIGH SCHOOL: MATH TESTS

These questions refer to the case study on page 488.

1. What type of standardized test is the SAT? Why might a student score high on an achievement test but not on the SAT?

2. Explain how a norm-referenced test, such as the SAT, can be used as a criterion-referenced test by colleges and universities for determining admissions.

3. Based on the information in the module about SAT scores, explain how much variability there was in the four students' test scores on the SAT math subscale as presented in the case.

4. Assume that another student received a score of 700 on the SAT math subscale. What would be the equivalent stanine score? What would be the equivalent z-score?

5. Assume that Trevor takes the SAT again next month and receives a score of 800 on the math subscale. What does the difference in his two scores indicate about the quality of the test scores?

Visit **edge.sagepub.com/durwin3e** to help you accomplish your coursework goals in an easy-to-use learning environment.

- Mobile-friendly **eFlashcards**
- Mobile-friendly practice **quizzes**
- A complete online **action plan**

- Chapter **learning objectives**
- EXCLUSIVE! Access to full-text **SAGE journal articles**

HOW DOES *EdPsych* HELP YOU PREPARE FOR THE PRAXIS EXAM?

PRAXIS II™ TOPICS	WHERE TO REVIEW IN *EDPSYCH*
I. STUDENTS AS LEARNERS **A. Student Development and the Learning Process**	
1. *Theoretical foundations about how learning occurs: how students construct knowledge, acquire skills, and develop habits of mind*	Module 5: Brain Development Module 6: Cognitive Development Module 7: Language Development Module 8: Behavioral Learning Theories Module 9: Social Cognitive Theory Module 10: Information Processing Module 11: Metacognition Module 12: Transfer of Skills and Knowledge Module 13: Higher Order Thinking
Examples of important theorists: Jean Piaget Lev Vygotsky Howard Gardner Robert Sternberg Erik Erikson Lawrence Kohlberg Urie Bronfenbrenner B. F. Skinner Albert Bandura	Module 6: pp. 121–124 Module 6: pp. 121–124 Module 20: pp. 414–416 Module 20: pp. 416–417 Module 3: pp. 46–50 Module 4: pp. 67–69 Module 2: pp. 30–32 Module 8: p. 162 Module 9: pp. 174–175
Important terms related to learning theory: Conservation Constructivism Equilibration Co-construction Private speech Scaffolding Zone of Proximal Development Modeling Rote memorization Elaborative Rehearsal Rehearsal Automaticity	Module 6: pp. 117–118 Module 6: See "individual constructivism," p. 113; See "social constructivism," p. 113 Module 6: p. 113 Module 6: See "intersubjectivity," p. 120 Module 6: See "egocentric speech," p. 115 Module 6: p. 120 Module 6: p. 120 Module 9: p. 180 Module 12: p. 235 Module 10: p. 194 Module 12: p. 194 Module 21: p. 234
Learning (classical conditioning) Learning (operant conditioning) Learning (observational learning) Knowledge Memory Schemas Transfer	Module 8: pp. 159–162 Module 8: pp. 162–168 Module 9: pp. 175–179 Module 11: See "metacognitive knowledge," p. 215 Module 10: pp. 192–198 Module 10: p. 196 Module 12: Transfer of Skills and Knowledge
2. Human development in the physical, social, emotional, moral, and cognitive domains	Module 2: Contexts of Development Module 3: Social-Emotional Development Module 5: Brain Development Module 6: Cognitive Development Module 7: Language Development
Contribution of important theorists: Jean Piaget Lev Vygotsky Erik Erikson Lawrence Kohlberg Carol Gilligan	Module 6: pp. 121–124 Module 6: pp. 121–124 Module 3: pp. 46–50 Module 4: pp. 67–69 Module 4: pp. 69–70

Major progressions in each developmental domain and the ranges of individual variation within each domain Impact of students' physical, social, emotional, moral, and cognitive development on their learning and how to address these factors when making decisions How development in one domain, such as physical, may affect performance in another domain, such as social	Module 3: Social-Emotional Development Module 4: Moral Development Module 5: Brain Development Module 6: Cognitive Development Module 7: Language Development

B. STUDENTS AS DIVERSE LEARNERS

1. *Differences in the ways students learn and perform*	Specific coverage appears in the context of every module. Please see the diversity icon on page margins. Also see: • Module 1: Using Science to Inform Classroom Practices • Module 2: Contexts of Development • Module 7: See "Individual Differences in Language Acquisition," pp. 140–142 • Module 20: Intelligence and Giftedness • Module 21: Cognitive Disabilities • Module 22: Emotional, Social, and Behavioral Disorders

Important terms related to diversity:
  Differentiated instruction
  Learning styles
  Multiple intelligences
  Performance modes, including concrete operational thinking
 	
  Gender differences
  Cultural expectations and styles
	Module 18: p. 368
	Module 18: p. 368
	Module 20: pp. 414–416, 429–430
	Module 6: p. 117
	Module 20: See "Teaching for Successful Intelligence," pp. 430–431
	Specific coverage appears in the context of every module. Please see the diversity icon on page margins. Also see:
	Module 1: Using Science to Inform Classroom Practices
	Module 2: Contexts of Development

2. Areas of exceptionality in students' learning Important terms related to exceptionality. Special physical or sensory challenges Learning disabilities ADHD Autism spectrum disorder Intellectual disability Bilingualism	Module 13: Higher Order Thinking Module 20: Intelligence and Giftedness Module 21: Cognitive Disabilities Module 22: Emotional, Social, and Behavioral Disorders Module 5: Brain Development Module 10: Information Processing Module 25: Standardized Tests and Scores Module 21: p. 445 Module 22: p. 463, pp. 469–472; Module 5: p. 100 Module 22: p. 463, pp. 473–474; Module 5: p. 101 Module 21: p. 442–443 Module 7: pp. 138–140
3. *Legislation and institutional responsibilities relating to exceptional students*	Module 21: Cognitive Disabilities Module 22: Emotional, Social, and Behavioral Disorders

Important terms related to exceptionality:
  Individuals with Disabilities Education Improvement Act (IDEA); Section 504 Protections for Students
  Inclusion
  Mainstreaming
  Least restrictive environment
	Module 22: pp. 439–440
	
	Module 21: p. 441
	Module 21: p. 440
	Module 21: p. 440

4. Approaches for accommodating various learning preferences, intelligences, or exceptionalities	Module 18 Module 20 Module 21 Module 22
Alternative assessment Testing modifications	Module 23: p. 494 Module 24: p. 515
5. Process of second language acquisition and strategies to support the learning of students	Module 7: Language Development
6. Understanding of influences of individual experiences, talents, and prior learning, as well as language, culture, family, and community values on students' learning	Specific coverage appears in the context of every module. Please see the diversity icon on page margins. Also see: Module 1: Using Science to Inform Classroom Practices Module 2: Contexts of Development Module 3: Social-Emotional Development Module 7: Language Development Module 20: Intelligence and Giftedness
Multicultural backgrounds	Module 1: Using Science to Inform Classroom Practices Module 2: Contexts of Development Module 3: Social-Emotional Development
Age-appropriate knowledge and behavior	Module 3: Social-Emotional Development Module 4: Moral Development Module 6: Cognitive Development
The student culture at school	Module 2: Contexts of Development Module 3: Social-Emotional Development Module 17: Classroom Management
Family backgrounds	Module 2: Contexts of Development Module 3: Social-Emotional Development
Linguistic patterns and differences	Module 7: Language Development

C. STUDENT MOTIVATION AND THE LEARNING ENVIRONMENT

1. Theoretical foundations of human motivation and behavior	Module 14: Behavioral Theory Module 15: Cognitive Theories Module 16: Self Theories
2. How knowledge of human motivation and behavior should influence strategies for organizing and supporting individual and group work in the classroom	Module 14 Module 15 Module 16 Module 17: Classroom Management Module 18: Instruction: Applying Behavioral, Cognitive, and Constructivist Approaches Module 19: Grouping Practices
3. Factors and situations that are likely to promote or diminish student's motivation to learn, and how to help students to become self-motivated	Module 14: Behavioral Theory Module 15: Cognitive Theories Module 16: Self Theories
4. Principles on effective classroom management and strategies to promote positive relationships, cooperation, and purposeful learning	Module 17: Classroom Management Module 18: Instruction: Applying Behavioral, Cognitive, and Constructivist Approaches Module 19: Grouping Practices
Establishing daily procedures and routines Establishing classroom rules Using natural and logical consequences Providing positive guidance Modeling conflict resolution, problem solving, and anger management	Module 17 Module 17 Module 8: Behavioral Learning Theories Module 17 Module 17

Using objective behavior descriptions	Module 17: Classroom Management
Responding to student behavior	Module 8: Behavioral Learning Theories
Arranging classroom space	Module 17

II. INSTRUCTION & ASSESSMENT
A. Instructional Strategies

1. Major cognitive processes	Module 11: Metacognition
	Module 12: Transfer of Skills and Knowledge
	Module 13: Higher Order Thinking

Critical thinking	Module 13: pp. 252–255
Creative thinking	Module 13: p. 262
Higher-order thinking	Module 13: pp. 250–252
Inductive and deductive thinking	Module 13: p. 253
Problem structuring and problem solving	Module 13: Higher Order Thinking
Memorization and recall	Module 12: p. 235
Social reasoning	Module 4: See "prosocial reasoning," pp. 70–72
Representation of ideas	Module 10: See "schemas" and "propositional networks," p. 196

2. Major categories, advantages, and appropriate uses of instructional strategies	Module 17: Classroom Management
	Module 18: Instruction: Applying Behavioral, Cognitive, and Constructivist Approaches
	Module 19: Grouping Practices

Cooperative learning	Module 18: pp. 376–378; Module 19: pp. 390–399
Direct instruction	Module 18: pp. 369–371
Discovery learning	Module 18: p. 373
Questioning	Module 18: pp. 379–380
Small-group work	Module 13: See "Problem-Based Learning," pp. 259–260
Project approach	Module 18: See "Methods Based on Constructivism," pp. 374–380

3. Principles, techniques, and methods associated with major instructional strategies	Module 17: Classroom Management
	Module 18: Instruction: Applying Behavioral, Cognitive, and Constructivist Approaches
	Module 19: Grouping Practices

| Direct instruction | Module 18: See "Teaching Methods Based on Behaviorism," pp. 369–372. |
| Student-centered methods | Module 18: See "Teaching Methods Based on Cognitive Learning Theory," pp. 372–374. Also see "Teaching Methods Based on Constructivism," pp. 374–380. |

4. Methods for enhancing student learning through the use of a variety of resources and materials	Module 18: Instruction: Applying Behavioral, Cognitive, and Constructivist Approaches
	Module 19: Grouping Practices
Computers, Internet resources, web pages, e-mail	Module 23: See "Parent-Teacher Communication," pp. 505–509
Service learning	Module 4: pp. 78–79

B. Planning Instruction

1. Techniques for planning instruction, including addressing curriculum goals, selecting content topics, incorporating learning theory, subject matter, curriculum development, and student development and interests	Module 17: Classroom Management
	Module 18: Instruction: Applying Behavioral, Cognitive, and Constructivist Approaches
	Module 19: Grouping Practices

Behavioral objectives: affective, cognitive, psychomotor, speech/language	Module 13: See "Bloom's taxonomy," p. 251.
	Module 18: See "Bloom's taxonomy," p. 367
Learner objectives and outcomes	Module 23: Assessing Student Learning
Anti-bias curriculum	Module 18: See "culturally responsive pedagogy," pp. 368–369

2. *Techniques for creating effective bridges between curriculum goals and students' experiences*	Module 10: Information Processing Module 11: Metacognition Module 12: Transfer of Skills and Knowledge Module 13: Higher-Order Thinking Module 18: Instruction: Applying Behavioral, Cognitive, and Constructivist Approaches Module 19: Grouping Practices Module 20: Intelligence and Giftedness
Modeling Independent practice, including homework	Module 9: p. 180 Module 18: See "Direct Instruction," pp. 369–371
Activating students' prior knowledge Encouraging exploration and problem solving	Module 10; Module 11; Module 12 Module 13: pp. 255–259
C. Assessment Strategies	
1. *Types of assessments*	Module 20: Intelligence and Giftedness Module 23: Assessing Student Learning Module 24: Test Construction and Use Module 25: Standardized Tests and Scores
2. *Characteristics of assessments*	Module 23: Assessing Student Learning Module 24: Test Construction and Use Module 25: Standardized Tests and Scores
3. *Scoring assessments*	Module 23: Assessing Student Learning Module 24: Test Construction and Use Module 25: Standardized Tests and Scores
4. *Uses of assessments*	Module 20: Intelligence and Giftedness Module 21: Cognitive Disabilities Module 23: Assessing Student Learning Module 24: Test Construction and Use Module 25: Standardized Tests and Scores
5. *Understanding of measurement theory and assessment–related issues*	Module 24: Test Construction and Use Module 25: Standardized Tests and Scores
6. Interpreting and communicating results of assessments	Module 20: Intelligence and Giftedness Module 23: Assessing Student Learning Module 25: Standardized Tests and Scores
III. COMMUNICATION TECHNIQUES	
A. Basic, effective verbal and nonverbal communication techniques	Module 17: Classroom Management Module 20: Intelligence and Giftedness
B. Effect of cultural and gender differences on communications in the classroom	Module 7 Module 20
C. Types of communications and interactions that can stimulate discussion in different ways for particular purposes	Module 11: Metacognition Module 7 Module 18
Probing for learner understanding	Module 12 Module 13
Helping students articulate their ideas and thinking processes	Module 10 Module 11 Module 12
Promoting risk taking and problem solving	Module 13
Facilitating factual recall	Module 10

Encouraging convergent and divergent thinking	Module 13
Stimulating curiosity	Module 13
	Module 14: See "Applications: Creating an Intrinsically Motivating Learning Environment," p. 287
Helping students to question	Module 13: Higher Order Thinking
	Module 11: See "Reading Comprehension," p. 221
	Module 18
	Module 16: See "Foster Relatedness in the Classroom," p. 331
Promoting a caring community	Module 17

IV. PROFESSION & COMMUNITY
A. The Reflective Practitioner

1. Types of resources available for professional development and learning	Module 1: Using Science to Inform Classroom Practices
2. Ability to read, understand, and apply articles and books about current research, views, ideas, and debates regarding best teaching practices	Module 1: Using Science to Inform Classroom Practices
3. Ongoing personal reflection on teaching and learning practices as a basis for making professional decisions	Module 1: Using Science to Inform Classroom Practices
	Module 12: Transfer of Skills and Knowledge
	Module 17: Classroom Management
	Also, reflective prompts are integrated throughout the text.

B. THE LARGER COMMUNITY

1. Role of the school as a resource to the larger community	Module 2: Contexts of Development
2. Factors in the students' environment outside of school (family circumstances, community environments, health and economic conditions) that may influence students' life and learning	Module 2: Contexts of Development
	Module 17
	Module 20: Intelligence and Giftedness. See "Socioeconomic and Cultural Factors," pp. 425–429
3. Develop and utilize active partnerships among teachers, parents/guardians and leaders in the community to support educational process	Module 2: Contexts of Development
4. Major laws related to students' rights and teacher responsibilities	Module 21: Cognitive Disabilities
	Module 22: Emotional, Social and Behavioral Disorders
Appropriate education for students with special needs	Module 21
	Module 22
	Module 25

GLOSSARY

A

Ability Grouping. A method of creating groups of students who are similar in achievement or ability level. (Module 19)

Academic Intrinsic Motivation. Motivation to learn characterized by curiosity, persistence, a desire to engage in challenging and novel tasks, and a focus on mastery of knowledge and skills. (Module 14; Module 15)

Academic Learning Time. Time students spend engaged in the learning process. (Module 17)

Academic Socialization. An aspect of parental involvement in which parents openly discuss the parents' values and expectations for academic success, assist with learning strategies, and foster future plans based on academic strengths and interests. (Module 17)

Acceleration. A method recommended for gifted students in which they move quickly through grades or receive instruction above grade level in one or two subjects. (Module 20)

Accommodation. A process of adaptation in Piaget's theory that involves modifying one's existing knowledge or creating new concepts when new information cannot fit into one's existing thinking. (Module 6)

Accommodations. Changes in the way standardized tests are administered or scored that do not change what is being measured. (Module 25)

Achievement Goal. A purpose for choosing to do a task and the standard that an individual constructs to evaluate performance on the task. (Module 15)

Active Learning. Any form of meaningful learning which involves constructing a rich knowledge base of interrelated concepts, prior knowledge, and real-life experiences. (Module 6)

Active Listening. Listening in a non-defensive way and responding by clarifying the message rather than criticizing. (Module 7)

ADHD. See Attention-Deficit/Hyperactivity Disorder. (Module 22)

Adolescent Egocentrism. Difficulty differentiating between one's own thoughts and the thoughts of others. (Module 11)

Advance Organizers. General information presented before instruction to provide the learner with prior knowledge and a structure in which to integrate new information. (Module 18)

Algorithm. A problem-solving strategy that provides a specific set of steps, which if followed, will result in a solution. (Module 13)

Alphabetic Principle. The knowledge that printed letters are represented by units of sound. (Module 21)

Alternative-Response Item. A declarative statement with dichotomous options, such as true-false, yes-no, and fact-opinion. (Module 24)

Alternatives. The choices in a multiple-choice item. (Module 24)

Amotivation. A lack of motivation; the least autonomous level of motivation in self-determination theory. See also self-determination. (Module 16)

Amygdala. A structure in the limbic system of the brain responsible for emotions such as anger, fear, happiness, and anxiety. (Module 5)

Analogical Thinking. A problem-solving strategy that focuses on exploring possible solutions that are similar to solutions used with similar problems. (Module 13)

Analogical Transfer. An example of high-road transfer involving creating or using an existing analogy to aid in understanding a new concept. (Module 12)

Analytic Rubric. Scoring tool used to evaluate separate, individual parts of a product or performance first, then sum the individual scores to obtain a total score. (Module 23)

Analytical Abilities. One of three abilities in Sternberg's theory of successful intelligence which is characterized by skills such as analyzing, evaluating, judging, or comparing and contrasting. See also creative abilities and practical abilities. (Module 20)

Androgynous. Having both masculine and feminine characteristics. (Module 3)

Anxiety. Mental thoughts related to worrying and negative emotions such as nervousness or tension, which can impair academic performance. (Module 15)

Anxiety Disorder. A disorder which involves distressingly unpleasant and maladaptive feelings, thoughts, behaviors, and physical reactions. (Module 22)

Appearance-Reality Distinction. An understanding that appearances can be deceiving or false. (Module 11)

Articulation Disorder. A speech disorder diagnosed when a familiar adult cannot understand a child's speech at age three, or when articulation errors are still evident at age eight. (Module 7)

Assessment. The process of obtaining information that is used for making decisions about curricula, students, programs, and educational policy. This term is also used to describe the actual tools (tests, papers, projects, etc.) used to gather information. (Module 23)

Assimilation. A process of adaptation in Piaget's theory that involves fitting new information or experiences into one's existing way of thinking. (Module 6)

Attainment Value. A component of expectancy-value theory referring to the importance of being good at a task. (Module 15)

Attention. The processing of focusing on certain aspects of the environment. (Module 10)

Attention-Deficit/Hyperactivity Disorder (Adhd). A neurological condition that impairs self-regulation, leading to problems maintaining attention, inhibiting impulsive or inappropriate responses, executive control over planning, monitoring progress, and selection of strategies in working memory. (Module 22)

Authoritarian Parenting. High level of control in which rules are enforced, yet emotional connectedness is lacking. (Module 2)

Authoritative Parenting. High levels of control or enforcing rules as well as high levels of emotional connectedness. (Module 2)

Autism Spectrum Disorder. A developmental disorder affecting social interaction, communication, and behavior. (Module 22)

Automatic Processing. Skills that are applied without conscious thought to accomplish fairly easy or familiar tasks. See also automaticity. (Module 10)

Automaticity. The ability to respond accurately, quickly, and using few cognitive resources such as attention and strategies while performing a mental or physical skill. (Module 12)

Automaticity Training. Practice aimed at improving the accuracy and speed of reading or math skills such as word recognition or math fact retrieval. (Module 21)

Autonomy. A component of self-determination theory referring to a feeling of having choice and control over one's actions. (Module 16)

B

Babbling. Repetitive consonant-vowel combinations produced by infants, such as dadadada. (Module 7)

Backward-Reaching Transfer. Deliberately looking for knowledge learned in the past that could be useful in a current situation. (Module 12)

Belief Perseverance. Tendency to hold onto existing ideas or beliefs even in the face of contradictory evidence. (Module 1; Module 13)

Best Practices. Evidence-based strategies determined by science to help inform decisions about instruction, classroom management, and assessment. (Module 1)

Best Work Portfolio. A carefully selected combination of materials that showcases examples of a student's best work and serves as final summative assessment. (Module 23)

Between-Class Ability Grouping. A practice typical in high school that involves using test scores or past performance to place students into curriculum tracks in which all their classes are with students of similar abilities. (Module 19)

Bloom's Taxonomy. A categorization of six learning objectives that includes lower-level objectives (remember, understand, apply) and higher-level objectives (analyze, evaluate, create). (Module 13)(Module 18)

Bottom-Up Processing. Type of processing that helps explain perception such that individuals begin with specific features of stimuli and automatically piece those features together without using conscious awareness to experience an entire object. (Module 6)

Brainstem. The lower part of the brain that regulates vital functions, such as heart rate, breathing, sleeping, and eating, and that is responsible for connections with sensory and motor systems in the body. (Module 5)

Broca's Area. Located in the frontal lobe of the left hemisphere of the brain, this area is primarily involved in the production of language, speech, and the control of facial neurons. (Module 5)

Bully Victims. Individuals who are both victims and perpetrators of bullying behavior. (Module 17)

Bullying. Intentional, repetitive aggression toward a person perceived as having less power. (Module 17)

C

Career or Educational Interest Inventories. Category of standardized tests that assess individual preferences toward certain types of activities. (Module 25)

Caring Orientation. Moral reasoning that focuses on responding to others' needs in intimate relationships. (Module 4)

Carry-Over Effect. A subjective error when scoring essays in which a teacher's evaluation of a student's response to one affects the evaluation of the student's response to a subsequent question, either positively to negatively. (Module 24)

Causal Attributions. Explanations for why events, such as success or failure, have occurred. (Module 15)

Central Executive. Subsystem of Baddeley's model of working memory that does not store information but manages or oversees the flow of information between the other three systems. (Module 10)

Central Tendency. A score that is typical or representative of the entire group. (Module 22)

Centration. An inability to focus on two dimensions simultaneously. (Module 6)

Cerebral Cortex. Extensive outer layer of neurons of the two cerebral hemispheres, largely responsible for higher brain functions, including sensation, voluntary muscle movement, thought, reasoning, and memory. (Module 5)

Cerebral Hemispheres. The two symmetrical halves of the cerebrum connected by a thick bundle of fibers called the corpus callosum. (Module 5)

Cerebrum. The largest part of the human brain consisting of two cerebral hemispheres; it is the last to develop, and is responsible for many higher-level functions. (Module 5)

Checklists. Scoring tools that list the behaviors or characteristics of a process or product for teachers to check whether or not the behaviors are present. (Module 23)

Child-Directed Speech. Language directed to infants and children characterized by high pitch, exaggerated intonations, elongated vowels, short and simple sentences, and repetition. (Module 7)

Chronosystem. Chronological nature of development within the individual as well as the surrounding environment. (Module 2)

Chunking. Organizing information into smaller units or meaningful bits of information. (Module 10)

Class Running Routines. Procedures for nonacademic or more administrative issues. (Module 17)

Classroom Tests. A type of formal assessment to measure student mastery in school subjects. (Module 23)

Cliques. Small peer groups of 2-8 people that are interaction-based. (Module 2)

Cluster Grouping. A grouping method for gifted students in which they are placed together in one classroom that also contains non-gifted students at various achievement levels. (Module 20)

Code Mixing. Bilingual individuals' use of words or phrases from one language as a substitute in the other language. (Module 7)

Cognitive Apprenticeship. An approach to learning cognitive skills within the context of authentic activities in which novices are guided, participate at a level commensurate with their ability, and gradually take over more responsibility with increasing skill. (Module 18)

Cognitive-Behavioral Treatment (CBT). Technique that teaches students to regulate their own behavior using a series of instructions that they memorize, internalize, and apply to different school tasks. (Module 22)

Collective Efficacy. Belief of success about a group or social system. (Module 9)

Commitment. Making decisions about areas of one's life such as educational and career goals, family obligations or goals, as well as political and religious beliefs. (Module 3)

Competency Belief. Belief that one has the ability to perform a task or succeed at an activity. (Module 15)

Completion Items. A type of constructed-response item that contains an incomplete statement and a blank for students to complete. (Module 24)

Concurrent Validity. Type of criterion-validity evidence that evaluates the relationship between the test score and another criterion assessed at approximately the same time. (Module 25)

Conditional Knowledge. Information about under what conditions or skills can be used. (Module 10)

Conditioned Response. The behavior that occurs due to conditioning; a learned response.

Conditioned Stimulus. The previously neutral stimulus that now evokes a conditioned response; a learned stimulus.

Conduct Disorder. Serious behavioral disorder that involves repeatedly and purposely violating rules or laws, the rights of others, or age-appropriate societal norms. (Module 22)

Confidence Interval. A range in which an individual's true score lies, based on the individual's score and the standard error of measurement for the test. (Module 25)

Consensual Assessment. Assessment of creativity that requires observers or judges to agree that an idea or product is creative.

Confirmation. Bias Tendency to search for information that confirms our existing ideas and beliefs. (Module 1)

Conservation. The understanding that quantity or amount remains the same even though appearance changes. (Module 6)

Consolidation. The neutral process that strengthens memories over time and can take days, weeks, and months to complete. (Module 10)

Construct Validity. The degree to which an unobservable, intangible quality or characteristic (construct) is measured accurately. (Module 25)

Constructed-Response. A type of item that requires students to formulate a response to a question or prompt, such as simple completion, short-answer items, and essays. (Module 24)

Constructivism. A psychological paradigm that characterizes learning as a process of actively constructing knowledge. (Module 6)

Content Validity. Type of validity evidence that is determined by how accurately test items or questions represent all possible items and questions for assessing a content domain. In a classroom context, an assessment with high content validity accurately represents a content domain and/or reflects what teachers have actually taught. (Module 24; Module 25)

Contiguity Learning. Learning by simple association. (Module 8)

Contingency Management. An approach to behavior modification involving the use of consequences that are tied to specific behaviors. See also contingency contract. (Module 22)

Continuous Schedule. Schedule of reinforcement in which consequences are provided after every single instance of the behavior. (Module 8)

Control. Behavioral aspect of parenting in which parents provide limits and discipline. (Module 2)

Controllability. Dimension of attributions in which the cause of an outcome is considered to be controllable by the individual or uncontrollable. (Module 15)

Conventional Level (of Moral Reasoning). Kohlberg's second level of moral reasoning that focuses on external authorities, such as the conventions and standards of society, for determining right and wrong. (Module 4)

Convergent Thinking. Reaching one conclusion or right answer. (Module 13)

Convergent Validity. Type of validity evidence that is determined by correlating the test score with another measure of the construct. (Module 25)

Cooperation. A dimension of the teacher-student relationship in which teachers are concerned for students' views, opinions and working as a team member. (Module 17)

Cooperative Learning. A method of grouping students together to work collaboratively characterized by five elements: positive interdependence, individual and group accountability, interpersonal skills, face-to-face interaction, and group processing. (Module 18; Module 19)

Corpus Callosum. A thick bundle of fibers that connects the left and right hemispheres, and allows communication between them. (Module 5)

Correlational Designs. Research design that attempts to make connections between two variables. (Module 1)

Cost. Component of expectancy-value theory referring to the expense of engaging in the activity. (Module 15)

Creative Abilities. One of three abilities in Sternberg's theory of successful intelligence, which is characterized by the ability to generate novel ideas and take risks in pursuing implementation of ideas. See also analytical abilities and practical abilities. (Module 20)

Creative-Productive Giftedness. Giftedness that reflects talents in generating creative ideas, problem-solving, or producing create products. (Module 20)

Creativity. A cognitive process that includes something new or unique that are appropriate in the context. (Module 13)

Criterion-Referenced Grading. A method of assigning grades in which scores on an assessment or a set of assessments are compared to a predetermined criterion (or standard) for what is considered A performance, B performance, and so on. (Module 23)

Criterion-Referenced Tests. Tests that are used to compare an individual score to a pre-set criterion for a learning objective. (Module 25)

Criterion-Related Validity. Type of validity evidence that is demonstrated by establishing a relationship between the test score and some criterion, usually an outcome that is thought to measure the variable of interest. (Module 25)

Critical Thinking. A set of cognitive abilities that allows one to evaluate and judge the accuracy and importance of information. (Module 13)

Cross-Grade Groupin. A procedure in which students from different grades but similar abilities are placed into homogeneous groups based on their reading or math achievement level, and each group works with different curricular materials and different methods. (Module 19; Module 20)

Crowd.s Large, reputation-based peer groups. (Module 2)

Cues. Nonverbal event that occurs prior to a behavior. (Module 8)

Cultural Test Bias Hypothesis. Tests are biased in some way for a categorical group such as gender, ethnicity, race, or socioeconomic status. (Module 25)

Curriculum Compacting. An approach to streamlining the curricular material for students who are gifted by teaching only content that has not been mastered, allowing for advanced instruction or enrichment activities in the time saved by eliminating already- learned content. (Module 20)

Cyberbullying. Relational aggression via texts, emails, and/or social media. (Module 17)

D

Declarative Knowledge. Information about facts, both personal facts (episodic memory) and general facts (sematic memory). (Module 10)

Decoding. The strategy of applying sounds to printed letters in order to identify unfamiliar words; referred to as sounding out. (Module 7; Module 21)

Deductive Reasoning. A type of reasoning that uses logic to determine specific outcomes or expectancies based on general information (Module 13)

Deficiency Needs. Lower level needs in Maslow's Hierarchy of Needs: physiological, safety, love, and self-esteem. (Module 16)

Deficit. Performance in a domain like reading or mathematics that is poorer than both same-age peers and younger children, indicating an impairment in which students process information in a qualitatively different way than other individuals. (Module 21)

Deliberate Practice. An intrinsic motivation to engage in extensive, long-term repetition of a skill with the desired goal of improving performance. (Module 12)

Descriptive Designs. Research design that provides basic information about behaviors without making connections between behaviors, events, or conditions. (Module 1)

Developmental Delay. Performance in a domain such as reading or mathematics that is poorer than same-age peers but similar to younger students, indicating a slower rate of development. (Module 21)

Deviation IQ. A standard score derived from raw scores; it indicates a test-taker's performance relative to all other test-takers having similar characteristics. (Module 20)

Direct Instruction. A teaching method based on behaviorist principles which uses teacher control, structured lessons, and extensive practice. (Module 18)

Disability. The inability to perform some behavior, task, or skill. (Module 1)

Discipline. To give instruction and teach. (Module 17)

Discovery Learning. An instructional method in which students discover and internalize a concept, rule, or principle by engaging in unstructured exploration of information without explicit guidance from the teacher. (Module 18)

Discriminant Validity. Type of validity evidence that demonstrates a test score is not correlated to another test score that assesses a different construct. (Module 25)

Discrimination. 1) Treating students differently based on prejudice feelings or biased beliefs about a particular group; 2) learning in classical conditioning that includes differentiating between similar, but different, stimuli. (Module 1; Module 8)

Disequilibrium. A discrepancy between one's existing knowledge and a new experience. (Module 6)

Distractor Analysis. An analysis to evaluate multiple-choice test items that examines how many students selected each alternative. (Module 24)

Distractors. Incorrect alternatives provided in a multiple choice item. (Module 24)

Divergent Thinking. A form of higher-order thinking that includes identifying several outcomes or solutions, usually from a single starting point. (Module 13)

Divided Attention. The ability to focus on multiple stimuli. (Module 10)

Doctrine of Formal Discipline. Theory proposing that studying disciplines which require logical thinking could improve general mental abilities, facilitating transfer of these abilities to learning of other subjects. (Module 12)

Dominance. A dimension of the teacher-student relationship that provides a clear purpose and strong guidance or support for both academic content as well as expected behavior. (Module 17)

Dual Coding Theory. A theory of long-term memory suggesting that we remember information better if we encode the information both verbal and visual information. (Module 10)

Dual Discrepancy Method. A method within the response-to- intervention approach to identify whether a student needs more intensive and/or more frequent intervention in which two criteria must be met: the student performs below average compared with grade-level expectations, and shows a slow rate of improvement toward benchmarks. (Module 21)

Dysfluency. A lack of fluency in speech production. (Module 7)

E

Educational Psychology. A discipline that links the science of psychology with educational practice. (Module 1)

Efficacy Expectations. Beliefs that individuals have the necessary knowledge or skills to achieve an outcome. (Module 16)

Effortful Processing. Providing conscious attention to difficult or new tasks. (Module 10)

Egocentric. Thinking about the world primarily from one's own physical or cognitive viewpoint. (Module 6)

Egocentric Speech. An example of egocentrism in which children talk from the perspective of their own interests and experiences without regard for the interests and conversational contributions of the listener. (Module 6)

Egocentrism. A focus on the self with little consideration for other people or their perspectives. (Module 4)

Elaborative Rehearsal. A memory strategy used to connect new information to information already learned. (Module 10)

Emotional Competence. The ability to express, understand, and regulate emotions within the self and others.

Emotional Disturbance. One of thirteen categories of disability specified by the Individuals with Disabilities Education Improvement Act. (Module 22)

Empathy. The ability to experience and understand the emotions or feelings of someone else. (Module 4)

Empathy-Based Guilt. The feeling of pain and regret for causing distress or pain in another person. (Module 4)

Encoding. The process by which information or stimuli enter our memory. (Module 10)

English Immersion. A sink-or-swim approach to teaching English-language learners in which students receive all instruction in English in classes with native English-speaking peers. (Module 7)

Enrichment. An approach designed to broaden and deepen the knowledge of students who are gifted while keeping them within their grade level. (Module 20)

Entity View of Ability. A pessimistic perception that one's ability is fixed (stable and uncontrollable) leading individuals to believe that their ability cannot change over time and they cannot control their level of ability. (Module 15; Module 16)

Episodic Buffer. A subsystem of Baddeley's model of working memory responsible for integrating information from the visuospatial sketchpad and phonological loop as well as linking information in working memory or long-term memory. (Module 10)

Episodic Memory. A type of long-term memory that includes personal information from "episodes" in one's own life. (Module 10)

Equilibration. A process of maintaining a cognitive balance between our existing knowledge and new experiences. (Module 6)

Ethnic Group. Group of people who share a similar culture or environment. (Module 1)

Ethnic Identity. Psychological attitudes and behaviors toward one's ethnic and racial group membership. (Module 3)

Evaluating. An executive process in cognition allowing individuals to appraise the outcomes of the cognitive strategies used; the process of making subjective judgments about a student's performance or product; the subjective interpretation of a measurement or test score. (Module 11, Module 25)

Evaluation. The act of making a value judgment about a student's product or performance, which can be based on measurement of performance or an observation. (Module 25)

Exosystem. Interaction among two or more environments, one of which does not directly include the individual. (Module 2)

Expansion. A method of interacting with children in which adults add to—or expand—children's incomplete statements. (Module 7)

Expectancy. A component of expectancy-value theory, which involves a student's expectation for success; "can I do this task?" See also value. (Module 15)

Experience-Dependent Plasticity. The modification of existing structures and neuronal connections already present in the brain and the creation of new connections that occurs as a result of an individual's life experiences. (Module 5)

Experience-Expectant Plasticity. The forming of biologically pre-programmed connections among neurons in response to environmental stimulation that the brain expects to receive based on evolution. (Module 5)

Experimental Designs. Research design that allows cause and effect between study variables to be inferred. (Module 1)

Exploration. A period of role experimentation and trying new behaviors, including contemplating morals and values. (Module 3)

Expository Teaching. A highly organized presentation of material from general principles to specific examples beginning with the activation of prior knowledge. (Module 18)

Extended-Response Essay. Test item that requires students to write essays in which they are free to express their thoughts and ideas, and to organize the information as they see fit. With this format, there is usually no single correct answer; rather correctness ends up being a matter of degree. (Module 24)

External Regulation. The least autonomous form of extrinsic motivation in self-determination theory in which a person performs behaviors to obtain external rewards. See also self-determination. (Module 16)

Extinction. Strategy used to decrease an inappropriate behavior by no longer providing reinforcement for that behavior, or ceasing to provide the pairing between stimuli and response. (Module 8)

Extrinsic Motivation. A motivational orientation in which individuals engage in an activity or behavior to obtain an external outcome such as a reward or praise. (Module 14; Module 15; Module 16)

F

Face-to-Face Interaction. A feature of cooperative learning that involves effective help and feedback to improve performance, exchanging resources effectively, challenging each other's reasoning, and motivating each other to achieve goals. (Module 19)

Fact-Retrieval Deficit. The most common deficit in mathematics disability characterized by the inability to commit facts to long-term memory and automatically retrieve them. (Module 21)

Failure-Accepting Students. Students who accept failure and give up trying to demonstrate their ability because of repeated failures to perform up to their expectations. (Module 16)

Failure-Avoiding Students. Students who are highly motivated to avoid failure have low motivation to approach success situations and value learning only if it makes them look competent. (Module 16)

Fairness. The degree to which all students have an equal opportunity to learn and demonstrate their knowledge and skill. (Module 23; Module 24)

False-Beliefs. Understanding that people can believe one thing but be wrong. (Module 11)

Family Educational Rights and Privacy Act. Legislation that protects the privacy of students' academic records by specifying that parents of children under 18 years of age may review the student's school records, but parents must provide written permission in order for the school to release information about a student's educational record. (Module 21; Module 23)

Far Transfer. Application of knowledge to a context that is very different from the learning context. (Module 12)

Feminine. Stereotypical female behaviors such as being affectionate, warm, gentle, cheerful, and loyal. (Module 3)

Fixed Percentage Method. A method of criterion-referenced grading in which scores on each course component are converted to a percentage correct (or a percent of total points), and then the percentages are combined and converted to letter grades using predetermined percentage ranges (e.g., A = 95–100%). (Module 23)

Flow. A feeling of intense engagement, enjoyment, and challenge in an activity that an individual feels is personally rewarding, causing the individual to feel at one with the task. (Module 14)

Fluency. The ability to read text quickly, accurately, and with proper expression, which is a problem for many students with reading disability. (Module 21)

Flynn Effect. A phenomenon in which IQ scores have increased over successive generations throughout the world. (Module 20)

Formal Assessmen. A pre-planned systematic attempt to discover what students have learned. (Module 23)

Formative Assessment. Given before or during instruction to provide feedback that helps the teacher guide students' learning. (Module 23)

Forward-Reaching Transfer. A principle or strategy is so well-learned or deeply understood that it becomes applicable in future learning situations. (Module 12)

Frequency Distribution. Simple list of all scores for a group. (Module 25)

Frontal Lobe. One of the last brain regions to develop, this area is involved in many executive functioning abilities, such as using working memory, planning, decision making, problem solving, implementing strategies, and inhibitory control. (Module 5)

Functional Fixedness. The inability to use objects or tools in a new way because we are "fixed" on using objects for their intended purpose and ignoring other potential uses. (Module 13)

G

Gender. Social definition including behaviors learned in the environment about being either male (masculine) or female (feminine) (Module 1; Module 3)

Gender Constancy. Knowledge that gender will remain the same regardless of behaviors. (Module 3)

Gender Identity. Knowledge that one is biologically male or female. (Module 3)

Gender Labeling. Being able to label one's self and others as male or female. (Module 3)

Gender-Role Attitude. The approval or disapproval toward societal expectations for each gender. (Module 3)

Gender-Role Flexibility. The ability to alter social expectations regarding gender of one's own and other's behaviors. (Module 3)

Gender-Role Identity. Knowledge that one behaves appropriately according to societal expectations for one's gender. (Module 3)

Gender-Stability. Knowledge that gender will not change over time. (Module 3)

Generalization. Learning can be expanded beyond a specific stimulus to other similar stimuli. (Module 8)

Giftedness. An elusive trait characterized by high achievement in one of a variety of domains. (Module 20)

Grade-Equivalent (GE) Scores. Scores based on the median score for a particular grade-level of the norm group. (Module 25)

Grading on the Curve Method. A method of norm-referenced grading in which teachers arrange scores from highest to lowest and then assign grades based on the ranked scores, with highest scores receiving an A grade, and so on. (Module 23)

Group Administered IQ Tests. An approach to IQ testing in which an examiner administers an IQ test to a group of individuals in a paper-and-pencil format. See also Individually administered IQ tests. (Module 20)

Group Processing. A feature of cooperative learning that involves reflecting on how well the group is functioning and how to improve it. (Module 19)

Group Work. A structure in which students work in groups but do not necessarily need to work cooperatively. (Module 19)

Group-Administered IQ Tests. An approach to IQ testing in which an examiner administers an IQ test to a group of individuals in a paper-and-pencil format. (Module 20)

Growth Needs. Higher level needs in Maslow's Hierarchy of Needs: intellectual competence, aesthetic appreciation, and self-actualization. (Module 16)

Growth Portfolios. A type of performance assessment in which students collect samples of their work that are not final products, accompanied by teacher comments and student self-reflections. (Module 23)

Guided Discovery. A variant of discovery learning in which the teacher provides enough guidance to ensure that students discover the rule or principle to be learned. (Module 18)

H

Halo Effect. A subtle bias when scoring subjective assessments, such as rating scales and rubrics, in which teachers' overall impression of a student subtly influences their ratings. (Module 23; Module 24)

Heterogeneity. Variation among individuals on an attribute, such as achievement or ability. (Module 19)

Heuristic. A general problem-solving strategy that are simple rules of thumb the aork in some situations but not always. (Module 13)

Higher-Order Thinking. More advanced or complex cognitive processes that may include integrating facts, applying knowledge and skills, as well as analyzing and evaluating information. (Module 13)

High-Road Transfer. Applying abstract knowledge learned in one context to a different situation. (Module 12)

Hippocampus. A structure in the limbic system responsible for the formation of new memories and retrieval of information from long-term memory. (Module 5)

Holistic Rubrics. Scoring tools that include scoring criteria requiring the teacher to score the overall process or product as a whole, without judging the component parts separately. (Module 23)

Holophrastic Speech. Use of single words to express a larger meaning. (Module 7)

Homogeneity. Little variation among individuals on an attribute, such as achievement or ability. (Module 19)

Hostile Attributional Bias. The tendency to interpret another person's intentions as hostile. (Module 4)

Humanistic Theories. Theories that emphasize factors intrinsic to the individual, such as needs, choice, self-determination, and self-actualization as sources of motivation. (Module 16)

Hypothesis Testing. Method of using data to determine if a suspected outcome or idea can be confirmed. (Module 13)

I

Identified Regulation. A slightly internalized form of regulation in self-determination theory in which individuals identify with the value of an activity and have accepted regulation of the activity as their own. See also self-determination. (Module 16)

Identity Achieved. Adolescents who have explored and made commitments in occupations, academic skills, friendships, and values and commit to certain goals and values. (Module 3)

Identity Constancy. Understanding that an object remains qualitatively the same even though its appearance changes. (Module 6)

Identity Diffusion. Adolescents who either have not yet begun the process of exploration (as you might expect for younger children) or have been through the exploration process but were unable to make commitments to their goals and values. (Module 3)

Identity Foreclosure. Adolescents who have parents that typically use an authoritarian style of parenting such as telling their adolescent who they are, what they will become, or where they will attend college are considered foreclosure. (Module 3)

IEP Team. A team of individuals responsible for writing and revising a student's IEP. See also Individualized Education Plan (IEP). (Module 21)

Ill-Defined Problem. A problem that does not have a clear goal or may have multiple correct answers. (Module 13)

Imaginary Audience. Adolescent's belief that others' thoughts are focused on him or her, just as their own thoughts are focused on themselves. (Module 11)

Inclusion. An approach to implementing the Least Restrictive Environment in which students with disabilities, even those with severe disabilities, are integrated within the regular education classroom. See also Least Restrictive Environment (LRE) and Mainstreaming. (Module 21; Module 22)

Incremental View of Ability. An optimistic view of ability in which one believes that ability is improvable (unstable and controllable). (Module 15; Module 16)

Individual and Group Accountability. A feature of cooperative learning that involves group goals (group accountability) and personal responsibility for helping other members and contributing to the group goal (individual accountability). (Module 19)

Individual Constructivism. A form of constructivism in which individuals construct meaning by themselves from their experiences. (Module 6)

Individual Interest. Interest in a particular subject or activity that is intrinsic to the individual. (Module 12)

Individualized Education Plan (IEP). A plan for students with disabilities who are eligible for special education, which outlines curricula, educational modifications, and provision of services intended to enhance or improve the student's academic, social, or behavioral skills. (Module 21; Module 22)

Individually-Administered IQ Tests. IQ testing in which an examiner tests an examinee one-on-one; the tester presents items orally, and sometimes uses pictures or materials such as blocks, and the examinee either responds orally or by manipulating materials. (Module 20)

Individuals With Disabilities Education Improvement Act (IDEA). A 2004 revision of the special educational law originally passed in 1975 as the Education for All Handicapped Children Act (PL 94-142) and later revised as the Individuals with Disabilities Act (PL 101-476), which requires states to provide appropriate public education to students with disabilities aged 3 to 21. (Module 21; Module 22)

Inductive Reasoning. A form of reasoning using specific information to make generalizations that focus on the probability of a conclusion rather than the absolute truth. (Module 13)

Informal Assessments. Techniques such as observations, interviews, or reading journal entries that are conducted for the purpose of providing feedback and do not involve scores or comparing students. (Module 23)

Inner Speech. Internalized speech for regulating one's thoughts and actions. (Module 8)

Inquiry Learning. An instructional activity that involves formulating research questions, collecting, analyzing and evaluating data, and communicating the results. (Module 18)

Instructional Conversations. A method of encouraging elementary school students' interaction with and comprehension of stories during reading lessons based on Vygotsky's Zone of Proximal Development. (Module 18)

Integrated Regulation. A form of regulation in self-determination theory in which an individual has fully internalized extrinsic regulations and now takes ownership of these values. See also self-determination. (Module 16)

Intellectual Disability. A disability characterized by significant limitations in intellectual functioning and adaptive behavior (formerly called mental retardation). (Module 21)

Interaction Routines. Procedures that provide students with instruction on how to communicate in the classroom. (Module 17)

Interference. A limitation in keeping information active in short-term memory because new information from sensory memory comes into short-term memory and overrides the activation of old information. (Module 10)

Intermittent Schedule. A schedule of reinforcement in which consequences are provided periodically for the behavior. (Module 8)

Internalization. A developmental process; in Vygotsky's theory of cognitive development it occurs when an individual progresses from performing cognitive processes with a more capable person, socially, to performing them independently and mentally (Module 6); in self-

determination theory it occurs when an individual moves from less self-determined to more self-determined. (Module 16)

Interpersonal Skills. A feature of cooperative learning that involves skills such as trust, communication, decision-making, leadership, and conflict resolution. (Module 19)

Interrater Reliability. Consistency in rating subjective assessments that is obtained if similar scores result from two teachers independently rating the same assessments. (Module 23; Module 24)

Intrarater Reliability. Consistency of the same rater over time when scoring subjective assessments. (Module 23; Module 24)

Intersubjectivity. Co-construction of knowledge where two individuals who begin a task with different knowledge perspectives come to a shared understanding, each adjusting to the perspective of the other. (Module 6)

Interviews. Type of measure used in research that includes verbal questions. (Module 1)

Intrinsic Motivation. A motivational orientation in which individuals engage in an activity or behavior that is rewarding in and of itself. (Module 14; Module 15; Module 16)

Intrinsic Value. A component of expectancy-value theory referring to interest in or enjoyment of an activity. (Module 15)

Introjected Regulation. A form of extrinsic motivation in self-determination theory in which individuals engage in an activity to comply with external pressure. See also self-determination. (Module 16)

Introspection. (Module 11)

IQ-Achievement Discrepancy. A method of diagnosing learning disabilities in which scores on standardized achievement tests in one or more academic subjects are significantly below what would be expected from the individual's IQ. (Module 21)

IQ Tests. See Group administered IQ tests and Individually administered IQ tests. (Module 20)

Item Analysis. The process of collecting, summarizing, and using information from student test responses to make decisions about whether test items are functioning properly. (Module 24)

Item Difficulty Index. An item analysis technique reporting the proportion of the group of test-takers who answered an item correctly. (Module 24)

Item Discrimination. An item analysis technique reporting the degree to which a particular test item is able to differentiate high-scoring from low-scoring students. (Module 24)

J

Joint Attention. A method of interacting with children in which adults label and talk about objects on which the child's attention is focused. (Module 7)

Joplin Plan. Most famous cross-grade grouping plan, originating in 1954, in which students were assigned to cross-grade, homogeneous groups based on reading-skill level. (Module 19)

Justice Orientation. Moral reasoning that focuses on the rights of individuals due to their focus on independence and individuality. (Module 4)

K

KWL Method. Asks students to list their knowledge about a topic and what questions they have before instruction and list what they learned after instruction. (Module 12)

L

Lateralization. Refers to the left and right hemispheres of the brain being specialized for different types of processing. (Module 5

Law of Effect. Behaviors that are associated with good consequences are more likely to occur, whereas behaviors that are associated with bad consequences are less likely to occur again. (Module 8)

Learned Helplessness. Phenomenon in which students give up trying because they attribute repeated failures to causes that they do not control. (Module 15)

Learning. Change in behavior or knowledge. (Module 8)

Learning Objective. Specific descriptions of what students will know or be able to do once they have completed the lesson. (Module 18)

Least Restrictive Environment (LRE). A legal requirement to place students with special needs in the regular classroom "to the maximum extent appropriate." (Module 21; Module 22)

Lesson Running Routines. Procedures that directly related to learning and academic isssues. (Module 17)

Limbic System. Surrounds the brainstem and contains structures such as the amygdala and hippocampus. (Module 5)

Live Models. Individuals that are observed directly. (Module 9)

Locus. A dimension of attributions in which the cause of an outcome is considered to be internal or external. (Module 15)

Locus of Control. An individual's belief that outcomes or events are caused by either external factors outside of one's control (external locus) or internal factors (internal locus). (Module 14)

Long-Term Memory. The component of memory that holds all the information we have learned or experienced. (Module 10)

Low-Road Transfer. Spontaneous, automatic transfer of highly practiced skills. (Module 12)

M

Macrosystem. Broader cultural patterns such as beliefs, customs, knowledge, and morals. (Module 2)

Mainstreaming. An approach to implementing the Least Restrictive Environment in which students with disabilities are placed with non-disabled peers in the general education classroom when appropriate (e.g., for music, gym, art) but remain in special education classrooms for most academic subjects. See also Least Restrictive Environment (LRE) and Inclusion. (Module 21; Module 22)

Maintenance Rehearsal. Repetition of information over and over to keep it activated in working memory. (Module 10)

Major Depressive Disorders. Mood disorders in which individuals experience at least two weeks of depressed mood or loss of interest, along with at least four additional depressive symptoms as specified in the DSM-IV-TR. (Module 22)

Masculine. Stereotypical male behaviors such as being athletic, aggressive, dominant, self-reliant, and independent. (Module 3)

Maslow's Hierarchy of Needs. A humanistic theory that emphasizes a need for self-actualization, which is obtained by first satisfying lower-level deficiency needs and being needs. (Module 16)

Mastery Goals. Goals that focus on mastery, improving intellectually, and acquiring new skills and knowledge. (Module 12)

Mastery Learning. An approach in which educational objectives are divided into small units, and students work at their own pace through each unit, progressing to the next unit only once they have achieved mastery on the current one. (Module 18)

Mastery-Approach Goals. An intrinsic motivation to focus on mastery, improvell intellectually, and acquire new skills and knowledge. (Module 15)

Mastery-Avoidance Goals. Motivation to avoid lack of mastery or looking incompetent according to one's own criteria of performance. (Module 15)

Matching Exercise. Test format that presents students with directions for matching a list of premises and a list of responses; the student must match each premise with one of the responses. (Module 24)

Matthew Effect. A rich-get-richer-poor-get-poorer phenomenon in which high achieving students increase their achievement at a faster rate than low-achieving students. (Module 19)

Mean. Measure of central tendency where all scores are summed and the sum is divided by the number of scores in the group (simple average). (Module 25)

Meaningful Learning. The process of actively constructing knowledge by selecting relevant information, organizing it, and connecting it to prior knowledge. (Module 18)

Means-End Analysis. A heuristic that focuses on dividing the problem into subgoals. (Module 13)

Measurement. A quantitative or descriptive number (score) assigned to describe the extent to which someone possesses a certain attribute or skill. (Module 23; Module 25)

Measurement Error. The accumulation of imperfections that are found in all measurements. (Module 25)

Median. Measure of central tendency that is the middle score in a list of all scores. (Module 25)

Mesosystem. Interaction between two or more microsystems. (Module 2)

Metacognition. Thinking about thinking; thinking about one's own and others' knowledge such as skills, memory capabilities, and the ability to monitor learning. (Module 11)

Metacognitive Knowledge. Knowledge about our own cognitive processes and our understanding of how to regulate those processes to maximize learning. (Module 11)

Metacognitive Regulation. The purposeful act of attempting to control one's own cognitions, beliefs, emotions, and values. (Module 11)

Metalinguistic Awareness. Knowledge about language and how it works. (Module 7)

Microsystem. Immediate environment surrounding the individual. (Module 2)

Mindful Abstraction. A defining feature of high-road transfer in which information that is consciously and actively learned is retrieved and applied to a new situation, guided by one's metacognition. (Module 12)

Minority Group. A group of people with less power in comparison to the majority group. (Module 1)

Misbehavior. Any student behavior that disrupts the learning environment of the classroom. (Module 17)

Mnemonics. Memory strategies used to help remember large amounts of information.

Mode. Measure of central tendency that is the most frequently occurring score among the group. (Module 25)

Model. Individual who performs a behavior that is being observed and can be imitated. (Module 9)

Monitoring. Checking on how well your plan is working through self-testing and revising or rescheduling cognitive strategies. (Module 11)

Moral Realism. Piaget's first stage of moral reasoning, which includes viewing right and wrong as being determined by the consequences of behavior given by adult authority figures. (Module 4)

Moral Reasoning. The thoughts or rationale for determining right and wrong. (Module 4)

Morality of Cooperation. Piaget's second stage of moral reasoning, which includes understanding certain situations or under particular circumstances rules can be bent. (Module 4)

Moratorium. Adolescents who are actively involved in the exploration process but have not yet made decisions or commitments. (Module 3)

Morphemic Inflections. Word endings. (Module 7)

Multiage Classrooms. A procedure where students of varying ages are flexibly grouped within a classroom based on their current achievement, motivation, and interests. (Module 19)

Multigrade Classes. An administrative tool in which students from different grades are put into the same class to address declining enrollments or uneven class sizes. (Module 19)

Multimodal Interventions. An approach that combines one or more of the following interventions: medication, contingency management, cognitive-behavior modification, and academic interventions. (Module 22)

Multiple-Choice Item. A question format in which students must choose the correct answer from among the list of response alternatives. (Module 24)

Myelin Sheath. A fatty layer that protects and insulates the axons of a

neuron, which speeds up electrical transmission along axons and makes transmitting of nerve impulses quicker and more efficient. (Module 5)

Myelination. The creation of myelin sheaths around axons. (Module 5)

N

Narrative Reports. Reports prepared by teachers to provide detailed, written accounts of each student's learning and performance in class. (Module 23)

Near Transfer. The application of prior knowledge to situations that are similar but not identical to the learning context. (Module 12)

Negative Transfer. Occurs when previous learning hinders learning on new task. (Module 12)

Neglected Youth. Individuals who are neither liked nor disliked by peers. (Module 2)

Network Theory. A theory of long-term memory suggesting that information is encoded in relation to other information (also referred to as semantic network, propositional network, or concept map). (Module 10)

Neuron. Nerve cell in the brain that sends and receives electrical signals over long distances within the body. (Module 5)

Neurotransmitters. Chemical substances that transmit nerve impulses across a synapse. (Module 5)

Neutral Stimuli. All events that do not evoke an automatic response. (Module 8)

Nongraded Plans. Grouping students flexibly into homogeneous groups across grade or age levels. Examples are the Joplin plan and multiage classrooms. (Module 19)

Norm Group. All other test-takers having characteristics similar to the individual taking a test, such as age, grade, gender, socioeconomic status, ethnic or racial status, or geographic region. (Module 20)

Norm Sample. A large group of individuals who represent the population of interest on numerous dimensions such as gender, age, race, and SES. (Module 25)

Norm-Referenced. An interpretation in which one evaluates the performance of an individual as compared to other similar test-takers. (Module 20)

Norm-Referenced Grading. Grades that are based on how a student has performed in comparison with other students in the class. (Module 23)

Norm-Referenced Tests. Tests that are used to compare an individual score to the scores of other students from a norm sample. (Module 25)

Normal Distribution. Frequency distribution of scores that is symmetrical and bell-shaped.

Number Sense. The ability to represent exact quantities or approximate magnitudes of objects, which is important for development of counting and arithmetic skills. (Module 21)

O

Object Permanence. Awareness that objects and people continue to exist even when not present. (Module 6)

Objective Data. Refers to a score having one interpretation, such as right or wrong. (Module 23)

Objective Tests. Tests containing items that have one correct answer and that can be scored without interpretation or judgment.

Observational Learning. Learning by observing and imitating others' (models) behaviors. (Module 9)

Observations. Type of measure used in research that includes watching or viewing the behavior of individuals. (Module 1)

Occipital Lobe. The area at the back of the cortex primarily involved in processing visual information. (Module 5)

Operations. Physical actions performed mentally. (Module 6)

Outcome Expectations. Beliefs that particular actions lead to particular outcomes in general. (Module 16)

Overcorrection. Behavioral strategy used to make restitution for an inappropriate behavior by having a student perform an appropriate behavior. (Module 8)

Overextensions. Using a word to apply to a range of concepts. (Module 7)

Overlearning. The process of continuing practice after students have become accurate at performing a skill. (Module 12)

Overregularizations. Making an irregular word form regular by applying a rule (adding -ed to break = breaked). (Module 7)

Overstrivers. Students who are motivated by a need to perform better than others to ensure their success and prove their ability. (Module 16)

Overt Aggression. Behaviors intended to harm someone physically. (Module 2)

P

Parental Involvement. Parents' participation in their children's education to promote academic success. (Module 17)

Parenting Practices. Patterns of discipline and affection parents display with their children.

Parietal Lobe. Located above the temporal lobe, the area responsible for spatial processing and integration of information from the senses. (Module 5)

Perceived Popularity. Having good social skills, but may not be well-liked by peers and may display aggressive behaviors. (Module 2)

Percentile Scores. Type of test score that denotes the percentage of people in the norm sample who scored below or equal to a raw score. (Module 25)

Perception. The interpretation of the sensory information we encounter that helps us understand the environment. (Module 10)

Performance Assessment. Any form of assessment that requires students to carry out an activity or develop a product in order to demonstrate skill or knowledge. (Module 23)

Performance Praise. Also called outcome praise; an evaluation of the end-product, such as what the student did well on an assignment. (Module 14)

Performance-Approach Goals. An intrinsic motivation to demonstrate ability and do better than others. (Module 15)

Performance-Avoidance Goals. Motivation to avoid lack of mastery or looking incompetent compared to the performance of peers. (Module 15)

Performance-Contingent Rewards. Rewards that are given for mastery or for a standard of performance, which provide the individual with information about his or her ability. (Module 14)

Permissive Parenting. Parenting practice that involves less control but a close connection to children.

Person Knowledge. Type of metacognitive knowledge referring to understanding our own capabilities.

Person Praise. A favorable judgment about a person's attributes or behaviors, such as being smart, or being a good speller, which implies a fixed ability that does not change. (Module 14)

Personal Fable. Adolescents' belief that they are unique, such that no one else can understand their situation.

Perspective Taking. Being able to appreciate that different people facing the same event may think or feel differently due to their unique backgrounds and qualities.

Phonological Awareness. Knowledge that spoken words can be divided into smaller units of sound. (Module 7 also Module 21)

Phonological Loop. A subsystem of Baddeley's model of working memory responsible for briefly processing verbal or auditory information. (Module 10)

Physical Aggression. Behaviors that intend to harm another physically. (Module 17)

Planning. Type of metacognitive regulation involving scheduling learning strategies and selecting which strategies to use in different contexts.

Plasticity. The flexibility of the brain in being able to be modified by new experiences. (Module 5)

Positive Interdependence. A feature of cooperative learning that involves members of the group working together and depending on one another so that all group members succeed. (Module 19)

Positive Practice. Behavioral strategy used to increase an appropriate behavior by having the person perform the right or appropriate behavior.

Positive Transfer. Occurs when previous learning facilitates learning on new task. (Module 12)

Postconventional Level (of moral reasoning). Kohlberg's final level of moral reasoning that includes moving beyond focusing on simply consequences and away from external authorities to an internal authority; establishing personal convictions about what is right and wrong.

PQ4R. Instructional strategy used to increase reading comprehension that includes several steps: preview, question, read, reflect, recite, and review. (Module 11)

Practical Abilities. One of three abilities in Sternberg's theory of successful intelligence, which is characterized by the ability to apply knowledge and to effectively implement solutions in real-life contexts. See also analytical abilities and creative abilities. (Module 20)

Practicality. The extent to which the development, administration, and scoring of assessments is economical and efficient. (Module 23)

Pragmatics. Knowledge of the purpose of language and how language is used in social interactions. (Module 7)

Praise. Positive feedback on an individual's behavior or performance in verbal or written form. (Module 14)

Praise-and-Ignore. Behavioral strategy used to increase an appropriate behavior by providing reinforcement and decrease inappropriate behavior by ignoring the behavior. (Module 8)

Preconventional Level. Kohlberg's first level of moral reasoning that includes an egocentric, self-interest view of right and wrong, not using the conventions or standards of society. (Module 4)

Predictive Validity. Type of criterion-validity evidence that uses the test score and another criterion assessed in the future. (Module 25)

Prejudice Feelings. Rigid and irrational generalizations about a group or category of people. (Module 1)

Premack Principle. Behavioral strategy used to increase an appropriate behavior by providing another behavior as reinforcement. (Module 8)

Private Speech. In Vygotsky's theory, a form of self-regulatory, internalized speech that helps individuals guide their thoughts and actions. (Module 6)

Problem. Any situation in which the desired goal is different for the initial state. (Module 13)

Problem Solving. Attempting to find a means of moving from the initial state to the desired goal. (Module 13)

Problem-Based Learning (PBL). An instructional strategy that includes a series of steps that begin with a problem rather than teaching content knowledge in order to allow students an opportunity to construct their own knowledge from real-world, complex problems. (Module 13)

Problem-Solving Transfer. A type of high-road transfer involving recall of a general strategy or principle learned from solving one type of problem to solve another type of problem. Module 12)

Procedural Delays. A developmental delay in the use of counting procedures. (Module 21)

Procedural Knowledge. Information about how to do tasks and skills. (Module 10)

Procedural Memory. (Module 10)

Procedures. Instructions for carrying out specific tasks that occur regularly (also referred to as routines). Specific descriptions of how to accomplish an activity or task in the classroom. (Module 17)

Process Praise. An evaluation of the process taken to complete a task such as strategies, procedures, methods, approaches, and subskills for performing the task. (Module 14)

Prompts. Verbal reminder that accompanies a cue. (Module 8)

Prosocial Behavior. Voluntary behavior intended to benefit others by helping or sharing. (Module 4)

Prosociality. An important aspect of social skills that focuses on others' needs and interests by helping or cooperating with individuals or groups based on social norms and expectations.

Pruning. The systematic elimination of excess or redundant synapses, which occurs at different times in different areas of the brain. (Module 5)

Psychological and Cultural Tools. Any symbolic system provided by culture, such as signs, language, mnemonics, concepts, activities, or social interactions. (Module 6)

Psychosocial Crisis. Psychological and social challenge with two developmental outcomes, one positive and one negative. (Module 3)

Psychosocial Moratorium. A time with few responsibilities and many opportunities for exploration of different roles. (Module 3)

Punishment. A consequence of a behavior that decreases the occurrence of that behavior. (Module 9; Module 17)

Q

Quasi-Experimental Designs. Research design that attempts to demonstrate a cause-effect relationship when random assignment is not possible and unclear manipulating the independent variable. (Module 1)

R

Racial Group. Group of people who share common biological traits. (Module 1)

Random Sample. Every person within the population has an equal chance of being included in the sample. (Module 1)

Range. Measure of variability that is the difference between the highest and the lowest score in a group of scores. (Module 25)

Rating Scales. A tool for scoring subjective assessments that provide a numerical score for varying levels or degrees of performance on one or more dimensions. (Module 23)

Raw Score. The number of correct answers. (Module 25)

Recall. The ability to remember information without being given any choices. (Module 10)

Recasting. A method of interacting with children in which adults reproduce children's utterances as a semantically similar expression that adds new information. (Module 7)

Reciprocal Questioning. A method for encouraging the social negotiation of conflicting perspectives by requiring students to generate questions based on expository material and take turns asking and answering each other's questions. (Module 18)

Reciprocal Teaching. A method of teaching metacognitive strategies to increase reading comprehension that includes several steps: summarizing, questioning, clarifying, and predicting. (Module 11; Module 18)

Recognition. The ability to remember information when presented with a list of choices. (Module 10)

Reflective Practice. Any technique that allows a learner to develop a conceptual understanding of content. (Module 12)

Region of Proximal Learning. Proposes that individuals will study items close to being learned but not yet mastered. (Module 11)

Regrouping. Placing students of the same grade into homogeneous groups only for reading or mathematics based on their current skill level and continually changing students' group placement based on re-evaluation of their skills. (Module 19)

Reinforcement. A consequence that is given after display of a behavior, which will increase the likelihood that an individual will perform the behavior again. (Module 8; Module 14; Module 15; Module 17)

Reinforcing Incompatible Behaviors. Behavioral strategy used to increase appropriate behavior by providing reinforcement and decrease an inappropriate behavior that cannot occur at the same time. (Module 8)

Rejected Youth. Individuals who do not have good social skills, display aggressive behaviors, and tend to be less well liked by peers. (Module 2)

Relatedness. A component of self-determination theory referring to the need to feel securely connected to others, which enables individuals to feel safe to explore their environment. (Module 16)

Relational Aggression. Behaviors specifically intended to damage another person's relationships. (Module 2; (Module 17)

Reliability. The consistency of the test score or results. (Module 23; Module 24; Module 25)

Repeated Reading. An approach to increase fluency that involves reading a text multiple times. (Module 21)

Reprimand. Behavioral strategy used to decrease an inappropriate behavior by providing undesired verbal criticisms of behavior. (Module 8)

Research Design. Method for investigating how and whether the variables selected are related.

Response Alternatives. List of alternatives in a multiple choice item from which students must choose a correct response. (Module 24)

Response Cost. Behavioral strategy used to decrease an inappropriate behavior by taking away something desired. (Module 8)

Response-to-Intervention. A method of diagnosing learning disabilities in which students identified as at risk for learning disabilities are given appropriate instructional interventions. Those who fail to respond to increasingly intensive interventions would be considered to have a learning disability. (Module 21)

Responsiveness. Emotional component of parenting such as affection, acceptance, and caring. (Module 2)

Restricted-Response Essay. Question format that limits the content of students' answers as well as the form of their responses. (Module 24)

Retrieval. The process by which information is obtained from memory. (Module 10)

Reversibility. Ability to manipulate one's thinking in two directions. (Module 6)

Rote Memorization. Memorizing information without necessarily understanding it. (Module 12)

Rubric. A scoring tool that provides preset criteria for scoring student responses, making grading simpler and more transparent. (Module 23; Module 24)

Rules. Clear expectations for general conduct. (Module 17)

S

Sample. Smaller set of individuals from the population of interest who are included in the research study. (Module 1)

Satiation. Behavioral strategy used to decrease an inappropriate behavior by having a student perform the behavior until it is no longer reinforcing. (Module 8)

Scaffolding. Temporary social support provided by an adult or more capable peer for a child to accomplish a task. (Module 6)

Schema Theory. A theory of long-term memory suggesting that information contained within a script, or typical pattern of events, is easier to understand and encode. (Module 10)

Schemes. Organized patterns of physical action. (Module 6)

Schoolhouse Giftedness. Giftedness that reflects high overall cognitive ability, high achievement in particular subjects, or efficiency in processing information and learning new things. (Module 21)

Section 504 of the Rehabilitation Act Of 1973. A federal anti-discrimination law protecting the rights of individuals with mental and physical disabilities. (Module 22)

Section 504 Plan. A curriculum plan for students with disabilities, required by Section 504 of the Rehabilitation Act of 1973, which outlines the type of education and services needed for the student to function as adequately as non-disabled students. See also Section 504 of the Rehabilitation Act of 1973. (Module)

Seductive Details. Very interesting parts of a text that convey nonessential information. (Module 12)

Selected Response. A test format that requires students to select a response from information given in the test item, such as selecting true or false.

Selective Attention. The ability to focus on one stimuli and ignore others. (Module 10)

Self-Actualization. The highest level of motivation in Maslow's Hierarchy of Needs characterized by a need to satisfy one's full potential. (Module 16)

Self-Concept. A cognitive aspect in which an individual has a perception or description about themselves. (Module 3)

Self-Determination. Autonomy, or the feeling of having choice in one's actions rather than being controlled or pressured; also refers to a theory of motivation in which individuals are motivated intrinsically by needs for autonomy, competence, and relatedness. (Module 16)

Self-Efficacy. One's belief about or expectation for success on a particular task. (Module 9; Module 16)

Self-Esteem. An affective aspect in which an individual evaluates components of him or herself and feels either good or bad. (Module 3)

Self-Evaluation. Determining the quality of the judgment (good or bad) and possibly providing self-imposed consequences. (Module 9)

Self-Fulfilling Prophecy. A groundless expectation that becomes true simply because it was expected. (Module 2; Module 20)

Self-Interrogation. Asking one's self questions to help gauge whether newly learned material has been mastered.

Self-Judgment. Comparing one's own performance to a predetermined goal or standard. (Module 10

Self-Observation. Viewing one's own behavior including possibly recording one's own behavior. (Module 9)

Self-Referenced Grading. A method in which teachers assign grades by comparing students' performance to past performance or to the teacher's perceptions of their ability. (Module 23)

Self-Regulation. The ability to control one's emotions, cognitions, and behaviors by providing consequences to oneself. (Module 9; Module 16)

Self-Worth. One's overall evaluation of worth as a person; also refers to a theory of motivation in which feelings of competence affect one's self-worth and consequently motivation to achieve in school. (Module 16)

Semantic Memory. Information we have that is not tied directly to our personal experiences, including information about language and the meaning of concepts. (Module 10)

Semantics. A component of language referring to how meaning is communicated and interpreted. (Module 7)

Semiotic Functions. An ability to use signs and symbols to represent an object. (Module 6)

Sensitive Periods. Periods in development that involve subtle changes in the brain's ability to be shaped by sensory input at a particular stage. (Module 5)

Sensory Memory. All the sensory information experienced before that information is processed. (Module 10)

Sex. The biological status of male (penis) or female (vagina). (Module 1; Module 3)

Sexual Orientation. Term used to denote homosexuality, heterosexuality, and bisexuality. (Module 1)

Shaping. Behavioral strategy used to increase an appropriate behavior by reinforcing small steps toward the behavior. (Module 8)

Short-Answer Item. Test item format that requires filling in a short response, usually consisting of a word or phrase. (Module 24)

Short-Term Memory. The memory system that temporarily holds information from sensory memory that we are attending to, until the information is either no longer attended to or moved to long-term memory (also referred to as working memory). (Module 10)

Situational Interest. Immediate interest in a particular topic that a teacher creates. (Module 12)

Skewness. The symmetry or asymmetry of a frequent distribution. (Module 25)

Sleeper Effect. Negative effects of divorce seem dormant for many years only to arise again during adolescence. (Module 2)

SOAR Method. Study strategy with four components (1) selection, (2) organization, (3) association, and (4) regulation.

Sociability. An important aspect of social skills that includes one's level of social participation, such as maintaining relationships and interactions with others.

Social Competence. The outcomes, skills, and processes involved in successful social interactions. (Module 3)

Social Constructivism. A form of constructivism in which individuals construct meaning by interacting with others within a social and cultural context. (Module 6)

Social Isolation (Time-Out). Behavioral strategy used to decrease an inappropriate behavior by removing an individual from a setting that includes reinforcement to a setting in which reinforcement is denied. (Module 8)

Social Skills. The ability to reason, think through, pick up cues, and make appropriate decisions with respect to interpersonal relationships. (Module 3)

Socialized Speech. Speech used for communicating in a social context with adults. (Module 6)

Socioeconomic Status (SES). Status of a family household that relies on the education level and occupation of family members rather than their level of income. (Module 1)

Sociometric Popularity. Being well-liked by peers as well as having good social skills. (Module 2)

Sociomoral Developmental Delay. Self-centered, egocentric orientation that is not replaced by the more typical advanced moral development. (Module 4)

Specific Determiners. Extraneous clues to the answer of an alternative-response item. (Module 24)

Specific Language Impairment. A disorder in which language development is significantly below age level because of difficulties in receptive and expressive language, despite normal hearing, average nonverbal intelligence, and an absence of developmental disabilities. (Module 7)

Specific Learning Disabilities. The largest special education category of disability served under the Individuals with Disabilities Education Improvement Act. (Module 21)

Spreading Activation. Memory process where accessing one concept can lead to activation of other related concepts. (Module 10)

Stability. A dimension of attributions in which the cause of an outcome is considered to be stable (unchangeable) or unstable (changeable). (Module 15; Module 16)

Standard Deviation (SD). The degree of variability in a group of scores or how much the scores deviate from or vary from around the average score. (Module 20; Module, 25)

Standard Deviation Method. A type of norm-referenced grading in which teachers use the standard deviation of a set of scores (which indicates the variability of scores around the average) to mark segments of the score distribution corresponding to letter grades. (Module 23)

Standard Error of Measurement (SEM). Estimated amount of error expected on a given test. (Module 25)

Standard Scores. Scores that are created by converting raw scores, typically using the mean and standard deviation, into scores that more easily and accurately describe score differences as compared to some other types of scores. (Module 25)

Standardized Achievement Tests. Tests that assess learning outcomes and skills for broad or domain-specific learning. (Module 25)

Standardized Aptitude Tests. Tests that assess future potential or capacity to learn in general or in a specific domain. (Module 25)

Standardized Tests. Tests that are created by numerous experts in the field, focus on broad areas of learning, and have standard procedures and scoring. (Module 23; Module 25)

Standards-Based Grades. A method of grade reporting that lists the standards (or expectations for mastery) in each subject and performance level descriptors for each standard, such as "advanced," "proficient," "basic," "below basic," which are similar to descriptors used on state standards-based assessments. (Module 23,)

Stanine Scores. Type of standard score which converts raw scores to a single-digit system from 1 to 9. (Module 25)

Stem. An introductory statement or question in a multiple-choice item that calls for a response. (Module 24)

Stereotype Threat. An unconscious, automatic activation of prior knowledge about a stereotype which hinders performance on cognitive tasks. (Module 20)

Storage. The process in which information is held or kept between encoding and retrieval. (Module 10)

Strategy Knowledge. Knowledge about which strategies are available to aid in learning information and under what conditions or when it is best to use a particular strategy. (Module 11)

Structured English Immersion. English-language learners learn subjects in English in classes separate from native-English speakers for typically one year, and teachers use materials and methods designed to accommodate students who are learning the language. Also called sheltered immersion. (Module 7)

Student Engagement. A student's motivation and effort to learn, interest in specific topics, and connectedness to the school or classroom. (Module 17)

Students at Risk. A group of students considered to be at risk for not meeting standard achievement levels at school. (Module 25)

Study-Time Allocation. The amount and distribution of studying. (Module 11)

Subjective Data. Referring to data from assessments that are open to interpretation such as scores on an essay or ratings of a skill. (Module 23)

Subjective Tests. A test format where the scoring is open to interpretation. (Module 24)

Success-Oriented Students. Students who are intrinsically motivated, and define success in terms of becoming the best they can be, regardless of the achievements of others. (Module 16)

Summative Assessment. A form of assessment that helps the teacher evaluate students' progress, as well as the effectiveness of instructional methods, at the end of a unit or grading period. (Module 23; Module 24)

Sustaining Expectation Effect. An effect whereby teachers sometimes fail to notice students' skill improvement, and therefore do not change their group placement, which inadvertently sustains students' achievement at their current level. (Module 19)

Symbolic Models. Individuals who are observed indirectly through various forms of the media. (Module 9)

Synapses. A gap between two neurons that allows transmission of messages. (Module 5)

Synaptogenesis. The growth of new connections in the brain, which continues throughout life as individuals adapt to changing life conditions and experiences. (Module 5)

Syntax. The rules for combining components of language. (Module 7)

Systematic Desensitization. A technique that combines relaxation training with gradual exposure to an anxiety-provoking stimulus to reduce anxieties and fears. (Module 22)

Systematic Phonics Instruction. A program that focuses on teaching children to recognize and manipulate phonemes and to then explicitly apply that knowledge to letter-sound correspondences and decoding. (Module 21)

T

Table of Specifications. A test blueprint in the form of a matrix specifying the number and type of items to include on a test, based on the number of learning objectives and the class time spent on each of the objectives. (Module 23)

Task Knowledge. Knowledge about the difficulty or ease of a task. (Module 11)

Task-Contingent Rewards. Rewards that are given for participating in an activity or for completing an activity without regard to performance level. (Module 14)

Teacher Efficacy. A teacher's belief that he or she has the capabilities to transmit knowledge and manage the classroom in order to teach all students effectively. (Module 9; Module 16)

Telegraphic Speech. A way of ordering words according to the grammatical rules of one's language. (Module 7)

Temporal Lobe. Located on the sides of the brain (where your ears are), the area responsible for functions such as hearing, language, and long-term memories. (Module 5)

Test Bias. Systemic error in a test score that may or may not be a function of cultural variations. (Module 25)

Test Fairness. An ethical issue of how to use tests appropriately. (Module 25)

Tests and Surveys. Types of measure used in research that are typically paper-and-pencil and include a number of questions. (Module 1)

Theories. Sets of ideas used to explain phenomena and make predictions about behavior. (Module 1)

Theory of Identical Elements. A theory proposing that transfer between two learning tasks will occur if the tasks share common elements. (Module 12)

Theory of Mind. Early development of children's attempt to understand the mind and mental world. (Module 11)

Theory of Multiple Intelligences. A theory of intelligence proposed by Howard Gardner consisting of eight separate but interacting intelligences. (Module 20)

Theory of Successful Intelligence. A theory proposed by Robert Sternberg in which success is defined as the ability to succeed in life and involves finding ways to effectively balance one's analytical, creative, and practical abilities. (Module 20)

Theory-Based Validity. Type of validity evidence that demonstrates the test score is consistent with a theoretical aspect of the construct. (Module 25)

Three-Ring Conception of Giftedness. A theoretical model of giftedness, proposed by Joseph Renzulli, that giftedness is composed of three behaviors: above-average ability, high levels of task commitment, and high levels of creativity. (Module 20)

Top-Down Processing. Conscious use of our prior knowledge, expectations, or context to perceive stimuli. (Module 10)

Total Points Method. A method of criterion-referenced grading in which teachers decide the total amount of points to be earned across a set of assessments, then assign letter grades for the subject based on the number of total points a student accumulated over a marking period. (Module 23)

Transfer. The application of previously learned knowledge, skills, or strategies to new contexts. (Module 12)

Transitional Bilingual Education. A method of bilingual instruction in which students learn subjects in their native language (as well as English-language instruction) while they are acquiring the second language. (Module 7)

T-Score. Type of standard score based on the units of standard deviation with a mean of 50 and standard deviation of 10. (Module 25)

Two-Factor Theory of Intelligence. One of the first theories of intelligence, which posited that performance on intelligence tests could be attributed to a general mental ability, *g,* and abilities in specific domains, *s.* See also other theories of intelligence: theory of multiple intelligences and theory of successful intelligence. (Module 20)

Two-Way Immersion. A method of bilingual instruction in which students who speak English and students who speak a non-English language are combined in one class to learn academic subjects in both languages. (Module 7)

U

Unconditioned Response. The behavior that automatically occurs due to an unconditioned stimulus. (Module 8)

Unconditioned Stimulus. The behavior that evokes an automatic response. (Module 8)

Underextensions. Limiting the use of a word to a subset of objects it refers to. (Module 7)

Uninvolved Parenting. Lacks both control and responsiveness. (Module 2)

Utility Value. A component of expectancy-value theory referring to the usefulness of a task for meeting short-term and long-term goals. (Module 15)

V

Validity. The extent to which a test or assessment actually measures what it is intended to measure, so that meaningful interpretations can be derived from the test score. (Module 23; Module 24; Module 25)

Value. A component of expectancy-value theory referring to reasons for undertaking a task; "do I want to do this task?" See also expectancy. (Module 15)

Variability. Measure of how widely scores are distributed. (Module 25)

Variables. The events, characteristics, or behaviors of interest in a research study. (Module 1)

Vicarious Punishment. Behaviors are displayed less frequently if a model has been punished for those behaviors. (Module 9)

Vicarious Reinforcement. Behaviors are displayed more frequently if a model has been reinforced for those behaviors. (Module 9)

Visual Perspective-Taking. Understanding that another person can see something in a different way or from a different view than one's own. (Module 11)

Visuospatial Sketchpad. A subsystem of Baddeley's model of working memory responsible for briefly processing visual information. (Module 10)

Volunteer Bias. The tendency for those who choose to participate in research studies to be different in some way from others who decline the invitation to participate. (Module 1)

W

Well-Defined Problem. A problem with a clear initial state, goal, and constraints with only one correct answer. (Module 13)

Wernicke's Area. Part of the left temporal lobe of the brain that surrounds the auditory cortex and is thought to be essential for understanding and formulating speech. Damage in Wernicke's area causes deficits in understanding spoken language. (Module 5)

Within-Class Ability Grouping. Forming groups of students in a self-contained classroom in which groups are of similar ability. (Module 19)

Withitness. A teacher's ability to remain aware of and responsive to students' behaviors at all times. (Module 17)

Word Recognition. The act of identifying or recognizing individual words while reading. (Module 21)

Work-Avoidance Goal. Motivation to avoid academic work and prefer easy tasks. (Module 15)

Working Memory. The memory system that temporarily holds information from sensory memory that we are attending to, until the information is either no longer attended to or moved to long-term memory (also referred to as short-term memory). (Module 10)

Working-Backward Strategy. A heuristic in which you start with the end goal and determine the steps needed by thinking backward (Module ,)

Z

Zero Transfer. Occurs when previous learning has no effect on a new task. (Module 12,)

Zone of Proximal Development (ZPD). The difference between what an individual can accomplish independently and what he or she can learn with assistance from more capable individuals. (Module 6,)

Z-Score. Standard score based on units of standard deviation ranging from -4.0 to +4.0. (Module 25,)

REFERENCES

Module 1

Caro, D. H., McDonald, J. T., & Willms, J. D. (2009). Socio-economic status and academic achievement trajectories from childhood to adolescence. *Canadian Journal of Education, 32*(3), 558–590.

Council of Chief State School Officers. (2011, April). Interstate Teacher Assessment and Support Consortium (InTASC) Model Core Teaching Standards: A Resource for State Dialogue. Washington, DC: Author. Retrieved from http://www.ccsso.org/Documents/2011/InTASC_Model_Core_Teaching_Standards_2011.pdf

Dawson-McClure, S., Calzada, E., Huang, K., Kamboukos, D., Rhule, D., Kolawole, B., . . . Brotman, L. M. (2015). A population-level approach to promoting healthy child development and school success in low-income, urban neighborhoods: Impact of parenting and child conduct problems. *Preventive Science, 16,* 279–290.

Doyle, A., & Aboud, F. (1995). A longitudinal study of white children's racial prejudice as a social cognitive development. *Merrill-Palmer Quarterly, 41,* 213–223.

Garcia-Mila, M., & Anderson, C. (2008). Argumentation in science education: An overview. In S. Erduran & M. P. Jiménez-Aleixandre (Eds.), *Argumentation in science education: Perspectives from classroom-based research* (pp. 3–28). New York, NY: Springer.

Goodman, R., & Burton, D. (2012). What is the nature of the achievement gap, why does it persist and are government goals sufficient to create social justice in the education system? *Education 3–13: International Journal of Primary, Elementary and Early Years Education, 40*(5), 500–514.

Katz, P. A. (2003). Racists or tolerant multiculturalists? How do they begin? *American Psychologist, 58,* 897–909.

Mercier, H. (2011). Reasoning serves argumentation in children. *Cognitive Development, 26,* 177–191.

Monteiro, M. B., de França, D. X., & Rodrigues, R. (2009). The development of intergroup bias in childhood: How social norms can shape children's racial behaviours. *International Journal of Psychology, 44*(1), 29–39.

Moya, P. M. L., & Markus, H. R. (2010). Doing race: An introduction. In H. R. Markus & P. M. Moya (Eds.), *Doing race: 21 essays for the 21st century* (pp. 1–102). New York, NY: W. W. Norton.

National Center for Education Statistics. (2015, February). *Early high school dropouts: What are their characteristics?* (Report No. NCES-2015-066). Washington, DC: U.S. Department of Education, Office of Educational Research and Improvement.

Nickerson, R. S. (1998). Confirmation bias: A ubiquitous phenomenon in many guises. *Review of General Psychology, 2*(2), 175–220.

Raabe, T., & Beelmann, A. (2011). Development of ethnic, racial and national prejudice in childhood and adolescence: A multinational meta-analysis of age differences. *Child Development, 82*(6), 1715–1737.

Sanetti, L. M. H., Collier-Meek, M. A., Long, A. C. J., Kim, J., & Kratochwill, T. R. (2014). Using implementation planning to increase teachers' adherence and quality to behavior support plans. *Psychology in the Schools, 51*(8), 879–895.

Savion, L. (2009). Clinging to discredited beliefs: The larger cognitive story. *Journal of the Scholarship of Teaching and Learning, 9*(1), 81–92.

Spencer, S. (2014). *Race and ethnicity: Culture, identity, and representation* (2nd ed.). New York, NY: Taylor & Francis.

Module 2

Adler, P. A., & Adler, P. (1998). *Peer power: Preadolescent culture and identity.* New Brunswick, NJ: Rutgers University Press.

Amato, P. R., & Cheadle, J. E. (2008). Parental divorce, marital conflict and children's behavior problems: A comparison of adopted and biological children. *Social Forces, 86*(3), 1139–1161.

Amato, P. R., Kane, J. B., & James, S. (2011). Reconsidering the "good divorce." *Family Relations, 60*(5), 511–524.

Amato, P. R., & Keith, B. (1991). Parental divorce and the well-being of children: A meta-analysis. *Psychological Bulletin, 110*(1), 26–46.

Bagwell, C. L., Coie, J. D., Terry, R. A., & Lochman, J. E. (2000). Peer clique participation and social status in preadolescence. *Merrill-Palmer Quarterly, 46,* 280–305.

Bagwell, C. L., & Schmidt, M. E. (2011). *Friendships in childhood and adolescence.* New York, NY: Guilford Press.

Barone, F. J. (1997). Bullying in school: It doesn't have to happen. *Phi Delta Kappan, 79,* 80–82.

Bascoe, S. M., Davies, P. T., Cummings, E. M., & Sturge-Apple, M. L. (2009). Children's representations of family relationships, peer information processing, and school adjustment. *Developmental Psychology, 45*(6), 1740–1751.

Baumrind, D. (1966). Effects of authoritative parental control and child behavior. *Child Development, 37,* 887–907.

Becker, S. J., & Curry, J. F. (2014). Testing the effects of peer socialization versus selection on alcohol and marijuana use among treated adolescents. *Substance Use and Misuse, 49*(3), 234–242.

Beeri, A., & Lev-Wiesel, R. (2012). Social rejection by peers: A risk factor for psychological distress. *Child and Adolescent Mental Health, 17*(4), 216–221.

Bellmore, A. (2011). Peer rejection and unpopularity: Associations with GPAs across the transition to middle school. *Journal of Educational Psychology, 103*(2), 282–295.

Belsky, J., Vandell, D. L., Burchinal, M., Clarke-Stewart, K. A., McCartney, K., & Owen, M. T. (2007). Are there long-term effects of early child care? *Child Development, 78,* 681–701.

Bing, N. M., Nelson, W. M. III., & Wesolowski, K. L. (2009). Comparing the effects of amount of conflict on children's adjustment following parental divorce. *Journal of Divorce and Remarriage, 50*(3), 159–171.

Borman, G. D., & Dowling, M. (2010). Schools and inequality: A multilevel analysis of Coleman's equality of educational opportunity data. *Teacher College Record, 112*(5), 1201–1246.

Brechwald, W. A., & Prinstein, M. J. (2011). Beyond homophily: A decade of advances in understanding peer influence processes. *Journal of Research on Adolescence, 21*(1), 166–179.

Bronfenbrenner, U. (1994). Ecological models of human development. *International Encyclopedia of Education, 3,* 1643–1647.

Bronfenbrenner, U. (2005). *Making human beings human: Bioecological perspectives on human development.* Thousand Oaks, CA: SAGE.

Brooks-Gunn, J., Han, W. J., & Waldfogel, J. (2002). Maternal employment and child cognitive outcomes in the first three years of life: The NICHD study of early child care. *Child Development, 73,* 1052–1072.

Brown, B. B. (1990). Peer groups and peer cultures. In S. S. Feldman & F. R. Elliot (Eds.), *At the threshold: The developing adolescent.* Cambridge, MA: Harvard University Press.

Brown, B. B. (2004). Adolescents' relationships with peers. In R. M. Lerner & L. Steinberg (Eds.), *Handbook of adolescent psychology* (2nd ed., pp. 363–394). New York, NY: Wiley.

Brown, B. B., & Braun, M. T. (2013). Peer relations. In C. Proctor & P. A. Linley (Eds.), *Research applications, and interventions for children and adolescents: A positive psychology perspective* (pp. 149–164). New York, NY: Springer.

Brown, B. B., & Klute, C. (2006). Friendships, cliques, and crowds. In G. R. Adams & M. D. Berzonsky (Eds.), *Blackwell handbook of adolescence* (pp. 330–348). Oxford, UK: Blackwell.

Brown, B. B., & Larson, J. (2009). Peer relationships in adolescence. In R. M. Lerner & L. Steinberg (Eds.), *Handbook of adolescent development* (Vol. 2, pp. 74–103). New York, NY: Wiley.

Burchinal, M. R., Lowe Vandell, D., & Belsky, J. (2014). Is the prediction of adolescent outcomes from early child care moderated by later maternal sensitivity? Results from the NICHD study of early child care and youth development. *Developmental Psychology, 50*(2), 542–553.

Burr, J. E., Ostrov, J. M., Jansen, E. A., Cullerton-Sen, C., & Crick, N. R. (2005). Relational aggression and friendship during early childhood: "I won't be your friend!" *Early Education and Development, 16*(2), 161–183.

Chen, C., & Stevenson, H. W. (1995). Motivation and mathematics achievement: A comparative study of Asian-American, Caucasian-American, and East Asian high school students. *Child Development, 66,* 1215–1234.

Choi, N., Chang, M., Kim, S., & Reio, T. G. (2015). A structural model of parent involvement with demographic and academic variables. *Psychology in the Schools, 52*(2), 154–167.

Cillessen, A. H. N., & Rose, A. J. (2005). Understanding popularity in the peer system. *Current Directions in Psychological Science, 14*(2), 102–105.

Copen, C. E., Daniels, K., Vespa, J., & Mosher, W. D. (2012). First marriages in the United States: Data from the 2006–2010 National Survey of Family Growth. *National Health Statistics Reports, 49,* 1–22.

Crick, N. R., & Grotpeter, J. K. (1995). Relational aggression, gender and social-psychological adjustment. *Child Development, 66,* 710–722.

Crouter, A. C., Bumpus, M. F, Maguire, M. C., & McHale, S. M. (1999). Linking parents' work pressure and adolescent's well-being: Insights into dynamics in dual-earner families. *Developmental Psychology, 35*(6), 1453–1461.

Crouter, A. C., & McHale, S. (2005). The long arm of the job revisited: Parenting in dual-earner families. In T. Luster & L. Okagaki (Eds.), *Parenting: An Ecological Perspective* (2nd ed., pp. 275–296). Mahwah, NJ: Lawrence Erlbaum.

Davies, P. T., & Windle, M. (2001). Interparental discord and adolescent adjustment trajectories: The potentiating and protective role of intrapersonal attributes. *Child Development, 72*(4), 1163–1178.

de Bruyn, E. H., & Cillessen, A. H. N. (2006). Popularity in early adolescence: Prosocial and antisocial subtypes. *Journal of Adolescent Research, 21*(6), 607–627.

De la Torre-Cruz, M. J., García-Linares, M. C., & Casanova-Arias, P. F. (2014). Relationship between parenting styles and aggressiveness in adolescents. *Electronic Journal of Research in Educational Psychology, 12*(1), 147–170.

Demo, D. H., & Acock, A. C. (1996). Family structure, family process, and adolescent well-being. *Journal of Research on Adolescence, 6,* 457–488.

Denham, S. A., Blair, K. A., DeMulder, E., Levitas, J., Sawyer, K., Auerbach-Major, S., & Queenan, P. (2003). Preschool emotional competence: Pathway to social competence? *Child Development, 74*(1), 238–256.

Dijkstra, J. K., Lindenberg, S., Verhulst, F. C., Ormel, J., & Vennstra, R. (2009). The relation between popularity and aggressive, destructive, and norm-breaking behaviors: Moderating effects of athletic abilities, physical attractiveness, and prosociality. *Journal of Research on Adolescence, 19*(3), 401–413.

Dornbusch, S. M., Carlsmith, J. M, Bushwall, S. J., Ritter, P. L, Leiderman, H., Hastorf, A. H., & Gross, R. T. (1985). Single parents, extended households, and the control of adolescents. *Child Development, 56,* 326–341.

Duchesne, S., & Ratelle, C. (2010). Parental behaviors and adolescents' achievement goals at the beginning of middle school: Emotional problems as potential mediators. *Journal of Educational Psychology, 102*(2), 497–507.

Eamon, M. K. (2001). Poverty, parenting, peer and neighborhood influences on young adolescent antisocial behavior. *Journal of Social Service Research, 28*(1), 1–23.

Esmaeili, N. S., Yaacob, S. N., Juhari, R., & Mansor, M. (2011). Post-divorce parental conflict, economic hardship and academic achievement among adolescents of divorced families. *Asian Social Science, 7*(12), 119–124.

Estell, D. B., Farmer, T. W., Irvin, M. J., Crowther, A., Akos, P., & Boudah, D. J. (2009). Students with exceptionalities and the peer group context of bullying and victimization in late elementary school. *Journal of Child and Family Studies, 18,* 136–150.

Farmer, T. W., Estell, D. B., Bishop, J. L., O'Neal, K. K., & Cairns, B. D. (2003). Rejected bullies or popular leaders? The social relations of aggressive subtypes of rural African American early adolescents. *Developmental Psychology, 39*(6), 992–1004.

Farmer, T. W., Hall, C. M., Petrin, R., Hamm, J. V., & Dadisman. (2010). Evaluating the impact of a multicomponent interventional model on teachers' awareness of social networks at the beginning of middle school in rural communities. *School Psychology Quarterly, 25*(2), 94–106.

Fine, M. A., & Harvey, J. H. (2006). Divorce and relationship dissolution in the 21st century. In M. A. Fine & J. H. Harvey (Eds.), *Handbook of Divorce and Remarriage* (pp. 3–11). Mahwah, MJ: Lawrence Erlbaum.

Flashman, J. (2012). Academic achievement and its impact on friend dynamics. *Sociology of Education, 85*(1), 61–80.

Forehand, R., Thomas, A. M., Wierson, M., Brody, G., & Fauber, R. (1990). Role of maternal functioning and parenting skills in adolescent functioning following parental divorce. *Journal of Abnormal Psychology, 99*(3), 278–283.

Hamm, J. V. (2000). Do birds of a feather flock together? The variable bases for African American, Asian American and European American adolescents' selection of similar friends. *Developmental Psychology, 36*(2), 209–219.

Hartup, W. W. (1996). The company they keep: Friendships and their developmental significance. *Child Development, 67,* 1–13.

Hatfield, B. E., Lower, J. K., Cassidy, D. J., & Faldowski, R. A. (2015). Inequities in access to quality early care and education: Associations with funding and community context. *Early Childhood Research Quarterly, 30*(B), 316–326.

Helms, S. W., Choukas-Bradley, S., Giletta, M., Cohen, G. L., & Prinstein, M. J. (2014). Adolescents misperceive and are influenced by high-status peers' health risk, deviant, and adaptive behavior. *Developmental Psychology, 50*(12), 2697–2714.

Hetherington, E. M. (1991). The role of individual differences and family relationships in children's coping with divorce and remarriage. In P. A. Cowan & M. Hetherington (Eds.), *Family transitions* (pp. 165–194). Hillsdale, NJ: Lawrence Erlbaum.

Hetherington, E. M. (1993). An overview of the Virginia longitudinal study of divorce and remarriage with a focus on early adolescence. *Journal of Family Psychology, 7*(1), 39–56.

Hetherington, E. M., Bridges, M., & Insabella, G. M. (1998). What matters? What does not? Five perspectives on the association between marital transitions and children's adjustment. *American Psychologist, 53*(2), 167–184.

Hetherington, E. M., Henderson, S. H., Reiss, D., Anderson, E. R., Bridges, M., Chan, R. W., . . . Taylor, L. C. (1999). Adolescent siblings in stepfamilies: Family functioning and adolescent adjustment. *Monographs of the Society for Research in Child Development, 64*(4, Serial No. 295).

Hoffman, L. W. (1974). Effects of maternal employment on the child—A review of the research. *Developmental Psychology, 10*(2), 204–228.

Jeynes, W. H. (2008). Effects of parental involvement on experiences of discrimination and bullying. *Marriage and Family Review, 43*(3/4), 255–268.

Jones, M. H., Audley-Piotrowski, S. R., & Kiefer, S. M. (2011). Relationships among adolescents' perceptions of friends' behaviors, academic self-concept, and math performance. *Journal of Educational Psychology, 104*(1), 19–31.

Kang, Y., & Moore, J. (2011). Parenting style and adolescents' school performance in mainland China. *US-China Education Review, B1,* 133–138.

Kurdek, L. A., & Sinclair, R. J. (1988). Relation of eighth graders' family structure, gender, and family environment with academic performance and school behavior. *Journal of Educational Psychology, 80*(1), 90–94.

Ladd, G. W. (2013). Peer influences in elementary school. In J. Hattie & E. M. Anderman (Eds.), *International guide to student achievement* (pp. 205–207). New York, NY: Taylor & Francis.

LaFontana, K. M., & Cillessen, A. H. N. (2002). Children's perceptions of popular and unpopular peers: A multi-method assessment. *Developmental Psychology, 38,* 635–647.

Li, Y., & Wright, M. F. (2012). Adolescents' social status goals: Relationships to social status insecurity, aggression, and prosocial behavior. *Journal of Youth and Adolescence, 43,* 146–160.

Lucas-Thompson, R. G., Goldberg, W. A., & Prause, J. (2010). Maternal work early in the lives of children and its distal associations with achievement and behavior problems: A meta-analysis. *Psychological Bulletin, 136*(6), 915–942.

Luyckx, K., Tildesley, E. A., Soenens, B., Andrews, J. A., Hampson, S. E., Peterson, M., & Duriez, B. (2011). Parenting and trajectories of children's maladaptive behaviors: A 12-year prospective community study. *Journal of Clinical Child & Adolescent Psychology, 40*(3), 468–478.

Mandara, J. (2006). The impact of family functioning on African American males' academic achievement: A review and clarification of the empirical literature. *Teachers College Record, 108*(2), 206–223.

Mathieson, L. C., & Crick, N. R. (2010). Reactive and proactive subtypes of relational and physical aggression in middle childhood: Links to concurrent and longitudinal adjustment. *School Psychology Review, 39*(4), 601–611.

McCartney, K., Burchinal, M., Clarke-Steward, A., Bub, K. L., Owen, M. T., Belsky, J. & NICHD Early Child Care Research Network. (2010). Testing a series of causal propositions relating time in child care to children's externalizing behavior. *Developmental Psychology, 46*(1), 1–17.

Nair, H., & Murray, A. D. (2005). Predictors of attachment security in preschool children from intact and divorced families. *The Journal of Genetic Psychology, 166*(3), 245–263.

Naumann, L. P., Guillaume, E. M., & Funder, D. C. (2012). The correlates of high parental academic expectations: An Asian-Latino comparison. *Journal of Cross-Cultural Psychology, 43*(4), 515–520.

Nesdale, D., & Pickering, K. (2006). Teachers' reactions to children's aggression. *Social Development, 15*(1), 109–127.

Newman, B. M., & Newman, P. R. (2001). Group identity and alienation: Giving the we its due. *Journal of Youth and Adolescence, 30,* 515–538.

Nyarko, K. (2011). The influence of authoritative parenting style on adolescents' academic achievement. *American Journal of Social and Management Sciences, 2*(3), 278–282.

Ogbu, J. U. (1994). Racial stratification and education in the United States: Why inequality persists. *Teachers College Record, 96*(2), 264–298.

Ogbu, J. U. (2003). *Black American students in an affluent suburb: A study of academic disengagement.* Mahwah, NJ: Lawrence Erlbaum.

Ojanen, T., & Findley-Van Nostrand, D. (2014). Social goals, aggression, peer preference, and popularity: Longitudinal links during middle school. *Developmental Psychology, 50*(8), 2134–2143.

Ostrov, J. M., & Crick, N. R. (2007). Forms and functions of aggression during early childhood: A short-term longitudinal study. *School Psychology Review, 36*(1), 22–43.

Platt, B., Kadosh, K. C., & Lau, J. T. F. (2013). The role of peer rejection in adolescent depression. *Depression and Anxiety, 30,* 809–821.

Pluess, M., & Belsky, J. (2010). Differential susceptibility to parenting and quality of child care. *Developmental Psychology, 46*(2), 379–390.

Pong, S. (1997). Family structure, school context, and eighth-grade math and reading achievement. *Journal of Marriage and the Family, 59*(3), 734–746.

Pong, S. (1998). The school compositional effect of single parenthood on 10th-grade achievement. *Sociology of Education, 71*(1), 23–43.

Pong, S., Johnston, J., & Chen, V. (2009). Authoritarian parenting and Asian adolescent school performance: Insights from the US and Taiwan. *International Journal of Behavioral Development, 34*(1), 62–72.

Potter, D. (2010). Psychosocial well-being and the relationship between divorce and children's academic achievement. *Journal of Marriage and Family, 72*(4), 933–946.

Prinstein, M. J., & La Greca, A. M. (2002). Peer crowd affiliation and internalizing distress in childhood and adolescence: A longitudinal follow-back study. *Journal of Research on Adolescence, 12*(3), 325–351.

Puckett, M. B., Aikins, J. W., & Cillessen, A. H. N. (2008). Moderators of the association between relational aggression and perceived popularity. *Aggressive Behavior, 34*(6), 563–576.

Risser, S. D. (2013). Relational aggression and academic performance in elementary school. *Psychology in the Schools, 50*(1), 13–26.

Rose, A. J., Swenson, L. P., & Carlson, W. (2004). Friendships of aggressive youth: Considering the influences of being disliked and of being perceived as popular. *Journal of Experimental Child Psychology, 88,* 25–45.

Santiago, C. D., Wadsworth, M. E., & Stump, J. (2011). Socioeconomic status, neighborhood disadvantage, and poverty-related stress: Prospective effects of psychological syndromes among diverse low-income families. *Journal of Economic Psychology, 32,* 218–230.

Sarigiani P. A., & Spierling, T. (2011). Sleeper effect of divorce. In S. Goldstein & J. A. Naglieri (Eds.), *Encyclopedia of child behavior and development* (pp. 1378–1385). New York, NY: Springer.

Scarr, S. (1998). American child care today. *American Psychologist, 53,* 95–108.

Schaefer, D. R., Simpkins, S. D., Vest, A. E., & Price, C. D. (2011). The contribution of extracurricular activities to adolescent friendships: New insights through social network analysis. *Developmental Psychology, 47*(4), 1141–1152.

Shek, D. T. L. (2005). Paternal and maternal influences on the psychological well-being, substance abuse, and delinquency of Chinese adolescents experience economic disadvantage. *Journal of Clinical Psychology, 61*(3), 219–234.

Simons-Morton, B., & Chen, R. (2009). Peer and parent influences on school engagement among early adolescents. *Youth and Society, 41*(1), 3–25.

Steinberg, L. S. (1996). *Beyond the classroom: Why school reform has failed and what parents need to do.* New York, NY: Simon & Schuster.

Sullivan, T. N., Farrell, A. D., & Kliewer, W. (2006). Peer victimization in early adolescence: Association between physical and relational victimization and drug use, aggression, and delinquent behaviors among urban middle school students. *Development and Psychopathology, 18,* 119–137.

Sun, Y., & Li, Y. (2009). Postdivorce family stability and changes in adolescents' academic performance. *Journal of Family Issues, 30*(11), 1527–1555.

Sun, Y., & Li, Y. (2011). Effects of family structure type and stability on children's academic performance trajectories. *Journal of Marriage and Family, 73,* 541–556.

Sussman, S., Pokhrel, P., Ashmore, R. D., & Brown, B. B. (2007). Adolescent peer group identification and characteristics: A review of the literature. *Addictive Behaviors, 32,* 1602–1627.

Vaillancourt, T., & Hymel, S. (2006). Aggression and social status: The moderating roles of sex and peer-valued characteristics. *Aggressive Behavior, 32,* 396–408.

Vandell, D. L., Belsky, J., Burchinal, M., Steinberg, L., & Vandergrift, N. (2010). Do effects of early child care extend to age 15 years? Results from the NICHD study of early child care and youth development. *Child Development, 81*(3), 737–756.

Walker, J. M. T., & Hoover-Dempsey, K. V. (2006). Research on parental involvement important to classroom management. In C. M. Evertson & C. S. Weinstein (Eds.), *Handbook of classroom management: Research, practice, and contemporary issues.* Mahwah, NJ: Lawrence Erlbaum.

Werner, N. E., & Crick, N. R. (2004). Maladaptive peer relationships and the development of relational and physical aggression during middle childhood. *Social Development, 13*(4), 495–514.

Windle, M., Brener, N., Cuccaro, P., Dittus, P., Kanouse, D. E., Murray, N., . . . Schuster, M. A. (2010). Parenting predictors of early-adolescents' health behaviors: Simultaneous group comparisons across sex and ethnic groups. *Journal of Youth and Adolescence, 39,* 594–606.

Xie, H., Cairns, B. D., & Cairns, R. B. (2005). The development of aggressive behaviors among girls: Measurement issues, social functions, and differential trajectories. In D. J. Pepler, K. C. Madsen, C. Webster, & K. S. Levene (Eds.), *The development and treatment of girlhood aggression.* Mahwah, NJ: Lawrence Erlbaum.

Xie, H., & Shi, B. (2009). Gender similarities and differences in preadolescent peer groups. *Merrill-Palmer Quarterly, 55*(2), 157–183.

Youniss, J., McLellan, J. A., & Strouse, D. (1994). "We're popular, but we're not snobs": Adolescents describe their crowds. In R. Montemayor, G. R. Adams, & T. P. Gullotta (Eds.), *Personal relationships during adolescence* (pp. 101–122). Thousand Oaks, CA: SAGE.

Yu, T., Pettit, G. S., Lansford, J. E., Dodge, K. A., & Bates, J. E. (2010). The interactive effects of marital conflict and divorce on parent-adult children's relationships. *Journal of Marriage and Family, 72*(2), 282–292.

Zimmer-Genbeck, M. J., Nesdale, D., McGregor, L., Mastro, S., Goodwin, B., & Downey, G. (2013). Comparing reports of peer rejection: Associations with rejection sensitivity, victimization, aggression, and friendship. *Journal of Adolescence, 36,* 1237–1246.

Module 3

Allington, R. (1980). Teacher interruption behaviors during primary-grade oral reading. *Journal of Educational Psychology, 71,* 371–377.

Anthony, L. G., Anthony, B. J., Glanville, D. N., Naiman, D. Q., Waanders, C., & Shaffer, S. (2005). The relationships between parenting stress, parenting behaviour and preschoolers' social competence and behaviour problems in the classroom. *Infant and Child Development, 14,* 133–154.

Arnold, D. H., Kupersmidt, J. B., Voegler-Lee, M. E., & Marshall, N. A. (2012). The association between preschool children's social functioning and their emergent academic skills. *Early Childhood Research Quarterly, 27,* 376–386.

Attili, G., Vermigli, P., & Roazzi, A. (2010). Children's social competence, peer status, and the quality of mother-child and father-child relationships: A multidimensional scaling approach. *European Psychologist, 15*(1), 23–33.

Bachman, J. G., O'Malley, P. M., Freedman-Doan, P., Trzesniewski, K. H., & Donnellan, M. B. (2011). Adolescent self-esteem: Differences by race/ethnicity, gender, and age. *Self-Identity, 10*(4), 445–473.

Bem, S. L. (1974). The measurement of psychological androgyny. *Journal of Consulting and Clinical Psychology, 42,* 115–162.

Bem, S. L. (1975). Sex role adaptability: One consequence of psychological androgyny. *Journal of Personality and Social Psychology, 31,* 634–643.

Benner, A. D., & Crosnoe, R. (2011). The racial/ethnic composition of elementary schools and young children's academic and socioemotional functioning. *American Educational Research Journal, 48*(3), 621–646.

Bohlmann, N. L., & Weinstein, R. S. (2013). Classroom, context, teacher expectations, and cognitive level: Predicting children's math ability judgments. *Journal of Applied Developmental Psychology, 34,* 288–298.

Bornholt, L. J. (2005). Aspects of self-knowledge about activities: An integrated model of self-concepts. *European Journal of Psychological Assessment, 21*(3), 156–164.

Bornholt, L. J., & Wilson, R. (2007). A general mediated model of aspects of self-knowledge (M-ASK): Children's participation in learning activities across social contexts. *Applied Psychology: An International Review, 56*(2), 302–318.

Bowlby, J. (1969). *Attachment and loss, vol. 1. Attachment.* New York, NY: Basic Books.

Bowlby, J. (1973). *Attachment and loss, vol. 2. Separation.* New York, NY: Basic Books.

Brown, C. S., & Chu, H. (2012). Discrimination, ethnic identity, and academic outcomes of Mexican immigrant children: The importance of school context. *Child Development, 83*(5), 1477–1485.

Byrne, B. M., & Shavelson, R. J. (1986). On the structure of adolescent self-concept. *Journal of Educational Psychology, 78,* 474–481.

Cairns, R. (1986). A contemporary perspective on social development. In P. S. Strain, M. J. Gurlankick, & H. M. Walker (Eds.), *Children's social behavior: Development, assessment, and modification* (pp. 352–387). Orlando, FL: Academic Press.

Cassidy, J., Jones, J. D., & Shaver, P. R. (2013). Contributions of attachment theory and research: A framework for future research, translation, and policy. *Developmental Psychopathology, 25,* 1415–1434.

Chen, X., Li, D., Li, Z., Li, B., & Liu, M. (2000). Sociable and prosocial dimensions of social competence in Chinese children: Common and unique contributions to social, academic, and psychological adjustment. *Developmental Psychology, 36*(3), 302–214.

Chen, Y., Thompson, M. S., Kromrey, J. D., & Chang, G. H. (2011). Relations of student perceptions of teacher oral feedback with teacher expectancies and student self-concept. *The Journal of Experimental Education, 79*(4), 452–477.

Corenblum, B. (2014). Relationships between racial-ethnic identity, self-esteem and in-group attitudes among first nation children. *Journal of Youth and Adolescence, 43,* 387–404.

Cotugno, A. J. (2009). Social competence and social skills training and intervention for children with autism spectrum disorders. *Journal of Autism & Developmental Disorders, 39,* 1268–1277.

Deci, E. L., Koestner, R., & Ryan, R. M. (1999). A meta-analytic review of experiments examining the effects of extrinsic rewards on intrinsic motivation. *Psychological Bulletin, 125*(6), 627–668.

Denham, S. A., Blair, K. A., DeMulder, E., Levitas, J., Sawyer, K, Auerbach-Major, S., & Queenan, P. (2003). Preschool emotional competence: Pathway to social competence? *Child Development, 74*(1), 238–256.

Denham, S. A., Way, E., Kalb, S. C., Warren-Khot, H. K., & Bassett, H. H. (2013). Preschoolers' social information processing and early school success: The challenging situations task. *British Journal of Developmental Psychology, 31,* 180–197.

Ding, Y., Xu, X., Wang, Z., Li, H., & Wang, W. (2014). The relation of infant attachment to attachment and cognitive and behavioral outcomes in early childhood. *Early Human Development, 90,* 459–464.

Dion, K. K., & Dion, K. L. (2004). Gender, immigrant generation, and ethnocultural identity. *Sex Roles, 50*(5/6), 347–355.

Durlak, J. A., Weissberg, R. P., Dymnicki, A. B., Taylor, R. D., & Schellinger, K. B. (2011). The impact of enhancing students' social and emotional learning: A meta-analysis of school-based universal interventions. *Child Development, 82*(1), 405–432.

Dusek, J. B., & McIntyre, J. G. (2006). Self-Concept and self-esteem development. In G. R. Adams & M. D. Berzonsky (Eds.), *Blackwell handbook of adolescence* (pp. 290–310). Malden, MA: Blackwell.

Eisenberg, N., Fabes, R., & Murphy, B. C. (1996). Parents' reactions to children's negative emotions: Relationship to children's social competence and comforting behavior. *Child Development, 67,* 2227–2247.

Eisenberg, N., Martin, C. L., & Fabes, R. (1996). Gender development and gender effects. In D. C. Berliner & R. C. Calfee (Eds.), *Handbook of educational psychology* (pp. 358–396). New York, NY: Macmillan.

Elias, M. J., & Haynes, N. M. (2008). Social competence, social support, and academic achievement in minority, low-income, and urban elementary school children. *School Psychology Quarterly, 23*(4), 474–495.

Elias, M. J., & Weissberg, R. P. (2000). Primary prevention. Educational approaches to enhance social and emotional learning. *Journal of School Health, 70,* 186–190.

Elias, M. J., Zins, J. E., Weissberg, R. P., Frey, K. S., Greenberg, M. T., Haynes, N. M., . . . Shriver, T. P. (1997). *Promoting social and emotional learning: Guidelines for educators.* Alexandria, VA: Association for Supervision and Curriculum Development.

Erikson, E. H. (1980). *Identity and the life cycle.* New York, NY: W. W. Norton. (Original work published 1959)

Falci, C. D. (2011). Self-esteem and mastery trajectories in high school by social class and gender. *Social Science Research, 40,* 586–601.

Gagnon, S. G., Huelsman, T. J., Reichard, A. E., Kidder-Ashley, P., Griggs, M. S., Struby, J., & Bollinger, J. (2014). Help me play! Parental behaviors, child temperament, and preschool peer play. *Journal of Child and Family Studies, 23,* 872–884.

Galambos, N. L., Berenbaum, S. A., & McHale, S. M. (2009). Gender development in adolescence. In R. M. Lerner & L. Steinberg (Eds.), *Handbook of adolescent psychology* (3rd ed., pp. 305–357). New York, NY: Wiley.

Garner, P. W., Jones, D. C., & Miner, J. L. (1994). Social competence among low-income preschoolers: Emotion socialization practices and social cognitive correlates. *Child Development, 65,* 622–637.

Gentile, B., Grabe, S., Dolan-Pascoe, B., Twenge, J. M., Wells, B. E., & Maitino, A. (2009). Gender differences in domain-specific self-esteem: A meta-analysis. *Review of General Psychology, 13*(1), 34–45.

Goleman, D. (1995). *Emotional intelligence.* New York, NY: Bantam Books.

Gray-Little, B., & Hafdahl, A. R. (2000). Factors influencing racial comparisons of self-esteem: A quantitative review. *Psychological Bulletin, 126,* 26–54.

Gresham, F. M., Vance, M. J., & Chenier, J. (2013). Improving academic achievement with social skills. In J. Hattie & E. M. Anderman (Eds.), *International guide to student achievement* (pp. 327–344). New York, NY: Taylor & Francis.

Han, S. S., Catron, T., Weiss, B., & Marciel, K. K. (2005). A teacher-consultation approach to social skills training for pre-kindergarten children: Treatment Model and short-term outcome effects. *Journal of Abnormal Child Psychology, 33,* 681–693.

Harter, S. (1990). Self and identity development. In S. S. Feldman & G. R. Elliott (Eds.), *At the threshold: The developing adolescent* (pp. 352–387). Cambridge, MA: Harvard University Press.

Harter, S. (2012). *The construction of self: Developmental and sociocultural foundations* (2nd ed.). New York, NY: Guilford Press.

Harter, S., Waters, P., & Whitesell, N. R. (1998). Relational self-worth: Differences in perceived worth as a person across interpersonal contexts among adolescents. *Child Development, 69,* 756–766.

Hayashi, H., & Shiomi, Y. (2015). Do children understand that people selectively conceal or express emotion? *International Journal of Behavioral Development, 39*(1), 1–8.

Hope, E. C., Chavous, T. M., Jagers, R. J., & Sellers, R. M. (2013). Connecting self-esteem and achievement: Diversity in academic identification and dis-identification patterns among black college students. *American Educational Research Journal, 50*(5), 1122–1151.

Hubbard, J. A., & Coie, J. D. (1994). Emotional correlates of social competence in children's peer relationships. *Merrill-Palmer Quarterly, 40,* 1–20.

Hwang, H. S., & Matsumoto, D. (2012). Ethnic differences in display rules are mediated by perceived relationship commitment. *Asian American Journal of Psychology, 3*(4), 254–262.

Jaffari-Bimmel, N., Juffer, F., van Ijxendoorn, M. H., Bakermans-Kranenburg, M. J., & Mooijaart, A. (2006). Social development from infancy to adolescence: Longitudinal and concurrent factors in an adoption sample. *Developmental Psychology, 42,* 1143–1153.

Jones, M. H., Irvin, M. J., & Kibe, G. W. (2012). Does geographic setting alter the roles of academically supportive factors? African American adolescents' friendships, math self-concept, and math performance. *The Journal of Negro Education, 81*(4), 319–337.

Jones, S. M., Brown, J. L., & Aber, J. L. (2011). Two-year impacts of a universal school-based social-emotional and literacy intervention: An experiment in translational developmental research. *Child Development, 82*(2), 533–554.

Josselson, R. (1988). The embedded self: I and thou revisited. In D. K. Lapsley & E. C. Power (Eds.), *Self, ego, and identity: Integrative approaches* (pp. 91–108). New York, NY: Springer.

Jussim, L. (2013). Teachers' expectations. In J. Hattie & E. M. Anderman (Eds.), *International guide to student achievement* (pp. 243–246). New York, NY: Taylor & Francis.

Kling, K. C., Hyde, J. S., Showers, C. J., & Buswell, B. N. (1999). Gender differences in self-esteem: A meta-analysis. *Psychological Bulletin, 125,* 470–500.

Kress, J. S., & Elias, M. J. (2013). Consultation to support sustainability of social and emotional learning initiative in schools. *Consulting Psychology Journal: Practice and Research, 65*(2), 149–163.

La Freniere, P., & Sroufe, L. A. (1985). Profiles of peer competence in the preschool interrelations between measures, influence of social ecology, and relation to attachment history. *Developmental Psychology, 21,* 56–69.

Lam, R. S. Y., & Tam, V. C. W. (2011). Correlates of identity statuses among Chinese adolescents in Hong Kong. *International Journal of Adolescent Medical Health, 23*(1), 51–58.

Lester, A. L. (1994). Psychology (5th ed.). Boston, MA: Allyn and Bacon.

Liao, Z., Li, Y., & Su, Y. (2014). Emotion understanding and reconciliation in overt and relational conflict scenarios among preschoolers. *International Journal of Behavioral Development, 38*(2), 111–117.

Liem, G. A. D., Marsh, H. W., Martin, A. J., McInerney, D. M., & Yeung, A. S. (2013). The big-fish-little-pond effect and a national policy of within-school ability streaming: Alternative frames of reference. *American Educational Research Journal, 50*(2), 326–370.

Lindsay, G., Dockrell, J., Letchford, B., & Mackie, C. (2002). Self esteem of children with specific speech and language difficulties. *Child Language Teaching and Therapy, 18,* 125–143.

Luyckx, K., Klimstra, T. A., Schwartz, S. J., & Duriez, B. (2013). Personal identity in college and the work context: Developmental trajectories and psychological functioning. *European Journal of Personality, 27,* 222–237.

Maccoby, E. E. (1990). The role of gender identity and gender constancy in sex-differentiated development.

New Directions for Child Development, 47, 5–20.

MacPhee, D., Farro, S., & Canetto, S. S. (2013). Academic self-efficacy and performance of underrepresented STEM majors: Gender, ethnic, and social class patterns. *Analyses of Social Issues and Public Policy, 13*(1), 347–369.

Marcia, J. E. (1966). Development and validation of ego-identity status. *Journal of Personality and Social Psychology, 3,* 551–558.

Marcia, J. E. (1987). The identity status approach to the study of ego identity development. In T. Honess & K. Yardley (Eds.), *Self and identity: Perspectives across the lifespan.* New York, NY: Routledge & Kegan Paul.

Marcia, J. E. (1994). The empirical study of ego identity. In H. A. Bosma, T. L. G. Graafsma, J. D. Grotevant, & D. J. de Levita (Eds.), *Identity and development: An interdisciplinary approach* (pp. 67–80). Thousand Oaks, CA: SAGE.

Marsh, H. W., Abduljabbar, A. S., Morin, A. J. S., Parker, P., Abdelfattah, F., Nagengast, B., & Abu-Hilal, M. M. (2015). The big-fish-little-pond effect: Generalizability of social comparison processes over two age cohorts from Western, Asian, and Middle Eastern Islamic countries. *Journal of Educational Psychology, 107*(1), 258–271.

Martin, A. J., Marsh, H. W., McInerney, D. M., Green, J., & Dowson, M. (2007). Getting along with teachers and parents: The yields of good relationships for students' achievement motivation and self-esteem. *Australian Journal of Guidance & Counseling, 17,* 109–125.

Matsumoto, D. (2009). Display rules. In H. Reis & S. Sprecher (Eds.), *Encyclopedia of human relationships* (pp. 432–434). Thousand Oaks, CA: SAGE.

Meeus, W. (2011). The study of adolescent identity formation 2000–2010: A review of longitudinal research. *Journal of Research on Adolescence, 21*(1), 75–94.

Moksnes, U. K., & Espnes, G. A. (2013). Self-esteem and life satisfaction in adolescents-gender and age as potential moderators. *Quality of Life Research, 22*(10), 2921–2928.

Moller, E. L., Majdandzic, M., Vriends, N., & Bogels, S. M. (2014). Social referencing and child anxiety: The evolutionary based role of fathers' versus mothers' signals. *Journal of Child and Family Studies, 23,* 1268–1277.

Montroy, J. J., Bowles, R. P., Skibbe, L. E., & Foster, T. D. (2014). Social skills and problem behaviors as mediators of

the relationship between behavioral self-regulation and academic achievement. *Early Childhood Research Quarterly, 29,* 298–309.

Morales, M. I. J., & Zafra, E. L. (2013). The impact of students' perceived emotional intelligence, social attitudes and teacher expectations on academic performance. *Electronic Journal of Research in Educational Psychology, 11*(1), 75–97.

O'Mara, A. J., Marsh, H. W., Craven, R. G., & Debus, R. L. (2006). Do self-concept interventions make a difference? A synergistic blend of construct validation and meta-analysis. *Educational Psychologist, 41,* 181–206.

Orlofsky, J. L., Marcia, J. E., & Lesser, R. M. (1973). Ego identity status and the intimacy versus isolation crisis of young adulthood. *Journal of Personality and Social Psychology, 27,* 211–219.

Ostberg, M., & Hagekull, B. (2013). Parenting stress and external stressors as predictors of maternal ratings of child adjustment. *Scandinavian Journal of Psychology, 54,* 213–221.

Park, K. A., & Walters, E. (1989). Security of attachment and preschool friendships. *Child Development, 60,* 1076–1081.

Parker, A. K. (2010). A longitudinal investigation of young adolescents' self-concepts in the middle grades. *Research in Middle Level Education, 33*(10), 1–13.

Phinney, J. S. (1989). Stages of ethnic identity in minority group adolescents. *Journal of Early Adolescence, 9, 163–173.*

Phinney, J. S. (1990). Ethnic identity in adolescents and adults: Review of research.

Psychological Bulletin, 108(3), 499–514.

Phinney, J. S., & Balderlomar, O. A. (2011). Identity development in multiple cultural contexts. In J. A. Jennsen (Ed.), *Bridging cultural and developmental approaches to psychology: New syntheses in theory, research, and policy* (pp. 161–186). New York, NY: Oxford University Press.

Pickar, D. B., & Tori, C. D. (1986). The learning disabled adolescent: Eriksonian psychosocial development, self-concept, and delinquent behavior. *Journal of Youth and Adolescence, 15*(5), 429–440.

Reese, E., Bird, A., & Tripp, G. (2007). Children's self-esteem and moral self: Links to parent-child conversations regarding emotion. *Social Development, 16*(3), 460–478.

Richardson, R. C., Tolson, H., Huang, T., & Lee, Y. (2009). Character education: Lessons for teaching social and emotional competence. *Child & Schools, 31*(2), 71–78.

Rivas-Drake, D., Syed, M., Umana-Taylor, A., Markstrom, C., French, S., Schwartz, S. J., & Lee, R. (2014). Feeling good, happy, and proud: A meta-analysis of positive ethnic-racial affect an adjustment. *Child Development, 85*(1), 77–102.

Robinson-Cimpian, J. P., Lubienski, S. T., Ganley, C. M., & Copur-Gencturk, Y. (2014). Teachers' perceptions of students' mathematics proficiency may exacerbate early gender gaps in achievement. *Developmental Psychology, 50*(4), 1262–1281.

Rodeiro, C. L. V., Emery, J. L., & Bell, J. F. (2012). Emotional intelligence and academic attainment of British secondary school children: A cross-sectional study. *Educational Studies, 38*(5), 521–539.

Rosenberg, M., Schooler, C., Schoenbach, C., & Rosenberg, F. (1995). Global self-esteem and specific self-esteem: Difference concepts, different outcomes. *American Sociological Review, 60,* 141–156.

Rosenthal, R. (1995). Critiquing Pygmalion: A 25-year perspective. *Current Directions in Psychological Science, 4,* 171–172.

Saarni, C. (1979). Children's understanding of display rules for expressive behavior. *Developmental Psychology, 15,* 424–429.

Seaton, M., Parker, P., Marsh, H. W., Craven, R. G., & Yeung, A. S. (2014). The reciprocal relations between self-concept, motivation and achievement: juxtaposing academic self-concept and achievement goal orientations for mathematics success. *Educational Psychology: An International Journal of Experimental Educational Psychology, 34*(1), 49–72.

Sheridan, S. M., Hungelmann, A., & Maughan, D. P. (1999). A contextualized framework for social skills assessment, intervention, and generalization. *School Psychology Review, 28,* 84–103.

Simmon, R. G. (1987). Self-esteem in adolescence. In T. Honess & K. Yardley (Eds.), *Self and identity: Perspectives across the lifespan* (pp. 172–192). New York, NY: Routledge & Kegan Paul.

Steffens, M. C., Jelenec, P., & Noack, P. (2010). On the leaking math pipeline: Comparing implicit math-gender stereotypes and math withdrawal in female and male children and adolescents. *Journal of Educational Psychology, 102*(4), 947–963. doi:10.037/a0019920

Streitmatter, J. L. (1989). Identity development and academic achievement in early adolescence.

Journal of Early Adolescence, 9, 99–111.

Twenge, J. M., & Campbell, W. K. (2002). Self-esteem and socioeconomic status: A meta-analytic review. *Personality and Social Psychology Review, 6*(1), 59–71.

Twenge, J. M., & Campbell, W. K. (2008). Increases in positive self-views among high school students: Birth-cohort changes in anticipated performance, self-satisfaction, self-liking, and self-competence. *Psychological Science, 19*(11), 1082–1086.

Umana-Taylor, A. J., Gonzales-Backen, M. A., & Guimond, A. B. (2009). Latino adolescents' ethnic identity: Is there a developmental progression and does growth in ethnic identity predict growth in self-esteem? *Child Development, 80*(2), 391–405.

van Laar, C. (2000). The paradox of low academic achievement but high self-esteem in African American students: An attributional account. *Educational Psychology Review, 12*(1), 33–61.

Webster-Stratton, C., & Reid, M. J. (2013). Supporting social and emotional development in preschool children. In V. Buysse & E. S. Peisner-Feinberg (Eds.), *Handbook of response to intervention in early childhood* (pp. 265–282). London, UK: Brookes.

Wilkins, J. L. M. (2004). Mathematics and science self-concept: An internal investigation. *The Journal of Experimental Education, 72*(4), 331–346.

Zins, J. E., Bloodworth, M. R., Weissberg, R. P., & Walberg, H. J. (2004). The scientific base linking social and emotional learning to school success. In J. Zins, M. Bloodworth, R. Weissberg, & H. Walberg (Eds.), *Building academic success on social and emotional learning: What does the research say?* (pp. 3–22). New York, NY: Teachers College Press.

Zorza, J. P., Marino, J., de Lemus, S., & Mesas, A. A. (2013). Academic performance and social competence of adolescents: Predictions based on effortful control and empathy. *Spanish Journal of Psychology, 16,* 1–12.

Module 4

Bacchini, D., Affuso, G., & De Angelis, G. (2013). Moral vs. non-moral attribution in adolescence: Environmental and behavioral correlates. *European Journal of Developmental Psychology, 10*(2), 221–238.

Berkowitz, M. W. (2012). Moral and character education. In K. R. Harris,

S. Graham, T. Urdan, S. Graham, J. M. Royer, & M. Zeidner (Eds.), *APA educational psychology handbook. Vol. 2: Individual differences and cultural and contextual factors* (pp. 247–264). Washington, DC: American Psychological Association.

Berkowitz, M. W., & Grych, J. H. (1998). Fostering goodness: Teaching parents to facilitate children's moral development. *Journal of Moral Education, 27,* 371–391.

Billig, S. H. (2013). Service-learning. In J. Hattie & E. M. Anderman (Eds.), *International guide to student achievement* (pp. 158–160). New York, NY: Taylor & Francis.

Boom, J., Brugman, D., & van der Heijden, P. G. M. (2001). Hierarchical structure of moral stages assessed by a sorting task. *Child Development, 72,* 535–548.

Bradshaw, C. P., Rodgers, C. R. R., Ghandour, L. A., Garbarino, J. (2009). Social-cognitive mediators of the association between community violence exposure and aggressive behavior. *School Psychology Quarterly, 24*(3), 199–210.

Bronstein, P., Fox, B. J., Kamon, J. L., & Knolls, M. L. (2007). Parenting and gender as predictors of moral courage in late adolescence: A longitudinal study. *Sex Roles, 56,* 661–674.

Carlo, G. (2014). The development and correlates of prosocial moral behaviors. In M. Killen & J. Smetana (Eds.), *Handbook of moral development* (2nd ed., pp. 208–234). New York, NY: Psychology Press.

Carpendale, J. I. M. (2000). Kohlberg and Piaget on stages and moral reasoning. *Developmental Review, 20,* 181–205.

Crick, N. R., & Dodge, K. A. (1994). A review and reformulation of social information-processing mechanisms in children's social adjustment. *Psychological Bulletin, 115,* 74–101.

Crick, N. R., & Dodge, K. A. (1996). Social information-processing mechanisms in reactive and proactive aggression. *Child Development, 67,* 993–1002.

Colby, A., & Kohlberg, L. (1987). *The measurement of moral judgment (Vol. 1): Theoretical foundations and research validation.* Cambridge, UK: Cambridge University Press.

Colby, A., Kohlberg, L., Gibbs, J., & Lieberman, M. (1983). A longitudinal study of moral judgment. *Monographs of the Society for Research in Child Development, 48*(1–2, Serial No. 200).

Damon, W. (1988). *The moral child: Nurturing children's natural moral growth.* New York, NY: Free Press.

Dunn, J. (2014). Moral development in early childhood and social interaction in the family. In M. Killen & J. Smetana (Eds.), *Handbook of moral development* (2nd ed., pp. 135–160). New York, NY: Psychology Press.

Eisenberg, N. (1986). *Altruistic emotion, cognition and behavior*. Hillsdale, NJ: Lawrence Erlbaum.

Eisenberg, N., Eggum, N. D., & Di Giunta, L. (2010). Empathy-related responding: Associations with prosocial behavior, aggression, and intergroup relations. *Social Issues and Policy Review, 4*(1), 143–180.

Eisenberg, N., & Fabes, R. A. (1998). Prosocial development. In W. Damon (Series Ed.) & N. Eisenberg (Vol. Ed.), *Handbook of child psychology: Vol. 3. Social, emotional, and personality development* (5th ed., pp. 701–778). New York, NY: Wiley.

Eisenberg, N., Morris, A. S., McDaniel, B., & Sprinrad, T. L. (2009). Moral cognitions and prosocial responding in adolescence. In R. M. Lerner & L. Steinberg (Eds.), *Handbook of adolescent psychology* (3rd ed., Vol. 1, pp. 229–265). New York, NY: Wiley.

Eisenberg, N., Shell, R. Pasternack, J., Lennon, R. Beller, R., & Mathy, R. M. (1987). Prosocial development in middle childhood: A longitudinal study. *Developmental Psychology, 23,* 712–718.

Eisenberg, N., Spinrad, T. L., & Morris, A. (2014). Empathy-related responding in children. In M. Killen & J. Smetana (Eds.), *Handbook of moral development* (2nd ed., pp. 184–207). New York, NY: Psychology Press.

Eisenberg, N., Spinrad, T., & Sadovsky, A. (2006). Empathy-related responding in children. In M. Killen & J. Smetana (Eds.), *Handbook of moral development* (pp. 517–549). Mahwah, NJ: Lawrence Erlbaum.

Espelage, D. L., Low, S., Polanin, J. R., & Brown, E. C. (2013). The impact of a middle school program to reduce aggression, victimization, and sexual violence. *Journal of Adolescent Health, 53,* 180–186.

Fontaine, F. G., Fida, R., Paciello, M., Tisak, M. S., & Caprara, G. V. (2014). The mediating role of moral disengagement in the developmental course from peer rejection in adolescence to crime in early adulthood. *Psychology, Crime, & Law, 20*(1), 1–19.

Gagnon, J., McDuff, P., Daelman, S., & Fournier, S. (2015). Is hostile attributional bias associated with negative urgency and impulsive behaviors? A social-cognitive conceptualization of impulsivity. *Personality and Individual Differences, 72,* 18–23.

Gehlbach, H. (2004). A new perspective on perspective taking: A multidimensional approach to conceptualizing an aptitude. *Educational Psychology Review, 16,* 207–234.

Gibbs, J. C. (1991). Sociomoral developmental delay and cognitive distortion: Implications for the treatment of antisocial youth. In W. M. Kurtines & J. L. Gewirtz (Eds.), *Handbook of moral behavior and development: Application* (Vol. 3, pp. 95–110). Hillsdale, NJ: Lawrence Erlbaum.

Gibbs, J. C., Potter, G. B., & DiBiase, A. (2013). Sociomoral development for behaviorally at-risk youth: Mac's group meeting. In C. Proctor & P. A. Linley (Eds.), *Research, applications, and interventions for children and adolescents: A positive psychology perspective* (pp. 225–245). New York, NY: Springer.

Gilligan, C. (1977). In a different voice: Women's conception of the self and of morality. *Harvard Educational Review, 47,* 481–517.

Hoffman, M. L. (2000). *Empathy and moral development: Implications for caring and justice.* New York, NY: Cambridge University Press.

Jones, S. M., Brown, J. L., & Aber, J. L. (2011). Two-year impacts of a universal school-based social-emotional and literacy intervention: An experiment in translational developmental research. *Child Development, 82*(2), 533–554.

Jorgensen, G. (2006). Kohlberg and Gilligan: Duet or duel? *Journal of Moral Education, 35,* 179–196.

Kanacri, B. P. L., Pastorelli, C., Eisenberg, N., Zuffiano, A., & Caprara, G. V. (2013). The development of prosociality from adolescence to early adulthood: The role of effortful control. *Journal of Personality, 81,* 302–312.

Kaplan, U., Crockett, C. E., & Tivnan, T. (2014). Moral motivation of college students through multiple developmental structures: Evidence of intrapersonal variability in a complex dynamic system. *Motivation and Emotion, 38,* 336–352.

Kohlberg, L. (1963). The development of children's orientations toward moral order: Sequence in the development of moral thought. *Vita Humans, 6,* 11–33.

Kohlberg, L. (1975). The cognitive-developmental approach to moral education. *Phi Delta Kappan, 57,* 670–677.

Kohlberg L. (1981). *Essays in moral development: The philosophy of moral development* (Vol. 1). San Francisco, CA: Harper & Row.

Lam, C. B., Solmeyer, A. R., & McHale, S. M. (2012). Sibling relationships and empathy across the transition to adolescence. *Journal of Youth and Adolescence, 41,* 1657–1670.

Langdon, P. E., Clare, I. C. H., & Murphy, G. H. (2010). Developing an understanding of the literature relating to the moral development of people with intellectual disabilities. *Developmental Review, 30,* 273–293.

Lapsley, D. K. (2006). Moral stage theory. In M. Killen & J. Smetana (Eds.), *Handbook of moral development* (pp. 37–66). Mahwah, NJ: Lawrence Erlbaum.

Lies, J. M., Bock, T., Brandenberger, J., & Trozzolo, T. A. (2012). The effects of off-campus service learning on the moral reasoning of college students. *Journal of Moral Education, 41*(2), 189–199.

Maite, G. (2009). A comparative analysis of empathy in childhood and adolescence: Gender differences and associated socio-emotional variables. *International Journal of Psychology & Psychological Therapy, 9*(2), 217–235.

Malti, T., Eisenberg, N., Kim, H., & Buchman, M. (2013). Developmental trajectories of sympathy moral emotion attributions, and moral reasoning: The role of parental support. *Social Development, 22*(4), 773–793.

Malti, T., Gasser, L., & Buchmann, M. (2009). Aggressive and prosocial children's emotion attributions and moral reasoning. *Aggressive Behavior, 35,* 95–102.

McDonald, K. L., Malti, T., Killen, M., & Rubin, K. H. (2014). Best friends' discussions of social domains. *Journal of Youth and Adolescence, 43,* 233–244.

McDonough, G. P. (2005). Moral maturity and autonomy: Appreciating the significance of Lawrence Kolberg's Just Community. *Journal of Moral Education, 34,* 199–213.

Molano, A., Jones, S. M., Brown, J. L., & Aber, J. L. (2013). Selection and socialization of aggressive and prosocial behavior: The moderating role of social-cognitive processes. *Journal of Research on Adolescence, 23*(3), 424–436.

Murray-Close, D., Crick, N. R., & Galotti, K. M. (2006). Children's moral reasoning regarding physical and relational aggression. *Social Development, 15*(3), 345–372.

Nucci, L. (2006). Education for moral development. In M. Killen & J. Smetana (Eds.), *Handbook of moral development* (pp. 657–682). Mahwah, NJ: Lawrence Erlbaum.

Palmer, E. J. (2005). The relationship between moral reasoning and aggression, and the implications for practice. *Psychology, Crime & law, 11,* 353–361.

Patrick, R. B., & Gibbs, J. C. (2012). Inductive discipline, parental expression of disappointed expectations, and moral identity in adolescence. *Journal of Youth and Adolescence, 41,* 973–983.

Piaget, J. (1932). *The moral judgment of the child.* London, UK: Routledge & Kegan Paul.

Pornari, C., & Wood, J. (2010). Peer and cyber aggression in secondary school students: The role of moral disengagement, hostile attribution bias, and outcome expectancies. *Aggressive Behavior, 36*(2), 81–94.

Rest, J. R., Thomas, S. J., & Edwards, L. (1997). Designing and validating a measure of moral judgment: Stage preference and stage consistency approaches. *Journal of Educational Psychology, 89,* 5–28.

Rizzo, K., & Bosacki, S. (2013). Social cognitive theory and practice of moral development in educational settings. In B. J. Irby, G. Brown, R. Lara-Alecio, & S. Jackson (Eds.), *The handbook of educational theories* (pp. 595–606). Charlotte, NC: Information Age.

Selman, R. L. (1971). The relation of role taking to the development of moral judgment in children. *Child Development, 42,* 79–91.

Shaffer, D. R. (2000). *Social and personality development* (4th ed.). Belmont, CA: Wadsworth.

Speicher, B. (1994). Family patterns of moral judgment during adolescence and early adulthood. *Developmental Psychology, 30,* 624–632.

Spivak, A. L., & Farran, D. C. (2012). First-grade teacher behaviors and children's prosocial actions in classrooms. *Early Education and Development, 23*(5), 623–639.

Solomon, D., Watson, M. S., & Battistich, V. A. (2001). Teaching and schooling effects on moral/prosocial development. In V. Richardson (Ed.), *Handbook for research on teaching* (pp. 566–603). Washington, DC: American Educational Research Association.

Taylor, Z. E., Eisenberg, N., Spinrad, T. L., Eggum, N. D., & Sulik, M. J. (2013). The relations of ego-resiliency and emotion socialization to the development of empathy and prosocial behavior across early childhood. *Emotion, 13*(5), 822–831.

Tisak, M. S., Tisak, J., & Goldstein, S. E. (2006). Aggression, delinquency, and morality: A social-cognitive perspective. In M. Killen & J. Smetana (Eds.), *Handbook of moral development* (pp. 611–632). Mahwah, NJ: Lawrence Erlbaum.

Turiel, E. (1983). *The development of social knowledge: Morality and convention.* San Francisco, CA: Jossey-Bass.

Vaish, A., Carpenter, M., & Tomasello, M. (2009). Sympathy through affective perspective taking and its relation to prosocial behavior in toddlers. *Developmental Psychology, 45*(2), 534–543.

Van Cleemput, K., Vadenbosch, H., & Pabian, S. (2014). Personal characteristics and contextual factors that determine "helping," "joining in," and "doing nothing" when witnessing cyberbullying. *Aggressive Behavior, 40*(5), 383–396.

Walker, L. J. (2006). Gender and morality. In M. Killen & J. Smetana (Eds.), *Handbook of moral development* (pp. 93–115). Mahwah, NJ: Lawrence Erlbaum.

Watson, M., & Ecken, L. (2003). *Learning to trust: Transforming difficult elementary classrooms through developmental discipline.* San Francisco, CA: Jossey-Bass.

Yeager, D. S., Miu, A. S., Powers, J., & Dweck, C. S. (2013). Implicit theories of personality and attributions of hostile intent: A meta-analysis, an experiment, and a longitudinal intervention. *Child Development, 84*(5), 1651–1667.

Module 5

Adolphs, R., Tranel, D., & Damasio, A. R. (1998). The human amygdala in social judgment. *Nature, 393,* 470–473.

Amodio, D. M., & Frith, C. D. (2006). Meeting of minds: The medial frontal cortex and social cognition. *Nature Reviews Neuroscience, 7,* 268–277.

Arsalidou, M., & Taylor, M. J. (2011). Is 2 + 2 = 4? Meta-analyses of brain areas needed for numbers and calculations. *NeuroImage, 54,* 2382–2393.

Ashkenazi, S., Rosenberg-Lee, M., Tenison, C., & Menon, V. (2012). Weak task-related modulation and stimulus representations during arithmetic problem solving in children with developmental dyscalculia. *Developmental Cognitive Neuroscience, 2S,* S152–S166.

Aylward, E. H., Richards, T. L., Berninger, V. W., Nagy, W. E., Field, K. M., Grimme, A. C., . . . Cramer, S. C. (2003). Instructional treatment associated with changes in brain activation in children with dyslexia. *Neurology, 61*(2), 212–219.

Aytaclar, S., Tarter, R. E., Kirisci, L., & Lu, S. (1999). Association between hyperactivity and executive cognitive functioning in childhood and substance use in early adolescence. *Journal of*

the *American Academy of Child and Adolescent Psychiatry, 38,* 172–178.

Baird, A., Fugelsang, J., & Bennett, C. (2005, April). *What were you thinking: An fMRI study of adolescent decision-making.* Poster presented at Cognitive Neuroscience Society meeting, New York, NY.

Barkley, R. A. (1997). Behavioral inhibition, sustained attention, and executive functions: constructing a unifying theory of ADHD. *Psychological Bulletin, 121*(1), 65–94.

Barkley, R. A. (2007). School interventions for attention deficit hyperactivity disorder: Where to from here? *School Psychology Review, 36*(2), 279–286.

Bechara, A., Damasio, H., Tranel, D., & Damasio, A. R. (1997). Deciding advantageously before knowing the advantageous strategy. *Science, 275*(5304), 1293–1295.

Bjorklund, D. F. (2012). *Children's thinking* (5th ed.). Belmont, CA: Cengage.

Blair, C., & Razza, R. P. (2007). Relating effortful control, executive function, and false belief understanding to emerging math and literacy ability in kindergarten. *Child Development, 78,* 647–663.

Blair, R. J. R., Morris, J. S., Frith, C. D., Perrett, D. I., & Dolan, R. J. (1999). Dissociable neural responses to facial expressions of sadness and anger. *Brain, 122,* 883–893.

Blackwell, L. S., Trzesniewski, K., & Dweck, C. S. (2007). Implicit theories of intelligence predict achievement across an adolescent transition: A longitudinal study and an intervention. *Child Development, 78,* 246–263.

Blakemore, S.-J., & Choudhury, S. (2006). Development of the adolescent brain: implications for executive function and social cognition. *Journal of Child Psychology and Psychiatry, and Allied Disciplines, 47*(3–4), 296–312.

Bodini, B., Iacoboni, M., & Lenzi, G. L. (2004). Acute stroke effects on emotions: An interpretation through the mirror system. *Current Opinion in Neurology, 17,* 55–60.

Booth J. R., Burman, D. D., Meyer J. R., Lei, Z., Trommer, B. L., Davenport, N. D., . . . Mesulam, M. M. (2003). Neural development of selective attention and response inhibition. *NeuroImage, 20*(2), 737–751.

Brainerd, C. J. (2003). Jean Piaget, learning research, and American education. In B. J. Zimmerman & D. H. Schunk (Eds.), *Educational psychology: A century of contributions* (pp. 251–287). Mahwah, NJ: Lawrence Erlbaum.

Bruer, J. T. (1997). A bridge too far. *Educational Researcher, 26,* 1–13.

Bunge, S. A., Dudukovic, N. M., Thomason, M. E., Vaidya, C. J., & Gabrielli, J. D. E. (2002). Immature frontal lobe contributions to cognitive control in children: Evidence from fMRI. *Neuron, 33,* 301–311.

Butterworth, B., Varma, S., & Laurillard, D. (2011). Dyscalculia: From brain to education. *Science, 332*(6033), 1049–1053.

Bzdok, D., Schilbach, L., Vogeley, K., Schneider, K., Laird, A. R., Langner, R., & Eickhoff, S. B. (2012). Parsing the neural correlates of moral cognition: ALE meta-analysis on morality, theory of mind, and empathy. *Brain Structure and Function, 217,* 783–796.

Cantlon, J. F., Libertus, M. E., Pinel, P., Dehaene, S., Brannon, E. M., & Pelphrey, K. A. (2008). The neural development of an abstract concept of number. *Journal of Cognitive Neuroscience, 21,* 2217–2229.

Caplan, D. (2006). Why is Broca's area involved in syntax? *Cortex, 42*(4), 469–471.

Carr, L., Iacoboni, M., Dubeau, M. C., Mazziotta, J. C., & Lenzi, G. L. (2003). Neural mechanisms of empathy in humans: A relay from neural systems for imitation to limbic areas. *Proceedings of the National Academy of Science, 100,* 5497–5502.

Casey, B. J., Giedd, J. N., & Thomas, K. M. (2000). Structural and functional brain development and its relation to cognitive development. *Biological Psychology, 54,* 241–257.

Casey B. J., Jones, R. M., & Hare, T. A. (2008). The adolescent brain. *Annals of the New York Academy of Sciences, 1124,* 111–126.

Changeux, J.-P., & Danchin, A. (1976, December 23). Selective stabilisation of developing synapses as a mechanism for the specification of neuronal networks. *Nature, 264,* 705–712.

Chein, J., Albert, D., O'Brien, L., Uckert, K., & Steinberg, L. (2011). Peers increase adolescent risk taking by enhancing activity in the brain's reward circuitry. *Developmental Science, 14,* F1–10.

Chong, S. L., & Siegel, L. S. (2008). Stability of computational deficits in math learning disability from second through fifth grades. *Developmental Neuropsychology, 33*(3), 300–317.

Code, C. (1987). *Language, aphasia, and the right hemisphere.* New York, NY: Wiley.

Cohen, L., & Dehaene, S. (2004). Specialization within the ventral stream: The case for the visual word form area. *NeuroImage, 22,* 466–476.

Crewe, T., Bornkessel, I., Zysset, S., Wiese, R., Yves von Cramon, D., & Schlesewksy, M. (2005). The emergence of the unmarked: A new perspective on the language-specific function of Broca's area. *Human Brain Mapping 26*(3), 178–190.

Dapretto, M., Davies, M. S., Pfeifer, J. H., Scott, A. A., Sigman, M., Bookheimer, S. Y., & Iacoboni, M. (2006). Understanding emotions in others: Mirror neuron dysfunction in children with autism spectrum disorders. *Nature Neuroscience, 9,* 28–30.

Davis, N., Cannistraci, C. J., Rogers, B. P., Gatenby, J. C., Fuchs, L. S., Anderson, A. W., & Gore, J. C. (2009). Aberrant functional activation in school age children at-risk for mathematical disability: A functional imaging study of simple arithmetic skill. *Neuropsychologia, 47,* 2470–2479.

Dawson, P., & Guare, R. (2010). *Executive skills in children and adolescents: A practical guide to assessment and intervention* (2nd ed.). New York, NY: Guilford Press.

Dehaene, S., Cohen, L., Sigman, M., & Vinckier, F. (2005). The neural code for written words: A proposal. *Trends in Cognitive Sciences, 9,* 335–341.

Dehaene, S., Pegado, F., Braga, L. W., Ventura, P., Nunes, F. G., Jobert, A., . . . Cohen, L. (2010). How learning to read changes the cortical networks for vision and language. *Science, 330*(6009), 1359–1364.

Dehaene, S., Piazza, M., Pinel, P., & Cohen, L. (2003). Three parietal circuits for number processing. *Cognitive Neuropsychology, 20,* 487–506.

Dehaene, S., Spelke, E., Pinel, P., Stanescu, R., & Tsivkin, S. (1999). Sources of mathematical thinking: Behavioral and brain-imaging evidence. *Science, 284,* 970–974.

Dickstein, S. G., Bannon, K., Castellanos, F. X., & Milham, M. P. (2006). The neural correlates of attention deficit hyperactivity disorder: An ALE meta-analysis. *Journal of Child Psychology and Psychiatry and Allied Disciplines, 10,* 1051–1062.

Donohoe, C., Topping, K., & Hannah, E. (2012). The impact of an online intervention (Brainology) on the mindset and resiliency of secondary school pupils: A preliminary mixed methods study. *Educational Psychology, 32*(5), 641–655.

Dubinsky, J. M., Roehrig, G., & Varma, S. (2013). Infusing neuroscience into teacher professional development. *Educational Researcher, 42*(6), 317–329.

Duncan, G. J., Dowsett, C. J., Claessens, A., Magnuson, K., Huston, A. C., Klebanov, P., . . . Japel, C. (2007). School readiness and later achievement. *Developmental Psychology, 43,* 1428–1446.

Eisenberg, N., Morris, A. S., McDaniel, B., & Sprinrad, T. L. (2009). Moral cognitions and prosocial responding in adolescence. In R. M. Lerner & L. Steinberg (Eds.), *Handbook of adolescent psychology* (3rd ed., pp. 229–265). New York, NY: Wiley.

Emerson, R. W., & Cantlon, J. F. (2015). Continuity and change in children's longitudinal neural responses to numbers. *Developmental Science, 18,* 314–326.

Fiez J. A. (1997). Phonology, semantics, and the role of the left inferior prefrontal cortex. *Human Brain Mapping, 5,* 79–83.

Fletcher, J. M., Shaywitz, S. E., Shankweiler, D. P., Katz, L., Liberman, I. Y., Stuebing, K. K., . . . Shaywitz, B. A. . (1994). Cognitive profiles of reading disability: Comparisons of discrepancy and low achievement definitions. *Journal of Educational Psychology, 86*(1), 6–23.

Friedman, N. P., Miyake, A., Young, S. E., Defries, J. C., Corley, R. P., & Hewitt, J. K. (2008). Individual differences in executive functions are almost entirely genetic in origin. *Journal of Experimental Psychology: General, 137*(2), 201–225.

Fuster, J. M. (2000). Executive frontal functions. *Experimental Brain Research, 133,* 66–70.

Gallagher, M. (2000). The amygdala and associative learning. In J. P. Aggleton (Ed.), *The amygdala: A functional analysis* (pp. 311–330). New York, NY: Oxford University Press.

Galvan, A., Hare, T., Voss, H., Glover, G., & Casey, B. J. (2007). Risk-taking and the adolescent brain: Who is at risk? *Developmental Science, 10*(2), F8–F14.

Galvan, A., Hare, T. A., Parra, C. E., Penn, J., Voss, K., Glover, G., & Casey, B. J. (2006). Earlier development of the accumbens relative to orbitofrontal cortex might underlie risk-taking behavior in adolescents. *The Journal of Neuroscience, 26*(25), 6885–6892.

Gardner M., & Steinberg, L. (2005). Peer influence on risk taking, risk preference, and risky decision making in adolescence and adulthood: An experimental study. *Developmental Psychology, 41,* 625–635.

Geary, D. C. (1994). *Children's mathematical development: Research and practical applications.* Washington, DC: American Psychological Association.

Giedd, J. N. (2004). Structural magnetic resonance imaging of the adolescent brain. In R. E. Dahl & L. P. Spear (Eds.), *Adolescent brain development: Vulnerabilities and opportunities. Annals of the New York Academy of Sciences* (Vol. 1021, pp. 77–85).

New York, NY: New York Academy of Sciences.

Giedd, J. N., Blumenthal, J., Jeffries, N. O., Castellanos, F. X., Liu, H., Zijdenbos, A., . . . Rapoport, J. L. (1999). Brain development during childhood and adolescence: A longitudinal MRI study. *Nature Neuroscience, 2*(10), 861–863.

Gogtay, N., Sporn, A., Clasen, L. S., Nugent, T. F., Greenstein, D., Nicolson, R., . . . Rapoport, J. L. (2004). Comparison of progressive cortical gray matter loss in childhood-onset schizophrenia with that in childhood-onset atypical psychoses. *Archives of General Psychiatry, 61,* 17–22.

Goswami, U. (2006). Neuroscience and education: from research to practice? *Nature Reviews Neuroscience, 7*(5), 406–411.

Goswami, U. (2008). Principles of learning, implications for teaching: A cognitive neuroscience perspective. *Journal of Philosophy of Education, 42*(3–4), 381–399.

Gu, X., Gao, Z., Wang, X., Liu, X., Knight, R. T., Hof, P. R., . . . Fan, J. (2012). Anterior insular cortex is necessary for empathic pain perception. *Brain, 135,* 2726–2735.

Hamann, S. B., Ely, T. D., Hoffman, J. M., & Kilts, C. D. (2002). Ecstasy and agony: Activation of the human amygdala in positive and negative emotion. *Psychological Science: A Journal of the American Psychological Society/APS, 13*(2), 135–141.

Harnishfeger, K. K., & Pope, R. S. (1996). Intending to forget: The development of cognitive inhibition in directed forgetting. *Journal of Experimental Child Psychology, 62,* 292–315.

Hart, A. J., Whalen, P. J., Shin, L. M., McInerney, S. C., Fischer, H., & Rauch, S. L. (2000). Differential response in the human amygdala to racial outgroup vs ingroup face stimuli. *NeuroReport: For rapid communication of neuroscience research, 11*(11), 2351–2355.

Haskell, R. E. (2001). *Transfer of learning: Cognition, instruction, and reasoning.* San Diego, CA: Academic Press.

Hebb, D. O. (1949). *The organization of behavior: A neuropsychological theory.* Hoboken, NJ: Wiley.

Hillman, C. H., Buck, S. M., Themanson, J. R., Pontifex, M. B., & Castelli, D. M. (2009). Aerobic fitness and cognitive development: Event-related brain potential and task performance indices of executive control in preadolescent children. *Developmental Psychology, 45,* 114–129.

Hoffman, M. L. (2000). *Empathy and moral development: Implications for caring and justice.* New York, NY: Cambridge University Press.

Holmes, J., Gathercole, S. E., & Dunning, D. L. (2009). Adaptive training leads to sustained enhancement of poor working memory in children. *Developmental Science, 12,* F9–F15.

Hooker, C. I., Verosky, S. C., Germine, L. T., Knight, R. T., & D'Esposito, M. (2008). Mentalizing about emotion and its relationship to empathy. *Social Cognitive and Affective Neuroscience, 3,* 204–217.

Hruby, G. G., Goswami, U., Frederiksen, C. H., & Perfetti, C. A. (2011). Neuroscience and reading: A review for reading education researchers. *Reading Research Quarterly, 46*(2), 156–172.

Hughes, C., & Ensor, R. (2009). Executive function and theory of mind: Predictive relations from ages 2 to 4. *Developmental Psychology, 43,* 1447–1459.

Huttenlocher, P. R., & Dabholkar, A. S. (1997). Regional differences in synaptogenesis in human cerebral cortex. *Journal of Comparative Neurology, 387,* 167–178.

Ischebeck, A., Zamarian, L., Schocke, M., & Delazer, M. (2009). Flexible transfer of knowledge in mental arithmetic—An fMRI study. *NeuroImage, 44*(3), 1103–1112.

James, K. H. (2007, March–April). *Perceptual-motor interactions in letter recognition: fMRI evidence.* Paper presented at the biennial meeting of the Society for Research in Child Development, Boston.

Johnson, M. H. (2007). The social brain in infancy: A developmental cognitive neuroscience approach. In D. Coch, K. W. Fischer, & G. Dawson (Eds.), *Human behavior, learning, and the developing brain: Typical development* (pp. 115–137). New York, NY: Guilford.

Jordan N. C., Hanich, L. B., & Kaplan, D. (2003a). Arithmetic fact mastery in young children: A longitudinal investigation. *Journal of Experimental Child Psychology, 85,* 103–119.

Jordan, N. C., Hanich, L., & Kaplan, D. (2003b). A longitudinal study of mathematical competencies in children with specific mathematics difficulties versus children with comorbid mathematics and reading difficulties. *Child Development, 74,* 834–850.

Knudsen, E. I. (2004). Sensitive periods in the development of the brain and behavior. *Journal of Cognitive Neuroscience, 16,* 1412–1425.

Keysers C., & Gazzola, V. (2006). Towards a unifying neural theory of social cognition. *Progress in Brain Research, 156,* 379–401.

Kolb, B. (1995). *Brain plasticity and behavior.* New York, NY: Worth.

Konrad K., Firk C., Uhlhaas P. J (2013). Brain development during adolescence: Neuroscientific insights into this developmental period. *Deutsches Arzteblatt International, 110*(25), 425–431.

Kroger, J. K., Sabb, F. W., Fales, C. L., Bookheimer, S. Y., Cohen, M. S., & Holyoak, K. J. (2002). Recruitment of anterior dorsolateral prefrontal cortex in human reasoning: A parametric study of relational complexity. *Cerebral Cortex, 12,* 477–485.

Kucian, K., Loenneker, T., Dietrich, T., Dosch, M., Martin, E., & von Aster, M. (2006). Impaired neural networks for approximate calculation in dyscalculic children: A functional MRI study. *Behavioral and Brain Functions, 2,* 31.

Kuhn, J-T. (2015). Developmental dyscalculia: Neurobiological, cognitive, and developmental perspectives. *Zeitschrift Für Psychologie, Special Issue: Developmental Dyscalculia, 223*(2), 69–82.

Lamendella, J. T. (1977). General principles of neurofunctional organization and their manifestation in primary and nonprimary language acquisition. *Language and Learning, 27,* 155–196.

Lehman, E. B., McKinley-Pace, M. J., Wilson, J. A., Savsky, M. D., & Woodson, M. E. (1997). Direct and indirect measures of intentional forgetting in children and adults: Evidence for retrieval inhibition and reinstatement. *Journal of Experimental Child Psychology, 64,* 295–316.

Lenroot, R. K., & Giedd, J. N. (2006). Brain development in children and adolescents: Insights from anatomical magnetic resonance imaging. *Neuroscience and Biobehavioral Reviews, 30,* 718–729.

Levy, R., & Goldman-Rakic, P. S. (2000). Segregation of working memory functions within the dorsolateral prefrontal cortex. *Experimental Brain Research, 133,* 23–32.

Lyon, G. R. (1995). Toward a definition of dyslexia. *Annals of Dyslexia, 45,* 3–27.

Mechelli, A., Gorno-Tempini, M. L., & Price, C. J. (2003). Neuroimaging studies of word and pseudoword reading: Consistencies, inconsistencies, and limitations. *Journal of Cognitive Neuroscience, 15,* 260–271.

Moffitt, T. E., Arseneault, L., Belsky, D., Dickson, N., Hancox, R. J., Harrington, H., . . . Caspi, A. (2011). A gradient of childhood self-control predicts health, wealth, and public safety. *PNAS Proceedings of the National*

Academy of Sciences, 108(7), 2693–2698.

Morris, J. S., Frith, C. D., Perrett, D. I., Rowland, D., Young, A. W., Clader, A. J., & Dolan, R. J. (1996). A differential neural response in the human amygdala to fearful and happy facial expressions. Nature, 383, 812–815.

Morrison, S. E., & Salzman, C. D. (2010). Re-valuing the amygdala. Current Opinion in Neurobiology, 20(2), 221–230.

Munakata, Y., & McClelland, J. L. (2003). Connectionist models of development. Developmental Science, 6, 413–429.

Nelson, C. A., Thomas, K. M., & Dehaan, M. (2006). Neural bases of cognitive development. In D. Kuhn & R. S. Siegler (Vol. Eds.), Cognition, perception, and language (Vol. 2, pp. 3–57), in W. Damon & R. M. Lerner (Gen. Eds.), Handbook of child psychology (6th ed.). New York, NY: Wiley.

Nieder, A., & Dehaene, S. (2009). Representation of number in the brain. Annual Review of Neuroscience, 32, 185–208.

Nielsen, J. A., Zielinski, B. A., Ferguson, M. A., Lainhart, J. E., & Anderson, J. S. (2013). An evaluation of the left-brain vs. right-brain hypothesis with resting state functional connectivity magnetic resonance imaging. PLoS ONE, 8(8), e71275.

Nolte, J. (2009). The human brain: An introduction to its functional anatomy (6th ed.). Philadelphia, PA: Mosby/Elsevier.

Organization for Economic Cooperation and Development. (2002). Understanding the brain: Towards a new learning science. Paris, France: OECD.

Paulesu, E., Démonet, J.-F., Fazio, F., McCrory, E., Chanoine, V., Brunswick, N., . . . Frith, U. (2001). Dyslexia: Cultural diversity and biological unity. Science, 291(5511), 2165–2167.

Penhune, V. B. (2011). Sensitive periods in human development: Evidence from musical training. Cortex, 47, 1126–1137.

Perkins, D., Jay, E., & Tishman, S. (1993). New conceptions of thinking: From ontology to education. Educational Psychologist, 28(1), 67–85.

Phelps, E. A., O'Connor, K. J., Cunningham, W. A., Funayama, E. S., Gatenby, J. C., Gore, J. C., & Banaji, M. (2000). Performance on indirect measures of race evaluation predicts amygdala activation. Journal of Cognitive Neuroscience, 12, 729–738.

Piaget, J. (1970). Piaget's theory. In P. H. Mussen (Ed.), Carmichael's manual of child psychology (pp. 703–732). New York, NY: Wiley.

Piaget, J. (1972). Intellectual evolution from adolescence to adulthood. Human Development, 15, 1–12.

Price, C. J., Winterburn, D., Giraud, A. L., Moore, C. J., & Noppeney, U. (2003). Cortical localisation of the visual and auditory word form areas: A reconsideration of the evidence. Brain Language, 86, 272–286.

Pugh, K. (2006). A neurocognitive overview of reading acquisition and dyslexia across languages. Developmental Science, 9(5), 448–450.

Qin, S., Cho, S., Chen, T., Rosenberg-Lee, M., Geary, D. C., & Menon, V. (2014). Hippocampal-neocortical functional reorganization underlies children's cognitive development. Nature Neuroscience, 17, 1263–1269.

Rakic, P. (1995). Corticogenesis in human and nonhuman primates. In M. S. Gazzaniga (Ed.), The cognitive neurosciences (pp. 127–145). Cambridge, MA: The MIT Press.

Rakic, P. (2002). Neurogenesis in adult primate neocortex: An evaluation of the evidence. Nature Reviews Neuroscience, 3, 65–71.

Richards, T. L., & Berninger, V. W. (2008). Abnormal fMRI connectivity in children with dyslexia during a phoneme task: Before but not after treatment. Journal of Neurolinguistics, 21(4), 294–304.

Rivera, S. M., Reiss, A. L., Eckert, M. A., & Menon, V. (2005). Developmental changes in mental arithmetic: Evidence for increased functional specialization in the left inferior parietal cortex. Cerebral Cortex, 15(11), 1779–1790.

Romer, D. (2003). Reducing adolescent risk: Toward an integrated approach. Thousand Oaks, CA: SAGE.

Romer, D. (2010). Adolescent risk taking, impulsivity, and brain development: Implications for prevention. Developmental Psychobiology, 52, 263–276.

Rubia, K., Russell, T., Overmeyer, S., Brammer, M. J., Bullmore, E. T., Sharma, T., . . . Taylor, E. (2001). Mapping motor inhibition: Conjunctive brain activations across different versions of go/no-go and stop tasks. NeuroImage, 13, 250–261.

Rueda, M. R., Fan, J., McCandliss, B. D., Halparin, J., Gruber, D. B., Lercari, L. P., & Posner, M. I. (2004). Development of attentional networks in childhood. Neuropsychologia, 42(8), 1029–1040.

Rykhlevskaia, E., Uddin, L. Q., Kondos, L., & Menon, V. (2009). Neuroanatomical correlates of developmental dyscalculia: Combined evidence from morphometry and tractography. Frontiers in Human Neuroscience, 3, 51.

Schoenbaum, G., Chiba, A. A., & Gallagher, M. (1998). Orbitofrontal cortex and basolateral amygdala encode expected outcomes during learning. Nature Neuroscience, 1, 155–159.

Schumann, C. M., Hamstra J., Goodlin-Jones, B. L., Lotspeich, L. J., Kwon, H., Buonocore, M. H., . . . Amaral, D. G. (2004). The amygdala is enlarged in children but not adolescents with autism; the hippocampus is enlarged at all ages. Journal of Neuroscience, 24, 6392–6401.

Segalowitz, S. J., & Davies, P. L. (2004). Charting the maturation of the frontal lobe: An electrophysiological strategy. Brain Cognition, 55, 116–133.

Shamay-Tsoory, S. G. (2011). The neural bases for empathy. Neuroscientist, 17, 18–24.

Shatz, C. J. (1992). The developing brain. Scientific American, 267(3), 60–67.

Shaw, P., Eckstrand, K., Sharp, W., Blumenthal, J., Lerch, J. P., Greenstein, D., . . . Rapoport, J. L. (2007). Attention-deficit/hyperactivity disorder is characterized by a delay in cortical maturation. Proceedings of the National Academy of Sciences, 104, 19649–19654.

Shaw, P., Greenstein, D., Lerch, J., Clasen, L., Lenroot, R., Gogtay, N., . . . Giedd, J. (2006). Intellectual ability and cortical development in children and adolescents. Nature, 440, 676–679.

Shaywitz, B. A., Shaywitz, S. E., Blachman, B. A., Pugh, K. R., Fulbright, R. K., Skudlarski, P., . . . Gore, J. C. (2004). Development of left occipitotemporal systems for skilled reading in children after a phonologically-based intervention. Biological Psychiatry, 55, 926–933.

Shaywitz, B. A., Shaywitz, S. E., Pugh, K. R., Mencl, W. E., Fulbright, R. K., Skudlarski, P., . . . Gore, J. C. (2002). Disruption of posterior brain systems for reading in children with developmental dyslexia. Biological Psychiatry, 52(2), 101–110.

Shaywitz, S., & Shaywitz, B. (2005). Dyslexia (specific reading disability). Biological Psychiatry, 57, 1301–1309.

Shaywitz, S. E., Mody, M., & Shaywitz, B. A. (2006). Neural mechanisms in dyslexia. Current Directions in Psychological Science, 15(6), 278–281.

Shors, T. J. (2014). The adult brain makes new neurons, and effortful learning keeps them alive. Current Directions in Psychological Science, 23(5), 311–318.

Siegler, R. S., DeLoache, J. S., Eisenberg, N., & Saffron, J. (2014). How children develop (4th ed.). New York, NY: Worth.

Simos, P. G., Fletcher, J. M., Bergman, E., Breier, J. I., Foorman, B. R., Castillo, E. M., . . . Papanicolaou, A. C. (2002). Dyslexia-specific brain activation profile becomes normal following successful remedial training. *Neurology, 58,* 1203–1213.

Spear, L. P. (2010). *The behavioral neuroscience of adolescence.* New York, NY: Norton.

Squire, L. R., Stark, C. E., & Clark, R. E. (2004). The medial temporal lobe. *Annual Review of Neuroscience, 27,* 279–306.

Stanovich, K. E., & Siegel, L. S. (1994). Phenotypic performance profile of children with reading disabilities: A regression-based test of the phonological-core variable-difference model. *Journal of Educational Psychology, 86*(1), 24–53.

Steinberg, L. (2004). Risk taking in adolescence: What changes and why? In R. E. Dahl & L. P. Spear (Eds.), *Adolescent brain development: Vulnerabilities and opportunities. Annals of the New York Academy of Sciences* (Vol. 1021, pp. 51–58). New York, NY: New York Academy of Sciences.

Stiles, J. (2008). *The fundamentals of brain development: Integrating nature and nurture.* Cambridge, MA: Harvard University Press.

Tan, L. H., Spinks, J. A., Gao, J. H., Liu, H. L., Perfetti, C. A., Xiong, J., . . . Fox, P. T. (2000). Brain activation in the processing of Chinese characters and words: A functional MRI study. *Human Brain Mapping, 10*(1), 16–27.

Temple, E., Deutsch, G. K., Poldrack, R. A., Miller, S. L., Tallal, P., Merzenich, M. M., & Gabrieli, J. D. (2003). Neural deficits in children with dyslexia ameliorated by behavioral remediation: Evidence from functional MRI. *Proceedings of the National Academy of Sciences, 100*(5), 2860–2865.

Turkeltaub, P., Gareau, L., Flowers, D. L., Zeffiro, T. A., & Eden, G. F. (2003). Development of neural mechanisms for reading. *Nature Neuroscience, 6,* 767–773.

Uttal, W. R. (2001). *The new phrenology: The limits of localizing cognitive processes in the brain.* Cambridge, MA: The MIT Press.

Varma, S., McCandliss, B. D., & Schwartz, D. L. (2008). Scientific and pragmatic challenges for bridging education and neuroscience. *Educational Researcher, 37,* 140–152.

Weisberg, D. S., Keil, F. C., Goodstein, E. R., & Gray, J. R. (2008). The seductive allure of neuroscience explanations. *Journal of Cognitive Neuroscience, 20*(3), 470–477.

Winner, E., & Gardner, H. (1977). The comprehension of metaphor in brain-damaged patients. *Brain, 100,* 717–729.

Winston, J. S., Strange, B. A., O'Doherty, J., & Dolan, R. J. (2002) Automatic and intentional brain response during evaluation of trustworthiness of faces. *Nature, 5,* 277–283.

Zamarian, L., Ischebeck, A., & Delazer, M. (2009). Neuroscience of learning arithmetic: Evidence from brain imaging studies. *Neuroscience and Biobehavioral Reviews, 33*(6), 909–925.

Zecevic, N., & Rakic, P. (2001). Development of layer I neurons in the primate cerebral cortex. *Journal of Neuroscience, 21,* 5607–5619.

Zelazo P. D., & Müller, U. (2002). Executive function in typical and atypical development. In U. Goswami (Ed.), *Handbook of childhood cognitive development* (pp. 445–469). Oxford, UK: Blackwell.

Zigler, E., & Gilman, E. (1998). The legacy of Jean Piaget. In G. A. Kimble & M. Wertheimer (Eds.), *Portraits of pioneers in psychology* (pp. 145–160). Washington, DC: American Psychological Association.

Module 6

Alexander, R. D. (1989). Evolution of the human psyche. In P. Mellers & C. Stringer (Eds.), *The human revolution: Behavioural and biological perspectives on the origins of modern humans* (pp. 455–513). Princeton, NJ: Princeton University Press.

Ashton, P. T. (1975). Cross-cultural Piagetian research: An experimental perspective. *Harvard Educational Review, 45,* 475–506.

Au, T. K., Sidle, A. L., & Rollins, K. B. (1993). Developing an intuitive understanding of conservation and contamination: Invisible particles as a plausible mechanism. *Developmental Psychology, 29,* 286–299.

Baillargeon, R. (1991). Reasoning about the height and location of a hidden object in 4.5- and 6.5-month-old infants. *Cognition, 38,* 13–42.

Baltes, P. (1987). Theoretical propositions of life-span developmental psychology: On the dynamics between growth and decline. *Developmental Psychology, 23,* 611–626.

Barron, B. J. S., Schwartz, D. L., Vye, N. J., Moore, A., Petrosino, A., Zech, L., & Bransford, J. D. (1998). Doing with understanding: Lessons from research on problem- and project-based learning. *The Journal of the Learning Sciences, 7*(3–4), 271–311.

Behrend, D. A., Rosengren, K., & Perlmutter, M. (1989). A new look at children's private speech: The effects of age, task difficulty, and parent presence. *International Journal of Behavioral Development, 12,* 305–320.

Berk, L. E. (1986). Relationship of elementary school children's private speech to behavioral accompaniment to task, attention, and task performance. *Developmental Psychology, 22,* 671–680.

Berk, L. E. (1992). Children's private speech: An overview of theory and the status of research. In R. M. Diaz & L. E. Berk (Eds.), *Private speech: From social interaction to self-regulation* (pp. 17–53). Hillsdale, NJ: Lawrence Erlbaum.

Berk, L. E., & Spuhl, S. T. (1995). Maternal intervention, private speech, and task performance in preschool children. *Early Childhood Research Quarterly, 10,* 145–169.

Best, J. R. (2012). Exergaming immediately enhances children's executive function. *Developmental Psychology, 48*(5), 1501–1510.

Bjorklund, D. F., & Pellegrini, A. D. (2000). Child development and evolutionary psychology. *Child Development, 71,* 1687–1708.

Bodrova, E., & Leong, D. (1997). *Tools of the mind: The Vygotskian approach to early childhood education.* Upper Saddle River, NJ: Prentice Hall.

Brainerd, C. J. (1978). Learning research and Piagetian theory. In L. S. Siegel & C. J. Brainerd (Eds.), *Alternatives to Piaget: Critical essays on the theory* (pp. 69–109). New York, NY: Academic Press.

Brainerd, C. J. (2003). Jean Piaget, learning research, and American education. In B. J. Zimmerman & D. H. Schunk (Eds.), *Educational psychology: A century of contributions* (pp. 251–287). Mahwah, NJ: Lawrence Erlbaum.

Bransford, J. D., & Schwartz, D. L. (1999). Rethinking transfer: A simple proposal with multiple implications. In A. Iran-Nejad & P. D. Pearson (Eds.), *Review of research in education* (pp. 61–100). Washington, DC: American Educational Research Association.

Brown, A. L., & Ferrara, R. A. (1985). Diagnosing zones of proximal development. In J. V. Wertsch (Ed.), *Culture, communication, and cognition: Vygotskian perspectives* (pp. 273–305). New York, NY: Cambridge University Press.

Brown, A. L., & Kane, M. J. (1988). Preschool children can learn to transfer: Learning to learn and learning from example. *Cognitive Psychology, 20,* 493–523.

Brown, A. L., & Palincsar, A. S. (1989). Guided, cooperative learning and individual knowledge acquisition. In L. B. Resnick (Ed.), *Knowing, learning, and instruction: Essays in honor of Robert Glaser* (pp. 393–451). Hillsdale, NJ: Lawrence Erlbaum.

Bruning, R. H., Schraw, G. J., Norby, M. M., & Ronning, R. R. (2004). *Cognitive psychology and instruction* (4th ed.). Columbus, OH: Merrill.

Campione, J. C., & Brown, A. L. (1990). Guided learning and transfer: Implications for approaches to assessment. In N. Frederiksen, R. Glaser, A. Lesgold, & M. Shafto (Eds.), *Diagnostic monitoring of skill and knowledge acquisition* (pp. 141–172). Hillsdale, NJ: Lawrence Erlbaum.

Chandler, M. A., & Chapman, M. (Eds.). (1991). *Criteria for competence*. Hillsdale, NJ: Lawrence Erlbaum.

Das, J. P. (1995). Some thoughts on two aspects of Vygotsky's work. *Educational Psychologist, 30*(2), 93–97.

Dasen, P. R. (1977). Introduction in Piagetian psychology. In P. R. Dasen (Ed.), *Piagetian psychology: Cross-cultural contributions* (pp. 1–25). New York, NY: Gardner.

Davydov, V. V. (1972). *The types of generalization in learning*. Moscow, Russia: Pedagogika.

Davydov, V. V. (1988). The concept of theoretical generalization. *Studies in Soviet Thought, 36,* 169–202.

Day, J. D., & Cordon, L. A. (1993). Static and dynamic measures of ability: An experimental comparison. *Journal of Educational Psychology, 85,* 75–82.

Dennen, V. P. (2004). Cognitive apprenticeship in educational practice: Research on scaffolding, modeling, mentoring, and coaching as instructional strategies. In D. H. Jonassen (Ed.), *Handbook of research on educational communications and technology* (2nd ed., pp. 813–828). Mahwah, NJ: Lawrence Erlbaum.

DeVries, R. (1969). Constancy of generic identity in the years three to six. *Monographs of the Society for Research in Child Development, 34*(Serial 127).

Duncan, R., & Tarulli, D. (2009). On the persistence of private speech: Empirical and theoretical considerations. In A. Winsler, C. Fernyhough, & I. Montero (Eds.), *Private speech, executive functioning, and the development of verbal self-regulation* (pp. 176–187). Cambridge, UK: Cambridge University Press.

Fedewa, A. L., & Ahn, S. (2011). The effects of physical activity and physical fitness on children's achievement and cognitive outcomes: A meta-analysis. *Research Quarterly for Exercise and Sport, 82*(3), 521–535.

Fromberg, D. P. (2002). *Play and meaning in early childhood education*. Boston, MA: Allyn & Bacon.

Goncu, A. (1993). Development of intersubjectivity in social pretend play. *Human Development, 36,* 185–198.

Goodnow, J. J. (1962). A test of milieu effects with some of Piaget's tasks. *Psychological Monographs, 76*(36, Whole No. 555).

Greenfield, P. M. (1976). Cross-cultural research and Piagetian theory: Paradox and progress. In K. Riegel & J. Meacham (Eds.), *The developing individual in a changing world* (pp. 322–333). The Hague, Netherlands: Mouton.

Griffin, P., & Cole, M. (1999). Current activity for the future: The zo-ped. In P. Lloyd & C. Fernyhough (Eds.), *Lev Vygotsky: Critical assessments* (pp. 276–295). London, UK: Routledge.

Grigorenko, E. L., & Sternberg, R. J. (1998). Dynamic testing. *Psychological Bulletin, 124,* 75–111.

Harris, P. L. (2006). Hard work for the imagination. In A. Gönçü & S. Haskins (Eds.), *Play and development: Evolutionary, sociocultural and functional perspectives* (pp. 205–226). Mahwah, NJ: Lawrence Erlbaum.

Haskell, R. E. (2001). *Transfer of learning: Cognition, instruction, and reasoning*. San Diego, CA: Academic Press.

Hirsh-Pasek, K., Golinkoff, R. M., Berk, L. E., & Singer, D. G. (2008). *A mandate for playful learning in preschool: Presenting the evidence*. New York, NY: Oxford University Press.

Inhelder, B., & Piaget, J. (1955). *The growth of logical thinking from childhood to adolescence*. Paris, France: Presses Universitaires de France.

Inhelder, B., Sinclair, H., & Bovet, M. (1974). *Learning and the development of cognition*. Cambridge, MA: Harvard University Press.

Jacobs, J. E., & Eccles, J. S. (2000). Parents, task values, and real-life achievement-related choices. In C. Sansone & J. M. Harackiewicz (Eds.), *Intrinsic and extrinsic motivation: The search for optimal motivation and performance* (pp. 405–439). San Diego, CA: Academic Press.

Karpov, Y. V. (2006). Neo-Vygotskian activity theory: Merging Vygotsky's and Piaget's theories of cognitive development. In M. A. Vanchevsky (Ed.), *Frontiers in cognitive psychology* (pp. 31–51). Hauppauge, NY: Nova Science Publishers.

Karpov, Y. V., & Bransford, J. D. (1995). L. S. Vygotsky and the doctrine of empirical and theoretical learning. *Educational Psychologist, 30*(2), 61–66.

Kohlberg, L. (1984). *Essays in moral development, Vol. 2*. New York, NY: Harper & Row.

Kohlberg, L., Yaeger, J., & Hjertholm, E. (1968). Private speech: Four studies and a review of theories. *Child Development, 39,* 691–736.

Laurendeau-Bendavid, M. (1977). Culture, schooling, and cognitive development: A comparative study of children in French Canada and Rwanda. In P. R. Dasen (Ed.), *Piagetian psychology: Cross-cultural contributions* (pp. 123–168). New York, NY: Gardner Press.

Lawton, J. T., & Hooper, F. H. (1978). Piagetian theory and early childhood education: A critical analysis. In L. S. Siegel & C. J. Brainerd (Eds.), *Alternatives to Piaget: Critical essays on the theory* (pp. 169–199). New York, NY: Academic Press.

Leontiev, A. N. (1961). Learning as a problem in psychology. In N. O'Connor (Ed.), *Recent Soviet psychology* (pp. 227–246). New York, NY: Liveright.

Leontiev, A. N., & Luria, A. R. (1972). Some notes concerning Dr. Fodor's "reflections on L.S. Vygotsky's thought and language." *Cognition, 1,* 311–316.

Lourenço, O., & Machado, A. (1996). In defense of Piaget's theory: A reply to 10 common criticisms. *Psychological Review, 103*(1), 143–164.

Mayer, R. E. (2003). *Learning and instruction*. Upper Saddle River, NJ: Prentice Hall.

Mayer, R. E. (2004). Should there be a three-strikes rule against pure discovery learning? The case for guided methods of instruction. *American Psychologist, 59*(1), 14–19.

Miller, K., & Baillargeon, R. (1990). Length and distance: Do preschoolers think that occlusion brings things together? *Developmental Psychology, 26,* 103–114.

Moll, L. C. (2001). Through the mediation of others: Vygotskian research on teaching. In V. Richardson (Ed.), *Handbook of research on teaching* (4th ed., 111–129). Washington, DC: American Educational Research Association.

Moshman, D. (1997). Pluralist rational constructivism. *Issues in Education: Contributions from Educational Psychology, 3,* 229–234.

Murphy, P. K., & Woods, B. S. (1996). Situating knowledge in learning and instruction. *Educational Psychologist, 31,* 141–145.

Newson, J., & Newson, E. (1975). Intersubjectivity and the transmission of culture: On the social origins of symbolic functioning. *Bulletin of the British Psychological Society, 28,* 437–446.

Palincsar, A. S. (1998). Social constructivist perspectives on teaching and learning. In J. T., Spence, J. M. Darley, & D. J. Foss (Eds.), *Annual review of psychology* (pp. 345–375). Palo Alto, CA: Annual Reviews.

Paris, S. G., Byrnes, J. P., & Paris, A. H. (2001). Constructing theories, identities, and actions of self-regulated learners. In B. J. Zimmerman & D. H. Schunk (Eds.), *Self-regulated learning and academic achievement: Theoretical perspectives* (2nd ed., pp. 253–287). Mahwah, NJ: Lawrence Erlbaum.

Pellegrini, A. (2009). Research and policy on children's play. *Child Development Perspectives, 3*(2), 131–136.

Pellegrini, A., & Galda, L. (1993). Ten years after: A reexamination of symbolic play and literacy research. *Reading Research Quarterly, 28,* 163–175.

Pellegrini A., & Smith, P. K. (1993). School recess. *Review of Educational Research, 63,* 51–67.

Pellegrini, A. D., & Bohn, C. M. (2005). The role of recess on children's cognitive performance and school adjustment. *Educational Researcher, 34*(1), 13–19.

Pellegrini, A. D., Huberty, P. D., & Jones, I. (1995). The effect of recess timing on children's classroom and playground behavior. *American Educational Research Journal, 32,* 845–864.

Piaget, J. (1924). *Judgment and reasoning in the child.* Neuchatel, Switzerland: Delachaux et Niestle.

Piaget, J. (1926). *The child's conception of the world.* Paris, France: Alcan.

Piaget, J. (1932). *The moral judgment of the child.* Paris, France: Alcan.

Piaget, J. (1962). *Play, dreams, and imitation in childhood.* New York, NY: Norton. (Original work published 1945)

Piaget, J. (1950). *The psychology of intelligence.* London, UK: Routledge & Kegan Paul.

Piaget, J. (1962). *Comments on Vygostky's critical remarks concerning "the language and thought of the child," and "judgment and reasoning in the child."* Boston, MA: The MIT Press.

Piaget, J. (1970). Piaget's theory. In P. H. Mussen (Ed.), *Carmichael's manual of child psychology* (pp. 703–732). New York, NY: Wiley.

Piaget, J. (1972a). Intellectual evolution from adolescence to adulthood. *Human Development, 15,* 1–12.

Piaget, J. (1972b). *Problems of genetic psychology.* Paris, France: Gonthier.

Piaget, J. (1976a). Postscript. *Archives de Psychologie, 44,* 223–228.

Piaget, J. (1976b). *The grasp of consciousness: Action and concept in the young child.* Cambridge, MA: Harvard University Press.

Piaget, J. (1985). *The equilibration of cognitive structures: The central problem of intellectual development* (T. Brown & K. L. Thampy, Trans.) Chicago, IL: The University of Chicago Press.

Renkl, A., Mandl, H., & Gruber, H. (1996). Inert knowledge: Analyses and remedies. *Educational Psychologist, 31,* 115–121.

Rogoff, B., & Chavajay, P. (1995). What's become of research on the cultural basis of cognitive development? *American Psychologist, 50,* 859–877.

Rowe, S. M., & Wertsch, J. V. (2002). Vygotsky's model of cognitive development. In U. Goswami (Ed.), *Blackwell handbook of childhood cognitive development* (pp. 538–554). Malden, MA: Blackwell.

Salomon, G., & Perkins, D. (1989). Rocky roads to transfer: Rethinking mechanisms of a neglected phenomenon. *Educational Psychologist, 18,* 42–50.

Siegler, R. S., & Alibali, M. W. (2005). *Children's thinking* (4th ed.). Upper Saddle River, NJ: Prentice Hall.

Singer, D. G., & Singer, J. L. (2006). Fantasy and imagination. In D. P. Fromberg & D. Bergen (Eds.), *Play from birth to 12: Contexts, perspectives, and meanings* (pp. 371–378). New York, NY: Routledge.

Smith, L. (2002). Piaget's model. In U. Goswami (Ed.), *Blackwell handbook of childhood cognitive development* (pp. 515–537). Malden, MA: Blackwell.

Smith, L. (1993). *Necessary knowledge: Piagetian perspectives on constructivism.* Hillsdale, NJ: Lawrence Erlbaum.

Smolucha, L., & Smolucha, F. (1998). The social origins of mind: Post-Piagetian perspectives on pretend play. In O. N. S. B. Saracho (Ed.), *Multiple perspectives on play in early childhood education.* SUNY series: *Early childhood education: Inquiries and insights* (pp. 34–58). Albany: State University of New York Press.

Spiro, R., Feltovich, P. J., Jacobson, M. J., & Coulson, R. L. (1992). Cognitive flexibility, constructivism, and hypertext: Random access instruction for advanced knowledge acquisition in ill-structured domains. In T. M. Duffy, & D. H. Jonassen (Eds.), *Constructivism and the technology of instruction: A conversation*

(pp. 57–75). Mahwah, NJ: Lawrence Erlbaum.

Sternberg, R. J. (Ed.). (1990). *Wisdom: Its nature, origins, and development.* Cambridge, UK: Cambridge University Press.

Sternberg, R. J. (2002). Individual differences in cognitive development. In U. Goswami (Ed.), *Blackwell handbook of childhood cognitive development* (pp. 600–619). Malden, MA: Blackwell.

Sternberg, R. J. (2003). Intelligence. In D. K. Freedheim (Ed.), *Handbook of psychology: History of psychology, Vol. 1* (pp. 135–156). New York, NY: Wiley.

Tharp, R. G. (1989). Psychocultural variables and constants: Effects on teaching and learning in schools. *American Psychologist, 44,* 349–359.

Tharp, R. G., & Gallimore, R. (1988). *Rousing minds to life: Teaching, learning, and schooling in social context.* Cambridge, UK: Cambridge University Press.

Tudge, J., & Scrimsher, S. (2003). Lev S. Vygotsky on education: A cultural-historical, interpersonal, and individual approach to development. In B. J. Zimmerman & D. H. Schunk (Eds.), *Educational psychology: A century of contributions* (pp. 207–228). Mahwah, NJ: Lawrence Erlbaum.

van Joolingen, W. R., de Jong, T., Lazonder, A. W., Savelsbergh, E. R., & Manlove, S. (2005). Co-Lab: Research and development of an online learning environment for collaborative scientific discovery learning. *Computers in Human Behavior, 21*(4), 671–688.

Vygotsky, L. S. (1962). *Thought and language.* Cambridge, MA: The MIT Press.

Vygotsky, L. S. (1978). *Mind in society: The development of higher psychological processes.* Cambridge, MA: Harvard University Press.

Vygotsky, L. S. (1987). *The collected works of L. S. Vygotsky: Vol. 1. Problems of general psychology* (R. W. Rieber & A. S. Carton, Vol. Eds.; N. Minick, Trans.). New York, NY: Plenum.

Vygotsky, L. S. (1993). *The collected works of L. S. Vygotsky: Vol. 2. The fundamentals of defectology (abnormal psychology and learning disabilities).* (R. W. Rieber, & A. S. Carton, Vol. Eds.; N. Minick, Trans.). New York, NY: Plenum (Chapters originally written between 1924 and 1935)

Vygotsky, L. S. (1994). The problem of the environment. In R. van der Veer & J. Valsiner (Eds.), *The Vygotsky reader* (pp. 338–354). Oxford, UK: Blackwell (Original work published 1935)

Vygotsky, L. S. (1998). *The collected-works of L. S. Vygotsky: Vol. 5. Child psychology* (R. W. Rieber, Vol Ed.; M. J. Hall, Trans.). New York, NY: Plenum (Chapters originally written between 1930 and 1934)

Webb, N. M., & Palincsar, A. S. (1996). Group processes in the classroom. In D. C. Berliner & R. C. Calfee (Eds.), *Handbook of educational psychology* (pp. 841–873). New York, NY: Prentice Hall.

Whitington, V., & Floyd, I. (2009). Creating intersubjectivity during socio-dramatic play at an Australian kindergarten. *Early Child Development and Care, 179*(2), 143–156.

Windschitl, M. (2002). Framing constructivism in practice as the negotiation of dilemmas: An analysis of the conceptual, pedagogical, cultural, and political challenges facing teachers. *Review of Educational Research, 72*, 131–175.

Wink, J., & Putney, L. (2002). *A vision of Vygotsky.* Boston, MA: Allyn & Bacon.

Winsler, A. (2009). Still talking to ourselves after all these years: A review of current research on private speech. In A. Winsler, C. Fernyhough, & I. Montero (Eds.), *Private speech, executive functioning, and the development of verbal self-regulation* (pp. 3–41). Cambridge, UK: Cambridge University Press.

Winsler, A., & Naglieri, J. (2003). Overt and covert verbal problem-solving strategies: Developmental trends in use, awareness, and the relations with task performance in children aged 5 to 17. *Child Development, 74*, 659–678.

Wood, D. J. (1989). Social interaction as tutoring. In M. H. Bornstein & J. S. Bruner (Eds.), *Interaction in human development* (pp. 59–80). Hillsdale, NJ: Lawrence Erlbaum.

Wood, D. J., Bruner, J. S., & Ross, G. (1976). The role of tutoring in problem solving. *Journal of Child Psychology and Psychiatry, 17*, 89–100.

Zigler, E., & Gilman, E. (1998). The legacy of Jean Piaget. In G. A. Kimble & M. Wertheimer (Eds.), *Portraits of pioneers in psychology* (pp. 145–160). Washington, DC: American Psychological Association.

Module 7

Aarnoutse, C., & van Leeuwe, J. (1998). Relation between reading comprehension, vocabulary, reading pleasure, and reading frequency. *Educational Research and Evaluation, 4*(2), 143–166.

Abrahamsen, E., & Rigrodsky, S. (1984). Comprehension of complex sentences in children at three levels of cognitive development. *Journal of Psycholinguistic Research, 13,* 333–350.

Adams, M. J. (1990). *Beginning to read: Thinking and learning about print.* Cambridge, MA: The MIT Press.

Anglin, J. (1993). Vocabulary development: A morphological analysis. *Monographs of the Society for Research in Child Development, 58*(10, Serial No. 238).

Arnold, D. H., Lonigan, C. J., Whitehurst, G. J., & Epstein, J. N. (1994). Accelerating language development through picture book reading: Replication and extension to a videotape training format. *Journal of Educational Psychology, 86*(2), 235–243.

Baldie, B. (1976). The acquisition of the passive voice. *Journal of Child Language, 3,* 331–348.

Barnett, W. S., Yarosz, D. J., Thomas, J., Jung, K., & Blanco, D. (2007). Two-way monolingual English immersion in preschool education: An experimental comparison. *Early Childhood Research Quarterly, 22*(3), 277–293.

Bauer, D. J., Goldfield, B. A., & Reznick, J. S. (2002). Alternative approaches to analyzing individual differences in the rate of early vocabulary development. *Applied Psycholinguistics, 23,* 313–335.

Bauer, E. B., & Manyak, P. C. (2008). Creating language-rich instruction for English-language learners. *The Reading Teacher, 62*(2), 176–178.

Behne, T., Liszkowski, U., Carpenter, M., & Tomasello, M. (2012). Twelve-month-olds' comprehension and production of pointing. *British Journal of Developmental Psychology, 30,* 359–375.

Benedict, H. (1979). Early lexical development: Comprehension and production. *Journal of Child Language, 6,* 183–200.

Bereiter, C., & Scardamalia, M. (1987). *The psychology of written composition.* Hillsdale, NJ: Lawrence Erlbaum.

Berko Gleason, J., Hay, D., & Cain, L. (1988). Social and affective determinants of language acquisition. In M. L. Rice & R. L. Schiefelbusch (Eds.), *The teachability of language* (pp. 171–186). Baltimore, MD: Brookes.

Bernstein, D. (1989). Language development: The school-age years. In D. Bernstein & E. Tiegerman (Eds.), *Language and communication disorders in children* (2nd ed., pp. 127–154). Upper Saddle River, NJ: Prentice Hall.

Bhatnagar, J. K. (1980). Linguistic behavior and adjustment of immigrant children in French and English schools in Montreal. *International Review of Applied Psychology, 2,* 141–158.

Bialystok, E. (2001). *Bilingualism in development: Language, literacy, & cognition.* Cambridge, UK: Cambridge University Press.

Bloom, L. (1973). *One word at a time: The use of single word utterances before syntax.* The Hague, the Netherlands: Mouton.

Boyd, F., Sullivan, M., Popp, J., & Hughes, M. (2012). Vocabulary instruction in the disciplines. *Journal of Adolescent and Adult Literacy, 56*(1), 18–20.

Brisk, M. E. (1991). Toward multilingual and multicultural mainstream education. *Journal of Education, 173*(2), 114–129.

Brown, R. (1973). *A first language: The early stages.* Cambridge, MA: Harvard University Press.

Brown, R., & Bellugi, U. (1964). Three processes in children's learning of syntax [Special issue]. *Harvard Educational Review, 34,* 133–151.

Brown, R., & Fraser, C. (1963). The acquisition of syntax. In C. N. Cofer & B. Musgrave (Eds.), *Verbal behavior and learning: Problems and processes* (pp. 158–201). New York, NY: McGraw-Hill.

Brown, R., & Hanlon, C. (1970). Derivational complexity and order of acquisition. In J. R. Hayes (Ed.), *Cognition and the development of language* (pp. 11–54). New York, NY: Wiley.

Büchel, C., & Sommer, M. (2004, February). Unsolved mystery: What causes stuttering? *PLoS Biology, 2*(2), 0159–0163.

Campbell, A., & Namy, L. (2003). The role of social referential context and verbal and nonverbal symbol learning. *Child Development, 74,* 549–563.

Carlo, M. S., & Royer, J. M. (1999). Cross-language transfer of reading skills. In D. A. Wagner, R. L. Venezky, & B. V. Street (Eds.), *Literacy: An international handbook* (pp. 148–154). Boulder, CO: Westview Press.

Caselli, M. C., Bates, E. Casadio, P., Fenson, J., Fenson, L., Sanderl, L., & Weir, J. (1995). A cross-linguistic study of early lexical development. *Cognitive Development, 10,* 159–199.

Cherry-Wilkinson, L., & Dollaghan, C. (1979). Peer communication in first grade reading groups. *Theory Into Practice, 18,* 267–274.

Cisero, C. A., & Royer, J. M. (1995). The development and cross-language transfer of phonological awareness.

Contemporary Educational Psychology, 20, 275–303.

Collier, V. P., & Thomas, W. P. (2004). *The astounding effectiveness of dual language education for all. NABE Journal of Research and Practice, 2(1), 1–20.*

Cook, R., Tessier, A., & Armbruster, V. (1987). *Adapting early childhood curricula for children with special needs* (2nd ed.). Upper Saddle River, NJ: Prentice Hall.

Crago, M. (1992). Communicative interaction and second language acquisition: The Inuit example. *TESOL Quarterly, 26,* 487–505.

Cronk, B. C., Lima, S. D., & Schweigert, W. A. (1993). Idioms in sentences: Effects of frequency, literalness, and familiarity. *Journal of Psycholinguistic Research, 22,* 59–82.

DaSilva Iddlings, A. C. (2005). Linguistic access and participation: English language learners in an English-dominant community of practice. *Bilingual Research Journal, 29(1),* 165–183.

Davidson, D., Raschke, V. R., & Pervez, J. (2010). Syntactic awareness in young monolingual and bilingual (Urdu-English) children. *Cognitive Development, 25,* 166–182.

Dean Qualls, C., O'Brien, R. M., Blood, G. W., & Scheffner Hammer, C. (2003). Contextual variation, familiarity, academic literacy, and rural adolescents' idiom knowledge. *Language, Speech, and Hearing Services in Schools, 34,* 69–79.

de Boysson-Bardies, B. (1999). *How language comes to children: From birth to two years.* Cambridge, MA: The MIT Press.

DeTemple, J. (2001). Parents and children reading books together. In D. Dickinson & P. Tabors (Eds.), *Beginning literacy with language: Young children learning at home and school* (pp. 31–51). Baltimore, MD: Brookes.

Dixon, M., Stuart, M., & Masterson, J. (2002). The relationship between phonological awareness and the development of orthographic representations. *Reading and Writing: An Interdisciplinary Journal, 15,* 295–316.

Ely, R., & McCabe, A. (1994). The language play of kindergarten children. *First Language, 14,* 19–35.

Farris, P., Fuhler, C., & Walther, M. (2004). *Teaching reading: A balanced approach for today's classrooms.* Boston, MA: McGraw-Hill.

Fenson, L., Dale, P. S., Reznick, J. S., Bates, E., Thal, D. J., & Pethick, S. J. (1994). Variability in early communicative development.

Monographs of the Society for Research in Child Development, 59(5, Serial No. 242).

Fernald, A. (1992). Human maternal vocalizations to infants as biologically relevant signals: An evolutionary perspective. In J. H. Barkow, L. Cosmides, & J. Tooby (Eds.), *The adaptive mind: Evolutionary psychology and the generation of culture* (pp. 391–428). New York, NY: Oxford University Press.

Fernald, A., Marchman, V. A., & Weisleder, A. (2013). SES differences in language processing skill and vocabulary are evident at 18 months. *Developmental Science, 16*(2), 234–248.

Fey, M., Long, S., & Finestack, L. (2003, February). Ten principles of grammar facilitation for children with specific language impairments. *American Journal of Speech-Language Pathology, 12,* 3–15.

Flavell, J. H., Miller, P. H., & Miller, S. A. (2002). *Cognitive development* (4th ed.). Upper Saddle River, NJ: Prentice Hall.

Ford-Connors, E., & Paratore, J. R. (2015). Vocabulary instruction in fifth grade and beyond: Sources of word learning and productive contexts for development. *Review of Educational Research, 85*(1), 50–90.

Fraser, J., Goswami, U., & Conti-Ramsden, G. (2010). Dyslexia and specific language impairment: The role of phonology and auditory processing. *Scientific Studies of Reading, 14*(1), 8–29.

Fujiki, M., Brinton, B., Morgan, M., & Hart, C. H. (1999). Withdrawn and sociable behavior of children with language impairment. *Language, Speech, and Hearing Services in Schools, 30,* 183–195.

Garcia, E. E. (1992). "Hispanic" children: Theoretical, empirical, and related policy issues. *Educational Psychology Review, 4*(1), 69–93.

Gathercole, V. C. M. (2002). Grammatical gender in bilingual and monolingual children: A Spanish morphosyntactic distinction. In D. Kimbrough Oller & R. E. Eilers (Eds.), *Language and literacy in bilingual children* (pp. 207–219). Cleveland, OH: Multilingual Matters Limited.

Genesee, F., & Nicoladis, E. (1995). Language development in bilingual preschool children. In E. E. Garcia & B. McLaughlin (Eds.), *Meeting the challenge of linguistic and cultural diversity in early childhood education* (pp. 18–33). New York, NY: Teachers College Press.

Genesee, F., Paradis, J., & Crago, M. (2004). *Dual language development & disorders: A handbook on*

bilingualism & second language learning. Baltimore, MD: Brookes.

Ginsburg, G. E, & Kilbourne, B. K. (1988). Emergence of vocal alternation in mother-infant interchanges. *Journal of Child Language, 15,* 221–235.

Goldfield, B. E., & Snow, C. E. (2005). Individual differences: Implications for the study of language acquisition. In J. B. Gleason (Ed.), *The development of language* (6th ed., pp. 292–303). Boston, MA: Pearson.

Goldin-Meadow, S., & Morford, M. (1985). Gesture in early child language: Studies of deaf and hearing children. *Merrill-Palmer Quarterly, 31,* 145–176.

Goldin-Meadow, S., & Mylander, C. (1983). Gestural communication in deaf children: Noneffect of parental input on language development. *Science, 221,* 372–374.

Gopnik, A., Meltzoff, A. N., & Kuhl, P. K. (1999). *The scientist in the crib: What early learning tells us about the mind.* New York, NY: Perennial/HarperCollins.

Gottwald, S., Goldbach, P., & Isack, A. (1985). Stuttering: Prevention and detection. *Young Children, 41*(1), 9–16.

Gutiérrez, K. D., Baquedano-López, P., & Asato, J. (2001). English for the children: The new literacy of the old word order, language policy, and education reform. *Bilingual Research Journal, 24*(1–2), 87–112.

Hart, B., & Risley, T. (1995). *Meaningful differences in the everyday experience of young American children.* Baltimore, MD: Brookes.

Hart, B., & Risley, T. (1999). *The social world of children learning to talk.* Baltimore, MD: Brookes.

Hart, B., & Risley, T. R. (2003). The early catastrophe. The 30 million word gap. *American Educator, 27*(1), 4–9.

Hirata-Edds, T. (2011). Influence of second language Cherokee immersion on children's development of past tense in their first language, English. *Language Learning, 61*(3), 700–733.

Hoff, E. (2003a). The specificity of environment influence: Socioeconomic status affects early vocabulary development via maternal speech. *Child Development, 74*(5), 1368–1378.

Hoff, E. (2003b). Causes and consequences of SES related differences in parent to child speech. In M. Bornstein & R. Bradley (Eds.), *Socioeconomic status, parenting, and child development* (pp. 147–160). Mahwah, NJ: Lawrence Erlbaum.

Holowka, S., & Petitto, L. A. (2002). Left hemisphere cerebral specialization for babies while babbling. *Science, 297,* 1515.

Horgan, D. (1978). The development of the full passive. *Journal of Child Language, 5,* 65–80.

Howard, E. R., Christian, D., & Genesee, F. (2004). *The development of bilingualism and biliteracy from grade 3 to 5: A summary of findings from the CAL/CREDE study of two-way immersion education.* Santa Cruz, CA: CREDE, University of California at Santa Cruz.

Howard, E. R., Sugarman, J., & Christian, D. (2003). *Trends in two-way immersion education: A review of the research.* Washington, DC: Center for Applied Linguistics.

Hulit, L. M., Fahey, K. R., & Howard, M. R. (2015). *Born to talk: An introduction to speech and language development* (6th ed.). Boston, MA: Pearson.

Hurtado, N., Marchman, V. A., & Fernald, A. (2008). Does input influence uptake? Links between maternal talk, processing speed and vocabulary size in Spanish-learning children. *Developmental Science, 11*(6), 31–40.

Huttenlocher, J., Waterfall, H., Vasilyeva, M., Vevea, J., & Hedges, L. V. (2010). Sources of variability in children's language growth. *Cognitive Psychology, 61,* 343–365.

Huttenlocher, P. (2002). *Neural plasticity: The effects of environment on the development of the cerebral cortex.* Cambridge, MA: Harvard University Press.

Irwin, J., & Moore, D. (2014). *Preparing children for reading success: Hands-on activities for librarians, educators, and caregivers.* Lanham, MD: Rowman & Littlefield.

Jalava, A. (1988). Mother tongue and identity: Nobody could see that I was a Finn. In T. Skutnabb-Kangas & J. Cummins (Eds.), *Minority education: From shame to struggle* (pp. 161–166). Bristol, PA: Multilingual Matters.

James, S. (1990). *Normal language acquisition.* Austin, TX: PRO-ED.

Johnson, C. J., & Anglin, J. M. (1995). Qualitative developments in the content and form of children's definitions. *Journal of Speech and Hearing Research, 38*(3), 612–629.

Justice, L. M., Bowles, R. P., Pence Turnbull, K. L., & Skibbe, L. E. (2009). School readiness among children with varying histories of language difficulties. *Developmental Psychology, 45,* 460–476.

Kelley, J. G., Lesaux, N. K., Kieffer, M. J., & Faller, S. E. (2010). Effective academic vocabulary instruction in the urban middle school. *Source: The Reading Teacher, 64*(1), 5–14.

Kent, R. D., & Miulo, G. (1995). Phonetic abilities in the first year of life. In P. Fletcher & B. MacWhinney (Eds.), *The handbook of child language* (pp. 303–334). Cambridge, MA: Blackwell.

Kim, Y. K., Hutchison, L. A., & Winsler, A. (2015). Bilingual education in the United States: An historical overview and examination of two-way immersion. *Educational Review, 67*(2), 236–252.

Kogan, E. (2001). *Gifted bilingual students.* New York, NY: Peter Lang.

Kostelnik, M., Soderman, A., & Whiren, A. (2004). *Developmentally appropriate curriculum: Best practices in early childhood education.* Upper Saddle River, NJ: Prentice Hall.

Kuhl, P. K. (2004). Early language acquisition: Cracking the speech code. *Neuroscience, 5,* 831–843.

Le, H.-N. (2000). Never leave your little one alone: Raising an Ifaluk child. In J. S. DeLoache & A. Gottlieb (Eds.), *A world of babies: Imagined childcare guides for seven societies* (pp. 199–220). New York, NY: Cambridge University Press.

Lessow-Hurley, J. (2000). *The foundations of dual language instruction* (3rd ed.). White Plains, NY: Longman.

Liberman, I. Y., Shankweiler, D., Camp, L., Blachman, B., & Werfelman, M. (1980). Steps toward literacy. In P. Levinson & C. Sloan (Eds.), *Auditory processing and language: Clinical and research perspectives* (pp. 189–215). New York, NY: Grune & Stratton.

Liberman, I. Y., Shankweiler, D., & Liberman, A. M. (1989). The alphabetic principle and learning to read. In D. Shankweiler, & I. Y. Liberman, (Eds.), *Phonology and reading disability: Solving the reading puzzle* (pp. 1–33). Ann Arbor: University of Michigan Press.

Lindholm-Leary, K. J. (2001). *Dual language education.* Avon, UK: Multilingual Matters.

Lindholm-Leary, K. J. (2004–2005). The rich promise of two-way immersion. *Educational Leadership, 62*(4), 56–59.

Locke, J. L. (1983). *Phonological acquisition and change.* New York, NY: Academic Press.

Locke, J. L. (1995). Development of the capacity for spoken language. In P. Fletcher & B. MacWhinney (Eds.), *The handbook of child language* (pp. 278–302). Cambridge, MA: Blackwell.

Loizou, M., & Stuart, M. (2003). Phonological awareness in monolingual and bilingual English and Greek five-year-olds. *Journal of Research in Reading, 26*(1), 3–18.

Maclean, M., Bryant, P. E., & Bradley, L. (1987). Rhymes, nursery rhymes, and reading in early childhood. *Merrill-Palmer Quarterly, 33,* 255–281.

Mancilla-Martinez, J., & Lesaux, N. K. (2011). Early home use and later vocabulary development. *Journal of Educational Psychology, 103*(3), 535–546.

Marcus, G. E., Pinker, S., Ullman, M., Hollander, M., Rosen, T. J., & Xu, F. (1992). Overregularization in language acquisition. *Monographs of the Society for Research in Child Development, 57*(Serial No. 228).

Marsh, H. W., Hau, K. T., & Kong, C. K. (2002). Multilevel causal ordering of academic self-concept and achievement: Influence of language of instruction (English compared with Chinese) for Hong Kong students. *American Educational Research Journal, 39,* 727–763.

Martinez-Roldan, C. M., & Lopez-Robertson, J. M. (2000). Initiating literature circles in a first-grade bilingual classroom. *The Reading Teacher, 53*(4), 270–281.

Masataka, N. (1992). Pitch characteristics of Japanese maternal speech to infants. *Journal of Child Language, 19,* 213–224.

McLean, J., & Snyder-McLean, L. (1999). *How children learn language.* San Diego, CA: Singular Publishing.

McMurray, B. (2007). Defusing the childhood vocabulary explosion. *Science, 317,* 631.

McNeill, J., & Fowler, S. (1996). Using story reading to encourage children's conversations. *Teaching Exceptional Children, 28*(4), 43–47.

Menyuk, P. (1988). *Language development: Knowledge and use.* Glenview, IL: Scott, Foresman/Little, Brown.

Montgomery, J. (2002). Understanding the language difficulties of children with specific language impairments: Does verbal working memory matter? *American Journal of Speech-Language Pathology, 11,* 77–91.

Morrisette, P., Ricard, M., & Gouin-Decarie, T. (1995). Joint visual attention and pointing in infancy: A longitudinal study of comprehension. *British Journal of Developmental Psychology, 13,* 163–177.

Morrow, L. (1989). *Literacy development in the early years.* Upper Saddle River, NJ: Prentice Hall.

Murphy, P. K., Wilkinson, I. A., Soter, A. O., Hennessey, M. N., & Alexander, J. F. (2009). Examining the effects of classroom discussion on students' comprehension of text: A meta-analysis. *Journal of Educational Psychology, 101*(3), 740–764.

National Reading Panel. (2000). *Teaching children to read: An evidence-based assessment of the scientific research literature on reading and its* implications for reading instruction (NIH Pub. No. 00–4769). Washington, DC: National Institutes of Health.

Nelson, K. E., Welsh, J. A., Vance Trup, E. M., & Greenberg, M. T. (2011). Language delays of impoverished preschool children in relation to early academic and emotion recognition skills. *First Language, 31,* 164–194.

Nicholas, H., Lightbown, P. M., & Spada, M. (2001). Recasts as feedback to language learners. *Language Learning, 51*(4), 719–758.

Nicoladis, E., & Genesee, F. (1996). Word awareness in second language learners and bilingual children. *Language Awareness, 5*(2), 80–90.

Nicoladis, E., & Genesee, F. (1997). Language development in preschool bilingual children. *Journal of Speech-Language Pathology and Audiology, 21*(4), 258–270.

Nippold, M., & Duthie, J. (2003). Mental imagery and idiom comprehension: A comparison of school-age children and adults. *Journal of Speech, Language, and Hearing Research, 46,* 788–799.

Nippold, M. A., Moran, C., & Schwartz, I. E. (2001). Idiom understanding in preadolescents: Synergy in action. *American Journal of Speech-Language Pathology, 10,* 169–179.

Ochs, E., & Schieffelin, B. B. (1984). Language acquisition and socialization: Three developmental stories and their implications. In R. Shweder & R. LeVine (Eds.), *Developmental pragmatics* (pp. 276–320). New York, NY: Academic Press.

Omoteso, B. A., & Sadiku, F. A. (2013). Effectiveness of PQ4R study technique on performance of students in chemistry: Child & adolescent therapy and e-therapy. *IFE Psychologia: An International Journal: Psychotherapy: Unity in Diversity, 21*(3), 238–244.

Otto, B. (2006). *Language development in early childhood* (2nd ed.). Upper Saddle River, NJ: Prentice Hall.

Otto, B. (2014). *Language development in early childhood education* (4th ed.). Boston, MA: Pearson.

Owens, R. E., Jr. (1988). *Language development.* Upper Saddle River, NJ: Prentice Hall.

Owens, R. E., Jr. (2005). *Language development: An introduction* (6th ed.). Boston, MA: Allyn & Bacon.

Owens, R. E, Jr. (2012). *Language development: An introduction* (8th ed.). Boston, MA: Pearson.

Palincsar, A. S. (2003). Ann L. Brown: Advancing a theoretical model of learning and instruction. In B. J. Zimmerman & D. H. Schunk (Eds.), *Educational psychology: A century of*

contributions (pp. 459–475). Mahwah, NJ: Lawrence Erlbaum.

Patterson, K., & Wright, A. (1990). The speech, language or hearing-impaired child: At-risk academically. *Childhood Education, 67*(2), 91–95.

Payne, A., Whitehurst, G., & Angell, A. (1994). The role of home literacy environment in the development of language ability in preschool children from low-income families. *Early Childhood Research Quarterly, 9*(3–4), 427–440.

Pearson, B. (1998). Assessing lexical development in bilingual babies and toddlers. *International Journal of Bilingualism, 2*(3), 347–372.

Pepicello, W., & Weisberg, R. (1983). Linguistics and humor. In P. McGhee & J. Goldstein (Eds.), *Handbook of humor research: Volume 1. Basic issues* (pp. 59–83). New York, NY: Springer-Verlag.

Perez, B. (2004). *Becoming biliterate: A study of two-way bilingual immersion education.* Mahwah, NJ: Lawrence Erlbaum.

Petitto, L. A., Holowka, S., Sergio, L. E., & Ostry, D. (2001). Language rhythms in baby hand movements. *Nature, 413,* 35–36.

Petitto, L. A., Katerelos, M., Levy, B. G., Gauna, K., Tetreault, K., & Ferraro, V. (2001). Bilingual signed and spoken language acquisition from birth: Implications for the mechanisms underlying early bilingual language acquisition. *Journal of Child Language, 28*(2), 453–496.

Proctor, C. P., August, D., Carlo, M. S., & Snow, C. E. (2006). The intriguing role of Spanish language vocabulary knowledge in predicting English reading comprehension. *Journal of Educational Psychology, 98*(1), 159–169.

Raphael, T., & Hiebert, E. (1996). *Creating an integrated approach to literacy instruction.* Fort Worth, TX: Harcourt Brace College.

Ratner, N. (2004, January). Caregiver-child interactions and their impact on children's fluency: Implications for treatment. *Language, Speech and Hearing Services in Schools, 35,* 46–56.

Redcay, E., Haist, F., & Courchesne, E. (2008). Functional neuroimaging of speech perception during a pivotal period in language acquisition. *Developmental Science, 11,* 237–252.

Rijlaarsdam, G., Van den Bergh, H., Couzijn, M., Janssen, T., Braaksma, M., Tillema, M., . . . Raedts, M. (2012). Writing. In K. R. Harris, S. Graham, T. Urdan, A. G. Bus, S. Major, & H. L. Swanson (Eds.), *APA educational psychology handbook. Volume 3:*

Application to learning and teaching (pp. 189–227). Washington, DC: American Psychological Association.

Ritchie, W. C., & Bhatia, T. K. (Eds.). (1999). *Handbook of child language acquisition.* Orlando, FL: Academic Press.

Rollins, P. (2003). Caregivers' contingent comments to 9-month-old infants: Relationship with later language. *Applied Psycholinguistics, 24,* 221–234.

Rowe, M. L. (2012). A longitudinal investigation of the role of quantity and quality of child-directed speech vocabulary development. *Child Development, 83*(5), 1762–1774.

Rowe, M. L., & Goldin-Meadow, S. (2000, February 13). Differences in early gesture explain SES disparities in child vocabulary size at school entry. *Science, 323,* 951–953.

Roy, P., & Chiat, S. (2013). Teasing apart disadvantage from disorder. In C. R. Marshall (Ed.), *Current issues in developmental disorders* (pp. 125–150). London, UK: Psychology Press.

Rupley, W. H., Blair, T. R., & Nichols, W. D. (2009). Effective reading instruction for struggling readers: The role of direct/explicit teaching. *Reading and Writing Quarterly, 25*(2–3), 125–138.

Sachs, J. (1989). Communication development in infancy. In J. Berko Gleason (Ed.), *The development of language* (2nd ed., pp. 35–58). Upper Saddle River, NJ: Prentice Hall.

Santiago, R. (1994). The interdependence between linguistic and cognitive performance among bilingual preschoolers with differing home language environments. In D. MacLaughlin & S. McEwen (Eds.), *Proceedings of Boston University Conference on Language Development* (pp. 511–520). Somerville, MA: Cascadilla Press.

Saunders, W., & Goldenberg, C. (1999). The effects of instructional conversations and literature logs on limited- and fluent-English-proficient students' story comprehension and thematic understanding. *The Elementary School Journal, 99*(4), 277–301.

Scherer, N., & Olswang, L. (1984). Role of mothers' expansions in stimulating children's language production. *Journal of Speech and Hearing Research, 27,* 387–396.

Schickedanz, J., York, M., Stewart, I., & White, D. (1990). *Strategies for teaching young children.* Upper Saddle River, NJ: Prentice Hall.

Schieffelin, F., & Ochs, E. (1986). Language socialization. *Annual Review of Anthropology, 15,* 163–246.

Schneider, B. A., Trehub, S. E., & Bull, D. (1979). The development of basic auditory processes in infants. *Canadian Journal of Psychology, 33,* 306–319.

Scott, L. (2007). *The child who stutters at school: Notes to the teacher.* Retrieved from The Stuttering Foundation website: http://www.stutteringhelp.org/Portals/english/0042NT.pdf

Shankweiler, D., & Fowler, A. E. (2004). Questions people ask about the role of phonological processes in learning to read. *Reading and Writing: An Interdisciplinary Journal, 17,* 483–515.

Skinner, B. F. (1957). *Verbal behavior.* Upper Saddle River, NJ: Prentice Hall.

Siegler, R. S., & Alibali, M. W. (2005). *Children's thinking* (4th ed.). Upper Saddle River, NJ: Prentice Hall.

Snow, C. E. (1986). Conversations with children. In P. Fletcher & M. Garman (Eds.), *Language acquisition: Studies in first language development* (pp. 69–89). Cambridge, UK: Cambridge University Press.

Snow, C. E., & Goldfield, B. A. (1983). Turn the page please: Situation-specific language learning. *Journal of Child Language, 10,* 551–569.

Snow, C. E., Tabors, P. O., & Dickinson, D. K. (2001). Language development in the preschool years. In D. K. Dickinson & P. O. Tabors (Eds.), *Beginning literacy with language* (pp. 1–25). Baltimore, MD: Brookes.

Spelke, E. S., & Newport, E. L. (1998). Nativism, empiricism, and the development of knowledge. In W. Damon (Series Ed.) & D. Kuhn & R. S. Siegler (Vol. Eds.), *Handbook of child psychology. Vol. 2. Cognition, perception, and language* (5th ed., pp. 275–340). New York, NY: Wiley.

Squibb, B., & Dietz, S. (2000). *Learning activities for infants and toddlers: An easy guide for everyday use.* Washington, DC: Children's Resources International.

Stiles, J. (2008). *The fundamentals of brain development.* Cambridge, MA: Harvard University Press.

Stiles, J., & Thal, D. (1993). Linguistic and spatial cognitive development following early focal brain injury: Patterns of deficit and recovery. In M. H. Johnson (Ed.), *Brain development and cognition: A reader* (2nd ed., pp. 643–664). Oxford, UK: Blackwell.

Swan, A. (1993). Helping children who stutter: What teachers need to know. *Childhood Education, 69*(3), 138–141.

Tamis-LeMonda, C. S., Bornstein, M. H., & Baumwell, L. (2001). Maternal responsiveness and children's achievement of language milestones. *Child Development, 72*(3), 748–767.

Tardif, T., Fletcher, P., Liang, W., Zhang, Z., Kaciroti, N., & Marchman, V. A. (2008). Baby's first 10 words. *Developmental Psychology, 44,* 929–938.

Thomas, W. P., & Collier, V. P. (2002). *A national study of school effectiveness for language minority students' long-term academic achievement.* Honolulu, HI: Center for Research on Education, Diversity & Excellence.

Tomasello, M. (2005). *Constructing a language: A usage-based theory of language acquisition.* Cambridge, MA: Harvard University Press.

Tomasello, M. (2006). Acquiring linguistic constructions. In D. Kuhn & R. Siegler (Vol. Eds.), *Handbook of child psychology: Cognition, perception, and language* (Vol. 2, pp. 255–298). New York, NY: Wiley.

Tomblin, J. B., Zhang, X., Buckwalter, P., & O'Brien, M. (2003). The stability of primary language disorder: Four years after kindergarten diagnosis. *Journal of Speech, Language, and Hearing Research, 46,* 1283–1296.

Torgesen, J. K., & Mathes, P. G. (2000). *A basic guide to understanding and teaching phonological awareness.* Austin, TX: Pro-Ed.

Verhoeven, L., van Leeuwe, J., & Vermeer, A. (2011). Vocabulary growth and reading development across the elementary school years. *Scientific Studies of Reading, 15*(1), 8–25.

Wagner, R. K., Torgesen, J. K., & Rashotte, C. A. (1994). The development of reading-related phonological processing abilities: New evidence of bi-directional causality from a latent variable longitudinal study. *Developmental Psychology, 30,* 73–87.

Warren-Leubecker, A., & Bohannon, J. N. (1983). The effects of verbal feedback and listener type on the speech of preschool children. *Journal of Experimental Child Psychology, 35,* 540–548.

Weir, E., & Bianchet, S. (2004). Developmental dysfluency: Early intervention is key. *Canadian Medical Association Journal, 170*(12), 1790–1791.

Whitehurst, G., & Lonigan, C. (1998). Child development and emergent literacy. *Child Development, 69,* 848–872.

Whitehurst, G. J., Arnold, D. S., Epstein, J. N., Angell, A. L., Smith, M., & Fischel, J. E. (1994). A picture book reading intervention in day care and home for children from low-income families. *Developmental Psychology, 30*(5), 679–689.

Wing, C., & Scholnick, E. (1981). Children's comprehension of pragmatic concepts expressed in "because," "although," "if" and "unless." *Journal of Child Language, 8,* 347–365.

Wolvin, A., & Coakley, C. (1985). *Listening.* Dubuque, IA: William C. Brown.

Yairi, E., & Ambrose, N. (2005). *Early childhood stuttering: For clinicians by clinicians.* Austin, TX: Pro-Ed.

Yopp, H. K., & Yopp, R. H. (2009). Phonological awareness is child's play! *Young Children, 64*(1), 12–28.

Zevenbergen, A. A., & Whitehurst, G. J. (2003). Dialogic reading: A shared picture book reading intervention for preschoolers. In A. van Kleeck, S. A. Stahl, & E. B. Bauer (Eds.), *On reading books to children: Parents and teachers* (pp. 177–200). Mahwah, NJ: Lawrence Erlbaum.

Module 8

Alberto, P. A., & Troutman, A. C. (2012). *Applied Behavior Analysis for Teachers* (9th ed.). London, UK: Pearson.

American Academy of Pediatrics. (2013). The crucial role of recess in school. *Pediatrics, 131*(1), 183–188.

Anderson, J., & Le, D. D. (2011). Abatement of intractable vocal stereotype using an overcorrection procedure. *Behavioral Interventions, 26,* 134–146.

Barros, R. M., Silver, E. J., & Stein, R. E. K. (2009). School recess and group classroom behavior. *Pediatrics, 123*(2), 431–436.

Beaman, R., & Wheldall, K. (2000). Teachers' use of approval and disapproval in the classroom. *Educational Psychology, 20,* 431–446.

Becker, D. R., McClelland, M. M., Loprinzi, P., & Trost, S. G. (2014). Physical activity, self-regulation, and early academic achievement in preschool children. *Early Education and Development, 25*(1), 56–70.

Becker, W. C., Madsen, C. H., Arnold, C. R., & Thomas, D. R. (1967). The contingent use of teacher attention and praise in reducing classroom behavior problems. *The Journal of Special Education, 1,* 287–307.

Bohn-Gettler, C. M., & Pellegrini, A. D. (2014). Recess in primary school: The disjuncture between educational policy and scientific research. In B. H. Bornstein & R. L. Wiener (Eds.), *Justice, conflict and wellbeing: Multidisciplinary perspectives* (pp. 313–336). New York, NY: Springer.

Cheyne, J. A., & Walters, R. H. (1970). Punishment and Prohibition: Some origins of self-control. *New Directions in Psychology, 4,* 281–366.

Cook-Cottone, C. P., Tribole, E., & Tylka, T. L. (2013). *Healthy eating in schools.* Washington, DC: American Psychological Association.

Corno, L. (1996). Homework is a complicated thing. *Educational Researcher, 25,* 27–30.

Damon, S., Riley-Tillman, T. C., & Fiorello, C. (2008). Comparing methods of identifying reinforcing stimuli in school consultation. *Journal of Educational & Psychological Consultation, 18*(1), 31–53.

Davis, G. A., & Thomas, M. A. (1989). *Effective schools and effective teachers.* Boston, MA: Allyn & Bacon.

DeLeon, I. G., Bullock, C. E., & Catania, A. C. (2013). Arranging reinforcement contingencies in applied settings: Fundamentals and implications of recent basic and applied research. In G. J. Madden (Ed.), *APA handbook of behavior analysis, vol. 2* (pp. 47–75). Washington, DC: American Psychological Association.

Donaldson, J. M., Vollmer, T. R., Yakich, T. M., & Van Camp, C. (2013). Effects of a reduced time-out interval on compliance with the time-out instruction. *Journal of Applied Behavioral Analysis, 46,* 369–378.

Everett, G. E., Hupp, S. D. A., & Olmi, J. (2010). Time-out with parents: A descriptive analysis of 30 years of research. *Educational and Treatment of Children, 33(2),* 235–259.

Flood, W. A., Wilder, D. A., Flood, A. L., & Masuda, A. (2002). Peer-mediated reinforcement plus prompting as treatment for off-task behavior in children with attention deficit hyperactivity disorder. *Journal of Applied Behavior Analysis, 35,* 199–204.

Freeland, J. T., & Noell, G. H. (1999). Maintaining accurate math responses in elementary school students: The effects of delayed intermittent reinforcement and programming common stimuli. *Journal of Applied Behavior Analysis, 32,* 211–215.

Gibson, P. A., Wilson, R., Haight, W., Kayama, M., & Marshall, J. M. (2014). The role of race in the out-of-school suspensions of black students: The perspectives of students with suspensions, their parents and educators. *Children and Youth Services Review, 47,* 274–282.

Gootman, M. E. (1998). Effective in-house suspension. *Educational Leadership, 56,* 39–41.

Hodge, G. K., & Nelson, N. H. (1991). Demonstrating differential reinforcement by shaping classroom participation. *Teaching of Psychology, 18,* 239–241.

Holmes, R. M., Pellegrini, A. D., & Schmidt, S. L. (2006). The effects of different recess timing regimens on preschoolers' classroom attention. *Early Child Development and Care, 176*(7), 735–743.

Homme, L. E., DeBaga, P. C., Devine, J. V., Steinhorst, R., & Rickert, E. J. (1963). Use of the Premack Principle in controlling the behavior of nursery school children. *Journal of the Experimental Analysis of Behavior, 6,* 544.

Huff, J. A. (1988). Personalized behavior modification: An in-school suspension program that teaches students how to change. *The School Counselor, 35*(3), 210–214.

Jimura, K., Myerson, J., Hilgard, J., Keighley, J., Braver, T. S., & Green, L. (2011). Domain independence and stability in young and older adults' discounting of delayed rewards. *Behavioral Processes, 87,* 253–259.

Kazdin, A. E. (2001). *Behavior modification in applied settings* (6th ed.). Belmont, CA: Wadsworth.

Kimble, G. A. (2000). Behaviorism and unity in psychology. *Current Directions in Psychological Science, 9,* 208–212.

Krezmien, M. P., Leone, P. E., & Achilles, G. M. (2006). Suspension, race, and disability: Analysis of statewide practices and reporting. *Journal of Emotional & Behavioral Disorders, 14*(4), 217–226.

Krumboltz, J. D., & Krumboltz, H. B. (1972). *Changing children's behaviors.* Englewood Cliffs, NJ: Prentice Hall.

Kulik, J. A., & Kulik, C. C. (1988). Timing of feedback and verbal learning. *Review of Educational Research, 58,* 79–97.

Lerman, D. C., & Iwata, B. A. (1995). Prevalence of the extinction burst and its attenuation during treatment. *Journal of Applied Behavior Analysis, 28,* 93–94.

Locke, J. (1892). Some thoughts concerning education. In R. H. Quick (Ed.), *Locke on education* (pp. 1–236). Cambridge, UK: Cambridge University Press. (Original work published in 1690)

Maag, J. W. (2001). Rewarded by punishment: Reflections on the disuse of positive reinforcement in schools. *Exceptional Children, 67,* 173–186.

Maag, J. W. (2012). School-wide discipline and the intransigency of exclusion. *Children and Youth Services Review, 34,* 2094–2100.

Mackenzie, M. J., Nicklas, E., Waldfogel, J., & Brooks-Gunn, J. (2013). Spanking and child development across the first decade of life. *Pediatrics, 132*(5), 1118–1125.

Madsen, C. H., Becker, W. C., & Thomas, D. R. (1968). Rules, praise, and ignoring: Elements of elementary classroom control. *Journal of Applied Behavior Analysis, 1,* 139–150.

Mahar, M. T. (2011). Impact of short bouts of physical activity on attention-to-task in elementary school children. *Preventive Medicine, 52,* 560–564.

McComas, J. J., Thompson, A., & Johnson, L. (2003). The effects of precession attention on problem behavior maintained by different reinforcers. *Journal of Applied Behavior Analysis, 36,* 297–307.

McGoey, K. E., & DuPaul, G. J. (2000). Token reinforcement and response cost procedures: Reducing the disruptive behavior of preschool children with attention-deficit/hyperactivity disorder. *School Psychology Quarterly, 15,* 330–343.

Milo, J., Mace, F. C., & Nevin, J. A. (2010). The effects of constant versus varied reinforcers on preference and resistance to change. *Journal of Experimental Analysis of Behavior, 93,* 385–394.

Morawska, A., & Sanders, M. (2011). Parental use of time out revisited: A useful or harmful parenting strategy? *Journal of Child Family Studies, 20,* 1–8.

O'Leary, K. D., Kaufman, K. F., Kass, R. E., & Drabman, R. S. (1970). The effects of loud and soft reprimands on the behavior of disruptive students. *Exceptional Children, 37,* 145–155.

Oliver, P., & Brady, M. P. (2014). Effects of covert audio coaching on parents' interactions with young children with Autism. *Behavioral Analysis Practice, 7,* 112–116.

Pavlov, I. (1960). *Conditioned reflexes: An investigation of the physiological activity of the cerebral cortex.* Oxford, UK: Oxford University Press. (Original work published 1927)

Peters, L. C., & Thompson, R. H. (2013). Some indirect effects of positive practice overcorrection. *Journal of Applied Behavioral Analysis, 46,* 613–625.

Pfiffner, L. J., & Barkley, R. A. (1998). Treatment of ADHD in school settings. In R. Barkley (Ed.), *Attention-Deficit hyperactivity disorder: A handbook for diagnosis and treatment* (2nd ed., pp. 458–490). New York, NY: Guilford Press: New York.

Premack, D. (1959). Toward empirical behavioral laws: I. Positive reinforcement. *Psychological Review, 66,* 219–233.

Premack D. (1965). Reinforcement theory. In D. Levine (Ed.), *Nebraska Symposium on Motivation* (pp. 123–180). Lincoln: University of Nebraska Press.

Rapport, M. D., Murphy, H. A., & Bailey, J. S. (1982). Ritalin vs. response cost in the control of hyperactive children: A within-subject comparison. *Journal of Applied Behavior Analysis, 15,* 205–216.

Rescorla, R. A. (1988). Pavlovian conditioning: It's not what you think. *American Psychologist, 43,* 151–160.

Ridgway, A., Northup, J., Pellegrin, A., LaRue, R., & Hightshoe, A. (2003). Effects of recess on the classroom behavior of children with and without attention-deficit hyperactivity disorder. *School Psychology Quarterly, 18,* 253–268.

Robinson, D. H., Funk, D. C., Beth, A., & Bush, A. M. (2005). Changing beliefs about corporal punishment: Increasing knowledge about ineffectiveness to build more consistent moral and informational beliefs. *Journal of Behavioral Education, 14,* 117–139.

Rotenberg, K. J., & Mayer, E. V. (1990). Delay of gratification in native and white children: A cross-cultural comparison. *International Journal of Behavioral Development, 13,* 23–30.

Seaver, J. L., & Bouret, J. C. (2014). An evaluation of response prompts for teaching behavior chains. *Journal of Applied Behavioral Analysis, 47,* 777–792.

Shabani, D. B., Katz, R. C., Wilder, D. A., Beauchamp, K., Taylor, C. R., & Fischer, K. J. (2002). Increasing social initiations in children with autism: Effects of a tactile prompt. *Journal of Applied Behavior Analysis, 35,* 79–83.

Shea, T. M., & Bauer, A. M. (2012). *Behavior management: A practical approach for educators* (10th ed.). London, UK: Pearson.

Skiba, R. J., Horner, R. H., Chung, C., Rausch, M. R., May, S. L., & Tobin, T. (2011). Race is not neutral: A national investigation of African American and Latino disproportionality in school discipline. *School Psychology Review, 40*(1), 85–107.

Skinner, B. F. (1953). *Science and human behavior.* New York, NY: Macmillan.

Skinner, B. F. (1954). The science of learning and the art of teaching. *Harvard Education Review, 14,* 86–97.

Sullivan, M. A., & O'Leary, S. G. (1990). Maintenance following reward and cost token programs. *Behavior Therapy, 21,* 139–149.

Tafa, E. M. (2002). Corporal punishment: The brutal face of Botswana's authoritarian schools. *Educational Review, 54,* 17–26.

Thorndike, E. L. (1898). Animal Intelligence: An experimental study of the associate processes in animals. *Psychological Review Monograph Supplement, 2,* 1–8.

Vanderveldt, A., Green, L., & Myerson, J. (2014). Discounting of monetary rewards that are both delayed and probabilistic: Delay and probability combine multiplicatively, not additively. *Journal of Experimental Psychology: Learning, Memory, and Cognition, 41*(1), 148–162.

Van Houten, R., Nau, P. A., MacKenzie-Keating, S. E., Sameoto, D., & Colavecchia, B. (1982). An analysis of some variables influencing the effectiveness of reprimands. *Journal of Applied Behavior Analysis, 15,* 65–83.

Watson, J. B. (1913). Psychology as the behaviorist views it. *Psychological Review, 20,* 158–177.

Watson, J. B., & Rayner, R. (1920). Conditioned emotional reactions. *Journal of Experimental Psychology, 3,* 1–14.

Woolfolk, A. E., & Brooks, D. M. (1985). The influence of teachers' nonverbal behaviors on students' perceptions and performance. *The Elementary School Journal, 85,* 513–528.

Module 9

Akinsola, M. J., & Awofala, A. O. A. (2009). Effect of personalization of instruction on students' achievement and self-efficacy in mathematics word problems. *International Journal of Mathematical Education in Science & Technology, 40*(3), 389–404.

Bandura, A. (1977). Self-efficacy: Toward a unifying theory of behavioral change. *Psychological Review, 84,* 191–215.

Bandura, A. (1982). Self-efficacy mechanism in human agency. *American Psychologist, 37,* 122–147.

Bandura, A. (1986). *Social foundations of thought and action.* Englewood Cliffs, NJ: Prentice Hall.

Bandura, A. (1989). Social cognitive theory. *Annals of Child Development, 6,* 1–60.

Bandura, A. (1997). *Self-Efficacy: The exercise of control.* New York, NY: Freeman.

Bandura, A. (2002). Social cognitive theory in cultural context. *Applied Psychology: An International Review, 51,* 269–290.

Bandura, A., Ross, D., & Ross, S. (1961). Transmission of aggression through imitation of aggressive models. *Journal of Abnormal and Social Psychology, 63,* 575–582.

Basak, R., & Ghosh, A. (2014). Perception of mathematics self-efficacy and achievement of primary school students. *Journal of the Indian Academy of Applied Psychology, 40*(1), 113–120.

Belfi, B., Gielen, S., De Fraine, B., Verschueren, K., & Meredith, C. (2015). School-based social capital: The missing link between schools' socioeconomic composition and collective teacher efficacy. *Teaching and Teacher Education, 45,* 33–44.

Braaksma, M. A. H., Rijlaarsdam, G., van den Bergh, H., & van Hout-Wolters, B. H. A. M. (2004). Observational learning and its effects on the orchestration of writing processes. *Cognition and Instruction, 22,* 1–36.

Bussey, K., & Bandura, A. (1999). Social cognitive theory of gender development and differentiation. *Psychological Review, 106,* 676–713.

Butler, D. L. (1998). The strategic content learning approach to promoting self-regulated learning: A report of three studies. *Journal of Educational Psychology, 90,* 682–697.

Chatzistamatiou, M., & Dermitzaki, I. (2013). Teaching mathematics with self-regulation and for self-regulation: Teachers' reports. *Hellenic Journal of Psychology, 10,* 253–274.

Edwards, L. A. (2014). A meta-analysis of imitation abilities in individuals with autism spectrum disorders. *Autism Research, 7,* 363–380.

Fouad, N. A., & Smith, P. L. (1996). A test of a social cognitive model for middle school students: Math and science. *Journal of Counseling Psychology, 43,* 338–346.

Goldstein, N. E., Arnold, D. H., Rosenber, J. L., Stowe, R. M., & Ortiz, C. (2001). Contagion of aggression in day care classrooms as a function of peer and teacher responses. *Journal of Educational Psychology, 93,* 708–719.

Horner, S. L. (2004). Observational learning during shared book reading: The effects on preschoolers attention to print and letter knowledge. *Reading Psychology, 25,* 167–188.

Kurt, T., Duyar, I., & Calik, T. (2011). Are we legitimate yet? A closer look at the casual relationship mechanisms among principal leadership, teacher self-efficacy, and collective efficacy. *Journal of Management Development, 31*(1), 71–86.

Labuhn, A. S., Zimmerman, B. J., & Hasselhorn, M. (2010). Enhancing students' self-regulation and mathematics performance: The influence of feedback and self-evaluative standards. *Metacognition Learning, 5,* 173–194.

Lee, J., Yu, H., & Choi, S. (2012). The influences of parental acceptance and parental control on school adjustment and academic achievement for South Korean children: The mediation role of self-regulation. *Asia Pacific Education Review, 13,* 227–237.

Linnenbrink, E. A., & Pintrich P. R. (2003). The role of self-efficacy beliefs in student engagement and learning in the classroom. *Reading and Writing Quarterly, 19,* 119–137.

Markova, G., & Legerstee, M. (2015). The role of maternal behavior in children's pretense during the second year of life. *Cognitive Development, 34,* 3–15.

Mayo, M. W., & Christenfeld, N. (1999). Gender, race, and performance expectations of college students. *Journal of Multicultural Counseling & Development, 27,* 93– 104.

Moolennaar, N. M., Sleegers, P. J. C., & Daly, A. J. (2012). Teaming up: Linking collaboration networks, collective efficacy, and student achievement. *Teaching and Teacher Education, 28,* 251–262.

Mucherah, W., & Yoder, A. (2008). Motivation for reading and middle school students' performance on standardized testing in reading. *Reading Psychology, 29*(3), 214–235.

Odden, H., & Rochat, P. (2004). Observational learning and enculturation. *Educational and Child Psychology, 21,* 39–50.

Pastorelli, C., Caprara, G. V., Barbaranelli, C., Rola, J., Rozsa, S., & Bandura, A. (2001). The structure of children's perceived self-efficacy: A cross-national study. *European Journal of Psychological Assessment, 17,* 87–97.

Paulas, M. (2014). How and why do infants imitate? An ideomotor approach to social and imitative learning in infancy (and beyond). *Psychonomics Bulletin & Review, 21,* 598. doi:10.3758/s1342301405981

Schunk, D. (2001). Social cognitive theory and self-regulated learning. In B. J. Zimmerman & D. H. Schunk (Eds.), *Self-regulated learning and academic achievement: Theoretical perspectives* (2nd ed., pp.125–152). Mahwah, NJ: Lawrence Erlbaum.

Schunk, D. (2003). Self-efficacy for reading and writing: Influence of modeling, goal setting, and self-evaluation. *Reading and Writing Quarterly, 19,* 159–172.

Schunk, D., & Hanson, A. R. (1989). Self-modeling and children's cognitive skill learning. *Journal of Educational Psychology, 81,* 155–163.

Schunk, D., & Zimmerman, B. (1997). Social origins of self-regulatory competence. *Educational Psychologist, 32,* 195–208.

Schunk, D., & Zimmerman, B. (2007). Influencing children's self-efficacy and self-regulation of reading and writing through modeling. *Reading and Writing Quarterly, 23,* 7–25.

Schunk, D. H. (2012). *Learning theories: An educational perspective*

(4th ed.). Upper Saddle River, NJ: Pearson.

Schunk, D. H., & DiBenedetto, M. K. (2014). Academic self-efficacy. In M. J. Furlong, R. Gilman, & E. S. Huebner (Eds.), *Handbook of positive psychology in schools* (2nd ed., pp. 115–130). New York, NY: Taylor & Francis.

Schunk, D. H., & Pajares, F. (2002). The development of academic self-efficacy. In A. Wigfield & J. Eccles (Eds.), *Development of achievement motivation* (pp. 15–31). San Diego, CA: Academic Press.

Tella, A., Tella, A., & Adeniyi, O. (2009). Locus of control, interest in schooling, self-efficacy, and academic achievement. *Cypriot Journal of Educational Sciences, 4*(3), 168–182.

Viel-Ruma, K., Houchins, D., Jolivette, K., & Benson, G. (2010). Efficacy beliefs of special educators: The relationships among collective efficacy, teacher self-efficacy, and job satisfaction. *Teacher Education & Special Education, 33*(3), 225–233.

Weiser, D. A., & Riggio, H. R. (2010). Family background and academic achievement: Does self-efficacy mediate outcomes? *Social Psychology of Education, 13*(3), 67–383.

Woolfolk, A. E., & Hoy, W. K. (1990). Prospective teachers' sense of efficacy and beliefs about control. *Journal of Educational Psychology, 82,* 81–91.

Zimmerman, B. J. (1998). Academic studying and the development of personal skill: A self-regulatory perspective. *Educational Psychologist, 33*(3), 73–86.

Zimmerman, B. J. (2001). Theories of self-regulated learning and academic achievement: An overview and analysis. In B. J. Zimmerman & D. H. Schunk (Eds.), *Self-regulated learning and academic achievement: Theoretical perspectives* (2nd ed., pp. 1–38). Mahwah, NJ: Lawrence Erlbaum.

Zimmerman, B. J., & Labuhn, A. S. (2012). Self-regulation of learning: Process approaches to personal development. In K. R. Harris, S. Graham, T. Urdan, C. B. McCormick, G. Sinatra, & J. Sweller (Eds.), *APA educational psychology handbook, vol. 1: Theories, constructs, and critical issues* (pp. 399–425). Washington, DC: American Psychological Association.

Zimmerman, B. J., & Martinez-Pons, M. (1990). Student differences in self-regulated learning: Relating grade, sex, and giftedness to self-efficacy and strategy use. *Journal of Educational Psychology, 82,* 51–59.

Zimmerman, B. J., & Schunk, D. H. (2001). *Self-regulated learning and academic achievement: Theoretical perspectives* (2nd ed.). Mahwah, NJ: Lawrence Erlbaum.

Zimmerman, B. J., & Schunk, D. H. (2011). Self-regulated learning and performance: An introduction and an overview. In B. J. Zimmerman & D. H. Schunk (Eds.), *Handbook of self-regulation learning and performance* (pp. 1–15). New York, NY: Taylor & Francis.

Module 10

Allen, R. J., Havelka, J., Falcon, T., Evans, S., & Darling, S. (2015). Modality specificity and integration in working memory: Insights form visuospatial bootstrapping. *Journal of Experimental Psychology, 41*(3), 820–830.

Anderson, J. R. (1983). A spreading activation theory of memory. *Journal of Verbal Learning and Verbal Behavior, 22*(3), 261–295.

Anderson, J. R., & Bower, G. H. (1973). *Human associative memory.* Washington, DC: Winston.

Ashcraft, M. H., & Rudig, N. O. (2012). Higher cognition is altered by noncognitive factors: How affect enhances and disrupts mathematics performance in adolescence and young adulthood. In V. F. Reyna, S. B. Chapman, M. R. Dougherty, & J. Confrey (Eds.), *The adolescent brain: Learning, reasoning, and decision making* (pp. 243–264). Washington, DC: American Psychological Association.

Atkinson, R. C., & Shiffrin, R. M. (1968). Human memory: A proposed system and its control processes. In K. W. Spence & J. T. Spence (Eds.). *The psychology of learning and motivation: Advances in research and theory* (Vol. 2, pp. 89–195). New York, NY: Academic Press.

Baddeley, A. D. (1992). Working memory. *Science, 255,* 556–559.

Baddeley, A. D. (1998). Recent developments in working memory. *Current Opinion in Neurobiology, 8,* 234–238.

Baddeley, A. D. (2000). The episodic buffer: A new component of working memory? *Trends in Cognitive Sciences, 4,* 417–423.

Baddeley, A. D. (2012). Working memory: Theories, models, and controversies. *Annual Review of Psychology, 63,* 1–29.

Baddeley, A. D., & Hitch, G. J. (1974). Working memory. In G. H. Bower

(Ed.), *The psychology of learning and motivation: Advances in research and theory* (Vol. 8, pp. 47–89). New York, NY: Academic Press.

Bebko, J. M., McMorris, C. A., Metcalfe, A., Ricciuti, C., & Goldstein, G. (2014). Language proficiency and metacognition as predictors of spontaneous rehearsal in children. *Canadian Journal of Experimental Psychology, 68*(1), 46–58.

Bjork, R. A., & Bjork, E. L. (1992). A new theory of disuse and an old theory of stimulus fluctuation. In A. Healy, S. Kosslyn, & R. Shiffrin (Eds.), *From learning processes to cognitive processes: Essays in honor of William K. Estes* (Vol. 2, pp. 35–67). Hillsdale, NJ: Lawrence Erlbaum.

Blunt, J. R., & Karpicke, J. D. (2014). Learning with retrieval-based concept mapping. *Journal of Educational Psychology, 106*(3), 849–858.

Bradley, C., & Pearson, J. (2012). The sensory components of high-capacity iconic memory and visual working memory. *Frontiers in Psychology, 3*(Article 355), 1–8.

Brown, L. A., & Wesley, R. W. (2013). Visual working memory is enhanced by mixed strategy use and semantic coding. *Journal of Cognitive Psychology, 25*(3), 328–338.

Cepeda, N. J., Coburn, N., Rohrer, D., Wixted, J. T., Mozer, M. C., & Pashler, H. (2009). Optimizing distributed practice theoretical analysis and practical implications. *Experimental Psychology, 56*(4), 236–246.

Cepeda, N. J., Pashler, H., Vul, E., Wixted, J. T., & Rohrer, D. (2006). Distributed practice in verbal recall tasks: A review and quantitative synthesis. *Psychological Bulletin, 132*(3), 354–380.

Clark, J. M., & Paivio, A. (1991). Dual coding theory and education. *Educational Psychology Review, 3*, 149–210.

Craik, F. I. M., & Tulving, E. (1975). Depth of processing and the retention of words in episodic memory. *Journal of Experimental Psychology: General, 104*, 268–294.

Darling, S., Parker, M. J., Goodall, K. E., Havelka, J., & Allen, R. J. (2014). Visuospatial bootstrapping: implicit binding of verbal working memory to visuospatial representations in children and adults. *Journal of Experimental Child Psychology, 119*, 112–119.

Darwin, C. T., Turvey, M. T., & Crowder, R. G. (1974). An auditory analogue of the Sperling partial report procedure: Evidence for brief auditory storage. *Cognitive Psychology, 3*, 255–267.

Erviti, M., Semal, C., Wright, B. A., Amestoy, A., Bouvard, M. P., Demany,

L. (2015). A late-emerging auditory deficit in Autism. *Neuropsychology, 29*(3), 454–462.

Fisher, A. V., Godwin, K. E., & Seltman, H. (2014). Visual environment, attention allocation, and learning in young children: When too much of a good thing may be bad. *Psychological Science, 1–9*. doi:10.1177/0956797614533801

Glanzer, M., & Cunitz, A. R. (1966). Two storage mechanisms in free recall. *Journal of Verbal Learning and Verbal Behavior, 5*, 351–360.

Halpern, D. F. (2000). *Sex differences in cognitive abilities* (3rd ed.). Mahwah, NJ: Lawrence Erlbaum.

Halpern, D. F., & LaMay, M. L. (2000). The smarter sex: A critical review of sex differences in intelligence. *Educational Psychology Review, 12*, 229–246.

Henry, L. A. (2010). The episodic buffer in children with intellectual disabilities: An exploratory study. *Research in Developmental Disabilities, 31*, 1609–1614.

Hu, Y., Hitch, G. J., Baddeley, A. D., Zhang, M., & Allen, R. J. (2014). Executive perceptual attention play different roles in visual working memory: Evidence from suffix and strategy effects. *Journal of Experimental Psychology: Human Perception and Performance, 40*(4), 1665–1678.

Jenkins, J. B., & Dallenbach, K. M. (1924). Oblivescence during sleep and waking. *American Journal of Psychology, 35*, 605–612.

Jolles, D., Kleibeuker, S., Rombouts, S. A. R. B., & Crone, E. A. (2011). Developmental differences in prefrontal activation during working memory maintenance and manipulation for different memory loads. *Developmental Science, 14*, 713–724.

Kahneman, D. (1973). *Attention and effort*. Englewood Cliffs, NJ: Prentice Hall.

Karpicke, J. D. (2012). Retrieval-based learning: Active retrieval promotes meaningful learning. *Current Directions in Psychological Science, 21*(3), 157–163.

Karpicke, J. D., & Bauernschmidt, A. (2011). Spaced retrieval: Absolute spacing enhances learning regardless of relative spacing. *Journal of Experimental Psychology: Learning, Memory, and Cognition, 37*(5), 1250–1257.

Karpicke, J. D., & Grimaldi, P. J. (2012). Retrieval-based learning: A perspective for enhancing meaningful learning. *Educational Psychology Review, 24*(3), 401–418.

Keating, D. (2004). Cognitive and brain development. In R. Lerner & L. Steinberg (Eds.), *Handbook of adolescent psychology* (2nd ed., pp. 45–84). New York, NY: Wiley.

Kirschner, P. A., & van Merrienboer, J. J. G. (2013). Do learners really know best? Urban legends in education. *Educational Psychologist, 48*(3), 169–183.

McMorris, C. A., Brown, S. M., & Bebko, J. M. (2013). An examination of iconic memory in children with Autism spectrum disorders. *Journal of Autism Developmental Disorders, 43*, 1956–1966.

Melton, A. W. (1970). The situation with respect to the spacing of repetitions and memory. *Journal of Verbal Learning and Verbal Behavior, 9*, 596–606.

Miller, G. A. (1956). The magical number seven, plus or minus two: Some limits on our capacity for processing information. *Psychological Review, 63*, 81–97.

Miller, G. R. (1967). *An evaluation of the effectiveness of mnemonic devices as aids to study* (Cooperative Research Project No. 5–8438). El Paso, University of Texas.

Mizuno, K., Tanaka, M., Fukuda, S., Sasabe, T., Imai-Matsumura, K., & Watanabe, Y. (2011). Changes in cognitive functions of students in the transitional period from elementary school to junior high school. *Brain and Development, 33*(5), 412–420.

Peterson, L. R., & Peterson, M. J. (1959). Short-term retention of individual verbal items. *Journal of Experimental Psychology, 58*, 193–198.

Pyc, M. A., & Rawson, K. A. (2012). Why is test-restudy practice beneficial for memory? An evaluation of the mediator shift hypothesis. *Journal of Experimental Psychology: Learning, Memory, and Cognition, 38*(3), 737–746.

Quinn, J. G., & McConnell, J. (1996). Irrelevant pictures in working memory. *Quarterly Journal of Experimental Psychology, 49A*, 200–215.

Recht, D. R., & Leslie, L. (1988). Effect of prior knowledge on good and poor readers' memory of text. *Journal of Educational Psychology, 80*(1), 16–20.

Roberts, G., Scammacca, N., Osman, D. J., Hall, C., Mohammed, S. S., & Vaughn, S. (2014). Team-based learning: Moderating effects of metacognitive elaborative rehearsal and middle school history content recall. *Educational Psychology Review, 26*, 9266. doi:10.1007/s1064801492662

Roediger, H. L. III, & Pyc, M. A. (2012). Inexpensive techniques to improve education: Applying cognitive psychology to enhance educational practice. *Journal of Applied Research in Memory and Cognition, 1,* 242–248.

Sinclair, R. J., & Burton, H. (1996). Discrimination of vibrotactile frequencies in a delayed pair comparison task. *Perception & Psychophysics, 58,* 680–692.

Smith, S. M., & Vela, E. (2001). Environmental context-dependent memory: A review and meta-analysis. *Psychonomic Bulletin & Review, 8,* 203–220.

Sperling, G. (1960). The information available in brief visual presentations. *Psychological Monographs, 74*(498), 1–29.

Sprondel, V., Kipp, K. H., & Mecklinger, A. (2011). Developmental changes in item and source memory: evidence from an ERP recognition memory student with children, adolescents, and adults. *Child Development, 82,* 1638–1653.

Stickgold, R., Hobson, J. A., Fosse, H. R., & Fosse, M. (2001). Sleep, learning, and dreams: Off-line memory processing. *Science, 294,* 1052–1057.

Strayer, D. L., & Johnston, W. A. (2001). Driven to distraction: Dual-task studies of simulated driving and conversing on a cellular telephone. *Psychological Science, 12,* 462–466.

Talarico, J. M., & Rubin, D. C. (2003). Confidence, not consistency, characterizes flashbulb memories. *Psychological Science, 14,* 455–461.

Tam, H., Jarrold, C., Baddeley, A. D., & Sabatos-DeVito. M. (2010). The development of memory maintenance: Children's use of phonological rehearsal and attentional refreshment in working memory tasks. *Journal of Experimental Child Psychology, 107*(3), 306–324.

Treisman, A. M., & Gelade, G. (1980). A feature integration theory of attention. *Cognitive Psychology, 12,* 97–136.

Treisman, A. M., Sykes, M., & Gelade, G. (1977). Selective attention and stimulus integration. In S. Dornic (Ed.), *Attention and performance IV* (pp. 333–361). Hillsdale, NJ: Lawrence Erlbaum.

Warrington, E. K., & Weiskrantz, L. (1970). Amnesic syndrome: Consolidation or retrieval. *Nature, 228,* 628–630.

Wilson, K., & Korn, J. H. (2007). Attention during lectures: Beyond ten minutes. *Teaching of Psychology, 34*(2), 85–89.

Wixted, J. T. (2010). The role of retroactive interference and consolidation in everyday forgetting. In S. Della Sala (Ed.), *Forgetting* (pp. 285–312). Psychology Press, East Sussex, UK.

Module 11

Aiken, E. G., Thomas, G. S., & Shennum, W. A. (1975). Memory for a lecture: Effects of notes, lecture rate and informational density. *Journal of Educational Psychology, 67,* 439–444.

Alberts, A., Elkind, D., & Ginsberg, S. (2007). The personal fable and risk-taking in early adolescence. *Journal of Youth and Adolescence, 36*(1), 71–76.

Anderson, J. R. (1990). *Cognitive psychology and its implications* (3rd ed.). New York, NY: Freeman.

Artelt, C., & Schneider, W. (2015). Cross-country generalizability of the role of metacognitive knowledge for students' strategy use and reading competence. *Teachers College Record, 117,* 1–32.

Askell-Williams, H., Lawson, M. J., & Skrzypiec, G. (2012). Scaffolding cognitive and metacognitive strategy instruction in regular class lessons. *Instructional Science, 40*(2), 413–443.

Baker, L. (2013). Metacognitive strategies. In J. Hattie & E. M. Anderman (Eds.), *International guide to student achievement.* New York, NY: Taylor & Francis.

Beal, C. R., & Fleisig, W. E. (1987, April). *Preschoolers' preparation for retrieval of object relocation tasks.* Paper presented at the biennial meeting of the Society for research in Child Development, Baltimore, MD.

Beck, I. L., & McKeown, M. G. (2001). Inviting students into the pursuit of meaning. *Educational Psychology Review, 13*(3), 225–241.

Bereiter, C., & Scardamalia, M. (1987). *The psychology of written composition.* Hillsdale, NJ: Lawrence Erlbaum.

Berninger, V. W., Mizokawa, D. T., & Bragg, R. (1991). Theory-based diagnosis and remediation of writing disabilities. *Journal of School Psychology, 29,* 57–79.

Boyle, J. R., & Rivera, T. Z. (2012). Note-taking techniques for students with disabilities A systematic review of the research. *Learning Disability Quarterly, 35*(3), 131–143.

Brown, A. (1987). Metacognition, executive control, self-regulation and other more mysterious mechanisms. In F. E. Weinert & R. H. Kluwe (Eds.), *Metacognition, motivation, and understanding.* Hillsdale, NJ: Lawrence Erlbaum.

Brown, A. L., Bransford, J. D., Ferrara, R. A., & Campione, J. C. (1983). Learning, remembering, and understanding. In J. H. Flavell & E. M. Markman, *Handbook of child psychology, vol. III: Cognitive development.* New York, NY: Wiley & Sons.

Brown, A. L., Day, J. D., & Jones R. S. (1983). The development plans for summarizing texts. *Child Development, 54,* 968–979.

Bruning, R. H., Schraw, G. J., & Ronning, R. R. (1995). *Cognitive psychology and instruction* (2nd ed.). Englewood Cliffs, NJ: Prentice Hall.

Bui, D. C., & Myerson, J. (2014). The role of working memory abilities in lecture note-taking. *Learning and Individual Differences, 33,* 12–22.

Chi, M. T. H. (1987). Representing knowledge and metaknowledge: Implications for interpreting metamemory research. In F. E. Weinert & R. H. Kluwe (Eds.), *Metacognition, motivation, and understanding.* Hillsdale, NJ: Lawrence Erlbaum.

Conner, L. N. (2007). Cueing metacognition to improve researching and essay writing in final year high school biology class. *Research in Science Education, 37*(1), 1–16. Hamilton, A. F., Brindley, R., & Frith, U. (2009). Visual perspective taking impairment in children with autistic spectrum disorder. *Cognition, 113*(1), 37–44.

Dunlosky, J., & Hertzog, C. (1998). Training programs to improve learning later in adulthood: Helping older adults educate themselves. In D. J. Hacker, J. Dunloksy, & A. C. Graesser (Eds.), *Metacognition in educational theory and practice.* Mahwah, NJ: Lawrence Erlbaum.

Elkind, D. (1967), Egocentrism in adolescence. *Child Development, 38,* 1025–1034.

Engle, R. W., Nations, J. K., & Cantor, J. (1990). Is "working memory capacity" just another name for word knowledge? *Journal of Educational Psychology, 82*(4), 799–804.

Flavell, J. H. (2000). Development of children's knowledge about the mental world. *International Journal of Behavioral Development, 24,* 15–23.

Flavell, J. H. (2004). Theory-of-mind development: Retrospect and prospect. *Merrill-Palmer Quarterly, 50,* 274–290.

Flavell, J. H., Flavell, E. R., & Green, F. L. (1983). Development of the appearance-reality distinction. *Cognitive Psychology, 15,* 95–120.

Flavell, J. H., Green, F. L., & Flavell, E. R. (1995). *Young children's knowledge about thinking, Monographs of the Society for Research in Child Development.*

Flavell, J. H. Green, F. L., & Flavell, E. R. (2000). Development of children's awareness of their own thoughts. *Journal of Cognition and Development, 1,* 97–112.

Flavell, J. H., Miller, P. H., & Miller, S. A. (2002). *Cognitive development* (4th ed.). Upper Saddle River, NJ: Prentice Hall.

Frankenberger, K. D. (2000). Adolescent egocentrism: A comparison among adolescents and adults. *Journal of Adolescence, 23,* 343–354.

Gajria, M., Jitendra, A. K., Sood, S., & Sacks, G. (2007). Improving comprehension of expository text in students with LD: A research synthesis. *Journal of Learning Disabilities, 40*(3), 210–225.

Garcia-Mila, M., & Anderson, C. (2007). Developmental change in notetaking during scientific inquiry. *International Journal of Science Education, 29*(8), 1035–1058.

Gavazzi, S., & Sabatelli, R. M. (1990). Family system dynamics, the individuation process, and psychosocial development. *Journal of Adolescent Research, 5,* 500–519.

Hamilton, A. F., Brindley R., & Frith, U. (2009). Visual perspective taking impairment in children with autistic spectrum disorder. *Cognition*, 113(1), 37–44.

Haynes, J. M., McCarley, N. G., & Williams, J. L. (2015). An analysis of notes taken during and after a lecture presentation. *North American Journal of Psychology, 17*(1), 175–186.

Hertzog, C., & Robinson, A. E. (2005). Metacognition and intelligence. In O. Wilhelm & R. W. Engle (Eds.), *Handbook of understanding and measuring intelligence.* Thousand Oaks, CA: SAGE.

Hirsch Jr, E. D., & Hansel, L. (2013). Why content is king. *Educational Leadership, 71*(3), 28–33.

Hooper, S. R., Wakely, M. B., de Kruif, R. E., & Swartz, C. W. (2006). Aptitude-treatment interactions revisited: Effect of metacognitive intervention on subtypes of written expression in elementary school students. *Developmental Neuropsychology, 29,* 217–241.

Jacobs, G. M. (2004). A classroom investigation of the growth of metacognitive awareness in kindergarten children through the writing process. *Early Childhood Education Journal, 32,* 17–23.

Jairam, D., & Kiewra, K. A. (2009). An investigation of the SOAR study method. *Journal of Advanced Academics, 20*(4), 602–629.

Jairam, D., & Kiewra, K. A. (2010). Helping students soar to success on computers: An investigation of the SOAR study method for computer-based learning. *Journal of Educational Psychology, 102*(3), 601–614.

Jairam, D., Kiewra, K. A., Rogers-Kasson, S., Patterson-Hazley, M., & Marxhausen, K. (2014). SOAR versus SQ3R: A test of two study systems. *Instructional Science, 42*(3), 409–420.

Karlen, Y., Merki, K. M., & Ramseier, E. (2014). The effect of individual differences in the development of metacognitive strategy knowledge. *Instructional Science, 42*(5), 777–794.

Krebs, S. S., & Roebers, C. M. (2010). Children's strategic regulation, metacognitive monitoring, and control processes during test-taking. *British Journal of Educational Psychology, 80*(3), 325–340.

Kiewra, K. A. (1985). Investigating notetaking and review: A depth of processing alternative. *Educational Psychologist, 20,* 23–32.

Kiewra, K. A. (2002). How classroom teachers can help students learn and teach them how to learn. *Theory Into Practice, 41,* 71–80.

Kiewra, K. A., DuBois, N. F., Christian, D., McShane, A., Meyerhoffer, M., & Roskelley, D. (1991). Note-taking functions and techniques. *Journal of Educational Psychology, 83,* 240–245.

Kistner, S., Rakoczy, K., Otto, B., Dignath-van Ewijk, C., Büttner, G., & Klieme, E. (2010). Promotion of self-regulated learning in classrooms: investigating frequency, quality, and consequences for student performance. *Metacognition and Learning, 5,* 157–171.

Kornell, N., & Metcalfe, J. (2006). Study efficacy and the region of proximal learning framework. *Journal of Experimental Psychology: Learning, Memory, and Cognition, 32,* 609–622.

Kucan, L., Palinscar, A. S., Khasnabis, D., & Chang, C. (2009). The video viewing task: A source of information for assessing and addressing teacher understanding of text-based discussion. *Teaching and Teacher Education, 25,* 415–423.

Kuhura-Kojima, K., & Hatano, G. (1991). Contribution of content knowledge and learning ability to the learning of facts. *Journal of Educational Psychology, 83*(2), 253–263.

Lapsley, D. K. (1993). Toward an integrated theory of adolescent ego development: The "new look" at adolescent egocentrism. *American Journal of Orthopsychiatry, 63,* 562–571.

Laranjo, J., Bernier, A., Meins, E., & Carlson, S. M. (2014). The roles of maternal mind-mindedness and infant security of attachment in predicting preschoolers' understanding of visual perspective taking and false belief. *Journal of Experimental Child Psychology, 125,* 48–62.

Lecce, S., Caputi, M., & Pagnin, A. (2015). False-belief understanding at age 5 predicts beliefs about learning in year 3 of primary school. *European Journal of Developmental Psychology, 12*(1), 40–53.

Lockl, K., & Schneider, W. (2007). Knowledge about the mind: Links between theory of mind and later metamemory. *Child Development, 78*(1), 148–167.

Lundberg, I., & Reichenberg, M. (2013). Developing reading comprehension among students with mild intellectual disabilities: An intervention study. *Scandinavian Journal of Educational Research, 57*(1), 89–100.

Manning, B. H. (1991). *Cognitive self-instruction for classroom processes.* Albany, NY: New York Press.

Merki, K. M., Ramseier, E., & Karlen, Y. (2013). Reliability and validity analyses of a newly developed test to assess learning strategy knowledge. *Journal of Cognitive Education and Psychology, 12*(3), 391–408.

Metcalfe, J. (2000). Metamemory: Theory and data. In E. Tulving, & F. I. M. Craik (Eds.), *The Oxford handbook of memory.* Oxford: University Press.

Metcalfe, J. (2002). Is study time allocated selectively to a region of proximal learning? *Journal of Experimental Psychology: General, 131,* 349–363.

Metcalfe, J., & Finn, B. (2008). Evidence that judgments of learning are causally related to study choice. *Psychonomic Bulletin & Review, 15*(1), 174–179.

Metcalfe, J., & Finn, B. (2013). Metacognition and control of study choice in children. *Metacognition and Learning, 8*(1), 19–46.

Metcalfe, J., & Kornell, N. (2005). A region of proximal learning model of study time allocation. *Journal of Memory and Language, 52,* 463–477.

Nader-Grosbois, N. (2014). Self-perception, self-regulation and metacognition in adolescents with intellectual disability. *Research in Developmental Disabilities, 35*(6), 1334–1348.

Omoteso, B. A., & Sadiku, F. A. (2013). Effectiveness of PQ4R study technique on performance of students in chemistry: Child & adolescent therapy and e-therapy. *IFE PsychologIA: An International Journal: Psychotherapy: Unity in Diversity, 21*(3), 238–244.

Palincsar, A. S. (2003). Ann L. Brown: Advancing a theoretical model of learning and instruction. In B. J. Zimmerman & D. H. Schunk (Eds.), *Educational psychology: A century of contribution.* Mahwah, NJ: Lawrence Erlbaum.

Palincsar, A. S. (2013). Reciprocal teaching. In J. Hattie & E. M. Anderman (Eds.), *International guide to student achievement.* New York, NY: Taylor & Francis.

Palincsar, A. S., & Brown, A. L. (1984). Reciprocal teaching of comprehension-fostering and comprehension-monitoring activities. *Cognition & Instruction, 1,* 117–175.

Palincsar, A. S., Brown, A. L., & Martin, S. M. (1987). Peer interaction in reading comprehension instruction. *Educational Psychologist, 22,* 231–253.

Peterson, P. L. (1988). Teachers' and students' cognitional knowledge for classroom teaching and learning. *Educational Researcher, 17*(5), 5–14.

Peverly, S. T., Brobost, K. E., Graham, M., & Shaw, R. (2003). College adults are not good at self-regulation: A study on the relationship of self-regulation, note taking, and test taking. *Journal of Educational Psychology, 95,* 335–346.

Quadrel, M. J., Fischhoff, B., & Davis, W. (1993). Adolescent (in)vulnerability. *American Psychologist, 48,* 102–116.

Rijlaarsdam, G., Van den Bergh, H., Couzijn, M., Janssen, T., Braaksma, M., Tillema, M. … Raedts, M. (2012). Writing. In Harris, K. R., Graham, S., Urdan, T., Bus, A. G., Major, S., & Swanson, H. L. *APA educational psychology handbook, volume 3: Application to learning and teaching,* (pp. 189–227). Washington, DC: American Psychology Association.

Risch, N. L., & Kiewra, K. A. (1990). Content and form variations in note taking: Effects among junior high students. *Journal of Educational Research, 83,* 355–357.

Ritter, K. (1978). The development of knowledge of an external retrieval cue strategy. *Child Development, 49,* 1227–1230.

Robinson, R. P. (1961). *Effective study.* New York, NY: Harper & Row.

Rosenshine, B., & Meister, C. (1994). Reciprocal teaching: A review of the research. *Review of Educational Research, 64*(4), 479–530.

Sabatelli, R. M., & Mazor, A. (1985). Differentiation, individuation, and identity formation: The integration of family system and individual developmental perspectives. *Adolescence, 20,* 619–633.

Scardamalia, M., & Bereiter, C. (1985). Fostering the development of self-regulation in children's knowledge processing. In S. F. Chipman, J. W. Segal, & R. Glaser (Eds.), *Thinking and learning skills: Research and open questions* (pp. 563–577). Hillsdale, NJ: Lawrence Erlbaum.

Scardamalia, M., Bereiter, C., & Steinbach, R. (1984). Teachability of reflective processes in written composition. *Cognitive Science, 8,* 173–190.

Schewel, R. H., & Waddell, J. G. (1986). Metacognitive skills: Practical strategies. *Academic Therapy, 22,* 19–25.

Schünemann, N., Spörer, N., & Brunstein, J. C. (2013). Integrating self-regulation in whole-class reciprocal teaching: A moderator–mediator analysis of incremental effects on fifth graders' reading comprehension. *Contemporary Educational Psychology, 38*(4), 289–305.

Schunk, D. H. (2012). *Learning theories: An educational perspective* (6th ed.). Boston, MA: Pearson.

Schuwerk, T., Vuori, M., & Sodian, B. (2015). Implicit and explicit theory of mind reasoning in autism spectrum disorders: The impact of experience. *Autism, 19*(4), 459–468.

Shimamura, A. P. (1994). The neuropsychology of metacognition. In J. Metcalfe & A. P. Shimamura (Eds.), *Metacognition: Knowing about knowing.* Cambridge: The MIT Press.

Szczepanski, S. M., & Knight, R. T. (2014). Insights into human behavior from lesions to the prefrontal cortex. *Neuron, 83*(5), 1002–1018.

Tajika, H., Nakatsu, N., Nozaki, H., Neumann, E., & Maruno, S. (2007). Effects of self-explanation as a metacognitive strategy for solving mathematical word problems. *Japanese Psychological Research, 49*(3), 222–233.

Thomas, E. L., & Robinson, H. A. (1972). *Improving reading in every class: A sourcebook for teachers.* Boston, MA: Allyn & Bacon.

Van Meter, P., Yokoi, L., & Pressley, M. (1994). College students' theory of note-taking derived from their perceptions of note-taking. *Journal of Educational Psychology, 86,* 323–338.

Module 12

Adams, L., Kasserman, J., Yearwood, A., Perfetto, G., Bransford, J., & Franks, J. (1988). The effects of facts versus problem-oriented acquisition. *Memory & Cognition, 16,* 167–175.

Adey, P., & Shayer, M. (1993). An exploration of long-term far-transfer effects allowing an extended intervention program in the high school science curriculum. *Cognition and Instruction, 11*(1), 1–29.

Ainley, M., Hidi, S., & Berndorff, D. (2002). Interest, learning, and the psychological processes that mediate their relationship. *Journal of Educational Psychology, 94,* 545–561.

Alfieri, L., Nokes-Malach, T. J., & Schunn, C. D. (2013). Learning through case comparisons: A meta-analytic review. *Educational Psychologist, 48*(2), 87–113.

Al-Khateeb, O. S. M., & Idrees, M. W. K. (2010). The impact of using KWL strategy on grade ten female students' reading comprehension of religious concepts in Ma'an city. *European Journal of Social Sciences, 12,* 471–489.

Anderson, J. R. (1982). Acquisition of cognitive skills, *Psychological Review, 89*(4), 369–406.

Barnett, M. S., & Ceci, S. J. (2002). When and where do we apply what we learn? A taxonomy for far transfer. *Psychological Bulletin, 128,* 612–637.

Bereiter, C. (1995). A dispositional view of transfer. In A. McKeough, J. Lupart, & A. Marini (Eds.), *Teaching for transfer: Fostering generalization in learning* (pp. 21–34). Mahwah, NJ: Lawrence Erlbaum.

Bergin, D. A. (1999). Influences on classroom interest. *Educational Psychologist, 34,* 87–98.

Bransford, J. D., & Schwartz, D. L. (1999). Rethinking transfer: A simple proposal with multiple implications. In A. Iran-Nejad & P. D. Pearson (Eds.), *Review of Research in Education* (pp. 61–100). Washington, DC: American Educational Research Association.

Bransford, J. D., Zech, L., Schwartz, D. L., Barron, B. J., Vye, N., & CTGV. (2000). Design environments that invite and sustain mathematical thinking. In P. Cobb (Ed.), *Symbolizing and communicating in mathematics classrooms* (pp. 275–324). Mahwah, NJ: Lawrence Erlbaum.

Brooks, L. W., & Dansereau, D. F. (1987). Transfer of information: An instructional perspective. In S. M. Cormier & J. D. Hagman (Eds.), *Transfer of learning: Contemporary research and applications* (pp. 121–150). New York, NY: Academic Press.

Brown, A. L., Campione, J. C., Webber, L. S., & McGilly, K. (1992). Interactive learning environments: A new look at assessment and instruction. In B. R. Gifford & M. C. O'Connor (Eds.). *Changing assessments: Alternative view of aptitude, achievement, and instruction* (pp. 37–75). Boston, MA: Kluwer Academic.

Bugg, J. M., & McDaniel, M. A. (2012). Selective benefits of question self-generation and answering for remembering expository text. *Journal of Educational Psychology, 104*(4), 922–931.

Cantrell, R. J., Fusaro, J. A., & Dougherty, E. A. (2000). Exploring the effectiveness of journal writing on learning social studies: A comparative study. *Reading Psychology, 21,* 1–11.

Case, R. (1985). *Intellectual development: Birth to adulthood.* Orlando, FL: Academic Press.

Catrambone, R., & Holyoak, K. S. (1989). Overcoming contextual limitations on problem-solving transfer. *Journal of Experimental Psychology: Learning, Memory, and Cognition, 15,* 1147–1156.

Champagne, A. B., Gunstone, R. F., & Klopfer, L. E. (1985). Effecting changes in cognitive structures among physics students. In H. T. West & A. L. Pines (Eds.), *Cognitive structure and conceptual change* (pp. 163–187). Orlando, FL: Academic Press.

Chen, Z., & Klahr, D. (1999). All other things being equal: Acquisition and transfer of the Control of Variables Strategy. *Child Development, 70*(5), 1098–1120.

Chi, M. T. H. (2000). Self-explaining expository texts: The dual process of generating inferences and repairing mental models. In R. Glaser (Ed.), *Advances in instructional psychology* (Vol. 5, pp. 161–238). Mahwah, NJ: Lawrence Erlbaum.

Chi, M. T. H., & VanLehn, K. A. (2012). Seeing deep structure from the interactions of surface features. *Educational Psychologist, 47*(3), 177–188.

Choo, T. O. L., Eng, T. K., & Ahmad, N. (2011). Effects of reciprocal teaching strategies on reading comprehension. *Reading Matrix: An International Online Journal, 11*(2), 140–149.

Ciani, K., Ferguson, Y., Bergin, D., & Hilpert, J. (2010). Motivational influences on school-prompted interest. *Educational Psychology, 30,* 377–393.

Colquitt, J. A., LePine, J. A., & Noe, R. A. (2000). Toward an integrative theory of training motivation: A meta-analytic path analysis of 20 years of research. *Journal of Applied Psychology, 85,* 678–707.

Covington, M. V. (2000). Intrinsic versus extrinsic motivation in schools: A reconciliation. *Current Directions in Psychological Science, 9,* 22–25.

Day, S. B., & Goldstone, R. L. (2012). The import of knowledge export: Connecting findings and theories of transfer of learning. *Educational Psychologist, 47*(3), 153–176.

Del Favero, L., Boscolo, P., Vidotto, G., & Vicentini, M. (2007). Classroom discussion and individual problem-solving in the teaching of history: Do different instructional approaches affect interest in different ways? *Learning and Instruction, 17,* 635–657.

Duckworth, A. L., Kirby, T. A., Tsukayama, E., Berstein, H., & Ericsson, K. A. (2011). Deliberate practice spells success: Why grittier competitors triumph at the National Spelling Bee. *Social Psychological and Personality Science, 2*(2), 174–181.

Duncker, K. (1945). On problem solving. *Psychological Monographs, 58*(5, Whole No. 270).

Durnin, J. H., Perrone, A. E., & MacKay, L. (1997). Teaching problem solving in elementary school mathematics. *Journal of Structural Learning and Intelligent Systems, 13,* 53–69.

Elliot, A. J., & Murayama, K. (2008). On the measurement of achievement goals: Critique, illustration, and application. *Journal of Educational Psychology, 100,* 613–628.

Engle, R. A., Lam, D. P., Meyer, X. S., & Nix, S. E. (2012). How does expansive framing promote transfer? Several proposed explanations and a research agenda for investigating them. *Educational Psychologist, 47*(3), 215–231.

Ericsson, A. (2006). The influence of experience and deliberate practice on the development of superior expert performance. In K. A. Ericsson, N. Charness, P. J. Feltovich, & R. R. Hoffman (Eds.), *The Cambridge handbook of expertise and expert performance* (pp. 683–703). Cambridge, UK: Cambridge University Press.

Ericsson, K. A., & Ward, P. (2007). Capturing the naturally occurring superior performance of experts in the laboratory : Toward a science of expert and exceptional performance. *Current Directions in Psychological Science, 16*(6), 346–350.

Fuchs, L. S., Fuchs, D., Kams, K., Hamlett, C. L., & Karzaroff, M. (1999). Mathematics performance assessment in the classroom: Effects on teacher planning and student problem solving. *American Educational Research Journal, 36,* 609–646.

Fuchs, L. S., Fuchs, D., Prentice, K., Burch, M., Hamlett, C. L., Owen, R., Hosp, M., & Jancek, D. (2003). Explicitly teaching for transfer: Effects on third-grade students' mathematical problem solving. *Journal of Educational Psychology, 95,* 293–305.

Gage, N. L., & Berliner, D. C. (1992). *Educational psychology* (5th ed.). Boston, MA: Houghton Mifflin.

Gajria, M., Jitendra, A. K., Sood, S., & Sacks, G. (2007). Improving comprehension of expository text in students with LD: A research synthesis. *Journal of Learning Disabilities, 40*(3), 210–225.

Geary, D. C. (1994). *Children's mathematical development: Research and practical applications.* Washington, DC: American Psychological Association.

Gentner, D., & Namy, L. L. (2004). The role of comparison in children's early word learning. In S. R. Waxman & D. G. Hall (Eds.), *Weaving a lexicon* (pp. 533–568). Cambridge, MA: The MIT Press.

Gentner, D., Loewenstein, J., & Thompson, L. (2003). Learning and transfer: A general role for analogical encoding. *Journal of Educational Psychology, 95*(2), 393–405.ree

Ghorbani, M. R., Gangeraj, A. A., & Alavi, S. Z. (2013). Reciprocal teaching of comprehension strategies improves EFL learners' writing ability. *Current Issues in Education, 16*(1), 1–13.

Gick, M. L., & Holyoak, K. J. (1980). Analogical problem solving. *Cognitive Psychology, 12,* 306–355.

Gick, M. L., & Holyoak, K. J. (1983). Schema induction and analogical transfer. *Cognitive Psychology, 15,* 1–38.

Glynn, S. M., Britton, B. K., Muth, D., & Dogan, N. (1982). Writing and revising persuasive documents: Cognitive demands. *Journal of Educational Psychology, 74,* 557–567.

Grant, H., & Dweck, C. S. (2003). Clarifying achievement goals and their impact. *Journal of Personality and Social Psychology, 85,* 541–553.

Harp, S. F., & Mayer, R. E. (1998). How seductive details do their damage: A theory of cognitive interest in science learning. *Journal of Educational Psychology, 90,* 414–34.

Haskell, R. E. (2001). *Transfer of learning: Cognition, instruction, and reasoning.* San Diego, CA: Academic Press.

Hayes, J. R. (1985). Three problems in teaching general skills. In S. F. Chipman, J. W. Segal, & R. Glaser (Eds.), *Thinking and learning skills: Vol. 1: Research and open questions* (pp. 391–406). Hillsdale, NJ: Lawrence Erlbaum.

Hayes, J. R., & Simon, H. A. (1977). Psychological differences among problem isomorphs. In N. J. Castellan, P. B. Pisoni, & G. R. Potts (Eds.), *Cognitive theory* (Vol. 2, pp. 21–41). Hillsdale, NJ: Lawrence Erlbaum.

Holyoak, K. J., & Koh, K. (1987). Surface and structural similarity in analogical transfer. *Memory and Cognition, 15,* 332–340.

Hübner, S., Nückles, M., & Renkl, A. (2010). Writing learning journals: Instructional support to overcome learning-strategy deficits. *Learning and Instruction, 20,* 18–29.

Hulleman, C. S., Durik, A. M., Schweigert, S. A., & Harackiewicz, J. M. (2008). Task values, achievement goals, and interest: An integrative analysis. *Journal of Educational Psychology, 100,* 398–416.

Jee, B. D., Uttal, D. H., Gentner, D., Manduca, C. J., Shipley, T. F., & Sageman, B. (2013). Finding faults: Analogical comparison supports spatial concept learning in geoscience. *Cognitive Processes, 14,* 175–187.

Kelly, M., Moore, D. W., & Tuck, B. F. (1994). Reciprocal teaching in regular primary school classroom. *Journal of Educational Research, 88*(1), 53–61.

Kourilsky, M. L., & Wittrock, M. C. (1992). Generative teaching: An enhancement strategy for the learning of economics in cooperative groups. *American Educational Research Journal, 29*(4), 861–876.

Kyun, S., Kalyuga, S., & Sweller, J. (2013). The effect of worked examples when learning to write essays in English literature. *Journal of Experimental Education, 81*(3), 385–408.

Langer, E. J. (1993). A mindful education. *Educational Psychologist, 28*(1), 43–50.

Larkin, J. H. (1989). What kind of knowledge transfers? In L. B. Resnick (Ed.), *Knowing, learning, and instruction* (pp. 283–305). Hillsdale, NJ: Lawrence Erlbaum.

Lave, J. (1988). *Cognition in practice.* Cambridge, UK: Cambridge University Press.

Lederer, J. M. (2000). Reciprocal teaching of social studies in inclusive elementary classrooms. *Journal of Learning Disabilities, 33*(1), 91–106.

Linnenbrink-Garcia, L., Durik, A. M., Conley, A. M., Barron, K. E., Tauer, J. M., Karabenick, S. A., & Harackiewicz, J. M. (2010). Measuring situational interest in academic domains. *Educational and Psychological Measurement, 70,* 647–671.

Linnenbrink-Garcia, L., Patall, E. A., & Messersmith, E. E. (2013). Antecedents and consequences of situational interest. *British Journal of Educational Psychology, 83*(4), 591–614.

Lundberg, I., & Reichenberg, M. (2013). Developing reading comprehension among students with mild intellectual disabilities: An intervention study. *Scandinavian Journal of Educational Research, 57*(1), 1–12.

Mackenzie, A. A., & White, R. T. (1982). Fieldwork in geography and long-term memory structures. *American Educational Research Journal, 19*(4), 623–632.

Mayer, D. P. (1998). Do new teaching standards undermine performance on old tests? *Educational Evaluation and Policy Analysis, 15,* 1–16.

Mayer, R. E., Griffith, E., Jurkowitz, I. T. N., & Rothman, D. (2008). Increased interestingness of extraneous details in a multimedia science presentation leads to decreased learning. *Journal of Experimental Psychology: Applied, 14,* 329–339.

Mayer, R. E., Quilici, J. L., & Moreno, R. (1999). What is learned in an after-school computer club? *Journal of Educational Computing Research, 20,* 223–235.

Mayer, R. E., & Wittrock, M. C. (1996). Problem-solving transfer. In D. C. Berliner & R. C. Calfee (Eds.), *Handbook of educational psychology* (pp. 47–62). New York, NY: Simon & Schuster Macmillan.

Means, M. B., & Knapp, M. S. (1994). Cognitive approaches to teaching advanced skills to educationally disadvantaged students. In H. F. Clarizio, W. A. Mehrens, & Hapkiewicz, W. G. (Eds.), *Contemporary issues in educational psychology* (6th ed., pp. 180–190). New York, NY: McGraw-Hill.

Montessori, M. (1964). *Advanced Montessori method.* Cambridge, MA: Bentley.

Moyer, P. S. (2002). Are we having fun yet? How teachers use manipulatives to teach mathematics. *Educational Studies in Mathematics, 47,* 175–197.

Nickerson, R. S., Perkins, D. N., & Smith, E. E. (1985). *The teaching of thinking.* Hillsdale, NJ: Lawrence Erlbaum.

Nokes-Malach, T. J., VanLehn, K., Belenky, D. M., Lichtenstein, M., & Cox, G. (2013). Coordinating principles and examples through analogy and self-explanation. *European Journal of Psychology of Education, 28*(4), 1237–1263.

Ogle, D. S. (2009). Creating contexts for inquiry: From KWL to PRC2. *Knowledge Quest, 38*(1), 56–61.

Osborne, R. J., & Wittrock, M. C. (1983). Learning science: A generative process. *Science Education, 67,* 489–504.

Ostovar-Namaghi, S. A., & Shahhosseini, M.-R. (2011). On the effect of reciprocal teaching strategy on EFL learners' reading proficiency. *Journal of Language Teaching and Research, 2*(6), 1238–1243.

Owen, P., & Sweller, J. (2008). Cognitive load theory and music instruction. *Educational Psychology, 28,* 29–45.

Palincsar, A. S., & Brown, A. L. (1984). Reciprocal teaching of comprehension-monitoring activities. *Cognition and Instruction, 1,* 117–175.

Palmer, D. H. (2009). Student interest generated during an inquiry skills lesson. *Journal of Research in Science Teaching, 46,* 147–165.

Pea, R. D. (1987). Socializing the knowledge transfer problem. *International Journal of Educational Research, 11,* 639–663.

Peled, Z., & Wittrock, M. C. (1990). Generative meanings in the comprehension of word problems in mathematics. *Instructional Science, 19,* 171–205.

Perfetti, C. A. (1992). The representation problem in reading acquisition. In P. B. Gough, L. Ehri, & R. Treiman (Eds.), *Reading acquisition* (pp. 145–174). Hillsdale, NJ: Lawrence Erlbaum.

Perkins, D., Jay, E., & Tishman, S. (1993). New conceptions of thinking: From ontology to education. *Educational Psychologist, 28*(1), 67–85.

Perkins, D. N., & Salomon, G. (2012). Knowledge to go: A motivational and dispositional view of transfer. *Educational Psychologist, 47*(3), 248–258.

Perry, M. (1991). Learning and transfer: Instructional conditions and conceptual change. *Cognitive Development, 6,* 449–468.

Prawat, R. S. (1989). Promoting access to knowledge, strategy, and disposition in students: A research synthesis. *Review of Educational Research, 59,* 1–41.

Pugh, K. J., & Bergin, D. A. (2006). Motivational influences on transfer. *Educational Psychologist, 41*(3), 147–160.

Reed, S. K. (1987). A structure-mapping model for word problems. *Journal of Experimental Psychology: Learning, Memory, and Cognition, 13*(1), 124–139.

Reed, S. K., Ernst, G. W., & Banerji, R. (1974). The role of analogy in transfer between similar problem states. *Cognitive Psychology, 6,* 436–450.

Renkl, A. (2005). The worked-out-example principle in multimedia learning. In R. Mayer (Ed.), *Cambridge handbook of multimedia learning* (pp. 229–246). Cambridge, UK: Cambridge University Press.

Renkl, A., & Atkinson, R. K. (2010). Learning from worked-out examples and problem solving. In J. Plass, R. Moreno, & R. Brünken (Eds.), *Cognitive load theory and research in educational psychology* (pp. 91–108). New York, NY: Cambridge University Press.

Renkl, A., Atkinson, R. K., & Maier, U. H. (2000). From studying examples to solving problems: Fading worked-out solution steps helps learning. In L. Gleitman & A. K. Joshi (Eds.), *Proceeding of the 22nd Annual Conference of the Cognitive Science Society* (pp. 393–398). Mahwah, NJ: Lawrence Erlbaum.

Richland, L. E., Zur, O., & Holyoak, K. J. (2007). Cognitive supports for analogies in the mathematics classroom. *Science, 316,* 1128–1129.

Rosenshine, B., & Meister, C. (1994). Reciprocal teaching: A review of the research. *Review of Educational Research, 64*(4), 479–530.

Ross, B. H. (1987). This is like that: The use of earlier problems and the separation of similarity effects. *Journal of Experimental Psychology: Learning, Memory, and Cognition, 13,* 629–639.

Ross, B. H. (1989). Distinguishing types of superficial similarities: Different effects on the access and use of earlier problems. *Journal of Experimental Psychology: Learning, Memory, and Cognition, 15,* 456–468.

Salomon, G., & Globerson, T. (1987). Skill may not be enough: The role of mindfulness in learning and transfer. *International Journal of Educational Research, 11,* 623–637.

Salomon, G., & Perkins, D. (1989). Rocky roads to transfer: Rethinking mechanisms of a neglected phenomenon. *Educational Psychologist, 24(2),* 113–142.

Saxe, G. B. (2002). Candy selling and math learning. In C. Desforges & R. Fox (Eds.), *Teaching and learning: The essential readings* (pp. 86–106). Malden, MA: Blackwell.

Scardamalia, M., Bereiter, C., & Goelman, H. (1982). The role of production factors in writing ability. In M. Nystrand (Ed.), *What writers know* (pp. 173–210). New York: Academic Press.

Schliemann, A. D., & Acioly, N. M. (1989). Mathematical knowledge developed at work: The contribution of practice versus the contribution of schooling. *Cognition and Instruction, 6,* 185–221.

Schneider, W. (1985). Training high-performance skills: Fallacies and guidelines. *Human Factors, 27*(3), 285–300.

Schwartz, D. L., Bransford, J. D., & Sears, D. L. (2005). Efficiency and innovation in transfer. In J. Mestre (Ed.), *Transfer of learning from a modern multidisciplinary perspective* (pp. 1–51). Greenwich, CT: Information Age.

Silver, E. A., Ghousseini, H., Gosen, D., Charalambous, C., & Strawhun, B. (2005). Moving from rhetoric to praxis: Issues faced by teachers in having students consider multiple solutions for problems in the mathematics classroom. *Journal of Mathematical Behavior, 24,* 287–301.

Singley, M. K., & Anderson, J. R. (1989). *The transfer of cognitive skill.* Cambridge, MA: Harvard University Press.

Smith, L., Ping, R. M., Matlen, B. J., Goldwater, M. B., Gentner, D, & Lvine, S. (2014). Mechanisms of spatial learning: Teaching children geometric categories. *Spatial Cognition, 9,* 325–337.

Sweller, J., Ayres, P., & Kalyuga, S. (2011). *Cognitive load theory.* New York, NY: Springer.

Tajika, H., & Nakatsu, N. (2005). Using a metacognitive strategy to solve mathematical problems. *Bulletin of the Aichi University of Education, 54,* 1–9.

Tajika, H., Nakatsu, N., Nozaki, H., Neumann, E., & Maruno, S. (2007). Effects of self-explanation as a metacognitive strategy for solving mathematical word problems. *Japanese Psychological Research, 49*(3), 222–233.

Terwel, J., van Oers, B., van Dijk, I., & van den Eeden, P. (2009). Are representations to be provided or generated in primary mathematics education? Effects on transfer. *Educational Research and Evaluation, 15*(1), 25–44.

Thorndike, E. L. (1923). The influence of first-year Latin upon the ability to read English. *School and Society, 17,* 165–168.

Thorndike, E. L. (1924). Mental discipline in high school studies. *Journal of Educational Psychology, 15,* 1–22, 83–98.

Tok, Ş., T. (2013). Effects of the know-want-learn strategy on students' mathematics achievement, anxiety, and metacognitive skills. *Metacognition Learning, 8,* 193–212.

Tsai, Y., Kunter, M., Ludtke, O., Trautwein, U., & Ryan, R. M. (2008). What makes lessons interesting? The role of situational and individual factors in three school subjects. *Journal of Educational Psychology, 100,* 460–472.

Vendetti, M. S., Matlen, B., J., Richland, L. E., & Bunge, S. A. (2015). Analogical reasoning in the classroom: Insights from cognitive science. *Mind, Brain, and Education, 9*(2), 100–106.

Weinstein, Y., McDermott, K. B., & Roediger, H. L. (2010). A comparison of study strategies for passages: rereading, answering questions, and generating questions. *Journal of Experimental Psychology: Applied, 16*(3), 308–316.

Wittwer, J., & Renkl, A. (2008). Why instructional explanations often do not work: a framework for understanding the effectiveness of instructional explanations. *Educational Psychologist, 43*(1), 49–64.

Wolters, C. (2004). Advancing achievement goal theory: Using goal structures and goal orientations to predict students' motivation, cognition, and achievement. *Journal of Educational Psychology, 96,* 236–250.

Woodward, J., & Baxter, J. (1997). The effects of an innovative approach to mathematics on academically low-achieving students in inclusive settings. *Exceptional Children, 63,* 373–388.

Youssef-Shalala, A., Ayres, P., & Schubert, C. (2014). Using a general problem-solving strategy to promote transfer. *Journal of Experimental Psychology: Applied, 20*(3), 215–231.

Zepeda, C. D., Richey, J. E., Ronevich, P., & Nokes-Malach, T. J. (2015). Direct instruction of metacognition benefits adolescent science learning, transfer, and motivation: An in vivo study. *Journal of Educational Psychology.* Advance online publication.

Module 13

Abrami, P. C., Bernard, R. M., Borokhovski, E., Waddington, D. I., Wade, C. A., & Persson, T. (2015). Strategies for teaching students to think critically a meta-analysis. *Review of Educational Research, 85*(2), 275–314.

Alexander, P. A. (2014). Thinking critically and analytically about critical-analytic thinking: An introduction. *Educational Psychology Review, 26*(4), 469–476.

Alfonso-Benlliure, V., Meléndez, J. C., & García-Ballesteros, M. (2013). Evaluation of a creativity intervention program for preschoolers. *Thinking Skills and Creativity, 10,* 112–120.

Amabile, T. M. (1996). *Creativity in context: Update to the social psychology of creativity.* Boulder, CO: Westview.

Anderson, L. W., & Krathwohl, D. R. (Eds.). (2001). *A taxonomy for learning, teaching, and assessing.* New York, NY: Longman.

Beghetto, R. A., & Kaufman, J. C. (2011). Teaching for creativity with disciplined improvisation. In K. Sawyer (Ed.), *Structure and improvisation in creative teaching* (pp. 94–109). New York, NY: Cambridge University Press.

Beghetto, R. A. & Kaufman, J. C. (2014). Classroom contexts for creativity. *High Ability Studies, 25*(1), 53–69.

Beghetto, R. A., Kaufman, J. C., & Baer, J. (2015). *Teaching for creativity in the common core classroom.* New York, NY: Teachers College Press.

Bloom, B. S., Englehart, M. D., Frost, E. J., Hill, W. H., & Krathwohl, D. R. (1956). *Taxonomy of educational objectives.* New York, NY: David McKay.

Bransford, J. D., & Stein, B. S. (1993). *The IDEAL problem solver: A guide for improving thinking, learning, and creativity* (2nd ed.). New York, NY: Freeman.

Colzato, L. S., Szapora, A., Pannekoek, J. N., & Hommel, B. (2013). The impact of physical exercise on convergent and divergent thinking. *Frontiers in human neuroscience, 7,* 1–6.

Delialioğlu, Ö. (2012). Student engagement in blended learning environments with lecture-based and problem-based instructional approaches. *Journal of Educational Technology & Society, 15*(3), 310–322.

Duncker, K. (1945). On problem solving (trans. by L. S. Lees). *Psychological Monographs, 58* (5), whole # 270.

Facione, P. A., (2013). *Critical thinking: What it is and why it counts.* 2013 Update. Milbrae, CA: California Academic Press.

Garcia-Mila, M., & Anderson, C. (2008). Argumentation in science education: An overview. In S. Erduran & M. P. Jiménez-Aleixandre (Eds.), *Argumentation in science education: Perspectives from classroom-based research* (pp. 3–28). New York, NY: Springer.

Giacumo, L. A., Savenye, W., & Smith, N. (2013). Facilitation prompts and rubrics on higher-order thinking skill performance found in undergraduate asynchronous discussion boards. *British Journal of Educational Technology, 44*(5), 774–794.

Halpern, D. F. (1998). Teaching critical thinking for transfer across domains: Disposition, skills, structure training, and metacognitive monitoring. *American Psychologist, 53*(4), 449.

Hammond, H. L., Skidmore, L. E., Wilcox-Herzog, A., & Kaufman, J. C. (2013). Creativity and Creativity Programs. In J. Hattie & E. M. Anderman (Eds.), *International guide to student achievement.* New York, NY: Taylor & Francis.

Hmelo-Silver, C. E. (2012). International perspectives on problem-based learning: Contexts, cultures, challenges, and adaptations. *Interdisciplinary Journal of Problem-Based Learning, 6*(1), 3.

Hung, W. (2015). Cultivating creative problem solvers: the PBL style. *Asia Pacific Education Review, 16*(2), 237–246.

Jensen, J. L., McDaniel, M. A., Woodard, S. M., & Kummer, T. A. (2014). Teaching to the test . . . or testing to teach: exams requiring higher order thinking skills encourage greater conceptual understanding. *Educational Psychology Review, 26*(2), 307–329.

Kaufman, J. C., & Beghetto, R. A. (2009). Beyond big and little: The four c model of creativity. *Review of General Psychology, 13*(1), 1.

Kaufman, J. C., & Beghetto, R. A. (2013). In praise of Clark Kent: Creative metacognition and the importance of teaching kids when (not) to be creative. *Roeper Review, 35*(3), 155–165.

Liu, M., Horton, L., Olmanson, J., & Toprac, P. (2011). A study of learning and motivation in a new media enriched environment for middle school science. *Educational Technology Research and Development, 59*(2), 249–265. doi:10.1007/s11423-011-9192-7

Liu, M., Rosenblum, J. A., Horton, L., & Kang, J. (2014). Designing science learning with game-based approaches. *Computers in the Schools, 31*(1–2), 84–102.

Loyens, S. M., Kirschner, P. A., & Paas, F. (2012). Problem-based learning. In K. R. Harris, S. Graham, T. Urdan, A. G. Bus, S. Major, H. L. Swanson, . . . H. L. Swanson (Eds.), *APA educational psychology handbook, Vol 3: Application to learning and teaching* (pp. 403–425). Washington, DC: American Psychological Association.

Maier, N. R. F. (1931). Reasoning in humans: II. The solution of a problem and its appearance in consciousness. *Journal of Comparative Psychology, 12,* 181–194.

Molnár, G., Greiff, S., & Csapó, B. (2013). Inductive reasoning, domain specific and complex problem solving: Relations and development. *Thinking Skills and Creativity, 9,* 35–45.

Muehlenkamp, J. J., Weiss, N., & Hansen, M. (2015). Problem-Based learning for introductory psychology: Preliminary supporting evidence. *Scholarship of Teaching and Learning in Psychology, 1*(2), 125–136.

Pang, W. (2015). Promoting creativity in the classroom: A generative view. *Psychology of Aesthetics, Creativity, and the Arts, 9*(2), 122.

Paul, R., & Elder, L. (2014). *The miniature guide to critical thinking: Concepts and tools* (7th ed.). Dillon, Beach, CA: Foundation for Critical Thinking.

Plucker, J. A., Beghetto, R. A., & Dow, G. T. (2004). Why isn't creativity more important to educational psychologists? Potentials, pitfalls, and future directions in creativity research. *Educational Psychologist, 39*(2), 83–96.

Scherer, R., & Tiemann, R. (2014). Evidence on the effects of task interactivity and grade level on thinking skills involved in complex problem solving. *Thinking Skills and Creativity, 11,* 48–64.

Schmidt, H. G. (1983). Problem-based learning: Rationale and description. *Medical education, 17*(1), 11–16.

Schmidt, H. G., van der Molen, H. T., Te Winkel, W. W., & Wijnen, W. H. (2009). Constructivist, problem-based learning does work: A meta-analysis of curricular comparisons involving a single medical school. *Educational Psychologist, 44*(4), 227–249.

Sternberg, R. J. (2006). Creating a vision of creativity: The first 25 years. *Psychology of Aesthetics, Creativity, and the Arts,* (1), 2.

Sternberg, R. J. (2015). Teaching for creativity: The sounds of silence. *Psychology of Aesthetics, Creativity, and the Arts, 9*(2), 115.

Strom, P. S., & Strom, R. D. (2013). *Thinking in childhood and adolescence.* Charlotte, NC: Information Age Publishing.

Torrance, E. P. (1972). Predictive validity of the Torrance Tests of Creative Thinking. *Journal of Creative Behavior, 6*(4), 236–252.

Torrance, E. P. (2000). Preschool creativity. *The psychoeducational assessment of preschool children, 3,* 349–363.

Wason, P. C. (1960). On the failure to eliminate hypotheses in a conceptual task. *Quarterly Journal of Experimental Psychology, 12,* 129–140.

Wason, P. C., & Johnson-Laird, P. N. (1972). *Psychology of reasoning: Structure and content.* London, UK: Batsford.

Yi, X., Hu, W., Plucker, J. A., & McWilliams, J. (2013). Is there a developmental slump in creativity in China? The relationship between organizational climate and creativity development in Chinese adolescents. *The Journal of Creative Behavior, 47*(1), 22–40.

Module 14

Ainley, M., Hidi, S., & Berndorff, D. (2002). Interest, learning, and the psychological processes that mediate their relationship. *Journal of Educational Psychology, 94,* 545–561.

Amabile, T. M., DeJong, W., & Lepper, M. (1976). Effects of externally imposed deadlines on intrinsic motivation. *Journal of Personality and Social Psychology, 34,* 92–98.

Anderman, E. M., & Maehr, M. L. (1994). Motivation and schooling in the middle grades. *Review of Educational Research, 64*(2), 287–309.

Anderson, L., Evertson, C., & Brophy, J. (1979). An experimental study of effective teaching in first-grade reading groups. *Elementary School Journal, 79,* 193–223.

Assor, A., Kaplan, H., Kanat-Maymon, Y., & Roth, G. (2005). Directly controlling teacher behaviors as predictors of poor motivation and engagement in girls and boys: The role of anger and anxioty. *Learning and Instruction, 15,* 397–413.

Beaman, R., & Wheldall, K. (2000). Teachers' use of approval and disapproval in the classroom. *Educational Psychology, 20,* 431–446.

Brockner, J., & Vasta, R. (1981). Do causal attributions mediate the effects of extrinsic rewards on intrinsic interest? *Journal of Research in Personality, 15,* 201–209.

Brophy, J. (1981). Teacher praise: A functional analysis. *Review of Educational Research, 51*(1), 5–32.

Brophy, J. (2008). Developing students' appreciation for what is taught in school. *Educational Psychologist, 43*(3), 132–141.

Brown, J. S., Collins, A., & Duguid, P. (1989). Situated cognition and the culture of learning. *Educational Researcher, 18*(1), 32–42.

Brummelman, E., Thomaes, S., Overbeek, G., Orobio de Castro, B., van den Hout, M. A., & Bushman, B. J. (2014). On feeding those hungry for praise: Person praise backfires in children with low self-esteem. *Journal of Experimental Psychology: General, 143*(1), 9–14.

Cameron, J. (2001). Negative effects of reward on intrinsic motivation—A limited phenomenon: Comment on Deci, Koestner, and Ryan (2001). *Review of Educational Research, 71*(1), 29–42.

Collins, A., Hawkins, J., & Carver, S. M. (1991). In B. Means, C. Chelemer, & M. S. Knapp (Eds.), *Teaching advanced skills to at-risk students* (pp. 173–194). San Francisco, CA: Jossey-Bass.

Cordova, D. I., & Lepper, M. R. (1996). Intrinsic motivation and the process of learning: Beneficial effects of contextualization, personalization and choice. *Journal of Educational Psychology, 88,* 715–730.

Corpus, J. H., & Lepper, M. R. (2007). The effects of person versus performance praise on children's motivation: Gender and age as moderating factors. *Educational Psychology, 27*(4), 487–508.

Corpus, J. H., & Wormington, S. V. (2014). Profiles of intrinsic and extrinsic motivations in elementary school: A longitudinal analysis. *The Journal of Experimental Education, 82*(4), 480–501.

Covington, M. V. (2000). Intrinsic versus extrinsic motivation in schools: A reconciliation. *Current Directions in Psychological Science, 9,* 22–25.

Craske, M. L. (1985). Improving persistence through observational learning and attribution retraining. *British Journal of Educational Psychology, 55,* 138–147.

Csikszentmihalyi, M. (1990). *Flow: The psychology of optimal experience.* New York, NY: HarperCollins.

Csikszentmihalyi, M. (1997). *Finding flow: The psychology of engagement with everyday life. Masterminds series.* New York, NY: Basic Books.

Csikszentmihalyi, M. (2000). *Beyond boredom and anxiety: Experiencing flow in work and play* (2nd ed.). San Francisco, CA: Jossey-Bass.

deCharms, R. (1968). *Personal causation: The internal affective determinants of behavior.* New York, NY: Academic.

deCharms, R. (1968). *Personal causation: The internal affective determinants of behavior.* New York, NY: Academic Press.

Deci, E. L. (1971). Effects of externally mediated rewards on intrinsic motivation. *Journal of Personality and Social Psychology, 18,* 105–115.

Deci, E. L., Eghrari, H., Patrick, B. C., & Leone, D. R. (1994). Facilitating internalization: The self-determination perspective. *Journal of Personality, 62,* 119–142.

Deci, E. L., Koestner, R., & Ryan, R. M. (1999a). A meta-analytic review of experiments examining the effects of extrinsic rewards on intrinsic motivation. *Psychological Bulletin, 125*(6), 627–668.

Deci, E. L., Koestner, R., & Ryan, R. M. (1999b). The undermining effect is a reality after all—Extrinsic rewards, task interest, and self-determination: Reply to Eisenberger, Pierce, and Cameron (1999) and Lepper, Henderlong, and Gingras (1999). *Psychological Bulletin, 125*(6), 692–700.

Deci, E. L., Koestner, R., & Ryan. R. M. (2001). Extrinsic rewards and intrinsic motivation in education: Reconsidered once again. *Review of Educational Research, 71*(1), 1–27.

Deci, E. L., & Ryan, R. M. (1985). *Intrinsic motivation and self-determination in human behavior.* New York, NY: Plenum Press.

Deci, E. L., & Ryan, R. M. (1992). The initiation and regulation of intrinsically motivated learning and achievement. In A. K. Boggiano & T. S. Pittman (Eds.), *Achievement and motivation: A social-developmental perspective* (pp. 9–36). New York, NY: Cambridge University Press.

Deci, E. L., & Ryan, R. M. (2000). The "what" and the "why" of goal pursuits: Human needs and the self-determination of behavior. *Psychological Inquiry, 11,* 227–268.

Deci, E. L., Ryan, R. M., & Koestner, R. (2001). The pervasive negative effects of rewards on intrinsic motivation: Response to Cameron (2001). *Review of Educational Research, 71*(1), 43–51.

Dotterer, A. M., McHale, S. M., & Crouter, A. C. (2009). The development and correlates of academic interests from childhood through adolescence. *Journal of Educational Psychology, 101*(2), 509–519.

Driscoll, M. P. (2005). *Psychology of learning for instruction.* Boston, MA: Allyn & Bacon.

Dweck, C. S. (2006). *Mindset: The new psychology of success.* New York, NY: Random House.

Dweck, C. S., & Master. A. (2008). Self-theories motivate self-regulated learning. In D. H. Schunk & B. J. Zimmerman (Eds.), *Motivation and self-regulated learning: Theory, research, and applications* (pp. 31–51). Mahwah, NJ: Lawrence Erlbaum.

Eccles, J. S., Wigfield, S., & Schiefele, U. (1998). Motivation to succeed. In N. Eisenberg (Ed.), *Handbook of child psychology: Vol. 3. Social, emotional, and personality development* (5th ed., pp. 1017–1095). New York, NY: Wiley.

Fryer, J. W., & Elliot, A. J. (2008). Self-regulation of achievement goal pursuit. In D. H. Schunk & B. J. Zimmerman (Eds.), *Motivation and self-regulated learning: Theory, research, and applications* (pp. 53–75). Mahwah, NJ: Lawrence Erlbaum.

Gottfried, A. E., Fleming, J. S., & Gottfried, A. W. (1994). Role of parental motivational practices in children's academic intrinsic motivation and achievement. *Journal of Educational Psychology, 86,* 104–113.

Gottfried, A. E., Fleming, J. S., & Gottfried, A. W. (1998). Role of cognitively stimulating home environment in children's academic intrinsic motivation: A longitudinal study. *Child Development, 69*(5), 1448–1460.

Gottfried, A. E., Fleming, J. S., & Gottfried, A. W. (2001). Continuity of academic intrinsic motivation from childhood through late adolescence: A longitudinal study. *Journal of Educational Psychology, 93,* 3–13.

Gottfried, A. E., & Gottfried, A. W. (1996). A longitudinal study of academic intrinsic motivation in intellectually gifted children: Childhood through early adolescence. *Gifted Child Quarterly, 40,* 179–183.

Gunderson, E. A., Gripshover, S. J., Romero, C., Dweck, C. S., Goldin-Meadow, S., & Levine, S. C. (2013). Parent praise to 1- to 3-year-olds predicts children's motivational frameworks 5 years later. *Child Development, 84*(5), 1526–1541.

Haimovitz, K., & Corpus, J. H. (2011). Effects of person versus process praise on student motivation: Stability and change in emerging adulthood. *Educational Psychology, 31*(5), 595–609.

Harackiewicz, J., Manderlink, G., & Sansone, C. (1984). Rewarding pinball wizardry: The effects of evaluation on intrinsic interest. *Journal of Personality and Social Psychology, 47,* 287–300.

Harter, S. (1978). Effectance motivation reconsidered: Toward a developmental model. *Human Development, 21,* 34–64.

Harter, S., & Jackson, B. K. (1992). Trait vs. nontrait conceptualizations of intrinsic/ extrinsic motivational orientation. *Motivation and Emotion, 16,* 209–230.

Haselhuhn, C. W., Al-Mabuk, R., Gabriele, A., Groen, M., & Galloway, S. (2007). Promoting positive achievement in the middle school: A look at teachers' motivational knowledge, beliefs, and teaching practices. *Research in Middle Level Education, 30,* 1–20.

Hayenga, A. O., & Corpus, J. H. (2010). Profiles of intrinsic and extrinsic motivations: A person-centered approach to motivation and achievement in middle school. *Motivation and Emotion, 34*(4), 371–383.

Henderlong, J., & Lepper, M. R. (2002). The effects of praise on children's intrinsic motivation: A review and synthesis. *Psychological Bulletin, 128*(5), 774–795.

Hidi, S. (2000). An interest researcher's perspective: The effects of intrinsic and extrinsic factors on motivation. In C. Sansone & J. M. Harackiewicz (Eds.), *Intrinsic and extrinsic motivation: The search for optimal motivation and performance* (pp. 309–339). San Diego, CA: Academic Press.

Hughes, B., Sullivan, H., & Mosley, M. (1985). External evaluation, task difficulty, and continuing motivation. *Journal of Educational Research, 78,* 210–215.

Jacobs, J. E., Lanza, S., Osgood, D. W., Eccles, J. S., & Wigfield, A. (2002). Changes in children's self-competence and values: Gender and domain differences across grades one through twelve. *Child Development, 73,* 509–527.

Kamins, M., & Dweck, C. S. (1999). Person vs. process praise and criticism: Implications for contingent self-worth and coping. *Developmental Psychology, 35,* 835–847.

Kast, A., & Connor, K. (1988). Sex and age differences in response to informational and controlling feedback. *Personality and Social Psychology Bulletin, 14,* 514–523.

Koestner, R., Ryan, R. M., Bernieri, F., & Holt, K. (1984). Setting limits on children's behavior: The differential effects of controlling versus informational styles on intrinsic motivation and creativity. *Journal of Personality, 52,* 233–248.

Koestner, R., Zuckerman, M., & Koestner, J. (1987). Praise, involvement, and intrinsic motivation. *Journal of Personality and Social Psychology, 53,* 383–390.

Koestner, R., Zuckerman, M., & Koestner, J. (1989). Attributional focus of praise and children's intrinsic motivation: The moderating role of gender. *Personality and Social Psychology Bulletin, 15,* 61–72.

Lepper, M. R., Corpus, J. H., & Iyengar, S. S. (2005). Intrinsic and extrinsic motivational orientations in the classroom: Age differences and academic correlates. *Journal of Educational Psychology, 97*(2), 184–196.

Lepper, M. R., & Greene, D. (1978). *The hidden costs of reward.* Hillsdale, NJ: Lawrence Erlbaum.

Lepper, M. R., & Henderlong, J. (2000). Turning "play" into "work" and "work" into "play": 25 years of research on intrinsic versus extrinsic motivation. In C. Sansone & J. M. Harackiewicz (Eds.), *Intrinsic and extrinsic motivation: The search for optimal motivation and performance* (pp. 257–307). New York, NY: Academic Press.

Malone, M. R., & Lepper, M. R. (1983). Making learning fun. In R. E. Snow & J. F. Marshall (Eds.), *Aptitude, learning, and instruction: Cognitive and affective process analyses* (Vol. 3, pp. 223–253). Hillsdale, NJ: Lawrence Erlbaum.

Manderlink, G., & Harackiewicz, J. (1984). Proximal vs. distal goal setting and intrinsic motivation. *Journal of Personality and Social Psychology, 47,* 918–928.

Marinak, B. A., & Gambrell, L. B. (2008). Intrinsic motivation and rewards: What sustains young children's engagement with text? *Literacy Research and Instruction, 47,* 9–26.

Martin, A. J. (2009). Motivation and engagement across the academic life span: A developmental construct validity study of elementary school, high school, and university/ college students. *Educational and Psychological Measurement, 69,* 794–825.

Marzano, R. J., Pickering, D. J., & Pollack, J. E. (2005). *Classroom instruction that works: Research-based strategies for increasing student achievement.* Englewood Cliffs, NJ: Prentice Hall.

Mehan, H. (1974). Accomplishing classroom lessons. In A. Cicourel, K. Jennings, S. Jennings, K. Leiter, R. MacKay, H. Mehan, & D. Roth (Eds.), *Language use and school performance* (pp. 76–142). New York, NY: Academic Press.

Miller, D., & Hom, H. (1997). Conceptions of ability and the interpretation of praise, blame, and material rewards. *The Journal of Experimental Education, 65,* 163–177.

Mueller, C. M., & Dweck, C. S. (1998). Praise for intelligence can undermine children's motivation and performance. *Journal of Personality and Social Psychology, 75,* 33–52.

O'Leary, K., & O'Leary, S. (Eds.). (1977). *Classroom management: The successful use of behavior modification* (2nd ed.). Elmsford, NY: Pergamon.

Otis, N., Grouzet, F. M. E., & Pelletier, L. G. (2005). Latent motivational change in an academic setting: A 3-year longitudinal study. *Journal of Educational Psychology, 97*(2), 170–183.

Patall, E. A. (2013). Constructing motivation through choice, interest, and interestingness. *Journal of Educational Psychology, 105*(2), 522–534.

Patall, E. A., Cooper, H., & Robinson, J. C. (2008). The effects of choice on intrinsic motivation and related outcomes: A meta-analysis of research findings. *Psychological Bulletin, 134,* 270–300.

Patall, E. A., Cooper, H., & Wynn, S. R. (2010). The effectiveness and relative importance of providing choices in the classroom. *Journal of Educational Psychology, 102,* 896–915.

Piaget, J. (1954). *The construction of reality in the child.* New York, NY: Basic Books.

Piaget, J. (1963). *Origins of intelligence in children.* New York, NY: W. W. Norton.

Piaget, J. (1985). *The equilibration of cognitive structures: The central problem of intellectual development* (T. Brown & K. L. Thampy, Trans.) Chicago, IL: The University of Chicago Press.

Pittman, T. S., Cooper, E. E., & Smith, T. W. (1977). Attribution of causality and the overjustification effect. *Personality and Social Psychology Bulletin, 3,* 280–283.

Plant, R., & Ryan, R. M. (1985). Intrinsic motivation and the effects of self-consciousness, self-awareness, and ego-involvement: An investigation of internally controlling styles. *Journal of Personality, 53,* 435–449.

Pomerantz, E. M., & Kempner, S. G. (2013). Mothers' daily person and process praise: Implications for children's theory of intelligence and motivation. *Developmental Psychology, 49*(11), 2040–2046.

Premack, D. (1959). Toward empirical behavior laws: I. Positive reinforcement. *Psychological Review, 66,* 219–233.

Premack, D. (1963). Rate differential reinforcement in monkey manipulation. *Journal of Experimental Analysis of Behavior, 6,* 81–89.

Randall, J., & Engelhard, G. (2009). Differences between teachers' grading practices in elementary and middle schools. *Journal of Educational Research, 102,* 175–185.

Reeve, J., & Deci, E. L. (1996). Elements of the competitive situation that affect intrinsic motivation. *Personality and Social Psychology Bulletin, 22,* 24–33.

Rolland, R. G. (2012). Synthesizing the evidence on classroom goal structures in middle and secondary schools: A meta-analysis and narrative review. *Review of Educational Research, 82*(4), 396–435.

Rotter, J. (1966). Generalized expectancies for internal versus external control of reinforcement. *Psychological Monographs, 1*(Whole No. 609).

Rotter, J. (1990). Internal versus external control of reinforcement: A case history of a variable. *American Psychologist, 45,* 489–493.

Ryan, R. M., & Deci, E. L. (2000). Self-determination theory and the facilitation of intrinsic motivation, social development and well-being. *American Psychologist, 55,* 68–78.

Ryan, R. M., Mims, V., & Koestner, R. (1983). Relation of reward contingency and interpersonal context to intrinsic motivation: A review and test using cognitive evaluation theory. *Journal of Personality and Social Psychology, 45,* 736–750.

Ryan, R. M., & Stiller, J. (1991). The social contexts of internalization: Parent and teacher influences on autonomy, motivation, and learning. In M. L. Maehr & P. L. Pintrich (Eds.), *Advances in motivation and achievement* (Vol. 7, pp. 115–149). Greenwich, CT: JAI.

Schweinle, A., Turner, J. C., & Meyer, D. K. (2008). Understanding young adolescents' optimal experiences in academic settings. *The Journal of Experimental Education, 77*(2), 125–143.

Seligman, M., & Maier, S. (1967). Failure to escape traumatic shock. *Journal of Experimental Psychology, 74,* 1–9.

Seligman, M. E. P. (1994). *What you can change and what you can't.* New York, NY: Knopf.

Shernoff, D. J., Csikszentmihalyi, M., Schneider, B., & Shernoff, E. S. (2003).

Student engagement in high school classrooms from the perspective of flow theory. *School Psychology Quarterly, 18*(2), 158–176.

Skinner, B. F. (1953). *Science and human behavior.* New York, NY: Macmillan.

Silvia, P. J. (2005). What is interesting? Exploring the appraisal structure of interest. *Emotion, 5,* 89–102.

Silvia, P. J. (2006). *Exploring the psychology of interest.* New York, NY: Oxford University Press.

Stipek, D. (2002). *Motivation to learn: Integrating theory and practice* (4th ed.). Boston, MA: Allyn & Bacon.

Stipek, D. J. (1996). Motivation and instruction. In D. C. Berliner & R. C. Calfee (Eds.), *Handbook of educational psychology* (pp. 85–113). New York, NY: Simon & Schuster.

Turner, J., & Paris, S. G. (1995). How literacy tasks influence children's motivation for literacy. *The Reading Teacher, 48*(8), 662–673.

Urdan, T., Midgley, C., & Anderman, E. M. (1998). The role of classroom goal structure in students' use of self-handicapping strategies. *American Educational Research Journal, 35*(1), 101–122.

Van Overwalle, F., & De Metsenaere, M. (1990). The effects of attribution-based intervention and study strategy training on academic achievement in college freshmen. *British Journal of Educational Psychology, 60,* 299–311.

Vansteenkiste, M., & Deci, E. L. (2003). Competitively contingent rewards and intrinsic motivation: Can losers remain motivated? *Motivation and Emotion, 27*(4), 273–299.

Vansteenkiste, M., Sierens, E., Soenens, B., Luyckx, K., & Lens, W. (2009). Motivational profiles from a self-determination perspective: The quality of motivation matters. *Journal of Educational Psychology, 101*(3), 671–688.

Vansteenkiste, M., Simons, J., Lens, W., Sheldon, K. M., & Deci, E. L. (2004). Motivating learning, performance, and persistence: The synergistic effects of intrinsic goal contents and autonomy-supportive contexts. *Journal of Personality and Social Psychology, 87,* 246–260.

Vygotsky, L. S. (1978). *Mind in society: The development of higher psychological processes.* Cambridge, MA: Harvard University Press.

Weiner, B. (1990). History of motivational research in education. *Journal of Educational Psychology, 82*(4), 616–622.

White, R. W. (1959). Motivation reconsidered: The concept of competence. *Psychological Review, 66,* 297–333.

Wigfield, A., Eccles, J. S., Schiefele, U., Roeser, R. W., & Davis-Kean, P. (2006). Development of achievement motivation. In W. Damon & R. M. Lerner (Eds.), *Handbook of child psychology* (pp. 933–1002). Hoboken, NJ: Wiley.

Wigfield, A., & Wagner, A. L. (2005). Competence, motivation, and identity development during adolescence. In A. J. Elliot & C. S. Dweck (Eds.), *Handbook of competence and motivation* (pp. 222–239). New York, NY: Guilford Press.

Wormington, S. V., Corpus, J. H., & Anderson, K. G. (2012). A person-centered investigation of academic motivation and its correlates in high school. *Learning and Individual Differences, 22*(4), 429–438.

Zentall, S. R., & Morris, B. J. (2010). "Good job, you're so smart:" The effects of inconsistency of praise type on young children's motivation. *Journal of Experimental Child Psychology, 107,* 155–163.

Module 15

Ames, C. A. (1990). Motivation: What teachers need to know. *Teachers College Record, 91*(3), 409–421.

Ames, C. A. (1992). Classrooms: Goals, structures, and student motivation. *Journal of Educational Psychology, 84*(3), 261–271.

Anderman, E. M., Cupp, P. K., & Lane, D. (2009). Impulsivity and academic cheating. *Journal of Experimental Education, 78,* 135–150.

Anderman, E. M., & Maehr, M. L. (1994). Motivation and schooling in the middle grades. *Review of Educational Research, 64(2),* 287–309.

Arunkumar, R., Midgley, C., & Urdan, T. (1999). Perceiving high or low home-school dissonance: Longitudinal effects on adolescent emotional and academic well-being. *Journal of Research on Adolescence, 9,* 441–466.

Ball, S. (1995). Anxiety and test performance. In C. Spielberger & P. Vagg (Eds.), *Test anxiety: Theory, assessment, and treatment* (pp. 107–113). Washington, DC: Taylor & Francis.

Banks, J. A., & Banks, C. A. M. (1995). *Handbook of research on multicultural education.* New York, NY: Macmillan.

Barker, G., & Graham, S. (1987). Developmental study of praise and blame as attributional cues. *Journal of Educational Psychology, 79,* 62–66.

Barron, K. E., & Harackiewicz, J. M. (2000). Achievement goals and optimal motivation: A multiple goals approach. In C. Sansone & J. M. Harackiewicz (Eds.), *Intrinsic and* extrinsic motivation: The search for optimal motivation and performance (pp. 229–254). San Diego, CA: Academic Press.

Barron, K. E., & Harackiewicz, J. M. (2001). Achievement goals and optimal motivation: Testing multiple goal models. *Journal of Personality and Social Psychology, 80,* 706–722.

Beilock, S. L., Gunderson, E. A., Ramirez, G., & Levine, S. C. (2010). Female teachers' math anxiety affects girls' math achievement. *PNAS Proceedings of the National Academy of Sciences of the United States of America, 107*(5), 1860–1863.

Benita, M., Roth, G., & Deci, E. L. (2014). When are mastery goals more adaptive? It depends on experiences of autonomy support and autonomy. *Journal of Educational Psychology, 106*(1), 258–267.

Blackwell, L. S., Trzesniewski, K., & Dweck, C. S. (2007). Implicit theories of intelligence predict achievement across an adolescent transition: A longitudinal study and an intervention. *Child Development, 78,* 246–263.

Bleeker, M. M., & Jacobs, J. E. (2004). Achievement in math and science: Do mothers' beliefs matter 12 years later? *Journal of Educational Psychology, 96*(1), 97–109.

Blumenfeld, P., Hamilton, V., Bossert, S., Wessels, K., & Meece, J. (1983). Teacher talk and student thought: Socialization into the student role. In J. M. Levine & M. C. Wang (Eds.), *Teacher and student perceptions: Implications for learning* (pp. 143–192). Hillsdale, NJ: Lawrence Erlbaum.

Blumenfeld, P., Pintrich, P., Meece, J., & Wessels, K. (1982). The formation and role of self-perceptions of ability in elementary classrooms. *Elementary School Journal, 82,* 401–420.

Bong, M. (2009). Age-related differences in achievement goal differentiation. *Journal of Educational Psychology, 101,* 879–896.

Brophy, J. (1981). Teacher praise: A functional analysis. *Review of Educational Research, 51*(1), 5–32.

Brophy, J. (1999). Toward a model of the value aspects of motivation in education: Developing appreciation for particular learning domains and activities. *Educational Psychologist, 34,* 75–85.

Brophy, J. (2008). Developing students' appreciation for what is taught in school. *Educational Psychologist, 43*(3), 132–141.

Brophy, J., & Good, T. (1974). *Teacher-student relationships: Causes and consequences.* New York, NY: Holt, Rinehart & Winston.

Brown-Wright, L., & Tyler, K. M. (2010). The effects of home–school dissonance on African American male high school students. *Journal of Negro Education, 79*(2), 125–136.

Bruch, M., Juster, H., & Kaflowitz, N. (1983). Relationships of cognitive components of test anxiety to test performance: Implications for assessment and treatment. *Journal of Counseling Psychology, 30,* 527–536.

Canning, E. A, & Harackiewicz, J. M. (2015). Teach it, don't preach it: The differential effects of directly-communicated and self-generated utility-value information. *Motivation Science, 1*(1), 47–71.

Cole, J. S., Bergin, D. A., & Whittaker, T. A. (2008). Predicting student achievement for low stakes testing with effort and task value. *Contemporary Educational Psychology, 33,* 609–624.

Corpus, J. H., & Wormington, S. V. (2014). Profiles of intrinsic and extrinsic motivations in elementary school: A longitudinal analysis. *The Journal of Experimental Education, 82*(4), 480–501.

Covington, M. V., & Omelich, C. L. (1979). Effort: The double-edged sword in school achievement. *Journal of Educational Psychology, 71,* 169–182.

Covington, M., V., & Omelich, C. L. (1984a). An empirical examination of Weiner's critique of attribution research. *Journal of Educational Psychology, 76,* 1214–1225.

Covington, M. V., & Omelich, C. L. (1984b). Task-oriented versus competitive learning structures: Motivational and performance consequences. *Journal of Educational Psychology, 76,* 1038–1050.

Craske, M. L. (1985). Improving persistence through observational learning and attribution retraining. *British Journal of Educational Psychology, 55,* 138–147.

Cury, F., Elliot, A. J., Da Fonseca, D., & Moller, A. C. (2006). The social cognitive model of achievement motivation and the 2 x 2 achievement-goal framework. *Journal of Personality and Social Psychology, 90,* 666–679.

Daniels, L. M., Haynes, T. L., Stupnisky, R. H., Perry, R. P., Newall, N., & Pekrun, R. (2008). Individual differences in achievement goals: A longitudinal study of cognitive, emotional, and achievement outcomes. *Contemporary Educational Psychology, 33,* 584–608.

Darnon, C., Butera, F., Mugny, G., Quiamzade, A., & Hulleman, C. (2009). "Too complex for me!" Why do performance-approach and performance-avoidance goals predict performance? *European Journal of Psychology of Education, 24,* 423–434.

Debacker, T. K., & Nelson, R. M. (2000). Motivation to learn science: Differences related to gender, class type, and ability. *Journal of Educational Research, 93,* 245–254.

Dekker, S., Krabbendam, L., Lee, N. C., Boschloo, A., de Groot, R., & Jolles, J. (2013). Sex differences in goal orientation in adolescents aged 10–19: The older boys adopt work-avoidant goals twice as often as girls. *Learning and Individual Differences, 26,* 196–200.

Denissen, J. J., Zarrett, N. R., & Eccles, J. S. (2007). I like to do it, I'm able, and I know I am: Longitudinal couplings between domain specific achievement, self-concept, and interest. *Child Development, 78,* 430–447.

Diener, C. I., & Dweck, C. S. (1978). An analysis of learned helplessness: Continuous changes in performance, strategy, and achievement cognitions after failure. *Journal of Personality and Social Psychology, 36,* 451–462.

Diseth, A. (2011). Self-efficacy, goal orientations and learning strategies as mediators between preceding and subsequent academic achievement. *Learning and Individual Differences, 21,* 191–195.

Dowson, M., & McInerney, D. M. (2001). Psychological parameters of students' social and work avoidance goals: A qualitative investigation. *Journal of Educational Psychology, 93*(1), 35–42.

Durik, A. M., Shechter, O. G., Noh, M., Rozek, C. S., & Harackiewicz, J. M. (2015). What if I can't? Success expectancies moderate the effects of utility value information on situational interest and performance. *Motivation and Emotion, 39,* 104–118.

Durik, A. M., Vida, M., & Eccles, J. S. (2006). Task values and ability beliefs as predictors of high school literacy choices: A developmental analysis. *Journal of Educational Psychology, 98*(2), 382–393.

Dweck, C. (2000). *Self-theories: Their role in motivation, personality, and development.* Philadelphia, PA: Psychology Press.

Dweck, C., Davidson, W., Nelson, S., & Enna, B. (1978). Sex differences in learned helplessness: II. The contingencies of evaluative feedback in the classroom and III. An experimental analysis. *Developmental Psychology, 14,* 268–276.

Dweck, C., & Goetz, T. (1978). Attributions and learned helplessness. In W. Harvey & R. Kidd (Eds.), *New directions in attribution research.*

Vol. 2 (pp. 157–179). Hillsdale, NJ: Lawrence Erlbaum.

Dweck, C. S. (2002). The development of ability conceptions. In A. Wigfield & J. S. Eccles (Eds.), *Development of achievement motivation* (pp. 57–88). New York, NY: Academic Press.

Dweck, C. S. (2007). The perils and promises of praise. *Educational Leadership, 65*(2), 34–39.

Dweck, C. S., & Bush, E. S. (1976). Sex differences in learned helplessness: I. Differential debilitation with peer and adult evaluators. *Developmental Psychology, 12*, 147–156.

Dweck, C. S., Chiu, C., & Hong, Y. (1995). Implicit theories and their role in judgments and reactions: A world from two perspectives. *Psychological Inquiry, 6*, 267–285.

Dweck, C. S., & Leggett, E. L. (1988). A social-cognitive approach to motivation and personality. *Psychological Review, 95*, 256–273.

Dweck, C. S., & Master, A. (2008). Self-theories motivate self-regulated learning. In D. H. Schunk & B. J. Zimmerman (Eds.), *Motivation and self-regulated learning: Theory, research, and applications* (pp. 31–51). Mahwah, NJ: Lawrence Erlbaum.

Dweck, C. S., & Sorich, L. (1999). Mastery-oriented thinking. In C. R. Snyder (Ed.), *Coping* (pp. 232–251). New York, NY: Oxford University Press.

Eccles, J., Barber, B., Jozefowicz, D., Malenchuk, O., & Vida, M. (2000). Self-evaluations of competence, task values, and self-esteem. In N. Johnson, M. Roberts, & J. Worrell (Eds.), *Girls and adolescence* (pp. 53–84). Washington, DC: American Psychological Association.

Eccles, J. S. (2005). Subjective task value and the Eccles et al. model of achievement-related choices. In A. J. Elliot & C. S. Dweck (Eds.), *Handbook of competence and motivation* (pp. 105–121). New York, NY: Guilford Press.

Eccles, J. S., Adler, T. F., Futterman, R., Goff, S. B., Kaczala, C. M., & Meece, J. L. (1983). Expectancies, values and academic behaviors. In J. T. Spence (Ed.), *Achievement and achievement motives* (pp. 75–146). San Francisco, CA: Freeman.

Eccles, J. S., Wigfield, A., & Schiefele, U. (1998). Motivation to succeed. In N. Eisenberg (Ed.), *Handbook of child psychology: Vol. 3. Social, emotional, and personality development* (5th ed., pp. 1017–1095). New York, NY: Wiley.

Elliot, A. J., & Church, M. A. (1997). A hierarchical model of approach and avoidance achievement motivation. *Journal of Personality and Social Psychology, 72*, 218–232.

Elliot, A. J., & McGregor, H. A. (2001). A 2 x 2 achievement goal framework. *Journal of Personality and Social Psychology, 80*(3), 501–519.

Elliot, A. J., McGregor, H. A., & Gable, S. (1999). Achievement goals, study strategies, and exam performance. A meditational analysis. *Journal of Educational Psychology, 91*(3), 549–563.

Elliot, A. J., & Moller, A. C. (2003). Performance-approach goals: Good or bad forms of regulation? *International Journal of Educational Research, 39*, 339–356.

Elliot, A. J., & Murayama, K. (2008). On the measurement of achievement goals: Critique, illustration, and application. *Journal of Educational Psychology, 100*, 613–628.

Fletcher, K. L., Shim, S. S., & Wang, C. (2012). Perfectionistic concerns mediate the relationship between psychologically controlling parenting and achievement goal orientations. *Personality and Individual Differences, 52*, 876–881.

Folmer, A. S., Cole, D. A., Sigal, A. B., Benbow, L. D., Satterwhite, L. F., Swygert, K. E., & Ciesla, J. A. (2008). Age-related changes in children's understanding of effort and ability: Implications for attribution theory and motivation. *Journal of Experimental Child Psychology, 99*(2), 114–134.

Frattaroli, J., Thomas, M., & Lyubomirsky, S. (2011). Opening up in the classroom: Effects of expressive writing on graduate school entrance exam performance. *Emotion, 11*, 691–696.

Fredericks, J., & Eccles, J. S. (2002). Children's competence and value beliefs from childhood through adolescence: Growth trajectories in two male sex-typed domains. *Developmental Psychology, 38*, 519–533.

Freedman-Doan, C., Wigfield, A., Eccles, J., Blumenfeld, P., Arbreton, A., & Harold, R. (2000). What am I best at? Grade and gender differences in children's beliefs about ability improvement. *Journal of Applied Developmental Psychology, 21*, 379–402.

Frenzel, A. C., Pekrun, R., & Goetz, T. (2007). Girls and mathematics—A "hopeless" issue? A control-value approach to gender differences in emotions towards mathematics. *European Journal of Psychology of Education, 22*, 497–514.

Friedel, J. M., Cortina, K. S., Turner, J. C., & Midgley, C. (2007). Achievement goals, efficacy beliefs and coping strategies in mathematics: The roles of perceived parent and teacher goal

emphases. *Contemporary Educational Psychology, 32*, 434–458.

Fryer, J. W., & Elliot, A. J. (2008). Self-regulation of achievement goal pursuit. In D. H. Schunk & B. J. Zimmerman (Eds.), *Motivation and self-regulated learning: Theory, research, and applications* (pp. 53–75). Mahwah, NJ: Lawrence Erlbaum.

Gaspard, H., Dicke, A.-L., Flunger, B., Schreier, B., Häfner, I., Trautwein, U., & Nagengast, B. (2015). More value through greater differentiation: Gender differences in value beliefs about math. *Journal of Educational Psychology, 107*(3), 663–677.

Gonida, E. N., Voulala, K., & Kiosseoglou, G. (2009). Students' achievement goal orientations and their behavioral and emotional engagement: Co-examining the role of perceived school goal structures and parent goals during adolescence. *Learning and Individual Differences, 19*, 53–60.

Good, C., Aronson, J., & Inzlicht, N. (2003). Improving adolescents' standardized test performance: An intervention to reduce the effects of stereotype threat. *Journal of Applied Developmental Psychology, 24*, 645–662.

Gottfried, A. E., Fleming, J. S., & Gottfried, A. W. (1994). Role of parental motivational practices in children's academic intrinsic motivation and achievement. *Journal of Educational Psychology, 86*, 104–113.

Gottfried, A. E., Fleming, J. S., & Gottfried, A. W. (2001). Continuity of academic intrinsic motivation from childhood through late adolescence: A longitudinal study. *Journal of Educational Psychology, 93*, 3–13.

Gottfried, A. E., & Gottfried, A. W. (1996). A longitudinal study of academic intrinsic motivation in intellectually gifted children: Childhood through early adolescence. *Gifted Child Quarterly, 40*, 179–183.

Graham, S. (1984). Communicating sympathy and anger to black and white students: The cognitive (attributional) consequences of affective cues. *Journal of Personality and Social Psychology, 47*, 40–54.

Graham, S. (1990). Communicating low ability in the classroom: Bad things good teachers sometimes do. In S. Graham & V. Folkes (Eds.), *Attribution theory: Applications to achievement, mental health, and interpersonal conflict* (pp. 17–36). Hillsdale, NJ: Lawrence Erlbaum.

Graham, S., & Barker, G. P. (1990). The down-side of help: An attributional-developmental analysis of helping behavior as a low-ability cue.

Journal of Educational Psychology, 82, 7–14.

Graham, S., & Weiner, B. (1996). Theories and principles of motivation. In D. C. Berliner & R. C. Calfee (Eds.), *Handbook of educational psychology* (pp. 63–84). New York, NY: Macmillan.

Graham, S., & Williams, C. (2009). An attributional approach to motivation in school. In K. R. Wentzel & A. Wigfield (Eds.), *Handbook of motivation at school* (pp. 11–33). New York, NY: Routledge/Taylor & Francis.

Gunderson, E. A., Gripshover, S. J., Romero, C., Dweck, C. S., Goldin-Meadow, S., & Levine, S. C. (2013). Parent praise to 1- to 3-year-olds predicts children's motivational frameworks 5 years later. *Child Development, 84*(5), 1526–1541.

Haimovitz, K., Wormington, S. V., & Corpus, J. H. (2011). Dangerous mindsets: How beliefs about intelligence predict motivational change. *Learning and Individual Differences, 21*(6), 747–752.

Harackiewicz, J. M., Barron, K. E., Pintrich, P. R., Elliot, A. J., & Thrash, T. M. (2002). Revision of achievement goal theory: Necessary and illuminating. *Journal of Educational Psychology, 94*(3), 638–645.

Harackiewicz, J. M., Barron, K. E., Tauer, J. M., Carter, S. M., & Elliot, A. J. (2000). Short-term and long-term consequences of achievement goals: Predicting interest and performance over time. *Journal of Educational Psychology, 92*(2), 316–330.

Heine, S. J., & Hamamura, T. (2007). In search of East Asian self-enhancement. *Personality and Social Psychology Review, 11*, 1–24.

Heine, S. J., Kitayama, S., Lehman, D. R., Takata, T., Ide, E., Leung, C., & Matsumoto, H. (2001). Divergent consequences of success and failure in Japan and North America: An investigation of self-improving motivations and malleable selves. *Journal of Personality and Social Psychology, 81*(4), 599–615.

Henderlong, J., & Lepper, M. R. (2002). The effects of praise on children's intrinsic motivation: A review and synthesis. *Psychological Bulletin, 128*(5), 774–795.

Henderson, V., & Dweck, C. S. (1990). Achievement and motivation in adolescence: A new model and date. In S. Feldman & G. Elliott (Eds.), *At the threshold: The developing adolescent* (pp. 308–329). Cambridge, MA: Harvard University Press.

Hong, Y. Y., Chiu, C., Dweck, C. S., Lin, D., & Wan, W. (1999). Implicit theories, attributions, and coping: A meaning system approach. *Journal of Personality and Social Psychology, 77*, 588–599.

Horner S., & Gaither, S. (2006). Attribution retraining with a second grade class. *Early Childhood Education Journal, 31*, 165–170.

Hulleman, C. S., Durik, A. M., Schweigert, S. A., & Harackiewicz, J. M. (2008). Task values, achievement goals, and interest: An integrative analysis. *Journal of Educational Psychology, 100*, 398–416.

Hulleman, C. S., & Harackiewicz, J. M. (2009). Promoting interest and performance in high school science classes. *Science, 326*, 1410–1412.

Hulleman, C. S., Schrager, S. M., Bodmann, S. M., & Harackiewicz, J. M. (2010). A meta-analytic review of achievement goal measures: Different labels for the same constructs or different constructs with similar labels? *Psychological Bulletin, 136*(3), 422–449.

Hulleman, C. S., & Senko, C. (2010). Up and around the bend: Forecasts for achievement goal theory and research in 2020. In T. C. Urdan & S. A. Karabenick (Eds.), *The decade ahead: Theoretical perspectives on motivation and achievement* (Vol. 16A, pp. 71–104). Bradford, UK: Emerald Group.

Hynd, C., Holschuh, J., & Nist, S. (2000). Learning complex science information: Motivation theory and its relation to student perceptions. *Reading and Writing Quarterly, 16*, 23–58.

Jacobs, J. E., Lanza, S., Osgood, D. W., Eccles, J. S., & Wigfield, A. (2002). Changes in children's self-competence and values: Gender and domain differences across grades one through twelve. *Child Development, 73*, 509–527.

Jansen, A. (2006). Seventh graders' motivations for participating in two discussion-oriented mathematics classrooms. *Elementary School Journal, 106*, 409–428.

Juvonen, J. (2000). The social functions of attributional face-saving tactics among early adolescents. *Educational Psychology Review, 12*, 15–32.

Karabenick, S. A. (2003). Seeking help in large college classes: A person-centered approach. *Contemporary Educational Psychology, 28*, 37–58.

Kim, J.-I., Schallert, D. L., & Kim, M. (2010). An integrative cultural view of achievement motivation: Parental and classroom predictors of children's goal orientations when learning mathematics in Korea. *Journal of Educational Psychology, 102*(2), 418–437.

Kumar, S., & Jagacinski, C. M. (2011). Confronting task difficulty in ego involvement: Change in performance goals. *Journal of Educational Psychology, 103*(3), 664–682.

Law, W., Elliot, A. J., & Murayama, K. (2012). Perceived competence moderates the relation between performance-approach and performance-avoidance goals. *Journal of Educational Psychology, 104*(3), 806–819.

Leondari, A., & Gonida, E. (2007). Predicting academic self-handicapping in different age groups: The role of personal achievement goals and social goals. *British Journal of Educational Psychology, 77*, 595–611.

Lindberg, S. M., Hyde, J. S., Peterson, J. L., & Linn, M. C. (2010). New trends in gender and mathematics performance: A meta-Analysis. *Psychological Bulletin, 136*(6), 1123–1135.

Linn, R. L., & Gronlund, N. E. (2000). *Measurement and assessment in teaching.* Upper Saddle River, NJ: Prentice Hall.

Linnenbrink, E. A., & Fredericks, J. A. (2007). Developmental perspectives on achievement motivation: Personal and contextual influences. In J. Y. Shah & W. L. Gardner (Eds.), *Handbook of motivation science: The social psychological perspective* (pp. 448–517). New York, NY: Guilford Press.

Luo, W., Hogan, D., & Paris, S. G. (2011). Predicting Singapore students; achievement goals in their English study: Self-construal and classroom goal structure. *Learning and Individual Differences, 21*(5), 526–535.

Maatta, S., & Nurmi, J. (2007). Achievement orientations, school adjustment, and well-being: A longitudinal study. *Journal of Research on Adolescence, 17*, 789–812.

Maehr, M. L., & Midgley, C. (1991). Enhancing student motivation: A schoolwide approach. *Educational Psychologist, 26*, 399–427.

Maehr, M. L., & Nicholls, J. G. (1980). Culture and achievement motivation: A second look. In N. Warren (Ed.), *Studies in cross-cultural psychology* (Vol. 2, pp. 221–267). New York, NY: Academic Press.

Maehr, M. L., & Zusho, A. (2009). Achievement goal theory: The past, present, and future. In K. R. Wentzel & A. Wigfield (Eds.), *Handbook of motivation in school* (pp. 77–104). New York, NY: Routledge/Taylor & Francis.

Malka, A., & Covington, M. V. (2005). Perceiving school performance as instrumental to future goal attainment: Effects on graded performance. *Contemporary Educational Psychology, 30,* 60–80.

Marshall, H. H., & Weinstein, R. S. (1984). Classroom factors affecting students' self-evaluations: An interactional model. *Review of Educational Research, 54,* 301–325.

Mau, W. C., & Bikos, L. H. (2000). Educational and vocational aspirations of minority and female students: A longitudinal study. *Journal of Counseling and Development, 78,* 186–194.

McLoyd, V. C. (1998). Socioeconomic disadvantage and child development. *American Psychologist, 53,* 185–204.

Meece, J. (1981). *Individual differences in the affective reactions of middle and high school students to mathematics: A social cognitive perspective* (Unpublished doctoral dissertation). University of Michigan, Ann Arbor.

Meece, J. L., Glienke, B. B., & Askew, K. (2009). Gender and motivation. In K. R. Wentzel & A. Wigfield (Eds.), *Handbook of motivation at school* (pp. 412–431). New York, NY: Routledge/ Taylor & Francis.

Meece, J. L., Glienke, B. B., & Burg, S. (2006). Gender and motivation. *Journal of School Psychology, 44,* 351–373.

Meece, J. L., & Miller, S. D. (2001). A longitudinal analysis of elementary school students' achievement goals in literacy activities. *Contemporary Educational Psychology, 26,* 454–480.

Meece, J. L., & Painter, J. (2008). Gender, self-regulation, and motivation. In D. H. Schunk & B. J. Zimmerman (Eds.), *Motivation and self-regulated learning: Theory, research, and applications* (pp. 339–367). Mahwah, NJ: Lawrence Erlbaum.

Meyer, W. U., Bachmann, M., Biermann, U., Hempelmann, M., Plöger, F. O., & Spiller, H. (1979). The informational value of evaluative behavior: Influences of praise and blame on perceptions of ability. *Journal of Educational Psychology, 71,* 259–268.

Mickelson, R. (1990). The attitude-achievement paradox among black adolescents. *Sociology of Education, 63,* 44–61.

Middleton, M., & Midgley, C. (1997). Avoiding the demonstration of lack of ability: An underexplored aspect of goal theory. *Journal of Educational Psychology, 89,* 710–718.

Midgley, C. (2002). *Goals, goal structures, and adaptive learning.* Mahwah, NJ: Lawrence Erlbaum.

Midgley, C., Anderman, E., & Hicks, L. (1995). Differences between elementary and middleschool teachers and students: A goal theory approach. *Journal of Early Adolescence, 15,* 90–113.

Moller A. C., & Elliot, A. J. (2006). The 2 x 2 achievement goal framework: An overview of empirical research. In A. Mittel (Ed.), *Focus on educational psychology* (pp. 307–326). New York, NY: Nova Science.

Mok, M. M. C., Kennedy, K. J., & Moore, P. J. (2011). Academic attribution of secondary students: Gender, year level and achievement level. *Educational Psychology, 31,* 87–104.

Molden, D., & Dweck, C. (2000). Meaning and motivation. In C. Sansone & J. Harackiewicz (Eds.), *Intrinsic and extrinsic motivation: The search for optimal motivation and performance* (pp. 131–159). San Diego, CA: Academic Press.

Mueller, C. M., & Dweck, C. S. (1998). Intelligence praise can undermine motivation and performance. *Journal of Personality and Social Psychology, 75,* 33–52.

Murayama, K., & Elliot, A. J. (2009). The joint influence of personal achievement goals and classroom goal structures on achievement-related outcomes. *Journal of Educational Psychology, 101,* 432–447.

Nagy, G., Trautwein, U., Baumert, J., Köller, O., & Garrett, J. (2006). Gender and course selection in upper secondary education: Effects of academic self-concept and intrinsic value. *Educational Research and Evaluation, 12,* 323–345.

Naveh-Benjamin, M. (1991). A comparison of training programs intended for different types of test-anxious students: Further support for an information processing model. *Journal of Educational Psychology, 83*(1), 134–139.

Naveh-Benjamin, M., McKeachie, W. J., & Lin, Y-G. (1987). Two types of test-anxious students: Support for an information processing model. *Journal of Educational Psychology, 79*(2), 131–136.

Ng, F. F. Y., Pomerantz, E. M., & Lam, S. F. (2007). European American and Chinese parents' responses to children's success and failure: Implications for children's responses. *Developmental Psychology, 43*(5), 1239–1255.

Niiya, Y., Crocker, J., & Bartmess, E. N. (2004). From vulnerability to resilience: Learning orientations buffer contingent self-esteem from failure. *Psychological Science, 15,* 801–805.

Nottlemann, E. D., & Hill, K. T. (1977). Test anxiety an off-task behavior in evaluative situations. *Child Development, 48,* 225–231.

Oakes, J., & Guiton, G. (1995). Matchmaking: the dynamics of high school tracking decisions. *American Educational Research Journal, 32,* 3–33.

Ogbu, J. U. (1994). Racial stratification and education in the United States: Why inequality persists. *Teachers College Record, 96*(2), 264–298.

Ogbu, J. U. (2003). *Black American students in an affluent suburb: A study of academic disengagement.* Mahwah, NJ: Lawrence Erlbaum.

Park, D., Ramirez, G., & Beilock, S. L. (2014). The role of expressive writing in math anxiety. *Journal of Experimental Psychology. Applied, 20*(2), 103–11.

Parker, P. D., Schoon, I., Tsai, Y. M., Nagy, G., Trautwein, U., & Eccles, J. S. (2012). Achievement, agency, gender, and socioeconomic background as predictors of postschool choices: A multicontext study. *Developmental Psychology, 48*(6), 1629–1642.

Payne, S. C., Youngcourt, S. S., & Beaubien, J. M. (2007). A meta-analytic examination of the goal orientation nomological net. *Journal of Applied Psychology, 92,* 128–150.

Peixoto, F. (2011). "Is it beneficial to stress grades to my child?" Relationships between parental attitudes towards academic achievement, motivation, academic self-concept and academic achievement. *International Journal about Parents in Education, 5,* 98–109.

Pintrich, P. R. (2000). An achievement goal theory perspective on issues in motivation terminology, theory, and research. *Contemporary Educational Psychology, 25,* 92–104.

Plaks, J., Stroessner, S., Dweck, C., & Sherman, J. (2001). Person theories and attention allocation: Preferences for stereotypic versus counterstereotypic information. *Journal of Personality and Social Psychology, 80,* 876–893.

Plass, J. A., & Hill, K. T. (1986). Children's achievement strategies and test performance: The role of time pressure, evaluation, anxiety, and sex. *Developmental Psychology, 22,* 31–36.

Ramirez, G., & Beilock, S. L. (2011). Writing about testing worries boosts exam performance in the classroom. *Science, 331*(6014), 211–213.

Rattan, A., Good, C., & Dweck, C. S. (2012). "It's ok — Not everyone can be good at math": Instructors with an entity theory comfort (and demotivate) students. *Journal of*

Experimental Social Psychology, 48(3), 731–737.

Reilly, D. (2012). Gender, culture, and sex-typed cognitive abilities. *PLoS ONE, 7*(7), e39904.

Reyna, C. (2000). Lazy, dumb, or industrious: When stereotypes convey attribution information in the classroom. *Educational Psychology Review, 12,* 85–110.

Reyna, C., & Weiner, B. (2001). Justice and utility in the classroom: An attributional analysis of the goals of teachers' punishment and intervention strategies. *Journal of Educational Psychology, 93,* 309–319.

Rholes, W., Blackwell, J., Jordan, C., & Walters, C. (1980). A developmental study of learned helplessness. *Developmental Psychology, 16,* 616–624.

Roeser, R., Eccles, J., & Sameroff, A. (1998). Academic and emotional functioning in early adolescence: Longitudinal relations, patterns, and predictions by experience in middle school. *Development and Psychopathology, 10,* 321–352.

Roeser, R., Eccles, J., & Sameroff, A. (2000). School as a context of early adolescents' academic and social-emotional development: A summary of research findings. *The Elementary School Journal, 100,* 443–471.

Rolland, R. G. (2012). Synthesizing the evidence on classroom goal structures in middle and secondary schools: A meta-analysis and narrative review. *Review of Educational Research, 82*(4), 396–435.

Rončević, B., & Kolić-Vehovec, S. (2014). Perceptions of contextual achievement goals: Contribution to high-school students' achievement goal orientation, strategy use, and academic achievement. *Studia Psychologica, 56*(2), 137–154.

Rose, M. (1989). *Lives on the boundary: The struggles and achievements of America's underprepared.* New York, NY: Free Press.

Rosenholtz, S. J., & Simpson, C. (1984). The formation of ability conceptions: Developmental trend or social construction? *Review of Educational Research, 54*(1), 31–63.

Sapp, M. (1999). *Test anxiety: Applied research, assessment, and treatment interventions* (2nd ed.). New York, NY: University Press of America.

Schunk, D. (1989). Self-efficacy and cognitive skill learning. In C. Ames & R. Ames (Eds.), *Research on motivation in education: Goals and cognitions* (Vol. 3, pp. 13–44). San Diego, CA: Academic Press.

Schunk, D. H. (2008). Attributions as motivators of self-regulated learning.

In D. H. Schunk & B. J. Zimmerman (Eds.), *Motivation and self-regulated learning: Theory, research, and applications* (pp. 245–266). Mahwah, NJ: Lawrence Erlbaum.

Sedek, G., & McIntosh, D. (1998). Intellectual helplessness: Domain specificity, teaching styles, and school achievement. In M. Kofta, G. Weary, & G. Sedek (Eds.), *Personal control in action: Cognitive and motivational mechanisms* (pp. 419–443). New York, NY: Plenum Press.

Seligman, M., & Maier, S. (1967). Failure to escape traumatic shock. *Journal of Experimental Psychology, 74,* 1–9.

Sieber, J., O'Neil, H., & Tobias, S. (2008). *Anxiety, learning, and instruction.* New York, NY: Routledge.

Simpkins, S. D., Davis-Kean, P. E., & Eccles, J. S. (2006). Math and science motivation: A longitudinal examination of the links between choice and beliefs. *Developmental Psychology, 42,* 70–83.

Simpkins, S. D., Fredricks, J. A., & Eccles, J. S. (2012). Charting the Eccles' expectancy-value model from mothers' beliefs in childhood to youths' activities in adolescence. *Developmental Psychology, 48,* 1019–1032.

Snyder, K. E., Malin, J. L., Dent, A. L., & Linnenbrink-Garcia, L. (2014). The message matters: The role of implicit beliefs about giftedness and failure experiences in academic self-handicapping. *Journal of Educational Psychology, 106*(1), 230–241.

Steinmayr, R., Bipp, T., & Spinath, B. (2011). Goal orientations predict academic performance beyond intelligence and personality. *Learning and Individual Differences, 21*(2), 196–200.

Steinmayr, R., & Spinath, B. (2010). Construction and validation of a scale for the assessment of school-related values. *Diagnostica, 56,* 195–211.

Stephanou, G. (2008). Students' value beliefs, performance expectations, and school performance: The effect of school subject and gender. *Hellenic Journal of Psychology, 5*(3), 231–257.

Stetsenko, A., Little, T. D., Gordeeva, T., Granshof, M., & Oettingen, G. (2000). Gender effects in children's beliefs about school performance: A cross-cultural study. *Child Development, 71,* 517–527.

Stipek, D. (1984). The development of achievement motivation. In R. Ames & C. Ames (Eds.), *Research on motivation in education* (Vol. 1, pp. 145–174). Orlando, FL: Academic Press.

Stipek, D. (2002). *Motivation to learn: Integrating theory and practice* (4th ed.). Boston, MA: Allyn & Bacon.

Stipek, D., & Tannatt, L. (1984). Children's judgments of their own and their peers' academic competence. *Journal of Educational Psychology, 76,* 75–84.

Stipek, D. J., & Daniels, D. H. (1990). Children's use of dispositional attributions in predicting the performance and behavior of classmates. *Journal of Applied Developmental Psychology, 11,* 13–28.

Sungur, S., & Senler, B. (2010). Students' achievement goals in relation to academic motivation, competence expectancy, and classroom environment perceptions. *Educational Research and Evaluation: An International Journal on Theory and Practice, 16*(4), 303–324.

Taylor, A. Z., & Graham, S. (2007). An examination of the relationship between achievement values and perceptions of barriers among low-SES African American and Latino students. *Journal of Educational Psychology, 99*(1), 52–64.

Thorkildsen, T. A., & Nicholls, J. G. (1998). Fifth graders' achievement orientations and beliefs: Individual and classroom differences. *Journal of Educational Psychology, 90,* 179–201.

Tobias, S. (1992). The impact of test anxiety cognition in school learning. In K. A. Hagtvet & T. B. Johnsen (Eds.), *Advances in test anxiety research* (Vol. 7, pp. 18–31). Amsterdam, the Netherlands: Swets & Zeitlinger.

Tollefson, N. (2000). Classroom applications of cognitive theories of motivation. *Educational Psychology Review, 12*(1), 63–83.

Topman, R., Kleijn, W., van der Ploeg, H., & Masset, E. (1992). Test anxiety, cognitions, study habits and academic performance: A prospective study. In K. Hagtvet & T. Johnsen (Eds.), *Advances in test anxiety research* (Vol. 7, pp. 239–259). Amsterdam, the Netherlands: Swets & Zeitlinger.

Tuominen-Soini, H., Salmela-Aro, K., & Niemivirta, M. (2008). Achievement goal orientations and subjective well-being: A person-centered analysis. *Learning and Instruction, 18,* 251–266.

Turner, J. C., Meyer, D. K., Midgley, C., & Patrick, H. (2003). Teacher discourse and sixth graders' reported affect and achievement behaviors in two high-mastery/high performance mathematics classrooms. *The Elementary School Journal, 103,* 357–378.

Turner, L. A., & Johnson, B. (2003). A model of mastery motivation for at-risk preschoolers. *Journal of Educational Psychology, 95*(3), 495–505.

Tyler, K., Brown-Wright, L., Stevens-Watkins, D., Thomas, D., Stevens, R., Roan-Belle, C., . . . Smith, L. T. (2010). Linking home-school dissonance to school-based outcomes for African American high school students. *Journal of Black Psychology, 36*(4), 410–425.

Urdan, T. (2004). Predictors of academic self-handicapping and achievement: Examining achievement goals, classroom goal structures, and culture. *Journal of Educational Psychology, 96,* 251–264.

Urdan T., & Mestas, M. (2006). The goals behind performance goals. *Journal of Educational Psychology, 98*(2), 354–365.

Urdan, T., Midgley, C., & Anderman, E. M. (1998). The role of classroom goal structure in students' use of self-handicapping strategies. *American Educational Research Journal, 35*(1), 101–122.

Vagg, P., & Spielberger, C. (1995). Treatment of test anxiety: Application of the transactional process model. In C. Spielberger & P. Vagg (Eds.), *Test anxiety: Theory, assessment, and treatment* (pp. 197–215). Washington, DC: Taylor & Francis.

Valentiner, D. P., Mounts, N. S., Durik, A. M., & Gier-Lonsway, S. L. (2011). Shyness mindset: Applying mindset theory to the domain of inhibited social behavior. *Personality and Individual Differences, 50,* 1174–1179.

van Laar, C. (2000). The paradox of low academic achievement but high self-esteem in African American students: An attributional account. *Educational Psychology Review, 12,* 33–61.

Van Overwalle, F., & De Metsenaere, M. (1990). The effects of attribution-based intervention and study strategy training on academic achievement in college freshmen. *British Journal of Educational Psychology, 60,* 299–311.

Vansteenkiste, M., Lens, W., Elliot, A. J., Soenens, B., & Mouratidis, A. (2014). Moving the achievement goal approach one step forward: Toward a systematic examination of the autonomous and controlled reasons underlying achievement goals. *Educational Psychologist, 49*(3), 153–174.

Vansteenkiste, M., Matos, L., Lens, W., & Soenens, B. (2007). Understanding the impact of intrinsic versus extrinsic goal framing on exercise performance: The conflicting role of task and ego involvement. *Psychology of Sport and Exercise, 8,* 771–794.

Vansteenkiste, M., Simons, J., Lens, W., Sheldon, K. M., & Deci, E. L. (2004). Motivating learning, performance, and persistence: The synergistic effects of intrinsic goal contents and autonomy-supportive contexts. *Journal of Personality and Social Psychology, 87,* 246–260.

Wagner, T., Kegan, R., Lahey, L. L., Lemons, R. W., Garnier, J., Helsing, D., . . . Rasmussen, H. T. (2006). *Change leadership: A practical guide to transforming our schools.* San Francisco, CA: Jossey-Bass.

Watt, H. M. (2004). Development of adolescents' self-perceptions, values, and task perceptions according to gender and domain in 7th through 11th-grade Australian students. *Child Development, 75,* 1556–1574.

Watt, H. M., Shapka, J. D., Morris, Z. A., Durik, A. M., Keating, D. P., & Eccles, J. S. (2012). Gendered motivational processes affecting high school mathematics participation, educational aspirations, and career plans: A comparison of samples from Australia, Canada, and the United States. *Developmental Psychology, 48,* 1594–1611.

Weiner, B. (1982). An attributionally based theory of motivation and emotion: Focus, range, and issues. In N. T. Feather (Ed.), *Expectations and actions* (pp. 163–204). Hillsdale, NJ: Lawrence Erlbaum.

Weiner, B. (1994). Integrating social and personal theories of achievement striving. *Review of Educational Research, 64,* 557–573.

Weiner, B. (2000). Intrapersonal and interpersonal theories of motivation from an attributional perspective. *Educational Psychology Review, 12,* 1–14.

Weiner, B. (2010). The development of an attribution-based theory of motivation: A history of ideas. *Educational Psychologist, 45*(1), 28–36.

Weinstein, R. S. (1993). Children's knowledge of differential treatment in school: Implications for motivation. In T. M. Tomlinson (Ed.), *Motivating students to learn: Overcoming barriers to high achievement* (pp. 197–224). Berkeley, CA: McCutchan.

Wigfield, A., & Cambria, J. (2010a). Expectancy-value theory: Retrospective and prospective. In T. C. Urdan & S. A. Karabenick (Eds.), *The decade ahead: Theoretical perspectives on motivation and achievement* (pp. 35–70). Bradford, UK: Emerald Group.

Wigfield, A., & Cambria, J. (2010b). Students' achievement values, goal orientations and interest: Definitions, development, and relations to achievement outcomes. *Developmental Review, 30,* 1–35.

Wigfield, A., & Eccles, J. S. (1989). Test anxiety in elementary and secondary students. *Educational Psychologist, 24*(2), 159–183.

Wigfield, A., & Eccles, J. (1994). Children's competence beliefs, achievement values, and general self-esteem: Change across elementary and middle school. *Journal of Early Adolescence, 14,* 107–137.

Wigfield, A., & Eccles, J. S. (2000). Expectancy-value theory of achievement motivation. *Contemporary Educational Psychology, 25,* 68–81.

Wigfield, A., & Eccles, J. S. (2002). The development of competence beliefs, expectancies for success, and achievement values from childhood through adolescence. In A. Wigfield & J. S. Eccles (Eds.), *Development of achievement motivation* (pp. 91–120). San Diego, CA: Academic Press.

Wigfield, A., Eccles, J. S., Schiefele, U., Roeser, R. W., & Davis-Kean, P. (2006). Development of achievement motivation. In W. Damon & R. M. Lerner (Eds.), *Handbook of child psychology* (pp. 933–1002). New York, NY: Wiley.

Wigfield, A., Eccles, J., Yoon, K., Harold, R., Arbreton, A., Freedman-Doan, C., & Blumenfeld, P. (1997). Changes in children's competence beliefs and subjective task values across the elementary school years: A three-year study. *Journal of Educational Psychology, 89*(3), 451–469.

Wigfield, A., Tonks, S., & Klauda, S. L. (2009). Expectancy-value theory. In K. R. Wentzel & A. Wigfield (Eds.), *Handbook of motivation at school* (pp. 55–75). New York, NY: Routledge/Taylor & Francis.

Wolters, C. A., & Daugherty, S. G. (2007). Goal structures and teachers' sense of efficacy: Their relation and association to teaching experience and academic level. *Journal of Educational Psychology, 99*(1), 181–193.

Wood, D., Kaplan, R., & McLoyd, V. C. (2007). Gender differences in the educational expectations of urban, low-income African American youth: The role of parents and the school. *Journal of Youth Adolescence, 36,* 417–427.

Zalta, A. K., & Chambless, D. L. (2012). Understanding gender differences in anxiety: The mediating effects of instrumentality and mastery. *Psychology of Women Quarterly, 36*(4), 488–499.

Zeidner, M., & Nevo, B. (1992). Test anxiety in examinees in a college admissions testing situation: Incidence, dimensionality, and cognitive correlates. In K. Hagtvet & T. Johnsen (Eds.), *Advances in test anxiety research* (Vol. 7, pp. 288–303).

Amsterdam, the Netherlands: Swets & Zeitlinger.

Zusho, A., & Pintrich, P. R. (2003). A process-oriented approach to culture: Theoretical and methodological issues in the study of culture and student motivation in a multicultural context. In F. Salili & R. Hoosain (Eds.), *Teaching, learning, and motivation in a multicultural context* (pp. 33–65). Greenwich, CT: Information Age.

Module 16

Alvernini, F., Lucidi, F., & Manganelli, S. (2008). Assessment of academic motivation: A mixed methods study. *International Journal of Multiple Research Approaches, 2*(1), 71–82.

Ames, C. A. (1990). Motivation: What teachers need to know. *Teachers College Record, 91*(3), 409–421.

Ames, R., & Ames, C. (1984). Introduction. In R. Ames & C. Ames (Eds.), *Research on motivation in education* (Vol. 2, pp. 13–51). New York, NY: Academic Press.

Anderman, E. M., & Maehr, M. L. (1994). Motivation and schooling in the middle grades. *Review of Educational Research, 64*(2), 287–309.

Anderman, E. M., & Midgley, C. (1997). Changes in achievement goal orientations, perceived academic competence, and grades across the transition to middle-level schools. *Contemporary Educational Psychology, 22,* 269–298.

Anderman, E. M., & Young, A. J. (1994). Motivation and strategy use in science: Individual differences and classroom effects. *Journal of Research in Science Teaching, 31*(8), 811–831.

Anderman, L. H., & Anderman, E. M. (1999). Social predictors of changes in students' achievement goal orientations. *Contemporary Educational Psychology, 24,* 21–37.

Ashton, P., & Webb, R. (1986). *Making a difference: Teachers' sense of efficacy and student achievement.* New York, NY: Longman.

Assor, A., Kaplan, H., Kanat-Maymon, Y., & Roth, G. (2005). Directly controlling teacher behaviors as predictors of poor motivation and engagement in girls and boys: The role of anger and anxiety. *Learning and Instruction, 15,* 397–413.

Assor, A., Kaplan, H., & Roth, G. (2002). Choice is good but relevance is excellent: Autonomy-enhancing and suppressing teacher behaviours in

predicting students' engagement in school work. *British Journal of Educational Psychology, 72,* 261–278.

Bandura, A. (1977). Self-efficacy: Toward a unifying theory of behavioral change. *Psychological Review, 84,* 191–215.

Bandura, A. (1982). Self-efficacy mechanism in human agency. *American Psychologist, 37,* 122–147.

Bandura, A. (1986). *Social foundations of thought and action: A social cognitive theory.* Englewood Cliffs, NJ: Prentice Hall.

Bandura, A. (1997). *Self-efficacy: The exercise of control.* New York, NY: Freeman.

Bandura, A. (2001). Social cognitive theory: An agentic perspective. *Annual Review of Psychology, 52,* 1–26.

Bandura, A., & Locke, E. (2003). Negative self-efficacy and goal effects revisited. *Journal of Applied Psychology, 88,* 87–99.

Bandura, A., & Schunk, D. H. (1981). Cultivating competence, self-efficacy, and intrinsic interest through proximal self-motivation. *Journal of Personality and Social Psychology, 41,* 586–598.

Bleeker, M. M., & Jacobs, J. E. (2004). Achievement in math and science: Do mothers' beliefs matter 12 years later? *Journal of Educational Psychology, 96*(1), 97–109.

Bong, M., & Skaalvik, E. M. (2003). Academic self-concept and self-efficacy: How different are they really? *Educational Psychology Review, 15,* 1–40.

Bouffard-Bouchard, T., Parent, S., & Larivee, S. (1991). Influence of self-efficacy on self-regulation and performance among junior and senior high-school age students. *International Journal of Behavioral Development, 14,* 153–164.

Britner, S. L., & Pajares, F. (2006). Sources of science self-efficacy beliefs of middle school students. *Journal for Research in Science Teaching, 43,* 485–499.

Brown, J. S., Collins, A., & Duguid, P. (1989). Situated cognition and the culture of learning. *Educational Researcher, 18*(1), 32–42.

Burden, P. (2003). *Classroom management: Creating a successful learning community* (2nd ed.). New York, NY: John Wiley & Sons.

Butler, R. (1998). Determinants of help seeking: Relations between perceived reasons for classroom help-avoidance and help seeking behaviors in an experimental context. *Journal of Educational Psychology, 90,* 630–643.

Caprara, G., Barbaranelli, C., Steca, P., & Malone, P. (2006). Teachers' self-efficacy beliefs as determinants of job

satisfaction and students' academic achievement: A study at the school level. *Journal of School Psychology, 44,* 473–490.

Chirkov, V., Ryan, R. M., & Willness, C. (2005). Cultural context and psychological needs in Canada and Brazil: Testing a self-determination approach to the internalization of cultural practices, identity, and well-being. *Journal of Cross-Cultural Psychology, 36,* 423–443.

Collie, R. J., Shapka, J. D., & Perry, N. E. (2012). School climate and social–emotional learning: Predicting teacher stress, job satisfaction, and teaching efficacy. *Journal of Educational Psychology, 104*(4), 1189–1204.

Collins, A., Hawkins, J., & Carver, S. M. (1991). In B. Means, C. Chelemer, & M. S. Knapp (Eds.), *Teaching advanced skills to at-risk students* (pp. 173–194). San Francisco, CA: Jossey-Bass.

Corpus, J. H., & Lepper, M. R. (2007). The effects of person versus performance praise on children's motivation: Gender and age as moderating factors. *Educational Psychology, 27*(4), 487–508.

Cousins, J., & Walker, C. (2000). Predictors of educators' valuing of systematic inquiry in schools [Special issue]. *Canadian Journal of Program Evaluation, 15,* 25–53.

Covington, M. (1992). *Making the grade: A self-worth perspective on motivation and school reform.* Cambridge, UK: Cambridge University Press.

Covington, M. (1998). *The will to learn: A guide for motivating young people.* New York, NY: Cambridge University Press.

Covington, M. (2009). Self-worth theory. In K. R. Wentzel & A. Wigfield (Eds.), *Handbook of motivation at school* (pp. 142–169). New York, NY: Routledge/Taylor & Francis.

Covington, M., & Beery, R. (1976). *Self-worth and school learning.* New York: Holt, Rinehart & Winston.

Covington, M. V. (1984). The motive for self worth. In R. Ames & C. Ames (Eds.), *Research on motivation in education: Student motivation* (Vol. 1, pp. 77–113). San Diego, CA: Academic Press.

Covington, M. V., & Müeller, K. J. (2001). Intrinsic versus extrinsic motivation: An approach/avoidance reformulation. *Education Psychology Review, 13*(2), 157–176.

Covington, M. V., & Omelich, C. L. (1979). Effort: The double-edged sword in school achievement. *Journal of Educational Psychology, 71,* 169–182.

Covington, M. V., & Omelich, C. L. (1984). Task-oriented versus competitive learning structures: Motivational and performance consequences. *Journal of Educational Psychology, 76,* 1038–1050.

Covington, M. V., & Omelich, C. L. (1985). Ability and effort valuation among failure-avoiding and failure-accepting students. *Journal of Educational Psychology, 77,* 446–459.

Covington, M. V., & Omelich, C. L. (1991). Need achievement revisited: Verification of Atkinson's original 2 x 2 model. In C. D. Spielberger, I. G. Sarason, Z. Kulcsar, & G. L. Van Heck (Eds.), *Stress and emotion* (Vol. 14, pp. 85–105). New York, NY: Hemisphere.

DeBacker, T. K., & Nelson, R. M. (1999). Variations on an expectancy-value model of motivation in science. *Contemporary Educational Psychology, 24,* 71–94.

De Bruyckere, P., Kirschner, P. A., & Hulshof, C. D. (2015). *Urban myths in learning and education.* New York, NY: Academic Press.

De Castella, K., Byrne, D., & Covington, M. (2013). Unmotivated or motivated to fail? A cross-cultural study of achievement motivation, fear of failure, and student disengagement. *Journal of Educational Psychology, 105*(3), 861–880. deCharms, R. (1976). *Enhancing motivation.* New York, NY: Irvington.

deCharms, R. (1976). *Enhancing motivation: Change in the classroom.* New York, NY: Irvington.

Deci, E. L., Eghrari, H., Patrick, B. C., & Leone, D. R. (1994). Facilitating internalization: The self-determination theory perspective. *Journal of Personality, 62,* 119–142.

Deci, E. L., Hodges, R., Pierson, L., & Tomassone, J. (1992). Autonomy and competence as motivational factors in students with learning disabilities and emotional handicaps. *Journal of Learning Disabilities, 25,* 457–471.

Deci, E. L., & Ryan, R. M. (1985). *Intrinsic motivation and self-determination in human behavior.* New York, NY: Plenum.

Deci, E. L, & Ryan, R. M. (1992). The initiation and regulation of intrinsically motivated learning and achievement. In A. K. Boggiano & T. S. Pittman (Eds.), *Achievement and motivation: A social-developmental perspective* (pp. 9–36). New York, NY: Cambridge University Press.

Deci, E. L., Vallerand, R. J., Pelletier, L. G., & Ryan, R. M. (1991). Motivation and education: The self-determination perspective. *Educational Psychologist, 26,* 325–346.

Dweck, C. S. (1999). *Self-theories: Their role in motivation, personality and development.* Philadelphia, PA: Taylor & Francis.

Eccles, J. S., Early, D., Frasier, K., Belansky, E., & McCarthy, K. (1996). The relation of connection, regulation, and support for autonomy to adolescents' functioning. *Journal of Adolescent Research, 12,* 263–286.

Eccles, J. S., & Midgley, C. (1989). Stage-environment fit: Developmentally appropriate classrooms for young adolescents. In C. Ames, & R. Ames (Eds.), *Research on motivation in education* (Vol. 3, pp. 139–186). San Diego, CA: Academic Press.

Eccles, J. S., Midgley, C., Wigfield, A., Miller-Buchannan, C., Reuman, D., Flanagan, C., & MacIver, D. (1993). Development during adolescence: The impact of stage-environment fit on young adolescents' experiences in schools and families. *American Psychologist, 48,* 90–101.

Friedel, J. M., Cortina, K. S., Turner, J. C., & Midgley, C. (2010). Changes in efficacy beliefs in mathematics across the transition to middle school: Examining the effects of perceived teacher and parent goal emphases. *Journal of Educational Psychology, 102*(1), 102–114.

Gibson, S., & Dembo, M. (1984). Teacher efficacy: A construct validation. *Journal of Educational Psychology, 76,* 569–582.

Gottfried, A. E., Fleming, J. S., & Gottfried, A. W. (2001). Continuity of academic intrinsic motivation from childhood through late adolescence: A longitudinal study. *Journal of Educational Psychology, 93,* 3–13.

Graham, S. (1990). Communicating low ability in the classroom: Bad things good teachers sometimes do. In S. Graham & V. Folkes (Eds.), *Attribution theory: Applications to achievement, mental health, and interpersonal conflict* (pp. 17–36). Hillsdale, NJ: Lawrence Erlbaum.

Graham, S. (1994). Motivation in African Americans. *Review of Educational Research, 64*(1), 55–117.

Graham, S., & Weiner, B. (1993). Attributional applications in the classroom. In T. M. Tomlinson (Ed.), *Motivating students to learn: Overcoming barriers to high achievement* (pp. 179–195). Berkeley, CA: McCutchan.

Grolnick, W. S., Deci, E. L., & Ryan, R. M. (1997). Internalization within the family: The self-determination perspective. In J. E. Grusec & L. Kuczynski (Eds.), *Parenting and children's internalization of values: A handbook of contemporary theory* (pp. 135–161). New York, NY: Wiley.

Grolnick, W. S., Gurland, S. T., Jacob, K. F., & DeCourcey, W. (2002). The development of self-determination in middle childhood and adolescence. In A. Wigfield & J. Eccles (Eds.), *Development of achievement motivation* (pp. 147–171). New York, NY: Academic Press.

Halmovitz, K., & Corpus, J. H. (2011). Effects of person versus process praise on student motivation: Stability and change in emerging adulthood. *Educational Psychology, 31*(5), 595–609.

Hampton, N. Z., & Mason, E. (2003). Learning disabilities, gender, sources of efficacy, self-efficacy beliefs, and academic achievement in high school students. *Journal of School Psychology, 41,* 101–112.

Harari, O., & Covington, M. V. (1981). Reactions to achievement behavior from a teacher and student perspective: A developmental analysis. *American Educational Research Journal, 18,* 15–28.

Harter, S. (1974). Pleasure derived from cognitive challenge and mastery. *Child Development, 45,* 661–669.

Harter, S. (1978). Pleasure derived from challenge and the effects of receiving grades on children's difficulty level choices. *Child Development, 49,* 788–799.

Harter, S. (1992). The relationship between perceived competence, affect, and motivational orientation within the classroom: Process and patterns of change. In A. Boggiano & T. Pittman (Eds.), *Achievement and motivation: A social-developmental perspective* (pp. 77–114). Cambridge, UK: Cambridge University Press.

Harter, S., Whitesell, N., & Junkin, L. (1998). Similarities and differences in domain-specific and global self-evaluations of learning-disabled, behaviorally disordered, and normally achieving adolescents. *American Educational Research Journal, 35,* 653–680.

Harter, S., Whitesell, N., & Kowalski, P. (1992). Individual differences in the effects of educational transitions on young adolescent's perceptions of competence and motivational orientation. *American Educational Research Journal, 29,* 777–807.

Hines, M. T., & Kritsonis, W. A. (2010). The interactive effects of race and teacher self-efficacy on the achievement gap in school. *National Forum of Multicultural Issues Journal, 7*(1), 1–14.

Howes, C., Phillipsen, L., & Peisner-Feinberg, E. (2000). The consistency of perceived teacher-child relationships between preschool and kindergarten. *Journal of School Psychology, 38,* 113–132.

Jang, H., Reeve, J., & Deci, E. L. (2010). Engaging students in learning activities: It's not autonomy support or structure, but autonomy support and structure. *Journal of Educational Psychology, 102*(3), 588–600.

Jang, H., Reeve, J., Ryan, R. M., & Kim, A. (2009). Can self-determination theory explain what underlies the productive, satisfying learning experiences of collectivistically-oriented Korean adolescents? *Journal of Educational Psychology, 101*(3), 644–661.

Kast, A., & Connor, K. (1988). Sex and age differences in response to informational and controlling feedback. *Personality and Social Psychology Bulletin, 14,* 514–523.

Katz, I., & Assor, A. (2007). When choice motivates and when it does not. *Educational Psychology Review, 19,* 429–442.

Kim, J. S., & Sunderman, G. L. (2005). Measuring academic proficiency under the No Child Left Behind Act: Implications for educational equity. *Educational Researcher, 34*(8), 3–13.

Koestner, R., Ryan, R. M., Bernieri, F., & Holt, K. (1984). Setting limits on children's behavior: The differential effects of controlling versus informational styles on intrinsic motivation and creativity. *Journal of Personality, 52,* 233–248.

Lay, R., & Wakstein, J. (1985). Race, academic achievement, and self-concept of ability. *Research in Higher Education, 22,* 43–64.

Legault, L., Green-Demers, I., & Pelletier, L. (2006). Why do high school students lack motivation in the classroom? Toward an understanding of academic amotivation and the role of social support. *Journal of Educational Psychology, 98*(3), 567–582.

Lent, R. W., Lopez, F. G., Brown, S. D., & Gore, P. A. (1996). Latent structure of the sources of mathematics self-efficacy. *Journal of Vocational Behavior, 49,* 292–308.

Leondari, A., & Gonida, E. (2007). Predicting academic self-handicapping in different age groups: The role of personal achievement goals and social goals. *British Journal of Educational Psychology, 77,* 595–611.

Lepper, M. R., Corpus, J. H., & Iyengar, S. S. (2005). Intrinsic and extrinsic motivational orientations in the classroom: Age differences and academic correlates. *Journal of Educational Psychology, 97*(2), 184–196.

Lepper, M. R., Sethi, S., Dialdin, D., & Drake, M. (1997). Intrinsic and extrinsic motivation: A developmental perspective. In S. S. Luthar, J. A. Burack, D. Cicchetti, & J. R. Weisz (Eds.), *Developmental psychopathology: Perspectives on adjustment, risk, and disorder* (pp. 23–50). New York, NY: Cambridge University Press.

Levesque, C., Zuehike, A. N., Stanek, L. R., & Ryan, R. M. (2004). Autonomy and competence in German and American university students: A comparative study based on self-determination theory. *Journal of Educational Psychology, 96,* 68–84.

MacIver, D., Stipek, D., & Daniels, D. (1991). Explaining within-semester changes in student effort in junior high school and senior high school courses. *Journal of Educational Psychology, 83,* 201–211.

Malmberg, L.-E. (2000). Student teachers' achievement goal orientations during teacher studies: Antecedents, correlates and outcomes. *Learning and Instruction, 18*(4), 438–452.

Martin, A. J. (2001). The Student Motivation Scale: A tool for measuring and enhancing motivation. *Australian Journal of Education, 14,* 34–49.

Martin, A. J. (2009). Motivation and engagement across the academic life span: A developmental construct validity study of elementary school, high school, and university/college students. *Educational and Psychological Measurement, 69,* 794–825.

Martin, A. J., & Marsh, H. W. (2003). Fear of failure: Friend or foe? *Australian Psychologist, 38*(1), 31–38.

Martin, A. J., Marsh, H. W., & Debus, R. L. (2001a). A quadripolar need achievement representation of self-handicapping and defensive pessimism. *American Educational Research Journal, 38,* 583–610.

Martin, A. J., Marsh, H. W., & Debus, R. L. (2001b). Self-handicapping and defensive pessimism: Exploring a model of predictors and outcomes from a self-protection perspective. *Journal of Educational Psychology, 93,* 87–102.

Maslow, A. H. (1943). A theory of human motivation. *Psychological Review, 50,* 370–396.

Maslow, A. H. (1954). *Motivation and personality.* New York, NY: Harper.

Maslow, A. H. (1987). *Motivation and personality* (3rd ed.). Delhi, India: Pearson Education.

McLoyd, V. C. (1998). Socioeconomic disadvantage and child development. *American Psychologist, 53,* 185–204.

McMullin, D., & Steffen, J. (1982). Intrinsic motivation and performance standards. *Social Behavior and Personality, 10,* 47–56.

Meece, J. L., Glienke, B. B., & Askew, K. (2009). Gender and motivation. In K. R. Wentzel & A. Wigfield (Eds.), *Handbook of motivation at school* (pp. 412–431). New York, NY: Routledge/Taylor & Francis.

Midgley, C. (2002). *Goals, goal structures, and adaptive learning.* Mahwah, NJ: Lawrence Erlbaum.

Midgley, C., & Feldlaufer, H. (1987). Students' and teachers' decision-making fit before and after the transition to junior high school. *Journal of Early Adolescence, 7,* 225–241.

Mucherah, W., & Yoder, A. (2008). Motivation for reading and middle school students' performance on standardized testing in reading. *Reading Psychology, 29,* 214–235.

Mueller, C. M., & Dweck, C. S. (1998). Intelligence praise can undermine motivation and performance. *Journal of Personality and Social Psychology, 75,* 33–52.

Oakes, J., & Guiton, G. (1995). Matchmaking: the dynamics of high school tracking decisions. *American Educational Research Journal, 32,* 3–33.

Otis, N., Grouzet, F. M. E., & Pelletier, L. G. (2005). Latent motivational change in an academic setting: A 3-year longitudinal study. *Journal of Educational Psychology, 97*(2), 170–183.

Pajares, F., & Johnson, M. J. (1996). Self-efficacy beliefs in the writing of high school students: A path analysis. *Psychology in the Schools, 33,* 163–175.

Pajares, F., Johnson, M. J., & Usher, E. L. (2007). Sources of writing self-efficacy beliefs of elementary, middle, and high school students. *Research in the Teaching of English, 42,* 104–120.

Pajares, F., & Kranzler, J. (1995). Self-efficacy beliefs and general mental ability in mathematical problem solving. *Contemporary Educational Psychology, 20,* 426–443.

Pajares, F., & Valiante, G. (2001). Influence of self-efficacy on elementary students' writing. *Journal of Educational Research, 90*(6), 353–360.

Patall, E. A. (2013). Constructing motivation through choice, interest, and interestingness. *Journal of Educational Psychology, 105*(2), 522–534.

Patall, E. A., Cooper, H., & Robinson, J. C. (2008). The effects of choice on intrinsic motivation and related outcomes: A meta-analysis of research findings. *Psychological Bulletin, 134,* 270–300.

Patall, E. A., Cooper, H., & Wynn, S. R. (2010). The effectiveness and relative importance of choice in the classroom. *Journal of Educational Psychology, 102*(4), 896–915.

Pintrich, P. R., & De Groot, E. V. (1990). Motivational and self-regulated learning components of classroom academic performance. *Journal of Educational Psychology, 82,* 33–40.

Pintrich, P. R., & Garcia, T. (1991). Student goal orientation and self-regulation in the college classroom. In M. L. Maehr & P. R. Pintrich (Eds.), *Advances in motivation and achievement: Goals and self-regulatory processes* (Vol. 7, pp. 371–402). Greenwich, CT: JAI.

Pintrich, P. R., & Schunk, D. H. (2002). *Motivation in education: Theory, research, and applications* (2nd ed.). Upper Saddle River, NJ: Prentice Hall.

Plaks, J., Stroessner, S., Dweck, C., & Sherman, J. (2001). Person theories and attention allocation: Preferences for stereotypic versus counterstereotypic information. *Journal of Personality and Social Psychology, 80,* 876–893.

Pugh, K. J., & Bergin, D. A. (2006). Motivational influences on transfer. *Educational Psychologist, 41*(3), 147–160.

Rattan, A., Good, C., & Dweck, C. S. (2012). "It's ok — Not everyone can be good at math": Instructors with an entity theory comfort (and demotivate) students. *Journal of Experimental Social Psychology, 48*(3), 731–737.

Reeve, J. (2009). Why teachers adopt a controlling motivating style toward students and how they can become more autonomy supportive. *Educational Psychologist, 44*(3), 159–175.

Reeve, J., & Jang, H. (2006). What teachers say and do to support students' autonomy during a learning activity. *Journal of Educational Psychology, 98,* 209–218.

Reeve, J., Jang, H., Carrell, D., Barch, J., & Jeon, S. (2004). Enhancing high school students' engagement by increasing their teachers' autonomy support. *Motivation and Emotion, 28,* 147–169.

Reyna, C. (2000). Lazy, dumb, or industrious: When stereotypes convey attribution information in the classroom. *Educational Psychology Review, 12,* 85–110.

Rhodewalt, F., & Davison, J. (1986). Self-handicapping and subsequent performance: Role of outcome valance and attributional certainty. *Basic and Applied Social Psychology, 7,* 307–322.

Rolland, R. G. (2012). Synthesizing the evidence on classroom goal structures in middle and secondary schools: A meta-analysis and narrative review. *Review of Educational Research, 82*(4), 396–435.

Ross, J., & Bruce, C. (2007). Professional development effects on teacher efficacy: Results of randomized field trial. *Journal of Educational Research, 101*(1), 50–60.

Ross, J. A. (1998). The antecedents and consequences of teacher efficacy. In J. Brophy (Ed.), *Research on teaching* (Vol. 7, pp. 49–74). Greenwich, CT: JAI.

Roth, G., Assor, A., Kanat-Maymon, Y., & Kaplan, H. (2007). Autonomous motivation for teaching: How self-determined teaching may lead to self-determined learning. *Journal of Educational Psychology, 99*(4), 761–774.

Ryan, R. M. (1995). Psychological needs and the facilitation of integrative processes. *Journal of Personality, 63,* 397–427.

Ryan, R. M., Connell, J. P., & Deci, E. L. (1985). A motivational analysis of self-determination and self-regulation in education. In C. Ames & R. Ames (Eds.), *Research on motivation in education* (Vol. 2, pp. 13–51). San Diego, CA: Academic Press.

Ryan, R. M., & Deci, E. L. (2000a). Self-determination theory and the facilitation of intrinsic motivation, social development, and well-being. *American Psychologist, 55*(1), 68–78.

Ryan, R. M., & Deci, E. L. (2000b). Intrinsic and extrinsic motivation: Classic definitions and new directions. *Contemporary Educational Psychology, 25,* 54–67.

Ryan, R. M., Deci, E. L., & Grolnick, W. S. (1995). Autonomy, relatedness, and the self: Their relation to development and psychopathology. In D. Cicchetti & D. J. Cohen (Eds.), *Developmental psychopathology: Vol. I. Theory and methods* (pp. 618–655). New York, NY: Wiley.

Ryan, R. M., Mims, V., & Koestner, R. (1983). Relation of reward contingency and interpersonal context to intrinsic motivation: A review and test using cognitive evaluation theory. *Journal of Personality and Social Psychology, 45,* 736–750.

Scholz, U., Dona, B. G., Sud, S., & Schwarzer, R. (2002). Is general self-efficacy a universal construct? Psychometric findings from 25 countries. *European Journal of Psychological Assessment, 18*(3), 242–251.

Schunk, D., & Hanson, A. (1985). Peer models: Influence on children's self-efficacy and achievement. *Journal of Educational Psychology, 77,* 313–322.

Schunk, D. H. (1981). Modeling and attributional feedback effects on children's achievement: A self-efficacy analysis. *Journal of Educational Psychology, 74,* 93–105.

Schunk, D. H. (1987). Peer models and children's behavioral change. *Review of Educational Research, 57,* 149–174.

Schunk, D. H., & Meece, J. L. (2006). Self-efficacy development in adolescence. In F. Pajares & T. Urdan (Eds.), *Self-efficacy beliefs of adolescents* (pp. 71–96). Greenwich, CT: Information Age.

Schunk, D. H., & Miller, S. D. (2002). Self-efficacy and adolescents' motivation. In F. Pajares & T. Urdan (Eds.), *Academic motivation of adolescents* (pp. 29–52). Greenwich, CT: Information Age.

Schunk, D. H., & Pajares, F. (2009). Self-efficacy theory. In K. R. Wentzel & A. Wigfield (Eds.), *Handbook of motivation at school* (pp. 35–53). New York, NY: Routledge/Taylor & Francis.

Schunk, D. H., Pintrich, P. R., & Meece, J. L. (2008). *Motivation in education. Theory, research, and applications.* Upper Saddle River, NJ: Prentice Hall.

Seijts, G. H., & Latham, G. P. (2001). The effect of learning, outcome, and proximal goals on a moderately complex task. *Journal of Organizational Behavior, 22,* 291–302.

Sierens, E., Vansteenkiste, M., Goossens, L., Soenens, B., & Dochy, F. (2009). The synergistic relationship of perceived autonomy support and structure in the prediction of self-regulated learning. *British Journal of Educational Psychology, 79,* 57–68.

Snyder, K. E., Malin, J. L., Dent, A. L., & Linnenbrink-Garcia, L. (2014). The message matters: The role of implicit beliefs about giftedness and failure experiences in academic self-handicapping. *Journal of Educational Psychology, 106*(1), 230–241.

Soenens, B., & Vansteenkiste, M. (2005). Antecedents and outcomes of self-determination in three life domains: The role of parents' and teachers' autonomy support. *Journal of Youth and Adolescence, 34,* 589–604.

Stevens, T., Olivárez, A., Jr., & Hamman, D. (2006). The role of cognition, motivation, and emotion in explaining the mathematics achievement gap between Hispanic and white students. *Hispanic Journal of Behavior Sciences, 28,* 161–186.

Stevens, T., Olivárez, A., Lan, W. Y., & Tallent-Runnels, M. K. (2004). Role of mathematics self-efficacy and motivation in mathematics performance across ethnicity. *Journal of Educational Research, 97*(4), 208–221.

Stevenson, H. W., Chen, C., & Uttal, D. H. (1990). Beliefs and achievement: A study of black, white, and Hispanic children. *Child Development, 61,* 508–523.

Stipek, D. (2002). *Motivation to learn: Integrating theory and practice* (4th ed.). Boston, MA: Allyn & Bacon.

Stipek, D. (2012). Effects of student characteristics and perceived administrative and parental support on teacher self-efficacy. *The Elementary School Journal, 112*(4), 590–606.

Sungur, S., & Senler, B. (2010). Students' achievement goals in relation to academic motivation, competence expectancy, and classroom environment perceptions. *Educational Research and Evaluation: An International Journal on Theory and Practice, 16*(4), 303–324.

Supovitz, J. A., & Turner, H. M. (2000). The effects of professional development on science teaching practices and classroom culture. *Journal of Research in Science Teaching, 37*(9), 963–980.

Tollefson, N. (2000). Classroom applications of cognitive theories of motivation. *Educational Psychology Review, 12*(1), 63–83.

Tschannen-Moran, M., & Woolfolk Hoy, A. (2001). Teacher efficacy: Capturing an elusive construct. *Teaching and Teacher Education, 17,* 783–805.

Tschannen-Moran, M., Woolfolk Hoy, A., & Hoy, W. K. (1998). Teacher efficacy: Its meaning and measure. *Review of Educational Research, 68,* 202–248.

Urdan, T., Midgley, C., & Anderman, E. M. (1998). The role of classroom goal structure in students' use of self-handicapping strategies. *American Educational Research Journal, 35*(1), 101–122.

Usher, E. L., & Pajares, F. (2006a). Inviting confidence in school: Invitations as a critical source of the academic self-efficacy beliefs of entering middle school students. *Journal of Invitational Theory and Practice, 12,* 7–16.

Usher, E. L., & Pajares, F. (2006b). Sources of academic and self-regulatory efficacy beliefs of entering middle school students. *Contemporary Educational Psychology, 31,* 125–141.

Usher, E. L., & Pajares, F. (2008). Sources of self-efficacy in school: Critical review of the literature and future directions. *Review of Educational Research, 78*(4), 751–796.

Valentine, J. C., DuBois, D. L., & Cooper, H. (2004). The relation between self-beliefs and academic achievement: A meta-analytic review. *Educational Psychologist, 39,* 111–133.

Valeski, T., & Stipek, D. (2001). Young children's feelings about school. *Child Development, 72*(4), 1198–1213.

Vallerand, R. J., Pelletier, L. G., Blais, M. R., Brière, N. M., Senécal, C., & Vallières, E. F. (1993). On the assessment of intrinsic, extrinsic, and amotivation in education: Evidence on the concurrent and construct validity of the academic motivation scale. *Educational and Psychological Measurement, 53,* 159–172.

Vansteenkiste, M., Lens, W., & Deci, E. L. (2006). Intrinsic versus extrinsic goal contents in self-determination theory: Another look at the quality of academic motivation. *Educational Psychologist, 41*(1), 19–31.

Vansteenkiste, M., Lens, W., Dewitte, S., De Witte, H., & Deci, E. L. (2004). The "why" and "why not" of job search behavior: Their relation to searching, unemployment experience and well-being. *European Journal of Social Psychology, 34,* 345–363.

Vansteenkiste, M., Niemiec, C. P., & Soenens, B. (2010). The development of the five mini-theories of self-determination theory: An historical overview, emerging trends, and future directions. In T. C. Urdan & S. A. Karabenick (Eds.), *The decade ahead: Theoretical perspectives on motivation and achievement* (Volume 16A, pp. 105–165). Somerville, MA: Emerald Group.

Vansteenkiste, M., Simons, J., Lens, W., Sheldon, K. M., & Deci, E. L. (2004). Motivating learning, performance, and persistence: The synergistic effects of intrinsic goal contents and autonomy-supportive contexts. *Journal of Personality and Social Psychology, 87,* 246–260.

Vansteenkiste, M., Zhou, M., Lens, W., & Soenens, B. (2005). Experiences of autonomy and control among Chinese learners. Vitalizing or immobilizing? *Journal of Educational Psychology, 97,* 468–483.

Wahlstrom, K., & Louis, K. (2008). How teachers experience principal leadership: The roles of professional community, trust, efficacy, and shared responsibility. *Educational Administration Quarterly, 44,* 458–495.

Weiner, B. (1994). Integrating social and personal theories of achievement striving. *Review of Educational Research, 64,* 557–573.

White, R. W. (1959). Motivation reconsidered: The concept of competence. *Psychological Review, 66,* 297–333.

Wigfield, A., & Cambria, J. (2010). Expectancy-value theory: Retrospective and prospective. In T. C. Urdan & S. A. Karabenick (Eds.), *The decade ahead: Theoretical perspectives on motivation and achievement* (pp. 35–70). Somerville, MA: Emerald Group.

Wininger, S. R., & Norman, A. D. (2010). Assessing coverage of Maslow's theory in educational psychology textbooks: A content analysis. *Teaching Educational Psychology, 6*(1), 33–48.

Wolters, C., & Daugherty, S. (2007). Goal structures and teachers' sense of efficacy: Their relation and association to teaching experience and academic level. *Journal of Educational Psychology, 99,* 18–193.

Woolfolk, A. E., Rosoff, B., & Hoy, W. K. (1990). Teachers' sense of efficacy and their beliefs about managing students. *Teaching and Teacher Education, 6*(2), 137–148.

Wormington, S. V., Corpus, J. H., & Anderson, K. G. (2012). A person-centered investigation of academic motivation and its correlates in high school. *Learning and Individual Differences, 22*(4), 429–438.

Zhou, N., Lam, S.-F., & Chan, K. C. (2012). The Chinese classroom paradox: A cross-cultural comparison of teacher controlling behaviors. *Journal of Educational Psychology, 104*(4), 1162–1174.

Zimmerman, B. J. (2000). Self-efficacy: An essential motive to learn. *Contemporary Educational Psychology, 25,* 82–91.

Zimmerman, B. J., Bandura, A., & Martinez-Pons, M. (1992). Self-motivation for academic attainment: The role of self-efficacy beliefs and personal goal setting. *American Educational Research Journal, 29,* 663–676.

Zimmerman, B. J., & Martinez-Pons, M. (1990). Student differences in self-regulated learning: Relation of grade, sex, and giftedness to self-efficacy and strategy use. *Journal of Educational Psychology, 82,* 51–59.

Module 17

Ackerman, P. L. (2013). Engagement and opportunity to learn. In J. Hattie & E. M. Anderman (Eds.), *International guide to student achievement* (pp. 39–41). New York, NY: Taylor & Francis.

Adler, P. A., & Adler, P. (1998). *Peer power: Preadolescent culture and identity.* New Brunswick, NJ: Rutgers University Press.

Albdour, M., & Krouse, H. J. (2014). Bullying and victimization among African American adolescents: A literature review. *Journal of Child and Adolescent Psychiatric Nursing, 27*(2), 68–82.

Alberto, P. A., & Troutman, A. C. (2012). *Applied behavior analysis for teachers* (9th ed.). Upper Saddle River, NJ: Pearson Education.

American Academy of Pediatrics. (2013). The crucial role of recess in school. *Pediatrics, 131*(1), 183–188.

Ayenibiowo, K. O., & Akinbode, G. A. (2011). Psychopathology of bullying and emotional abuse among school children. *Ife Psychologia, 19*(2), 127–141.

Baly, M. W., Cornell, D. G., & Lovegrove, P. (2014). A longitudinal investigation of self- and peer reports of bullying victimization across middle school. *Psychology in the Schools, 51*(3), 217–240.

Bradshaw, C. P. (2015). Translating research to practice in bullying prevention. *American Psychologist, 70*(4), 322–332.

Brophy, J. (1998). Classroom management as socializing students into clearly articulated roles. *The Journal of Classroom Interaction, 45*(1), 1–4.

Chen, C., & Stevenson, H. W. (1995). Motivation and mathematics achievement: A comparative study of Asian-American, Caucasian-American, and East Asian high school students. *Child Development, 66*, 1215–1234.

Chen, P. Y., & Schwartz, I. S. (2012). Bullying and victimization experiences of students with autism spectrum disorders in elementary schools. *Focus on Autism and Other Developmental Disabilities, 27*(4), 200–212.

Cheyne, J. A., & Walters, R. H. (1970). Punishment and prohibition: Some origins of self-control. *New Directions in Psychology, 4*, 281–366.

Choi, N., Chang, M., Kim, S., & Reio, T. G. (2015). A structural model of parent involvement with demographic and academic variables. *Psychology in the Schools, 52*(2), 154–167.

Cook, C. R., Williams, K. R., Guerra, N. G., Kim, T. E., & Sadek, S. (2010). Predictors of bullying and victimization in childhood and adolescence: A meta-analytic investigation. *School Psychology Quarterly, 25*(2), 65–83.

Cook-Cottone, C. P., Tribole, E., & Tylka, T. L. (2013). *Healthy eating in schools.* Washington, DC: American Psychological Association.

Cooper, K. S. (2013). Eliciting engagement in the high school classroom: A mixed-methods examination of teaching practices. *American Educational Research Journal, 51*(2) 363–402.

Corno, L. (1996). Homework is a complicated thing. *Educational Researcher, 25*, 27–30.

Couvillon, M. A., & Ilieva, V. (2011). Recommended practices: A review of schoolwide preventative programs and strategies on cyberbullying. *Preventing School Failure: Alternative Education for Children and Youth, 55*(2), 96–101.

Crick, N. R., & Grotpeter, J. K. (1995). Relational aggression, gender and social-psychological adjustment. *Child Development, 66*, 710–722.

Davis, G. A., & Thomas, M. A. (1989). *Effective schools and effective teachers.* Boston, MA: Allyn & Bacon.

Deleon, I. G., Bullock, C. E., & Catania, A. C. (2013). Arranging reinforcement contingencies in applied settings: Fundamentals and implications of recent basic and applied research. In G. J. Madden (Ed.), *APA handbook of behavior analysis* (Vol. 2, pp. 47–75). Washington, DC: American Psychological Association.

Dijkstra, J. K., Lindenberg, S., Verhulst, F. C., Ormel, J., & Vennstra, R. (2009). The relation between popularity and aggressive, destructive, and norm-breaking behaviors: Moderating effects of athletic abilities, physical attractiveness, and prosociality. *Journal of Research on Adolescence, 19*(3), 401–413.

Elledge, L. C., Williford, A., Boulton, A. J., DePaolis, K. J., Little, T. D., & Salmivalli, C. (2013). Individual and contextual predictors of cyberbullying: The influence of children's provictim attitudes and teachers' ability to intervene. *Journal of Youth and Adolescence, 42*(5), 698–710.

Epstein, J. L. (1987). Toward a theory of family–school connections: Teacher practices and parent involvement. In K. Hurrelman, F. X. Kaufman, & F. Losel (Eds.), *Social intervention: Potential and constraints* (pp. 121–136). Berlin, Germany: de Gruyer.

Feldman, M. A., Ojanen, T., Gesten, E. L., Smith-Schrandt, H., Brannick, M., Totura, C. M. W., . . . Brown, K. (2014). The effects of middle school bullying and victimization on adjustment through high school: Growth modeling of achievement, school attendance, and disciplinary trajectories. *Psychology in the Schools, 51*(10), 1046–1062.

Finkelhor, D., Turner, H., Ormrod, R., & Hamby, S. L. (2010). Trends in childhood violence and abuse exposure: evidence from 2 national surveys. *Archives of Pediatrics & Adolescent Medicine, 164*(3), 238–242.

Fisher, A. V., Godwin, K. E., & Seltman, H. (2014). Visual environment, attention allocation, and learning in young children when too much of a good thing may be bad. *Psychological Science, 25*(7), 1362–1370.

Fredricks, J. (2013). Behavioral engagement in learning. In J. Hattie & E. M. Anderman (Eds.), *International guide to student achievement* (pp. 42–44). New York, NY: Taylor & Francis.

Freeland, J. T., & Noell, G. H. (1999). Maintaining accurate math responses in elementary school students: The effects of delayed intermittent reinforcement and programming common stimuli. *Journal of Applied Behavior Analysis, 32*, 211–215.

Freiberg, H. J. (2013). *Classroom management and student achievement.* In J. Hattie & E. M. Anderman (Eds.), *International guide to student achievement* (pp. 228–230). New York, NY: Taylor & Francis.

Gibson, P. A., Wilson, R., Haight, W., Kayama, M., & Marshall, J. M. (2014). The role of race in the out-of-school suspensions of black students: The perspectives of students with suspensions, their parents and educators. *Children and Youth Services Review, 47*, 274–282.

Gilboy, M. B., Heinerichs, S., & Pazzaglia, G. (2015). Enhancing student engagement using the flipped classroom. *Journal of Nutrition Education and Behavior, 47*(1), 109–114.

Good, T. L., & Brophy, J. E. (2008). *Looking in classrooms* (10th ed.). Boston, MA: Allyn & Bacon.

Goodstein, P. K. (2013). *How to stop bullying in classrooms and schools: Using social architecture to prevent, lessen, and end bullying.* New York, NY: Routledge.

Gonzalez, L., Borders, L. D., Hines, E., Villalba, J., & Henderson, A. (2013). Parental involvement in children's education: considerations for school counselors working with Latino immigrant families. *Professional School Counseling, 16*(3), 185–193.

Grolnick, W. S., Raftery-Helmer, J. N., & Flamm, E. S. (2013). Parent involvement in learning. In J. Hattie & E. M. Anderman (Eds.), *International guide to student achievement* (pp. 101–103). New York, NY: Taylor & Francis.

Harbour, K. E., Evanovich, L. L., Sweigart, C. A., & Hughes, L. E. (2015). A brief review of effective teaching practices that maximize student engagement. *Preventing School Failure: Alternative Education for Children and Youth, 59*(1), 5–13.

Harris, A. H., & Garwood, J. D. (2015). Beginning the school year. In W. G. Scarlett (Ed.), *The SAGE encyclopedia of classroom management* (pp. 88–92). Thousand Oaks, CA: SAGE.

Harter, S. (1996). Teacher and classmate influences on scholastic motivation, self-esteem, and level of voice in adolescents. In J. Juvonen & K. R. Wentzel (Eds.), *Social motivation: Understanding children's school adjustment* (pp. 11–42). New York, NY: Cambridge University Press.

Hill, N. E., & Tyson, D. F. (2009). Parental involvement in middle school: A meta-analytic assessment of the strategies that promote achievement. *Developmental Psychology, 45*(3), 740–763.

Hopson, L. M., Schiller, K. S., & Lawson, H. A. (2014). Exploring linkages between school climate, behavioral norms, social supports, and academic success. *Social Work Research, 38*(4), 197–209.

Hsu, L. M., & Mascolo, M. F. (2015). Interactive teaching. In W. G. Scarlett (Ed.), *The SAGE encyclopedia of classroom management* (pp. 431–433), Thousand Oaks, CA: SAGE.

Hymel, S., & Swearer, S. M. (2015). Four decades of research on school bullying: An introduction. *American Psychologist, 70*(4), 293–299.

Karıbayeva, A., & Boğar, Y. (2014). To what extent does parents' involvement in middle school influence children's educational progress? *Procedia-Social and Behavioral Sciences, 152,* 529–533.

Kounin, J. S. (1970). *Discipline and group management in classrooms.* New York: Holt, Rinehart & Winston.

Krezmien, M. P., Leone, P. E., & Achilles, G. M. (2006). Suspension, race, and disability: Analysis of statewide practices and reporting. *Journal of Emotional & Behavioral Disorders, 14*(4), 217–226.

Maag, J. W. (2001). Rewarded by punishment: Reflections on the disuse of positive reinforcement in schools. *Exceptional Children, 67,* 173–186.

Maag, J. W. (2012). School-wide discipline and the intransigency of exclusion. *Children and Youth Services Review, 34,* 2094–2100.

Marzano, R. J., Marzano, J. S., & Pickering, D. (2003). *Classroom management that works: Research-Based strategies for every teacher.* Alexandria, VA: Association for Supervision & Curriculum Development.

Mathieson, L. C., & Crick, N. R. (2010). Reactive and proactive subtypes of relational and physical aggression in middle childhood: Links to concurrent and longitudinal adjustment. *School Psychology Review, 39*(4), 601–611.

McComas, J. J., Thompson, A., & Johnson, L. (2003). The effects of precession attention on problem behavior maintained by different reinforcers. *Journal of Applied Behavior Analysis, 36,* 297–307.

Milo, J., Mace, F. C., & Nevin, J. A. (2010). The effects of constant versus varied reinforcers on preference and resistance to change. *Journal of Experimental Analysis of Behavior, 93,* 385–394.

Murray, C. (2015). Assessment of teacher-student relationships. In W. G. Scarlett (Ed.), *The SAGE encyclopedia of classroom management* (pp. 55–58). Thousand Oaks, CA: SAGE.

Naumann, L. P., Guillaume, E. M., & Funder, D. C. (2012). The correlates of high parental academic expectations: An Asian-Latino comparison. *Journal of Cross-Cultural Psychology, 43*(4), 515–520.

Ogbu, J. U. (1994). Racial stratification and education in the United States: Why inequality persists. *Teachers College Record, 96*(2), 264–298.

Ogbu, J. U. (2003). *Black American students in an affluent suburb: A study of academic disengagement.* Mahwah, NJ: Lawrence Erlbaum.

Olweus, D. (1978). *Aggression in the schools: Bullies and whipping boys.* Washington, DC: Hemisphere.

Ostrov, J. M., & Crick, N. R. (2007). Forms and functions of aggression during early childhood: A short-term longitudinal study. *School Psychology Review, 36*(1), 22–43.

Panferov, S. (2010). Increasing ELL parent involvement in our schools: Learning from the parents. *Theory Into Practice, 49,* 106–112.

Pianta, R. C. (2006). Classroom management and relationships between children and teachers: Implications for research and practice. *Handbook of Classroom Management: Research, Practice, and Contemporary Issues, 8,* 685–709.

Rose, C. A., Espelage, D. L., & Monda-Amaya, L. E. (2009). Bullying and victimization rates among students in general and special education: A comparative analysis. *Educational Psychology, 29,* 761–776.

Rose, C. A., & Monda-Amaya, L. E. (2011). Bullying and victimization among students with disabilities: Effective strategies for classroom teachers. *Intervention in School and Clinic, 47*(2), 99–107.

Shea, T. M., & Bauer, A. M. (2012). *Behavior management: A practical approach for educators* (10th ed.). London, UK: Pearson.

Skiba, R. J., Horner, R. H., Chung, C., Rausch, M. R., May, S. L., & Tobin, T. (2011). Race is not neutral: A national investigation of African American and Latino disproportionality in school discipline. *School Psychology Review, 40*(1), 85–107.

Smith, B. (2000). Quantity matters: Annual instructional time in an urban school system. *Educational Administration Quarterly, 36*(5), 652–682.

Steinberg, L. S. (1996). *Beyond the classroom: Why school reform has failed and what parents need to do.* New York, NY: Simon & Schuster.

Tarasawa, B., & Waggoner, J. (2015). Increasing parental involvement of English language learner families: What the research says. *Journal of Children and Poverty, 21*(2), 129–134.

Wang, M. C., Haertel, G. D., & Walberg, H. J. (1993). Toward a knowledge base for school learning. *Review of Educational Research, 63*(3), 249–294.

Wang, M. T., & Holcombe, R. (2010). Adolescents' perceptions of school environment, engagement, and academic achievement in middle school. *American Educational Research Journal, 47*(3), 633–662.

Weinstein, C. S., & Romano, M. E. (2015). *Elementary classroom management: Lessons from research and practice* (6th ed.). New York, NY: McGraw-Hill

Wentzel, K. R. (1998). Social relationships and motivation in middle school: The role of parents, teachers, and peers. *Journal of Educational Psychology, 90*(2), 202–209.

White, J. W. (2011). Resistance to classroom participation: Minority students, academic discourse, cultural conflicts, and issues of representation in whole class discussions. *Journal of Language, Identity & Education, 10*(4), 250–265.

Wubbels, T., Brekelmans, M., Den Brok, P., & Van Tartwijk, J. (2006). An interpersonal perspective on classroom management in secondary classrooms in the Netherlands. In C. Evertson & C. S. Weinstein (Eds.), *Handbook of classroom management: Research, practice and contemporary issues* (pp. 1161–1191). New York, NY: Lawrence Erlbaum.

Wubbels, T., & Levy, J. (1993). *Do you know what you look like? Interpersonal relationships in education.* London, UK: Falmer Press.

Yamamoto, Y. (2015). Asian American students. In W. G. Scarlett (Ed.), *The SAGE encyclopedia of classroom management* (pp. 41–44), Thousand Oaks, CA: SAGE.

Xie, H., Cairns, B. D., & Cairns, R. B. (2005). The development of aggressive behaviors among girls: Measurement issues, social functions, and differential trajectories. In D. J. Pepler, K. C. Madsen, C. Webster, & K. S. Levene (Eds.), *The development and treatment of girlhood aggression* (pp. 105–136). Mahwah, NJ: Lawrence Erlbaum.

Module 18

Akinbobola, A. O., Afolabi, F. (2009). Constructivist practices through guided discovery approach: The effect on students' cognitive achievements in Nigerian senior secondary school physics. *Bulgarian Journal of Science & Education Policy, 3*(2), 233–252.

Alfassi, M., Weiss, I., & Lifshitz, H. (2009). The efficacy of reciprocal teaching in fostering the reading literacy of students with intellectual disabilities. *European Journal of Special Needs Education, 24*(3), 291–305.

Alfieri, L., Brooks, P. J., Aldrich, N. J., & Tenenbaum, H. R. (2011). Does discovery-based instruction enhance learning? *Journal of Educational Psychology, 103*(1), 1–18.

Anderson, J. R., Corbett, A. T., Koedinger, K., & Pelletier, R. (1995). Cognitive tutors: Lessons learned. *Journal of the Learning Sciences, 4,* 167–207.

Anderson, L. W., & Krathwohl, D. R. (Eds.). (2001). *A taxonomy for learning, teaching, and assessing: A revision of Bloom's taxonomy of educational objectives.* New York, NY: Longman.

Au, K. (1979). Using the experience-text-relationship method with minority children. *Reading Teacher, 32*(6), 677–679.

Ausubel, D. P. (1963). *The psychology of meaningful verbal learning.* New York, NY: Grune & Stratton.

Ausubel, D. P. (2000). *The acquisition of retention of knowledge: A cognitive view.* Boston, MA: Kluwer Academic.

Balim, A. G. (2009). The effects of discovery learning on students' success and inquiry learning skills. *Eurasian Journal of Educational Research, 35,* 1–20.

Bearison, D. J. (1982). New directions in studies of social interactions and cognitive growth. In F. C. Sarafiea (Ed.), *Social-cognitive development in context* (pp. 199–221). New York, NY: Guilford Press.

Bloom, B. S. (1971). Mastery learning. In J. H. Block (Ed.), *Mastery learning: Theory and practice* (pp. 47–63). New York, NY: Holt, Rinehart & Winston.

Bloom, B. S., Englehart, M. D., Frost, E. J., Hill, W. H., & Krathwohl, D. R. (1956). *Taxonomy of educational objectives.* New York, NY: David McKay.

Brophy, J. E., & Evertson, C. M. (1976). *Learning from teaching: A developmental perspective.* Boston, MA: Allyn & Bacon.

Brown, A. L., & Palincsar, A. S. (1987). Reciprocal teaching of comprehension strategies: A natural history of one program for enhancing learning. In J. D. Day & J. Borkowski (Eds.), *Intelligence and exceptionality: New directions for theory, assessment and instructional practice* (pp. 81–132). Norwood, NJ: Ablex.

Brown, A. L., & Palincsar, A. S. (1989). Guided, cooperative learning and individual knowledge acquisition. In L. B. Resnick (Ed.), *Knowing, learning, and instruction: Essays in honor of Robert Glaser* (pp. 393–451). Hillsdale, NJ: Lawrence Erlbaum.

Brown, J. S., Collins, A., & Duguid, P. (1989). Situated cognition and the culture of learning. *Educational Researcher, 18*(1), 32–42.

Brown-Jeffy, S., & Cooper, J. E. (2011). Toward a conceptual framework of culturally relevant pedagogy: An overview of the conceptual and theoretical literature. *Teacher Education Quarterly, 38*(1), 65–84.

Bruner, J. (1961). The act of discovery. *Harvard Educational Review, 31,* 21–32.

Bruner, J. S. (1965). *The process of education.* Cambridge, MA: Harvard University Press.

Carroll, J. B. (1971). Problems of measurement related to the concept of learning for mastery. In J. H. Block (Ed.), *Mastery learning: Theory and practice* (pp. 29–46). New York: Holt, Rinehart & Winston.

Cepeda, N. J., Coburn, N., Rohrer, D., Wixted, J. T., Mozer, M. C., & Pashler, H. (2009). Optimizing distributed practice theoretical analysis and practical implications. *Experimental Psychology, 56*(4), 236–246.

Cepeda, N. J., Pashler, H., Vul, E., Wixted, J. T., & Rohrer, D. (2006). Distributed practice in verbal recall tasks: A review and quantitative synthesis. *Psychological Bulletin, 132*(3), 354–380.

Chi, M. T. H. (2009). Active-constructive-interactive: A conceptual framework for differentiating learning activities. *Topics in Cognitive Science, 1,* 73–105.

Cobb, P., & Bowers, J. (1999). Cognitive and situated learning: Perspective in theory and practice. *Educational Researcher, 28*(2), 4–15.

Coffield, F., Moseley, D., Hall, E., & Ecclestone, K. (2004). *Learning styles and pedagogy in post-16 learning. A systematic and critical review.* London, UK: Learning and Skills Research Centre.

Collins, A., Brown, J. S., & Newman, S. E. (1989). Cognitive apprenticeship: Teaching the crafts of reading, writing, and mathematics. In L. B. Resnick (Ed.), *Knowing, learning, and instruction: Essays in honor of Robert Glaser* (pp. 453–494). Hillsdale, NJ: Lawrence Erlbaum.

Collins, A., Hawkins, J., & Carver, S. M. (1991). In B. Means, C. Chelemer, & M. S. Knapp (Eds.), *Teaching advanced skills to at-risk students* (pp. 173–194). San Francisco, CA: Jossey-Bass.

Corkill, A. J. (1992). Advance organizers: Facilitators of recall. *Educational Psychology Review, 4,* 33–67.

Dansereau, D. F. (1988). Cooperative learning strategies. In C. E. Weinstein, E. T. Goetz, & P. A. Alexander (Eds.), *Learning and study strategies: Issues in assessment, instruction, and evaluation* (pp. 103–120). Orlando, FL: Academic Press.

Dean Jr., D., & Kuhn, D. (2007). Direct instruction vs. discovery: The long view. *Science Education, 91*(3), 384–397.

Denham, C., & Lieberman, A. (1980). *Time to learn.* Washington, DC: National Institute of Education.

Dennen, V. P. (2004). Cognitive apprenticeship in educational practice: Research on scaffolding, modeling, mentoring, and coaching as instructional strategies. In D. H. Jonassen (Ed.), *Handbook of research on educational communications and technology* (pp. 813–828). Mahwah, NJ: Lawrence Erlbaum.

Ebmeier, H., & Good, T. L. (1979). The effects of instructing teachers about good teaching on mathematics achievement of fourth grade students. *American Educational Research Journal, 16*(1), 1016.

Enkenberg, J. (2001). Instructional design and emerging models in higher education. *Computers in Human Behavior, 17,* 495–506.

Fantuzzo, J. W., Riggio, R. E., Connelly, S., & Dimeff, L. A. (1989). Effects of reciprocal peer tutoring on academic achievement and psychological adjustment: A component analysis. *Journal of Educational Psychology, 81,* 173–177.

Fisher, C. W., Berliner, D. C., Filby, N. N., Marliave, R., Ghen, L. S., & Dishaw, M. M. (1980). Teaching behaviors, academic learning time, and student achievement: An overview. In C. Denham & A. Lieberman (Eds.),

Time to learn (pp. 7–32). Washington, DC: National Institute of Education.

Fisher, K. R., Hirsh-Pasek, K., Newcombe, N., & Golinkoff, R. M. (2013). Taking shape: Supporting preschoolers' acquisition of geometric knowledge through guided play. *Child Development, 84*(6), 1872–1878.

Fletcher, J. D. (2009). From behaviorism to constructivism. In S Tobias & T. M. Duffy (Eds.), *Constructive theory applied to instruction: Success or failure?* (pp. 242–263). New York, NY: Taylor & Francis.

Furtak, E. M., Seidel, T., Iverson, H., & Briggs, D. C. (2012). Experimental and quasi-experimental studies of inquiry-based science teaching: A meta-analysis. *Review of Educational Research, 82*(3), 300–329.

Gajria, M., Jitendra, A. K., Sood, S., & Sacks, G. (2007). Improving comprehension of expository text in students with LD: A research synthesis. *Journal of Learning Disabilities, 40*(3), 210–225.

Gallimore, R., & Goldenberg, C. (1992). Mapping teachers' zone of proximal development: A Vygotskian perspective on teaching and teacher training. In F. Oser, A. Dick, & J.-L. Patry (Eds.), *Effective and responsible teaching: The new synthesis* (pp. 203–221). San Francisco, CA: Jossey-Bass.

Gallimore, R., & Tharp, R. (1990). Teaching mind in society: Teaching, schooling, and literate discourse. In L. C. Moll (Ed.), *Vygotsky and education* (pp. 175–205). Cambridge, UK: Cambridge University Press.

Gardner, R., & Mayes, R. D. (2013). African American learners. *Preventing School Failure: Alternative Education for Children and Youth, 57*(1), 22–29.

Gay, G. (2010). *Culturally responsive teaching: Theory, research, and practice* (2nd ed.). New York, NY: Teachers College Press.

Gillani, B. B. (2003). *Learning theories and the design of e-learning environments.* Lanham, MD: University Press of America.

Glachan, M., & Light, P. H. (1982). Peer interaction and learning. In G. E. Butterworth & P. H. Light (Eds.), *Social cognition: Studies of the development of understanding* (pp. 238–260). Brighton, UK: The Harvester Press.

Goldenberg, C. (1987). Low-income Hispanic parents' contributions to their first-grade children's word-recognition skills. *Anthropology and Education Quarterly, 18,* 149–179.

Goldenberg, C. (1992/1993). Instructional conversations: Promoting comprehension through discussion. *The Reading Teacher, 46*(4), 316–326.

Good, T. L., Biddle, B. J., & Brophy, J. E. (1975). *Teachers make a difference.* New York, NY: Holt, Rinehart & Winston.

Guskey, T. R., & Jung, L. A. (2011). Response-to-intervention and mastery learning: Tracing roots and seeking common ground. *The Clearing House, 84,* 249–255.

Guskey, T. R., & Pigott, T. D. (1988). Research on group-based mastery learning programs: A meta-analysis. *Journal of Educational Research, 81,* 197–216.

Holmes, R. M., Pellegrini, A. D., & Schmidt, S. L. (2006). The effects of different recess timing regimens on preschoolers' classroom attention. *Early Child Development and Care, 176*(7), 735–743.

Johnson, D. W., & Johnson, R. T. (1985). Motivational processes in cooperative, competitive, and individualistic learning situations. In C. Ames & R. Ames (Eds.), *Attitudes and attitude change in special education: Its theory and practice* (pp. 249–286). New York, NY: Academic Press.

Johnson, D. W., & Johnson, R. T. (1986). Mainstreaming and cooperative learning strategies. *Exceptional Children, 52*(6), 553–561.

Johnson, D. W., & Johnson, R. T. (1990). Cooperative learning and achievement. In S. Sharan (Ed.), *Cooperative learning: Theory and research* (pp. 23–37). New York, NY: Praeger.

Johnson, D. W., & Johnson, R. T. (1998). Cooperative learning and social interdependence theory. In R. S. Tindale, L. Heath, J. Edwards, E. J. Posavac, F. B. Bryant, and Y. Suarez-Balcazar (Eds.), *Theory and research on small groups* (pp. 9–35). New York, NY: Plenum Press.

Johnson, D. W., & Johnson, R. T. (1999). *Learning together and alone: Cooperative, competitive, and individualistic learning.* Boston, MA: Allyn & Bacon.

Johnson, D. W., & Johnson, R. T. (2000). Cooperative learning, values, and culturally plural classrooms. In M. Leicester, C. Mogdill, & S. Mogdill (Eds.), *Values, the classroom, and cultural diversity* (pp. 15–28). London, UK: Cassell.

Johnson, D. W., & Johnson, R. T. (2002). Learning together and alone: Overview and meta-analysis. *Asia Pacific Journal of Education, 22,* 95–105.

Johnson, D. W., & Johnson, R. T. (2009). An educational psychology success story: Social interdependence theory and cooperative learning. *Educational Researcher, 38*(5), 365–379.

Johnson, D. W., Johnson, R. T., & Smith, K. A. (2014). Cooperative learning: Improving university

instruction by basing practice on validated theory. *Teacher Education Quarterly, 4*(1), 291–304.

Joyce, B., Weil, M., & Calhoun, E. (2004). *Models of teaching* (7th ed.). Boston, MA: Allyn & Bacon.

Kierstad, J. (1985). Direct instruction and experiential approaches: Are they really mutually exclusive? *Educational Leadership, 42*(8), 25–30.

King, A. (1990). Enhancing peer interaction and learning in the classroom. *American Educational Research Journal, 27,* 664–687.

King, A. (1991). Effects of training in strategic questioning on children's problem-solving performance. *Journal of Educational Psychology, 83*(3), 307–317.

King, A. (2002). Structuring peer interaction to promote high-level cognitive processing. *Theory Into Practice, 41*(1), 33–39.

Kirschner, P. A., Sweller, J., & Clark, R. E. (2006). Why minimal guidance does not work: An analysis of failure of constructivist, discovery, problem-based, experiential, and inquiry-based teaching. *Educational Psychologist, 41*(2), 75–86.

Kirschner, P. A., & van Merriënboer, J. J. G. (2013). Do learners really know best? Urban legends in education. *Educational Psychologist, 48*(3), 169–183.

Klahr, D., & Carver, S. M. (1988). Cognitive objectives in a LOGO debugging curriculum: Instruction, learning, and transfer. *Cognitive Psychology, 20,* 362–404.

Klahr, D., & Nigam, M. (2004). The equivalence of learning paths in early science instruction effects of direct instruction and discovery learning. *Psychological Science, 15*(10), 661–667.

Klingner, J., & Soltero-González, L. (2011). Culturally and linguistically responsive literacy instruction for English language learners with learning disabilities. *Multiple Voices for Ethnically Diverse Exceptional Learners, 12*(1), 4–20.

Kulik, C. C., Kulik, J. A., & Bangert-Drowns, R. L. (1990). Effectiveness of mastery learning programs: A meta-analysis. *Review of Educational Research, 60,* 265–299.

Lave, J., & Wenger, E. (1991). *Situated learning: Legitimate peripheral participation.* Cambridge, UK: Cambridge University Press.

Lazonder, A. W., & Egberink, A. (2014). Children's acquisition and use of the control-of-variables strategy: Effects of explicit and implicit instructional guidance. *Instructional Science, 42,* 291–304.

Luiten, J., Ames, W., & Ackerson, G. (1980). A meta-analysis of the effects of advance organizers on learning and retention. *American Educational Research Journal, 17*(2), 211–218.

Mandel, E., Osana, H. P., & Venkatesh, V. (2013). Addressing the effects of reciprocal teaching on the receptive and expressive vocabulary of 1st-Grade students. *Journal of Research in Childhood Education, 27*(4), 407–426.

Mastropieri, M. A., Scruggs, T. E., & Butcher, K. (1997). How effective is inquiry learning for students with mild disabilities? *The Journal of Special Education, 31*(2), 199–211.

Mastropieri, M. A., Scruggs, T. E., Hamilton, S. L., Wolfe, S., Whedon, C., & Canevaro, A. (1996). Promoting thinking skills of students with learning disabilities: Effects on recall and comprehension of expository prose. *Exceptionality, 6*, 1–11.

Mayer, R. E. (1992). Guiding students' cognitive processing of scientific information. In M. Pressley, K. Harris, & J. Guthrie (Eds.), *Promoting academic competence and literacy: Cognitive research and instructional innovation* (pp. 243–258). Orlando, FL: Academic Press.

Mayer, R. E. (2003). *Learning and instruction.* Upper Saddle River, NJ: Prentice Hall.

Mayer, R. E. (2004). Should there be a three-strikes rule against pure discovery learning? The case for guided methods of instruction. *American Psychologist, 59*(1), 14–19.

McCaslin, M., & Good, T. (1996). The informal curriculum. In D. Berliner & R. Calfee (Eds.), *Handbook of educational psychology* (pp. 622–670). New York, NY: Macmillan.

McFaul, S. A. (1983). An examination of direct instruction. *Educational Leadership, 40*(7), 67–69.

McMaster, K., & Fuchs, D. (2002). Effects of cooperative learning on the academic achievement of students with learning disabilities: An update of Tateyama-Sniezek's review. *Learning Disabilities Research and Practice, 17*, 107–117.

Means, M. B., & Knapp, M. S. (1991). Cognitive approaches to teaching advanced skills to educationally disadvantaged students. *Phi Delta Kappan, 73*(4), 282–289.

Medley, D., Soar, R., & Coker, H. (1984). *Measurement-based evaluation of teacher performance.* New York, NY: Longman.

Meyer, K. (2014). Making meaning in mathematics problem-solving using the reciprocal teaching approach. *Literacy Learning, 22*(2), 7–15.

Moll, L. C. (2001). Through the mediation of others: Vygotskian research on teaching. In V. Richardson (Ed.), *Handbook of research on teaching* (pp. 111–129). Washington, DC: American Educational Research Association.

Morin, V. A., & Miller, S. P. (1998). Teaching multiplication to middle school students with mental retardation. *Education & Treatment of Children, 21*, 22–36.

Nieto, S., & Boder, P. (2008). *Affirming diversity: The sociopolitical context of multicultural education* (5th ed.). Boston, MA: Allyn & Bacon.

Palincsar, A. S. (2003). Ann L. Brown: Advancing a theoretical model of learning and instruction. In B. J. Zimmerman & D. H. Schunk (Eds.), *Educational psychology: A century of contribution* (pp. 459–475). Mahwah, NJ: Lawrence Erlbaum.

Parker, W. C., Mosborg, S., Bransford, J., Vye, N., Abbott, R., & Wilkerson, J. (2011). Rethinking advanced high school coursework: Tackling the depth/breadth tension in the AP US government and politics course. *Journal of Curriculum Studies, 43*, 553–559.

Pashler, H., McDaniel, M., Rohrer, D., & Bjork, R. (2009). Learning styles: Concepts and evidence. *Psychological Science in the Public Interest, 9*(3), 105–119.

Polleck, J., & Shabdin, S. (2013). Building culturally responsive communities. *The Clearing House: A Journal of Educational Strategies, Issues and Ideas, 86*(4), 142–149.

Poncy, B. C., McCallum, E., & Schmitt, A. J. (2010). A comparsion of behavioral and constructivist interventions for increasing math-fact fluency in a second-grade classroom. *Psychology in the Schools, 47*(9), 917–930.

Reddy, G. L., Ramar, R., & Kusama, A. (2000). *Education of children with special needs.* New Delhi, India: Discovery Publishing House.

Reilly, Y., Parsons, J., & Bortolot, E. (2009). Reciprocal teaching in mathematics. *Proceedings of the Mathematics of Prime Importance Conference*, 182–189. Retrieved from http://www.mav.vic.edu.au/files/conferences/2009/13Reilly.pdf

Renne, C. H. (1997). *Excellent classroom management.* Belmont, CA: Wadsworth.

Robinson, D. H. (1998). Graphic organizers as aids to test learning. *Reading Research and Instruction, 37*, 85–105.

Rogoff, B. (1990). *Apprenticeship in thinking.* New York, NY: Oxford University Press.

Rohrer, D., & Pashler, H. (2012). Learning styles: Where's the evidence? *Medical Education, 46*(7), 634–635.

Rohrbeck, C. A., Ginsburg-Block, M. D., Fantuzzo, J. W., & Miller, T. R. (2003). Peer assisted learning interventions with elementary school students: A meta-analytic review. *Journal of Educational Psychology, 94*(2), 240–257.

Rosenshine, B. (1971). *Teaching behaviours and student achievement.* London, UK: National Foundation for Educational Research.

Rosenshine, B. (1979). Content, time, and direct instruction. In P. Peterson & H. Wahlberg (Eds.), *Research on teaching: Concepts, findings, and implications* (pp. 28–56). Berkeley, CA: McCutchan Publishing.

Rosenshine, B. (1985). Direct instruction. In T. Husen & T. N. Postlethwaite (Eds.), *International encyclopedia of education* (Vol. 3, pp. 1395–1400). Oxford, UK: Pergamon Press.

Rosenshine, B., & Meister, C. (1994). Reciprocal teaching: A review of the research. *Review of Educational Research, 64*(4), 479–530.

Saunders, W., & Goldenberg, C. (1992, April). *Instructional conversations on transition students' concepts of "friendship": An experimental study.* Paper presented at the annual meeting of the American Educational Research Association, San Francisco, CA.

Saunders, W., & Goldenberg, C. (1999). The effects of instructional conversations and literature logs on limited- and fluent-English-proficient students' story comprehension and thematic understanding. *The Elementary School Journal, 99*(4), 277–301.

Schmidt, P. R., & Ma, W. (2006). *50 literacy strategies for culturally responsive teaching, K-8.* Thousand Oaks, CA: Corwin.

Slavin, R. E. (1990). Mastery learning re-reconsidered. *Review of Educational Research, 60*(2), 300–302.

Slavin, R. E., Lake, C., Chambers, B., Cheung, A., & Davis, S. (2009). Effective reading programs for the elementary grades: A best-evidence synthesis. *Review of Educational Research, 79*(4), 1391–1466.

Solomon, D., & Kendall, A. J. (1976). Individual characteristics and children's performance in "open" and "traditional" classroom settings. *Journal of Educational Psychology, 65*, 613–625.

Tharp, R., & Gallimore, R. (1988). *Rousing minds to life: Teaching, learning, and schooling in social context.* Cambridge, UK: Cambridge University Press.

Turnbull, R., Turnbull, A., Shank, M., Smith, S., & Leal, D. (2002). *Exceptional lives: Special education in today's schools* (3rd ed.). Upper Saddle River, NJ: Prentice Hall.

Utley, C. A., Obiakor, F. E., & Bakken, J. P. (2011). Culturally responsive practices for culturally and linguistically diverse students with learning disabilities. *Learning Disabilities: A Contemporary Journal, 9*(1), 5–18.

Wambugu, P. W., & Changeiywo, J. M. (2008). Effects of mastery learning approach on secondary school students' physics achievement. *Eurasia Journal of Mathematics, 4*(3), 293–302.

Webb, N. M. (1989). Peer interaction and learning in small groups. *International Journal of Educational Research, 13,* 21–39.

Whalon, K., & Hanline, M. F. (2008). Effects of a reciprocal questioning intervention on the question generation and responding of children with autism spectrum disorder. *Education & Training in Developmental Disabilities, 43*(3), 367–387.

Yilmaz, K. (2011). The cognitive perspective on learning: Its theoretical underpinnings and implications for classroom practices. *The Clearing House: A Journal of Educational Strategies, Issues and Ideas, 84*(5), 204–212.

Module 19

Adelson, J. L., & Carpenter, B. D. (2011). Grouping for achievement gains: For whom does achievement grouping increase kindergarten reading growth? *Gifted Child Quarterly, 48,* 7–20.

Allen, B. A., & Boykin, A. W. (1992). African-American children and the educational process: Alleviating cultural discontinuity through prescriptive pedagogy. *School Psychology Review, 21,* 586–596.

Allington, R. L. (1980). Teacher interruption behaviors during primary-grade oral reading. *Journal of Educational Psychology, 72,* 371–374.

Allington, R. L. (1983). The reading instruction provided readers of differing reading abilities. *Elementary School Journal, 83,* 548–559.

Allington, R. L. (1984). Content coverage and contextual reading in reading groups. *Journal of Reading Behavior, 16*(2), 85–96.

Amspaugh, L. B. (1975). Teachers' perceptions of various characteristics of first grade children and reading group placement. *Dissertation Abstracts International, 35A,* 4999.

Anderson, R. H., & Pavan, B. N. (1993). *Nongradedness: Helping it to happen.* Lancaster, PA: Technomic Publishing.

Applebee, A. N., Langer, J., Nystrand, M., & Gamoran, A. (2003). Discussion-based approaches to developing understanding: Classroom instruction and student performance in middle and high school English. *American Educational Research Journal, 40,* 685–730.

Aronson, E. (2000). *Nobody left to hate: Teaching compassion after Columbine.* New York, NY: Worth.

Aronson, E., Blaney, N., Stephan, C., Sikes, J., & Snapp, M. (1978). *The jigsaw classroom.* Beverly Hills, CA: SAGE.

Banks, J. A. (2006). *Cultural diversity and education: Foundations, curriculum, and teaching* (5th ed.). Boston, MA: Pearson Education.

Barr, R. (1995). What research says about grouping in the past and present and what it suggests about the future. In M. Radencich & L. McKay (Eds.), *Flexible grouping for literacy in the elementary grades* (pp. 1–24). Boston, MA: Allyn & Bacon.

Barr, R., & Dreeben, R. (1983). *How schools work.* Chicago, IL: The University of Chicago Press.

Bertucci, A., Conte, S., Johnson, D. W., & Johnson, R. T. (2010). The impact of size of cooperative group on achievement, social support, and self-esteem. *The Journal of General Psychology, 137*(3), 256–272.

Bertucci, A., Johnson, D. W., Johnson, R. T., & Conte, S. (2012). Influence of group processing on achievement and perception of social and academic support in elementary inexperienced cooperative learning groups. *The Journal of Educational Research, 105*(5), 329–335.

Biemiller, A. (1977/1978). Relationships between oral reading rates for letters, words, and simple text in the development of reading achievement. *Reading Research Quarterly, 13*(2), 223–253.

Boaler, J., & Staples, M. (2008). Creating mathematical futures through an equitable teaching approach. *Teachers College Record, 110*(3), 608–645.

Boekaerts, M. (2009). Goal-directed behavior in the classroom. In K. R. Wentzel, & A Wigfield (Eds.), *Handbook of motivation at school* (pp. 105–122). New York, NY: Taylor & Francis.

Brown, R. G. (1993). *Schools of thought.* San Francisco, CA: Jossey-Bass.

Butler, R. (2008). Ego-involving and frame of reference effects of tracking on elementary school students' motivational orientations and help seeking in math class. *Social Psychology of Education, 11,* 5–23.

Buttaro, A., Catsambis, S., Mulkey, L. M., & Steelman, L. C. (2010). An organizational perspective on the origins of instructional segregation: School composition and the use of within-class ability grouping in American kindergartens. *Teachers College Record, 112*(5), 1300–1337.

Carbonaro, W. (2005). Tracking, students' effort, and academic achievement. *Sociology of Education, 78,* 27–49.

Catsambis, S., Mulkey, L. M., Buttaro, A., Steelman, L. C., & Koch, P. R. (2012). Examining gender differences in ability group placement at the onset of schooling: The role of skills, behaviors, and teacher evaluations. *The Journal of Educational Research, 105*(1), 8–20.

Catsambis, S., Mulkey, L., & Crain, R. L. (1999). To track or not to track? The social effects of gender and middle school tracking. *Research in Sociology of Education and Socialization, 12,* 135–163.

Catsambis, S., Mulkey, L., & Crain, R. L. (2001). For better or for worse? A nationwide study of the social psychological effects of gender and ability grouping in mathematics. *Social Psychology of Education, 5,* 83–115.

Chait, R., Muller, R. D., Goldware, S., & Housman, N. G. (2007). *Academic interventions to help students meet rigorous standards: State policy options.* Washington, DC: The National High School Alliance at the Institute for Educational Leadership.

Chang, M., Singh, K., & Filer, K. (2009). Language factors associated with achievement grouping in math classrooms: a cross-sectional and longitudinal study. *School Effectiveness and School Improvement, 20*(1), 27–45.

Chiu, D., Beru, Y., Watley, E., Wubu, S., Simson, E., Kessinger, R., . . . Wigfield, A. (2008). Influences of math tracking on seventh-grade students' self-beliefs and social comparisons. *The Journal of Educational Research, 102*(2), 125–136.

Chorzempa, B. F., & Graham, S. (2006). Primary-grade teachers' use of within-class ability grouping in reading. *Journal of Educational Psychology, 98*(3), 529–541.

Clark, B. (1990). An update on ability grouping and its importance for gifted learners. *Communicator, 20*(5), 1, 20–21.

Condron, D. J. (2008). An early start: Skill grouping and unequal reading gains in the elementary years. *Sociological Quarterly, 49*(2), 363–394.

Darling-Hammond, L. (1995). Inequality and access to knowledge. In J. A. Banks & C. A. M. Banks (Eds.),

Handbook of research on multicultural education (pp. 465–483). New York, NY: Macmillan.

DeVries, D., & Edwards, K. (1974). Student teams and learning games: Their effects on cross-race and cross-sex interaction. *Journal of Educational Psychology, 66*(5), 741–749.

Eder, D. (1983). Ability grouping and students' academic self-concepts: A case study. *Elementary School Journal, 84,* 149–161.

Epstein, J. L., & MacIver, D. J. (1992). *Opportunities to learn: Effects on eighth graders of curriculum offerings and instructional approaches* (Report No. 34). Baltimore, MD: Center for Research on Elementary and Middle Schools, Johns Hopkins University.

Feldhusen, J. F., & Moon, S. M. (1992). Grouping gifted students: Issues and concerns. *Gifted Child Quarterly, 36,* 63–67.

Fielder, E. D., Lange, R. E., & Winebrenner, S. (1993). In search of reality: Unraveling the myths about tracking, ability grouping and the gifted. *Roeper Review, 16,* 4–7.

Filby, N. N., & Barnett, B. G. (1982). Student perceptions of "better readers" in elementary classrooms. *Elementary School Journal, 82,* 435–449.

Floyd, C. (1954). Meeting children's reading needs in the middle grades: A preliminary report. *Elementary School Journal, 55,* 99–103.

Gamoran, A. (1993). Alternative uses of ability grouping in secondary schools: Can we bring high-quality instruction to low-ability classes? *American Journal of Education, 102*(1), 1–22.

Gamoran, A. (2010). Tracking and inequality: New directions for research and practice. In M. Apple, S. J. Ball, & L. A. Gandin (Eds.), *The Routledge international handbook of the sociology of education* (pp. 213–228). London, UK: Routledge.

Gamoran, A., & Weinstein, M. (1998). Differentiation and opportunity in restructured schools. *American Journal of Education, 106,* 385–415.

García, E. E. (1992). "Hispanic" children: Theoretical, empirical, and related policy issues. *Educational Psychology Review, 4*(1), 69–93.

Gillies, R. (2003). The behaviors, interactions, and perceptions of junior high school students during small-group learning. *Journal of Educational Psychology, 95,* 137–147.

Gillies, R. M. (2008). The effects of cooperative learning on junior high school students' behaviours, discourse, and learning during a science-based learning activity.

School Psychology International, 29(3), 328–347.

Goldsmith, P. R. (2011). Coleman revisited: School segregation, peers, and frog ponds. *American Educational Research Journal, 48,* 508–535.

Goodlad, J. I., & Anderson, R. H. (1987). *The non-graded elementary school.* New York, NY: Teachers College Press.

Gutiérrez, R., & Slavin, R. E., (1992). Achievement effects of the nongraded elementary school: A best evidence synthesis. *Review of Educational Research, 62*(4), 333–376.

Hallinan, M. T., & Sorensen, A. B. (1985). Class size, ability group size, and student achievement. *American Journal of Education, 94*(1), 71–89.

Hinnant, J. B., O'Brien, M., & Ghazarian, S. R. (2009). The longitudinal relations of teacher expectations to achievement in the early school years. *Journal of Educational Psychology, 101*(3), 662–670.

Huang, M. H. (2009). Classroom homogeneity and the distribution of student math performance: A country-level fixed-effects analysis. *Social Science Research, 38*(4), 781–791.

Johnson, D., Maruyama, G., Johnson, R., Nelson, D., & Skon, L. (1981). Effects of cooperative, competitive, and individualistic goal structures on achievement. *Psychological Bulletin, 89*(1), 47–62.

Johnson, D. W., & Johnson, R. (1975). *Learning together and alone: Cooperation, competition, and individualization.* Englewood Cliffs, NJ: Prentice Hall.

Johnson, D. W., & Johnson, R. (1978). Cooperative, competitive, and individualistic learning. *Journal of Research and Development in Education, 12,* 3–15.

Johnson, D. W., & Johnson, R. T. (1985). Motivational processes in cooperative, competitive, and individualistic learning situations. In C. Ames & R. Ames (Eds.), *Attitudes and attitude change in special education: Its theory and practice* (pp. 249–286). New York, NY: Academic Press.

Johnson, D. W., & Johnson, R. T. (1986). Mainstreaming and cooperative learning strategies. *Exceptional Children, 52*(6), 553–561.

Johnson, D. W., & Johnson, R. T. (1990). Cooperative learning and achievement. In S. Sharan (Ed.), *Cooperative learning: Theory and research* (pp. 23–37). New York, NY: Praeger.

Johnson, D. W., & Johnson, R. T. (1998). Cooperative learning and social interdependence theory. In

R. S. Tindale, L. Heath, J. Edwards, E. J. Posavac, F. B. Bryant, & Y. Suarez-Balcazar (Eds.), *Theory and research on small groups* (pp. 9–35). New York, NY: Plenum Press.

Johnson, D. W., & Johnson, R. T. (2009). An educational psychology success story: Social interdependence theory and cooperative learning. *Educational Researcher, 38*(5), 365–379.

Johnson, D. W., Johnson, R. T., & Smith, K. (2007). The state of cooperative learning in postsecondary and professional settings. *Educational Psychology Review, 19,* 15–29.

Johnson, D. W., Johnson, R. T., & Smith, K. A. (2014). Cooperative learning: Improving university instruction by basing practice on validated theory. *Journal on Excellence in College Teaching, 25*(3&4), 85–118.

Juel, C. (1988). Learning to read and write: A longitudinal study of fifty-four children from first through fourth grades. *Journal of Educational Psychology, 80,* 437–447.

Kalogrides, D., & Loeb, S. (2013). Different teachers, different peers: The magnitude of student sorting within schools. *Educational Researcher, 42*(6), 304–316.

Kemple, J. J., Herlihy, C. M., & Smith, T. J. (2005). *Making progress toward graduation: Evidence from the talent development high school model.* New York, NY: MDRC.

Kirk, S. A., Gallagher, J. J., Anastasiow, N. J., & Coleman, M. R. (2006). *Educating exceptional children* (11th ed.). Boston, MA: Houghton Mifflin.

Kuklinski, M. R., & Weinstein, R. S. (2001). Classroom and developmental differences in a path model of teacher expectancy effects. *Child Development, 72*(5), 1554–1578.

Kulik, J., & Kulik, C. (1987). Effects of ability grouping on student achievement. *Equity and Excellence, 23*(1–2), 22–30.

Kulik, J. A. (1992). *An analysis of the research on ability grouping: Historical and contemporary perspectives.* Storrs: The National Research Center on the Gifted and Talented, University of Connecticut.

Kulik, J. A., & Kulik, C. C. (1992). Meta-analytic findings on grouping programs. *Gifted Child Quarterly, 36*(2), 73–77.

Kulik, J. A., & Kulik, C. C. (2004). Meta-analytic findings on grouping programs. In L. E. Brody (Ed.), *Grouping and acceleration practices in gifted education* (pp. 105–114). Thousand Oaks, CA: Corwin.

Ladd, G. W., Kochenderfer-Ladd, B., Visconti, K. J., Ettekal, I., Sechler, C. M., &

Cortes, K. I. (2013). Grade-school children's social collaborative skills: Links with partner preference and achievement. *American Educational Research Journal, 51*(1), 152–183.

Lavasani, M. G., Afzali, L., & Afzali, F. (2011). Cooperative learning and social skills. *Cypriot Journal of Educational Information & Communication Technologies, 4,* 186–193.

Lleras, C., & Rangel, C. (2009). Ability grouping practices in elementary school and African American/Hispanic achievement. *American Journal of Education, 115,* 279–304.

Lloyd, L. (1999). Multi-age classes and high ability students. *Review of Educational Research, 69*(2), 187–212.

Lomawaima, K. T. (2003). Educating Native Americans. In J. A. Banks & C. A. M. Banks (Eds.), *Handbook of research on multicultural education* (2nd ed., pp. 441–461). New York, NY: John Wiley & Sons.

Lou, Y., Abrami, P. C., Spence, J. C., Poulsen, C., Chambers, B., & d'Apollonia, S. (1996). Within-class grouping: A meta-analysis. *Review of Educational Research, 66*(4), 423–458.

Loveless, T. (1999). Will tracking reform promote social equity? *Educational Leadership, 56*(7), 28–32.

Loveless, T. (2013). *The resurgence of ability grouping and persistence of tracking* (Part II of the Brown Center Report on American Education, pp. 12–20). Washington, DC: Brookings Institution.

Lynch, S., & Mills, C. (1990). The skills reinforcement program (SRP): An academic program for high potential minority youth. *Journal for the Education of the Gifted, 21,* 95–102.

Marzano, R. J., Pickering, D. J., & Pollack, J. E. (2005). *Classroom instruction that works: Research-based strategies for increasing student achievement.* Upper Saddle River, NJ: Prentice Hall.

Mason, D. A., & Good, T. L. (1993). Effects of two-group and whole-class teaching on regrouped elementary students' mathematics achievement. *American Educational Research Journal, 30,* 328–360.

McCaslin, M., & Good, T. (1996). The informal curriculum. In D. Berliner & R. Calfee (Eds.), *Handbook of educational psychology* (pp. 47–62). New York, NY: Macmillan.

McKown, C., & Weinstein, R. S. (2008). Teacher expectations, classroom context, and the achievement gap. *Journal of School Psychology, 46*(3), 235–261.

Merton, R. K. (1948). The self-fulfilling prophecy. *Antioch Review, 8,* 193–210.

Mills, C. J., & Durden, W. G. (1992). Cooperative learning and ability grouping: An issue of choice. *Gifted Child Quarterly, 36*(1), 11–16.

Moore, D., & Davenport, S. (1988). *The new improved sorting machine.* Madison, WI: National Center on Effective Secondary Schools.

Mulkey, L. M., Catsambis, S., Steelman, L. C., & Crain, R. L. (2005). The long-term effects of ability grouping in mathematics: A national investigation. *Social Psychology of Education, 8,* 137–177.

Nagy, W., & Anderson, R. C. (1984). How many words are there in printed school English? *Reading Research Quarterly, 19,* 304–330.

Nomi, T. (2010). The effects of within-class ability grouping on academic achievement in early elementary years. *Journal of Research on Educational Effectiveness, 3,* 56–92.

Nomi, T., & Allensworth, E. (2009). "Double-Dose" algebra as an alternative strategy to remediation: Effects on students' academic outcomes. *Journal of Research on Educational Effectiveness, 2*(2), 111–148.

Oakes, J. (1992). Can tracking research inform practice? Technical, normative, and political considerations. *Educational Researcher, 27*(4), 12–21.

Oakes, J. (2005). *Keeping track: How schools structure inequality* (2nd ed.). New Haven, CT: Yale University Press.

Oakes, J., & Wells, A. S. (2002). Detracking for high student achievement. In L. Abbeduto (Ed.), *Taking sides: Clashing views and controversial issues in educational psychology* (2nd ed., pp. 26–30). Guilford, CT: Dushkin.

Preckel, F., Götz, T., & Frenzel, A. (2010). Ability grouping of gifted students: Effects on academic self-concept and boredom. *British Journal of Educational Psychology, 80*(3), 451–472.

Puma, M. J., Jones, C. C., Rock, D., & Fernandez, R. (1993). *Prospects: The congressionally mandated study of educational growth and opportunity* (Interim Report). Bethesda, MD: Abt Associates.

Quail, A., & Smyth, E. (2014). Multigrade teaching and age composition of the class: The influence on academic and social outcomes among students. *Teaching and Teacher Education, 43,* 80–90.

Rist, R. (1970). Student social class and teacher expectations: The self-fulfilling prophecy in ghetto education. *Harvard Educational Review, 40,* 411–451.

Robinson, A. (1990). Point-counterpoint: Cooperation or exploitation? The argument against cooperative learning for talented students. *Journal for the Education of the Gifted, 14,* 9–27.

Rogers, K. B. (1991). *The relationship of grouping practices to the education of the gifted and talented learner.* Storrs: The National Research Center on the Gifted and Talented, University of Connecticut.

Rogers, K. B. (1993). Grouping the gifted and talented: Questions and answers. *Roeper Review, 16,* 8–12.

Rohrbeck, C. A., Ginsburg-Block, M. D., Fantuzzo, J. W., & Miller, T. R. (2003). Peer assisted learning interventions with elementary school students: A meta-analytic review. *Journal of Educational Psychology, 94*(2), 240–257.

Rosenbaum, J. E. (1980). Social implications of educational grouping. *Review of Research in Education, 8,* 361–401.

Rosenbaum, J. E. (1999). If tracking is bad, is detracking better? *American Educator, 23*(4), 24–29, 47.

Rowan, B., & Miracle, A. W., Jr. (1983). Systems of ability grouping and the stratification of achievement in elementary schools. *Sociology of Education, 56,* 133–144.

Rubin, B. C. (2008). Detracking in context: How local constructions of ability complicate equity. *Teachers College Record, 110*(3), 646–699.

Sáenz, L., Fuchs, L. S., & Fuchs, D. (2005). Peer-assisted learning strategies for English language learners with learning disabilities. *Exceptional Children, 71,* 231–247.

Saleh, M., Lazonder, A. W., & Jong, T. D. (2005). Effects of within-class ability grouping on social interaction, achievement, and motivation. *Instructional Science, 33,* 105–119.

Schachar, H. (2003). Who gains what from cooperative learning: An overview of eight studies. In R. Gillies & A. Ashman (Eds.), *Cooperative learning: The social and intellectual outcomes of learning in groups* (pp. 103–118). London, UK: Routledge/Falmer.

Schwalbe, M. L., & Staples, C. L. (1991). Gender differences in sources of self-esteem. *Social Psychology Quarterly, 54,* 158–168.

Shields, C. (1995). A comparison study of student attitudes and perceptions in homogeneous and heterogeneous classrooms. *Roeper Review, 17,* 234–238.

Slavin, R. E. (1978). Student teams and achievement divisions. *Journal of Research and Development in Education, 12,* 39–49.

Slavin, R. E. (1980). Cooperative learning. *Review of Educational Research, 50*(2), 315–342.

Slavin, R. E. (1986). *Using student team learning* (3rd ed.). Baltimore, MD: Center for Research on Elementary and Middle Schools, Johns Hopkins University.

Slavin, R. E. (1987a). Grouping for instruction in elementary school. *Educational Psychologist, 22*(2), 109–127.

Slavin, R. E. (1987b). Ability grouping and student achievement in elementary schools: A best-evidence synthesis. *Review of Educational Research, 57*(3), 293–336.

Slavin, R. E. (1990). Achievement effects of ability grouping in secondary schools: A best-evidence synthesis. *Review of Educational Research, 60,* 471–499.

Slavin, R. E. (1991). Synthesis of research on cooperative learning. *Educational Leadership, 48*(5), 71–82.

Slavin, R. E., Lake, C., Chambers, B., Cheung, A., & Davis, S. (2009). Effective reading programs for the elementary grades: A best-evidence synthesis. *Review of Educational Research, 79*(4), 1391–1466.

Slavin, R. E., Leavey, M., & Madden, N. A. (1984). Combining cooperative learning and individualized instruction: Effects on student mathematics achievement, attitudes and behaviors. *Elementary School Journal, 84,* 409–422.

Slavin, R. E., & Madden, N. (1989). What works for students at risk: A research synthesis. *Educational Leadership, 46*(5), 4–13.

Slavin, R. E., Madden, N. A., & Stevens, R. J. (1990). Cooperative learning models for the 3 R's. *Educational Leadership, 47*(4), 22–28.

Smith, D. D. (2006). *Introduction to special education: Teaching in an age of opportunity* (5th ed.). Boston, MA: Allyn & Bacon.

Smith, K., Johnson, D. W., & Johnson, R. (1982). Effects of cooperative and individualistic instruction on the achievement of handicapped, regular, and gifted students. *The Journal of Social Psychology, 116,* 277–283.

Smith, N. B., & Robinson, H. A. (1980). *Reading instruction for today's children.* New York, NY: Prentice Hall.

Solomon, D., Watson, M. S., & Battistich, V. A. (2001). Teaching and schooling effects on moral/prosocial development. In V. Richardson (Ed.), *Handbook of research on teaching* (4th ed., pp. 566–603). Washington, DC: American Educational Research Association.

Sorhagen, N. S. (2013). Early teacher expectations disproportionately affect poor children's high school performance. *Journal of Educational Psychology, 105*(2), 465–477.

Stanovich, K. E. (1986). Matthew effects in reading: Some consequences of individual differences in the acquisition of literacy. *Reading Research Quarterly, 21*(4), 360–406.

Stevens, R. J., Madden, N. A., Slavin, R. E., & Farnish, A. M. (1987). Cooperative integrated reading and composition: Two field experiments. *Reading Research Quarterly, 22,* 433–454.

Tach, L. M., & Farkas, G. (2006). Learning-related behaviors, cognitive skills, and ability grouping when schooling begins. *Social Science Research, 35*(4), 1048–1079.

Tarim, K. (2009). The effects of cooperative learning on preschoolers' mathematics problem-solving ability. *Educational Studies in Mathematics, 72,* 325–340.

Thijs, J., Verkuyten, M., & Helmond, P. (2010). A further examination of the big-fish–little-pond effect. *Sociology of Education, 83,* 333–345.

Tsay, M., & Brady, M. (2010). A case study of cooperative learning and communication pedagogy: Does working in teams make a difference? *Journal of the Scholarship of Teaching and Learning, 10*(2), 78–89.

Veenman, S. (1995). Cognitive and noncognitive effects of multigrade and multiage classes: A best-evidence synthesis. *Review of Educational Research, 65*(4), 319–381.

Veenman S. (1997). Combination classrooms revisited. *Educational Research and Evaluation, 3*(3), 262–276.

Watanabe, M. (2007). Lessons from a teacher inquiry group about tracking: Perceived student choice in course-taking and its implications for detracking reform. *Teachers College Record, 109,* 2136–2170.

Watanabe, M. (2008). Tracking in the era of high-stakes accountability reform: Case studies of classroom instruction in North Carolina. *Teachers College Record, 110,* 489–533.

Webb, N. M. (1984). Sex differences in interaction and achievement in cooperative small groups. *Journal of Educational Psychology, 74,* 475–484.

Webb, N. M. (1985). Gender differences in small group interaction and achievement in high- and low-achieving classes. In L. C. Wilkinson & C. B. Marrett (Eds.), *Gender differences in classroom interaction* (pp. 209–236). New York, NY: Academic Press.

Webb, N. M. (1991). Task-related verbal interaction and mathematics learning in small groups. *Journal of Research in Mathematics Education, 22,* 366–369.

Webb, N. M. (2008). Learning in small groups. In T. L. Good (Ed.), *21st century education: A reference handbook* (pp. 203–211). Thousand Oaks, CA: SAGE.

Weinstein, R. (1993). Children's knowledge of differential treatment in school: Implications for motivation. In T. Tomlinson (Ed.), *Motivating students to learn: Overcoming barriers to high achievement* (pp. 197–224). Berkeley, CA: McCutchan Publishing.

Yonezawa, S., Wells, A. S., & Serna, I. (2002). Choosing tracks: "Freedom of choice" in detracked schools. *American Educational Research Journal, 39,* 37–67.

Module 20

Adelson, J. L., & Carpenter, B. D. (2011). Grouping for achievement gains: For whom does achievement grouping increase kindergarten reading growth? *Gifted Child Quarterly, 48,* 7–20.

American Educational Research Association, American Psychological Association, & National Council on Measurement in Education. (2014). *Standards for educational and psychological testing.* Washington, DC: American Educational Research Association.

Baker, D. P., Eslinger, P. J., Benavides, M., Peters, E., Dieckmann, N. F., & Leon, J. (2015). Intelligence The cognitive impact of the education revolution: A possible cause of the Flynn effect on population IQ. *Intelligence, 49,* 144–158.

Barnett, W. S. (2004). Does Head Start have lasting cognitive effects? The myth of fade-out. In E. Zigler & S. J. Styfco (Eds.), *The Head Start debates* (pp. 221–249). Baltimore, MD: Brookes.

Beaver, K. M., Schwartz, J. A., Connolly, E. J., Nedelec, J. L., Al-Ghamdi, M. S., & Kobeisy, A. N. (2013). The genetic and environmental architecture to the stability of IQ: Results from two independent samples of kinship pairs. *Intelligence, 41*(5), 428–438.

Beilock, S. L., Gunderson, E. A., Ramirez, G., & Levine, S. C. (2010). Female teachers' math anxiety affects girls' math achievement. *PNAS Proceedings of the National Academy of Sciences of the United States of America, 107*(5), 1860–1863.

Bianco, M., Harris, B., Garrison-Wade, D., & Leech, N. (2011). Gifted girls: Gender bias in gifted referrals. *Roeper Review, 33*(3), 170–181.

Bleeker, M. M., & Jacobs, J. E. (2004). Achievement in math and science: Do mothers' beliefs matter 12 years later? *Journal of Educational Psychology, 96*(1), 97–109.

Bonner, F. A. II. (2000). African American giftedness. *Journal of Black Studies, 30*(5), 643–663.

Borland, J. H., & Wright, L. (1994). Identifying young, potentially gifted economically disadvantaged students. *Gifted Child Quarterly, 38,* 164–171.

Bradley, R. H., & Caldwell, B. M. (1984). 174 children: A study of the relationship between home environment and cognitive development during the first 5 years. In A. W. Gottfried (Ed.), *Home environment and early cognitive development: Longitudinal research* (pp. 5–56). San Diego, CA: Academic Press.

Brown, R. P., & Day, E. A. (2006). The difference isn't black and white: Stereotype threat and the race gap on Raven's advanced progressive matrices. *Journal of Applied Psychology, 91,* 979–985.

Brulles, D., Peters, S. J., & Saunders, R. (2012). Schoolwide mathematics achievement within the gifted cluster grouping model. *Journal of Advanced Academics, 23,* 200–216.

Brulles, D., Saunders, R., & Cohn, S. J. (2010). Improving performance for gifted students in a cluster grouping model. *Journal for the Education of the Gifted, 34*(2), 327–350.

Brulles, D., & Winebrenner, S. (2013). The schoolwide cluster grouping model. *Gifted Child Today, 34*(4), 35–46.

Campbell, L. (1997). How teachers interpret MI theory. *Educational Leadership, 55*(1), 14–19.

Carroll, J. B. (1993). *Human cognitive abilities: A survey of factor-analytic studies.* New York, NY: Cambridge University Press.

Cattell, R. B. (1963). Theory of fluid and crystallized intelligence: A critical experiment. *Journal of Educational Psychology, 54,* 1–22.

Chart, H., Grigorenko, E. L., & Sternberg, R. J. (2008). Identification: The Aurora battery. In J. A. Plucker & C. M. Callahan (Eds.), *Critical issues and practices in gifted education* (pp. 281–301). Waco, TX: Prufrock Press.

Cohen, R. J., Swerdlik, M. E., & Sturman, E. D. (2013). *Psychological testing and assessment: An introduction to tests and measurement* (8th ed.). New York, NY: McGraw-Hill.

Colangelo, N., & Assouline, S. (2009). Acceleration: Meeting the academic and social needs of students. In L. V. Shavinina (Ed.), *International handbook on giftedness* (pp. 1085–1098). New York, NY: Springer.

Coleman, M. R., Gallagher, J. J., & Job, J. (2012). Developing and sustaining professionalism within gifted education. *Gifted Child Today, 35*(1), 27–36.

Creel, C., & Karnes, F. A. (1988). Parental expectations and young gifted children. *Roeper Review, 11,* 48–50.

Croizet, J.-C., Desert, M., Dutrevis, M., & Leyens, J.-P. (2001). Stereotype threat, social class, gender, and academic underachievement: When our reputation catches up to us and takes over. *Social Psychology of Education, 4,* 295–310.

Davidson, J., & Davisdon, B. (2004). *Genius denied: How to stop wasting our brightest young minds.* New York, NY: Simon & Schuster.

Davis, G. A., Rimm, S. B., & Siegle, D. (2011). *Education of the gifted and talented* (6th ed.). Boston, MA: Pearson.

Donovan, M. S., & Cross, C. T. (Eds.). (2002). *Minority students in special education.* Washington, DC: The National Academies Press.

Duncan, G. J., & Brooks-Gunn, J. (2000). Family poverty, welfare reform, and child development. *Child Development, 71,* 188–196.

Eccles, J., Barber, B., Jozefowicz, D., Malenchuk, O., & Vida, M. (2000). Self-evaluations of competence, task values, and self-esteem. In N. Johnson, M. Roberts, & J. Worrell (Eds.), *Girls and adolescence* (pp. 53–84). Washington, DC: American Psychological Association.

Else-Quest, N. M., Hyde, J. S., & Linn, M. C. (2010). Cross-national patterns of gender differences in mathematics: A meta-analysis. *Psychological Bulletin, 136*(1), 103–127.

Ferrando, M., Ferrandiz, C., Prieto, M. D., Bermejo, M. R., & Sainz, M. (2008). Creativity in gifted & talented children. *The International Journal of Creativity & Problem Solving, 18*(2), 35–47.

Flynn, J. R. (1984). The mean IQ of Americans: Massive gains 1932 to 1978. *Psychological Bulletin, 95,* 29–51.

Flynn, J. R. (2007). *What is intelligence?* New York, NY: Cambridge University Press.

Freedman-Doan, C., Wigfield, A., Eccles, J., Blumenfeld, P., Arbreton, A., & Harold, R. (2000). What am I best at? Grade and gender differences in children's beliefs about ability improvement. *Journal of Applied Developmental Psychology, 21,* 379–402.

Gallagher, J. J. (2005, May 25). Commentary: National security and educational excellence. *Education Week, 24*(38), 32–33, 40.

Gardner, H. (1983). *Frames of mind: The theory of multiple intelligences.* New York, NY: Basic Books.

Gardner, H. (1991). *The unschooled mind: How children think and how schools should teach.* New York, NY: Basic Books.

Gardner, H. (1993). *Frames of mind: The theory of multiple intelligences* (10th anniversary edition with new Introduction). New York, NY: Basic Books.

Gardner, H. (1995). Reflections on multiple intelligences: Myths and messages. *Phi Delta Kappan, 77*(3), 200–203.

Gardner, H. (1999). *Intelligence reframed: Multiple intelligences for the 21st century.* New York, NY: Basic Books.

Gardner, H. (2006). *Multiple intelligences: New horizons.* New York, NY: Basic Books.

Gardner, H., & Connell, M. (2000). Response to Nicholas Allix. *Australian Journal of Education, 44,* 288–293.

Gardner, H., & Moran, S. (2006). The science of multiple intelligences theory: A response to Lynn Waterhouse. *Educational Psychologist, 41*(4), 227–232.

Garlick, D. (2003). Integrating brain science research with intelligence research. *Current Directions in Psychological Science, 12*(5), 185–189.

Geary, D. C., Saults, S. J., Liu, F., & Hoard, M. K. (2000). Sex differences in spatial cognition, computational fluency, and arithmetical reasoning. *Journal of Experimental Child Psychology, 77* (4), 337–353.

Geiser, C., Lehmann, W., & Eid, M. (2008). A note on sex differences in mental rotation in different age groups. *Intelligence, 36,* 556–563.

Gentry, M., & MacDougall, J. (2008). Total school cluster grouping: Model, research, and practice. In J. S. Renzulli & E. J. Gubbins (Eds.), *Systems and models for developing programs for the gifted and talented* (2nd ed., pp. 211–234). Mansfield Center, CT: Creative Learning Press.

Gilman, B. (2008). *Challenging highly gifted learners.* Waco, TX: Prufrock Press.

Greenfield, P. M. (1997). You can't take it with you: Why ability assessments don't cross cultures. *American Psychologist, 52*(10), 1115–1124.

Grigorenko, E. L., Jarvin, L., & Sternberg, R. J. (2002). School-based tests of the triarchic theory of intelligence: Three settings, three samples, three syllabi. *Contemporary Educational Psychology, 27,* 167–208.

Gross, M. (1993). *Exceptionally gifted children.* London, UK: Routledge.

Grotzer, T. A., & Perkins, D. A. (2000). Teaching of intelligence: A performance conception. In R. J. Sternberg (Ed.), *Handbook of intelligence* (pp. 492–515). New York, NY: Cambridge University Press.

Gubbins, E. J., Callahan, C. M., & Renzulli, J. S. (2014). Contributions to the impact of the Javits Act by the National Research Center on the Gifted and the Talented. *Journal of Advanced Academics, 25*(4), 422–444.

Guilford, J. P (1956). The structure of intellect. *Psychological Bulletin, 53,* 267–293.

Guilford, J. P (1988). Some changes in the structure-of-intellect model. *Educational and Psychological Measurement, 48,* 1–4.

Gustafsson, J. E. (1994). Hierarchical models of intelligence and educational achievement. In A. Demetriou & A. Efklides (Eds.), *Intelligence, mind, and reasoning: Structure and development* (pp. 45–73). Amsterdam, the Netherlands: North-Holland/Elsevier Science.

Hallinan, M. T., & Sorensøn, A. B. (1987). Ability grouping and sex differences in mathematics achievement. *Sociology of Education, 60,* 63–72.

Halpern, D. (2011). *Sex differences in cognitive abilities* (4th ed.). New York, NY: Psychology Press.

Halpern, D. F. (1997). Sex differences in intelligence: Implications for education. *American Psychologist, 52*(10), 1091–1101.

Halpern, D. F., & LaMay, M. L. (2000). The smarter sex: A critical review of sex differences in intelligence. *Educational Psychology Review, 12*(2), 229–246.

Hammond, D. R., McBee, M. T., & Hébert, T. P. (2007). Motivational aspects of giftedness. *Roeper Review, 29*(3), 197–205.

Harry, B., & Klingner, J. (2006). *Why are so many minority students in special education? Understanding race & disability in schools.* New York, NY: Teachers College Press.

Hart, B., & Risley, T. R. (2003). The early catastrophe. *Education Review, 17*(1), 110–118.

Hogan, T. P. (2015). *Psychological testing: A practical introduction* (3rd ed.). Hoboken, NJ: Wiley.

Horn, J. L. (1994). Theory of fluid and crystallized intelligence. In R. J. Sternberg (Ed.), *The encyclopedia of human intelligence* (Vol. 1, pp. 443–451). New York, NY: Macmillan.

Housand, A., & Reis, S. M. (2008). Self-regulated learning in reading: Gifted pedagogy and instructional settings. *Journal of Advanced Academics, 20*(1), 108–136.

Hyde, J. S. (2005). The gender similarities hypothesis. *American Psychologist, 60*(6), 581–592.

Hyde, J. S. (2014). Gender similarities and differences. *Annual Review of Psychology, 65*(1), 373–398.

Hyde, J. S., Lindberg, S. M., Linn, M. C., Ellis, A. B., & Williams, C. C. (2008). Gender similarities characterize math performance. *Science, 321,* 494–495.

Iaria, G., Petrides, M., Dagher, A., Pike, B., & Bohbot, V. D. (2003). Cognitive strategies dependent on the hippocampus and caudate nucleus in human navigation: Variability and change with practice. *Journal of Neuroscience, 23,* 5945–5952.

Jacobs, J., Davis-Kean, P., Bleeker, M., Eccles, J., & Malanchuk, O. (2005). "I can, but I don't want to": The impact of parents, interests, and activities on gender differences in math. In A. Gallagher & J. Kaufman (Eds.), *Gender differences in mathematics: An integrative psychological approach* (pp. 73–98). New York, NY: Cambridge University Press.

Jarvin, L., & Sternberg, R. J. (2003). Alfred Binet's contributions to educational psychology. In B. J. Zimmerman & D. L. Schunk (Eds.), *Educational psychology: A century of contributions* (pp. 65–79). Mahwah, NJ: Lawrence Erlbaum.

Johnson, A. P. (2000). *Up and out: Creative and critical thinking skills to enhance learning.* Boston, MA: Allyn & Bacon.

Kaplan, R. M., & Saccuzzo, D. P. (2013). *Psychological testing: Principles, applications, and issues* (8th ed.). Belmont, CA: Wadsworth/Cengage.

Kaufman, A. S. (2010). '"In what way are apples and oranges alike?"' A critique of Flynn's interpretation of the Flynn effect. *Journal of Psychoeducational Assessment, 28*(5) 382–398.

Klein, P. S., Adi-Japha, E., & Hakak-Benizri, S. (2010). Mathematical thinking of kindergarten boys and girls: Similar achievement, different contributing processes. *Educational Studies in Math, 73,* 233–246.

Korenman, S., Miller, J., & Sjaastad, J. (1995). Long-term poverty and child development in the United States: Results from the NLSY. *Children and Youth Services Review, 17,* 127–155.

Kornhaber, M., Fierros, E., & Veenema, S. (2004). *Multiple intelligences: Best ideas from research and practice.* Boston, MA: Allyn & Bacon.

Kulik, J. (2003). Grouping and tracking. In N. Colangelo & G. Davis (Eds.), *Handbook of gifted education* (pp. 268–281). Boston, MA: Allyn & Bacon.

Kulik, J. A., & Kulik, C. C. (2004). Meta-analytic findings on grouping programs. In L. E. Brody (Ed.), *Grouping and acceleration practices in gifted education* (pp. 105–114). Thousand Oaks, CA: Corwin.

Lazar, I., & Darlington, R. (1982). Lasting effects of early education: A report from the consortium for longitudinal studies. *Monographs of the Society for Research in Child Development, 47*(2–3, Serial No. 195).

Lindberg, S. M., Hyde, J. S., & Hirsch, L. M. (2008). Gender and mother-child interactions during mathematics homework. *Merrill-Palmer Quarterly, 54,* 232–255.

Lindberg, S. M., Hyde, J. S., Petersen, J. L., & Linn, M. C. (2010). New trends in gender and mathematics performance: A meta-analysis. *Psychological Bulletin, 136*(6), 1123–1135.

LoCicero, K. A., & Ashbly, J. S. (2000). Multidimensional perfectionism in middle school age gifted students: A comparison to peers from the general cohort. *Roeper Review, 22*(3), 182–185.

Maeda Y., & Yoon, S. Y. (2013). A meta-analysis on gender differences in mental rotation ability measured by the Purdue Spatial Visualization Tests: Visualization of rotations (PSVT:R). *Educational Psychology Review, 25,* 69–94.

Mayer, R. (2000). Intelligence and education. In R. J. Sternberg (Ed.), *Handbook of intelligence* (pp. 519–533). New York, NY: Cambridge University Press.

McLoyd, V. C. (1998). Economic disadvantage and child development. *American Psychologist, 53,* 185–204.

Merton, R. K. (1948). The self-fulfilling prophecy. *Antioch Review, 8,* 193–210.

Miller, R., & Gentry, M. (2010). Developing talents among high-potential students from low-income families in an out-of-school enrichment program. *Journal of Advanced Academics, 21*(4), 594–627.

Miyake A., Kost-Smith, L. E., Finkelstein, N. D., Pollock, S. J., Cohen, G. L., & Ito, T. A. (2010). Reducing the gender achievement gap in college science: A classroom study of values affirmation. *Science, 330,* 1234–1237.

Muzzatti, B., & Agnoli, F. (2007). Gender and mathematics: Attitudes and stereotype threat susceptibility in Italian children. *Developmental Psychology, 43,* 747–759.

National Science Foundation. (2012). *Science and engineering indicators 2012.* Retrieved from http://www.nsf.gov/statistics/seind12/c1/c1s2.htm

Nisbett, R. E., Aronson, J., Blair, C., Dickens, W., Flynn, J., Halpern, D. F., & Turkheimer, E. (2012). Intelligence: New findings and theoretical developments. *American Psychologist, 67*(2), 130–159.

Oakes, J. (1990). Opportunities, achievement, and choice: Women and minority students in science and math. *Review of Research in Education, 16,* 153–222.

Okagaki, L., & Sternberg, R. J. (1993). Parental beliefs and children's school performance. *Child Development, 64,* 36–56.

Parker, W. D. (1997). An empirical typology of perfectionism in academically talented children. *American Educational Research Journal, 34,* 545–562.

Pesta, B. J., & Poznanski, P. J. (2014). Only in America: Cold winters theory, race, IQ and well-being. *Intelligence, 46,* 271–274.

Pfeiffer, S. I., & Blei, S. (2008). Gifted identification beyond the IQ test: Rating scales and other assessment procedures (pp. 177–198). In S. Pfeiffer (Ed.), *Handbook of giftedness in children: Psychoeducational theory, research, and best practices.* New York, NY: Springer.

Piaget, J. (1972). *The psychology of intelligence.* Totowa, NJ: Littlefield Adams.

Pierce, R. L., Cassady, J. C., Adams, C. M., Neumeister, K. L. S., Dixon, F. A., & Cross, T. L. (2011). The effects of clustering and curriculum on the development of gifted learners' math achievement. *Journal for the Education of the Gifted, 34*(4), 569–594.

Postma, A., Jager, G., Kessels, R. P. C., Koppeschaar, H. P. F., & van Honk, J. (2004). Sex differences for selective forms of spatial memory. *Brain Cognition, 54,* 24–34.

Preckel, F., Götz, T., & Frenzel, A. (2010). Ability grouping of gifted students: Effects on academic self-concept and boredom. *British Journal of Educational Psychology, 80*(3), 451–472.

Ramey, C. T. (1994). Abecedarian project. In R. J. Sternberg (Ed.), *Encyclopedia of human intelligence* (Vol. 1, pp. 1–3). New York, NY: Macmillan.

Reilly, D. (2012). Gender, culture, and sex-typed cognitive abilities. *PLoS ONE, 7*(7), e39904.

Reilly, D., Neumann, D. L., & Andrews, G. (2015). Sex differences in mathematics and science achievement: A meta-analysis of National Assessment of Educational Progress assessments. *Journal of Educational Psychology, 107*(3), 645–662.

Reis, S. M., & Boeve, H. (2009). How academically gifted elementary, urban students respond to challenge in an enriched, differentiated reading program. *Journal for the Education of the Gifted, 33*(2), 203–240.

Reis, S. M., & Purcell, J. H. (1993). An analysis of content elimination and strategies used by elementary classroom teachers in the curriculum compacting process. *Journal for the Education of the Gifted, 16*(2), 147–170.

Reis, S. M., & Renzulli, J. S. (2004). Current research on the social and emotional development of gifted and talented students: Good news and future possibilities. *Psychology in the Schools, 41*(1), 119–130.

Renzulli, J. S. (1978a). What makes giftedness? Reexamining a definition. *Phi Delta Kappan, 60,* 180–184, 261.

Renzulli, J. S. (1978b). *The compactor.* Mansfield Center, CT: Creative Learning Press.

Renzulli, J. S. (1988). *Technical report of research studies related to the enrichment triad/revolving door model* (3rd ed.). Storrs: University of Connecticut, Bureau of Educational Research.

Renzulli, J. S. (1990). A practical system for identifying gifted and talented students. *Early Child Development and Care, 63,* 9–18.

Renzulli, J. S. (1999). What is this thing called giftedness, and how do we develop it? A twenty-five year perspective. *Journal for the Education of the Gifted, 23*(1), 3–54.

Renzulli, J. S. (2002). Emerging conceptions of giftedness: Building a bridge to the new century. *Exceptionality, 10*(2), 67–75.

Renzulli, J. S. (2011). Kappan classic: What makes giftedness?: Reexamining a definition. *Phi Delta Kappan, 92*(8), 81–88.

Renzulli, J. S., & Reis, S. M. (1991). The reform movement and the quiet crisis in gifted education. *Gifted Child Quarterly, 35,* 26–35.

Renzulli, J. S., & Reis, S. M. (2004). Curriculum compacting: A research-based differentiation strategy for culturally diverse talented students. In D. Boothe & J. C. Stanley (Eds.), *In the eyes of the beholder: Critical issues for diversity in gifted education* (pp. 87–100). Waco, TX: Prufrock Press.

Resing, W. C. M., & Tunteler, E. (2007). Children becoming more intelligent: Can the Flynn effect be generalized to other child intelligence tests? *International Journal of Testing, 7*(2), 191–208.

Rindermann, H., & Baumeister, A. E. E. (2015). Parents' SES vs. parental educational behavior and children's development: A reanalysis of the Hart and Risley study. *Learning and Individual Differences, 37,* 133–138.

Robinson, J. P., & Lubienski, S. T. (2011). The development of gender achievement gaps in mathematics and reading during elementary and middle school examining direct cognitive assessments and teacher ratings. *American Educational Research Journal, 48,* 268–302.

Rogers, K. B. (1993). Grouping the gifted and talented: Questions and answers. *Roeper Review, 16,* 8–12.

Roid, G. (2003). *Stanford-Binet Intelligence Scales, fifth edition.* Itasca, IL: Riverside Publishing.

Rosenthal, R., & Jacobson, L. (1968). *Pygmalion in the classroom: Teacher expectation and pupils' intellectual development.* New York, NY: Holt, Rinehart & Winston.

Rushton, J., & Jensen, A. (2005). Thirty years of research on race differences in cognitive ability. *Psychology, Public Policy, and Law, 11,* 235–294.

Sadker, M., Sadker, D., & Klein, S. (1991). The issue of gender in elementary and secondary education. In G. Grant (Ed.), *Review of research in education* (pp. 269–334). Washington, DC: American Educational Research Association.

Schmader, T., & Johns, M. (2003). Converging evidence that stereotype threat reduces working memory capacity. *Journal of Personality and Social Psychology, 85,* 440–452.

Schmidt, W. H., McKnight, C. C., & Raizen, S. A. (2002). *A splintered vision: An investigation of U.S. science and mathematics education.* Rotterdam, the Netherlands: Springer.

Schoon, I., Jones, E., Cheng, H., & Maughan, B. (2012). Family hardship, family instability, and cognitive development. *Journal of Epidemiology and Community Health, 66,* 716–722.

Silverman, I., Choi, J., & Peters, M. (2007). The hunter-gatherer theory of sex differences in spatial abilities: Data from 40 countries. *Archives of Sexual Behavior, 36,* 261–268.

Spearman, C. E. (1904). General intelligence objectively determined and measured. *American Journal of Psychology, 15,* 201–293.

Spearman, C. E. (1927). The nature of "intelligence" and the principles of cognition (2nd ed.). London, UK: Macmillan.

Spencer, S. J., Steele, C. M., & Quinn, D. M. (1999). Stereotype threat and women's math performance. *Journal of Experimental Social Psychology, 35,* 4–28.

Steele, C. M. (1997). A threat is in the air: How stereotypes shape intellectual identity and performance. *American Psychologist, 52,* 613–629.

Steele, C. M., & Aronson, J. (1995). Stereotype threat and the intellectual test performance of African Americans. *Journal of Personality and Social Psychology, 69,* 797–811.

Steiner, H. H., & Carr, M. (2003). Cognitive development in gifted children: Toward a more precise understanding of emerging differences in intelligence. *Educational Psychology Review, 15*(3), 215–246.

Stemler, S. E., Grigorenko, E. L., Jarvin, L., & Sternberg, R. J. (2006). Using the theory of successful intelligence as a basis for augmenting AP exams in psychology and statistics. *Contemporary Educational Psychology, 31,* 344–376.

Stemler, S. E., Sternberg, R. J., Grigorenko, E. L., Jarvin, L., & Sharpes, K. (2009). Using the theory of successful intelligence as a framework for developing assessments in AP physics. *Contemporary Educational Psychology, 34,* 195–209.

Sternberg, R. J. (1996). *Successful intelligence.* New York, NY: Simon & Schuster.

Sternberg, R. J. (1997). What does it mean to be smart? *Educational Leadership, 54*(6), 20–24.

Sternberg, R. J. (1998). Principles of teaching for successful intelligence. *Educational Psychologist, 33*(2–3), 65–72.

Sternberg, R. J. (1999). The theory of successful intelligence. *Review of General Psychology, 3*(4), 292–316.

Sternberg, R. J. (Ed.). (2000). *Handbook of intelligence.* New York, NY: Cambridge University Press.

Sternberg, R. J. (2002). Individual differences in cognitive development. In U. Goswami (Ed.), *Blackwell handbook of childhood cognitive development* (pp. 600–619). Malden, MA: Blackwell.

Sternberg, R. J. (2003). Contemporary theories of intelligence. In W. M. Reynolds & G. E. Miller (Eds.), *Handbook of psychology: Educational psychology* (Vol. 7, pp. 23–45). New York, NY: Wiley.

Sternberg, R. J. (2004). Culture and intelligence. *American Psychologist, 59*(5), 325–338.

Sternberg, R. J. (2006). How can we simultaneously enhance both academic excellence and diversity? *College and University, 81*(1), 17–23.

Sternberg, R. J. (2007). Who are the bright children? The cultural context of being and acting intelligent. *Educational Researcher, 36*(3), 148–155.

Sternberg, R. J. (2010a). WICS: A new model for cognitive education. *Journal of Cognitive Education and Psychology, 9*(1), 36–47.

Sternberg, R. J. (2010b). Assessment of gifted students for identification purposes: New techniques for a new millennium. *Learning and Individual Differences, 20,* 327–336.

Sternberg, R. J. (2014). Teaching about the nature of intelligence. *Intelligence, 42*(1), 176–179.

Sternberg, R. J., & Coffin, L. A. (2010). Kaleidoscope: Admitting and developing new leaders for a changing world. *New England Journal of Higher Education, 24*(3), 12–13.

Sternberg, R. J., Conway, B. E., Ketron, J. L., & Bernstein, M. (1981). People's conceptions of intelligence. *Journal of Personality and Social Psychology, 41,* 37–55.

Sternberg, R. J., & Grigorenko, E. L. (2004). Successful intelligence in the classroom. *Theory Into Practice, 43,* 274–280.

Sternberg, R. J., Grigorenko, E. L., Ferrari, M., & Clinkenbeard, P. (1999). A triarchic analysis of an aptitude-treatment interaction. *European Journal of Psychological Assessment, 15*(1), 1–11.

Sternberg, R. J., Grigorenko, E. L., & Zhang, L.-F. (2008). Styles of learning and thinking matter in instruction and assessment. *Perspectives on Psychological Science, 3*(6), 486–506.

Sternberg, R. J., & Kaufman, J. C. (1998). Human abilities. *Annual Review of Psychology, 49,* 479–502.

Sternberg, R. J., Torff, B., & Grigorenko, E. L. (1998a). Teaching for successful intelligence raises school achievement. *Phi Delta Kappan, 79,* 667–669.

Sternberg, R. J., Torff, B., & Grigorenko, E. L. (1998b). Teaching triarchically improves school achievement. *Journal of Educational Psychology, 90,* 1–11.

Subotnik, R. F., Olszewski-Kubilius, P., & Worrell, F. C. (2011). Rethinking giftedness and gifted education: A proposed direction forward based on psychological science. *Psychological Science in the Public Interest, 12*(1), 3–54.

Subotnik, R. F., Olszewski-Kubilius, P., & Worrell, F. C. (2012). A proposed direction forward for gifted education based on psychological science. *Gifted Child Quarterly, 56*(4), 176–188.

Suzuki, L. A., & Valencia, R. R. (1997). Race-ethnicity and measured intelligence. *American Psychologist, 52*(10), 1103–1114.

Thurstone, L. L. (1938). *Primary mental abilities.* Chicago, IL: The University of Chicago Press.

Thurstone, L. L. (1947). *Multiple-factor analysis.* Chicago, IL: The University of Chicago Press.

Titze, C., Jansen, P., & Heil, M. (2010). Mental rotation performance in fourth graders: No effects of gender beliefs (yet?). *Learning and Individual Differences, 20,* 459–463.

Uttal, D. H., Meadow, N. G., Tipton, E., Hand, L. L., Alden, A. R., Warren, C., & Newcombe, N. S. (2013). The malleability of spatial skills: A meta-analysis of training studies. *Psychological Bulletin, 139,* 352–402.

VanTassel-Baska, J. (1998). *Excellence in educating gifted and talented learners* (3rd ed.). Denver, CO: Love Publishing.

VanTassel-Baska, J. (2015). Theories of giftedness: Reflections on James Gallagher's work. *Journal for the Education of the Gifted, 38*(1), 18–23.

VanTassel-Baska, J., Feng, A. X., Swanson, J. D., Quek, C., & Chandler, K. (2009). Academic and affective profiles of low-income, minority, twice exceptional gifted learners: The role of gifted program membership in enhancing self. *Journal of Advanced Academics, 20*(4), 702–739.

Voyer D. (2011). Time limits and gender differences on paper-and-pencil tests of mental rotation: A meta-analysis. *Psychonomic Bulletin Review, 18,* 267–277.

Vygotsky, L. S. (1978). *Mind in society: The development of higher mental process.* Cambridge, MA: Harvard University Press.

Wai, J., Cacchio, M., Putallaz, M., & Makel, M. C. (2010). Sex differences in the right tail of cognitive abilities: A 30-year examination. *Intelligence, 38,* 412–423.

Waterhouse, L. (2006). Multiple intelligences, the Mozart effect, and emotional intelligence: A critical review. *Educational Psychologist, 41*(4), 207–225.

Wechsler, D. (2014). *WISC-V administration and scoring manual.* Bloomington, MN: Pearson.

White, K. R. (1982). The relation between socioeconomic status and academic achievement. *Psychological Bulletin, 91,* 461–481.

Wigfield, A., & Cambria, J. (2010a). Expectancy-value theory: Retrospective and prospective. In T. C. Urdan & S. A. Karabenick (Eds.), *The decade ahead: Theoretical perspectives on motivation and achievement* (pp. 35–70). Bingley, UK: Emerald Group.

Wigfield, A., Eccles, J. S., Schieffele, U., Roeser, R. W., & Davis-Kean, P. (2006). Development of achievement motivation. In W. Damon & R. M. Lerner (Eds.), *Handbook of child psychology* (pp. 933–1002). Hoboken, NJ: Wiley.

Winebrenner, S., & Brulles, D. (2008). *The cluster grouping handbook: A schoolwide model.* Minneapolis, MN: Free Spirit.

Winner, E. (1996). *Gifted children: Myths and realities.* New York, NY: Basic Books.

Winner, E. (2000). The origins and ends of giftedness. *American Psychologist, 55*(1), 159–169.

Worrell, F. C. (2009). What does gifted mean? Personal and social identity perspectives on giftedness in adolescence. In F. D. Horowitz, R. F. Subotnik, & D. J. Matthews (Eds.), The development of giftedness and talent across the lifespan (pp. 131–152). Washington, DC: American Psychological Association.

Zigler, E., & Berman, W. (1983). Discerning the future of early childhood intervention. *American Psychologist, 38,* 894–906.

Module 21

Aaron, P. G., Joshi, M., Gooden, R., & Bentum, K. (2008). Diagnosis and treatment of reading disabilities based on the component model of reading: An alternative to the discrepancy model of LD. *Journal of Learning Disabilities, 41,* 67–84.

Abbott, M., & Wills, H. (2012). Improving the upside-down response-to-intervention triangle with a systematic, effective elementary school reading team. *Preventing School Failure: Alternative Education for Children and Youth, 56*(1), 37–46.

Abbott, M., Wills, H. P., Kamps, D., Greenwood, C. R., Kaufman, J., & Filingim, D. (2008). The process of implementing a reading and behavior three-tier model: A case study in a Midwest elementary school. In C. R. Greenwood, R. Horner, T. Kratochwill, & I. Oxaal (Eds.), *Elementary school-wide prevention models: Real models and real lessons learned* (pp. 215–265). New York, NY: Guilford Press.

Acton, H. M., & Zabartany, L. (1988). Interaction and performance within groups: Effects on handicapped and nonhandicapped students' attitudes toward their mildly mentally retarded peers. *American Journal of Mental Retardation, 93,* 16–23.

Adams, M. J. (1990). *Beginning to read: Thinking and learning about print.* Cambridge, MA: The MIT Press.

Alfassi, M., Weiss, I., & Lifshitz, H. (2009). The efficacy of reciprocal teaching in fostering the reading literacy of students with intellectual disabilities. *European Journal of Special Needs Education, 24*(3), 291–305.

Al Otaiba, S., Connor, C. M., Folsom, J. S., Wanzek, J., Greulich, L., Schatschneider, C., & Wagner, R. K. (2014). To wait in tier 1 or intervene immediately: A randomized experiment examining first-grade response to intervention in reading. *Exceptional Children, 81*(1), 11–27.

Al Otaiba, S., & Fuchs, D. (2002). Characteristics of children who are unresponsive to early literacy intervention: A review of the literature. *Remedial and Special Education, 23,* 300–316.

Al Otaiba, S., & Fuchs, D. (2006). Who are the young children for whom best practices in reading are ineffective? An experimental and longitudinal study. *Journal of Learning Disabilities, 39,* 414–431.

American Psychiatric Association. (2014). *Diagnostic and statistical manual of mental disorders, fifth edition.* Washington, DC: Author.

Andersson, U. (2010). Skill development in different components of arithmetic and basic cognitive functions: Findings from a 3-year longitudinal study of children with different types of learning difficulties. *Journal of Educational Psychology, 102*(1), 115–134.

Ashman, A. (1998). Students with intellectual disabilities. In A. Ashman & J. Elkins (Eds.), *Educating children with special needs* (3rd ed.). Englewood Cliffs, NJ: Prentice Hall.

Axtell, P. K., McCallum, R. S., & Bell, S. M. (2009). Developing math automaticity using a classwide fluency building procedure for middle school students: A preliminary study. *Psychology in the Schools, 46*(6), 526–538.

Bartelet, D., Ansari, D., Vaessen, A., & Blomert, L. (2014). Cognitive subtypes of mathematics learning difficulties in primary education. *Research in Developmental Disabilities, 35*(3), 657–670.

Beach, K. D., & O'Connor, R. E. (2015). Early response-to-intervention measures and criteria as predictors of reading disability in the beginning of third grade. *Journal of Learning Disabilities, 48*(2), 196–223.

Berkeley, S., Bender, W. N., Peaster, L. G., & Saunders, L. (2009). Implementation of response to intervention: A snapshot of progress. *Journal of Learning Disabilities, 42*(1), 86–95.

Blanchett, W. (2006). Disproportionate representation of African American students in special education: Acknowledging the role of white privilege and racism. *Educational Researcher, 35*(6), 24–28.

Brown, J. S., & Burton, R. R. (1978). Diagnostic models for procedural bugs in basic mathematical skills. *Cognitive Science, 2*(2), 155–192.

Butterworth, B. (2005). The development of arithmetical abilities. *Journal of Child Psychology and Psychiatry, 46,* 3–18.

Cain, K. (2010). *Reading development and difficulties.* Oxford, UK: Wiley-Blackwell.

Cakiroglu, O. (2015). Response to intervention : Early identification of students with learning disabilities. *International Journal of Early Childhood Special Education, 7*(1), 170–182.

Callinan, S., Cunningham, E., & Theiler, S. (2013). Revisiting discrepancy theory in learning disabilities: What went wrong and why we should go back. *Australian Journal of Guidance & Counselling, 23*(1), 1–17.

Carreker, S., & Joshi, M. (2010). Response to intervention: Are the emperor's clothes really new? *Psicothema, 22*(4), 943–948.

Caspi, A., Taylor, A., Moffitt, T. E., & Plomin, R. (2000). Neighborhood deprivation affects childrens' mental health: Environmental risks identified in a genetic design. *Psychological Science, 11,* 338–342.

Cates, G. L., Blum, C., & Swerdlik. M. E. (2011). *Effective RTI training and practice: Helping school and district teams improve academic performance and social behavior.* Champaign, IL: Research Press.

Chan, B. M., & Ho, C. S. (2010). The cognitive profile of Chinese children with mathematics difficulties. *Journal of Experimental Child Psychology, 107,* 260–279.

Chan, L., & Dally, K. (2001). Learning disabilities: Literacy and numeracy development. *Australian Journal of Learning Disabilities, 6*(1), 12–19.

Cisero, C. A., Royer, J. M., Marchant, H. G., & Jackson, S. J. (1997). Can the Computer-Based Academic Assessment System (CAAS) be used to diagnose reading disability in college students? *Journal of Educational Psychology, 89*(4), 599–620.

Clarke, P., Snowling, M. J., Truelove, E., & Hulme, C. (2010). Ameliorating children's reading comprehension difficulties: A randomised controlled trial. *Psychological Science, 21,* 1106–1116.

Compton, D. L., & Carlisle, J. F. (1994). Speed of word recognition as a distinguishing characteristic of reading disabilities. *Educational Psychology Review, 6*(2), 115–140.

Compton, D. L., Gilbert, J. K., Jenkins, J. R., Fuchs, D., Fuchs, L. S., Cho, E., . . . Bouton, B. (2012). Accelerating chronically unresponsive children to tier 3 instruction: What level of data is necessary to ensure selection accuracy? *Journal of Learning Disabilities, 45*(3), 204–216.

Compton, D. L., Miller, A. C., Elleman, A. M., & Steacy, L. M. (2014). Have we forsaken reading theory in the name of "quick fix" interventions for children with reading disability? *Scientific Studies of Reading, 18*(1), 55–73.

Denton, C. A. (2012). Response to intervention for reading difficulties in the primary grades: Some answers and lingering questions. *Journal of Learning Disabilities, 45,* 232–243.

Duff, F. J., & Clarke, P. J. (2011). Practitioner review: Reading disorders: What are the effective interventions and how should they be implemented and evaluated? *Journal of Child Psychology and Psychiatry and Allied Disciplines, 52*(1), 3–12.

Elleman, A. M., Lindo, E. J., Morphy, P., & Compton, D. L. (2009). The impact of vocabulary instruction on passage-level comprehension of school-age children: A meta-analysis. *Journal of Research on Educational Effectiveness, 2,* 1–44.

Evans, G. W., & English, K. (2002). The environment of poverty: Multiple stressor exposure, psychophysiological stress, and socioemotional adjustment. *Child Development, 73,* 1238–1248.

Finch, M. E. H. (2012). Special considerations with response to intervention and instruction for students with diverse backgrounds. *Psychology in the Schools, 49*(3), 285–296.

Fleischner, J. E. (1994). Diagnosis and assessment of mathematics learning disabilities. In G. R. Lyon (Ed.), *Frames of reference for the assessment of learning disabilities: New views on measurement issues* (pp. 459–472). Baltimore, MD: Brookes.

Fletcher, J. M., Barth, A. E., & Stuebing, K. K. (2011). A response to intervention (RTI) approach to SLD identification. In D. P. Flanagan & V. C. Alfonso (Eds.), *Essentials of specific learning disability and identification* (pp. 115–144). Hoboken, NJ: Wiley.

Fletcher, J. M., Lyon, G. R., Fuchs, L. S., & Barnes, M. A. (2007). *Learning disabilities: From identification to intervention.* New York, NY: Guilford Press.

Foorman, B. R., Francis, D. J., Winikates, P. M., Schatschneider, C., & Fletcher, J. M. (1997). Early interventions for children with reading disabilities. *Scientific Studies of Reading, 1*(3), 255–276.

Fuchs, D., & Deshler, D. D. (2007). What we need to know about responsiveness to intervention (and shouldn't be afraid to ask). *Learning Disabilities Research and Practice, 22*(2), 129–136.

Fuchs, D., & Fuchs, L.S. (2006). Introduction to response to intervention: What, why and how valid is it? *Reading Research Quarterly, 41,* 93–99.

Fuchs, L. S., & Fuchs, D. (2007). A model for implementing responsiveness to intervention. *Teaching Exceptional Children, 39,* 14–20.

Garnett, K. (1992). Developing fluency with basic number facts: Intervention for students with learning disabilities. *Learning Disabilities Research & Practice, 7,* 210–216.

Geary, D. (1990). A componential analysis of an early learning deficit in mathematics. *Journal of Experimental Child Psychology, 33,* 386–404.

Geary, D. C. (1993). Mathematical disabilities: Cognitive, neuropsychological, and genetic components. *Psychological Bulletin, 114,* 345–362.

Geary, D. C. (1994). *Children's mathematical development: Research and practical applications.* Washington, DC: American Psychological Association.

Geary, D. C. (2004). Mathematics and learning disabilities. *Journal of Learning Disabilities, 37*(1), 4–15.

Geary, D. C. (2010). Mathematical disabilities: Reflections on cognitive, neuropsychological, and genetic components. *Learning and Individual Differences, 20,* 130–133.

Geary, D. C. (2011). Consequences, characteristics, and causes of mathematical learning disabilities and persistent low achievement in mathematics. *Journal of Developmental Behavioral Pediatrics, 32*(3), 250–263.

Geary, D. C. (2013). Early foundations for mathematics learning and their relations to learning disabilities. *Current Directions in Psychological Science, 22*(1), 23–27.

Geary D. C., Hoard, M. K., Byrd-Craven, J., Nugent, L., & Numtee, C. (2007). Cognitive mechanisms underlying achievement deficits in children with mathematical learning disability. *Child Development, 78,* 1343–1359.

Geary, D. C., Hoard, M. K., Nugent, L., & Bailey, D. H. (2012). Mathematical cognition deficits in children with learning disabilities and persistent low achievement: A five-year prospective study. *Journal of Educational Psychology, 104*(1), 206–223.

Gersten, R., Chard, D. J., Jayanthi, M., Baker, S. K., Morphy, P., & Flojo, J. (2009). Mathematics instruction for students with learning disabilities: A meta-analysis of instructional components. *Review of Educational Research, 79*(3), 1202–1242.

Gersten, R., Fuchs, L. S., Williams, J. P., & Baker, S. (2001). Teaching reading comprehension strategies to students with learning disabilities: A review of research. *Review of Educational Research, 71,* 279–320.

Gordon, S. (2006). Making sense of the inclusion debate under IDEA. *Brigham Young University Education & Law Journal, 1,* 189–225.

Halberda J., Mazzocco, M. M. M., & Feigenson, L. (2008). Individual differences in non-verbal number acuity correlate with math achievement. *Nature, 455,* 665–668.

Hallahan, D. P., & Kauffman. J. (2000). *Exceptional learners* (8th ed.). Boston, MA: Allyn & Bacon.

Hale, J. B., Wycoff, K. L., & Fiorello, C. A. (2011). RTI and cognitive hypothesis testing for identification and intervention of specific learning disabilities. In D. P. Flanagan & V. C. Alfonso (Eds.), *Essentials of specific learning disability identification* (pp. 173–201). Hoboken, NJ: Wiley.

Hauerwas, L. B., Brown, R., & Scott, A. M. Y. N. (2013). Specific learning disability and response to intervention: State-level guidance. *Exceptional Children, 80*(I), 101–120.

Hiebert, E. H. (2003). *The role of text in developing fluency: A comparison of two interventions.* Ann Arbor, MI: Center for the Improvement of Early Reading Achievement.

Hiebert, E. H., & Fisher, E. W. (2002, April). *Text matters in developing reading fluency.* Paper presented at the annual convention of the International Reading Association, San Francisco, CA.

Hosp, J. L., & Reschly, D. (2004). Disproportionate representation of minority students in special education: Academic, demographic, and economic predictors. *Exceptional Children, 70*(2), 185–199.

Iuculano, T., Tang, J., Hall, C. W. B., & Butterworth, B. (2008). Core information processing deficits in developmental dyscalculia and low numeracy. *Developmental Science, 11,* 669–680.

Johnson, D. W., & Johnson, R. T. (2009). An educational psychology success story: Social interdependence theory and cooperative learning. *Educational Researcher, 38*(5), 365–379.

Jordan, N. C. (1995). Clinical assessment of early mathematics disabilities: Adding up the research findings. *Learning Disabilities Research & Practice, 10*(1), 59–69.

Jordan N. C., Hanich, L. B., & Kaplan, D. (2003a). Arithmetic fact mastery in young children: A longitudinal investigation. *Journal of Experimental Child Psychology, 85,* 103–119.

Jordan, N. C., Hanich, L. B., & Kaplan, D. (2003b). A longitudinal study of mathematical competencies in children with specific mathematics difficulties versus children with comorbid mathematics and reading difficulties. *Child Development, 74,* 834–850.

Jordan, N. C., & Montani, T. O. (1997). Cognitive arithmetic and problem solving: A comparison of children with specific and general mathematics difficulties. *Journal of Learning Disabilities, 30*(6), 624–634.

Kavale, K. (2005). Identifying specific learning disability: Is responsiveness to intervention the answer? *Journal of Learning Disabilities, 38,* 553–562.

Kavale, K. A., Kauffman, A. S., Bachmeier, R. J., & LeFevers, G. B. (2008). Response-to-intervention: Separating the rhetoric of self-congratulation from the reality of specific learning disability identification. *Learning Disabilities Quarterly, 31,* 135–150.

Kim, A., Vaughn, S., Wanzek, J., & Wei, S. (2004). Graphic organizers and their effects on reading comprehension of students with learning disabilities: A synthesis of research. *Journal of Learning Disabilities, 37,* 105–118.

Klingner, J. K., Vaughn, S., & Boardman, A. (2007). *Teaching reading comprehension to students with learning difficulties: What works for special-needs learners.* New York, NY: Guilford Press.

Kroeger, L. A., Brown, R. D., & O'Brien, B. A. (2012). Connecting neuroscience, cognitive, and educational theories and research to practice: A review of mathematics intervention programs. *Early Education & Development, 23*(1), 37–58.

Kroesbergen, E. H., & Van Luit, J. E. H. (2005). Constructivist mathematics education for students with mild mental retardation. *European Journal of Special Needs Education, 27*(1), 107–116.

Kuhn, M. R., & Stahl, S. A. (2003). Fluency: A review of developmental and remedial practices. *Journal of Educational Psychology, 95,* 3–21.

Lam, E. A., & McMaster, K. L. (2014). Predictors of responsiveness to early literacy intervention: A 10-year update. *Learning Disability Quarterly, 37*(3), 134–147.

Lipson, M. Y., Chomsky-Higgins, P., & Kanfer, J. (2011). Diagnosis: The missing ingredient in RTI assessment. *Reading Teacher, 65*(3), 204–208.

Lyon, R., Shaywitz, S. E., & Shaywitz, B. A. (2003). A definition of dyslexia. *Annals of Dyslexia, 53,* 1–14.

MacMillan, D. L., & Siperstein, G. N. (2002). Learning disabilities as operationally defined in schools. In R. Bradley, L. Danielson, & D. P. Hallahan (Eds.), *Identification of learning disabilities: Research to practice* (pp. 287–333). Mahwah, NJ: Lawrence Erlbaum.

Madaus, J. W., & Shaw, S. F. (2006). The impact of the IDEA 2004 on transition to college for students with learning disabilities. *Learning Disabilities Research and Practice, 21*(4), 273–281.

Mastropieri, M. A., & Scruggs, T. E. (1984). Generalization: Five effective strategies. *Academic Therapy, 19*(4), 427–431.

Mastropieri, M. A., & Scruggs, T. E. (2005). Feasibility and consequences of response to intervention: Examination of the issues and scientific evidence as a model for the identification of individuals with learning disabilities. *Journal of Learning Disabilities, 38,* 525–531.

Mazzocco, M. M. M., Devlin, K. T., & McKenney, S. J. (2008). Is it a fact? Timed arithmetic performance of children with mathematical learning disabilities (MLD) varies as a function of how MLD is defined. *Developmental Neuropsychology, 33*(3), 318–344.

Mazzocco, M. M. M., Feigenson, L., & Halberda, J. (2011). Impaired acuity of the approximate number system underlies mathematical learning disability (dyscalculia). *Child Development, 82*(4), 1224–1237.

McCandliss, B., Beck, I. L., Sandak, R., & Perfetti, C. (2003). Focusing attention on decoding for children with poor reading skills: Design and preliminary tests of the word building intervention. *Scientific Studies of Reading, 7,* 75–104.

McGee, A., & Johnson, H. (2003). The effect of inference training on skilled and less skilled comprehenders. *Educational Psychology, 23,* 49–59.

McKinney, E., Bartholomew, C., & Gray, L. (2010). RTI and SWPBIS: Confronting the problem of disproportionality. *NASP Communiqué, 38*(6), 1–5.

Meese, R. L. (2001). *Teaching learners with mild disabilities: Integrating research and practice* (2nd ed.). Belmont, CA: Wadsworth-Thomson.

Mellard, D., McKnight, M., & Jordan, J. (2010). RTI tier structures and instructional intensity. *Learning Disabilities Research & Practice, 25*(4), 217–225.

Mercer, C. D., Jordan, L., Allsopp, D. H., & Mercer, A. R. (1996). Learning disabilities definitions and criteria used by state education departments. *Learning Disability Quarterly, 19,* 217–232.

Moll, K., Kunze, S., Neuhoff, N., Bruder, J., & Schulte-Körne, G. (2014). Specific learning disorder: Prevalence and gender differences. *PLoS One, 9,* e103537.

National Institute of Child Health and Human Development. (2000). *Report of the National Reading Panel* (NIH Publication No. 00–4754). Washington, DC: Government Printing Office.

National Research Council. (2001). *Adding it up: Helping children learn mathematics* (J. Kilpatrick, J. Swafford, & B. Findell, Eds.). Washington, DC: The National Academies Press.

O'Connor, R., & Fuchs, L. S. (2013). Responsiveness to intervention in the elementary grades: Implications for early childhood education. In V. Buysse, E. Peisner-Feinberg, & J. Cantler (Eds.), *Handbook of response to intervention (RTI) in early childhood education* (pp. 41–56). Baltimore, MD: Brookes.

Ostad, S. A. (1998). Developmental differences in solving arithmetic word problems and simple number-fact problems: A comparison of mathematically normal and mathematically disabled children. *Mathematical Cognition, 4,* 1–19.

Parkhurst, J., Skinner, C. H., Yaw, J., Poncy, B., Adcock, W., & Luna, E. (2010). Efficient class-wide remediation: Using technology to identify idiosyncratic math facts for additional automaticity drills. *International Journal of Behavioral Consultation and Therapy, 6*(2), 111–124.

Perfetti, C. A. (1985). *Reading ability.* New York, NY: Oxford University Press.

Perfetti, C. A. (1992). The representation problem in reading acquisition. In P. B. Gough, L. Ehri, & R. Treiman (Eds.), *Reading acquisition* (pp. 145–174). Hillsdale, NJ: Lawrence Erlbaum.

Piazza, M., Facoetti, A., Trussardi, A. N., Berteletti, I., Conte, S., Lucangeli, D., . . . Zorzi, M. (2010). Developmental trajectory of number acuity reveals a severe impairment in developmental dyscalculia. *Cognition, 116,* 33–41.

Poncy, B., Fontenelle, S. F. IV, & Skinner, C. H. (2013). Using detect, practice, and repair (DPR) to differentiate and individualize math fact instruction in a class-wide setting. *Journal of Behavioral Education, 22,* 211–228.

Poncy, B. C., Skinner, C. H., & Axtell, P. K. (2010). An investigation of detect, practice, and repair to remedy math-fact deficits in a group of third-grade students. *Psychology in the Schools, 47*(4), 342–352.

Poncy, B. C., Skinner, C. H., & O'Mara, T. (2006). Detect, practice, and repair: The effects of a classwide intervention on elementary students' math-fact fluency. *Journal of Evidence-Based Practices for Schools, 7*(1), 47–68.

Pressley, M., Gaskins, I. W., & Fingeret, L. (2006). Instruction and development of reading fluency in struggling readers. In S. J. Samuels & A. E. Farstrup (Eds.), *What research has to say about fluency instruction* (pp. 47–69). Newark, DE: International Reading Association.

Price, G., & Ansari, D. (2013). Dyscalculia: Characteristics, causes, and treatments. *Numeracy, 6*(1), 1–16.

Raghubar, K., Cirino, P., Barnes, M., Ewing-Cobbs, L., Fletcher, J., & Fuchs, L. (2009). Errors in multi-digit arithmetic and behavioral inattention in children with math difficulties. *Journal of Learning Disabilities, 42,* 356–371.

Räsänen, P., Salminen, J., Wilson, A. J., Aunio, P., & Dehaene, S. (2009). Computer-assisted intervention for children with low numeracy skills. *Cognitive Development, 24,* 450–472.

Reddy, G. L., Ramar, R., & Kusama, A. (2000). *Education of children with special needs.* New Delhi, India: Discovery Publishing.

Reid, D. K., & Knight, M. G. (2006). Disability justifies exclusion of minority students: A critical history grounded in disability studies. *Educational Researcher, 35*(6), 18–23.

Reschly, D. J., & Hosp, J. L., (2004). State SLD policies and practices. *Learning Disability Quarterly, 27,* 197–213.

Reynolds, C. R. (2008). RTI, neuroscience, and sense: Chaos in the diagnosis and treatment of learning disabilities. In E. Fletcher-Janzen & C. R. Reynolds (Eds.), *Neuropsychological perspectives on learning disabilities in the era of RTI* (pp. 14–27). Hoboken, NY: John Wiley & Sons.

Reynolds, C. R., & Shaywitz, S. E. (2009). Response to intervention: Ready or not? Or, from wait-to-fail to watch-them-fail. *School Psychology Quarterly, 24,* 130–145.

Roberts, G., Torgesen, J. K., Boardman, A., & Scammacca, N. (2007). Evidence-based strategies for reading instruction of older students with learning disabilities. *Learning*

Disabilities Research & Practice, 23(2), 63–69.

Robinson, C., Menchetti, B., & Torgesen, J. (2002). Toward a two-factor theory of one type of mathematics disabilities. *Learning Disabilities Research & Practice, 17,* 81–89.

Roid, G. (2003). *Stanford-Binet Intelligence Scales, fifth edition.* Itasca, IL: Riverside Publishing.

Rosenshine, B. (1979). Content, time, and direct instruction. In P. Peterson & H. Wahlberg (Eds.), *Research on teaching: Concepts, findings, and implications* (pp. 28–56). Berkeley, CA: McCutchan.

Rosenshine, B. (1988). Explicit teaching. In D. Berliner & B. Rosenshine (Eds.), *Talks to teachers* (pp. 75–92). New York, NY: Random House.

Rosenshine, B., & Meister, C. (1994). Reciprocal teaching: A review of the research. *Review of Educational Research, 64,* 479–530.

Rosenshine, B., & Stevens, R. (1986). Teaching functions. In M. Wittrock (Ed.), *Handbook of research on teaching* (3rd ed., pp. 376–391). New York, NY: Macmillan.

Rousselle, L., & Noël, M.-P. (2007). Basic numerical skills in children with mathematical learning disabilities: A comparison of symbolic vs. non-symbolic number magnitude processing. *Cognition, 102,* 361–395.

Royer, J. M. (1997). A cognitive perspective on the assessment, diagnosis, and remediation of reading skills. In G. Phye (Ed.), *Handbook of academic learning* (pp. 199–234). New York, NY: Academic Press.

Royer, J. M., & Sinatra, G. M. (1994). A cognitive theoretical approach to reading diagnostics. *Educational Psychology Review, 6*(2), 81–113.

Royer, J. M., & Tronsky, L. N. (1998). Addition practice with math disabled students improves subtraction and multiplication performance. *Advances in Learning and Behavioral Disabilities, 12,* 185–217.

Rubinsten, O., & Henik, A. (2009). Developmental dyscalculia: Heterogeneity might not mean different mechanisms. *Trends in Cognitive Sciences, 13,* 92–99.

Russell, R. L., & Ginsburg, H. P. (1984). Cognitive analysis of children's mathematical difficulties. *Cognition and Instruction, 1,* 217–244.

Salend, D., & Sonnenschein, P. (1989). Validating the effectiveness of a cooperative learning strategy through direct observation. *Journal of School Psychology, 27*(1), 47–58.

Schalock, R. L., Borthwick-Duffy, S. A., Bradley, V. J., Buntinx, W. H. E., Coulter, D. L., Craig, E. M., . . .

Yeager, M. H. (2010). *Intellectual disability: Definition, classification, and systems of supports* (11th ed.). Washington, DC: American Association on Intellectual & Developmental Disabilities.

Scott, A. N., Hauerwas, L. B., & Brown, R. D. (2014). State policy and guidance for identifying learning disabilities in culturally and linguistically diverse students. *Learning Disability Quarterly, 37*(3), 172–185.

Semrud-Clikeman, M. (2005). Neuropsychological aspects for evaluating learning disabilities. *Journal of Learning Disabilities, 38,* 563–568.

Shifrer, D., Muller, C., & Callahan, R. (2011). Disproportionality and learning disabilities: Parsing apart race, socioeconomic status, and language. *Journal of Learning Disabilities, 44*(3), 246–257.

Snowling, M. J., & Hulme, C. (2013). Children's reading impairments: From theory to practice. *Japanese Psychological Research, 55*(2), 186–202.

Sparrow, S. S., Cicchetti, D. V., & Balla, D. A. (2005). *Vineland Adaptive Behavior Scales, second edition.* San Antonio, TX: Pearson Assessments.

Stahl, S. (1998). Teaching children with reading problems to decode: Phonics and "not-phonics" instruction. *Reading & Writing Quarterly: Overcoming Learning Difficulties, 14*(2), 165–188.

Stanovich, K. E. (1990). Concepts in developmental theories of reading skill: Cognitive resources, automaticity, and modularity. *Developmental Review, 10,* 72–100.

Stanovich, K. E. (1991a). Conceptual and empirical problems with discrepancy definitions of reading disability. *Learning Disability Quarterly, 14,* 269–280.

Stanovich, K. E. (1991b). Discrepancy definitions of reading disability: Has intelligence led us astray? *Reading Research Quarterly, 26*(1), 7–29.

Stanovich, K. E. (1993). A model for studies of reading disability. *Developmental Review, 13,* 225–245.

Stanovich, K. E., & Siegel, L. S. (1994). Phenotypic performance profile of children with reading disabilities: A regression-based test of the phonological-core variable-difference model. *Journal of Educational Psychology, 86*(1), 24–53.

Stock, P., Desoete, A., & Roeyers, H. (2010). Detecting children with arithmetic disabilities from kindergarten: Evidence from a 3-year longitudinal study on the role of preparatory arithmetic abilities.

Journal of Learning Disabilities, 43, 250–268.

Stuebing, K. K., Barth, A., Cirino, P. T., Francis, D. J., & Fletcher, J. M. (2008). A response to the recent reanalyses of the national reading panel report: Effects of systematic phonics instruction are practically significant. *Journal of Educational Psychology, 100,* 123–134.

Taylor, R. L., Sternberg, L., & Richards, S. B. (1995). *Exceptional children: Integrating research and teaching* (2nd ed.). San Diego, CA: Singular Publishing.

Thornton, C. A., & Toohey, M. A. (1985). Basic math facts: Guidelines for teaching and learning. *Learning Disabilities Focus, 1*(1), 44–57.

Torgesen, J. K. (1998). Catch them before they fall: Identification and assessment to prevent reading failure in young children. *American Educator, 22*(1–2), 32–40.

Torgesen, J. K. (2000). Individual differences in response to early interventions in reading: The lingering problem of treatment resisters. *Learning Disabilities Research & Practice, 15*(1), 55–64.

Torgesen, J. K. (2005). Recent discoveries on remedial interventions for children with dyslexia. In M. J. Snowling & C. Hulme (Eds.), *The science of reading* (pp. 521–537). Oxford, UK: Blackwell.

Torgesen, J. K., Alexander, A. W., Wagner, R. K., Rashotte, C. A., Voeller, K. K. S., & Conway, T. (2001). Intensive remedial instruction for children with severe reading disabilities: Immediate and long-term outcomes from two instructional approaches. *Journal of Learning Disabilities, 34*(1), 33–58, 78.

Torgesen, J. K., Wagner, R. K., & Rashotte, C. A. (1997). Prevention and remediation of severe reading disabilities: Keeping the end in mind. *Scientific Studies of Reading, 1*(3), 217–234.

Torgesen, J. K., Wagner, R. K., Rashotte, C. A., Herron, J., & Lindamood, P. (2010). Computer-assisted instruction to prevent early reading difficulties in students at risk for dyslexia: Outcomes from two instructional programs. *Annals of Dyslexia, 60,* 40–56.

Torgesen, J. K., Wagner, R. K., Rashotte, C. A., Lindamood, P., Rose, E., Conway, T., & Garvan, C. (1999). Preventing reading failure in young children with phonological processing disabilities: Group and individual differences to instruction. *Journal of Educational Psychology, 91,* 579–593.

Turnbull, R., Turnbull, A., Shank, M., Smith, S., & Leal, D. (2002). *Exceptional lives: Special education in today's schools* (3rd ed.). Upper Saddle River, NJ: Prentice Hall.

U.S. Department of Education. (2009). *Twenty-eighth annual report to Congress on the implementation of the Individuals with Disabilities Education Act, 2006, vol. 1.* Office of Special Education and Rehabilitative Services. Washington, DC: U.S. Government Printing Office.

U.S. Department of Education. (2014). *Thirty-sixth annual report to Congress on the implementation of the Individuals with Disabilities Education Act, 2014, vol. 1.* Office of Special Education and Rehabilitative Services. Washington, DC: U.S. Government Printing Office.

Van Der Heyden, A. M., & Burns, M. (2010). *Essentials of response to intervention.* Hoboken, NJ: Wiley.

Vaughn, S., Linan-Thompson, S., & Hickman, P. (2003). Response to instruction as a means of identifying students with reading/learning disabilities. *Exceptional Children, 69,* 391–409.

Vellutino, F. R., Fletcher, J. M., Snowling, M. J., & Scanlon, D. M. (2004). Specific reading disability (dyslexia): What have we learned in the past four decades? *Journal of Child Psychology and Psychiatry, 45*(1), 2–40.

Volker, M. A., Lopata, C., & Cook-Cottone, C. (2006). Assessment of children with intellectual giftedness and reading disabilities. *Psychology in the Schools, 43*(8), 855–869.

Wagner, R. K., Torgesen, J. K., & Rashotte, C. A. (1994). The development of reading-related phonological processing abilities: New evidence of bi-directional causality from a latent variable longitudinal study. *Developmental Psychology, 30,* 73–87.

Wechsler, D. (2014). *WISC-V administration and scoring manual.* Bloomington, MN: Pearson.

Westwood, P. (2003). *Commonsense methods for children with special educational needs: Strategies for the regular classroom* (4th ed.). New York, NY: Routledge.

Wilson, A. J., Dehaene, S., Dubois, O., & Fayol, M. (2009). Effects of an adaptive game intervention on accessing number sense in low-socioeconomic-status kindergarten children. *Mind, Brain, and Education, 3,* 224–234.

Wilson, A. J., Revkin, S. K., Cohen, D., Cohen, L., & Dehaene, S. (2006). An open trial assessment of The Number Race, an adaptive computer game for remediation of dyscalculia. *Behavioral and Brain Functions, 2,* 20–35.

Yuill, N. M., & Oakhill, J. V. (1988). Effects of inference awareness training in poor reading comprehension. *Applied Cognitive Psychology, 2,* 33–45.

Zigler, E., Hodapp, R. M., & Edison, M. R. (1990). From theory to practice in the care and education of mentally retarded individuals. *American Journal on Mental Retardation, 95,* 1–12.

Zirkel, P. A., & Thomas, L. B. (2010). State laws for RTI: An updated snapshot. *Teaching Exceptional Children, 42*(1), 56–63.

Module 22

Achenbach, T. M. (1992). *Manual for the Child Behavior Checklist/2–3 and 1992 Profile.* Burlington: University of Vermont, Department of Psychiatry.

Albano, A. M., Chorpita, B. F., & Barlow, D. H. (2003). Childhood anxiety disorders. In E. J. Mash & R. A. Barkley (Eds.), *Child psychopathology* (2nd ed., pp. 279–329). New York, NY: Guilford Press.

American Psychiatric Association. (2013). *Diagnostic and statistical manual of mental disorders* (5th ed.). Washington, DC: Author.

Barkley, R. A. (1997). Behavioral inhibition, sustained attention, and executive functions: Constructing a unifying theory of ADHD. *Psychological Bulletin, 121*(1), 65–94.

Barkley, R. A. (2003). Attention-deficit/hyperactivity disorder. In E. J. mash & R. A. Barkley (Eds.), *Child Psychopathology* (2nd edition, pp. 75–143).

Broadhead, M. A., Hockaday, A., Zahra, M., Francis, P. J., & Crichton, C. (2009). Scallywags—An evaluation of a service targeting conduct disorders at school and at home. *Educational Psychology in Practice, 25*(2), 167–179.

Bryson, S. E. (1997). Epidemiology of autism: Overview and issues outstanding. In D. J. Cohen & F. R. Volkmar (Eds.), *Handbook of autism and pervasive developmental disorders* (2nd ed., pp. 41–46). New York, NY: Wiley.

Burgess, A. F., & Gutstein, S. E. (2007). Quality of life for people with autism: Raising the standard for evaluating successful outcomes. *Child and Adolescent Mental Health, 12*(2), 80–86.

Carrero, K. M., & Lusk, M. E. (2014). Educating culturally diverse students with challenging behaviors: A review of literature. *Multicultural Learning and Teaching, 9*(1), 15–32.

Cartledge, G., Kea, C., & Simmons-Reed, E. (2002). Serving culturally diverse children with serious emotional disturbance and their families. *Journal of Child and Family Studies, 11*(1), 113–126.

Centers for Disease Control and Prevention. (2009). Prevalence of autism spectrum disorders—Autism and developmental disabilities monitoring network, United States, 2006. *MMWR Surveillance Summaries, 58*(10), 1–20.

Chilakamarri, J. K., Filkowski, M. M., & Ghaemi, S. N. (2011). Misdiagnosis of bipolar disorder in children and adolescents: A comparison with ADHD and major depressive disorder. *Annals of Clinical Psychiatry, 23,* 25–29.

Connor, D. F. (2002). *Aggression and antisocial behavior in children and adolescents: Research and treatment.* New York, NY: Guilford Press.

Coo, H., Ouellette-Kuntz, H., Lloyd, J. E. V., Kasmara, L., Holden, J. J. A., & Lewis, M. E. S. (2008). Trends in autism prevalence: Diagnostic substitution revisited. *Journal of Autism & Developmental Disorders, 38,* 1036–1046.

Cullinan, D. (2007). *Students with emotional and behavioral disorders: An introduction for teachers and other helping professionals* (2nd ed.). Upper Saddle River, NJ: Prentice Hall.

Curchack-Lichtin, J. T., Chacko, A., & Halperin, J. M. (2014). Changes in ADHD symptom endorsement: Preschool to school age. *Journal of abnormal child psychology, 42*(6), 993–1004.

Davis, T. E., Ollendick, T. H., & Nebel-Schwalm, M. (2008). Intellectual ability and achievement in anxiety-disordered children: A clarification and extension of the literature. *Journal of Psychopathology & Behavioral Assessment, 30,* 43–51.

DeVoe, J. F., Peter, K., Kaufman, P., Ruddy, S. A., Miller, A. K., Planty, M., . . . Rand, M. R. (2003). *Indicators of school crime and safety: 2003* (NCES 2004-004/NCJ 201257). Washington, DC: U.S. Departments of Education and Justice.

DuPaul, G. J., Eckert, T. L., & Vilardo, B. (2012). The effects of school-based interventions for attention deficit hyperactivity disorder: A meta-analysis 1996–2010. *School Psychology Review, 41*(4), 387–412.

DuPaul, G. J., & Langberg, J. M. (2015). Educational impairments in children with ADHD. In R. A. Barkley (Ed.), *Attention-Deficit hyperactivity disorder* (4th ed.). New York, NY: Guilford Press.

DuPaul, G. J., & Stoner, G. (2014). ADHD in the schools: Assessment and intervention strategies (3rd ed.) New York, NY: Guilford Press.

Eacott, C., & Frydenberg, E. (2009). Promoting positive coping skills for rural youth: Benefits for at-risk young people. *Australian Journal of Rural Health, 17,* 338–345.

Egger, H. L., Costello, E. J., Erkanli, A., & Angold, A. (1999). Somatic complaints and psychopathology in children and adolescents : Stomach aches, musculoskeletal pains, and headaches. *Journal of the American Academy of Child and Adolescent Psychiatry, 38,* 852–860.

Ehlers, S., & Gillberg, C. (1993). The epidemiology of Asperger syndrome. A total population study. *Journal of Child Psychology and Psychiatry, 34,* 1327–1350.

Eikeseth, S. (2009). Outcome of comprehensive psycho-educational interventions for young children with autism. *Research in Developmental Disabilities, 30*(1), 158–178.

Ellison-Wright, I., Ellison-Wright, Z., & Bullmore, E. (2008). Structural brain change in attention-deficit hyperactivity disorder identified by meta-analysis. *BMC Psychiatry, 8,* 51.

Fabiano, G. A., Pelham, W. E., Coles, E. K., Gnacy, E. M., Chronis-Tuscano, A., & O'Connor, B. C. (2009). A meta-analysis of behavioral treatments for attention-deficit/hyperactivity disorder. *Clinical Psychology Review, 29,* 129–140.

Fabiano, G. A., Vujnovic, R. K., Pelham, W. E., Waschbusch, D. A., Massetti, G. M., Pariseau, M. E., . . . Volker, M. (2010). Enhancing the effectiveness of special education programming for children with attention deficit hyperactivity disorder using daily report card. *School Psychology Review, 39*(2), 219–239.

Fanti, K. A., & Henrich, C. C. (2010). Trajectories of pure and co-occurring internalizing and externalizing problems from age 2 to age 12: Findings from the National Institute of Child Health and Human Development Study of Early Child Care. *Developmental Psychology, 46*(5), 1159–1175.

Filipek, P. A., Accardo, P. J., Baranek, G. T., Cook, E. H. Jr., Dawson, G., Gordon, B., . . . Volkmar, F. R. (1999). The screening and diagnosis of autism spectrum disorders. *Journal of Autism and Developmental Disorders, 29*(6), 439–484.

Foster, S. L. (2005). Aggression and antisocial behavior in girls. In D. J. Bell, S. L. Foster, & E. J. Mash (Eds.), *Handbook of behavioral and emotional problems in girls* (pp. 149–180). New York, NY: Kluwer Academic/Plenum.

Frick, P. J. (2012). Developmental pathways to conduct disorder: Implications for future directions in research, assessment, and treatment. *Journal of Clinical Child & Adolescent Psychology, 41*(3), 378–389.

Garber, J., & Horowitz, J. L. (2002). Depression in children. In C. L. Hammen & I. H. Gotlib (Eds.), *Handbook of depression* (pp. 510–540). New York, NY: Guilford.

Graziano, P. A., Slavec, J., Hart, K., Garcia, A., & Pelham, W. E. (2014). Improving school readiness in preschoolers with behavior problems: Results from a summer treatment program. *Journal of Psychopathology and Behavioral Assessment, 36*(4), 555–569.

Gresham, F. M., & Kern, L. (2004). Internalizing behavior problems in children and adolescents. In R. B. Rutherford Jr., M. M. Quinn, & S. Mathur (Eds.), *Handbook of research in behavioral disorders* (pp. 262–281). New York, NY: Guilford.

Gresham, F. M., Lane, K. L., & Beebe-Frankenberger, M. (2005). Predictors of hyperactive-impulsive-inattention and conduct problems: A comparative follow-back investigation. *Psychology in the Schools, 42*(7), 721–736.

Grover, R. L., Ginsburg, G. S., & Ialongo, N. (2007). Psychosocial outcomes of anxious first graders: A seven-year follow-up. *Depression and Anxiety, 24,* 410–420.

Hammen, C. L., Rudolph, K. D., & Abaied, J. L. (2014). Child and adolescent depression. In E. J. Mash & R. A. Barkley (Eds.), *Child psychopathology* (3rd ed.). New York, NY: Guilford Press.

Harrington, R. (2002). Affective disorders. In M. Rutter & E. Taylor (Eds.), *Child and adolescent psychiatry* (4th ed., pp. 463–485). Malden, MA: Blackwell Science.

Higa-McMillan, C. K., Francis, S. E., & Chorpita, B. F. (2014). Anxiety disorders. In E. J. Mash & R. A. Barkley (Eds.), *Child psychopathology* (3rd Edition). New York: Guildford Press.

Hinshaw, S. P., & Lee, S. S. (2003). Conduct and oppositional defiant disorders. In E. J. Mash & R. A. Barkley (Eds.), *Child psychopathology* (2nd ed., pp. 144–198). New York, NY: Guilford.

Holmes, J., Gathercole, S. E., Place, M., Dunning, D. L., Hilton, K. A., & Elliott, J. G. (2010). Working memory deficits can be overcome: Impacts of training and medication on working memory in children with ADHD. *Applied Cognitive Psychology, 24,* 827–836. doi:10.1002/acp.1589

Holmes, J., Hilton, K. A., Place, M., Alloway, T. P., Elliott, J. G., & Gathercole, S. E. (2014). Children with low working memory and children with ADHD: Same or different? *Frontiers in Human Neuroscience, 8*(976), 116–128.

Howard, R., Finn, P., Jose, P., & Gallagher, J. (2012). Adolescent-onset alcohol abuse exacerbates the influence of childhood conduct disorder on late adolescent and early adult antisocial behaviour. *Journal of Forensic Psychiatry & Psychology, 23*(1), 7–22.

Howlin, P., Mawhood, L., & Rutter, M. (2000). Autism and developmental receptive language disorder—A follow-up comparison in early adult life. II: Social, behavioral, and psychiatric outcomes. *Journal of Child Psychology and Psychiatry, 41,* 561–578.

Jensen, M. M. (2005). *Introduction to emotional and behavioral disorders: Recognizing and managing problems in the classroom.* Upper Saddle River, NJ: Prentice Hall.

Jensen, P. S., Hinshaw, S. P., Kraemer, H. C., Lenora, N., Newcorn, J. H., Abikoff, H. B., . . . Vitiello, B. (2001). ADHD comorbidity findings from the MTA study: Comparing comorbid subgroups. *Journal of the American Academy of Child Adolescent Psychiatry, 40*(2), 147–158.

Jitendra, A. K., DuPaul, G. J., Someki, F., & Tresco, K. E. (2008). Enhancing academic achievement for children with attention-deficit hyperactivity disorder: Evidence form school-based intervention research. *Developmental Disabilities Research Reviews, 14,* 325–330.

Johnston, C., & Chronis-Tuscano, A. (2015). Families and ADHD. In R. A. Barkley (Ed.), *Attention-Deficit hyperactivity disorder* (4th ed.). New York, NY: Guilford Press.

Kendall, P. C., Cummings, C. M., Villabø, M. A., Narayanan, M. K., Treadwell, K., Birmaher, B., . . . Gosch, E. (2016). Mediators of change in the Child/Adolescent Anxiety Multimodal Treatment Study. *Journal of Consulting and Clinical Psychology, 84*(1), 1–14.

King, S., Waschbusch, D. A., Pelham, W. E., Frankland, B. W., Corkum, P. V., & Jacques, S. (2009). Subtypes of aggression in children with attention deficit hyperactivity disorder: Medication effects and comparison with typical children. *Journal of Clinical Child & Adolescent Psychology, 38*(5), 619–629.

Kirkovski, M., Enticott, P. G., & Fitzgerald, P. B. (2013). A review of the role of female gender in autism spectrum disorders. *Journal of Autism and Developmental Disorders, 43*(11), 2584–2603.

Kohler, F. W., Anthony, L. J., Steighner, S. A., & Hoyson, M. (2001). Teaching social interaction skills in the integrated preschool: An examination of naturalistic tactics. *Topics in Early Childhood Special Education, 21*(2), 93–103.

Lane, K. L., Gresham, F. M., & O'Shaughnessy, T. E. (2002). *Interventions for children with or at risk for emotional and behavioral disorders.* Boston, MA: Allyn & Bacon.

Lang, R., Mahoney, R., El Zein, F., Delaune, E., & Amidon, M. (2011). Evidence to practice: Treatment of anxiety in individuals with autism spectrum disorders. *Neuropsychiatric Disease and Treatment, 7,* 27–30.

Lee, S-H., Simpson, R. L., & Shogren, K. A. (2007). Effects and implications of self-management for students with autism: A meta-analysis. *Focus on Autism and Other Developmental Disabilities, 22*(1), 2–13.

Lewinsohn, P. M., & Essau, C. A. (2002). Depression in adolescents. In C. L. Hammen & I. H. Gotlib (Eds.), *Handbook of depression* (pp. 541–559). New York, NY: Guilford.

Mansell, W., & Morris, K. (2004). A survey of parents' reactions to the diagnosis of autistic spectrum disorder by a local service. *Autism, 8,* 387–407.

Marcotte, D., Lévesque, N., & Fortin, L. (2006). Variations of cognitive distortions and school performance in depressed and non-depressed high school adolescents: A two-year longitudinal study. *Cognitive Therapy Research, 30,* 211–225.

Martin, A. J. (2014). The role of ADHD in academic adversity: Disentangling ADHD effects from other personal and contextual factors. *School Psychology Quarterly, 29*(4), 395–408.

Martinussen, R., Hayden, J., Hogg-Johnson, S., & Tannock, R. (2005). A meta-analysis of working memory impairments in children with attention-deficit/hyperactivity disorder. *Journal of the American Academy of Child & Adolescent Psychiatry, 44*(4), 377–384.

McGoey, K. E., Schneider, D. L., Rezzetano, K. M., Prodan, T., & Tankersley, M. (2010). Classwide intervention to manage disruptive behavior in the kindergarten classroom. *Journal of Applied School Psychology, 26,* 247–261.

McQuade, J. D., & Hoza, B. (2015). Peer relationships of children with ADHD. In R. A. Barkley (Ed.), *Attention-Deficit hyperactivity disorder* (4th ed.). New York, NY: Guilford Press.

Morrier, M. J., & Hess, K. L. (2010). Ethnic differences in autism eligibility in the United States public schools. *The Journal of Special Education, 46*(1) 49–63.

Mrug, S., Molina, B. S., Hoza, B., Gerdes, A. C., Hinshaw, S. P., Hechtman, L., & Arnold, L. E. (2012). Peer rejection and friendships in children with attention-deficit/

hyperactivity disorder: Contributions to long-term outcomes. *Journal of Abnormal Child Psychology, 40*(6), 1013–1026.

Nail, J. E., Christofferson, J., Ginsburg, G. S., Drake, K., Kendall, P. C., McCracken, J. T., . . . Sakolsky, D. (2015). Academic impairment and impact of treatments among youth with anxiety disorders. *Child & Youth Care Forum, 44*(3) 327–342.

Naoi, N., Yokoyama, K., & Yamamoto, J. (2007). Intervention for tact as reporting in children with autism. *Research in Autism Spectrum Disorders, 1,* 174–184.

Nelson, J. R., Benner, G. J., & Bohaty, J. (2014). Addressing the academic problems and challenges of students with emotional and behavioral disorders. In H. M. Walker & F. M Gresham (Eds.), *Handbook of evidence-based practices for emotional and behavioral disorders: Applications in schools* (pp. 363–377). New York, NY: Guilford Press.

Nishina, A., Juvonen, J., & Witkow, M. R. (2005). Sticks and stones may break my bones, but names will make feel sick: The psychosocial, somatic, and scholastic consequences of peer harassment. *Journal of Clinical Child and Adolescent Psychology, 34,* 37–48.

Osher, D., Cartledge, G., Oswald, D., Sutherland, K. S., Artiles, A. J., & Coutinho, M. (2004). Cultural and linguistic competency and disproportionate representation. In R. B. Rutherford, M. M. Quinn, & S. B. Mathur (Eds.), *Handbook of research in emotional and behavioral disorders* (pp. 54–77). New York, NY: Guilford Press.

Owens, M., Stevenson, J., Hadwin, J. A., & Norgate, R. (2012). Anxiety and depression in academic performance: An exploration of the mediating factors of worry and working memory. *School Psychology International, 33*(4), 433–449.

Parrish, T. (2002). Racial disparities in the identification, funding, and provision of special education. In D. Losen (Ed.), *Minority issues in special education* (pp. 15–38). Cambridge, MA: Harvard Education Press.

Pliszka, S. R. (2015) Comorbid psychiatric disorders in children with ADHD. In R. A. Barkley (Ed.), *Attention-Deficit hyperactivity disorder* (4th ed.). New York, NY: Guilford Press.

Quiroga, C. V., Janosz, M., Bisset, S., & Morin, A. J. (2013). Early adolescent depression symptoms and school dropout: Mediating processes involving self-reported academic competence and achievement. *Journal of Educational Psychology, 105*(2), 552–560.

Read, K. L., Puleo, C. M., Wei, C., Cummings, C. M., & Kendall, P. C. (2013). Cognitive–Behavioral treatment for pediatric anxiety disorders. In R. A. Vasa & A. K. Roy (Eds.), *Pediatric anxiety disorders: A clinical guide* (pp. 269–287). New York, NY: Springer.

Ridgway, A., Northup, J., Pellegrini, A., La Rue, R., & Hightshoe, A. (2003). Effects of recess on the classroom behavior of children with and without attention-deficit hyperactivity disorder. *School Psychology Quarterly, 18*, 253–268.

Schachar, R., & Tannock, R. (2002). Syndromes of hyperactivity and attention deficit. In M. Rutter & E. Taylor (Eds.), *Child and Adolescent Psychiatry* (4th edition, pp. 399–418). Malden, MA: Blackwell Science.

Sciutto, M. J., & Eisenberg, M. (2007). Evaluating the evidence for and against the overdiagnosis of ADHD. *Journal of Attention Disorders, 11*(2), 106–113.

Skiba, R. J., Middelerg, L. V., & McClain, M. B. (2014). Multicultural issues for school and students with emotional and behavioral disorders: Disproportionality in discipline and special education. In H. M. Walker & F. M Gresham (Eds.), *Handbook of evidence-based practices for emotional and behavioral disorders: Applications in schools* (pp. 54–70). New York, NY: Guilford Press.

Smith, B. H., & Shapiro, C. J. (2015). Combined treatments for ADHD. In R. A. Barkley (Ed.), *Attention-Deficit hyperactivity disorder* (4th ed.). New York, NY: Guilford Press.

Stone, L. B., Uhrlass, D. J., & Gibb, B. E. (2010). Co-rumination and lifetime history of depressive disorders in children. *Journal of Clinical Child & Adolescent Psychology, 39*(4), 597–602.

Swan, A. J., Cummings, C. M., Caporino, N. E., & Kendall, P. C. (2014). Evidence-based intervention approaches for students with anxiety and related disorder. In H. M. Walker & F. M Gresham (Eds.), *Handbook of evidence-based practices for emotional and behavioral disorders: Applications in schools* (pp. 324–343). New York, NY: Guilford Press.

Thomas, L. E. (2013). Spatial working memory is necessary for actions to guide thought. *Journal of Experimental Psychology: Learning, Memory, and Cognition, 39*(6), 1974–1981.

Tillfors, M., Persson, S., Willén, M., & Burk, W. J. (2012). Prospective links between social anxiety and adolescent peer relations. *Journal of Adolescence, 35*(5), 1255–1263.

Tobin, R. M., & House, A. E. (2016). *DSM-5 diagnosis in the schools.* New York, NY: Guilford Press.

Towle, P. O., Visintainer, P. F., O'Sullivan, C., Bryan, N. E., & Busby, S. (2009) Detecting autism spectrum disorder from early intervention charts: Methodology and preliminary findings. *Journal of Autism Disorder, 39*, 444–452.

Treatment for Adolescents with Depression Study Team. (2004). Fluoxetine, cognitive-behavioral therapy, and their combination for adolescents with depression: Treatment for Adolescents with Depressions Study (TADS) randomized controlled trial. *Journal of the American Medical Association, 292*, 807–820.

U.S. Department of Education. (2014). *Thirty-sixth annual report to Congress on the implementation of the Individuals with Disabilities Education Act.* Office of Special Education and Rehabilitative Services. Washington, DC: U.S. Government Printing Office.

Vaidya, C. J. (2013). Attention Deficit/Hyperactivity disorder (ADHD). In K. Ochsner & S. M. Koslyn, (Eds.), *The Oxford handbook of cognitive neuroscience: Vol. 2: The cutting edges* (pp. 421–433). New York, NY: Oxford University Press.

Walker, H. M., Seeley, J. R., Small, J., Severson, H. H., Graham, B. A., Feil, E. G., . . . Forness, S. R. (2009). A randomized controlled trial of the First Step to Success Early Intervention: Demonstration of program efficacy outcomes in a diverse, urban school district. *Journal of Emotional and Behavioral Disorders, 17*(4), 197–212.

Walkup, J. T., Albano, A. M., Piacentini, J., Birmaher, B., Compton, S. N., Sherrill, J. T., . . . Kendall, P. C. (2008). Cognitive behavioral therapy, sertraline, or a combination in childhood anxiety. *New England Journal of Medicine, 359*(26), 2753–2766.

Wehmeier, P. M., Schacht, A., & Barkley, R. A. (2010). Social and emotional impairment in children and adolescents with ADHD and the impact on quality of life. *Journal of Adolescent Health, 46*, 209–217.

Weiss, M., & Weiss, G. (2002). Attention deficit hyperactivity disorder. In M. Lewis (Ed.), *Child and Adolescent Psychiatry: A comprehensive textbook* (3rd edition, pp. 645–670). Philadelphia: Lippincott Williams & Wilkins.

Weller, E. B., Weller, R. A., Rowan, A. B., & Svadjian, H. (2002). Depressive disorders in children and adolescents. In M. Lewis (Ed.), *Child and adolescent psychiatry: A comprehensive textbook* (3rd ed., pp. 767–781). Philadelphia, PA: Lippincott Williams & Wilkins.

Wiley, A. L., Brigham, F. J., Kauffman, J. M., & Bogan, J. E. (2013). Disproportionate poverty, conservatism, and the disproportionate identification of minority students with emotional and behavioral disorders. *Education and Treatment of Children, 36*(4), 29–50.

Wood, J. (2006). Effect of anxiety reduction on children's school performance and social adjustment. *Developmental Psychology, 42*(2), 345–349.

Wood, J. J., Chiu, A. W., Hwang, W., Jacobs, J., & Ifekwunigwe, M. (2008). Adapting cognitive-behavioral therapy for Mexican-American students with anxiety disorders: Recommendations for school psychologists. *School Psychology Quarterly, 23*(4), 515–532.

Wood, J. J., Drahota, A., Sze, K., Har, K., Chiu, A., & Langer, D. A. (2009). Cognitive behavioral therapy for anxiety in children with autism spectrum disorders: A randomized, controlled trial. *Journal of Child Psychology and Psychiatry, 50*(3), 224–234.

Zentall, S. S. (1993). Research on the educational implications of attention deficit hyperactivity disorder. *Exceptional Children, 60*(2), 143–153.

Zimmermann, F., Schütte, K., Taskinen, P., & Köller, O. (2013). Reciprocal effects between adolescent externalizing problems and measures of achievement. *Journal of Educational Psychology, 105*(3), 747–761.

Module 23

Anderson, L. W., & Krathwohl (Eds.). (2001). *A taxonomy for learning, teaching, and assessing: A revision of Bloom's taxonomy of educational objectives.* New York, NY: Longman.

Bagley, S. S. (2008). High school students' perceptions of narrative evaluations as summative assessment. *American Secondary Education, 36*(3), 15–32.

Bean, J. C. (2011). *Engaging ideas: The professor's guide to integrating writing, critical thinking, and active learning in the classroom* (2nd ed.). San Francisco, CA: Wiley.

Bennett, R. E. (2011). Formative assessment: A critical review. *Assessment in Education: Principles, Policies, & Practice, 18*, 5–25.

Bergman, P. L. S. (2015). *Parent-child information frictions and human capital investment: Evidence from a field experiment* (CESifo Working Paper No. 5391). Retrieved from http://www.econstor.eu/handle/10419/110891

Bloom, B. S., Englehart, M. D., Frost, E. J., Hill, W. H., & Krathwohl, D. R. (1956). *Taxonomy of educational objectives.* New York, NY: David McKay.

Bonner, S. M. (2013). Validity in classroom assessment: Purposes, properties, and principles. In J. H. McMillan (Ed.), *SAGE handbook of research on classroom assessment* (pp. 87–106). Thousand Oaks, CA: SAGE.

Brookhart, S. (2012). Preventing feedback fizzle. *Educational Leadership, 70*(1), 24–29.

Brookhart, S. (2013). The use of teacher judgement for summative assessment in the USA. *Assessment in Education: Principles, Policy & Practice, 20*(1), 69–90.

Brookhart, S. M. (2011). Educational assessment knowledge and skills for teachers. *Educational Measurement: Issues and Practice, 30*(1), 3–12.

Brookhart, S. M. (2015). Making the most of multiple choice: How to use multiple-choice to uncover students' critical thinking skills. *Educational Leadership, 73*(1), 36–39.

Brookhart, S. M., & Chen, F. (2015). The quality and effectiveness of descriptive rubrics. *Educational Review, 67*(3), 343–368.

Brookhart, S. M., & Nitko, A. J. (2014). *Educational assessment of students* (7th ed.). Boston, MA: Pearson.

Carey, T., & Carifio, J. (2012). The minimum grading controversy: Results of a quantitative study of seven years of grading data from an urban high school. *Educational Researcher, 41*(6), 201–208.

Cizek, G. J. (2009). Reliability and validity of information about student achievement: Comparing large-scale and classroom testing contexts. *Theory Into Practice, 48*(1), 63–71.

Cohen, R. J., Swerdlik, M. E., & Sturman, E. D. (2013). *Psychological testing and assessment: An introduction to tests and measurement* (8th ed.). New York, NY: McGraw-Hill.

Corpus, J. H., & Lepper, M. R. (2007). The effects of person versus performance praise on children's motivation: Gender and age as moderating factors. *Educational Psychology, 27*(4), 487–508.

Gullickson, A. R., & Ellwein, M. C. (1985). Post hoc analysis of teacher-made tests: The goodness-of-fit between prescription and practice. *Educational Measurement: Issues and Practice, 4*(1), 15–18.

Guo, Y. (2010). Meetings without dialogue: A study of ESL parent-teacher interactions at secondary schools parents' nights. *The School Community Journal, 20*(1), 121–140.

Guskey, T. R. (2009). *Practical solutions for serious problems in standards-based grading*. Thousand Oaks, CA: Corwin.

Hambleton, R. K., & Murphy, E. (1992). A psychometric perspective on authentic measurement. *Applied Measurement in Education, 5,* 1–16.

Humphry, S. M., & Heldsinger, S. A. (2014). Common structural design features of rubrics may represent a threat to validity. *Educational Researcher, 43*(5), 253–263.

Kraft, M. A., & Rogers, T. (2014). *The underutilized potential of teacher-to-parent communication: Evidence from a field experiment* (Faculty Research Working Paper Series). Retrieved from https://research.hks.harvard.edu/publications/workingpapers/Index.aspx

Lane, S. (2013). Performance assessment. In J. H. McMillan (Ed.), *SAGE handbook of research on classroom assessment* (pp. 313–329). Thousand Oaks, CA: SAGE.

Lane, S., Parke, C., & Moskal, B. (1992). *Principles for developing performance assessments*. Paper presented at the annual meeting of the American Educational Research Association, San Francisco, CA.

Linn, R. L. (1993). Educational assessment: Expanded expectations and challenges. *Educational Evaluation and Policy Analysis, 15,* 1–16.

Marzano, R. J. (2006). *Classroom assessment and grading that work*. Alexandria, VA: ASCD.

Marzano, R. J., & Heflebower, T. (2011). Grades that show what students know. *Educational Leadership, 69*(3), 35–39.

McKenzie, W. (2005). Constructing a rubric. In R. L. Bell (Ed.), *National educational technology standards for students curriculum series: Social studies units for grades 9–12* (pp. 25–29). Eugene, OR: International Society for Technology in Education.

McLesky, J., & Waldron, N. L. (2002). Inclusion and school change: Teacher perceptions regarding curricular and instructional adaptations. *Teacher Education and Special Education, 25*(1), 41–54.

McMillan, J. H. (2014). *Classroom assessment: Principles and practice for effective standards-based education* (6th ed.). Boston, MA: Pearson.

McMillan, J. H., Myran, S., & Workman, D. (2002). Elementary teachers' classroom assessment and grading practices. *Journal of Educational Research, 95*(4), 203–213.

Mertler, C. A. (2000). Teacher-centered fallacies of classroom assessment validity and reliability. *MidWestern Educational Researcher, 13*(4), 29–35.

Miller, M. D., & Seraphine, A. E. (1993). Can test scores remain authentic when teaching to the test? *Educational Assessment, 1,* 119–129.

Morris, C. D., Bransford, J. D., & Franks, J. J. (1977). Levels of processing versus transfer appropriate processing. *Journal of Verbal Learning & Verbal Behavior, 16*(5), 519–533.

Moss, C. M. (2013). Research on classroom summative assessment. In J. H. McMillan (Ed.), *SAGE handbook of research on classroom assessment* (pp. 235–255). Thousand Oaks, CA: SAGE.

Naylor, C. (1993). *The views of parents of ESL students concerning the B.C. education system*. Vancouver, Canada: British Columbia Teachers' Federation.

Nitko, A. J., & Brookhart, S. M. (2011). *Educational assessment of students* (6th ed.). Boston, MA: Pearson.

Ogbu, J. (1982). Cultural discontinuities and schooling. *Anthropology and Education Quarterly, 13,* 290–307.

Osborne, A. B. (1996). Practice into theory into practice: Culturally relevant pedagogy for students we have marginalized and normalized. *Anthropology and Education Quarterly, 27,* 285–314.

Parkes, J. (2007). Reliability as argument. *Educational Measurement: Issues and Practice, 26*(4), 2–10.

Pomerantz, E. M., & Kempner, S. G. (2013). Mothers' daily person and process praise: Implications for children's theory of intelligence and motivation. *Developmental Psychology, 49*(11), 2040–2046.

Quinlan, A. M. (2012). *A complete guide to rubrics: Assessment made easy for teachers of K-college* (2nd ed.). New York, NY: Rowman & Littlefield.

Randall, J., & Engelhard, G. (2010). Examining the grading practices of teachers. *Teaching and Teacher Education, 26*(7), 1372–1380.

Randel, B., & Clark, T. (2013). Measuring classroom assessment practices. In J. H. McMillan (Ed.), *SAGE handbook of research on classroom assessment* (pp. 145–163). Thousand Oaks, CA: SAGE.

Reynolds, C. R., & Livingston, R. B. (2012). *Mastering modern psychological testing: Theory & methods*. Boston, MA: Pearson.

Rodriguez, M. C., & Haladyna, T. M. (2013). Writing selected-response items for classroom assessment. In J. H. McMillan (Ed.), *SAGE handbook of research on classroom assessment* (pp. 293–311). Thousand Oaks, CA: SAGE.

Rudner, L. M., & Boston, C. (1994). Performance assessment. *The ERIC Review, 3*(1), 2–12.

Sanders, P. (2011). The purpose of testing. In P. Sanders (Ed.), *Testing at school* (pp. 9–20). Arnhem, the Netherlands: Cito.

Shavelson, R. J., & Baxter, G. P. (1991). Performance assessment in science. *Applied Measurement in Education, 4,* 347–362.

Shepard, L. A. (2006). Classroom assessment. In R. L. Brennan (Ed.), *Educational measurement* (4th ed., pp. 624–646). Westport, CT: Praeger.

Stevens, D. D., & Levi, A. J. (2013). *Introduction to rubrics: An assessment tool to save grading time, convey effective feedback, and promote student learning* (2nd ed.). Sterling, VA: Stylus Publishing.

Thompson, B. C., Mazer, J. P., Grady, E. F. (2015). The changing nature of parent-teacher communication: Mode selection in the smartphone era. *Communication Education, 64*(2), 187–207.

Tierney, R. D. (2013). Fairness in classroom assessment. In J. H. McMillan (Ed.), *SAGE handbook of research on classroom assessment* (pp. 125–144). Thousand Oaks, CA: SAGE.

Tulving, E., & Thomson, D. M. (1973). Encoding specificity and retrieval processes in episodic memory. *Psychological Review, 80,* 352–373.

Van der Kleij, F. M., Vermeulen, J. A., Schildkamp, K., & Eggen, T. J. H. M. (2015). Integrating data-based decision-making, assessment for learning and diagnostic testing in formative assessment. *Assessment in Education: Principles, Policy, and Practice, 22*(3), 324–343.

Waugh, C. K., & Gronlund, N. E. (2013). *Assessment of student achievement* (10th ed.). Boston, MA: Pearson.

Wormeli, R. (2006). *Fair isn't always equal: Assessing and grading in the differentiated classroom.* Portland, ME: Stenhouse Publishers.

Wright, R. J. (2008). *Educational assessment: Tests and measurements in the age of accountability.* Thousand Oaks, CA: SAGE.

Zentall, S. R., & Morris, B. J. (2010). "Good job, you're so smart:" The effects of inconsistency of praise type on young children's motivation. *Journal of Experimental Child Psychology, 107,* 155–163.

Module 24

Anderson, L.W., & Krathwohl (Eds.). (2001). *A taxonomy for learning, teaching, and assessing: A revision of Bloom's taxonomy of educational objectives.* New York, NY: Longman.

Bloom, B. S., Englehart, M. D., Frost, E. J., Hill, W. H., & Krathwohl, D. R. (1956). *Taxonomy of educational objectives.* New York. NY: David McKay.

Bonner, S. M. (2013). Validity in classroom assessment: Purposes, properties, and principles. In J. H. McMillan (Ed.), *SAGE handbook of research on classroom assessment* (pp. 87–106). Thousand Oaks, CA: SAGE.

Brookhart, S. M. (2015). Making the most of multiple choice: How to use multiple-choice to uncover students' critical thinking skills. *Educational Leadership, 73*(1), 36–39.

Brookhart, S. M., & Nitko, A. J. (2014). *Educational assessment of students* (7th ed.). Boston, MA: Pearson.

Cizek, G. J., Fitzgerald, S. M., & Rachor, R. E. (1995). Teachers' assessment practices: Preparation, isolation, and the kitchen sink. *Educational Assessment, 32*(2), 159–179.

Fives, H., & DiDonato-Barnes, N. (2013). Classroom test construction: The power of a table of specifications. *Practical Assessment, Research & Evaluation, 18*(3), 2. Retrieved from http://pareonline.net/getvn.asp?v=18&n=3

Frey, B. B., & Schmitt, V. L. (2010). Teachers' classroom assessment practices. *Middle Grades Research Journal, 5*(3), 107–117.

Frisbie, D. A., & Becker, D. F. (1990). An analysis of textbook advice about true-false tests. *Applied Measurement in Education, 4,* 67–83.

Gregory, R. J. (2013). *Psychological testing: History, principles, and applications* (7th ed.). Boston, MA: Pearson.

Gronlund, N. E. (2003). *Assessment of student achievement* (7th ed.). Boston, MA: Allyn & Bacon.

Haladyna, T. M., Downing, S. M., & Rodriguez, M. C. (2002). A review of multiple-choice item-writing guidelines for classroom assessment. *Applied Measurement in Education, 15*(3), 309–334.

McMillan, J. H., Myran, S., & Workman, D. (2002). Elementary teachers' classroom assessment and grading practices. *Journal of Educational Research, 95*(4), 203–213.

Morris, C. D., Bransford, J. D., & Franks, J. J. (1977). Levels of processing versus transfer appropriate processing. *Journal of Verbal Learning & Verbal Behavior, 16*(5), 519–533.

Notar, C. E., Zuelke, D. C., Wilson, J. D., & Yunker, B. D. (2004). The table of specifications: Insuring accountability in teacher made tests. *Journal of Instructional Psychology, 31,* 115–129.

Randel, B., & Clark, T. (2013). Measuring classroom assessment practices. In J. H. McMillan (Ed.), *SAGE handbook of research on classroom assessment* (pp. 145–163). Thousand Oaks, CA: SAGE.

Reynolds, C. R., & Livingston, R. B. (2012). *Mastering modern psychological testing: Theory & methods.* Boston, MA: Pearson.

Rodriguez, M. C., & Haladyna, T. M. (2013). Writing selected-response items for classroom assessment. In J. H. McMillan (Ed.), *SAGE handbook of research on classroom assessment* (pp. 293–311). Thousand Oaks, CA: SAGE.

Shepard, L. A. (2013). Validity for what purpose? *Teachers College Record, 115,* 1–11.

Tierney, R. D. (2013). Fairness in classroom assessment. In J. H. McMillan (Ed.), *SAGE handbook of research on classroom assessment* (pp. 125–144). Thousand Oaks, CA: SAGE.

Tulving, E., & Thomson, D. M. (1973). Encoding specificity and retrieval processes in episodic memory. *Psychological Review, 80,* 352–373.

Waugh, C. K., & Gronlund, N. E. (2013). *Assessment of student achievement* (10th ed.). Boston, MA: Pearson.

Wright, R. J. (2008). *Educational assessment: Tests and measurements in the age of accountability.* Thousand Oaks, CA: SAGE.

Module 25

American Educational Research Association. (2014). *Standards for educational and psychological testing.* Washington, DC: American Educational Research Association, American Psychological Association, National Council on Measurement in Education.

Brookhart, S. M., & Nitko, A. J. (2014). *Educational assessment of students* (7th ed.). Boston, MA: Pearson.

Chatterji, M. (2003). *Designing and using tools for educational assessment.* Boston, MA: Pearson.

Finch, H., Baron, K., Meyer, P. (2009). Differential item functioning analysis for accommodated versus non-accommodated students. *Educational Assessment, 14,* 38–56.

Gregory, R. J. (2013). *Psychological testing: History, principles, and applications* (7th ed.). Boston, MA: Pearson.

Haladyna, T. M. (2002). *Essentials of standardized achievement testing: Validity and accountability.* Boston, MA: Pearson.

Lissitz, R. W., & Schafer, W. D. (2002). *Assessment in educational reform: Both means and ends.* Boston, MA: Allyn & Bacon.

Popham, W. J. (2006). *Assessment for educational leaders.* Boston, MA: Pearson Education.

Reynolds, C. R., Livingston, R. B., & Willson, V. (2009). *Measurement and assessment in education* (2nd ed.). Boston, MA: Pearson.

Sullivan, J. R., Winter, S. M., Sass, D. A., & Svenkerud, N. (2014). Assessing growth in young children: A comparison of raw, age-equivalent, and standard scores using the Peabody Picture Vocabulary Test. *Journal of Research in Childhood Education, 28*(2), 277–291.